ביאור תניא

THE STEINSALTZ TANYA

VOLUME I

Steinsaltz Center

מגיד
MAGGID

THE MAGERMAN EDITION

THE STEINSALTZ TANYA

LIKKUTEI AMARIM 1–32

COMMENTARY & TRANSLATION BY

RABBI ADIN EVEN-ISRAEL STEINSALTZ

Steinsaltz Center
Maggid Books

The Steinsaltz Tanya:
Likkutei Amarim, Volume 1
First edition, 2022

Maggid Books
An imprint of Koren Publishers Jerusalem Ltd.

POB 8531, New Milford, CT 06776-8531, USA
& POB 4044, Jerusalem 9104001, Israel
www.maggidbooks.com

This book was published in cooperation with
the Israeli Institute for Talmudic Publications.

We acknowledge with gratitude the generous support of
Terri and Stephen Geifman, *who made possible an earlier edition of this commentary.*

Steinsaltz Center is the parent organization of institutions
established by Rabbi Adin Even-Israel Steinsaltz
POB 45187, Jerusalem 91450 ISRAEL
Telephone: +972 2 646 0900, Fax +972 2 624 9454
www.steinsaltz-center.org

Cover design by Tani Bayer

ISBN 978-1-59264-585-5, hardcover

Printed and bound in ROT

Executive Director, Steinsaltz Center
Rabbi Meni Even-Israel

Editor-in-Chief
Rabbi Jason Rappoport

Translators
Noam Harris
Sara Fenton

Editors
Suri Brand, Senior Editor
Rabbi Simcha Mirvis
Noam Harris
Rabbi Zalman Margolin

Proofreader
Dvora Rhein

Hebrew Proofreader
Avichai Gamdani

Hebrew Edition Editors
Rabbi Meir Hanegbi, Senior Editor
Rabbi Hillel Mondshein
Rabbi David Brokner

Hebrew Vocalization
Rabbi Hillel Mondshein

Technical Staff
Adena Frazer
Adina Mann
Avi Steinhart

Dedicated to

my wife, **Debra,**

and my children,
Elijah, Zachary, Sydney, and **Lexie.**

May this new translation of the Tanya,
along with the commentary from Rabbi Steinsaltz (*z"l*),
bring us closer to hasidic teaching and
help us connect with the mystical meaning
behind the Torah.

May all the children of Israel use
the Tanya's knowledge and wisdom
to work together to hasten the coming of Mashiaḥ.

David M. Magerman

צַדִּיק כַּתָּמָר יִפְרָח כְּאֶרֶז בַּלְּבָנוֹן יִשְׂגֶּה:
שְׁתוּלִים בְּבֵית ה׳ בְּחַצְרוֹת אֱלֹקֵינוּ יַפְרִיחוּ:
עוֹד יְנוּבוּן בְּשֵׂיבָה דְּשֵׁנִים וְרַעֲנַנִּים יִהְיוּ:
לְהַגִּיד כִּי יָשָׁר ה׳ צוּרִי וְלֹא עַוְלָתָה בּוֹ:

(תהילים צב:יג-טז)

The righteous man flourishes like a palm tree;
like a cedar in Lebanon he grows tall.
Planted in the House of the Lord,
they blossom in the courts of our God.
They will continue to yield fruit even in old age;
they will remain full and fresh,
to tell that the Lord is upright.
He is my rock, and there is no wrongdoing in Him.

(Ps. 92:13–16)

We dedicate this *sefer* in loving memory of our beloved grandfather and great-grandfather HaRav Avraham ben Uszer and Chana Feldman, *zichrono livracha.*

He was a true tzaddik and exemplified the beautiful words of King David. We pray that our children, Baruch Aryeh, Ezra Yishayahu, Rut Chana, Shmaryahu Yisrael, and Yitzchak Eliyahu will be the "fresh fruit" of the tree of Torah, and that along with their cousins, they will proudly carry his legacy forward.

May they take the lessons from the Ba'al HaTanya to heart and treat each other and all of Israel as brothers with love and have long lives filled with Torah, mitzvot, and joy.

כָּל יִשְׂרָאֵל ״אַחִים״ מַמָּשׁ, מִצַּד שׁוֹרֶשׁ נַפְשָׁם בַּה׳ אֶחָד

All Jews are literally called brothers on account of their collective soul's common root in the one God.

– Tanya, chap. 32

Maeira and Michel Werthenschlag

ספר התניא מלמד אותנו שהנפש האלוקית מסורה כל כולה לקב"ה והיא מבחינה זו חסרת אנוכיות או תחושת ישות. הנפש הבהמית לעומת זאת מרוכזת בעצמה ומסורה לקיומה הנפרד.

לפיכך לימד אותנו האדמו"ר האמצעי שכאשר שני יהודים לומדים או משוחחים בענייני עבודת ה׳ הרי אלו שתי נשמות אלוקיות כנגד נפש בהמית אחת. הנפש הבהמית לא מצטרפת עם חבירתה משום שכאמור היא מסורה לעצמה אבל הנפשות האלוקיות מצטרפות יחד בלי כל חציצה או הבדל.

(מתוך: "היום יום" כ׳ לטבת)

לזכות
משה ליב בן זיסל שיחי׳ לאויש"ט
שולמית בת זהרה שתחי׳ לאויש"ט

The *Tanya* teaches us that the divine soul is fully devoted to G-d, and therefore it is selfless. By contrast, the animal soul is selfish, devoted only to maintaining its own existence.

The Mitteler Rebbe, Rabbi Dovber of Lubavitch, taught that when two Jews learn or discuss matters pertaining to service of God, there are two divine souls against one animal soul. The animal soul thinks only of itself and will not attach itself to the animal soul of the other. But the two divine souls are joined together with no division or barrier.

(Cited from *HaYom Yom*, 20 Tevet)

In the merit of
Moshe Leib ben Zisel
Shulamit bat Zohara

A blessing from the Lubavitcher Rebbe, Rabbi Menachem Mendel Schneerson, regarding Rabbi Steinsaltz's unique commentary on the *Tanya*, dated 21 Av 5721 (August 3, 1961):

(ושאלות ותשובות – כהמצורף למכתבו) בעניינים המובאים בתניא, כן ביאור קצר או גם ארוך, ובסגנונו, ערוכים בלשון בני דורנו...

בברכה לבשו"ט

In December 2012, the final volume of the Hebrew edition of *The Steinsaltz Tanya* was published. That year, at a hasidic gathering, Rabbi Adin Steinsaltz shared why he wrote the book. He explained that Rabbi Shneur Zalman of Liadi, the author of the *Tanya*, had poured his entire soul, his love and awe, his soul-wrenching oneness with God into that concise book, into pages that obscured his immense spirit so well. Through his commentary, Rabbi Steinsaltz strove to reveal to us this spirit, that powerful fire just barely contained by the words of the *Tanya*.

And he certainly succeeded. Yet he failed to mask his own burning spirit, his own love, awe, and closeness to God, as he had attempted to do his entire life.

The publication of this English edition of *The Steinsaltz Tanya* is the fulfillment of Rabbi Steinsaltz's vision to make the teachings of the *Tanya* accessible to every single individual. At the height of the preparations for this edition, our teacher Rabbi Adin Even-Israel passed away.

In this book, one learns how the life of the tzaddik lives on in this world, in those who learn his works. It is through those students who are open to receiving his teachings and are inspired to build upon his words that his light remains with us. We pray that this commentary of Rabbi Steinsaltz will introduce many generations of Jews to the world of the *Tanya* and to the path of authentic devotion to God.

May it serve to elevate his soul.

Contents

For the Hebrew Tanya Vilna edition, open from the Hebrew side of the book.

Publisher's Preface

The insights and elucidations of this seminal commentary were adapted from weekly lectures on the *Tanya* that Rabbi Steinsaltz delivered to a small group of Jerusalemites from 1977 to 1980, as well as classes broadcast on the Israeli radio station Kol Yisrael. Those teachings were later transcribed, edited, and published as a commentary to the *Tanya* in Hebrew. The commentary was well received and has since been revised and reprinted.

This series, the Steinsaltz commentary on the *Tanya*, will ultimately consist of six volumes spanning the five sections that comprise the Tanya. The first section of the *Tanya*, *Likkutei Amarim* (A Compilation of Teachings), has been divided into two volumes. The third volume of the series contains two self-contained sections of the *Tanya*: *Sha'ar HaYiḥud VeHa'emuna* (The Gate of Unity and Faith) and *Iggeret HaTeshuva* (Letter on Repentance). The fourth and fifth sections of the *Tanya*, *Iggeret HaKodesh* (The Holy Epistle) and *Kuntres Aḥaron* (Last Tract), comprise volumes 4–6.

The Steinsaltz Tanya offers the original Hebrew *Tanya* text, an English translation of the *Tanya*, and a running commentary by Rabbi Steinsaltz. Care was taken that both the *Tanya* text and the commentary be true to the original, though it is important to bear in mind that the translation necessarily has to relinquish some of the pungency of the original discourses.

The Commentary

Rabbi Steinsaltz's commentary on the *Tanya* reverberates with authenticity, expressing the ideas and spirit of Jewish thought in a way that is simultaneously traditional and yet profoundly original. His style passes freely from one topic to another and then returns to the original idea without belaboring it. He also employs a wide variety of modes of explanation, including philosophical logic, textual exegesis, and scientific illustration, as well as symbolism, story, and parable.

This is not a commentary that aims for the comfort of being spoon-fed the simple explanation of each line. Instead, one gains an appreciation of the profundity and brilliance of the *Tanya,* as well as the penetrating insights and genuine perspective that Rabbi Steinsaltz lends to it.

The commentary is comprised of two sections. The main body is a running elucidation of the *Tanya* text, one segment at a time. As a supplement, we have included a companion section of additional insights, which can be found in the gray boxes that run across the bottom of the pages. This supplemental material provides a broader context and a deeper look at the concepts presented in the main body of the commentary. Here the reader will find hasidic teachings, tangents from other disciplines, such as physics and mathematics, and analogies and hasidic stories.

At the end of each section there is an outline that summarizes the flow of ideas throughout the chapters.

The Hebrew *Tanya* Text

This volume presents the original Hebrew text of the *Tanya* in two formats. In accordance with the Chabad hasidic tradition, and by specific directive from the Lubavitcher Rebbe to the author, we have included the Hebrew text as it was printed in the Vilna edition in 1900, without vocalization or punctuation. This unembellished *Tanya* text, which can be found at the end of this book, connects and anchors the modern commentary with the authentic chain of hasidic teachings, originating with the author of the *Tanya* himself. In addition, it furnishes the reader the opportunity to reflect on the text as one uninterrupted unit, affording a person a broad perspective on the flow of ideas.

Second, to make the *Tanya* text more accessible to the contemporary reader, a vocalized and punctuated version of the Hebrew text is provided. This text is presented alongside the English translation of the *Tanya* and is divided into phrases according to the content of the commentary. This version also furnishes sources for citations, and abbreviations and acronyms have been expanded.

Both versions of the *Tanya* text contain the *Moreh Shiur*, the annual calendar for daily study of the *Tanya*.

The English *Tanya* Text

One of the major contributions of this work is a groundbreaking English translation of the Hebrew *Tanya* text. The *Tanya* is a classic, canonic work, and its author invested deep meaning into the minutiae of its language and style. The outcome is an esoteric and dense text, which presents a formidable challenge when rendering the *Tanya* into contemporary English.

This rendition, in the tradition of previous classic Steinsaltz translations, combines rigorous fidelity to the nuances of the original text along with clear and contemporary English translation. Careful effort was invested to represent each word of the original Hebrew in the translation using bold font, while interlacing words in nonbold to clarify the meaning and flow of the text.

Certain expressions in the original, common to the style of rabbinic Hebrew, would have obscured the clarity of the English rendition. Such words, such as *beḥinat, yitbarakh, barukh hu,* and *hineh,* are not always rendered into English or represented in a different form. For example, *yitbarakh,* used as a term of reverence referring to God, has been rendered most often as "God's." Thus, instead of rendering עצמותו יתברך as "His essence, may He be blessed," the phrase was rendered as "God's essence."

In addition, although the original text was written as a flowing discourse with no punctuation, we have composed the English translation according to conventional syntax, inserting transitions in non-bold where necessary.

The English translations of verses and passages from the *Tanakh* and Talmud cited in this work were taken from *The Steinsaltz Tanakh* and *The Koren Talmud Bavli*, the Steinsaltz English edition of the Talmud. In several instances, context dictated minor variations to those translations.

The English *Tanya* text is presented in segments that serve as headings for each passage of commentary. The division of the text follows the content of the commentary. Therefore, each segment does not necessarily constitute a single self-contained thought. The reader may find it worthwhile to first read several English segments of *Tanya* at a time, skipping over the commentary, to digest the overall idea of the *Tanya* and then return to each segment to delve into the commentary itself.

Naturally, all these features – the translation, the punctuation, and the sources – are a reflection of Rabbi Steinsaltz's interpretation of the *Tanya*.

A Note on Gender

For the sake of convenience, this book was written using male pronouns to refer to individuals and not because it is a book for men only, which it is not. Neutral language was used wherever possible when it did not interfere with the accuracy or clarity of the content.

Acknowledgments

This commentary comprises an "oral Torah" that emerged from a series of weekly classes in Chabad Hasidism and, in a different fashion, from *Tanya* classes broadcast over *Kol Yisrael,* the Israeli State radio station. The participants in these *Tanya* classes added so much – through their questions, their comments, and even their very listening. For all the many ways they have enriched me and my classes, I am deeply grateful.

A project of this magnitude could not have been realized without the support of Debra and David Magerman. Thank you for your generous contribution to this edition of the *Tanya.*

I reserve a special thanks for my friend Rabbi Meir Hanegbi, the adapter and editor of this material. With immense dedication and extreme effort, he took all of this oral material and turned it into a book, adding many comments, explanations, source references, and an extensive bibliography. Due to his efforts, its end is certainly better than its beginning.

He merited to learn in order to teach, and to teach in order to actualize – and for this, may he be blessed with continued fortitude.

Rabbi Adin Even-Israel Steinsaltz

Introduction

The author of the *Tanya*, Rabbi Shneur Zalman of Liadi, was among the greatest Jewish personalities of his time: great in Torah, both in its exoteric or revealed aspect (that is, Talmud and *halakha*) and in its esoteric dimension. He was also learned in secular knowledge, a virtuoso of the Hebrew language, a master writer and editor, a born leader, and superb administrator, an ecstatic mystic, and a composer of music. In each of his creative fields, he wrote books of permanent value that have become classic works of hasidic thought, particularly Chabad Hasidism, for all generations.

Rabbi Shneur Zalman was born on 18 Elul 5505 (1745) in the town of Liozna in White Russia (now Belarus). His father was Rabbi Barukh, a descendant of the famed Maharal, Rabbi Loewe of Prague.

From his early childhood, Rabbi Shneur Zalman's genius and prodigious Torah knowledge were widely recognized. A few years after his marriage in 1760, he decided to study Torah at one of the great Torah centers. The two centers he considered were Vilna, home to the famed Gaon of Vilna, and Mezeritch, where the great Maggid, Rabbi Dov Ber, successor to the Ba'al Shem Tov (founder of the hasidic movement), taught. Feeling that he knew a little about how to study Torah but virtually nothing about how to pray, he decided to go to Mezeritch.

Rabbi Shneur Zalman arrived in Mezeritch in 1764. Despite his student's youth, the Maggid soon counted him among his inner circle of disciples. The Maggid greatly appreciated his talents and Torah knowledge, giving the young man the task of compiling a new and updated *Shulḥan Arukh*, the Code of Jewish Law. Rabbi Shneur Zalman labored at this task for many years, but tragically most of the work was destroyed by fire. Only a part of it – most of *Oraḥ Ḥayyim* and a few chapters from the other three sections – survived and was published after his death. The book, which is not a specifically hasidic work, is known as *Shulḥan Arukh HaRav*. It is a halakhic masterpiece, adapting and condensing the gist of Torah law up to that time, and it serves as the basic halakhic source for hasidim in general and Chabad hasidim in particular. Were it not for the violent opposition to Hasidism that prevailed at the time, it would doubtless have earned a more central position in halakhic literature.

In 1767, Rabbi Shneur Zalman was appointed Maggid in his hometown of Liozna, and beginning in 1772, highly talented young men began to come to him for instruction in Torah and the service of God. Rabbi Shneur Zalman arranged these disciples in three *chadarim* ("rooms" or classes), instructing each according to his level. According to Chabad tradition, this is when Rabbi Shneur Zalman began to consolidate his unique Chabad philosophy and approach, and it is thus considered the founding year of Chabad Hasidism.

In 1774, following the death of the Maggid, the hasidic community accepted the central leadership of Rabbi Menaḥem Mendel of Vitebsk. But in 1777, under the pressure of persecution and excommunication by the opponents of Hasidism, which were directed mainly against the hasidim of White Russia, Rabbi Menaḥem Mendel and a large group of hasidim emigrated to the Land of Israel. Rabbi Shneur Zalman, who was initially in the group, was persuaded to return home and he became one of the leaders of the hasidic community in White Russia, together with Rabbi Yisrael of Plotsk and Rabbi Yissachar Dov of Lubavitch. In 1788, Rabbi Menaḥem Mendel, in a letter from the Land of Israel, appointed Rabbi Shneur Zalman as the sole leader of the hasidim in this region.

This was merely a confirmation of the de facto state of affairs, because Rabbi Shneur Zalman's comprehensive educational endeavors, both written and oral, and his impressive success in many public debates with Hasidism's opponents (including the famous disputation in Minsk in 1783) had made him the most important hasidic leader in White Russia. Moreover, by this time his teachings had also consolidated into a unique system within Hasidism, the system of "Chabad" (an acronym for *ḥokhma, bina, da'at* – wisdom, understanding, knowledge).

Rabbi Shneur Zalman's influence continued to grow. Copies of his writings on hasidic teachings circulated widely, and his published works, initially published anonymously, added considerably to the spread of the Chabad approach and to the author's reputation. If his *Hilkhot Talmud Torah* ("Laws of Torah Study," published anonymously in 1794) demonstrated his knowledge of *halakha* and of Torah in general, his *Tanya* (published in 1797) was a lucid and systematic articulation of the fundamentals of hasidic thought.

His influence spread not only throughout White Russia but increasingly also in Lithuania and even in Vilna itself, to the extent that several community leaders in this bastion of opposition to Hasidism were among his followers. This aroused the wrath of the *mitnagdim*, the opponents of Hasidism. They realized that their old recourse of excommunication would be ineffective, so they availed themselves of their last remaining weapon: informing against Rabbi Shneur Zalman to the Russian government, which had recently annexed White Russia and Poland. The chief rabbi of Pinsk brought a formal complaint to the Russian authorities, accusing a number of hasidic leaders, and in particular Rabbi Shneur Zalman, of various offenses, both religious and political: sending money to the sultan of Turkey (actually funds raised for the support of the hasidic community in the Holy Land, then under Turkish rule) and the creation of a new religious sect, which Russian law strictly forbade.

In 1798, as a result of these accusations, Rabbi Shneur Zalman was arrested and brought as a criminal offender to St. Petersburg. After a secret trial, whose details only fully came to light in recent years, he was exonerated of all charges and released from prison on the nineteenth of Kislev of that year. This day came to symbolize the public victory of Hasidism over its opponents and was established, in the lifetime of Rabbi Shneur Zalman, as a festival of redemption.

That day came to represent a watershed in the development of Hasidism: From that point, it grew stronger, accelerated its spread, and gained tens of thousands of new followers. Hasidim viewed the Russian authorities' verdict as, in its inner essence, the supernal verdict. The earthly court's decision to free Rabbi Shneur Zalman merely echoed the decision of the heavenly court, expressing the supernal vindication of Hasidism. Thus, Chabad Hasidim celebrate the nineteenth of Kislev as the New Year's Day for Hasidism to this day.

The nineteenth of Kislev also marks a new period in Rabbi Shneur Zalman's teachings and works. Before St. Petersburg, Rabbi Shneur Zalman did not convey his esoteric teachings openly and clearly, leaving much to allusion. After St. Petersburg, the trickling wellspring became the great river of Chabad Hasidism, because Rabbi Shneur Zalman then felt that there was no longer any divine impediment to the teaching of Hasidism, and the time had come to elaborate on it and disseminate it without inhibition.

Following further slanderous accusations, Rabbi Shneur Zalman was summoned to a second interrogation in St. Petersburg in 1800, and after a lengthy imprisonment, though under much easier conditions, he was finally released by command of the new czar, Alexander I. On his return from prison, he moved to the town of Liadi and thus came to be known as Rabbi Shneur Zalman of Liadi.

After Rabbi Shneur Zalman had largely overcome the opposition to Hasidism from without, a bitter dispute broke out within the hasidic community, mainly over the intellectual nature of the Chabad system. The leader of the dispute was Rabbi Avraham of Kalisk, a disciple of Rabbi Menaḥem Mendel of Vitebsk, who was later joined by Rabbi Barukh of Medzibozh, the Ba'al Shem Tov's grandson. This dispute caused Rabbi Shneur Zalman deep sorrow, but it did not affect his standing. Instead, it actually highlighted the uniqueness of his personality and his philosophy.

When Napoleon invaded Russia in 1812, Rabbi Shneur Zalman was among the fiercest opponents of the French conquest. He feared that French rule would grant emancipation to the Jews and accelerate assimilation, and he therefore supported Russia with all his power. As the French army advanced, he was forced to flee behind the Russian army to the interior of the country. He fell ill on the journey, and on 24 Tevet 5573 (1812), he died in the remote village of Piena. He was buried in the nearby town of Haditz.

The *Tanya*

Rabbi Shneur Zalman left behind a great legacy that formed the underpinnings of Hasidism, and particularly Chabad Hasidism: his halakhic masterwork *Shulḥan Arukh HaRav* on one hand and his mystical work of ethics, the *Tanya,* on the other. If it is at all possible to define a work such as the *Tanya,* then its best description lies in the words of the sixth Lubavitcher Rebbe, Rabbi Yosef Yitzḥak of Lubavitch, who said, "*Tanya* is the 'Written Torah' of hasidim, and studying it is like studying *Ḥumash*: Everyone studies it, from the greatest scholars to the most simple of folk; each, according to his level, understands what he understands, and no one understands it at all."

At first glance, the *Tanya* seems to affect the style of an ordinary book of *mussar,* practical advice intended to direct people in the path of God's service and of self-perfection. In truth, it takes an original approach to the fundamental elements of self-improvement, applying the principles of Hasidism to reveal the root causes of human failings and to devise comprehensive solutions. The *Tanya* seeks to demonstrate to every man or woman that knowledge of God is there for the taking, that spiritual growth to ever higher levels is real and immanent, if one is willing to engage in the struggle.

The *Tanya* is not only one of the fundamental works of Hasidism, but it is also one of the greatest books of moral teaching of all time. Although the author of the *Tanya* modestly describes himself as a "compiler," this is a most original work, both in its basic premise as well as in the many ideas and insights it expresses parenthetically. And though the author repeatedly notes that the book is intended for a select audience, for "those who know me personally," it strives to solve the dilemmas with a most broad and comprehensive approach – an approach that is not specific to a particular person, time, or outlook. The *Tanya* does not, in the main, address specific problems but delves into their root causes, seeking to distill the predicaments of humankind down to their most elementary maxims and to solve them in the most comprehensive way.

But these points, despite their centrality to the work, do not summarize the *Tanya.* This is a book in which the incidental ideas, as well as the supporting chapters surrounding the central theme, are no less important than the main topics. The more one studies this book, the more one discovers illuminating thoughts and ideas, a comprehensive outlook on life, insight into the structure of Jewish history, and moral guidance on countless issues. This short book encapsulates an entire philosophy and guide to life. As Rabbi Levi Yitzḥak of Berditchev expressed it, "How did he put such a great and awesome God into such a small book?"

לִקּוּטֵי אֲמָרִים

Likkutei Amarim

A Compilation of Teachings

Preface to *Likkutei Amarim*

There are very few passages in this work that inspire spiritual excitement or an immediate feeling of transcendence. The ideas are intentionally presented in a deceivingly simple way. One does not experience sudden flashes of inspiration, prompting him to exclaim, "Beautiful! Incredible!" One who studies the *Tanya* discovers the beauty of it only by deepening his understanding through repeated review. Only through sincere effort will one crack through the understated style to reveal the profound content and depth of emotion concealed therein.

Upon a second perusal, one uncovers more than he did in his first reading, and upon his third reading, more than the second. The power and beauty of the *Tanya* lies beneath the surface of a writing style that resembles that of Rambam: simple, with minimal usage of technical terms, limited only to instances that demand it, yet it is infused with a depth and intensity that waxes and wanes. One will not find lofty and effusive expressions overflowing with emotion, not because that emotion does not exist, but rather because the author of the *Tanya* restrains his fervor, allowing only a hint of it to emerge.

The *Tanya* is built, to a large degree, in a format that invites a person to put the ideas and messages it contains into practice. Only after applying the ideas found here can a person internalize them and integrate them into the very fabric of his soul. Then, upon further study, he will reap layers of added meaning the more he learns. As the Sages put it, "As for the rest, go and learn it."

The author of the *Tanya* would say that he worked very hard, not just to convey the meaning of the ideas, but also to fine-tune their precise wording. It is said that he sat and analyzed every single letter, considering whether to add or delete the conjunctive *vav*, whether or not to insert a comma. This precision is not necessarily apparent in the structure of the wording, but it demands of the reader a deeper analysis.

Due to the degree to which the ideas herein are condensed and packed with meaning, one who studies the *Tanya* will grapple with the subtleties of the wording and ponder both that which is said and that which is not said. The one who studies the *Tanya* in this way cannot help but develop an appreciation for the beautifully crafted, classic writing style that demands serious application before it will unveil its hidden dimensions to the reader.

Most *mussar* works focus on clarifying particular issues and the ways in which a person can achieve specific goals in specific areas. The advantage in such an individualized approach is that it deals with the specific questions that a person might ask himself, and the answers supplied are likewise specific and definitive. On the other hand, the book is limited to the specific problems it raises and is of actual help only to certain individuals. Others might be impressed by the book's profundity, yet they will always feel that it does not speak to them. It fails to answer their problems or take into account their specific personalities and circumstances.

The *Tanya,* by contrast, does not address specific problems but delves into their root causes, seeking to distill the predicaments of humankind down to their most elementary maxims and solve them in the most comprehensive way. The crux of the book is an in-depth summation of the workings of the inner soul and an analysis of good and evil as fundamental forces at play in the soul and the primary sources of its dissonance.

Although written with great restraint, the *Tanya* – and particularly its first section, *Likkutei Amarim* – energetically and dramatically depicts human life as an immense battle between good and evil that one endures throughout one's lifetime, a battle between the forces that drag the soul down and the forces that strive heavenward. In describing this battle, the author of the *Tanya* offers a completely new approach. The battle in a person's soul is actually not between good and evil, expressions the author rarely uses, except when he needs to clarify a point by using the ordinary semantics of these terms, but between the two elements within the human soul: the divine soul and the animal soul.

The divine soul is the part of a person that aspires to the Divine, in all its connotations. The animal soul is the part that relates to a person's physical identity and his involvement in the material world. These are not merely alternative terms for "good" and "evil" or for "body" and "soul." They draw a far subtler distinction. The animal soul is not negative in essence, nor is it necessarily hedonistic. It can become refined and wise and achieve much in the life of the spirit yet remain animal.

The animal soul is the soul of a human being as a biological creature, as a specific level of development in the zoological system. Even in this sense, humans are superior to other creations in their ability to attain great heights in the realms of thought and feeling, yet still they could remain an animal among animals – if not for the other side to the human being. It is in the divine soul, in its aspiration to the Divine, that man's uniqueness lies. The divine soul yearns to cleave to the Divine and be subsumed by it, and only by this aspiration, by the constant struggle of the divine soul to transcend its own desires, even its very self, in order to attain identification with the divine light, does one achieve a true identity as a human being.

This is the inner struggle of the human soul, between the desires of the animal soul and the yearnings of the divine soul. Yet this is not a war to the death, in which a person tries to destroy and obliterate a part of the self. Since the animal soul is not fundamentally evil, the battle against it is essentially a battle of education. A person's task is to train the animal soul, to elevate it to a higher level of awareness and understanding, until it is unified, both in its objectives and in its aspirations, with the divine soul. In this way, one achieves full harmony of body and soul, of earthliness and transcendence.

The perpetual battle in the human soul, which stems from its dual nature, also has moral and pragmatic implications. The teachers of *mussar* have always recognized the almost vital need for a person to achieve total inner identification with his deeds and actions. The assumption is that a purely mechanical act has a low moral and spiritual value. Yet few individuals are capable of truly attaining such an inner identification. This leaves to most the choice of either giving up the spiritual struggle or descending to hypocrisy and self-delusion. The author of the *Tanya*, by delving into the nature of the relationship between a person's two souls, finds an approach that is very different, even revolutionary. It readily acknowledges that not everyone is able to achieve complete victory for the divine soul over the animal – but not everyone is required to do so.

A state of war within the human soul, says the author of the *Tanya*, is not a negative thing. A person might achieve perfection with respect to his deeds, his speech, and even his thoughts without achieving complete perfection within the inner recesses of the soul. The author requires a person to achieve perfection in these "garments" of the soul, in his thoughts, speech, and actions, but not at his soul's essence.

Thus, the author of the *Tanya* removes the veil of hypocrisy that has cloaked many a soul as a result of the demand to be elevated beyond one's capacity. The recognition of the intrinsic duality of the soul enables a person to understand that his moral imperfection need in no way impede his aspiration and ability to fulfill his divinely ordained role. Once a person knows that his undesirable lusts and thoughts emanate from a fundamental source within himself that might not be within his power and duty to uproot, its presence within is not tragic, nor will it necessarily bring about an unsolvable inner crisis. On the contrary, a person can achieve perfection precisely through this knowledge. One can be righteous in all the particulars of his life and at the same time be engaged in the constant struggle within his soul.

The *Tanya* assigns to this spiritual person a new moral status, that of the *beinoni*, an intermediate level that renders a person neither righteous nor wicked in the strictest sense.

The *beinoni* is the hero of this book: It addresses him, discusses him, and carries his name (one of the titles the author gave the *Tanya* is *Sefer shel Beinonim*, "Book of *Beinonim*"). The *beinoni* is described in this work as "one who serves God," whose entire life is a perpetual battle for the sake of the Divine, whose inner struggle is a hymn of praise to his Creator. The concept of the *beinoni* as an ideal to which every person should aspire. It opens the door to everyone, regardless of spiritual status, to be counted among those who aspire to true greatness – those who serve God in truth.

The Title Page

THE STUDY OF THE *TANYA* CUSTOMARILY BEGINS HERE, from the book's title page, because the author of the *Tanya* wrote it himself (though he calls himself the "compiler") and because it perfectly characterizes the essence of the book.

סֵפֶר לִקּוּטֵי אֲמָרִים ***Sefer Likkutei Amarim*** 19 Kislev

חֵלֶק רִאשׁוֹן **Part 1**

Traditionally, the *Tanya* by Rabbi Shneur Zalman of Liadi consists of five parts. The first section is called *Likkutei Amarim*, "A Compilation of Teachings," or *Sefer shel Beinonim*, "The Book of *Beinonim*," as delineated in the text of the title page below. Yet still in the author's time, it became known simply as the *Tanya*, after the word that begins the book.[1]

This section, *Likkutei Amarim*, which was published first, is the most central part of the book. Consisting of fifty-three chapters, it is the most complete section. According to Chabad tradition, the fifty-three chapters of *Likkutei Amarim*, along with the introduction, correspond to the fifty-four *parashot* in the Torah, supporting the claim that the *Tanya* is indeed the "Written Torah of Hasidism." ☞

הַנִּקְרָא בְּשֵׁם סֵפֶר שֶׁל בֵּינוֹנִים **entitled *Sefer shel Beinonim***

THE SECTIONS OF THE TANYA

☞ The second section of the *Tanya*, *Sha'ar HaYiḥud VeHa'emuna*, also called *Ḥinukh Katan*, "Education of a Child," was originally meant to be equal in length to

1. See chap. 1 below.

This title, provided by the author of the *Tanya,* expresses the uniqueness of the book. The establishment of the concept of the *beinoni,* the intermediate-level individual, is undoubtedly its novel axis. While the idea of the *beinoni* is not new, the author of the *Tanya* gives the term an additional meaning that differs from the foundational position of most approaches in *mussar* (moral and ethical conduct).

The ideal personality portrayed in *mussar* works is that of the tzaddik, the righteous person, which is presented as an attainable goal. This book, on the other hand, was written for *beinonim,* for those who are neither tzaddik nor *rasha,* neither righteous nor wicked. The *Tanya,* then, relinquishes that ideal image, postulating that such a goal is in fact unattainable for most people and is not expected of them. Instead, the *beinoni* is presented as the ideal that every person can and must attain. ☞

מְלוּקָט מִפִּי סְפָרִים וּמִפִּי סוֹפְרִים קְדוֹשֵׁי עֶלְיוֹן נִשְׁמָתָם עֵדֶן,

Compiled from the works and teachings of the **holy masters, whose souls are in** the Garden of **Eden,**

As was the practice of other authors who conducted themselves with modesty, the author of the *Tanya* does not state that he wrote this book but merely compiled it. Nevertheless, without a doubt, the *Tanya* is obviously not a compilation. Though he certainly has sources for every idea he presents, the author offers an original perspective and line of thinking, with very few quotations from other places. Those few that

the first part, comprising fifty-three chapters, but for various reasons the author of the *Tanya* did not complete it. Consisting of twelve chapters, *Sha'ar HaYiḥud VeHa'emuna* deals primarily with divine providence, a doctrine that teaches that God is within the world and that isolating even one aspect of the universe from the Divine, no matter how small, fundamentally negates the entire paradigm of God's existence.

The third part, *Iggeret HaTeshuva,* "Letter on Repentance," deals entirely with the topic of repentance. It too is not complete, consisting, like *Sha'ar HaYiḥud VeHa'emuna,* of twelve chapters.

The fourth part, *Iggeret HaKodesh,* "The Holy Epistle," consists of a collection of letters. Most were not printed in their entirety in the book; only those parts that bear relevance to hasidim in general were included.

The fifth part, *Kuntres Aḥaron,* "Last Treatise," consists of a series of essays and supplements to topics addressed in the previous sections.

he does cite are presented in a novel way, adding an angle and approach that is uniquely his.

It is commonly accepted that the "works" mentioned here, besides the basic canonical texts (the *Tanakh*, Talmud, *Zohar*, *Shulḥan Arukh*, and writings of the Arizal), refer to the works of the Maharal of Prague, the author's direct paternal ancestor by seven generations, *Shenei Luḥot HaBerit* by Rabbi Yeshaya HaLevi Horowitz, and *Reshit Ḥokhma* by Rabbi Eliyahu de Vidas.

The "masters" refer primarily to the author's rabbis and mentors: the Maggid of Mezeritch, Rabbi Shneur Zalman's foremost mentor; Rabbi Menaḥem Mendel of Vitebsk, the Maggid's disciple and successor; and the Maggid's son, Rabbi Avraham, famously known as Rabbi Avraham HaMalakh (Rabbi Avraham the Angel), who was both a peer and

THE *BEINONI*

☞ The concept of the *beinoni* acquires unique significance here. He is not just an average person, someone who is not totally righteous yet not entirely evil. His level is not simply one of compromise or a blend of good and wicked. Rather, it is a unique quality in and of itself.

All the works of *mussar* that discuss the *beinoni* see it as a temporary stage that one needs to move beyond, a phase of spiritual entanglement that will stabilize in time. Yet this book defines the essence of the *beinoni* as perpetual: Every day of his life a person engages in the spiritual struggle for his self-actualization on the journey toward holiness, never reaching the final resolution of his soul's challenges. The *beinoni* transcends the level of average men and even seems like a complete tzaddik relative to others, yet within he fights a constant battle, enduring the perpetual pain of imperfection.

Although the *beinoni* has not reached the level of tzaddik because he cannot attain a constant state of holiness and control over his evil inclination, he certainly merits authentic closeness with God. When he achieves that union, that is his ultimate truth, his authentic reality. And if he falls from that level of closeness, that too is his ultimate truth.

In contrast to the tzaddik, who maintains an equilibrium, a constant state of holiness, the *beinoni* finds himself perpetually off balance. In a certain sense, the overall goal of the *Tanya* is to show the *beinoni* how to maintain his equilibrium, how to remain on the level where he must still grapple with his evil inclination and restrain himself from sinning in action, speech, and thought.

This characterization of the *beinoni* occupies the central focus of the entire book and the theological infrastructure that is built on it. It is the central cornerstone from which the book emerges and to which it returns. This does not mean it is an easier book to understand, but this work undoubtedly differs drastically from other works of *mussar* by portraying attainable, practical goals.

disciple of the author. It is told that the Maggid instructed the two to make a trade: Rabbi Shneur Zalman would teach Rabbi Avraham Talmud and *halakha* for two hours every day in exchange for receiving two hours of tutelage in the wisdom of Kabbala.[2] Due to his unique relationship with the "Angel," Rabbi Shneur Zalman felt that he had a deep, loving connection – almost familial – with Rabbi Avraham's father, the great Maggid. He used to say that he attained the inner dimension of the Torah of Hasidism from the Maggid and his son, meaning that he received it from the Maggid like a son from his father.

Some count the Ba'al Shem Tov among the masters mentioned here. Although Rabbi Shneur Zalman did not learn from him in person, he considered him his spiritual grandfather and felt as if he had learned Torah from him, not through the intermediary of *sefarim*, books, but directly, as if the Ba'al Shem Tov was one of his *sofrim*, masters, and teachers.

מְיוּסָּד עַל פָּסוּק: "כִּי קָרוֹב אֵלֶיךָ הַדָּבָר מְאוֹד בְּפִיךָ וּבִלְבָבְךָ לַעֲשׂוֹתוֹ" (דברים ל, יד),

based on the verse "Rather, the matter is very near to you, in your mouth and in your heart, to perform it" (Deut. 30:14),

This verse serves as the premise for the entire book. Far more than a decorative catch phrase, it is the central motif woven throughout the work, from page to page, from one chapter to the next.

This verse expresses two essential ideas. First, that which is incumbent on man is attainable, and second, that "the matter is very near to you, in your mouth and in your heart." The key message of the book lies in its optimism, in the premise that man can not only practice the methods described therein but can even draw close to God in the process and transform himself, through his words and thoughts, evoking emotions and experiences that allow him to blaze a new spiritual path.

לְבָאֵר הֵיטֵב אֵיךְ הוּא קָרוֹב מְאֹד,

to thoroughly clarify how this matter **is** indeed **very near,**

2. See *Beit Rebbe*, vol. 1, chap. 2; *Sefer HaMa'amarim* 5708, p. 177.

The author of the *Tanya* will proceed to explain how the word of God, and God Himself, are truly very close to every individual. He will explore how it is possible to attain lofty spiritual levels and to elevate oneself so that one may cleave to the Divine through the particular avenue of divine service that he outlines in this book.

בְּדֶרֶךְ אֲרוּכָּה וּקְצָרָה, through a long yet **short path,**

These three words are perhaps the most condensed description of the author of the *Tanya*'s entire approach. They are borrowed from the famous story in the Talmud in which Rabbi Yehoshua ben Ḥananya said, "In all my days, no person ever defeated me except for a woman, a young boy, and a young girl."[3] He goes on to relate how he encountered a young boy at a crossroads and asked him how to get to the city. The boy answered, "This path is short yet long, and that path is long yet short." Rabbi Yehoshua chose the short, long path and found that though it was short it did not actually lead into the city. It led to the city's outskirts, to a place surrounded by gardens and orchards that blocked the trails leading to the city. He had to return and choose the long, short way.

The shorter yet longer path seems like a shortcut, but it is riddled with impediments and ultimately prevents passage. Conversely, the longer yet shorter way is more tiring and complicated, but ultimately it proves to be the safer path that leads to the desired destination. The path of divine service that the author of the *Tanya* presents here is the "long yet short path." ☞

בְּעֶזְרַת ה׳ יִתְבָּרַךְ. with the help of God

By using this common phrase, the author of the *Tanya* did not intend only that he would explain the ideas herein with God's help, but also

THE LONG YET SHORT PATH

☞ Theoretically, there are shorter pathways through which one can jump beyond the known boundaries of normalcy and quickly cover immense distances through spiritual shortcuts. The problem with these shortcuts is that they are unreliable. Some

3. *Eiruvin* 53b.

that the goals put forth in this work can be attained with God's help. Although the path that is delineated is long and demands serious effort and investment of time, one encounters God's help to assist him. Even this path does not consist solely of one's own toil and suffering from below, but offers glimmerings of hope from above and windows of divine assistance along the way.

harbor the highest conceivable level of danger. Some are totally theoretical and, for all intents and purposes, impassable.

A person seeking enlightenment may kindle the spiritual equivalent of a pile of straw in his eagerness for illumination. Though it ignites instantaneously, it is quickly extinguished and he remains as he was – on the same level, in the same place. The path presented by the author of the *Tanya* is the "long" way, a path that does not guarantee immediate spiritual heights.

This is not a path where one may leap from one level to the next, skipping from one idea to another. It is not a way through which an individual becomes catapulted from a simple person to one who is lofty. It is instead a path that demands serious work, practice, and training, with very few revelatory experiences. One must invest focused effort with his cognitive attributes, with his wisdom, understanding, and knowledge, in order to build an awareness and the proper emotional framework. This path works from the ground up, not relying on inspiration from above. It is considered long on the one hand, while short on the other, because at the end of the day it is a thoroughly dependable system with a solid base.

Though it is attainable and entirely possible to achieve, the shortest path is indeed the longer one, and one should be prepared to invest effort and time to achieve it.

Approbations

הַסְכָּמַת הָרַב הֶחָסִיד הַמְפוּרְסָם אִישׁ אֱלֹהִי קָדוֹשׁ יֵאָמֵר לוֹ מוֹרֵנוּ הָרַב רַבִּי מְשׁוּלָּם זוּסִיל מֵאָנִיפָּאלִי:

Approbation of the famous rabbi and hasid, a Godly man of saintly renown, our master and teacher Rabbi Meshulam Zusil of Anipoli:

הִנֵּה בִּרְאוֹתִי אֶת הַכְּתָבִים שֶׁל הָרַב הַאי גָּאוֹן אִישׁ אֱלֹקִים קָדוֹשׁ וְטָהוֹר אַסְפַּקְלַרְיָא הַמְּאִירָה וְטוֹב אֲשֶׁר עָשָׂה וַאֲשֶׁר הִפְלִיא ה׳ חַסְדּוֹ וְנָתַן בְּלִבּוֹ הַטָּהוֹר לַעֲשׂוֹת אֶת כָּל אֵלֶּה לְהַרְאוֹת עַם ה׳ דְּרָכָיו הַקְּדוֹשִׁים. וּרְצוֹנוֹ הָיָה שֶׁלֹּא לְהַעֲלוֹת אֶת הַכְּתָבִים הָהֵם לְבֵית הַדְּפוּס מֵחֲמַת שֶׁאֵין דַּרְכּוֹ בְּכָךְ. רַק מֵחֲמַת הִתְפַּשְּׁטוּת הַקּוּנְטְרֵסִים הָהֵם בְּקֶרֶב כָּל יִשְׂרָאֵל בְּהַעְתָּקוֹת רַבּוֹת מִידֵי סוֹפְרִים מְשׁוּנִּים וּמֵחֲמַת רִיבּוּי הַעְתָּקוֹת שׁוֹנוֹת רַבּוּ הַטָּעֻיּוֹת סוֹפֵר בִּמְאֹד. וְהוּכְרַח לְהָבִיא הַקּוּנְטְרֵסִים הָהֵם לְבֵית הַדְּפוּס.

I have seen the writings of this rabbi and luminary, a man of God, saintly and pure, a leading light, and I assert that **he has done well. God has been incredibly kind and has inspired his pure heart to do all this** and **to show God's people His holy ways.** The author initially **intended to not have these writings published, for it is not his way. But he** reconsidered his position **on account of the widespread dissemination of many copies of these pamphlets among the entire Jewish people by various scribes, and as a result of the copious errors among the many copies,** the author **was compelled to have these pamphlets printed.**

וְהֵעִיר ה׳ אֶת רוּחַ הַשּׁוּתָּפִים הַמְלֻמָּד הַמְכֻבָּד הָרַבָּנִי הַמּוּפְלָג

God has thus **inspired the** two business **partners – the outstanding, distinguished scholar, our teacher**

הַוָּתִיק מוֹרֵנוּ הָרַב רַבִּי שָׁלוֹם שֶׁכְנָא בֶּן מוֹרֵנוּ הָרַב רַבִּי נֹחַ וְהַמְלֻמָּד הַמְכֻבָּד הָרַבָּנִי הַמּוּפְלָג הַוָּתִיק מוֹרֵנוּ הָרַב רַבִּי מָרְדְּכַי בֶּן מוֹרֵנוּ הָרַב רַבִּי שְׁמוּאֵל הַלֵּוִי לְהָבִיא הַקּוּנְטְרֵסִים הָהֵם לְבֵית הַדְּפוּס בִּסְלָאוִויטָא וּלְפָעֳלָא טָבָא אָמַרְתִּי יִישַׁר חֵילָא אַךְ עָלוּ בִּלְבָבָם מָגוֹר מִסָּבִיב מִן הַדְּפוּסִים אֲשֶׁר רַבּוּ שֶׁדַּרְכָּן לְהַזִּיק וּלְקַלְקֵל הַמְאוּשָּׁרִים אִי לָזֹאת גָּמַרְנוּ בִּלְבֵּינוּ לִיתֵּן הַסְכָּמָה לְבַל יָרִים אִישׁ אֶת יָדוֹ וְאֶת רַגְלוֹ לִגְרוֹם לְהַמַּדְפִּיסִים הַנִּזְכָּר לְעֵיל שׁוּם הֵיזֵק חַס וְשָׁלוֹם בְּהַשָּׂגַת גְּבוּל בְּשׁוּם אוֹפֶן. וְאָסוּר לְשׁוּם אָדָם לִדְפּוֹס הַסֵּפֶר הַנִּזְכָּר לְעֵיל בִּלְתִּי יְדִיעַת הַמַּדְפִּיסִים הַנִּזְכָּרִים לְעֵיל עַד מֶשֶׁךְ חָמֵשׁ שָׁנִים רְצוּפִים מִיּוֹם דִּלְמַטָּה.

and master Rabbi Shalom Shakhna, son of our teacher and master Rabbi Noaḥ, and the outstanding, distinguished scholar, our teacher and master Rabbi Mordekhai, son of our teacher and master Rabbi Shmuel HaLevi – to publish these pamphlets in Slavita. I congratulate them on this good deed. Yet their hearts were filled with apprehension with regard to the printing houses that have proliferated, which tend to cause damage and ruin the reputable ones. In light of this, we have decided to grant our approval so that no one may make any move to cause the aforementioned printers even the slightest amount of damage, God forbid, by infringing upon their exclusive **rights in any manner. It is forbidden for anyone to print the aforementioned book without the consent of the aforementioned printers for a period of five consecutive years from the date** given **below.**

וְשׁוֹמֵעַ לִדְבָרַי אֵלֶּה יָבֹא עָלָיו בִּרְכַּת טוֹב. הַכֹּל דִּבְרֵי הַדּוֹרֵשׁ זֹאת לִכְבוֹד הַתּוֹרָה הַיּוֹם יוֹם ג׳ שֶׁנִּכְפַּל בּוֹ כִּי טוֹב פָּרָשַׁת תָּבֹא שְׁנַת פְּדוּתֵינוּ לִפְרָט קָטָן.

Those who adhere to these words of mine will be blessed with good. These are the words of one who demands this for the honor of the Torah today, Tuesday, which is doubly blessed **with good, of the** week in which ***Parashat Ki Tavo*** is read, in **the year 5556** (1796).

הַקָּטָן מְשׁוּלָּם זוּסִיל מֵאָנִיפָּאלִי

The lowly Meshulam Zusil of Anipoli

הַסְכָּמַת הָרַב הֶחָסִיד הַמְפוּרְסָם אִישׁ אֱלֹהִי קָדוֹשׁ יֵאָמֵר לוֹ מוֹרֵנוּ הָרַב רַבִּי יְהוּדָא לֵיבּ הַכֹּהֵן:

Approbation of the famous rabbi and hasid, a Godly man of saintly renown, our master and teacher Rabbi Yehuda Leib HaKohen:

חָכְמַת אָדָם תָּאִיר פְּנֵי הָאָרֶץ בִּרְאוֹתִי יְדֵי קֹדֶשׁ הַמְחַבֵּר הָרַב הַגָּאוֹן אִישׁ אֱלֹקִים קָדוֹשׁ וְטָהוֹר חָסִיד וְעָנָיו אֲשֶׁר מִכְּבָר נִגְלָה מִסְתָּרָיו יוֹשֵׁב בַּשֶּׁבֶת תַּחְכְּמוֹנִי אֵצֶל אֲדוֹנֵינוּ מוֹרֵינוּ וְרַבֵּינוּ גְּאוֹן עוֹלָם וְדָלָה מַיִם מִבְּאֵר מַיִם חַיִּים וְכָעֵת יִשְׂמַח יִשְׂרָאֵל בְּהִגָּלוֹת דִּבְרֵי קָדְשׁוֹ הַמְחוּבָּר לְהָבִיא לְבֵית הַדְּפוּס לְלַמֵּד לְעַם ה׳ דַּרְכֵי קֹדֶשׁ כַּאֲשֶׁר כָּל אֶחָד יֶחֱזֶה בִּפְנִימִיּוּת דְּבָרָיו וְהַמְפוּרְסָם אֵין צָרִיךְ רְאָיָה רַק מֵחֲשַׁשׁ קִלְקוּל הַדָּבָר שֶׁלֹּא יִגְרוֹם הֶיזֵּק לַמַּדְפִּיסִים בָּאתִי לִיתֵּן תּוֹקֶף וְאַזְהָרָה לְבַל יָרִים אִישׁ אֶת יָדוֹ וְרַגְלוֹ לִדְפּוֹס עַד מֶשֶׁךְ חָמֵשׁ שָׁנִים מִיּוֹם דִּלְמַטָּה.

A man's wisdom illuminates the face of the earth. This is evident **as I peruse the holy work of the author, the rabbi and luminary, a man of God, saintly and pure, pious and humble, whose hidden** greatness **was revealed long ago when he sat in the council of the wise, by our master, teacher, and rabbi, a luminary of the world,** the Maggid of Mezeritch, **and drew waters** of wisdom **from the wellspring. Now let the Jewish people rejoice as** the author's **holy words, which have been collated in preparation for printing, are to be revealed in order to teach the nation of God the ways of holiness, which each individual will see** for themselves **by studying the meaning inherent in** the author's **words.** This point need not be belabored, as **that which is obvious requires no proof, but it is only out of concern that something may go awry and cause harm to the printers that I** have written this approbation and **hereby demand and warn that no one should make any move to print** this book **for a period of five years from the date** given **below.**

וְשׁוֹמֵעַ לְדִבְרֵי אֵלֶּה יָבוֹא עָלָיו בִּרְכַּת טוֹב. הַכֹּל דִּבְרֵי הַמְדַבֵּר זֹאת לִכְבוֹד הַתּוֹרָה הַיּוֹם יוֹם ג׳ פָּרָשַׁת תָּבֹא תקנ״ו לִפְרָט קָטָן.

Those who adhere to these words of mine will be blessed with good. These are the words of one who speaks thus for the honor of the Torah, today, Tuesday, which is doubly blessed **with good, of the** week in which ***Parashat Ki Tavo*** is read, in **the year 5556** (1796).

יְהוּדָה לֵיב הַכֹּהֵן.

Yehuda Leib HaKohen

These two approbations, which are learned by many and are even included in the daily *Tanya* learning schedule instituted by the sixth Lubavitcher Rebbe, Rabbi Yosef Yitzḥak Schneerson, were written by two colleagues of the author of the *Tanya,* disciples of the Maggid of Mezeritch. Though they were not the most famous of the Maggid's students, the author of the *Tanya* asked these colleagues in particular to endorse his book.

20 Kislev (leap year)

הַסְכָּמַת הָרַבָּנִים שֶׁיִּחְיוּ בְּנֵי הַגָּאוֹן הַמְחַבֵּר זִכְרוֹנוֹ לִבְרָכָה נוּחוֹ עֵדֶן.

Approbation of the rabbis, may they live long, the **sons of the eminent author, of blessed memory, whose soul is in the Garden of Eden:**

הֱיוֹת שֶׁהוּסְכַּם אֶצְלֵינוּ לִיתֵּן רְשׁוּת וְהַרְמָנָא לְהַעֲלוֹת עַל מִכְבַּשׁ הַדְּפוּס לְזִכָּרוֹן לִבְנֵי יִשְׂרָאֵל כְּתוּב דִּבְרֵי יוֹשֶׁר וֶאֱמֶת דִּבְרֵי אֱלֹקִים חַיִּים שֶׁל אֲדוֹנֵנוּ אָבִינוּ מוֹרֵנוּ וְרַבֵּנוּ זִכְרוֹנוֹ לִבְרָכָה כְּתוּבִים בִּכְתַב יָדוֹ הַקְּדוֹשָׁה בְּעַצְמוֹ וּלְשׁוֹנוֹ הַקָּדוֹשׁ שֶׁכָּל דְּבָרָיו כְּגַחֲלֵי אֵשׁ בּוֹעֲרוֹת יַלְהִיבוּ הַלְּבָבוֹת לְקָרְבָן לַאֲבִיהֶן שֶׁבַּשָּׁמַיִם. וּבְשֵׁם אִגֶּרֶת הַקֹּדֶשׁ נִקְרְאוּ שֶׁרוּבָּם הָיוּ אִגֶּרֶת שָׁלוּחַ מֵאֵת כְּבוֹד

We have hereby agreed to grant permission and authorization, as a remembrance for the children of Israel, to publish these **words written with integrity and truth, words of the living God, by our master, father, teacher, and rabbi, of blessed memory, penned by his own holy hand and in his holy language, whose every word is like burning, fiery coals, igniting the hearts** of the Jewish people **to bring them close to their Father in Heaven. These** writings, which will be appended in this

קָדְשָׁתוֹ לְהוֹרוֹת לְעַם ה׳ הַדֶּרֶךְ יֵלְכוּ בָהּ וְהַמַּעֲשֶׂה אֲשֶׁר יַעֲשׂוּן.

printing to the first three sections of the *Tanya,* **are titled** ***Iggeret HaKodesh*** (The Holy Epistle), **since most of the letters** contained therein **were sent by his holy honor,** our father, **to instruct the nation of God regarding the proper path they should walk and the mode of conduct to which they should adhere.**

וּמֵחֲמַת שֶׁבְּכַמָּה מְקוֹמוֹת הִצִּיב לוֹ צִיּוּנִים בְּסֵפֶר לִקּוּטֵי אֲמָרִים שֶׁלּוֹ וְדִבְרֵי תוֹרָה עֲנִיִּים בְּמָקוֹם אֶחָד וַעֲשִׁירִים בְּמָקוֹם אַחֵר וּמַה גַּם בִּשְׁבִיל דָּבָר שֶׁנִּתְחַדֵּשׁ בּוֹ קוּנְטְרֵס אַחֲרוֹן עַל אֵיזֶה פְּרָקִים אֲשֶׁר כָּתַב בְּעֵת חִיבְּרוֹ הַסֵּפֶר לִקּוּטֵי אֲמָרִים פִּלְפּוּל וְעִיּוּן עָמוֹק עַל מַאַמְרֵי זֹהַר וְעֵץ חַיִּים וּפְרִי עֵץ חַיִּים שֶׁנִּרְאִים כְּסוֹתְרִים זֶה אֶת זֶה וּבְרוּחַ מְבִינָתוֹ מְיַשְּׁבָם כָּל דִּיבּוּר עַל אוֹפַנָּיו שֶׁכָּתַב בְּלִקּוּטֵי אֲמָרִים.

In several places in *Iggeret HaKodesh,* our father **referred to his book** ***Likkutei Amarim,*** **and since words of Torah are scarce in one place while plentiful in another,** complementary sources are necessary to gain a complete picture of the subject. **Moreover,** these writings **contain new material, a last treatise** known as *Kuntres Aḥaron* (Last Treatise), **on certain chapters, which he penned while writing the book** ***Likkutei Amarim.*** This last treatise represents **a profound analysis and inquiry pertaining to passages in the** ***Zohar, Etz Ḥayyim,*** **and Pri** ***Etz Ḥayyim*** **that seem contradictory. With his understanding spirit,** our father **reconciles each statement in its context, based on what he wrote in** ***Likkutei Amarim.***

רָאוֹ רָאִינוּ שֶׁרָאוּי וְנָכוֹן לְחַבְּרָם עִם סֵפֶר לִקּוּטֵי אֲמָרִים וְאִגֶּרֶת הַתְּשׁוּבָה שֶׁל כְּבוֹד קְדֻשַּׁת אֲדוֹנֵנוּ אָבִינוּ מוֹרֵנוּ וְרַבֵּנוּ זִכְרוֹנוֹ לִבְרָכָה.

We have therefore deemed it fit and proper to attach *Iggeret HaKodesh* and *Kuntres Aharon* as addendums **to** this **book,** ***Likkutei Amarim*** **and** ***Iggeret HaTeshuva,*** written **by his holy honor, our master, father, teacher, and rabbi, of blessed memory.**

אִי לָזֹאת בָּאנוּ לְהַטִּיל גּוּדָא רַבָּה וּגְזֵרַת נְחָ״שׁ דְּרַבָּנָן דְּלֵית לָהּ אַסְוָותָא שֶׁלֹּא יָרִים אִישׁ אֶת יָדוֹ לְהַדְפִּיס כְּתַבְנִיתָם אוֹ זֶה בְּלֹא זֶה מֶשֶׁךְ חֲמִשָּׁה שָׁנִים מִיּוֹם דִּלְמַטָּה.

In view of this, we hereby impose a prohibition and a decree of excommunication of rabbinic status, for which its violation **has no remedy: that no one may make a move to print** these writings **in their present form, or one without the other, for a period of five years from the date** given **below.**

בְּרַם כְּגוֹן דָּא צָרִיךְ לְאוֹדוֹעֵי שֶׁבַּעֲוֹנוֹתֵינוּ הָרַבִּים סָפוּ תַּמּוּ כִּתְבֵי יָדוֹ הַקְּדוֹשָׁה בְּעַצְמוֹ אֲשֶׁר הָיוּ בְּדִקְדּוּק גָּדוֹל לֹא חָסֵר וְלֹא יָתֵר אוֹת אַחַת וְלֹא נִשְׁאַר כִּי אִם זֶה הַמְעַט מֵהַרְבֵּה אֲשֶׁר נִלְקְטוּ אֶחָד לְאֶחָד מֵהַעְתָּקוֹת הַמְפוּזָּרִים אֵצֶל הַתַּלְמִידִים וְאִם הִמָּצֵא תִּמָּצֵא אֵיזֶה טָעוּת שְׁגִיאוֹת מִי יָבִין יִמָּצֵא הַטָּעוּת דְּמוּכָח מִטָּעוּת סוֹפֵר וְהַכַּוָּנָה תִּהְיֶה בְּרוּרָה:

However, this must be made known: Unfortunately, our father's **manuscripts,** written **by his own holy hand with great precision, without one extraneous or omitted letter, have been lost. There remain only but these few** writings **out of many, which were collected one by one from copies scattered among** our father's **disciples. In the event that any error whatsoever is found, as this is inevitable, the obvious mistake should be attributed to a scribal error, but the meaning will be clear.**

הַיּוֹם יוֹם ה׳ כ״ב אִיָּיר תקע״ד לִפְרָט קָטָן

Thursday, 22 Iyar 5574 (1814)

נְאוּם

Signed

דּוֹב בֶּער בֶּן אֲדוֹנִי אָבִי מוֹרֵנוּ וְרַבֵּנוּ הַגָּאוֹן הֶחָסִיד קְדוֹשׁ יִשְׂרָאֵל מָרָנָא וְרַבָּנָא שְׁנֵיאוֹר זַלְמָן זִכְרוֹנוֹ לִבְרָכָה נִשְׁמָתוֹ בְּגִנְזֵי מְרוֹמִים.

Dovber, son of my master, father, teacher, and rabbi, the eminent and pious saint of Israel, our master and teacher, Shneur Zalman, of blessed memory, whose soul is in the hidden chambers of Heaven.

Signed	**וְנְאוּם**
Ḥayyim Avraham, son of my master, father, teacher, and rabbi, our eminent and pious master and teacher, Shneur Zalman, may the memory of the righteous be blessed, whose soul is in the hidden chambers of Heaven.	**חַיִּים אַבְרָהָם בֶּן אֲדוֹנִי אָבִי מוֹרֵנוּ וְרַבֵּנוּ הַגָּאוֹן הֶחָסִיד מָרָנָא וְרַבָּנָא שְׁנֵיאוּר זַלְמָן זֵכֶר צַדִּיק לִבְרָכָה נִשְׁמָתוֹ בְּגִנְזֵי מְרוֹמִים.**
Signed	**וְנְאוּם**
Moshe, son of my master, father, teacher, and rabbi, the eminent and pious Shneur Zalman, of blessed memory, whose soul is in the hidden chambers of Heaven.	**מֹשֶׁה בֶּן אֲדוֹנִי אָבִי מוֹרֵנוּ וְרַבֵּנוּ הַגָּאוֹן הֶחָסִיד שְׁנֵיאוּר זַלְמָן זִכְרוֹנוֹ לִבְרָכָה נִשְׁמָתוֹ בְּגִנְזֵי מְרוֹמִים.**

The author of the *Tanya,* Rabbi Shneur Zalman of Liadi, is not mentioned by name in the approbations to the original edition, because initially the book was published anonymously so that he would not promote his own fame and also so that the work would be judged on its own merits. The author of the *Tanya* suspected that his involvement in the conflict between the hasidim and their opponents would prevent certain camps from reading it. If printed anonymously, all streams would be more open to learning it.

And so it was. Many who studied the early editions praised the book effusively without knowing the identity of its author.

Compiler's Introduction

THIS INTRODUCTION CONTAINS TWO PARTS. THE FIRST cautions against relying just on written works of *mussar* to improve one's service of God. This is why hasidim must travel to the Rebbe and not suffice with studying his written works to benefit from his teachings. The second part explains the reason why, despite this warning, the author of the *Tanya* wrote this type of book.

וְהִיא אִגֶּרֶת הַשְּׁלוּחָה לִכְלָלוּת אַנְשֵׁי שְׁלוֹמֵינוּ יִשְׁמְרֵם צוּרָם וְגוֹאֲלָם:

The following **is a letter sent to all the members of our community** of hasidim, may God, **their Rock and Redeemer, protect them:** 20 Kislev / 21 Kislev (leap year)

This introduction was taken from an open letter addressed to all hasidim, not just one specific community or person. But though the author of the *Tanya* is addressing a readership outside his immediate circle, he is certainly also directing these words inward, since this work provoked, to a certain degree, even his own hasidic colleagues. The complaint was not just against what they considered to be an overly rational approach, but against the very act of committing the ideas herein to writing in a formulaic way.

The hasidic movement thrived via the direct, personal relationship between Rebbe and hasid, and writing down any teachings seemed to breach this unique connection. The written word contains a lifeless element that is incapable of truly healing the ailments of the soul. Teaching prepared Torah, and furthermore, writing it down, was therefore considered an act of petrification.

In this vein, early hasidim interpreted the verse "And you shall inquire [*vedarashta*] diligently, and behold, it is true, the matter is correct, this abomination was performed in Israel" (Deut. 17:4) as saying: When the teaching [*derasha*] is good, even containing words of truth, but "the matter" was prepared in advance (the word *nakhon*, "correct," from the verse and *hakhana*, "preparation," share the same root), then "an abomination was performed in Israel."

Due to this dilemma, the Ba'al Shem Tov and the Maggid of Mezeritch, as well many other hasidic leaders in the earlier generations, avoided writing entirely. They felt that the written word did not serve as an effective medium for transmitting hasidic teachings from one soul to another. Writing may succeed in communicating other topics but not Hasidism.

This introduction comes to clarify that the author of the *Tanya* did not approach the writing of this book lightly. He had a clear awareness of the limitations and dangers entailed in constructing the concepts of hasidic *mussar* into one unified edifice. He even responds to some of these inherent obstacles throughout the work, as will be explained below. ☞

אֲלֵיכֶם אִישִׁים אֶקְרָא, שִׁמְעוּ אֵלַי רוֹדְפֵי צֶדֶק מְבַקְשֵׁי ה׳, וְיִשְׁמַע אֲלֵיכֶם אֱלֹקִים לְמִגָּדוֹל וְעַד קָטָן כָּל אַנְשֵׁי שְׁלוֹמֵנוּ דִּמְדִינָתֵינוּ וּסְמוּכוֹת שֶׁלָּהּ, אִישׁ עַל מְקוֹמוֹ יָבוֹא לְשָׁלוֹם וְחַיִּים עַד הָעוֹלָם נֶצַח סֶלָה וָעֶד, אָמֵן כֵּן יְהִי רָצוֹן.

To you, men, I call! Heed me, pursuers of righteousness, seekers of God, and may God listen to you, both great and small, all the members of our community of hasidim **in our country and in the surrounding regions. May each man in his place attain peace and eternal life! Amen, may this be** His **will.**

TRANSCRIBING HASIDIC TEACHINGS

☞ The story is told that the Ba'al Shem Tov saw a demon holding a book in a dream. The Ba'al Shem Tov asked, "What book are you holding?"

The demon answered, "This is the book that you authored."

The next day, the Ba'al Shem Tov gathered his disciples and demanded, "Who is writing Torah in my name?"

One of the students admitted that he had collected some of the Ba'al Shem Tov's teachings and written them down. The Ba'al Shem Tov asked him to show him the writings. He studied them and said, "I never said one word written here!"

As the author of the *Tanya* will clarify below, this book is geared toward particular people. Unsure of whether the book will be as impactful for those outside the demographic that he outlines, he addresses "all the members of our community [of hasidim] in our country and in the surrounding regions" – that is, the hasidim of White Russia and its environs, a group that, at this stage, was only vaguely identified as Chabad hasidim.

הִנֵּה מוּדַעַת זֹאת כִּי מַרְגְּלָא בְּפוּמֵי דְאִינְשֵׁי בְּכָל אַנְשֵׁי שְׁלוֹמֵנוּ לֵאמֹר כִּי אֵינָהּ דּוֹמָה שְׁמִיעַת דִּבְרֵי מוּסָר לִרְאִיָּה וּקְרִיאָה בִּסְפָרִים,

It is well known that throughout our community of hasidim **people are accustomed to saying that hearing words of moral guidance is not the same as seeing and reading** them **in books.**

This hasidic saying is a play on the talmudic statement "Hearing should not be greater than seeing" (*Rosh HaShana* 25b), conveying the opposite message from that of the Talmud. When it comes to awakening the heart to service of God, it is hearing that is superior to seeing – that is, to reading books. One should not suffice solely with studying the works of tzaddikim and leaders of past generations, but rather a person must journey to the living sage in his time to hear those words directly.

שֶׁהַקּוֹרֵא קוֹרֵא לְפִי דַּרְכּוֹ וְדַעְתּוֹ וּלְפִי הַשָּׂגַת וּתְפִיסַת שִׂכְלוֹ בַּאֲשֶׁר הוּא שָׁם.

For a reader reads a book **according to his inclination and mindset and in accordance with his intellect's ability to comprehend and grasp** the concepts therein **at that moment.**

No book, even the greatest and holiest among them, is capable of adapting itself to its reader. The reader himself determines how he reads and what he understands. As the author of the *Tanya* points out, every reader is limited by two essential restrictions.

First, he reads "according to his inclination and mindset." No person reads passively; he registers the subject matter according to his understanding and interpretation. What he gleans passes through the lens of his spiritual tendencies, mood, and status at the moment that he is reading the book. Two people, reading the same work, experience it uniquely. They may read the same line, yet they will be affected in totally different ways. Every person has his personal predisposition, outlook, and unique life experience, which can distort his understanding of what he sees. This conceptual and emotional distortion is impossible to ignore.

The second limitation confines the reader to "his intellect's ability to comprehend and grasp [the concepts therein]." Even if he aligns his soul with the true meaning of the words he is reading, he remains incapable of absorbing its message in the optimal way if he lacks the intellectual aptitude to comprehend it.

וְאִם שִׂכְלוֹ וְדַעְתּוֹ מְבוּלְבָּלִים, **If one's intellect or mind is confused,**

The inability to "comprehend and grasp [the concepts therein]" does not only indicate a lack of cognitive aptitude. A person can also be in a state of confusion. There are two aspects to this befuddlement: that of the intellect and that of the mind. A befuddled intellect entails confusion and distortion in one's ability to think clearly. A confused mind implies confused ideas, warped theories, and a distorted world outlook. This stems from a person's failure to understand himself. He does not know what he is seeking and therefore cannot determine which path to take.

וּבַחֲשֵׁיכָה יִתְהַלָּכוּ בַּעֲבוֹדַת ה׳, **and he proceeds in darkness in the service of God,**

Even a wise, educated, and otherwise sharp individual may be confused when it comes to matters of divine service because connection to God does not just demand intellectual understanding. It also touches on that which is the most transcendent and lofty while penetrating to the most subtle stirrings of the soul.

The risk of erring and deceiving oneself in these matters, which are so complex and nuanced, is high. The slightest distortion in one's soul or mind propels a person into total darkness. These matters demand significant work and immense divine assistance until they unleash even a glimmer of light.

בְּקוֹשִׁי יָכוֹל לִרְאוֹת אֶת הָאוֹר כִּי טוֹב הַגָּנוּז בַּסְּפָרִים, אַף כִּי מָתוֹק הָאוֹר לָעֵינַיִם וּמַרְפֵּא לַנֶּפֶשׁ.

it will be difficult to perceive the "light that was good" hidden within the books, though the light is sweet to the eyes and a remedy for the soul.

Although the *Tanya* contains few quotations, its liberal use of biblical phrases and adages of the Sages serves to make connections and to add additional layers of meaning. Here the author of the *Tanya* seamlessly weaves in the verse "God saw the light that it was good" (Gen. 1:4) and alludes to a statement of the Midrash that divulges that God hid away the light that He created during the six days of Creation – a light that He declares as "good" – for the righteous.[1] The Ba'al Shem Tov teaches that God hid this light within the Torah.[2] This implies that every holy book contains a powerful light, the light of Creation, the light of God, within its pages. But since one who studies a holy book sees its content through the lens of his understanding and awareness, he himself may occlude his perception of that delightful, divine light.

No matter how objectively sacred a topic, committing it to writing makes it susceptible to the whims of the reader, who may warp its message in one way or another. As a result, he may not be moved by it because he is missing its hidden sweetness. He is unaware of its capacity to serve as a "remedy for the soul." He does not understand its healing power, which is sought out by spiritual seekers so they may take refuge in its pages.

The problem lies in the transmission of a written, abstract topic to personal application. While intellectual comprehension can be problematic as well, it poses less of an issue. The dilemma lies more in palpably relating to the subject and actually implementing the ideas in the particulars of one's life.

The reader of a book finds himself necessarily confined to the limitations of his intrinsic subjectivity. Blind to his own deficiencies, man is incapable of recognizing the cures for his ailment. How can he find the way if he does not know where he erred? Learning directly from one's

1. *Bereshit Rabba* 3:6; *Shemot Rabba* 35:1.
2. See *Ba'al Shem Tov al HaTorah, Parashat Bereshit* 27, 45.

rabbi allows the teacher to tailor the subject matter to the particular spiritual needs of his student at that moment in time. Furthermore, the seeker can query and clarify misunderstandings until he reaches a thorough apprehension.

By contrast, when a person reads from a book, he could be totally unaware that he misunderstands the subject matter and that through his mistake he is straying from the correct path. He risks remaining as he was, while the illumination contained in the book does not endow him with the benefit and transformation that it could have engendered.

וּבַר מִן דֵּין, **Besides this** limitation,

Even if one has minimized his intrinsic bias with regard to the subject matter, and he has the capacity to understand it, making him a worthy vessel to be illuminated, the hidden light itself has a certain inherent limitation that prevents it from being transmitted to him.

הִנֵּה סִפְרֵי הַיִּרְאָה הַבְּנוּיִים עַל פִּי שֵׂכֶל אֱנוֹשִׁי **books that cultivate fear** of God **based on human intellect**

Many *mussar* works are philosophical in nature, consisting mainly of human thought and logic. Though indisputably crucial, even a great work such as *Ḥovot HaLevavot* is built to a large degree on the intellect and mindset of the author.

בְּוַודַּאי אֵינָן שָׁוִין לְכָל נֶפֶשׁ, כִּי אֵין כָּל הַשְּׂכָלִים וְהַדֵּעוֹת שָׁוֹות, וְאֵין שֵׂכֶל אָדָם זֶה מִתְפַּעֵל וּמִתְעוֹרֵר מִמַּה שֶּׁמִּתְפַּעֵל וּמִתְעוֹרֵר שֵׂכֶל חֲבֵירוֹ, **are certainly not equally appropriate for every individual, for not all intellects and minds are identical. That which profoundly affects and inspires one individual's intellect does not affect and inspire the intellect of another,**

Theoretically, every intellect is rational and therefore capable of rational comprehension, and anything that is logical can be apprehended through logic. However, the difference between people lies, not in their raw cognitive faculties, but rather in the bridge between the concept and the person. Ideas affect different people in different ways. An idea that may speak very deeply to the mind and heart of one person may not move another at all. What may inspire one person to the highest level of excitement and spiritual transcendence may not engender a significant response in another.

The questions posed in a book of *mussar*, as great as it may be in its own right, are not necessarily those that a person from a different time or culture might ask. The answers offered therein, even if true, may not speak to the reader and so will fail to awaken his soul. He will walk away without any notable inspiration to grow because of what he read.

This is not a denial of the holiness of these works but rather notes their inherent limitation. A book that is written on the basis of human apprehension speaks to its author and to those who have some resonance with it, while there will always be those who are unaffected by it. ☞

וּכְמוֹ שֶׁאָמְרוּ רַבּוֹתֵינוּ ז״ל גַּבֵּי בִּרְכַּת חֲכַם הָרָזִים עַל שִׁשִּׁים רִיבּוֹא מִיִּשְׂרָאֵל, שֶׁאֵין דֵּעוֹתֵיהֶם דּוֹמוֹת זוֹ לָזוֹ וכו׳ (ברכות נח, א),

as our Rabbis stated with regard to the blessing of *ḥakham harazim*, "blessed is He who knows all secrets," which is recited **upon** seeing **six hundred thousand Jews** at once, "One recites this blessing because he sees a whole nation **whose minds are unlike each other...**" (*Berakhot* 58a),

MUSSAR FROM ASTRONOMY

☞ In Rambam's *Mishneh Torah*, there is a section of *Hilkhot Yesodei HaTorah* (chap. 4) that could be referred to as a "book that cultivates fear of God based on human intellect." There Rambam teaches an astronomy lesson and concludes, "When a person contemplates these matters, becoming familiar with all the creations...his love for God increases. His soul will thirst and his flesh will yearn to love God, blessed be He" (*Hilkhot Yesodei HaTorah* 4:12).

Some people (including people like Einstein and Kant), the more they see and know the wonders of the created universe, the more their souls are stirred. Yet there are many who learn astronomy, but their flesh does not yearn to love God. While these topics may evoke fear and love in the heart of the author, not every reader experiences that same spiritual inspiration.

This blessing expresses praise to God, who created an immense number of different people, and awe that He alone is *ḥakham harazim*, "He who knows all secrets," who knows intimately the consciousness of every single individual. Among six hundred thousand people, no two are identical. Six hundred thousand people, six hundred thousand different opinions, approaches, and ways of functioning in the world.[3] A book written with human intellect cannot adapt to every single one of the six hundred thousand Jewish souls. It can, perhaps, adapt to a limited number of people in a particular place and time.

וּכְמוֹ שֶׁכָּתַב הָרַמְבַּ"ן ז"ל בְּ'מִלְחָמוֹת' שָׁם,

and as Ramban, of blessed memory, wrote there in *Milḥamot* Hashem

In his work *Milhamot Hashem*, Ramban elucidates a novel angle of this blessing based on a story brought there in the Talmud.[4] The story is told that Rav Ḥanina, son of Rav Ika, recited this blessing upon seeing Rav Pappa and Rav Huna, son of Rabbi Yehoshua. Apparently he deemed it appropriate to also recite this blessing at the sight of an accomplished sage who contains within him all opinions. Though Ramban does not include this circumstance in his conclusive halakhic parameters for the recitation of this blessing, this idea still grants one "a window into the foundations of wisdom," as Ramban puts it.

בְּפֵירוּשׁ הַסִּפְרִי גַּבֵּי יְהוֹשֻׁעַ שֶׁנֶּאֱמַר בּוֹ: "אִישׁ אֲשֶׁר רוּחַ בּוֹ" (במדבר כז, יח), **"שֶׁיָּכוֹל לַהֲלוֹךְ נֶגֶד רוּחוֹ שֶׁל כָּל אֶחָד וְאֶחָד"** וכו'.

regarding the *Sifri*'s explanation of the verse **describing Joshua as "a man in whom there is spirit"** (Num. 27:18): "Joshua **was able to attune himself to the spirit of each and every individual...."**

Moses had requested, "May the Lord, God of the spirits of all flesh, appoint a man over the congregation" (Num. 27:16), that is, as leader of the children of Israel. God responded in the affirmative and commanded Moses to appoint Joshua, characterizing him as "a man in

3. Six hundred thousand is the archetypal number of the Jewish nation as a collective. See below, where the author of the *Tanya* also refers to six hundred thousand root souls of Israel.

4. *Berakhot* 58b.

whom there is spirit." According to the *Sifri*, this crucial prerequisite for leadership meant the capacity to consider the *ruaḥ*, the spirit or opinion, of each of his subjects.

A leader must understand his subordinates, grasp the inner workings of their souls, and comprehend the outlook of each and every person. This defines true leadership: a person capable of considering the spirit of six hundred thousand individual souls of Israel.

By contrast, it is impossible to commit an idea to writing in a way that will resonate with each and every single individual. A live teacher can align himself to the spirit of the listener and counterbalance any initial incompatibility. A rabbi who teaches the concepts of Torah and *mussar* correctly, but does not adapt himself to the student, fails to fulfill his role. He must sense the spirit of the listener and align himself accordingly. Through familiarizing himself with the listener's basic assumptions, challenges of comprehension, and modes of expression, the teacher can speak in a way that will be absorbed and heard. It follows that speaking to two people is immeasurably harder than speaking to one, and all the more so speaking to a group or writing a book. A true leader must have the gift of speaking in the language of every individual so that each will truly hear the message the leader wants to impart. ☞

A TRUE LEADER

☞ Solomon Maimon relates an interesting story (and since he was a heretic through and through, his testimony is certainly reliable). He went to see the Maggid of Mezeritch and observed the Maggid receiving his guests. The Maggid sat at the head of the table and called on each guest by name and city. He then instructed the guest to say the first verse that came to mind. After each guest offered his biblical verse, the Maggid thought for a moment and then delivered a sermon woven from each of those verses. Incredibly, every person felt that the Maggid was addressing him directly, focusing on his verse, and addressing his personal situation with his particular life challenges.

The crucial point here lies not in his knowing the names of the guests, but rather in his ability to speak in a way that every person heard exactly what he needed to hear.

The phenomenon of a leader who can speak to fifty or a thousand people yet resonate with each one, imparting that which specifically relates to him, is impossible to achieve with a book. No book can bridge the gap between vastly different eras in time, place, and culture. Even a great sage who understands the depth of the

אֶלָּא אֲפִילּוּ בְּסִפְרֵי הַיִּרְאָה אֲשֶׁר יְסוֹדוֹתָם בְּהַרְרֵי קוֹדֶשׁ, מִדְּרָשֵׁי חֲכָמֵינוּ ז״ל אֲשֶׁר רוּחַ ה׳ דִּבֶּר בָּם וּמִלָּתוֹ עַל לְשׁוֹנָם.

Even those **books that cultivate fear** of God **whose foundations are** rooted **in the holy mountains,** that is, they are based on **the midrashic writings of our Sages, through whom the spirit of God spoke and His word was on their tongues,** are not equally appropriate for every individual.

The problem of human diversity arises not only in works written through the confines of the author's human comprehension, but also those that were written with divine illumination. We believe that the words of our Sages are not just words of deep wisdom, but they were actually inspired by some degree of prophetic intuition. The Divine spoke through their mouths and can be found in their words. This applies not only to the early sages but also to later sages.

It is said in the name of the Ba'al Shem Tov that every holy book up to and including the *Maharsha* was written with divine intuition.[5] Even if one cannot understand the deep meaning behind every single word, he can nevertheless trust that the words of Torah sages, even in recent generations, come from a holy source.

When a person is aligned with the Torah and his intentions are pure, the spirit of God speaks through him. Even if the decisive halakhic ruling is not in accordance with the opinion of a certain sage, and the world does not accept his practice as custom, still "these and those [opinions] are the words of the living God." The sage is endowed with the power and illumination of the words uttered to Moses at Mount Sinai.

Yet even those works that include the words of such Torah sages may not resonate with every individual.

concepts is writing from his personal perspective with people who share the same time period, place, and worldview. Others studying his work may feel like foreigners to those concepts conveyed in his book and will be unable to relate to them.

5. *Keter Shem Tov, Hosafot* 217; *Ba'al Shem Tov al HaTorah, Parashat Shoftim* 4.

וְאוֹרַיְיתָא וְקוּדְשָׁא בְּרִיךְ הוּא כּוּלָּא חַד וְכָל שִׁשִּׁים רִבּוֹא נִשְׁמוֹת כְּלָלוּת יִשְׂרָאֵל וּפְרָטֵיהֶם וּפְרָטֵי פְּרָטֵיהֶם,

It is true that **the Torah and the Holy One, blessed be He, are all one, and all six hundred thousand** root **souls of the collective of Israel, as well as** the souls' **derivatives and their derivatives' derivatives,**

Just as God is eternal and all-encompassing, the Torah is eternal and includes within it the spirit of every Jewish soul.

Six hundred thousand, the number of Jews who left Egypt, constitutes the archetypical number of the Jewish nation as a collective. It is the number of the root souls of Israel. These root souls are basic identities that divide into an infinite number of derivative souls, each with its unique qualities.[6] Therefore, although there are only six hundred thousand souls in Israel, the divine promise that the Jewish people will be "so many they cannot be counted" (Gen. 32:12) can still be fulfilled. Yet the multitude of souls that exist in the nation are not new souls but rather are microcosmic shards of the root souls.

עַד נִיצוֹץ קַל שֶׁבְּקַלִּים וּפְחוּתֵי הָעֵרֶךְ שֶׁבְּעַמֵּנוּ בְּנֵי יִשְׂרָאֵל,

even the spark that vivifies **the most unworthy and the least estimable among our nation, the children of Israel,**

These six hundred thousand root souls encompass the entire collective of the Jewish people, from its greatest leader to the unlearned individual who lacks any spiritual assets, neither Torah wisdom nor fear of God nor the commandments.

כּוּלְּהוּ מִתְקַשְּׁרָאן בְּאוֹרַיְיתָא וְאוֹרַיְיתָא הִיא הַמְקַשֶּׁרֶת אוֹתָן לְהַקָּדוֹשׁ בָּרוּךְ הוּא,

are all connected to the Torah, and the Torah is what connects them to the Holy One, blessed be He,

Every aspect of each of the six hundred thousand souls is connected to the Torah. Some are aware of that connection, and some even dedicate every waking hour and conscious thought to the study of Torah. Yet

---

6. See chap. 37 below.

the emphasis here, conveying that everyone shares a connection with the Torah, serves to highlight that even a person who does not study any Torah, and even someone who is not even interested in Torah, is bound to it nevertheless.

The Torah serves as a path of connection with God, and so every person, no matter what, has a bond with the Torah.

כַּנּוֹדָע בַּזֹּהַר הַקָּדוֹשׁ (חלק ג עג, א). **as is known from the holy *Zohar*** (3:73a).

The *Zohar* states, "Three dimensions are bound to each other: God, the Torah, and Israel." The Torah is God's Torah and clearly bound to Him. Therefore, it is an intrinsically holy entity. The Torah is also inseparable from the essence of the Jewish people, bound to each Jew, no matter what. Torah is the medium, the intermediary, through which every single soul of Israel connects to God.

The Torah speaks to every individual soul and obligates it to serve God. The words of the Torah, whether those of the Written Torah or the words of the Sages in the Oral Torah, or anything stemming from them, are not an expression of the individual personality of the author, but rather contain wisdom that draws from the all-inclusive source of the Jewish souls themselves. Every person can thus unearth his association with those holy words and resonate with them.

A written book that channels the power of the Torah, whose foundation lies in the words of the Sages, should theoretically be equally meaningful to all, since all the souls of Israel are bound to the Torah. The implication of this is that not one Jew, not even "the most unworthy and the least estimable," should be able to claim that the Torah is not for him or that the Torah does not speak to him.

הֲרֵי זֶה דֶּרֶךְ כְּלָלוּת לִכְלָלוּת יִשְׂרָאֵל. Nevertheless, **this** bond between the Torah and Israel applies **in a general way to Israel as a collective.**

The Torah as a whole is bound to the Jewish people as a collective. The 613 Torah commandments are 613 general categories that include all the commandments that are relevant to the entirety of Israel. This sum total does not pertain to every individual; it is actually impossible for a single person to perform every mitzva. Some commandments pertain to *kohanim*, or priests, while others only to non-*kohanim*. Some mitzvot are incumbent only upon men, while others apply only to women. And some apply only to the king.

While the Torah in its entirety speaks to the essence of the Jewish people, and it resides deep within each and every Jew, the individual is connected to only a portion of the Torah. In light of this, we request in our prayers, "Grant us our portion in Torah"[7] – guide us to the part of Torah that pertains particularly to us.

וְאַף שֶׁנִּיתְּנָה הַתּוֹרָה לִידָּרֵשׁ בִּכְלָל וּפְרָט

Even **though the Torah is meant to be expounded** both **on a general and specific** level,

This is not a reference to one of the thirteen methods of deriving *halakhot* from the Torah. Rather, it is used in the figurative sense. It means that every aspect of Torah not only bears meaning to a collective group but also serves as a personalized message to each individual.

וּפְרָטֵי פְּרָטוֹת לְכָל נֶפֶשׁ פְּרָטִית מִיִּשְׂרָאֵל הַמּוּשְׁרֶשֶׁת בָּהּ,

from which can be further derived **the most individualized meaning** that resonates **with each particular Jewish soul rooted** in the Torah,

The soul of every Jew is bound to the Torah. He draws from the Torah and receives essential vitality from it. The Torah speaks to him in the most intimate, personal way, uniquely coalescing to relate to his exact disposition and situation.

הֲרֵי אֵין כָּל אָדָם זוֹכֶה לִהְיוֹת מַכִּיר מְקוֹמוֹ הַפְּרָטִי שֶׁבַּתּוֹרָה.

not everyone is privileged to recognize his specific place in the Torah.

In truth, the Torah communicates to each of us all the time, through every occurrence, through every experience, through every vicissitude

7. Shabbat *Amida*.

of life. But not every person merits studying Torah through this lens, picking up on the messages it whispers to his heart, to the inner recesses of his unique self. ☞

וְהִנֵּה אַף בְּהִלְכוֹת אִיסּוּר וְהֶיתֵּר הַנִּגְלוֹת לָנוּ וּלְבָנֵינוּ, מָצָאנוּ רָאִינוּ מַחֲלוֹקֶת תַּנָּאִים וַאֲמוֹרָאִים מִן הַקָּצֶה אֶל הַקָּצֶה מַמָּשׁ,

Even with regard to *halakhot* delineating that which is prohibited and permitted, which have been revealed to us and to our children, we find and see disputes among **the *tanna'im* and *amorai'm*,** the talmudic Sages, **literally ranging from one end** of the spectrum **to the other.**

This applies not only to elusive spiritual matters that are difficult to express and grasp, but even to concrete matters, which are easy to define and determine. Even then, disputes can arise. There is no difference whether the debate involves details or general principles, whether foundations of faith or the specifics of Jewish law. Disputes emerge in both, "literally ranging from opposite ends of the spectrum."

For example, according to the opinion of Beit Shammai, it is a mitzva to perform a levirate marriage with one's daughter's co-wife, while according to Beit Hillel, performing a levirate marriage in this case is forbidden and warrants the punishment of *karet*, premature death and excision from the World to Come.

ONE'S TORAH PORTION

☞ Every person needs to know which is his relevant portion of Torah, what he needs to do right now at this unique moment, but not every person is aware of this. After the death of Rabbi Moshe Kordevero (famously known as the Ramak), Rabbi Yosef Karo, author of the *Shulḥan Arukh*, went to study Kabbala from the Arizal, but he would fall asleep as soon as the Arizal began speaking. Finally the Arizal told him that Lurianic Kabbala was not Rabbi Karo's portion in Torah. Similarly, the Arizal told Rabbi Moshe Alsheikh to engage in homiletics and not Kabbala, and as a result Rabbi Alsheikh wrote *Torat Moshe*, a masterpiece of Torah homiletics.

The prayer "Grant us our portion in Torah," then, can be understood not just as a request to acquire a portion of the Torah, but as a plea to know our particular portion of the Torah. A person can and must study Torah, but if he immerses himself in Torah that is not his (although he is still fulfilling the commandment to study Torah), he does not receive the same spiritual benefit as he would if he would delve into his portion.

This illustrates how two sages can approach the same measurable, explicable Torah issue and arrive at conclusions that not only differ from each other but diametrically oppose one another.

וְאֵלּוּ וְאֵלּוּ דִּבְרֵי אֱלֹהִים חַיִּים, לְשׁוֹן רַבִּים, עַל שֵׁם מְקוֹר הַחַיִּים לְנִשְׁמוֹת יִשְׂרָאֵל,

Yet **both these and those** opinions **are the words of God,** the bestower **of life.** The Hebrew word for life, *ḥayyim,* is **expressed in the plural form,** alluding to **the source of life for the souls of Israel,**

The Sages use this axiom, "These and those [opinions] are the words of God..." (*Eiruvin* 13b), regarding the differing positions of Hillel and Shammai. The word *ḥayyim* here does not serve as an adjective describing God as the living God but rather as a transitive verb: God who gives life, God as the source of life. This is why *ḥayyim* is in the plural form: to denote that God endows a plurality and diversity of life. Each soul receives a unique influx of life and portion of the Torah different from every other, each one receiving its fitting endowment.

הַנֶּחְלָקוֹת דֶּרֶךְ כְּלָל לִשְׁלֹשָׁה קַוִּין: יָמִין וּשְׂמֹאל וְאֶמְצַע, שֶׁהֵם חֶסֶד וּגְבוּרָה וכו׳.

which are divided into three broad arrays: right, left, and center, corresponding to the attributes of ***Ḥesed*** (Kindness), ***Gevura*** (Restraint), and *Tiferet* (Beauty).

The ten *sefirot,* the divine attributes through which God created the world and sustains it, can be grouped into three arrays. The one on the right includes *Ḥokhma* (Wisdom), *Ḥesed,* and *Netzaḥ* (Dominance). On the left is *Bina* (Understanding), *Gevura,* and *Hod* (Splendor), while the middle array includes *Da'at* (Knowledge), *Tiferet, Yesod* (Foundation), and *Malkhut* (Kingship).

Each array of *sefirot* shares commonalities embodied by one characteristic *sefira.* The right array is characterized by the *sefira* of *Ḥesed,* the left by the *sefira* of *Gevura,* and the one in the middle by *Tiferet. Ḥesed,* the attribute of Kindness, embodies the right hand that draws close,

Gevura, Restraint, the left hand that pushes away, and *Tiferet*, Beauty, embodies the middle way, the synthesis of *Ḥesed* and *Gevura*.

וּנְשָׁמוֹת שֶׁשָּׁרְשָׁן מִמִּדַּת חֶסֶד, הַנְהָגָתָן גַּם כֵּן לְהַטּוֹת כְּלַפֵּי חֶסֶד לְהָקֵל כו',

The tendency of souls rooted in the attribute of *Ḥesed*, Kindness, **is to incline toward kindness, ruling leniently** in matters of *halakha* and so on,

The root of a person's soul influences the way he functions throughout the course of his life, the way he processes phenomena, and the decisions he makes. This principle is at play in the realm of Torah as well. Here the author of the *Tanya* explains that the tendency of a sage to rule more strictly or more leniently stems from the root of his soul. If his soul is rooted in *Gevura*, in constriction and limitation, he tends toward strictness. If the source of his soul lies in *Ḥesed*, expansiveness and openness, then he will tend to be lenient. ☞ ☞

כַּנּוֹדָע.

as is well known.

Anyone who has studied the Talmud and *halakha* knows that the sheer quantity of opinions and controversies regarding revealed matters is huge and that the differences between some halakhic reasonings are stark.

THE VERDICT OF THE OX

☞ This principle comes to the fore in the example of a rabbi who, according to his legal understanding, rules that a particular chicken is unfit to eat and thereby causes the owner loss, monetary or otherwise. This position aligns with the attribute of *Gevura*, of judgment and the energy of concealment and constriction, the opposite of *Ḥesed*.

Below, in chapter 7, the author of the *Tanya* discusses the concepts of the prohibited and the permissible in another, more esoteric light. When a rabbi permits something, he in essence extracts it from the dimension of impurity and places it in the realm of holiness, infusing it with the potential to become sanctified. Hence the term *mutar*, permitted, which literally means to release.

By contrast, when a rabbi prohibits something, he binds it to the realm of impurity and decrees upon it eternal death, as it were. Hence the word *assur*, prohibited, literally means bound.

The story is told of a rabbi who rendered a lenient legal decision regarding the kosher status of a slaughtered animal in opposition to the ruling of Rabbi Shabtai HaKohen, famously known as the Shakh. When asked how he could disagree with such a great authority, he answered, "When I stand before the supernal court in the World of Truth, I prefer to stand against the Shakh than the ox."

וְכָל שֶׁכֵּן וְקַל וָחוֹמֶר בְּ״הַנִּסְתָּרוֹת לַה׳ אֱלֹהֵינוּ״ (דברים כט, כח),

Surely, all the more so will there be different interpretations **concerning** matters that are referred to as "**the concealed aspects, which are for the Lord our God**" (Deut. 29:28),

As the author of the *Tanya* pointed out above, regarding clear, rational issues, whose factors are exposed for all to see, we find differences of opinion due to varying worldviews and methods of legal arbitration. All the more so with regard to the subtleties of the soul, "the concealed aspects, which are for the Lord our God," one finds that every person is unique and multifaceted. It is virtually impossible to debate these issues by way of generalities.

דְּאִינּוּן דְּחִילוּ וּרְחִימוּ דְּבְמוֹחָא וְלִבָּא דְּכָל חַד וְחַד לְפוּם שִׁיעוּרָא דִּילֵיהּ, לְפוּם מַה דִּמְשַׁעֵר בְּלִיבֵּיהּ כְּמוֹ שֶׁכָּתוּב בַּזֹּהַר הַקָּדוֹשׁ (חלק א קג, א) עַל פָּסוּק ״נוֹדָע בַּשְּׁעָרִים בַּעְלָהּ״ וְגוֹ׳ (משלי לא, כג).

namely, fear and love of God, **which** are latent **in the mind and heart of each and every individual,** each **commensurate with his own capacity** [*shiur*], **according to his heart's capacity** to conceive God, **as the holy** *Zohar* **(1:103a) comments regarding the verse "Her husband,** that is, God, **is renowned at the gates** [*she'arim*]..." (Prov. 31:23).

LENIENCY IN THE SCHOOL OF SHAMMAI

☞ The truth is that people are not products of a single array, but rather are syntheses of several. No person is completely *Ḥesed,* nor entirely *Gevura,* but is made up of an assortment of attributes: *Ḥesed* in the context of *Gevura,* for example, or *Gevura* in the context of *Ḥesed.* Although Beit Shammai is generally more stringent and Beit Hillel more lenient, one finds some rulings in which Beit Shammai is lenient while others rely on the stringencies of Beit Hillel. Sages known as very stringent will occasionally present a lenient view, even when others arrive at stringent conclusions.

The salient point here is that even in matters that demand rational consideration, the soul causes one's inclination to shift from one extreme to the other. One person may reason in one way, while another person reasons very differently, influenced by the root of his soul.

The extent to which one feels love and awe of God hinges on how much he knows God. God is great, awesome, or loved depending on the person's own conception. Impossible to explain or learn, this matter depends on intimate, personal, inexpressible awareness.

One hasidic master expounds on the words of the verse "I know the Lord is great" (Ps. 135:5), with an emphasis on the words "I know": "Only I know how great God is to me, and no other person can grasp that. I am no better or worse than others; I am simply unique. Therefore, the awareness in my heart of God's greatness – only I know."[8]

Matters of a revealed nature are communicable from one person to another. They are disputable and debatable. By contrast, it is impossible to express to another person how one imagines and senses the greatness of God in his heart. The same is true with regard to the Torah. The way in which each person comprehends the Torah is totally unique, like his utterly unique soul-root, like his singular personal reality.

In summary, the author of the *Tanya* has explained in the first part of this introduction why it is impossible to comprehend the Torah from books. Even if it truly expresses the word of God, a book is incapable of adjusting to the unique spiritual alignment of the reader. A person can immerse himself in studying holy books, knowing their content very well and understanding thoroughly how others responded to them, yet if they are not in line with his soul-root, they may not be pertinent to his unique way of serving God. Rather, a person must seek out direct contact with a living teacher, someone with whom he can connect, and not be satisfied with books alone.

After the author of the *Tanya* has explained at length why one should not write books of *mussar*, he goes on to explain why he nevertheless wrote this book.

21 Kislev

22 Kislev (leap year)

אַךְ בְּיוֹדְעַיי וּמַכִּירַיי קָאָמֵינָא,

However, I am directing my words to those who know me and are acquainted with me,

As discussed above, the underlying limitation of any book is that the author engages primarily in self-reflection. He cannot relate to the reader because he does not know him. For this reason, the author of

8. See *Likkutei Moharan* 1:72, s.v. "*ki yesh kama beḥinot.*"

the *Tanya* here states that he is addressing those he knows. This book is not intended for the public at large but rather targets specific people: those who already sought private counsel from him and bared their souls to him, sharing their secrets with him.

Yet Chabad hasidim maintain that these words, "those who know me and are acquainted with me," include every person throughout all the generations who studies and will study the *Tanya*. Each one can find within it the answers to his personal questions.[9] ☞

הֵם כָּל אֶחָד וְאֶחָד מֵאַנְשֵׁי שְׁלוֹמֵנוּ שֶׁבִּמְדִינוֹתֵינוּ וּסְמוּכוֹת שֶׁלָּהּ. אֲשֶׁר הָיָה הַדִּבּוּר שֶׁל חִיבָּה מָצוּי בֵּינֵינוּ וְגִילּוּ לְפָנַי כָּל תַּעֲלוּמוֹת לִבָּם וּמוֹחָם בַּעֲבוֹדַת ה׳

namely, each and every one of the members of our community of hasidim **in our country and its surrounding regions, with whom it was**

"THOSE WHO KNOW ME"

☞ That the author of the *Tanya* is addressing only followers whom he knew personally obviously cannot be taken literally. His whole prerogative in writing this book was to reach those who would not come to learn his teachings directly from him. One could posit that the author of the *Tanya* knew with prophetic intuition all the people who would ever study his book and thus geared his words toward each and every one of them. In other words, since the author of the *Tanya* did not direct his words to some theoretical audience from the outset, but rather to specific people, addressing real-life issues and questions that people had actually asked him, the *Tanya* relates to those specific circumstances, those issues and questions, and those particular people. It never departs into the realm of the purely theoretical but remains rooted in reality. Though this manner of writing may come across as less organized and diverges into particulars, the risks outlined in the first half of this introduction are minute.

Moreover, when the author of the *Tanya* associated with those he knew, he forged a connection with them that permeated the inner essence of their souls. That place of unification is also the place of unity with all the souls of the people of Israel. Through this deep connection with his followers when they were face-to-face, the author of the *Tanya* could access the essence of every person who would ever open the *Tanya* and resonate with him, no matter when he would live. That being said, the degree to which a reader resonates with the ideas and teachings that can be found in the *Tanya* still depends on him, as explained above. However, the potential for a direct experience of receiving from the author remains embedded within its pages.

---

9. See *Likkutei Biurim LaTanya*; Rabbi Shalom Dovber Schneerson, *Torat Shalom, Sefer HaSiḥot*, p. 71.

הַתְּלוּיָה בַּלֵּב, אֲלֵיהֶם תִּטּוֹף מִלָּתִי וּלְשׁוֹנִי עֵט סוֹפֵר בְּקוּנְטְרֵיסִים אֵלּוּ הַנִּקְרָאִים בְּשֵׁם לִקּוּטֵי אֲמָרִים,

common to exchange affectionate conversations and who divulged to me all the innermost recesses of their hearts and minds pertaining to the service of God, which is contingent on the heart. It is to them that my words pour forth, my tongue serving as **a pen** in the hands **of a scribe, in these pamphlets titled *Likkutei Amarim*.**

The author of the *Tanya* addresses those hasidim with whom he had a deep, inner connection. They poured out their hearts to him and told him, not their mundane problems,[10] but rather their internal spiritual struggles, the obstacles on their journey toward heartfelt divine service, and their efforts to achieve a real connection with God.

מְלוּקָּטִים מִפִּי סְפָרִים וּמִפִּי סוֹפְרִים קְדוֹשֵׁי עֶלְיוֹן נִשְׁמָתָם עֵדֶן הַמְפוּרְסָמִים אֶצְלֵינוּ, וּקְצָת מֵהֶם נִרְמָזִין לַחֲכִימִין בְּאִגְּרוֹת הַקֹּדֶשׁ מֵרַבּוֹתֵינוּ שֶׁבְּאֶרֶץ הַקֹּדֶשׁ תִּבָּנֶה וְתִכּוֹנֵן בִּמְהֵרָה בְיָמֵינוּ אָמֵן. וּקְצָתָם שָׁמַעְתִּי מִפִּיהֶם הַקָּדוֹשׁ בִּהְיוֹתָם פֹּה עִמָּנוּ.

These writings **were compiled from the works and** teachings of **the holy masters, whose souls are in the Garden of Eden, who are well known to us. The wise will find allusions to some of these** teachings **in the holy letters** sent to us **from our rabbis in the Holy Land, may it be swiftly built and established in our days, amen. I heard some** of these teachings **from their holy mouths while they were here with us.**

The author of the *Tanya* now revisits the idea put forth in the title page above, emphasizing that while the *Tanya* aims to reach certain people

10. This was a common practice that the author of the *Tanya* strongly critiqued. See *Iggeret HaKodesh*, epistle 22.

whom he knew, the concepts are nonetheless based on the teachings of his teachers, the leaders of Hasidism.

וְכוּלָּם, הֵן תְּשׁוּבוֹת עַל שְׁאֵלוֹת רַבּוֹת אֲשֶׁר שׁוֹאֲלִין בְּעֵצָה כָּל אַנְשֵׁי שְׁלוֹמֵנוּ דִּמְדִינָתֵינוּ תָּמִיד כָּל אֶחָד לְפִי עֶרְכּוֹ,

All the teachings in this work **are responses to the many questions that the members of our community** of hasidim **in our country continually posed in search of advice, each one commensurate with his stature,**

The *Tanya* is essentially a book of frequently asked questions and corresponding answers that various people asked according to their spiritual challenges and struggles in forging a pathway toward God.

The quantity of questions that the author of the *Tanya* received during his leadership was countless. Among hasidim, there were thousands who asked, each with his particular life situation. The question of a person who has already achieved a certain spiritual level and refined his soul to some degree does not compare to that of someone who is just beginning to embark on the struggle toward true self-awareness and perception of God's light.

לָשִׁית עֵצוֹת בְּנַפְשָׁם בַּעֲבוֹדַת ה',

in order **to give them counsel regarding the service of God.**

The path of divine service, on which every person must toil, is a tortuous road riddled with obstacles. This is true not only in the realm of practical *halakha,* but primarily in the dimension of authentic spiritual growth, because divine service is in essence a labor of the heart. How should one react to his challenges? What should he do with his spiritual angst? From where can he draw spiritual energy to continue serving God, day in and day out, and to constantly intensify and deepen his connection?

An immensely crucial part of the role of a hasidic leader, a Rebbe, was to counsel people in relation to such questions, to be with them in their struggles, to listen and to guide them in their spiritual quests.

לִהְיוֹת כִּי אֵין הַזְּמַן גְּרָמָא עוֹד לְהָשִׁיב לְכָל אֶחָד וְאֶחָד עַל שְׁאֵלָתוֹ בִּפְרָטוּת,

Since time no longer allows me **to provide an answer to each individual's specific question,**

Initially, when the number of hasidim was still small, every person was able to talk to the Rebbe privately, present his question at length and in detail, and receive a tailor-made, personal answer. When the numbers of hasidim increased exponentially, it became impossible to designate to each the necessary private discussion time.

וְגַם הַשִּׁכְחָה מְצוּיָה, **and also** since **forgetfulness is common,**

One's private audience was packed with meaning. Every word was important; every point, each subtle way of phrasing, was loaded with life-changing significance. Yet a large degree of the meaning behind the words lay beyond the comprehension of the student, becoming decipherable only later, sometimes years later. The hasid may have disregarded details that at the time did not seem relevant and failed to pay attention to all the peripheral messages being communicated to him.

Therefore, even when a person would receive personal advice, he often could not register the multifaceted breadth and scope of it.

עַל כֵּן רָשַׁמְתִּי כָּל הַתְּשׁוּבוֹת עַל כָּל הַשְּׁאֵלוֹת **I therefore recorded all the responses to all the questions**

Ostensibly, these words imply that the *Tanya* is simply a collection of answers, an assortment of notes answering questions asked at different times by various people. Yet, as one can see, the structure of the *Tanya* does not resemble a collection of answers to questions at all. It is far more than a work that weaves disparate ideas together into a unified literary arrangement.

The *Tanya* works on two different planes. First, it is structured as a classic work of *mussar*. It presents and develops in-depth questions about abstract issues that arise regarding the service of God and touches on everything related to man's struggles in the world and with himself as he strives to cultivate love and fear of God. This motif, however, serves as an outward template that conceals the second plane: the *Tanya*'s internal structure, which constitutes answers to actual questions by specific people.

In view of this, the author of the *Tanya* explains that the intended benefit of the book is not to serve as an all-inclusive work of abstract thought that one person authored from his inner resources (often as an expression of himself), but rather as a nexus of specific, extremely sensitive, personal questions asked by many people. Since the questions are countless, the answers must be formulated in a general format so that they will resonate with the masses. ☞

לְמִשְׁמֶרֶת לְאוֹת לִהְיוֹת לְכָל אֶחָד וְאֶחָד לְזִכָּרוֹן בֵּין עֵינָיו וְלֹא יִדְחוֹק עוֹד לִיכָּנֵס לְדַבֵּר עִמִּי בִּיחִידוּת, כִּי בָּהֶן יִמְצָא מַרְגּוֹעַ לְנַפְשׁוֹ וְעֵצָה נְכוֹנָה לְכָל דָּבָר הַקָּשֶׁה עָלָיו בַּעֲבוֹדַת ה׳.

so that this work may serve **as a keepsake** and **sign to be remembered in each one's mind. One will no longer need to push to come and speak with me in a private audience, since in these** teachings **one will find tranquility for his soul and sound advice for any difficulty one may encounter in his service of God.**

To study the *Tanya* as an answer to a question is to discover its power. But if one has not clarified the question, or is not bothered by it at all, he will not understand, let alone relate, to the answer. This deficiency is its benefit: The *Tanya* is more than a book; it is the Rebbe's private audience with each of his hasidim.[11]

THE *TANYA*'S APPROACH

☞ The aim of this book far transcends an attempt to develop a theory, philosophy, theology, or even ethics. More than that, it addresses particular challenges in the service of God. The *Tanya* is not aimed toward the public, addressing problems in general and in the abstract as they apply to people in general like other *mussar* works. Rather, it consists of responses to living, palpable issues. Not the writer's issues – the reader's. The reader can find the answer to his particular dilemma because it is there; he need only search for it. He may find it in a sentence, or in a cluster of sentences, in one place or in several places, in what is said and sometimes in what is not said, and, occasionally, in the particular style chosen to present a concept.

11. Rabbi Shalom Dovber Schneerson, *Torat Shalom, Sefer HaSiḥot*, p. 56.

וְנָכוֹן יִהְיֶה לִבּוֹ בָּטוּחַ בַּה׳ גּוֹמֵר בַּעֲדֵינוּ.

His heart will then be steadfast, trusting in God, who completes our work **for us.**

Upon careful examination of these words, one finds more than just flowery well-wishes. They guide the reader to bolster his heart to be confident not just in God, but in "God who completes [our work] for us."

The meaning behind these words is related to the talmudic statement "Everything is in the hands of Heaven except for fear of Heaven" (*Berakhot* 33b). In everything that relates to divine service, one must not rely upon the help of Heaven. One may expect divine assistance or additional enlightenment, but one must not expect that God will actually do the work for him. If we begin, if we make the effort, we can anticipate that at most God will complete it for us.

Until this point, the author of the *Tanya* has explained why he wrote this book: It was written as a substitute for a private audience with the Rebbe. The reader should see it as a beginning and continuation of a personal discussion to uncover his own questions and discover the answers hidden within.

But since the questions and answers are not always apparent, and the book imparts content that is not simple to understand, the reader may frequently find it difficult to personally connect with the matters discussed. The author of the *Tanya* therefore adds the following paragraph.

וּמִי שֶׁדַּעְתּוֹ קְצָרָה לְהָבִין דְּבַר עֵצָה מִתּוֹךְ קוּנְטְרֵיסִים אֵלּוּ,

As for one whose intellect is too limited to derive a word of counsel from these pamphlets,

If the *Tanya* were arranged as a list of questions and answers, it would perhaps be easier for a person to retrieve the personal advice he needs. Yet that would necessitate going into the details of the problems to the extent that the answers would be too personal and particularized, effective only for that particular person and for only one of his issues. In order that these matters will be meaningful for a wide array of people and various circumstances, the book is arranged in a different format.

Many people ask the same question in different ways, yet they need to receive the same answer. The common denominator of the book, then, is answers, not questions. The all-inclusive structure of the book is comprehensive answers, while each reader holds his time-sensitive, situation-based question in his soul. The problem arises in the bridge between the burning question in the reader's heart at that very moment and the written answer that the reader must discover for himself. Not every person can find that connection.

יְפָרֵשׁ שִׂיחָתוֹ לִפְנֵי הַגְּדוֹלִים שֶׁבְּעִירוֹ וְהֵם יְבוֹנְנוּהוּ.

he should discuss his spiritual quandaries **with the sages of his city, who will grant** the questioner **the ability to understand** the answers on his own.

To overcome this problem, the author suggests that a person who feels that the *Tanya* does not directly address his issues should discuss his issues with the hasidic leaders in his city. They will give him the understanding to grasp the answer to his questions on his own.

וַאֲלֵיהֶם בַּקָּשָׁתִי שֶׁלֹּא לָשׂוּם יָד לַפֶּה, לְהִתְנַהֵג בַּעֲנָוָה וּשְׁפָלוּת שֶׁל שֶׁקֶר חַס וְשָׁלוֹם.

I implore these sages **to not remain silent on the pretense of false humility and self-deprecation, God forbid.**

If a person comprehends something, yet in the name of modesty he says, "Who am I to explain this to others?" his response is actually a show of false humility. A person needs to cultivate humility. Every *mussar* work praises this characteristic. But a person who knows the answer to a question but does not offer it because he reasons that responding will seem like arrogance is not displaying true humility because he is acting in contradiction to the truth. Humility must not be an impediment that prevents a person from expressing his gifts.

True humility lies in self-evaluation, in assessing how much one has succeeded in manifesting his highest self. At the same time, someone who understands an issue must explain it, not as a right to showcase his superiority, but rather as an obligation.

וְכַנּוֹדַע עוֹנֶשׁ הַמַּר עַל מוֹנֵעַ בַּר,

The bitter punishment for one who is competent to teach others yet **withholds "grain,"** that is, Torah knowledge, **is well known,**

The Sages state that anyone who withholds a *halakha* from being studied by a student, even fetuses in their mother's womb curse him, as it says, "The withholder of grain, the nation will curse him" (Prov. 11:26).[12] Meaning, he who withholds the goodness, or the "grain" of the Torah, from those ready to receive it will suffer the bitter consequences.

וְגוֹדֶל הַשָּׂכָר, מִמַּאֲמַר רַבּוֹתֵינוּ ז"ל (תמורה טז, א) עַל פָּסוּק (משלי כט, יג): "מֵאִיר עֵינֵי שְׁנֵיהֶם ה'".

and so is the immense reward for granting such knowledge, as we learn **from the teaching of our Rabbis** (*Temura* 16a) **regarding the verse "The Lord enlightens the eyes of both of them"** (Prov. 29:13).

Extensive reward is granted to a person when he dedicates his life to teaching those whose knowledge is inferior to his. The *Tanya* cites the Sages' teaching that when a student goes to his teacher and says to him, "Teach me Torah," and the teacher agrees to teach him, then "the Lord enlightens the eyes of both of them." In other words, God not only helps the student understand what he wants to know but also enlightens the teacher further as payment for enlightening the student.

כִּי יָאִיר ה' פָּנָיו אֲלֵיהֶם אוֹר פְּנֵי מֶלֶךְ חַיִּים. וּמְחַיֶּה חַיִּים יְזַכֵּנוּ וִיחַיֵּינוּ לְיָמִים אֲשֶׁר לֹא יְלַמְּדוּ עוֹד אִישׁ אֶת רֵעֵהוּ וְגוֹ' כִּי כוּלָּם יֵדְעוּ אוֹתִי וְגוֹ' כִּי מָלְאָה הָאָרֶץ דֵּעָה אֶת ה' אָמֵן כֵּן יְהִי רָצוֹן.

God will shine His countenance toward them with **the light of the countenance of the King who bestows life. May He who bestows life grant us life and let us merit** seeing **days in which man will no longer teach his neighbor** nor each man his brother, saying, "Know God," **for all of them will know Me…, for the earth will be filled with the knowledge of God. Amen, may it be** His **will.**

12. *Sanhedrin* 91b.

The author of the *Tanya* concludes with a wondrous tapestry of quotes from *Tanakh* that complement the topics he addressed in this introduction.[13] After explaining the need to write this book, he concludes with heartfelt yearning that the final redemption should arrive, when God will reveal Himself completely to every individual, each in his own unique way. Then people will no longer need to learn from one another or to write books about how to serve God.

וְהִנֵּה אַחַר שֶׁנִּתְפַּשְּׁטוּ הַקּוּנְטְרֵיסִים הַנִּזְכָּרִים לְעֵיל בְּקֶרֶב כָּל אַנְשֵׁי שְׁלוֹמֵנוּ הַנִּזְכָּרִים לְעֵיל, בְּהַעְתָּקוֹת רַבּוֹת מִיְּדֵי סוֹפְרִים שׁוֹנִים וּמְשׁוּנִּים, הִנֵּה עַל יְדֵי רִיבּוּי הַהַעְתָּקוֹת שׁוֹנוֹת רַבּוּ כְּמוֹ רַבּוּ הַטָּעֻיוֹת סוֹפְרִים בִּמְאוֹד מְאוֹד. וְלָזֹאת נָדְבָה רוּחָם שֶׁל אֲנָשִׁים אֶפְרָתִים הַנְּקוּבִים הַנִּזְכָּרִים לְעֵיל מֵעֵבֶר לַדַּף לִטְרוֹח בְּגוּפָם וּמְאוֹדָם לְהָבִיא אֶת קוּנְטְרֵיסִים הַנִּזְכָּרִים לְעֵיל לְבֵית הַדְּפוּס, מְנוּקִּים מִכָּל סִיג וְטָעוּת סוֹפֵר וּמוּגָּהִים הֵיטֵב. וְאָמֵינָא לְפָעֳלָא טָבָא יִישַׁר חֵילָא,

After many copies of the aforementioned pamphlets were distributed among all our aforementioned members of our community of hasidim **by various and diverse copyists, these many copies have become rife with an exceedingly immense number of textual errors. In light of this, the distinguished men mentioned above** by Reb Meshulam Zusil **on the previous page generously dedicated themselves personally and financially to having these aforementioned pamphlets printed** after **having been cleared of any distortion or copyists' errors and properly proofread. I congratulate them on this good deed.**

וְלִהְיוֹת כִּי מִקְרָא מָלֵא דִּבֵּר הַכָּתוּב: "אָרוּר מַסִּיג גְּבוּל רֵעֵהוּ" (דברים כז, יז), וְאָרוּר בּוֹ קְלָלָה בּוֹ נִדּוּי חַס וְשָׁלוֹם וכו', עַל כֵּן כִּיהוּדָה וְעוֹד לִקְרָא קָאָתֵינָא לְמִשְׁדֵי גוּדָא רַבָּא עַל כָּל הַמַּדְפִּיסִים שֶׁלֹּא לְהַדְפִּיס קוּנְטְרֵיסִים הַנִּזְכָּרִים

Since there is already an explicit verse that states, "Cursed [*arur*] is one who moves his neighbor's boundary" (Deut. 27:17), and the term *arur* **contains** "an element of **ostracism within** it and an element **of curse within it…"** (*Shevuot* 36a), **God forbid, I therefore** merely **come in the same way** the

13. Num. 6:25; Prov. 16:15; Jer. 31:33; Isa. 11:9.

לְעֵיל לֹא עַל יְדֵי עַצְמָן וְלֹא עַל יְדֵי גִּירָא דִּילְהוֹן בִּלְתִּי רְשׁוּת הַנְּקוּבִים הַנִּזְכָּרִים לְעֵיל מֶשֶׁךְ חָמֵשׁ שָׁנִים מִיּוֹם כְּלוֹת הַדְּפוּס. וְלַשּׁוֹמְעִים יוּנְעַם וְתָבוֹא עֲלֵיהֶם בִּרְכַּת טוֹב.

custom of **Judea** is cited to **bolster a scriptural prohibition** (based on *Kiddushin* 6a) **to impose a strict prohibition on all printers that neither they, nor their agents, may print the aforementioned pamphlets without permission from the publishers specified above for a period of five years from the completion of** this **printing. For those who adhere** to this warning, **it will be pleasant, and a blessing of goodness will come upon them.**

כֹּה דִּבְרֵי הַמְלַקֵּט לִקּוּטֵי אֲמָרִים הַנִּזְכָּרִים לְעֵיל.

This concludes **the** introductory **remarks of the compiler of the aforementioned *Likkutei Amarim*.**

These closing words refer not to the writing of the book but rather to its printing. The author of the *Tanya* explains that producing hand-copied versions caused a multitude of mistakes and therefore gave permission to print the book, granting copyright to the publishers so that they would not incur losses through other printings. Thousands of copies of the book were printed, and another edition was even printed shortly after.

In summary, the *Tanya* is essentially a response. Though written in a general way, within an extremely sophisticated structure, it is nonetheless a response to the problems and questions of the individual.

Herein lies the challenge of the book and the difficulty in understanding it. One must study it time and time again to disclose the insight it intends to transmit. Every individual must toil to accurately hone in on the articulation of his own question so that he may arrive at his personal answer.

This introduction serves, in many respects, as a general introduction to other books that have been written in this way, as an oral Torah that has taken on written form. This preserves the feeling of live, personal, intimate discussion between the Rebbe and his followers, as palpable as interpersonal contact.

Chapter 1

THE *TANYA* BEGINS IN THE SAME MANNER AS MOST hasidic texts, with several aphorisms from the Sages. These sources serve as a springboard for most of the author's questions and the ideas that follow. Although this book is not designed specifically to answer those questions, he opens with them to anchor the discussion in source material and to show that through in-depth study one can arrive at the same conclusions on one's own.

22 Kislev | 24 Kislev (leap year)

תַּנְיָא [בְּסוֹף פֶּרֶק ג דְּנִדָּה] (ל, ב):

It was taught in a *baraita* (**at the conclusion of the third chapter of *Nidda*** [30b]):

Although the Talmud there quotes an *amora*, Rabbi Samlai, and not a *baraita*, which is a teaching of a *tanna*, the term *tanya* can still be attached to this citation. According to some, there were two Sages who shared this name and the one mentioned here was indeed a *tanna*. In addition, Rabbi Samlai lived in the bridge generation between the *tanna'im* and *amora'im*, and a few of their teachings became codified in *beraitot*.

"מַשְׁבִּיעִים אוֹתוֹ, תְּהִי צַדִּיק וְאַל תְּהִי רָשָׁע. וַאֲפִילוּ כָּל הָעוֹלָם כּוּלּוֹ אוֹמְרִים לְךָ צַדִּיק אַתָּה - הֱיֵה בְּעֵינֶיךָ כְּרָשָׁע".

"The angels **administer an oath** to the soul prior to its descent into the fetus: **Be righteous and do not be wicked. And even if the entire world says to you, 'You are righteous,' consider yourself like a wicked person."**

There are two elements to the oath that the angels have the soul swear. The first is that one should be righteous and not wicked, and the second is that one should always consider himself wicked, even if everyone else insists that he is righteous. ☞

וְצָרִיךְ לְהָבִין, דְּהָא תְּנַן [אָבוֹת פֶּרֶק ב משנה יג]: "וְאַל תְּהִי רָשָׁע בִּפְנֵי עַצְמְךָ".

This statement **demands explanation, for it was taught** in a mishna, **"Do not be wicked in your own estimation"** (*Avot* 2:13).

Clearly, the second part of the oath demands explanation: Why do the angels administer such an oath, giving the person a heavenly, inalterable directive that he should always regard himself as wicked? This poses a contradiction between the sources. In the *baraita*, man is advised to view himself as wicked, while the Mishna states that one should not consider himself wicked.

וְגַם אִם יִהְיֶה בְּעֵינָיו כְּרָשָׁע - יֵרַע לְבָבוֹ וְיִהְיֶה עָצֵב וְלֹא יוּכַל לַעֲבוֹד ה' בְּשִׂמְחָה וּבְטוּב לֵבָב. וְאִם לֹא יֵרַע לְבָבוֹ כְּלָל מִזֶּה - יָכוֹל לָבוֹא לִידֵי קַלּוּת חַס וְשָׁלוֹם.

Furthermore, if one views himself as wicked, he will feel distraught and saddened, in which case **he will be unable to serve God with joy and gladness.** On the other hand, **if he will not feel distraught at all by this,** by finding a fault during his self-assessment, **he could be led to frivolity, God forbid.**

This challenge does not just demand the reconciliation of these two sources, but rather poses an essential, existential issue. On the one hand, a person who views himself as defective, flawed, and wicked will be prone to sadness and despair. On the other hand, a person who is not affected by his shortcomings will not feel the weight of transgression.

THE OATH

☞ The oath that the soul takes before birth, that one will be righteous and not wicked, alludes to a spiritual force that comes from above, from the perspective of the soul's surrounding light, a spiritual force that is not internalized or intellectually comprehensible by the person. This force imbues the unborn child with the spiritual strength to subjugate his evil inclination and avoid becoming wicked during his lifetime (Tzemaḥ Tzedek).

When one does not engage in self-evaluation at all, or if he always concludes that for one reason or another he is justified in his actions, while avowing that others – the world at large, society, or God – are in the wrong, then he is liable to take his obligations lightly.

Much more than a question of textual study, the author of the *Tanya* is posing a foundational issue: Should man view himself as perfect, imperfect, or essentially defective? This question has nothing to do with reputation or public opinion but rather probes the depths of one's soul, independent of whatever titles one has earned or attributed to himself.

אַךְ הָעִנְיָן, כִּי הִנֵּה מָצִינוּ בַּגְּמָרָא ה' חֲלוּקוֹת: צַדִּיק וְטוֹב לוֹ, צַדִּיק וְרַע לוֹ, רָשָׁע וְטוֹב לוֹ, רָשָׁע וְרַע לוֹ, וּבֵינוֹנִי.

However, the truth of the **matter is that we find five distinctions** regarding the righteous and the wicked **in the Talmud: a righteous person who prospers, a righteous person who suffers, a wicked person who prospers, a wicked person who suffers, and a *beinoni*,** an intermediate-level person.

To understand this issue, the fundamental definitions of tzaddik and *rasha*, righteous person and wicked person, must be clarified. Piecing together several talmudic sources, the author of the *Tanya* arrives at five general categories that describe five types of people.[1]

וּפֵירְשׁוּ בַּגְּמָרָא (ברכות ז, א): "צַדִּיק וְטוֹב לוֹ – צַדִּיק גָּמוּר, צַדִּיק וְרַע לוֹ – צַדִּיק שֶׁאֵינוֹ גָּמוּר".

The Sages in the **Talmud offer an explanation: "The righteous** person **who prospers is a completely righteous** person. **The righteous** person **who suffers is** one who is **not a completely righteous** person" (*Berakhot* 7a).

The Talmud goes on to say that a wicked person who prospers is not completely wicked, while a wicked person who suffers is completely

1. See *Berakhot* 7a, 61b.

wicked. These categorizations are not based on the set of life circumstances dealt to a person in this world. It is not that the tzaddik who prospers and the tzaddik who suffers are on the same spiritual level, and it is only that the latter is a tzaddik who has a life filled with hardship and suffering, while the former is both righteous and enjoys a life of prosperity. Rather, this categorization refers to distinctly different types of people based on their personal inner world and their struggles with their evil inclination.

Essentially, the five distinctions listed in the Talmud are five levels that classify all human beings within life's vast spectrum from one extreme to the other.[2]

וּבְרַעְיָא מְהֵימְנָא, פָּרָשַׁת מִשְׁפָּטִים (חלק ב קיז, ב) פֵּירֵשׁ צַדִּיק וְרַע לוֹ, שֶׁהָרַע שֶׁבּוֹ כָּפוּף לַטּוֹב וכו'.

In ***Raya Meheimna, Parashat Mishpatim*** (*Zohar* 2:117b), **it is explained** that **a righteous person who suffers,** literally, "who possesses evil," means **that the evil within him is subservient to the good** within him **and so forth.**

A tzaddik who suffers refers to a tzaddik who still grapples with evil but dominates it. For this reason, he is not considered a complete tzaddik. A complete tzaddik has no vestige of evil within him at all. In this light, a wicked person who prospers refers to a wicked person who is not thoroughly evil and still has glimmerings of good within, but his evil urge prevails over them.

וּבַגְּמָרָא סוֹף פֶּרֶק ט דִּבְרָכוֹת (סא, ב): "צַדִּיקִים יֵצֶר טוֹב שׁוֹפְטָן כו' רְשָׁעִים יֵצֶר הָרַע שׁוֹפְטָן, בֵּינוֹנִים זֶה וָזֶה שׁוֹפְטָן וכו'

In the Talmud, at the conclusion of the ninth chapter of ***Berakhot*** (61b), it states, **"The good inclination rules the righteous.... The evil inclination rules the wicked....** ***Beinonim*** **are ruled by both** inclinations....

The word for rule, *shofet,* also connotes to judge. This talmudic teaching is thus derived from the verse "For He stands at the right hand of the

2. See also chap. 11 below.

needy to deliver him from those who judge him" (Ps. 109:31). Two judges adjudicate in the inner consciousness of one's being: one's good inclination and one's evil inclination. The difference between people on various spiritual levels, between a tzaddik and a *rasha*, is their ultimate, decisive inner authority, despite other dissenting inner voices. In the tzaddik, it is the good inclination that has decisive power, while the wicked person's evil inclination dominates. The *beinoni* grapples with a more complex inner reality, as will be explored below.

אָמַר רַבָּה: כְּגוֹן אֲנָא - בֵּינוֹנִי.

Rabba said: I, for example, am a *beinoni*.

Tzaddik and *rasha* are clearly defined levels, whereas the *beinoni* is a complex intermediate level difficult to delineate. It is for this reason that Rabba presented himself as an example of the *beinoni*, to help clarify this elusive category.

אָמַר לֵיהּ אַבַּיֵּי: לָא שָׁבֵיק מָר חַיֵּי לְכָל בְּרִיָּה" וכו'.

Abaye said to him: If the Master claims that he is merely a *beinoni*, **he does not leave** room for **any creature to live."**

Rabba claims that he himself is a *beinoni*, but as the head of the yeshiva of Pumbedita, Rabba is not an average person. He was one of the greatest of the *amora'im* in Babylon, so holy that even the angel of death had no power over him.[3] It is no wonder that Abaye, Rabba's nephew and prize student, protests and responds, "If you are a *beinoni*, then the standard that you are establishing does not leave any room for anyone else. No one can possibly achieve the level of tzaddik, and we are necessarily wicked."[4]

וּלְהָבִין כָּל זֶה בֵּאֵר הֵיטֵב,

In order to understand all this, a thorough explanation is needed.

The author of the *Tanya* now embarks on an exploration of these three distinctions, tzaddik, *rasha*, and *beinoni*. He will show how these definitions lie at the very bedrock of divine service, crucial to

3. *Bava Metzia* 86a.
4. See commentary of Rabbi Shmuel Gronem Esterman.

the questions that every person must ask himself when he chooses his spiritual path.

וְגַם לְהָבִין מַה שֶּׁאָמַר אִיּוֹב [בָּבָא בַּתְרָא פֶּרֶק א] (טז, א): "רִבּוֹנוֹ שֶׁל עוֹלָם, בָּרָאתָ צַדִּיקִים, בָּרָאתָ רְשָׁעִים" כו'.

It is **also** important **to understand Job's statement** (cited in **the first chapter of *Bava Batra*** [16a]), "**Master of the universe, You created righteous people** and **You created wicked people...,**"

Job's grievous complaint against God, as quoted in the Talmud, is not a protest regarding his own personal plight but rather the lack of fairness in the creation of the world: "You created the ox with split hooves [making it kosher], and You created the donkey with closed hooves [making it forbidden]. You created the Garden of Eden, and You created Gehenna; You created righteous people, and You created wicked people. Who can restrain You?"

Job makes a claim against God that He created all His handiwork according to a predetermined form that forces it to function accordingly. Every created entity must live within the confines of its genetic makeup, in accordance with the immutable gifts with which it was endowed. In light of this, Job's complaint concerns the unfairness of judgment. As Rashi explains, "Sinners act under compulsion."[5] If man is born with a particular innate character, either righteous or wicked, he cannot really be blamed for his actions.

וְהָא "צַדִּיק וְרָשָׁע לָא קָאָמַר" (נדה טז, ב).

for "**he does not say:** Will he be **righteous or wicked?**" (*Nidda* 16b).

Job's declaration implies that God created every human being from the outset to be either righteous or wicked. Yet the talmudic statement in tractate *Nidda* relates what happens before a person is even born: The angel appointed over conception takes a drop of seed, presents it before God, and asks, "Master of the universe, what will be with this drop? Will the person fashioned from it be mighty or weak, wise or foolish, wealthy or poor?" The Talmud then notes that the angel does

5. Rashi, *Bava Batra* 16a.

not ask God, nor does God disclose, whether this particular person will be righteous or wicked, because "everything is in the hand of Heaven except for fear of Heaven."

Every person inherits certain characteristics, including his skills, abilities, talents, and selected areas of excellence. He is even handed a particular life trajectory that engenders either wealth or poverty, success or wretchedness. But the choice between good and evil, whether to be a tzaddik or a *rasha*, remains absolutely in a person's control every moment of his life.

The question, then, becomes, how could Job claim that "You created righteous people, and You created wicked people"?

The answer is that it is true that He created the ox with split hooves, rendering it kosher, and the donkey without, rendering it forbidden, so that the donkey is incapable of transforming into a pure animal, and the ox is powerless to become impure. Yet there is no predestined lot that forces a person to be righteous or wicked. God does not determine the spiritual level that any person may attain. This choice is totally up to each individual.

וְגַם לְהָבִין מַהוּת מַדְרֵגַת הַבֵּינוֹנִי,

It is **also** necessary **to understand the nature of the level of *beinoni*.**

Though the author of the *Tanya* listed five categories of individuals, his focus in this work is on the *beinoni*. As highlighted in the title page of the book, the *beinoni* serves as the axis around which the entire book revolves. In fact, this section of the *Tanya* is called *Sefer shel Beinonim*, "The Book of *Beinonim*," since the book deals primarily with "the nature of the level of *beinoni*." As will be explained, a difference is drawn between the *beinoni*'s nature and level. One can even argue that the whole book is based on the conflict between the two.

שֶׁבְּוַדַּאי אֵינוֹ מֶחֱצָה זְכֻיּוֹת וּמֶחֱצָה עֲוֹנוֹת,

It **certainly** does **not** mean that his deeds are **half meritorious and half sinful.**

The general concept of *beinoni*, which literally means "average" or "medium," is difficult to apply. Not every phenomenon can be divided in half with the demarcation of a third, independent realm. There are many pairs that do not have a meaningful average or middle. They can either be one way or the other. Yet, as outlined below, one way that the concept of *beinoni* can be understood is figuratively, by delineating an average, a person who has equal merits and demerits.

Yet this definition poses certain difficulties. One cannot posit that the essential nature of a tzaddik is someone who possesses mostly mitzvot, while a *rasha* is one who mostly sins, and the *beinoni* is someone who has an equal number of merits and transgressions.

שֶׁאִם כֵּן אֵיךְ טָעָה רַבָּה בְּעַצְמוֹ לוֹמַר שֶׁהוּא בֵּינוֹנִי,

If it were so, how could Rabba err concerning himself by saying that he is a *beinoni*?

If half the actions of the *beinoni* are characterized as mitzvot and half as transgressions, his transgressive behavior would be obvious. In that case, it is impossible that the behavior of a person of the stature of Rabba, who was a leader of his generation and who spent every waking hour studying Torah and performing endless acts of kindness, would lead him to believe he was a *beinoni*. On the other hand, one cannot make the claim that his self-assessment was merely a show of humility. A falsehood cannot be an expression of true humility. A person of great stature claiming to be lowly is not being humble. He is simply stating an untruth. ☞

וְנוֹדָע דְּלָא פְּסִיק פּוּמֵיהּ מִגִּירְסָא עַד שֶׁאֲפִילוּ מַלְאַךְ הַמָּוֶת לֹא הָיָה יָכוֹל לִשְׁלוֹט בּוֹ וְאֵיךְ הָיָה יָכוֹל

It is known that his mouth never ceased studying Torah **to the extent that even the angel of death was unable to best him. How, then, could he err** in determining **that**

TRUE HUMILITY

☞ True humility emerges in the way a person evaluates himself in relation to God and in relation to himself. This type of humility is actually found particularly in great people. They know the lofty quality of their souls and their talents, yet are always aware of the gap between their potential and how much they have actualized. This type of comparison, where a person measures his worth in relation to his own potential, is the source of true humility. However, when one evaluates his success and abilities objectively in the context of the success and abilities of others, denying his own merit is not true humility but instead a false and pretentious showcase of self-deprecation.

לְטָעוּת בְּמֶחֱצָה עֲוֹנוֹת חַס וְשָׁלוֹם?

half his deeds were **sinful, God forbid?**

Rabba did not even have time to commit transgressions because he never ceased studying Torah. The Talmud relates that the angel of death was sent from Heaven to take Rabba's life, but the angel could not even approach him because Rabba did not stop studying Torah for one instant.[6] Suddenly, a wind blew and howled between the branches. Rabba, thinking that an infantry battalion was about to capture him, surrendered his soul to death rather than be handed over to the enemy. Only then was the angel of death able to take his soul.[7]

וְעוֹד, שֶׁהֲרֵי בְּשָׁעָה שֶׁעוֹשֶׂה עֲוֹנוֹת נִקְרָא רָשָׁע גָּמוּר [וְאִם אַחַר כָּךְ עָשָׂה תְּשׁוּבָה נִקְרָא צַדִּיק גָּמוּר].

Furthermore, when one commits sins, he is categorized as a completely wicked person (**and,** conversely, **if he subsequently repents, he is categorized as a completely righteous person**).

It is clear from Rabba's description of himself and his great qualities that the *beinoni* cannot be characterized as someone who is half sinful. Rather, the *beinoni* must closely resemble a tzaddik to the point that one cannot differentiate between the two.

Yet the question of what defines the *beinoni* becomes even more pointed, because this distinction does not define a person's outer behavior but rather his internal essence, his nature. This leads to the crucial question of how there can exist an intermediate level between tzaddik and *rasha*. Is there really such a thing as an "intermediate" person? The moment a person commits a transgression, no matter what his prior merits were, he is considered an absolute *rasha*. If that same person repents, despite the number of merits or demerits he accrued, at that moment he becomes a complete tzaddik. In that case, when does a person become a *beinoni*?

6. This is reminiscent of the giving of the Torah, when the children of Israel merited being released even from the binds of the angel of death. The sin of the golden calf restored death to their reality. From here it can be deduced that death cannot affect a person who is studying Torah in holiness (*Torat Ḥayyim*).

7. *Bava Metzia* 86a.

וַאֲפִילוּ הָעוֹבֵר עַל אִיסּוּר קַל שֶׁל דִּבְרֵי סוֹפְרִים מִקְרֵי רָשָׁע, כִּדְאִיתָא בְּפֶרֶק ב׳ דִּיבָמוֹת (כ, א) וּבְפֶרֶק קַמָּא דְּנִדָּה (יב, א).

Even one who transgresses a minor prohibition of the Rabbis is categorized as a wicked person, as stated in the second chapter of *Yevamot* (20a) **and in the first chapter of *Nidda*** (12a).

It is also impossible to characterize the *beinoni* as one who performs only minor mitzvot and commits only minor transgressions because it is not just one who transgresses foundational tenets of the Written Torah who is considered a *rasha*. Even someone who transgresses a small aspect of an enactment of the Sages is considered wicked.

וַאֲפִילוּ מִי שֶׁיֵּשׁ בְּיָדוֹ לִמְחוֹת וְלֹא מִיחָה נִקְרָא רָשָׁע [בְּפֶרֶק ו דִּשְׁבוּעוֹת] (לט, ב).

Also, **even one who had the ability to protest** a transgression **and** nevertheless **he did not protest is categorized as a wicked person** (as stated **in the sixth chapter of *Shevuot*** [39b]).

A person may be deemed wicked, not only through his actions but also due to inaction in the face of a *rasha*, when he could have objected or prevented the *rasha* from causing harm.

וְכָל שֶׁכֵּן וְקַל וָחוֹמֶר בִּמְבַטֵּל אֵיזוֹ מִצְוַת עֲשֵׂה שֶׁאֶפְשָׁר לוֹ לְקַיְּימָהּ, כְּמוֹ כָּל שֶׁאֶפְשָׁר לוֹ לַעֲסוֹק בַּתּוֹרָה וְאֵינוֹ עוֹסֵק, שֶׁעָלָיו דָּרְשׁוּ רַבּוֹתֵינוּ ז״ל (סנהדרין צט, א): ״כִּי דְבַר ה׳ בָּזָה וגו׳ הִכָּרֵת תִּכָּרֵת״ וגו׳.

All the more so is this **certainly** true **regarding one who neglects to fulfill any positive commandment that he is capable of performing, such as someone who is able to study Torah yet does not do so. Concerning such a person, our Rabbis** (*Sanhedrin* 99a) **expound** the verse **"Because he scorned the word of the Lord** and he violated His commandment, that person **shall be excised..."** (Num. 15:31).

A person who is capable of performing a mitzva and fails to do so also moves into the realm of wicked. The fact that he did not commit a sin when he was supposed to perform a mitzva does not remove him from the category of *rasha*. A paradigmatic example of this is when a person could have studied Torah but instead engaged in some neutral activity that is neither good nor bad.[8]

וּפְשִׁיטָא דְּמִקְרֵי 'רָשָׁע' טְפֵי מֵעוֹבֵר אִיסּוּר דְּרַבָּנָן, וְאִם כֵּן עַל כָּרְחָךְ הַבֵּינוֹנִי אֵין בּוֹ אֲפִילּוּ עֲוֹן בִּיטּוּל תּוֹרָה, וּמִשּׁוּם הָכִי טָעָה רַבָּה בְּעַצְמוֹ לוֹמַר שֶׁהוּא בֵּינוֹנִי.

It is obvious that such a person **is categorized as wicked, more so than one who transgresses a rabbinic prohibition. If so, it must be that a *beinoni* does not possess even the sin of neglecting Torah** study. **It is on account of this that Rabba erred concerning himself by stating that he was a *beinoni*.**

Clearly a person who neglects his Torah study is considered wicked even more than one who transgresses an enactment of the Sages, since the Sages attach such neglect to the very severe punishment of *karet*, premature death and excision from the World to Come.

In summary, those who are considered a *rasha* include a person who transgresses a major or minor sin, a person who fails to protest against or prevent other people from sinning, and even one who could have performed a positive commandment, such as Torah study, yet failed to do so. In that case, a *beinoni* must be someone who commits no sins and fulfills every mitzva he possibly can in thought, speech, and action.

The *beinoni* is clearly not an average person. The central question then becomes, why is he called a *beinoni*? What does he lack that makes him undeserving of the title of tzaddik?

The author of the *Tanya* will go on to explain that what the *beinoni* lacks is not expressed in his actions, speech, or even thoughts but rather in the inner recesses of his soul. There, hidden from the purview of any onlooker, known only to himself, lies the distinction between tzaddik and *beinoni*.

הַגָּהָה: וּמַה שֶּׁכָּתוּב בַּזֹּהַר חלק ג׳ דף רל״א, א: ״כָּל שֶׁמְּמוּעָטִין עֲוֹנוֹתָיו״ וכו׳

Gloss: As for what is written in the *Zohar* (3:231a), that **"one who has fewer sins** than merits is categorized as a righteous person

8. See *Torah Or* 99b.

הִיא שְׁאֵלַת רַב הַמְנוּנָא לְאֵלִיָּהוּ. אֲבָל לְפִי תְּשׁוּבַת אֵלִיָּהוּ שָׁם, פֵּירוּשׁ "צַדִּיק וְרַע לוֹ" הוּא כְּמוֹ שֶׁכָּתוּב בְּרַעְיָא מְהֵימְנָא פָּרָשַׁת מִשְׁפָּטִים דִּלְעֵיל, "וְשִׁבְעִים פָּנִים לַתּוֹרָה".

who suffers," this seems to pose a contradiction to the aforementioned premise that a righteous person is one who never sins. **This is** actually **Rav Hamnuna's question to Elijah. But according to Elijah's response there, the definition of a righteous person who suffers accords with what is written in *Raya Meheimna, Parashat Mishpatim,*** cited **above.** Yet **the Torah has seventy facets.**

The definitions of tzaddik, *rasha,* and *beinoni* that are presented in this chapter seem to be contradicted by the definitions of these terms from another source in the *Zohar*. According to the *Zohar* there, even if a person has many sins, he is still considered righteous as long as his merits outnumber his transgressions. Since he is punished for his sins in this world, he is considered a righteous person who suffers. This understanding differs from the author of the *Tanya*'s approach here based on the *Zohar*'s statement in *Raya Meheimna*: A righteous person who suffers is not someone who has fewer sins than merits but rather is someone whose evil inclination is subjugated to his good inclination.

The contradiction is resolved by pointing out that the alternative explanation does not reflect the conclusion of the *Zohar* but rather was only presented in the form of a question by Rav Hamnuna. Elijah's answer is the authoritative conclusion, and it parallels the *Zohar*'s statement that the author of the *Tanya* quoted at the beginning of the chapter from *Raya Meheimna*.[9]

While the *Zohar* does not come to the same conclusion as Rav Hamnuna, the author of the *Tanya* notes the importance of taking his opinion into account, and so he concludes that "the Torah has

9. The Lubavitcher Rebbe, Rabbi Menaḥem Mendel Schneerson, explains that Rav Hamnuna posited that there is a facet of the Torah through which a person who has mostly merits can be viewed as righteous. However, in light of Elijah's response, such a perspective is not counted among the seventy facets of the Torah, and from that viewpoint the term "righteous" is merely figurative.

seventy facets." One must not view the plethora of opinions on a given statement from the Torah, especially with regard to mystical teachings, as correct or incorrect, but rather as various angles of the same point. Each angle reflects a certain context, relaying a particular message that speaks to a different aspect of the human experience.

וְהָא דְּאָמְרִינַן בְּעָלְמָא דְּמֶחֱצָה עַל מֶחֱצָה מִקְרֵי בֵּינוֹנִי, וְרוֹב זְכִיּוֹת מִקְרֵי צַדִּיק, הוּא שֵׁם הַמּוּשְׁאָל לְעִנְיַין שָׂכָר וְעוֹנֶשׁ, לְפִי שֶׁנִּדּוֹן אַחַר רוּבּוֹ וּמִקְרֵי צַדִּיק בְּדִינוֹ, מֵאַחַר שֶׁזּוֹכֶה בַּדִּין.

23 Kislev

25 Kislev (leap year)

As for the well-known statement that one whose deeds are **half** meritorious **and half** sinful **is categorized as a** ***beinoni*****, while** one who has accrued **a majority of merits is categorized as a tzaddik,** this does not define the person's intrinsic nature. Here "tzaddik" is merely **a figurative term** applied **in the context of reward and punishment, since one is judged** in Heaven **according to the majority** of his deeds, **and he is categorized as righteous with regard to his verdict since he was acquitted in the judgment.**

The common usage of the term *beinoni* as referring to a person whose merits and demerits are equal, an idea reflected in many sources,[10] is not the way the author of the *Tanya* is defining the term.

Some terms are nouns – in Hebrew called *shem etzem,* which literally means "name of essence" – such as man or table. Others are adjectives, such as wise or strong. Some nouns, essentially referring to one type of person, place, or thing, are used figuratively to describe another because the latter shares some facet with the essential thing.[11] A person may be a tzaddik in essence, while another person may not be a tzaddik in essence but is still deemed a tzaddik in the figurative sense because of his actions. He is a tzaddik with regard to his verdict in Heaven, just as *rasha* and *beinoni* can characterize

10. See *Rosh HaShana* 16b; *Kiddushin* 39b; Rambam, *Sefer HaMadda, Hilkhot Teshuva,* chap. 3.

11. See commentary of Rabbi Shmuel Gronem Esterman.

a person according to his deeds, weighing his performance of positive commandments against his transgressions. These distinctions focus solely on the deeds but are not an evaluation of the person's quintessential essence. ☞

אֲבָל לְעִנְיַן אֲמִיתַּת שֵׁם הַתּוֹאַר וְהַמַּעֲלָה שֶׁל מַעֲלַת וּמַדְרֵגוֹת חֲלוּקוֹת צַדִּיקִים וּבֵינוֹנִים,

However, with regard to delineating a **term that truly describes the different qualities and levels of tzaddikim and *beinonim*,**

When the tzaddik is defined as one whose merits outweigh his sins, and therefore is a tzaddik in the figurative sense, then there is no real difference between tzaddikim and *beinonim*. Yet the true definition of a tzaddik describes his intrinsic nature, which is indeed different from that of the *beinoni.*

In a certain sense, the author of the *Tanya* raises each of these categories by several levels. The *rasha* is anyone who committed even one transgression or failed to perform a viable positive commandment and has not yet repented. By our standard, the author of the *Tanya*'s definition of *rasha* is our conception of the average Jew. According to the author of the *Tanya,* the *beinoni* performs every possible good deed that he can and never committed a sin that he did not rectify. The question then becomes, what is a tzaddik?

The author of the *Tanya* goes on to explain.

THE FIGURATIVE TZADDIK

☞ A true evaluation of a person's nature based on his deeds must take into account quality along with quantity. Yet we have no way to assess a person's quality, nor can we surmise the power of his good deeds. We cannot tell whether or not a given mitzva makes a great impact or whether a particular transgression did or did not make a significant negative imprint.

In view of this, a pronouncement of meritorious does not indicate that the person in question is a tzaddik and upright at his essence. He is a tzaddik in the figurative sense, as in the verse "You shall not kill the innocent and the righteous" (Ex. 23:7). Here "righteous" does not refer to the person's intrinsic nature but rather to a person who was found innocent in judgment and so evaded capital punishment.

אָמְרוּ רַבּוֹתֵינוּ ז״ל (בתלמוד בברכות שם): ״צַדִּיקִים יֵצֶר טוֹב שׁוֹפְטָן, שֶׁנֶּאֱמַר: ׳וְלִבִּי חָלַל בְּקִרְבִּי׳״ (תהלים קט, כב), שֶׁאֵין לוֹ יֵצֶר הָרַע כִּי הֲרָגוֹ בְּתַעֲנִית.

our Rabbis state (*Berakhot* 61b), **"The good inclination** alone **rules the righteous, as the verse states, 'And my heart is dead within me'** (Ps. 109:22)." With this statement, King David was expressing **that he no longer had an evil inclination, because he killed it by fasting.**

The heart is the abode of desire and emotional impulse. When this desire is channeled toward evil, it becomes the seat of the evil inclination. The heart of the tzaddik, however, is "dead within him" – meaning empty and hollow. His heart does not contain an evil impulse. This is the essential quality of the tzaddik, who not only acts righteous like the *beinoni*, but he is a tzaddik at his core, with no evil inclination at all.

The difference between a tzaddik and a *beinoni* does not lie in their actions, speech, or even thoughts, because a person who sins even in the realm of thought by allowing forbidden thoughts to enter his mind defiles his soul and is considered a completely wicked person. (Sins of the mind may be even worse than transgressive behavior.) The *beinoni* does not even sin in thought, yet he still has an evil inclination. Although he does not allow it to manifest, it still exists palpably within him. By contrast, for the tzaddik, "his heart is dead within him." He has no evil inclination at all.

אֲבָל כָּל מִי שֶׁלֹּא הִגִּיעַ לְמַדְרֵגָה זוֹ, אַף שֶׁזְּכֻיּוֹתָיו מְרוּבִּים עַל עֲוֹנוֹתָיו, אֵינוֹ בְּמַעֲלַת וּמַדְרֵגַת צַדִּיק כְּלָל. וְלָכֵן אָמְרוּ רַבּוֹתֵינוּ ז״ל בַּמִּדְרָשׁ (יומא לח, ב): ״רָאָה הַקָּדוֹשׁ בָּרוּךְ הוּא בַּצַּדִּיקִים שֶׁהֵם מוּעָטִים, עָמַד וּשְׁתָלָן בְּכָל דּוֹר וָדוֹר וכו׳ וּכְמוֹ שֶׁכָּתוּב: ׳וְצַדִּיק יְסוֹד עוֹלָם׳ (משלי י, כה)״.

But whoever has not attained this level, where one has no evil inclination at all, **even though his merits outnumber his sins, is not at all of the status and level of a tzaddik. That is why our Rabbis expound in the Midrash** (*Yoma* 38b), **"The Holy One, blessed be He, saw that the righteous people were few,** so **He arose and planted** some of **them in each and every generation… as the verse states, 'But the tzaddik is the foundation of the world'** (Prov. 10:25)."

Tzaddikim uphold the world and, through their righteousness, justify its existence. It is in their merit that the world exists. Since there are but few tzaddikim, God distributed them throughout the generations so that the world would continue to exist.

Yet in this work the author of the *Tanya* focuses mainly on *beinonim*, not tzaddikim. As discussed above, the problem with other preexisting *mussar* works is the formulation of an ideal that is virtually impossible to attain. The innovation of the *Tanya* is in the portrayal of a new ideal: the *beinoni*.

Until this point, the concepts presented have been in the way of an introduction, presenting the concept of tzaddik, *rasha*, and *beinoni* from the sources along with an initial analysis. This point in the chapter marks the beginning of the organized, theoretical arrangement of the book: a delineation of the three levels of tzaddik, *rasha*, and *beinoni*, how they are attained, and how a person operates within the framework of these definitions.

אַךְ בֵּיאוּר הָעִנְיָן עַל פִּי מַה שֶּׁכָּתַב הָרַ׳ חַיִּים וִיטַל ז״ל בְּשַׁעַר הַקְּדוּשָּׁה (חלק א שער ב) [וּבְעֵץ חַיִּים שַׁעַר נ׳ פ״ב], דִּלְכָל אִישׁ יִשְׂרָאֵל, אֶחָד צַדִּיק וְאֶחָד רָשָׁע, יֵשׁ שְׁתֵּי נְשָׁמוֹת,

In fact, this matter can be explained in light of what Rabbi Ḥayyim Vital, of blessed memory, wrote in *Sha'ar HaKedusha* 1:2 **(and in *Etz Ḥayyim*** 50:2**), that within every Jew, whether righteous or wicked, there are two** distinct **souls,**

The basis of all that will be discussed below is the idea that every Jew has two souls (unlike non-Jews, which will be explained further on). The presence of these two souls is not contingent on the quality of a person – great or simple, righteous or wicked. Essentially, the presence of these two souls is an intrinsic component of each and every Jew no matter who he or she is. Their differing spiritual levels depend on the degree of expression of these two souls, which one is made more manifest, in what way, and to what degree in one's life and consciousness.

וּכְדִכְתִיב: ״וּנְשָׁמוֹת אֲנִי עָשִׂיתִי״ (ישעיה נז, טז), שֶׁהֵן שְׁתֵּי נְפָשׁוֹת.

as it is written, "And souls it was I who made" (Isa. 57:16) – "souls" in the plural, **referring to two souls.**

First and foremost, the author of the *Tanya* demonstrates that every Jew has two souls by citing a verse that uses the Hebrew word *neshamot,*[12] yet here he seems to emend that statement, explaining that those two souls are in essence two *nefashot.*

These two different words for soul, *nefesh* and *neshama,* are not synonymous. The term *nefesh* has a double meaning, both a particular one and in general. Its general definition is the spiritual being that enlivens every person and is distributed among five progressively higher levels. The particularized implication of the term *nefesh* refers to the lowest of these soul levels, that which is closest to the body, that which enlivens it most directly, while the level of soul called *neshama* is two levels above it. The remaining three levels are *ruaḥ* (the level between *nefesh* and *neshama*), *ḥaya,* and *yeḥida.*

Accordingly, saying that every Jew has two *neshamot* is not precise, and the author of the *Tanya* adds that the verse refers to two *nefashot* to clarify that the use of the term *neshama* in the verse does not refer to the level of *neshama* in the hierarchy within the framework of soul

---

12. On the surface, it would seem that the author of the *Tanya* could have adduced a more obvious source, one from the five books of the Torah, to prove this point. The verse states, "The Lord God formed [*vayitzer*] man of dust from the ground…" (Gen. 2:7). The Sages homiletically interpret the word *vayitzer,* which is spelled with a double *yod,* as alluding that God created two inclinations: a *yetzer tov* and a *yetzer hara,* a good inclination and an evil inclination (*Berakhot* 61a). This poses no difficulty, since it could be resolved based on the teaching recorded in *Torah Or* (63b) that explains that the good inclination refers only to the attributes of the divine soul, and the evil inclination denotes the attributes of the animal soul – the two souls referred to here by the author of the *Tanya.* In our context, however, the author of the *Tanya* teaches a novel idea about the root of these two souls, as he goes on to explain. See also *Likkutei Torah,* Deut. 37d. Rabbi Shmuel Gronem Esterman suggests, in his commentary on the *Tanya,* that the verse that the author of the *Tanya* cites here is not meant to serve as a concrete proof to the concept of two souls but rather functions as a mere support.

levels.[13] Rather, it refers to the *nefesh* in its broad sense of the spiritual force that enlivens the body.[14]

נֶפֶשׁ אַחַת מִצַּד הַקְּלִיפָּה וְסִטְרָא אָחֳרָא,

One soul is rooted in the *kelippa*, the husk of impurity, **and the *sitra aḥara*,** literally, "the other side," referring to the forces of impurity.

One of the two aforementioned souls stems from the *kelippa* and the *sitra aḥara,* the side of evil and impurity in opposition to the side of holiness.

In truth, *kelippa* and *sitra aḥara* are concepts that hasidic teachings, and particularly that of Chabad, do not elucidate too extensively. One reason is that one who is familiar with these forces knows of them, and if he is not familiar, why familiarize him? The main reason that hasidic teachings avoid going into too much detail is that one who delves into evil in any way, even to rectify it, is drawn into negativity, making contact and creating a familiarity that has many adverse repercussions.

In a very broad sense, without getting too specific, the world can be divided into two sides: the side of holiness and the other side. The side of holiness belongs to God and to anyone who acknowledges His presence and accepts His authority. The other side does not even have an independent name because it does not have its own essence. It is only "other," something that is other than holiness, and therefore it is viewed as negating holiness.

According to the author of the *Tanya,* a neutral position between

---

13. Rabbi Shmuel Gronem Esterman points out that this misnomer stems from the expression employed in the aforementioned verse, "And souls [*neshamot*] it was I who made." Yet there are seventy ways to interpret *Tanach*. Moreover, according to the Lubavitcher Rebbe, Rabbi Menaḥem Mendel Schneerson, this verse can be read to bear a precise meaning: The verse refers to the higher realms, where "it was I who made." For this reason, it refers to *neshamot*. Upon their descent into the lower realm to be enclothed within the body, they are delineated as *nefashot*.

14. This assertion is obvious, since the higher level, the *neshama,* is not necessarily found within every person, "both righteous and wicked." Only the lower level, the *nefesh,* is equally present in all people (Lubavitcher Rebbe, Rabbi Menaḥem Mendel Schneerson).

the holy and the unholy does not exist. Everything falls into either the category of holiness or the lack of holiness. A person who cleaves to God is on the side of holiness, and if he does not cleave to God, he finds himself on the other side. One who is not in favor is necessarily opposed.

This approach is also connected to the definition of the *beinoni* herein. As mentioned above, no average exists between tzaddik and *rasha*. One who is not a tzaddik, who is not connected to the side of holiness, necessarily belongs to the *sitra aḥara* and is essentially a *rasha*. In this light, the *beinoni* depicted by the author of the *Tanya* is like the tzaddik in that he does not sin and has no association whatsoever with the other side, and if he does sin, he belongs to an entirely different realm and becomes associated with the other side.

From the perspective of *halakha*, one finds a different approach. A whole dimension of Jewish law deals with situations that fall neither into the category of obligatory nor prohibited. There are commandments, prohibited actions, and permissible actions. Kabbala, on the other hand, views the dimension of the permissible, not as neutral, but rather as belonging to the *sitra aḥara*, that which has not yet been transformed into holiness and so by definition is "other." Though there is nothing that is not either holy or impure, there is a significant division within the realm of impurity: impurity that can be rectified and impurity that cannot. *Kelippa* that has no rectification, that cannot be elevated to holiness, falls into the category of that which is prohibited according to the *halakha*. That which is permissible in *halakha* is a paradigm of *kelippa* that bears the possibility of rectification, harboring the potential to be elevated to holiness. Belonging to the *sitra aḥara*, it can and must be transferred to the side of holiness. ☞

KELIPPA VERSUS *SITRA AḤARA*

☞ Another aspect of the *sitra aḥara* can be extrapolated by understanding another implication of the word *aḥara*. In addition to meaning "other," as in other side, the term also means "back" as in *panim ve'aḥor*, front and back, which relates to the other term used here for evil, *kelippa*.

Kelippa, which literally means husk or peel, is not just a label but rather an analogy lending insight into the relationship between good and evil. The fruit is good and desirable, and the function of the peel that surrounds it is merely to protect it. The peel itself is inedible. When the fruit reach-

וְהִיא הַמִּתְלַבֶּשֶׁת בְּדַם הָאָדָם לְהַחֲיוֹת הַגּוּף, וּכְדִכְתִיב: "כִּי נֶפֶשׁ הַבָּשָׂר בַּדָּם הִיא" (ויקרא יז, יא).

This soul **is clothed within a person's blood in order to animate the body, as it is written, "For the life of the flesh is in the blood"** (Lev. 17:11).

The first *nefesh* that the author of the *Tanya* describes is the vital, natural soul. It is the soul of life that provides man with vitality in every aspect of his natural, spiritual, and physical being. This is the "soul of flesh" that binds with the body by becoming enclothed in the blood and sustains a person as part of the global biological ecosystem. ☞

וּמִמֶּנָּה בָּאוֹת כָּל הַמִּדּוֹת רָעוֹת מֵאַרְבַּע יְסוֹדוֹת רָעִים שֶׁבָּהּ.

From this soul **stem all evil traits,** which emanate **from the four elements of evil contained within** this soul.

All negative human attributes stem from the vital soul, in accordance with the four basic elements that comprise it. These four foundational elements – fire, water, wind, earth – encapsulate the entire physical world, as was accepted in the ancient world and, to a certain degree, in Jewish thought. These are not the indivisible elements delineated in

es a certain level of ripeness, the peel becomes an impediment that must be eliminated.

In view of this, *kelippa* and *sitra aḥara* are not just two terms for the same phenomenon. *Sitra aḥara* is the characterization of one of two facets of existence, a realm that denies God and rejects His authority, as opposed to the other facet, the side of holiness. The term *kelippa* offers a glimpse into the dynamic between them. Instead of a structure that cuts all of reality diametrically into two, *kelippa* suggests a concentric structure. Holiness lies within, surrounded by a husk. When one breaks through the husk, he reaches holiness.

This dynamic does not present itself when discussing holiness as being on one side and impurity on the other, corresponding to positive and negative, light and darkness. One cannot reach the light by breaking through the darkness; the negative cannot engender the positive. But when the comparison is to a fruit and peel, the pathway becomes clear: Penetrate the peel to discover underlying holiness. As the author of the *Tanya* explains further on (chap. 29; see also *Iggeret HaTeshuva*, chap. 7), one needs to break, diminish, and crush the *kelippa* and *sitra aḥara* to dust until the light within bursts through.

chemistry but rather the four basic elements that constitute everything in the universe.[15]

Early commentators explain that these refer to four states of physical material – cold, wet, hot, and dry – or, in modern-day terms, solid, liquid, gas, and energy. Here the author of the *Tanya* discusses the parallel of these elements to the attributes of the soul that is attached to the body and the material world. Like the fabric of this soul, its attributes are evil in the sense that they are associated with the realm of the mundane, which is considered *kelippa.*

דְּהַיְינוּ, כַּעַס וְגַאֲוָה מִיסוֹד הָאֵשׁ שֶׁנִּגְבַּהּ לְמַעְלָה,	**Namely, anger and arrogance** emanate **from the element of fire, which rises upward.**

Anger and arrogance are intrinsically connected; one engenders the other. Here, however, the author of the *Tanya* is referring to their structural similarity. Like fire that perpetually rises upward, anger and arrogance are attributes that stem from an inflated ego and self-aggrandizement. Arrogance is a swollen sense of self, while anger is a

ENCLOTHED IN THE BLOOD

☞ "Enclothing" is not just a term used to imply a physical reality, but it may be understood in the same sense as clothing, a concept that includes both the elements of exposure and concealment simultaneously. A garment covers and hides a person while also serving to expose him to others.

The dynamic between speech and thought portrays how nonphysical clothing works. Thought becomes enclothed in speech, which means that speech simultaneously reveals and conceals the thought within because the listener relates only to the speech. This is also comparable to light and vessel, to a receptacle and its contents. The vessel serves as the medium through which the light manifests and functions, while at the same time the vessel conceals the light.

This is the way the vital animal soul is clothed in the blood of man: hiding within it, yet being revealed through it. This *nefesh* infuses the body with its spiritual life force through the blood, while at the same time it becomes obscured in the physical body.

15. See the Lubavitcher Rebbe, Rabbi Menaḥem Mendel Schneerson, *Iggerot Kodesh*, vol. 19, p. 239.

response to anything that disturbs one's sense of me and myself and no other. Like fire, which rises upward on its own, anger and arrogance are attributes that spontaneously surge up.

The more one engages in other negative attributes, the less he is captivated by them until they eventually dissipate. But when it comes to anger and arrogance, the more one engages in them, the more they increase. This is why the Hebrew term for each is in the reflexive form – *mitragez* and *mitga'eh*, to cause oneself to be angry and to cause oneself to be prideful. When a person allows himself to be prideful, the pride reverts back on him, making him even more arrogant. When a person gets angry and wallows in his anger, he works himself up even more. Arrogance and pride fuel themselves, inflaming and further igniting, just like fire, increasing and rising ever higher.

וְתַאֲוַת הַתַּעֲנוּגִים מִיסוֹד הַמַּיִם, כִּי הַמַּיִם מַצְמִיחִים כָּל מִינֵי תַּעֲנוּג,

The desire for pleasures emanates **from the element of water, for water causes the growth of all sorts of pleasures.**

"The desire for pleasures" does not necessarily imply mere lust or physical desire. All desire constitutes a drive for something specific. "The desire for pleasures" refers to the craving for anything that gives a person pleasure, whose roots lie in the element of water, the foundation of life, fertility, and delight felt by the animal soul. Water represents the faculties of kindness and love, which in their negative manifestations in the realm of *kelippa* lead to repugnant desires and destructive love, to lusting after pleasure simply for its own sake.

BOASTFULNESS VERSUS ARROGANCE

☞ The author of the *Tanya* makes a distinction between these two attributes, noting that boastfulness is rooted in the element of wind and differs from arrogance, which is rooted in the element of fire. Some people are clearly arrogant yet do not flatter themselves, while there are those who boast about themselves yet are not prideful. These are two distinct attributes not necessarily attributed to the same type of person.

וְהוֹלֵלוּת וְלֵיצָנוּת וְהִתְפָּאֲרוּת
וּדְבָרִים בְּטֵלִים מִיסוֹד הָרוּחַ,

Frivolity, scoffing, boastfulness, and idle talk all emanate **from the element of air,**

These attributes are vapid, wind-like characteristics, lacking any real substance. Scoffing, frivolity, and boastfulness express a degree of anarchy and irresponsibility. This is not a craving for greatness or pleasure, but only so much hot air. Something puffed up with air seems to be filled with content but actually contains nothing of substance. Similarly, a person exhibiting these attributes seems to be accomplished but is filled with nothing but air. ☞

וְעַצְלוּת וְעַצְבוּת מִיסוֹד הֶעָפָר.

and slothfulness and depression emanate **from the element of earth.**

Earth is the lowest element, drawing the vital soul down to inactivity. Whether stemming from lethargy or melancholy, laziness is a sensation of heaviness, of inability to motivate oneself to accomplish what one needs or wants. Sadness numbs the desire for productivity and creation even to the point where a person is paralyzed from functioning and responding to his surroundings.

The division of all negative attributes into four categories embodied by each of the four elements does not suggest that one person cannot exhibit all four. This is certainly possible. These categories resemble *avot,* principle categories in *halakha,* foundational theoretical structures, each one of which constitutes an edifice in and of itself. The *toledot,* derivatives that stem from an *av,* are each rooted in one element. Various *toledot* that stem from the same principle attribute can blend together and feed into each other. Attributes that are derivatives of different principles can exist within one person yet still remain distinct attributes. They are intrinsically two different attributes yet can reside within the same person. ☞

ATTRIBUTES AND ELEMENTS

☞ Although the negative attributes stem from the four elements that are contained in the vital soul, they are not identical to them. Various other religions and particular world outlooks tend to identify attributes, good and bad, with particular characteristics of the soul. For example, in many cultures, it is widely accepted that being sober

וְגַם מִדּוֹת טוֹבוֹת שֶׁבְּטֶבַע כָּל יִשְׂרָאֵל בְּתוֹלְדוֹתָם,

So too positive attributes that are innate within every Jew,

The vital soul is not inherently bad but rather defines the innate nature of an individual Jew. This vital, spiritual, and emotional force enlivens a person and may be channeled either for good or bad. ☞

כְּמוֹ רַחֲמָנוּת וּגְמִילוּת חֲסָדִים, בָּאוֹת מִמֶּנָּה.

such as compassion and kindheartedness, stem from the vital soul.

and sad is a good quality, while cheerfulness is considered a fault. This implies that sin comes about as a result of happiness and gaiety but not sadness and seriousness. By contrast, there is an opposing view that a good attribute is one that motivates action. Therefore, joy and cheerfulness are essentially positive attributes, while even anger and arrogance are not necessarily negative.

Clearly, the four elements have no bearing on the distinction between positive attributes and negative ones. The same attributes can be good in one circumstance and bad in another. It is not that one element is good and another is bad, but rather that the same element can be the root of both positive and negative attributes. Positive and negative attributes are not two different species but rather relate to each other like mirror images, as the verse says, "God made this corresponding to that" (Eccles. 7:14).

The distinction between negative and positive attributes is rooted, not in their nature and character, but rather in their application in given situations. Therefore, a person who exhibits one attribute or another is not necessarily good or bad. It depends on what he does with the energies of his soul and the choices that are laid before him. Even sadness, which all hasidic thinkers condemned, has a place in certain situations, and it can be channeled for good purposes (with great caution).

Similarly, one tzaddik related that one of his hasidim refrained from committing transgressions purely out of arrogance. How could a person of his caliber reduce himself to such a pitiful state as sin?!

This principle is at play in the world of nature as well. Even the most fatal poisons are not lethal in every manner and amount. Some are used in precise amounts and ways to formulate remedies.

THE VITAL SOUL OF MAN

☞ Every creation has a vital soul, which is not merely a nebulous energy but rather a complex, unique life force which makes that creation what it is, whether man, animal, or stone. Imprinted in the vital soul are the characteristics that comprise the uniqueness of a person: his desires, perspectives, and physical and spiritual tendencies.

The vital, or animal, soul informs one's biological makeup. In this sense, human thought and speech are also part of that definition. Even such higher functions as philosophical reasoning, a faculty of the mind, is part of a person's biological framework. In a Jew, this blueprint also includes positive character traits.

The degree to which a Jew actualizes his

The Talmud states, "There are three distinguishing marks to this nation [the Jewish people]: [They are] compassionate, bashful, and kind" (*Yevamot* 79a). These qualities are part of a Jew's identity to the extent that the Sages were wont to say that a person who does not display these characteristics is clearly not Jewish. A Jew is charitable not because he subjugated his negative inclination, or because he is an especially good person, but rather because it is part of his vital soul's DNA. Just as some people have particular weaknesses and are sympathetic to certain causes, so too a Jew has certain "weaknesses": he is humble, compassionate, and benevolent.

Some people have a musical sense yet are not better or worse human beings because of it. That Jews are humble, benevolent, and compassionate is an innate part of their makeup. They were born that way. These traits are hereditary, and this does not make them tzaddikim – it just makes them Jews.[16] ☞

כִּי בְּיִשְׂרָאֵל נֶפֶשׁ זוֹ דִּקְלִיפָּה הִיא מִקְּלִיפַּת נוֹגַהּ שֶׁיֵּשׁ בָּהּ גַּם כֵּן טוֹב,

For with regard to **a Jew, this soul of *kelippa*** stems **from the *kelippa*** called ***noga,* which also contains good** aspects.

inherent, unique potential to attain lofty spiritual heights is another question. The answer depends on his education, development, and, primarily, his willpower. This is also true regarding man in general. It is known that a child raised by wolves would barely develop human characteristics, and then only on the most rudimentary level.

In studies conducted with animals, it was found that the more sophisticated the creature, the more training it needed to function in the manner unique to its species. A fly does not have to learn. Everything it needs to know it figures out on its own. More advanced species, on the other hand, must learn. If they are not raised in the proper environment, a deviation from their intrinsic growth curve will develop, and they will not behave like the rest of their species.

BASHFULNESS

☞ The Lubavitcher Rebbe, Rabbi Menaḥem Mendel Schneerson, points out that the author of the *Tanya* mentions only two of the three attributes that are intrinsic to the Jewish people, compassion and kindheartedness, excluding the third, bashfulness.

Being compassionate and performing

16. See chap. 6 for further explanation regarding the good attributes intrinsic to the Jew's vital soul.

In general, there are four *kelippot*: the three impure *kelippot* and the *kelippa* of *noga,* which literally means glowing. Their names are extrapolated from a verse in Ezekiel's vision of the divine chariot: "I saw, and behold, a storm wind was coming from the north, a great cloud and fire igniting and an aura surrounding it..." (Ezek. 1:4). "Storm wind," "great cloud," and "fire igniting" correspond to the three impure *kelippot,* while "an aura surrounding it" refers to the fourth *kelippa* called *kelippat noga.*

The *kelippa* of *noga* is the realm between the world of impurity, which is entirely darkness and oblivion, and holiness, which is solely light. It is a *kelippa* and so it is dark, but it is a darkness with *noga* – a darkness illuminated by a glimmer of light. ☞

וְהִיא מִסּוֹד "עֵץ הַדַּעַת טוֹב וָרָע" (בראשית ב, ט).

This *kelippa* is derived **from the mystery of "the tree of the knowledge of good and evil"** (Gen. 2:9).

The tree of the knowledge of good and evil is the foundation and paradigm of *kelippat noga,* of the mixture of light and darkness, of good and evil in one working blend. When Adam ate from the tree of knowledge, he broke the global balance between good and evil, creating an intermediate reality between holiness and *kelippa.* From now on, they would struggle, receiving spiritual nourishment from each other, one influencing the other. This is a dangerous reality, wherein the *kelippa* receives its spiritual nourishment from the realm of holiness yet is also gradually rectified and refined by it. This is the reality of *kelippat noga* in this world, the realm where Jewish souls have been sent after Adam's sin, so that they may cultivate and rectify it.

מַה שֶּׁאֵין כֵּן נַפְשׁוֹת אוּמּוֹת הָעוֹלָם הֵן מִשְּׁאָר קְלִיפּוֹת

This is not the case with regard to **the souls of the** gentile **nations of the**

acts of kindness are characteristics inborn in their nature, but humility is a characteristic they developed. The Jewish people are naturally the most brazen of nations (*Beitza* 25b). When they received the Torah, it weakened their strength, and they became humble (see *Likkutei Biurim LaTanya*; Maharsha, *Yevamot* 79a).

טְמֵאוֹת שֶׁאֵין בָּהֶן טוֹב כְּלָל, כְּמוֹ שֶׁכָּתוּב בְּעֵץ חַיִּים שַׁעַר מ"ט פרק ג׳. "וְכָל טִיבוּ דְּעָבְדִין הָאוּמּוֹת - לְגַרְמַיְיהוּ עָבְדִין".

world, which are derived from the other, impure *kelippot*, which contain no good whatsoever, as it is written in *Etz Ḥayyim* 49:3. As the *Zohar* states, **"Any good** deed **performed by the nations is performed for their own** selfish purposes" (see *Tikkunei Zohar* 22a).

The entire *kelippa* system revolves around ego, where the "I" becomes the central axis of anything that is executed through its power. The starting point is always "How do I benefit?" In light of this, even the good that is accomplished flows from ulterior motives, whether out of pride or out of a desire to maintain the status quo of the world that revolves around me. It is not authentically good, which actually constitutes nullification of the self and giving to another.

THE *KELIPPA* OF *NOGA* VERSUS THE IMPURE *KELIPPOT*

☞ As will be explained, even the impure *kelippot* are not entirely lacking light. Nothing exists without some good mixed in with it. The essence of good, of holiness, and of a divine reality is foundationally one. Defining something as lacking all good entirely therefore negates its very existence. If something exists, it must contain some good.

In light of this, even the three impure *kelippot* possess a divine spark within (see Tzemaḥ Tzedek, end of *Derekh Mitzvotekha*). The significant difference between the three impure *kelippot* and the *kelippa* of *noga* lies in the capacity to release the good from them.

This is true in general. Certain good aspects can be extracted from some things, while from others, the good is inaccessible. This does not necessarily depend on the amount of good present but rather in the degree to which it can be extracted.

In industry, one of the materials in highest demand is aluminum. While aluminum is one of the most common elements in nature, present in almost every sample of earth, extracting it from ordinary earth is nearly impossible. Rather, one must mine the aluminum ore called bauxite and then extract it through a chemical process.

This represents to a certain degree the difference between the three impure *kelippot* and the *kelippa* of *noga*. In the former, the good is impossible to extract, while the mixture of good and bad in *noga* is more overt and therefore separable.

וְכִדְאִיתָא בַּגְּמָרָא (בבא בתרא י, ב) עַל פָּסוּק "וְחֶסֶד לְאוּמִּים חַטָּאת" (משלי יד, לד), שֶׁכָּל צְדָקָה וָחֶסֶד שֶׁאוּמּוֹת הָעוֹלָם עוֹשִׂין אֵינָן אֶלָּא לְהִתְיַיהֵר כו'.

This is supported by **the Talmud's statement regarding the verse "Kindness of nations is sin"** (Prov. 14:34): **"All the** acts of **charity and kindness that the nations of the world perform** are counted as a sin for them, since they perform them **only in order to glorify themselves…"** (*Bava Batra* 10b).

These statements are not quoted in order to denigrate the gentile nations but rather to provide background for the subject that the author of the *Tanya* is addressing here: the vital soul of the Jew. The chosenness of the Jewish people and their uniqueness amid the nations lies in the dimension of the vital soul and not in the divine soul, which Jews possess and non-Jews do not have at all. The souls of the nations of the world are like a tree trunk from which the animal soul of the Jew sprouts, both comparable and incomparable to the souls of gentiles. ☞ ☞

In this chapter, the author of the *Tanya* explained that there are two souls within man, the first of which animates the body and is known as the animal soul or the vital soul. Although this soul stems from *kelippa,* it does not embody the essence of evil nor is it synonymous

THE CHOSENNESS OF THE JEWISH PEOPLE

☞ The selection of the Jewish people as the chosen nation, described in the book of Genesis, may be compared to genomic selection of plants. Out of tens of thousands of grafts, three or four seedlings with desirable traits will emerge. When grafted with each other, again and again, a unique species, with new characteristics, naturally emerges.

The stories in Genesis may be viewed as telling a similar tale. God chooses one branch from millions of people. From that branch He chooses one offshoot, which He raises and nurtures with caution until it blossoms into a new species. This species is the product of natural mutation and emerges from thousands of possibilities. Since the "species" has been bred with specific innate qualities, members of this group do not need to go against their nature or overly exert themselves to achieve certain levels of goodness. Other groups of humans are also capable of accomplishing such levels, but they must expend greater effort, display focused intent, and undergo spiritual preparation to accomplish the same degree of good.

with the evil traits that emanate from it. On the contrary, it is also the source of the Jew's innate positive characteristics, his kindness and compassion.

Yet this soul's capacity, no matter how large, does not even remotely touch upon the dimension of holiness. No part of a person's vital soul propels him toward that which is holy. Even if a person were to refine his body and the vital soul that vivifies it to the ultimate degree, he would not encounter holiness, nor does a refined aesthetic sense or a powerful mental capacity, both faculties of this soul, necessarily engender holiness.

In the next chapter, the author of the *Tanya* will discuss the second facet of the Jewish soul: the divine soul.

A QUESTION ABOUT THE NATIONS

☞ The story is told that when Rabbi Shneur Zalman of Liadi, the author of the *Tanya*, was incarcerated, interrogators demanded that he answer many questions relating to the position of Hasidism on various issues. Among questions about various customs and the mystical dimension of Torah, there was one question regarding his statement here about the nations of the world. As described in the book *Beit Rebbe*, Rabbi Shneur Zalman answered all the inquiries to the interrogators' liking, but when they came to the question about the nations, he did not answer them at all. He only smiled. It is written there that those who understand will know the reason behind the smile.

Another source attests that he did answer them, saying, "After answering all the previous questions and proving to you that I am correct, must I answer this question as well? Better that we leave it be" (see *Sefer HaToledot Rabbi Shneur Zalman MiLiadi*, edited by Rabbi Avraham Ḥanokh Glitzenstein).

Chapter 2

IN THE PREVIOUS CHAPTER, THE AUTHOR OF THE *Tanya* described the animal soul, or vital soul, which stems from *kelippa*. The vital soul comprises only one facet of a person. There is another facet, one that gravitates toward holiness and guides the individual and the world toward the side of holiness. This aspect, the second soul that abides within man – what is called the divine soul – exists on a completely different plane of existence and is the focus of the second chapter.

24 Kislev / 26 Kislev (leap year)

וְנֶפֶשׁ הַשֵּׁנִית בְּיִשְׂרָאֵל הִיא חֵלֶק אֱלוֹ־הַּ מִמַּעַל מַמָּשׁ,

The second soul within a Jew is literally a portion of God on high,

This soul is the divine aspect of a person, comprised of divine essence that manifests within his being. The emphasis on the word "literally" indicates that this expression, "a portion of God on high," is not just a flowery phrase, but one that must be understood literally. The divine soul is literally a part of God. Not figuratively, but actually.

Given its supreme virtue and loftiness, it would seem that this soul should be the first in order of rank, yet the author of the *Tanya* deems it the "second soul within a Jew." One explanation for this is that this soul is chronologically second. Man is born with an evil inclination and only later receives his good inclination.[1] Although the divine soul gives life to a person even from birth, it does not manifest in the form of the good inclination until the age of maturity. For the expression and revelation of the divine soul, a developed receptacle is necessary. If the vessel

1. See *Kohelet Rabba*, Eccles. 4:13; Zohar 1:179a; *Shulḥan Arukh HaRav, Oraḥ Ḥayyim* 4, second edition.

lacks the required faculties, it will not be capable of containing the divine soul in a manifest way, but rather the soul will remain latent.

If the soul of man were to enter a stone, the union would be meaningless because the human soul cannot express itself through such a medium. The manifestation of every spiritual level demands a corresponding preliminary preparation. For the revelation of a Jew's divine soul, a portion of God above, the presence of the animal soul is necessary. Its cultivation enables the divine soul to merge with it, manifest within it, and refine it in a meaningful way.[2]

כְּמוֹ שֶׁכָּתוּב: "וַיִּפַּח בְּאַפָּיו נִשְׁמַת חַיִּים" (בראשית ב, ז), "וְאַתָּה נְפַחְתָּהּ בִּי". וּכְמוֹ שֶׁכָּתוּב בַּזֹּהַר: "מַאן דְּנָפַח מִתּוֹכֵיהּ נָפַח", פֵּירוּשׁ מִתּוֹכִיּוּתוֹ וּמִפְּנִימִיּוּתוֹ, שֶׁתּוֹכִיּוּת וּפְנִימִיּוּת הַחַיּוּת שֶׁבָּאָדָם מוֹצִיא בִּנְפִיחָתוֹ בְּכֹחַ.

as it is written, "And He blew into his nostrils the soul of life" (Gen. 2:7), and, similarly, in the morning blessings, "**You blew** it **into me.**" This concept is clarified by **the *Zohar*'s statement "One who blows, from within himself he blows," meaning from within His essence and innermost being, since by blowing forcefully, one emits the innermost essence of his life force.**

The life force that was manifest when God "blew into [Adam's] nostrils the soul of life" differs from the word of God, from the breath or life force that powers divine speech. God's speech created and constantly sustains the heavens, the earth, and everything in them, as will be explained in part 2, *Sha'ar HaYiḥud VeHa'emuna.* The exception to this rule is the human soul, about which it is written, "And He blew into his nostrils the soul of life." To understand the difference, one must explore the concepts of the breath of speech and blowing in the physical realm when employed by man.

When a person speaks, he exhales only a portion of the air within him, breathing as he is speaking. Speech is only a partial expression of a

2. In *Likkutei Biurim LaTanya,* the Lubavitcher Rebbe, Rabbi Menaḥem Mendel Schneerson, points out that the divine soul itself does not need to be rectified. The only reason it descends into the body is to refine the animal soul and the evil inclination. For this reason, the divine soul is called "second."

person's essence and self and therefore formulates something external to the speaker. By contrast, a person who blows, blows from within himself, as the quote from the *Zohar* indicates.[3] "He blew into His nostrils" does not constitute creation rooted in the external power of speech, as is the case with all other created entities, but rather God gave something of Himself, issuing from His essence the "soul of life" – the very soul of man, a portion of God on high.

"And He blew into his nostrils the soul of life" implies a connection to God that runs deeper than that of the rest of creation. The universe was created through God's speech, with only external air, as it were, while the human soul is literally the breath of God. Man, then, is sustained from the power of a "portion of God on high" in the innermost facet of his being present and active within him. ☞

כָּךְ עַל דֶּרֶךְ מָשָׁל, נִשְׁמוֹת יִשְׂרָאֵל עָלוּ בְּמַחֲשָׁבָה,

So too this is analogous to the souls of the Jewish people that **arose in** divine **thought,**

This sheds light on another facet of the words "He blew into his nostrils the soul of life." Having been created through God's word, all creative entities are bound to God in the same sense that speech is connected

A PORTION OF GOD WITHIN

☞ The fact that the human soul is a "portion of God on high" is not merely a theoretical idea. It is the conceptual key to unlocking the intense demands contained within this book. The book expects of the *beinoni* what others consider the level of a complete tzaddik: ultimate perfection. This can only be asked of a person who is a "portion of God on high."

One must keep in mind that the author of the *Tanya*'s objective is not to give a general theoretical picture, but rather to provide schemas that a person can employ in his service of God and in a lifetime of interpersonal interactions on the moral plane. To that end, a person needs to be aware that the most lofty, powerful, holy thing, a portion of God on high, exists within him. It is incumbent on him to do everything in his power to express it in actuality so that it will "literally" be manifest within his physical body.

3. See *Iggeret HaKodesh*, epistle 15, where this statement is also quoted. The Lubavitcher Rebbe, Rabbi Menaḥem Mendel Schneerson, notes that apparently this statement does not appear in our editions of the *Zohar* or the *Tikkunei Zohar*, but it does appear in other early works, some of which attribute this statement to the Sages.

to the speaker: externally. The Jewish soul, conversely, "arose in [divine] thought." Compared to speech, thought is internal, one's expression to himself.

כִּדְכְתִיב: "בְּנִי בְכוֹרִי יִשְׂרָאֵל" (שמות ד, כב), "בָּנִים אַתֶּם לַה' אֱלֹהֵיכֶם" (דברים יד, א). פֵּירוּשׁ, כְּמוֹ שֶׁהַבֵּן נִמְשָׁךְ מִמּוֹחַ הָאָב, כָּךְ כִּבְיָכוֹל נִשְׁמַת כָּל אִישׁ יִשְׂרָאֵל נִמְשְׁכָה מִמַּחֲשַׁבְתּוֹ וְחָכְמָתוֹ יִתְבָּרֵךְ,

as it is written, "My firstborn son is Israel" (Ex. 4:22), and **"You are children to the Lord your God"** (Deut. 14:1). **This means that just as a child** is created by being **drawn from the father's brain, so too the soul of each Jew is drawn from God's thought and wisdom, as it were,**

The relationship between father and child serves as yet another metaphor for the connection between the divine soul and God. This imagery, of the child being drawn from the father's mind, comes from the ancient medical theory that assumed that the drop of seed that the father contributes to the conceiving of a child originated in the father's mind as hyle, formless, almost spiritual, primal matter. According to this theory, this drop exits the mind and descends through the body, becoming increasingly solidified and physical until it finally takes shape and forms as a drop of seed that will grow and develop into the child. In that case, the connection between father and child far transcends the physical and touches on the roots of their being in spirit. Father and child are united at their essence, and only through the process of materialization does the child separate from the father to become an independent being.

This imagery implies that at the child's very inception, he is part and parcel of his father's psyche. Formed by the depths of the father's self through a complicated process, the child crystallizes into a being that is outwardly distinct but on the most basic level is part of the father's spiritual self-identity.

In this sense, a Jew is a child of God. The root of the divine soul within him, at its source, does not just result from a spark of divine will but rather is a constant manifestation of the Divine. This is the soul level known as *yeḥida*, the focal point where all souls are unified into one entity, where the soul lacks any independent existence and its reality as a "portion of God on high" emerges and all the disparate parts of the whole merge together and are subsumed within the Divine.

This is the basis for the hasidic concept of *deveikut*, literally "cleaving" or "attachment" to God. It is the process by which a person reverts back through the stages of his own creation until he arrives at the point where he ceases to be an independent being. He then achieves what the *Zohar* calls "being drawn into the King's body"[4] – being subsumed into the essence of the King, like a child who actually returned to the state where he was literally a portion of his father's thoughts. ☞

"דְּאִיהוּ חַכִּים וְלָא בְּחָכְמָה יְדִיעָא" (תיקוני זוהר יז:), אֶלָּא הוּא וְחָכְמָתוֹ - אֶחָד,

for "God **is wise, yet not with known wisdom**" (*Tikkunei Zohar* 17b), **but rather, He and His wisdom are one,**

The soul of every Jew is drawn from God's wisdom, which the *Zohar* describes as wisdom that is not known.[5] In other words, we cannot understand or even relate to God's wisdom. Man's wisdom, understanding,

DRAWN FROM THE MIND OF THE FATHER

☞ If one were to describe this process in modern-day terms, one would describe how the pituitary gland secretes hormones that instruct the reproductive glands to produce a certain number of sperm cells. The pituitary gland does not function automatically but is activated by the senses and the power of thought, which are engendered by the consciousness. There is a progressive chain of cause and effect between the initial kernel of consciousness that arises in the thoughts and its physical manifestation, where the totally immaterial translates into sensations and thoughts, activating physiological mechanisms in the brain. This sparks various bodily responses until the actual sperm cells are formed. The technical details of the process are, of course, more complex, involving many stages of transition and progression from one phase to another, but the idea is the same: According to the scientific lens as well, there is a connection between the father's mind and the sperm cell.

Irrespective of one's preferred terminology, the relationship between father and son is one of unity at their source, and even when they become two separate beings, at their root they are essentially one.

4. See *Zohar* 1:217b.

5. This refers to the *Ḥokhma* that is manifest in the world of *Atzilut*, the world that is the most spiritual, as opposed to the *Ḥokhma* that is manifest in the worlds

and consciousness are essentially additional and in a sense outside him. Man generally knows that which is external and separate from him, so his knowledge is distinct from him. Certainly he connects with what he knows, is affected by it, and even changes due to its influence, yet still his essence remains separate from his wisdom.

This is not the case with God. Since there is nothing other than Him, His knowledge is necessarily an inseparable part of His being.

וּכְמוֹ שֶׁכָּתַב הָרַמְבַּ"ם: "שֶׁהוּא הַמַּדָּע וְהוּא הַיּוֹדֵעַ" כו'.

as Rambam stated, "He is the known, He is the knower…" (see *Sefer HaMadda, Hilkhot Yesodei HaTorah* 2:10).

Rambam posits that knowledge can be divided into three categories: the knower, the object being known, and the knowledge itself.[6] With regard to God, these three categories are one. He is not only the knower, but He is also the object being known and the knowledge itself.

הַגָּהָה: וְהוֹדוּ לוֹ חַכְמֵי הַקַּבָּלָה,

Gloss: The sages of Kabbala concur with him,

There were sages who disagreed with Rambam on this point,[7] but most kabbalists, regardless of the degree to which their world outlook diverged from Rambam's, agreed with him on two points. First, God's wisdom is essentially different in every way from every level and semblance of human wisdom, and second, God's wisdom is not separate

of *Beria, Yetzira,* and *Asiya,* which is a wisdom that can be described as known. (Each of the ten *sefirot* is manifest in each of the four worlds.) See *Torah Or* 10c.

6. To understand why the author of the *Tanya* here omitted the third category, knowledge, from this quote of Rambam, and why the order of the categories presented here differs from the author's citation of Rambam in chapter 4 below, see the letter of the sixth Lubavitcher Rebbe, Rabbi Yosef Yitzḥak Schneerson, printed in *Kitzurim VeHe'arot,* p. 118. See also *Sha'ar HaYiḥud VeHa'emuna,* chap. 7, where this concept is discussed at length.

7. See Maharal, *Gevurot Hashem,* Introduction; *Derekh Mitzvotekha, Mitzvat Ha'amanat Elokut,* chap. 3, and *Shoresh Mitzvat HaTefilla,* chap. 25.

from Him, but rather is unified with Him in absolute unity and totally removed from anything we are able to fathom.

כְּמוֹ שֶׁכָּתוּב בְּפַרְדֵּס מֵהָרַמַ"ק. וְגַם לְפִי קַבָּלַת הָאֲרִ"י ז"ל יַצִּיבָא מִילְּתָא בְּסוֹד הִתְלַבְּשׁוּת אוֹר אֵין סוֹף בָּרוּךְ הוּא עַל יְדֵי צִמְצוּמִים רַבִּים בִּכְלִים דְּחָכְמָה בִּינָה דַּעַת דַּאֲצִילוּת, אַךְ לֹא לְמַעְלָה מֵהָאֲצִילוּת.

as stated in *Pardes Rimmonim* (4:3) by Rabbi Moshe Kordevero. According to the kabbalistic teachings of the Arizal, of blessed memory, as well, this concept is correct specifically as **it pertains to the mystery of the light of *Ein Sof*, blessed be He, which is clothed by means of many constrictions in the vessels of** the *sefirot* of ***Ḥokhma, Bina,*** and ***Da'at*** **of** the world of ***Atzilut*** (Emanation), **though not above *Atzilut*.**

According to the teachings of the Arizal, who attained loftier levels than even Rabbi Moshe Kordevero, Rambam's statement regarding the identical nature of the knower, the known, and the knowledge is only partially accurate. It is incorrect when related to the divine essence itself (substantiating the Maharal's standpoint that one cannot equate the divine essence with wisdom, just as it is impossible to equate it with any other defined thing). Rambam's assertion pertains only to the divine essence as it is manifest in the realm of *Atzilut* through the *sefira* of *Ḥokhma*, Wisdom. There His infinite divine essence is clothed, through numerous constrictions, within the attribute of *Ḥokhma*. It is only regarding that constricted divine light clothed in *Ḥokhma* that one might say that the Divine is unified with *Ḥokhma*, like one being, that it is the knowledge, the knower, and the known object itself.

וּכְמוֹ שֶׁנִּתְבָּאֵר בְּמָקוֹם אַחֵר, שֶׁאֵין סוֹף בָּרוּךְ הוּא מְרוֹמָם וּמִתְנַשֵּׂא רוֹמְמוּת אֵין קֵץ לְמַעְלָה מַעְלָה מִמַּהוּת וּבְחִינַת חָכְמָה בִּינָה דַּעַת, עַד שֶׁמַּהוּת וּבְחִינַת חָכְמָה בִּינָה דַּעַת

This conforms with what **is explained elsewhere** (*Sha'ar HaYiḥud Veha'emuna*, chap. 9), **that *Ein Sof*, blessed be He, is infinitely exalted and lofty, above and beyond the essence and level of *Ḥokhma, Bina,* and *Da'at* to the extent that the essence and level of *Ḥokhma*,**

נֶחֱשֶׁבֶת כַּעֲשִׂיָּיה גּוּפָנִיּוּת אֶצְלוֹ יִתְבָּרֵךְ, כְּמוֹ שֶׁכָּתוּב: "כֻּלָּם בְּחָכְמָה עָשִׂיתָ" (תהלים קד, כד).

***Bina,* and *Da'at* are considered like physical action in relation to God, as it is written, "In wisdom have You made them all"** (Ps. 104:24).

"He and His wisdom are one" does not reflect the relationship between God's wisdom and His essence, but rather conveys the connection between the vessel of supernal wisdom and the divine light that is constricted and manifest through it. The relationship between divine wisdom and the divine essence, between divine wisdom and *Ein Sof*, is incomprehensible and impossible to articulate except to say that God's wisdom relative to Him is like physical action is to us.

To us, wisdom is the absolute upper limit in the highest reaches of the spectrum of our reality, while physical action is the lowest. The distance between them is the greatest span that we can possibly comprehend. Though the range between God's wisdom and His divine essence is immeasurably more immense, we utilize this example to appreciate the unfathomable scope of God. Just as one's essential being, one's core self, far transcends a physical action that one may do, God's wisdom is the lower aspect of His being, encapsulating a negligible degree of His divine essence. His essence far transcends His attributes, the *sefirot,* and their various manifestations. The divine essence itself cannot be equated at all with the medium through which it manifests.

וְדָבָר זֶה אֵין בִּיכוֹלֶת הָאָדָם לַהֲבִינוֹ עַל בּוּרְיוֹ כו',

Rambam continues: **"This is something that is not within the human capacity to comprehend clearly...,"**

A person can apprehend only that which exists within him to some degree.[8] Man lacks anything that resembles a consciousness that encompasses all and includes all, that is not external to himself, but internal, deep within, like divine knowledge. Therefore, man is incapable of understanding this concept properly.

8. See commentary on *Sha'ar HaYiḥud VeHa'emuna,* chap. 8.

כִּדְכְתִיב: ״הַחֵקֶר אֱלוֹהַּ תִּמְצָא״ (איוב יא, ז), וּכְתִיב: ״כִּי לֹא מַחְשְׁבוֹתַי מַחְשְׁבוֹתֵיכֶם״ וגו׳ (ישעיה נה, ח).

as it is written, "Can you discover the understanding of God?" (Job 11:7), **and it is written, "For My thoughts are not your thoughts...** and your ways are not My ways – the utterance of the Lord" (Isa. 55:8).

"For My thoughts are not your thoughts" does not mean that God thinks about other, more important things but rather refers to the way in which God thinks, so to speak. In the words of the *Zohar*, which the author of the *Tanya* quoted above, "Not with known wisdom." His wisdom does not share the nature and fabric of our wisdom in any way whatsoever but is rather of a distinctly incomprehensible quality.

וְאַף שֶׁיֵּשׁ רְבָבוֹת מִינֵי חִלּוּקֵי מַדְרֵגוֹת בַּנְּשָׁמוֹת,

Granted, there are myriad types of distinct levels of souls,

The second soul of every Jew is a portion of God on high, a spark of the divine essence, the light of the Divine. Although at their root all souls are seamlessly one with the divine essence in perfect unity, when they manifest corporeally they become divided into innumerable gradations and levels.

גָּבוֹהַּ מֵעַל גָּבוֹהַּ לְאֵין קֵץ,

one **higher than the next, without end.**

As stated in the introduction, people differ from each other in their character, in their overall ability, in their capacity for understanding, and in their attitude. Here the author of the *Tanya* presents another distinguishing feature among people: their soul level. There are lower souls and infinitely higher souls. This distinction between levels does not stem from the Jewish soul's root, from the place where it is literally a portion of God and one with every other Jewish soul, but rather in the place where the ethereal divine soul manifests as a particular person. The level at which the soul finds itself on the vast, infinite spectrum, from its root in the Divine until its manifestation in a corporeal body, is embodied in the person's consciousness and unique personality.

כְּמוֹ גּוֹדֶל מַעֲלַת נִשְׁמוֹת הָאָבוֹת וּמֹשֶׁה רַבֵּינוּ עָלָיו הַשָּׁלוֹם עַל נִשְׁמוֹת דּוֹרוֹתֵינוּ אֵלֶּה דְּעִקְבֵי מְשִׁיחָא שֶׁהֵם בְּחִינַת עֲקֵבַיִים מַמָּשׁ לְגַבֵּי הַמּוֹחַ וְהָרֹאשׁ.

For example, **the souls of the forefathers and Moses, our teacher, may he rest in peace, are immensely superior to the souls** of the people **in our generations,** which are described as **the heels of the Messiah, since they are literally like heels in relation to the brain and the head.**

The "heels of the Messiah" is not just a figurative phrase implying that Messiah's arrival is imminent, that his footsteps can be heard in our generation. It is also a description of the nature of this era and the quality of the souls in it. Every soul is a complete structural analogue, a composite whole that corresponds to the structure of the body it wears. It has a "head" – that is, it possesses the faculties of consciousness, *Hokhma*, *Bina*, and *Da'at* – Wisdom, Understanding, and Knowledge – which are the sources of the rest of the attributes. The soul also has elements that correspond to the arms, torso, legs, and feet, with its heels being the lowest extremity of a person's character with hardly any vitality.

On a broader scale, all the souls living in one generation together also constitute a complete structural analogue and as a collective form a manifestation of a single being. On a broader scale still, all the Jewish souls that ever lived and ever will live, throughout all the generations, constitute their own complete structural analogue – that of Adam, the first man.

The Midrash explains that every soul existed in the soul of Adam, some in his head, others in his arm, others in his feet, and so on. One generation of souls were those rooted in Adam's head, while another generation consisted of souls from Adam's feet. As the days of the Messiah become more imminent, the souls of the generations come from an increasingly lower place, down to the heels. The souls of the most recent generations are thus deemed the "heels of the Messiah."[9] There are therefore myriad levels and gradations between generations, between an era that sprouts giants and one that generates dwarfs.

9. See the commentaries of Rabbi Shmuel Gronem Esterman and Rabbi Yaakov Kidaner.

Elsewhere, the author of the *Tanya* discusses how the analogue of all Jewish souls as a collective resembles the limbs of the body. Just as every limb has a purpose, a function particular to it, so does every soul. The head cannot walk; a leg cannot think. So too, different things are demanded of each person, each soul, and people on different levels are not held accountable for the same things. Even in the realm of mitzva performance, in which every person, from Moses to the simplest Jew, is equally obligated, there is a vast difference in the way each person is meant to perform them. It is told that a certain tzaddik said to his wagon driver, "You merely put *tefillin* on your head, whereas I put *tefillin* in my head."

Another crucial point emerges from this understanding of the interconnectedness of every soul: The difference between souls lies in their roles, not in the inherent value of the soul's essence.[10] ☞

וְכֵן בְּכָל דּוֹר וָדוֹר יֵשׁ רָאשֵׁי אַלְפֵי יִשְׂרָאֵל שֶׁנִּשְׁמוֹתֵיהֶם הֵם בְּחִינַת רֹאשׁ וּמוֹחַ לְגַבֵּי נִשְׁמוֹת הֶהָמוֹן וְעַמֵּי הָאָרֶץ.

Likewise, in each and every generation there are the heads, or leaders, **of the thousands of Israel. Their souls constitute the head and brain in relation to the souls of the masses and the ignorant.**

Every generation in and of itself is a complete structural analogue, consisting of souls on various levels, from the heads of thousands, which function like the mind in relation to the limbs, to lower souls,

THE LOFTY SOUL

☞ The differences between one person and the next, between a person of lesser attainment and one of great attainment, between the souls of the forefathers and the souls of our generation, is not a difference of more or less intelligence. The level of a soul, whether it is lofty or lowly, refers to a particular characteristic of the soul, namely, its capacity for holiness.

The most simple person, not wise or learned at all, may have a tremendously holy soul, while a wise person, brilliant and learned, may have an extremely lowly soul. A person could be talented in every area but inferior in holiness. The level of holy soul constitutes that unique sense, that special ability to make contact with the Divine.

10. See chap. 32, where this concept is discussed at length.

which resemble heels relative to the head. The heads of the nation are not simply higher souls, but they also interact with the other souls of their time as the mind does with the body.

There are therefore distinctions between souls within every generation that span an entire spectrum from one extreme to the other, from the head to the heels. Likewise, there is a commensurate scope of distinctions between different generations. When these two ranges of distinctions are combined, the intersection of the analogue of a single generation and that of all time constitute "myriad types of distinct levels of souls," as the author of the *Tanya* asserts above. ☞

וְכֵן נְפָשׁוֹת לְגַבֵּי נְפָשׁוֹת, כִּי כָּל נֶפֶשׁ כְּלוּלָה מִנֶּפֶשׁ רוּחַ וּנְשָׁמָה.

Similarly, there are distinctions between the ***nefesh*** levels within some souls **in relation to** the ***nefesh*** levels within other souls, **for every soul is comprised of a *nefesh*** level, **a *ruaḥ*** level, **and a *neshama*** level.

THE UNIQUENESS OF EVERY SOUL

☞ Another corollary of this concept is that every Jew has a unique quality and particular role that he must fill. One of the first questions that every person must ask himself is "What is my function? What is that special thing that only I must do?"

The story is told of a hasid who was both a fabulously wealthy man and a Torah scholar who studied Torah all day. He was also incredibly stingy. One time, his Rebbe said to him, "You should know that you are in grave danger!"

The hasid was astounded, and the Rebbe continued, "In every army there are special units. If a soldier abandons his unit to go to a different one, he is considered a deserter and deserves the death penalty. You belong to the squadron of dispensers of charity, yet since you are fleeing and deserting to the platoon of Torah scholars, your life is at risk!"

This idea of the uniqueness of every person is expressed in rabbinic language as a question posed in the Talmud: "In what area was your father especially vigilant?" (*Shabbat* 118b). Even though it is taught that every Jew must live through multiple lifetimes until he fulfills all 613 mitzvot, he must give preference to a specific mitzva and be scrupulous to the utmost degree with that particular area, which corresponds to the unique essence of his soul.

On the one hand, each Jew stands alone; he is a whole world unto himself. On the other hand, he must fulfill his role in the context of the entirety of the Jewish nation. He must familiarize himself well with his specific function and execute it with exceptional effort and meticulousness, since he was appointed to fulfill this particular mitzva in the most powerful way. If he fails to actualize his unique role, no one else will.

A person has three levels of soul within him: *nefesh, ruaḥ,* and *neshama.* Just as people vary with regard to their highest soul level, their *neshama,* so too the level of their *nefesh,* the lowest rung of their soul, varies greatly. How can this be so? After all, the level of *nefesh* represents the everyday perspective of this physical world of *Asiya* (Action) and of the body, and in the world of *Asiya* all Jews are equal. For example, every Jew is obligated to don *tefillin* irrespective of his soul level. Nevertheless, as the *Tanya* asserts, there can still be distinctions between individuals on the *nefesh* level, since every soul consists not only of a *nefesh,* but also a *ruaḥ* and *neshama.* The interconnectedness between the higher levels of *ruaḥ* and *neshama* and the *nefesh* level breeds the "[distinctions between the] *nefesh* [levels within some souls] in relation to [the] *nefesh* [levels within other souls]."[11]

מִכָּל מָקוֹם, שֹׁרֶשׁ כָּל הַנֶּפֶשׁ רוּחַ נְשָׁמָה כּוּלָּם, מֵרֹאשׁ כָּל הַמַּדְרֵיגוֹת עַד סוֹף כָּל דַּרְגִּין, הַמְלוּבָּשׁ בְּגוּף עַמֵּי הָאָרֶץ וְקַל שֶׁבַּקַּלִּים,

Nevertheless, the root of every *nefesh, ruaḥ,* and *neshama,* all of them, from the highest of all levels to the lowest of all levels that are clothed within the bodies of the ignorant and the most unworthy,

The *am ha'aretz,* or ignorant person, refers to the most extreme ignoramus, far removed from knowledge and awareness of the Divine. Practically speaking, his soul exists on a low level, lacking the manifestation of the higher levels of his soul, his *ruaḥ* and *neshama.*

"The most irreverent" refers to those who commit transgressions liberally and carelessly, mocking anything that is holy.

נִמְשָׁךְ מִמּוֹחַ הָעֶלְיוֹן שֶׁהִיא חָכְמָה עִילָּאָה כִּבְיָכוֹל,

is drawn down, as it were, from the supernal mind, which is supernal wisdom.

11. This is similar to the idea stated above, that even in the realm of the physical performance of a mitzva, there is a difference between people in the way they perform the mitzva. The intent with which they perform the deed is the spirit that they infuse within the physical action. The purer the intent, the more spiritual the deed.

Both the highest and the lowest of souls stem from the same source – the supernal divine wisdom – and every soul is a unique expression of that same divine wisdom.

כְּמְשַׁל הַבֵּן הַנִּמְשָׁךְ מִמּוֹחַ הָאָב,

This is **analogous to the child who is drawn from the father's brain.**

Just as the initial inception of the child is in the mind of the father, so too every Jewish soul is drawn from God's supernal wisdom. And just as the children of the same father differ from each other, so too there are differences between souls. Though it is said of all the Jewish people that "you are children to the Lord" (Deut. 14:1), that does not mean that all Jews are equal. There are good children and rebellious children; some are smart and some are not. Yet still, beyond all the differences and levels, each one is still God's child.

שֶׁאֲפִילוּ צִפָּרְנֵי רַגְלָיו נִתְהַווּ מִטִּפָּה זוֹ מַמָּשׁ עַל יְדֵי שֶׁהָיְתָה תִּשְׁעָה חֳדָשִׁים בְּבֶטֶן הָאֵם וְיָרְדָה מִמַּדְרֵגָה לְמַדְרֵגָה לְהִשְׁתַּנּוֹת וּלְהִתְהַוּוֹת מִמֶּנָּה צִפָּרְנַיִם, וְעִם כָּל זֶה עוֹדֶנָּה קְשׁוּרָה וּמְיוּחֶדֶת בְּיִחוּד נִפְלָא וְעָצוּם בְּמַהוּתָהּ וְעַצְמוּתָהּ הָרִאשׁוֹן שֶׁהָיְתָה טִפַּת מוֹחַ הָאָב.

Even his toenails were literally brought into existence from this drop of semen **by his gestating in the mother's womb for nine months, having descended level by level,** constantly **morphing, until even nails were formed. Despite this,** the drop is **still connected and unified in a wondrous and awesome unity with its original essence and being, namely, the drop** of semen as it originated **in the father's brain.**

That which passes from the essence of the father to enliven the child (in modern-day terms, his genetic code) informs the entirety of the child's being: his personality, his talents, his mind, and even his toenails. That very same essential life force expresses itself on all levels, and the lower the level, the more physical and concrete its form. The toenails are not only far from the control center of the body, but it has the least vitality of all body parts. Yet it is still created from the same life force that forms the more sublime aspects of a person, the same life force that gives him the ability to create music, learn philosophy, or study science.

Likewise, a defect in the first cell that passes from father to child may cause a defect in the child's nails. Despite the vast distance between them, the toenail too is bound to the initial source in the father's mind. The first stimulus happens there, in the seed of the child's formation, and that nucleus includes the entirety of the child's being.

וְגַם עַכְשָׁיו, בַּבֵּן, יְנִיקַת הַצִּפָּרְנַיִם וְחַיּוּתָם נִמְשֶׁכֶת מֵהַמּוֹחַ שֶׁבָּרֹאשׁ. כִּדְאִיתָא בַּגְּמָרָא [נִדָּה שָׁם] (לא, א): "לוֹבֶן שֶׁמִּמֶּנּוּ גִּידִים וַעֲצָמוֹת וְצִפָּרְנַיִם"

Even now, in the child, the nourishment and life force that the nails receive are drawn from the brain that is in the head, as the Talmud states, "There are three partners in the creation of a person: the Holy One, blessed be He, his father, and his mother. His father emits **the white seed, from which** the following body parts are formed: the **sinews,** the **bones,** the **nails,** the brain that is in its head, and the white of the eye" (***Nidda*** 31a).

To clarify, the nails receive nourishment from the brain in the child's head, not the father's head. This metaphor corresponds to connection between the souls of simple people in comparison to the souls of the leaders of Israel. The *nefesh, ruaḥ,* and *neshama* of simple Jews are like the toenails of God's firstborn child. They receive their vitality from the *nefesh, ruaḥ,* and *neshama* of the heads of the Jewish people in their generation, which correspond to their brain.[12]

[וּכְמוֹ שֶׁכָּתוּב בְּעֵץ־חַיִּים שַׁעַר הַחַשְׁמַל, בְּסוֹד לְבוּשִׁים שֶׁל אָדָם הָרִאשׁוֹן בְּגַן־עֵדֶן, שֶׁהָיוּ צִפָּרְנַיִם מִבְּחִינַת מוֹחַ תְּבוּנָה].

(It is likewise written in *Etz Ḥayyim, Sha'ar HaḤashmal,* with regard to the mystery of Adam's garments in the Garden of Eden, that they were made of **nails** originating **from the brain's** faculty of ***tevuna,*** insight.**)**

In kabbalistic terms, the word used here for the faculty of understanding, *tevuna,* is the external aspect of the attribute of *Bina*. *Bina* is the

12. The Lubavitcher Rebbe, Rabbi Menaḥem Mendel Schneerson.

understanding itself, while *tevuna* is the cognitive response toward reality that exists outside the mind, as opposed to objects of the intellect. *Tevuna* functions as a type of garment, or outward expression, for *Bina*, and that is why it corresponds to the nails, which were Adam's garment in the Garden of Eden, and to the nails of all humans today, which encase the fingers and toes.

וְכָכָה מַמָּשׁ כִּבְיָכוֹל It is literally the same, as it were,

Just as there is an extremely complex and obscure relationship between the initial drop of life in the father's mind and his child's toenails, the same is true of the connection between the souls of Israel and their Father in Heaven. The various limbs of the body are on differing levels, serving varying functions, yet each one stems from the same drop of seed in the father's mind. So too the souls of Israel, with all their varying levels, from the highest strata corresponding to the heads of Israel such as the forefathers and Moses to the most extreme ignoramuses, sinners, and heretics, are all, at their deepest root, a portion of God on high. ☞

"LITERALLY THE SAME, AS IT WERE"

☞ This phrase, which appears frequently in the *Tanya*, is a strange combination that seems to be an oxymoron. Appending the modifier "as it were" to any expression indicates that it is not entirely accurate. Conversely, saying that something is "literally the same" means that it is exactly that, without embellishment. It is not symbolic with a loose meaning but rather conveys that the thing is literally that. The expression "it is literally the same, as it were" implies that the metaphor includes both connotations.

When we say that every Jewish soul is a portion of God on high whose roots lie in supernal divine wisdom, that is literally the case. Yet with regard to the metaphor used here, that the child's entire being, even his toenails, are bound to the mind of the father, one must add "as it were." The distance between the mind of the father and the toenails of the child is negligible compared to the infinitely immense gap between a person's soul and the supernal divine wisdom.

The combination of these two implications in one phrase serves to verify and strengthen the fact that the soul is a "portion of God above." Although incomprehensible, it is literal, while any metaphor offered to explain it can only be described with the expression "as it were."

בְּשֹׁרֶשׁ כָּל הַנֶּפֶשׁ רוּחַ וּנְשָׁמָה שֶׁל כְּלָלוּת יִשְׂרָאֵל לְמַעְלָה בִּירִידָתוֹ מִמַּדְרֵגָה לְמַדְרֵגָה עַל יְדֵי הִשְׁתַּלְשְׁלוּת הָעוֹלָמוֹת, אֲצִילוּת בְּרִיאָה יְצִירָה עֲשִׂיָּה, מֵחָכְמָתוֹ יִתְבָּרֵךְ,

with regard to the root of every *nefesh*, *ruaḥ*, and *neshama* of the collective of Israel on high. When the soul **descends level by level, by means of the unfolding progression of the worlds of *Atzilut*** (Emanation), ***Beria*** (Creation), ***Yetzira*** (Formation), **and *Asiya*** (Action), **from God's wisdom,** where it originates,

The essence and nature of the soul root that originates in the supernal wisdom does not shine at its full strength in every person, just as the energy of the father does not manifest at its full strength in every limb of the child. Just as the father's creative material must descend level by level and become clothed in garment after garment until it solidifies into a particular physical cell, the divine spark that is the root of every Jewish soul's *nefesh*, *ruaḥ*, and *neshama* undergoes a similar progression. The divine spark descends and is clothed in garment after garment until it is manifest in the physical body.

כִּדְכְתִיב: "כּוּלָּם בְּחָכְמָה עָשִׂיתָ" (תהלים קד, כד),

as it is written, "In wisdom have You made them all" (Ps. 104:24),

Hokhma is the key to creation, the first *sefira* in the whole order of progression from conception to physical reality. It constitutes the manifestation of the divine light in the creation of the worlds.

נִתְהַוּוּ מִמֶּנּוּ נֶפֶשׁ רוּחַ וּנְשָׁמָה שֶׁל עַמֵּי הָאָרֶץ וּפְחוּתֵי הָעֵרֶךְ, וְעִם כָּל זֶה עוֹדֶינָּה קְשׁוּרוֹת וּמְיוּחָדוֹת בְּיִחוּד נִפְלָא וְעָצוּם בְּמַהוּתָן וְעַצְמוּתָן הָרִאשׁוֹן שֶׁהִיא הַמְשָׁכַת חָכְמָה עִילָּאָה,

the *nefesh*, *ruaḥ*, and *neshama* of the ignorant and those who are inferior come into existence through it, the soul's descent. **Nonetheless,** their *nefesh*, *ruaḥ*, and *neshama* **are still connected and unified in a wondrous and awesome unity with their original essence and being, which is drawn from supernal wisdom,**

Even one who has fallen lower than the inferior and ignorant among Israel, until there is nowhere else to fall, even the heretic who says that he has no Father in Heaven, has a *nefesh, ruaḥ,* and *neshama* that are bound and unified to their primary source, which is drawn from the supernal wisdom. Whether a person admits or denies the reality of his father does not change the essential bond between them. It just offers insight into the type of person he is. It does not change the fact that his father is his father.

כִּי יְנִיקַת וְחַיּוּת נֶפֶשׁ רוּחַ וּנְשָׁמָה שֶׁל עַמֵּי הָאָרֶץ הוּא מִנֶּפֶשׁ רוּחַ וּנְשָׁמָה שֶׁל הַצַּדִּיקִים וְהַחֲכָמִים רָאשֵׁי בְּנֵי יִשְׂרָאֵל שֶׁבְּדוֹרָם.

because the nourishment and life force of the *nefesh, ruaḥ,* and *neshama* of the ignorant are drawn **from the *nefesh, ruaḥ,* and *neshama* of the righteous and the sages,** who serve as **the heads of Israel in their generation.**

The Jewish people of a given generation are, as explained above, a complete structural analogue comparable to the human body. It is composed of a head – the leaders of the generation – as well as those who correspond to the feet and toenails of the nation. Every limb is connected on two levels: It works in conjunction with the mind (and

THE TZADDIK CONNECTION

☞ This concept, that all Jewish souls are like the limbs of one body, with certain select souls serving as the head, is the central axis of the concept of tzaddik in hasidic thought. The tzaddik, or Rebbe, does not earn his title because he is a more accomplished Torah scholar but rather because his soul is truly a head of Israel. The public that calls upon him are those who feel that connection with him, who yearn to be nourished by him.

This connection works both ways. Not only are amputated appendages incapable of survival without connection to the body, the same is true of its severed head. After the incident of the golden calf, God said to Moses, "Go, descend, for your people...have acted corruptly" (Ex. 32:7). The Talmud elaborates: "The Holy One, blessed be He, said to Moses, 'Moses, descend from your greatness. Isn't it only for the sake of Israel that I granted you prominence? And now that Israel has sinned, why do I need you?'" (*Berakhot* 32a).

When the nation sinned, Moses could not be Moses. He was great irrespective of his role as leader of Israel, but he could never reach the apex of his potential only by comprehending lofty ideas through prophecy and relating God's word to the nation. His greatness lay in the fact that he was the leader of the Jewish people, in his connection and association with them.

A defect in the nation also affects the head. If "your nation has acted corruptly," then "go descend" – descend from your greatness.

the rest of the limbs) as a component of the entire bodily structure, and it is also directly bound to the primary creative force that originates in the father.

In light of this, the father's life force exists equally in every limb, yet it is manifest in the head more than in the feet. The feet, the arms, and the rest of the limbs are subjugated to the mind from which they receive their vitality.

While all Jewish souls are "children of God," a complex interrelationship operates among them. The "heads of Israel" sense and channel the divine life force to every Jewish soul, each according to its capacity and function.

Like the dynamic between the head and the body, the connection between a leader and a Jewish soul is not one way. Just as the head feels the pain of the feet, so too a "head" of Israel empathizes with every person, even those who are like the feet of the nation.

It is related about a famous tzaddik that if a woman was birthing three hundred miles away, he would not be able to sleep because he felt her pain. If a Jewish leader does not feel the pain of every part of his "body," he is clearly not a true "head."

This pathway of connection does not just flow to and from the head, but in a certain sense courses between all the organs. As long as a limb is connected to the body, it interacts with all the other organs. The suffering of one limb necessarily must affect every other organ in some way given the reciprocal flow between them. Yet the degree to which each limb senses the pain and pleasure of all the others is not the same as that of the head. The connection between the organs is not a conscious one, while the head is acutely aware of this bond, and it is that awareness that makes it worthy of being a head. ☞ ☞

LOVE OF THE JEWISH PEOPLE

☞ This concept is discussed elsewhere (see, e.g., chap. 32) in the context of cultivating love of the Jewish people. Each and every Jew is a limb in the structural analogue of the entire nation. All are responsible for each other and dependent on each other. In view of this, love of a fellow Jew becomes synonymous with self-love, no different from the way one loves himself and the limbs of his own body. A person cannot hate his hand. He cannot ignore the pain in his foot and say, "That's my foot's problem, not mine." This is the degree to which a Jew loves his fellow Jew.

וּבָזֶה יוּבַן מַאֲמַר רַבּוֹתֵינוּ ז״ל (כתובות קיא, ב) עַל פָּסוּק ״וּלְדָבְקָה בוֹ״ (דברים ל, כ): ״שֶׁכָּל הַדָּבֵק בְּתַלְמִידֵי חֲכָמִים מַעֲלֶה עָלָיו הַכָּתוּב כְּאִלּוּ נִדְבַּק בַּשְּׁכִינָה מַמָּשׁ״, כִּי עַל יְדֵי דְבִיקָה בְּתַלְמִידֵי חֲכָמִים קְשׁוּרוֹת נֶפֶשׁ רוּחַ וּנְשָׁמָה שֶׁל עַמֵּי הָאָרֶץ וּמְיוּחָדוֹת בְּמַהוּתָן הָרִאשׁוֹן וְשָׁרְשָׁם שֶׁבְּחָכְמָה עִילָּאָה, שֶׁהוּא יִתְבָּרֵךְ וְחָכְמָתוֹ אֶחָד, וְהוּא הַמַּדָּע כו׳.

With this we can understand our Rabbis' statement regarding the verse "To love the Lord your God, to heed His voice, **and to cleave to Him**" (Deut. 30:20): "But is it possible to cleave to the Divine Presence?... **Rather, anyone who cleaves to Torah scholars, the verse ascribes him credit as though he is literally cleaving to the Divine Presence**" (*Ketubot* 111b). **By cleaving to Torah scholars, the *nefesh*, *ruaḥ*, and *neshama* of the ignorant are connected and unified with their original essence and root in supernal wisdom,** and thereby with God Himself, **since God and His wisdom are one, and He is the known,** He is the knower, and He is the knowledge itself (as cited above from Rambam, *Sefer HaMadda*, *Hilkhot Yesodei HaTorah* 2:10).

Even when a person who is utterly ignorant cleaves to the leaders of his generation, he receives the life force that flows through them directly from the primary source, that portion of God on high, which originates in God's supernal wisdom. Yet though this is true of those who are ignorant and even inferior, the same cannot be said of sinners and rebels.

[וְהַפּוֹשְׁעִים וּמוֹרְדִים בְּתַלְמִידֵי חֲכָמִים, יְנִיקַת נֶפֶשׁ רוּחַ וּנְשָׁמָה שֶׁלָּהֶם מִבְּחִינַת אֲחוֹרַיִים שֶׁל נֶפֶשׁ רוּחַ וְנִשְׁמַת תַּלְמִידֵי חֲכָמִים.]

(**However, those who sin deliberately and those who rebel against Torah scholars,** and consequently dissociate themselves from the generation's leaders, **the nourishment of their *nefesh*, *ruaḥ*, and *neshama* comes from the back side of the *nefesh*, *ruaḥ*, and *neshama* of Torah scholars.**)

Those who sin intentionally and rebel against the generation's leaders cannot receive their spiritual nourishment directly from the souls of those leaders. Granted, no creation is completely cut off from holiness. This is certainly true of the Jewish soul. Every Jewish soul is bound at his primal root to the heads of Israel. The difference between people lies in the nature of the connection.

A person who is aware of his connection to the leader of his generation has a face-to-face relationship with him, as it were, drawing his vitality directly from the leader in a conscious way. Someone who is unaware of his connection to the leader of the generation receives his vitality in an indirect, "backward" way.

Along the same lines, the author of the *Tanya* explains the nature of repentance elsewhere through the following analogy:[13] Two people are standing close together. When they face each other, they are as close as can be. When they turn away from each other and stand back to back, they are as far as could be from each other, even though they are literally right next to each other.

Repentance is as simple as a change in direction: One need only turn and face God. Someone who transgresses and rebels against the leaders of his generation cannot disconnect from them, even if he does not wish to accept their leadership. He is still a Jew and is bound to them, receiving vitality from them, just as the limbs receive vitality from the brain. But the rebel does not want that connection; he turns his back on them. Since it cannot be that he will not receive vitality from them, he receives it from the back side. ☞

FRONT AND BACK

☞ The concept of "front" represents intention aimed directly toward a goal, while "back" entails the usage of extrinsic means in order to attain that target. This principle can be seen in the physical realm as well. Consider the usage of a knife. The sharp edge, the side that slices, is geared toward the fulfillment of the knife's purpose, while the back of the knife, the dull edge, is only a byproduct: There cannot be a front without a back.

Hasidic teachings give the parable of a king who throws a banquet for all his officers and servants. His intention, of course, is to honor the distinguished ministers with fine food and drink. Yet to honor them

13. *Likkutei Torah*, Lev. 26d.

וּמַה שֶּׁכָּתוּב בַּזֹּהַר וּבְזֹהַר חָדָשׁ שֶׁהָעִיקָּר תָּלוּי שֶׁיִּתְקַדֵּשׁ עַצְמוֹ בִּשְׁעַת תַּשְׁמִישׁ דַּוְקָא, מַה שֶּׁאֵין כֵּן בְּנֵי עַמֵּי הָאָרֶץ כו',

As for what is written in the ***Zohar*** **and** ***Zohar Ḥadash*****, that the primary** spiritual makeup of the child **is specifically contingent on whether one sanctifies himself during intercourse, whereas this is not the case with** regard to **children of the ignorant,** who do not sanctify themselves,

Ostensibly, one can infer from the *Zohar* that the makeup of the child depends mainly on one factor: his parents. That is, who they are and whether their intentions at the decisive moment of cohabitation were holy or not (according to their level). In view of this, a person's essence is determined solely by inheritance. It seems that a holy person can be born only to parents who themselves are on that level. However, this seems to contradict the theme of this chapter, that all Jews have divine souls that share a common source in the supernal wisdom. How, then, can the *Zohar* state that a person's spiritual makeup is dependent on his father and mother?

הַיְינוּ מִשּׁוּם שֶׁאֵין לְךָ נֶפֶשׁ רוּחַ וּנְשָׁמָה שֶׁאֵין לָהּ לְבוּשׁ מִנֶּפֶשׁ דְּעַצְמוּת אָבִיו וְאִמּוֹ.

this is because there is no ***nefesh, ruaḥ,*** **and** ***neshama*** **that does not have a garment** that stems **from the essence of one's father and mother.**

To understand this, we must differentiate between the essential soul and its garments. The essential soul is a portion of God on high, totally independent of one's parents, education, and environment. The garment of the soul, meaning the way in which the soul appears and

appropriately, he must invite other people who will also receive food and drink. Their enjoyment of the banquet is not the king's primary, intrinsic will. They enjoy the banquet as an indirect consequence of the king's wishes, from the back side.

A more abstract example is when two people hear the same thing and one remembers the essential content while the other recalls all the illustrations, the metaphors and jokes. While both glean something from the speech, the former receives the inner intention while the latter gleans the "back" of the intended message, the means utilized by the speaker, not the end itself.

manifests, depends on one's parents and, later, on the way in which a person was raised. As the Mishna states, "The father transmits to the child beauty, strength, wealth, wisdom, and years" (*Eduyyot* 2:9).

While parents pass their own characteristics down to their children, they do not transmit their children's souls. The "portion of God on high" is not inherited from one's father or mother. Yet the garments that parents give the soul are highly significant and encompass both physical as well as emotional characteristics, spiritual faculties, and the capacity to achieve that which it is capable of accomplishing. All these qualities combine to give the child his personality through which he lives and functions. Yet we need to remember that the garment, as significant as it is, is not the soul itself and does not control the soul itself. Its importance lies in the way it affects the manner in which the soul operates.

וְכָל הַמִּצְוֹת שֶׁעוֹשֶׂה הַכֹּל עַל יְדֵי אוֹתוֹ הַלְּבוּשׁ כו׳,

All the mitzvot that the soul **performs are all** performed **through that garment and so forth.**

The soul does not perform mitzvot by itself. Mitzvot are not performed in a vacuum, but rather through that with which the soul has no direct point of contact. The soul needs the intermediaries of physical and spiritual instruments through which it can operate in the world. These instruments are the garments of the soul and include intellectual ability, basic axiomatic beliefs, modes of interpersonal interaction, and ways of interacting with phenomena and understanding them. These garments are influenced by a person's parents, mostly through inheritance and partially through education and training.

וַאֲפִילוּ הַשֶּׁפַע שֶׁנּוֹתְנִים לוֹ מִן הַשָּׁמַיִם הַכֹּל עַל יְדֵי לְבוּשׁ זֶה.

Moreover, **even the** life-giving **sustenance that one is granted from Heaven is entirely by means of this garment.**

The soul does not act only through these garments; it receives through them as well. When a person receives the life-giving sustenance from above, that influx must be clothed in these garments – in the person's way of thinking, his ideas, how he relates to himself and others – in order to be drawn down.

וְאִם יְקַדֵּשׁ אֶת עַצְמוֹ יַמְשִׁיךְ לְבוּשׁ קָדוֹשׁ לְנִשְׁמַת בְּנוֹ, וַאֲפִילוּ הִיא נְשָׁמָה גְּדוֹלָה צְרִיכָה לְקִידּוּשׁ אָבִיו כו׳.

Therefore, **if one sanctifies himself** during intercourse, **he will draw down a holy garment for his child's** divine **soul. Even if the** child's divine **soul is great, it requires the sanctification of the father and so forth.**

The garments of the soul that parents draw down to their child are not just physical qualities but the entirety of his personality. It is not only the father's particular abilities that are important to his child but also his level of holiness throughout his life. Even a great soul needs holy garments that stem from the level of sanctification engendered by the parent.

It is related that Rabbi Uri of Strelisk, famously known as the Saraf, who came from a simple family, said that if his father had immersed in a *mikveh* (a ritual bath designed for ritual purification) even once in his life, it is inestimable how much easier it would have been for him to grow in his divine service. The Zidichover Rebbe's mother would wake up her five children every night to recite *Tikkun Ḥatzot*, yet one of her children said that if his mother had not eaten cooked cabbage from the non-Jewish neighbor when she was pregnant, he would have had significantly fewer obstacles in his divine service.

A person cannot separate himself from his inherited soul-garb. Even a great soul, a tzaddik by nature, is incapable of disconnecting entirely from the garments of his soul. If his garb is of a low quality, it will hinder him. Alternatively, a person who merits holy garments from his parents, even if he has a low-level soul, will find it easier to accomplish great things in the realm of holiness. ☞

THE VALUE OF GOOD LINEAGE

☞ This point provides fundamental justification for the importance placed on family lineage. Although parents do not bequeath the soul to their child, they do pass down the soul's garments, which endow the soul with particular qualities and capabilities. The child inherits these garments even if an aspect of his essential nature tends toward other directions. Even a child who is intrinsically of the lowest caliber can inherit holy garments. In that case, even if he wants to engage in every type of impurity, this garment hinders him from doing so. It is not a function of his upbringing, but rather an inherent mark emblazed on his soul wherever he may find himself.

אֲבָל הַנְּשָׁמָה עַצְמָהּ, הִנֵּה לִפְעָמִים נִשְׁמַת אָדָם גָּבוֹהַּ לְאֵין קֵץ בָּא לִהְיוֹת בְּנוֹ שֶׁל אָדָם נִבְזֶה וְשָׁפֵל כו׳, כְּמוֹ שֶׁכָּתַב הָאֲרִ״י ז״ל כָּל זֶה בְּלִיקּוּטֵי תוֹרָה פָּרָשַׁת וַיֵּרָא וּבְטַעֲמֵי מִצְוֹת פָּרָשַׁת בְּרֵאשִׁית.

But with regard to **the soul itself, there are times when the soul of a person of infinitely lofty stature comes to be the child of a despicable and lowly person and so forth. The Arizal states all this in *Likkutei Torah, Parashat Vayera,* and in *Ta'amei HaMitzvot, Parashat Bereshit.***

Jewish history offers many examples of great souls with dubious lineage. The *tanna* Rabbi Meir apparently descended from a family of Roman caesars, which is certainly a wretched lineage in terms of holiness. A soul like his, which came from Esau, could not come to our world in any other way than through a convert.

Rabbi Akiva too came from a family of converts. They say about him that a soul of his caliber, which in several respects was commensurate with that of Moses, had to have been born particularly of such lineage. That is the only way to extract such a soul from its origin in the realm of *kelippa.* Even the lineage of Moses himself includes a subtle blemish, not entirely from the realm of holiness.

Yet the most blatant example of dubious ancestry is that of the soul of the Messiah. From the beginning, there were problems: Judah and Tamar, Boaz and Ruth, David and Batsheva, Solomon and Na'ama the Amonitess. The soul of King David, deemed the fourth leg of the chariot from Ezekiel's vision, and the soul of his offspring, the Messiah, are the most lofty of souls. Yet these souls were in captivity in the *kelippa.* To escape, they needed to traverse the border between holiness and impurity, which was enabled by the less than pristine relationships of their progenitors. These souls are like pearls found only in refuse. The great leaders of Israel do not rummage around in the garbage, even if to extract a pearl; it is not their way. The people who are drawn to those dirtier places, who generally take things from the trash heap, usually

There are people among us who inherited a soul garment from their pious forebears that does not allow them to actually sin or enjoy a misdeed. Behind the scenes of their unfolding life story, this inseparable garment of the soul directs their lives from generation to generation.

find only trash. Yet when a pearl has been lost there, they end up taking possession of it as well.

In short, parents do not create the soul, only its garb. As the Talmud states, "There are three partners in the creation of a person: the Holy One, blessed be He, his father, and his mother. His father emits the white seed ... his mother emits red seed ... and the Holy One, blessed be He, inserts into him a spirit, a soul ...." God endows the child with a soul and does not always consult with His partners on which type they prefer. As in the common analogy of a duck hatching goose eggs, some parents may be disappointed with a holy child while others are dissatisfied with a child who is anything less. Yet at the end of the day, it does not depend on them.

This chapter explains how every Jew, even the most unworthy and insignificant, is a portion of God on high. Every Jew is a child of God. Yet each person is distinguished by the soul garments with which his parents endow him and the way in which his soul manifests and expresses itself. Like siblings in the same family, there is the successful child and the less successful one, the wise one and the foolish one, yet beyond these differences there is a plane where all are equal, all are children. This immutable fact is not affected by a person's actions or even by the greatness or lowliness of his soul.

Chapter 3

IN THE PREVIOUS CHAPTER, THE AUTHOR OF THE *TANYA* introduced the divine soul, an actual portion of God on high that exists within every Jew. This chapter discusses the qualities and faculties of that soul.

The divine soul itself is not made up of constituent parts, but rather it is a simple, seamless, indivisible light. Viewing the soul as being comprised of various components negates its existence as a singular, distinct entity. If it were multifaceted, then there would be no such thing as a single soul but rather a mere assortment of individual characteristics.

Since the soul that lies at the core of every person is one singular, unchanging entity, its essence is beyond the scope of comprehension, intrinsically unknowable. It is a "portion of God on high," and just as one cannot fathom the divine essence, one cannot grasp the nature of this indivisible, incomprehensible, seamlessly singular soul. Rather, one may only cultivate an awareness of its existence.

The author of the *Tanya* thus does not attempt to analyze the essence of the soul itself but rather suffices with analyzing its faculties and the way they work together. It is through these faculties that the soul's light is manifest, and it is these faculties that comprise the content of this chapter.

וְהִנֵּה כָּל בְּחִינָה וּמַדְרֵגָה מִשָּׁלֹשׁ אֵלּוּ, נֶפֶשׁ רוּחַ וּנְשָׁמָה,

Each of these three facets and levels, ***nefesh, ruaḥ,*** **and** ***neshama,*** 25 Kislev / 27 Kislev (leap year)

The *nefesh*, or soul, in the broadest sense of the term, encompasses three foundational levels: *nefesh, ruaḥ*, and *neshama.* Each of these levels is different from each other to the extent that two people, each with his respective soul, differ from each other.

כְּלוּלָה מֵעֶשֶׂר בְּחִינוֹת כְּנֶגֶד עֶשֶׂר סְפִירוֹת עֶלְיוֹנוֹת שֶׁנִּשְׁתַּלְשְׁלוּ מֵהֶן,

contains ten faculties corresponding to the ten supernal *sefirot* from which they devolved.

Despite the distinctions between these soul levels, each of the three soul levels shares these ten faculties, which correspond to the ten *sefirot*.

The ten *sefirot* are supernal manifestations, or aspects of the Divine, through which the Divine interacts with the world. They serve as the creative forces of existence comprising the very fabric of the entire universe. These creative forces infuse the universe with life and sustain it.

Every created entity in the world likewise possesses ten faculties that correspond to these ten *sefirot*. This is particularly true of the human soul. As a portion of God on high, forged "in His image and likeness," the human soul possesses ten faculties that mirror the ten supernal *sefirot*. ☞

"GARMENTS" AND "ADORNMENTS"

☞ Elsewhere, the author of the *Tanya* explains that these faculties of the soul are not, as might have been understood here and, below, in chapter 12, the essence and being of the divine soul but rather mere "garments" for the soul (see *Torah Or* 13c; *Likkutei Torah*, Lev. 4b). In that case, one must distinguish between these garments referred to by the author of the *Tanya* as the soul's faculties and the garments of the soul discussed in the next chapter: thought, speech, and action.

In the broader sense of the term, all manifestations of the soul are garments, and this includes the faculties discussed in this chapter. But the term is usually used more narrowly to designate the three most external manifestations of the soul. Despite the vast difference between the more internal garment of thought and the more external garments of speech and action, every one of these three garments is equal in the sense that there is no true, essential connection between the garment and the wearer. Just as a garment reveals something of its wearer's essence yet garment and wearer each retain distinct and separate identities, these garments serve the soul and reveal its powers but are never identified with it. Even thought, the most intimate of the three external garments, only expresses the soul's will, desires, and feelings and merely translates these into the language of conscious thought. Thought translates the content it receives from the soul yet is not synonymous with it.

הַנֶּחֱלָקוֹת לִשְׁתַּיִם, שֶׁהֵן "שָׁלֹשׁ אִמּוֹת וְשֶׁבַע כְּפוּלוֹת".

These ten faculties are **subdivided into two** general categories, **namely, "three mothers and seven doubles"** (*Sefer Yetzira* 2:3).

Sefer Yetzira refers to the ten *sefirot* as "three mothers and seven doubles" and correlates them to letters of the Hebrew alphabet. The three mothers correspond to the letters *alef, mem,* and *shin,* representing the span of the Hebrew alphabet, being the first, middle, and last letters.[1] Likewise, these three *sefirot* are the foundational *sefirot* making up the entire infrastructure of reality. These *sefirot,* as they operate in the

There is, however, another level of the soul's manifestations, expressions of the soul that are more intimately related to its being, figuratively referred to as *tikkunim,* or "adornments." This term comes from the *Tikkunei Zohar* (17a), which states, "You brought forth ten *tikkunim.*" They too are referred to as garments (see *Torah Or* 13c, s.v. "*Pataḥ Eliyahu,*" and the commentary of Rabbi Sholom Dovber Schneerson, the fifth Lubavitcher Rebbe, on this discourse, in *Sefer Ma'amarim* 5658). This type of garment not only reveals the soul's inner essence but to a certain extent is unified with it. Through it, inner content and outer expression literally become one to the extent that the revealed and the revealer become inseparable – they are utterly identical.

The term *tikkun* connotes a decorative piece of jewelry. A woman is more intimately connected with her jewelry than with any other type of garb; it reflects her essence and mood. This piece of jewelry, this *tikkun* or adornment, has two facets. On the one hand, it is extrinsic to that which it reveals, the soul, separate and distinct from the essence it expresses. On the other hand, an outside observer does not separate between the decoration and the one who wears it. The moment essence is revealed through the *tikkun* – when the soul is manifest through a particular attribute – soul and attribute appear to be virtually synonymous. The soul's mode of manifestation becomes its identity.

Although the soul might manifest itself at different times through various *tikkunim,* at that moment it assumes that particular attribute as its personality, in the same way that the body unifies with its adorning garb and that garment becomes a fixture of the body that is wearing it.

In this sense, the ten faculties – the cognitive and the emotive attributes that will be explored in this chapter – are the *tikkunim* of the soul. In relation to the soul itself, they are only garments, but relative to the garments of the soul discussed later on – thought, speech, and action – they constitute the essence and being of the soul.

1. The *shin* is actually the second-to-last letter, coming before *tav,* which represents one of the seven emotive attributes.

soul, are the cognitive faculties that determine the scope and content of a person's awareness. Yet they are not only tools for intellectual conception and cognitive processing; they represent the soul's capacity to perceive and assimilate reality.

This explains why they are called "mothers." No flicker of mental or emotional experience can happen without that initial awareness of relating to something in some way. These cognitive faculties are necessary to generate the other faculties of the soul, like a mother who produces offspring.

The "seven doubles" refer to the attributes of *Ḥesed, Gevura, Tiferet, Netzaḥ, Hod, Yesod,* and *Malkhut,* which correspond to the letters *bet, gimmel, dalet, khaf, peh, resh,* and *tav*. These seven letters serve a double function: Each has both a hard and soft pronunciation. Likewise, these seven attributes have an intrinsic diametric nature and can diverge into two possible directions: either holy expressions or that of *kelippa,* the forces of impurity.[2] While these *sefirot* have a particular character and way of operating in the world, they have no intrinsic objective. Whether channeled for holiness or the opposite is not predetermined.

פֵּירוּשׁ, חָכְמָה בִּינָה וָדַעַת, The "three mothers" **refers to *Ḥokhma, Bina,* and *Da'at,***

Although generally *Keter, Ḥokhma,* and *Bina* (Crown, Wisdom, and Understanding) are regarded as the first three *sefirot,* the author of the *Tanya* here enumerates *Ḥokhma, Bina,* and *Da'at* (Wisdom, Understanding, and Knowledge) as the initial three. The two versions, one positioning *Ḥokhma* as the first *sefira* and the other listing *Keter* as first, stems from a difference of opinion in Kabbala regarding the nature of the *sefira* of *Keter*. When discussing the *sefirot* in broad terms, the author of the *Tanya* himself counts *Keter* as the first, but in the context of the soul, the structure that he presents as being first is *Ḥokhma, Bina,* and *Da'at.*

Understanding this distinction calls for an examination of these three *sefirot.*

The manifestation of the *sefira* of *Keter* in the soul has two facets.

---

2. In keeping with the principle that God made one corresponding to the other. See *Torah Or* 29a.

Its external aspect is the person's simple will, which defies any rational definition. The internal dimension of this faculty is pleasure, which also inherently lies beyond the realm of human comprehension. One cannot understand these aspects of his own being and certainly cannot control them. Conscious self-awareness begins only with the faculty of wisdom, the manifestation of the *sefira* of *Ḥokhma* in the soul.

On a subjective level, wisdom is the starting point of everything that transpires within a person. An outside observer may notice that conscious intellectual faculties are not the only determining factor that cause him to act in a certain way. But that deeper inner *Keter* mechanism is not within the purview of the person's own subjective awareness.

From this perspective, we relate to the "three mothers" of every thought as being within the person's scope of awareness. We therefore do not consider the faculty of the primal will that transcends consciousness and imposes itself upon the intellect like a *keter*, or crown. Rather, the will that is born of cognitive process, that which we refer to as *Da'at*, is derived from the cognitive process, the end product of the faculties of wisdom and understanding. For this reason, the foundational points of inception, the "mothers" in one's soul, are the faculties that correspond to the *sefirot* of *Ḥokhma*, *Bina*, and *Da'at*.

וְשִׁבְעַת יְמֵי הַבִּנְיָן, חֶסֶד גְּבוּרָה תִּפְאֶרֶת כו'.

and the seven "doubles," known as **"the seven days of building,"** are ***Ḥesed*, *Gevura*, *Tiferet*,** *Netzaḥ*, *Hod*, *Yesod*, and *Malkhut*.

These *sefirot* are called the "seven days of building" because the world was created through them during the six days of Creation. As the building blocks of Creation, they create and sustain all of existence at every moment, both during the six days of the week and on Shabbat. The first day of Creation is sustained by the attribute of *Ḥesed*, the second by the attribute of *Gevura*, and so on. But this does not mean that each of the *sefirot* operates only within the confines of its particular day in time, since the *sefirot* do not operate in their pure states. Rather, the *Ḥesed* of the first day encompasses elements of the other *sefirot* as well: *Gevura* in the context of *Ḥesed*, *Tiferet* in the context of *Ḥesed*, and so forth. In essence, the reality of the entire world is built from an admixture of these seven manifestations, which form every dimension and facet of reality.

וְכָךְ בְּנֶפֶשׁ הָאָדָם שֶׁנֶּחֱלֶקֶת לִשְׁתַּיִם: שֵׂכֶל וּמִדּוֹת.

It is the same within the human soul, that the ten faculties **are** also **subdivided into two** classes: the **cognitive** faculties **and** the emotive **attributes.**

The division of the ten *sefirot* into "three mothers" and "seven doubles," or the "seven days of building," refers to the categorization of the supernal *sefirot* themselves. A parallel division exists in a person's soul but with human parameters. The "three mothers" correspond to the cognitive attributes, those of the intellect, the attributes of the mind, while the "seven doubles" parallel the attributes and emotions, the attributes of the heart.

The essence of the intellect is awareness. Intelligence and cognition are only one facet of its capacity, not its sum, which is primarily the faculty of perception, the basic awareness of every thing in every way.

Though the other seven attributes are emotive, they are not synonymous with emotion, but rather are seven impulses or drives, seven forces that motivate human behavior and elicit an emotional response in the person. Emotions such as love or fear are the attributes' imprint on a person's thoughts and awareness. The attributes themselves are fundamental elements that operate in certain ways, but only when combined with the power of thought do they form actual emotions.

An emotion is actually a composite entity that includes perceptive elements, sensual components, and tactile responses. For example, the emotion of fear includes, in addition to the actual feeling of fear, a perception and recognition of the cause of the fear, as well as the reactions and responses spawned by the fear. In our experience, we never encounter a pure attribute, or even a pure emotion, but a compound of emotions, just as chemical elements are rarely found in a pure form but in various compounds. The attribute, then, is only the drive, the vector of a certain emotive direction in the heart of man. As such, the attributes in their pure form are not found in reality, but rather they operate within certain emotional structures.

הַשֵּׂכֶל כּוֹלֵל חָכְמָה, בִּינָה וָדַעַת, וְהַמִּדּוֹת הֵן: אַהֲבַת ה׳ וּפַחְדּוֹ וְיִרְאָתוֹ וּלְפָאֲרוֹ כוּ׳.

The cognitive faculties **comprise wisdom, understanding, and knowledge, and the** emotive **attributes,** which correspond to the seven *sefirot,* **are love of God, trepidation and awe of Him, the glorification of Him, and so on.**

Since this is an exploration of the divine soul, whose point of reference is its relationship with God, its seven attributes are channeled toward God. Its love, which is derived from the attribute of *Ḥesed,* is therefore embodied by love of God.[3] Likewise, its fear is embodied by trepidation and awe of God, which is aligned with the *sefira* of *Gevura,* and its glory, corresponding to the *sefira* of *Tiferet,* is channeled toward the glorification of God.

The author of the *Tanya* here differentiates between two types of fear, awe and trepidation. *Yira,* awe, is a sensation that a person feels after rationally apprehending the reality of something great and powerful. It is the resultant caution that he takes to maintain a distance from it, but not due to an emotional reaction. Rather, awe is an awareness in the mind. *Paḥad,* trepidation, on the other hand, is a feeling in the heart that has a visceral effect. The person is frightened even if he doesn't understand why.[4]

3. See *Iggeret HaKodesh,* epistle 15.

4. Similarly, *Kitzurim VeHe'arot LeSefer Likkutei Amarim* (p. 89) states, "Trepidation in the heart and awe in the mind." See also the comment of the fifth Lubavitcher Rebbe, Rabbi Sholom Dovber Schneerson, there, p. 113. In addition, in his commentary to the *Tanya,* Rabbi Shmuel Gronem Esterman points out that it is for this reason that the author of the *Tanya* precedes awe with trepidation, yet later in the chapter, in the context of their cultivation, he places awe before trepidation.

וְחָכְמָה בִּינָה דַּעַת נִקְרָאוּ אִמּוֹת וּמָקוֹר לַמִּדּוֹת, כִּי הַמִּדּוֹת הֵן תּוֹלְדוֹת חָכְמָה בִּינָה דַּעַת.

The cognitive faculties of **wisdom, understanding,** and **knowledge are called "mothers" and are the source of the** emotive **attributes because the** emotive **attributes are the offspring of wisdom, understanding,** and **knowledge.**

Every attribute, every emotional experience, must be preceded by some sort of perception that stems from the wisdom, understanding, and knowledge of the soul. Without perception, not necessarily in the intellectual sense but in the sense of an awareness of the reality to which the soul relates, there is no context for emotion. This does not imply that every emotion is sparked by intellectual apprehension. Certainly, some emotions seem absurd and totally illogical. Yet there must be some awareness of the thing that elicits the emotion. ☞

26 Kislev
28 Kislev (leap year)

וּבֵיאוּר הָעִנְיָן, כִּי הִנֵּה הַשֵּׂכֶל שֶׁבַּנֶּפֶשׁ הַמַּשְׂכֶּלֶת, שֶׁהוּא הַמַּשְׂכִּיל כָּל דָּבָר, נִקְרָא בְּשֵׁם חָכְמָה, כֹּ״חַ מָ״ה.

The explanation of the matter, the basic definitions of the cognitive faculties, is as follows: **The intellectual faculty in the rational soul, that which** rationally **comprehends every matter, is called *ḥokhma*,** wisdom, which is comprised of two words: ***ko'aḥ***, potential, and ***ma***, what.

DERIVATIVES OF THE INTELLECT

☞ It is important to note that while the "attributes are the 'offspring' of wisdom, understanding, and knowledge," one should not err and assume that the mind itself generates the attributes. The mind creates the object regarding which a person feels emotion. Without that awareness, the attributes, the emotions, could not exist, but that does not mean that the mind creates them. Even if they are latent and the mind activates them, causing their emergence, they were not generated by the mind.

The essence of the mind inherently differs from the essential nature of the attributes, and each has its own source in the soul. Elsewhere, in a deeper analysis of this concept, the author of the *Tanya* explains that while the world at large attributes greater importance to the intellect, the root of the emotive attributes is more potent and powerful than the cog-

Before a person registers anything, whether sensory or rational, he gets a general perception of that thing, a light-bulb gist of it. This initial flash of awareness is called *ḥokhma,* wisdom.

The role of wisdom in the cognitive process parallels the manner in which the senses perceive physical reality. The senses perceive pure data devoid of significance and direction, but this is the very beginning of any connection to the perceived object. Similarly, the faculty of wisdom transmits the perceived object to the self that perceives it. Without the mediation of wisdom, the other faculties could not be activated.

Wisdom is compared to an illuminating flash, an indivisible iota of time, an experience that cannot be broken down into phases. In the same way, wisdom registers reality as a singular entity, without differentiating details. The faculty of wisdom grasps the full picture in an intuitive way, viewing its components as a complete template. This can be compared to the way a person views an abstract drawing: as patches of light and color but without being able to associate that picture with any known object. The person perceives an idea, but does not quite understand what it is. This is wisdom: perception without understanding. It in itself is not strictly a cognitive faculty, but rather the link between the mind and that which lies beyond the mind.

Along these lines, the author of the *Tanya* points out that the word for wisdom, *ḥokhma,* is comprised of the Hebrew words *ko'aḥ* and *ma,* meaning the potential, or power, of "what." The expression *ma* is not merely a word that connotes a question, but in the broader sense it is an

nitive faculties (see *Torah Or* 19b; *Likkutei Torah*, Song 46d; *Ma'amarei Admor HaZaken* 5568, first discourse).

The intellect vis-à-vis the emotive attributes could more accurately be described, not as a birth mother, but as a midwife. The attributes are intrinsic to every soul, existing within it in a latent, potential form, and the mind merely facilitates their birth, drawing them out from their latent form in the recesses of the soul so that they emerge as palpable emotions.

The mind is fundamentally a faculty that is capable of grasping and being aware of reality, whether external or internal. The attributes are impulses inherent in every person from his inception, existing in potential: the potential to love and to hate, for example, or the impulse to feel drawn to something or repelled by it. On their own, these impulses are blind, because they lack the objects to which they should be applied. Only when the mind, as the instrument of comprehension and cognitive reception, clarifies the object of the person's impulses is his fundamental relationship toward them determined. Then the soul's emotional impulses can be activated and manifest as actual feelings.

expression of *ayin*, of nothingness. The question of "what" is always the first question one asks when confronted with the total lack of knowledge about a given thing. When Moses said, "And what are we?" (Ex. 16:7), a question on the surface, in a deeper sense his words could be understood as a statement pronouncing, "We are 'what' – we are nothing."

That wisdom is the "potential of what" means that it is the potential inherent in nothingness. It is the first faculty of the soul, the point where perception begins from a state of non-conception, an awareness that does not stem from previous perception but rather begins from zero, the transition from absolute nothingness into existence.

The flash of wisdom is also the touchstone of every idea. The veracity of an idea comes, not through intellectual analysis or comparison (which is the *bina* process, that of understanding), but from that flash of perception that is wisdom, where a person attains instant clarity, a resonance with the idea, the gut feeling that it is true.

This capacity for distinction that wisdom wields is also the ability to distinguish between truth and falsity. This explains the kabbalistic phrase "Through wisdom it will be clarified,"[5] meaning that the faculty of wisdom is what distinguishes between good and evil. ☞

THE POWER OF SELF-ABNEGATION

☞ Hasidic teachings discuss at length the concept of wisdom as the power of self-nullification. The more a person can nullify himself, the greater his capacity to grasp a thing on the level of wisdom. One who lacks the ability to divest himself of ego cannot grasp anything.

This faculty can be compared to the dark chamber of a camera or the black pupil of the eye. Since it is empty and devoid of light, it can serve as the optimal vessel for absorbing the light that enters it from outside.

This is the connection between wisdom and humility. Someone who lacks humility cannot comprehend anything. A person who is full of himself, who thinks he knows everything, cannot learn. It is not by chance that Moses, who merited the loftiest revelation ever apprehended, whose illuminating flash was so frequent that it became constant, was also "very humble, more than any person on the face of the earth" (Num. 12:3). They were but two sides of the same coin, Moses's humility and his immense wisdom, which surpassed that of any human being.

5. See, e.g., *Iggeret HaKodesh*, epistles 26, 28.

וּכְשֶׁמּוֹצִיא כֹּחוֹ אֶל הַפּוֹעַל, שֶׁמִּתְבּוֹנֵן בְּשִׂכְלוֹ לְהָבִין דָּבָר לַאֲשׁוּרוֹ וּלְעָמְקוֹ מִתּוֹךְ אֵיזֶה דָּבָר חָכְמָה הַמּוּשְׂכָּל בְּשִׂכְלוֹ - נִקְרָא בִּינָה.

When one brings forth the idea **from its potential** in wisdom **into actuality by contemplating with his intellect** in order **to thoroughly and deeply apprehend something from a concept conceived through wisdom in his mind, this is referred to as understanding.**

Wisdom is that initial flash. A person registers that he grasped something, but he does not yet know what it is. He cannot define or transmit what he has ascertained to another. Only when the idea that he has perceived becomes actualized through a process of dissection, analysis, and synthesis, through breaking down the concept into its primary focal points and their particulars, stringing each detail together into meaningful units, only then is the intellectual process complete. This is the level of understanding.

Every point of apprehension is built from two stages: The first phase is the flash of wisdom, and the second is the development of that point through the process of understanding until it becomes a fully comprehensible and relatable topic. The intellect, then, in its familiar sense, begins with understanding.

The dynamic between wisdom and understanding is analogous to the difference between seeing and hearing and, more particularly, between seeing an event and hearing about it after the fact. Seeing grants a complete picture in an instant, offering every detail simultaneously. By contrast, hearing presents the picture one detail at a time.

Wisdom is the direct sighting of a concept, creating a full picture of all its principles and particulars. From wisdom, this picture passes through the "thirty-two paths of wisdom,"[6] thirty-two avenues that narrate the picture to the faculty of understanding. Understanding receives its information not only secondhand but in a mode that is essentially different from the manner of perception attained through wisdom. With understanding, one grasps the details of the original picture that wisdom grasped in one flash and organizes and arranges them anew.

---

6. See *Sefer Yetzira* 1:1.

The definition of wisdom as an illuminating flash accords with Rambam's metaphor for the nature of prophecy that appears at the beginning of *Guide of the Perplexed*: Most people walk in absolute darkness, with no light. The prophet receives a flash of illumination and insight through which he grasps the truth. According to the definition of wisdom put forth by the author of the *Tanya,* this illuminating flash is not the exclusive domain of prophets alone but rather is the inception of every single cognitive process on every level. The object of thought first lies in total darkness, and the initial moment of cognitive awareness is that primary illuminating flash: wisdom. Only after this fundamental perception enters the mind can the thought process develop in an organized fashion. Wisdom, then, is the sheer power of comprehension, that initial grasp of a concept before it is analyzed and understood. ☞

וְהֵן הֵם אָב וָאֵם

These cognitive faculties of wisdom and understanding **are** known, respectively, as **father and mother,**

The most common imagery used to describe the dynamic between wisdom and understanding is the interaction between a father and a

ḤOKHMA VERSUS *BINA*

☞ Distinguishing between the faculty of wisdom and that of understanding is no simple task. First and foremost, these processes occur with such speed that a person is unable to follow what is happening within his own mind. He is aware of the contents of his mind but not of its processes. A person becomes accustomed to the dynamics of his own mind, and like any phenomenon one is born with, it is extremely difficult for him to analyze what is actually unfolding. It is easier for one to define that which occurs outside oneself than to describe what is happening in his own mind, because external stimuli are alien, allowing him to contemplate them objectively.

Second, the faculties of wisdom and understanding are intrinsically inseparable. Kabbalistic works refer to the pair as "two friends who never part," whose union is constant and eternal. All of reality derives from this union, just as the entire spectrum of the soul's activities, rational or emotional, is a byproduct of the unification of wisdom and understanding.

Practically speaking, the distinction between them is purely theoretical because one never exists without the other. The nucleus of every conceived idea is in and of itself incomprehensible because the qualities that facilitate its understanding have yet to be developed. By the same token, mother, both with regard to their relationship, which involves mutual giving and receiving, and with regard to their engendering the rest of the attributes. The father contributes one drop, the raw, unformed nucleus, and the mother develops it into a multifaceted entity, a complete analogue.

The content of that initial seed is not merely a miniature human being that only needs to be blown up into larger dimensions. Rather, it is the code that encompasses the entirety of an organism within a single cell. For this singular unit to develop into that organism, it needs a mother to carry it, reminiscent of pregnancy in the womb, so that it will not only grow in size but also qualitatively, each component evolving, transforming, and correlating with its other parts.

The physical development of a fetus thus resembles the process of cognitive development on the spiritual level. It starts with cohabitation, the mating of the faculties of wisdom and understanding, which leads to the development of the "fetus" for a period of time (nine months in physical pregnancy, and as much as forty years or more in the spiritual womb of the mind), followed by a nursing stage until it reaches cognitive maturity.

There are three aspects to physical pregnancy that are also present in the faculty of understanding: duration, construction, and growth.

understanding, the faculty of analysis and apprehension, has no meaning without an object to analyze and comprehend.

Still, there are certain conditions where one's thought processes can be slowed enough to make some degree of analysis of these stages possible. When a person wakes from a deep slumber or emerges from the effects of anesthesia, when all his bodily processes are working slowly, he can occasionally follow his cognitive processes and distinguish between his faculty of wisdom and that of understanding.

Another instance, cited in many Chabad works, is where a person is struggling to understand a very difficult concept. When he must invest a concentrated effort to conceptualize the idea and understand it, he can distinguish between the various stages of his cognitive awareness. At first, the concept eludes him completely. His mind is blank. Then, out of the blue, comes a flash of awareness: "I've got it! I understand the concept!" In that one instant, the whole concept becomes clear. Yet if an outsider were to ask him to explain what he understood, he would only be able to say that he grasped the concept but would not be able to explain anything about it. This is the stage of wisdom that precedes understanding. This apprehension is all-encompassing, like pure intuition, that is not susceptible to articulation or categorization, neither to others nor to oneself.

Duration lends the quality of time. While the illuminating flash of wisdom does not exist in the confines of time, the faculty of understanding embodies a process that demands a particular amount of time. Although time might be required to create the conditions for the flash of wisdom to occur, this period of time is not factored as part of the spark of wisdom itself. Yet from the moment the faculty of understanding receives the initial cognitive seed, it adapts, develops, and brings to fruition a bona fide, complete, understandable concept. Through this process, a particular period of time passes. These are the concept's "months of pregnancy."

The faculty of understanding also builds. Wisdom lends the seed, the fundamental inception, that overarching snapshot that lacks any demarcation of "limbs" or "organs." The process of understanding extracts details from that seed and builds it into a working structure wherein each part functions in mutual interdependence. The various parts of an idea that, at first, are nothing but scattered seeds of formless potential, become integrated in the process of understanding and come together as a system whose constituent parts function with a beginning, middle, and end. Understanding receives the individual components from wisdom but in a condensed form. To become a complete, comprehensible idea, the faculty of understanding must expand on them and distinguish one from the next. Not only does every detail become interconnected with every other detail, but every component is substantiated so that each one can stand on its own within the system. This is the quality of growth that the faculty of understanding possesses.

Growth is part of the construction process but also involves a creative element: Every newborn idea must be fleshed out and expanded with additional material so that it will exist as a distinct and meaningful point on its own. Only after the constructive and growth processes have been accomplished can we speak of a concept, something that may be understood, articulated, and communicated to others. ☞

Wisdom is the father, the masculine, active, giving element of the mind, while understanding is the mother, the feminine, passive, receptive element. However, there is another facet to these faculties that implies the opposite dynamic.

The Sages distinguish between a wise person and an understanding person.[7] A wise person understands that which he learns, while an

THE DIMENSIONS OF *BINA*

☞ *Ḥokhma*, wisdom, is but a flash, a spark, that has no dimensions. *Bina*, wisdom, on the other hand, is said to possess actual dimensions: length, width, and depth.

The depth of understanding is the ability to delve into the roots of a concept. The width of understanding refers to the expansion of ideas, to inferring various conclusions and corollaries of a given premise. The length of an idea corresponds to the ability to extend one's understanding and apply it to other realms in one's life.

The depth of understanding refers to analytic ability, while width of understanding is the power of synthesis. The faculty of understanding constructs a concept first through analyzing the spark of wisdom and then synthesizing and building these flashes to form a fresh, complete structure. These two powers, that of analysis and synthesis, in the faculty of understanding make up its two poles: receiving and giving. When the faculty of understanding receives the flash from wisdom, it makes use of its analytic faculty, disassembling the entirety of the flash into derivatives, each distinctly intelligible in and of itself, while being comprehensible in the context of their interrelationship.

This is the source of the power of understanding – and of all organized human thought. In this sense, the work of the faculty of understanding is comparable to making a square out of a circle, which from a mathematical standpoint is like transforming a system of transcendental numbers into a system of rational numbers. The faculty of understanding takes the singular snapshot acquired through wisdom and dissects it into a sequence of individually understandable, rational concepts. The ability to pinpoint the beginning and end of a straight line is the mission of the faculty of understanding. To distinguish between the causes and effects, the primary from the secondary, is impossible to do in a perfect circle.

At the same time, understanding also entails the power of expansion, the ability to synthesize. Not only does understanding transform the shape of that flash of wisdom by dissecting it, but it also adds brand-new content, expanding the wellspring of wisdom and turning it into a broad, rushing river.

The length of understanding is the ability to clarify an idea and to explain it, not just on its own plane of reality, but also at more basic levels. Every descent from one level to the next demands particular changes in form while retaining the content. The capacity to reduce concepts to more simple ideas many degrees removed from the complexity of the original idea is one of the measures of true understanding. The great wisdom of King Solomon was that he could articulate three thousand proverbs (I Kings 5:12). The author of the *Tanya* explains that he could convey every idea with three thousand metaphors (*Torah Or* 12c; *Likkutei Torah*, Lev. 57b). To formulate three thousand metaphors, one more relatable than the next, in order to simplify an idea even a few levels, let alone three thousand, demands the clearest of understanding.

7. See Rashi, Deut. 1:13.

understanding person infers one thing from another. An understanding person is thus greater than a wise one. Not only does he grasp what is being learned, but he also derives new ideas from what he has learned. Hasidism speaks of this hierarchy as well. The constituent words that comprise the term *ḥokhma, ko'aḥ ma,* the potential of "what," mentioned above, imply absolute nullification, which implies total passivity, simply being receptive and open to grasping an idea. The faculty of understanding, on the other hand, has substance. It has the essential nature of active innovation.

This facet comes to the fore when one considers, not the mutual relationship between wisdom and understanding, but rather the nature of each of these faculties, how each one independently receives particular content. The greater the mind's capacity for self-abnegation, the greater its wisdom. The faculty of wisdom does not create that initial flash but simply registers and absorbs it. A person who has wisdom but not understanding grasps the insight but does not generate or develop it. By contrast, the more creative the person, the less his capacity to receive concrete concepts. For a person to attain the "potential of 'what,'" he must emulate Moses, who declared, "What are we?"

The essence of understanding, on the other hand, does not entail silent reception but rather its capacity to analyze, to dissect, in order to create something new. The understanding person "infers one concept from another." He analyzes what he knows and formulates something new from it. In light of this, the *sefira* of *Bina* corresponds to the world of *Beria,* wherein phenomena take on new shape and form, coming into existence from nothingness as distinct entities in their own right.

From here one can understand how wisdom is the father, the giver, only in light of its relationship with understanding, where understanding plays the feminine role of receiver. But as far as their nature and function, wisdom is the passive receiver, while understanding plays the active, creative role.

Wisdom and understanding are perpetually interfacing with each other. They are "two friends who never part." Their connection fuels all of existence, and any separation between the two is a taste of death, because it suspends renewal, movement, and growth. Their union, like birth itself, is the most powerful sign of life. ☞

הַמּוֹלִידוֹת אַהֲבַת ה׳ וְיִרְאָתוֹ וּפַחְדּוֹ. כִּי הַשֵּׂכֶל שֶׁבַּנֶּפֶשׁ הַמַּשְׂכֶּלֶת כְּשֶׁמִּתְבּוֹנֵן וּמַעֲמִיק מְאֹד בִּגְדוּלַּת ה׳,

which produce love of God, on one hand, **and,** on the other, **awe and trepidation of Him, for when the intellect in the rational soul contemplates and ruminates exceedingly on the greatness of God,**

The faculties of wisdom and understanding engender an awareness of God's greatness, which evokes the emotions of love or fear. When a person contemplates the greatness of God, and he arrives at a clear apprehension, this will inevitably trigger an emotional response. To "contemplate and ruminate exceedingly" is challenging work, but if one succeeds and cultivates a clear awareness, he can rest assured that the faculties of his soul, his capacity for love and awe, will be automatically activated. If a person spends time thinking about the

A WISE AND UNDERSTANDING PERSON

☞ As in every creative arena, whether the arts or sciences, there is a stage or point in time that heralds a paradigm shift. These achievements depend on the degree to which an individual or group can attain the level of "what are we?" – as if lacking any and all prior knowledge, empty of every preconceived notion. This is why children are so wise: They are not yet filled with an overflowing sense of self. This is also why in fields that demand this type of intellectual creativity, such as modern physics, people stop being inventive at a very young age. When a person loses the ability to abnegate himself in order to receive creative insight from outside his conscious self, he loses the ability to create or make discoveries.

On the other end of the spectrum, people who get stuck in the mode of "what" remain confined to undeveloped intuitive flashes. A person like this may grasp everything, but he cannot explain himself. He sees the world with the eyes of an artist, but he cannot create art. Capturing his vision on canvas depends on his faculty of understanding.

The wise person who has no understanding perceives external stimuli that come his way, but it is the understanding person who can infer the salient element from that which he has internalized. He can then analyze and expand on it, transforming a seed into an entire tree.

Obviously, no one functions purely with wisdom or only with understanding. They are abstractions. Even people who display one of the two in a more prominent way employ a combination of both faculties. It is the interrelationship between the two faculties within an individual that determines whether he tends more toward being a wise person or one more adept at understanding.

greatness of God from various angles so that he may come to a clear apprehension of it, he will arrive at love and fear of God. On the other side of the spectrum, if a person is constantly dwelling on the temptations that he is confronted with, he will inevitably give in to his desires and sin.

When a person constantly ruminates on anything, an emotional response will arise within him automatically. The problem is that realistically it is much easier to imagine life's temptations than to envision the greatness of God. Rabbi Levi Yitzḥak of Berditchev famously said, "Master of the universe! You placed material temptations right here before our eyes, while people must learn about Gehenna from the book *Reshit Ḥokhma*. I guarantee that if the opposite had been the case, and You had placed the horrors of Gehenna in plain view, while worldly desires were described in *Reshit Ḥokhma*, no one would sin!"

אֵיךְ הוּא מְמַלֵּא כָּל עָלְמִין וְסוֹבֵב כָּל עָלְמִין וְכוּלָּא קַמֵּיהּ כְּלָא חֲשִׁיב,

how He fills all worlds and encompasses all worlds, and how **everything before Him is considered as nothingness,**

The author of the *Tanya* notes three aspects of this contemplation: God fills all worlds, vivifying and sustaining the worlds from His being. He encompasses all the worlds, surrounding them and transcending reality, because His existence extends above and beyond creation. Finally, both aspects, His light that fills and His light that surrounds, are negligible compared to His essence so that relative to Him they have no consequence whatsoever.

נוֹלְדָה וְנִתְעוֹרְרָה מִדַּת יִרְאַת הָרוֹמְמוּת בְּמוֹחוֹ וּמַחֲשַׁבְתּוֹ לִירָא וּלְהִתְבּוֹשֵׁשׁ מִגְּדוּלָּתוֹ יִתְבָּרֵךְ שֶׁאֵין לָהּ סוֹף וְתַכְלִית וּפַחַד ה׳ בְּלִבּוֹ.

then the attribute of awe at God's **exaltedness is produced and awakened in one's mind and thoughts, so that one feels awe and shame before God's infinite and limitless greatness, as well as fear of God in one's heart.**

Contemplating God's incalculable greatness engenders an appreciation of the vast distance between man and God. It is the conscious awareness of the Exalted One, of awe at God's eminence, that brings with it a shrinking of one's own sense of self. This awe engendered in the mind then engenders an emotion: "fear of God in one's heart."

וְשׁוּב יִתְלַהֵב לִבּוֹ בְּאַהֲבָה עַזָּה כְּרִשְׁפֵּי אֵשׁ בַּחֲשִׁיקָה וַחֲפִיצָה וּתְשׁוּקָה וְנֶפֶשׁ שׁוֹקֵקָה לִגְדוּלַּת אֵין סוֹף בָּרוּךְ הוּא.

In turn, one's heart will be ignited with a love of God **as fierce as sparks of fire, with longing, desire, and yearning, and a soul that thirsts for** connection to **the greatness of *Ein Sof*, blessed be He.**

One's contemplation will engender love for God as well. The author of the *Tanya* uses four expressions to describe this love, which are found in the writings of the Sages, each with its own unique connotation.[8] *Ḥashika,* longing, implies the directionality of the love, the gravitation toward a particular object. *Ḥafitza,* desire, signifies one's inner desire, not as it relates to an external reality but rather in and of itself. *Teshuka,* yearning, and *nefesh shokeka,* a thirsting soul, describe that burning sensation that fills one's soul, that feeling that a person cannot survive without a connection with God.[9]

וְהִיא כְּלוֹת הַנֶּפֶשׁ,

This level of love **is** known as the **pining of the soul,**

Love of God at its highest level is called the "pining of the soul." The soul's desire for God, to the point that it would be subsumed into *Ein Sof,* is so immense that the soul would lose its independent existence. This is why it is called the pining of the soul: because the soul perishes due to its love. (The term for "pining of the soul," *kelot hanefesh,* literally means the expiration of the soul.)

8. See *Bereshit Rabba* 80:7.

9. In his commentary, Rabbi Shmuel Gronem Esterman explains, citing Rabbi Hillel Malisov of Paritch, that these four terms correspond to four aspects rooted in the divine soul's quality of fire – that is, its attribute of love – reflecting the four hues of a flame.

כדכתיב: "נכספה וגם כלתה נפשי" וגו' (תהלים פד, ג), וכתיב: "צמאה נפשי לאלהים" וגו' (שם מב, ג), וכתיב: "צמאה לך נפשי" וגו' (שם סג, ב).

as it is written, "My soul longs, indeed it yearns…" (Ps. 84:3), **and it is written, "My soul thirsts for God…"** (Ps. 42:3), **and it is written, "My soul thirsts for You…"** (Ps. 63:2).

The three verses that the author of the *Tanya* quotes here correspond to the three vantage points of contemplation he outlined above: "how He fills all worlds and encompasses all worlds, and [how] everything before Him is considered as nothing." The first verse parallels God's filling of all of the worlds, the second, His encompassing all worlds, while the third points to His essence, which transcends both.[10]

והצמאון הוא מיסוד האש שבנפש האלהית, וכמו שכתבו הטבעיים, וכן הוא בעץ חיים, שיסוד האש הוא בלב ומקור המים והליחות מהמוח, וכמו שכתוב בעץ חיים שער נ', שהיא בחינת חכמה שנקרא מים שבנפש האלהית.

The thirst for God **stems from the element of fire in the divine soul. As stated** in the works of **the natural scientists, and similarly it is written in *Etz Ḥayyim*, the element of fire is in the heart, while the source of** the element of **water and moisture is in the brain. As explained in *Etz Ḥayyim*, chapter 50, that** source of the element of water **is the level of wisdom, which is called water that is within the divine soul.**

There is a distinction between the fiery and watery aspects of the soul. Fire moves upward and expresses the impassioned excitement and

10. In his commentary on the *Tanya*, Rabbi Shmuel Gronem Esterman, as well as Rabbi Nissan Nemanov, state that this correlation can be explained as follows: "My soul longs, indeed it yearns" describes the pining of the soul, when the light that fills the vessel desires to leave it to be subsumed into the transcendent light. "My soul thirsts for God" is the movement of "returning" from the encompassing light to the vessel. "My soul thirsts for You" relates to God's essence, to "You," as explained in several hasidic sources.

fervor of the heart. It is also the source of the soul's thirst, inspired by love, to ascend and become subsumed in the Divine.

Water, on the other hand, is the rational element of the soul. Like water, the intellect is cold and damp (as opposed to the heart, which is hot and dry). Water moves downward, just as wisdom descends from the supernal heights to all points of existence.

וּשְׁאָר הַמִּדּוֹת כּוּלָּן הֵן עַנְפֵי הַיִּרְאָה וְהָאַהֲבָה וְתוֹלְדוֹתֵיהֶן, כְּמוֹ שֶׁנִּתְבָּאֵר בְּמָקוֹם אַחֵר (אגרת הקודש טו).

All the other emotive **attributes are offshoots and derivatives of fear and love, as explained elsewhere** (*Iggeret HaKodesh*, epistle 15).

Love and fear are the foundational emotions of the soul, two poles that direct the soul's trajectory. Love, which corresponds to the attribute of *Ḥesed,* moves from the inside out, expanding and breaking through boundaries; it is the desire to give without limit. The attribute of fear, which corresponds to the attribute of *Gevura,* moves from the outside inward; it represents the constriction and restraint from giving. It is the capacity to set boundaries and confine oneself within them. Thus love and fear define the two poles of the soul: expansion and contraction, giving and abstention.

The attribute of compassion is an expression of *Tiferet,* and in this context it constitutes giving to one who needs it. It is not a new, additional direction in the soul but rather a composite of love and fear, a middle point between undifferentiated giving and absolute restraint from giving. The other attributes, *Netzaḥ, Hod,* and *Yesod,* are also not primary attributes like *Ḥesed* and *Gevura* – but rather are secondary attributes that characterize, direct, and adjust the primary attributes.

וְהַדַּעַת, הוּא מִלְּשׁוֹן: "וְהָאָדָם יָדַע אֶת חַוָּה" (בראשית ד, א),

Da'at, the cognitive faculty of knowledge, **has the same connotation as** the expression in the verse "**And the man had been intimate** [*yada*] **with Eve,** his wife" (Gen. 4:1)

Da'at is the third of the cognitive faculties. Wherever the word *da'at* is used in *Tanakh,* it always implies connection, as in the verse "For

I love him [*yedativ*], so that he shall command his children and his household after him" (Gen. 18:19). Rashi explains that the word *yedativ* connotes affection, as in "Naomi had an acquaintance [*muda*] of her husband" (Ruth 2:1, 3:2), meaning that the person referred to was not a stranger; he was connected to Naomi in some way. Another example is with regard to Moses: "You have found favor in My eyes, and I have known you [*ve'eda'akha*] by name" (Ex. 33:17).

וְהוּא לְשׁוֹן הִתְקַשְּׁרוּת וְהִתְחַבְּרוּת,

and is an expression of bonding and connection.

Da'at is the third *sefira* among the "mothers" introduced by the author of the *Tanya* in this chapter: *Ḥokhma, Bina,* and *Da'at.* As explained above, *Ḥokhma* is the faculty of apprehending the initial flash of perception. *Bina* is the analytic, synthesizing faculty. *Da'at* is the capacity to form connections with the subject at hand. *Da'at* is not an intellectual faculty but rather the bridge between the mind and the emotions, relating the concept that was perceived by *Ḥokhma* and understood by *Bina* to the emotive attributes of the soul. Through *Da'at,* one stimulates an emotional experience toward that given concept. ☞

שֶׁמְּקַשֵּׁר דַּעְתּוֹ בְּקֶשֶׁר אַמִּיץ וְחָזָק מְאֹד וְיִתְקַע מַחֲשַׁבְתּוֹ בְּחוֹזֶק בִּגְדוּלַּת אֵין סוֹף בָּרוּךְ הוּא וְאֵינוֹ

One binds his knowledge with a supremely mighty and powerful bond and firmly applies his thoughts to the contemplation of **the greatness of *Ein Sof,* blessed be He, without diverting his**

THE *SEFIRA* OF *DA'AT*

☞ *Da'at* does not have the same level of importance as *Ḥokhma* and *Bina*. *Ḥokhma* and *Bina* are not only *sefirot*; they are *partzufim* (literally, "countenances"), meaning that they are entire structures or configurations, each encompassing all the other *sefirot*. *Da'at*, on the other hand, is only an auxiliary attribute that serves as a connector between the *partzufim*. Although it does not build awareness, it is significant in that it activates the emotive attributes of the soul. *Da'at* determines the degree to which the awareness born in *Ḥokhma* and understood in *Bina* affects the soul. What is perceived and understood is acquired only by *Da'at*. Along these lines, the Midrash states, "If you have acquired knowledge, what do you lack? Without knowledge, what do you have?" (*Vayikra Rabba* 1:6).

מַסִּיחַ דַּעְתּוֹ. כִּי אַף מִי שֶׁהוּא חָכָם וְנָבוֹן בִּגְדוּלַּת אֵין סוֹף בָּרוּךְ הוּא, הִנֵּה אִם לֹא יְקַשֵּׁר דַּעְתּוֹ וְיִתְקַע מַחֲשַׁבְתּוֹ בְּחוֹזֶק וּבְהַתְמָדָה לֹא יוֹלִיד בְּנַפְשׁוֹ יִרְאָה וְאַהֲבָה אֲמִיתִּית כִּי אִם דִּמְיוֹנוֹת שָׁוְא.

focus from that connection, **for even one who is wise and understanding regarding the greatness of *Ein Sof*, blessed be He, will not engender true fear and love in his soul if he does not firmly and constantly bind his knowledge and apply his thoughts** to the contemplation of God's greatness, **only futile illusions.**

Da'at forges one's connection to a concept. It brings to the fore the connection of the self, the feeling that "this speaks to me. I care about this." A person forms this bond by "binding his knowledge and firmly and constantly fixing his thoughts." He concentrates his thoughts on the given concept and connects to it until it becomes part of the fabric of his being.

This connection must be constant. If the person diverts his attention from the concept, then he no longer has knowledge of it and the concept ceases to be bound to his soul. Diversion means that one's thoughts are no longer actively engaged with the concept. It does not mean that his understanding is lost; it means that his knowledge of the concept – his spiritual bond with the concept – dissipates. As a result, his intellect fails to generate either love or fear within his being.

וְעַל כֵּן הַדַּעַת הוּא קִיּוּם הַמִּדּוֹת וְחַיּוּתָן וְהוּא כּוֹלֵל חֶסֶד וּגְבוּרָה, פֵּירוּשׁ אַהֲבָה וַעֲנָפֶיהָ וְיִרְאָה וַעֲנָפֶיהָ.

Thus, knowledge provides the sustenance and vitality of the emotive **attributes, and it incorporates** the attributes of **kindness and restraint, meaning love and its offshoots and fear and its offshoots.**

The faculty of knowledge also has an active function: the ability to draw conclusions. The perpetual activity of wisdom and understanding does not produce deductions, not even of an intentional thought process, but only alerts one to the existence of something, to an awareness of that which exists within his soul or in the supernal world. Knowledge is the capacity to reach a conclusion about that awareness, to impart meaning to the ideas engendered by the faculties of wisdom and understanding so that one reacts to it emotionally and even takes a course of action.

Knowledge actualizes the abstract awareness that comes about through wisdom and understanding. A person may be extremely smart or gifted at deductive reasoning, but if he lacks *da'at*, the faculty of knowledge, he will be incapable of applying those insights in a personal way. Although the faculty of knowledge does not add anything to the core insight, it plays a critical and decisive role. The deductions and conclusions formulated by the faculty of knowledge is the ability to generate emotion, whether it is one of attraction (love) or compulsion (fear). It is the faculty of knowledge that formulates one's likes and dislikes, the impulse to desire or to hate, ideals and pitfalls. Since knowledge is that which determines how a person relates to every aspect of his life, it "provides the sustenance and vitality of the [emotive] attributes."

Da'at, then, is, in a certain sense, the root of the soul's emotive attributes.

In this chapter, the author of the *Tanya* discussed the ten faculties of the soul, which correspond to the ten supernal attributes, or *sefirot*. These faculties are referred to as the soul's *tikkunim*, "adornments." Yet although these faculties serve as "adornments," in a sense extrinsic to the soul's actual essence, when the soul is manifest through a particular *tikkun* or faculty, the soul and attribute appear synonymous. The faculties personify the soul in such a way that, as perceived from without, the soul's inner essence and its expression through its attributes are one. This is the way the personality of the soul reveals itself not only to the outside world but also how it manifests itself internally to the soul's "garments" – thought, speech, and action. It is the garments of the divine soul that the author of the *Tanya* discusses in the next chapter.

Chapter 4

IN CHAPTER 3, THE AUTHOR OF THE *TANYA* DISCUSSED the ten faculties of the soul, which correspond to the ten *sefirot*. It is through these faculties – through wisdom, understanding, kindness, restraint, and so on – that the soul functions within the body and with the world at large.

These faculties are mere glimmers of the soul yet are unified with its essence, just as the ten supernal *sefirot* are unified with the divine essence. Each of these faculties can only express the soul's intrinsic essence, its wisdom, understanding, or kindness – the inner world of the soul. The "garments" of the soul, on the other hand – thoughts, speech, or actions – through which the soul is also manifest, express not only the soul's essential self but also its grasp of that which is extrinsic to it. Not only does the soul possess wisdom or understanding in and of itself, but through a particular thought, statement, or deed, it manifests its understanding or kindness toward the person's consciousness and other external phenomena.

וְעוֹד יֵשׁ לְכָל נֶפֶשׁ אֱלֹהִית שְׁלֹשָׁה לְבוּשִׁים, שֶׁהֵם מַחֲשָׁבָה דִּבּוּר וּמַעֲשֶׂה

Furthermore, each divine soul possesses three garments, which are thought, speech, and action

29 Kislev (leap year)

(In a 29-day month, study also the portion for 30 Kislev.)

Thought, the faculty by which a person's soul expresses itself to the conscious self, is the innermost of the garments. Speech is the soul's vehicle of expression to others through words, whereas deed is the expression of the soul by way of the tools of the material world.

These garments are the means through which the soul expresses itself, just as the clothes a person wears are an expression of who he is. The metaphor of garment stresses the dual nature of revelation: To manifest something is to both reveal it and conceal it. The garment facilitates a person's revelation of himself to others; without his garments, he would not show himself. At the same time, it conceals the wearer. One sees not the person but the garments.

Another aspect of the analogy is the synonymy between the person and his clothes: The clothes mirror the person. They are external to the person, yet they reflect the character of the wearer.

Here lies the difference between the garment and other tools a person might use. A tool does not imitate its user, whereas a garment alludes to the shape of its wearer even as it conceals him. Similarly, speech is the garment of thought, expressing the thought, its words mirroring the letters and images of the thought, even as it veils its deeper dimensions. ☞

שֶׁל תַּרְיַ"ג מִצְוֹת הַתּוֹרָה. **of the 613 mitzvot of the Torah.**

The garments of the divine soul are the 613 commandments of the Torah. Each soul, like every other aspect of reality, expresses itself through those garments that facilitate the revelation of its particular

GARMENTS VERSUS ADORNMENTS

☞ Unlike the *tikkunim*, or "adornments" – the soul's ten faculties – the garments constitute the outer expressions of the soul and are distinct from it. The soul has the choice of whether to dress itself in them or not, just as a person can clothe himself in a garment or remove it without effecting any change in himself. This is not the case with the more internal faculties, which, to extend the analogy, are more like a body to the soul. Though in essence the body and the soul are two different entities, in many respects body and soul appear to comprise a single entity. A soul cannot remove or change its body without itself changing.

Similarly, the soul's faculties are integrally bound to the soul's essence. Moreover, just as the soul's essence is immutable, so are its attributes. Kindness cannot be transformed into restraint and vice versa, just as the soul cannot remove and don its body at will. Moreover, the integral bond between the soul and its faculties means that the very essence of the soul is present in each of them.

The garments, on the other hand, are separate from the soul's essence. The faculties of thought, speech, and action can change their function from one extreme to the other, expressing love one moment, for instance, and fear a moment later (see *Torah Or* 13b; *Derekh Mitzvotekha* 155b).

nature. The animal soul expresses itself through garments whose content and form are akin to its physical and material nature. By contrast, the garments of the divine soul are affiliated with all that is holy – namely, the thoughts, speech, and deeds that constitute the 613 commandments of the Torah.

That holiness is manifest through the 613 commandments of the Torah has a twofold implication: Holiness is attained by fulfilling the mitzvot, and it cannot be attained in any other way. This axiom has far-reaching implications: that holiness, that which is absolute good, does not contain anything that is not connected to the Torah.

There are many important things in the world, but they are not necessarily holy. There is no meaning to such expressions as "the sanctity of the law," "the sanctity of the state," or "the sanctity of labor." People involved in a profession or an ideal acquire a love for it and attribute to it a sort of holiness. But holiness is not merely a matter of extreme regard, that because something is important or valuable, it is perforce holy. Rather, holiness by definition is something that pertains to the Divine, and the only way to connect with the Divine is through the Torah and mitzvot. ☞

THE PATH TO HOLINESS

☞ Can holiness be attained in some other way? Is it possible to create new types of holiness other than through Torah and mitzvot?

The author of the *Tanya*, Rabbi Shneur Zalman of Liadi, wrote a letter (printed in some Chabad prayer books) regarding certain hasidic groups who, in order to raise their spirits and awaken their souls to prayer, would sit around telling jokes. Rabbi Shneur Zalman sharply condemned this practice, referring to it as "a mitzva that comes through a sin" (see *Berakhot* 47b), and as the joy of those who are "extremely wicked and sinful to the Lord" (Gen. 13:13, a phrase that refers to the people of Sedom), and similar expressions.

Holiness cannot be manufactured by man. Holiness means relationship with God, but finite man cannot, by his own power, relate to God, who is infinite, as neither he nor anything he generates can be of intrinsic significance to the Divine. People tend to attribute things they have created to God and then expect Him to regard those things as holy. A person might create something that is very important, very great, very inspiring, and that creation might even represent a great sacrifice on his part, in the sense that he has devoted his time and his very self to it, but none of that makes it in any way connected with the Divine. Between the infinite and the finite is an infinite gap; between *Ein Sof* and man is a chasm that man cannot bridge. However high a man rises, whatever ef-

שֶׁכְּשֶׁהָאָדָם מְקַיֵּים בְּמַעֲשֶׂה כָּל מִצְוֹת מַעֲשִׂיּוֹת, וּבְדִבּוּר הוּא עוֹסֵק בְּפֵירוּשׁ כָּל תַּרְיַ״ג מִצְוֹת וְהִלְכוֹתֵיהֶן, וּבְמַחֲשָׁבָה הוּא מַשִּׂיג כָּל מַה שֶּׁאֶפְשָׁר לוֹ לְהַשִּׂיג בְּפַרְדֵּ״ס הַתּוֹרָה, הֲרֵי כְּלָלוּת תַּרְיַ״ג אֵבָרֵי נַפְשׁוֹ מְלוּבָּשִׁים בְּתַרְיַ״ג מִצְוֹת הַתּוֹרָה.

When a person fulfills all the action-related commandments with his deeds, and with his **speech he engages in expounding all the 613 commandments and their** ***halakhot*****, and with** his **thoughts he apprehends all that he is capable of apprehending of the** ***peshat*** (plain meaning), ***remez*** (allusion), ***derush*** (homiletic exposition), and ***sod*** (mystical aspects) **of the Torah, then the entirety of the 613 limbs of his soul are clothed within the 613 commandments of the Torah.**

The human body consists of 248 organs and 365 sinews. The soul too contains 613 "limbs," the spiritual counterparts of the 613 limbs of the body. Each of the 613 limbs of the human soul has a corresponding garment, which constitutes one of the 613 commandments of the Torah. ☞

fort he makes, the gap between him and the Divine remains. From his side, it cannot be closed.

From the time of Adam, the temptation has existed to be "as God, knowers of good and evil" (Gen. 3:5). Artists, writers, and scientists are tempted by the belief that there is some ruse, some hidden trail, some new invention, whereby a person can cross a certain line and become Godly. But although a person can, with his own efforts, achieve great things, even taste of the fruit of the tree of knowledge and know good and evil, he cannot, on his own, touch the Divine.

As will be explained, the only way such contact can be achieved is when God creates this contact, when He extends His hand, so to speak, across the chasm to grant man the ability to connect with Him. This is not an awakening from above that is initiated by an awakening from below – from man. It is a higher level of influence, that which comes from God Himself, that no one individual's awakening can achieve. The gap that separates the finite from the infinite can be bridged only by the infinite God, by *Ein Sof*.

The hand that God extends to us is the Torah. The Torah is not merely words of wisdom but rather its essence constitutes the Creator's communication to man in a way that man can hear, comprehend, and thereby connect with Him. The Torah is thus a manifestation of the Divine, a ray of the infinite light penetrating the infinite abyss. It, and it alone, constitutes the garments with which the divine soul may manifest itself.

ובִפְרָטוּת, בְּחִינוֹת חָכְמָה בִּינָה דַּעַת שֶׁבְּנַפְשׁוֹ מְלוּבָּשׁוֹת בְּהַשָּׂגַת הַתּוֹרָה שֶׁהוּא מַשִּׂיג בְּפַרְדֵּ״ס כְּפִי יְכוֹלֶת הַשָּׂגָתוֹ וְשֹׁרֶשׁ נַפְשׁוֹ לְמַעְלָה.

To be specific, the cognitive **faculties of wisdom, understanding, and knowledge in one's soul are clothed within the apprehension of Torah that one apprehends through** the four levels of ***peshat, remez, derush,*** and ***sod,*** **commensurate with** both **his intellectual capacity and the root of his soul on high.** 30 Kislev (leap year)

Comprehension of the Torah, on the level at which a person understands, connects, and unites with it, serves as the garment for the cognitive faculties of the divine soul, which desires to connect and cleave to God. This comprehension has two components: a person's intellectual capacity and the supernal root of his soul.

There are areas of Torah that many are incapable of comprehending

FULFILLING ALL 613 COMMANDMENTS

☞ In truth, no single individual can actually observe all 613 commandments, not only because conditions might not allow it, but because there is no individual to whom all of them apply. Some mitzvot are commanded exclusively to women, others exclusively to men. Some apply only to the king or the High Priest.

Yet every Jew has some connection with each of the mitzvot and, in a certain sense, can observe them all. One way he can do so is through the agent of another. For example, the High Priest or the king fulfills his mitzvot on his own behalf and on behalf of all of Israel. As explained in chapter 3, all of Israel in a particular generation and, in a broader sense, of all generations, constitutes a singular unit, just as the human body, with its various limbs and organs, constitutes a single organism. Israel, in this sense, is a multidimensional being, in time as well as in space, its various generations and communities composing an integrated whole. Each generation is a cross section of the greater body, personifying the totality in its specific way. Each individual, therefore, as a part of the whole, shares in the mitzvot that every other part observes.

Another way in which a person can fulfill all the mitzvot is that those mitzvot that he cannot observe physically he can observe on another plane, in speech and thought. A person who cannot fulfill the commandments that apply only to kings, for instance, can still fulfill them, in a way, by thinking and speaking about them. Though merely talking and thinking about a mitzva does not constitute its true fulfillment (aside from those mitzvot that are fulfilled through thought and speech), in some cases it may be enough for a person to develop that part of the garment that clothes the 613 limbs of his soul.

strictly because of their intellectual limitations. Not every mind can understand the complexities of Talmud with the commentary of *Tosafot*. Every person has his limits as to how much he can comprehend of the four levels through which the Torah is interpreted, limits set by his intellectual ability.

The second factor in the acquisition of Torah is the supernal root of a person's soul. Even someone who is intellectually able to understand a certain area of the Torah will not grasp it completely unless it relates to the root of his soul. Only then will its concepts resonate with him and have an impact on him to their fullest extent. To comprehend something requires intellectual ability, but it also requires an affinity with the concept, which derives from the soul's rootedness in this area of Torah. If a person lacks this identification with that part of the Torah, the matter might be explained to him or illustrated to him by means of metaphors and analogies, but he will not truly connect to it. Conversely, some possess a lofty soul, sensitive to great and lofty things, but lack the intellectual talent to fully understand them. Such a person relates to these things intuitively, even without the tools to rationally comprehend them. ☞

THE SOUL'S SUPERNAL ROOT

☞ The Talmud touches on this phenomenon when it speaks of those with the capacity to "draw conclusions according to the *halakha*" (*Yoma* 26a). This ability is a special talent, almost intuitive, that is not necessarily connected with a person's greatness in the comprehension of Torah. Though obviously one must be proficient in order to derive halakhic conclusions, he may not necessarily be the greatest scholar.

The works of such individuals, who exhibited an acute ability to meet the needs of the time, have become widely accepted and revered, even though they were not among the leading scholars of their generation. While the author of *Kitzur Shulḥan Arukh* was certainly a great rabbi, he was generally not considered the greatest of his time, neither in his own eyes nor in the eyes of others. Yet even the most brilliant scholars of the time did not merit achieving what he achieved. Not only was he able to write in a style that was accessible to the people, but he intuitively knew how to hone in on the essentials of Torah law that the common Jew of his generation needed to know.

When the root of a person's soul is attuned to a certain area of Torah, it leads him there even if he is unable to fully explain or even understand it.

וְהַמִּדּוֹת, שֶׁהֵן יִרְאָה וְאַהֲבָה וְעַנְפֵיהֶן וְתוֹלְדוֹתֵיהֶן, מְלוּבָּשׁוֹת בְּקִיּוּם הַמִּצְוֹת בְּמַעֲשֶׂה,

The emotive **attributes, namely, fear and love and their offshoots and derivatives, are clothed within the fulfillment of the commandments in deed**

Although there are six emotive attributes, love and fear are considered the roots of them all since they exemplify the two affinities to which the attributes are associated: giving and drawing close versus preservation and distancing. These two faculties are the two spiritual energies that cause a person to either commit a particular act or refrain from doing it. In the context of the divine soul, love motivates the performance of positive commandments, while fear impels a person to abstain from violating a prohibition.

וּבְדִבּוּר, שֶׁהוּא תַּלְמוּד תּוֹרָה שֶׁכְּנֶגֶד כּוּלָּן.

and in speech, referring specifically **to Torah study, which is the equivalent of all** the commandments.

Though other examples of such mitzvot exist, such as the recitation of the *Shema* and Grace after Meals, the author of the *Tanya* singles out Torah study as the example of a mitzva that is fulfilled through the garment of speech because it is the most prestigious of the mitzvot, the equivalent of them all.[1]

כִּי הָאַהֲבָה הִיא שֹׁרֶשׁ כָּל רמ"ח מִצְוֹת עֲשֵׂה וּמִמֶּנָּה הֵן נִמְשָׁכוֹת וּבִלְעָדָהּ אֵין לָהֶן קִיּוּם אֲמִיתִּי, כִּי הַמְקַיְּימָן בֶּאֱמֶת הוּא הָאוֹהֵב אֶת שֵׁם ה' וְחָפֵץ לְדָבְקָה בּוֹ בֶּאֱמֶת,

For love is the root of all 248 positive commandments and the source **from which they are drawn. Without this** love, the commandments one fulfills **have no true substance, for one who fulfills** the commandments **in truth is one who loves God's name and truly desires to cleave to Him,**

The 613 mitzvot consist of 248 positive commandments, such as giving charity or donning *tefillin,* and 365 prohibitions, such as murder or

1. See *Mishna Pe'a* 1:1.

adultery. These correspond to the 248 organs and 365 sinews of the body and the corresponding limbs of the soul, as mentioned above.

It is through the 248 positive commandments that a person expresses his love for God. Thus the positive commandments stem from the soul's love of God in the sense that love of God is the feeling that motivates and drives their observance.

For the mitzvot to have enduring substance, a person has to perform them. Yet it is not enough to fulfill the mitzvot merely out of habit or simply because he was trained to do so from childhood. This is not a true fulfillment of the mitzvot, but a casual, extrinsic deed with no relation to the person's inner being. "One who fulfills [the commandments] in truth" is one who does so out of a genuine desire and love.

וְאִי אֶפְשָׁר לְדָבְקָה בּוֹ בֶּאֱמֶת כִּי אִם בְּקִיּוּם רמ"ח פִּקּוּדִין,

and it is impossible to truly cleave to God **except through the fulfillment of the 248** positive **commandments,**

It is a frequently recurring question: How can one cleave to God? We know how to unite with something physical, such as a human being, but how can we unite with something infinite and undefinable, something that has no physical form – indeed, no form at all? A person may feel love for God, may yearn for God, may proclaim, "My soul thirsts for God!" (Ps. 42:3), but this only expresses his yearning. It does not consummate his love; it does not join him to God. At times, a person might feel attached to God, but such a feeling, by definition, is virtually never genuine.

The way to attach oneself to God in truth is not by means of a self-generated feeling of yearning for God but, as the author of the *Tanya* states here, by fulfilling the 248 positive commandments. It is with this concept that he will explain Isaiah's statement "Ho, everyone thirsty, go to water" (Isa. 55:1).[2] On the face of it, the verse does not seem to be telling us anything. Obviously, one who is thirsty should go and drink water, and so the author of the *Tanya* interprets the verse metaphorically as a reference to the Torah.[3] The author of the *Tanya* explains that the verse is telling us a profound truth regarding man's

2. See chap. 40.
3. Based on *Bava Kamma* 17a.

efforts to relate to God: Whoever thirsts for God, for connection to the Divine, should go to the water, to the Torah.

One who is physically thirsty knows that he needs water, but one who thirsts for God does not necessarily know that he needs Torah. He yearns for God, yet he is told to go and study about the "bull that gored the cow"![4] This approach to relating to God is far from self-evident. It even runs contrary to one's natural inclinations. So the prophet proclaims, "Let whoever thirsts go to the water!" In other words, "it is impossible to truly cleave [to God] except through the fulfillment of the 248 [positive] commandments." Just as there is no genuine fulfillment of the mitzvot without love of God, there is no true significance to love of God without fulfillment of the mitzvot. A person who yearns to cleave to God and yet is sated with the spiritual experience of yearning for God will never achieve true connection to the Divine. When a person merely desires but does not do, even if the desire is genuine and faultless, this alone will never bring about the realization of the desire.

which are the 248 "limbs" of the King, as it were, as explained elsewhere (chap. 23).

שֶׁהֵם רמ"ח אֵבָרִין דְּמַלְכָּא כִּבְיָכוֹל, כְּמוֹ שֶׁנִּתְבָּאֵר בְּמָקוֹם אַחֵר.

The *Tikkunei Zohar* teaches that the 248 positive commandments correspond not only to the 248 organs of the human body but also to the metaphorical body of the supernal King.[5] Kabbalistic thought describes the divine manifestations that reveal God as creator and vitalizer of the world in terms of an anatomical configuration.[6] This divine configuration is the spiritual source of the mitzvot that have been given to us.[7]

When a person fulfills the mitzvot in thought, speech, and deed,

4. These are opening words of chap. 4 of tractate *Bava Kamma*.

5. *Tikkunei Zohar* 74a.

6. See *Iggeret HaKodesh*, epistle 23; *Etz Hayyim*, *Sha'ar HaShemot*, chap. 7; *Yahel Or*, p. 573.

7. The creation of man in the divine image also relates to this concept. Thus, the 248 parts of the human body mirror the spiritual structure of the divine anatomical structure.

when he attaches himself to them and cleaves to them, he thereby cleaves to the 248 limbs of God, so to speak. Human beings express love by embracing and kissing the limbs of the beloved. When a person loves God with great desire and craving, and wishes to come close to Him and cleave to Him, the way to consummate this love is by embracing the "limbs of the King," the 248 positive commandments that constitute the revelation of the Divine in this world.

וְהַיִּרְאָה הִיא שֹׁרֶשׁ לְשס"ה לֹא תַעֲשֶׂה,

The fear of God **is the root of the 365 prohibitions,**

There are many factors that may prevent a person from committing a transgression, but the root of them all is fear. The essence of the emotion of fear is a movement inward, a withdrawal, self-retraction, and introversion, in contrast to love, which is the movement from the self outward in order to connect with another. Fear is when a person refrains from doing a certain thing and does not reach out for it.

כִּי יָרֵא לִמְרוֹד בְּמֶלֶךְ מַלְכֵי הַמְּלָכִים הַקָּדוֹשׁ בָּרוּךְ הוּא.

for one who fears God **is afraid to rebel against the King of kings, the Holy One, blessed be He.**

Fear can assume many forms. One of them is the fear of rebellion. A deliberate sin is an act of rebellion, a scorning of the divine authority, as indicated by the verse "The person that acts with a high hand… it is the Lord that he blasphemes…" (Num. 15:30). Man is prevented

SHAME-DRIVEN FEAR VERSUS AWE-INSPIRED FEAR

☞ Elsewhere, the author of the *Tanya* speaks of yet another type of fear: *yirat haromemut*, fear inspired by awe. This too is a deeper, more internal level of fear but of a different character than the shame-driven awe, or *yirat boshet*, mentioned here.

The difference between them is one of personality. *Yirat haromemut* is predicated upon a sense of distance. One is struck by how lofty and removed the awed object is from one's lowly self, so it applies more to people inclined to view things objectively. *Yirat boshet*, on the other hand, includes an element of connection and intimacy, connoting a relationship in which one experiences the shame of inadequacy. When considering God's greatness, some feel overawed and paralyzed; others feel shame. It is told of Rabbi Nachman of Breslov that as a young child, whenever he did or thought of doing something wrong, he would blush in shame before God.

from sinning out of fear of rebelling against God, not merely fear of punishment and reprisal, but because the very thought of rebelling against the King of all kings is a frightening prospect.

אוֹ יִרְאָה פְּנִימִית מִזּוֹ, שֶׁמִּתְבּוֹשֵׁשׁ מִגְּדוּלָּתוֹ לַמְרוֹת עֵינֵי כְבוֹדוֹ

Alternatively, there exists **a deeper** level of **fear, where one is ashamed in the face of** God's **greatness to defy the eyes of His glory**

This is a deeper, more internal level of fear, because the feeling that affects the person is not the dread of the King's might, but rather a feeling of awe in the face of God Himself. Because he is so aware of God's greatness, he is literally ashamed to contravene His will. He feels "the eyes of His glory" – that God is ever present, watching him. ☞

וְלַעֲשׂוֹת הָרַע בְּעֵינָיו, כָּל תּוֹעֲבַת ה׳ אֲשֶׁר שָׂנֵא, הֵם הַקְּלִיפּוֹת וְסִטְרָא אָחֳרָא אֲשֶׁר יְנִיקָתָם מֵהָאָדָם הַתַּחְתּוֹן וַאֲחִיזָתָם בּוֹ הוּא בְּשַׁס״ה מִצְוֹת לֹא תַעֲשֶׂה.

and do that which is evil in His eyes, all that is abominable and hateful to God, which is in the realm of ***kelippa*** **and** ***sitra aḥara,*** **whose nourishment comes from man below and whose hold on him** comes about **through** his transgression of **the 365 prohibitions.**

An evil deed is not merely an act that is contrary to a system of conventions, that violates the rules of a game or some arbitrary set of laws. Evil is evil in essence. The evil deed is an act that nourishes the cosmic evil, a conduit that feeds power and vitality to *kelippa*. The existence of evil is inherent in the nature of creation, but its nourishment, its source of power and growth, comes from man down here on earth. ☞

NOURISHING THE *KELIPPA*

☞ Man is the sole source of the *kelippa*'s nourishment, expansion, and growth. No other creature, spiritual or physical, relates in any way to the distinction between good and evil. The leopard is no worse than the lamb; both are created with a certain nature that cannot be defined as good or evil. The leopard that preys on the lamb has committed no transgression of the divine will, nor does the devoured lamb become a martyred saint because it was eaten.

In this sense, even the supernal angels,

28 Kislev
1 Tevet (leap year)

וְהִנֵּה שְׁלֹשָׁה לְבוּשִׁים אֵלּוּ מֵהַתּוֹרָה וּמִצְוֹתֶיהָ, אַף שֶׁנִּקְרָאִים לְבוּשִׁים לְנֶפֶשׁ רוּחַ וּנְשָׁמָה,

These three garments that are derived from the Torah and its commandments, although called mere **garments for the *nefesh, ruaḥ,* and *neshama,***

As explained above, the soul clothes itself in the mitzvot it fulfills, each of the 613 commandments enclothing one of the 613 limbs that constitute the human soul. Collectively, the 613 commandments form an overall garment that the *Zohar* refers to as the "garment of the sages,"[8] enveloping the three levels of the soul – *nefesh, ruaḥ,* and *neshama* – from every angle. Thus, the commandments are mere vestments for the soul, garments that it dons from time to time.

עִם כָּל זֶה, גָּבְהָה וְגָדְלָה מַעֲלָתָם לְאֵין קֵץ וָסוֹף עַל מַעֲלַת נֶפֶשׁ רוּחַ וּנְשָׁמָה עַצְמָן.

nevertheless possess an infinite and endlessly higher and greater stature than the stature of the *nefesh, ruaḥ,* and *neshama* themselves.

The Torah and commandments serve as the soul's garments, the means by which it expresses its relationship with God, but they are more than

whose holiness far surpasses that of man, have the capacity neither for good nor for evil. An angel cannot do good or bad. It is an agent, an emissary, without the capacity for independent choice. To attribute good or evil to an angel is like attributing free choice to a machine.

Only man, who lives in this world, a world where the Divine is concealed and he is always tempted to commit evil, has been granted the capacity to choose between transcending it or succumbing to it. Only he can act wicked; only he can nourish evil and increase its power. The 365 prohibitions of the Torah delineate the ways in which evil can gain a hold on man. When a person transgresses one of the prohibitions, he nourishes its corresponding aspect of evil.

Elsewhere, the author of the *Tanya* describes evil as a parasite that lives off man, coexisting with him in a symbiotic relationship (see *Torah Or* 74b). Evil exists wherever man allows it to exist, wherever he allows it to feed off the divine life force that flows to him. In this way, the divine vitality is diverted from holiness – the soul of man – to *kelippa.* The 365 prohibitions can thus be seen as a sort of delineation that defines the various ways in which man nourishes evil, from those in the mind and heart to those in speech and action.

8. See *Likkutei Torah,* Num. 44b.

auxiliary tools of the soul. Qualitatively, they are loftier than the soul itself. As the author of the *Tanya* will go on to explain, it is precisely because of their loftiness that the soul clothes itself in them in order to connect with God. Because the Torah is higher than the soul, it is able to serve as a bridge between the soul and God.

כְּמוֹ שֶׁכָּתוּב בַּזֹּהַר (ב, ס, א) דְּאוֹרַיְיתָא וְקוּדְשָׁא בְּרִיךְ הוּא כּוּלָּא חַד. פֵּירוּשׁ, דְּאוֹרַיְיתָא הִיא חָכְמָתוֹ וּרְצוֹנוֹ שֶׁל הַקָּדוֹשׁ בָּרוּךְ הוּא,

As the *Zohar* (2:60a) states, the Torah and the Holy One, blessed be He, are all one. This means that the Torah, which is the wisdom and will of the Holy One, blessed be He,

The Torah and God are one in the sense that the Torah is the supernal wisdom of God, and the commandments of the Torah reveal the divine will, expressing God's desire as to what should be done and what should not be done.

וְהַקָּדוֹשׁ בָּרוּךְ הוּא בִּכְבוֹדוֹ וּבְעַצְמוֹ כּוּלָּא חַד, כִּי הוּא הַיּוֹדֵעַ וְהוּא הַמַּדָּע וכו׳ כְּמוֹ שֶׁנִּתְבָּאֵר לְעֵיל בְּשֵׁם הָרַמְבַּ״ם.

and the Holy One, blessed be He, Himself in all His glory, are all one, since He is the knower, He is the known, and He is the knowledge itself, **as explained above** (chap. 2) **in the name of Rambam.**

The Torah is God's wisdom, which, like all the *sefirot*, is synonymous with God Himself. Similarly, God's knowledge is His knowledge of Himself, so all three aspects of knowledge – the object of His knowledge, the knowledge He possesses, and He, the knower – are one and the same. In view of this, the person who studies Torah, fusing his own mind to its concepts, achieves a bond with the Divine and thereby with God Himself. ☞

LOFTIER THAN THE SOUL

☞ An examination of a statement in the *Tanya* above (chap. 2) raises a question: Here we say that the Torah and mitzvot are loftier than the soul because they represent the divine will and wisdom. Yet in chapter 2 we said that the soul is "literally a portion of God on high" because the soul itself derives from *Ḥokhma*, the super-

וְאַף דְּהַקָּדוֹשׁ בָּרוּךְ הוּא נִקְרָא אֵין סוֹף, וְלִגְדוּלָּתוֹ אֵין חֵקֶר וְלֵית מַחֲשָׁבָה תְּפִיסָא בֵּיהּ כְּלָל,

Yet the Holy One, blessed be He, is referred to as *Ein Sof*, God's infinite being, **and His greatness is unfathomable, and no thought can grasp Him at all,**

Not only is our earthly intellect an inadequate tool to comprehend God, but no thought at all, not even the spiritual perception of the angels on high, can possibly comprehend Him, because the infinite is, by definition, incomprehensible.

nal attribute of wisdom. In what way, then, is the Torah superior to the soul?

One explanation is that above, the author of the *Tanya* speaks of the soul's essence, whereas here he is speaking of the soul's ten faculties discussed in chapter 3. In other words, although the essence of the soul derives from the divine wisdom, the soul's attributes are on a lower level. Its garments, on the other hand, the Torah and its mitzvot, also derive directly from the supernal wisdom. While the garments are extrinsic to the faculties, they constitute, in and of themselves, a loftier manifestation of the Divine.

In his commentary on the *Tanya*, Rabbi Shmuel Gronem Esterman explains that at its source, where it is unified with the supernal wisdom, the soul is at its most pure, the soul at the level of *Atzilut*. However, as it passes through worlds, descending to the world of *Asiya*, it undergoes a series of metamorphoses, where it is invested in a physical body. It is now a creature with a character and physical self. Regarding the Torah and commandments, the reverse is true: It is the divine will that the commandments be fulfilled on earth below, so it is in the world of *Asiya* that the Torah is most synonymous with the divine wisdom. The soul as it exists in the physical world is in a state of descent and distance from its source and achieves connection with God only by enclothing itself in the thought, speech, and deeds of the Torah.

Accordingly, the author of the *Tanya* refers to the soul as a "portion of God on high," implying that it has parted and descended from its source in the supernal wisdom. This is not the case with the Torah and commandments, which are the express will of God as they exist in the physical world.

Moreover, the *Zohar* states that "Torah emerges from wisdom" (*Zohar* 2:121a). Although the Torah emerges from the supernal wisdom, and the attribute of wisdom is the agent of its revelation, its true source is *Keter*, which is a higher manifestation of Godliness than *Ḥokhma*. Thus, the soul descends to the physical world in order to clothe itself in the thought, speech, and action of the Torah and thereby elevate its level of connection with God from *Ḥokhma* to *Keter*.

וְכֵן בִּרְצוֹנוֹ וְחָכְמָתוֹ, כְּדִכְתִיב: "אֵין חֵקֶר לִתְבוּנָתוֹ" (ישעיה מ, כח), וּכְתִיב: "הַחֵקֶר אֱלוֹ־הַּ תִּמְצָא" (איוב יא, ז), וּכְתִיב: "כִּי לֹא מַחְשְׁבוֹתַי מַחְשְׁבוֹתֵיכֶם" (ישעיה נה, ח),

and the same applies with regard to His will and wisdom, as it is written, "There is no scrutinizing His understanding" (Isa. 40:28). **It is also written, "Can you discover the understanding of God?"** (Job 11:7), **and it is written, "For My thoughts are not your thoughts"** (Isa. 55:8).

The author of the *Tanya* is raising a question: If God's wisdom and will are as infinite and unfathomable as Himself, how can the Torah, which we do comprehend, be the wisdom of God, and the mitzvot, which we enact in our daily lives, be His will? How can we possibly grasp and relate to His wisdom and will?

הִנֵּה עַל זֶה אָמְרוּ: "בִּמְקוֹם שֶׁאַתָּה מוֹצֵא גְּדוּלָּתוֹ שֶׁל הַקָּדוֹשׁ בָּרוּךְ הוּא שָׁם אַתָּה מוֹצֵא עַנְוְתָנוּתוֹ" (מגילה לא, א). וְצִמְצֵם הַקָּדוֹשׁ בָּרוּךְ הוּא רְצוֹנוֹ וְחָכְמָתוֹ בְּתַרְיַ"ג מִצְוֹת הַתּוֹרָה וּבְהִלְכוֹתֵיהֶן וּבְצֵירוּפֵי אוֹתִיּוֹת תַּנַ"ךְ וּדְרָשׁוֹתֵיהֶן שֶׁבָּאַגָּדוֹת וּמִדְרְשֵׁי חֲכָמֵינוּ ז"ל,

Regarding this conundrum, the Sages **stated, "Wherever you find** a reference to **the greatness of the Holy One, blessed be He, you** also **find** a reference to **His humility"** (*Megilla* 31a). **The Holy One, blessed be He, constricted His will and wisdom within the 613 commandments of the Torah and their *halakhot*, and within the combination of letters in** the verses of ***Tanakh*** **and their homiletical expositions** of these verses found **in the aggadot and midrashic works of our Sages,**

No human being, whoever the person may be, can comprehend the divine wisdom itself in its purity. Yet the Talmud states, "Wherever you find His greatness"[9] – wherever God's infinity is referred to in *Tanakh* – "you find His humility." In that very same place, you read of how God constricts and confines Himself to a specific place. And

9. The standard talmudic text reads *gevurato*, "His might," but certain manuscripts have *gedulato*, "His greatness."

wherever you find His might, His infinite power to constrict His own infinity, there you find His humility; there you find Him manifesting Himself in the minutiae of reality.

As the Talmud there states further, where He is described as the "God of gods and the Lord of lords" (Deut. 10:17), He is also described as "He who executes justice for the orphan and the widow" (Deut. 10:18). Where He is described as "the Exalted and Most High, who dwells forever, and Holy is His name" (Isa. 57:15), this is followed by "Exalted and holy I will dwell, and I will be with the downtrodden and humble to revive the spirit of the humble and to revive the heart of the downtrodden." We also find that God, whom "the heavens and the heaven of heavens cannot contain" (I Kings 8:27), constricted His presence between the carrying poles of the ark.[10] This is God's greatness, and this is His might. He is not merely great but infinite, and it is His very infinity and omnipotence that enables the expression of His wisdom in finite words and forms.[11]

Even if those elements of Torah to which we have access are but "the residue of *Ḥokhma*,"[12] representing but a paltry fraction of the supernal wisdom, they are nevertheless the written expression of the divine wisdom. If a concept were to be expressed in a series of formulas, each outlining a deeper aspect of the concept, even the most superficial formula is correct, although layer upon layer of deeper formulations exist. Likewise, the Torah is the divine truth at whatever level it appears, in whatever world or stratum of reality it is articulated. The letters and words of the Written Torah, the demarcations and categories that define the legal details of each mitzva, this is the wisdom and will of God as expressed in the obscurities, limitations, and contradictions of our material world. ☞

10. See *Bereshit Rabba* 4:4.

11. In his commentary on the *Tanya*, Rabbi Yaakov Kadiner explains that one might venture to say that because God is infinite and without limit, He cannot manifest Himself through a finite medium. But this in itself imposes a limit on Him! It is specifically His infinity that enables Him to clothe Himself in finite garments. He can do anything – even constrict Himself. This is what the Talmud means when it says, "Wherever you find His greatness, you find His humility."

12. See *Midrash Rabba*, Bereshit 44:17.

בְּכְדֵי שֶׁכָּל הַנְּשָׁמָה אוֹ רוּחַ וְנֶפֶשׁ שֶׁבְּגוּף הָאָדָם תּוּכַל לְהַשִּׂיגָן בְּדַעְתָּהּ וּלְקַיְּימָן כָּל מַה שֶּׁאֶפְשָׁר לְקַיֵּים מֵהֶן בְּמַעֲשֶׂה דִּבּוּר וּמַחֲשָׁבָה, וְעַל יְדֵי זֶה תִּתְלַבֵּשׁ בְּכָל עֶשֶׂר בְּחִינוֹתֶיהָ בִּשְׁלֹשָׁה לְבוּשִׁים אֵלּוּ.

so that each *neshama*, or even the lower soul levels of ***ruaḥ* and *nefesh*, within the human body may apprehend them** with its own **intellect and fulfill them as much they can possibly be fulfilled in action, speech, and thought. By this means, each** soul level, **with all its ten faculties, can become clothed within these three garments.**

The constriction of the divine will within the 613 commandments of the Torah is not meant for the pure soul as it exists in the higher worlds, but rather for the lower levels of the soul that are enclothed in a physical body and a physical world. When outside the body, existing in the abstract, spiritual realm, the soul itself is infinite and has no need for the constriction of the divine will within the Torah's words and action-related mitzvot. The soul's limitations stem from its bond with the body and its dependence on the body's tools for navigating this physical world, the senses, and the mind.

וְלָכֵן נִמְשְׁלָה הַתּוֹרָה לְמַיִם - מַה מַּיִם יוֹרְדִים מִמָּקוֹם גָּבוֹהַּ לְמָקוֹם נָמוּךְ, כָּךְ הַתּוֹרָה יָרְדָה מִמְּקוֹם כְּבוֹדָהּ שֶׁהִיא רְצוֹנוֹ וְחָכְמָתוֹ יִתְבָּרֵךְ, וְאוֹרַיְיתָא וְקוּדְשָׁא בְּרִיךְ הוּא כּוּלָּא חַד וְלֵית מַחֲשָׁבָה תְּפִיסָא בֵּיהּ כְּלָל.

Therefore, the Torah is likened to water. Just as water descends from an elevated place to a lower one, so too the Torah descended from its place of honor, for it is God's will and wisdom, and the Torah and the Holy One, blessed be He, are all one, and no thought can grasp Him at all. 2 Tevet (leap year)

WHEREVER YOU FIND HIS HUMILITY...

☞ Whenever you encounter God's greatness in nature, in a piece of wisdom, in an expression of His loving-kindness, or in a situation that demonstrates His strength, you are essentially encountering His humility. God constricted His infinity into such intensely confined parameters so that we could recognize Him. The inverse is true as well: Wherever you find His humility – in the nuances of the mitzvot and in the way He relates to every single person exactly as he is – this is God's greatness!

In its loftier incarnation, the soul is, like God, inherently unattainable and incomprehensible since the Torah is the wisdom of God. But it does not remain at this level. The entire point of the Torah is that the divine wisdom, while remaining inherently incomprehensible, should progressively be rearticulated, level after level, until it is rendered into a formulation to which every person can in some way relate. We cannot fully comprehend the former rearticulations, because they relate to the divine reality rather than to ours, but we can all relate to the version presented to us, each person on his own level. ☞

וּמִשָּׁם נָסְעָה וְיָרְדָה בְּסֵתֶר הַמַּדְרֵגוֹת

From its place of honor, where it is unified with God, **it traveled and descended through concealed stages**

The words *beseter hamadregot,* "through concealed stages," is a reference to the verse "My dove, in the clefts of the rock, in the covert of the terrace [*beseter hamadrega*]" (Song 2:14). "My dove" refers to the soul at its source, in its highest manifestation, united with God, and the Hebrew word for terrace in the verse, *madrega,* also means level or stage. The verse, then, may read, "God's 'dove,' the Jewish soul, descends 'through stages of concealment.'" That the soul descends from level to level means that it undergoes increasing constrictions, becoming more and more hidden.

Another way to understand the soul's "concealed stages" is that the distance between the soul after it descends to the world of *Asiya* and the soul as it exists in the level above this realm is so immense

THE TORAH'S DESCENT

☞ To understand this, we can use another analogy. Consider a computer. One can understand a computer on many levels. The most fundamental level, the theory of how the computer operates, is extremely complex and requires specialized expertise that few people are able to master. On more superficial levels, one can, with a minimum of intellectual ability, achieve a certain mastery of the computer. If one wanted the computer to multiply a two-digit number to the power of six, the programming behind this operation would be beyond the understanding of the vast majority of people, but the computer has an operating system that translates this process into a simple problem that most everyone can solve: Which keys do I punch?

The Torah is incomprehensible at its

that the higher level of soul is essentially invisible in the physical realm. Similarly, here below we learn the *halakha* – do this; don't do that – yet the divine wisdom and will that are behind it are hidden from our purview.

מִמַּדְרֵגָה לְמַדְרֵגָה בְּהִשְׁתַּלְשְׁלוּת הָעוֹלָמוֹת, **from level to level, through the progression of the worlds,**

The Torah is manifest in all the worlds, from its source in divine wisdom in the world of *Atzilut* throughout the worlds of *Beria, Yetzira,* and *Asiya,* step by endless step. Each world has a corresponding level of Torah that relates to the spiritual reality of that level, and the Torah reveals itself in each world according to its essence.

עַד שֶׁנִּתְלַבְּשָׁה בִּדְבָרִים גַּשְׁמִיִּים וְעִנְיְינֵי עוֹלָם הַזֶּה, **until it became clothed within physical things and worldly matters,**

In our material world, the Torah manifests itself in physical phenomena, and in the interrelationship between them, encompassing the whole gamut of this worldly existence. In this way, the Torah reveals divine wisdom within the context of our reality. And our reality is a reality that a person can grasp, a reality to which the body can relate so that the soul that dwells and operates within the body can experience it, resonate with it, and fuse with it. While the Torah constitutes infinite divine wisdom, it is also definitive and intelligible to man.

שֶׁהֵן רוֹב מִצְוֹת הַתּוֹרָה כְּכוּלָּם וְהִלְכוֹתֵיהֶן, **which comprise the majority of commandments of the Torah and their** respective ***halakhot,***

elemental level, but much of it translates into deeds and rules, dos and don'ts, to which anyone can relate. Were the Torah to remain in the supernal worlds, as abstract wisdom, the ordinary person could not relate to it. When the Torah successively reformulates itself to the point that, for example, it instructs that we must give gifts to the poor on Purim, everyone knows what to do.

The Torah is the path to God, a path that ascends without limit. On the other hand, it descends all the way down here below, to a level where it will resonate with every person at all times, no matter who they are.

While there are certain commandments that are fundamentally spiritual in nature, the vast majority of them entail physical action with the use of material objects. Even if a commandment does not entail a physical action per se, it still requires some interaction with the physical reality. Not only is the body required for the handling of a physical object, but even an intangible thought or feeling must be thought and felt by the body within this world.

וּבְצֵרוּפֵי אוֹתִיּוֹת גַּשְׁמִיּוֹת בִּדְיוֹ עַל הַסֵּפֶר, עֶשְׂרִים וְאַרְבָּעָה סְפָרִים שֶׁבַּתּוֹרָה נְבִיאִים וּכְתוּבִים,

and within the physical letter combinations written **with ink on parchment, comprising the twenty-four books of** the **Torah, Prophets, and Writings.**

Another example of the physical embodiment of the Torah, besides the physical actions of the mitzvot, is the Torah scroll, in which the books of the Written Torah are inscribed. Their content, their wording, the shape of the letters, and even the quality of the ink with which they are written (all of which is governed by a series of *halakhot*) are all expressions of the divine will and wisdom.

כְּדֵי שֶׁתְּהֵא כָּל מַחֲשָׁבָה תְּפִיסָא בָּהֶן.

This descent occurred **in order that every** human **thought could grasp** God's will and wisdom.

When unified with God in the higher worlds, the supernal wisdom cannot be apprehended by any conceivable thought. But when the supernal wisdom is embodied in the Torah here in our world, in physical concepts and realities, every mind can apprehend it.

וַאֲפִילּוּ בְּחִינוֹת דִּבּוּר וּמַעֲשֶׂה שֶׁלְּמַטָּה מִמַּדְרֵגַת מַחֲשָׁבָה, תְּפִיסָא בָּהֶן וּמִתְלַבֶּשֶׁת בָּהֶן.

Even speech and action, which are lower than the level of thought, can grasp them and be clothed within them.

The Torah clothes itself not only in concepts that relate to our world, but also in words we can speak and deeds we can do. We can relate to it not only through abstract thoughts but also through concrete speech and deeds. Not only can we understand the Torah, we can also speak it and do it, investing our very bodies in the very act of a mitzva.

וּמֵאַחַר שֶׁהַתּוֹרָה וּמִצְוֹתֶיהָ מַלְבִּישִׁים כָּל עֶשֶׂר בְּחִינוֹת הַנֶּפֶשׁ,

Since the Torah and its commandments enclothe all ten facets of the soul,

The ten faculties of the soul, which correspond to the ten *sefirot*, constitute a person's internal infrastructure.[13] For each faculty, there is a corresponding garment of Torah. *Ḥokhma, Bina,* and *Da'at* clothe themselves in the wisdom of the Torah, *Ḥesed* in the performance of the positive commandments, *Gevura* in the observance of the prohibitions, and so on with regard to the rest of the soul's ten faculties.

וְכָל תַּרְיַ"ג אֵבָרֶיהָ, מֵרֹאשָׁהּ וְעַד רַגְלָהּ, הֲרֵי כּוּלָּהּ צְרוּרָה בִּצְרוֹר הַחַיִּים אֶת ה' מַמָּשׁ,

as well as all its 613 limbs from head to foot, it, the soul, **is literally bound completely within the bond of life, with God,**

Not only the soul's ten primary faculties but also each of its 613 particular limbs (which correspond to the 613 limbs and sinews of the body) has its corresponding mitzva in the Torah: There are 613 mitzvot for the soul's 613 components. Moreover, since such a perfect correlation exists between the soul and the Torah, the soul can clothe itself in the Torah to the point that "it is literally bound completely within the bond of life, with God."[14] The soul can delve into the Torah, becoming utterly united and identified with it, a union that involves the soul's every trait and faculty. It becomes enveloped in a mantle of divinity, totally bound with God.

---

13. See chap. 3.
14. This phrase is based on I Sam. 25:29.

וְאוֹר ה׳ מַמָּשׁ מַקִּיפָהּ וּמַלְבִּישָׁהּ מֵרֹאשָׁהּ וְעַד רַגְלָהּ, כְּמוֹ שֶׁכָּתוּב: "צוּרִי אֶחֱסֶה בּוֹ" (תהלים יח, ג), וּכְתִיב: "כַּצִּנָּה רָצוֹן תַּעְטְרֶנּוּ" (שם ה, יג),

and the light of God literally encompasses and enclothes it from head to foot, as it is written, "My mighty Rock, I take refuge in Him" (Ps. 18:3), **and it is written, "Surrounding him with** His **will, like a shield"** (Ps. 5:13),

Hence, we have a bilateral relationship between the soul and the Torah: The soul is bound with God, entering the Torah – the light of God – and uniting with it, clothing its every limb in a divine command: "My mighty Rock, I take refuge in Him." At the same time, the divine light of the Torah embraces and envelops the soul like a protective fortress.

Along the same lines, the soul is "surrounded with [God's] will, like a shield." The Torah originates in the divine will, which is even higher than the supernal wisdom. When one delves into the Torah, the divine will, which is the inner essence of Torah, surrounds the person and envelops him on all sides, like a shield.[15]

שֶׁהוּא רְצוֹנוֹ וְחָכְמָתוֹ יִתְבָּרֵךְ הַמְלוּבָּשִׁים בְּתוֹרָתוֹ וּמִצְוֹתֶיהָ.

referring to God's will and wisdom, which are clothed within His Torah and its commandments.

This will is the supernal will of God, which God enclothed in the Torah and its commandments. The Torah, then, is the divine will and wisdom at every level of its evolution. Although the Torah is not revealed to us in the full scope of its loftiest level, whatever is revealed to us is of the divine will itself, and its study and observance constitute the true and ultimate attachment to God, even if the form it has assumed is lowly and physical.

Furthermore, it is precisely because the divine wisdom and will is expressed in such mundane and physical terms that man, who inhabits a material reality, can truly relate to it and unite with it. In this way, he is able to unite with the divine wisdom and will, which is fully present in the Torah's earthly manifestation.

---

15. See *Iggeret HaKodesh*, epistle 1.

וְלָכֵן אָמְרוּ: "יָפָה שָׁעָה אַחַת בִּתְשׁוּבָה וּמַעֲשִׂים טוֹבִים בָּעוֹלָם הַזֶּה מִכָּל חַיֵּי עוֹלָם הַבָּא" (אבות פרק ד משנה יז). כִּי עוֹלָם הַבָּא הוּא שֶׁנֶּהֱנִין מִזִּיו הַשְּׁכִינָה, שֶׁהוּא תַּעֲנוּג הַהַשָּׂגָה, וְאִי אֶפְשָׁר לְשׁוּם נִבְרָא, אֲפִילוּ מֵהָעֶלְיוֹנִים, לְהַשִּׂיג כִּי אִם אֵיזוֹ הֶאָרָה מֵאוֹר ה',

Therefore, our Sages **stated, "One hour of repentance and good deeds in this world is more precious than an entire lifetime in the World to Come"** (Mishna *Avot* 4:17), **for the World to Come is where one derives pleasure from** a mere **glimmer of the Divine Presence, which is the pleasure of apprehending** the Divine, **and it is impossible for any created beings, even those on high, to apprehend but a mere ray of God's light.**

Only in this physical world can one perform a mitzva and thus unite with the divine will and wisdom, which is a revelation of the divine essence. By contrast, though the World to Come is a spiritual world and thus on a higher plane than our physical reality, there one can only "derive pleasure from a glimmer of the Divine Presence." In the words of the Sages, "In the World to Come, there is no eating, no drinking, no procreation, no business negotiations.... Rather, the righteous sit with their crowns upon their heads, enjoying a glimmer of the Divine Presence" (*Berakhot* 17a).

"Enjoying a glimmer of the Divine Presence," explains the author of the *Tanya*, refers to the pleasure derived from the apprehension of holiness, of the Divine. But any apprehension, be it intellectual or emotional, is by definition finite and definitive, even if we are speaking of apprehension by a wholly spiritual being, such as an angel or a disembodied soul that has achieved its ultimate level of purity and refinement. Every apprehension is still only a "mere ray of God's light." No thought can comprehend the actual luminary or even its light but rather only a glimmer of a glimmer of that light. When a person sees light but cannot see its source, when the light source does not reach him at all, then what he is viewing is not the light itself but rather the light refracting off of something else. If a person can attain a sufficient level of purity and refinement, he may be able to relate to these glimmers and reflections, but his mind will never be able to fathom the essence itself. On every spiritual level, what he grasps is but a "mere ray of God's light."

וְלָכֵן נִקְרָא בְּשֵׁם 'זִיו הַשְּׁכִינָה'. אֲבָל הַקָּדוֹשׁ בָּרוּךְ הוּא בִּכְבוֹדוֹ וּבְעַצְמוֹ לֵית מַחֲשָׁבָה תְּפִיסָא בֵּיהּ כְּלָל.

It is therefore referred to as a "glimmer of the Divine Presence." However, with regard to **the Holy One, blessed be He, Himself in all His glory, no thought can grasp Him at all.**

The pleasure of the righteous in the World to Come constitutes the apprehension of only a glimmer of the Divine Presence, a mere reflection of the divine reality, rather than the essence of the Divine itself. They cannot apprehend the luminary, the source of the light – God Himself – nor even the light, the direct and utter expression of the luminary's essence, but only a reflection of the light. This is the most that a created entity of the highest order can grasp, on its own, of the divine reality.

Thought, no matter how refined, can grasp only the illumination of a particular projection of a thing as it is manifest in reality. Therefore, it grasps only an echo of the glimmer of the supernal essence, while the essence itself cannot be apprehended by the mind at all.

כִּי אִם כַּאֲשֶׁר תְּפִיסָא וּמִתְלַבֶּשֶׁת בַּתּוֹרָה וּמִצְוֹתֶיהָ, אֲזַי הִיא תְּפִיסָא בָּהֶן* וּמִתְלַבֶּשֶׁת בְּהַקָּדוֹשׁ בָּרוּךְ הוּא מַמָּשׁ, דְּאוֹרַיְיתָא וְקוּדְשָׁא בְּרִיךְ הוּא כּוּלָּא חַד.

* בכתב יד ליתא תיבת בהן

Only when the thought **grasps and becomes enclothed within the Torah and its commandments, then it grasps them and literally becomes clothed within the Holy One, blessed be He, since the Torah and the Holy One, blessed be He, are all one.**

The only way that a person can apprehend the divine essence itself and thus unite with it, surmounting the quantum boundary that no level of apprehension can cross, is through his assimilation of the concepts of the Torah and his involvement in the performance of mitzvot. When a person performs a mitzva, he becomes bound up in the mitzva. When he studies Torah, he unites with the Commander of the mitzva, with the Giver of the Torah.

The Torah is not merely a compilation of God's directives to man but a manifestation of the divine essence. It is not a reflection of divine light, nor even a reflection of the Divine, but the Divine itself. Apprehending Torah, attachment and union with it, is an apprehension of and union with God Himself.

וְאַף שֶׁהַתּוֹרָה נִתְלַבְּשָׁה בִּדְבָרִים תַּחְתּוֹנִים גַּשְׁמִיִּם, הֲרֵי זֶה כִּמְחַבֵּק אֶת הַמֶּלֶךְ דֶּרֶךְ מָשָׁל, שֶׁאֵין הֶפְרֵשׁ בְּמַעֲלַת הִתְקָרְבוּתוֹ וּדְבֵיקוּתוֹ בַּמֶּלֶךְ בֵּין מְחַבְּקוֹ כְּשֶׁהוּא לָבוּשׁ לְבוּשׁ אֶחָד בֵּין שֶׁהוּא לָבוּשׁ כַּמָּה לְבוּשִׁים, מֵאַחַר שֶׁגּוּף הַמֶּלֶךְ בְּתוֹכָם.

Although the Torah is clothed in lowly, physical things, one who studies Torah **is likened, by way of analogy, to one who embraces the king. There is no distinction between the quality of one's closeness and attachment to the king whether one embraces** the king **when he is garbed in one garment or when he is garbed in multiple garments, since the king's body is inside them.**

One who studies Torah is like one who embraces a king. Is the number of garments that the king is wearing in any way relevant to the degree of intimacy and love that the embrace represents? Obviously not. What is significant is that he is embracing the king.

When a person grasps the Torah, when he envelops the Torah in his mind, he is in effect embracing God, whose will and wisdom are implicit within it. True, the Torah is draped in many garments, its

THE GARMENTS OF THE TORAH

☞ Again and again, we return to the paradox that to study Torah and fulfill commandments is to involve oneself with mundane and material things: oxen and donkeys, wool and linen, and so on. Granted, man's connection and identification with the mundane are tangible and complete. A person who gives charity becomes at that moment a tool for the mitzva of charity. The man who dons *tefillin* becomes an implement of the mitzva of *tefillin,* which could not have been fulfilled without a physical, human arm. One who studies a page of Talmud dealing with an ox and a donkey can fully grasp and comprehend his subject; they are familiar to him, abstract essence garbed in various formulations and euphemisms, but the clothes are only clothes, and the King Himself is inside them. ☞

וְכֵן אִם הַמֶּלֶךְ מְחַבְּקוֹ בִּזְרוֹעוֹ, גַּם שֶׁהִיא מְלוּבֶּשֶׁת תּוֹךְ מַלְבּוּשָׁיו, כְּמוֹ שֶׁכָּתוּב: "וִימִינוֹ תְּחַבְּקֵנִי" (שיר השירים ח, ג),

The same is true if the king embraces him with his arm, although it too is garbed in the king's **garments, as it is written, "His right embraces me"** (Song 8:3),

As the author of the *Tanya* will explain in the forthcoming chapter, one who studies Torah not only encompasses it with his mind but is also encompassed by it. In this sense, it is comparable to one who embraces the king while the king embraces him. He envelops the Torah, while at the same time the Torah envelops him.

שֶׁהִיא הַתּוֹרָה שֶׁנִּתְּנָה מִיָּמִין, שֶׁהִיא בְּחִינַת חֶסֶד וּמַיִם.

which refers to the Torah, given by God's **right** hand, **which corresponds to the attribute of kindness and water.**

and he can therefore fully identify with the problems under discussion. But however complete his grasp, he has grasped material things. How can we say that this, however profound, is the essence of divine wisdom?

The author of the *Tanya* explains that these things, however lowly and material, are indeed the will and wisdom of God. They are not merely a reflection of His will but constitute the divine will itself translated into the language of the material.

The Torah itself does not undergo change; rather, it descends through stages of concealment, from level to level, assuming at each level the garments that relate to that plane of reality. Within these garments, however, is the Torah itself, which is one with God and remains His unadulterated will and wisdom at every level. One can say that the Torah undergoes a series of translations: a translation into the language of the spiritual entities called seraphim, a translation into the language of the angels, a translation into the language of the soul that resides in the physical body. These "languages" are merely garments for the essence of the Torah, which remains unchanged at every level.

Divine wisdom can therefore be envisioned as an extremely abstract, axiomatic formula that embodies within it laws relating to a broad spectrum of systems of all types and forms, yet this formula is so abstract that no particular system can fully express it. The Torah must descend and be translated into a great variety of languages, including the language of our physical existence. The formula itself is neither altered nor diminished but acquires a definitive and contracted form so that we can comprehend its meaning in our reality.

According to Kabbala, the "right hand" is a reference to the embodiment of kindness, which is analogous to water. The giving of the Torah "by [God's] right [hand]"[16] is an expression of great kindness to whoever receives it. Like water, the Torah emerged from a lofty place and naturally flows downward, reaching the lowest conceivable places, as explained above. God's giving of the Torah is thus an expression of His infinite love and desire to draw near and unify with His loved ones through it. Because of that desire for closeness with us, He designed the Torah to reach every person in every situation, no matter what.

In this chapter, the author of the *Tanya* discussed the garments of the divine soul. The divine soul achieves the ultimate realization of its holiness and greatness through these garments, which are the thoughts, speech, and actions of the Torah and commandments.

Furthermore, the Torah and commandments are not only garments of the soul, but they are also the garments and expression of the Divine, so to speak, within which God can be found. Since it is impossible for any created entity, let alone those who inhabit this physical world, to apprehend the divine essence itself, God has contracted His will and wisdom within the Torah and commandments in a series of stages or successive rearticulations. The last of these formulations is the Torah as we know it, formulated as a doctrine and philosophy comprehensible to the physical mind and as a guide to life in this material reality.

Thus, on the one hand, the Torah is garbed within mundane and material matters with which the soul, vested in the material body, can identify and unite. On the other hand, "the Torah and God are one." When a person immerses his mind in the study of Torah, and when his 613 limbs and sinews are involved in the performance of the 613 commandments, he is at that moment cleaving to God Himself, with no intermediary and no partition in between. Although the Torah is garbed in many garments, these are but veiled expressions of the divine essence. These, in turn, become garments for the divine soul, which itself is literally "a portion of God on high."

---

16. See Deut. 33:2.

Chapter 5

THE PREVIOUS CHAPTER DISCUSSED THE GARMENTS OF the divine soul – specifically the thoughts, speech, and actions of the commandments. The author of the *Tanya* explained that although these garments have descended to this world so that the soul may be clothed within them, in and of themselves they are loftier than the soul, united with the divine essence itself.

Clothed in these garments, the soul is enveloped in the sublime embrace of the divine essence. Yet garments are still external to the soul, and as a result the soul is unable to apprehend and internalize that divine wisdom. This chapter addresses how the divine illumination may penetrate the soul and, like the food one eats, be absorbed within and become one's veritable flesh.

וּלְתוֹסֶפֶת בֵּיאוּר בַּאֵר הֵיטֵב לְשׁוֹן תְּפִיסָא שֶׁאָמַר אֵלִיָּהוּ "לֵית מַחֲשָׁבָה תְּפִיסָא בָּךְ" כו':

To explain further and fully elucidate the expression *tefisa*, "grasp," **stated by Elijah** in the phrase **"No thought can grasp You** at all…":

30 Kislev

4 Tevet (leap year)

In the previous chapter, the author of the *Tanya* quoted a statement from the introduction to *Tikkunei Zohar*, which quotes Elijah as saying of God, "No thought can grasp You at all." The apprehension that this refers to is primarily intellectual, absorbed within the mind and the senses of a person.

הִנֵּה כָּל שֵׂכֶל כְּשֶׁמַּשְׂכִּיל וּמַשִּׂיג בְּשִׂכְלוֹ אֵיזֶה מוּשְׂכָּל, הֲרֵי הַשֵּׂכֶל

When any intellect intellectually perceives and apprehends in the mind a particular concept, the

תּוֹפֵס אֶת הַמּוּשְׂכָּל וּמַקִּיפוֹ בְּשִׂכְלוֹ, **mind grasps the concept and encompasses it with its intellect,**

The author of the *Tanya* uses the terms "encompasses" here figuratively. Clearly, the mind and the concept are not physical objects occupying specific points in space in such a way that one might be placed within the other.

The grasping of the concept is the initial contact between the mind and the concept it conceives, the flash point of wisdom.[1] The mind's encompassing of the concept, as opposed to merely touching the idea, occurs in the next stage, that of understanding. At this phase, it can be said that the object of the mind's interest, the concept being apprehended, exists within the mind, and is encompassed by it.

At first, the mind only touches the concept tangentially. As comprehension develops, the mind covers more sides of the concept until it completely encloses it and relates to its every facet. At this stage, when the concept is encompassed by the intellect, it is internalized by the person and becomes part and parcel of him, essentially united with him. It is now his own understanding and knowledge; this is what he thinks.

וְהַמּוּשְׂכָּל נִתְפָּס וּמוּקָּף וּמְלוּבָּשׁ בְּתוֹךְ הַשֵּׂכֶל שֶׁהִשִּׂיגוֹ וְהִשְׂכִּילוֹ. **and the concept is grasped, encompassed, and clothed within the mind that apprehended and perceived it.**

TO APPREHEND A CONCEPT IS FOR IT TO BE APPREHENDED

☞ The Lubavitcher Rebbe, Rabbi Menaḥem Mendel Schneerson, points out that even if this statement contained nothing novel, the author of the Tanya states it explicitly since it is necessary to encapsulate the subject, which teaches that this apprehension is a "wondrous union," as the author states below. Moreover, this is, in fact, an innovative insight with regard to the Torah study of someone who does not study Torah for its own sake, or even for someone about whom the verse states, "But to the wicked one God says: What right have you to speak of My statutes...?" (Ps. 50:16), and the Talmud states that the Torah he studied "becomes a potion of death for him" (*Yoma* 72b). Nevertheless, if only his intellect apprehends the Torah he has studied, it is apprehended and internalized to the extent that it becomes as his flesh and blood.

1. See chap. 3.

This clause is somewhat perplexing: It appears to be completely superfluous. If the mind apprehends and encompasses a particular concept, it is obvious that the concept is apprehended and encompassed within the intellect. Yet there is reason to delineate this point, since one might think that this is the subjective experience of the mind alone. Perhaps it only appears to it that it has apprehended and encompassed the concept when in fact this is not the case. This additional statement comes to clarify that a characteristic and faculty of the intellect is its capacity to apprehend and encompass a particular concept truly and perfectly to the degree that it is as if the concept were actually enclosed within the mind. ☞ ☞

Moreover, the mind is also clothed within the concept at the same time it apprehends it and grasps it intellectually. For example, when a person thoroughly and clearly understands and apprehends a particular *halakha* in the Mishna or Talmud, his mind grasps and encompasses that *halakha*, and his mind is also simultaneously clothed within it.

וְגַם הַשֵּׂכֶל מְלוּבָּשׁ בַּמּוּשְׂכָּל בְּשָׁעָה שֶׁמַּשִּׂיגוֹ וְתוֹפְסוֹ בְּשִׂכְלוֹ. דֶּרֶךְ מָשָׁל, כְּשֶׁאָדָם מֵבִין וּמַשִּׂיג אֵיזוֹ הֲלָכָה בַּמִּשְׁנָה אוֹ בַּגְּמָרָא לַאֲשׁוּרָהּ עַל בּוּרְיָהּ, הֲרֵי שִׂכְלוֹ תּוֹפֵס וּמַקִּיף אוֹתָהּ וְגַם שִׂכְלוֹ מְלוּבָּשׁ בָּהּ בְּאוֹתָהּ שָׁעָה.

There is yet another astounding phenomenon with regard to the mind's apprehension of a concept: At the very same moment that the mind clothes the concept and encompasses it within itself, the opposite

A CONCEPT ONCE APPREHENDED CAN BE TRANSMITTED

☞ When comprehension is complete, so that the concept is totally encompassed by the mind, it may now be transmitted to others. As explained in chapter 3, a garment is the medium through which a thing relates to realities outside itself. When we say that the mind clothes a concept, this means that the concept can now be further extended, that the mind can now serve as the garment by which the concept is related to other concepts.

This is the basis of the assumption that the inability to explain something well shows a deficiency in understanding. There are other factors, not connected with understanding, that interfere with the ability to pass things on, such as difficulty in communicating. But a true and full explanation is not possible without a complete understanding, whereas a person who truly and fully understands something will inevitably find a way to pass it on.

process also takes place, in which the mind is itself clothed within the concept. Just as the mind serves as a garment for the concept – that is, as its medium of expression, as well as the screen that obscures its essence and allows only a certain expression of it to be manifest – so does the concept serve as the garment of the mind.

When the mind is engaged and absorbed in a certain subject, it expresses itself at that moment through that concept. One can say that the mind is clothed in the concept it is contemplating because it is now manifesting itself through this particular garment, and the garment is obscuring its quintessential qualities. In other words, the mind is now not an independent mind per se but a mind as expressed through the particulars of the concept within which it has invested itself. The mind is not only pondering the idea, but it is also being "thought" by it, in the sense that the mind is now perceived exclusively in the context of the particular idea.

This is true of every mind and every concept at any level, from the simplest to the most complex. The process of thought is always a process in which the mind and the object of its contemplation encompass and are encompassed by one another.

וְהִנֵּה הֲלָכָה זוֹ הִיא חָכְמָתוֹ וּרְצוֹנוֹ שֶׁל הַקָּדוֹשׁ בָּרוּךְ הוּא,

This *halakha* is the wisdom and will of the Holy One, blessed be He,

When a person achieves an understanding of a concept in the Mishna or Talmud, or comprehends a ruling set forth by the halakhic authorities, this is no ordinary thought but the "wisdom and will" of God. The author of the *Tanya* is not speaking here about the *halakha* as practical instruction but about its essence, an expression of the divine wisdom and will.

שֶׁעָלָה בִּרְצוֹנוֹ שֶׁכְּשֶׁיִּטְעוֹן רְאוּבֵן כָּךְ וְכָךְ, דֶּרֶךְ מָשָׁל, וְשִׁמְעוֹן כָּךְ וְכָךְ - יִהְיֶה הַפְּסָק בֵּינֵיהֶם כָּךְ וְכָךְ. וְאַף אִם לֹא הָיָה

for it arose in His will that when Reuven claims thus, for example, and Shimon thus, the ruling between them should be such and such. Even if such a situation, where litigants **come to court on account of these claims and charges, never was and**

וְלֹא יִהְיֶה הַדָּבָר הַזֶּה לְעוֹלָם לָבֹא לְמִשְׁפָּט עַל טְעָנוֹת וּתְבִיעוֹת אֵלּוּ, מִכָּל מָקוֹם, מֵאַחַר שֶׁכָּךְ עָלָה בִּרְצוֹנוֹ וְחָכְמָתוֹ שֶׁל הַקָּדוֹשׁ בָּרוּךְ הוּא, שֶׁאִם יִטְעוֹן זֶה כָּךְ וְזֶה כָּךְ - יִהְיֶה הַפְּסָק כָּךְ,

never will occur, nevertheless since such a scenario **arose in the will and wisdom of the Holy One, blessed be He, where should this** person **claim thus and this** other person claim **thus, the** halakhic **ruling will be such and such,**

In physics and mathematics, complicated systems are constructed to solve theoretical problems, and the question of whether such a situation could ever arise in practice is considered beside the point. The scientist is seeking to uncover a truth: What is the reality? What is the quintessential state of things in a given situation? The purpose is not to solve a practical problem but to gain a comprehensive understanding of a truth, to learn the nature of things.

When the Talmud discusses a financial dispute between two parties, citing their arguments and counterarguments, it is not necessarily relating an actual case that occurred or ever will occur. Rather, it is presenting an abstract, theoretical model. It is endeavoring to discover what God's will would be in such a situation. The purpose is not to solve a particular dispute between two individuals but to see how this point relates to the universal order, to the inner life of creation, to learn what it is that God wants from us as we navigate His world.

הֲרֵי כְּשֶׁאָדָם יוֹדֵעַ וּמַשִּׂיג בְּשִׂכְלוֹ פְּסָק זֶה כַּהֲלָכָה הָעֲרוּכָה בְּמִשְׁנָה אוֹ גְּמָרָא אוֹ פּוֹסְקִים - הֲרֵי זֶה מַשִּׂיג וְתוֹפֵס וּמַקִּיף בְּשִׂכְלוֹ רְצוֹנוֹ וְחָכְמָתוֹ שֶׁל הַקָּדוֹשׁ בָּרוּךְ הוּא.

then, when a person knows and apprehends in his mind this ruling as the *halakha* set forth in the Mishna, Talmud, or the works of **the halakhic authorities, this** person **apprehends, grasps, and encompasses in his mind the will and wisdom of the Holy One, blessed be He,**

Obviously, one who comprehends a halakhic ruling does not assimilate the whole of the divine wisdom related to this matter. Even when he understands the entire array of legal principles and processes that relate to this law and how it all derives from the Torah, he comprehends the subject on only one plane. He does not understand the many strata of meaning that lie beyond the grasp of human reason or even the full significance of the law. But in understanding a particular aspect of it at a particular level, he grasps a point of truth, even if it is only a particle of the divine truth.

By way of example, the equations $A + B = C$ and $1 + 1 = 2$ in effect say the same thing. The first is general and abstract, and the second is specific; the first sets up a principle, and the second provides a particular example of that principle. When teaching a small child, one teaches the specific case, because the child can learn and understand that specific example thoroughly, but he cannot comprehend the general principle. Yet, despite the fact that the abstract equation is beyond the child's comprehension, when he comprehends that an apple and another apple make two apples, he has grasped something of the truth of the formula.

By the same token, when a person studies a *halakha* about an ox and a donkey, he is assimilating not a mere expression or analogue of the divine wisdom but something of its very essence.

דְּלֵית מַחֲשָׁבָה תְּפִיסָא בֵּיהּ וְלֹא בִּרְצוֹנוֹ וְחָכְמָתוֹ, כִּי אִם בְּהִתְלַבְּשׁוּתָם בַּהֲלָכוֹת הָעֲרוּכוֹת לְפָנֵינוּ,

for no thought can grasp Him at all, nor His will and His wisdom, unless they are clothed within the *halakhot* set forth before us.

Since no thought can grasp God at all, there is no way to comprehend this particle of truth except by comprehending Torah. The divine wisdom cannot be attained by contemplating abstract truths. Such contemplation yields, at best, false visions and, in other cases, self-deception. Apprehending the truth of God's wisdom, if merely a tiny grain of truth on a particular level, practical or theoretical, is possible only through the comprehension of the Torah. The *halakhot* that have been spelled out to us in the Torah are that aspect of its divine wisdom that is humanly attainable. When a person comprehends a teaching of the Torah, even if it is not an inspirational teaching, it is an articulation of absolute truth, a point of divine wisdom related to a particular problem.

וְגַם שִׂכְלוֹ מְלוּבָּשׁ בָּהֶם. At the same time, **one's mind is also clothed within them.**

When a person's mind grasps and enclothes a concept of the Torah, when one apprehends something of the divine wisdom, his mind is simultaneously enclothed within the concept, as explained above. His mind envelops that divine wisdom, and the divine wisdom envelops his mind. The divine wisdom becomes a part of him, and he becomes part of it.

וְהוּא יִחוּד נִפְלָא שֶׁאֵין יִחוּד כָּמוֹהוּ וְלֹא כְּעֶרְכּוֹ נִמְצָא כְּלָל בְּגַשְׁמִיּוּת, לִהְיוֹת לַאֲחָדִים וּמְיוּחָדִים מַמָּשׁ מִכָּל צַד וּפִנָּה. **This constitutes a wondrous union, of which no likeness or** equal **estimation can be found at all in the physical realm,** a union where the human intellect and divine wisdom of the Torah **are literally one and the same from every side and angle.**

When the thinking mind and the concept it is thinking about encompass each other, what happens is not just contact between them but reciprocal unity, a merging together of the mind and the concept. Whether it is an abstract concept, a story, or a legal ruling, when a person's mind is occupied with that thought, which he understands from every angle and from every side, his mind is fused with that thought in a wonderful union – a union that has no parallel to any of the other unions we know.

In the material world, we encounter certain intrinsic barriers that we cannot surmount. The encloser and the enclosed, the self and the other, cannot be united because their inherent differences, which are part and parcel of a material existence, separate them. By contrast, in the sphere of conscious ideas, in the relationship between the one who comprehends and that which is comprehended, the encloser can also

A WONDROUS UNION

☞ The "wondrous union" that the author of the *Tanya* refers to is unique in that one achieves it through the comprehension of Torah. Aside from the fact that it is the be the enclosed. The differences between them become diffused until they merge together from every angle in total union. ☞

1 Tevet וְזֹאת מַעֲלָה יְתֵרָה גְּדוֹלָה וְנִפְלָאָה לְאֵין קֵץ אֲשֶׁר בְּמִצְוַת יְדִיעַת הַתּוֹרָה וְהַשָּׂגָתָהּ עַל כָּל הַמִּצְוֹת מַעֲשִׂיּוֹת

This is the infinitely superior, great, and wondrous quality that the commandment of knowing and apprehending Torah contains over all action-related commandments

Although one establishes a connection with God through all the mitzvot, only the comprehension and knowledge of Torah achieves the wonderful union that occurs between a mind and the object of its contemplation.

וַאֲפִילּוּ עַל מִצְוֹת הַתְּלוּיוֹת בְּדִבּוּר וַאֲפִילּוּ עַל מִצְוַת תַּלְמוּד תּוֹרָה שֶׁבְּדִבּוּר.

and even over speech-dependent commandments and even over the mitzva of oral **Torah study,** which is fulfilled **through speech.**

The mitzva of Torah study has two aspects. One is the commandment to "speak of them" (Deut. 6:7) – to speak words of Torah, to articulate them with one's mouth even if one does not understand their meaning. In this sense, the mitzva of Torah study – that is, articulating the words of Torah, reciting them repeatedly, and elucidating them – is akin to other action-related mitzvot, such as donning *tefillin* or giving charity. But another aspect of this mitzva is knowing Torah – studying it and

divine wisdom of the Torah that the mind is uniting with as opposed to mundane disciplines, the very nature of the union itself is more wonderful when it is rooted in Torah than in those other disciplines.

When a person understands some other subject, he unites with the idea of the subject but not with the subject itself. For instance, when he studies the orbits of the stars, his mind unites with the concept of the moving stars and not with the movement of the stars itself. Torah, on the other hand, is not merely the understanding of a certain reality but the source of the realities it explains. In the words of the Sages, "God looked into the Torah and created the world" (*Zohar* 2:161b). When a mind unites with the Torah, it is one not only with the understanding of a concept but also with the thing itself, because Torah is the essence of the thing's very existence (*Torat Menaḥem* 18, pp. 313–314; see also *Likkutei Biurim LaTanya*).

comprehending it in accordance with one's intellectual capacity. With regard to this aspect, the mitzva of Torah study is "infinitely superior, greater, and more wondrous" than all other mitzvot. It is this that allows for the wondrous union that is unique to the mitzva of Torah study.

כִּי עַל יְדֵי כָּל הַמִּצְוֹת שֶׁבְּדִבּוּר וּמַעֲשֶׂה - הַקָּדוֹשׁ בָּרוּךְ הוּא מַלְבִּישׁ אֶת הַנֶּפֶשׁ וּמַקִּיפָהּ אוֹר ה׳ מֵרֹאשָׁהּ וְעַד רַגְלָהּ.

For through all speech-and action-related commandments, the Holy One, blessed be He, clothes the soul and encompasses it in the **light of God from its head to its toe.**

When a person is involved in the performance of a mitzva, it becomes the manner in which he expresses himself, and it can be said that he is enclothed in the mitzva. When he extends his hand to give charity, the faculty of action implicit in his hand is manifest in the form of a charitable deed: The mitzva of charity is enclothing his hand. The same applies to all other mitzvot. A certain faculty of the soul is manifest by a particular medium, that of a certain mitzva, and when a person reveals the faculties of his soul through the mitzva in which he is enclothed, the person, or a certain part of him, is essentially enclothed in the divine will and wisdom.

וּבִידִיעַת הַתּוֹרָה - מִלְּבַד שֶׁהַשֵּׂכֶל מְלוּבָּשׁ בְּחָכְמַת ה׳, הִנֵּה גַּם חָכְמַת ה׳ בְּקִרְבּוֹ,

As for the knowledge of Torah, aside from the mind being clothed within God's wisdom, God's wisdom is also within that person

When it comes to knowing Torah, a person gains an additional advantage. As with every mitzva, when a person's mind is engaged in Torah, he is clothed within the wisdom of the Torah, which, at that very moment, is the arena in which his mind is functioning. The mind is now involved in the wisdom of Torah and is expressing its prowess through this medium. This is the quality that Torah study shares with all other mitzvot. In this sense, there is no difference whether the hand is enclothed in the act of charity, the head in *tefillin*, or the brain in a Torah idea. But when it comes to the mitzva to know Torah, there is something more, an aspect that is not found with regard to action-based mitzvot: The divine wisdom not only clothes the mind that is contemplating it, but at the same time, the mind enclothes it. When a person understands and grasps a concept of Torah, he encloses it within him.

מַה שֶּׁהַשֵּׂכֶל מַשִּׂיג וְתוֹפֵס וּמַקִּיף בְּשִׂכְלוֹ מַה שֶּׁאֶפְשָׁר לוֹ לִתְפּוֹס וּלְהַשִּׂיג מִידִיעַת הַתּוֹרָה אִישׁ כְּפִי שִׂכְלוֹ וְכֹחַ יְדִיעָתוֹ וְהַשָּׂגָתוֹ בְּפרד״ס.

in accordance with the mind's capacity to apprehend, grasp, and encompass with its intellect whatever it can grasp and apprehend of the knowledge of the Torah, each person according to his intellectual capacity and ability to know and apprehend of the *peshat* (plain meaning), ***remez*** (allusion), ***derush*** (homiletic exposition), and **sod** (mystical aspects) of the Torah.

What is significant is not the magnitude of the concept that the mind has grasped, whether it is great or small, but the fact that it has grasped Torah. When a person acquires a knowledge of some item of Torah – a story, a complex *halakha,* or even a small detail – his mind is then clothed in this item of Torah and encompassed by it. At the same time, this item expresses itself through his mind, is encompassed by his mind, and becomes an integral part of it. A complete union is formed between the subject of the person's thoughts and his thought process. The thinker and the thought become one.

וּלְפִי שֶׁבִּידִיעַת הַתּוֹרָה הַתּוֹרָה מְלוּבֶּשֶׁת בְּנֶפֶשׁ הָאָדָם וְשִׂכְלוֹ וּמוּקֶּפֶת בְּתוֹכָם,

Since it is specifically **through the knowledge of Torah,** and not its performance, that **the Torah is clothed within a person's soul and mind and is encompassed within them,**

When a person physically performs the commandments of the Torah, he becomes connected to it and associated with it. By contrast, when he uses his mind and intellect to know and apprehend the Torah, it literally becomes his very own. He does not merely enter the realm of the Torah he studies, but that knowledge of Torah now enters him and becomes, at that moment, his own thought, something unique to his soul. Now this piece of Torah constitutes his own thoughts. From now on, it is an expression of himself, and he can identify himself with it.

לָכֵן נִקְרֵאת בְּשֵׁם לֶחֶם וּמְזוֹן הַנֶּפֶשׁ.

the Torah **is therefore referred to as the bread and nourishment of the soul.**

The Torah is compared to bread in several places in *Tanakh*, as in the verse "Come, partake of My bread" (Prov. 9:5). The Torah that a person learns is absorbed and assimilated by his mind, just as physical food is absorbed and assimilated by the body.

כִּי כְּמוֹ שֶׁהַלֶּחֶם הַגַּשְׁמִי זָן אֶת הַגּוּף כְּשֶׁמַּכְנִיסוֹ בְּתוֹכוֹ וְקִרְבּוֹ מַמָּשׁ וְנֶהְפַּךְ שָׁם לִהְיוֹת דָּם וּבָשָׂר כִּבְשָׂרוֹ, וַאֲזַי יִחְיֶה וְיִתְקַיֵּים, כָּךְ בִּידִיעַת הַתּוֹרָה וְהַשָּׂגָתָהּ בְּנֶפֶשׁ הָאָדָם, שֶׁלּוֹמְדָהּ הֵיטֵב בְּעִיּוּן שִׂכְלוֹ עַד שֶׁנִּתְפֶּסֶת בְּשִׂכְלוֹ וּמִתְאַחֶדֶת עִמּוֹ וְהָיוּ לַאֲחָדִים,

Just as physical bread nourishes the body when one actually ingests it, whereupon it is transformed into blood and flesh of his own flesh and then the body **can live and be sustained, so too with regard to the knowledge and apprehension of Torah by the soul of the person who studies it thoroughly, concentrating his intellect** on it, **until his mind grasps it and unites with it, so that** the Torah knowledge and the person's soul **become one.**

The process by which bread (or any food, for that matter) nourishes the body has two stages. First, the food enters the person and is digested. Second, it ceases to be a distinct entity and becomes "blood and flesh of his own flesh," whereupon it sustains and nourishes the body.

The same applies to Torah knowledge. Here the author of the *Tanya* is not referring to the positive commandment to study Torah with one's speech, certainly a great mitzva, but rather the focus is on accruing Torah knowledge, on "ingesting" it by deeply apprehending it. The process through which a person apprehends Torah is similar to the process of ingesting food. In the first stage, the concept enters the mind and is chewed and digested. The idea is transferred from the form in which it existed outside the person to the form in which he absorbs it by breaking it down to its particulars and processing it in his mind.

When a person digs deep as he studies Torah, toiling until his mind grasps it, he achieves the next stage, where the concept becomes part and parcel of the structure of his mind and thought processes, the mind and the Torah that he is studying becoming one.

נַעֲשָׂה מָזוֹן לַנֶּפֶשׁ וְחַיִּים בְּקִרְבָּהּ מֵחַיֵּי הַחַיִּים אֵין סוֹף בָּרוּךְ הוּא הַמְלוּבָּשׁ בְּחָכְמָתוֹ וְתוֹרָתוֹ שֶׁבְּקִרְבָּהּ.

The Torah then **becomes nourishment for the soul and** a source of **life within it from the Bestower of life,** ***Ein Sof*****, blessed be He,** who is **clothed within His wisdom and Torah that are within** the soul of the one studying.

When a person studies Torah and achieves an intellectual union with it, he not only unites with the revealed Torah as we understand it but also with the essence of the Torah, the divine light of *Ein Sof*.

וְזֶהוּ שֶׁכָּתוּב: "וְתוֹרָתְךָ בְּתוֹךְ מֵעָי" (תהלים מ, ט).

This is the meaning of **the verse "Your Torah is in my belly"** (Ps. 40:9).

The Torah becomes like food that a person has eaten and digested. It is no longer distinct from him, external to him, but something that has been absorbed by the body and has become a part of it.

וּכְמוֹ שֶׁכָּתוּב בְּעֵץ חַיִּים שַׁעַר מ"ד פֶּרֶק ג', שֶׁלְּבוּשֵׁי הַנְּשָׁמוֹת בְּגַן עֵדֶן הֵן הַמִּצְוֹת,

Likewise, it is written in ***Etz Ḥayyim*** **44:3 that the garments of the souls in the Garden of Eden are the commandments,**

The soul relates to the reality in which it exists through its garments. In the physical world, the soul clothes itself in the physical faculties of the body in order to interact with the material reality within which it resides. But in a higher world, in the spiritual reality of the Garden of Eden, it has other garments, appropriate for relating to that environment. These spiritual garments are generated by the mitzvot that a person performed in this world. Ungraspable by our material senses, these garments become, in a higher and loftier reality, the sole garments of the soul, facilitating its interaction with its spiritual environment.

וְהַתּוֹרָה הִיא הַמָּזוֹן לַנְּשָׁמוֹת שֶׁעָסְקוּ בָּעוֹלָם הַזֶּה בַּתּוֹרָה לִשְׁמָהּ, וּכְמוֹ שֶׁכָּתוּב בְּזֹהַר וַיַּקְהֵל דַּף ר״י.

and the Torah is the nourishment for the souls of those **who engaged in Torah** study **for its own sake in this world, as stated in the *Zohar*,** *Vayak'hel* 210a.

The Torah that a person studied in this world becomes food for his soul in the Garden of Eden. The soul's food in the Garden of Eden, generated by the Torah it studied in the physical world, not only provides a way for the soul to interact with the reality in which it finds itself, as the garments do, but it serves a more intrinsic role: It allows the soul to internalize and assimilate the spiritual reality of the Garden of Eden into itself, literally making it a part of its own essence.

וְ'לִשְׁמָהּ' - הַיְינוּ כְּדֵי לְקַשֵּׁר נַפְשׁוֹ לַה' עַל יְדֵי הַשָּׂגַת הַתּוֹרָה

Torah study **for its own sake means** study **in order to bind one's soul to God through apprehending the Torah,**

There are various definitions for what constitutes Torah study "for its own sake." Here the author of the *Tanya* presents what, in a certain sense, is the most basic meaning of the term: study for the sake of "binding one's soul to God through apprehending the Torah" – His wisdom.

The novelty presented here is that even this most basic level of studying Torah for its own sake suffices to unite the person's soul with the Torah studied, just as food is absorbed and united with the body. Yet if a person does not study Torah for its sake at all, his soul does not merit being united with God through the Torah study.[2]

אִישׁ כְּפִי שִׂכְלוֹ, כְּמוֹ שֶׁכָּתוּב בִּפְרִי עֵץ חַיִּים (שער הנהגת הלימוד).

each person according to his intellect, as it is written in *Pri Etz Ḥayyim* (*Sha'ar Hanhagat HaLimud*).

---

2. Yearning to unite with God is not to be understood as an exercise in self-fulfillment but as the desire to give pleasure to God, who derives great satisfaction from a soul's reunion with its source. This is elucidated below by the *Tanya*'s analogy of a king's joy when his only child is freed from captivity (see chap. 41).

Not all minds are created equal. One person's comprehension of Torah differs from that of another. But when one becomes united with the Torah commensurate with his soul's level of comprehension, and he does so "for its own sake" – that is, in order to thereby become united with God – then the Torah becomes food for his soul.

[וְהַמָּזוֹן הִיא בְּחִינַת אוֹר פְּנִימִי

(**The nourishment** of the soul **constitutes the inner light,**

"Inner light" is the kabbalistic term for the light of the Divine, the aspect of God's will and wisdom embodied in the Torah, that a person may imbibe and internalize, that he can absorb and integrate into his being. Food is the analogy for this inner light because both are ingested and absorbed within.

וְהַלְּבוּשִׁים בְּחִינַת מַקִּיפִים.

while the garments constitute the surrounding light.

Garments are the analogy for what Kabbala terms the "surrounding light." The garments are external to the person not only in the sense that they exist outside of him but also in terms of the manner in which they affect him. Their influence on the person is not direct and palpable; it is not internalized and consciously assimilated. Though they affect a person and the reality around him, it is a less intimate influence. A soul's garments facilitate the relationship between the soul and its environment, but they affect the soul and its functions without it being conscious of it.

וְלָכֵן אָמְרוּ רַבּוֹתֵינוּ ז"ל (פאה פרק א משנה א) שֶׁתַּלְמוּד תּוֹרָה שָׁקוּל כְּנֶגֶד כָּל הַמִּצְוֹת, לְפִי שֶׁהַמִּצְוֹת הֵן לְבוּשִׁים לְבַד,

Therefore, our Rabbis stated that Torah study is equivalent to all the commandments (Mishna *Pe'a* 1:1), **since the commandments are only garments,**

A physical mitzva, such as *tzitzit, lulav,* or *tefillin,* is an action that a person does but not something that merges with him and becomes a part of his being. A person can fulfill a mitzva out of deep, heartfelt feelings, out of love and awe of God, out of a yearning for a deep spiritual attachment to God, yet the mitzva itself remains external to the person, a reality distinct from himself, a surrounding reality. That reality envelops a person – he exists within it and deeply relates to it – but he cannot internalize it and assimilate its essence.

For this reason, the Sages have said that a mitzva protects a person from harm only at the instant he is performing it,[3] because no perceivable trace of the mitzva remains after the person performed it.

וְהַתּוֹרָה הִיא מָזוֹן וְגַם לְבוּשׁ לַנֶּפֶשׁ הַמַּשְׂכֶּלֶת, שֶׁמִּתְלַבֵּשׁ בָּהּ בְּעִיּוּנָהּ וְלִימּוּדָהּ.

whereas the Torah constitutes both **nourishment and also the garment of the rational soul, which becomes clothed within it by means of its in-depth study and scholarship.**

By contrast, the Torah is food for the soul, entering the being of the person who studies it and becoming part of his inner self, his essence.

Furthermore, the Torah is not only food for the soul but also a garment for the soul. As the author of the *Tanya* explained at length in this chapter, when a person studies Torah, not only does his mind enclose the concept and make it a part of him, but the concept also clothes and encloses his mind. So the Torah serves as nourishment, being absorbed within and becoming a part of the soul's essence, and it also serves as a garment, since it enclothes the person who studies it, becoming the manner of the soul's expression at the time he is engaged in its study, as is the case with all mitzvot.

וְכָל שֶׁכֵּן כְּשֶׁמּוֹצִיא בְּפִיו בְּדִבּוּר,

All the more so when one articulates the words of Torah **with his mouth and speech,**

In addition to all that has been said about the virtue of knowing and apprehending Torah, there is also the act associated with Torah study, which is the mitzva to "speak of them" (Deut. 6:7), to verbally discuss and recite words of Torah, as the verse states, "This book of the Torah shall not depart from your mouth" (Josh. 1:8)

3. *Sukka* 21a.

שֶׁהֶבֶל הַדִּיבּוּר נַעֲשֶׂה בְּחִינַת אוֹר מַקִּיף, כְּמוֹ שֶׁכָּתוּב בִּפְרִי עֵץ חַיִּים.]

in which case the breath from the speech that emerges when he studies the Torah **assumes the quality of** the **surrounding light** of the soul, **as it is written in *Pri Etz Ḥayyim*.**)

Torah acts as a garment for the soul even when it merely remains in one's thoughts, when the mind apprehends and knows Torah. But this is the case even more so when one articulates it verbally, introducing a dimension of action to the mitzva. Then the physical substance of the breath or air that carries the words at the time of study becomes a surrounding light for the soul.

When a person performs a mitzva, the material substance of the mitzva is transformed into a spiritual light that envelops its performer – the surrounding light. When one studies Torah aloud, it is the physical air that carries the sound of his learning that constitutes the material substance of the mitzva, which in turn generates that surrounding light.

On this basis alone (without even considering the special qualities of Torah study in their own right), we can explain why study of Torah is equal to all the mitzvot: All mitzvot serve only the role of garment for the soul, whereas Torah study is both food and garment. We acquire and grasp Torah through the mind, so that while it is tackling an idea, it encloses it and is enclosed by it. Thus, the Torah that a person learns is imbibed as food for the soul, as something that becomes a part of his inner self and at the same time envelops him as a garment. Furthermore, in studying Torah out loud, the breath that carries the words of Torah becomes a surrounding light, as is the case with all material substances with which a physical mitzva is performed.

This chapter picked up the thread of the previous chapter and elaborated at length on the garments of the divine soul – the thoughts, speech, and actions in the Torah and its mitzvot. This chapter focused on the study, knowledge, and understanding of the Torah, which become nourishment for the divine soul and constitute the divine illumination that not only reaches man but enters the soul and unites with it, just as food enters the body.

The importance of this topic, and the author of the *Tanya*'s fondness for it, so evident in his tone, means that this chapter deviated from the progression of ideas in the book and went on at length to explain the absolutely unique and wondrous union – one that is not extant in any of the other worlds – that is generated when one apprehends and knows the Torah. This wondrous union occurs when the Torah, which is God's will and wisdom, enters the person who studies it while simultaneously drawing him into it as well.

Chapter 6

THE PREVIOUS CHAPTERS DISCUSSED THE DIVINE SOUL and its garments. Now, to complete the picture of the human soul, the author of the *Tanya* discusses the animal soul, as well as its ten faculties and three garments, mentioned briefly in the first chapter. The author will also touch on the way the animal soul is manifest in a person's life, which is in the realm of *kelippa*, literally, "husk," a term used to describe the forces of impurity, and *sitra aĥara*, literally, "the other side," referring to that which is not holy.

וְהִנֵּה זֶה לְעוּמַּת זֶה עָשָׂה אֱלֹהִים.

Now it is axiomatic that **God made this corresponding to that.**

2 Tevet

5 Tevet (leap year)

The whole of existence is structured on a correspondence between good and evil.[1] Not only is good as a whole contrasted with the phenomenon of evil, but every element and detail in the world of good has its corresponding negative counterpoint.

In truth, the framework of good is also the framework of evil, because evil is but a shadow, a duplicate, albeit a negative one, of good.

כִּי כְּמוֹ שֶׁנֶּפֶשׁ הָאֱלֹהִית כְּלוּלָה מֵעֶשֶׂר סְפִירוֹת קְדוֹשׁוֹת

Just as the divine soul contains ten holy ***sefirot***

As discussed in chapter 3, the divine soul possesses ten attributes that both correspond to the ten supernal *sefirot* and derive from them.

וּמִתְלַבֶּשֶׁת בִּשְׁלֹשָׁה לְבוּשִׁים קְדוֹשִׁים,

and is clothed in three holy garments,

1. See Eccles. 7:14, on which the author of the *Tanya*'s statement is based.

Since the divine soul is exclusively devoted to the endeavor of cleaving to God and uniting with Him, it is manifest through holy garments, which constitute the ideas, words, and deeds of the Torah and its precepts.

כָּךְ הַנֶּפֶשׁ דְּסִטְרָא אָחֳרָא מִקְּלִיפּוֹת נוֹגַהּ **so too the soul of the** ***sitra aḥara,*** which stems **from** the ***kelippa*** called ***noga***

This is the animal soul, or vital soul, which derives from the *sitra aḥara,* the "other side," and which in the Jew comes from *kelippat noga,* the "glowing husk," as opposed to the utterly impure *kelippot.* Though *kelippat noga* is a husk, something that obscures the divine light, it is not utterly dark. In a certain sense, it represents an intermediate state between impurity and holiness.[2]

הַמְּלוּבֶּשֶׁת בְּדַם הָאָדָם, and is **embodied in a person's blood,**

The animal soul is embodied in the blood in order to animate the body, as the verse states, "For the life [*nefesh*] of the flesh is in the blood (Lev. 17:11). Essentially, the blood serves as the nexus between the nonphysical soul and the corporeal body. The soul that is found in the blood is the animal soul that stems from *kelippat noga* and is that which provides a Jew with his vitality, his life force, along with his divine soul. In this sense, the animal soul serves as a bridge between the divine soul and the physical body, allowing the divine soul to connect with the body.

כְּלוּלָה מֵעֶשֶׂר כִּתְרִין דִּמְסָאֲבוּתָא, **is comprised of** the **ten crowns of impurity.**

Just as the divine soul possesses ten holy attributes, corresponding to the ten *sefirot,* the animal soul is comprised of ten "crowns of impurity." We refer to the attributes of the animal soul not as *sefirot* but as crowns in order to distinguish them from the holy attributes of the divine soul.

The term also has a deeper significance. In a certain sense, the forces of evil collectively relate to the attribute called *Keter,* Crown. The *sefira*

2. See chap. 7.

of *Keter* is not of a piece with the other *sefirot*, but is extrinsic to them and encompassing them, just as a crown encircles the head. By the same token, the forces of evil, which must also receive their life force from the side of holiness, receive their vitality in an external manner, in which the sustenance encompasses them from above, out of necessity, and not from a nurturing bestowal that reflects a desire for inner connection, as is the case with the supernal *sefirot*. Moreover, the power that evil holds over man derives not from comprehended and internalized truths but from base, unconscious drives that stem from the level of *Keter*, the level that represents the faculties of desire and will. ☞

שֶׁהֵן שֶׁבַע מִדּוֹת רָעוֹת הַבָּאוֹת מֵאַרְבַּע יְסוֹדוֹת רָעִים הַנִּזְכָּרִים לְעֵיל וְשֵׂכֶל הַמּוֹלִידָן,

These are the **seven evil attributes, which stem from the four aforementioned evil elements** (see chap. 1) **and the intellect that generates them.**

CROWNS OF IMPURITY

☞ The attributes of the divine soul are referred to as *sefirot*, derived from the term *sapir*, sapphire, used in the verse that describes the radiant gemstones embedded in the High Priest's breast plate (see Ex. 28:18). This conveys that the divine soul receives its life force from these *sefirot* in the optimal manner, described as a "shining countenance." By contrast, the life force of the *kelippa*'s attributes is in a state of exile, so to speak, encompassing rather than radiating from within. This indicates that the life force exists in a less than optimal state, analogous to a person who gives something begrudgingly to another by tossing it over his shoulder without facing the person.

It is for this reason that these attributes are dubbed "crowns." They allude to the nature of a crown, which merely encompasses the wearer's head. Granted, the concept of a crown applies to the highest realm of holiness as well, but there the term *keter* alludes to the highest level containing the divine light at such a magnitude that it is unable to radiate into the supernal vessels that are meant to receive and channel it but can only encompass them from without. By contrast, with regard to *kelippa*, the defect lies in the recipients themselves: They do not constitute suitable receptacles by which to receive any radiance and life force of holiness, except in the aspect of a crown – that is, external encompassment (*HaLekaḥ VeHalibuv*).

Another reason the attributes of the animal soul are called crowns is that *kelippat noga*, from which this soul is derived, is a crown in the sense that it is an intermediate level between holiness and *kelippa*. This is comparable to the way that the *Keter* of each of the four worlds is the intermediate level between its world and the world above it (see Rabbi Shmuel Gronem Esterman's commentary on the *Tanya*).

As is the case with the holy attributes of the divine soul, the evil attributes of the animal soul have their rationale. They too need a cognitive basis as a reference point in order for them to operate. Yet this intellect is not independent of the evil attributes, transcending them as with the intellectual faculties associated with the realm of holiness; there, the emotive attributes are generated by the cognitive attributes but are not an integral part of the intellect that produces them. On the other hand, the intellect that generates the evil attributes is embedded within the evil attribute itself. It cannot make a decision that runs contrary to the will of that attribute because it shares the same desire and inclination. Its only function is to produce and help develop the attribute's particular characteristics. In a sense, the evil attribute itself begets the intellect for its own selfish purposes in order to expand and achieve its desires.[3]

הַנֶּחֱלָק לְשָׁלֹשׁ שֶׁהֵן: חָכְמָה בִּינָה וָדַעַת - מְקוֹר הַמִּדּוֹת. כִּי הַמִּדּוֹת הֵן לְפִי עֵרֶךְ הַשֵּׂכֶל,

This intellect **is divided into three** aspects, **namely, wisdom, understanding, and knowledge,** which are **the source of the attributes, since the attributes are** expressed **commensurate with the quality of the intellect.**

In order for any attribute, any drive or impulse, to be manifest in reality and, more importantly, in order for it to acquire the characteristics that make it a full-fledged desire for a specific thing, the intellect must provide it with certain criteria: What should it desire? Why is the thing desirable? And how can it pursue its desire?

3. In his commentary on the *Tanya,* Rabbi Shmuel Gronem Esterman explains that the relationship between the emotive attributes and the intellect in the animal soul and the relationship between them in the divine soul are significantly different. The animal soul, as will be explained, is essentially characterized by impulse, and the attributes constitute the bulk of the animal soul's being, while the intellect is merely the attributes' catalyst. The attributes – love, anger, and so on – might manifest themselves of their own initiative, and in that case the role of the intellect is merely to give form to their expression. By contrast, in the divine soul, the emotive attributes are conceived, generated, and manifest by the intellect.

כִּי הַקָּטָן חוֹשֵׁק וְאוֹהֵב דְּבָרִים קְטַנִּים פְּחוּתֵי הָעֵרֶךְ, לְפִי שֶׁשִּׂכְלוֹ קָטָן וְקָצָר לְהַשִּׂיג דְּבָרִים יְקָרִים יוֹתֵר מֵהֶם.

This is empirically demonstrated as follows: **A child desires and loves trivial things of petty value since his intellect is too immature and deficient to apprehend things of greater value.**

A young child will make a small toy, a thing of little value, the object of his desire and envy. This is not because his desires are inherently directed toward such things but because his mind is not mature enough to appreciate things of greater and more abstract value. The object of his desire is confined to things he can relate to and understand. Things that an adult might desire are not things that appeal to a child, since the child does not yet possess a clear understanding of the nature of those items.

וְכֵן מִתְכַּעֵס וּמִתְקַצֵּף מִדְּבָרִים קְטַנִּים,

Likewise, he gets angry and annoyed on account of petty matters,

What is true of the attribute of kindness, which is expressed as love, is also the case with the attribute of restraint, which can be expressed as anger and fear. A child becomes angry over trivial things, because things that adults perceive as important and real are beyond the range of his understanding. A person will not be attracted to or repulsed by something he cannot perceive as desirable or repulsive. Such things will simply be neutral to him.

וְכֵן בְּהִתְפָּאֲרוּת

and likewise with regard to boastfulness

The same is true of the attribute of beauty, or *tiferet,* which can be negatively expressed as boastfulness and self-glorification. A child prides himself on petty achievements because these are comprehensible to his intellect.

וּשְׁאָר מִדּוֹת.

and the **other attributes.**

The same dynamic applies to all other attributes: The framework of evil is exactly the same as the framework of good, down to the smallest detail.

וְעֶשֶׂר בְּחִינוֹת אֵלּוּ הַטְּמֵאוֹת, כְּשֶׁאָדָם מְחַשֵּׁב בָּהֶן אוֹ מְדַבֵּר אוֹ עוֹשֶׂה – הֲרֵי מַחֲשַׁבְתּוֹ שֶׁבְּמוֹחוֹ, וְדִבּוּרוֹ שֶׁבְּפִיו וְכֹחַ הַמַּעֲשִׂיִּי שֶׁבְּיָדָיו וּשְׁאָר אֵיבָרָיו נִקְרָאִים "לְבוּשֵׁי מְסָאֲבוּ" לְעֶשֶׂר בְּחִינוֹת אֵלּוּ הַטְּמֵאוֹת, שֶׁמִּתְלַבְּשׁוֹת בָּהֶן בִּשְׁעַת מַעֲשֶׂה אוֹ דִּבּוּר אוֹ מַחֲשָׁבָה.

With regard to **these ten impure faculties, when a person employs them to think, speak, or act, then the thought in his brain, the speech in his mouth, and the power of action in his hands and his other limbs are referred to as the impure garments of these ten impure faculties, which clothe themselves in** these garments **during the act, speech, or thought.**

When a person activates the attributes of the animal soul, when he actualizes one of these impulses through one of the faculties of his body, whether thought, speech, or action, that faculty becomes a vehicle of expression for that evil attribute. The attribute is essentially spiritual and abstract, and the person is the means, the vessel, the garment – the medium – that expresses it in practice. When a person enclothes the attribute with his body, mouth, or mind, he becomes at that instant an instrument for impurity, a form of *kelippa*'s expression in the world.

וְהֵן הֵם כָּל הַמַּעֲשִׂים אֲשֶׁר נַעֲשִׂים תַּחַת הַשָּׁמֶשׁ,

These constitute all the actions that are performed in this world, **under the sun,**

The deeds, words, and thoughts that constitute an actualization of the animal soul's attributes include not only things that are commonly considered evil – thoughts, words, and acts of anger, of doing others harm, of rebellion against God, and so on – but comprise "all the actions that are performed under the sun" (an expression from Eccles. 1:14). Everything that can be found in the material world, everything that relates to the order of nature, that which constitutes the mundane, is encompassed in the phrase "under the sun."

אֲשֶׁר "הַכֹּל הֶבֶל וּרְעוּת רוּחַ" וּכְמוֹ שֶׁכָּתוּב בַּזֹּהַר בְּשַׁלַּח (חלק ב נט, א), שֶׁהֵן תְּבִירוּ דְּרוּחָא כו'.

which are "all futility and herding wind" (Eccles. 1:14), **and as the *Zohar*,** *Parashat* ***Beshalaḥ*** (2:59a), **states** regarding this verse, **these** actions **are the "breaking of the spirit…."**

The plain meaning of the expression "herding wind" evokes the image of a shepherd who pursues wind, an apparition, something that does not exist.

The *Zohar* lends a deeper layer of meaning to the Hebrew words for "herding wind," *re'ut ru'aḥ,* connecting *re'ut* to the word *ro'a,* to break, and interpreting the word *ruaḥ* as spirit instead of wind. This implies that the "actions that are performed under the sun" are all a ruination of the spirit, a blockage of the divine life force, an expression of *kelippa,* and a force that is contrary to that which is holy.

6 Tevet (leap year)

וְכֵן כָּל הַדִּבּוּרִים וְכָל הַמַּחֲשָׁבוֹת אֲשֶׁר לֹא לַה' הֵמָּה וְלִרְצוֹנוֹ וְלַעֲבוֹדָתוֹ.

The same applies to all speech and thoughts that are not dedicated **to God, His will, and His service.**

Not only blatant evil but also the entire array of material life and all that it entails is "futility and herding wind." There might be nothing inherently negative about these things, but their deficiency lies in that they are not directed toward "God, His will, and His service." They are merely matters that pertain to this world, bearing no divine meaning or direction. As such, they are relegated to the realm of the *sitra aḥara.*[4]

שֶׁזֶּהוּ פֵּירוּשׁ לְשׁוֹן סִטְרָא אָחֳרָא, פֵּירוּשׁ צַד אַחֵר שֶׁאֵינוֹ צַד הַקְּדוּשָּׁה.

This is the meaning of the term *sitra aḥara,* literally, "the other side," namely, anything **that is not on the side of holiness.**

Sitra aḥara is the kabbalistic term for evil, but the expression literally means "the other side," that is, not the side of holiness. On the most basic level, there are two aspects to reality: the side of holiness and the other side. Unlike the domain of *halakha,* which contains a broad realm known as *reshut,* that which is neither virtuous nor sinful, neither

4. In the beginning of the chapter, the author of the *Tanya* referred to thoughts, speech, and actions that were expressions of the evil attributes. Here the author refers to deeds that aren't necessarily evil but are simply not channeled toward divine service. In the next chapter, the author will distinguish between thoughts, speech, and actions that stem from the three *kelippot,* the forces of pure evil, which constitute transgressions of the 365 prohibitions, and those that stem from the *kelippa* of *noga,* which are neutral. The latter can be directed toward God, in which case they become holy, or toward the other side, which makes them evil.

mitzva nor transgression, in the kabbalistic division of reality, there is no middle ground. Nothing is truly neutral. There cannot be anything that does not relate, positively or negatively, to God. Anything that is not actively directed toward God is automatically of the other side. ☞

וְצַד הַקְּדוּשָּׁה אֵינוֹ אֶלָּא הַשְׁרָאָה וְהַמְשָׁכָה מִקְּדוּשָּׁתוֹ שֶׁל הַקָּדוֹשׁ בָּרוּךְ הוּא,

The side of holiness in nothing other than the manifestation and channeling of the holiness of the Holy One, blessed be He.

There is no inherent holiness other than that of God. This reality constitutes the nature of the side of holiness. Something might be of value in the practical sense, but it is not holy. Holiness belongs exclusively to God, and the side of holiness contains no realities that are inherently holy on their own, only realities that derive their holiness from God.

וְאֵין הַקָּדוֹשׁ בָּרוּךְ הוּא שׁוֹרֶה אֶלָּא עַל דָּבָר שֶׁבָּטֵל אֶצְלוֹ יִתְבָּרֵךְ,

The Holy One, blessed be He, dwells only within something that is abnegated to Him,

The author of the *Tanya* explains elsewhere that the indwelling of the Divine Presence is not present in everything.[5] In truth, the Divine Presence is everywhere, and the entire world is filled with it. There

THE SIDE OF HOLINESS

☞ The realm of holiness is a world of unity, a world that manifests the truth that "there is no other besides Him" (Deut. 4:35). The conception of God as *Ein Sof*, the infinite, does not merely imply that He is infinitely great but that He is the infinite being without limit and definition, so that there can be nothing else.

By contrast, the other side is rooted in the world of disunity, in which the light of *Ein Sof* is not manifest, where the exclusive reality of God is not recognized. This is the essence of the *sitra aḥara*: the implication that there is, so to speak, something else besides Him. In its initial, most basic form, the other side does not deny the existence of holiness, nor is it hostile to it. It merely deigns to constrict holiness, to confine it within a set of parameters. It is willing to accept the existence of a lofty and superior realm of holiness. What it does not accept is the exclusivity of holiness, and it presumes that there are other things of significance as well.

5. See *Iggeret HaKodesh*, epistles 23, 25.

are no boundaries or limits to the truth that "there is no other besides Him." But when speaking of the indwelling of the Divine Presence, we are speaking of a manifest revelation of Godliness, of a thing becoming a vessel for the Divine, something that visibly relates to God. The indwelling of the Divine Presence within a certain object or reality implies that the Divine Presence is not only there but that it operates and manifests itself through that thing. Not everything can serve as a conduit for the Divine. It must have a certain quality that makes it a vessel. This quality is utter self-abnegation to God. ☞

בֵּין בְּפוֹעַל מַמָּשׁ כְּמַלְאָכִים עֶלְיוֹנִים **whether actually and literally, as in the case of the supernal angels,**

The angels are holy because, as higher creatures, without corporeal bodies that obscure the Divine, they are exposed directly to the divine light. They have no identity of their own and exist in a perpetual state of complete abnegation to God.

בֵּין בְּכֹחַ כְּכָל אִישׁ יִשְׂרָאֵל לְמַטָּה or **whether potentially, as in the case of every Jew below.**

The Jew, as a physical being on earth, might not be in a state of self-abnegation at all times, but he possesses the potential to utterly negate his very existence to God.

"WHERE IS GOD?"

☞ Rabbi Yitzḥak Meir Alter of Gur, the author of *Ḥiddushei HaRim*, once asked his hasidim, "Where is God?"

What a question! the hasidim thought. *God is everywhere!*

Their Rebbe replied, "That is not precisely true. God can be found only where He is allowed to enter."

This story is a characteristically sharp and concise formulation of the concept discussed here: God dwells only wherever there is self-abnegation to Him. When one does not allow Him to enter, where He is confined to a specific date and time or to certain conditions, God does not enter at all. For holiness to permeate, one must be a receptacle for holiness. God's presence infiltrates every corner of reality, leaving no place for any other existence, so the only way to relate to Him is from the standpoint of utter self-abnegation. The closer to Him one approaches, the more meaningful one's relationship to Him, the more one's own being is negated and the more the supernal holiness dwells and manifests itself in one's life.

שֶׁבְּכֹחוֹ לִהְיוֹת בָּטֵל מַמָּשׁ לְגַבֵּי הַקָּדוֹשׁ בָּרוּךְ הוּא בִּמְסִירַת נַפְשׁוֹ עַל קְדוּשַּׁת ה׳.

He has the potential to actually submit to the Holy One, blessed be He, by sacrificing his life for the sake of sanctifying God's name.

A Jew is holy, not because he is more clever, more compassionate, or more successful, but because he has the capacity to negate himself to God. Elsewhere, the author of the *Tanya* describes a Jew as one who, at a moment of truth, is prepared to sacrifice his life rather than disrupt, even for a moment, his bond with God.[6] A Jew is one in whom union with God and self-abnegation to Him are implanted in his soul. Should anyone ever attempt to separate him from God, this latent bond will be invoked in all its intensity, to the point of self-sacrifice. It is from this potential for utter self-abnegation, implicit even in the most wicked and sinful Jew, that the holiness of the Jew derives.

וְלָכֵן אָמְרוּ רַבּוֹתֵינוּ ז״ל שֶׁאֲפִילּוּ אֶחָד שֶׁיּוֹשֵׁב וְעוֹסֵק בַּתּוֹרָה שְׁכִינָה שְׁרוּיָה כו׳ (אבות פרק ג משנה ו),

Therefore, our Rabbis stated that "even when only **one** person **sits and engages in Torah** study, **the Divine Presence is with him…"** (Mishna *Avot* 3:6).

When a Jew studies Torah, he realizes this potential, nullifying himself to the divine wisdom that he enclothes and in which he is enclothed. At such a time, the Divine Presence actually dwells in him.

The author of the *Tanya* refers specifically to Torah study as a means of abnegating oneself to God.[7] As he mentions elsewhere,[8] the virtue of the giving of the Torah at Sinai constituted, on a deeper level, the granting of the potential for each Jew to abnegate himself to the words of Torah that he verbally articulates. When one speaks the words of Torah, it effectuates a reality in which God is speaking through him and he is merely repeating the words after Him, so to speak.

The same is true of one's understanding and knowledge of Torah.

---

6. See chaps. 18, 25.

7. Although a person also actively subordinates himself to God while praying, this is not utter self-abnegation, because in prayer one also asks God for his personal needs.

8. See, e.g., *Torah Or, Parashat Yitro*.

They are nullified in the face of the wisdom and knowledge of God, the Giver of the Torah. This state is, in effect, a veritable continuation of the Jewish people's state at the giving of the Torah, wherein the Divine Presence literally and truly dwelled in each and every Jew.

וְכָל בֵּי עֲשָׂרָה שְׁכִינְתָּא שַׁרְיָא לְעוֹלָם (סנהדרין לט, א).

Moreover, **"the Divine Presence always dwells** in **any place where there are ten** Jews" (*Sanhedrin* 39a).

Even if the ten Jews are not actually studying Torah, the Divine Presence dwells with them. Ten Jews together have the potential to constitute a *minyan*, a quorum that can recite prayers sanctifying God's name. Wherever ten Jews congregate, even if they are unaware of their holiness, even if they defile it, the Divine Presence, as well as the supernal congregation of Israel referred to as *Kenesset Yisrael* (essentially a gathering of the collective's souls), dwells with them.[9]

אֲבָל כָּל מַה שֶּׁאֵינוֹ בָּטֵל אֶצְלוֹ יִתְבָּרֵךְ, אֶלָּא הוּא דָּבָר נִפְרָד בִּפְנֵי עַצְמוֹ,

However, anything that is not abnegated to God, but rather is its own, independent entity, 3 Tevet

How the entity defines itself is irrelevant, whether it considers its own worth as great or insignificant, as lofty or lowly. The point is that it relates to itself as a distinct entity, as something other and separate from God.

אֵינוֹ מְקַבֵּל חַיּוּת מִקְּדוּשָּׁתוֹ שֶׁל הַקָּדוֹשׁ בָּרוּךְ הוּא, מִבְּחִינַת פְּנִימִית הַקְּדוּשָּׁה וּמַהוּתָהּ וְעַצְמוּתָהּ בִּכְבוֹדָהּ וּבְעַצְמָהּ, אֶלָּא מִבְּחִינַת אֲחוֹרַיִים,

does not receive its **life force from the holiness of the Holy One, blessed be He, from the inner aspect, essence, and core of holiness in all its glory. Rather,** it receives its life force **from the back side** of God's will.

Ultimately, such an entity does receive life and existence from God because there is no created being that is not sustained by His power,

9. See *Iggeret HaKodesh*, epistle 23; *Likkutei Torah*, Deut. 98b.

no existence that is not derived from His existence. But it does not receive its vitality from the inner or "front" aspect of God's holiness, but rather only from the back side.

God is the sole source of existence in all its forms and manifestations. Yet there is a profound difference between an existence that is sustained from the inner holiness of God, because the entity desires God and God desires it, and an existence where the being does not desire a bond with God and the complete self-abnegation it requires. In that case, the entity receives its vitality, not from the core of the divine will, but from its external element or "back." ☞

שֶׁיּוֹרְדִים מִמַּדְרֵגָה לְמַדְרֵגָה רִבְבוֹת מַדְרֵגוֹת בְּהִשְׁתַּלְשְׁלוּת הָעוֹלָמוֹת דֶּרֶךְ עִלָּה וְעָלוּל וְצִמְצוּמִים רַבִּים,

This life force **descends level by level** through **myriad levels, in the unfolding succession of the worlds by way of cause and effect and numerous constrictions,**

The divine life force that derives from the back side, or the external aspect of the divine will, passes through a multiphased process of concealment and diminution known as the unfolding succession of the worlds. These worlds, or levels of reality, devolve one from the other, descending like the links of a chain, the top of one world linked through the bottom of the one above it. Each world derives from its predecessor not by a quantum leap but by a link of cause and effect. This serves to even further conceal the divine source of creation.

THE FRONT AND BACK OF GOD'S WILL

☞ Consider a container, which has an inside and an outside. One doesn't need the outside of the container in and of itself. The container's purpose and function is filled by the part containing its contents, the inside. Yet no container can possibly consist only of an inside. By necessity, the inside will always have an outside.

By the same token, the part of a knife that is needed is its cutting edge, but it is impossible for there to be a sharp edge without the dull edge. Though the dull edge of the knife is unimportant and unnecessary, there can't be a sharp edge without it. Along the same lines, in order to realize a goal, we often need to build an entire organization that includes many auxiliary elements. The auxiliary elements might be far greater, quantitatively, than the part of the organization that actual-

עַד שֶׁנִּתְמַעֵט כָּל כָּךְ הָאוֹר וְהַחַיּוּת מִיעוּט אַחַר מִיעוּט עַד שֶׁיָּכוֹל לְהִתְצַמְצֵם וּלְהִתְלַבֵּשׁ בִּבְחִינַת גָּלוּת תּוֹךְ אוֹתוֹ דָּבָר הַנִּפְרָד

until the light and life force become so diminished, diminution upon diminution, that they may be constricted and clothed, in exile, within that independent entity

Each link in the chain of the unfolding succession of the worlds is a screen that dims the light of the divine life force, until at the last screen only the life force that sustains that specific entity in this reality is manifest. The divine element that is the inner source of every creation is blurred or completely obscured, and the divine light can then be said to be in exile. It is not apparent to that created entity that it receives its life from the divine life force that grants it life and sustains it. It might even deny its very existence.

A person in exile is someone who finds himself in a place where he does not want to be and is forced to remain there and operate under alien and confining circumstances. While there, he is compelled to function through the place's "garments" – his material lifestyle, thought processes, culture, and other garments of his soul – which neither belong to him nor does he want anything to do with them. In this sense, the divine light that sustains the material world is in exile. It has descended through worlds and undergone numerous constrictions that obscure the Divine and make it possible for a created entity to even deny its existence, even though the Divine is that entity's source of life and it could not be alive otherwise.

ly fulfills its purpose. A great and complex system might exist just for the sake of a minuscule unit.

In this sense, the realm of holiness is the inner element of creation, the realm in which is invested the core of the divine will. God relates to the realm of holiness in an intimate manner because this is His inner will, the essence of His desire. The other, that which is not holy, is the scaffolding and infrastructure, the setting and the background, for the holy core. It is not because God desires it in the sense of a fundamental will that it exists, but because it is necessary to the existence of the universe, which is only the background to the inner desire. This immense structure, the physical world and whatever it contains, is sustained not by the inner will of God but circuitously, by way of its back. It is the mundane world of the other, unholy side – that of *kelippat noga*.

לְהַחֲיוֹתוֹ וּלְקַיְּימוֹ מֵאַיִן לְיֵשׁ שֶׁלֹּא יַחֲזוֹר לִהְיוֹת אַיִן וָאֶפֶס כְּבַתְּחִלָּה מִקּוֹדֶם שֶׁנִּבְרָא.

to grant it life and sustain it, bringing it forth **from nothingness into existence,** in order **that it not revert to absolute nothingness, as it was prior to its creation.**

Every entity, including the creation that considers itself a thing in its own right, separate from God, requires the divine light to keep it alive and grant it its very existence.

In view of this, holiness and *kelippa* are not antagonists in essence but are two sides of the same reality. It is a reality that has both a facet that is conscious of its divine source, as well as *kelippa,* which also receives its life force and existence from the same holy source, though it is unaware of it. ☞

7 Tevet (leap year)

וְלָכֵן נִקְרָא עוֹלָם הַזֶּה וּמְלוֹאוֹ עוֹלַם הַקְּלִיפּוֹת וְסִטְרָא אָחֳרָא.

Therefore, this world, and all that it contains, is referred to as the world of the *kelippot* and *sitra aḥara*.

TWO SIDES OF THE SAME REALITY

☞ God is the essence of all existence, good and evil, darkness and light. The difference between these two categories is wholly a matter of perspective on the part of the creations themselves. The creations of the side of holiness perceive themselves as naught before God, whereas the creations of the other side do not sense the divine light within them, do not abnegate themselves to the Divine. Rather, they see themselves as independent entities.

The creations of the side of holiness are an expression of the divine will's inner essence and constitute the core and purpose of creation. The creations of the other side, as explained above, constitute the scaffolding and infrastructure, the setting and background that enables the actualization of the inner point of holiness. The other side is bigger and more abundant than the side of holiness because the maintenance of a single being of significance, of a single inner reality, requires an entire world of ancillary structures that enable that inner reality to manifest.

Still, even without being aware of it, the entity that perceives itself as independent also receives its vitality from the source of holiness. If that holiness, which is in exile within it, ceased to exist, that entity would cease to exist as well, utterly vanishing from reality.

We see a similar phenomenon throughout history. Great structures have suddenly collapsed and no longer exist. In the same vein, it very well may be that a person toiled to construct great edifices, entire life structures, in his soul, and for whatever reason, they have suddenly disappeared from his life and no longer exist.

As a rule, the physical world and the creatures that inhabit it, including mankind, do perceive themselves as a separate reality that is not subordinate to God. In the spiritual worlds, the inner core of holiness occupies a greater and more prominent part of that world, so the Divine is sensed and manifest more clearly. Our world is not only more tactile but also lower down on the chain from the divine source, consisting almost entirely of *kelippa* and *sitra aḥara*. Overall, this world is primarily a world of the other side, a world in which holiness is not manifest at all and the other side dominates.

וְלָכֵן כָּל מַעֲשֵׂה עוֹלָם הַזֶּה קָשִׁים וְרָעִים וְהָרְשָׁעִים גּוֹבְרִים בּוֹ, כְּמוֹ שֶׁכָּתוּב בְּ"עֵץ חַיִּים" שַׁעַר מ"ב סוֹף פֶּרֶק ד'.

As a result, all affairs of this world are harsh and evil, and the wicked are dominant in it, as stated in *Etz Ḥayyim* 42, end of chapter 4.

Here the author of the *Tanya* quotes the conception expressed in the kabbalistic work *Etz Ḥayyim*, whose general view of our world seems to be one of hardened realism, even pessimism. Ours is a world characterized by an almost total concealment of the Divine, a world whose visible components are overwhelmingly *kelippa* and *sitra aḥara*. It is small wonder that it is not filled with brightness and light. ☞

THE HARSH REALITY OF THIS WORLD

☞ In a world that is basically *kelippa*, evil has the natural advantage and the wicked prevail. But this picture is not completely pessimistic because things can be put right. The precise definition of our world is "the darkest possible world that can still be illuminated anew." It is a world that descended exceedingly far from the divine source, yet in a manner by which it can yet ascend once more.

The optimistic aspect of this world is that when it does eventually ascend and become rectified and illuminated, it will actually be elevated and exalted above all the other worlds. This is akin to the advantage that light possesses when viewed in contrast to darkness, to that of the penitent over the completely righteous.

All this means that there is a way to transform the world to the extent that it itself illuminates all the other worlds of holiness and fills them with goodness and increased holiness. But this does not happen automatically. It requires diligent and constant work by man, work that entails change and rectification.

הַגָּהָה: עִם הֱיוֹת בְּתוֹכוֹ עֶשֶׂר סְפִירוֹת דַּעֲשִׂיָּה דִקְדוּשָּׁה, וּכְמוֹ שֶׁכָּתוּב בְּ"עֵץ חַיִּים" שַׁעַר מ"ג, וּבְתוֹךְ עֶשֶׂר סְפִירוֹת דַּעֲשִׂיָּה אֵלּוּ הֵן עֶשֶׂר סְפִירוֹת דִּיצִירָה, וּבְתוֹכָן עֶשֶׂר סְפִירוֹת דִּבְרִיאָה, וּבְתוֹכָן עֶשֶׂר סְפִירוֹת דַּאֲצִילוּת שֶׁבְּתוֹכָן אוֹר אֵין סוֹף בָּרוּךְ הוּא. וְנִמְצָא אוֹר אֵין סוֹף בָּרוּךְ הוּא מְלֹא כָל הָאָרֶץ הַלָּזוּ הַתַּחְתּוֹנָה עַל יְדֵי הִתְלַבְּשׁוּתוֹ בְּעֶשֶׂר סְפִירוֹת דְּאַרְבַּע עוֹלָמוֹת - אֲצִילוּת בְּרִיאָה יְצִירָה עֲשִׂיָּה, כְּמוֹ שֶׁכָּתוּב בְּ"עֵץ חַיִּים" שַׁעַר מ"ז פֶּרֶק ב' וּבְ"סֵפֶר גִּלְגּוּלִים" פֶּרֶק כ'.

Gloss: Yet this world **does contain within it the ten holy** ***sefirot*** **of** the world of ***Asiya,*** **as stated in** ***Etz Ḥayyim*** **43, and** subsumed **within these ten** ***sefirot*** **of** ***Asiya*** **are the ten** ***sefirot*** **of** the world of ***Yetzira,*** **and** subsumed **within them are the ten** ***sefirot*** **of** the world of ***Beria,*** **and** subsumed **within them are the ten** ***sefirot*** **of** the world of ***Atzilut,*** **within which is the light of** ***Ein Sof.*** **Consequently, the light of** ***Ein Sof,*** **blessed be He, permeates this entire lower world through its being clothed in the ten** ***sefirot*** **of the four worlds,** ***Atzilut, Beria, Yetzira,*** and ***Asiya,*** **as stated in** ***Etz Ḥayyim*** **47:2 and in** ***Sefer Gilgulim,*** **chapter 20.**

This gloss, which is based on a teaching from *Etz Ḥayyim,* explains that notwithstanding the darkness enshrouding this world, in its deepest depths there exists a tiny, inner point of sublime holiness. To be more precise, it is not a mere point; it is a beam of the light of *Ein Sof* that threads its way through each of the worlds at the degree of holiness extant in each of them.

The view presented here maintains that each world and level of existence possesses ten holy *sefirot* that are manifest according to that world's spiritual level, from the corporeal world of *Asiya* all the way up to the most sublime world of *Atzilut.* Thus, the ten *sefirot* of each world are linked to the ten *sefirot* of *Atzilut* and its loftiest point, the *sefira* of *Ḥokhma* – a level that is impervious to the pernicious touch of any *kelippa.*

It is clear that the aforementioned beam of light likewise refers to the constricted beam that channels the light of *Ein Sof* into all the worlds through *Ḥokhma* and the other *sefirot,* from *Atzilut* to *Beria,* down to *Yetzira,* and finally, to the corporeal world of *Asiya.* Despite this deep descent, the beam remains intact, so to speak, and in view of this, whatever initially descended can reascend in the same way. It may not reascend immediately, nor is its reascent inevitable, yet the potential to do so exists.

The constriction, or descent, of the beam of divine light itself creates the potential for its own subsequent reascent and expansion at a future point in time; it creates a connection between the worlds and the Divine that allows for both descent from above and ascent from below. Most significantly, at this very moment, it is already forming the wondrous reality in which this polarity coexists: the lowest descent and yet the opportunity for the highest ascent. Whether or not the ascent will occur is dependent on us: Will there be meaning and justification for all the suffering and extreme concealment? Will it result in the revelation that justifies it all? Is this revelation already emerging now, as we speak, to the extent that we will be able to say, in the World to Come, "Indeed, it was very difficult, but it was worthwhile"?

אֶלָּא שֶׁהַקְּלִיפּוֹת הֵן נֶחֱלָקוֹת לִשְׁתֵּי מַדְרֵגוֹת זוֹ לְמַטָּה מִזּוֹ.

However, the *kelippot* are divided into two categories, one lower than the other.

Both the *kelippot* and the *sitra aḥara* possess a distinct lack of holiness. From this perspective, these terms are interchangeable. Yet each expression conveys a different aspect of this absence. *Kelippa* indicates that it is an external, extrinsic element, serving as a peel or husk for the fruit, protecting and preserving the inner content. By contrast, *sitra aḥara* is a generalized description, expressing only the concept of what this realm is not – not holy but "other." We do not speak of various levels in a phenomenon that is defined solely in terms of what it is not. There is only the side of holiness and the other side. *Kelippa*, on the other hand, expresses what it is, describing the function of the nonholy elements of creation. In this context, we can distinguish between various forms of this function and discuss two primary levels of *kelippa*.

הַמַּדְרֵגָה הַתַּחְתּוֹנָה הִיא שָׁלֹשׁ קְלִיפּוֹת הַטְּמֵאוֹת וְרָעוֹת לְגַמְרֵי וְאֵין בָּהֶם טוֹב כְּלָל, וְנִקְרְאוּ בְּמֶרְכָּבָה יְחֶזְקֵאל (יחזקאל א, ד): "רוּחַ סְעָרָה", וְ"עָנָן גָּדוֹל"

The lower level of *kelippa* is comprised of **the three utterly impure and evil *kelippot*, containing no good whatsoever. In Ezekiel's** vision of the divine **chariot, they are referred to as "storm wind," "great cloud,"** and "fire igniting"

וגו׳, וּמֵהֶן נִשְׁפָּעוֹת וְנִמְשָׁכוֹת נַפְשׁוֹת כָּל אוּמּוֹת הָעוֹלָם וְקִיּוּם גּוּפָם, וְנַפְשׁוֹת כָּל בַּעֲלֵי חַיִּים הַטְּמֵאִים וַאֲסוּרִים בַּאֲכִילָה וְקִיּוּם גּוּפָם, וְקִיּוּם וְחַיּוּת כָּל מַאֲכָלוֹת אֲסוּרוֹת מֵהַצּוֹמֵחַ, כְּמוֹ עָרְלָה וְכִלְאֵי הַכֶּרֶם כו׳, וּכְמוֹ שֶׁכָּתוּב בְּ״עֵץ חַיִּים״ שַׁעַר מ״ט פֶּרֶק ו׳.

(Ezek. 1:4). **From these** three impure *kelippot* **issue forth and are drawn down the souls of all the nations of the world and the sustaining force of their bodies, as well as the souls of the impure living creatures, whose consumption is prohibited, and the sustaining force of their bodies. The existence and life force of all prohibited vegetable foods, such as *orla*,** the fruit of a tree in its first three years, **and *kilei hakerem*,** mixtures of diverse kinds in a vineyard**, and so on,** also stem from these *kelippot*, **as stated in *Etz Ḥayyim* 49:6.**

The author of the *Tanya* elaborates on the three impure *kelippot* that he alluded to briefly in chapter 1. They are what he calls the lower level of *kelippa*, based on a vision perceived by the prophet Ezekiel. These *kelippot* are utterly evil, and they are the root of whatever manifests itself as evil.

וְכֵן קִיּוּם וְחַיּוּת כָּל הַמַּעֲשֶׂה דִּבּוּר וּמַחֲשָׁבָה שֶׁל כָּל שס״ה לֹא תַעֲשֶׂה וְעַנְפֵיהֶן, כְּמוֹ שֶׁכָּתוּב שָׁם סוֹף פֶּרֶק ה׳.

Likewise, the existence and life force of every action, spoken word, and thought that constitute a transgression **of each of the 365 prohibitions and their corollaries,** stem from the three *kelippot*, **as stated there,** in *Etz Ḥayyim* 49, **end of chapter 5.**

As the author of the *Tanya* will go on to explain in the next chapter, the Jew's connection to the three utterly impure *kelippot* is manifest through the prohibitions detailed in the Torah. At his essence and nature, a Jew bears no relation to these impure *kelippot*, since his animal soul stems from the other level of *kelippa*, *kelippat noga*,[10] yet if he were to violate either a biblical or rabbinic prohibition, he opens

10. See chap. 1.

the pathway by which he receives the energy of the impure *kelippot* and is impacted by it. In turn, the *kelippot* themselves receive energy from the transgressor and thus are the beneficiaries of the life force and sustenance deriving from holiness.

In other words, when a person sins, he receives the life force stemming from the impure *kelippot,* while concurrently opening the figurative pathway for the life force of holiness to power and energize those impure *kelippot,* which, unbridled, will continue to have a deleterious effect on him. ☞

This chapter revolves around the faculties and garments of the animal soul. These faculties comprise one's negative traits and the intellect that generates them, while its garments are the mundane thoughts, speech, and actions that do not pertain to holiness, the service of God, Torah, or mitzvot. This realm, which is not attached to holiness, is referred to as the *sitra aḥara,* the "other side" that is contrary to holiness and derives nourishment from the back or external aspect of the divine will. It also constitutes *kelippa,* the husk that surrounds and obscures the inner core of creation.

THE *BEINONI* AND THE IMPURE *KELIPPOT*

☞ On the surface, it is puzzling: Why did the author of the *Tanya* deem it necessary for the *beinoni,* for whom this book was written, to be made aware of the three completely impure *kelippot,* considering that his life bears no relation to them whatsoever? Rather, it is structured around the beam of holiness described in the gloss that has the capacity to descend and ascend.

The *beinoni* is associated only with *kelippat noga,* which has the potential to be incorporated into the realm of holiness, and never even committed a transgression, nor will he ever commit one, not even violating a minor rabbinic prohibition. He is so meticulous in his divine service that he will not even passively neglect to fulfill a positive commandment.

Why, then, is it necessary to discuss the impure *kelippot* at all?

Granted, the *beinoni* never sinned nor will sin, and his arena of divine service will never extend to include the three impure *kelippot.* Nevertheless, these *kelippot* exist in potential as a looming threat in his life, a constant possibility – the possibility of his falling. At the same time, there also exists the possibility of his ascending and elevating others.

Chapter 7

THE PREVIOUS CHAPTER CONCLUDED BY ESTABLISHING that *kelippa* comprises two basic levels. The lower level includes the three utterly impure *kelippot,* which contain no good at all. The higher level, which will be discussed in this chapter, is *kelippat noga,* the "luminescent husk," in which some good is mixed and has the potential to manifest itself as holiness.

4 Tevet
8 Tevet (leap year)

אַךְ נֶפֶשׁ הַחִיּוּנִית הַבַּהֲמִית שֶׁבְּיִשְׂרָאֵל שֶׁמִּצַּד הַקְּלִיפָּה הַמְלוּבֶּשֶׁת בְּדַם הָאָדָם כַּנִּזְכָּר לְעֵיל, וְנַפְשׁוֹת בְּהֵמוֹת וְחַיּוֹת וְעוֹפוֹת וְדָגִים טְהוֹרִים וּמוּתָּרִים בַּאֲכִילָה, וְקִיּוּם וְחַיּוּת כָּל הַדּוֹמֵם וְכָל הַצּוֹמֵחַ הַמּוּתָּר בַּאֲכִילָה,

However, the vital animal soul within a Jew that stems from *kelippa,* which is embodied in a person's blood, as stated above (chaps. 1, 6), is not derived from the three thoroughly impure *kelippot,* nor do **the souls of domesticated animals, undomesticated animals, birds, and fish** that are deemed **pure and permitted for consumption, nor the existence and life force of all inanimate matter and all vegetation that is permitted for consumption.**

The animal or vital soul that the author of the *Tanya* discussed in chapter 1 is not animalistic in the base sense of the word. Rather, it is referred to as animal soul because it is a part of the world of all living creatures, of animals both domesticated and undomesticated. The drives and desires of this soul, like those of all other living creatures, are not inherently evil; they are simply part of the biological stratum of creation: The animal soul in man is the life force that vivifies the human being, infusing him with the same basic vitality he shares with all other living things. It is only that a human being's brain is larger (relative to his body) and more highly developed than that of other animals. As a result, what we might call the animalism in him differs from that which is inherent in other creatures, even though he is part of the same stratum.

וְכֵן קִיּוּם וְחַיּוּת כָּל הַמַּעֲשֶׂה דִּבּוּר וּמַחֲשָׁבָה בְּעִנְיְנֵי עוֹלָם הַזֶּה שֶׁאֵין בָּהֶם צַד אִיסּוּר, לֹא שֹׁרֶשׁ וְלֹא עָנָף מִשְּׁסַ״ה מִצְוֹת לֹא תַעֲשֶׂה וְעַנְפֵיהֶן דְּאוֹרַיְיתָא וּדְרַבָּנָן, רַק שֶׁאֵינָן לְשֵׁם שָׁמַיִם, אֶלָּא רְצוֹן הַגּוּף וְחֶפְצוֹ וְתַאֲוָתוֹ,

The same is true with regard to **the existence and life force of each action, word, and thought pertaining to matters of this world that contain no trace of prohibition, neither a root nor an offshoot of one of the 365 prohibitions and their corollaries,** whether prohibited **by Torah law or by rabbinic law, yet are not** performed **for the sake of Heaven but rather** are **the will, desire, and passion of the body.**

The author of the *Tanya* is differentiating between that which stems from the utterly impure *kelippot* – the animal souls of non-Jews and the life force of animals that are prohibited for consumption – and that which stems from the fourth type of *kelippa*: *kelippat noga*. Included in this category, along with the animal soul of a Jew and the sustaining force of animals permitted for consumption, are all things or actions in existence that have no moral fault or prohibited aspect, but also do not possess, in and of themselves, any aspect of mitzva, of divine service. This broad spectrum is not the domain of the dark, the prohibited, or the corrupt, but the sphere of the nonholy and the neutral, that which is neither mitzva nor sin. Yet since those actions or things do not belong to the realm of holiness, they fall under the category of *kelippa*.

There is no middle ground between the holy and the profane, no gray area that is neither one nor the other. A thing is either holy and devoted to God, or it is profane. So all the acts listed, though kosher and permissible, are *kelippa,* because they are not directly and solely committed to the fulfillment of God's will but to the fulfillment of the will and desire of the body. The difference is that they do not belong to the purely evil *kelippot* but to *kelippat noga* and can potentially be rectified. ☞

וַאֲפִילּוּ הוּא צוֹרֶךְ הַגּוּף וְקִיּוּמוֹ וְחַיּוּתוֹ מַמָּשׁ, אֶלָּא שֶׁכַּוָּונָתוֹ אֵינָהּ לְשֵׁם שָׁמַיִם, כְּדֵי לַעֲבוֹד אֶת ה' בְּגוּפוֹ,

Even when an action, speech, or thought **is necessary to literally sustain and vivify the body, yet one does not have the intention** that it is **for the sake of Heaven, in order to serve God with one's body,**

Kelippat noga includes not only luxuries or superfluous pleasures but even the slice of bread that keeps one alive so that he will not die of starvation. If a person eats it as an animal would, just to sustain the body, that act of eating does not belong to the side of holiness and by definition belongs to the other side. A person can live in utter conformity with Torah law, even modestly and ascetically, but entirely for himself. He can be a glutton, for instance, even while leading a most simple and modest existence. He need not feast like a king but eat only a dry crust of bread followed by a sip of water while wearing sackcloth, and still that act would belong to the realm of *kelippa,* because any action that is not expressly directed toward holiness belongs to the other side. On the other hand, a person can wear clothes of silk and gold, consume

KELIPPA VERSUS *KELIPPA*

☞ An old hasidic saying states, "What is forbidden, one must not, and what is permitted, one need not" (*HaYom Yom*, 25 Adar Sheni, cited in the name of Rabbi Mordekhai of Horodok, who heard it from the author of the *Tanya* himself). What is prohibited is impure, wholly of the other side, but what is permitted is also in the realm of *kelippa* and *sitra aḥara.* The permissible is not intrinsically holy and therefore belongs to the other side, since the other side includes all that is not holy. What is not a mitzva, what is not actively holy – that is, subservient to the Divine – is "husk," something extraneous to the divine essence of creation. The difference between the prohibited and the permitted is not the difference between holiness and *kelippa* but the difference between levels of *kelippa,* between *kelippa* that can be rectified and *kelippa* that cannot be rectified.

the finest meats, and drink the most exquisite wines, and in so doing be serving God. ☞

לָא עֲדִיפֵי מַעֲשֶׂה דִּבּוּר וּמַחֲשָׁבוֹת אֵלּוּ מִנֶּפֶשׁ הַחִיּוּנִית הַבַּהֲמִית בְּעַצְמָהּ.

then **these actions, words, and thoughts are no better than the vital, animal soul itself.**

As explained above, the nature of the animal soul does not imply that man is reduced to the moral level of animals, but merely places man in the category of a creation. Just as the animal soul itself is neither good nor evil, so too its thoughts, speech, and deeds, whether sophisticated or simple, elevated or base, whether connected with essential needs or mere desires, are neither good nor evil in and of themselves. Yet since these deeds, speech, and thoughts do not constitute the fulfillment of a mitzva, since they are not done for the sake of serving God, they are as neutral as the animal soul itself.

וְהַכֹּל כַּאֲשֶׁר לַכֹּל נִשְׁפָּע וְנִמְשָׁךְ מִמַּדְרֵגָה הַשֵּׁנִית שֶׁבַּקְּלִיפּוֹת וְסִטְרָא אָחֳרָא שֶׁהִיא קְלִיפָּה רְבִיעִית הַנִּקְרֵאת קְלִיפַּת נוֹגַהּ,

The totality of all these actions **issues forth and stems from the second level of the *kelippot* and *sitra aḥara*, which is the fourth *kelippa* referred to as the *kelippa* of *noga*.**

In Ezekiel's vision of the divine chariot, we find a description of the *kelippot*: "a storm wind coming from the north, a great cloud and fire igniting, and an aura surrounding it" (Ezek. 1:4). "Storm wind," "great cloud," and "fire igniting" refer to the three impure *kelippot*, while the

DRESSED IN SACKCLOTH

☞ The story is told of a certain learned Jew whose own brand of piety entailed fasting and other ascetic practices such as wearing sackcloth underneath his clothes. One day he went to visit a great tzaddik. He wanted the tzaddik to know how pious he was, so he unbuttoned his jacket so that the sackcloth would be visible.

The tzaddik looked at him and said, "How clever he is! How clever he is!"

He repeated this several times until the man had to ask, "Who is so clever?"

The tzaddik answered, "The evil inclination, who took a man such as yourself and put him into a sack!"

fourth *kelippa* is alluded to by the words "an aura [*noga*] surrounding it," indicating that this *kelippa* is not entirely dark but contains a glimmer of light.[1]

The *kelippa* of *noga*, literally, "the glowing husk," is not as gross as the other husks, yet it is a husk nonetheless. By way of analogy, some fruits come encased in a double covering: a tough outer shell that is completely unfit for consumption and a finer, inner rind that can, with the proper preparation, be eaten. That is the nature of *kelippat noga*, a *kelippa* from which some good can be extracted. ☞

שֶׁבָּעוֹלָם הַזֶּה הַנִּקְרָא עוֹלַם הָעֲשִׂיָּה - רוּבּוֹ כְּכוּלּוֹ רַע, רַק מְעַט טוֹב מְעוֹרָב בְּתוֹכָהּ

In this physical **world, referred to as the world of *Asiya*,** the *kelippa* of *noga* **is mostly evil, apart from a modicum of good intermingled within it**

The *kelippa* of *noga* is the luminescent husk, a veil of darkness that nevertheless contains a glimmer of light. It is a *kelippa* that is not entirely evil but also has some good in it. ☞

THE DESIRE FOR THE PERMITTED

☞ The desire associated with *kelippat noga*, such as the desire to eat kosher meat, is described in the next chapter as a "Jewish demon." By contrast, the desire to eat pork is a "foreign demon," a desire associated with the three impure *kelippot.* Even the Jewish demon, the lust for what is kosher and permitted, is *kelippa.* It is not decidedly evil, but for that very reason it is even more difficult to overcome. Distinguishing between that which is permitted and that which is prohibited is easier than distinguishing between holiness and *kelippa* within the sphere of the permitted. A person can do everything he is obligated to do and avoid every prohibition and still, without realizing it, be immersed in *kelippa* all his life.

THE GOOD ELEMENT

☞ The extent of the good that the *kelippa* of *noga* contains varies in the four worlds that constitute the phases by which our material world devolved. In the highest link of the chain, the world of *Atzilut*, the *kelippa* is entirely good. In the world of *Beria*, it is mostly good, but something of an obscuring husk has already been formed. In the world of *Yetzira*, it is equal parts light and darkness, while in our world of *Asiya*, it is virtually dark, manifesting but the faintest glimmer of divine light.

1. See also chap. 6, where this description from Ezekiel's vision is discussed.

[שֶׁמִּמֶּנָּה בָּאוֹת מִדּוֹת טוֹבוֹת שֶׁבְּנֶפֶשׁ הַבַּהֲמִית שֶׁבְּיִשְׂרָאֵל, כְּמוֹ שֶׁנִּתְבָּאֵר לְעֵיל].

(from which stem the positive attributes that are in the animal soul of a Jew, as explained above [chap. 1]**).**

As the author of the *Tanya* discussed above, the Jewish people possess the traits of bashfulness, compassion, and kindheartedness. These traits do not stem from their divine souls but rather are intrinsic to their nature, deriving from the animal soul. Just as a certain family or race might pass down the trait of aggression or a talent for writing poetry to its members, the Jew possesses these traits as a part of his natural, genealogical composition and not as a result of the holiness of his divine soul. ☞

וְהִיא בְּחִינָה מְמוּצַּעַת בֵּין שָׁלֹשׁ קְלִיפּוֹת הַטְּמֵאוֹת לְגַמְרֵי וּבֵין בְּחִינַת וּמַדְרֵגַת הַקְּדוּשָּׁה, וְלָכֵן פְּעָמִים שֶׁהִיא נִכְלֶלֶת בְּשָׁלֹשׁ קְלִיפּוֹת הַטְּמֵאוֹת [כְּמוֹ שֶׁכָּתוּב בְּעֵץ חַיִּים שַׁעַר מ"ט רֵישׁ פֶּרֶק ד' בְּשֵׁם הַזֹּהַר], וּפְעָמִים שֶׁהִיא

***Kelippat noga* is the intermediate category between the three completely impure *kelippot* and the category and level of holiness. Consequently, at times it is incorporated in the three impure *kelippot* (as stated in *Etz Ĥayyim* 49, beginning of chapter 4, citing the *Zohar*), and at times it is**

THE POSITIVE TRAITS OF THE ANIMAL SOUL

☞ Citing the verse "Who teaches us through the animals of the earth and makes us wiser from the birds of the sky?" (Job 35:11), the Talmud explains (*Eiruvin* 106b) that we could have learned certain positive traits – modesty from the cat, respect for another person's property from the ant, and so on – from animals had the Torah not been given. In a certain sense, the positive traits of a Jew's animal soul can be compared to the positive traits of these animals. However, the modesty of the cat (evident by the way it covers its excrement) is not a result of the cat's awareness of the divine omnipresence impelling it to modesty. It is part of the cat's immutable nature. By the same token, one might learn the practice of *netilat yadayim* (ritual washing of the hands) from the raccoon, which appears to wash its hands in water before eating, but the raccoon does not do this because it is mandated by the *Shulḥan Arukh*. This is not a practice deriving from the divine soul's desire to fulfill God's will but rather an inherited characteristic in the nature of the particular animal. In a certain sense, the good traits that mark the Jewish nation are like the good traits of these animals.

נִכְלֶלֶת וְעוֹלָה בִּבְחִינַת וּמַדְרֵגַת הַקְּדוּשָּׁה.

incorporated in and elevated to the category and level of holiness.

Note the precise terminology used here. The author of the *Tanya* does not say that the *kelippa* of *noga* is the intermediate category between impurity and holiness but rather between "the three completely impure *kelippot*" and the "category and level of holiness." By definition, that which is not holy is *kelippa* and impure. A thing is either one or the other, and there is no intermediate level between holiness and *kelippa*. The *kelippa* of *noga* is an intermediate level not because it contains both holy and unholy elements but only in the sense that the elements in its domain can be transferred from one side to the other. A person may, with the proper preparation and focused action, elevate that which is in the domain of *kelippat noga* to the "category and level of holiness."

In light of this, the difference between the *kelippat noga* and the three impure *kelippot* lies in the potential of those elements that are in the province of *kelippat noga* to be rectified by man and thus redirected and transferred to the province of holiness. That which is in the realm of the three impure *kelippot*, on the other hand, is off-limits to such efforts and entirely unrectifiable.

דְּהַיְינוּ כְּשֶׁהַטּוֹב הַמְעוֹרָב בָּהּ נִתְבָּרֵר מֵהָרַע וְגוֹבֵר וְעוֹלֶה וְנִכְלָל בַּקְּדוּשָּׁה.

That is, when the good intermingled within it is distilled from the evil and overpowers that evil, it then **ascends and becomes incorporated in** the level of **holiness.**

The elevation of the *kelippat noga* to the level of holiness is achieved by extracting the good implicit within it. Extracting the good means, first of all, achieving a distinction between good and evil, because in the realm of *kelippat noga*, the boundary between good and evil is blurred, which leaves room for error. The next stage, after defining what is good and what is evil, is to intensify the good so that it separates from the evil and ascends to the level of holiness.

כְּגוֹן דֶּרֶךְ מָשָׁל, הָאוֹכֵל בִּשְׂרָא שְׁמֵינָא דְּתוֹרָא וְשׁוֹתֶה יַיִן

For example, to illustrate: One who consumes marbled beef and drinks

מְבוּשָּׂם, לְהַרְחִיב דַּעְתּוֹ לַה׳ וּלְתוֹרָתוֹ, **spiced wine to expand one's mind for** the service of **God and His Torah,**

For every individual, there are certain conditions, dictated by his particular nature, that enable him to make the most of his potential. When a person is hungry or thirsty, or experiencing some bodily or psychological torment, his ability to function is obviously impaired. But some individuals require special foods, things commonly regarded as luxuries, for their peace of mind. If they lack these things, their concentration and clarity of mind are adversely affected.

כִּדְאָמַר רָבָא: ״חַמְרָא וְרֵיחָא״ כו׳, **as Rava said, "Wine and good scents** make me wise" (*Yoma* 76b),

The effect that these ostensible luxuries had on Rava was to open his mind to Torah study. A person such as Rava, who was extremely sensitive so that even something minor disturbed him to the extent that he could not continue studying Torah, can "eat marbled beef and drink spiced wine" and elevate them to holiness, since he does this in order to "expand his mind [for the service of] God and His Torah."

This extreme example illustrates the extent to which proper intentions can elevate elements that are in and of themselves *kelippa*. The person is not only partaking of the material world but of luxuries, of things that are not meant to serve the body's basic needs but whose only purpose is to give pleasure. Yet because he is doing this for a particular and expressly intended goal, for the purpose of serving God, he raises these elements to the level of holiness. ☞

KELIPPA OF *NOGA* IN THE SERVICE OF HEAVEN

☞ Obviously, a person does not have carte blanche to indulge in every pleasure with the justification that it is to "expand his mind for [the service of] God and His Torah." For an act to elevate a material substance to holiness, it must be permeated with an awareness that is both thorough and constant. If the performance of a mitzva requires acute awareness and focused intent, this is even more crucial when attending to one's mundane business. When it comes to a mitzva, the act itself is holy, so the awareness and intent that must accompany it are mainly to prevent one's thoughts from getting distracted. But in the case of non-mitzva activities, the awareness and intent themselves sanctifiy the act. If eating and drinking are to have holy significance, they require an active elevation into the realm of holiness.

או בִּשְׁבִיל כְּדֵי לְקַיֵּם מִצְוַת עֹנֶג שַׁבָּת וְיוֹם טוֹב,

or in order to fulfill the commandment of delighting in the Sabbath and festivals,

Eating three meals on the Sabbath may be a mitzva and a holy act in itself, but intent plays a crucial role in elevating the food to the realm of holiness. The mitzva entails delighting in the Sabbath, not simply experiencing physical pleasure. If a person who indulges in meat and fine wine without a constant awareness and intent that the enjoyment he is experiencing is for the sake of the Sabbath rather than for the pleasure of filling his stomach, it remains a pleasure for the stomach and does not ascend to holiness.

A person eats and enjoys his food because it is his nature, as a biological creature, to eat. In this sense, he is no different from other animals, regardless of his advanced level of development. The point of transfer to holiness, the point at which a person truly differs from other creatures, depends on his awareness: Why am I doing this? What is the significance of my actions? Eating is unequivocally a permitted act, but a person who eats for himself, who is thinking only of his own pleasure, belongs at that moment to *kelippa*. He has not transcended his material and biological nature. To emerge from that realm to that which is holy requires more than cleverness and feeling good. Holiness is not cleverness nor a feeling of inspiration. Holiness is attachment to God.

In the realm of holiness, there is no concept or sense of self, only self-abnegation. The person who negates himself before God and cleaves to Him transfers himself and everything in his life into the realm of holiness. A person – any person – who does not do so belongs to the other side, to the *sitra aḥara*. If the eating is intended to serve as an instrument of holiness, then not only the food but even the pleasure it provides become part of what ascends to the Divine, to God Himself.

אֲזַי נִתְבָּרֵר חַיּוּת הַבָּשָׂר וְהַיַּיִן שֶׁהָיָה נִשְׁפָּע מִקְּלִיפַּת נוֹגַהּ וְעוֹלֶה לַה׳ כְּעוֹלָה וּכְקָרְבָּן.

then the life force within **the meat and the wine, which stem from the *kelippa* of *noga*, will become distilled** from the evil **and will** then **ascend to God like a sacrificial offering.**

An offering to God is something that is taken from the domain of the ordinary and nonholy and elevated to the realm of holiness. In this sense, any ordinary act involving a mundane object that is done with the intent of elevating it to the realm of holiness is an offering, since it elevates a mundane resource and makes it a part of the holy realm, like the sacrifices that were offered in the Temple. An act of eating may not be intrinsically holy (when it is not a mitzva act), but it is *mutar*, permitted and "unbound" to the realm of *kelippa*, and is therefore freely transportable by the intent of the person to wherever he directs it, whether to holiness or impurity. ☞

וְכֵן הָאוֹמֵר מִילְתָא דִבְדִיחוּתָא לְפַקֵּחַ דַּעְתּוֹ וּלְשַׂמֵּחַ לִבּוֹ לַה' וּלְתוֹרָתוֹ וַעֲבוֹדָתוֹ,

The same applies to one who says something humorous in order to sharpen his mind and make his heart rejoice for God, His Torah, and His service,

Even something that appears to be closer to the realm of evil than eating, such as telling a joke, can be an offering to God. If a person tells a joke for his own enjoyment, because he cannot resist displaying his wit, then his act indeed belongs to a very lowly *kelippa*. But if he does it

REFINEMENT AND ELEVATION

☞ When a person performs a mitzva, his awareness and intent affect only the quality of the mitzva but not the very fact that it is a mitzva. A mitzva by definition is an act that constitutes the fulfillment of a divine command, an act that is inherently and objectively holy, regardless of the performer's intent. But in the case of an act that is not in itself a mitzva, such as eating an ordinary meal, the holiness of the act depends on intent. Without the appropriate intent, it has no holiness and is pure *kelippa*. Moreover, the higher the level of the intent, the greater its honesty and sincerity, the higher the level of holiness the act achieves, until it reaches such a high level that it is equivalent to a sacrifice offered in the Temple.

The Talmud states (*Ḥagiga* 27a) that when the Temple existed, the altar atoned for a person, and now that the Temple is gone, a person's table atones for him. Hence the custom to place salt on the table as a reminder of the salt that was brought with every offering. Likewise, it is customary to remove the knives from the table before the Grace after Meals because the altar's purpose was to prolong a person's life span by providing atonement, while a knife shortens a person's life span (see *Shulḥan Arukh HaRav, Oraḥ Ḥayyim* 167:8, 180:6). Yet for the table to atone, placing salt on it is not sufficient. One must maintain a constant, active awareness that one is eating for the sake of Heaven.

for God, to raise his spirits and open his heart the better to serve Him, and he is conscious of this at the time, he elevates the very words of the joke to a level of holiness.

שֶׁצְּרִיכִים לִהְיוֹת בְּשִׂמְחָה, **which must be** done **with joy,**

In addition to the pragmatic performance of a mitzva, it must be accompanied by joy. Extraordinary things have been said, by both the talmudic Rabbis and later sages, with regard to the virtue of engaging in Torah study and the performance of mitzvot with joy. In several places, the author of the *Tanya* cites the novel interpretation suggested by the Arizal regarding the verse stated in the context of the punishments that would be incurred if the people failed to serve God: "Because you did not serve the Lord your God with joy and with gladness of heart, due to the abundance of everything" (Deut. 28:47).[2] He explains that the verse must be understood on a deeper level than its simple meaning that the punishments befell the Jewish people because they failed to serve God while in a state of happiness and complacency. The verse also means that although the Jews performed the mitzvot, they failed to do so with joy.

The Arizal adds that the end of the verse, "due to the abundance of everything," teaches that the joy one must have while serving God ought to exceed the joy felt in every other context in one's life.[3] The significance inherent in the joy involved in performing a mitzva is related to the way the person becomes a veritable partner with the One who commanded the mitzva, not only in the person's fulfillment itself but in both the intention and spiritual virtues. He not only rejoices in his personal joy, but in the joy of God, as it were. ☞

THE VIRTUE OF JOY

☞ It is said in the name of many hasidic masters that there is something that is not listed in the Torah as a sin yet is worse than any sin, and there is something that

2. See chap, 26 below; see also *Shenei Luḥot HaBerit,* citing the Arizal; Rambam, *Sefer Zemanim,* end of *Hilkhot Lulav.*
3. See *Shemoneh She'arim* 7, p. 10b.

וּכְמוֹ שֶׁעָשָׂה רָבָא לְתַלְמִידָיו, שֶׁאָמַר לִפְנֵיהֶם מִילְּתָא דִּבְדִיחוּתָא תְּחִלָּה - וּבָדְחֵי רַבָּנָן.

as Rava demonstrated for his disciples by first saying something humorous to them, and the students would be cheered.

The Talmud relates that it was Rava's custom to preface his discourse with a joke, and after his disciples had laughed in merriment, he would wrap himself in his *tallit* and begin teaching them in a most solemn and awe-inspiring manner.[4] Precisely because he wanted them to absorb the words of Torah with awe and reverence, he felt the need to first lighten the atmosphere with a witticism and clear away the cobwebs of mundane worries and heavy-heartedness. The students were then able to approach the Torah lesson with true awe and fear of Heaven.

When this is the way a joke is employed, it is possible for even a joke to be a holy matter. The same applies to every permissible act, word, or thought. If a person's intention is to serve God, he is taking something that belonged to the realm of *kelippa* and elevating it to the realm of holiness. ☞

is technically not a mitzva yet is greater than all mitzvot. Nowhere does the Torah expressly forbid sadness and depression, yet this is the most virulent of sins since it stifles the heart and mind, closing them to the service of God. Neither is joy an express mitzva but it is the greatest of mitzvot, because it opens a person's heart and mind, enabling him to perform all the mitzvot and to make a mitzva of everything.

The Talmud relates (*Ta'anit* 22a) that Rabbi Beroka was often found in the marketplace, and Elijah the prophet would often appear to him. Once, Rabbi Beroka asked Elijah, "Is there anyone in this market worthy of the World to Come?" Elijah answered no. As they spoke, two men entered the marketplace, and Elijah said that these two were worthy. Rabbi Beroka ran after them and asked what their profession was. They told him that they were jesters, and their job was to cheer up the downhearted. This is what made them worthy of the World to Come.

4. See *Shabbat* 30b.

5 Tevet
9 Tevet (leap year)

אַךְ מִי שֶׁהוּא בְּזוֹלְלֵי בָשָׂר וְסוֹבְאֵי יַיִן לְמַלֹּאת תַּאֲוַת גּוּפוֹ וְנַפְשׁוֹ הַבַּהֲמִית, שֶׁהוּא בְּחִינַת יְסוֹד הַמַּיִם מֵאַרְבַּע יְסוֹדוֹת הָרָעִים שֶׁבָּהּ, שֶׁמִּמֶּנּוּ מִדַּת הַתַּאֲוָה,

However, someone who is among those who devour meat and guzzle wine to satisfy the lusts of his body and animal soul, behavior **that embodies the element of water,** one **of the four evil elements in** the animal soul, **from which the trait of lust originates,**

As the author of the *Tanya* discussed above,[5] the animal soul comprises four elements, corresponding to the four elements of fire, air, water, and earth. The element of water in the animal soul is the source of lust, desire that is not directed to a higher goal but is an end in itself, desire

DIVINE SERVICE IN THE REALM OF *KELIPPAT NOGA*

☞ A certain tzaddik said that it is easier to study an entire tractate of Talmud than to eat a single meal. When navigating one's way through the Talmud, the boundaries are clearly marked, and one walks along a well-trodden and well-defined path. Eating is far more complicated, requiring a concentrated effort, a perpetual awareness of what one is doing. It is not only harder work than studying Torah or performing a mitzva but also more dangerous because one is involved with *kelippa*, with the other side.

Granted, elevating material things and mundane acts to holiness is a lofty endeavor, but if one should fail to do so, if he does not infuse it with the proper intent and awareness, his act remains in the realm of *kelippa*. Not only will it not be holy, but it will be an impure act. Whatever a person does unthinkingly, without conscious intent, automatically belongs to the realm of unholiness, and the neutral state of *kelippat noga* is transferred to the realm of impurity.

The other categories of *kelippa* may be lowlier than that of *kelippat noga*, but there is a negative aspect to the *kelippa of noga* that does not exist even in the utterly impure *kelippot*: the feeling of dejection when something that could have been elevated has been degraded into something even worse, that a human being who possesses the potential to attain holiness could end up being no more than an intelligent ape. To avoid that feeling of disappointment, a person's every deed, his every bite of food, and his every experience of pleasure must be governed by a conscious endeavor to direct it toward holiness.

Can this degree of awareness and control be demanded of every person? The author of the *Tanya* insists that, yes, this is humanly possible. This is the essence of the

5. Chap. 1.

for the sake of the pleasure that comes from the fulfillment of desire. Lust itself is *kelippa,* even if the desired object is not prohibited. The desire for it is negative if it has no higher objective than self-satiation. Thus the food a person consumes only to satisfy his lust remains in *kelippa* and cannot ascend to the side of holiness.

הִנֵּה עַל יְדֵי זֶה יוֹרֵד חַיּוּת הַבָּשָׂר וְהַיַּיִן שֶׁבְּקִרְבּוֹ וְנִכְלָל לְפִי שָׁעָה בְּרַע גָּמוּר שֶׁבְּשָׁלֹשׁ קְלִיפּוֹת הַטְּמֵאוֹת,

then due to this the life force of the meat and wine that is now **inside** this person's body **descends and is temporarily incorporated in the utter evil of the three impure *kelippot.***

The vital essence of permitted food derives from *kelippat noga,* but when a person eats merely to satisfy his desire for food, he degrades himself, as well as the food he has eaten, to the level of the utterly impure *kelippot.* In this sense, he descends even lower than the food itself. A man who, possessing the potential to transcend the level of an animal, chooses to eat like an animal is worse than the animal, which

beinoni, around whom the book revolves. By no means is it easy, but it is within the realm of the possible for every individual. A person does not have to be an exceptional human being in order to achieve this level. But it involves a constant effort of unceasing awareness that whatever one does must be toward this aim. The higher the degree of awareness, the higher the levels of holiness one can attain.

The Midrash relates (*Midrash Talpiyot,* s.v. "Ḥanokh") that Ḥanokh, the father of Mehuselah, sewed leather into shoes, and with each stitch he would say, "Blessed is the name of His glorious kingdom forever and ever." This statement of the Midrash has many levels of meaning, the most basic of which is that when an ordinary shoemaker, a simple man engaged in the mundane pursuits of material life, dedicates each and every stitch for the sake of Heaven, he becomes an angel in his lifetime (as is told of Ḥanokh, who was taken to Heaven alive). After all, he is living like an angel already, even in this world. The materiality of the world is transparent to him; he sees through it to its divine function.

Stories are told of individuals who led such an existence, whose every movement was filled with focused intent as they channeled every deed, word, and thought heavenward. Such service of God is not the exclusive prerogative of the tzaddik, but pertains to everyone, even if not as fully. Everyone can attain a certain degree of awareness of his individual existence and direct it to the service of God.

can only be what it is, and he imposes this sub-animal status upon the flesh of the animal that he has eaten.

וְגוּפוֹ נַעֲשֶׂה לָהֶן לְבוּשׁ וּמֶרְכָּבָה,

This person's **body becomes a garment and vehicle for** the forces of evil,

One who eats and drinks merely to satisfy his bodily desires, or acts similarly in other respects, becomes a vehicle, an instrument and expression, for the forces of evil. ☞

לְפִי שָׁעָה, עַד אֲשֶׁר יָשׁוּב הָאָדָם וְיַחֲזוֹר לַעֲבוֹדַת ה׳ וּלְתוֹרָתוֹ, כִּי לְפִי שֶׁהָיָה בְּשַׂר הֶיתֵּר וְיַיִן כָּשֵׁר, לָכֵן יְכוֹלִים לַחֲזוֹר וְלַעֲלוֹת עִמּוֹ בְּשׁוּבוֹ לַעֲבוֹדַת ה׳.

at least **temporarily, until the person repents and returns to the service of God and His Torah. Since the meat was permitted and the wine was kosher, therefore they are able to return and ascend with him** to a state of holiness, **when he returns to the service of God.**

The meat one eats and the wine one drinks, even if not for the sake of serving God, become part of his body, part of the vital force that empowers him to function and achieve. When he subsequently engages in Torah study and mitzvot, he does this with the body and the energy that the meat and wine generate.

SITTING IN THE PLATE

☞ It is told of Rabbi Yissachar Dov Ber Baron, famously known as the Sabba Kaddisha of Radoshitz, that in his youth, before he became a Rebbe, he was terribly poor and often had nothing to eat. One year, when he had eaten nothing from Yom Kippur until the day before Sukkot, his wife sold a piece of her jewelry and bought candles, ḥalla, and potatoes for the festival. When he saw the candles and challa on his return from the synagogue, he was very happy, recited the *Kiddush*, washed his hands, and sat down to eat.

Being very hungry, he ate ravenously, until he suddenly stopped and chastised himself, "Berel, you are not sitting in the *sukka* but in the plate!"

Someone can be tending to the most basic needs of his body, and may even have the intent of observing the mitzva of eating in the *sukka*, yet still be "sitting" in the dish and not in the mitzva.

Thus, when a person elevates himself to the realm of holiness, all that has sustained his life is elevated along with him. Just as he previously served as a garment and vehicle for *kelippa* when he ingested the food like an animal, he can now revert to being a garment and vehicle for holiness, redirecting the material substances he had previously ingested to serve his Torah study, prayer, and performance of mitzvot. This can be done even though he did not ingest those substances for this purpose, provided that the food was permissible for consumption.

שֶׁזֶּהוּ לְשׁוֹן הֶיתֵּר וּמֻתָּר, כְּלוֹמַר שֶׁאֵינוֹ קָשׁוּר וְאָסוּר בִּידֵי הַחִיצוֹנִים, שֶׁלֹּא יוּכַל לַחֲזוֹר וְלַעֲלוֹת לַה׳.

This is the meaning of the Hebrew **expressions for permitted, *heter*** **and *mutar*,** literally "unbound." That is, the consumed food **is neither tied nor bound by the power of the external forces** of impurity, **so that it would not be able to return and ascend to God.**

AN EARTHLY ANALOGY

☞ The difference between the permitted and the prohibited is between what can and what cannot be separated from *kelippa*. By way of analogy, minerals are found in nature in various forms and compounds. Some can be used as they are. Some require extraction, processing, and refinement. Others cannot be used at all, because the useful element cannot be extracted from its ore. The latter are analogous to things that are *assur*, forbidden and bound by Torah law. A halakhic ruling on whether something is prohibited or permitted determines whether it is bound forever to the domain of *kelippa* or whether it is unbound and extractable.

This explains why there are so many more halakhic prohibitions nowadays than there were in earlier periods, such as in the time of the Talmud. One certainly cannot say that the talmudic scholars ate forbidden food and that only we eat what is kosher. Permitted and prohibited are functions of our capacity to extract the positive essence of a thing from its impure embodiment. A lesser person has a lesser capacity, so for him there are fewer things that can be elevated and set free from the bounds of *kelippa*. The lower the spiritual stature of a generation, the more things are prohibited to it. The greater a person is, the greater his capacity to elevate things that lie in the twilight zone that borders on the forbidden.

But particularly in this zone, one must exercise extreme caution. The relationship

The permissible is that which is not bound to *kelippa*, that which can be freed and separated from *kelippa*. The permissible may serve as an instrument of *kelippa*, as a vehicle of expression for evil, but it is not bound to it and is always free to move and change direction from the realm of the impure to that of the holy and vice versa. For this reason, although a person who lives like an animal, only to satisfy his desires, becomes a part of the realm of *kelippa*, he can subsequently transfer himself and all his eating, drinking, and other worldly pleasures to the realm of holiness. ☞

רַק שֶׁהָרְשִׁימוּ מִמֶּנּוּ נִשְׁאָר בַּגּוּף, **However, a trace** of evil still **remains in the body.**

When a person eats like an animal, for no other purpose than to sustain his physical existence, he belongs to the other side, to the universal

between one who influences and one who is influenced is never one-sided. When a person eats, he transforms the food, and the food transforms him. When a person tells a joke, the joke has an effect on the one who told it. The more ambiguous the line between the permissible and the prohibited, the greater the danger that instead of the person elevating the object or force with which he involves himself, the object or force will drag him down.

The greatest people of history are no exception. Rabbi Elazar ben Arakh, of whom the Talmud attests, "If all the sages of Israel were on one side of a balance scale, and Rabbi Elazar ben Arakh on the other, he would outweigh them all" (Mishna *Avot* 2:8), is also reputed to have forgotten all his learning because he pursued a life of luxury. Not that he became involved in anything that was definitively prohibited, but he indulged in Phrygian wine and Roman baths, which, although permitted, can be dangerous (*Shabbat* 147b).

All influence is bilateral, and the more a person is involved with a particular thing, the more he is drawn to it, so that he often fails to maintain the approach to it that he had when he first began his involvement. We say of God, "You extend Your hand to sinners" (*Amida* of *Ne'ila*), because only God can extend a hand to an iniquitous person without the risk of being sullied by the contact. The problem with all contact with *kelippa* is that a relationship is never one-sided: The influenced influences, and the influencer is influenced.

Due to these dangers, safety fences, in the form of ordinances and rabbinic prohibitions, must be established. The need for these fences varies. In times past, many things in the twilight zone of *kelippat noga* had to be declared out of bounds. At other times, the spiritual state of the generation was such that they could involve themselves with matters that were on the border of holiness and still remain within the realm of the holy.

order of the profane. At that moment (or hour or day), he is part of the other, nonholy world. This moment creates a vacuum in his holy existence, a vacuum that leaves its mark even when he subsequently returns to the service of God. The lapse can be put right, the wound can be healed, but the scar it leaves behind can never be erased, or, at least, only with great difficulty. Practically everything can be repaired – a broken dish can be fixed, a torn limb reattached – but it is much more difficult, if not impossible, to remove all traces of the fact that, sometime in the past, something had been in a state of disrepair.

וְעַל כֵּן צָרִיךְ הַגּוּף לְחִיבּוּט הַקֶּבֶר, כְּמוֹ שֶׁיִּתְבָּאֵר לְקַמָּן.

Therefore, the body requires torments of the grave, as will be explained below (chap. 8).

A dead body is a primary source of impurity, yet the Sages say that the bodies of the righteous do not contaminate.[6] The source of impurity does not lie in the human body itself but is generated in the course of a person's lifetime. Every mundane act, each bite of food or uttered word that is not intended for a holy purpose, even if later elevated to holiness, leaves its imprint on the body. In the words of the prophet Ezekiel, "Their iniquities are upon their bones" (Ezek. 32:27). This residue of *kelippa* that accumulates in the body must eventually be cleansed. A bucket used to carry out slops can be emptied, cleaned, and used for other purposes, but when it is used time and again, the grime and stench become absorbed in its walls, and it must be thoroughly scoured before it can be reused. The "torments of the grave" is this scouring. ☞

וְכֵן הַחַיּוּת שֶׁבְּטִפּוֹת זֶרַע שֶׁיָּצְאוּ מִמֶּנּוּ בְּתַאֲוָה בַּהֲמִית, שֶׁלֹּא קִדֵּשׁ עַצְמוֹ בִּשְׁעַת תַּשְׁמִישׁ עִם אִשְׁתּוֹ טְהוֹרָה.

Likewise, this applies to **the life force that is within the drops of semen that emitted from the body in** a state of **animal lust, when one did not sanctify himself during intercourse** even **with his** ritually **pure wife.**

6. See *Zohar* 1:268b; *Midrash Mishlei* 9; *Yalkut Shimoni* 544. This also bears halakhic relevance, since it pertains to the question of whether the graves of the righteous transmit impurity; see *Shulḥan Arukh, Yoreh De'a* 372; *Pitḥei Teshuva, Yoreh De'a* 372:2.

Like eating, this is a permissible act, done when one's wife was in a pure state. Yet if its sole purpose is the satisfaction of one's physical desires, this too is an act that belongs to *kelippa*.

Thus far, the author of the *Tanya* has explored the permissible realm of *kelippat noga*. Now he will examine the garments of the animal soul – thought, speech, and action – that are found in the forbidden realm of the utterly impure *kelippot*.

מַה שֶׁאֵין כֵּן בְּמַאֲכָלוֹת אֲסוּרוֹת וּבִיאוֹת אֲסוּרוֹת, שֶׁהֵן מִשָּׁלֹשׁ קְלִפּוֹת הַטְּמֵאוֹת לְגַמְרֵי, הֵם אֲסוּרִים וּקְשׁוּרִים בִּידֵי הַחִיצוֹנִים לְעוֹלָם וְאֵין עוֹלִים מִשָּׁם

This is not the case with regard to prohibited foods and forbidden acts of **sexual intercourse, which stem from the three completely impure** ***kelippot*** and **are** therefore **forever bound and tied to the external forces** of impurity **and never ascend from there**

The "external forces" refers to the other side, that which is neither holy nor a true expression of God's inner will in His world. An object that is *assur*, prohibited – literally, "bound" – is something that cannot break free of its connection with the other side. When a person is tied to the other side, the realm of the external forces, through a permitted act, he can be released from there, as explained above. The possibility of severing this bond and attaining a connection with holiness belongs only to the permitted, which is freely transportable from level to level by the way in which one uses it. But that which is prohibited remains profane. If a person eats a forbidden food, deliberately or accidentally, it remains bound to the other side, regardless of the person's intentions and subsequent actions. A pig

THE TORMENTS OF THE GRAVE

☞ The "torments of the grave" (referring to the angels' beating of one's body after his burial) refers to one of the stages in a process that the body and soul undergo after death in order to scour and purge them of the mundane life lived in this world. The torments of the grave specifically serve to scour the body because the traces of physical lusts remain in the body – the soul's vessel or container in this world – while it is quite possible that no vestige of one's former lusts remain in the remorseful inner recesses of the soul that repented.

remains a pig and cannot be converted into something pure and permissible. ☞

עַד כִּי יָבוֹא יוֹמָם וִיבוּלַּע הַמָּוֶת לָנֶצַח, כְּמוֹ שֶׁכָּתוּב: "וְאֶת רוּחַ הַטֻּמְאָה אַעֲבִיר מִן הָאָרֶץ" (זכריה יג, ב),	**until their day** of release **arrives and death will be eliminated for all eternity, as it is written, "And I will remove the spirit of impurity from the land"** (Zech. 13:2),

One cannot rectify that which is prohibited by having the intent that one is performing the act for the sake of Heaven. The prohibition is bound to evil by definition, and its rectification involves the uprooting of evil from its source. This will occur at the end of time, when God will transform the essence of the entire world so that evil will disappear from existence. Only then, when "I will remove the spirit of impurity from the land," will everything – even those things that were "bound" to utter evil – be rectified.

אוֹ עַד שֶׁיַּעֲשֶׂה תְּשׁוּבָה גְּדוֹלָה כָּל כָּךְ שֶׁזְּדוֹנוֹת נַעֲשׂוּ לוֹ כִּזְכֻיּוֹת מַמָּשׁ,	**or until one achieves such** a **great** level of **repentance to the extent that his intentional sins actually become like merits for him.**

There is one exception to the rule that the positive essence buried within those objects and acts that are expressly prohibited by the Torah cannot be extracted by man. The exception is *teshuva*, repentance, which, at its highest level, has the power to elevate elements that derive from the three utterly impure *kelippot* to holiness.

MITZVOT AND TRANSGRESSIONS: ONE DOES NOT OFFSET THE OTHER

☞ What is prohibited remains *kelippa* even if a person uses it to perform a mitzva. A mitzva is a mitzva, and a transgression is a transgression, and one cannot be offset against the other. A person cannot align his transgressions and mitzvot as two columns of figures that amount to a deficit or surplus of virtue. Each occurs on a different plane and has its effect on the person regardless of what transpires on the other plane. A virtuous act does not reduce the negativity of a sinful act that preceded it, nor is it reduced by it. So even the most wicked of the wicked, even a heretic or an apostate, is duty bound to fulfill every commandment of the Torah.

The Talmud speaks of two levels of repentance: a level on which one's intentional sins are regarded as unintentional sins and a higher level where one's intentional sins are regarded as merits.[7] On the first level, a person's sins, even if done deliberately, are regarded as no more than mistakes. One of the explanations of this phenomenon, given in the name of the Ba'al Shem Tov, is that when a person repents, he attains a higher level of awareness. He now knows what he did not know previously, so that a deed that may have been considered intentional according to his previous state of mind is now a deed bereft of knowledge and understanding in his current state of awareness.

The Sages say that "a man commits a transgression only if a spirit of folly enters him" (*Sota* 3a). A penitent is someone who cures himself of this insanity, who now realizes that he performed his previous actions without a true understanding of their significance. He would not have committed those transgressions if he had attained his current state of awareness. With such repentance, he severs himself from his past and attains a new perspective about himself and his life, about his past and his future.

The second level of repentance involves a much more radical change: It transforms the very essence of the deed. There is not merely a change of awareness regarding the sin but a transformation of the sin into a merit. It is not only a change in the degree of the sin, from deliberate to something less than deliberate, but constitutes its complete reversal into a positive phenomenon.

To achieve this level of repentance, a person has to effect a change in his personal existence that is akin to the universal transformation at the end of days when "I will remove the spirit of impurity from the land." He has to undergo a transformation so drastic that his entire being, and all his deeds and thoughts, acquire a new and different significance. In effect, he passes into a new field of reality, where everything is completely different from what it was.

At this level of repentance, a person elevates to holiness not only the permitted elements of *kelippat noga* but even acts of outright evil. His transgressions are not merely mitigated but are completely transformed

7. *Yoma* 86b.

into good. In this way, what is prohibited and utterly impure can, in certain circumstances, be rectified even before the end of days. ☞

שֶׁהִיא תְּשׁוּבָה מֵאַהֲבָה **This is** achieved through **repentance out of love**

How is such repentance achieved? This higher level of repentance, where transgressions are transformed into merits, must be effected specifically through love, as opposed to standard repentance, which is motivated by one of the various levels of awe and fear.

מֵעוּמְקָא דְלִבָּא **from the depths of the heart,**

The "depths of the heart" refers to what a person truly desires, as opposed to the things he desires only with the more external aspects of the heart. A person might say, "I want to study," "I want to pray," or "I want to perform mitzvot," but that might not be what he truly desires. The depths of the heart is what a person would do if nothing were compelling him to act in any specific way, if he were truly free to do whatever he wishes. Repentance from the depths of the heart is a *teshuva* that reaches to the very core of a person's being, transforming his will all the way down to its deepest essence. In its shallower forms, repentance achieves a change in the garments of the penitent's heart, redirecting some of the expressions of his will. With repentance from the depths of the heart, the very essence of his will is transformed.

TRANSFORMING TRANSGRESSIONS INTO MERITS

☞ One of the most complicated problems in symmetry is to transform something right-handed into its left-handed symmetrical counterpart. Effecting a transformation from one configuration to another is nearly always possible, but transforming right to left involves completely dislodging the thing from its coordinates and reversing it. The only way to turn a right-hand glove into a left-hand glove is to turn it inside out. The transformation from *kelippa* to holiness, from deliberate sin to virtue, likewise involves turning everything in one's personal world completely inside out.

Another analogy is the reversal of clay under the seal (see Job 38:14), where there is a reversal from left to right, from engraving to embossing. This is the mystical concept of the seal referred to in kabbalistic writings, the mystical concept of inversion.

בְּאַהֲבָה רַבָּה **with a great love,**

Ahava rabba, "a great love," is love that is greater than life and before which life itself pales into insignificance. This love is greater than any love of this world, greater than reality. It is the soul's striving for the essence of God that transcends creation, the soul's yearning to dissolve its very being within God, its Father, as He is in essence.[8]

וַחֲשִׁיקָה וְנֶפֶשׁ שׁוֹקֵקָה לְדָבְקָה בּוֹ יִתְבָּרֵךְ. **longing, and a soul yearning to cleave to God.**

The love of God that this level of repentance requires constitutes the longing and yearning of the soul to cleave to God in the same way that a person craves material things, with the same fervor that he lusts for physical pleasures. ☞

וְצָמְאָה נַפְשׁוֹ לַה׳ כְּאֶרֶץ עֲיֵפָה וְצִיָּה לִהְיוֹת כִּי עַד הֵנָּה הָיְתָה נַפְשׁוֹ בְּאֶרֶץ צִיָּה וְצַלְמָוֶת, הִיא הַסִּטְרָא אַחֲרָא, וּרְחוֹקָה **One's soul thirsts for God as a parched and thirsty land** thirsts for water, **for until now his soul had been in a thirsty and shadow-ridden land, namely, the** ***sitra aḥara,*** **and had been utterly dis**

A SOUL YEARNING FOR GOD

☞ It is told that Rabbi Levi Yitzḥak of Berditchev was unable to sleep on the first night of Sukkot because of his anticipation of making the blessing on the *etrog*. All night he gazed at the *etrog*, which sat in a glass-paned cabinet, and waited for morning so that he could recite the blessing over it. When morning came, he could wait no longer. He ran to the case, plunged his hand through the glass, and took out the *etrog*, oblivious to the blood streaming from his hand.

It is said that his animal soul had been transformed into a divine soul, that he had a lust for mitzvot in the same way that others lust for worldly pleasures. When a person has a physical desire, he might also lie awake all night with longing and yearning, and he is prepared to crash through glass to satisfy his desire. Such is the love and desire for God on the level of repentance out of love.

---

8. See *Torah Or* 86b, which goes on to state that through such love, which transcends the order of creation, a person transforms his entire nature, negates his very being, and is reborn as an entirely new creature. See *Ma'amarei Admor HaZaken* 5562, p. 222).

מֵאוֹר פְּנֵי ה' בְּתַכְלִית, וְלָזֹאת צָמְאָה נַפְשׁוֹ בְּיֶתֶר עָז מִצִּמָּאוֹן נַפְשׁוֹת הַצַּדִּיקִים, כְּמַאֲמָרָם ז"ל: "בִּמְקוֹם שֶׁבַּעֲלֵי תְשׁוּבָה עוֹמְדִים" כו' (ברכות לד, ב).

tant from the light of God's countenance. That is why his soul possesses a more intense thirst for God **than the thirst of the souls of the righteous, as the Sages state, "In the place where penitents stand,** even the full-fledged righteous do not stand" (*Berakhot* 34b).

The tzaddik too yearns and craves to cleave to God, but the penitent who attains a love for God experiences this desire far more intensely. The tzaddik, who is immersed in holiness all his life and can, at all times, satiate his desire to cleave to God, cannot truly thirst for God. He cannot feel the acute craving that is born of lack. Only one who traverses a spiritually arid land, who knows true thirst, can experience

THE REPENTANCE OF RABBI ELAZAR BEN DURDAYA

☞ The Talmud tells the story of a penitent who is an exemplar of such repentance (*Avoda Zara* 17a). Elazar ben Durdaya was said to have never encountered a harlot without committing a sin with her, until one of them remarked to him that he was beyond repentance. He took her words to heart and decided that he would repent. First, he approached the hills and mountains and said, "Mountains and hills, pray for mercy on my behalf," but they refused. They said to him, "Before we pray for mercy on your behalf, we must pray for mercy on our behalf," as the verse states, "For the mountains will move, and the hills will collapse" (Isa. 54:10).

After receiving similar responses from the heavens and the earth and the sun and the moon, Rabbi Elazar ben Durdaya concluded, "If such is the case, the matter depends solely on myself." He dropped his head between his knees and began to weep, and he wept until his soul departed from his body. A voice from Heaven promptly announced, "Rabbi Elazar ben Durdaya is destined for life in the World to Come."

When Rabbi Yehuda HaNasi heard this story of Rabbi Elazar ben Durdaya, he wept and said, "There are those who acquire their share in the World to Come only after many years of toil, and there are those who acquire their share in the World to Come in a single moment."

Rabbi Elazar ben Durdaya's repentance constituted a return to God out of "great love," which transformed all his sins into merits to the extent that the heavenly voice referred to him as "Rabbi" and proclaimed that he was granted a place in the World to Come. In a single instant, he had created for himself a virtuous life. He had no need to afflict himself for his sins, but rather so great was his anguish that he simply could not continue living. His yearning on the one hand and his sense of lack on the other affected him so deeply that in a single explosive moment, with a single wrenching turnaround, he underwent a complete transformation.

the full intensity of the soul's thirst for God. The penitent's love for God is the product of his distance, the result of his having been in "a thirsty and shadow-ridden land." One who undergoes such repentance, then, has his sins transformed into merits. The very sin he committed, his very disconnection and alienation from God, is what now fuels his greater and more intense love of God.

If a person wants to do *teshuva* simply in order to fulfill his obligation to repent for his sins or to become an accepted member of the community, the rules for this sort of repentance are found in the *Shulḥan Arukh*. On the other hand, repentance of the sort that transforms sins into merits does not give a person any certificate of respectability. On the contrary, it only deepens his awareness of his sins, rousing him to yet a higher level of repentance and a greater yearning to cleave to God. And the lower he sunk in committing the transgression, the greater – by the same ratio – his desire for God.

The higher a dam is built, the greater the pressure of water accumulating behind it. The greater a person's sins, the higher a dam it is, stymieing his soul's desire to cleave to God and increasing its pressure and intensity. The desire for God that in a tzaddik's life finds instant and immediate realization accumulates in the soul of the penitent for ten, twenty, or fifty years of sin, and the pressure of the accumulation of sins is so great that he can never alleviate it, until this unceasing pressure becomes a part of the structure of his soul and is transformed into an incessant striving toward holiness. ☞ ☞

THE REPENTANCE OF KING DAVID

☞ The chapter of Psalms that describes King David's repentance begins with the words "When Natan the prophet came to him after he had been with Bathsheba" (Ps. 51:2). It does not say that Natan came to rebuke him "on account of" his being with Bathsheba but "after" – or, more literally, "when" – he had been with Bathsheba. True repentance entails the craving to return to God with the same intensity, with the same turmoil, as the craving one experienced at the time of his sin. The sin does not become a mitzva as a consequence, but the repentance redirects it to function as a mitzva does: as an impetus to bring the person closer to God.

In the same psalm, David proclaims, "My sin is always before me" (Ps. 51:5). The ultimate rectification of a sin is not to neutralize it, not to remove it as a factor in one's life, but for it to continue to act upon the person. That he sinned continually

וְעַל תְּשׁוּבָה מֵאַהֲבָה רַבָּה זוֹ אָמְרוּ שֶׁזְּדוֹנוֹת נַעֲשׂוּ לוֹ כִּזְכֻיּוֹת, הוֹאִיל וְעַל יְדֵי זֶה בָּא לְאַהֲבָה רַבָּה זוֹ.

It is regarding this level of **repentance out of a great love** of God **that** the Sages **stated that** one's **intentional sins become like merits for him, since it was** specifically **through this** place of distance **that he came to this** level of **great love** of God.

Through this level of repentance, through this endless love and intense yearning, a person's entire life is transformed. His sojourn in the "thirsty and shadow-driven land" has become a lever that lifts him to a more profound awakening and greater closeness to God. All his past failings become the instruments of his attainments in holiness. Such repentance is not merely a good deed to counteract past evil but leads to the employment of the evil in such a way that each past sin is now an impetus to a greater desire and a greater love for God. When intentional sins become the instrument for a love of God that is more powerful than the love of a tzaddik, the very laws of reality are transformed. Evil becomes a force for good; a deliberate sin becomes a merit.

This person has undergone a process akin to that of the end of days.

impels him to attain the highest level of repentance, so that his repentance transcends his previous attempts at repentance.

The sin is like a stain that penetrates many layers. As each layer is peeled away, the next layer is revealed showing that the stain has permeated all the layers above it and penetrated ever deeper. By the same token, after the sin is rectified on one level, one achieves the recognition that it still exists on a deeper, subtler level, and one is driven to achieve yet greater repentance.

The story is told of a peasant who once insulted the king, but because he did not understand the gravity of what he did, he could not be properly punished. He was invited to the palace and given a position in the royal court. He was promoted, gradually rising in rank, and began to appreciate the significance of royalty, the honor due to a king, and the gravity of his offense. As he rose in rank, his appreciation grew. With each higher position he attained came deeper regret over his deed.

By the same token, the higher a person ascends in holiness, the more he comprehends the depth of his sin. The greater his recognition of his sin, the greater its power to elevate him to holiness. Repentance is thus not a onetime act but a perpetual process, and as the penitent attains each higher level of repentance, he understands, each time with greater intensity, how he must begin the process of repentance all over again.

Though he has not brought redemption to the entire world, he achieves redemption in his own private world, removing the "spirit of impurity" from his individual pathway through life.

אֲבָל תְּשׁוּבָה שֶׁלֹּא מֵאַהֲבָה זוֹ, אַף שֶׁהִיא תְּשׁוּבָה נְכוֹנָה וַה׳ יִסְלַח לוֹ, מִכָּל מָקוֹם לֹא נַעֲשׂוּ לוֹ כִּזְכֻיּוֹת,

But repentance that is not done **through this** great **love, although it is proper repentance and God will forgive him, nevertheless** his intentional sins **do not become like merits for him,**

Not everyone merits nor possesses the spiritual capacity to effect such repentance. A person may repent, and God may pardon him for his sins, but his repentance will not necessarily entail the transformation of those sins into merits. As the author of the *Tanya* explains in the first chapter of *Iggeret HaTeshuva*, "The mitzva of repentance [as stipulated] by the Torah consists of no more than abandoning the sin.... That is, one must wholeheartedly decide to never again revert to the folly of rebelling against God's kingship." Such a penitent truly severs himself from his past deeds and is no longer responsible for the evil he has perpetrated in the world. But even if his past can no longer cast a shadow on his present, he cannot transform and sublimate it. The evil deed remains evil and has not been transformed into good.

וְאֵין עוֹלִים מֵהַקְּלִיפָּה לְגַמְרֵי עַד עֵת קֵץ, שֶׁיְּבוּלַּע הַמָּוֶת לָנֶצַח.

and they will not completely ascend from ***kelippa*** **until the end of time, when death,** or evil, **will be eliminated for eternity.**

Only at the end of time, when evil will be obliterated, will every element of creation be rectified: the permissible and the prohibited, the repented sins and the unrepented sins. Until that time, the prohibited and bound remain prohibited and bound. A person can alleviate the gravity of his offense against God by changing his relationship with evil and even setting his iniquitous life on an opposite course, but the evil remains evil. Only repentance done out of such great, driving, and potent love can transform reality in the manner of the messianic era, when death will forever be eradicated.

To illustrate, the author of the *Tanya* now cites an exception to this rule that illuminates the general rule.

6 Tevet

10 Tevet (leap year)

אַךְ הַחַיּוּת שֶׁבְּטִפּוֹת זֶרַע שֶׁיָּצְאוּ מִמֶּנּוּ לְבַטָּלָה, אַף שֶׁיָּרְדָה וְנִכְלְלָה בְּשָׁלֹשׁ קְלִיפּוֹת הַטְּמֵאוֹת, הֲרֵי זוֹ עוֹלָה מִשָּׁם בִּתְשׁוּבָה נְכוֹנָה

However, the life force in the drops of semen that were wastefully emitted from him, although it has descended and become incorporated in the three completely **impure** ***kelippot*****, can nevertheless ascend from there by means of proper repentance**

The wasteful emission of semen is a grave prohibition that, like other prohibitions, causes a descent into the three impure *kelippot*. Nevertheless, this particular sin is the exception to the rule, since the wasted semen can indeed be rescued and released from the clutches of the three *kelippot* through "proper repentance." This type of repentance, though regarded as a higher level of repentance,[9] is not the level of repentance where one's deliberate sins become merits, and it would not suffice for other prohibited (or "bound") acts. This does not mean that someone who transgressed a prohibition has no option to repent, since there is nothing that repentance does not remedy. But a distinction must be drawn between rectification of the sinner and rectification of the illicit act itself. Through ordinary, "proper" repentance, a person may disassociate himself from the onus attached to the sin he committed, yet the forbidden act remains forbidden. The semen absorbed during an illicit act of sexual intercourse, for example, like prohibited food, cannot be released from the grip of the *kelippot* through the level of "proper repentance." The one who sinned can fix himself but not the act; he cannot change the reality of the situation.

וּבְכַוָּונָה עֲצוּמָה בִּקְרִיאַת שְׁמַע שֶׁעַל הַמִּטָּה, כַּנּוֹדָע מֵהָאֲרִ"י ז"ל וּמְרוּמָּז בַּגְּמָרָא: "כָּל הַקּוֹרֵא קְרִיאַת שְׁמַע עַל מִטָּתוֹ כְּאִלּוּ

and by reciting the bedtime ***Shema*** **with intense concentration, as is known from** the teachings of **the Arizal. This is hinted at in the Talmud** (*Berakhot* 5a), which states, **"Anyone who recites the** ***Shema*** **on his,**

9. See *Iggeret HaTeshuva*, chap. 4.

אוֹחֵז חֶרֶב שֶׁל שְׁתֵּי פִּיּוֹת" כוּ' (ברכות ה, א),

bed it is as if he holds a double-edged sword…"

The Talmud goes on to quote the verse "Let the devoted ones exult in honor; let them sing for joy in their beds. Exaltation of the Almighty is in their throats, and a double-edged sword in their hand" (Ps. 149:5–6). Those who not only sing the praises of God in their beds by reciting the *Shema* before retiring for the night, but do so with intense concentration, have a double-edged sword in their hands.[10]

לַהֲרוֹג גּוּפוֹת הַחִיצוֹנִים שֶׁנַּעֲשׂוּ לְבוּשׁ לַחַיּוּת שֶׁבַּטִּפּוֹת, וְעוֹלָה הַחַיּוּת מֵהֶם כַּיָּדוּעַ לְיוֹדְעֵי ח"ן.

with which to slay the bodies of the external forces of impurity **that have become garments for the life force in the drops** of semen. **The life force** then **ascends from them, as is known to those initiated in the esoteric wisdom** of Kabbala.

The Sages teach in reference to the verse "These are the descendants of Noah" (Gen. 6:9) that "a person's descendants are his mitzvot and good deeds" (Rashi). The same is true of his sins and evil deeds. A person generates deeds that translate into realities both good and evil, all of which are his "children." The spiritual essence of a good deed is an angel, a person's emissary on high; the spiritual essence of a sin is a demon, a corrupter and agent of destruction. Angel or demon, they remain bound to him and dependent on him. They pursue him and call after him, "You are our father! You created us, and it is your responsibility to sustain us!"

All afflictions of man, all his suffering and ills, are demons of his creation. He made them, and he is the source of their vitality. They leech on to him, suck out his life, and destroy him step by step. *Teshuva*, proper repentance, helps to sever this link, and in certain cases, it even kills these demons and blots them entirely out of existence.

וְלָכֵן לֹא הוּזְכַּר עֲוֹן זֶרַע לְבַטָּלָה בַּתּוֹרָה בִּכְלַל בִּיאוֹת אֲסוּרוֹת,

Therefore, the sin of wasteful emission of semen is not mentioned in the Torah among the illicit acts of **sexual intercourse,**

10. See *Pri Etz Ḥayyim, Sha'ar Keriat Shema She'al HaMita.*

The Torah contains a detailed list of prohibited unions but does not mention the wasteful emission of semen among them. The only reference is in the story of Judah's sons Er and Onan,[11] and even there not as an explicit law but implicit within a story.[12]

אַף שֶׁחָמוּר מֵהֶן וְגָדוֹל עֲוֹנוֹ, בִּבְחִינַת הַגַּדְלוּת וְרִבּוּי הַטּוּמְאָה וְהַקְּלִיפּוֹת שֶׁמּוֹלִיד וּמַרְבֶּה בִּמְאֹד מְאֹד בְּהוֹצָאַת זֶרַע לְבַטָּלָה יוֹתֵר מִבִּיאוֹת אֲסוּרוֹת, רַק שֶׁבְּבִיאוֹת אֲסוּרוֹת מוֹסִיף כֹּחַ וְחַיּוּת בִּקְלִיפָּה טְמֵאָה בְּיוֹתֵר עַד שֶׁאֵינוֹ יָכוֹל לְהַעֲלוֹת מִשָּׁם הַחַיּוּת בִּתְשׁוּבָה.

though it is more egregious than them, and his sin is far **greater in terms of the magnitude and enormity of the impurity and *kelippot* that he produces and causes to increase exponentially through the wasteful emission of semen more so than through illicit** acts of **sexual intercourse. It is only that illicit** acts of **sexual intercourse add power and life force to an extremely impure *kelippa* to the extent that one is unable to elevate the life force from there through** ordinary **repentance.**

Waste, destruction, and death are fundamental characteristics of evil, and these elements are present in every forbidden union. In this sense, every forbidden union is a destruction of life, and the sin of wasteful emission is worse than any forbidden union because it entails utter waste. The vital potential in the drops is completely wasted, so this sin possesses a negativity that is greater and more profound than any prohibited relations.

הַגָּהָה: מִפְּנֵי שֶׁנִּקְלְטָה בִּיסוֹד דְּנוּקְבָא דִּקְלִיפָּה הַמְקַבֶּלֶת וְקוֹלֶטֶת הַחַיּוּת מֵהַקְּדוּשָּׁה. מַה

Gloss: This is because semen emitted during an act of illicit intercourse **is absorbed in** the level of ***Yesod* by the feminine** element **of *kelippa*, which receives and absorbs the life force from the** place of **holiness. This is not**

11. Gen. 38.

12. However, some halakhic authorities include this prohibition among the 613 mitzvot; see *Derekh Mitzvotekha* 2b.

שֶׁאֵין כֵּן בְּזֶרַע לְבַטָּלָה שֶׁאֵין שָׁם בְּחִינַת נוּקְבָא דִקְלִיפָּה רַק שֶׁכֹּחוֹתֶיהָ וְחַיָּילוֹתֶיהָ מַלְבִּישִׁים לַחַיּוּת שֶׁבַּטִּפּוֹת, כַּיָּדוּעַ לְיוֹדְעֵי חֵן.

so with regard to wastefully emitted semen, in which case there is no feminine aspect of *kelippa* to receive the life force. **It is only** the *kelippa's* **forces and battalions that clothe the life force that is in the drops** of semen and not the *kelippa* itself, **as is known to those initiated in the esoteric wisdom** of Kabbala.

That it is possible to rectify the sin of wasteful emission is not because it is less serious a sin. On the contrary, the impurity engendered by this sin is more profound than that of other sexual sins, and it touches on the very essence of evil. Yet precisely because this sin entails such utter destruction, precisely because there is no vessel that receives it, it can more readily be rectified. Because it was not absorbed by another being, it also does not become part of any other reality. Its severity lies in the fact that it is wholly one-directional, being an emission of life that is not received by any vessel (that is, any female element), yet it is for that very reason that it does not become rooted in reality. On the other hand, since other prohibited unions do not entail utter destruction, because the life force is received by a female element, the sin is etched in reality. There remains a black hole, a blot of evil, and this blot cannot be eradicated with ordinary repentance.

In light of this, a person can, with proper repentance, entirely obliterate the negative embodiment of this sin, which is spiritual rather than physical. He cannot transform it and redirect it (as repentance performed out of great love transforms sins into merits), but he can destroy it and render it utterly nonexistent, as if it never was.

אֶלָּא אִם כֵּן יַעֲשֶׂה תְּשׁוּבָה מֵאַהֲבָה רַבָּה כָּל כָּךְ עַד שֶׁזְּדוֹנוֹת נַעֲשׂוּ לוֹ כִּזְכֻיּוֹת. וּבָזֶה יוּבַן מַאֲמַר רַבּוֹתֵינוּ ז״ל (חגיגה פרק א משנה ז): אֵיזֶהוּ מְעֻוָּת שֶׁ״לֹּא יוּכַל לִתְקוֹן״ (קהלת א, טו) - זֶה שֶׁבָּא עַל הָעֶרְוָה

One cannot elevate an illicit act of sexual intercourse **unless one repents out of a great love** for God, **so much so that one's deliberate sins become like merits for him. In light of this, one can understand our Rabbis' statement "Who is 'warped that cannot be mended'** (Eccles. 1:15)? **One who**

וְהוֹלִיד מַמְזֵר. שֶׁאָז גַּם אִם יַעֲשֶׂה תְּשׁוּבָה גְּדוֹלָה כׇּל כָּךְ, אִי אֶפְשָׁר לוֹ לְהַעֲלוֹת הַחַיּוּת לִקְדוּשָּׁה מֵאַחַר שֶׁכְּבָר יָרְדָה לָעוֹלָם הַזֶּה וְנִתְלַבְּשָׁה בְּגוּף בָּשָׂר וָדָם.

engaged in illicit **sexual intercourse and fathered a** *mamzer*" (*Ḥagiga* 1:7). **Then, even were one to achieve such a great** level of **repentance, it is not possible for him to elevate the life force to** a place of **holiness, since it already descended into this** physical **world and became clothed within a body of flesh and blood.**

When it is said of a particular sin that a person cannot repent for it, this does not mean that he cannot repent and be forgiven for his wrongdoing. A person can always repent so that his sins will no longer be recalled to his detriment, and he can always wrench himself from the vicious cycle where "one sin leads to another," but the sin itself is not blotted out.

Thus the Talmud speaks of sins such as theft and robbery as a warped act that can be mended, since that which was stolen can be restored, whereas murder and begetting a *mamzer* (illegitimate child) are examples of what King Solomon calls "that which is warped that cannot be mended." The existence of a *mamzer* implies that the sin has become rooted in reality, and the sinner cannot uproot it. However lofty his repentance, however it might elevate him to holiness, the reality of his sin cannot be undone. His deed has taken on a physical, living form and has assumed an objective reality of its own.

The more spiritual a sin is, the uglier and more negative it is likely to be and the more likely to reach to the very essence of evil. At the same time, repenting for such a sin is easier, as nothing physical has to be changed. On the other hand, a sin whose consequences are physically recognizable within our reality remains "that which is warped that cannot be mended." Even if the sinner achieves rectification and is absolved of all responsibility for the deed, the deed itself is not rectified.

The focus of the author of the *Tanya* in this chapter is not to detail types of sin and their appropriate repentance. That is not the subject nor the nature of this book. The purpose of the book is to explain the unique role of man in the various realms, on the side of holiness and the other side. For man to know how to wage the war of life, he requires a map to guide him: Here is the holy side; here is the other side. Yet one cannot know the demarcation of good and evil solely from the halakhic definitions delineated in the *Shulḥan Arukh*. One must also consider a person's thoughts and intentions when he performs mitzvot or commits transgressions. Intent can degrade great mitzvot or elevate minor mitzvot. They can also elevate the neutral world of *kelippat noga* to the realm of holiness.

At the end of the chapter, the author of the *Tanya* touches on the distinction between what is prohibited and "bound" (*assur*) and what is permitted and "unbound" (*mutar*), between the three utterly impure *kelippot* and *kelippat noga*. But this is for the purposes of definition only: The *Tanya* does not revolve around that which is prohibited. Yet evil is an integral aspect of reality, and its presence cannot be ignored. Since it must be mentioned, the topic of the unparalleled power of repentance and its levels, including repentance that transforms one's deliberate sins into merits, must also be noted.

Chapter 8

THE PREVIOUS CHAPTER FOCUSED ON THE *KELIPPOT*, particularly the difference between *kelippat noga* and the three utterly impure *kelippot*. The realm of the permitted in *kelippat noga* and the realm of the prohibited in the three impure *kelippot* do not differ in essence, because permitted things that are not done with holy intent also belong to *kelippa*. The difference between those things that are prohibited and permitted things done without holy intent is only in whether or not they can be subsequently rectified and elevated to a place of holiness.

This chapter will explore other distinctions between that which is prohibited and that which is permissible yet not done with holy intent, by considering both the evil inclination that influences such acts and the methods one can employ to be rectified and purified of the evil. The second part of this chapter will examine an intermediate state, which the author of the *Tanya* illustrates with the example of "permissible idle chatter," as well as a discussion of one who studies non-Torah subjects.

וְעוֹד זֹאת בְּמַאֲכָלוֹת אֲסוּרוֹת, שֶׁלְּכָךְ נִקְרָאִים בְּשֵׁם אִיסּוּר, מִפְּנֵי שֶׁאַף מִי שֶׁאָכַל מַאֲכָל אִסּוּר בְּלֹא הוֹדַע, לְשֵׁם שָׁמַיִם, לַעֲבוֹד ה׳ בְּכֹחַ אֲכִילָה הַהִיא, וְגַם פָּעַל וְעָשָׂה כֵּן, וְקָרָא וְהִתְפַּלֵּל בְּכֹחַ אֲכִילָה הַהִיא,

7 Tevet

11 Tevet (leap year)

There is an additional aspect **with regard to prohibited foods. They are referred to by the term** ***issur***, literally, "something that is bound," **because even if one unwittingly ate a prohibited food,** not knowing that it was prohibited and even intending to eat it **for the sake of Heaven, in order to serve**

אֵין הַחַיּוּת שֶׁבָּהּ עוֹלָה וּמִתְלַבֶּשֶׁת בְּתֵיבוֹת הַתּוֹרָה וְהַתְּפִלָּה כְּמוֹ הַהֶיתֵּר, מִפְּנֵי אִיסוּרָהּ בִּידֵי הַסִּטְרָא אָחֳרָא מִשָּׁלֹשׁ קְלִיפּוֹת הַטְּמֵאוֹת.

God through the energy gained from **this** act of **eating, and he even acted on it,** for example, **he studied** Torah **and prayed using the energy** gained **from that act of eating,** nevertheless **the life force contained within it does not ascend and become clothed in the words of Torah and prayer, as** is the case with **that which is permitted** for consumption, **since** the life force **is bound in the grasp of the *sitra aḥara* of the three impure *kelippot*.**

The author of the *Tanya* now presents another type of prohibited act: one done with holy intent. When one performs a permitted action without the intention that it should be for the sake of Heaven, the action falls into the realm of *kelippat noga*. What is the status of one who did something prohibited yet all the while intended the act to be for the sake of Heaven?

Had he done this with a permitted act, it would have been as virtuous an act as can be. As explained in the previous chapter, such an act is akin to bringing a sacrifice, an offering brought on the altar in the Temple, a mundane object elevated to holiness. Yet because this was a forbidden act, such as eating non-kosher food, even if he was in error or completely blameless because he did not know that it was prohibited, it cannot ascend to the realm of holiness. Although there is no willful transgression on the person's part, the offering to God is not accepted.

Certain laws govern which type of offering is fit and which is not fit to ascend from the altar, and if something that is not fit is offered, even in error, even if the one who offers it is completely blameless, God does not accept the offering. By the same token, the life force within the non-kosher food cannot ascend to holiness, since it is fettered to the *sitra aḥara* of the three impure *kelippot*.

Issur and *heter*, that which is prohibited and that which is permitted, are not subjective concepts. They do not relate to the person, nor does the person define them by his knowledge and awareness. A person's knowledge or ignorance does not alter the basic definition of a thing as prohibited or permitted. A positive intention, such as intent for the sake of Heaven, for a holy purpose, does not prevent something prohibited from being prohibited. The prohibition is objective, relating to the composition, nature, and characteristics of the thing itself and not to what someone happens to think about it. ☞

וַאֲפִילּוּ הוּא אִיסּוּר דְּרַבָּנָן, שֶׁחֲמוּרִים דִּבְרֵי סוֹפְרִים יוֹתֵר מִדִּבְרֵי תוֹרָה כו'.

Even if it is a rabbinic prohibition, the life force does not ascend, **since there is greater stringency with regard to the words of the Sages,** to rabbinic law, **than with regard to words of the Torah,** such as prohibitions, **and so on.**

This applies not only to items that the Torah itself prohibits, which we can more readily view as an objective definition, but also to rabbinic prohibitions, which appear to be subjective, human definitions. This is based on the assumption (which the author of the *Tanya* does not

THE OBJECTIVE REALITY OF THE PERMITTED AND THE PROHIBITED

☞ This conception of good and evil rejects the emotional and subjective view many have of these definitions, where everything is assessed according to a person's intentions. This view does not recognize the concept of an act that is intrinsically evil, only acts that derive from the intention to do evil. The act itself, the reality of its being done or not, is devoid of significance. But the concept of a prohibited act or thing as defined here is not a factor of the person's intent but an intrinsic quality of the act or thing itself. Even if done unwittingly, the act itself is evil. Evil intention, a deliberate rebellion against God, is a sin in its own right, but it does not in any way define what is in the realm of the forbidden.

This is not to diminish the significance of intent. Intent has the power to elevate something that is merely permitted into the realm of holiness or to degrade it to the lowest levels of *kelippa*. But intent cannot transform prohibited into permitted. A person who intends to take a drink of water but inadvertently drinks poison had no adverse intentions, and the fact that it was a totally blameless mistake (for example, the poison was in a bottle marked as water) might subjectively justify his action, but none of this can alter the fact that he drank poison. The Torah's prohibition of something is a definition of its nature. Just as there are healthy foods and poisonous substances, so too there are things that are objectively holy and things that are objectively prohibited.

discuss here) that the Rabbis have the power to decree that from this point onward this or that thing is prohibited – objectively evil – so that it now belongs to the realm of the three utterly impure *kelippot.*

וְלָכֵן גַּם הַיֵּצֶר הָרַע וְכֹחַ הַמִּתְאַוֶּה לִדְבָרִים הָאֲסוּרִים הוּא שֵׁד מְשֵׁידִין נוּכְרָאִין, שֶׁהוּא יֵצֶר הָרַע שֶׁל אוּמּוֹת הָעוֹלָם, שֶׁנַּפְשׁוֹתֵיהֶם מִשָּׁלֹשׁ קְלִיפּוֹת הַטְּמֵאוֹת.

Therefore, the evil inclination and impulse that lusts for things that are prohibited is also one of the foreign demons, which is the evil inclination of the nations of the world, whose souls stem from the three impure *kelippot.*

The impulse that drives a person to do an evil act that belongs to the three impure *kelippot,* an act that cannot be rectified, is an alien impulse, an impulse that belongs to a non-Jewish soul, which derives from those *kelippot.* The animal soul of the Jew derives from *kelippat noga,* so its negative impulses are *kelippat noga* impulses – impulses for deeds that, though negative, can be rectified since they are not expressly defined by the Torah as evil and prohibited. The essence of the Jew is rectification, so everything related to a Jew is rectifiable. This is not to say that a Jew cannot sin with something that is prohibited. The reality

UGLY SINS

☞ The Midrash in *Tanna deVei Eliyahu* speaks extensively of "ugly" sins versus "non-ugly" sins, a distinction that is not halakhic but intrinsic. In light of this, some sins, in addition to being prohibited, are repulsive when committed by a Jew. Even in our generation, in which the lines between good and evil, right and wrong, are blurred, some desires are still considered abnormal – sins and deeds that are considered aberrant for a human being, as being outside the norms of human behavior.

In this sense, "Jewish demons" are temptations that are a part of the struggle within the Jewish soul and the challenges a Jew faces in his service of God. This is part of normal Jewish life. By contrast, "foreign demons" are unrectifiable temptations and thus beyond the context of the Jew's mission in life. A Jew who is tempted by them is behaving in a way that is beyond the definition of Jewish behavior. One who lives within the Jewish norm, whose struggles and doubts are all within the context of his Jewishness, is one whose lusts and even sins are confined to the sphere of *kelippat noga.*

is that he can commit such a transgression, but he is behaving as the opposite of a Jew. ☞

מַה שֶּׁאֵין כֵּן הַיֵּצֶר הָרַע וְכֹחַ הַמִּתְאַוֶּה לִדְבָרִים הַמּוּתָּרִים לְמַלֹּאת תַּאֲוָתוֹ - הוּא שֵׁד מִ'שֵּׁדִין יְהוּדָאִין',

By contrast, the evil inclination and impulse that lusts for permitted things not for the sake of Heaven but rather solely **to gratify its lusts is one of the Jewish demons,**

Some demons are "Jewish" demons, products of the Jewish experience. These demons are experts in Torah, acting entirely within the framework of *halakha* and claiming that those acts are kosher. Since this act is still in the realm of the permitted, it is rectifiable and can be elevated to holiness. Jewish demons, then, are demons created with the Jewish inclination and Jewish sins, which derive not from the three impure *kelippot* but from *kelippat noga,* which is never completely severed from holiness. ☞

לְפִי שֶׁיָּכוֹל לַחֲזוֹר לִקְדוּשָּׁה, כִּדְלְעֵיל.

because the life force in that permitted thing **can return to** the realm of **holiness, as** explained **above** (chap. 7).

DEMONS

☞ One of the problems with demons is that they are usually represented in surreal forms so that we cannot identify them in actuality. Literature and art represent demons in half-comical forms, and when we look for the chicken's claw or the goat's horns, we fail to identify the very human demons in our life. The truth is that the demon is not a stranger to man; it does not come from without but from within. Man himself produced it with his thoughts, speech, and actions, and from that point on, the demon is attached to him. It is his offspring, it feeds on him, sucks him dry, and ultimately destroys him.

The verse "Sin crouches at the entrance, and its desire is for you" (Gen. 4:7) expresses the complex relationship between a person and evil. It is not a confrontational relationship but rather a complicated, mutual, love-hate relationship. Evil is a parasite that strives to attach itself to man, because man is its only source of nourishment. It devours man because it lives and feeds by consuming its host.

These products of evil are created by man, but then they assume an existence of their own, reproducing and multiplying until they strangle a person. This is not because they desire his demise but because they must destroy him in order to continue to exist.

Regardless of whether a person eats a prohibited or permitted food, if he eats it only to satisfy a physical need or desire, he is reduced to *kelippa* to the same degree. The difference is only that the act of eating a permissible food can be rectified.

On a deeper level, a rectifiable sin is essentially different from a sin that cannot be rectified. It is said in the name of several tzaddikim that a Jew never fully sins. The Jewish demon created by his transgressions is always missing one limb or another. It can never be wholly evil, because the act that generates it is never wholehearted. A sin committed by a Jew always contains an iota of good intent, and there is at least an assumption that the matter can be put right.

The author of the *Tanya* develops this idea later on as one of the principles of this book. A Jew cannot sin with a complete sense of abandonment of God. If he is capable of sin at all, it is only because he does not commit to it completely. In the recesses of his mind, he is aware that he is still a Jew and has a way back. ☞

אַךְ מִכָּל מָקוֹם, קוֹדֶם שֶׁחָזַר לִקְדוּשָּׁה הוּא סִטְרָא אָחֳרָא וּקְלִיפָּה. וְגַם אַחַר כָּךְ הָרְשִׁימוּ מִמֶּנּוּ נִשְׁאַר דָּבוּק בַּגּוּף, לִהְיוֹת כִּי מִכָּל מַאֲכָל וּמַשְׁקֶה נַעֲשֶׂה תֵּיכֶף דָּם וּבָשָׂר מִבְּשָׂרוֹ.

Nevertheless, prior to its return to the realm of **holiness, it is *sitra aḥara* and *kelippa*. Even after its return, the trace of it remains attached to the body, since any food or beverage** one consumes **immediately becomes blood and flesh of his flesh.**

A "JEWISH" SIN

☞ The story is told of two friends who in their youth were both disciples of the same Rebbe. In the course of time, one became a commissar in the Communist Party, while the other remained a God-fearing Jew. One day they met, and the latter asked the commissar, "I wonder, does anything remain with you of all the years we studied together?"

The commissar replied, "Sinning. I sin a lot, but I get no true satisfaction from it."

A Jew cannot fully enjoy his sins because he does not fully intend to sin. Paradoxically, what does not allow him to sin completely is what allows him to sin at all. That he does actually enjoy the act is his justification, his dispensation for committing the sin. The connecting thread between the Jew and God that is never completely severed turns the sin into something else. The sin is never complete, neither the pleasure nor the pain of it, because the possibility of rectification always remains.

In order for a person's eating to be holy, there must be holy intent. Otherwise, he allows the *sitra aḥara* to infiltrate his being. When that happens, this impure act leaves an impression on reality. A stain is formed that can never be completely removed. If the deed was permissible, it can be rectified, but the impurity it spawned has been ingrained in the person's body as "blood and flesh of his flesh."

By way of analogy, exposure to radiation beyond a certain intensity can prove fatal. But a lesser dose is also destructive in the long term. Although the person does not die immediately, a steady process of deterioration begins from the time of the exposure and onward. Or, to cite another example, some poisons, such as lead, ingested even in the smallest of quantities, can never be removed. Any immediate damage can usually be overcome, but the cumulative effect over time, as more and more of that material enters the body, can be extremely dangerous.

By the same token, every nonholy act, even if later permitted, even if rectified and elevated to holiness, leaves a mark. The steady accumulation of mundane actions is liable to draw him out of the realm of holiness. In this way, a person can degenerate spiritually even by doing things that are permitted according to the *Shulḥan Arukh*. A decent person who never deliberately commits a sin, who merely allows himself a so-called normal life, can in the half hour or afternoon he devoted to activities devoid of holiness, leave a mark of impurity in his body that cannot be removed.

Therefore, the body requires the **torments of the grave to cleanse and purify it of the impurity it received from the enjoyment and pleasures of this world,** which stem **from the impurity of the *kelippa* of *noga* and Jewish demons,**

וְלָכֵן צָרִיךְ הַגּוּף לְחִיבּוּט הַקֶּבֶר, לְנַקּוֹתוֹ וּלְטַהֲרוֹ מִטּוּמְאָתוֹ שֶׁקִּיבֵּל בַּהֲנָאַת עוֹלָם הַזֶּה וְתַעֲנוּגָיו מִטּוּמְאַת קְלִיפַּת נוֹגַהּ וְשֵׁדִין יְהוּדָאִין,

The "torments of the grave" is the suffering that the body endures in death through its deterioration and decomposition in the grave, which is a punishment and atonement for the body. It can also refer to the angels' beating of one's body after its burial.[1]

1. See chap. 7.

אֶלָּא אִם כֵּן מִי שֶׁלֹּא נֶהֱנָה מֵעוֹלָם הַזֶּה כָּל יָמָיו כְּרַבֵּינוּ הַקָּדוֹשׁ.

unless one never derived pleasure from this world his entire life, like the saintly Rabbeinu, Rabbi Yehuda HaNasi.

Rabbi Yehuda HaNasi, compiler of the Mishna, was an extremely wealthy man who lived his entire life surrounded by luxury and opulence. Yet before his passing, he was able to proclaim, "Master of the universe, it is revealed and known before You that I toiled with my ten fingers in the Torah, and I have never derived any benefit [from the material world] even with my small finger" (*Ketubot* 104a). This was not only about asceticism and self-denial, but the ability to refrain from partaking of anything in this world for one's own sake, to be surrounded by all the pleasure of this world and not enjoy it just to satisfy one's own desires and fulfill one's own wishes. A person who lives such a life is holy. His body too is holy and does not require the cleansing or purification that the torments of the grave provide.

The body is not impure in itself. It has become impure because it is contaminated, because it accumulates the residue of all the profane things that were done with it and that passed through it. These are not necessarily things that are prohibited by *halakha* but even things that can be – and have been – rectified. But because at some point the act belonged to *kelippa*, a stain of impurity remains, a remnant of filth, even when this point has passed and the act has been elevated. Sewage can be purified to make it drinkable, but a foul smell adheres to the machinery and vessels employed in the purification process. In this sense, the body, through which so much spiritual "sewage" passes in the course of a lifetime due to the animalistic, material existence it leads, is like a sewage-treatment plant and must be scoured to remove the stench that adheres to it.

On the other hand, the body of one who leads a wholly sacred life has no reason to be impure. This is why the bodies of the righteous do not contaminate. Their bodies no longer contain life, but there is none of the impurity normally associated with a dead body.[2]

2. See chap. 7. For the practical application of this idea, see *Torat Menaḥem* 5711, vol. 1, p. 172.

Up to this point, the author of the *Tanya* has discussed the *kelippa* that arises from physical enjoyments of the body, such as eating and drinking. Now he will address the concept of nonphysical *kelippot.*

וְעַל ׳דְּבָרִים בְּטֵלִים׳ בְּהֶיתֵּר, כְּגוֹן עַם הָאָרֶץ שֶׁאֵינוֹ יָכוֹל לִלְמוֹד,

With regard to permissible idle chatter and thoughts, **such as** in the case of **an ignoramus who is incapable of studying** Torah, 8 Tevet

The Jew is commanded to devote every available moment to Torah study, and failing to do so is a grave sin. It would therefore follow that engaging in idle chatter, in talk that serves no purpose, will always constitute a transgression. Here, however, the author of the *Tanya* wants to cite an example of talk that is *kelippat noga,* mundane but permissible. He cites the example of a Jew who is unable to study Torah, perhaps due to a lack of literacy or intellectual ability. His idle chatter is not a sin, because it does not take the place of Torah study, but neither is it directed toward a holy purpose.

צָרִיךְ לְטַהֵר נַפְשׁוֹ מִטּוּמְאָה זוֹ דִּקְלִיפָּה זוֹ עַל יְדֵי גִלְגּוּלָהּ בְּכַף הַקֶּלַע, כְּמוֹ שֶׁכָּתוּב בַּזֹּהַר פָּרָשַׁת בְּשַׁלַּח דַּף נ״ט.

he must have his soul purified from the impurity of this *kelippa,* through its being rolled around *in kaf hakela,* literally, "the hollow of a sling," **as the *Zohar* states in *Parashat Beshalaḥ* 59**a.

Just as the body requires the torments of the grave to cleanse and purify it because it served, even temporarily, as a channel for impurity, so must the soul be purified of the impurity that clings to it as a result of its misuse of permitted things. This purification is effected through *kaf hakela.* This is a concept taken from Avigayil's remarks to David: "May the soul of my lord be bound in the bond of life with the Lord your God, and the souls of your enemies may he cast away as from the hollow of a sling" (I Sam. 25:29). The Talmud explains that the souls of the wicked are "continuously tied up, and one angel stands at one end of the world and another angel at the other end of the world, and they sling the souls [of the wicked back and forth] to one another" (*Shabbat* 152b).

Elsewhere, the author of the *Tanya* explains that *kaf hakela* is the experience of the soul that is repeatedly confronted with its failings in the course of its lifetime in this world.[3] Over and over again, it is wrenched from its present state as a being aware of the divine truth that desires to cleave to God, drawn to its experiences of the past and the pettiness and profanity of its past actions.

In our experience, we know this as the agony of memory. Remembering and reexperiencing past traumas is a major factor in much of our spiritual suffering. In truth, though terribly painful, this allows a person to attain atonement and rectification. In *kaf hakela,* the soul is compelled to review its past life and relive it, this time not as a participant but merely as an objective observer. This process, apart from the pain it brings, is a process of purification (somewhat reminiscent of psychoanalysis), of recalling and reviewing the past in a new light. ☞

אֲבָל לְדִיבּוּרִים אֲסוּרִים כְּמוֹ לֵיצָנוּת וְלָשׁוֹן הָרַע וְכַיּוֹצֵא בָּהֶם, שֶׁהֵן מִשָּׁלֹשׁ קְלִיפּוֹת הַטְּמֵאוֹת לְגַמְרֵי,

But for forbidden speech, such as scoffing, malicious speech, and the like, which stem from the three completely impure *kelippot,*

When a person scoffs at things that it is forbidden to scoff at, such as insulting others, this is not just idle chatter but a sin in itself. It is unequivocally prohibited and cannot be rectified by holy intent.[4] Speaking

A TICKET TO EDEN

☞ All souls, except for those that never involved themselves in the mundane aspects of this world, must undergo the process of being purified through *kaf hakela*. This is not a punishment but rather a technical, almost automatic, stage in the soul's journey to a higher world.

A soul that formed an attachment to frivolous things while in the body remains attached to them also when it leaves it, and in that state it cannot enter the Garden of Eden. The Garden of Eden is a place where one basks in the radiance of the Divine Presence. The unpurified soul cannot appreciate or enjoy the divine radiance when its enjoyment still lies in earthly matters. Even if it were smuggled into the Garden of Eden, it would find the experience meaningless.

The story is told of a wagon driver who saved the life of a Jew. When this man died, the heavenly court did not know how to re-

3. See *Likkutei Torah,* Num. 75c.

4. This scoffing entails humiliation and is not synonymous with the scoffing

ill of someone else is another outright prohibition performed through speech. It is a grave sin not only to slander and defame a person by means of falsehoods but even to relate a truth that is to his detriment. This too is speech that is bound to the evil that stems from the three totally impure *kelippot*.

אֵין כַּף הַקֶּלַע [לְבַדּוֹ] מוֹעִיל לְטַהֵר וּלְהַעֲבִיר טוּמְאָתוֹ מֵהַנֶּפֶשׁ, רַק צְרִיכָה לֵירֵד לַגֵּיהִנֹּם.

the punishment of ***kaf hakela*** **alone is not effective for purifying and removing its impurity from the soul. Rather, it must** subsequently **descend to Gehenna.**

The soul of one who transgressed a veritable prohibition must descend to Gehenna, a far harsher fate than that of *kaf hakela*. This fate does not apply to someone who merely lacked the proper intent when performing a permitted action, such as in the example of idle chatter presented here.

The distinction lies in the degree of cleansing required for each respective act. *Kaf hakela* constitutes the reenactment of the experience wherein the idle chatter occurred, the purpose of which is to rectify that speech by incorporating proper intentions. By contrast, Gehenna

ward him. He had performed a great mitzva, but being a boor and a very coarse man, he would not be able to appreciate the spiritual pleasures of the Garden of Eden as tzaddikim do. They decided to ask him what he would like. He asked for a new wagon with six mighty horses. To this day, he drives this wagon with its six horses along a straight, smooth road to infinity.

Without a certain reconditioning, a soul cannot enter the Garden of Eden, because there is nothing for it to do there. A person who does not appreciate music will not enjoy a free ticket to a concert. Likewise, a soul cannot simply be given a ticket to the Garden of Eden. If it does not have the capacity to appreciate what it will find there, it won't be in the Garden of Eden at all but in limbo. *Kaf hakela*, then, is not a punishment or chastisement but a refinement that the soul must undergo in order to proceed to its destination. The soul need not undergo any transformation – it is essentially and inherently divine. It needs only a process of divestment of the experiences of the material world in order to attain a higher level of existence.

---

mentioned at the end of chapter 1, which stems from the *kelippa* of *noga* and is regarded as idle chatter bearing no intrinsic prohibition. See *HaLekaḥ VeHalibuv*.

is where the soul experiences actual punishment and suffering, measure for measure, for its sins. As the author of the *Tanya* explains in *Iggeret HaTeshuva*, just as the suffering one undergoes in this world atones for his sins, so the pain experienced by the soul in Gehenna effects atonement. But whereas the suffering of this world is transient and bestowed with benevolence, the suffering of Gehenna is unmitigated and meted out in the strictest sense through the attribute of harsh judgment. Having said this, one must always bear in mind that this severe suffering in Gehenna can be avoided or mitigated if one performs proper repentance in this world.

וְכֵן מִי שֶׁאֶפְשָׁר לוֹ לַעֲסוֹק בַּתּוֹרָה וְעוֹסֵק בִּדְבָרִים בְּטֵלִים, אֵין כַּף הַקֶּלַע לְבַדּוֹ מוֹעִיל לְנַפְשׁוֹ לְמָרְקָהּ וּלְזַכְּכָהּ,

Similarly, *kaf hakela* alone cannot effectively scour and refine the soul of one who is capable of studying Torah yet engages in idle chatter,

For a person who is capable of Torah study, idle chatter is not a permissible mundane act but a prohibition. On this subject, the Talmud expresses itself quite vehemently, interpreting the verse "Those who forsake the Lord will perish" (Isa. 1:28) as referring to those who abandon their books of Torah and leave the study hall.[5] This is not just an act of omission, a failure to do something, but rather an act of commission, an active abandonment of the Torah. In that case, the rectification of *kaf hakela* is not enough to scour the soul of this transgression.

רַק עוֹנָשִׁים חֲמוּרִים שֶׁמַּעֲנִישִׁים עַל בִּיטּוּל תּוֹרָה בִּפְרָטוּת, מִלְּבַד עוֹנֶשׁ הַכְּלָלִי לְכָל בִּטּוּל מִצְוַות עֲשֵׂה מֵחֲמַת עַצְלוּת בְּגֵיהִנֹּם שֶׁל שֶׁלֶג, כַּמְבוֹאָר בְּמָקוֹם אַחֵר (ליקוטי תורה להאר"י ז"ל תחילת פרשת שמות, ובזהר חלק א סב, ב, רלז, ב, וחלק ב קנ, א).

only severe punishments that are administered specifically on account of neglecting Torah study, apart from the general punishment for neglecting a positive commandment out of indolence, which is **Gehenna of snow, as explained elsewhere** (Arizal, *Likkutei Torah, Parashat Shemot*; *Zohar* 1:62b, 1:237b, 2:150a).

5. *Berakhot* 8a.

On the spectrum of mitzvot, Torah study is unique in a number of aspects.[6] For one, it is regarded as tantamount to all other mitzvot altogether. Consequently, the neglect of Torah study is an egregious sin and as such is not treated the same as neglecting the performance of other positive commandments. The punishment for such a sin, and its accompanying methods of rectification, are commensurately severe and complex.

The assumption is that a person who is able to study Torah and does something else instead neglects his Torah study out of laziness, and the punishment for laziness is the Gehenna of snow. There are two types of Gehenna: one of fire (intense heat) and one of snow (intense cold). The Gehenna of fire is the punishment for possessing too much ardor, for having wanted too much, having done too much, and having pursued what one should not have pursued. The Gehenna of snow is the punishment for not possessing enough ardor, for not having desired, not having done, and not having pursued all the mitzvot that one ought to have desired, done, and pursued.

וְכֵן הָעוֹסֵק בְּחָכְמוֹת אוּמּוֹת הָעוֹלָם - בִּכְלַל דְּבָרִים בְּטֵלִים יֵחָשֵׁב לְעִנְיַן עֲוֹן בִּיטּוּל תּוֹרָה, כְּמוֹ שֶׁכָּתוּב בְּ׳הִלְכוֹת תַּלְמוּד תּוֹרָה׳ (פרק ג סעיף ז).

Likewise, one who studies the wisdom of the nations of the world is considered in the category of one who engages in **idle chatter and constitutes the sin of neglecting Torah** study, **as stated in *Hilkhot Talmud Torah*** (3:7).

The sin of neglecting Torah study is so severe that what a person does instead, whether nonsense or profound intellectual study, does not make any difference. There is no real difference between discussing the price of shoes and delving into philosophy if it is in place of the

THE LAWS OF TORAH STUDY

☞ *Hilkhot Talmud Torah*, published in Shklov in 1794, is the first published work of the author of the *Tanya*, preceding his halakhic masterwork, *Shulḥan Arukh HaRav*. The slim book was originally published anonymously with the goal of obtaining approbations from universally recognized Torah scholars who, had they known the true identify of its author, would not have written them and after which

6. See chaps. 5, 23.

pursuit of Torah. The author of the *Tanya* is not referring to prohibited subjects, those that are heretical or idolatrous. He refers to subjects that are inherently benign yet are nonetheless regarded as sinful because they occupy a person's time and soul instead of Torah study. ☞

וְעוֹד זֹאת יְתֵרָה טוּמְאָתָהּ שֶׁל חָכְמַת הָאוּמּוֹת עַל טוּמְאַת דְּבָרִים בְּטֵלִים, שֶׁאֵינוֹ מַלְבִּישׁ וּמְטַמֵּא רַק הַמִּדּוֹת מִיסוֹד הָרוּחַ הַקָּדוֹשׁ שֶׁבְּנַפְשׁוֹ הָאֱלֹהִית בְּטוּמְאַת קְלִיפַּת נוֹגַהּ שֶׁבִּדְבָרִים בְּטֵלִים, הַבָּאִים מִיסוֹד הָרוּחַ הָרַע שֶׁבִּקְלִיפָּה זוֹ בְּנַפְשׁוֹ הַבַּהֲמִית כִּדְלְעֵיל.

In addition, there is a greater degree of **impurity in the wisdom of the nations of the world than the impurity of idle chatter, which clothes and renders impure only the** emotive **attributes that stem from the holy element of air that is within one's divine soul.** These attributes are defiled **with the impurity of *kelippat noga* contained in idle chatter, which stems from the evil element of air that is within this *kelippa* in one's animal soul, as** discussed **above** (chap. 1).

Idle chatter is profane only because it is not uttered for the sake of Heaven, and anything that does not serve a holy purpose is *kelippa*. Just as a person can be either alive or dead, and cannot be in some intermediate state between the two, so too whatever is not for the sake of Heaven is impure, because the very definition of *kelippa* is that which is not holy. Idle chatter, devoid of all meaning and content, thus belongs to the realm of the impure, of *kelippa*. However, since it is not

they would no longer have been able to retract their support.

Hilkhot Talmud Torah is a unique and complete work in itself. More conceptually complete than even the laws of Torah study in Rambam's *Sefer HaMadda*, the work includes a philosophical overview of the qualities and significance of the Torah. Rambam, too, considers the theoretical side of the laws, but throughout *Sefer HaMadda* there is a certain lack of integration between the *halakhot* and the conceptual aspects of the laws. *Hilkhot Talmud Torah* has a greater unity and coherence, with the particular laws and conceptions of Torah and Torah study producing an integral, unified structure.

prohibited in and of itself, it belongs to the *kelippa* of *noga* and not the utterly impure *kelippot.*

וְלֹא בִּבְחִינוֹת חָכְמָה בִּינָה דַּעַת שֶׁבְּנַפְשׁוֹ, מֵאַחַר שֶׁהֵם דִּבְרֵי שְׁטוּת וּבוּרוּת שֶׁגַּם הַשּׁוֹטִים וְעַמֵּי הָאָרֶץ יְכוֹלִים לְדַבֵּר כֵּן.

The impurity of idle chatter, however, does **not** clothe **the faculties of wisdom, understanding, and knowledge in one's soul, since they are foolish and ignorant words such that even fools and the ignorant can speak that way.**

Idle chatter involves only the base, instinctive faculties of the soul, not its intellect. When a person occupies himself with idle chatter, he contaminates only the emotive attributes of his divine soul, while its cognitive faculties – wisdom, understanding, and knowledge – are not involved, compromised, or contaminated.

מַה שֶּׁאֵין כֵּן בְּחָכְמַת הָאוּמּוֹת הוּא מַלְבִּישׁ וּמְטַמֵּא בְּחִינוֹת חָכְמָה בִּינָה דַּעַת שֶׁבְּנַפְשׁוֹ הָאֱלֹהִית

This is not the case with regard to wisdom of the nations, with which one clothes and renders impure the faculties of wisdom, understanding, and knowledge that are in his divine soul

When a person studies philosophy, science, or any other secular pursuit that uses the intellectual powers of wisdom, understanding, and knowledge, his spiritual investment is far deeper. This is not just external involvement, as when someone speaks about superficial things, but involves all the faculties of the soul, including its cognitive attributes, to the extent that the soul itself is identified and unified with the unholy subject matter.

בְּטוּמְאַת קְלִיפַּת נוֹגַהּ שֶׁבְּחָכְמוֹת אֵלּוּ,

with the impurity of *kelippat noga* that is within these disciplines of **wisdom,**

As in the case of idle chatter, the author of the *Tanya* is speaking of secular disciplines that do not, in and of themselves, contain any prohibited element but are neutral, involving no transgression but also no holy purpose. As long as they are not used for the sake of the Divine, they belong to *kelippat noga*. For something to belong to *kelippat noga*, it need not be evil. It suffices that it contains no intrinsic holiness. Whenever a person involves himself in something that lacks holiness, even if it is intellectually lofty and profound, he contaminates his soul. More than that, the more lofty and profound the subject of study is, the more interesting and stimulating to the mind, the more a person invests his soul in it, and the more he contaminates the soul – involving not only his emotive attributes but his intellectual faculties as well.

שֶׁנָּפְלוּ שָׁמָּה בִּשְׁבִירַת הַכֵּלִים, מִבְּחִינַת אֲחוֹרַיִים שֶׁל חָכְמָה דִקְדֻשָּׁה, כַּיָּדוּעַ לְיוֹדְעֵי חֵן.

which fell into *kelippat noga* **through the shattering of the vessels from the back side of the wisdom of holiness, as known to those initiated in the esoteric wisdom** of Kabbala.

The source and nature of nonholy wisdom is a complex and somewhat problematic kabbalistic concept, which we cannot thoroughly deal with here. Generally speaking, according to the wisdom of Kabbala, the shattering of the vessels, which generated *kelippa*, occurred only in the realm of the seven emotive attributes but not that of the three cognitive attributes, the intellectual faculties of wisdom, understanding, and knowledge. According to this, the existence of impure wisdom seems impossible. This is why the author of the *Tanya* emphasizes that the sciences of the nations fell from the "back side" of supernal wisdom, not from its inner aspect, regarding which there is no death or fall to impurity, as implied by the verse "They die without wisdom" (Job 4:21).[7]

אֶלָּא אִם כֵּן עוֹשֶׂה אוֹתָן קַרְדּוֹם לַחְתּוֹךְ בָּהֶן, דְּהַיְינוּ כְּדֵי לְהִתְפַּרְנֵס מֵהֶן בְּרֶיוַח לַעֲבוֹד ה׳,

The wisdom of the nations renders impure the divine soul's cognitive faculties **unless one uses them as an ax with which to chop** wood, **meaning in order to earn a comfortable livelihood with which to serve God,**

7. See *Torah Ohr* 110d.

A person may pursue a secular science as a profession by which to earn his livelihood, just as another takes up shoemaking as his livelihood. The subject itself is not prohibited, but since it has no inherent holiness, it belongs to the realm of *kelippa* as long as it serves no holy purpose and represents an achievement in and of itself. Yet just as eating can be rectified and elevated by using it for holy purposes, in order to give one the strength and energy to serve God, so too a secular science can be rectified and elevated when a person uses it to support a life devoted to the service of God.

Furthermore, even if such a profession demands a spiritual involvement on the part of the person that is deeper than, say, a life of shoemaking, it is justified by the fact that it will earn him a more comfortable living. This is implied by the *Tanya*'s seemingly superfluous expression *berevaḥ*, implying a comfortable livelihood that would allow a person more time and energy to devote to his holy pursuits.

אוֹ שֶׁיּוֹדֵעַ לְהִשְׁתַּמֵּשׁ בָּהֶן לַעֲבוֹדַת ה׳ אוֹ לְתוֹרָתוֹ. וְזֶהוּ טַעֲמוֹ שֶׁל הָרַמְבַּ״ם וְרַמְבַּ״ן ז״ל וְסִיעָתָן שֶׁעָסְקוּ בָּהֶן.

or one knows how to employ these subject matters **for the service of God or for** understanding **His Torah. This is the reason that Rambam and Ramban, of blessed memory, and their colleagues, studied** such subjects.

Secular sciences can assist in the service of God not only indirectly, through providing a livelihood, but also directly if the knowledge itself is applied to the service of God. If a person studies philosophy to clarify for himself the ways of serving God, or astronomy to see how "the heavens declare the glory of God" (Ps. 19:2), or other sciences in order to devise ways of better fulfilling the mitzvot, his pursuit of these studies constitutes a part of his service of God.

The chapters on astronomy that Rambam included at the beginning

THE HEAVENS DECLARE THE GLORY OF GOD

☞ The greatness of the Creator can be inferred not only from astronomy but from other studies of nature as well. Observing a tiny worm in the sand, one rabbi remarked, "People think that only 'the heavens declare the glory of God,' but how much divine glory is there in a tiny worm!"

There is a saying attributed to the Vilna Gaon that states that when someone lacks one part in science, he lacks nine parts in of *Sefer HaMadda* are not a professional study of astronomy but part of his halakhic work, *Mishneh Torah*. Rambam's astronomy made him think not of Ptolemy but of God. His assumption was that the more one knows about creation, the more one knows about the Creator. ☞

This chapter can be viewed as a summary of the preceding chapters that explored man's animal soul, its faculties and garments. In contrast to the garments of the divine soul, which constitute the thoughts, speech, and actions that manifest the divine expression in this world through Torah and mitzvot, the garments of the animal soul are ensconced in worldly matters. This chapter completes the map delineating the boundaries of good and evil, holiness and *kelippa, kelippat noga* and the utterly impure *kelippot,* and also examines when and how these *kelippot* hinder one's divine service.

In the next chapter, the author of the *Tanya* discusses the person himself, the one in whom both the divine and animal souls reside side by side. He examines how these two opposing forces interact with one another, what difficulties arise as a result, and most importantly, what purpose each one has vis-à-vis the individual.

knowledge of Torah (see *Sefer HaToledot Rabbi Shneur Zalman MiLiadi*, p. 540). Science aids the understanding of Torah, and even the logical comparison of different systems can be a stimulating tool in studying Torah. When a person pursues secular knowledge in such a manner, he does to it what he does to the bread he eats for the sake of Heaven: He transforms *kelippa* into holiness.

Chapter 9

THE PREVIOUS CHAPTERS DESCRIBED THE TWO SOULS within man, the divine soul, with its faculties and holy garments, and the animal soul, with its traits and garments of *kelippa* through which it finds expression. They also described the domains of *kelippa* and holiness, establishing the points of reference for this pivotal chapter, which discusses the relationship between the two souls and the struggle between them.

וְהִנֵּה מְקוֹם מִשְׁכַּן נֶפֶשׁ הַבַּהֲמִית שֶׁמִּקְּלִיפַּת נוֹגַהּ בְּכָל אִישׁ יִשְׂרָאֵל הוּא בַּלֵּב בֶּחָלָל שְׂמָאלִי שֶׁהוּא מָלֵא דָּם, וּכְתִיב: "כִּי הַדָּם הוּא הַנָּפֶשׁ" (דברים יב, כג).

The abode of the animal soul, which stems from the *kelippa* of *noga* within every Jew, is in the heart, in the left chamber, which is filled with blood, as it is written, "As the blood is the soul" (Deut. 12:23).

9 Tevet

12 Tevet (leap year)

Just as a person wears clothes that fit his body, so is a body fitting for its soul. As a rule, the head is the abode and garment for the soul's intellectual faculties, while the heart is the abode and garment for the soul's emotive attributes. Moreover, the body's limbs and organs are tailor-made to correlate with the respective characteristics of its animal and divine souls, each finding expression through the corresponding limbs and organs of the body.

As the author of the *Tanya* points out, the animal soul specifically resides in the left chamber of the heart, "which is filled with blood." The imagery this evokes accords with the ancients' anatomical conception of the heart as consisting of two chambers, each with a different function: one chamber receiving air (oxygen) and the other being full of blood. Yet the *Tanya* is not a book of anatomy, and the author is not suggesting that the evil inclination can be removed by a surgical operation. The issue at hand is not where the animal soul resides in the anatomical sense but the relationship between the two souls and the central role that the animal soul plays in the inner life of a man.

When the author of the *Tanya* states that the animal soul resides in the heart – particularly in the part of the heart that relates to the blood and therefore the body – it is to convey that the animal soul is deeply connected to the heart and the emotions. Though the animal soul does not consist only of desires and feelings but is a complete entity containing also intellectual and abstract components, the center of gravity of the animal soul, the self, resides with the emotions, in the heart. In contrast to the essence of the intellect, to the mind, which perceives reality beyond itself, the characteristic of the emotive attributes is to first feel and experience the self and only then – through this lens – to experience reality. ☞

וְלָכֵן כָּל הַתַּאֲוֹת וְהִתְפָּאֲרוּת וְכַעַס וְדוֹמֵיהֶן	**Therefore, all lusts,** including those that are not physical, such as **boasting, anger, and the like,**

Boasting and anger are not desires in the conventional sense. Although a person might enjoy his conceit, and even his anger, the pleasure is not primary. Yet they too are quintessential expressions of the animal soul, not because they are the fulfillment of a desire but because they

THE EGO AND THE ANIMAL SOUL

☞ The difference between the two souls is brought into focus by the question, Where lies the center of life? In the animal soul, the axis of existence is the self, which is identified with the body and the physical life of man. The animal soul manifests itself in many forms, including some that are extremely refined and complex, but when these manifestations are traced to their source, it is consistently found to be the base instincts of man, in the left chamber of the heart, "which is filled with blood." From the perspective of the animal soul, life entails life for the sake of life itself rather than as an instrument for a higher purpose, as a passageway to a realm beyond this physical one. The blood is the soul, and the soul is the blood. The self is life, and life is the self. The self is the epicenter of existence; all derives from it, and all reverts to it.

This self-saturated being is not a holy thing. The experience of holiness is, by definition, separate from the experience of selfhood. Where there is ego, there cannot be holiness. Holiness can reside are an assertion of selfhood, pitting one's ego against another. In a sense, both are a sort of idolatry, of self-worship.

הֵן בַּלֵּב. **are** situated **in the heart.**

All these traits are in the heart in the sense that the heart is their primal cause. When a person's lusts, conceit, and anger are stripped of all rationalizations, what remains is the cause and motivation behind them, which is situated in the heart.

וּמֵהַלֵּב הֵן מִתְפַּשְּׁטוֹת בְּכָל הַגּוּף **From the heart, they spread throughout the entire body,**

These traits spread throughout the entire reality of the human experience – the totality of the soul and body that clothes it.

וְגַם עוֹלָה לַמּוֹחַ שֶׁבָּרֹאשׁ לְחַשֵּׁב וּלְהַרְהֵר בָּהֶן וּלְהִתְחַכֵּם בָּהֶן, **also rising to the brain in the head,** causing one **to think about and ponder them and,** in addition, **to devise a stratagem with regard to them,**

The crude impulse, the simple will that arises from the heart, is the nucleus around which the brain constructs an entire edifice. This edifice has two basic components. The first is "to think about and ponder them." The primal impulse is unformed, indistinct, one-dimensional.

only where there is a surrender of the "I," where the self is nullified before its supernal source. Holiness can never be a derivative or outgrowth of the ego.

Thus, the quality and sophistication of the animal soul is irrelevant to its holiness. A person can be small by the criteria of his animal soul yet be a holy person, or he might be great in humanistic terms but not holy at all. Yet the animal soul might determine the character of the holiness that is present in a person since the animal soul embodies the basic structure of the human personality, the self that permeates all the person's faculties and garments – his thoughts, speech, and actions. Though the person's holiness does not in itself derive from the animal soul, it assumes the scope and character of his animal soul. With regard to a great person – great in the conventional sense – his holiness will manifest itself in his greatness, whereas with regard to a person of modest capacities, his holiness will manifest itself in modest ways. But in and of itself, the animal soul is the antithesis of holiness, embodying the concept that "the blood is the soul," that the center of its existence is in the body itself.

The person is barely aware of what he wants. When the mind thinks of it, contemplates it, and ponders the what and how of the desire, the primitive, abstract impulse assumes a form, acquires the sophistication and richness of the imagination, and develops into a complex passion.

The second component of the rational edifice constructed around the impulses arising from the heart is that the person "devises a stratagem for them" – a stratagem for attaining his desire. In this way, the mind encompasses the desire to its rear and to its fore, erecting a system of rationalizations to back it up and support it, as well as a methodology to move it forward and realize it. Within this structure, the heart's elemental lust for food and drink assumes complex and sophisticated forms, which are given a base upon which they might be justified and a framework within which they can be implemented.

כְּמוֹ שֶׁהַדָּם מְקוֹרוֹ בַּלֵּב וּמֵהַלֵּב מִתְפַּשֵּׁט לְכָל הָאֵבָרִים, וְגַם עוֹלֶה לְהַמּוֹחַ שֶׁבָּרֹאשׁ.

just as the blood has its source in the heart and from the heart spreads to all the limbs, also rising to the brain in the head.

The analogy for the way these traits affect the thoughts and mind is the manner in which the blood, the metaphor for the animal soul, circulates through the body. Just as the blood spreads from the heart to all parts of the body, so too the heart's desires and emotions expand to all parts of the soul and its garments – to the thoughts, speech, and deeds.

אַךְ מְקוֹם מִשְׁכַּן נֶפֶשׁ הָאֱלֹהִית הוּא בַּמּוֹחִין שֶׁבָּרֹאשׁ,

However, the abode of the divine soul is in the consciousness and intellect of **the brain that is in the head,**

The brain is the seat of the cognitive faculties, wisdom, understanding, and knowledge. These are the faculties of the mind and intellect and, in a more general sense, the abode of a person's powers of perception and consciousness. Thus, the "headquarters" of the divine soul, the seat of awareness, is not in the blood, in the instinctive throb of physical life, but in a different though no less fundamental organ: the brain, the faculty of consciousness.

The basic difference between the heart and the mind is that the heart works to keep itself alive. The self is its ultimate point of reference and the ultimate objective of all its desires. By contrast, the brain, the faculty of perception, has the power to absorb and relate to matters that are outside and beyond the self. The basis of all perception is the surrender of the ego, of the self focused on the self. As long as the "I" is defined solely by the self and its own needs, it cannot assimilate any objective truths, anything that is beyond the self. For this reason, the abode of the divine soul in the human body is the brain, where there is abnegation of the self to another, higher reality. ☞

וּמִשָּׁם מִתְפַּשֶּׁטֶת לְכָל הָאֵבָרִים. **and from there, it spreads to all the limbs.**

The divine soul abides and is first expressed in the mind. From there,

SELF-ABNEGATION AND HOLINESS

☞ Elsewhere, the author of the *Tanya* defines the ultimate in impurity by quoting Pharaoh: "My river is mine, and I made myself" (Ezek. 29:3). When someone says, "This is mine," it constitutes a certain degree of impurity. When he adds, "and I made myself," it is the ultimate profanity. The circuit is closed completely; the *kelippa* is hermetically sealed. If I made myself for myself, then the "I" is the beginning and end of all existence, and that is the ultimate descent from holiness.

By contrast, each level of holiness is a level of self-negation. The highest level of holiness is that of the *merkava*, literally, "chariot," a state in which a person's individuality is completely negated and he operates as a vehicle, a mere tool, of the supernal will alone. Holiness is not merely the concept that I did not create myself, but also that the "river," the things that are ostensibly in my domain and control, does not belong to me. At this level, words such as "my" and "mine" are unutterable.

King David, upon offering an enormous donation to the future Temple, proclaimed, "For who am I, and who are my people, that we have the capacity to donate in this manner? For everything comes from You, and from Your own hand we have given to You" (I Chron. 29:14). As opposed to the essence of *kelippa*, which is "My river is mine, and I made myself," there is the essence of holiness: "For everything comes from You, and from Your own hand we have given to You."

The faculty for self-abnegation, the ability to be receptive to that which is outside the self, resides in the brain, in the power of perception, which is the capacity to absorb and receive information. *Ḥokhma*, wisdom, is *ko'aḥ ma*, the power of what. It is the power of self-negation, of humility, the power to be "what" – to be nothing (see chap. 3 and the commentary there). Wisdom can be compared to the faculty of sight, which is utterly passive: It entails the receptiveness of the eyes. Wisdom too does not emit light but only receives it. It does not exist by its own devices and presents no barrier to anything entering from without. Wisdom is thus the faculty most suitable to serve as a vessel for holiness.

clothed in consciousness and thought, it can spread to the other limbs by way of emotion and action.

וְגַם בַּלֵּב,

It **also** resides **in the heart,**

The divine soul has a residence in the heart, but this expression of the divine soul remains latent until awakened by the brain.

בֶּחָלָל הַיְמָנִי שֶׁאֵין בּוֹ דָּם. וּכְמוֹ שֶׁכָּתוּב: "לֵב חָכָם לִימִינוֹ" (קהלת י, ב).

in the right chamber, where there is no blood, as it is written, "The heart of the wise inclines to his right, and the heart of a fool inclines to his left" (Eccles. 10:2).

Man is not a homogenous creature but a dichotomous being, and thus his heart too is divided. In the right chamber of the heart reside emotions that belong to the realm of holiness – the desires of the divine soul. These do not manifest in the heart in a direct and spontaneous manner but by means of certain processes in the brain.

In the left chamber, which holds the blood that embodies the animal soul, is the home of the feelings and desires that derive from the person's physical, animal side – from *kelippa*.

Since the heart can contain contradictory drives, a person is perpetually faced with the question of where his true heart lies. Where does his heart of hearts, his ultimate self, reside? To the right or to the left?

וְהִיא אַהֲבַת ה' כְּרִשְׁפֵּי שַׁלְהֶבֶת מִתְלַהֶבֶת בְּלֵב מַשְׂכִּילִים הַמְּבִינִים וּמִתְבּוֹנְנִים בְּדַעְתָּם אֲשֶׁר בְּמוֹחָם בִּדְבָרִים הַמְעוֹרְרִים אֶת הָאַהֲבָה.

This manifestation of the divine soul is expressed as **love of God** as fierce **as sparks of a flame, burning in the heart of the wise, who understand and contemplate, with their minds, which are in their brains, matters that awaken the love.**

The human being also has fundamental desires that are of a holy, rather than an animal, nature, which express themselves as feelings of the heart that stem from the "right chamber." Just as there are emotions and impulses that belong to the animal sphere, there are emotions that are connected to the divine sphere. Love of God, as an emotional impulse, is no different from love that stems from the animal soul, as when one person loves another. The difference is that the feeling of love toward God is not normally evoked by itself. A higher machinery of perception and awareness is required to awaken it. This is not necessarily an intellectual awareness, like book knowledge, but rather a personal awareness, one's individual way of seeing, understanding, and sensing.

Every object of love requires some sort of imagery, whether visual, aural, or connected to some other sense, so that the natural feeling can latch onto it. When a person ponders matters that evoke love of God, this awakens a certain place in the heart – "the right chamber." This awareness does not remain a theoretical and intellectual experience but spreads throughout all the organs and limbs, as well as the heart, which has a place that is also open to such an emotion, to a love of God that burns like flaming coals.

וְכֵן שִׂמְחַת לֵבָב בְּתִפְאֶרֶת ה׳ וַהֲדַר גְּאוֹנוֹ, כַּאֲשֶׁר עֵינֵי הֶחָכָם אֲשֶׁר בְּרֹאשׁוֹ בְּמוֹחַ חָכְמָתוֹ וּבִינָתוֹ מִסְתַּכְּלִים בִּיקָרָא דְמַלְכָּא וְתִפְאֶרֶת גְּדוּלָּתוֹ עַד אֵין חֵקֶר וְאֵין סוֹף וְתַכְלִית, כַּמְבוֹאָר בְּמָקוֹם אַחֵר.

Similarly, another example of a holy emotion is **heartfelt joy in God's beauty and the glory of His majesty,** which is evoked in the heart **when the wise man's eyes that are in his head, in the faculty of his wisdom and understanding, gaze at the King's glory and the beauty of His majesty,** which are **beyond comprehension and without limits or bounds, as explained elsewhere** (*Torah Or* 47c).

The nature of these contemplations, what to meditate upon and how to meditate to evoke a particular emotion in the heart, is explained at length in hasidic thought. Here the author of the *Tanya* offers only a broad outline of the point of departure and the final goal. With respect to the divine soul, everything falls under the rubric of one topic: God, who is one. ☞

LOVE THAT STEMS FROM THE DIVINE SOUL

☞ A person's emotions are not all of one type. There are feelings of love and feelings of fear, feelings of joy and feelings of sadness and compassion. In the animal soul,

וְכֵן שְׁאָר מִדּוֹת קְדוֹשׁוֹת שֶׁבַּלֵּב, הֵן מֵחָכְמָה בִּינָה דַּעַת שֶׁבַּמּוֹחִין.

Likewise, the other holy attributes that are in the heart, such as fear and compassion, **are** evoked **through the wisdom, understanding,** and **knowledge that are in** the consciousness and intellect of **the brain.**

In later chapters, the author of the *Tanya* will clarify that we cannot simply say that the emotions that stem from the divine soul are always stimulated by the three cognitive faculties. There are some people who possess innate feelings of holiness and experience natural love and awe of God, feelings inherited with the "genes" of their soul and implanted in their subconscious. For various reasons, the author of the *Tanya* is not referring here to this type of love and awe of God but to the usual circumstances, where such emotions are derivatives of a person's consciousness. ☞

10 Tevet

13 Tevet (leap year)

אַךְ הִנֵּה כְּתִיב: "וּלְאוֹם מִלְאוֹם יֶאֱמָץ" (בראשית כה, כג),

However, it is written, "One nation will prevail over the other nation" (Gen. 25:23),

This verse appears in the Torah in relation to Rebecca's tumultuous pregnancy: "The children were agitated within her" (Gen. 25:22). Sensing that something was amiss, Rebecca "went to inquire of the Lord." The divine response was that "two peoples are in your womb, and two nations shall be separated from your innards; one nation will prevail over the other nation."

In a sense, this applies to every Jew, at any time. Every person senses

different emotions are aroused by different causes, be it of material or spiritual origin. By contrast, in the divine soul, the object of the emotions is always one and the same: God. Love is exclusively the love of God, and fear is always fear of God.

Unlike the objects of the animal soul's emotions, the divine essence is infinite, permeating every aspect of one's experience. The different feelings a person has toward God are only dependent on the manner in which he relates to Him. When approaching God from one perspective, a person is filled with awe and fear. From another perspective, he is suffused with love and yearning. The subject is always the one God, but depending on the person's manner of contemplation, God might evoke burning love, heartfelt joy, or fear and trepidation.

that there are two "children" struggling within him. When he passes a house of Torah, Jacob struggles to get out, and when he passes a house of idolatry, Esau struggles to get out. The reason for this is that "two peoples are in your womb." A person has within him not a single personality but two, each striving in a different direction and frequently in opposition to one another. The problem is that neither one is content with concerning itself with its own affairs. Each is constantly attempting to encroach on the domain of the other. Moreover, the relationship between them is such that "one nation will prevail over the other." Any increase in the strength of one side produces a reaction that increases the strength of the other.

It is a fierce, never-ending struggle.

The result is the extreme, agonizing spiritual upheavals that virtually every soul must contend with. A person attains a certain level of goodness or holiness, and then, at that very point, when he is anticipating a holy experience and a spiritual elevation, he experiences something that is the very opposite. He was involved in a holy pursuit – he truly was in a holy place – when suddenly a thought invaded his mind or a desire erupted in his heart that had no relation to the holy realm in which he had been, something that expresses the lowest and basest side of his personality.

THE BRAIN, THE HEART, AND THE SOURCE OF EMOTIONS

☞ There are two axes within man: the heart, which is the abode of the animal soul, and the brain, where the divine soul resides. The animal soul is primarily manifest through the emotions of the heart, the emotions that are of a piece with the biological or animal side of man. True, they do not remain at that simple level as with lower forms of animal life. In animals, impulses are simple desires without thought, refinement, or structure. Man can transform the emotions into the stuff of which great poetry is made. But even when they attain a high degree of sophistication and beauty, the true source and basis of all emotions of this type is the blood, the vitality that courses through the physical body.

By contrast, the brain is the seat of the intellect, of the faculties for perception and consciousness. It is also the abode for the divine soul. Though the brain, a physical organ, is by no means a perfect vessel for the divine soul, it is the vessel closest to holiness, and so it is the abode within the body that houses the sacred divine soul. The emotions evoked by the divine soul, though just as potent and sweeping as those of the animal soul, derive not from the materiality of man but from the human soul, whose closest bodily instrument is the brain.

At such moments, a person tends to see himself as even more base and lowly. It is therefore important that a person understand what is transpiring within him. He should understand that there are "two peoples in your womb" and "one nation will prevail over the other," that a person is not one but two, and when one becomes stronger, the other rallies in response.

Life is not a smooth and straight progression, and one should be prepared for sudden bursts of energy from one side or the other. As will be explained below, a person whose path in life is straight and smooth is not a normal person; he is a *tzaddik gamur*, a completely righteous individual. The tzaddik is a one-dimensional person: He has but one soul, one heart, which is directed toward Heaven. Only in such an individual are there no upheavals caused by the other side. ☞

כִּי הַגּוּף נִקְרָא עִיר קְטַנָּה וּכְמוֹ שֶׁשְּׁנֵי מְלָכִים נִלְחָמִים עַל עִיר אַחַת, שֶׁכָּל אֶחָד רוֹצֶה לְכָבְשָׁהּ וְלִמְלוֹךְ עָלֶיהָ, דְּהַיְינוּ לְהַנְהִיג יוֹשְׁבֶיהָ כִּרְצוֹנוֹ וְשֶׁיִּהְיוּ סָרִים לְמִשְׁמַעְתּוֹ בְּכָל אֲשֶׁר יִגְזוֹר עֲלֵיהֶם,

for the body is referred to as a "small city," and just as two kings wage war over one city, each one wishing to conquer and rule over it, that is, to govern its citizens according to his wishes, and that they obey whatever rules **he imposes on them,**

THE ONGOING STRUGGLE

☞ This conception of the human soul as consisting of two distinct souls is one of the most important innovations of the *Tanya*. The assumption in other books of *mussar* is that a person should be good and pious and show other virtues. Indeed, a person should be this way. But he is not always capable of doing so, and when he tries and fails, he feels like a failure. What is worse, he becomes convinced that the books are not speaking to him, that he is too lowly for the principles and axioms by which they operate to apply to him.

One of the classic works of *mussar*, written not long before the *Tanya*, is *Mesillat Yesharim* by Rabbi Moses Ḥayyim Luzzatto. The book, written in beautiful Hebrew, describes how someone can proceed from virtue to virtue, from diligence to alacrity, from alacrity to cleanliness, and so on, step by step, until he reaches the level of *ruaḥ hakodesh*, of prophetic intuition. Somewhere between diligence and alacrity, an ordinary person might regress, leaving him completely confused as to what level, if any, he now holds and feeling that what this book says is utterly impossible for him to implement.

By contrast, although the demands made herein may appear somewhat extreme, the *Tanya* takes into account human nature as we know it, with all its com-

The author of the *Tanya* borrows this metaphor from *Tanakh*.[1] The aim of these warring kings is not merely to physically occupy a place but to rule over it and influence it, to mold it and remake it to reflect their will.

כָּךְ שְׁתֵּי הַנְּפָשׁוֹת, הָאֱלֹהִית וְהַחִיּוּנִית-הַבַּהֲמִית שֶׁמֵּהַקְּלִיפָּה, נִלְחָמוֹת זוֹ עִם זוֹ עַל הַגּוּף וְכָל אֵבָרָיו.

so too the two souls, the divine soul **and the vital, animal** soul, **which stems from *kelippa*, wage war with one another** for control **over the body and all its limbs.**

The body and all its organs and limbs, including the heart and the brain, are neutral ground. Body and soul are not the conflicting representations of good and evil, holiness and impurity. The body in and of itself is not an expression of evil. Rather, the physical body is an instrument that might serve either the impure forces of *kelippa* or the holy forces of

plexities and problems. It explains to the person what is happening to him, how the inner upheavals he experiences are an integral part of him, of the basic duality of human nature. It explains that one must accept that this duality will exist within him until the day he dies. The duality can be moderated and can take on more refined forms, but he can never totally uproot it.

Similarly, the Mishna says, "We have neither the security of the wicked nor the afflictions of the righteous" (*Avot* 4:15). Apart from the very few individuals who happen to be either completely righteous or completely wicked, a person can be sure of one thing: His soul will give him no rest. Peace and tranquility might perhaps come after death, but in this world, as long as a person lives, he cannot experience tranquility. At times, one may earn a respite, a temporary cease-fire, but achieving complete and true inner peace is never possible. There is a permanent struggle within, and one should understand that his is an existence of conflict and the hope of attaining peace and tranquility is not realistic. With this knowledge, he is not disappointed about failing to attain peace, nor does he feel that his life has been wasted if he does not achieve a decisive victory in the battle of life.

A person must realize that everything he does involves a struggle, that life is a war in which "one nation will prevail over the other." The pendulum swings from side to side, and a person's task is to make every effort to emerge from the struggle in a better state than he entered it. In the course of this struggle, in between battles, he should make sure to move forward. Ultimately, this is all a human being can achieve.

1. Eccles. 9:14; see *Targum* there; see also *Nedarim* 32b.

the Divine. The battle between the two souls is therefore over the body: Which force should it serve and for what purpose? Should it serve the animal soul, which sees the body not as an instrument but as an end in itself? Should the instrument, then, be recast as an objective and thus become an expression of *kelippa*? Or should it serve the divine soul, which sees it as an instrument through which it can achieve a higher degree of attachment to God than it possesses on its own? ☞

שֶׁהָאֱלֹהִית חֶפְצָהּ וּרְצוֹנָהּ שֶׁתְּהֵא הִיא לְבַדָּהּ הַמּוֹשֶׁלֶת עָלָיו וּמַנְהִיגַתּוֹ, וְכָל הָאֵבָרִים יִהְיוּ סָרִים לְמִשְׁמַעְתָּהּ וּבְטֵלִים אֶצְלָהּ לְגַמְרֵי, וּמֶרְכָּבָה אֵלֶיהָ, וְיִהְיוּ לְבוּשׁ לְעֶשֶׂר בְּחִינוֹתֶיהָ וְג׳ לְבוּשֶׁיהָ הַנִּזְכָּרִים לְעֵיל,

The divine soul's **desire and wish is that it be the sole ruler and leader** of the body **and** that **all of the** body's **limbs obey** the divine soul's **wishes, be completely nullified to it, and** serve as **a vehicle for it so that** the body's limbs **may be a garment for its aforementioned ten attributes and its three garments** (see chaps. 3–4).

ATTACHMENT THROUGH THE PRACTICAL MITZVOT

☞ The fulfillment of a mitzva does not, in and of itself, possess moral significance. The practical mitzvot are not devices for attaining spirituality, love of God, and other spiritual aims. In fact, the mitzvot have no purpose, material or spiritual, beyond the single aim of attachment to God, and God is neither material nor spiritual but equally distant from both matter and spirit. The question of whether a person believes in God or denies Him is not of any greater concern to God than whether a person smokes on Shabbat.

Furthermore, as far as genuine attachment to God is concerned, it is the body that holds the greater potential for such attachment because, among other things, the vast majority of the mitzvot are physical deeds, and, as just mentioned, attachment is achieved through the fulfillment of mitzvot. The prevalent assumption that the spiritual is better suited to achieve attachment to God stems from the failure to distinguish between actual attachment and a feeling of attachment. The two are not synonymous. They can even be far apart and at times opposites. Attachment is an objective truth: A person is one with God, and it makes no difference whether the person experiences an uplifting of the spirit at that time or not. If the criterion is how one feels, if one's feelings determine what is good and what is bad, what is true and what is false, what is right and what is wrong, then this is not attachment to God but attachment to oneself.

In this sense, love is not synonymous with attachment. Love is a feeling, an expression of the emotions and excitement of the soul. Though such love must not be

In the terminology of Kabbala, *merkava,* literally a chariot, refers to a vehicle, a thing that possesses no will or identity of its own but merely serves a higher will, like a chariot controlled and directed by its driver. The Midrash states that the patriarchs, Abraham, Isaac, and Jacob were the divine chariot, comparing their self-negation before God to that of the horse under its rider.[2]

Another way of understanding the analogy is that just as the horse takes its rider to a place that he cannot reach on his own, so too the body, if it is a vehicle for the divine soul, can transport it to a place that it cannot reach on its own. This is why the divine soul wants the body to act as its chariot, a vehicle that negates itself exclusively to it and serves solely to express its nature and aims within the world.

underrated, attachment is not a feeling. It may sometimes be accompanied by deep emotion but may also be present without any emotion at all. The presence or absence of emotion is irrelevant to the reality of the bond.

It is told of one of the great hasidim, Rabbi Shmuel of Karov, a disciple of the Ḥozeh of Lublin, that on the first night of Passover he conducted the Seder with great excitement, diligently fulfilling all the observances with the appropriate focus and intent, and he felt that he was rising into worlds above worlds. The following day, exhausted by the immense effort of that Seder, he decided to rest a little before the second Seder. When he awoke, it was nearly midnight (the deadline for finishing the main part of the Seder), so he had to rush to set up the Seder plate and do whatever had to be done quickly so that he would complete it all in time. Understandably, he was very upset and depressed about this development.

Sometime later, he went to his Rebbe, who said, "*Nu,* so you held two Seders. At the first, you were flying around in the heavens. So you were flying around in the heavens. But the second Seder – the second Seder was a very good Seder indeed."

When someone has lofty experiences, this might make him feel very good about himself, but it has nothing to do with attachment to God. In a sense, the reverse may be true: Someone who is in a state of true attachment has no time to think about how much he loves and how he loves, whereas someone who feels good about himself should, perhaps, cast doubts on the authenticity of his attachment. The hasid who had to prepare the Seder in a hurry had no time to prime himself, to introspect, to ascertain the precise level he had attained. In those moments when he was acting, doing, he displayed his inner desire, and he was attached from within, genuinely and cleanly, with no superlative emotion and awareness.

2. *Bereshit Rabba* 47:6.

שֶׁיִּתְלַבְּשׁוּ כּוּלָּם בְּאֵבְרֵי הַגּוּף וְיִהְיֶה הַגּוּף כּוּלּוֹ מָלֵא מֵהֶם לְבַדָּם וְלֹא יַעֲבוֹר זָר בְּתוֹכָם חַס וְשָׁלוֹם.

It desires **that all of them be clothed within the limbs of the body and that the body be completely permeated with them alone, so that no foreigner will pass through them, God forbid.**

The divine soul wants to attain complete control over the totality of human existence. As has been explained, holiness resides only where nothing else exists. There is neither room for any extraneous emotion or intellectual prowess, nor is there space for a superfluous thought, word, or action. It reigns supreme in the presence of the Divine alone.

דְּהַיְינוּ תְּלַת מוֹחִין שֶׁבָּרֹאשׁ יִהְיוּ מְמוּלָּאִים מֵחָכְמָה בִּינָה דַּעַת שֶׁבַּנֶּפֶשׁ הָאֱלֹהִית,

That is, the three faculties of the brain in the head should be permeated with the wisdom, understanding, and knowledge of the divine soul,

In this way, all of a person's thoughts, and his very manner of thinking, will be in the sphere of holiness, linked with the Divine.

שֶׁהִיא: חָכְמַת ה׳ וּבִינָתוֹ לְהִתְבּוֹנֵן בִּגְדוּלָּתוֹ אֲשֶׁר עַד אֵין חֵקֶר וְאֵין סוֹף, וּלְהוֹלִיד מֵהֶם עַל יְדֵי הַדַּעַת הַיִּרְאָה בְּמוֹחוֹ וּפַחַד ה׳ בְּלִבּוֹ וְאַהֲבַת ה׳ כְּאֵשׁ בּוֹעֲרָה בְּלִבּוֹ כְּרִשְׁפֵּי שַׁלְהֶבֶת,

namely, the wisdom of God and His understanding, by contemplating His greatness, which is infinite and beyond comprehension, and generate through them, by means of the faculty of **knowledge, awe** of God **in his brain and fear of God in his heart and love of God like a burning fire in his heart** and **like sparks of a flame.**

Two types of fear are mentioned here. The first is *yira,* the sense of inadequacy generated in the mind when it is aware of an infinitely greater presence than itself, while the second is *paḥad,* the corresponding emotion in the heart, which is different from the more theoretical sense of awe.

לִהְיוֹת נִכְסְפָה וְגַם כָּלְתָה נַפְשׁוֹ בַּחֲשִׁיקָה וַחֲפִיצָה לְדָבְקָה בּוֹ בְּאֵין סוֹף בָּרוּךְ הוּא בְּכָל לֵב וָנֶפֶשׁ וּמְאֹד,

His soul will yearn and pine with a longing and desire to cling to Him, to *Ein Sof,* blessed be He, with all his **heart, soul, and might**

"Heart, soul, and might" is a reference to the second verse of the *Shema*: "You shall love the Lord your God with all your heart, and with all your soul, and with all your might" (Deut. 6:5). "With all your heart," as the Talmud interprets it,[3] means with both chambers of the heart. The heart should be driven to attach itself to God with the very same forces of longing and desire with which it is drawn to *kelippa*. "With all your soul" means that one's love of God permeates all attributes of the soul: its three cognitive faculties and seven emotive traits, as well as its three garments – thought, speech, and action. "With all your might" is interpreted with the connotation of *me'od* as meaning "more" or, more specifically, to go beyond. The person loves God to the extent that he is even willing to give up his very existence. It is a devotion that is beyond all rational thought, that transcends the soul's cognitive faculties of wisdom, understanding, and knowledge.

מֵעוּמְקָא דְלִבָּא שֶׁבֶּחָלָל הַיְמָנִי,

from the depths of the heart, from its **right chamber,**

The "depths of the heart" is what a person really and truly desires. On the other hand, a person might desire certain things and act upon these desires only in the periphery of his heart. In the routine of life, distinguishing between the two, between that which is central and that which is peripheral, is not always possible, but in a crisis that upsets the normal balance of his life, a person will divest himself of

THE DEPTHS OF THE HEART

☞ There is an oft-told story of the Jew who rushes to throw his *tallit* and *tefillin* overboard when his ship gets caught in a storm and the captain orders the passengers to throw some of their possessions into the sea to lighten the load. Obviously,

3. *Berakhot* 54a.

those things that he values only in the periphery of the heart. In those moments, his true desires in the recesses of his heart will express themselves. ☞

שֶׁיִּהְיֶה תּוֹכוֹ רָצוּף אַהֲבָה, מָלֵא וְגָדוּשׁ, to the extent **that its interior is inlaid with love, permeating** it **and overflowing.**

These are not mere expressions. "Inlaid" and "permeated" are two manners in which the divine soul's love of God fills the right chamber of the heart until it contains nothing else. "Overflowing" is the stage at which this love spills over from its natural place to the other side.

עַד שֶׁתִּתְפַּשֵּׁט גַּם לֶחָלָל הַשְּׂמָאלִי That love spills over **until it spreads to the left chamber as well,**

The divine soul does not suffice with consolidating its rule over those parts of the person that are its natural domain – the brain and the right chamber of the heart. It wants more: that the feelings of love and awe of God should spill over into the other side of the heart, into the realm of the animal soul in the left chamber, to the human, biological element of man. The divine soul's desire is to transform the entire human being into a being of holiness.

this fellow had other possessions, including things that were heavier than his *tallit* and *tefillin*, but those, it seems, were of greater value to him.

What a person desires from the depths of his heart, he does not throw away so quickly. As long as his life is running smoothly, he can hold on to everything he has, but when hard pressed, he sheds those things whose connection to him he now shows to have been only peripheral.

Conversely, times of extreme freedom, when a person finds himself in a position where everything is permitted, are also indicative of a person's true desires. Someone was once told that he was insane. The person understood this to mean that as a madman, he was exempt from all mitzvot. The feeling that everything was permitted to him could just as well have moved him to start praying for seven or eight hours every day, but this was not what he truly wanted in the "depths of his heart."

לְאַכְפְּיָא לְסִטְרָא אָחֳרָא יְסוֹד הַמַּיִם הָרָעִים שֶׁבָּהּ, שֶׁהִיא הַתַּאֲוָה שֶׁמִּקְּלִיפַּת נוֹגַהּ, לְשַׁנּוֹתָהּ וּלְהַפְּכָהּ מִתַּעֲנוּגֵי עוֹלָם הַזֶּה לְאַהֲבַת ה',

to subdue the ***sitra aḥara*** in the heart, **the element of evil water within it, which is the lust that stems from the** ***kelippa*** **of** ***noga*** (see chap. 1), **to change it and transform it from** a lust for **the pleasures of this world to the love of God,**

The left side of the heart contains one's love for mundane things. When the love harbored in the right side of the heart permeates the left, the love for the mundane and material is transformed into the love of God. That is not to say that this permeation renders the left side of the heart equivalent to the right in all respects. Rather, it means that the passion and burning desire for the mundane will now be redirected toward God.

The author of the *Tanya* details a two-stage process in the divine soul's effect on the animal soul: "to subdue the *sitra aḥara*" and "to change it and transform it." "Subduing" and "transforming" are basic concepts in divine service as expressed in hasidic thought. There is a major difference between subduing the other side and transforming and changing it, and it is explained that one stage follows the next. The first stage of subduing is primarily the divine service of self-abnegation, an act attainable by every person, and it is the service of the *beinoni*. The second stage, that of transforming, is not easily attainable by the common person and is thus primarily the divine service of the righteous.

כְּמוֹ שֶׁכָּתוּב: "בְּכָל לְבָבְךָ" (דברים ו, ה) - בִּשְׁנֵי יְצָרֶיךָ.

as it is written, "With all your heart" (Deut. 6:5) – that is, **with both your inclinations,**

In Hebrew, the word for "your heart" can assume two forms: *libkha,* spelled with a single *bet,* or *levavekha,* spelled with two *bets*. In the verse from the *Shema* quoted here, the word is written with two *bets*. The Sages interpret this as a reference to the two sides of the human heart, the right and the left, the inclination for good and the inclination for evil.[4] The Torah is telling us that we should love God with both sides of our heart, with both wills and inclinations.

וְהַיְינוּ שֶׁיַּעֲלֶה וְיָבֹא וְיַגִּיעַ לְמַדְרֵגַת 'אַהֲבָה רַבָּה' וְחִיבָּה יְתֵרָה, מִמַּדְרֵגַת 'אַהֲבָה עַזָּה כְּרִשְׁפֵּי אֵשׁ'.

so that it may ascend, come, and reach the level of great love and affection that surpasses the level of a "love of God as **fierce as sparks of fire"** (see chap. 3).

The love of God described as a fierce love that burns as fierce as "sparks of fire" is the love that develops as a result of the intellectual contemplation of the divine soul in the right chamber of the heart. But the loftier level of love described here as a "great love" cannot be attained by mere intellectual contemplation. It can be achieved only when the lower level of love spills over and permeates the left side of the heart, the locus of one's natural, inborn love, and redirects that love to holiness. This in turn reveals the natural, latent love of the divine soul. This love, newly manifest, is known by two designations: "great love" and "love of delights," as the author of the *Tanya* goes on to say.

The author appears to be charting the process by which the level of *ahava rabba*, "great love," can be attained. Although it is true that there is no fixed route or technique when it comes to such matters because people operate and develop emotionally in different ways, it is nevertheless possible to speak of a general route that is applicable to most people.

The first stage of this process is perception and contemplation of the Divine, which serve to awaken the love that is in the heart. This is a love like a burning fire, a thirst and yearning for God that first develops in the right chamber of the heart, the source of the heart's "holy" emotions, those feelings that are directed toward God alone. The love fills the right side of the heart and then spills over into the

LOVE LIKE FIRE, LOVE LIKE WATER

☞ Love like fire and love like water seem to work in opposite ways. Both are forms of love; both contain the general desire for relationship, contact, and affection. But beyond this, they are fundamentally different. Love like fire is the love of one who lacks. It is a love that is born of thirst, a love that drives the lover to the beloved. But as the

4. Mishna *Berakhot* 9:5; see also *Likkutei Torah*, Song 29b.

left, subduing the heart's love for the material and the mundane and ultimately transforming it into a love for God. When this is achieved, the person can graduate to the higher level of love called *ahava rabba*.

וְהִיא הַנִּקְרֵאת בַּכָּתוּב: "אַהֲבָה בַּתַּעֲנוּגִים" (שיר השירים ז, ז),	This great love **is referred to in *Tanakh* as "love of delights"** (Song 7:7),	14 Tevet (leap year)

Love has two seemingly contradictory modes of expression: love that is like sparks of fire and great love, or "love of delights," which, as noted in hasidic thought, is also known as love that is like water. ☞

לְהִתְעַנֵּג עַל ה' מֵעֵין עוֹלָם הַבָּא.	**wherein one delights in God,** which is **a semblance of the World to Come.**

A higher form of love is the second type of love: love like water or, as the verse calls it, "love of delights." The soul achieves this love when there is no longer any struggle between the divine soul and the animal soul, when all the person's desires are directed toward God. Unlike love that

lover approaches the object of his love, the thirst only grows stronger. This love is never sated. It is a quest, a longing, a craving. Predicated upon lack and distance, it generates an ever-growing tension: The closer one is to God, the more one senses how distant one truly is from Him.

Although this is a holy love, a love directed toward God, it shares with other loves a certain egotistical element. Most loves that we find in the world are, in essence, the love of self. A person loves himself, and for the sake of his self-love, he needs something. When a person plucks a flower and says that he loves flowers, he doesn't actually love flowers. He loves himself, and to satisfy his self-love, he needs flowers. The same is often true of love between people – between husband and wife and between parents and children. Hasidim used to point out that the Yiddish expression "*zey hoben zikh leib*" – they love one another – also connotes "they love themselves." In this sense, any love that is "like sparks of fire" is a form of self-love. The object of such love can be a great variety of things and can even be God, but such love of God can be said to be a desire like all other desires, because it is predicated on a human lack.

Obviously, the more mundane the object of the love, the more pronounced the lover's lust, and the more the so-called love of the object is shown to be a fallacy. When a person says he loves fish, we know that he means he loves to eat fish. When he says that he loves wisdom, we tend to view his love in less selfish terms. But even in its finer forms, a person's expression of love toward someone or something might be no more a love for that person or thing than a love of fish is a love for the fish. As long as love is driven by lack and need, its dominant feature is the lover's want.

By contrast, love that is like water, as the author of the *Tanya* goes on to illustrate, is a love that is focused not on the self but on the object of the love.

is like fire, which is based on the self and what it lacks, born of thirst and longing for the object of its desire, this is a love in which the lover is not aware of himself at all, only of the object of his love. When the self ceases to be significant, its needs, too, cease to be significant and no longer afflict the soul with thirst and yearning. Such love is satisfying because it makes no demands; it does not seek to dominate or exercise ownership over its object.

As long as love implies the desire to obtain something for oneself, the lack is only magnified with the intensity of the love. But when love belongs to a totally different type of relationship, in which the beloved is loved for its own sake, unconnected with the self of the one who loves, then the more one loves and the more one thinks about and occupies himself with the object of his love, the more satisfying that love becomes.

When a fiery love graduates into a "love of delights," there is a complete transformation: Love that was formerly characterized by agony and longing becomes a delightful love, akin to the soul's delight in God in the World to Come. No longer is there a sense of lack because one is focused entirely on God, the object of one's love, rather than on the self and its needs.

This love is a "semblance of the World to Come" because it bears no connection to this world, a place of struggle, labor, destruction, and creation. It is, instead, a semblance of the world that follows this one, a future world in which the summation of this present world and the true place of everything therein is clearly perceivable. The love of delights thus belongs solely to the World to Come, a reality in which there is no conflict, in which man becomes an integral, harmonious being whose

A LOVE THAT TRANSCENDS TIME

☞ The seven years that Jacob waited for Rachel were "in his eyes but a few days in his love for her" (Gen. 29:20). Usually, the reverse is the case: A few days of separation from one's beloved seem like seven years. Indeed, as long as love is what the self demands, as long as it is about what one lacks and requires, the time of separation progressively feels longer. Every day of separation creates stronger yearnings, which increase the feeling of lack, until a few days seem like several years. But Jacob's love for Rachel was of the other type: a love of delights that makes no claims, is satisfied by the mere fact that the object of love is there, and does not desire to possess it. When it comes to such love, seven years feel like a few days.

soul is entirely subsumed with the love of God. This love cannot be attained in this world through human effort but can only be granted as a gift from God, akin to the very nature of the World to Come. Yet even in this present world, the righteous – and at rare moments and, to a lesser degree, the *beinoni* – are privy to an illumination, a guiding light, from the World to Come. ☞

וְהָעֹנֶג הוּא בְּמוֹחַ חָכְמָה וְשֵׂכֶל הַמִּתְעַנֵּג בְּהַשְׂכָּלַת ה׳ וִידִיעָתוֹ כְּפִי הַשָּׂגַת שִׂכְלוֹ וְחָכְמָתוֹ.

The delight is experienced **in the brain,** the seat of **wisdom and** the **intellect, which delights in apprehending God and knowing Him, commensurate with the capacity of one's intellect and wisdom to apprehend** God.

As explained above, awareness is what defines feeling. Just as there is awareness that leads to fiery love, to desire, craving, and longing, so there is a type of awareness, deriving from the faculty of wisdom in the mind, by which the more one contemplates, the more delight one derives.

It appears that the love of delights in particular is associated with the intellect that generates it. More accurately, it is associated with the faculty of wisdom, not so much as an independent emotion born of consciousness, but more as an emotion inextricably bound to the faculty of wisdom that produces it. This bond is unobstructed by any interposing barriers, allowing for a single, unified state of love "in the brain, [the seat of] wisdom and [the] intellect, which delights in apprehending God…." As explained elsewhere,[5] this core level of delight is the experience of the light of *Ein Sof* prior to its becoming clothed in the faculties of the soul, a state that can be touched only by the faculty of wisdom in the soul.

וְהוּא בְּחִינַת הַמַּיִם וְזֶרַע אוֹר זָרוּעַ שֶׁבִּקְדוּשַּׁת נֶפֶשׁ הָאֱלֹהִית הַמְהַפֶּכֶת לְטוֹב אֶת בְּחִינַת הַמַּיִם שֶׁבַּנֶּפֶשׁ הַבַּהֲמִית שֶׁמֵּהֶם בָּאוּ תַּאֲוֹת תַּעֲנוּגֵי עוֹלָם הַזֶּה מִתְּחִלָּה.

This love of delights **has the quality of the water and seed of light that is sown in the holiness of the divine soul, which transforms to good the element of water in the animal soul from which the lusts for the delights of this world originated.**

5. See gloss in chap. 35, citing the Maggid of Mezeritch.

This love of delights is like water, which is always channeled from a higher place. It is the love of the divine soul that is channeled downward to the mundane love experienced by the animal soul, transforming the love for the mundane into love of God.

When a person attains the higher level of love of delights, he no longer needs to force himself to abandon worldly matters and desires, because he no longer desires them. In this state of being, the mere existence of God is a source of delight. From this vantage point, all other pleasures are sterile alternatives to the delight in their ultimate source. This is the transition from the stage of subduing to that of transforming, from the stage where one has to suppress the animal soul to where the animal soul itself desires holiness. This is the ultimate solution to all the problems of desire, in all its forms and expressions. On this level, the person has achieved a resolution to the problem of desire at its root, eliminating the necessity for all other solutions.

We are drawn to worldly pleasures only so long as we are not connected with the Source of all things. All secondary, tertiary, and other substitutes serve only to drown out our single, basic need: our intrinsic love for God. Unwittingly, our thirst for God is contorted into other

THE PATH TO THE LOVE OF DELIGHTS

☞ The scenario seems idyllic. A person has a straight path before him: He contemplates God's greatness, which leads him to a love for God that is as fierce as "sparks of fire." The desire increases until it fills his heart and overflows to its other side and he attains "love of delights." Now he no longer desires or needs anything else.

In actuality, it is never that simple. Each of these stages can take thirty or sixty years or a whole lifetime of toil, with ups and downs and without a moment's respite. The road itself is full of contradictions. There is love like fire on the one hand, a process of self-abnegation, and on the other a process of intensification of the ego – because the more a person loves, the more pronounced is the self that loves and desires. Progress is thus engulfed in crises.

Elsewhere, the author of the *Tanya* says that the road to love in delights passes through the stage of awe (see chaps. 42–43; *Iggeret HaKodesh*, epistle 18). Before a person can experience an attachment to God, he must first annul his very self, abnegating all his desires and aspirations. As long as the "I" desires, it lacks; and the more it desires, the more it lacks. To achieve a love that is more gratifying, a love that fulfills the craving of the soul, one must, in a sense, waive love itself. The juncture in the road to higher love is not a simple transition but involves the annihilation of the initial level of love so that the soul's lusts, which seem to offer a solution, to quench our thirst. But once we attain a "love of delights" for God, all these things cease to attract us. We no longer crave them; they no longer even exist for us. ☞

וּכְמוֹ שֶׁכָּתוּב בְּעֵץ חַיִּים שַׁעַר נ׳ פֶּרֶק ג׳ בְּשֵׁם הַזֹּהַר (חלק ג רעז, א), שֶׁהָרַע נֶהְפַּךְ לִהְיוֹת טוֹב גָּמוּר כְּמוֹ יֵצֶר טוֹב מַמָּשׁ בְּהָסִיר הַבְּגָדִים הַצּוֹאִים מִמֶּנּוּ, שֶׁהֵם תַּעֲנוּגֵי עוֹלָם הַזֶּה, שֶׁהוּא מְלוּבָּשׁ בָּהֶם.

Likewise, it is written in *Etz Ḥayyim* 50:3, citing the *Zohar* (3:277a), that the evil within the animal soul **is transformed and becomes completely good, literally like the good inclination, when divested of its soiled garments, which are the pleasures of this world, within which** the animal soul **is clothed.**

This form of divine service is fundamental to hasidic thought. The *Zohar* quoted here distinguishes between the perpetually positive inner motivating force behind desire and love themselves and the garments of the desire, the negative forms it assumes. Because it is possible to separate the two, to strip the essential desire of the animal soul of its "soiled garments," the desire can be transformed and redirected from

faculty for love can be reconstructed in a completely different manner.

It is told of the author of the *Tanya* that he would stand and declare before God, "I do not want Your Eden, I do not want Your World to Come – I want only You!" There is a level at which a person attains a lofty state and desires to delight in God, so he is given the chance to delight in God. But higher than this is the level at which a person desires nothing. He waives even the pleasure that is found in the love of God and wants only "to be drawn into the body of the King" (*Zohar* 1:217b) – to be completely subsumed within God.

A HOLY EDUCATION

☞ The transformation of the animal soul is not a transformation of its essence but a process of educating, training, and refocusing its desires. The will of the animal soul serves as the evil inclination within man only as long as it desires evil, but in and of itself, at its essence, it is not evil. It desires evil, not because it is evil, but because it conceives of it as good. A baby who eats garbage does not do so out of a corrupt inner nature but because he thinks that it's tasty. He simply doesn't know better; he has not yet been educated about what is edible and what is not good to eat.

Education begins the moment a child is aware of himself. Our problem is that in that initial stage, a person learns that the one extreme to the other. This means that one has to change, not the essence of one's animal nature and the inner forces operating in the animal soul, but only their object. ☞

וְכֵן שְׁאָר כָּל הַמִּדּוֹת שֶׁבַּלֵּב, שֶׁהֵן עַנְפֵי הַיִּרְאָה וְהָאַהֲבָה, יִהְיוּ לַה' לְבַדּוֹ.

Similarly, all the other attributes in the heart, which are the offshoots of fear and love, should also be solely for God.

The bulk of this chapter dealt with the emotion of love. But the same applies to the heart's other emotions. A person can also be educated properly with regard to all these, clothed with the proper garments and elevating them, level by level, to holiness.

material world is the only world of substance, and realities that cannot be visualized are discounted as insignificant and therefore not desirable. Because our initial perception of reality is that only the material is "material," material things automatically become the things that the person wants and desires.

Someone who lives by his desires has difficulty distinguishing between the desire itself and the desired object. Yet one may observe in others desires that do not pertain to him, and he can view these desires objectively, analyze them, and clearly see the difference between desire and object of desire. For instance, when a football team wins an "important" match, one can observe people mourning or celebrating something that has no true effect on their lives. They cheer and rejoice over something that has no real substance and requires a great degree of abstraction to relate directly to themselves. Why should it matter to Joe the taxi driver which way the ball went? What real impact does it have on his life?

Some say that people are self-centered and only want what they can enjoy and gives them gratification, but it is not that black and white. This is not to say that such absurdity has any virtue, but it can serve as a model to demonstrate that, with the proper conditioning, people can derive a great deal of satisfaction from something they never saw and does not supply them with any material benefit. There is no reason people should not get equally excited over matters of holiness if their environment and education impressed them with a different set of priorities.

Once we are able to draw the distinction, it becomes clear that the distortion lies with the "soiled garments" rather than the intrinsic drives of the animal soul. Therein lies the hope, the feasibility of the *Tanya*'s program. The garments can be changed, rectified, and improved, and the very same drives that previously fueled the lowliest of cravings can now impel the person in the loftiest pursuits, even to the point of self-sacrifice, with the same passion he had for material things and often with an even greater intensity.

וְכָל כֹּחַ הַדִּבּוּר שֶׁבַּפֶּה וְהַמַּחֲשָׁבָה שֶׁבַּמּוֹחַ יִהְיוּ מְמוּלָּאִים מִן לְבוּשֵׁי הַמַּחֲשָׁבָה וְהַדִּבּוּר שֶׁל נֶפֶשׁ הָאֱלֹהִית לְבַדָּהּ, שֶׁהֵן מַחֲשֶׁבֶת ה׳ וְתוֹרָתוֹ לִהְיוֹת שִׂיחָתוֹ כָּל הַיּוֹם, לָא פָּסֵיק פּוּמֵיהּ מִגִּירְסָא.

The entire faculty of speech in the mouth and the thought in the brain should be permeated solely with the garments of thought and speech of the divine soul, which are the thoughts of God and His Torah, so that it may be one's subject **of conversation all day, his mouth never ceasing from** Torah **study.**

When everything a person says or thinks revolves around the Torah, or even with things that are necessary for him to live so that he may study and practice Torah, it can be said that his thoughts and speech are "permeated" with Torah. Even if it is not possible for a person's thoughts and speech to be restricted to Torah alone, they can nevertheless be permeated with it: namely, when Torah constitutes his only true desire, a desire that suffuses the innermost recesses of his heart. If a thought or word is not Torah in its substance, then he thinks it or says it only because he must, only because it is essential to his existence – an existence dedicated to Torah – and then he immediately returns to his true and only interest: Torah. When this is the case, his faculties of thought and speech are indeed permeated with Torah.

וְכֹחַ הַמַּעֲשִׂיִּי שֶׁבְּיָדָיו וּשְׁאָר רמ״ח אֵבָרָיו יִהְיֶה בְּמַעֲשֵׂה הַמִּצְוֹת לְבַד, שֶׁהוּא לְבוּשׁ הַשְּׁלִישִׁי שֶׁל נֶפֶשׁ הָאֱלֹהִית.

The faculty of action in his hands and the rest of his 248 limbs should be engaged **solely in the act of** performing **the commandments,** action **being the third garment of the divine soul.**

The soul has three garments by which it expresses itself: thought, speech, and action. The desire of the divine soul is that these should exclusively be in its domain, that the person's thoughts, words, and deeds should serve only the divine soul, making the body the exclusive instrument of its will.

אַךְ נֶפֶשׁ הַבַּהֲמִית שֶׁמֵּהַקְּלִיפָּה רְצוֹנָהּ לְהֵפֶךְ מַמָּשׁ.

However, the will of the animal soul, which stems **from** ***kelippa,*** **is literally the opposite.**

The author of the *Tanya* does not elaborate on the specific ways that the body's faculties and garments should serve the animal soul alone as he does in the case of the divine soul, perhaps because we are already all too familiar with these details, and in any case there is no duty to teach them.

The idea that the animal soul desires the exact opposite of the divine soul implies that there is no room here for compromise. A person might arrive at some sort of middle ground between the two halves of his inner self in an attempt to effect a peaceful coexistence between them, but such compromise is inherently partial and temporary. Ultimately, both souls want one thing: complete domination. So inherently, there is no room for compromise. ☞

לְטוֹבַת הָאָדָם שֶׁיִּתְגַּבֵּר עָלֶיהָ וִינַצְּחֶנָּה,

This is ultimately **for man's benefit, so that he may overpower it and emerge victorious,**

NO COMPROMISE

☞ If all that were required of a Jew would merely be to go to synagogue and pray there at certain times, life would be far more simple. But the Jew is also required to leave the synagogue for the outside world, where he is faced with the real question: What happens then? It is impossible to make some sort of compromise, cutting life in two, half for holiness and half for the mundane or the profane, because the spheres of holiness and *kelippa* cannot live alongside each other peacefully. Inevitably, a struggle ensues in which one soul prevails.

Another problem is that the spheres are not clearly defined. Within the range of the animal soul's desires are also aesthetic, philosophical, and even religious cravings. The aim of the animal soul is to satisfy the ego, and if doing holy things makes a person feel good, the animal soul can also grant him the illusion of holiness. As long as a person wishes to serve God part-time, as a hobby, his animal soul will be fully supportive of the endeavor. It will provide him with all the accoutrements of holiness and holy feelings, as much as he desires, because the essence of the battle, the quintessential point over which the souls are fighting, is who should occupy the innermost point, the epicenter of the person.

The author of *Ḥiddushei HaRim*, Rabbi Yitzḥak Meir of Gur, used to say that once Satan has taken the inner kernel of truth from a person, he is prepared to leave him all the outer trappings. If the person wants to wear a *shtreimel* (the hasidic fur hat), he can wear it. If he wants to pray, let him pray. If he wants to be a hasid, let him be a hasid, because even so, he can remain just an animal. Perhaps he is a different animal, somewhat more refined, who enjoys different pastimes, such as attending concerts, perhaps even concerts exclusively devoted to *ḥazzanut*, but an animal nonetheless.

Here the author of the *Tanya* touches on a deeper point. He has defined a dualistic world: holiness on one side, *kelippa* on the other, each struggling over the neutral ground in between. But at its root, it is not a true duality. In essence, the animal soul too is a creation of God, and it too desires holiness. The animal soul struggles against the divine soul, but its innermost desire is for man to defeat it. The seduction practiced by the animal soul is really a contrived challenge to enable the divine soul to reach higher levels. ☞

כְּמְשַׁל הַזּוֹנָה שֶׁבַּזֹּהַר הַקָּדוֹשׁ (חלק ב קסג, א). **as in the parable of the harlot** given **in the holy *Zohar*** (2:163a).

The *Zohar* relates the parable of a king who was extremely fond of his only son, and out of his love for him instructed him to stay away from

THE ANIMAL SOUL'S CHALLENGE FOR MAN

☞ A soul on its own, denuded of the body and the accoutrements of physical life, is a holy entity, but it is also a static entity, because it has nothing to overcome. Some hasidic masters would say that if God had merely desired love or study of Torah, He would have created a few million angels to love Him and to sit and study, but because there is no challenge in this, He does not desire it. Angels are static; they are what they are and do not change. It is for this reason that they are called *omdim*, "standing" (Zech. 3:7).

The pure soul is likewise static. In order to be truly desirable to God, in order that its service of God be significant, it requires a challenge, and the animal soul provides that challenge. The animal soul, in its primal state, is not evil in the destructive and negative sense but a kind of challenge that arises from the duality of human nature and the possibility of free will, a challenge that enables a person to achieve what even the pure soul cannot achieve.

Elsewhere, the author of the *Tanya* states that some souls descend to this world for the sole purpose of suffering. From these souls, God desires neither Torah nor divine service, only that they should suffer all their lives. This may seem cruel, but from a different standpoint, it represents a conception of reality that is not oriented toward achievement. What is important is not how many pages of Talmud the person has studied, or even how many mitzvot he has performed on a particular day, but the success of the soul in overcoming its challenges. Although such souls are completely befuddled by their situation and may not be able to pray at all, this is better for them than had they prayed with utter self-abnegation, since this spiritual refinement mitigates and rectifies any evil that must be scoured from the soul. What is important is what a person does despite all the challenges that confront him. As Rabbi Levi Yitzḥak of Berditchev would interject with great emphasis when promiscuous women.[6] One day the king decided to test his son. The king hired a prostitute and instructed her to seduce his son. The harlot had to try her best to faithfully perform the task for which she was employed, but she knew that her greatest reward would come if she failed. She also knew that if the prince succeeded at resisting her, he would rise in greatness, and she would be the cause of it.

By the same token, the task of the animal soul is to seduce a person, but it too knows that God's intention is that the person should overcome it. The animal soul does everything in its power to seduce the person, but it takes no pleasure in its victories. On the contrary, its true satisfaction comes from its failures.

This chapter, which revolves around the battle between the animal soul and the divine soul, concludes with a parable about the prostitute from the holy *Zohar*, a parable that puts a whole different perspective on the war. In truth, there is no war at all. It seems to be a battle between life and death when in fact it is the joint work of the two souls to attain a higher spiritual level than that which could be achieved had they been functioning independently of one another.

he sang the *Hoshana* prayer, "[The Jewish people] are exiled and rebellious, yet despite it all, they are [as virtuously beautiful] as the date palm."

The Sages have declared that a person is never subjected to a test that he has not been granted the capacity to withstand. The more difficult the test, the more emphatic the implied message: "You have what it takes to overcome this and grow from it." The degree of the test's difficulty is proof of the soul's ability to rise higher. From this perspective, there are no greater or stronger individuals. Each and every individual possesses a divine soul and an animal soul that are precisely matched so that there should be an ongoing challenge and a perpetual struggle that he can meet and overcome, so that he can constantly achieve – "despite it all."

6. See chap. 29, where this parable is also presented.

Chapter 10

AFTER EXTENSIVE DISCUSSION REGARDING THE TWO souls, the author of the *Tanya* returns to the person himself, in whom the two souls coexist. The previous chapter spoke of the perpetual and uncompromising battle between the divine soul and the animal soul, each of which desires to gain total mastery over the body, and essentially over the individual himself. Though it may have no resolution, at some point a certain equilibrium is achieved in every person's life, a spiritual front line around which the war takes place. What determines this line depends on the innate qualities of the person's soul, the events in his life, and the education he received.

Apart from the people, events, and vicissitudes unique to the life of each individual, people can be defined by the same general categories, which are the five ranks that were delineated in the first chapter: the completely righteous person, the righteous person who is not completely righteous, the completely wicked person, the wicked person who is not completely wicked, and the *beinoni*. This chapter is the first in a series of chapters in which these categories will be described one by one.

וְהִנֵּה כְּשֶׁהָאָדָם מַגְבִּיר נַפְשׁוֹ הָאֱלֹהִית וְנִלְחָם כָּל כָּךְ עִם הַבַּהֲמִית עַד שֶׁמְּגָרֵשׁ וּמְבָעֵר הָרַע שֶׁבָּהּ מֵחָלָל הַשְּׂמָאלִי, כְּמוֹ שֶׁכָּתוּב: "וּבִעַרְתָּ הָרָע מִקִּרְבֶּךָ" (דברים כא, כא),

11 Tevet

15 Tevet (leap year)

When a person fortifies his divine soul and fights so vigorously with the animal soul **that he drives out and eliminates its evil from the left chamber** of his heart, **as it is written, "You shall eliminate the evil from your midst"** (Deut. 21:21),

The literal meaning of this verse is in the social context, referring to the elimination of an evil individual from the community. Here the author of the *Tanya* is presenting it as an injunction to eliminate the evil element within oneself.

וְאֵין הָרַע נֶהְפַּךְ לְטוֹב מַמָּשׁ, נִקְרָא צַדִּיק שֶׁאֵינוֹ גָּמוּר, וְצַדִּיק וְרַע לוֹ, דְּהַיְינוּ שֶׁיֵּשׁ בּוֹ עֲדַיִין מְעַט מִזְּעֵר רַע בְּחָלָל הַשְּׂמָאלִי

yet the evil did not transform into actual good, he is referred to as an incomplete tzaddik, or by the parallel term, **a righteous person who suffers,** literally, "a righteous person who possesses evil." **That is, he still has a minuscule amount of evil in the left chamber** of his heart, the abode of the animal soul.

In its most literal sense, the phrase *tzaddik vera lo*, or "a righteous person who suffers," relates to the issue of reward and punishment and the age-old question, why do the righteous suffer? Why do they experience evil? But the phrase also has a deeper meaning: It refers to the tzaddik who still possesses some evil, which relates to the inner composition of the incomplete tzaddik.

אֶלָּא שֶׁכָּפוּף וּבָטֵל לַטּוֹב מֵחֲמַת מִיעוּטוֹ, וְלָכֵן נִדְמֶה לוֹ כִּי וַיְגָרְשֵׁהוּ וַיֵּלֶךְ לוֹ כּוּלּוֹ לְגַמְרֵי. אֲבָל בֶּאֱמֶת אִלּוּ חָלַף וְהָלַךְ לוֹ לְגַמְרֵי כָּל הָרַע שֶׁבּוֹ, הָיָה נֶהְפַּךְ לְטוֹב מַמָּשׁ.

Yet on account of its minuteness, the evil within him **is subservient and nullified by the good. It therefore seems to him that he has driven it out and it has gone wholly and completely, but in truth, had all the evil in him disappeared and was gone completely, it would have transformed into actual good.**

There is no outward difference, in deed, speech, or thought, between a complete tzaddik and an incomplete tzaddik. A person who acts in full conformity with the divine will might be completely righteous, but he might also be an incomplete tzaddik or even, as will be explained, not a tzaddik at all but a *beinoni*. The difference is internal and invisible and might even elude the person himself. One cannot always know whether one has achieved a complete transformation within.

The definition of a tzaddik, complete or otherwise, is someone who has no internal struggle against evil. His divine soul has achieved a decisive victory over his animal soul, and if this has not happened, he is not a tzaddik. To distinguish between the complete tzaddik and the incomplete tzaddik, one requires some sign, some indication, to tell him whether the tzaddik has truly overcome his evil inclination. If he had indeed driven out all evil from within, the animal soul would not have merely submitted to the divine soul. Something more drastic would have occurred: The evil would have been converted into absolute good.

Complete victory implies more than mere conquest of *kelippa* by the divine soul, more than the neutralization of the animal soul's ability to tempt the person with material pleasures. It implies a complete transformation so that the animal soul itself has become a force for holiness. So long as a person has not yet achieved this fundamental change, a residue of evil remains within him, and he is still in the category of a "righteous person who possesses evil." ☞

FOR WHOM WAS THE *TANYA* WRITTEN?

☞ A scenario where a person does not even have any evil thoughts seems completely divorced from reality, or certainly does not apply to the majority of people, to say the least. To whom, then, is this book directed?

Rabbi Shneur Zalman's followers included ordinary people, but also many who had attained great heights in Torah scholarship and spirituality even before they came to him. To be accepted even into the lowest of his study groups (called *ḥadarim*, these groups were classified according to the rank of its participants; see *Sefer HaToledot Rabbi Shneur Zalman MiLiadi*, chap. 11), one had to be thoroughly versed in both the Babylonian and Jerusalem Talmuds, *Zohar*, and the basic works of *mussar* and Jewish philosophy. For them, the terms "tzaddik" and "complete tzaddik" and their own relationship to these terms were not completely disconnected from the reality.

Furthermore, although the concept of tzaddik as defined in this book might be extremely difficult to attain, it is a standard that any seeker of truth can study and use to measure himself. On the most basic level, one who commits any negative act, or even feels drawn to commit evil, cannot be called a tzaddik.

There is a popular joke that tells of a hasid who was confined to his deathbed in a foreign country where he was totally unknown. The local Jews suggested that he perform the deathbed confession. The hasid replied that he had nothing to confess. But they pressed him: How can a Jew die without first confessing? He finally acquiesced, asked for a prayer book, opened it, and began to recite the confession.

"'*Ashamnu*,'" he began. "We have been

וּבֵיאוּר הָעִנְיָן, כִּי הִנֵּה צַדִּיק גָּמוּר שֶׁנֶּהְפַּךְ הָרַע שֶׁלּוֹ לְטוֹב וְלָכֵן נִקְרָא צַדִּיק וְטוֹב לוֹ, הוּא עַל יְדֵי הֲסָרַת הַבְּגָדִים הַצּוֹאִים לְגַמְרֵי מֵהָרַע, דְּהַיְינוּ לְמְאוֹס מְאֹד בְּתַעֲנוּגֵי עוֹלָם הַזֶּה, לְהִתְעַנֵּג בָּם בְּתַעֲנוּגוֹת בְּנֵי אָדָם לְמַלֹּאת תַּאֲוַת הַגּוּף בִּלְבַד וְלֹא לַעֲבוֹדַת ה׳, מִפְּנֵי הֱיוֹתָם נִמְשָׁכִים וְנִשְׁפָּעִים מֵהַקְּלִיפָּה וְסִטְרָא אָחֳרָא.

The explanation of the matter is as follows: **A complete tzaddik, whose evil has been transformed into good and, as such, is referred to as a righteous person who possesses** only **good**, effected this transformation **by completely removing the soiled garments from the evil. In other words,** the tzaddik **is exceedingly repulsed by the pleasures of this world, from gaining pleasure from human gratification, satisfying bodily lusts exclusively and not for the service of God, because** the pleasures **stem from and issue forth from the *kelippa* and *sitra aḥara*.**

That the person is disgusted by evil is the sign that he is a complete tzaddik, the indication that he has indeed removed all the "soiled garments." It is not only that he does not commit evil or even bear the temptations of evil, but he actually feels disgusted by it. That means that he cannot enjoy even a permissible thing that is not used for the sake of Heaven, and he certainly cannot commit any such action.

The idea that a person can engage in a physical activity simply to derive enjoyment from it, that a person can eat something simply because it is tasty, is an abomination that the complete tzaddik cannot bear. A hasid of our own generation, Rabbi Yitzḥak Horowitz, better known as "Reb Itche der Masmid," was sent to America by the sixth Lubavitcher Rebbe, Rabbi Yosef Yitzḥak Schneerson. In a letter that he sent home, Reb Itche wrote the profoundly shocking observation that

guilty." Then he paused, thought a little, and said, "No." He continued, "*Bagadnu*. We have been treacherous." Again he paused, thought, and said, "No." And so he continued throughout the alphabetical list until he came to "*Latznu*. We have scoffed," and said, "No. And what I have done in mocking the *mitnagdim* (opponents of Hasidism), I do not regret now either!"

The story is usually told as a joke against *mitnagdim*, but it also shows, from a serious angle, how a person on his deathbed, when every person conducts a true and honest self-assessment, can ask himself, "Have I sinned?" search his conscience, and answer, "No."

"here in America, people actually drink wine and eat meat for pleasure!" Thus we see that there is such a thing as a person who is shocked by the sight of people eating simply to enjoy themselves, without pangs of conscience and without even pretending that they are doing it for a holy purpose. ☞ ☞

THE COMPLETE TZADDIK WHO POSSESSES NO EVIL

☞ The existence of evil is like that of falsehood. There is no such thing as an utter falsehood. No lie can be sustained unless it contains a grain of truth. And when the lie is refined, when the element of truth is extracted from its embodiment of falsehood, the false embodiment disappears completely and one is left with the full, luminous truth.

This is the point of transition from the level of incomplete tzaddik to the level of complete tzaddik, the point at which evil is transformed completely into good. At that point, the person should feel as if the vital forces of his soul have been doubled – more than doubled, because the animal soul's drives are more passionate than those of the divine soul. All that he has done in the past seems to pale into insignificance compared to what he can do now, because now he has found the ultimate resolution to the struggles of life. The very nature of reality is transformed for him, and he functions as a totally different person.

It is said that there are two levels of tzaddik: the tzaddik who does God's will and the tzaddik whose every action is God's will. The latter is the level of the complete tzaddik. The incomplete tzaddik is never without a certain awareness that his mind must rule over his being and direct it toward the divine will. The complete tzaddik requires no such control. He can give free rein to his desires, because his desires always reflect the will of God. He requires no direction, because all directions his psyche might take are holy. Such a person does not inhabit a world where both good and evil are possible, because his entirety is a *merkava*, a vehicle for Godliness.

The hasidic master Rabbi Naḥum of Shtefanesht (son of Rabbi Yisrael of Ruzhin) once entered the study hall on Hanukkah and found his disciples enjoying a game of checkers. He asked them if they knew the rules of the game, but no one ventured a reply. Rabbi Naḥum promptly said, "I will tell you. The first rule is that you give up one in order to take two. The second rule is that you only move forward, and the third rule is that once you reach the end of the board, you can move any way you desire."

The implication is that the complete tzaddik has reached "the end of the board" in the battle of life. He can go whichever way he desires, because whichever route he takes is God's will. The tzaddik is simply incapable of acting any other way.

THE FREE WILL OF THE RIGHTEOUS

☞ Although the tzaddik is utterly free of the evil inclination that plagues the ordinary man, he is not devoid of free will. As long as he is in the human realm, he is free

וְכָל מַה שֶּׁהוּא מֵהַסִּטְרָא אָחֳרָא, הַצַּדִּיק גָּמוּר הוּא שׂוֹנְאוֹ בְּתַכְלִית הַשִּׂנְאָה, מֵחֲמַת גּוֹדֶל אַהֲבָתוֹ לַה׳ וּקְדוּשָּׁתוֹ בְּאַהֲבָה רַבָּה בְּתַעֲנוּגִים וְחִיבָּה יְתֵרָה הַנִּזְכָּרִים לְעֵיל, כִּי הֵם זֶה לְעוּמַּת זֶה, כְּדִכְתִיב: ״תַּכְלִית שִׂנְאָה שְׂנֵאתִים לְאוֹיְבִים הָיוּ לִי חָקְרֵנִי וְדַע לְבָבִי״ וגו׳ (תהלים קלט, כב-כג).

The complete tzaddik utterly hates anything that stems from the *sitra aḥara* on account of the magnitude of his love for God and His holiness, as manifest **by the aforementioned great love of delights and utmost affection** for Him, **since one corresponds to the other, as it is written, "I hate them with utter hatred; they have become my enemies. Search me, God, and know my heart…"** (Ps. 139:22–23).

The way to "search me and know my heart," to find out if one's love for God is indeed absolute, is to see whether one's regard of everything deriving from *kelippa* is such that "I hate them with utter hatred." The two are antithetical to each other. A desire, or even the slightest affinity, for *kelippa* indicates a less than complete desire for the Divine.

to choose and even err. Moreover, there are situations in which there is a fault to every available option. These are faults that do not arise from within the tzaddik but are inherent in the situation itself. Moses is recorded as having lost his temper on a number of occasions. Anger is certainly a fault, yet the situation made it impossible for him to act otherwise. It was the only educational means available to him to correct the problem. Moses, who was close to God more than anyone else before or since, faced choices. He chose, mistakenly or not, to do something that was counted against him as his great sin.

Situations arise in which perfection is not possible, in which the very structure of reality and the relationship between a person, the world, and God are such that no perfect solution exists. In such a situation, even a tzaddik can reach an erroneous decision. King David's sin with Bathsheba was a tragedy for Uriya, for David, and for Bathsheba, but from the greater perspective of Jewish history, it gave rise to one of the greatest moments of *teshuva*, repentance, as described in Psalms 51.

Virtually every person sins, and when a sinner reads the words of the psalm – "When Natan the prophet came to him [David] after he had been with Bathsheba…" – he has something to relate to. Considering that David is the fourth leg of the divine chariot of Ezekiel's vision, David's sin might be the only way that certain people can relate to him. In this sense, the failings of the righteous are our path to elevation.

וּכְפִי עֶרֶךְ גּוֹדֶל הָאַהֲבָה לַה'
כָּךְ עֶרֶךְ גּוֹדֶל הַשִּׂנְאָה לְסִטְרָא
אָחֳרָא וְהַמִּיאוּס בָּרַע בְּתַכְלִית,
כִּי הַמִּיאוּס הוּא הֵפֶךְ הָאַהֲבָה
מַמָּשׁ, כְּמוֹ הַשִּׂנְאָה.

Commensurate with the magnitude of one's love for God, so is the magnitude of one's hatred toward the *sitra aḥara* and one's **utter repulsion of evil, for repulsion is literally the opposite of love, as is hatred.**

Every person hates what is contrary to that which he loves. Since the tzaddik has love only for God, he abhors what is contrary to it: the *sitra aḥara*, the other side that is antithetical to holiness. Such a measure of the heart's desires is not limited to complete tzaddikim. In every society and in every individual's inner moral scale are certain things that are simply not done, certain limits that are not to be exceeded no matter what, things that are utterly despised because they are antithetical to everything that society or that the individual understands to be right and desirable. These things are not only not done, they are unthinkable. They are not temptations that need to be resisted because they are so totally abhorred that no possibility of temptation exists.

The idea of murdering someone in order to rob him of his money was once unheard of in Israeli society; there were thieves, but killing for money was taboo. Today, that boundary has been breached, and Israeli society has, so to speak, become receptive to the idea that such things are possible. People might still utterly reject the idea of killing for money, but they no longer feel the horror and abomination that the very thought once evoked, because the act has entered the realm of possibility.

In our society, the idea of eating human flesh is unthinkable. If we hear of a case of cannibalism, our reaction is one of total abhorrence and extreme contempt toward the one who did such a deed. Yet there are places in the world where even if people do not practice cannibalism daily, the idea is not unthinkable.

There are things that people would never do, sins they would never commit, yet the possibility is not unthinkable, and the temptation or at least the thought of doing them might occasionally arise in their hearts. But for every person, there are certain sins regarding which his heart is utterly pure, sins he would never even consider as a possibility. This is the way the complete tzaddik relates to everything belonging to the sphere of that which is unholy, in every shape and form. He does not comprehend them; they do not enter his mind. His mind and soul are attuned to that which is holy and yearn for God alone. Worldly pleasures of any kind are inconceivable to him, and he fails to understand how they can be conceivable to anyone else. ☞

16 Tevet (leap year)

וְצַדִּיק שֶׁאֵינוֹ גָּמוּר, הוּא שֶׁאֵינוֹ שׂוֹנֵא הַסִּטְרָא אָחֳרָא בְּתַכְלִית הַשִּׂנְאָה, וְלָכֵן אֵינוֹ מוֹאֵס גַּם כֵּן בָּרַע בְּתַכְלִית, וְכָל שֶׁאֵין הַשִּׂנְאָה וְהַמִּיאוּס בְּתַכְלִית - עַל כָּרְחָךְ נִשְׁאָר אֵיזֶה שֶׁמֶץ אַהֲבָה וְתַעֲנוּג לְשָׁם, וְלֹא הוּסְרוּ הַבְּגָדִים הַצּוֹאִים לְגַמְרֵי מִכֹּל וָכֹל. וְלָכֵן לֹא נֶהְפַּךְ לְטוֹב מַמָּשׁ מֵאַחַר שֶׁיֵּשׁ לוֹ אֵיזֶה אֲחִיזָה עֲדַיִן בַּבְּגָדִים הַצּוֹאִים, אֶלָּא שֶׁהוּא בָּטֵל בְּמִיעוּטוֹ וּכְלָא חֲשִׁיב, וְלָכֵן נִקְרָא צַדִּיק וְרַע כָּפוּף וּבָטֵל לוֹ.

An incomplete tzaddik is one who does not utterly hate the *sitra aḥara*, and therefore also is not utterly repulsed by evil, and as long as the hatred and repulsion of evil **are not absolute, there must necessarily remain a shred of love and pleasure toward it. The soiled garments were not completely removed through and through, and therefore** the evil **did not transform into actual good, since it still has a grip, however slight, on the soiled garments. Rather, it is nullified on account of its insignificance and is reckoned as if it were nothing, and therefore he is referred to as a tzaddik who possesses evil that is subservient and nullified** within him.

ABHORRENCE OF EVIL

☞ Rabbi Yeḥiel Michel of Zlotchov, one of the disciples of the Ba'al Shem Tov, was known as a complete tzaddik who possessed *ruaḥ hakodesh*, a level of divine perception akin to prophecy, which reputedly had been in his family for ten generations. A wagon driver in his town once desecrated the Sabbath, regretted his sin, and approached the local rabbi to see what amends he could make. The rabbi saw that the man's penitence was sincere and told him that if he donated a pound of candles to the synagogue, his sin would be forgiven. When Rabbi Yeḥiel Michel heard this, he did not approve: How could a pound of candles compensate for a breach of the Sabbath?

That Friday afternoon, when the wagon driver came and placed his candles in the appropriate place, a large dog entered

The incomplete tzaddik behaves like a complete tzaddik in every way. He too has passed the stage of inner doubt, torment, and struggle. He too is not tempted by evil and experiences no urge for anything that is not holy. The difference between them is in the innermost recesses of their hearts, in the ultimate transformation of evil to good. The incomplete tzaddik differs from the complete tzaddik in that he has not yet achieved this quintessential transformation. As long as this transformation has not occurred, there is a part of his soul that is not dedicated to the service of God. Although he has succeeded in suppressing that part of himself, and he serves God in all his deeds and ways, he serves Him without feeling an utter hatred for evil, not because he is likely to sin, God forbid, but because his soul still contains a shred of something contrary to that which is holy, albeit in the most subtle and diminished of forms.

As long as a person possesses a vestige of evil within him, he is vulnerable to it, even though he might never actually act on it. The very fact that he is not overcome with revulsion at the thought of it, that he can accept its possibility with equanimity, indicates that it is not

the synagogue, snatched the candles, and ate them before they could be used. The wagon driver was brokenhearted. He went back to the rabbi and told him that God has not accepted his atonement. The rabbi assured him that it was just an unfortunate coincidence. If he brought candles to the synagogue the following week, his sin would be forgiven.

The following week, another mishap occurred, and again the week following, until the rabbi conceded that something was amiss. He sent the penitent to the Ba'al Shem Tov, who realized that Rabbi Yeḥiel Michel was involved somehow and sent for him.

The Ba'al Shem Tov's home in Medzibozh was only a few hours' journey away, but the horses pulling Rabbi Yeḥiel Michel's wagon turned off the road and got lost in the forest. Then an axle broke, and one trouble followed another, so that by the time Rabbi Yeḥiel Michel entered Medzibozh, it was late on Friday afternoon and the sun was setting. The tzaddik feared that he had violated the Sabbath by traveling on the holy day, and when he came to the Ba'al Shem Tov, crushed and broken in spirit and beside himself, the Ba'al Shem Tov called out, "Come here, sinner! Until now you did not know how a Jew who has sinned feels, how brokenhearted he is. Now you will realize that a pound of candles is sufficient!"

Before, Rabbi Yeḥiel Michel, who had ascended all the rungs in the ladder of holiness, could not comprehend how anyone could sin, how one could possibly rebel against God. What others know from within themselves, the tzaddik has to be taught.

completely inconceivable to him. If it were truly beyond possibility for him, it would provoke a sharp negative reaction: "Utterly impossible!" Since the person does not possess an absolute hatred and revulsion of the other side, the potential for the expression of the forces of impurity still exists within him and he is called an incomplete tzaddik.

וְעַל כֵּן גַּם אַהֲבָתוֹ לַה' אֵינָהּ בְּתַכְלִית, וְלָכֵן נִקְרָא צַדִּיק שֶׁאֵינוֹ גָּמוּר.

Consequently, his love for God too is not perfect, and he is therefore referred to as an incomplete tzaddik.

Just as the person's hatred and repulsion for evil is not absolute, his love for God also is not perfect. Since he does not have a perfect hold on that which is holy, he is not completely disassociated from evil. The evil within him has been silenced but has not been converted into a positive force in his divine service. His love of God is thus incomplete, because it is fueled by less than one hundred percent of his potential, by less than the combined forces of his divine and animal souls.

12 Tevet

וְהִנֵּה מַדְרֵגָה זוֹ מִתְחַלֶּקֶת לְרִבְבוֹת מַדְרֵגוֹת בְּעִנְיַן בְּחִינַת מִיעוּט הָרָע הַנִּשְׁאָר מֵאַחַת מֵאַרְבַּע יְסוֹדוֹת הָרָעִים,

This rank of incomplete tzaddik **can be divided into myriad levels** based on **the quality of the shred of remaining evil that stems from one of the four evil elements** of the animal soul

Only one type of complete tzaddik exists: the person who possesses not the slightest trace of evil, having effected its complete conversion into good. By contrast, the incomplete tzaddik still possesses some evil, which comes in many shapes and forms. This translates into myriad types and levels of incomplete tzaddik, defined by the quality and quantity of evil still within him.

וּבְעִנְיַן בִּטּוּלוֹ בְּמִיעוּטוֹ בְּשִׁשִּׁים עַל דֶּרֶךְ מָשָׁל, אוֹ בְּאֶלֶף וּרְבָבָה וְכַיּוֹצֵא עַל דֶּרֶךְ מָשָׁל.

and based on its nullification on account of its insignificance, whether in sixty times as much good, **for example, or, for example, in one thousand or ten thousand and so forth.**

Here the author of the *Tanya* employs halakhic terminology. *Batel beshishim* refers to a circumstance where a small amount of prohibited food that is accidentally mixed with permitted food may in some cases be considered negligible if it is less than one part in sixty. In other cases, the *halakha* raises the question of whether certain foods might be nullified if it is less than one part in a thousand. In the realm of *halakha*, these might not result in different degrees of nullification. When a thing is nullified, it is nullified.

Similarly, there is no practical difference between an incomplete tzaddik whose evil is nullified by sixty and one whose evil is nullified by a thousand. In either case, the evil has been suppressed to the point that it has no effect on his behavior or his inclinations. But in terms of the person's inner truth, in terms of the quality of his love for God and his proximity to his ultimate perfection, there are differences between lesser and greater ratios of nullification.

וְהֵן הֵם בְּחִינַת צַדִּיקִים הָרַבִּים שֶׁבְּכָל הַדּוֹרוֹת, כִּדְאִיתָא בַּגְּמָרָא (סוכה מה, ב): דִּתְמַנֵּיסַר אַלְפֵי צַדִּיקֵי קַיְּימֵי קַמֵּיהּ הַקָּדוֹשׁ בָּרוּךְ הוּא. אַךְ עַל מַעֲלַת צַדִּיק גָּמוּר - הוּא שֶׁאָמַר רַבִּי שִׁמְעוֹן בֶּן יוֹחַאי: "רָאִיתִי בְּנֵי עֲלִיָּה וְהֵם מוּעָטִים" כו'.

These incompletely righteous individuals **constitute the rank of many tzaddikim throughout all the generations, as the Talmud states, "There are eighteen thousand righteous individuals who stand before the Holy One, blessed be He"** (*Sukka* 45b). **Yet with regard to the rank of complete tzaddik, Rabbi Shimon ben Yoḥai said, "I have seen lofty men,** literally, 'men of ascent,' who are truly righteous, **and they are few...."**

In reference to the "eighteen thousand individuals who stand before the Holy One, blessed be He," the author of the *Tanya* states that the Talmud is speaking of incomplete tzaddikim. But with regard to the complete tzaddik, the Talmud quotes Rabbi Shimon bar Yoḥai as declaring that "they are few."

The talmudic statement said in the name of Rabbi Shimon bar Yoḥai continues: "If they number one thousand, I and my son are among them. If they number one hundred, I and my son are among them; and if they number two, I and my son are they." Thus, Rabbi Shimon is not sure that there are more than two complete tzaddikim in his entire generation.

שֶׁלָּכֵן נִקְרָאִים בְּנֵי עֲלִיָּה, שֶׁמְּהַפְּכִין הָרַע וּמַעֲלִים אוֹתוֹ לִקְדוּשָּׁה,

It is for this reason that they are referred to as "men of ascent," because they transform evil and cause it to ascend to holiness,

These lofty men, or "men of ascent," refer to those who have achieved more than mastery over evil. They have actually effected its ascent, having transformed the very composition of their souls so that the *kelippa* has been elevated to holiness.

כְּדְאִיתָא בַּזֹּהַר בַּהַקְדָּמָה (חלק א ד, א) שֶׁכְּשֶׁרָצָה רַבִּי חִיָּיא לַעֲלוֹת לְהֵיכַל רַבִּי שִׁמְעוֹן בֶּן יוֹחַאי שָׁמַע קָלָא נָפִיק וְאָמַר: "מַאן מִנְּכוֹן דִּי חֲשׁוֹכָא מְהַפְּכָן לִנְהוֹרָא וְטַעֲמִין מְרִירוּ לְמִתְקָא עַד לָא יֵיתוּן הָכָא" וכו'.

as stated in the introduction to the *Zohar* (1:4a), **that when Rabbi Ḥiyya wished to ascend to the** heavenly **chamber of Rabbi Shimon ben Yoḥai, he heard a voice issue forth and say, "Those among you who, prior to entering here, transform darkness to light and bitter tastes to sweetness,** only such an individual may enter the heavenly chamber of Rabbi Shimon ben Yoḥai."

Rabbi Shimon was the quintessential complete tzaddik. Those who wished to enter his domain in heaven had to exhibit a similar quality. They had to be more than an incomplete tzaddik; they had to be among the lofty men, the "men of ascent," who transform the evil within their soul into good, the darkness into light, the bitterness into sweetness. These tzaddikim do not merely sweeten the bitter; they transform its bitterness into a new kind of sweetness. They do not merely drive out the darkness; they convert darkness into light.

One who can transform darkness into light has no darkness in his world. The temptations and pains of the world no longer exist for him. For him, no concealment exists, no partition that separates the Divine from the earthly, no gap between the physical and the spiritual.

Rabbi Levi Yitzḥak of Berditchev once visited one of the hasidic masters of his time. The hasidim had been notified in advance of the prestigious guest and were enjoined to treat him with due reverence. Rabbi Levi Yitzḥak arrived for prayers wearing his *tallit* and *tefillin*, but instead of joining in the prayers, he asked after the whereabouts of the kitchen, where he inquired about what was being cooked and chatted at length with the simple folk employed there. The hasidim wanted to chastise the guest for his improper behavior but waited until the prayers were over. Then, to their amazement, they saw their Rebbe take the visitor, whom they had considered to be the most unworthy and inferior, sit with him, and eat with him out of the same plate, the greatest of honors. Their Rebbe then told them, "What this man does, he does in higher worlds."

The distinctions between the lowly and the lofty among ordinary people, between eating because one is hungry and one's spiritual activities vis-à-vis the higher worlds (if one is indeed on that level), do not apply to the complete tzaddik. The complete tzaddik is one whose every action reaches the higher worlds, to which he elevates the lowest and most mundane elements of material life, which is why he and the likes of him are called "men of ascent." With regard to this level, attained only by the rare perfect individual, the prophet Jeremiah said, "If you return, I will restore you, you will stand before Me, and if you extract that which is precious from the worthless, you shall be like My mouth…" (Jer. 15:19). The ability to "extract that which is precious from the worthless" is the unique level of "men of ascent" – that of the complete tzaddik.

וְעוֹד נִקְרָאִים בְּנֵי עֲלִיָּה, מִפְּנֵי שֶׁגַּם עֲבוֹדָתָם בִּבְחִינַת "וַעֲשֵׂה טוֹב", בְּקִיּוּם הַתּוֹרָה וּמִצְוֹתֶיהָ, הוּא לְצוֹרֶךְ גָּבוֹהַּ וּמַעֲלָה מַעֲלָה עַד רוּם הַמַּעֲלוֹת, וְלֹא כְּדֵי לְדָבְקָה בוֹ יִתְבָּרֵךְ בִּלְבַד

Furthermore, completely righteous individuals **are referred to as lofty men,** or "men of ascent," **because also their** divine **service pertaining to doing good, in their fulfillment of the Torah and its commandments, is for the sake of the Most High** and ascends **above and beyond, to the pinnacle of** all **heights, and is not solely in order to cleave to God,** 17 Tevet (leap year)

Two reasons are given as to why the completely righteous are known as "men of ascent." The first addressed the work of the righteous in relation to evil and darkness, which the complete tzaddik elevates to a state of good and light. The second reason, which will be explained further below, addresses how he relates to good. Since his aim is not just to cleave to God but rather to give Him the ultimate gratification, he elevates that good to an even higher place "above and beyond, to the pinnacle of all heights" – not merely to a higher level, but beyond all levels. He elevates it to a realm where nothing, not even he himself, exists. It is a realm in which only the Divine may be found.

This is another distinction between the complete tzaddik and the incomplete tzaddik. The complete tzaddik is one whose yearnings, dreams, and desires are directed, not inward to his own spiritual development, but upward – to God alone. That which is holy is his pleasure and his entire world. He is at such a high level that the basis of his service of God is God Himself. He, the servant, is completely irrelevant. His endeavor to cleave to God is not motivated by his own desire to achieve this state but by the fact that God desires it. ☞

לְרַוּוֹת צִמְאוֹן נַפְשָׁם הַצְּמֵאָה לַה', כְּמוֹ שֶׁכָּתוּב: "הוֹי כָּל צָמֵא לְכוּ לַמַּיִם" (ישעיה נה, א), וּכְמוֹ שֶׁמְּבוֹאָר בְּמָקוֹם אַחֵר.

to quench their parched souls, thirsting for God, as it states, "Ho, everyone thirsty, go to water" (Isa. 55:1), **and as explained elsewhere** (chap. 40).

In a later chapter, the author of the *Tanya* explains the verse "Ho, everyone thirsty, go to water" as referring to anyone who is thirsty

THE YEARNING FOR CLOSENESS

☞ Some say that the craving for closeness to God, to cleave to Him, is also a desire. Yet in order to truly experience it, one must first nullify all other desires. This desire is the most wonderful, the loftiest, and the holiest of all the soul's desires. But the complete tzaddik is one in whom even this desire is annulled. It is not that he no longer desires God but that this desire pales to insignificance before his purpose in life: to fulfill the divine will, as expressed in the verse "Nearness to God is good" (Ps. 73:28). In his all-consuming drive to serve God, he is utterly without any thought of himself, even of the self at its loftiest and holiest level, which manifests itself as his yearning for holiness. Yet even this lofty level no longer exists. His sole purpose and yearning is to serve God for the sake of God.

for God, and the way to quench that thirst is to go to the waters of Torah. The study of Torah and the fulfillment of its commandments are the only way to quench the soul's thirst for God. The complete tzaddik, however, is beyond all that. He studies Torah and fulfills the commandments not to slake his own thirst for God but for God's sake, because God desires that he do so. The complete tzaddik is not only devoid of all material ambitions; he is free of all spiritual ambition as well. His objective is not the elevation of his own spiritual self or the sublime pleasure of being close to God, but only the satisfaction of the divine will.

אֶלָּא כִּדְפֵירְשׁוּ בַּתִּיקּוּנִים (הקדמת תיקוני זהר): **"אֵיזֶהוּ חָסִיד - הַמִּתְחַסֵּד עִם קוֹנוֹ. עִם קַן דִּילֵיהּ, לְיַיחֲדָא קֻדְשָׁא בְּרִיךְ הוּא וּשְׁכִינְתֵּיהּ בַּתַּחְתּוֹנִים".**

Rather, their divine service **is in accordance with the explanation** stated **in the** ***Tikkunei*** *Zohar* (1b): **"Who is a pious person? One who is benevolent toward his Maker** [*Kono*], meaning, **with his Source,** literally "his Nest" [*ken dileih*], which entails **unifying the Holy One, blessed be He, and His Divine Presence in the lower worlds."**

In the Talmud, the term *ḥasid,* literally a benevolent person, is used to connote an individual of great spiritual stature, equivalent to the complete tzaddik described in the *Tanya*. The *Tikkunei Zohar* explains that a ḥasid is "one who is benevolent toward his Maker," one whose every act is an act of benevolence toward God, whose motive in everything he does is not for his own sake, to achieve attachment and closeness with God, but to fulfill the divine will.

For the complete tzaddik, the fulfillment of this divine wish eclipses everything else. He completely forgets his own soul's cravings and desires, indeed his very sense of self, in the endeavor "to unite the Holy One, blessed be He, and His Divine Presence." ☞

TO RAISE THE HEAVENS

☞ The story is told of two disciples of one of the great hasidic masters who met after being separated for many years. One asked the other, "Why was man created?"

וּכְמוֹ שֶׁכָּתוּב בְּרַעְיָא מְהֵימְנָא פָּרָשַׁת תֵּצֵא (חלק ג רפא, א): "כִּבְרָא דְּאִשְׁתַּדֵּל בָּתַר אֲבוֹי וְאִימֵּיהּ דְּרָחִים לוֹן יַתִּיר מִגַּרְמֵיהּ וְנַפְשֵׁיהּ וְרוּחֵיהּ וְנִשְׁמָתֵיהּ כו' וּמָסַר גַּרְמֵיהּ לְמִיתָה עֲלַיְיהוּ לְמִיפְרַק לוֹן" כו', וּכְמוֹ שֶׁנִּתְבָּאֵר בְּמָקוֹם אַחֵר

It is also written in *Raya Meheimna, Parashat* *Ki Tetze* (3:281a), describing the service of the righteous, **"As a son who tends to his father and mother, loving them more than himself,** more than **his *nefesh, ruaḥ,*** and ***neshama*... and gives up his own life for their sakes to redeem them from captivity...,"** as is also **explained elsewhere** (chap. 41).

A complete tzaddik is one who abnegates not only the desires of his animal soul but also those of his divine soul, because the only desire that drives him is that which God desires. Such self-sacrifice is greater than physical martyrdom, when a person sacrifices his life for a certain cause. When a person gives up his life, he is sacrificing his body, but when a person forgoes the positive and holy desires of his soul for the sake of Heaven, the sacrifice is much greater.

At one level, a tzaddik desires to withdraw from all worldly affairs and cleave to God, but at a higher level, he is prepared to waive even this desire because God wants him to be in the world. This is the highest form of self-sacrifice, sacrifice of the divine soul's desire to enjoy the closeness of God.

[וּשְׁנֵיהֶם עוֹלִים בְּקָנֶה אֶחָד,

(These two explanations **go hand in hand,**

Both reasons given here regarding why complete tzaddikim are called "men of ascent" go hand in hand. That they transform evil into good and

"To refine himself" was the other's reply.

Said the first, "Have you forgotten what we learned? Man was created to raise the heavens!" – not to think about himself at all but only to "unite the Holy One and His Divine Presence."

One who serves God in order to attach himself to God achieves a level of self-improvement, but the one who serves to "unite the Holy One and His Divine Presence" (see chap. 41) raises the heavens. He does not think of self-improvement, not because such a thing does not exist, but because it is insignificant compared to the essence of his mission in life: to "raise the heavens."

darkness to light, elevating them to the realm of holiness, and that their only motivation is toward Heaven alone without any self-consideration, even for the divine soul, are in essence two aspects of the same truth.

כִּי עַל יְדֵי הַבֵּירוּרִים שֶׁמְּבָרְרִים מִנּוֹגַהּ

since by means of the refinement achieved through distilling the *kelippa* of ***noga,***

Man's service of God in the physical world consists primarily of what kabbalists call the work of refinement, the extraction of the kernel of divine vitality within the *kelippa* of *noga* and its elevation to holiness. The mitzvot, physical deeds involving physical objects, are performed within the realm of *kelippat noga*, the realm of the mundane. They reveal the holiness within *noga*, extracting it from its husk and elevating it to its source in God. This is what happens when a physical item is made into an object of holiness, such as a *tallit*, *shofar*, or *lulav*. It is also what happens to the person's very body and animal soul when he directs his physical life toward service of the Divine.

מַעֲלִים מַיִין נוּקְבִין וְנַעֲשִׂים יִחוּדִים עֶלְיוֹנִים לְהוֹרִיד מַיִין דְּכוּרִין,

one causes feminine waters to ascend, effecting supernal unifications, and thereby **causing masculine waters to descend.**

The most primary and basic division in reality is that which is between upper and lower, a division that appears in the very first stages of the Creation in the form of the separation of the upper waters from the lower waters. The upper waters belong to the heavenly reality and are what the kabbalists call "masculine waters," waters that provide. The kabbalists call the lower waters, belonging to the lower reality, that of the created worlds, "feminine waters," waters that receive. The act of Creation entailed the separation of the two, and its ultimate purpose is their reunification. But in order for the upper waters to descend and permeate the lower waters, the lower waters must first ascend. When the lower waters surge upward, when they well up in yearning toward their separated mate, the upper waters are drawn downward to effuse divine influence in the world, until complete unification is achieved.

In view of this, the aforementioned work of refinement, in which a person takes a piece of the world and reveals its inherent holiness, is a rising of the lower waters. At that moment, a spark is unleashed, a flash of holiness that rises to its source on high. When the lower waters ascend, they bring about a supernal union. They unite with the upper waters, stimulating them to meet their ascent with a descent of their own.

שֶׁהֵם הֵם מֵימֵי הַחֲסָדִים שֶׁבְּכָל מִצְוָה וּמִצְוָה מֵרמ"ח מִצְוֹת עֲשֵׂה, שֶׁכּוּלָּן הֵן בְּחִינַת חֲסָדִים וּמַיִין דְּכוּרִין, דְּהַיְינוּ הַמְשָׁכַת קְדוּשַּׁת אֱלֹהוּתוֹ יִתְבָּרֵךְ מִלְמַעְלָה לְמַטָּה לְהִתְלַבֵּשׁ בַּתַּחְתּוֹנִים, כְּמוֹ שֶׁנִּתְבָּאֵר בְּמָקוֹם אַחֵר].

Those masculine waters **are none other than the waters of kindness within each and every one of the 248 positive commandments, all of which embody the quality of kindness and the masculine waters, that is, the drawing down of God's holiness from above to below to become clothed in the lower worlds, as explained elsewhere** [chap. 41].)

There are two aspects to a mitzva. The first is its elevating effect: The mitzva has an effect on the "lower waters," upon the profane world of *kelippat noga*. The person performing the mitzva takes a material substance, a part of the lower realm of creation, refines it, wholly or partially, and elevates it to the realm of holiness. In this sense, the mitzva act is an ascension of the feminine waters. But this is only one aspect of a mitzva. The elevation of material matter, by which the physical world raises itself on tiptoe in an effort to reach for the heavens, is met by a supernal response, a descent of masculine waters, an effusion of divine lifegiving sustenance to the lower realm of creation.

The essence of a mitzva, then, is a joining, or *tzavta*, of the terrestrial with the supernal, a collaboration of the human and the Divine in a single act, the act of the mitzva. The mitzva is more than an ascent of the lower reality. It is also a spurt of divinity from above, in which the divine immanence is revealed within the physical reality. In this way, the supernal and the lowly are joined and united.

This confluence of forces constitutes the union of the Holy One and His Divine Presence implicit in every mitzva. Every act of Torah study, prayer, or charity is an ascent of "feminine waters" evoking a descent of "masculine waters." This dynamic is also referred to as "an awakening from below that evokes an awakening from above."

The part that the lower realm plays, that of elevation of the mundane to the higher realm, constitutes the creation of a vessel. The vessel is made up of will, of a conscious desire on the part of lower waters that says, "We want to ascend." Then comes the flow and descent of the upper waters, which unite with the lower waters, completing the mitzva.

A mitzva is not just a human action. It is a revelation of the Divine, a flash of divinity in the world. The physical act creates the body of the mitzva, the vessel, the physical conductor that attracts and captures the flash of divinity from above.

So the two interpretations of the phrase *benei aliya,* literally, "men of ascent"– that the complete tzaddik elevates material existence and that his concern lies not with his self-development but with the divine endeavor of "uniting the Holy One with His Divine Presence" – are not contradictory but complementary. The occupation of the tzaddik in this world, the process of transformation that he generates, is itself the union of the immanent and transcendent aspects of the Divine. The perfect and absolute nature of his elevation of *kelippa* is necessarily for the sake of God and not for his own sake.

The divine service of one who is not a complete tzaddik might be an escape from the material, in which the person takes things from the world and runs off with them toward closeness with God. But the complete tzaddik never runs away from the world, because he takes everything in the world and raises it to holiness. He is not satisfied with gratifying his own soul's craving for God but elevates everything with which he comes into contact, because everything he does is an act of transformation. ☞

THE TZADDIK'S MISSION

☞ A tzaddik who isolates himself and escapes the world ceases, at that moment, to fulfill his duty as a tzaddik. The tzaddik's mission in life, his duty to his fellow man and to God, is to involve himself with the world and elevate it. The story is told of a tzaddik who once fell ill and sent a request for a blessing to one of the hasidic masters of the time. In response, the Rebbe instructed him to eat a large meal of milk products in order to be cured. The Rebbe subsequently explained that this tzaddik

This chapter discusses two categories of tzaddik: the complete tzaddik and the incomplete tzaddik. As the author of the *Tanya* will explain later in the book, one cannot possibly attain these states by one's own efforts. If a person is not born with the unique ability to achieve total mastery over his animal soul, there is no way that he can make himself a tzaddik. The rank of tzaddik, on either level, is beyond the range of the ordinary person. It is even beyond the range of the *beinoni*. Nonetheless, the author describes these states in order to present the larger picture, so that a person can achieve a true estimate of his inner state.

Another reason that the author of the *Tanya* presents these unique levels is so that even if most people cannot fully attain the level of the righteous, they can from time to time experience and do things that resemble, albeit on a microscale, that which the righteous do and feel. By no means does the experience of a righteous person make a person righteous, but it is important that every individual have the concepts and words to define what happens to the righteous, and what sometimes happens to him, so that he can properly relate to that experience and perpetuate the good and the energy he can glean from it.

never ate cheese, and it was the cheese's accusation against the tzaddik – that he had neglected to elevate it to holiness – that led to his illness. His cure would therefore be to eat cheese so that the accusation would be withdrawn.

For the tzaddik, it is a great act of self-sacrifice not to neglect to elevate even a single corner of his world. The tzaddik is free of all internal evil. He has no need for any further transformation, no need for any contact with the bitter and the abhorrent. If he forgoes his state of perfect union with God to involve himself with the mundane and the profane, it is only to rectify God's world, to unite the Holy One with His Divine Presence. This is the meaning of the statement "Who is a pious one? He who is benevolent toward his Maker."

Chapter 11

THE PREVIOUS CHAPTER DESCRIBED TWO TYPES OF tzaddikim: the completely righteous person, the tzaddik who possesses only a good inclination, and one who is not completely righteous, who retains a vestige of evil. This chapter describes the corresponding ranks at the other end of the spectrum: the person who is not completely wicked because there is still a trace of good in him and the one who is completely wicked because no good remains within.

וְזֶה לְעוּמַּת זֶה: רָשָׁע וְטוֹב לוֹ לְעוּמַּת צַדִּיק וְרַע לוֹ.

One thing corresponds to another: The wicked person who prospers, that is, who possesses a trace of good, **corresponds to the righteous person who suffers,** that is, who possesses a vestige of evil.

13 Tevet

18 Tevet (leap year)

This expression, taken from the verse "God made this corresponding to that" (Eccles. 7:14), is often used to express the correspondence between good and evil.[1] In the previous chapter, the author of the *Tanya* described the tzaddik who possesses a trace of evil, who is righteous in essence yet has not completely eradicated the evil within him. This vestige of evil, however, is *lo*, "to him," subjugated and nullified by the good that defines his being. Mirroring the incomplete tzaddik is the incomplete *rasha*, the wicked person who possesses some good.

1. See also chap. 6 above.

דְּהַיְינוּ שֶׁהַטּוֹב שֶׁבְּנַפְשׁוֹ הָאֱלֹהִית שֶׁבְּמוֹחוֹ וּבֶחָלָל הַיְמָנִי שֶׁבְּלִבּוֹ כָּפוּף וּבָטֵל לְגַבֵּי הָרַע מֵהַקְּלִיפָּה שֶׁבֶּחָלָל הַשְּׂמָאלִי.

That is, the good that is in his divine soul, which resides **in his brain and in the right chamber of his heart, is subservient and nullified to the evil** that stems **from the *kelippa* that is in the left chamber** of the heart.

Although both good and evil reside in the heart of the wicked person who possesses a trace of good, he is called a *rasha*, wicked, because the evil in him has gained mastery over him and has become embedded in his identity.

וְזֶה מִתְחַלֵּק גַּם כֵּן לְרִבְבוֹת מַדְרֵגוֹת חֲלוּקוֹת בְּעִנְיַן כַּמּוּת וְאֵיכוּת הַבִּטּוּל וּכְפִיפַת הַטּוֹב לָרַע חַס וְשָׁלוֹם.

This rank **is likewise divided into myriad levels based on the quantity and quality of the nullification and subservience of the evil to the good, God forbid.**

As is the case with the incomplete tzaddik, the incomplete *rasha*, the wicked person who possesses a vestige of good, is a broad category. It includes an immense range of types that differ in the quantity of the good within them and the degree to which it is subjugated to *kelippa*.[2]

יֵשׁ מִי שֶׁהַכְּפִיפָה וְהַבִּיטּוּל אֶצְלוֹ מְעַט מִזְּעֵר, וְאַף גַּם זֹאת אֵינוֹ בִּתְמִידוּת וְלֹא תָּדִיר לִפְרָקִים קְרוֹבִים, אֶלָּא לְעִתִּים רְחוֹקִים מִתְגַּבֵּר הָרַע עַל הַטּוֹב וְכוֹבֵשׁ אֶת הָעִיר קְטַנָּה הוּא הַגּוּף,

There is one in whom the subservience and nullification of good to evil **is minuscule, and even then, it is neither constant nor does it recur at frequent intervals. Rather, on rare occasions the evil overpowers the good and conquers the "small city," which is the body.**

In his description of the various levels of incomplete *rasha*, the author of the *Tanya* begins at the top, with the one who is least evil. An

2. See chap. 10, where the author of the *Tanya* explains that there are myriad types and levels of incomplete tzaddik depending on how much the vestige of evil within him is nullified in the good. Here the author tells us that the same is true of the incomplete *rasha*.

incomplete *rasha*, a wicked person who retains a vestige of good, is someone in whom the evil rules over the good, but this rule may be temporary, occasional, or incomplete. Such a person may commit a sin, but he does not do so wholeheartedly nor with any pleasure. Inside, good and evil are in a state of equilibrium that is unstable, that every now and then it is prone to lose its balance.

The highest level of incomplete *rasha*, which the author of the *Tanya* describes here, is no ordinary individual. Such a *rasha* would probably even be considered a tzaddik nowadays. Yet if he but once transgressed the divine will, on however slight a matter, and he has not yet repented and rectified it properly, he is at that moment in the category of a wicked person in whom there is a vestige of good.

אַךְ לֹא כּוּלּוֹ אֶלָּא מִקְצָתוֹ לְבַד שֶׁיִּהְיֶה סָר לְמִשְׁמַעְתּוֹ וְנַעֲשָׂה לוֹ מֶרְכָּבָה וּלְבוּשׁ לְהִתְלַבֵּשׁ בּוֹ אֶחָד מִשְּׁלֹשָׁה לְבוּשֶׁיהָ הַנִּזְכָּרִים לְעֵיל. דְּהַיְינוּ, אוֹ בְּמַעֲשֶׂה לְבַד לַעֲשׂוֹת עֲבֵירוֹת קַלּוֹת וְלֹא חֲמוּרוֹת חַס וְשָׁלוֹם,

Yet it does **not** prevail over the body **entirely, but rather only** over **part of it, so that** the body **might be obedient to its demands and become a vehicle for it and a garment with which to clothe** only **one of** the animal soul's **three garments discussed above** (chap. 6). **That is to say,** the evil holds sway **over either actions alone, so that one may commit minor transgressions,** for instance, **and not severe ones, God forbid,**

The garments of the animal soul are the thoughts, speech, and actions of *kelippa*. In the wicked person who is not entirely evil, the evil does not prevail over every one of the soul's garments; it does not exert total dominance over his entire existence. For example, he may commit an evil deed without the premeditation of thought and discussion. When

A MINOR TRANSGRESSION

☞ A minor transgression is not necessarily one that has no effect on the sinner. On the contrary, the more righteous a person is, the more sensitive he becomes to sin. The Talmud recounts how the strap of Rav Huna's *tefillin* once got twisted so that the black side, which should be exposed, was turned inward. To rectify this "sin," Rav the deed is not premeditated, the person does not identify as deeply with his actions. In that case, the deed only superficially relates to the inner self of its doer and so constitutes a minor sin, even the most subtle of sins. ☞

אוֹ בְּדִיבּוּר לְבַד, לְדַבֵּר אֲבַק לָשׁוֹן הָרָע וְלֵיצָנוּת וּכְהַאי גַּוְונָא,

or over speech alone, so that one may speak but **a trace of malicious speech or** engage in **scoffing and the like,**

The wicked person's transgression might have been in the realm of speech and not necessarily actual slander, which is a most severe prohibition but only *avak lashon hara*, literally, "the dust of slander," words that border on slander but don't constitute actual slander. The person may have said the words unintentionally, or the words themselves may not be prohibited, but one might have inferred something derogatory about someone else from his manner of speech.

אוֹ בְּמַחֲשָׁבָה לְבַד,

or else it holds sway **over thought alone,**

Even if no actual deed was committed nor any word uttered, but a person only thought about committing a sin or simply pondered the matter in an innocuous way, he is nevertheless under the influence of the evil inclination within him.

הִרְהוּרֵי עֲבֵירָה הַקָּשִׁים מֵעֲבֵירָה.

through **thoughts of transgression, which are worse than transgression** itself.

Huna fasted forty fasts (*Mo'ed Katan* 25a). This was an extremely minor matter, done inadvertently, and from which he certainly derived no physical or spiritual pleasure. Yet to Rav Huna, this minute flaw in the manner of his fulfillment of a mitzva was nothing less than devastating.

Rabbi Elimelekh of Lizhensk was one of the greatest hasidic leaders. It is said that he would often go into the forest and sit on an anthill until the ants stopped biting him and would then cry, "Meilekh, Meilekh! Even the ants no longer want to bite you!" He frequently cried, "I am the most wicked man in the world!" Once, one of his followers said to him, "Rebbe, whom are you trying to fool? You know that is not true!" Rabbi Elimelekh replied, "The finer the needle, the more it pierces."

Even for the perfect tzaddik, there can be something that he will experience as a sin, and that can be so slight that someone else might not be aware of it, but the finer it is, the more piercing it is to the lofty soul.

The Talmud states that thoughts of transgression are worse than transgression itself.[3] Commentators offer various explanations for this statement. Rashi comments that the Talmud is not saying that a sinful thought is more severe than an actual transgression but is speaking of the severity of the temptation: The temptation to indulge in a sinful thought is often greater than the temptation to actually commit the sin. What is more, a person always has the opportunity to contemplate committing a sin, so this occurs more often than the actual commission, for which the opportunity does not always arise.

The *Or HaḤayyim* suggests that because the contemplation of sin never sates the thinker's desire, he is less likely to experience remorse and repent for it than for a sin actually committed. On a deeper level, it is said that the contemplation of a sin, involving the most intimate of the soul's three garments, affects the soul to a greater extent and, in a certain sense, contaminates the soul even more than actually committing the sin.

וְגַם אִם אֵינוֹ מְהַרְהֵר בַּעֲבֵירָה לַעֲשׂוֹתָהּ אֶלָּא בְּעִנְיַן זִיווּג זָכָר וּנְקֵיבָה בָּעוֹלָם, שֶׁעוֹבֵר עַל אַזְהָרַת הַתּוֹרָה: "וְנִשְׁמַרְתָּ מִכֹּל דָּבָר רָע" (דברים כג, י), שֶׁ"לֹּא יְהַרְהֵר בַּיּוֹם" כו' (כתובות מו, א)

Even if one does not contemplate a transgression in order to commit it but rather ponders, for example, **relations between a man and woman in general, one** thereby **transgresses the Torah prohibition "You shall be vigilant from every evil thing"** (Deut. 23:10), regarding which our Sages say **that "a person should not think** impure thoughts **by day** and thereby come by night to impurity…" (*Ketubot* 46a).

A sinful thought need not involve the thought of actually committing the sin. As the Talmud indicates, one should not contemplate a sin even as an abstract idea and even without any intention of committing it. At the end of the day, thoughts can lead to action. The Sages say that one "shall be vigilant from every evil thing" because "impure thoughts by day" can result in impure emission at night, a physical act.

---

3. *Yoma* 29a.

אוֹ שֶׁהִיא שְׁעַת הַכּוֹשֶׁר לַעֲסוֹק בַּתּוֹרָה וְהוּא מְפַנֶּה לִבּוֹ לְבַטָּלָה, כִּדְתְנַן בְּאָבוֹת (פרק ג משנה ד): הַנֵּיעוֹר בַּלַּיְלָה כו' וּמְפַנֶּה לִבּוֹ כו',

Alternatively, it may be an opportune time to study Torah, yet instead one turns his heart toward idle matters, as the Mishna **taught in *Avot*** (3:4) with regard to the severity of **one who remains awake at night** and instead of studying Torah **turns his heart** to idle matters.

This is a person who has the opportunity to study Torah but instead wastes his time thinking idle thoughts. Though these thoughts are not forbidden in themselves, they constitute a transgression in that he engages in them instead of studying Torah.

שֶׁבְּאַחַת מִכָּל אֵלֶּה וְכַיּוֹצֵא בָּהֶן נִקְרָא רָשָׁע בָּעֵת הַהִיא, שֶׁהָרַע שֶׁבְּנַפְשׁוֹ גּוֹבֵר בּוֹ וּמִתְלַבֵּשׁ בְּגוּפוֹ, וּמַחֲטִיאוֹ וּמְטַמְּאוֹ.

With regard to any one of these or similar transgressions, **one is referred to as a wicked person at that time, because the evil in his soul overpowers him and becomes clothed in his body, causing it to sin and defiling it.**

Technically speaking, a transgression is considered as such only when the soul is clothed within the body, as a body alone cannot sin. Any of the transgressions involving one of the three garments of the soul – thought, speech, or action – or any similar minor sin deems the transgressor a *rasha* at the moment of its commission, irrespective of the severity of the sin or its attendant punishment. ☞

SMALL SINS COUNT

☞ The author of the *Tanya* has already emphasized that the division of existence into holy elements and *kelippa* elements is a division with no neutral or intermediary ground. Every entity in existence must, by necessity, belong either to holiness or to *kelippa*. If a thing is not holy, it is profane. So ultimately the degree or extent of a sin is irrelevant. The moment a person turns to the *sitra aḥara*, the moment he is no longer within the realm of holiness, he has entered the realm of *kelippa*.

וְאַחַר כָּךְ גּוֹבֵר בּוֹ הַטּוֹב שֶׁבְּנַפְשׁוֹ הָאֱלֹהִית וּמִתְחָרֵט וּמְבַקֵּשׁ מְחִילָה וּסְלִיחָה מֵה' - וַה' יִסְלַח לוֹ, אִם שָׁב בִּתְשׁוּבָה הָרְאוּיָה עַל פִּי עֲצַת חֲכָמֵינוּ ז"ל בִּשְׁלֹשָׁה חִלּוּקֵי כַּפָּרָה שֶׁהָיָה רַבִּי יִשְׁמָעֵאל דּוֹרֵשׁ כו' (יומא פו, א) כְּמוֹ שֶׁנִּתְבָּאֵר בְּמָקוֹם אַחֵר.

Afterward, the good in his divine soul prevails over him, and he is remorseful and asks God for pardon and forgiveness. God then **forgives him, provided that he repented properly by following our Sages' counsel,** with one of **the three categories of atonement expounded by Rabbi Yishmael and so forth** (*Yoma* 86a), **as explained elsewhere** (*Iggeret HaTeshuva*, chap. 1).

Because we are speaking of a wicked person who still possesses a vestige of good, the incomplete *rasha*, one in whom the supremacy of evil occurs only in a fleeting moment of weakness, the good eventually prevails and he feels remorse for the evil act he committed. This leads him to repent and earn God's forgiveness. With regard to this, the author of the *Tanya* refers to the various categories of atonement expounded by Rabbi Yishmael in the Talmud (and which the author expounds in *Iggeret HaTeshuva*): "If one neglected [to perform] a positive commandment and [then] repents, he is forgiven even before he has moved from his place.... If one violated a prohibition and [then] repents, repentance suspends [his punishment] and Yom Kippur atones [for his sin].... If one committed [a transgression punishable

We can compare this to an act of treason, whose ultimate significance is that the person who commits it is no longer on "our side" but has gone over to the enemy. In this regard, the substance of the act is irrelevant. The person might not have engaged in espionage or sabotage but in something much less consequential. The triviality of the deed may be a consideration for leniency when he is judged and punished for his actions, but in terms of the ultimate significance of his deed, the fact that he has crossed over to the other side, the precise act that he committed to aid the enemy makes no difference.

Similarly, anyone touched by sin, anyone who still carries the imprint of a transgression for which he has not yet fully repented, exists at that moment outside the realm of holiness and constitutes a part of the world of *kelippa*.

by] *karet* or [one of] the court-imposed death penalties, repentance and Yom Kippur suspend [his punishment], and suffering absolves [him of his sin]."

But even after the incomplete *rasha* ceases his act of transgression, even after he repents properly and is completely forgiven for his sin, he is still not a tzaddik or even a *beinoni* but a *rasha* – a *rasha* who possesses a vestige of good.

In chapter 1, the author of the *Tanya* explained that there are two methods of classifying a righteous or wicked person. The first, more commonly employed method is where the terms "righteous" and "wicked" respectively describe one who is innocent or guilty in a court of law. The author of the *Tanya* stresses there that in this sense these terms are merely borrowed expressions in relation to reward and punishment but do not define the person's essence. The second method, employed by the author of the *Tanya*, defines a person by his quintessential nature: Is his essence that of tzaddik or is it that of *rasha*?

A wicked person who is not a complete *rasha* – who does not possess only evil – does not always act as a *rasha* but only occasionally. Such a person might, in terms of actual behavior, be great in Torah and good deeds, but in terms of his quintessential identity, he is a *rasha*.

In the ultimate sense of the term, a *rasha* is not defined by his deeds but by his psychological state, by his capacity for transgression. A person can be a "wicked person who possesses good" without actually committing a single transgression. It is only that the balance between his divine soul and his animal soul is unstable, so that even if he actually commits no sin, the possibility for sin always exists.[4] ☞

A POTENTIAL *RASHA* IS STILL A *RASHA*

☞ The definition of *rasha* applies not only to the actual *rasha* but also to the potential *rasha*. A person might remain a potential *rasha* all his life without ever having committed a sin simply because the opportunity never presented itself. Similarly, a person can be a thief in essence without ever actually stealing anything simply because he has never seen anything he wanted to steal. He only thinks about "big money," which has never come his way,

4. On the surface, it would seem that upon performing proper repentance,

וְיֵשׁ מִי שֶׁהָרַע גּוֹבֵר בּוֹ יוֹתֵר וּמִתְלַבְּשִׁים בּוֹ כָּל שְׁלֹשָׁה לְבוּשִׁים שֶׁל הָרַע, וּמַחֲטִיאוֹ בַּעֲבֵירוֹת חֲמוּרוֹת יוֹתֵר וּבְעִתִּים קְרוֹבִים יוֹתֵר.

There is a lower level of wicked person who possesses a vestige of good: **one whose evil overpowers him more** than in the aforementioned instances **and in whom all three garments of evil,** thought, speech, and action, **are clothed. This causes him to commit more egregious transgressions and at more frequent intervals.**

Above the author of the *Tanya* spoke of a *rasha* who, when he commits a transgression, allows only one of the evil garments of the animal soul to clothe itself in his body, whether the garment of thought, the garment of speech, or the garment of deed. Worse is one who sins with all three garments of the soul, indicating a far greater dominance

but given an opportunity worth his while, he would steal.

It is said that "one who sits and does not transgress receives a reward as one who performs a mitzva" (*Kiddushin* 39b). Since the Torah includes 365 prohibitions, most of which the vast majority of people do not commit day after day, everyone ought to be credited with countless mitzvot in their lifetime. But the author of the *Tanya* explains the statement as referring to a sin for which one has both opportunity and temptation.

For instance, one of the 365 prohibitions is the commandment that involves the breast piece worn by the High Priest when he served in the Temple. The Torah states, "The breast piece shall not be detached from upon the ephod" (Ex. 28:28). One must ensure that the breast piece may not budge from its assigned place atop another of the priestly garments. Today this is not a sin that people have committed, nor even considered doing so, not because they prevailed over their evil impulse but because they have never been presented with the opportunity or temptation.

There are also sins for which one has ample opportunity but virtually no temptation and vice versa. Many people are quite prepared to gossip but have no one to gossip with. Such people refrain from the sin of slander, not because they have overcome their evil inclination, but because they lack an appropriate audience.

---

one would no longer remain on the level of a wicked person, even one who still possesses some good, but would assume the higher status of *beinoni*. The Lubavitcher Rebbe, Rabbi Menaḥem Mendel Schneerson, suggests that the author of the *Tanya* is referring to a limited form of repentance in which the penitent remains with a perpetual potential for sin. It follows that there is a loftier level of repentance that can elevate the wicked person who possesses good to the status of *beinoni*.

of the evil within him. It intimates more than a momentary weakness, more than an occasional succumbing to temptation. This is a sinner who is fully involved in his sin, who primes himself psychologically to it, plans it, discusses it, and subsequently commits it in practice. Yet even this person is still a *rasha* who possesses some good, whose good inclination is still manifest and active within him.

אַךְ בֵּינְתַיִים מִתְחָרֵט וּבָאִים לוֹ הִרְהוּרֵי תְשׁוּבָה מִבְּחִינַת הַטּוֹב שֶׁבְּנַפְשׁוֹ שֶׁמִּתְגַּבֵּר קְצָת בֵּינְתַיִים,

In the interim, however, he is remorseful and visited by thoughts of repentance due to the good that is in his soul, which somewhat prevails over the evil **between** each transgression.

Between sins, between waves of the *kelippa*'s domination of his self, the good within this wicked person awakens, expressed by the feelings of remorse and repentance that plague any Jew who commits a transgression.

אֶלָּא שֶׁאֵין לוֹ הִתְגַּבְּרוּת כָּל כָּךְ לְנַצֵּחַ אֶת הָרַע לִפְרוֹשׁ מֵחֲטָאָיו לְגַמְרֵי לִהְיוֹת מוֹדֶה וְעוֹזֵב.

However, the good within him **does not prevail sufficiently** over the evil **so that he may defeat the evil,** enabling him **to completely disassociate from his sins** and **to be** considered **one who confesses** his transgressions **and forsakes** them.

The wicked person has thoughts of repentance, perhaps even many such thoughts, but they do not actualize to the extent that the supremacy of the good over the evil becomes the true and permanent state of his soul.

וְעַל זֶה אָמְרוּ רַבּוֹתֵינוּ ז״ל: רְשָׁעִים מְלֵאִים חֲרָטוֹת,

With regard to this category of the wicked, **our Rabbis stated, "The wicked are full of remorse."**

This dictum of the Sages[5] refers to the wicked person who commits a sin and yet, while feeling remorseful and penitent, does not fully abandon his sinful ways. Were this person to refrain from sinning, his

5. Cited in *Shevet Mussar*, chap. 25.

mind would be replete with thoughts of performing good deeds instead of being full of remorse. Yet he is stuck in a loop of sinning, remorse, and repentance.[6] Such a person repeatedly sins and regrets, sins and regrets. Such regrets are a sign not of hypocrisy or self-deception but of the inner struggle between the two forces that dichotomize his inner self, between his divine soul and his animal soul. The feelings of regret and the thoughts of repentance are the divine soul's reaction to the triumph of the animal soul. It is proof that there is one part of his soul that will never give him rest.

שֶׁהֵם רוֹב הָרְשָׁעִים שֶׁיֵּשׁ בְּחִינַת טוֹב בְּנַפְשָׁם עֲדַיִין.

This represents the majority of wicked people, who still possess an element of good in their souls.

Most wicked people belong to the ranks of the wicked person who possesses some good. The good within them is still active and repeatedly roused to combat the evil and influence the person. These surges of good cause the *rasha* to experience thoughts of repentance, and even to actually repent, but they fail to effect a qualitative change in the inner structure of his life.

The incomplete *rasha* thus inhabits a life of sins and regrets, in which the sins are sins and the regrets are regrets. The remorse may be sincere, deep, and very painful, yet he remains a *rasha,* even at the moment of his remorse. ☞

THE "ALIEN THOUGHTS" OF THE WICKED

☞ As the author of the *Tanya* will go on to explain, not only a *rasha* but even a person who is not wicked can succumb to sin. The difference is whether the person happens to have a weak moment, whether the transgression is incidental, or whether it is a natural result of his life's makeup.

Along these lines, the hasidic literature gave advice on how to deal with unwanted thoughts that enter the mind during prayer (see, e.g., *Ba'al Shem Tov al HaTorah, Parashat Noaḥ*). The author of the *Tanya* remarks (in chap. 28) that these thoughts are alien to a tzaddik but not to other people, who encounter such thoughts during the course of the entire day. On the contrary, when they think of praying properly, that is an "alien thought"! In this sense, to the wicked, a sin is not alien, even if committed only once. It is integral to his nature, a constant possibility that exists within his soul.

6. See *Ba'al Shem Tov al HaTorah, Parashat Ekev* 10.

אַךְ מִי שֶׁאֵינוֹ מִתְחָרֵט לְעוֹלָם וְאֵין בָּאִים לוֹ הִרְהוּרֵי תְשׁוּבָה כְּלָל - נִקְרָא רָשָׁע וְרַע לוֹ, שֶׁהָרַע שֶׁבְּנַפְשׁוֹ הוּא לְבַדּוֹ נִשְׁאָר בְּקִרְבּוֹ,

However, one who never experiences remorse, nor is visited by thoughts of repentance at all, is referred to as a wicked person who possesses evil, meaning **the evil in his soul is the only** force **that remains** active **within him**

"A wicked person who possesses evil" describes a state of being in which the good in the person no longer operates and is no longer a factor within his personality. Such a person never experiences regret over his evil deeds.

כִּי גָּבַר כָּל כָּךְ עַל הַטּוֹב עַד שֶׁנִּסְתַּלֵּק מִקִּרְבּוֹ וְעוֹמֵד בִּבְחִינַת מַקִּיף עָלָיו מִלְמַעְלָה.

because the evil **overpowered the good to such an extent that it withdrew from within him and** now **hovers** over him, **surrounding him from above.**

When contrasting the righteous and the wicked, the axiom with which our chapter began, that "God made this corresponding to that," is not applicable in its strict sense. No absolute symmetry exists between the complete tzaddik and the complete *rasha*. The complete tzaddik has succeeded in utterly driving out the evil within him so that he possesses no evil whatsoever. The complete *rasha*, on the other hand, cannot completely banish his divine soul so that he no longer possesses any good at all. ☞

UTTER EVIL AND UTTER FALSEHOOD

☞ In a sense, the complete *rasha* is a purely theoretical concept that cannot exist in actuality, because something that is completely of the other side cannot exist. One can create a small lie or a big lie but not a complete lie. Every lie has some factual component and therefore is not a complete lie. A complete falsehood is something one can talk about theoretically, but in actuality no such thing exists. The same is true of evil. If a person could reach the state of a complete *rasha* in the ultimate sense, a state in which he is wholly evil and possesses no good whatsoever, that would be the point of death.

"The wicked, even during their lives, are called dead," says the Talmud (*Berakhot* 18b), because every degree of evil is a degree of spiritual death. If a person were to come to a state of absolute evil,

There are two ways of affecting the animal soul. The first is to push it into a corner. This is what the incomplete tzaddik, the righteous person who possesses a trace of evil, does. He still has some shred of evil within him, but he has suppressed it so that it can no longer assert itself or exert any influence over him. The other way is to transform it so that it no longer functions as an animal soul but as a divine soul. This is the level of the complete tzaddik, the righteous individual who possesses only good. No evil remains within him because it has been entirely transformed into good.

By contrast, the *rasha* can repress his divine soul, reducing it to a state of subordination to the animal soul, but he cannot annihilate it entirely, as the tzaddik can do to his animal soul.

A person's soul actually exists at various levels, one above the other. There are five levels to the soul: *nefesh, ruaḥ, neshama, ḥaya,* and *yeḥida.* As a rule, only the lowest of them, the *nefesh,* operates in the realm of consciousness, while the others lie beyond the conscious reach of most people. A person's ascent to a higher level is his ability to consciously identify himself with a higher level of his soul. The highest level a person can reach is an awareness of the highest essence of his soul, which at its primary source is the "portion of the God on high" that is identified with God Himself. No one can drive out this aspect of his soul completely. Man cannot uproot this soul, his divine essence, because that would uproot his very existence. A person can, however, reach the stage where he is no longer aware of the existence of the divine soul, because it has ceased to operate within the realm of his consciousness. When in such a state, the divine soul encompasses him from above. It still exists, but the person has no conscious connection with it. He can then live an utterly animalistic life, completely discon-

he would be dead in every respect, because he would no longer have any hold on the essence of life, his connection to God. The other side is something that is negative in essence. Were it to exist in an absolute form, it would be absolute negativity – nothing – and total negativity negates everything, including its very self.

In actuality, the *rasha* who possesses only evil, the complete *rasha,* is not really completely evil, because he cannot drive out the last kernel of good from himself. As long as he exists, some good exists within him. But he has banished it from his internal self so that it "surrounds him from above."

nected from the higher levels of his soul: He does not encounter them, and they do not interfere with his life. ☞

וְלָכֵן אָמְרוּ רַבּוֹתֵינוּ ז״ל (סנהדרין לט, א): ״אַכָּל בֵּי עַשְׂרָה שְׁכִינְתָּא שַׁרְיָא״.

Therefore, our Rabbis stated, "The Divine Presence dwells upon any place where there are ten Jews" (*Sanhedrin* 39a).

The Divine Presence rests wherever ten Jews congregate. Who they are or what they are doing is irrelevant. Whether they are ten perfect

THE IMMUTABLE ESSENCE OF A JEW

☞ In 1927, the sixth Lubavitcher Rebbe, Rabbi Yosef Yitzḥak Schneerson, was arrested and imprisoned because the Soviet authorities wanted to put a stop to his work of teaching and spreading Judaism. Like many others, he was brought to the cellars of the NKVD (forerunner of the KGB), his captors intent on never letting him see the light of day again.

When he was brought into the interrogation chamber, he turned to his interrogators, all Jews and members of the infamous Yevsektzia, and said, "This is the first time I have entered a room where there are Jews who do not rise when I enter!"

The interrogators were shaken; they did not know what to do with a person whose spirit was not broken. The Rebbe added that he wished to tell them a story. When they objected, he said that when he told a story, even the *mitnagdim* listened! Then he said:

"My great-grandfather (the Tzemaḥ Tzedek) once said to an apostate Jew, 'In the book of Esther, the word for Jews, *Yehudim*, is sometimes spelled with one *yud* after the *dalet* and sometimes with two. This implies that there are two types of "*yud*" – two types of Jews: righteous Jews and wicked Jews. Sometimes only Jews of the first category consider themselves Jews, but when there is a decree such as that of Haman, it affects both, and then they all remember that they are Jews.

"'If you contract a fever,' my great-grandfather went on to say, 'you too will remember that you are a Jew!'

"Subsequently, that Jew contracted a fever that lasted a full year, as a result of which he had thoughts of repentance."

Rabbi Yosef Yitzḥak then turned to his interrogators and said, "And when you will contract a fever, you too will remember that you are Jews."

One may assume that in the following decade, the years of the great purges, when countless Jews were "removed" by Stalin, the interrogators too "caught a fever." If any one of them survived, he must have given weighty consideration to the question of what type of Jew he was.

Even if the Jew's self-awareness is modeled entirely on his animal self, it would be impossible for him to completely uproot his divine self. His essence as a Jew, his "portion of God on high," cannot be blotted out, even if he is totally unaware of it, even if it is no longer a component of his inner being but merely "surrounds him from above."

tzaddikim or completely wicked, it is impossible for the Divine Presence not to rest in that place.

The Talmud, however, stresses that the Divine Presence rests "upon" these ten individuals. It hovers over them but does not necessarily affect them.[7] Otherwise, one would be overwhelmed with holiness when one sits in a café or theater containing more than ten Jews. The Divine Presence is there, but in order to feel it, a person must be receptive to it.

Here is the essential difference between the tzaddik and the *rasha*: To what extent is he receptive? To what extent is he open to the divine essence of his own soul?

The story is told of the Kotzker Rebbe who once asked his disciples, "Where is God?"

They responded in surprise, "What do you mean? He is everywhere!"

"No," he replied. "He is wherever we allow Him to enter." ☞

REWARD AND PUNISHMENT AND THE TZADDIK AND *RASHA*

☞ The categories of tzaddik and *rasha* that have been the topic of the previous two chapters were delineated in the first chapter as categories that define the essence of the person and not in terms of reward and punishment, as the Talmud renders them. In truth, the tzaddik and *rasha* as defined in terms of reward and punishment – a righteous person who prospers or suffers and a wicked person who prospers or suffers – and the author of the *Tanya*'s definition of these terms are interconnected.

The complete tzaddik is a tzaddik who possesses good in the literal, material sense as well, because he is a person who is incapable of experiencing anything as negative. The reverse is true of the *rasha* who possesses evil. Negative things can be experienced as such only by someone who is receptive to evil and who reacts to evil. This applies not only to mental suffering but to physical suffering as well.

When Rabbi Shmuel HaLevi Horowitz of Nikolsburg and his brother, Rabbi Pinḥas HaLevi Horowitz, the author of *Hafla'a*, visited the Maggid of Mezeritch, they asked him how it is possible to "recite a blessing for the bad just as one recites a blessing over good" (Mishna *Berakhot* 9:5), and what is more, to do it "with joy" (*Berakhot* 60b). The Maggid pointed to Reb Zusha of Anipoli, who was sitting in the study hall, and said, "Ask him."

7. See *Iggeret HaKodesh,* epistle 25, for the distinction between the indwelling and revelation of the Divine Presence.

In this chapter, the author of the *Tanya* did not elaborate at length on the two levels of *rasha,* just as he did not elaborate on the two levels of tzaddik in the previous chapter, because this book is not intended for either the *rasha* or the tzaddik. *The Book of Beinonim* is intended for every person, and not everyone is able to attain the level of tzaddik, while everyone is expected to avoid the state of *rasha.* It is only in the next chapter that the author of the *Tanya* finally focuses his attention on the level attainable by all: that of the *beinoni.*

They posed their question to Reb Zusha, a lifelong pauper who was afflicted with countless misfortunes. "I don't know why the Rebbe sent you to me," he said, "a person who has never had a bad day in his life!"

This same Reb Zusha was once reduced to such poverty that he lacked even bread. He turned to God and said, "Master of the universe! Thank you for giving me an appetite!"

In view of this, the complete *rasha* is someone who possesses evil because he is totally nonreceptive to anything good. To receive something good and experience it as such, one has to be in a certain frame of mind. A person who has driven out his divine element, who has driven out the good within him, has also driven out the capacity to enjoy even material things. The more of a *rasha* a person becomes, the more he allows the evil within him to pervade his being, the more evil he experiences. Just as the complete tzaddik cannot experience evil, the complete *rasha* has destroyed his capacity to experience good.

The good things in life, the things from which we derive pleasure, are not objectively good. Our enjoyment of them depends on how receptive our soul is to their goodness. Pleasure, for the most part, derives from the fulfillment of a need. To enjoy the pleasure, we must first feel the need. Otherwise, life turns into an ever-escalating cycle of suffering and, even more than that, a growing lack of enjoyment in life. A person who has been granted wealth and honor, whose worldly desires are satisfied, finds that the more he pursues them, the less he enjoys and appreciates these assets. The more he exploits them, the more he destroys the vitality they contain, the good that is hidden within them, and their ability to give him pleasure. Such a person develops an increasing tendency toward perversion in an attempt to reach extremes where he can still build a life that contains good and bad so that he might find some meaning and pleasure amid the emptiness. Such a person may even be led to repent, out of dread of the emptiness that the evil has brought him.

Chapter 12

THE PREVIOUS TWO CHAPTERS DISCUSSED THE TWO types of righteous individuals at one end of the spectrum and the two types of wicked individuals at the other. After describing these two extremes – that which cannot be reached (by most people) and that which should not be reached (by anyone) – the author of the *Tanya* will now discuss the level that pertains to every individual,[1] a state that every person can and should achieve. This chapter thus focuses on the *beinoni* and how difficult, yet how possible, it is to achieve this rank.

14 Tevet
19 Tevet (leap year)

וְהַבֵּינוֹנִי הוּא שֶׁלְּעוֹלָם אֵין הָרַע גּוֹבֵר כָּל כָּךְ לִכְבּוֹשׁ אֶת הָעִיר קְטַנָּה לְהִתְלַבֵּשׁ בַּגּוּף לְהַחֲטִיאוֹ. דְּהַיְינוּ שֶׁשְּׁלֹשָׁה לְבוּשֵׁי נֶפֶשׁ הַבַּהֲמִית, שֶׁהֵם מַחֲשָׁבָה דִּבּוּר וּמַעֲשֶׂה שֶׁמִּצַּד הַקְּלִיפָּה - אֵין גּוֹבְרִים בּוֹ עַל נֶפֶשׁ הָאֱלֹהִית לְהִתְלַבֵּשׁ בַּגּוּף: בַּמּוֹחַ וּבַפֶּה וּבִשְׁאָר רמ"ח אֵבָרִים לְהַחֲטִיאָם וּלְטַמְּאָם חַס וְשָׁלוֹם.

The *beinoni* is one in whom **the evil never prevails to such an extent that it conquers the "small city" by clothing** itself **in the body** and **causing it to sin. This means that the three garments of the animal soul, namely, thought, speech, and action** stemming **from the side of *kelippa*, do not overpower the divine soul within him by becoming clothed in the body,** specifically **in the brain, in the mouth, and in the other 248 limbs, causing them to sin and defiling them, God forbid.**

1. See chap. 14.

Above, the author of the *Tanya* spoke of the war between the two opposing forces within man: the divine soul and the animal soul.[2] The consequences of this war define the quintessential essence of each particular person: When the animal soul is victorious, the person is categorized as wicked; when the divine soul triumphs, he is categorized as righteous. What about the *beinoni*, the main subject of this book?

The first thing that defines the *beinoni* is that he never commits a transgression. That is, the *beinoni* does not sin in any realm: action, speech, or thought. The brain, mouth, and 248 limbs referred to by the author of the *Tanya* are thus the specific parts of the body employed by these three garments. The garment of thought requires a physical brain in order to manifest itself; the garment of speech, a mouth; and the garment of action is expressed with the entire body.

רַק שְׁלֹשָׁה לְבוּשֵׁי נֶפֶשׁ הָאֱלֹהִית הֵם לְבַדָּם מִתְלַבְּשִׁים בַּגּוּף, שֶׁהֵם מַחֲשָׁבָה דִּבּוּר וּמַעֲשֶׂה שֶׁל תרי״ג מִצְוֹת הַתּוֹרָה,

Only the three garments of the divine soul alone become clothed within the body, namely, the thoughts, speech, and actions of the 613 commandments of the Torah,

Not only does the *beinoni* completely avoid transgression, but he also does good, fulfilling the 613 commandments of the Torah. In this way, the *beinoni*'s every thought, word, and deed is utterly devoted to fulfilling the divine will as expressed through the mitzvot.

וְלֹא עָבַר עֲבֵירָה מִיָּמָיו, וְלֹא יַעֲבוֹר לְעוֹלָם, וְלֹא נִקְרָא עָלָיו שֵׁם רָשָׁע אֲפִילּוּ שָׁעָה אַחַת וָרֶגַע אֶחָד כָּל יָמָיו.

and he never in his life committed a transgression, nor will he ever commit one. **He was never in his life, not even temporarily,** not even **for a moment, categorized as a wicked person.**

This is not to say that a person who once in his lifetime committed a sin can never become a *beinoni* or even a tzaddik. Rather, it means

2. See chap. 9.

that one who does achieve the level of *beinoni* exists in a state of mind that is utterly removed from transgression, present, past, or future. If he committed any sins in the past, he has repented to such an extent that those sins are no longer a part of his life. It is as if his negative past belongs to someone else. ☞

Why isn't such a person, who has never sinned and never will sin, whose every act is either a mitzva or in service of a mitzva, considered a complete tzaddik? What is missing? Why isn't he considered even an incomplete tzaddik but rather in the intermediate state between *rasha* and tzaddik called *beinoni*?

To understand this, we must first distinguish between the garments of the *beinoni*'s soul and the essence of his soul. Everything we have said thus far about the *beinoni* pertains only to the garments of his soul, the manner in which his inner self expresses itself in his behavior.

20 Tevet (leap year)

אַךְ מַהוּת וְעַצְמוּת נֶפֶשׁ הָאֱלֹהִית, שֶׁהֵן עֶשֶׂר בְּחִינוֹתֶיהָ, לֹא לָהֶן לְבַדָּן הַמְּלוּכָה וְהַמֶּמְשָׁלָה בָּעִיר קְטַנָּה,

However, the essence and being of the divine soul, namely, its ten faculties, do not have exclusive rulership and dominion over the "small city," the body,

RELATING TO OUR PAST

☞ Every person experiences examples of such disconnection from the past. Often something a person did, said, or thought in the past no longer relates to the person he is now. They might belong to his past in the factual and historical sense, but in terms of his present identity and experience, the connection is purely theoretical. They are no more his than they are someone else's. There is a severance from his past self, as if he were two different people. A person might look at things he has written or remember things he has done and say to himself, "These things were done by someone else, not by me. The person I am now would never have done such acts."

In truth, every person feels this way when he ceases to be a child. As children, we do things, good and bad, that as adults we could not do. We remember things that we saw and did as children, but they are like memories that belong to someone else.

If a *beinoni* has sinned in the past, he has repented to such an extent that he relates to his past in the same way: "That was someone else, not me." This does not mean that the *beinoni* is inherently incapable of sinning, but his present state is such that actually committing a sin is impossible, inconceivable. It creates no resonance within his soul (see *Iggerot Kodesh*, vol. 19, letter 7083).

The side of holiness rules the *beinoni*'s life in practice, but it does not change the inner makeup of his soul. He does not actually sin, but the conflict within his soul has not been resolved. The *beinoni* is in a perpetual state of tension: The good in him prevails over the evil only because of his active involvement in the struggle between them. His victory over the evil within is never complete. At best, he achieves a temporary cease-fire but never a full truce. The *beinoni* spends his life in an endless struggle. He cannot relax his vigil for a single instant, because the moment he does so, the enemy will rally and topple him. ☞☞

כִּי אִם בְּעִתִּים מְזוּמָּנִים, כְּמוֹ בִּשְׁעַת קְרִיאַת שְׁמַע וּתְפִלָּה, שֶׁהִיא שְׁעַת מוֹחִין דְּגַדְלוּת לְמַעְלָה.

with the exception of certain times, such as while reciting the *Shema* or praying, when there is a state of expanded consciousness on high.

Only at specific times can the *beinoni*, after expending the requisite effort, temporarily achieve that complete and perfected state in his soul and in his divine service. The designated time for reciting the *Shema* and for prayer is a time of expanded consciousness on high, when the supernal intellect manifests itself in its utmost radiance and potency. By contrast, there are times of constricted consciousness, when the illumination is partial and dimmed, connoting a state of reduced consciousness and perception at all levels of creation.

THE *BEINONI* AND THE "SMALL CITY"

☞ The *beinoni* must constantly guard his frontiers and does so successfully. The *rasha* is one whose frontier has breaches, whereas the tzaddik has no frontiers at all. The tzaddik has achieved a permanent peace: No battles rage within him because there are no frontiers; there are no two domains, because all is one domain.

In terms of the author of the *Tanya's* analogy of the body as a "small city," the tzaddik has eradicated the enemy so that he no longer poses a threat and the city need no longer be guarded. The *rasha*, even the one who possesses some good, even if he spends most of his life engaged in Torah study and good deeds, finds that the enemy keeps entering the city. The *beinoni* rules over the city and does not allow the enemy to enter, but he has to keep constant vigil because the other side besieges his city without pause, looking for a weak spot at which to force an entry. Yet he never wavers. In the *beinoni*, the other side is no less powerful than it is in the *rasha*, but the *beinoni* has full control of the city and never allows the other side in.

וְגַם לְמַטָּה הִיא שְׁעַת הַכּוֹשֶׁר לְכָל אָדָם, **It is also an auspicious time for every person below,**

The times deemed by *halakha* as suitable for prayer are also the times when prayer is most effective. When there is a revelation of the supernal intellect on high, a state of expanded consciousness, this is also a propitious time for a person to achieve an expanded consciousness on a personal level – to achieve a full and clear awareness of the Divine in his own mind in the reality in which he finds himself.

THE INTRINSIC VALUE OF THE *BEINONI*

☞ The tzaddik and the *beinoni* are not phases of one continuum, where at point A one is categorized as a *beinoni*, and upon reaching point B he is classified as a righteous person. Rather, they constitute two distinct states of being, like a road that forks into two different paths. The *beinoni* takes one path, while the righteous person takes the other. These are not rungs on the same ladder, where one climbs from the rung of the *beinoni* to a higher one in order to become a tzaddik, but two different roads through life. The importance of this book lies in its establishment of the state of *beinoni* as an end in itself to which one should aspire and regard as his goal in life. Even if one never achieves inner peace and tranquility, this does not mean that he has not attained anything. Even if one never achieves a full and decisive victory in the battle of life, one can still realize his objective in life, which is to maintain the struggle to the very end and never give ground.

Elsewhere (chap. 27), the author of the *Tanya* states that God creates two types of people and makes different demands on each. Only a few people are given the ability to achieve inner peace and tranquility in their lives, and only they are expected to achieve this. Most people are not granted the possibility; they are not required to attain this state and never will. We are not speaking, of course, of the peace and tranquility a soul gains in the World to Come in reward for its labors in this world, regarding which it is said, "According to the labor is the reward" (Mishna *Avot* 5:23). The *beinoni* may even obtain a greater reward there than the tzaddik, because he struggles harder and suffers more pain.

The struggle between good and evil is constant. The moment there is a lull in the battle, the *beinoni* must grow alarmed, because it is a sure sign that something is amiss. To the *beinoni* applies the talmudic rule "One should always incite his good inclination against his evil inclination" (*Berakhot* 5a). The evil within him against which he must struggle is not a negative sign but an indication that he is a *beinoni*, and the existence of struggle is a positive sign.

The *beinoni*'s divine soul never gives him a moment's rest. If the *beinoni* ever experiences peace and tranquility, he must worry that it originates from the other side. God neither requires nor desires of him to achieve such peace. He desires the *beinoni*'s struggles and expects him to continue with the struggle throughout his life. Indeed, the state of *beinoni* is not so much a goal but a path, a way of life to which everyone can aspire and in which every individual can walk.

שֶׁאָז מְקַשֵּׁר חָכְמָה בִּינָה דַּעַת שֶׁלּוֹ לַה׳ לְהַעֲמִיק דַּעְתּוֹ בִּגְדוּלַּת אֵין סוֹף בָּרוּךְ הוּא וּלְעוֹרֵר אֶת הָאַהֲבָה כְּרִשְׁפֵּי אֵשׁ בֶּחָלָל הַיְמָנִי שֶׁבְּלִבּוֹ,

because during those moments one binds his wisdom, understanding, and **knowledge to God, focusing his mind on the greatness of *Ein Sof,* blessed be He.** This leads one **to evoke the love** for God that is as fierce **as sparks of fire in the right chamber of his heart,**

It is through the faculty of *da'at,* knowledge, that a person identifies with a concept that he apprehends to the point that it affects and transforms him on an emotional level as well.[3] When a person meditates on the greatness of God and applies to it not only his faculties for abstract perception and analysis but also his *da'at,* his faculty for personalized and subjective apprehension, he will come to feel a fierce love for God.[4]

לְדָבְקָה בּוֹ בְּקִיּוּם הַתּוֹרָה וּמִצְוֹתֶיהָ מֵאַהֲבָה.

so that He may cleave to Him by fulfilling the Torah and its commandments out of love.

Prayer is a time to awaken the divine soul, not only through the appropriate meditations, but also through the stimulation of the divine soul's emotive faculties, as well as the person's innate receptiveness to goodness and holiness. The combination of all this impels the person to cleave to God and His Torah, which entails the fulfillment of the mitzvot, not out of a sense of duty to God, but out of love for Him, out of the desire to be close to Him and to cleave to Him.

שֶׁזֶּהוּ עִנְיַן הַמְבוֹאָר בִּקְרִיאַת שְׁמַע, דְּאוֹרַיְיתָא, וּבִרְכוֹתֶיהָ שֶׁלְּפָנֶיהָ וּלְאַחֲרֶיהָ, שֶׁהֵן מִדְּרַבָּנָן, הֵן הֲכָנָה לְקִיּוּם הַקְּרִיאַת שְׁמַע כְּמוֹ שֶׁמְּבוֹאָר בְּמָקוֹם אַחֵר.

This is the idea expressed in the biblically mandated recitation of the *Shema* and the blessings that precede and follow it, which are rabbinically mandated. These blessings **are a preparation for the fulfillment of the recitation of the *Shema,* as explained elsewhere** (chap. 49).

---

3. See chap. 3.
4. See chap. 9.

The *Shema* is essentially the manifesto of the divine soul. The first verse, "Hear, Israel: The Lord is our God, the Lord is one," is the divine soul's declaration of the awareness that pervades its cognitive faculties, its faculties of perception. The second verse, "And you shall love the Lord your God with all your heart...," is its declaration of love for God. Yet to actually achieve a love of God "with all your heart," a love that derives from both the divine soul in the heart's right chamber and the animal soul in its left, a declaration of principles by the divine soul is not enough. The animal soul too must be affected. For this purpose, the Sages instituted the preliminary blessings of the *Shema*, to prime the soul so that the principles contained in the *Shema* should take root in it and have their desired effect.

The first blessing, *Yotzer Or*, describes the greatness of God's creation, the supernal worlds and the angels that populate them, and the manner in which they all serve their Creator, in order to impress on the animal soul, which stems from that realm, that it too is nullified before God. The second blessing, *Ahavat Olam*, describes God's love for us and is meant to awaken our love for Him in response "as water reflects a face to a face." Thus the blessings of the *Shema* are intended to bring a person to a state of awareness and emotional stimulus from which one can truly relate to the truths he expresses when he proclaims, "Hear, Israel: The Lord is our God, the Lord is one."

וְאָז, הָרַע שֶׁבֶּחָלָל הַשְּׂמָאלִי כָּפוּף וּבָטֵל לַטּוֹב הַמִּתְפַּשֵּׁט בֶּחָלָל הַיְמָנִי מֵחָכְמָה בִּינָה דַּעַת שֶׁבַּמּוֹחַ, הַמְקוּשָּׁרִים בִּגְדוּלַּת אֵין סוֹף בָּרוּךְ הוּא.

Then the evil in the left chamber of his heart **is subservient and nullified to the good that spreads throughout the right chamber** of his heart **from the wisdom, understanding,** and **knowledge in the brain, which are** all **bound to the greatness of *Ein Sof*, blessed be He.**

Above, the author of the *Tanya* described the process by which the divine soul's love for God is stimulated to the point that it spills over into the left chamber of the heart, the abode of the animal soul, transforming the animal soul's passions into a love for God.[5] In the

5. See chap. 9.

tzaddik, this process is complete and is now the permanent state of affairs. The *beinoni* achieves this only at special times, such as during prayers or the recitation of the *Shema*. At such times, the dominion of the *beinoni* over the evil is not merely external, through control of his actions, speech, and conscious thoughts, but involves the entire soul – both its cognitive perceptions and its emotive faculties – alive and ardent in striving for the Divine. The passions of the other element in his soul are stilled, and he has no wish or desire other than to give himself completely over to his Creator and pour out his soul to God.

אֲבָל אַחַר הַתְּפִלָּה, בְּהִסְתַּלְּקוּת הַמּוֹחִין דְּגַדְלוּת אֵין סוֹף בָּרוּךְ הוּא, הֲרֵי הָרַע חוֹזֵר וְנֵיעוֹר בֶּחָלָל הַשְּׂמָאלִי וּמִתְאַוֶּה תַּאֲוָה לְתַאֲווֹת עוֹלָם הַזֶּה וְתַעֲנוּגָיו.

However, after the prayers, when the expanded consciousness of the greatness of *Ein Sof*, blessed be He, is withdrawn, the evil is reawakened in the left chamber of his heart, **and he lusts for the pleasures and delights of this world.**

When the time of prayer and the distinct spiritual opportunity it represents concludes, the *beinoni* again becomes like everyone else. Again the *beinoni* is tempted by worldly pleasures, each according to his nature and the manner in which the animal soul relates to the material world. The time of prayer was a time of slumber and submission for the evil within, a submission that entailed not an absolute negation, not an essential transformation, but only a temporary departure. Immediately after his prayers, the *beinoni* reverts to his previous state, with the evil within again rising against the good in battle.

15 Tevet / 21 Tevet (leap year)

רַק מִפְּנֵי שֶׁלֹּא לוֹ לְבַדּוֹ מִשְׁפַּט הַמְּלוּכָה וְהַמֶּמְשָׁלָה בָּעִיר, אֵינוֹ יָכוֹל לְהוֹצִיא תַּאֲוָתוֹ מִכֹּחַ אֶל הַפּוֹעַל,

However, since the evil **does not maintain exclusive rights to the rulership and dominion over the** "small **city," it is incapable of bringing its latent lusts to fruition**

The *beinoni* has a desire for the pleasures of the material world, but he is not a *rasha*. There is a basic, quintessential difference between the two. When the wicked person lusts for something, he actually carries out his desire, if not in deed, then in conscious, willful thought. On the other hand, the animal soul of the *beinoni* is incapable of giving expression to those lusts.

The initial urge, the craving, transpires in the *beinoni* with the same intensity and force that it does in the *rasha,* but for the initial urge to be implemented in practice, it must gain control of the person, and the *beinoni* never allows that to happen. The ultimate verdict of the internal tribunal as to what should actually be done is not in the hands of evil, and without the divine soul's consent, it is unable to carry out its desires.

לְהִתְלַבֵּשׁ בְּאֵבְרֵי הַגּוּף בְּמַעֲשֶׂה דִּבּוּר וּמַחֲשָׁבָה מַמָּשׁ, לְהַעֲמִיק מַחֲשַׁבְתּוֹ בְּתַעֲנוּגֵי עוֹלָם הַזֶּה אֵיךְ לְמַלֹּאוֹת תַּאֲוַת לִבּוֹ.

by actually becoming clothed in the body's limbs, in action, speech, and thought, so that it may contemplate the pleasures of this world, devising **how to gratify his heart's cravings,** theoretically or practically,

There are several stages whereby evil becomes clothed in the mind. The *beinoni* has no control over the initial stage, because a person is completely unaware of any impulses that occur prior to entering his mind. He is not conscious of the drives and urges rising within him until they somehow express themselves in the form of a conscious thought. Once this impulse has entered his consciousness, however, he has the willpower to control his thoughts.

There is a world of difference between one who willfully thinks sinful thoughts, whether thoughts of actually committing a sin or simply contemplation of the sin itself, and one in whom sinful thoughts arise that he immediately banishes the moment they enter his awareness. The *beinoni* is able to exercise such control.

כִּי הַמּוֹחַ שַׁלִּיט עַל הַלֵּב [כְּמוֹ שֶׁכָּתוּב בְּרַעְיָא מְהֵימְנָא פָּרָשַׁת פִּנְחָס (זהר, חלק ג רכד, א)] בְּתוֹלַדְתּוֹ וְטֶבַע יְצִירָתוֹ. שֶׁכָּךְ נוֹצַר הָאָדָם בְּתוֹלַדְתּוֹ, שֶׁכָּל אָדָם יָכוֹל בִּרְצוֹנוֹ שֶׁבְּמוֹחוֹ

because the brain controls the heart (as stated in *Raya Meheimna, Parashat Pinḥas* [*Zohar* 3:224a]), through its inborn, natural character. This is how every person is inherently created, so that every person is capable of using the will

לְהִתְאַפֵּק וְלִמְשׁוֹל בְּרוּחַ תַּאֲוָתוֹ שֶׁבְּלִבּוֹ שֶׁלֹּא לְמַלֹּאת מִשְׁאֲלוֹת לִבּוֹ בְּמַעֲשֶׂה דִּבּוּר וּמַחֲשָׁבָה, וּלְהַסִּיחַ דַּעְתּוֹ לְגַמְרֵי מִתַּאֲוַת לִבּוֹ אֶל הַהֵפֶךְ לְגַמְרֵי,

in his brain to restrain himself and control the spirit of lust in his heart by not gratifying his heart's desires in action, speech, and thought. Rather, he is able **to completely divert his mind from** fulfilling **his heart's lusts,** redirecting it instead **to the completely opposite** direction,

This axiom is fundamental to this chapter and to the entire book: The brain can control the heart, not only as a result of special training or extraordinary effort on the part of the mind but because this is the way a person was created.

A fundamental quality of the human being grants his mind the power to rule over the desires of the heart, certainly in his speech and actions but even in his thoughts. This does not mean that exercising this innate ability is easy, that all one needs to do is to think a certain thought and the heart will automatically follow the mind. It means that a person can consciously compel himself not to think certain thoughts. He cannot prevent them from entering his mind, but he has sufficient control to prevent their realization. If, for instance, someone is told not to think about polar bears, he cannot stop the thought of them from coming to mind, but he can prevent himself from thinking about them by immediately turning his mind to something else as soon as the thought arises.

That "the brain controls the heart" does not imply that the mind can stop any activity of the heart or develop it by force of will alone. Rather, it expresses the axiom that a person in a state of awareness and consciousness can supervise himself and refrain from certain actions and certain thoughts by not completing every thought that arises in his mind. This ability not to think through every thought but rather to disrupt it at a certain point is an innate advantage of the mind over the heart, of conscious will over unconscious drives.

The *beinoni* is the one who uses this power to repel thoughts that arise from the evil in his soul. Unlike the tzaddik, the *beinoni* cannot prevent the eruption of these impulses, but he can prevent them from reaching fruition, rejecting them as soon as they sprout and rise. ☞

וּבִפְרָט אֶל צַד הַקְּדוּשָּׁה, כְּדִכְתִיב: "וְרָאִיתִי שֶׁיֵּשׁ יִתְרוֹן לַחָכְמָה מִן הַסִּכְלוּת כִּיתְרוֹן הָאוֹר מִן הַחוֹשֶׁךְ" (קהלת ב, יג).

in particular to the side of holiness, as it is written, "I saw that there is advantage to wisdom over folly, like the advantage of light over darkness" (Eccles. 2:13).

In addition to the general power of the mind to control the heart, the divine soul has an advantage in its struggle to overpower desires originating in the animal soul. The nature of that additional advantage is expressed in the quote from Ecclesiastes, which compares the superiority of wisdom over folly – that is, of good over evil – to the superiority of light over darkness.

פֵּירוּשׁ, כְּמוֹ שֶׁהָאוֹר יֵשׁ לוֹ יִתְרוֹן וּשְׁלִיטָה וּמֶמְשָׁלָה עַל הַחוֹשֶׁךְ, שֶׁמְּעַט אוֹר גַּשְׁמִי דּוֹחֶה הַרְבֵּה מִן הַחֹשֶׁךְ, שֶׁנִּדְחֶה מִמֶּנּוּ מֵאֵלָיו וּמִמֵּילָא,

This means that **just as light has an advantage over darkness, utterly dominating it,** so that **a little physical light banishes a great amount of darkness, which is automatically banished from** the light **as a natural consequence,**

The advantage of light over darkness is not merely qualitative in the sense that light is better than darkness, nicer, more useful, and more

THE MIND'S CONTROL

☞ The principle stating that the mind governs the heart applies only when the mind is functioning normally, in situations that are experientially normative and where the individual functions as usual, as a sentient person. But in an abnormal situation, once a certain limit of provocation is exceeded, a person loses the ability to control the spread and surge of the heart's desires. Everyone, beyond a certain point, is dragged into a complex of emotions that is liable to draw him to do anything – for better or worse. In such situations, he might even be aware, sometimes very clearly, that he is about to do something that is self-destructive, that runs contrary to all that is true, right, and good, yet he is powerless to stop himself.

All the same, the control the mind exerts on the heart is complete and decisive. The situations in which control is lost do not occur on their own. A person loses control when he allows himself to cross a certain threshold. If he allows an emotion or relationship to develop beyond all manageable proportions, he is liable to reach a point of no return. He then becomes subject to emotions and desires that he can no longer stop.

pleasant, but it is also quantitative: Only a little light banishes a large amount of darkness. Light possesses an innate superiority over darkness, the superiority of positivity over negativity. Light need not battle darkness because with its very appearance it repels not only an equal amount of darkness but a great deal of darkness. When two substances that have no advantage over another are brought into contact, such as when a solid is immersed in water, the volume of water displaced exactly equals the volume of the solid immersed. But when one takes a small candle into a dark room, the volume of darkness displaced greatly exceeds the volume of the candle's flame.

כָּךְ נִדְחֶה מִמֵּילָא סִכְלוּת הַרְבֵּה שֶׁל הַקְּלִיפָּה וְסִטְרָא אָחֳרָא שֶׁבֶּחָלָל הַשְּׂמָאלִי [כְּמַאֲמַר רַבּוֹתֵינוּ ז״ל (סוטה ג, א): ״אֵין אָדָם עוֹבֵר עֲבֵירָה אֶלָּא אִם כֵּן נִכְנַס בּוֹ רוּחַ שְׁטוּת״ וכו׳]

so too a great deal of the folly of the *kelippa* **and** *sitra aḥara* located **in the left chamber** of the heart **is banished as a natural consequence (in accordance with our Rabbis' statement** "A man commits a transgression **only if a spirit of folly enters him...**" [*Sota* 3a])

Elsewhere, the author of the *Tanya* further develops this concept,[6] stating that no one who has any true awareness of what he is doing, however weak-minded he might be, would ever sin unless a spirit of folly entered him. At such a time, he can commit acts that fill him with shame and self-abhorrence when he regains his awareness, perhaps immediately after his deed or even in the midst of his deed. In retrospect, he cannot bear to think that he has done such a thing, yet he has done it because "a spirit of folly enters him."

מִפְּנֵי הַחָכְמָה שֶׁבַּנֶּפֶשׁ הָאֱלֹהִית שֶׁבַּמּוֹחַ, אֲשֶׁר רְצוֹנָהּ לִמְשׁוֹל לְבַדָּהּ בָּעִיר

by the wisdom in the divine soul that is in the brain, which is compared to light. The divine soul **desires to exercise exclusive control over the** small **city**

The faculty of wisdom in the divine soul has the power to repel the spirit of folly that stems from *kelippa* for two reasons. First, wisdom

6. See chaps. 24, 25.

is light in contrast to the darkness of folly. Folly operates in a space of conscious darkness: It has no explanation and justification but is only lust and sometimes mere blind foolishness. Second, wisdom is in fact the wisdom of the holy divine soul and has the advantage of holiness and good over *kelippa* and evil. The light embodied by the faculty of wisdom wishes not merely to overpower but specifically to "exercise exclusive control" over the body. There exists no middle ground between holiness and spiritual impurity wherein a compromise can be reached.

וּלְהִתְלַבֵּשׁ בִּשְׁלֹשָׁה לְבוּשֶׁיהָ הַנִּזְכָּרִים לְעֵיל בְּכָל הַגּוּף כּוּלּוֹ כַּנִּזְכָּר לְעֵיל, שֶׁהֵם: מַחֲשָׁבָה דִּבּוּר וּמַעֲשֶׂה שֶׁל תרי"ג מִצְוֹת הַתּוֹרָה כַּנִּזְכָּר לְעֵיל.

by being clothed in its aforementioned three garments, namely, the thoughts, speech, and actions of the 613 commandments of the Torah, as mentioned above (chap. 4), permeating **the entire body, as mentioned above** (chap. 9).

The thoughts, speech, and actions of the Torah's commandments are the exclusive garments of the divine soul. Only in these expressions of the soul, of the Torah and the mitzvot, can the holy divine soul be clothed and manifest. The author of the *Tanya* emphasizes the 613 mitzvot, that is, the entire gamut of mitzvot, to convey that it is specifically through fulfilling all the commandments that the entirety of the 613 "limbs" of the divine soul become clothed and manifest. The resultant revelation of holiness is complete, leaving no room for the evil of the other side.

וְאַף עַל פִּי כֵן אֵינוֹ נִקְרָא צַדִּיק כְּלָל

Nevertheless, he is not at all categorized as a tzaddik, 16 Tevet / 22 Tevet (leap year)

The *beinoni* immediately rejects all thought of transgression and never performs a sinful act. Moreover, his actions and thoughts are clothed only in the holy garments of Torah and mitzvot. Yet, despite the fact that the *beinoni* never transgresses even the most subtle of sins, he is not a tzaddik. There is still a great distance and a most fundamental difference between the two.

מִפְּנֵי שֶׁיִּתְרוֹן הַזֶּה אֲשֶׁר לְאוֹר נֶפֶשׁ הָאֱלֹהִית עַל הַחוֹשֶׁךְ וְסִכְלוּת שֶׁל הַקְּלִיפּוֹת הַנִּדְחֶה מִמֵּילָא, אֵינוֹ אֶלָּא בִּשְׁלֹשָׁה לְבוּשִׁים הַנִּזְכָּרִים לְעֵיל, וְלֹא בְּמַהוּתָהּ וְעַצְמוּתָהּ, עַל מַהוּתָהּ וְעַצְמוּתָהּ שֶׁל הַקְּלִיפָּה.

because this advantage that the light of the divine soul possesses over the darkness and folly of the *kelippa*, which is automatically banished, is only in its three aforementioned garments but not in the essence and being of the divine soul, which has no advantage **over the essence and being of the *kelippa*.**

The *beinoni* exercises the advantage of light over darkness, of wisdom over folly, only in the expressions of his soul but not in the essence of his soul. When two thoughts of equal magnitude, one of holiness and the other of the profane, struggle for supremacy, the former will oust the latter. But even if a person spends his entire lifetime thinking only holy thoughts, this will in no way banish the underlying forces of evil in his soul. The *beinoni* has transformed the external face of his soul, the manner in which his soul expresses itself outwardly (speech and deed) and inwardly (thought), but the soul itself has not been changed, not its unfathomable depths nor its consciously felt wishes, desires, and passions. These exist within the *beinoni* exactly as they exist within the *rasha,* the only difference being that the *beinoni* prevents the implementation and fruition of any evil desires in practice.

כִּי מַהוּתָהּ וְעַצְמוּתָהּ שֶׁל נֶפֶשׁ הַבַּהֲמִית שֶׁמֵּהַקְּלִיפָּה שֶׁבֶּחָלָל הַשְּׂמָאלִי לֹא נִדְחֶה כְּלָל מִמְּקוֹמוֹ בַּבֵּינוֹנִי אַחַר הַתְּפִלָּה,

This is **because the essence and being of the animal soul,** which stems **from the *kelippa* in the left chamber** of the heart, **is not at all banished from its place in the *beinoni* upon the conclusion of** his **prayers,**

During his prayers, the *beinoni* was completely engrossed in holy matters, completely consumed by his fervor, by a single-minded, self-negating bond with God. The love of God burned in his heart, extinguishing all other loves. The subjugation of evil to good was not merely in practice but in essence. His entire being lay within the realm of holiness. But the *beinoni* does not pray all day. There remain the hours after the conclusion of his prayers. ☞

שֶׁאֵין רִשְׁפֵּי אֵשׁ אַהֲבַת ה׳ בְּהִתְגַּלּוּת לִבּוֹ בֶּחָלָל הַיְמָנִי,

when the fiery sparks of love for God are not manifest in the right chamber of his heart.

All that the *beinoni* experienced during prayer recedes as if it never was. Earlier, when he was consumed by love and expressed it in his prayers, his experience was genuine. At the time, his heart truly and wholly belonged to God. However, this is not the *beinoni*'s normal state of being but a state brought on by a special effort to rouse in himself an all-consuming love for God. After the prayer, all that remains within him is the potential for such love.

כִּי אִם תּוֹכוֹ רָצוּף אַהֲבָה מְסוּתֶּרֶת, שֶׁהִיא אַהֲבָה הַטִּבְעִית שֶׁבְּנֶפֶשׁ הָאֱלֹהִית, כְּמוֹ שֶׁיִּתְבָּאֵר לְקַמָּן.

Instead, only **his interior is inlaid with** latent, **concealed love, which is the innate love that is in the divine soul, as will be explained below** (chap. 18 and onward).

The hidden love, though it may not manifest as an emotional experience, implies a very deep relationship. It represents a fundamental, quintessential bond between a person and God that exists beyond consciousness and, in a certain sense, is deeper and more basic than any experience of love.

THE POST-PRAYER HOURS

☞ The notion of "post-prayer" time is a concept in the *Tanya* that expresses the difference between the tzaddik and the *beinoni*. If during prayers the *beinoni* prays as a saintly man should pray, he is like the tzaddik. But upon the conclusion of his prayers, he reverts to being like the wicked, with an evil impulse, challenges, and doubts. It is during those post-prayer hours that the *beinoni* is put to the test. These hours serve as the proving ground for the tools with which the author of the *Tanya* equips the *beinoni* to engage in the battle over his soul.

וַאֲזַי, יָכוֹל לִהְיוֹת סִכְלוּת הַכְּסִיל הָרַע בְּהִתְגַּלּוּת לִבּוֹ בֶּחָלָל הַשְּׂמָאלִי לְהִתְאַוֹּת תַּאֲוָה לְכָל עִנְיְינֵי גַשְׁמִיּוּת עוֹלָם הַזֶּה, בֵּין בְּהֶיתֵּר בֵּין בְּאִיסּוּר חַס וְשָׁלוֹם, כְּאִלּוּ לֹא הִתְפַּלֵּל כְּלָל,

Then it is possible for the folly of the evil fool to be revealed in the left chamber of his heart, lusting after all physical matters of this world, be it permissible or prohibited, God forbid, as if he had never prayed at all.

Because this love is not experienced openly by the soul, because it does not manifest itself in the form of an actual craving and passion to cleave to God, now that the revealed love the *beinoni* experienced during prayer has receded, the "evil fool" – the evil inclination – can once again rear its ugly head.

When holiness is not expressed in its full intensity and maximal revelation in the *beinoni*'s heart, then the "spirit of folly" is manifest, which allows the forces of evil to rise up in his soul. The experience of holiness can linger in the *beinoni* after his prayers, and the author of the *Tanya* will discuss the various ways in which the *beinoni* might prime himself so that this experience will leave a mark on the soul and manifest itself as a tangible feeling. But in essence, the love that is evoked in the *beinoni* during prayer is confined to a specific time frame, after which it is no longer operative. When the divine soul ceases to manifest itself throughout his being, the *beinoni* is again exposed to rising alien passions, which exist within him as they do in the *rasha*.

The time of prayer has effected a change in him, but the change is temporary and does not effect a fundamental change in the *beinoni*'s soul. Immediately afterward he reverts to the person he had been before as if he had never prayed. ☞

A PRAYER'S IMPRINT

☞ The author of the *Tanya* does not intend to say that prayer effects no change at all in the soul of the *beinoni*. What he felt during prayer was so profound that it certainly made an impression on him. Yet the *beinoni*, and in fact every human being, is constructed in such a way that this impression may disappear from his consciousness as if it never existed, just as the divine soul itself could disappear from his life, from his conscious awareness, as if it never was. The task of the *beinoni* is to remember what he experienced and take it with him in such a manner that it will influence his life even during those post-prayer hours.

אֶלָּא שֶׁבְּדָבָר אִיסּוּר אֵינוֹ עוֹלֶה בְּדַעְתּוֹ לַעֲשׂוֹת הָאִיסּוּר בְּפוֹעַל מַמָּשׁ חַס וְשָׁלוֹם.

However, with regard to a prohibited matter, it does not occur to him at all to carry out the prohibition in practice, God forbid.

One of the definitions of a *beinoni* is that he is so far removed from certain things – that which is prohibited outright by the Torah – that they do not occur to him as practical possibilities. In this sense, the thought of something that is prohibited can perhaps occur even to the *beinoni*, yet the thought of actually carrying out that outright prohibited act in practice never occurs to him. He knows that for him it is completely and forever out of the realm of possibility. He bears no connection to such an act in the slightest. ☞

אֶלָּא הִרְהוּרֵי עֲבֵירָה הַקָּשִׁים מֵעֲבֵירָה

Yet thoughts of transgression, which are worse than transgression itself,

Even though it never occurs to the *beinoni* to actually commit a prohibited act, he nevertheless thinks about it. Such thoughts are regarded as more severe than transgression itself[7] because they involve the faculty of thought, the most intimate of the soul's garments.

יְכוֹלִים לִפְעוֹל לַעֲלוֹת לְמוֹחוֹ וּלְבַלְבְּלוֹ מִתּוֹרָה וַעֲבוֹדָה.

can manage to rise to his mind and distract him from Torah study **and the service** of God.

BEYOND THE REALM OF POSSIBILITY

☞ In truth, everyone has certain limits that he will never exceed and that he is unable to even consider exceeding, things for which any desire or lust is merely theoretical. These limits vary from individual to individual and from society to society, but every type of personality precludes certain acts as inconceivable. Ibn Ezra, explaining the last of the Ten Commandments, "You shall not covet" (Ex. 20:14), brings an example of a simple peasant who happens to see the king's daughter. He may think of her as beautiful and desirable, but he will never even think of trying to obtain her, because he knows that she is unattainable. Along the same lines, the thought of something that is prohibited might arise in the mind of a *beinoni* but not the thought of actually doing it, because he knows that this is something he can never do.

7. See *Yoma* 29a.

Thoughts of sin, even if they are devoid of any possibility of execution, are extremely damaging to the soul. Even if the circumstances are such that preclude any possibility of the thought being translated into action, it evokes basic lusts and confuses a person who was occupied at that time with Torah study and mitzvot.

וְכִמַאֲמַר רַבּוֹתֵינוּ ז״ל: ״ג׳ עֲבֵירוֹת אֵין אָדָם נִיצּוֹל מֵהֶן בְּכָל יוֹם: הִרְהוּר עֲבֵירָה וְעִיּוּן תְּפִלָּה״ כו׳.

As our Rabbis state, "There are **three sins from which** any **person is not spared each day.** They are having **sinful thoughts,** committing sins concerning **deliberation in prayer,** and uttering malicious speech" (*Bava Batra* 164b).

"Sinful thoughts" are not thoughts of actually committing a sin in practice but merely the contemplation of sinful things. A sin pertaining to "deliberation in prayer" is the failure to properly concentrate on one's prayers due to distractions. "Malicious speech" in this context does not actually refer to speaking ill of others, which is an outright sin that one can and must avoid at all times, but the semblance of slander, talk that might, in some roundabout way, imply something negative about another.

These transgressions are not committed intentionally, and they are extremely difficult to avoid even with a concentrated effort and the mind's control over the heart. Their occurrence is inherent to the state of *beinoni,* whose inner self has not undergone any fundamental change, for whom the evil within is dominated by the good but has not been transformed into good. The evil continues to ferment within him and gives him no rest. In the same way that the good remains within the wicked person and fills him with remorse, giving him no rest, so too does the evil in the *beinoni* constantly plague him, exposing him daily to the "three sins."

17 Tevet
23 Tevet (leap year)

רַק שֶׁלָּזֶה מוֹעִיל הָרְשִׁימוּ בְּמוֹחִין

However, it is for this **that the impression** remaining **in his intellect** after prayer **proves beneficial,**

When a person studies and prays and attains a state of love and attachment to God, even if only temporarily, the memory of it remains. Even if he does not repeat the experience, the impression of that occasion lingers within him This impression is an expression of the fact that the experience still exists in the recesses of his soul and that it only needs to be revealed and revived.

Moreover, even after the feeling is no longer manifest and felt in the heart, it leaves marks in the brain in the form of memories. The mind, which is a partner in the experience of love, took notes in the wake of that experience that could be applied in the future: What does this experience mean? What are the practical implications? In what manner do people act when in love? How does one maintain feelings of love? Equipped with these points in his mind, one can forge ahead even when the experience of love and connection to God is not active. These markers are so powerful that they allow the person to even reevoke those feelings of love.[8]

וְיִרְאַת ה׳ וְאַהֲבָתוֹ הַמְּסוּתֶּרֶת בְּחָלָל הַיְמָנִי

in addition to **the fear and love of God concealed in the right chamber** of his heart:

In addition to the impression remaining in the soul of the *beinoni* from the experience of prayer, a latent sense of awe and love of God inherent to the essence of the soul exists within every person at all times.

לְהִתְגַּבֵּר וְלִשְׁלוֹט עַל הָרַע הַזֶּה הַמִּתְאַוֶּה תַּאֲוָה, שֶׁלֹּא לִהְיוֹת לוֹ שְׁלִיטָה וּמֶמְשָׁלָה בָּעִיר לְהוֹצִיא תַּאֲוָתוֹ מִכֹּחַ אֶל הַפּוֹעַל לְהִתְלַבֵּשׁ בְּאֵבְרֵי הַגּוּף.

that he may prevail and exercise control over this evil that evokes lust, preventing the evil **from exercising control and dominating the** "small **city" by translating its lusts from potentiality to actuality and becoming clothed in the body's limbs.**

Through the combination of the impression left by the experience of love and awe in prayer and the latent potential for love and awe in

8. *Torah Or* 83d.

every soul, it is within the *beinoni*'s grasp to attain love and awe in their truest sense. He is now able to prevail over the evil within him, and the *beinoni*'s power is such that even without the ongoing experience of love and awe of God that the tzaddik experiences, he can draw strength from the impression left by his prayers and from his latent love of God to completely control every aspect of his life, never allowing his animal soul to bring its lusts to fruition.

וַאֲפִילּוּ בַּמּוֹחַ לְבַדּוֹ לְהִרְהֵר בָּרַע, אֵין לוֹ שְׁלִיטָה וּמֶמְשָׁלָה לְהִרְהֵר חַס וְשָׁלוֹם בִּרְצוֹנוֹ שֶׁבְּמוֹחוֹ,

Even in the mind alone, in terms of thinking evil thoughts, evil **has neither the control nor dominion** to cause him **to consciously think** such thoughts **in his mind, God forbid,**

So great is the power of the *beinoni* that even sinful thoughts never develop into conscious, structured thoughts.

שֶׁיְּקַבֵּל בִּרְצוֹן חַס וְשָׁלוֹם הִרְהוּר זֶה הָרַע הָעוֹלֶה מֵאֵלָיו מֵהַלֵּב לַמּוֹחַ כַּנִּזְכָּר לְעֵיל,

so that he would willingly accept this evil thought that automatically rises from the heart to the mind, God forbid, as mentioned above (chap. 9).

These thoughts arise spontaneously within the *beinoni* because the divided heart with which he was born has not been rectified. His heart is like that of every person: He desires what everyone desires and lusts after what everyone lusts after, each according to his tastes and station.

אֶלָּא מִיָּד בַּעֲלִיָּיתוֹ לְשָׁם דּוֹחֵהוּ בִּשְׁתֵּי יָדַיִם וּמַסִּיחַ דַּעְתּוֹ מִיָּד שֶׁנִּזְכַּר שֶׁהוּא הִרְהוּר רַע, וְאֵינוֹ מְקַבְּלוֹ בִּרְצוֹן אֲפִילּוּ לְהִרְהֵר בּוֹ בִּרְצוֹן, וְכָל שֶׁכֵּן לְהַעֲלוֹתוֹ עַל הַדַּעַת לַעֲשׂוֹתוֹ חַס וְשָׁלוֹם.

Rather, as soon as the unwanted thought merely **rises there** in his consciousness, **he utterly rejects it, and immediately diverts his mind** to other matters **when he recalls that this is an evil thought. He does not willingly accept it, even to** merely **entertain it willingly and all the more so to consider** actually **committing** the transgression, **God forbid,**

Despite the *beinoni*'s inability to prevent these kinds of thoughts from entering his heart, he is capable of repelling them immediately upon their entering his consciousness. Not only is he capable of doing so, but he does so in practice. He certainly does not entertain the thought of actually committing a prohibited act, a more egregious stage where one no longer confines the thought to his imagination but consciously schemes how to commit the act. This is similar to the distinction between consciously thinking of committing the act and thinking about how to actually implement it.

אוֹ אֲפִילּוּ לְדַבֵּר בּוֹ, כִּי הַמְהַרְהֵר בְּרָצוֹן נִקְרָא רָשָׁע בְּאוֹתָהּ שָׁעָה, וְהַבֵּינוֹנִי אֵינוֹ רָשָׁע אֲפִילּוּ שָׁעָה אַחַת לְעוֹלָם. וְכֵן בִּדְבָרִים שֶׁבֵּין אָדָם לַחֲבֵירוֹ,

or even speaking about it, because one who willingly thinks about committing a transgression **is considered wicked at that time, and a *beinoni* is never** categorized as **wicked, even for a moment. The same applies to matters between one person and another.**

Up to now, the discussion has dwelled on sinful desires that relate to man's duties toward God, such as the desire for non-kosher food. But the same applies to negative desires and behaviors in all that pertains to a person's relationship with others.

מִיָּד שֶׁעוֹלֶה לוֹ מֵהַלֵּב לַמּוֹחַ אֵיזוֹ טִינָא וְשִׂנְאָה, חַס וְשָׁלוֹם, אוֹ אֵיזוֹ קִנְאָה אוֹ כַּעַס אוֹ קְפֵידָא, וְדוֹמֵיהֶן, אֵינוֹ מְקַבְּלָן כְּלָל בְּמוֹחוֹ וּבִרְצוֹנוֹ.

The moment any animosity and hatred toward another **rises from his heart to his mind, God forbid, or any envy, anger, or a grudge, and the like, he does not accept them in his mind and will at all.**

The *beinoni* is not a person who never gets angry. But he has sufficient control over himself not to indulge his anger and allow it to take root and develop into a full-fledged emotion.

וְאַדְּרַבָּה, הַמּוֹחַ שַׁלִּיט וּמוֹשֵׁל בָּרוּחַ שֶׁבְּלִבּוֹ לַעֲשׂוֹת הֵיפֶךְ מַמָּשׁ, לְהִתְנַהֵג עִם חֲבֵירוֹ בְּמִדַּת חֶסֶד וְחִיבָּה יְתֵרָה מוּדַעַת לוֹ

On the contrary, the mind controls and dominates the spirit in his heart, causing him **to do the exact opposite, treating his friend with kindness and displaying extra affection toward him,**

לִסְבּוֹל מִמֶּנּוּ עַד קָצֶה הָאַחֲרוֹן וְלֹא לִכְעוֹס חַס וְשָׁלוֹם, וְגַם שֶׁלֹּא לְשַׁלֵּם לוֹ כְּפָעֳלוֹ חַס וְשָׁלוֹם, אֶלָּא אַדְּרַבָּה לִגְמוֹל לְחַיָּיבִים טוֹבוֹת, כְּמוֹ שֶׁכָּתוּב בַּזֹּהַר (חלק א רא, א) לִלְמוֹד מִיּוֹסֵף עִם אֶחָיו.

tolerating him to the utter extreme and not becoming angry, God forbid, nor taking revenge, God forbid, but rather, on the contrary, bestowing favors on offenders, as it is written in the ***Zohar*** (1:201a) that one should **learn from** the way **Joseph** conducted himself **with his brothers.**

Even if the *beinoni* was hurt in some way by another, he possesses the inner fortitude to not retaliate against the perpetrator,[9] but rather to demonstrate a disproportionately kind attitude toward him.

The *beinoni* is someone whose divine soul successfully controls his animal soul. Although he experiences all forms of temptation, such as anger, hatred, and lust, in exactly the same way that the wicked person experiences them, he will not succumb to them, even in his mind. In his conscious thoughts, and certainly in his speech and deeds, he expresses only the goodness and holiness of his divine soul.

9. The Torah prohibits this outright; see Lev. 19:18.

Chapter 13

THE PREVIOUS CHAPTER OFFERED A GENERAL DESCRIPtion of the *beinoni*, an intermediate level between the tzaddik, the righteous person, and the *rasha*, a wicked individual. Yet the *beinoni* is no happy medium, blending tzaddik and *rasha* in one person. Rather, he is one in whom these two extremes coexist.

To all appearances, in deed and even in thought, he is like a tzaddik, but in his inner desires and makeup, he resembles a *rasha*. His intermediate state balances the two: In his inner world, he is no different from any *rasha*; his outer behavior, the path he follows in practice, is that of a tzaddik. This is no sleight of hand, no lie that he is telling himself. It is the unique reality arising from his continual struggle with himself, his sole purpose and aim to strive as a servant of God.

This is not the straightforward existence of the tzaddik, but a complex reality that emerges particularly due to the constant struggle between these two sides of himself. It is the contest between his impulses and desires, which are the same as that of a *rasha*, and the superstructure of the tzaddik's existence lived every day of his life. This tug-of-war is the *beinoni*'s reality.

This complex figure that is the *beinoni* requires more explanation than the tzaddik and *rasha*. He is the particular subject of this chapter and the one that follows, and in a larger scope he is the focus of the entire book.

18 Tevet
24 Tevet (leap year)

וּבָזֶה יוּבַן לְשׁוֹן מַאֲמַר רַבּוֹתֵינוּ ז״ל (ברכות סא, ב): ״בֵּינוֹנִים זֶה וָזֶה שׁוֹפְטָן״ [פֵּירוּשׁ, יֵצֶר טוֹב וְיֵצֶר הָרַע] דִּכְתִיב: ״כִּי יַעֲמוֹד לִימִין אֶבְיוֹן לְהוֹשִׁיעַ מִשּׁוֹפְטֵי נַפְשׁוֹ״ (תהלים קט, לא).

On this basis, we can understand the language employed **in the** following statement **of our Rabbis** (*Berakhot* 61b): "The good inclination judges the righteous.... The evil inclination judges the wicked.... ***Beinonim* are judged by both" [meaning,** both **the good and evil inclinations], as it is written, 'For He stands at the right hand of the needy to deliver him from those who judge him'** (Ps. 109:31)."

After explaining at length the essential levels of tzaddik, *rasha*, and *beinoni*, the author of the *Tanya* returns to the questions he raised in the first chapter, quoting this very talmudic statement. The Hebrew word *shofet* used in the talmudic statement, often translated as "rule," actually connotes to judge. The plural usage of the word in the verse that the Sages quote, "to deliver him from those who judge him," introduces us to those individuals, the *beinonim*, who encounter two internal judges, not one.

וְלֹא אָמְרוּ זֶה וָזֶה מוֹשְׁלִים חַס וְשָׁלוֹם, כִּי כְּשֶׁיֵּשׁ אֵיזוֹ שְׁלִיטָה וּמֶמְשָׁלָה לַיֵּצֶר הָרַע בָּעִיר קְטַנָּה, אֲפִילוּ לְפִי שָׁעָה קַלָּה - נִקְרָא רָשָׁע בְּאוֹתָהּ שָׁעָה.

The Rabbis **did not say that both this,** the good inclination, **and that,** the evil inclination, **rule** over him, **God forbid,** employing the word *moshel,* **because were the evil inclination to have any dominion and rule over the** *beinoni*'s **"small city," even for a short while, he would be categorized as wicked at that time.**

The Sages use a word that connotes to judge, *shofet,* rather than the word *moshel,* which would connote dominion or dictatorship. When the evil nature holds sway over the "small city" – that is, the physical body, or the infrastructure of the self[1] – even for a moment, he is no

1. See Eccles. 9:14; *Nedarim* 32b.

longer designated as a *beinoni*. In his outward conduct, the *beinoni* resembles the tzaddik, utterly without evil for even a moment, but once the evil inclination takes over, this definition can no longer apply.

אֶלָּא הַיֵּצֶר הָרַע אֵינוֹ רַק עַל דֶּרֶךְ מָשָׁל כְּמוֹ שׁוֹפֵט וְדַיָּין הָאוֹמֵר דַּעְתּוֹ בְּמִשְׁפָּט, וְאַף עַל פִּי כֵן יָכוֹל לִהְיוֹת שֶׁלֹּא יִהְיֶה פְּסַק הֲלָכָה כָּךְ לְמַעֲשֶׂה מִפְּנֵי שֶׁיֵּשׁ עוֹד שׁוֹפֵט וְדַיָּין הַחוֹלֵק עָלָיו,

Rather, the evil inclination acts, **by way of analogy, only as a judge and jurist who expresses his opinion in a court case. Nevertheless, it may well be that** his **ruling is not final in practice, since there is another judge and jurist who contends with him.**

There can be only one ruler, but it is possible to have more than one judge. The dichotomy within the *beinoni* lies in the realm of his two inner magistrates and their respective beliefs. Yet each magistrate merely states his opinion. The final verdict need not be in agreement with the magistrate's view.

וְצָרִיךְ לְהַכְרִיעַ בֵּינֵיהֶם וַהֲלָכָה כְּדִבְרֵי הַמַּכְרִיעַ.

It is then **necessary to arbitrate between them, and the verdict will follow** the decision of **the arbiter.**

It is an arbiter's task to decide the final verdict. Once he does, the preceding debate vanishes, never to be mentioned again. With regard to the person's inner struggle, the debate disappears from any subsequent thought, speech, or action.

כָּךְ הַיֵּצֶר הָרַע אוֹמֵר דַּעְתּוֹ בֶּחָלָל הַשְּׂמָאלִי שֶׁבַּלֵּב

Similarly, the evil inclination expresses his opinion in the left chamber of the heart,

As noted earlier,[2] the animal soul's dwelling place is the blood and, in particular, in the part of the heart filled with blood, its left chamber. In the spiritual context, it dwells in the emotional plane of one's con-

2. Chap. 9.

sciousness where it expresses its likes and dislikes, its beliefs and wishes. This plane of consciousness is fully present in the *beinoni*, representing one of his inner magistrates.

וּמֵהַלֵּב עוֹלֶה לַמּוֹחַ לְהַרְהֵר בּוֹ,

and from the heart it rises to the mind for contemplation.

The evil inclination generates an impulse, an evil desire in the heart and emotions. For it to be actualized and developed, there must be a degree of awareness and recognition of the desire in the mind.

וּמִיָּד חוֹלֵק עָלָיו הַשּׁוֹפֵט הַשֵּׁנִי, שֶׁהוּא הַנֶּפֶשׁ הָאֱלֹהִית שֶׁבַּמּוֹחַ הַמִּתְפַּשֵּׁט בֶּחָלָל הַיְמָנִי שֶׁבַּלֵּב מְקוֹם מִשְׁכַּן הַיֵּצֶר טוֹב.

However, the moment the impulse reaches the mind, **it is immediately disputed by the second judge, the divine soul that is in the brain, which extends to the right chamber of the heart, the abode of the good inclination.**

Although the divine soul's sphere of influence also extends to the heart, the arena where it challenges the animal soul is the brain. In sheer strength, the animal soul predominates in the emotions. The brain, on the other hand, possesses the "advantage of wisdom over folly" (Eccles. 2:13),[3] and it launches the divine soul's instant counterresponse in this battle of wills, refusing to fall prey to the proclivities of the animal soul that rise from the left chamber of the heart.

וַהֲלָכָה כְּדִבְרֵי הַמַּכְרִיעַ, הוּא הַקָּדוֹשׁ בָּרוּךְ הוּא הָעוֹזְרוֹ לְהַיֵּצֶר טוֹב, כְּמַאֲמַר רַבּוֹתֵינוּ ז״ל: ״אִלְמָלֵא הַקָּדוֹשׁ בָּרוּךְ הוּא עוֹזְרוֹ – אֵין יָכוֹל לוֹ״ (קידושין ל, ב).

The verdict must then **follow the opinion of the arbiter, this being the Holy One, blessed be He, who assists the good inclination, in accordance with our Rabbis' statement "If not** for the fact that **the Holy One, blessed be He, assists** each person in battling his evil inclination, **he could not** overcome **it**" (*Kiddushin* 30b).

3. See chap. 12.

When it comes to the *beinoni*, the verdict will always be in accord with the arbiter – with God. This is the implication of the verse cited by the aforementioned talmudic dictum to demonstrate that the *beinoni* is judged by both inclinations: "For He stands at the right hand of the needy," that is, the divine soul, which dwells in the right side of the heart, "to deliver him from those who judge him" (Ps. 109:31). The divine soul is referred to as "needy" since it regards itself as nothing, as if it itself does not exist as a separate entity in the presence of God. Due to its utter self-abnegation, God ultimately helps the divine soul in its ongoing struggle against the animal soul.

וְהָעֵזֶר הִיא הַהֶאָרָה שֶׁמֵּאִיר אוֹר ה׳ עַל נֶפֶשׁ הָאֱלֹהִית לִהְיוֹת לָהּ יִתְרוֹן וּשְׁלִיטָה עַל סִכְלוּת הַכְּסִיל וְיֵצֶר הָרַע, כִּיתְרוֹן הָאוֹר מִן הַחוֹשֶׁךְ כַּנִּזְכָּר לְעֵיל.

This assistance constitutes the illumination that God's light casts upon the divine soul, so that it may possess an advantage and dominate the folly of the fool, the evil inclination, like the advantage that light has over darkness, as stated above (chap. 12).

God's intervention on behalf of the divine soul should not be regarded as a miraculous reshuffling of the natural order. In the head-to-head confrontation between the souls, the divine light that illuminates the divine soul tilts the balance in its favor. This illumination is nothing supernatural but rather a logical consequence: Light always chases away the darkness. The illumination cast by the divine light on the divine soul is not extrinsic, but rather it is inherent within the very essence of the divine soul, an essence that is utterly nullified in the presence of the Divine. Without this illumination, neither side possesses an inherent advantage over the other. It is through God's intercession alone that the *beinoni*'s ceaseless internal struggle yields positive results.

אַךְ מֵאַחַר שֶׁהָרַע שֶׁבֶּחָלָל הַשְּׂמָאלִי בַּבֵּינוֹנִי הוּא בְּתָקְפּוֹ כְּתוֹלַדְתּוֹ לְהִתְאַוּוֹת תַּאֲוָה לְכָל תַּעֲנוּגֵי עוֹלָם הַזֶּה, וְלֹא נִתְבַּטֵּל בְּמִיעוּט לְגַבֵּי הַטּוֹב וְלֹא נִדְחָה מִמְּקוֹמוֹ כְּלָל, רַק שֶׁאֵין לוֹ

25 Tevet (leap year) **Nevertheless, the evil in the left chamber of the *beinoni*'s heart maintains its innate potency to crave all the pleasures of this world and is not** sufficiently **minute that it is nullified by the good. Moreover, it is not banished from its place at all. It is only that** the

שְׁלִיטָה וּמֶמְשָׁלָה לְהִתְפַּשֵּׁט בְּאֵבְרֵי הַגּוּף, מִפְּנֵי הַקָּדוֹשׁ בָּרוּךְ הוּא הָעוֹמֵד לִימִין אֶבְיוֹן וְעוֹזֵר וּמֵאִיר לַנֶּפֶשׁ הָאֱלֹהִית,

evil **does not attain dominion or rule so that it may spread to the body's limbs. This** inability **is due to the Holy One, blessed be He, who "stands at the right hand of the needy," assisting and illuminating the divine soul.**

Though the arbiter's verdict blocked the animal soul's intentions, its power is neither negated nor diminished. Evil in full array persists in the *beinoni* no less than in the *rasha*, though it has no outlet for expression. This is in contrast to the tzaddik, in whom evil ceases to exist in the presence of overwhelming good. The only reason that the evil does not prevail in the *beinoni* as it does in the *rasha* is not because it is limited by the good inclination's restraining power but due to the assistance that the divine soul receives from above.

לָכֵן נִקְרָא "כְּרָשָׁע", כְּמַאֲמַר רַבּוֹתֵינוּ ז"ל: "אֲפִילוּ כָּל הָעוֹלָם כּוּלּוֹ אוֹמְרִים לְךָ צַדִּיק אַתָּה - הֱיֵה בְעֵינֶיךָ כְּרָשָׁע" (נידה ל, ב), וְלֹא רָשָׁע מַמָּשׁ, אֶלָּא שֶׁיַּחֲזִיק עַצְמוֹ לְבֵינוֹנִי,

The *beinoni* is **therefore referred to as being "like a wicked person" in accordance with our Rabbis' statement "Even** if **the entire world says to you, 'You are righteous,' consider yourself like a wicked person"** (*Nidda* 30b), **but not actually wicked. Rather, one should regard himself as a *beinoni*,**

The author of the *Tanya* returns to another question that he raised in the first chapter. He notes a nuance in this talmudic teaching that he quoted there: It states that one should view himself as being "like a wicked person." His evil inclination remains within him with the same lethal potential as the wicked person, yet the *beinoni* is regarded as being only like the wicked and not actually wicked, since he never sins in practice. By contrast, a truly wicked person is someone who commits evil and has evil thoughts.

This particular emphasis, that the *beinoni* should regard himself as being like a wicked person, is important because one of the foundations of the *beinoni*'s divine service is knowing his true place. This is crucial because the *beinoni* appears exactly like a righteous person: Neither ever commit a sin. It is imperative that the *beinoni* exercise caution and avoid deceiving himself by falsely thinking he has attained a spiritual rank that is beyond him. This concern, voiced a number of times throughout the book, is precisely the reason the author of the *Tanya* emphasizes this point.

וְלֹא לְהַאֲמִין לְהָעוֹלָם שֶׁאוֹמְרִים שֶׁהָרַע שֶׁבּוֹ נִתְבַּטֵּל לְגַבֵּי הַטּוֹב, שֶׁזּוֹ מַדְרֵגַת צַדִּיק. אֶלָּא יִהְיֶה בְּעֵינָיו כְּאִלּוּ מַהוּתוֹ וְעַצְמוּתוֹ שֶׁל הָרַע הוּא בְּתָקְפּוֹ וּבִגְבוּרָתוֹ בֶּחָלָל הַשְּׂמָאלִי כְּתוֹלַדְתּוֹ, וְלֹא חָלַף וְהָלַךְ מִמֶּנּוּ מְאוּמָה.

and he should not believe the people of **the world who say that the evil within him has become nullified by the good, which is the level of a tzaddik. Rather, he should view** his situation **as though the essence and core of the evil has maintained its innate potency and strength in the left chamber** of his heart **and has neither gone nor left him in the slightest.**

While others might think the *beinoni* has attained a level of essential goodness, having eliminated evil like the tzaddik, he should not believe this about himself. He must consider himself a *rasha* whose internal reality remains unresolved.

וְאַדְּרַבָּה, נִתְחַזֵּק יוֹתֵר בְּהֶמְשֵׁךְ הַזְּמַן שֶׁנִּשְׁתַּמֵּשׁ בּוֹ הַרְבֵּה בַּאֲכִילָה וּשְׁתִיָּה וּשְׁאָר עִנְיְנֵי עוֹלָם הַזֶּה.

On the contrary, it has gained strength with the passage of time, because he utilized the animal soul **extensively by eating and drinking and** engaging in **other mundane affairs.**

There is yet another reason that one should regard himself as a *rasha*. In our physical existence, in eating, drinking, and everything else, no matter how impeccably we act, we have to use our animal soul and physical body. Left to its own devices, the divine soul is unable to access this world. It cannot eat or drink. It cannot act or speak. It cannot even think. In all this, it needs an animal soul and a physical body in order to be effective. But with the passage of time, despite the mitzvot that the person performs, these pursuits give strength to the animal soul and reinforce it.

19 Tevet וְאַף מִי שֶׁבְּתוֹרַת ה׳ חֶפְצוֹ וְיֶהְגֶּה בָּהּ יוֹמָם וָלַיְלָה לִשְׁמָהּ - אֵין זוֹ הוֹכָחָה כְּלָל שֶׁנִּדְחָה הָרַע מִמְּקוֹמוֹ, אֶלָּא יָכוֹל לִהְיוֹת שֶׁמַּהוּתוֹ וְעַצְמוּתוֹ הוּא בְּתָקְפּוֹ וּבִגְבוּרָתוֹ בִּמְקוֹמוֹ בֶּחָלָל הַשְּׂמָאלִי.

Even with regard to **one whose desire is God's Torah, which he studies day and night for its own sake, this does not at all prove that the evil has been banished from its place** in the body. **Rather, it may well be that the essence and core of the evil is at its** utmost **potency and strength in its place in the left chamber** of the heart.

Even if a person's life revolves around Torah study and the service of God, without even the slightest interest elsewhere, this is not evidence of a true inner transformation, the sea change we expect to find in a tzaddik. The fact that one acts only positively, doing, speaking, and thinking properly, is itself no proof of a no-evil zone inside. The surface oil can float calmly over the tempest raging in one's psychic basement, the impulses and darkness in a person's soul.

רַק שֶׁלְּבוּשָׁיו, שֶׁהֵם מַחֲשָׁבָה דִּבּוּר וּמַעֲשֶׂה שֶׁל נֶפֶשׁ הַבַּהֲמִית, אֵינָן מִתְלַבְּשִׁים בַּמּוֹחַ וְהַפֶּה וְהַיָּדַיִם וּשְׁאָר אֵבְרֵי הַגּוּף מִפְּנֵי ה׳ שֶׁנָּתַן שְׁלִיטָה וּמֶמְשָׁלָה לַמּוֹחַ עַל הַלֵּב. וְלָכֵן נֶפֶשׁ הָאֱלֹהִית שֶׁבַּמּוֹחַ מוֹשֶׁלֶת בְּעִיר קְטַנָּה, אֵבְרֵי הַגּוּף כּוּלָּם, שֶׁיִּהְיוּ לְבוּשׁ וּמֶרְכָּבָה לִשְׁלֹשָׁה לְבוּשֶׁיהָ שֶׁיִּתְלַבְּשׁוּ בָּהֶם, שֶׁהֵם מַחֲשָׁבָה דִּבּוּר וּמַעֲשֶׂה שֶׁל תרי״ג מִצְוֹת הַתּוֹרָה.

However, the garments of the evil inclination, **which are the thoughts, speech, and actions of the animal soul, are not clothed in the brain, mouth, hands, and the rest of the body's limbs because of God, who granted the mind control and dominion over the heart. Therefore, the divine soul in the brain rules over the "small city,"** namely, **all the body's limbs, so that they function as the garment and vehicle in which** the divine soul's **three garments, which are the thoughts, speech, and actions of the 613 commandments of the Torah, are clothed.**

Two souls coexist within the *beinoni,* one never being fully ousted by the other. Yet when the two sides collide, the divine soul prevails over the other since its abode is in the mind, which was given dominion over the heart. Since the mind rules the heart, one can always subjugate unwanted impulses. Moreover, as stated, God assists the divine soul in this struggle. The *beinoni* is thus empowered and equipped to constantly suppress the evil impulses that attempt to dominate him, to the extent that he may not even be conscious of evil's existence within him. ☞

אֲבָל מַהוּתָהּ וְעַצְמוּתָהּ שֶׁל נֶפֶשׁ הָאֱלֹהִית - אֵין לָהּ שְׁלִיטָה וּמֶמְשָׁלָה עַל מַהוּתָהּ וְעַצְמוּתָהּ שֶׁל נֶפֶשׁ הַבַּהֲמִית בַּבֵּינוֹנִי,

But with regard to the *beinoni,* the essence and core of the divine soul exercises neither control nor dominion over the essence and core of the animal soul,

Such control lies in the tzaddik's domain alone, and a tzaddik is someone else completely, the Jewish version of a superman. But not the iconic Superman character nor Nietzsche's *Ubermensch.* He is someone made of different stuff from the rest of us, someone to whom the boundaries and expressions that rule us do not apply. Yet this is not the *Book of Tzaddikim* but the *Book of Beinonim.* It is directed toward everyone, including those for whom the ideal of constant and essential control by the divine soul over the animal soul is unrealistic.

APPEARANCES CAN BE DECEIVING

☞ One may be unaware of the evil within him and may not recognize the struggle within, the battle between good and evil, but that does not mean that he has become a tzaddik. Perhaps he has not had the opportunity for self-discovery. Perhaps he is not rebellious by nature. Perhaps in his daily life, negative impulses rarely, if ever, intrude. He may be someone whom everyone supposes, and on occasion he himself believes (and rightfully so), to live completely on the side of good.

In that case, he may discover cracks in himself when he encounters a new situation where he is expected to break through and aspire beyond his potential. It might just be a new and unaccustomed position in life that is enough to unearth other dimensions in his soul. Then it will become clear that the scenario in which he acts and thinks like a tzaddik is merely circumstantial.

כִּי אִם בְּשָׁעָה שֶׁאַהֲבַת ה׳ הוּא בְּהִתְגַּלּוּת לִבּוֹ בְּעִתִּים מְזוּמָּנִים, כְּמוֹ בִּשְׁעַת הַתְּפִלָּה וְכַיּוֹצֵא בָּהּ.

with the exception of certain times when his **love for God is revealed in his heart, such as during prayer and the like.**

The *beinoni*, like the tzaddik, studies Torah and performs mitzvot without interruption, and this service is certainly rooted in his love and awe of God. Yet these feelings are not the *beinoni*'s predominant experience. Only occasionally and at set times, such as during prayer, does the *beinoni* have a breakthrough, an intense love of God that sears his emotions.

וְאַף גַּם זֹאת הַפַּעַם אֵינָהּ רַק שְׁלִיטָה וּמֶמְשָׁלָה לְבַד,

Yet even then, the divine soul **exercises only** temporary and superficial **dominion and rule** over the animal soul,

Even when his love of God is manifest, when through self-refinement he senses the divine soul's dominion over his emotions, that moment is no more than a temporary subjugation of his animal soul. It does not mean that his animal soul has been converted into good.

כִּדְכְתִיב: ״וּלְאוֹם מִלְאוֹם יֶאֱמָץ״ (בראשית כה, כג), כְּשֶׁזֶּה קָם זֶה נוֹפֵל וּכְשֶׁזֶּה קָם כו׳.

as it is written, "One nation will prevail over the other nation" (Gen. 25:23), meaning, **when this one rises, the other will fall, and when the** other **one rises,** this one will fall.

The struggle between Jacob and Esau that began in their mother's womb, and ensues in the historical conflict between Israel and the nation of Edom, symbolizes the contest between the twin realities within each of us: the divine and animal souls. Just as the conflict with Edom will conclude only at the end of days, so will the struggle between the two souls continue unabated until that time. This never-ending struggle is embedded in the very fabric of the Jew, long before one's own personal existence. It is one in which "one nation" attempts to "prevail over the other nation," in which a greater exertion on the part of one meets a corresponding effort by its adversary. Even when one side overpowers the other, when one rises or falls depending on which force prevails, that can never produce a fundamental change, a banishment of the evil within. ☞

שֶׁנֶּפֶשׁ הָאֱלֹהִית מִתְאַמֶּצֶת וּמִתְגַּבֶּרֶת עַל נֶפֶשׁ הַבַּהֲמִית בִּמְקוֹר הַגְּבוּרוֹת שֶׁהִיא בִּינָה,

This means to say **that the divine soul prevails over and overpowers the animal soul at the source of the forces of restraint, which is *Bina*,**

The divine soul cannot overpower the animal soul in the realm of the emotive attributes, since it is countered there by an equal yet opposing emotion of the animal soul. Moreover, the animal soul reigns supreme in the realm of the emotions, which are experienced in the heart, the abode of the animal soul, where its powers are most potent and indomitable. The potential for the divine soul to gain the upper hand over the animal soul is possible only at the root of the forces of restraint and strict judgment: *Bina*.

In simplified terms, the *sefirot* are arranged in three arrays. The array on the right consists of the *sefirot* of *Ḥokhma*, *Ḥesed*, and *Netzaḥ*. The left comprises *Bina*, *Gevura*, and *Hod*. The middle contains *Da'at*, *Tiferet*, and *Yesod*. Accordingly, the source for *Gevura* is *Bina*, as the

TWO IN ONE

☞ The Midrash relates (*Bereshit Rabba* 63:6) that Rebecca felt like a wrestling match was taking place in her womb when she was pregnant. Whenever she passed the entrance to the study hall, Jacob tried to emerge. When she passed the doorway of a place of idolatry, Esau pushed hard to exit. Rebecca sought counsel from God, fearing that the one attempting to go to the study hall was the same one rushing to idolatry. When God informed her, "Two peoples are in your womb," she sighed in relief.

The awareness of two opposing forces clashing in our consciousness is no major cause for concern. True, it would unhinge us if we thought that the internal strife that we feel springs from a single source, a single soul. Our spirits would falter whenever the evil inclination exposed itself. While one is in the middle of prayer surrounded by an aura of holiness, a dozen of the worst thoughts imaginable arise. If a person believes that he has only one soul, that the soul that prays in holiness is the same one contemplating destructive thoughts, he will despair. But when he knows that "two peoples are in your womb," that not one but two souls are struggling inside and that "one nation will prevail over the other," when he realizes that he stands in the middle of a struggle that by definition cannot reach a resolution, then the ups and downs take on a different significance. Then he understands that he has the capacity to perceive that which is holy while being utterly unaware of the other side's existence, and still he must be cognizant that the other side is alive and well. He must know, in addition, that evil can manifest itself within him to such an extent that he forgets the experience of holiness. Nevertheless, he must keep in mind that holiness is there, inside, and that he need only uncover it.

verse states, "I am understanding [*Bina*]; might [*Gevura*] is mine" (Prov. 8:14). *Ḥokhma*, Wisdom, does not generate the forces of restraint, but rather it generates kindness. *Ḥokhma* is the beginning, the state of nothingness that gives rise to countless realities and supplies the infinite energies to operate them. In other words, it creates *ḥasadim*, the forces of giving. On the other hand, the attribute of *Gevura*, restraint and constriction, can interact only with an already extant reality deriving from *Bina*.

The same is true of the faculties of the human soul. The faculty of wisdom can produce that sense of astonishment and breakthrough, the streaming of energy that is kindness. The faculty of understanding, by contrast, creates the possibility for restraint and empowerment, because only a lucid and ordered understanding enables one to rule over his animal soul. This occurs through the concentration and contraction of the soul's powers to a workable scale, an application of *Gevura*, the power of restraint.

לְהִתְבּוֹנֵן בִּגְדוּלַּת ה׳ אֵין סוֹף בָּרוּךְ הוּא,

by meditating on the greatness of God, *Ein Sof*, blessed be He,

The work of prevailing over the animal soul at the source of the forces of restraint is accomplished through meditation, which entails directing one's thoughts toward one subject, in this case the greatness of God. Such contemplation evokes a love of God and subdues the *sitra aḥara*.

וּלְהוֹלִיד אַהֲבָה עַזָּה לַה׳ כְּרִשְׁפֵּי אֵשׁ בֶּחָלָל הַיְמָנִי שֶׁבְּלִבּוֹ, וְאָז אִתְכַּפְיָא סִטְרָא אָחֳרָא שֶׁבֶּחָלָל הַשְּׂמָאלִי.

and thereby **generating a love for God as fierce as sparks of fire in the right chamber of one's heart, whereupon the *sitra aḥara* in the left chamber is subdued.**

At certain times, the *beinoni* can also reach lofty heights. In those moments, when his understanding becomes crystal clear and his insight is heightened, his heart overflows with the love and awe of God and the evil inclination is subjugated. This not only entails the external control of his soul's garments but a deep and fundamental submissiveness, a lull in the battle.

אֲבָל לֹא נִתְבַּטֵּל לְגַמְרֵי בַּבֵּינוֹנִי, אֶלָּא בַּצַּדִּיק שֶׁנֶּאֱמַר בּוֹ: "וְלִבִּי חָלַל בְּקִרְבִּי" (תהלים קט, כב),

But the evil **is not completely nullified in the *beinoni*, only in the tzaddik, regarding whom the verse states, "My heart is hollow within me"** (Ps. 109:22).

The victory is only temporary and partial, far from a complete nullification and uprooting of evil. In a tzaddik, on the other hand, there is a total eradication of the animal soul's urgings. His heart can be emptied of them, "hollow" within him.

וְהוּא מוֹאֵס בָּרָע וְשׂוֹנְאוֹ

The righteous person **is repulsed by evil and despises it,**

The tzaddik's level precludes any enticements on the part of evil. Having no attraction to evil, he need not struggle against it. The desires of the body and the animal soul do not rise in his thoughts. If they do on occasion, it is only as an object of scorn.

בְּתַכְלִית הַשִּׂנְאָה וְהַמִּיאוּס אוֹ שֶׁלֹּא בְּתַכְלִית הַשִּׂנְאָה כַּנִּזְכָּר לְעֵיל, אֲבָל בַּבֵּינוֹנִי הוּא דֶּרֶךְ מָשָׁל כְּאָדָם שֶׁיָּשֵׁן, שֶׁיָּכוֹל לַחֲזוֹר וְלֵיעוֹר מִשְּׁנָתוֹ.

either **with an utter hatred and repulsion or not with such an utter hatred, as discussed above** (chap. 10). **But with regard to the *beinoni*,** the evil **is analogous to someone who is sleeping and can be reawakened from his sleep.**

Whether the righteous person feels utter hatred toward the evil or not, whether completely righteous or not completely righteous, either way he is on the rank of tzaddik. Within the *beinoni*, by contrast, even during moments of spiritual revelation and elevation, such as during prayers, the evil has not been totally eradicated.

כָּךְ הָרָע בַּבֵּינוֹנִי הוּא כְּיָשֵׁן בֶּחָלָל הַשְּׂמָאלִי בִּשְׁעַת קְרִיאַת שְׁמַע וּתְפִלָּה, שֶׁלִּבּוֹ בּוֹעֵר בְּאַהֲבַת ה',

Similarly, the evil in the *beinoni* is regarded as if it were asleep in the left chamber of his heart **during the recitation of *Shema* and prayers,** or during any other time **when his heart burns with love for God,**

Though the *beinoni* does not achieve an essential mastery of good, he can attain something comparable: an inundation of good, an experience of love and awe of God that permeates his entire soul. This is not a regular event but something that occurs during his service to God, in particular while reciting the *Shema* and other prayers that inspire this feeling. When it comes, it is no mere emotional peak; it is the blossoming of a true love for God. At that moment, it might appear that the evil inside him has died, that his heart is void of negative energy. The evil, though, is only slumbering and can ultimately be reawakened.

וְאַחַר כָּךְ יָכוֹל לִהְיוֹת חוֹזֵר וְנֵיעוֹר.

in which case **it can subsequently be reawakened.**

The *beinoni*, then, has a phase when evil can be asleep, when the internal war can pause, moments of holy intensity when the adversary does not challenge him in combat. A person who recites the *Shema* in his heart – not for five minutes but for three hours – can have a furlough from the war zone. If he studies Torah with dedication and enthusiasm, cleaving to the Torah's source, it may very well be that he will not sense the enticement of evil at all nor the need to fight it. He might even be a *beinoni* living out his days in the company of a somnolent sparring partner.

וְלָכֵן הָיָה רַבָּה מַחֲזִיק עַצְמוֹ כְּבֵינוֹנִי, אַף דְּלָא פָּסֵיק פּוּמֵיהּ מִגִּירְסָא,

Therefore, Rabba regarded himself as a *beinoni* even though he never ceased studying Torah,

The author of the *Tanya* returns here to another question that he asked in the first chapter. To explain what a *beinoni* is, Rabba said, "I, for example, am a *beinoni*" (*Berakhot* 61b). And the question was, how could someone of Rabba's stature be described as a *beinoni*?

NOT A CASE OF FALSE HUMILITY

☞ Clearly, Rabba's declaration did not come from a sense of false humility, which is just as negative as pride or perhaps worse. Hasidim say, regarding pride, that one at least knows it is unacceptable. With false humility, one not only finds himself faultless, but he also deludes himself into thinking that he is performing a mitzva.

It is in this vein that the Ba'al Shem Tov (*Keter Shem Tov* 315) quotes the verse "And

He never ceased studying Torah. His entire life consisted exclusively of Torah and mitzvot. If even the angel of death had no power over him,[4] how could he consider himself a *beinoni*? ☞

וּבְתוֹרַת ה׳ חֶפְצוֹ יוֹמָם וָלַיְלָה, בַּחֲפִיצָה וַחֲשִׁיקָה וּתְשׁוּקָה וְנֶפֶשׁ שׁוֹקֵקָה לַה׳ בְּאַהֲבָה רַבָּה,

and his desire was God's Torah day and night with a desire, longing, and yearning, his soul yearning for God with a great love,

Rabba's Torah study was not only uninterrupted but was also something he pursued with complete dedication, with a longing and yearning for God.

כִּבְשְׁעַת קְרִיאַת שְׁמַע וּתְפִלָּה. וְנִדְמֶה בְּעֵינָיו כְּבֵינוֹנִי הַמִּתְפַּלֵּל כָּל הַיּוֹם, וּכְמַאֲמַר רַבּוֹתֵינוּ ז״ל: ״הַלְוַאי שֶׁיִּתְפַּלֵּל אָדָם כָּל הַיּוֹם כּוּלּוֹ״ (ברכות כא, א).

such as that experienced **when reciting *Shema* and praying.** Rabba therefore **regarded himself as a *beinoni* who prays all day, in accordance with our Rabbis' statement "If only a person would pray throughout the entire day"** (*Berakhot* 21a).

Even though Rabba's heart burned with the love of God and he resembled a tzaddik in every way, he followed the talmudic injunction quoted at the beginning of chapter 1: "Even if the entire world says to you, 'You are righteous,' consider yourself like a wicked person" (*Nidda* 30b). As noted above, one should not consider himself as actually wicked but as though he were wicked, like someone with the full potential for evil but not at all sensing it. His waking hours, his entire consciousness, were

his concubine, whose name was Re'uma..." (Gen. 22:24) to describe corrupted humility, such as humility that a person wishes to display to others. The term *ma* signifies self-nullification, true humility, as we find Moses declaring, "And what [*ma*] are we?" (Ex. 16:7). By contrast, Re'uma implies a false show of humility, the word *re'u* meaning to see and *ma* meaning nothing, so that the name could be translated to mean "See that I am nothing." This is a false humility, a humility of *kelippa*. It follows that someone like Rabba would not diminish himself unless he honestly believed it was the case.

4. See *Bava Metzia* 86a.

wholly dedicated to Torah study with love and yearning for God so that there was no opportunity for evil to surface. Had Rabba paused in his studies and service of God for even a moment, perhaps his evil inclination might have instantly revealed itself.

Rabba considered himself a *beinoni*, as one who was unaware of the evil within him because he prayed all day, fully caught up in an occupation that generates love and awe of God and effectively sedates evil. Yet his all-encompassing love of God, his lack of desire for anything else, does not indicate that any essential change had transpired within him. He neither knew nor was able to know whether he had been able to uproot the evil inside him and replace it with something altogether good. Perhaps the evil remained in the left side of his heart, blocked from self-expression. ☞

20 Tevet

וְהִנֵּה מִדַּת אַהֲבָה זוֹ הָאֲמוּרָה בַּבֵּינוֹנִים בִּשְׁעַת הַתְּפִלָּה עַל יְדֵי הִתְגַּבְּרוּת הַנֶּפֶשׁ הָאֱלֹהִית כו׳

This level of love attributed to *beinonim* during prayer through the divine soul prevailing over the animal soul **and so forth,**

At times of prayer and other special moments, the *beinoni* attains a love of God that causes his other side to go into hiding. The love is

CAN ONE DISCERN WHETHER HE IS RIGHTEOUS?

☞ An individual who lives in an environment of holiness, with a holy occupation and a holy matrix of experience, can no longer discern what is truly holy and what is façade. It is said that the Vilna Gaon was very fond of the Maggid of Dubno and would invite him to visit from time to time. On one occasion, the Vilna Gaon told him, "You chastise everywhere you go. Why don't you chastise me as well?"

The Maggid became instantly ill at ease. How could he rebuke someone as revered as the Vilna Gaon? But the Vilna Gaon was insistent. Finally, the Maggid said, "Rabbi, you sit at home with the shutters so tightly closed that not even sunlight can enter. Is it any wonder, then, that you're a tzaddik? Perhaps if you wandered around the marketplace all day, you wouldn't be so righteous."

It is said that angels complain that humans commit transgressions, yet when angels descend to our world, they sin and cause others to sin, just as people do. The renowned hasid Rabbi Moshe of Kobrin was accustomed to sing:

Angel, angel, you have no wife or children,
You don't worry about making a living –
That's why you're an angel.
But if you had a wife and children
And worried about making a living –
Would you still be an angel?

deeply felt. It is not only manifest in his immediate awareness but encompasses his full reality. He loves God with all his heart without reservation, without misgivings.

הִנֵּה לְגַבֵּי מַדְרֵגַת הַצַּדִּיקִים עוֹבְדֵי ה׳ בֶּאֱמֶת לַאֲמִיתּוֹ - מִמְּקוֹמוֹ, אֵלָא יָכוֹל לִהְיוֹת שֶׁמַּהוּתוֹ וְעַצְמוּתוֹ הוּא בְּתָקְפּוֹ וּבִגְבוּרָתוֹ בִּמְקוֹמוֹ בֶּחָלָל הַשְּׂמָאלִי.

when compared to the rank of the righteous, who serve God with absolute truth, this level of love achieved by the *beinoni* **is not called "true service" at all since it is fleeting and is gone after the prayers, and it is written, "The language of truth will be established forever, but a tongue of falsehood is only for a moment"** (Prov. 12:19).

Here the author of the *Tanya* touches on a philosophical question that he seldom endeavors to address – a question about the truth of an experience. How we determine whether an experience is true, and how true, is not a simple matter, neither with regard to this subject nor any other. For this reason, the author of the *Tanya* broadens the question: What is truth?

Truth has many definitions, but here the author takes the strictest viewpoint. His definition of truth is not about whether someone deceives others or even himself. Rather, truth constitutes that which is "established forever," that which endures. In that case, the level of love achieved by the *beinoni* during times of prayer is not considered "true service" because that love is fleeting and does not last. Truth is eternal. Something transient and given to change cannot be called true. The litmus test of truth is in its endurance, not only under particular conditions but perpetually.

This concept of truth, incidentally, is rooted in the Hebrew language. The term *naḥal akhzav*, literally, a "deceptive stream," is so called because it does not always flow with water. The Mishna speaks of deceptive waters that fail to flow once in seven years.[5] A single failing once in seven years places it outside the bounds of truth.

---

5. *Para* 8:9.

Truth, then, is synonymous with the eternal. If it is not true forever, in every instance, in every dimension, it is not truth. ☞

וְאַף עַל פִּי כֵן לְגַבֵּי מַדְרֵגַת הַבֵּינוֹנִים נִקְרֵאת עֲבוֹדָה תַּמָּה בֶּאֱמֶת לַאֲמִיתּוֹ שֶׁלָּהֶם, אִישׁ אִישׁ כְּפִי מַדְרֵגָתוֹ בְּמַדְרֵגַת הַבֵּינוֹנִים.

Nevertheless, in relation to the rank of the *beinonim*, it is deemed a perfect service in terms of their level of **absolute truth, each one according to his level among** the various gradations of ***beinonim*.**

Though the expression "a perfect service in terms of their [level of] absolute truth," seems paradoxical, it bears great significance. Truth in the exact sense defined here does not change whatever the situation. It stands up under the objective scrutiny of eternity and allows no substitutes. The phrase "their absolute truth," on the other hand, implies relative, partial truth, the subjective outlook of a particular individual. Tomorrow it may not be true, but today it is absolute. Just as there is one truth, universal, constant, and unvarying in every situation, so too there is a truth that is valid in the present state of affairs, a situational truth that can and perhaps must change tomorrow.

In this sense, the *beinoni* can also reach a personal truth in his subjective experience. It may be neither absolute nor eternal, but not

DOES ABSOLUTE TRUTH EXIST?

☞ The words of the *Tanya* here present a problem. Within these austere limits, where can one hope to locate truth in our low-fidelity universe? How many actual truths are there within our experience of reality?

Rambam begins *Mishneh Torah* with a definition of truth in accordance with the words of the prophet Jeremiah: "But my Lord God is truth" (Jer. 10:10). Only God can be identified as true, for He alone is constant and unchanging. All other truths evolve, in Rambam's words, from "the truth of His being" (see *Sefer HaMadda, Hilkhot Yesodei HaTorah* 1:1, 4). Every other truth is built on God's truth and, consequently, is true only relative to Him.

In this sense, the definition of a true feeling is one that remains without fading away. Whatever cannot meet this standard fails the truth test. Subjectively speaking, the *beinoni*'s experience in prayer is genuine. But if, after the prayers, he returns to his former self, if the experience vanishes as a dream without a trace, then he has failed the test.

According to this, the criterion of a true experience cannot be measured in real time, but only afterward, when one can detect a lasting residue, an element that remains in the soul. We gauge the truth of an experience not by its intensity but by the footprints it leaves.

because it is imaginary nor contrived but rather because the *beinoni* himself has not achieved in his soul the balance and wholeness that are imperative for perfect truth. If he could achieve this internal perfection, he would no longer be a *beinoni* but a tzaddik. The *beinoni*'s truth, when he prays, when he feels something, is his subjective truth. It is not false, but it is strictly his own, each one according to his level as a *beinoni*.

Indeed, I consider their love achieved **during their prayers also as "the language of truth** that **will be established forever,"**

וַהֲרֵינִי קוֹרֵא בְּאַהֲבָתָם שֶׁבִּתְפִלָּתָם גַּם כֵּן "שְׂפַת אֱמֶת תִּכּוֹן לָעַד"

The *beinoni*'s love, though inconstant, except for such times as prayer, is also called "the language of truth [that] will be established forever." It is not truth in its most absolute sense, yet it is a "language of truth," or literally, "the edge of truth." It is the tip or taste of truth, which for him is the absolute truth.

since it is within the power of their divine soul to always reawaken this level of love by increasing its strength during prayers on a daily basis

הוֹאִיל וּבְכֹחַ נַפְשָׁם הָאֱלֹהִית לַחֲזוֹר וּלְעוֹרֵר בְּחִינַת אַהֲבָה זוֹ לְעוֹלָם בְּהִתְגַּבְּרוּתָהּ בִּשְׁעַת הַתְּפִלָּה מִדֵּי יוֹם בְּיוֹם

The truth test is constant: "The language of truth will be established forever." There is no room for concession, but there can be a slight broadening of the parameters. The *beinoni*'s love, though it is only the tip of the truth, in its own way it too is "established forever." This love is no unexpected, sudden event reached by happenstance. It is there, available and accessible in his soul, ready to be reexperienced at any time. The issue is an inability to alter his innate nature, the essential design of his inborn desires. For that reason, he cannot maintain the experience continually.

At the same time, while one cannot therefore label the experience absolute truth, from the standpoint of the *beinoni*, it is not possible to call it false because he can relive it. The fact that he can reexperience it, time after time, whenever he wishes, indicates that his soul possesses something steadfast, something forever and true, that can sustain it.

But this definition of truth as well is not easy to live up to, since it does not forgo the stringent requirement that the definition of absolute truth sets forth. Though the uppermost human achievement is only relative truth, the core truth of that particular individual, there is a demand here for an almost scientific validation of the matter. Scientific proof can be repeated. An experiment that cannot be replicated is merely an isolated phenomenon and cannot enter the realm of truth. This replicable truth is what the author of the *Tanya* seeks from the *beinoni*. The experience of a soul that has been awakened to love of God can happen to anyone but not on demand, whenever he wishes. The author of the *Tanya* expects from the *beinoni* the attainment of truth, that he have the ability, at the least, to return to this experience anytime he exercises this desire.

עַל יְדֵי הַהֲכָנָה הָרְאוּיָה לְכָל נֶפֶשׁ כְּפִי עֶרְכָּהּ וּמַדְרֵגָתָהּ.

by means of the preparation befitting each soul, commensurate with its quality and level.

The *beinoni* can reexperience love and awe of God, not automatically, but through the appropriate effort and preparation compatible with

PREPARING TO PRAY

☞ It is not by chance that hasidim devote so much time to preparations prior to prayer. The hasidim of Kotzk, who so fiercely demanded truth of themselves, said the prayers themselves quickly. Yet often the morning prayers began late in the afternoon. Preparing their souls to articulate truth could take up the whole day.

Rabbi Akiva Eiger's grandson, Rabbi Leibele Eiger, became a Kotzker hasid. He once asked the Kotzker Rebbe, "What shall I tell my grandfather when he questions me about our customs for prayer?"

The Rebbe replied, "Tell him the explicit *halakha*: A laborer hired to chop wood who spends most of the day sharpening his ax receives a full day's wages."

That was Kotzk: Most of the day was preparation, fine-tuning the ax blade. Once it was sharp, when the lips were lips of truth, the prayers could be recited in short order.

Preparations for truth have no set time span. It all depends on the person, his time, and his place. Rabbi Yitzḥak Meir of Gur prayed five or six hours a day. Once, after completing his prayers in a single hour and seeing his attendant's surprised expression, he said, "You think we always have to pray for six hours? Sometimes you can reach your destination in a short time without obstructions."

his soul's level. Some can reach this point in an instant; others require hours or even days. Still, when a person attains this level, it can be termed "the edge of truth [that] will be established forever." ☞

<table><tr><td>כִּי הִנֵּה מִדַּת אֱמֶת הִיא מִדָּתוֹ שֶׁל יַעֲקֹב,</td><td>Indeed, the attribute of truth is the attribute of Jacob,</td></tr></table>

The triad of higher attributes – *Ḥesed, Gevura,* and *Tiferet* – are related to the three forefathers. *Ḥesed* is linked with Abraham, *Gevura* to Isaac, and *Tiferet,* which is also the attribute of truth, to Jacob, as the verse states, "You will give truth to Jacob" (Mic. 7:20).[6]

<table><tr><td>הַנִּקְרָא בְּרִיחַ הַתִּיכוֹן, הַמַּבְרִיחַ "מִן הַקָּצֶה אֶל הַקָּצֶה" (שמות כו, כח),</td><td>who is called "the central bar inside the boards from end to end" (Ex. 26:28).</td></tr></table>

Three sets of bars secured the vertical beams of the Tabernacle: the upper bars, the lower bars, and a middle bar. Kabbala associates them with the three arrays of *sefirot.* The right array is that of *Ḥesed,* the kindness of Abraham; the left array is that of *Gevura,* Isaac's attribute; and the middle array is that of *Tiferet,* the attribute of Jacob.[7] In the Tabernacle, the upper and lower bars were fastened onto the outer face of the beams. Each bar had two sections, each of which extended halfway across the wall. The middle bar, by contrast, passed through an opening inside the beams and extended the entire width of the

---

6. This statement is somewhat perplexing, as it implies that the divine attributes of *Ḥesed* and *Gevura* do not embody truth. The fifth Lubavitcher Rebbe, Rabbi Sholom Dovber Schneerson, explains that both attributes indeed exemplify truth, yet not the quality of absolute truth. *Tiferet,* on the other hand, does possess this quality. Synonymous with compassion, it does not have an opposing attribute. Rather, it takes the judgment of *Gevura* into account, acknowledging that mercy is not necessarily deserved. It also incorporates *Ḥesed* by leaning toward kindness. Thus *Tiferet,* as the synthesis of *Ḥesed* and *Gevura,* exemplifies absolute truth (*Sefer HaMa'amarim* 5666, p. 434).

7. See Mic. 7:20; Gen. 31:42.

wall. In the spiritual realm, as well, the middle bar – the attribute of truth – penetrates all levels "from end to end."[8]

מֵרוּם הַמַּעֲלוֹת וּמַדְרֵגוֹת עַד סוֹף כָּל דַּרְגִּין, וּבְכָל מַעֲלָה וּמַדְרֵגָה מַבְרִיחַ תּוֹךְ נְקוּדָה הָאֶמְצָעִית שֶׁהִיא נְקוּדַּת וּבְחִינַת מִדַּת אֱמֶת שֶׁלָּהּ.

This attribute passes **from the loftiest ranks and levels to the lowest of all levels. It passes through the central point of each rank and level, which is the point and quality of** that level's unique **attribute of truth.**

On one hand, truth resides at the unattainable zenith, the quintessence of perfection. On the other hand, it penetrates "within the beams." Every point of reality contains an element of truth, which constitutes its own truth. This is why truth reaches from infinite heights to fathomless depths and penetrates reality's innermost dimensions. It is a line that is all-pervasive. From the uppermost level of reality to the lowest level, everything has its point of truth, whatever it may be.

וּמִדַּת אֱמֶת הִיא נַחֲלָה בְּלִי מְצָרִים וְאֵין לָהּ שִׁיעוּר לְמַעְלָה עַד רוּם הַמַּעֲלוֹת,

The attribute of truth is a boundless inheritance, with no upper limit, extending **to the loftiest heights,**

The Talmud states that Jacob's portion is a boundless inheritance,[9] as the verse states, "And you shall spread to the west, to the east, to the north, and to the south" (Gen. 28:14). In contrast to other, more limited attributes, truth is boundless. In the aforementioned words of Rambam, quoting Jeremiah, only "my Lord God is truth." All other realities derive from the truth of God's being, and their truth is a mere reflection of His. The attribute of absolute truth, then, is God's attribute, a "boundless inheritance," since its boundaries are the borders of the infinite, extending without cessation.

8. This is accentuated by the Talmud's assertion that the middle bar ran along the length and width of the Tabernacle, in which case it was miraculously bent through the beams on three sides. See *Shabbat* 98b.

9. *Shabbat* 118a.

וְכָל מַעֲלוֹת וּמַדְרֵגוֹת שֶׁלְּמַטָּה הֵם כְּאַיִן לְגַבֵּי מַעֲלוֹת וּמַדְרֵגוֹת שֶׁלְּמַעְלָה מֵהֶן.

and all lower ranks and levels are as nothing relative to the ranks and levels above them.

Truth is in everything. But truth is boundless, and whatever the truth of something, there is always a higher truth, so that relative to that higher truth the former is not true at all. Truth has no upper limit. Only God's truth can be referred to as absolute truth, so anything that does not constitute this level of truth can grow toward this ultimate truth. When a person calls a table a table, this is truth. But tomorrow or next year, it will not be a table; it will be a ruin. It can be true for a year or a century, but even a million years' truth is ephemeral before God's truth. Since truth is infinite, one will never really be able to attain it. The best one can do is reach a level where one realizes that everything until then was untrue. As one rises higher, he reaches again and again the point where everything before is untrue compared to his present-day awareness. He advances by steps, moving in dimensions that dwarf whoever he was and whatever he has accomplished. Each time, once again, one stands at "Go," the starting point, in the face of God's truth. ☞

RELATIVE TRUTH DOES NOT EQUAL FALSEHOOD

☞ It must be noted that the concept of relative truth in no way negates the existence of black-and-white truth and falsehood. Though we may not reach absolute truth, and our truth is only relative, there is still a clear distinction between truth and falsehood within this relativistic realm. The demand made of the *beinoni*, then, is twofold: He must be aware of the shortcomings and kaleidoscopic variations in his service to God, while at the same time he is not absolved of seeking the truth, of attempting at every moment to actualize his individual truth.

One year, Rabbi Levi Yitzḥak of Berditchev was unable to lead the prayers on Yom Kippur. The hasidim pleaded with him, to no avail. "Last year," he told them, "I promised God that I would achieve complete repentance, and look, the year passed by, and I still haven't repented. How can I possibly lead the prayers again?"

Finally, his son said to him, "Father, last year it was not true, but this time it will be!"

Hearing those words, the tzaddik took heart and began the prayers.

Last year's truth could not stand the endurance test, but that does not mean it was untrue at the time, only that now more is demanded. One knows that one did not fulfill last year's promise, that his past repentance is far from the truth of who he is now. But that does not contradict his ability now to promise that he will change with sincerity.

[כַּיָּדוּעַ לְיוֹדְעֵי חֵן שֶׁבְּחִינַת רֹאשׁ וּמוֹחִין שֶׁל מַדְרֵגוֹת תַּחְתּוֹנוֹת הֵן לְמַטָּה מִבְּחִינַת עֲקֵבַיִים וְרַגְלֵי מַדְרֵגוֹת עֶלְיוֹנוֹת מֵהֶן, וּכְמַאֲמַר רַבּוֹתֵינוּ ז״ל: ״רַגְלֵי הַחַיּוֹת כְּנֶגֶד כּוּלָּן״ (חגיגה יג, א)].

(As is known to those initiated in the esoteric wisdom of Kabbala, **the head and intellects of the lower levels are beneath the heels and feet of the levels above them, in accordance with our Rabbis' statement "The feet of the divine creatures correspond** in distance **to all** the firmaments" [*Ḥagiga* 13a].)

The Sages teach that the distance from earth to heaven spans the course of five hundred years, and the expanse of each firmament in heaven is five hundred years, as is the distance from one firmament to the next. There are seven such firmaments, one above the other. Above the heavens are the holy angels called *ḥayot,* and "the feet of the divine creatures correspond to all [the firmaments]" – the feet of the angels, their lowest part, exceed in size all the worlds and heavens beneath them.

This principle, with which the author of the *Tanya* concludes this chapter, is that the lower level of a higher world is always loftier than the higher level of the world beneath it. The sign of real development, then, is that one's previous level no longer holds true for him. When one genuinely grows, his current personal truth must surpass all his previous truths so that by comparison they are not true at all. The author of the *Tanya* is demanding that the *beinoni* pursue his individual truth at all times. Yesterday's heavens should be today's earth, and he must know: There is a truth still higher than this.

In this chapter, the author of the *Tanya* reexamined several questions that were asked in the first chapter. In answering these questions, the author explores the nature of the *beinoni* further: What makes him tick? What internal and external forces act on him?

Essentially, the *beinoni* is an intermediate level between the ranks of righteous and wicked, but is in no way a golden mean hovering between them. Though caught between two poles, between his essential character, which remains forever imperfect, and his unblemished conduct, he does not compromise. Rather, he struggles for a lifetime, never to act in accordance with the first and always to fully implement the second.

Chapter 14

IN THIS CHAPTER, THE AUTHOR OF THE *TANYA* CONTINUES painting a detailed portrait of the *beinoni*. As noted at the conclusion of the previous chapter, the divine service of the *beinoni* must be performed commensurate with his subjective absolute truth. This requirement seems almost impossible, as it demands that the *beinoni* withstand the unremitting stress of constant self-assessment of his ever-changing inner truth, climbing an ever-rising ladder, where yesterday's uppermost rung becomes today's lowest. This chapter therefore opens with a reassurance: The level of *beinoni* is attainable by all. As the author of the *Tanya* declares, "Any person can become a *beinoni* at any given moment."

It sounds like a reassurance, and indeed it is, but again – as with all matters pertaining to the *beinoni* – the assertion that this is possible also carries with it the demand: If it is possible, it is also required. Caught between two poles, between the awareness that he is both not able and not expected to achieve perfection and the relentless demand that he live his life with utter perfection to whatever extent he is able, the divine service of the *beinoni* is no simple feat.

וְהִנֵּה מִדַּת הַבֵּינוֹנִי הִיא מִדַּת כָּל אָדָם וְאַחֲרֶיהָ כָּל אָדָם יִמְשׁוֹךְ, שֶׁכָּל אָדָם יָכוֹל לִהְיוֹת בֵּינוֹנִי בְּכָל עֵת וּבְכָל שָׁעָה,

The level of the *beinoni* is a level that pertains to every person, and each person should strive for it, because any person can become a *beinoni* at any given moment, 21 Tevet / 26 Tevet (leap year)

Not everyone has the merit or the potential to become a tzaddik. It is not dependent on one's efforts but rather on the anatomy of his soul. Only one who is given the internal parameters that are capable of transforming evil into good can become a tzaddik. The *beinoni,* by contrast, is a normal person like anyone else, one whose soul is not capable of such radical change. His distinction lies not in his soul's structure or content but in his ability to take advantage of the potential existing in every person and channel it in the service of God.

For this reason, the rank of *beinoni* is attainable by all. Everyone is able to be a *beinoni,* never committing transgressions, neither in action, speech, nor thought. Whether he is doing good or turning from evil, he conducts himself, without exception, to the utmost of his ability in the path of holiness with the aim of achieving perfection.

כִּי הַבֵּינוֹנִי אֵינוֹ מוֹאֵס בָּרַע, **since a *beinoni* does not abhor evil,**

As explained above,[1] despising evil is a trademark of the tzaddik. Possessing no evil of his own, he lacks any connection to it and utterly abhors it.[2] But the *beinoni,* having evil of his own, though he may not act on it, does not detest it.

שֶׁזֶּהוּ דָּבָר הַמָּסוּר לַלֵּב **which is a matter entrusted to the heart.**

The *beinoni* stands apart from the wicked person in his actions, words, and thoughts but not in his heart's desires.

וְלֹא כָּל הָעִתִּים שָׁווֹת. **Yet not all moments are the same.**

Yet, as the previous chapter described, the *beinoni* can still achieve a state in which he truly loves good and hates evil, but only at particular times such as during the recitation of the *Shema* or the *Amida* prayer, times when he can direct his heart with greater effect.

1. Chap. 10.
2. That is, if he is a complete tzaddik. An incomplete tzaddik still retains a trace of evil, so that his hatred is less than absolute.

אֶלָּא ׳סוּר מֵרָע וַעֲשֵׂה טוֹב׳, דְּהַיְינוּ בְּפוֹעַל מַמָּשׁ בְּמַעֲשֶׂה דִּבּוּר וּמַחֲשָׁבָה, שֶׁבָּהֶם הַבְּחִירָה וְהַיְכוֹלֶת וְהָרְשׁוּת נְתוּנָה לְכָל אָדָם לַעֲשׂוֹת וּלְדַבֵּר וְלַחְשׁוֹב גַּם מַה שֶּׁהוּא נֶגֶד תַּאֲוַת לִבּוֹ וְהֶפְכָּהּ מַמָּשׁ.

Rather, the *beinoni* **turns away from evil and does good, meaning, literally** and **actually, in action, speech, and thought, regarding which every person is granted** free **choice and the ability and permission to act, speak, and think even that which literally defies and opposes his heart's desires.**

Since not all moments are equal in the life of the *beinoni*, we do not take his measure on the basis of his revulsion toward evil during those special occasions. Rather, his pristine spiritual record can be attributed to his ability to avoid evil in action, speech, and thought. Unlike the soul's desires that are hidden within the heart, the revealed expressions of the soul – action, speech, and thought – are subject to conscious choice. One is not compelled to behave in any particular fashion; he is free to express himself as he wishes in all three areas of the soul's expression.

כִּי גַּם בְּשָׁעָה שֶׁהַלֵּב חוֹמֵד וּמִתְאַוֶּה אֵיזוֹ תַּאֲוָה גַּשְׁמִיּוּת, בְּהֶיתֵּר אוֹ בְּאִיסּוּר חַס וְשָׁלוֹם, יָכוֹל לְהִתְגַּבֵּר וּלְהַסִּיחַ דַּעְתּוֹ מִמֶּנָּה לְגַמְרֵי, בְּאָמְרוֹ לְלִבּוֹ: אֵינֶנִּי רוֹצֶה לִהְיוֹת רָשָׁע אֲפִילּוּ שָׁעָה אַחַת,

Even when the heart covets and desires some physical pleasure, whether permitted or prohibited, God forbid, he is able to prevail and completely divert his mind from it by telling himself, "I do not wish to be wicked even for a single moment,

Here the author of the *Tanya* touches on a decisive element of the *beinoni*'s service to God, which he will expand and develop later: When a person has a powerful desire to commit a transgression, he confronts a dual temptation. There is the siren call of the temptation itself and – its constant companion – an additional seductive voice whispering, "In truth, this isn't a transgression, and certainly not a serious transgression."

The basic principle at work here is that no one wishes to self-destruct, to undo his life's efforts for the sake of a transgression, small or large. No one would ever go astray were it not for the additional murmur in his ear: "Do it. Just for a minute. Afterward you can return to business as usual." That is why, in response to that tempter, the *beinoni* must say, "I do not wish to be wicked even for a single moment."

Yet this rationale, that one is not willing to be wicked even for a moment, is insufficient on its own. After all, why not be wicked for a moment? If I can act like a tzaddik for a moment, then why not be a *rasha* for a moment? The author of the *Tanya* goes on to delineate this assertion more precisely: What is the implication of being a *rasha* "even for a single moment"?

כִּי אֵינֶנִּי רוֹצֶה לִהְיוֹת מוּבְדָּל וְנִפְרָד חַס וְשָׁלוֹם מֵה׳ אֶחָד בְּשׁוּם אוֹפֶן, כִּדְכְתִיב: "עֲוֹנֹתֵיכֶם מַבְדִּילִים" וגו׳ (ישעיה נט, ב).

because under no circumstances do I want to be separated or disconnected, God forbid, from the one God, as it is written, 'Your iniquities have been separating between you and your God...' (Isa. 59:2).

Being a *rasha* is tantamount to being separated from God. Yet it is explained elsewhere that nothing, physical or spiritual, can be a barrier before Him.[3] The notion of a barrier that comes between God and us is meaningless. A barrier by definition suggests an entity that is "other," and what could be other than God? Everything that exists comes from Him and is filled with Him: "Do I not fill the heavens and the earth?" (Jer. 23:24). There is no free space between creation and Creator into which something else could interpose. Yet the prophet Isaiah says, "Your iniquities have been separating between you and your God."

There is a single exception to the notion that there are no barriers between a person and God. There is one thing capable of separating God and man: transgressing His will. As the author of the *Tanya* explains in *Iggeret HaTeshuva*, every created being is an extension, so to speak, of God's will. He willed it, and they came into existence; He wills it, and they are sustained in reality. Everything exists and functions through its connection to the divine will, which sustains it

3. See *Iggeret HaTeshuva*, chap. 5

and grants it the ability to function. Transgression, by contrast, is that which opposes God's will. Consequently, it alone forms the barrier, the separation, between God and man.

While God's will is not revealed explicitly in creation, it is revealed and accessible in the Torah, which says, "Do this. Don't do that." When a person transgresses God's will, which is so blatantly revealed, he effectively separates himself from the source of life. He generates a hole, an empty space, in creation, providing a place to exist, so to speak, for opposition to God's will. In this sense, every transgression is suicidal, severing the life flow between the soul and its source. ☞

רַק אֲנִי רוֹצֶה לְדָבְקָה בּוֹ נַפְשִׁי רוּחִי וְנִשְׁמָתִי, בְּהִתְלַבְּשָׁן בִּשְׁלֹשָׁה לְבוּשָׁיו יִתְבָּרַךְ, שֶׁהֵם מַעֲשֶׂה דִּבּוּר וּמַחֲשָׁבָה בַּה׳ וְתוֹרָתוֹ וּמִצְוֹתָיו, מֵאַהֲבָה מְסוּתֶּרֶת שֶׁבְּלִבִּי לַה׳ כְּמוֹ בְּלֵב כְּלָלוּת יִשְׂרָאֵל שֶׁנִּקְרְאוּ ׳אוֹהֲבֵי שְׁמֶךָ׳.

I desire instead to attach my *nefesh*, *ruaḥ*, and *neshama* to Him through their being clothed in His three garments, which are action, speech, and thought channeled **toward God, His Torah, and His commandments.** This desire stems **from the** latent, **concealed love for God in my heart, just as** it exists **in the heart of the collective of Israel, who are referred to as 'those who love Your name.'**

Every Jew is a "lover of Your name."[4] Tzaddikim, prophets, and leaders of the generation are active "lovers of Your name," fully alive in their

THE TIP OF THE *YOD*

☞ The name of *Havaya*, God's four-letter name, brings forth everything into existence out of nothingness, and the source of this name is God's will, which is hinted at by the tip of the *yod*, the first of this name's four letters. Itself less than a letter, a mere tip of the *yod*, it indicates that there exists something that is transcendent, something that is beyond the scope of the letters to express, and it is the essence of everything. This focal point of God's will, which transcends the forces of creation, above *Bina* (the letter *heh*) and even higher than *Ḥokhma* (the letter *yod*), the source of everything in creation, is harmed when one commits a transgression.

4. See Ps. 5:12.

conscious relationship with God. Yet in truth, the entire Jewish people are "lovers of Your name" at least passively, unwilling in any way to cut themselves off from God.

וַאֲפִילוּ קַל שֶׁבַּקַּלִּים יָכוֹל לִמְסוֹר נַפְשׁוֹ עַל קְדוּשַּׁת ה׳,

Even the most unworthy is willing and **able to sacrifice his life for the sanctification of God's name,**

There are innumerable accounts of individuals who throughout their lives regarded the Torah and mitzvot as irrelevant, who were utterly apathetic to what they should do and what they should not, but when the moment of truth arrived, they sacrificed themselves to sanctify God's name. Every Jew, even the most unlettered, totally ignorant of the Torah and mitzvot and oblivious to the love and awe of God, is still a "lover of Your name." True, his love of God is latent, invisible during his lifetime. But when the ultimate test presents itself, he will forfeit his earthly existence rather than be separated from his source.

וְלֹא נוֹפֵל אָנֹכִי מִמֶּנּוּ בְּוַדַּאי.

and I am certainly not inferior to him.

The *beinoni,* who struggles with his heart's cravings, permitted or prohibited, understands that he has the same potential of self-sacrifice for God as the "most unworthy," the one who is apathetic to the Torah and its mitzvot. He too has a love for God resonating within that compels him to say, "I am unwilling to be cut off from God for even a single moment."

This raises a question: If every Jew, even the most unworthy among the worthless, is prepared to sacrifice his life rather than turn against God's will and be separated from Him, why does an individual transgress?

אֶלָּא שֶׁנִּכְנַס בּוֹ רוּחַ שְׁטוּת וְנִדְמֶה לוֹ שֶׁבַּעֲבֵרָה זוֹ עוֹדֶנּוּ בְּיַהֲדוּתוֹ וְאֵין נִשְׁמָתוֹ מוּבְדֶּלֶת מֵאֱלֹהֵי יִשְׂרָאֵל.

It is only that a spirit of folly entered him so that it appears to him that even **by** committing **this sin, he still maintains his Jewishness, and his soul is not separated from the God of Israel.**

The Talmud teaches, "A man commits a transgression only if a spirit of folly enters him" (*Sota* 3a). The author of the *Tanya* tells us that this is not the foolishness relating to any particular transgression, which evokes shame and astonishment at oneself: How could I ever do such a thing? Rather, it is that touch of madness, the lunacy of self-deception on the bases of which men develop misconceptions by which they live their lives. The most unworthy among the worthless goes about his life doing whatever his heart desires while assuming with complete confidence that he is still a good Jew.

The starting point of a transgression is never an unspoken wish to discard everything and abandon Judaism, to sever oneself from God. It is always the foolish notion that one can transgress, desecrate the Sabbath, eat prohibited food, and still remain a good Jew – or, as one often hears, "In my heart, I'm a good Jew."

The spirit of folly, then, is the mental construct that takes hold of the transgressor, where he thinks he can still be considered among "those who love Your name."

וְגַם שׁוֹכֵחַ אַהֲבָתוֹ לַה׳ הַמְסוּתֶּרֶת בְּלִבּוֹ.	**He also forgets his love of God that is hidden in his heart.**

For the spirit of folly to effectively influence a man's soul, it is not enough for him to be a fool at that moment. He must also forget his love of God. A conscious love in his heart would never allow him to pursue such foolishness. But once a person's love of God is forgotten, when he becomes lost in other matters, his heart is susceptible to folly.[5]

Since every Jew has the innate ability and desire to attach himself to God, he also possesses the strength not to transgress, not to cut

5. In his commentary on the *Tanya*, Rabbi Shmuel Gronem Esterman notes the distinction between the two phrases employed by the author of the *Tanya*: "it appears to him" and "he forgets." Rabbi Esterman suggests that these respectively reflect the aspects of "turn away from evil" and "do good" (see Ps. 34:15). That is to say, when one commits a transgression under the assumption that he is still connected to God, he manifests a failed compliance with the injunction to steer clear of evil. On the other hand, when failing to adhere to the directive to do good, he forgets his innate love of God, which entails fulfilling His will.

himself off from God, unless he is foolish enough to think that even if he committed a transgression, he is still connected to God.

אֲבָל אֲנִי אֵינֶנִּי רוֹצֶה לִהְיוֹת שׁוֹטֶה כָּמוֹהוּ לִכְפּוֹר הָאֱמֶת.

But as for me, I do not wish to be a fool such as he to deny the truth."

The foolish man imagines that there is a distinction between a major transgression and a minor one. But the person who has a keen understanding is aware that essentially there is no difference, that every transgression severs one from God. There is no distinction between a small disconnection or a large disconnection. There is only disconnection. Every detour, every parting, is a denial of God's rule and essentially an act of self-destruction. Clearly, anyone with such an awareness would never sin. Everyone has desires and urges and is willing to pay a certain price to gratify them, but no one would toss away his entire life for a craving.

The *beinoni* has the capacity to acknowledge that a transgression is not worth the price, that of separation and self-ruin. The horror this evokes is enough to put him off from committing the sin. It is not that he lacks temptations, but rather he is able to overcome them.

27 Tevet (leap year)

מַה שֶּׁאֵין כֵּן בְּדָבָר הַמָּסוּר לַלֵּב. דְּהַיְינוּ, שֶׁיְּהֵא הָרַע מָאוּס מַמָּשׁ בַּלֵּב וְשָׂנאוּי בְּתַכְלִית שִׂנְאָה, אוֹ אֲפִילּוּ שֶׁלֹּא בְּתַכְלִית שִׂנְאָה,

This is not the case with regard to a matter entrusted to the heart, meaning that the evil is actually despised in the heart either with an utter hatred or even not with such an utter hatred.

The *beinoni*'s ability to prevail over his temptations is limited to actual deed since he does not allow temptation to have the upper hand either actively or passively. But the *beinoni* is incapable of experiencing feelings powerful enough to either utterly abhor evil, like the complete tzaddik, or even to not utterly abhor evil, like the incomplete tzaddik.

הִנֵּה זֶה אִי אֶפְשָׁר שֶׁיִּהְיֶה בֶּאֱמֶת לַאֲמִיתּוֹ,

It is impossible for this abhorrence of evil **to be manifest in its absolute, truest sense**

The advice here is not effective with desires of the heart, over which only the tzaddik has dominion. As will be explained, the *beinoni* can attain varying levels. He can rise to excellence and even righteousness because he not only fulfills his obligations but exceeds normal expectations in both quality and quantity. Someone like this who dedicates his life to Torah and mitzvot may, in the midst of his efforts, come to regard a particular transgression with disgust and its commission as utterly unthinkable. Nonetheless, he is unable to achieve a genuine revulsion toward evil so that his sense of revulsion is perpetually rooted in his soul, dominating any life challenge with which he may potentially be faced.

אֶלָּא עַל יְדֵי גּוֹדֶל וְתוֹקֶף הָאַהֲבָה לַה׳ בִּבְחִינַת אַהֲבָה בְּתַעֲנוּגִים לְהִתְעַנֵּג עַל ה׳ מֵעֵין עוֹלָם הַבָּא.

except by means of the magnitude and potency of the love for God on the level of "love of delights," wherein one delights in God, which is **a semblance of the World to Come.**

Hatred of evil never emerges on its own. It is always accompanied by an ecstatic love of God, the "love of delights."[6] It is impossible for them to not be connected. It follows that when someone imagines he feels an actual hatred of evil yet does not have the corresponding feeling of loving God with a "love of delights," that hatred cannot be counted as authentic, nor can one say that he loves God to such an extent without an accompanying abhorrence of evil. Even if one occasionally thinks that he actually abhors evil, yet it is not accompanied by a love for God, it is merely the natural revulsion that one experiences on encountering anything he regards as unpleasant. It is only when one directs himself entirely toward holiness and it becomes his permanent companion, when his longing for good is so deeply ingrained that it permeates his soul without effort and needs no reinforcement, that whatever opposes that good is despicable and loathsome in his eyes.

וְעַל זֶה אָמְרוּ רַבּוֹתֵינוּ ז״ל (ברכות יז, א): ״עוֹלָמְךָ תִּרְאֶה בְּחַיֶּיךָ״ כו׳.

With regard to this, our Rabbis stated, "May you see your world in your lifetime…" (*Berakhot* 17a).

6. See chap. 9 and the commentary there.

A person will see his true world, his World to Come, in his lifetime in this world when it becomes unequivocally apparent to him that his life is permeated with his love for God and his connection with Him. Then both his present and future worlds are one and the same. When a person feels the "love of delights," he wants for nothing, not even the World to Come. "Whom else do I have in heaven?" the psalmist says. "With You, I desire nothing on earth" (Ps. 73:25). When one loves God to this extent, one tangibly feels God's presence, an experience that approximates the pleasure of the World to Come.

וְאֵין כָּל אָדָם זוֹכֶה לָזֶה כִּי זֶהוּ כְּעֵין קִבּוּל שָׂכָר,

Not every person merits this because it bears a semblance to the receiving of reward,

When a person performs a mitzva and actually feels that "the reward of a mitzva is a mitzva" (Mishna *Avot* 4:2), he realizes that it is not only that by fulfilling one mitzva he earns the merit to fulfill another, but that the reward of the mitzva is the mitzva itself. The very delight and spiritual wealth that he experiences through the fulfillment of the mitzva is his reward in this world. Not everyone has the fortune to attain such a level.

וּכְדִכְתִיב: "עֲבוֹדַת מַתָּנָה אֶתֵּן אֶת כְּהֻנַּתְכֶם" וגו' (במדבר יח, ז), כְּמוֹ שֶׁיִּתְבָּאֵר בְּמָקוֹם אַחֵר.

as it is written, "As a service that is a gift I give your priesthood..." (Num. 18:7)**, as will be explained elsewhere** (chaps. 40, 43).

The author of the *Tanya* understands that the service referred to in the verse is a gift that God has granted, not a reward. It is a gift because the individual derives great pleasure every moment that he is engaged in it and because he is incapable of performing this service solely with his own efforts. He can receive it only as a present from above. He must be born with this rank and cannot achieve it by his own efforts.[7]

7. See also *Pesaḥim* 73a; *Siddur Admor HaZaken, He'ara LeTikkun Ḥatzot*; *Iggeret HaKodesh*, epistles 6, 18; *Shulḥan Arukh HaRav, Hilkhot Talmud Torah* 4:6.

Therefore, Job said, "You created righteous people, and You created wicked people…" (*Bava Batra* 16a).

וְלָכֵן אָמַר אִיּוֹב: "בָּרָאתָ צַדִּיקִים" כו' (בבא בתרא טז, א).

Here the author of the *Tanya* answers another question he raised in the first chapter: How could Job say that God created people who were, at the outset, wicked or righteous, if we believe that the choice to be righteous or wicked is in a person's own hands?

According to the author of the *Tanya*, "You created righteous people" refers to those people who have the potential to be tzaddikim, and "You created wicked people" refers to those who do not have the potential to be tzaddikim. The latter are the very ones who are able to become *beinonim*. Accordingly, there are two distinct types of individuals. There are tzaddikim, a rare breed with souls equipped to transform their human essence to the extent that they may be intimate with God with the love of delights. These individuals have the potential to reach a level in which they experience the World to Come, the reward for their efforts, here in this world.

The second category, which comprises the majority of people, will never achieve perfection in this world because in their hearts they resemble the wicked. Nonetheless, by valiantly waging war in a lifelong struggle within themselves, they can be like complete tzaddikim in practice, and their reward in the World to Come is vast.

As the *Tikkunei Zohar* (1b) states, there are many levels and degrees in the souls of Israel: pious ones, mighty ones who overcome their evil **inclinations, masters of Torah, prophets, and so on, righteous people, and so on. See there.**

וְכִדְאִיתָא בַּתִּיקּוּנִים (א, ב), **שֶׁיֵּשׁ בְּנִשְׁמוֹת יִשְׂרָאֵל כַּמָּה מִינֵי מַדְרֵגוֹת וּבְחִינוֹת: חֲסִידִים, גִּבּוֹרִים הַמִּתְגַּבְּרִים עַל יִצְרָם, מָארֵי תוֹרָה, נְבִיאִים כו', צַדִּיקִים כו', עַיֵּין שָׁם.**

Every soul's source above determines its nature and potential below. This is the implication of the statement "You created righteous people, and You created wicked people."[8]

8. In his commentary on the *Tanya*, Rabbi Shmuel Gronem Esterman explains

22 Tevet
28 Tevet (leap year)

וּבָזֶה יוּבַן כֶּפֶל לְשׁוֹן הַשְּׁבוּעָה "תְּהִי צַדִּיק וְאַל תְּהִי רָשָׁע" (נידה ל, ב).

With this, one can understand the double expression employed in **the oath "Be righteous and do not be wicked"** (*Nidda* 30b).

After reaching some resolution regarding the definition of a *beinoni*, the author of the *Tanya* returns to the opening subject of the book, the Talmud's description of the oath that the angels administer to a soul before it descends into a body.

The oath is not only an expectation of accountability but also a prenatal energy booster to make it through one's life and overcome obstacles. The Hebrew term *mashbi'im*, which means to make one swear an oath (when spelled with the letter *shin*), can also be understood here in the sense of *sova*, abundance (when spelled with the letter *sin*), as in the verse "Behold, seven years are coming; great plenty [*sava*] throughout the land of Egypt" (Gen. 41:29), and also in the Sages' statement "Why is Tishrei called the seventh [*shevi'i*] month? Because it is replete [*mesuba*] with mitzvot" (*Yalkut Shimoni, Emor* 645). In this sense, the administering of the oath can also connote the granting of a gift, the ability from above to prevail in the struggle to be righteous and not to be wicked. ☞

SWEARING OVER A COMMANDMENT

☞ In reality, the inner content of any oath, whether initiated by the oath taker himself or administered by others, is the imparting of strength, the reinforcement of something already extant. A person decides that he wants something, and to strengthen his resolve and infuse it with added significance and force, he takes an oath: "I have sworn and will fulfill my oath, to follow Your righteous laws" (Ps. 119:106). In light of this, Rambam rules (*Sefer Hafla'a, Hilkhot Shevuot* 11:3) that a person can take an oath to fulfill a mitzva, even though his soul already swore to fulfill the mitzvot at Mount Sinai, in order to strengthen his performance and invest greater energy in its performance.

---

these distinctions among Jewish souls by correlating them to the six *sefirot*: *ḥasidim*, pious men, correspond to the *sefira* of *Ḥesed*, mighty ones to *Gevura*, Torah scholars to *Tiferet*, prophets to *Netzaḥ* and *Hod*, and tzaddikim to *Yesod*.

דִּלְכְאוֹרָה תְּמוּהָ, כִּי מֵאַחַר שֶׁמַּשְׁבִּיעִים אוֹתוֹ תְּהִי צַדִּיק, לָמָּה צְרִיכִים לְהַשְׁבִּיעוֹ עוֹד שֶׁלֹּא יִהְיֶה רָשָׁע?

On the surface, it seems perplexing: If the angels **administer an oath** enjoining the soul **to be righteous, why must they administer an additional oath to not be wicked?**

If the oath is effective, the oath to be righteous would be adequate. If it is not, why bother to administer an additional oath not to be wicked?

אֶלָּא מִשּׁוּם שֶׁאֵין כׇּל אָדָם זוֹכֶה לִהְיוֹת צַדִּיק, וְאֵין לָאָדָם מִשְׁפַּט הַבְּחִירָה בָּזֶה כׇּל כָּךְ

Rather, it is because not everyone merits being righteous, nor does a person possess the full advantage of choice in this matter,

It is not possible for everyone to be righteous, to be one who can transform his essence and experience delight in God's presence while truly despising evil. That is why the oath to "be righteous" alone is impossible to administer to every person. Even as a reinforcement, a simple provider of added strength, such an oath has little point, since being righteous is not a matter of human choice. Yet, as we will see, through extraordinary effort and self-sacrifice, the *beinoni* might be able to rise to the level of tzaddik in a certain sense. An unrealistic expectation for most people, the matter hinges on unique situations and on strivings that exceed the normal spectrum of human choice.

לְהִתְעַנֵּג עַל ה׳ בֶּאֱמֶת וְשֶׁיִּהְיֶה הָרַע מָאוּס מַמָּשׁ בֶּאֱמֶת.

to **truly delight in God and for evil to be truly, actually abhorrent** to him.

This is the domain of the tzaddik: delight in God complemented by the abhorrence of evil. The *beinoni* can achieve greatness, approximating a tzaddik in all his ways and thoughts, but he cannot despise evil in its fullest sense. A tzaddik lives in a dimension that is seemingly beyond evil's horizons. Evil in itself, or the desire for it, is incomprehensible through the lens, however magnified, of his own existence. His view of someone committing a sin has much in common with the reactions of a normal person when visiting a mental institution. He observes individuals carrying on and he thinks, *How can this be?* He gazes in wonder at someone eating glass and struggles to understand the temptation to do such a thing.

וְלָכֵן מַשְׁבִּיעִים שֵׁנִית: אַל תְּהִי רָשָׁע עַל כָּל פָּנִים. שֶׁבָּזֶה מִשְׁפַּט הַבְּחִירָה וְהָרְשׁוּת נְתוּנָה לְכָל אָדָם לִמְשׁוֹל בְּרוּחַ תַּאֲוָתוֹ שֶׁבְּלִבּוֹ וְלִכְבּוֹשׁ יִצְרוֹ שֶׁלֹּא יִהְיֶה רָשָׁע אֲפִילּוּ שָׁעָה אַחַת כָּל יָמָיו,

Therefore, they administer an oath a **second time: At any rate, do not be wicked. In this respect, each person is granted the advantage of choice and the permission to control the spirit of lust in his heart and to vanquish his** evil **inclination so that he will not be** categorized as **wicked his entire life, even for one moment,**

One of the tzaddik's distinguishing features is his delight in God. Yet the demarcation is not absolutely clear-cut, since individuals who are not on the rank of tzaddik can also derive great pleasure from the Torah and mitzvot. At the same time, not even the swearing of an oath will transform a *beinoni* into a tzaddik. How, then, do we understand this oath to "be righteous and do not be wicked"? On the one hand, the rank of the righteous cannot apply to every individual; on the other, if the individual does swear to be righteous, why the need for the additional oath not to be wicked?

We can understand this oath as follows: "Be righteous." Exert

STRIVE TO BE RIGHTEOUS

☞ Although the book's title is *The Book of Beinonim*, the overriding goal is to be righteous. From the start, we must establish a lofty target for our aspirations, and for this reason the book speaks at such length about the rank of tzaddik. Yet not many individuals will reach this goal, nor is it a matter of choice. Still, no one is capable of knowing from the start if he is a tzaddik or *beinoni*. One cannot read a child's forehead for clues. This becomes clear only after subsequent effort and struggle. A child born a tzaddik comes into the world with only the potential for becoming a tzaddik. His actions are not perfect at first, and he is capable of transgression. His development can lead to becoming a tzaddik but can also lead, in the absence of the proper exertion, to not becoming one. Though not everyone has the option of being a tzaddik, one fortunate to be born with this capacity does have a choice: to be a tzaddik or a *rasha*.

If the choice to become a tzaddik is beyond the grasp of most people, nothing prevents them from trying. As the author of the *Tanya* explains at the chapter's closing, though it is far from usual, a radical yourself to the maximum as much as you are able. If you are unable, then at the least strive not to be wicked. ☞

בֵּין בִּבְחִינַת "סוּר מֵרָע" בֵּין בִּבְחִינַת "וַעֲשֵׂה טוֹב".

whether with regard to turning away from evil or with regard to doing good.

The capacity to reach for the heights is the first part of the oath, the pathway to fulfilling the oath to "be righteous." The second part of the oath is a spiritual firewall against descent to the depths: At the least, "do not be wicked." The injunctions "turn away from evil" and "do good" constitute the boundaries set around every individual's life, the breach of which violates the oath not to be wicked.

"וְאֵין טוֹב אֶלָּא תּוֹרָה" (אבות פרק ו משנה ג), דְּהַיְינוּ 'תַּלְמוּד תּוֹרָה שֶׁכְּנֶגֶד כּוּלָּן'.

"'Good' means nothing but Torah" (Mishna *Avot* 6:3), **that is, Torah study, which is equivalent to all** the commandments of the Torah.

Whereas turning away from evil and doing good are the fundamental boundaries effected by the oath not to be wicked, the author of the *Tanya*'s comment regarding the study of Torah provides additional depth to these injunctions. Turning away from evil has fixed boundaries. Someone who currently does not have an opportunity to transgress is not considered to be turning away from evil. On the other hand, in the realm of doing good, there is one mitzva that has no limits, that is unhampered by place, time, or quality: the mitzva of Torah study. Whenever one has no other mitzva opportunity, he can always study Torah. In light of this, there are no limits to being righteous. There are

change, a sort of mutation, can occur, and someone born a *beinoni* can pass through a crisis touching on his very essence and emerge as a tzaddik. There are no guarantees, and the author clearly does not build on it, but the possibility, real but distant, warrants consideration.

Not all of us can become an Abraham, Isaac, or Jacob, but the objective we pursue should exceed the role model that a good friend may present. It is against Abraham, Isaac, and Jacob that we must measure ourselves. Our forefathers bequeathed us a criterion of human potential that calls out: This is what is possible for men to achieve. To this you must aspire!

no quotas assigned to one's capabilities and potential. The scorecard for any given day has endless possibilities.

אַךְ אַף עַל פִּי כֵן צָרִיךְ לִקְבּוֹעַ לוֹ עִתִּים גַּם כֵּן לָשִׁית עֵצוֹת בְּנַפְשׁוֹ לִהְיוֹת מוֹאֵס בָּרַע,

Nonetheless, one must also designate specific **times for himself to devise stratagems for abhorring evil,**

The *beinoni* does not essentially despise evil. At any moment, his soul can yearn for any number of prohibited things, and he has no means whatsoever to prevent that yearning. Yet, despite his built-in powerlessness to avoid such longings, he can still simulate a virtual hatred of evil. He can visualize particular situations and, with sufficient practice, create an abhorrence that, while neither constant nor spontaneous, is eminently effective.

כְּגוֹן בַּעֲצַת חֲכָמֵינוּ ז"ל: "אִשָּׁה חֵמֶת מְלֵאָה צוֹאָה" כו' (שבת קנב, א) וּכְהַאי גַּוְונָא. וְכֵן כָּל מִינֵי מַטְעַמִּים וּמַעֲדַנִּים נַעֲשִׂים כָּךְ חֵמֶת מָלֵא כו',

for example, by contemplating **our Sages' advice "A woman is** essentially **a flask full of feces…"** (*Shabbat* 152a), **and the like. Likewise, all types of tasty foods and delicacies similarly become a "flask full** of feces."

Our perception of pleasure is based on one-dimensional vision. As we contemplate and open our eyes to additional facets of whatever it is we desire, it becomes impossible to maintain the attraction; it can even turn into something despicable. When a man has a desire for a woman, he is advised to picture the woman's body from the inside as well as

ADAM'S INDUCED SLUMBER

☞ The Talmud (*Sanhedrin* 39a) relates that the Roman emperor asked Rabban Gamliel why God caused Adam to sleep when He created Eve. Rabban Gamliel requested that a sizable chunk of raw meat be brought before them. He took the meat and, while the emperor looked on, rinsed it and roasted it on a spit. When it was done, he offered it to the emperor to eat.

"I cannot eat that," the emperor told him. "It is disgusting."

The emperor knew, of course, how meat is prepared, but after seeing how unsavory it was before roasting, he lost his appetite for it.

from the outside. At that moment, if his visualization powers are sufficient and he acts in all earnestness, his desire turns into disgust. ☞

וְכֵן כָּל תַּעֲנוּגֵי עוֹלָם הַזֶּה, הֶחָכָם רוֹאֶה הַנּוֹלָד מֵהֶן שֶׁסּוֹפָן לִרְקוֹב וְלִהְיוֹת רִמָּה וְאַשְׁפָּה.

So too with regard to **all the pleasures of this world, the wise person foresees what will become of them: that they are destined to decay and become worms and filth.**

Advertising agencies produce endless commercials displaying the beautiful, the attractive, and the enchanting side of their clients' products all in order to fuel our desires. The advice put forth by the author of the *Tanya* is based on the same principle but in the opposite direction: One should meditate on the other dimensions that do not appear in the ads. When a person devotes certain times to contemplating the seductive messages bombarding him and visualizes their objects in various states of disintegration, disrepair, destruction, fragmentation, and death, he discovers a new and loathsome world. In those moments, rather than lusting after the pleasures of this world, he will begin to despise them.

וְהַהֵפֶךְ, לְהִתְעַנֵּג וְלִשְׂמוֹחַ בַּה' עַל יְדֵי הִתְבּוֹנְנוּת בִּגְדוּלַּת אֵין סוֹף בָּרוּךְ הוּא כְּפִי יְכוֹלְתּוֹ.

Conversely, one must invest time in training himself **to delight and be joyous in God by meditating on the greatness of *Ein Sof*, blessed be He, to the best of his ability.**

Just as the *beinoni* must invest time and practice in scorning evil, he must also immerse himself in meditation leading to pleasure and delight in God. The author of the *Tanya* will expand on this theme considerably, in accordance with his usual practice of minimizing the negative.

אַף שֶׁיּוֹדֵעַ בְּנַפְשׁוֹ שֶׁלֹּא יַגִּיעַ לְמַדְרֵגָה זוֹ בֶּאֱמֶת לַאֲמִיתּוֹ, כִּי אִם בְּדִמְיוֹנוֹת,

Although he himself knows that he will not attain this level in its absolute, truest sense but rather only **in his imagination,**

A true feeling need not be supported by crutches or surrounded by scaffolding. It stands by itself, vital and self-validating. Truth's hallmarks are stability, consistency, and eternity. This is why a person who must direct his thoughts in a particular direction and enter a temporary mindset in order to generate certain feelings will fail to achieve a genuine revulsion for evil and a love of truth except in his imagination. He will experience the feelings, but they will never become an integral part of him.

אַף עַל פִּי כֵן, הוּא יַעֲשֶׂה אֶת שֶׁלּוֹ לְקַיֵּים אֶת הַשְּׁבוּעָה שֶׁמַּשְׁבִּיעִים: "תְּהִי צַדִּיק",

he must nevertheless do his part to fulfill the oath administered to him to **"be righteous,"**

Because the individual has taken the oath to be a tzaddik, he must endeavor to become one. Though he may never arrive there, that is nonetheless his destination. Not only within the halakhic pathways of turning away from evil and doing good must he exert himself, but he must internalize this turning away from evil and doing good until it becomes part of his consciousness, creating an appropriate internal imagery and landscape to comply with the terms of the oath to be righteous.

Each ephemeral self-made image may be a struggle, but his efforts are not wasted. Even if the image passes, it will not vanish without a trace, without leaving an impression. Whether in the physical plane or the spiritual, something always remains. Just as a trickle of water can slice through stone, a consistent thought pattern eventually affects one's soul. When someone spends more than a few moments daily in his imagination – when one invests hours – his thoughts carve into the

HOW THOUGHTS INFLUENCE THE SOUL

☞ It is common knowledge that anthropologists and diplomats must occasionally return home from their research or embassy postings. If they fail to do so, their environments become so deeply enmeshed in their awareness, and they identify with them to such an extent, that their missions are compromised. More than one researcher has arrived at a distant locale to study an exotic people and, though mindful of its ways and superstitions, after too long a stay has begun to accept some of the indigenous beliefs, fears, and general mindset. The regular involvement with the culture, the habitual attempt to imagine oneself in their place, all this influences the essence of one's soul.

very essence of his soul little by little. On occasion, they may change him completely. ☞

וַה׳ יַעֲשֶׂה הַטּוֹב בְּעֵינָיו.

and God will do that which is good in His eyes.

As the author pf the *Tanya* will go on to explain, being a tzaddik is not dependent solely on man's own efforts. Rather, it requires "an awakening from above," heavenly inspiration. One should do his part in fulfilling the oath to be righteous, but for that to actually happen, he needs God to "do that which is good in His eyes."

וְעוֹד, שֶׁהַהֶרְגֵּל עַל כָּל דָּבָר - שִׁלְטוֹן, וְנַעֲשֶׂה טֶבַע שֵׁנִי.

Furthermore, habit reigns supreme in all matters and becomes second nature.

When one becomes accustomed to something, habit becomes second nature. Though not as strong, perhaps, as "first nature," it nonetheless becomes inseparably embedded in his soul.

וּכְשֶׁיַּרְגִּיל לְמָאֵס אֶת הָרַע יִהְיֶה נִמְאָס קְצָת בֶּאֱמֶת, וּכְשֶׁיַּרְגִּיל לְשַׂמֵּחַ נַפְשׁוֹ בַּה׳ עַל יְדֵי הִתְבּוֹנְנוּת בִּגְדוּלַּת ה׳,

When one accustoms himself to abhorring evil, it will at least **in part become truly abhorrent.** Conversely, **when one accustoms himself to rejoicing in God, by contemplating God's greatness,**

When the abhorrence of evil and delighting in God becomes habit, these feelings will move from the realm of the theoretical into regular modes of thought, and the person's soul will gradually become altered, if not essentially, then at least partially. Though he will not detest evil entirely and essentially, but only to some extent, this loathing of evil will nonetheless be authentic.

הֲרֵי בְּאִתְעֲרוּתָא דִלְתַתָּא אִתְעֲרוּתָא דִלְעֵילָּא.

then an awakening from below will generate **an awakening from above.**

This principle, that through our efforts below we cause an awakening above, is the cornerstone of all human endeavor. The Ba'al Shem Tov famously expounded the verse "The Lord is your shadow by your right hand" (Ps. 121:5), as implying that God is, in a manner of speaking, like a person's shadow. Lower your hand, and your shadow lowers its hand; lift your hand, and your shadow's hand correspondingly rises. Do an act of charity and kindness, and God will reciprocate. If a person's actions are ugly, God ensures that the person will receive suitable recompense.[9] So too, when a person becomes inspired to reach upward and achieve a new level, even though it may be beyond his ability, an awakening is created above. When there is an awakening above, when a person receives divine assistance, everything becomes possible.

וְכוּלֵי הַאי וְאוּלַי, יֵעָרֶה עָלָיו רוּחַ מִמָּרוֹם, וְיִזְכֶּה לִבְחִינַת רוּחַ מִשֹּׁרֶשׁ אֵיזֶה צַדִּיק שֶׁתִּתְעַבֵּר בּוֹ,

From all this, perhaps a spirit will be poured on him from on high, and he will merit that the soul **level of *ruaḥ* originating in** the soul of **some tzaddik will be infused within him,**

From the awakening that was initiated below, then perhaps – though it is far from certain – a spirit from above will descend on him. The individual in question is not a tzaddik, nor does he possess the potential to become one, yet it is possible that "a spirit will be poured on him from on high."

THE INTEGRATION OF A SOUL

☞ Through this process, called "impregnation," where the soul level of *ruaḥ* originating in a tzaddik is integrated into the soul of a *beinoni*, the *beinoni*'s spiritual balance tilts. He becomes, for the duration that this energy is in force, a tzaddik. This bears some resemblance to the concept of dybbuk, which occurs when another soul, with a different consciousness, enters a person and, either occasionally or continually, takes control of his persona. At such times, the person's self, his speech and actions, become a vehicle for the consciousness of the soul that has attached itself to him.

"Impregnation," or the integration of another soul's *ruaḥ*, is also an attachment of one soul to another but is quite different in nature. The person receives additional energy, in complete or partial form, from another soul but without its consciousness. The other soul does not make jarring guest appearances but blends evenly into his own self. When a tzaddik's soul becomes attached to him, he will not sense that another persona has made an appear-

9. *Keter Shem Tov*, addendum 78; *Ba'al Shem Tov al Torah, Parashat Kedoshim* 21–23.

It can happen, then, that a person whose entire life and focus was that of a *beinoni* can undergo a revolution, a sudden, dramatic internal upheaval, and become a tzaddik. Such a change does not occur from within but from a new soul, a spark that originates in the root of some tzaddik's soul that he receives as a gift from above.[10] ☞

לַעֲבוֹד ה׳ בְּשִׂמְחָה אֲמִתִּית, כִּדְכְתִיב: ״שִׂמְחוּ צַדִּיקִים בַּה׳״ (תהלים צז, יב), וְתִתְקַיֵּים בּוֹ בֶּאֱמֶת הַשְּׁבוּעָה שֶׁמַּשְׁבִּיעִים: ״תְּהִי צַדִּיק״.

so that he may serve God with true joy, and not the man-made joy created through the imagination, **as it is written, "Rejoice in the Lord, you righteous ones"** (Ps. 97:12), **and the oath administered** to him, to **"be righteous," will truly be fulfilled.**

Someone who was born a *beinoni* is nearly certain to remain a *beinoni*. Yet he must swear to "be righteous." The oath is not meant as a requirement to reach that level but a requirement to aspire to it. The oath establishes the goal and the ideal, and the commitment to work toward it with one's best efforts. The Midrash teaches that every Jew must say, "When will my deeds reach the deeds of Abraham, Isaac, and Jacob?" (*Tanna deVei Eliyahu Rabba* 23). But is it possible for everyone's deeds to reach the stature of the forefathers? They were vehicles for God's presence in this world with every deed they performed. Yet we must

ance. The integration is seamless. It is only his own consciousness and awareness that will have expanded and changed.

Autobiographies are not widespread among Jews, especially not first-person accounts of soul integration. The few isolated narratives we have of such events describe how, without any preparation and regardless of time and place, a person feels that his mind has expanded. He feels different. He functions differently and sees things he never saw before. He is aware in a completely new way. There is no sensation of someone else being in control but rather that he himself has changed. This internal sensation might occasionally be one that others also perceive, and it may also be hidden from himself.

10. As the Lubavitcher Rebbe, Rabbi Menaḥem Mendel Schneerson, points out, the person's soul itself will not become transformed, so there is no contradiction to the aforementioned talmudic statement, "You have created righteous people...."

understand this in the same manner as we do the oath to be a tzaddik: It is a pinnacle, a goal whose outer limits we stand on tiptoes to touch.

Such an objective may be beyond a person's reach, but his efforts to achieve it are never misspent. Every step brings a person closer to the target. Even if he cannot overcome all his challenges, over time, with practice, the *beinoni* can at least moderate them and deal soberly with them.

We can understand the fulfillment of the oath to be a tzaddik, then, as a hands-on learning session, an introductory Tzaddik 101 course. The swimming instructor tells the beginner to envision himself as a fish, and that will help him swim, at the very least, like a human. One should imagine himself as a tzaddik and try, even a little, to act like one. Still, the second part of the oath is the *beinoni*'s primary focus: Under no circumstances, even if he does not become a tzaddik, is he to be a *rasha*.

In this chapter, the author of the *Tanya* concluded his overall picture of the *beinoni* and his explanation of how the *beinoni* differs from the tzaddik and the *rasha*. He returned to the book's starting point, the dual oath, "Be righteous and do not be wicked," expressing the two poles of the *beinoni*'s experience. Though his acts of goodness will never match that of the tzaddik, he must aspire to be a tzaddik and thereby always exceed his past performance. Even if he does not succeed in becoming a tzaddik, he should, at the least, avoid becoming a *rasha*. In the chapters to follow, the author of the *Tanya* will offer practical guidance as to how the *beinoni* can wend his way through the winding paths presented to him in pursuit of the Divine.

Chapter 15

AFTER EXPLAINING THE NATURE OF THE *BEINONI* IN general, the author of the *Tanya* now turns his focus on specific facets of the *beinoni*'s service of God. This will be the theme of the coming chapters – and, in a certain sense, throughout the remainder of the book: How can one attain the level of *beinoni*? What is the unremitting work demanded of him? As demonstrated in the previous chapters, the service of the *beinoni* is no simple feat. Though possible, it requires constant guidance and vigilance in the various aspects and methods pertaining to this service.

As noted in the previous chapter, the *beinoni* occupies the middle lane between "be righteous" and "do not be wicked," between, on one hand, his aspiration to be a tzaddik and grasp infinity and, on the other hand, the boundary that he may not cross: to not be wicked. This chapter will explore the first of the two poles: "Be righteous." That is, the aspiration to achieve great heights in divine service, to touch the infinite, day by day, which is an unabating process. Unlike the previous chapter, the context here is not focused on the pinnacle of divine service, but rather the emphasis is on the mundane, routine efforts that this path entails, where the ambition is seemingly limited, where the goal is not necessarily focused on reaching the level of the righteous, but that of the *beinoni*.

Yet the type of *beinoni* discussed here is of a higher caliber than the *beinoni* hitherto discussed. This *beinoni*, dubbed "one who serves God," must constantly strive to maintain his lofty status. It is this category of *beinoni* on which this chapter focuses.

23 Tevet
29 Tevet (leap year)

וּבָזֶה יוּבַן מַה שֶּׁכָּתוּב: "וְשַׁבְתֶּם וּרְאִיתֶם בֵּין צַדִּיק לְרָשָׁע, בֵּין עוֹבֵד אֱלֹהִים לַאֲשֶׁר לֹא עֲבָדוֹ" (מלאכי ג, יח).

With this description of the *beinoni*, **we can understand the verse "You will return and see the difference between the righteous and the wicked, between one who serves God and one who does not serve Him"** (Mal. 3:18).

This verse divides people into four categories: the righteous, the wicked, one who serves God, and one who does not serve Him. The Talmud discusses the apparent duplicate wording of "the righteous" and "one who serves God" and "the wicked" and "one who does not serve Him," concluding that the one who serves God and the one who does not represent two categories of tzaddikim.[1]

The author of the *Tanya* will proceed to fill in the picture with greater detail in accordance with his approach: The one who serves God and the one who does not serve Him can also be two categories of *beinoni.*

שֶׁהַהֶפְרֵשׁ בֵּין עוֹבֵד אֱלֹהִים לְצַדִּיק הוּא שֶׁעוֹבֵד הוּא לְשׁוֹן הוֶֹה, שֶׁהוּא בְּאֶמְצַע הָעֲבוֹדָה שֶׁהִיא הַמִּלְחָמָה עִם הַיֵּצֶר הָרַע לְהִתְגַּבֵּר עָלָיו וּלְגָרְשׁוֹ מֵהָעִיר קְטַנָּה, שֶׁלֹּא יִתְלַבֵּשׁ בְּאֵבְרֵי הַגּוּף, שֶׁהוּא בֶּאֱמֶת עֲבוֹדָה וְעָמָל גָּדוֹל לְהִלָּחֵם בּוֹ תָּמִיד - וְהַיְינוּ הַבֵּינוֹנִי.

The difference between one who serves God and the tzaddik is that the term for "serves," ***oved*****, is in the present tense,** implying **that he is in the midst of laboring** in his service of God, **which is the war** that he is waging **against the evil inclination,** wherein he struggles **to prevail over it and drive it out of the small city so that it will not become clothed in the limbs of the body. Constantly waging war against** the evil inclination **truly entails considerable labor and toil. This is the *beinoni.***

The *beinoni* is called, in the active present, "one who serves," because he is continually engaged in the battle with the evil inclination for control of his own body, the "small city." For the *beinoni*, this war is

1. See *Ḥagiga* 9b.

not a finite episode that occurred sometime in the past. It is ongoing, for the duration of his life.

אֲבָל הַצַּדִּיק נִקְרָא עֶבֶד ה׳ בְּשֵׁם הַתּוֹאַר, כְּמוֹ שֵׁם ׳חָכָם׳ אוֹ ׳מֶלֶךְ׳, שֶׁכְּבָר נַעֲשָׂה חָכָם אוֹ מֶלֶךְ. כָּךְ זֶה, כְּבָר עָבַד וְגָמַר לְגַמְרֵי עֲבוֹדַת הַמִּלְחָמָה עִם הָרַע עַד כִּי וַיְגָרְשֵׁהוּ וַיֵּלֶךְ לוֹ וְ׳לִבּוֹ חָלָל בְּקִרְבּוֹ׳.

But the tzaddik is referred to with the appellation "servant of God," similar to the title "sage" or "king," where one has already become a sage or king. So too this tzaddik **has already labored and completely finished the labor of waging war against the evil** within him **to the extent that he has driven it out and it is gone from him, and,** consequently, **his heart is "hollow" within him.**

The left side of the tzaddik's heart, the abode of the evil inclination, is empty.[2] The tzaddik is not one who is "serving" God, in a constant struggle against his evil nature, because he no longer has such a nature. He is called a "servant of God" since that describes his essence. He no longer has to work toward becoming one who serves. He is already there. The *beinoni*, by contrast, will never reach that plateau. His life is a work in progress. He is on the path, and he struggles. For that reason, he is called one who serves. He is constantly serving God throughout his life in the battle against his evil inclination.

The difference between a worker and a servant can illustrate this distinction. During the hours that a worker is active, he is called a worker. The moment he stops, he ceases to be a worker. A servant, on the other hand, need not be active in order to be called a servant. His entire identity is bound up with his service.

A king also does not have to do anything in particular to be called a king. He is the king because he already has that standing; he is a king at his essence. In this sense, the tzaddik is not one who serves. He has completed that phase of the struggle. Now he can be called a servant of God. His position regarding the service of God is static. Though he may not have attained perfection, he has closed a chapter of his life. Those challenges no longer exist for him.

---

2. See Ps. 109:22; chap. 13.

When a child learns the multiplication tables, he activates his conceptual thinking time and again: How much is six times seven? How much is seven times eight? Over time, though, he no longer has to drill himself in these exercises. The challenges cease being challenges; his efforts are unconscious. When learning to read or to master a new language, the student repeatedly practices forming letters and writing words. Yet he reaches a point at which these matters are no longer an issue, when ideas modulate into language without confusion. Similarly, a tzaddik has reached a stage where he no longer serves. His exertions are past history, and the battleground between good and evil is silenced.

Such a distinction is also found in the realm of the most basic human desires. A young child must be taught what to eat and what to avoid. Left to his own devices, he would eat anything. An adult, by contrast, need not be told to avoid harmful things. Lack of discernment is not an issue, because inedible substances already disgust him. Similarly, a tzaddik chooses good and shuns evil. Just as the thought of eating something dangerous or repulsive would never occur to a normal person, so too a tzaddik chooses good and never entertains a base thought. The likelihood that he will gossip or commit any other wrongdoing is as remote as a member of our culture dining on tainted food. ☞ ☞

ARE THE RIGHTEOUS INFALLIBLE?

☞ Though immune to performing a transgression consciously and intentionally, the tzaddik is liable to fall prey to mistakes. If he is unaware of the evil nature of something, he may stumble. Yet just as one finds people everywhere who sense instinctively what is inappropriate, so it is with the tzaddik when it comes to the boundaries of good and evil, the holy and the profane. He has an innate, almost visceral, withdrawal reflex, protecting him from error.

Rabbi Yitzḥak Meir of Gur, the author of *Ḥiddushei HaRim*, never ate meat if anyone had raised any sort of question regarding its *kashrut*. Even if a rabbi had judged the meat to be kosher, Rabbi Yitzḥak Meir would still avoid it because there had been an uncertainty about it. On one occasion, he was served meat and would not touch it. The cook was interrogated, and it was discovered that there had been a mistake and there was a halakhic question concerning the animal.

The hasidim were stunned. "How did you know?" they asked.

"Why are you so surprised?" he replied. "Anyone is capable of reaching this lev-

וּבַבֵּינוֹנִי יֵשׁ גַּם כֵּן שְׁתֵּי מַדְרֵגוֹת: 'עוֹבֵד אֱלֹהִים' וַ'אֲשֶׁר לֹא עֲבָדוֹ'. וְאַף עַל פִּי כֵן אֵינוֹ רָשָׁע, כִּי לֹא עָבַר מִיָּמָיו שׁוּם עֲבֵירָה קַלָּה וְגַם קִיֵּים כָּל הַמִּצְוֹת שֶׁאֶפְשָׁר לוֹ לְקַיְּימָן "וְתַלְמוּד תּוֹרָה כְּנֶגֶד כּוּלָּם" (פאה פרק א משנה א), וְלֹא פָּסִיק פּוּמֵיהּ מִגִּירְסָא,

1 Shevat (leap year)

There are also two levels in the category of ***beinoni*****: "one who serves God" and "one who does not serve Him." Nevertheless,** even the *beinoni* who is categorized as one who does not serve Him **is not wicked, since he never in his life transgressed** even **a minor sin, and he has also fulfilled all the mitzvot** in the Torah **that he is able to perform,** including **Torah study,** which **is equivalent to all** the commandments (*Pe'a* 1:1), **and his mouth never ceased from** the **study** of Torah.

el if he resolves, fully and sincerely that, if something prohibited were to touch his lips, he would choke on it. Then he would never make an error."

Another story is told of Reb Shmuel Munkes, a disciple of Rabbi Shneur Zalman of Liadi, the author of the *Tanya*. The hasidim once brought a pot of appetizing food to a *farbrengen* (an informal gathering of hasidim with refreshments and words of Torah), and they were eager to start eating. But Reb Shmuel kept them away from the pot. Again they swarmed around the pot, but he spilled its contents onto the ground. Meanwhile, the cook sent word that they should not eat the food. It turned out that the food was not kosher. On hearing this, the hasidim, who were known for their outstanding service of God, seized Reb Shmuel and prepared to beat him up for the offense of openly displaying *ruaḥ hakodesh*.

"What are you talking about?" Reb Shmuel said in his defense. "When I saw everyone's eyes light up with desire, I knew the dish was not from the side of holiness but from the side of *kelippa*."

SERVANT AND SERVING

☞ When referring to the *beinoni* who serves God, the name *Elokim*, the name associated with strict judgment, is attributed to his service, and he is called *oved Elokim*, "one who serves God." The tzaddik, by contrast, is an *eved Hashem*, a "servant of the Lord," associated with the name of *Havaya*, the name that indicates mercy and compassion. Why the distinction?

In *Sha'ar HaYiḥud VeHa'emuna* (chap. 4), the author of the *Tanya* expounds the verse "For the Lord God is a sun and a shield" (Ps. 84:12), which uses both names of God. He comments that the name of *Havaya* represents the revelation of the divine light, while the name *Elokim* stands for the constriction and concealment of this illumination to the extent that the world appears to have an independent existence (hence the name *Elokim* has the same numerical value as the Hebrew word *hateva*, "the nature"). The tzaddik's service involves

The *beinoni* "who does not serve God" also studies Torah whenever he is able, in between his performance of the mitzvot. Though at first glance he appears perfect in his turning away from evil and doing good, he is not a tzaddik but a *beinoni*, and a low-level *beinoni* at that, who is not "serving God."

אֶלָּא שֶׁאֵינוֹ עוֹשֶׂה שׁוּם מִלְחָמָה עִם הַיֵּצֶר לְנַצְּחוֹ עַל יְדֵי אוֹר ה׳ הַמֵּאִיר עַל נֶפֶשׁ הָאֱלֹהִית שֶׁבַּמּוֹחַ הַשַּׁלִּיט עַל הַלֵּב, כַּנִּזְכָּר לְעֵיל,

Yet he wages no war against the evil **inclination to vanquish it by means of God's light that illuminates the divine soul** that abides **in the brain, which governs the heart, as mentioned above** (chap. 12),

What is missing here is the struggle. Throughout his life, the *beinoni* turns away from evil and does good. He studies Torah and fulfills the mitzvot. Nevertheless, he does not wage war against his evil inclination. He serves God not from a burning inner love or awe but because he possesses a character that complements this lifestyle.

מִפְּנֵי שֶׁאֵין יִצְרוֹ עוֹמֵד לְנֶגְדּוֹ כְּלָל לְבַטְּלוֹ מִתּוֹרָתוֹ וַעֲבוֹדָתוֹ וְאֵין צָרִיךְ לִלְחוֹם עִמּוֹ כְּלָל.

because his evil **inclination does not oppose him at all to deter him from his Torah** study **and his** divine **service, and he has no need whatsoever to wage war against it.**

This flies in the face of conventional experience. For most, turning away from evil and doing good means struggling against an array of clashing urges and desires that are on a collision course with this goal. Yet one can be built differently. A person may fulfill the mitzvot with

the name of *Havaya*, bringing additional light into the creation. The *beinoni*, the "*oved Elokim*," strives to process and transform the concealment of the divine light in the world, to draw down the attribute of the name of *Havaya* into the attribute of *Elokim*. Hence the word *oved* can connote a process, as in the term *orot avudim*, processed animal hides. On an individual level, this constitutes the work of refining the animal soul within so that the divine light can shine through (*Likkutei Biurim LaTanya*; see also commentaries of Rabbi Yaakov Kaidaner and Rabbi Shmuel Gronem Esterman).

the utmost attention to detail, he may study Torah diligently, and he does not feel compromised in the least. His natural bent for divine service precludes any need for conflict to realign his priorities or wrestle with his animal soul to preserve his core values as a Jew. Living in accordance with the Torah puts him at ease, in perfect consonance with his nature and personality.

כְּגוֹן שֶׁהוּא מַתְמִיד בְּלִמּוּדוֹ בְּטִבְעוֹ מִתּוֹלַדְתּוֹ עַל יְדֵי תִּגְבּוֹרֶת הַמָּרָה שְׁחוֹרָה.

He may, for example, be diligent in his Torah **study by his inborn nature due to a predominance of melancholy.**

Some people tend toward melancholy by nature. A tempestuous life, whether in the realm of holiness or of impurity, holds no attraction for them. They are happy to stay in one place and focus on single occupation. Contentment lies in quiet continuity. If they have an intellectual bent and matters of the spirit interest them, then the coziest means for self-realization is to sit and study. This requires no self-sacrifice on their part. On the contrary, it is an expression of their unique personality, and they will act this way in whatever situation they find themselves.

Such a person is the quintessential bookworm. He does not struggle with devoting every spare moment to Torah study. There is no contest between the divine soul and the animal soul. This *is* his animal soul.

וְכֵן אֵין לוֹ מִלְחָמָה מִתַּאֲוַת נָשִׁים מִפְּנֵי שֶׁהוּא מְצוּנָּן בְּטִבְעוֹ. וְכֵן בִּשְׁאָר תַּעֲנוּגֵי עוֹלָם הַזֶּה הוּא מְחוּסַּר הֶרְגֵּשׁ הֲנָאָה בְּטִבְעוֹ.

Similarly, he may not battle against feelings of **lust for women because of his frigid temperament. The same is true of the other pleasures of this world: By nature, he lacks** any **feeling for** physical **enjoyment.**

The capacity to enjoy sensual pleasures differs from one person to the next. Yet a lack of sensuality is no indication of spiritual achievement or righteousness. A person may not pay any attention to what he eats or what he sees, and the same applies to sexual desire. Such an individual can sit in a study hall and be occupied with the fulfillment of mitzvot while the world around him presents no temptation. He gets dressed every morning, has his breakfast, and goes about his business. His single-minded focus on Torah study does not stem from a magnetic attraction to holiness. He is simply disinclined by nature to do anything else. He could be a clerk, a professor, or a rabbi. It makes no difference; his disposition would be the same.

וְלָכֵן אֵין צָרִיךְ לְהִתְבּוֹנֵן כָּל כָּךְ בִּגְדוּלַּת ה׳ לְהוֹלִיד מִבִּינָתוֹ רוּחַ דַּעַת וְיִרְאַת ה׳ בְּמוֹחוֹ לְהִשָּׁמֵר שֶׁלֹּא לַעֲבוֹר עַל מִצְוֹת ׳לֹא תַעֲשֶׂה׳, וְאַהֲבַת ה׳ בְּלִבּוֹ לְדָבְקָה בּוֹ בְּקִיּוּם הַמִּצְוֹת וְתַלְמוּד תּוֹרָה כְּנֶגֶד כּוּלָּן,

Therefore, in order to avoid being categorized as wicked, **he need not meditate so much on God's greatness to generate from his** faculty of **understanding a spirit of knowledge and fear of God in his mind** in order **to be vigilant not to transgress any prohibitions.** He also need not generate **a love for God in his heart** in order **to cleave to Him through the fulfillment of the commandments and the study of Torah,** which is **equivalent to all** the commandments.

One who does not have the temptations of the evil inclination does not have the need to employ his arsenal of knowledge and fear of God against it. Nor does he have to evoke feelings of love for God in order to perform mitzvot and study Torah. This is in contrast to a person who does not by nature desire to perform the mitzvot and study Torah. Such a person must evoke a living emotion of love for God by virtue of which he will engage in these pursuits.

אֶלָּא דַּי לוֹ בְּאַהֲבָה מְסוּתֶּרֶת אֲשֶׁר בְּלֵב כְּלָלוּת יִשְׂרָאֵל שֶׁנִּקְרָאוּ ״אוֹהֲבֵי שְׁמוֹ״ (תהלים סט, לז).

Rather, the latent, **concealed love** for God **that is in the heart of the collective of Israel, who are referred to as "those who love His name"** (Ps. 69:37), **suffices for him.**

A natural love for God is embedded in the heart of every Jew, referred to by the author of the *Tanya* as "concealed love." Here the author merely mentions the existence of such love and reserves a fuller treatment for ensuing chapters.[3] In this chapter, he merely mentions its

3. See chap. 18ff.

existence, because this love is a prerequisite. Without it, why should the no-nonsense intellectual, sensorially numb individual engage in Torah study rather than other disciplines? He does so only because he is a Jew with a latent love for God, an essential bond to Him and His Torah, irrespective of whether or not he is consciously aware of such love. The path upon which he embarks is the default of his being. Torah study and the meticulous fulfillment of mitzvot then generate positive feelings within him, not only on account of the extrinsic benefits he associates with his studies and mitzva performance, but even by virtue of their intrinsic holiness. Yet his dedication to holy matters is little more than a character trait, an inborn inclination. It is not a connection to God that results from his supreme efforts, but rather a connection formed from within his comfort zone and natural state of being. He is naturally immersed within a life of Torah and his Jewish heritage, and that is the only reason he is drawn to this path. This natural bent keeps him within the fold as a proper Jew. ☞

וְלָכֵן אֵינוֹ נִקְרָא עוֹבֵד כְּלָל, כִּי אַהֲבָה זוֹ הַמְסוּתֶּרֶת אֵינָהּ פְּעוּלָּתוֹ וַעֲבוֹדָתוֹ כְּלָל אֶלָּא הִיא יְרוּשָּׁתֵנוּ מֵאֲבוֹתֵינוּ לִכְלַל יִשְׂרָאֵל, וּכְמוֹ שֶׁיִּתְבָּאֵר לְקַמָּן.

Therefore, he is not at all considered one who serves God, **because this concealed love is not** a result of **his actions or efforts whatsoever, but rather it is our heritage from our forefathers to the Jewish people, as will be explained below** (chaps. 18, 44).

A NATURAL SCHOLAR

☞ The story is told of a scholar who traveled to the famed Rabbi Yaakov Orenstein, the author of *Yeshuot Yaakov*, to receive rabbinical ordination. Rabbi Orenstein's custom was to rely on his son to examine the character of a newcomer. On this occasion, after careful observation, his son recommended against granting ordination to their visitor. Yet after speaking with the man and being impressed with his Torah knowledge, Rabbi Orenstein decided to ordain him nonetheless.

"If so," Rabbi Orenstein's son told his father, "do it quickly. If he is not soon a rabbi, he will become a priest!"

The son's impression was that this individual was interested in becoming a rabbi only because it was his natural proclivity. Yet it was conceivable that given his basic nature and potential, he could switch tracks without undue effort.

His innate feeling of connection to God, by virtue of which he is a *beinoni,* is not really his. He was born with it; he received it as an inheritance without working for it. This person, then, who turns away from evil and does only good, lives within an opportune state of affairs – a box, as it were, in which his life unfolds in proper fashion. He is not a *beinoni* on the level of one who is serving God. For him, being a *beinoni* entails no work whatsoever. It is simply the normal lifestyle for someone of his nature.

וְכֵן אַף מִי שֶׁאֵינוֹ מַתְמִיד בְּלִמּוּדוֹ בְּטִבְעוֹ, רַק שֶׁהִרְגִּיל עַצְמוֹ לִלְמוֹד בְּהַתְמָדָה גְּדוֹלָה וְנַעֲשָׂה הַהֶרְגֵּל לוֹ טֶבַע שֵׁנִי, דַּי לוֹ בְּאַהֲבָה מְסוּתֶּרֶת זוֹ,

Similarly, even one who is not by nature diligent in his Torah **study but has trained himself to study with great diligence, and** this **habit has become second nature to him, can suffice with this concealed love,**

This category of *beinoni,* who "does not serve God" because he is naturally diligent and lacks a lustful temperament, may sound extreme. Not only do such people exist, but the category includes a broader population as well: Someone who is not studious by nature but who applies himself diligently over the course of years can reach a point where his inner struggles subside and his persistence becomes habitual. After years of regular study and prayer, his efforts are not conditional on his striving and desire. They have already become ingrained. His studies do not stem from love of God or from an appreciation of their importance but because he can no longer function without them.

The principle is universal. When anyone enters a new field of endeavor in his youth with enthusiasm, his newfound habits can rewrite the basis of his entire life. He may not be able to turn himself completely inside out, to change his actual essence, but he can transform it to the extent that he no longer requires an inner battle to act effectively. At that point, his inner, hidden love for God suffices to enable him to turn away from evil and do good and be categorized as a *beinoni.*

The author of the *Tanya* is telling us that even if one has slain dragons, waged wars, and overcome obstacles, even with real achievements to his credit, none of this means that he has reached the level of "one who serves God." We see situations in the physical world too in which there can be an equilibrium, a balance, on one particular level and the effort to reach equilibrium on the next level may require a great deal of energy. Yet after that new balance is achieved, there is no longer any essential change.

When a stone rests on the ground, nothing is required to keep it there. To lift it to the roof takes a good deal of effort, but once it gets there, no further exertion is needed. It is as comfortable up high as it was on the ground. Its new location is unnatural. Getting it there took much effort, and the stone's new placement presumably offers some advantage to those who brought it. But the stone itself is unchanged, as stable and motionless as it was on the ground.

So too in matters of the spirit. As long as the faculties of the soul are not diligently applied, one is liable to reach a stasis, a level plane, without progressing further. When that happens, the person slides back to the same position he occupied before: He is serving God out of habit, not through diligent effort. The instant something becomes second nature, one behaves as though it were "first" nature.

אֶלָּא אִם כֵּן רוֹצֶה לִלְמוֹד יוֹתֵר מֵרְגִילוּתוֹ.

unless he wishes to study more than his normal practice.

In that case, neither habit nor hidden love are enough. He has to awaken within himself a revealed, powerful, and all-embracing love of God and actively serve Him. In other words, he must become "one who serves God."

וּבָזֶה יוּבַן מַה שֶּׁכָּתוּב בַּגְּמָרָא (חגיגה ט, ב) דְּ'עוֹבֵד אֱלֹהִים' הַיְינוּ מִי שֶׁשּׁוֹנֶה פִּרְקוֹ מֵאָה פְּעָמִים וְאֶחָד, וְ'לֹא עֲבָדוֹ' הַיְינוּ מִי שֶׁשּׁוֹנֶה פִּרְקוֹ מֵאָה פְּעָמִים לְבַד.

24 Tevet / 2 Shevat (leap year)

With this we can now **understand the Talmud's statement that "one who serves God" refers to one who reviews his studies one hundred and one times, while "one who does not serve Him" reviews his studies only one hundred times** (*Ḥagiga* 9b).

The Talmud's statement has been explained in various ways, mostly by way of *derush* (homiletical interpretation) and *remez* (allusion).[4] The author of the *Tanya* focuses here on the basic point: It is not an issue

4. See *Maharsha, Ḥagiga* 9b; *Kitzurim VeHe'arot LeSefer Likkuetei Amarim*, pp. 92–93.

of one hundred or one hundred and one. The issue is the measure to which one is accustomed and the measure beyond that.

וְהַיְינוּ מִשּׁוּם שֶׁבִּימֵיהֶם הָיָה הָרְגִילוּת לִשְׁנוֹת כָּל פֶּרֶק מֵאָה פְּעָמִים.

This is because in those days it was the normal practice to review each teaching one hundred times.

We need to remember that in the times of the Sages, the Oral Torah had not yet been transcribed. To learn the teachings and embed them precisely in their memory, they would repeat them as many as one hundred times.

כִּדְאִיתָא הָתָם בַּגְּמָרָא: מָשָׁל מִשּׁוּק שֶׁל חַמָּרִים שֶׁנִּשְׂכָּרִים לְעֶשֶׂר פַּרְסֵי בְּזוּזָא וּלְאַחַד עֲשָׂר פַּרְסֵי בִּתְרֵי זוּזֵי

As the Talmud states there, this concept is **analogous to the market of donkey drivers, who were hired** to travel up to **ten parasangs for one dinar** yet traveled **eleven parasangs for two dinars**

The Talmud records that in those days the donkey drivers would require one coin in payment to transport a load a distance of ten parasangs. However, to transport the same load an extra parasang, the payment amounted to two coins. To put it simply, the rate to transport a load one extra parasang was doubled, in complete disproportion to the standard rate.

מִפְּנֵי שֶׁהוּא יוֹתֵר מֵרְגִילוּתָם.

because it was a departure from their normal practice.

The Talmud explains that the difference in payments reflected the boundaries set by habit. There are limits beyond which, even if one only slightly exceeds them, one must invest great effort. In exchange for that effort, a disproportionately greater compensation is necessary. The wagon driver is familiar with the ten-mile trip. To change the itinerary, to extend it at all, goes beyond his routine and requires hard work. Consequently, the price doubles, disproportionate to the per-unit price for the original distance. In this sense, for the person in the habit of reviewing his lesson one hundred times, those one hundred times do not tax his mind and are not at all on a par with the challenge presented by the single one hundred and first time.

וְלָכֵן זֹאת הַפַּעַם הַמֵּאָה וְאַחַת הַיְּתֵרָה עַל הָרְגִילוּת שֶׁהוּרְגַּל מִנְּעוּרָיו - שְׁקוּלָה כְּנֶגֶד כּוּלָּן, וְעוֹלָה עַל גַּבֵּיהֶן בְּיֶתֶר שְׂאֵת וְיֶתֶר עָז לִהְיוֹת נִקְרָא 'עוֹבֵד אֱלֹהִים',

Therefore, the one hundred and first time devoted to reviewing a teaching, **which exceeds the normal practice that one was accustomed to since his youth, is equivalent to all** the rest **of them.** Moreover, **it surpasses them in strength and power so that he may be categorized as one who serves God.**

Breaking one's habit is tantamount to breaking one's nature, whether his "first" nature or his second nature. It is that very effort and internal war against one's nature and habits that designate a person as "one who serves God." That struggle, that battle against his own nature, takes a quantum leap the one hundred and first time he prevails over his nature so that the reward for that one hundred and first time equals the sum of all his recompense until then. For this reason, he deserves to be called "one who serves God." ☞

ROUTINE AND HABIT IN THE SERVICE OF GOD

☞ Here the author of the *Tanya* touches on one of the most formidable challenges in the service of God: routine. It is the Achilles' heel of anyone who fears God. At a certain point, everything becomes habit, and at that moment, one is no longer serving God. A person may be able to do things that in the eyes of others are unimaginably difficult, but for him they are not service. They require no work or effort at all.

When we see someone poring over holy books day and night, there is no reason to assume that he is serving God more than his neighbor for whom the fulfillment of the mitzvot on a high level seems remote. Once a person reaches a certain level of effort, and he becomes accustomed to it and allows this to be his norm, he is no longer one who is serving God.

Perhaps he was once. Regarding the verse "Pinḥas son of Elazar had been the chief official over them in the past; the Lord was with him" (I Chron. 9:20), the Midrash states, "Earlier He was with him, but not now" (*Vayikra Rabba* 37:4). That "the Lord was with him" in the past tense does not mean that he strayed from the path. Rather, it means that currently he is no longer one who is actively serving God. Routine kills everything, and the *beinoni* is no exception. As difficult as it is to be a *beinoni*, to be constantly aware and always achieving, now he also faces the danger of not being one who actively serves God. Although that is infinitely preferable to being a *rasha*, such a *beinoni* is flawed.

מִפְּנֵי שֶׁכְּדֵי לְשַׁנּוֹת טֶבַע הָרְגִילוּת צָרִיךְ לְעוֹרֵר אֶת הָאַהֲבָה לַה׳

This is **because in order to change the nature of habit, one must** awaken his **love for God**

To change the overfamiliar path, as difficult as that path itself might be, of fulfilling one's obligations, one must do something even more strenuous: Step outside his life's routine. To accomplish this, he awakens his love of God, and when he does so, there is a natural accompanying urge to increase his commitment to God, to give more of himself than before.

עַל יְדֵי שֶׁמִּתְבּוֹנֵן בִּגְדוּלַּת ה׳ בְּמוֹחוֹ, לִשְׁלוֹט עַל הַטֶּבַע שֶׁבֶּחָלָל הַשְּׂמָאלִי הַמָּלֵא דַּם הַנֶּפֶשׁ הַבַּהֲמִית שֶׁמֵּהַקְּלִיפָּה שֶׁמִּמֶּנָּה הוּא הַטֶּבַע.

by contemplating God's greatness in his mind so that he may govern the nature that is in the left chamber of his heart, **which is filled with the blood of the animal soul that stems from the *kelippa* from which this nature originates.**

In order to serve God, one must change his habits. A change like this requires one to realign his essential nature. This nature, including its holy elements, stems from one's animal soul, which is sustained by the divine name *Elokim* (a word sharing the same numerical value as the Hebrew word for nature, *hateva*).

The emphasis here is on the phrase "by contemplating... in his mind." The divine service of the *beinoni* entails the utilization of his mental capabilities, employing his brain to contemplate God's greatness as it is manifest in this corporeal world to whatever extent he is able. It is specifically by virtue of this natural act of contemplation that one is able to dominate and modify the nature of his animal soul. One's utilization of his conscious, natural faculties, with the objective of effecting a soul change that will allow him to push beyond his base nature, is precisely the service of God – of *Elokim* – discussed here.

וְזוֹ הִיא עֲבוֹדָה תַּמָּה לְבֵינוֹנִי.

This is a perfect service for the *beinoni*.

It is the perfect service for the *beinoni* because at the very moment that he reaches a state of repose, of being content with his spiritual state, he is already meditating on God's greatness. This in turn leads to a renewed love and fear of God together with the sentiment *How can I take it easy? This is no time to rest on my laurels. Now is the time to do more than ever!* It is a "perfect service," because he will be constantly striving to reach the pinnacle of spiritual achievement.

It is an endless effort. The moment he has succeeded in actualizing his feelings of love, he further contemplates God's greatness, and with the resultant renewed emotions of love and awe, he resolves to draw even closer to God, exceeding all his previous exertions.

אוֹ לְעוֹרֵר אֶת הָאַהֲבָה הַמְּסוּתֶּרֶת שֶׁבְּלִבּוֹ לִמְשׁוֹל עַל יָדָהּ עַל הַטֶּבַע שֶׁבֶּחָלָל הַשְּׂמָאלִי, שֶׁזּוֹ נִקְרָא גַּם כֵּן עֲבוֹדָה, לְהִלָּחֵם עִם הַטֶּבַע וְהַיֵּצֶר עַל יְדֵי שֶׁמְּעוֹרֵר הָאַהֲבָה הַמְּסוּתֶּרֶת בְּלִבּוֹ.

Alternatively, the *beinoni* **may awaken the concealed love in his heart through which he can govern the nature that is in the left chamber** of his heart**, for this is also considered service,** since this entails **waging war against** his **nature and** evil **inclination by awakening the concealed love in his heart.**

In this case, the *beinoni* is unable to achieve the aforementioned "perfect service." That level of divine service is particularly difficult for the *beinoni* to attain due to the fluctuating nature of his inner struggles and personality. But even where the *beinoni*'s emotional state does not allow for perfect service, he can nevertheless access the concealed love in his heart.

In that case, the *beinoni* can still be considered one who serves God since he is involved in the struggle against his evil inclination. Even when a person is unable to rule over his animal soul and modify his habitual nature in order to reach the level of perfect service by generating an intense love of God, he can do so through sheer willpower. If he senses that he has fallen into a rut, even if he cannot summon the strength to advance, to do more, then that in itself signals him to press forward. The process may not be infused with the same emotional charge of the perfect service, but it restarts the struggle. It may not result in an intense feeling of love for God, but it takes advantage of the hidden love he naturally possesses and the resolve of every Jew who wants to be close to God and is unwilling to be separated from Him. He experiences no profound emotions, but at least he renews the quest to rise above himself with renewed strength to engage in the struggle and continue to serve God.

מַה שֶּׁאֵין כֵּן כְּשֶׁאֵין לוֹ מִלְחָמָה כְּלָל, אֵין אַהֲבָה זוֹ מִצַּד עַצְמָהּ נִקְרֵאת עֲבוֹדָתוֹ כְּלָל.

This is not the case when he wages no battle at all, for **this love in itself is not considered his** personal **service whatsoever.**

When the *beinoni* is attached to God and habitually studies Torah and performs mitzvot through this hidden love alone without making any undue effort, then it is not at all considered his service. It is instead, as mentioned above, simply the inheritance of every Jew from his forefathers.

This chapter's message lies in the verse quoted in its opening words: "You will return and see...." Though the distinction between the righteous and the wicked is self-evident, the prophet states, "You will return and see the difference between the righteous and the wicked." The *beinoni* is told time after time, "Look again. Look and see." He has already achieved the level of "Do not be wicked." He has achieved, as much as he is able, that of "Be righteous." As far as he is concerned, he is just fine. Then we tell him, "Look again!" The *beinoni* must examine himself once more, not only to see whether he is still a *beinoni,* whether he has transgressed any prohibition or failed to fulfill an injunction. On the contrary, if he feels so certain that he has not overlooked anything, even the fine print, this should cause warning lights to flash. He must look yet again to assess whether he is one who is serving God or one who is not serving Him.

The *beinoni* must always stride into battle. If he is not there, this does not mean that he has transgressed. Rather, it is evidence that he has ceased to live. His life centers on being one who actively serves God, and that means continual struggle, an unending progression, always taking more on himself, forever exceeding the limitations of habit and perception, doing whatever it takes. Then, and only then, is he considered "one who serves God."

Chapter 16

THE PREVIOUS CHAPTER DISCUSSED THE DISTINCTION between the *beinoni* "who serves God" and "one who does not serve Him." At the conclusion of the previous chapter, the author of the *Tanya* described the "perfect service" of the *beinoni* who actively serves God. By contemplating God's greatness, he awakens a new and intense love for God that is so powerful that it stymies all the temptations and weaknesses that threaten the *beinoni* in his quest for closeness to God, even breaking his good habits so that he may overcome the pitfalls of routine and habitual service, propelling him higher and higher.

The author of the *Tanya* also introduced another type of service, one that is imperfect, practiced by one who lacks the ability to generate this level of love for God. This chapter will further explore both these pathways of divine service and show how every person has the potential to achieve the status of *beinoni* through them, perhaps even attaining the level of *beinoni* who actively serves God out of love and awe, the one described as "one who serves God."

וְזֶה כְּלָל גָּדוֹל בַּעֲבוֹדַת ה' לַבֵּינוֹנִים: **This, then, is a primary principle pertaining to the *beinoni*'s service of God:** 25 Tevet / 3 Shevat (leap year)

The fundamental principle noted here refers to the first of the two types of divine service mentioned in the previous chapter: the perfect service. The second fundamental principle, that which applies to the imperfect service of the *beinoni*, is addressed later in this chapter. These two paths of divine service are indeed fundamental to the *beinoni*'s journey, and the author of the *Tanya* will expand on them at length throughout the rest of the book.

הָעִיקָּר הוּא לִמְשׁוֹל וְלִשְׁלוֹט עַל הַטֶּבַע שֶׁבֶּחָלָל הַשְּׂמָאלִי

The main thing is for the *beinoni* **to rule and govern the natural inclinations that abide in the left chamber** of his heart

As explained above, the abode of the animal soul is the left chamber of the heart.[1] In view of this, the author of the *Tanya* here is referring to gaining dominion over the attributes and faculties of the animal soul. These are not necessarily evil in and of themselves. Rather, they are inherent in the individual's nature, akin to biological functions.

עַל יְדֵי אוֹר ה׳ הַמֵּאִיר לַנֶּפֶשׁ הָאֱלֹהִית שֶׁבַּמּוֹחַ, וְלִשְׁלוֹט עַל הַלֵּב כְּשֶׁמִּתְבּוֹנֵן בְּמוֹחוֹ בִּגְדוּלַּת אֵין סוֹף בָּרוּךְ הוּא, לְהוֹלִיד מִבִּינָתוֹ רוּחַ דַּעַת וְיִרְאַת ה׳ בְּמוֹחוֹ,

through God's light, which illuminates the divine soul abiding in the brain and thereby enables him to **govern the heart.** This occurs **when he contemplates in his mind the greatness of *Ein Sof*, blessed be He,** in order **to generate a spirit of knowledge and fear of God in his mind through his** faculty of **understanding.**

In the most general terms, the *beinoni*'s task is to rule over his natural inclinations, his primal desires, through meditation on the greatness of *Ein Sof*.

As mentioned in the previous chapter, the proper and complete service of God that is appropriate for a *beinoni* should evolve from an internal fervor encompassing his whole being, not merely from the lowest, subliminal levels, from the latent, unconscious love embedded within every Jew. It should include a full awareness and rich emotional experience, and it should inform his everyday activities. This is of prime importance, because when a person does something while fully engaging his psyche, harnessing his consciousness and emotions, he relates entirely to whatever he does. This is the "perfect service" of

1. See chap. 9.

the *beinoni,* which entails "generating a spirit of knowledge and fear of God" through active, focused concentration and effort. When there is something lacking in his service of God, that missing element, whether awareness or feeling, is liable to belong to a realm other than that which is holy. ☞

לִהְיוֹת "סוּר מֵרָע" דְּאוֹרַיְיתָא וּדְרַבָּנָן, וַאֲפִילוּ אִיסּוּר קַל שֶׁל דִּבְרֵיהֶם חַס וְשָׁלוֹם,

This will lead him **to avoid evil with regard to both biblically and rabbinically mandated** prohibitions **and even a minor prohibition mandated by the Sages, God forbid.**

For a person's service of God to be optimal, there must be a full complement of awareness and feeling. For this reason, the author of the *Tanya* offers a "primary principle" pertaining to divine service, the path that is recommended for the *beinoni* from the very outset. This principle states that it is incumbent on a person to achieve a continually growing emotional awareness that gives rise to the love and awe of God. This, in turn, leads him to "turn away from evil" and avoid transgression.

FULLY ENGAGED IN DIVINE SERVICE

☞ When someone is hungry, his relationship to food totally engages him. According to the Talmud, "before a person eats and drinks, he has two hearts; after he eats and drinks, he has only one" (*Bava Batra* 12b). As long as a person is hungry, he cannot be fully immersed in anything else, because at least part of him is thinking about food. Once he is satiated, though, his full attention can be engaged in whatever he is doing: He knows what he must do, he wants to do it, and he does so, with the total engagement of his personality. This does not mean that whenever one eats, his metaphysical powers are involved as well, only that one's awareness and feelings of hunger and appetite meld seamlessly with whatever he is doing.

From another perspective, suppose one's dinner were served, his bread, salad, meat, and dessert, in one homogeneous slab. Nutritionally, of course, nothing would be absent, but anyone sitting down to such a meal would be hard pressed to give it his full attention. It is certainly healthy, he might conclude, and worth his while to eat. He does his duty, chewing and swallowing, but at best only a reluctant fraction of his consciousness is actively involved.

Something similar happens on occasion when a person dons *tefillin* and prays with reduced concentration and feeling. He knows that prayer is something he is obligated to do and that his soul will benefit. Yet to a significant degree, his heart, the full capacity of his psyche, is not in it.

The measure of the *beinoni*'s efforts, the more he works and toils, determines the boundaries of his holy existence, until the *beinoni* rejects anything that conflicts with it, which constitutes first and foremost anything prohibited by the Torah. Yet this applies not only to the Torah's strict prohibitions, where the very thought of violating them is instinctively repellent, but also to the detailed and more easily disregarded prohibitions instituted by the Sages.

וְאַהֲבַת ה׳ בְּלִבּוֹ בֶּחָלָל הַיְמָנִי בַּחֲשִׁיקָה וַחֲפִיצָה לְדָבְקָה בּוֹ בְּקִיּוּם הַמִּצְוֹת דְּאוֹרַיְיתָא וּדְרַבָּנָן, וְתַלְמוּד תּוֹרָה שֶׁכְּנֶגֶד כּוּלָּן.

Meditating on God's greatness also evokes feelings of **love for God in the right chamber of his heart, with a yearning and desire to cleave to Him by fulfilling the commandments, both biblically and rabbinically mandated, and** by engaging in **Torah study, which is equivalent to them all.**

When a heartfelt desire to fulfill the mitzvot is evoked in one's soul, he pursues all precepts, both those he may consider important and those he views as unimportant, those mandated by the Torah and those mandated by the Sages, to the best of his ability and with fervor.

The author of the *Tanya* goes on to highlight one particular mitzva, the study of Torah, which he points out is "equivalent to them all."[2] The obligation to study Torah has no limits; every individual is required to invest maximal time in this pursuit every day of his life.[3] In this sense, one's Torah study is equivalent to them all, because at every moment, even when he has no other mitzva to perform, he must nevertheless engage in Torah study. Someone who fulfills this commandment properly not only fulfills all the mitzvot; he does nothing else.[4]

2. See Mishna *Pe'a* 1:1.
3. See Rambam, *Mishneh Torah, Sefer HaMadda, Hilkhot Talmud Torah* 1:10.
4. See chap. 37 for additional explanations of this principle.

וְיָתֵר עַל כֵּן, צָרִיךְ לֵידַע כְּלָל גָּדוֹל בַּעֲבוֹדָה לַבֵּינוֹנִים, שֶׁגַּם אִם אֵין יַד שִׂכְלוֹ וְרוּחַ בִּינָתוֹ מַשֶּׂגֶת לְהוֹלִיד אַהֲבַת ה׳ בְּהִתְגַּלּוּת לִבּוֹ

Moreover, one must know another **primary principle pertaining to the** divine **service of the *beinoni*: Even if his mind and spirit of understanding are incapable of generating a conscious love for God in his heart**

As discussed in the previous chapter, the divine service appropriate for the *beinoni*, his "perfect service," is predicated on his ability to evoke emotion through rational thought, by consciously directing his mind to something specific and thereby become emotionally connected to it.

The assumption here is that everyone is capable of ruling over his thoughts. Yet even if one is also able to direct his thoughts toward something specific, which is not a simple thing in itself and requires much focus and practice, there is no guarantee of an emotional response. The *beinoni* must traverse a bridge – not at all self-evident – from intellectual comprehension to the realm of feelings. When a person is incapable of making this transition, mental acuity and an understanding of God's greatness are insufficient alone to engender a love of God in one's heart.

Chabad literature offers accounts of individuals who, after years and sometimes decades of striving and working on themselves achieved such an in-depth comprehension.[5] They posit that this is possible even for an ordinary Jew if he has a burning desire to achieve it and he works ceaselessly and energetically over the course of years. But this is totally dependent on single-minded striving, intense motivation, and mental preparations that go beyond most people's capacities. ☞

CROSSING THE BRIDGE

☞ The ability to bridge the gap between conceptual understanding and the realm of the emotions is, first of all, a matter of the intellect. Some individuals have the capacity to generate mental imagery so vivid that they can build an entire

5. See *Sefer HaToledot Rabbi Dovber* (5728), p. 54, regarding the hasid Reb Yekutiel Liepler.

שֶׁיִּהְיֶה לִבּוֹ בּוֹעֵר כְּרִשְׁפֵּי אֵשׁ וְחָפֵץ בַּחֲפִיצָה וַחֲשִׁיקָה וּתְשׁוּקָה מוּרְגֶּשֶׁת בַּלֵּב לְדָבְקָה בּוֹ,

to the extent **that his heart burns like sparks of fire and desires to cleave to God with palpable feelings of desire, yearning, and longing in the heart,**

The difference between desire and yearning pertains not to content but rather to emotional charge. Desire is one's inner longing, not the act of choosing the best in a given situation but the internally endorsed expression of one's will – what the individual truly wants. Yearning is not only a desire for something but also the sense that something is missing. The heart burns for that which it lacks. Everyone desires to eat, but one does not always yearn to do so. When hunger enters the picture, so does yearning, and when one is famished, one actually feels the yearning in his heart, the "palpable feelings of desire, yearning, and longing in the heart."[6] The same dynamic applies when a person is starved for holiness: He yearns to cleave to God.

superstructure of associations on it. Such imagery affects a person not only emotionally but even physically. Some people can make their hair literally stand on end, not by controlling otherwise involuntary muscle reflexes but by visualizing extreme cold or fear.

But many people, among them individuals with great wisdom and insight, lack the facility to create imagery that will put their emotions into play. They may grasp verbal abstractions, they may compose words and play with them, but no more than that. A convincing mental picture is beyond their reach.

In the artistic or purely intellectual spheres, it is not rare to encounter someone who is unable to feel what he sees or hears. It is not that he cannot process and understand the message being conveyed. He understands the words being said, he can identify the picture he sees, but he cannot create the requisite internal matrix that can act as a conceptual springboard so that he might relate the words or image to other, related ideas.

A common example: The earth is, of course, round. It might follow that people on one side of the planet stand with their heads above and their feet below, while people on the other side stand with their heads below and their feet above. Not everyone would arrive at this skewed picture, yet many might imagine something like it. Many people, even in our own times, could not construct a more comprehensive picture of space. It is not that they are unaware that wherever people are on the planet, they walk with their feet below, but their intellectual grasp falls short of con-

6. See also *Bereshit Rabba* 80:7 and commentary on chap. 3 above regarding the distinctions between these terms.

רַק הָאַהֲבָה מְסוּתֶּרֶת בְּמוֹחוֹ וְתַעֲלוּמוֹת לִבּוֹ he possesses **instead the love concealed in his mind and the hidden recesses of his heart.**

Every insight we have of the Divine evokes, to some degree or another, love or fear of God, yet it does not always awaken a powerful emotional feeling to the extent that it is accompanied by "palpable feelings of desire, yearning, and longing in the heart." It may be that the love or fear is manifest only in the mind and intellect, so that one may acknowledge the emotion without actually feeling it. In that event, the love is not manifest in the heart. Rather, it is confined to the mind and creates a conscious inclination toward the Divine.[7] This should not be confused with the latent love that every Jew harbors in his heart. That love is not

structing a tangible image at such a level of abstraction.

A similar problem confronts many people in visualizing three dimensions from a two-dimensional sketch. Those who cannot evoke such imagery may be quite adept at working with maps, copying them, and making decisions based on them without ever truly understanding what they are seeing.

Moreover, thought alone is not always sufficient to build a complete picture, and a faulty image cannot depict an objective reality to which one can relate with conscious love or fear. It is the intellect that creates visualizations, and an incorrect image indicates a flaw in the intellect's ability to achieve an accurate understanding.

A similar distinction can be found in the verse "He will say on that day: Behold, this is our God; we hoped for Him, and He will save us..." (Isa. 25:9). The commentaries explain that "on that day" refers to the day of revelation, when all will recognize the existence of the Divine. Then it will be possible to point one's finger and say, "This is where we have placed our hope all this time. This is what we have always believed in – it is Him! After all the time we spoke of Him, believed in Him, sacrificed our lives for Him, and saw nothing and felt nothing, now we can point and say, 'Behold, this is our God!'" (see *Ta'anit* 31a).

The transition from *hu* ("that day") to *zeh* ("this is our God") is a fundamental switch. Regarding *hu,* one can contemplate and articulate words. But regarding *zeh,* one points with his finger! The instant one's perception of God changes from *hu* to *zeh,* no further explanation is needed, neither about love nor about awe. It is self-evident.

But desire to reach this level alone is not enough. It cannot be accomplished except through the exhaustive efforts of the soul, and this is generally beyond most individuals to attain on their own.

7. The concept noted here is what is known as "understanding of the heart." The root of all emotions, before becoming manifest in the heart, is in the mind.

a product of the intellect but rather is the natural love that every Jew inherits, as will be explained below.

הַגָּהָה: וְהַסִּיבָּה לָזֶה הִיא מִפְּנֵי הֱיוֹת הַמּוֹחִין שֶׁלּוֹ וְנֶפֶשׁ רוּחַ וּנְשָׁמָה שֶׁלּוֹ מִבְּחִינַת עִיבּוּר וְהֶעְלֵם תּוֹךְ הַתְּבוּנָה וְלֹא מִבְּחִינַת לֵידָה וְהִתְגַּלּוּת, כַּיָּדוּעַ לְיוֹדְעֵי חֵ"ן.

Gloss: The reason that this is so is that his intellect and his *nefesh*, *ruaḥ*, and *neshama* stem from the state of gestation and concealment within the supernal faculty of **understanding and not from the state of birth and revelation, as known to those initiated in the esoteric wisdom** of Kabbala.

In this note, the author of the *Tanya* explains why someone's intellect might not lead to a revelation in his heart. The problem, he says, is not a lack of intellectual capacity or insufficient contemplation. Rather, this is a far more basic issue relating to the entire soul, one's *nefesh, ruaḥ,* and *neshama*.

It could be said that there are two stages in the development of emotions: pregnancy and birth.[8] Pregnancy is the stage of concealment and internal development, while birth is revelation and outward manifestation. For some, the soul is in a state of birth, so that their intellectual and emotional faculties are outwardly manifest. When their intellect is aroused, a wave of activity is automatically unleashed in their heart as well. In those whose souls are in a state of pregnancy, whose faculties are not revealed, their souls function on a hidden, less sentient level.

When the mind is in a state of gestation, of pregnancy, thoughts operate in creative mode. As long as this thought process ensues, no finalization is reached. No complete picture drawn from the mind's perceptions can be realized, nor will those perceptions evoke overt emotions.

All this depends on how well the soul in general, and not only

---

"Understanding of the heart" refers to the level where one attains an understanding of a particular idea or concept prior to its penetrating his heart, while it is still in the realm of the intellect. See *Kitzurim VeHe'arot LeSefer Likkutei Amarim*; *Likkutei Torah*, Num. 85b.

8. See *Torah Or* 55a; *Derekh Mitzvotekha, Korban Pesaḥ*.

its intellectual component, has developed. The more extensive its development, the greater the integration between a person's intellectual aspects and his emotions and actions. The less evolved the soul is, the wider the gap between the person's apprehension and the sensitivities and experiences that he manifests.

דְּהַיְינוּ שֶׁהַלֵּב מֵבִין בְּרוּחַ חָכְמָה וּבִינָה שֶׁבְּמוֹחוֹ גְּדוּלַּת אֵין סוֹף בָּרוּךְ הוּא דְּכוּלָּא קַמֵּיהּ כְּלָא חֲשִׁיב מַמָּשׁ. אֲשֶׁר עַל כֵּן יֶאֱתָה לוֹ יִתְבָּרֵךְ שֶׁתִּכְלֶה אֵלָיו נֶפֶשׁ כָּל חַי לִידָּבֵק וּלְהִכָּלֵל בְּאוֹרוֹ.

This means the heart comprehends, with the spirit of wisdom and understanding in the brain, the greatness of *Ein Sof*, blessed be He, namely, **that everything before Him is literally considered as nothingness, and it therefore befits God that the soul of every living being should pine for Him in order to cleave** to Him **and become subsumed in His light.**

Though the heart does not feel the yearning to cleave to God on an emotional plane, but rather it remains within its recesses, in its unborn state in the faculty of understanding, a person can intellectually understand something of God's greatness, that in relation to Him everything is as nothing. Although he can speak about this and teach it to others, he isn't actually experiencing it on a tangible level. He understands, but does not feel, that "behold, the Lord stood over him."[9] Nevertheless, though his heart may be unmoved, his mind resolves that "the soul of every living being should pine for Him in order to cleave [to Him] and become subsumed in His light." He comprehends that in the face of God's greatness, everything is nothingness, and so it is fitting to fear and love God to the point that the soul is completely nullified and subsumed in its cleaving to God. ☞

SURROGATE FEELINGS AND SOCIAL INTERACTION

☞ Practically speaking, normal personal relationships are based on feelings of this caliber. People talk about feelings, think about feelings, and act according to feelings when they have never actually gotten beyond this level, where they perceive that

9. Gen. 28:13; see also chap. 41.

וְגַם נַפְשׁוֹ וְרוּחוֹ אֲשֶׁר בְּקִרְבּוֹ - כָּךְ יָאֲתָה לָהֶן לִהְיוֹת כָּלוֹת אֵלָיו בַּחֲשִׁיקָה וַחֲפִיצָה לָצֵאת מִנַּרְתִּיקָן, הוּא הַגּוּף, לְדָבְקָה בּוֹ.

It is also fitting for his *nefesh* and *ruaḥ* within him to pine for God **with a yearning and desire to leave their casing, namely, the body, in order to cleave to Him.**

Though this individual cannot attain a love and awe that is actually felt in his heart, he can create a mental visualization of a certain feeling. This is not a direct feeling of the experience itself, the yearning to soar beyond boundaries, the longing that God will "draw me; after You we will run" (Song 1:4), but a sort of surrogate experience. He understands that this is the appropriate relationship. He cannot feel it, but he knows that this is how he should feel: to desire and yearn with his whole being to overcome the encasement of his heart and cleave to Him. ☞

such-and-such is how they should feel rather than how they actually feel. Whether love or hate, the feelings that people exhibit are not necessarily authentic. Rather, they are an intellectual group consensus that this is the correct way to react.

A person can pass through his entire life with normal, fine interrelationships. He feels that he loves and is loved in return. Others regard him as decent, generous, and compassionate. Yet not once in his lifetime did he experience a real live feeling instead of its surrogate. Perhaps he is unaware of this. A person can behave as though he were compassionate, believe he is compassionate, and possibly even try to feel that way, but never actually be compassionate. He has reached an awareness that being merciful is important, and now he is role-playing: performing the pertinent commandments, showing compassion, at times even with self-sacrifice, for less fortunate individuals, but without once feeling real compassion. Often it is only in exceptional crisis conditions that real emotion emerges, whether love, hate, or compassion.

THE WORK OF THE *BEINONI*

☞ This is a necessary reality check for the *beinoni*. He has to know that he is not a tzaddik, and he must therefore engage in a continual process of self-introspection and clarify what is a true feeling and what is not. At the same time, he needs to be cognizant that a feeling that is not authentic may be good enough for a life of truth. It is important for the *beinoni* to achieve the correct balance, where he is neither deceiving himself into believing that what he is feeling is real when it is not nor giving in to the frustration of not being able to move beyond superficial feelings. He must neither slip into false imaginings nor despair when he is unable to experience that which is beyond his capacity. He is restricted by both emotion and perception in his efforts to create convincing abstract visualizations, and that limits his ability for authentic emotions. Similitude, synthesized experience, is within his grasp, but it is far removed from the intensity of the real thing.

This limitation is necessarily the nature of the *beinoni*. If he had the resources to see that "behold, the Lord stood over him" (Gen. 28:13) tangibly and at all times, he would not be a *beinoni* but a tzaddik. In the same sense, the Sages relate that at the giving of the Torah at Mount Sinai, God held the mountain over the heads of the assembled multitudes like an overturned cask (*Shabbat* 88a). He coerced them, so to speak, to accept the Torah against their will. It is possible, however, to understand this in another way: If we attempt to envision the King of the universe revealing Himself with unconditional love, it is clear that at that moment we could hardly refuse. There was no possibility of free choice. God forced on them a mountain of love, and a mountain of love is no less compelling than a mountain-sized cask.

Theoretically, free choice is always present, but when an overwhelming sense of reality confronts us, free choice seems to vanish, for better or worse. If someone were put into a cage of lions, he would hypothetically have the choice to be afraid or not. Practically speaking, his choice is extremely limited. In the same way, a person whose reality is that God stands over him has no free choice at that moment. He is no longer a *beinoni* forever struggling between holiness and impurity, because the latter is irrelevant.

Yet the *beinoni* has a problem when presented with a revelation: The experience is fleeting and quickly passes. A moment later, it may happen, as it did immediately after the revelation at Sinai, that a golden calf is made. When a person comes to serve God the hard way, through internalized struggle, it is not possible to make a golden calf. But when he reaches such a level as a result of an outside revelation, then no change has occurred within his soul. He reached this level only because he could not say no. The next moment, when the revelation is gone, whatever internal structure he had also disappears, and that void is liable to be filled by a golden calf.

The first paragraph of the *Shulḥan Arukh* states that on waking one should contemplate that God, who fills the entire universe with His glory, is standing before him, and he should rise energetically to serve Him. One who can indeed bring this image to mind with its full tangible import need not be told to do anything. As a logical consequence, he will leap out of bed and rush to serve his Creator. The problem arises when his mental screen is blank, when he opens his eyes in the morning and, at best, knows that such a passage appears in the *Shulḥan Arukh*. Then he needs to be told, and must tell himself, what he should be feeling. On the strength of his knowing what he is supposed to feel, he can get up and do what is needed.

This is the difference between the tzaddik and the *beinoni*. The tzaddik need not be told that "nearness to God is good" (Ps. 73:28). He knows this deep within, and consequently there is no internal conflict. The *beinoni* is aware, at best, that such a verse appears in Psalms. Once the *beinoni* attains this awareness, he must apply himself to prevent this knowledge of what he ought to feel from becoming stagnant, from remaining superficial or confined to the intellectual realm, so that the feeling will become increasingly authentic. Rather than leaving in a state of cerebral gestation, he must facilitate their birth, their actualization as palpable emotion in his heart and soul.

The story is told of a young man who became attracted to hasidic teachings at

רַק שֶׁבְּעַל כָּרְחָן חָיוֹת הֵנָּה בְּתוֹךְ הַגּוּף וּצְרוּרוֹת בּוֹ כְּאַלְמְנוּת חַיּוּת.

However, they, the ***nefesh*** **and** ***ruaḥ,*** **are compelled to live in the body and are bound to it like widows of a living man.**

The soul is trapped in the body and cannot leave, like an abandoned wife who cannot remarry as long as her husband is alive and missing and, because he has forsaken her, cannot rejoin him.[10]

the dawn of Hasidism. He left his household to be with the Rebbe and remained there several years before returning home. His father-in-law was furious but at the same time rejoiced at his return. "Tell me," he said. "You spent so much time with your Rebbe. What did you learn?"

"I learned that God is everywhere!" his son-in-law replied.

His father-in-law bristled. "Are you mocking me?" He called over his maid and asked, "Where is God?"

"Everywhere," she answered.

The father-in-law turned to his son-in-law and said, "For this you were away all those years?"

"She says," his son-in-law answered. "But I know."

Such a distinction can take many years to acquire. Sometimes even a lifetime is not enough.

Along the same lines, the verse states, "The sound of my beloved is knocking" (Song 5:2). God knocks on one's door, and one must get up and open it. The person thinks to himself, *Now, when I'm lying in a warm bed, I have to get up?*

The person has a choice in this situation: Sometimes he gets up, sometimes not. But the next verse relates, "My Beloved put His hand on the latch." God has reached out His hand. He is coming into view! "My core was moved for Him," and immediately, "I arose to open for my Beloved." He gets up by himself and jumps out of bed, ready to serve God.

There are times when a person knows that God exists, and he will make his own calculations one way or the other. But at the moment of firsthand experience, when he experiences a revelation of the Divine, all his personal considerations evaporate. He jumps out of bed and runs to serve God, without allowing for any inner debates to arise.

---

10. This is a reference to the souls of Israel, referred to collectively as the "wife," while God is the "husband." These nomenclatures are alluded to in the verse "Her husband is renowned at the gates" (Prov. 31:23). Teachings of Kabbala homiletically expound this verse as follows: "Husband" alludes to God. The Hebrew word for "renowned," *noda,* connotes an intimate bond, and *she'arim,* "gates," has the same root as the term for "estimation," *mesha'er.* Thus the verse can be understood as saying, "Each [person] according to his [heart's] estimation can intimately bond with God." In our context, the author of the *Tanya* explains how these souls should be able to unite completely with God yet are barred from

וְלֵית מַחֲשָׁבָה דִילְהוֹן תְּפִיסָא בֵּיהּ כְּלָל **Their thoughts cannot grasp Him at all,**

While clothed in a body, no thought of the *nefesh* and *ruaḥ* can apprehend God. The soul dwells within the body. It acts, thinks, and feels within the confines of the body and cannot have any direct perception beyond the physical. The starting point of its thoughts depends on the body, and for this reason, it is difficult, indeed nearly impossible, for the soul to grasp abstractions. Here and there one can find people who are able to free themselves of the body partially, but the basic limitation exists at all levels, including the highest, even for someone like Moses, to whom God said, "Man shall not see Me and live" (Ex. 33:20).

In essence, we have no direct inner perception of God, neither in thought nor on the emotional, experiential plane. One knows how it should be, that "it is fitting…to pine [for God] with a yearning and desire," but he does not feel this directly or palpably. True attachment to God is beyond any wisdom or experience. Wanting it is not enough. Human souls possess neither the wisdom nor the emotional-experiential faculty to cleave to Him.

כִּי אִם כַּאֲשֶׁר תְּפִיסָא וּמִתְלַבֶּשֶׁת בַּתּוֹרָה וּבְמִצְוֹתֶיהָ, כְּמְשַׁל הַמְחַבֵּק אֶת הַמֶּלֶךְ הַנִּזְכָּר לְעֵיל. **except when they grasp and are clothed within the Torah and its commandments, analogous to one who embraces the king, as described above** (chap. 4).

It is impossible to embrace God Himself, nor can we cleave to Him. He is a consuming fire; no man can see Him and live. Yet because He has clothed Himself in the Torah and commandments in our world, when a person studies Torah and performs commandments, he, in effect, embraces God. True, the garments are so numerous and opaque that any sense of intimacy is ruled out.[11] But one can nevertheless know: At that moment, he is embracing God.

---

doing so as long as they are fettered by the corporeal body (see Rabbi Shmuel Gronem Esterman's commentary on the *Tanya*).

11. In chapter 4, the author of the *Tanya* explained how the Torah is clothed in

וְאִי לָזֹאת, יָאֲתָה לָהֶן לְחַבְּקוֹ בְּכָל לֵב וָנֶפֶשׁ וּמְאֹד,

As such, it befits them to embrace God with all their **heart, soul, and might.**

In this way, one fulfills the verse "You shall love the Lord your God with all your heart, and with all your soul, and with all your might" (Deut. 6:5).

What is this embrace that enables one to attach and unite himself with God so completely?

דְּהַיְינוּ קִיּוּם הַתַּרְיַ"ג מִצְוֹת בְּמַעֲשֶׂה וּבְדִבּוּר וּבְמַחֲשָׁבָה, שֶׁהִיא הַשָּׂגַת וִידִיעַת הַתּוֹרָה, כַּנִּזְכָּר לְעֵיל.

This means fulfilling the 613 commandments in action and speech, as well as in thought, which refers to the apprehension and knowledge of the Torah, as stated above (chap. 4).

When one fulfills the commandments of the Torah, he is able to embrace God. This entails performing the mitzvot with one's actions, speech, and thoughts. Though one could never apprehend God with his limited intellect, he can grasp God through the study of His Torah.

הִנֵּה, כְּשֶׁמַּעֲמִיק בְּעִנְיָן זֶה בְּתַעֲלוּמוֹת תְּבוּנוֹת לִבּוֹ וּמוֹחוֹ, וּפִיו וְלִבּוֹ שָׁוִין, שֶׁמְּקַיֵּים כֵּן בְּפִיו כְּפִי אֲשֶׁר נִגְמַר בִּתְבוּנַת לִבּוֹ וּמוֹחוֹ,

When one deeply ponders this matter in the hidden recesses of his heart's and mind's understanding, and his mouth and heart are in consonance in that he fulfills with his mouth in accordance with the conclusion he reached based on the understanding of his heart and mind,

In order for one's thinking to be substantive, a casual review is insufficient. One must seek ever greater clarity and depth in seeking to understand the matter at hand. He must unite with the subjects he studies "in the hidden recesses of his heart's and mind's understanding" and not merely pay lip service.

---

physical concepts, like a king clothed in many layers. Yet an embrace from the king is still an embrace, whether he is garbed in one garment or many.

דְּהַיְינוּ לִהְיוֹת בְּתוֹרַת ה׳ חֶפְצוֹ
וְיֶהְגֶּה בָּהּ יוֹמָם וָלַיְלָה בְּפִיו, וְכֵן
הַיָּדַיִם וּשְׁאָר אֵבָרִים מְקַיְּימִים
הַמִּצְוֹת כְּפִי מַה שֶּׁנִּגְמַר בִּתְבוּנַת
לִבּוֹ וּמוֹחוֹ,

namely, that his desire is God's Torah that he studies day and night using his mouth by speaking words of Torah, **while his hands and other limbs likewise fulfill the commandments in accordance with the conclusion he reached based on the understanding of his heart and mind,**

One must be prepared to shift from thoughts and feelings to word and deed. In the abstract, serving God could make good sense, but light-years can separate that notion from what one actually does. One may also connect those thoughts to himself and his experience, but he needs to take his internal experiences to heart and resolve to make them real by carrying out his resolve in speech and action.

הֲרֵי תְּבוּנָה זוֹ מִתְלַבֶּשֶׁת בְּמַעֲשֵׂה
דִּבּוּר וּמַחֲשֶׁבֶת הַתּוֹרָה וּמִצְוֹתֶיהָ
לִהְיוֹת לָהֶם בְּחִינַת מוֹחִין וְחַיּוּת,
וְגַדְפִּין לְפָרְחָא לְעֵילָּא כְּאִלּוּ עָסַק
בָּהֶם בִּדְחִילוּ וּרְחִימוּ מַמָּשׁ אֲשֶׁר
בְּהִתְגַּלּוּת לִבּוֹ

then this understanding is clothed in the actions, speech, and thoughts of the Torah and its commandments. This understanding then **serves as an intellectual impetus and life force for them,** providing them with **wings** with which **to soar upward, as if** the *beinoni* **engaged in** the Torah and its commandments **with actual fear and love that manifest themselves in his heart**

This mode of understanding awakens the soul. True, it is not a breathtaking flame that ascends by itself, without intermediaries, but it is an awakening in the sense that it impels and enlivens one's activities. It provides wings, so to speak, to the person's actions, speech, and thoughts, as the *Tikkunei Zohar* (25b) states, "Torah without awe and love of God does not rise on high," and as the author of the *Tanya* will explain, love and awe are the two wings that elevate Torah study and the commandments.[12] When one performs a mitzva with authentic feel-

12. See chap. 40.

ings of love and awe of God, the love and awe lift the action from this limited physical world to the spiritual sphere where that love and awe are revealed, each according to the spiritual landscape he inhabits.

[בַּחֲפִיצָה וַחֲשִׁיקָה וּתְשׁוּקָה מוּרְגֶּשֶׁת בְּלִבּוֹ וְנַפְשׁוֹ הַצְּמֵאָה לַה׳ מִפְּנֵי רִשְׁפֵּי אֵשׁ אַהֲבָתוֹ שֶׁבְּלִבּוֹ כַּנִּזְכָּר לְעֵיל],

(with palpable feelings of desire, longing, and yearning in his heart and soul that thirst for God on account of the love for Him in his heart that is as fierce as **sparks of fire, as mentioned above),**

Although this individual does not attain love and awe on the emotional plane, he nevertheless acquires a conceptual love and awe as an abstract intellectual experience. This is not a fierce emotion but rather the sense and awareness, albeit ill defined and halfway between genuine love and pure intellectual reckoning, that it is necessary to love God. But because his intention is actual implementation, it is far from abstract and irrelevant. His thinking is a reality that becomes a part of his life, an awareness that serving God with love and awe is fitting. As a result, that feeling, that cognizance, finds expression in his actions and speech, with alacrity and attention to detail as though his love of God were fully manifest in his heart.

The *beinoni*'s architecture limits him from having direct and complete experience of the Divine. Yet even with his reduced abilities, his achievements need not be inferior to those of the tzaddik. It is easier for the tzaddik, to be sure, and avenues and methods are open to him that are forever unattainable to a *beinoni*. But by virtue of his service and his endless effort, the *beinoni* brings about a spiritual tour de force that would normally be beyond the scope of his own soul's attachment to God and equal to that of a tzaddik.

Perhaps the *beinoni*'s constructs are not those of the classic tzaddik, but they too possess beauty and holiness, although of a different nature. The unique virtue of the *beinoni*'s service lies in his very limitations, that despite them, he serves God. For this reason, the *beinoni* must not invest himself in matters that do not present a challenge. He must not rely on habit or routine. He must arouse his heart's and mind's understanding at all times, pondering deeply all matters related to his divine service. Even when he cannot perceive them directly, he can ponder them in the "hidden recesses of his heart's understanding" on a level parallel to that which the tzaddik is able to attain.

הוֹאִיל וּתְבוּנָה זוֹ שֶׁבְּמוֹחוֹ וְתַעֲלוּמוֹת לִבּוֹ הִיא הַמְבִיאָתוֹ לַעֲסוֹק בָּהֶם, וְלוּלֵי שֶׁהָיָה מִתְבּוֹנֵן בִּתְבוּנָה זוֹ לֹא הָיָה עוֹסֵק בָּהֶם כְּלָל, אֶלָּא בְּצָרְכֵי גוּפוֹ לְבַד

since this understanding in his mind and the hidden recesses of his heart is precisely **that which prompts him to engage in** the Torah and its commandments. **If he had not contemplated** God's greatness **with his** faculty of **understanding, he would never have engaged in them at all, but** would have been occupied **solely with his bodily needs.**

When a person studies Torah and fulfills the commandments, he does so because he has love and awe of God. He simply wouldn't do it otherwise. Although his actions may not light up the sky with a powerful display of emotion, and the love and awe may lack spiritual clarity, the fact that he is engaged in Torah and commandments indicates beyond a doubt that they are present and active within him.

[וְגַם אִם הוּא מַתְמִיד בְּלִמּוּדוֹ בְּטִבְעוֹ,

(Even if by nature he is diligent in his studies,

The author of the *Tanya* notes that his words apply not only to a *beinoni* who serves God but even to a *beinoni* "who does not serve Him."[13] As the previous chapter described, someone apathetic yet intellectually inclined, comfortably ensconced in a Jewish lifestyle and studying Torah, who neither knows nor wishes to know anything else, may from time to time imagine himself to be perfect – a tzaddik. The author of the *Tanya* explained that not only is such a person not a tzaddik at all, but he is not even one who serves God.

13. See chap. 15.

אַף עַל פִּי כֵן, אוֹהֵב אֶת גּוּפוֹ יוֹתֵר בְּטִבְעוֹ].

nevertheless he naturally loves his body more.)

Though at first glance his service of God does not stem from love and awe but rather from habit, were it not for those two attributes, he would solely be occupied with his physical needs. A person's base nature, that of his animal soul, is to first and foremost forge an inextricable bond with his body. That is his first love. If he did not possess a latent capacity to love and fear God, his physical needs and desires would take center stage.

Even if he is intellectual by nature and relishes Torah study, he still must decide what, which way, and how much to learn. These choices are rooted in his service, commensurate with the measure of love and awe he possesses. Though in his present state he cannot reach the zenith of divine service, these qualities elevate him beyond the level of plain existence, propelling him toward the plane of holiness.

26 Tevet וְזֶה רָמְזוּ רַבּוֹתֵינוּ זַ״ל בְּאָמְרָם: "מַחֲשָׁבָה טוֹבָה הַקָּדוֹשׁ בָּרוּךְ הוּא מְצָרְפָהּ לְמַעֲשֶׂה" (קידושין מ, א). וַהֲוָה לֵיהּ לְמֵימַר: מַעֲלֶה עָלָיו הַכָּתוּב כְּאִלּוּ עֲשָׂאָהּ.

Our Rabbis alluded to this in their statement "The Holy One, blessed be He, links a good thought to an action" (*Kiddushin* 40a). **The** Talmud **should have said, "The verse ascribes him** credit **as if he had** actually **performed it."**

Most commentaries explain that this talmudic statement indicates that although a good thought might not be actualized, God will nevertheless consider it as done. As the Talmud continues, "Rav Asi said: Even if a person intended to perform a mitzva but due to circumstances beyond his control he did not perform it, the verse ascribes him credit as if he performed the mitzva." This explanation, however, is wanting. If that were the case, the original statement would have said, "The verse ascribes him credit as if he had actually performed it." Since the Talmud specifically chose instead the expression "links a good thought to an action," there must be another dimension of understanding to the statement.

אֶלָּא הָעִנְיָן כִּי דְּחִילוּ וּרְחִימוּ שֶׁבְּהִתְגַּלּוּת לִבּוֹ הֵם הַמִּתְלַבְּשִׁים

Rather, the explanation of the **matter lies in the fact that the fear and**

בְּמַעֲשֵׂה הַמִּצְוֹת לְהַחֲיוֹתָם לְפָרְחָא לְעֵילָא.

love that are manifest in his heart are those that clothe themselves in the performance of the commandments, imbuing them with vitality with which to soar upward.

As mentioned, the author of the *Tanya* distinguishes between love and fear that are manifest in the heart as live emotions and love and fear that are concealed within the heart, when there is only the conceptual awareness and knowledge that these feelings are appropriate. When love and fear are felt intensely, when they are "manifest in the heart," then they are embodied in the performance of the mitzvot and propel them upward. As the author of the *Tanya* will explain, love and fear are the commandments' wings.[14] Though not an integral part of the commandment, they lift it from the domain of worldly action to its highest levels.

But why, specifically, do commandments take wing through their combination with the feelings of the heart? Why does the intent bound up with the emotion join together with action, whereas the intent in thought is insufficient on its own?

כִּי הַלֵּב הוּא גַּם כֵּן חוּמְרִי כִּשְׁאָר אֵבָרִים שֶׁהֵם כְּלֵי הַמַּעֲשֶׂה,

This is **because the heart is also corporeal like the other organs, which are the implements of action.**

There is no fundamental difference between the heart and the other parts of the body. The heart, like the brain, is no less material than the hand or foot. The only distinction to be made between what a hand does, what the heart feels, or what the brain thinks is that one activity is carried out by a particular set of muscles, whereas the other is a function of cells of another type.

אֶלָּא שֶׁהוּא פְּנִימִי וְחַיּוּת לָהֶם,

Yet the difference is that **it is** more **internal and** functions as the source of **their vitality.**

14. See chap. 40.

The essential difference between the heart and the rest of the body lies in the function of the body's physical components, not in their composition. The heart acts as an engine, activating the other parts of the body. The feelings of the heart, its wishes and desires, are not only functions unique to it alone but are also the driving forces that energize the other limbs. The heart is an internal power plant that powers and enlivens from within the rest of the body's functions.

In this sense, the heart is different from the brain, which is also composed of tissue. The heart is the abode of the animal or vital soul, which powers the body's actions from within. By contrast, the mind, whose abode is the brain, as well as the cognitive love and fear residing in thought, is not necessarily attached to the body or this physical world. Although physical, it acts in a manner that transcends the body's limbs rather than working internally as emotions do.

וְלָכֵן יָכוֹל לְהִתְלַבֵּשׁ בָּהֶם לִהְיוֹת לָהֶם גַּדְפִּין לְהַעֲלוֹתָם.

Therefore, the heart **can clothe itself in** the performance of the mitzvot, **functioning as wings for them to elevate them.**

Emotional experience is almost physical. Though unlike a movement that one does with his hand or foot, it is physical in that it depends on the body's chemistry. In a sense, emotional experience is a joint effort between the soul and the body, without which there would be no experience. In different terms, experience is essentially a cocktail combining conscious spiritual processes with glandular secretions and neurophysiological responses. These functions are part of a person's material existence, but directed toward the love and fear of God, they take on a meaning of their own. The emotions that are revealed in the heart, then, are at the interface between the physical and the spiritual, and for this reason, they can interact with physical commandments, becoming their wings and lifting them to a higher reality.

אַךְ הַדְּחִילוּ וּרְחִימוּ שֶׁבְּתְבוּנוֹת מוֹחוֹ וְתַעֲלוּמוֹת לִבּוֹ הַנִּזְכָּרִים לְעֵיל, גָּבְהוּ דַּרְכֵיהֶם לְמַעְלָה מַעְלָה מִבְּחִינַת הַמַּעֲשֶׂה. וְאִי

However, the aforementioned fear and love in his mind's understanding and the hidden recesses of his heart are far beyond the level of action. Consequently, **it is impossible**

אֶפְשָׁר לָהֶם לְהִתְלַבֵּשׁ בִּבְחִינַת מַעֲשֵׂה הַמִּצְוֹת לִהְיוֹת לָהֶם בְּחִינַת מוֹחִין וְחַיּוּת לְהַעֲלוֹתָן לְפָרְחָא לְעֵילָּא,

for them to clothe themselves in the performance of the mitzvot, thereby **serving as intellectual impetus and vitality, to elevate them** and causing them **to soar upward,**

The love and fear that exist within the sphere of one's intellect are only a preface to the heart's emotions. By virtue of their connection with the inner thoughts of the soul itself, both internal and transcendent, they are not related to the implements of action or physical existence.

In light of this, this cognitive love and fear cannot be embodied by the performance of mitzvot in order to elevate the actions on high, as opposed to the emotional experience that is manifest in the heart. The love and fear that are manifest in the heart as clear emotions are not wholly spiritual but rather an admixture involving the body and its mechanisms. Consequently, when someone loves God, and this love becomes revealed in his heart as a true personal experience, when he feels the same passion for closeness to God that he has for the things of this world, then this love lends wings to his mitzva so that it may soar above the material world.

This is in contrast to the primal emotions of love and fear implanted in the inner recesses of the heart and the intellect of the mind. These hitherto subconscious emotions possess a wholly spiritual orientation, resulting in a tenuous and abstract relationship with the person's self, the part of his being that functions in the physical body and interacts with the material world. They are like a spiritual force that merely encompasses one's manifest faculties, existing in a general, conceptual sense but not experienced by the physical faculties that animate the body. ☞

REVEALED LOVE VERSUS LOVE IN THE RECESSES OF THE HEART

☞ A paradox seems to exist here. The love and fear hidden within one's mind and the inner recesses of one's heart can neither influence the body nor elevate the commandments. They are too lofty. The love and fear that are manifest as real emotions in the heart are more grounded, almost physical. Yet they, specifically, cause the commandments to rise.

When a person loves deeply and that

אִם לֹא שֶׁהַקָּדוֹשׁ בָּרוּךְ הוּא מְצָרְפָן וּמְחַבְּרָן לִבְחִינַת הַמַּעֲשֶׂה. וְהֵן נִקְרָאוֹת בְּשֵׁם "מַחֲשָׁבָה טוֹבָה" כִּי אֵינָן דְּחִילוּ וּרְחִימוּ מַמָּשׁ בְּהִתְגַּלּוּת לִבּוֹ כִּי אִם בְּתְבוּנַת מוֹחוֹ וְתַעֲלוּמוֹת לִבּוֹ כַּנִּזְכָּר לְעֵיל.

if not for the fact that the Holy One, blessed be He, links and joins them to the element of action. These are referred to as a "good thought" because they are not fear and love that are actually revealed in the heart, but rather in his mind's understanding and the hidden recesses of his heart, as stated above.

As the author of the *Tanya* quoted above, "The Holy One, blessed be He, links a good thought to an action." The "good thought" is the love and awe of God that exists within the mind alone, the notion that "yes, this is worthwhile." But because the thought is unconnected

love is "manifest in his heart," he will do something to express this feeling, but that emotion has no intrinsic advantage over whatever expression it calls forth. This feeling is essentially no different from any other physical function. By contrast, the love that is hidden within the heart, which can only be experienced metaphorically as an emotion in potential, finds no expression at all in the body. Its domain lies solely within the dynamics of the soul. It lies beyond the experiences of this world, close by but not within them. Therefore, it is expressly the love hidden within the heart, the potential to love, that is of a higher and more abstract order. The potential that can create love is, in essence, utterly spiritual and towers above the actual love one feels. On the other hand, it is the physical emotions, which draw the spiritual down to the physical, that can also elevate the physical to the spiritual.

By way of example, when a person writes or paints a picture, he uses his hand. Yet one's ability to paint does not exist in the hand, whose muscles merely carry out the work. There exists a similar distinction within the soul itself. There is the deep awareness of the content or image one wishes to write or paint, and then there are the lower emotive faculties of the soul, which possess the ability to translate that awareness into physical action, to motivate the body to physically paint the picture. Mere cognizance without interconnectedness with the emotions can never become manifest in the material reality. It is specifically the second, lower aspect of the soul, whose hint of corporeality obstructs it from internalizing the spiritual essence of the painting, that stimulates the hand to draw.

This distinction in the *nefesh* level of the soul also exists in the *neshama* level. Everyone's soul includes aspects of the most sublime nature: powers of prophecy, holiness, and purity. Yet they are abstractions, unrelated to the conscious self. The fact that one's soul is a portion of God on high may not always have a meaningful effect on our physical lives. True, the highest level of the soul, the *yeḥida,* is linked directly to God, but practically speaking this is irrelevant to our everyday lives. When does to any action one might do, but rather each is a discrete entity, God unites thought with deed, integrating them on an inner and essential level.

Some mitzvot already have wings. Others need to be outfitted with them by God, who takes the inherently distant love and awe – the wings – and joins them to action. ☞

it make a difference? When a person actualizes this aspect of his soul.

When people speak of a good person, they make no mention of the root of his soul, the pure soul with which he was imbued. They are referring to the expressions of his soul in a this-worldly context. The highest and most concealed levels of the soul have very little to do with the person's self, except for those occasions when one purposefully directs his attention to them. When a person does not employ his innermost soul to perform a tangible act, it is no more related to him than to any other individual.

The paradox, then – the fact that it is the fierce, almost physical emotions felt overtly in the heart that elevate one's mitzvot on high – is only ostensible. Consider the analogy of writing and painting, the incomprehensible spiritual dimension underlying these acts can be revealed only through the physical acts themselves, not through merely speaking or thinking about the subject. The same applies with regard to the soul. The revelation of the Divine occurs only by means of the lower, more corporeal emotions one experiences. More than the cognitive faculties, the emotive attributes can transmit, connect, and reveal those deeper spiritual aspects of the soul.

LINKING THOUGHT TO ACTION

☞ In kabbalistic terminology, the love and fear "in his mind's understanding and the hidden recesses of his heart" are the source of the latent attributes rooted in the *sefira* of *Bina* before they are manifest in deeds. That is, *Bina* extends only to the *sefira* of *Hod* (Splendor) but does not reach the *sefira* of *Yesod* (Foundation), which represents connection to physical actions (*Malkhut*). In this sense, these attributes of love and fear are, in kabbalistic parlance, gestating within *Bina*. As a result, they cannot be actualized as physical actions in and of themselves. In order to manifest the potential attributes in *Bina* as physical actions, a force higher than *Bina* is required. This force is the faculty of wisdom in the soul, also known in Kabbala as *Abba*, literally, "father," which is far-reaching, extending to the realm of physical action.

The attribute of *Ḥokhma* is described as "*koaḥ ma*" — the potential for what, for utter nullification. The power of nullifying oneself to God transcends understanding and apprehension, thus circumventing the limiting realm of *Bina* and reaching *Malkhut* – physical action. Only God Himself activates the attribute of *Ḥokhma*. As the author of the *Tanya* aptly expresses it, "the Holy One, blessed be He, links and joins them to the element of action."

הַגָּהָה: וּכְמוֹ שֶׁכָּתוּב בַּזּוֹהַר וְעֵץ חַיִּים, דִּתְבוּנָה אוֹתִיּוֹת בֵּ"ן וּבַ"ת, שֶׁהֵן דְּחִילוּ וּרְחִימוּ.

Gloss: As it is written in the *Zohar* and *Etz Ḥayyim*, the Hebrew word for understanding, ***tevuna*, is** comprised of **the letters** that spell the words ***ben* and *bat*,** son and daughter, **which are fear and love.**

The Hebrew word *ben*, son, represents love, and *bat*, daughter, indicates awe, and their letters appear in the word *tevuna*, understanding, which is the mother. *Tevuna* therefore encompasses the roots of love and awe, although not in their revealed form. It contains their letters alone, but not their actual combination of letters. The potential, the possibility, is there, to build the words and the revealed thoughts and emotions.

וְלִפְעָמִים הַתְּבוּנָה יוֹרֶדֶת לִהְיוֹת מוֹחִין בְּנוּקְבָא דִּזְעֵיר אַנְפִּין, שֶׁהֵן אוֹתִיּוֹת הַתּוֹרָה וְהַמִּצְוֹת.

Sometimes the *tevuna* descends to serve as the intellect for the feminine aspect of *Zeir Anpin*, which are the letters comprising the Torah and commandments.

The element of *tevuna* that is hidden within the "hidden recesses of the heart" has no inherent link to the physical action of mitzva performance, which in kabbalistic terms is the feminine aspect of *Zeir Anpin*,[15] corresponding to the *sefira* of *Malkhut*. On occasion they come together, since a person would not perform a particular action were it not for the thought telling him, "Yes, this is something you should do!" Such a thought, with its causal rather than experiential relationship to deed, is the "good thought" that God attaches to an action to provide it with wings and raise it to higher worlds.

וְהַמַּשְׂכִּיל יָבִין.

The intelligent person will understand.

This note, like most others in the book, hints at related subjects that, though not requisite for an understanding of the immediate topic,

15. *Zeir Anpin*, literally, "small countenance," is the kabbalistic term for the array of the six *sefirot* that correspond to the emotive attributes: *Ḥesed, Gevura, Tiferet, Netzaḥ, Hod*, and *Yesod*.

are worthwhile for experienced students of Kabbala and Hasidism to pursue.

אַךְ צֵירוּף זֶה מְצָרֵף הַקָּדוֹשׁ בָּרוּךְ הוּא כְּדֵי לְהַעֲלוֹת מַעֲשֵׂה הַמִּצְוֹת וְעֵסֶק הַתּוֹרָה הַנַּעֲשִׂים עַל יְדֵי מַחֲשָׁבָה טוֹבָה הַנִּזְכֶּרֶת לְעֵיל עַד עוֹלַם הַבְּרִיאָה, מְקוֹם עֲלִיַּית הַתּוֹרָה וְהַמִּצְוֹת הַנַּעֲשִׂים עַל יְדֵי דְחִילוּ וּרְחִימוּ שִׂכְלִיִּים אֲשֶׁר בְּהִתְגַּלּוּת לִבּוֹ מַמָּשׁ.

However, the Holy One, blessed be He, links the mind's understanding to deed **in order to elevate the act of** performing **the commandments and Torah study, which are accomplished with the aforementioned "good thought," to the world of *Beria*.** This world is **the place to which the Torah** study **and commandments ascend when performed with cognitive fear and love that are actually manifest in his heart.**

To which destination do the wings of love and awe carry Torah study and mitzvot?

All reality exists within a system of four worlds at successive levels of holiness: *Atzilut* (Emanation), *Beria* (Creation), *Yetzira* (Formation), and *Asiya* (Action). The place where we perform the commandments is the world of *Asiya* – more precisely, that of physical action.

The next, higher level is the world of *Yetzira*, also called the world of angels, which is the dimension of emotions within the realm of holiness. The pure reality of angels consists of feeling alone, of love, awe, or other emotions. In contrast to man, who is a collage of infinite components, the angel is a being of single focus with a singular unadulterated and powerful emotion. For instance, every angel of the camp of Michael represents a particular aspect of love, whereas the angels in the camp of Gabriel express specific aspects of awe.

Above them is *Beria*, the world of consciousness and the domain of the seraphim, beings of pure perception far removed from the complexity of human existence. This is the realm to which the mitzvot ascend.

A mitzva is an act performed in the physical realm of *Asiya*. By giving charity, for example, we transfer money or an item from one place to another. The mitzva of *lulav*, performed on the festival of Sukkot, entails taking palm branches, binding them together, and shaking them back and forth. Other than rearranging objects in a physical world, we do not appear to be doing much. In truth, as long as the higher soul levels are uninvolved, there is no impact beyond the material world; the action remains below in the physical world of *Asiya*. Yet when a spiritual element is infused in the act, when it is accompanied by Heaven-directed feeling and cognizance, the mitzva assumes significance and rises to a higher level.

When one's performance of mitzvot is fully experienced by the soul, when love and awe are more than intellectualizations and a full awareness awakens real emotions, this fusion of intellect and feeling elevate the mitzva to the world of *Beria*, the world of consciousness and pure perception. When it comes to cognitive fear and love, there is a fusion of emotion and intellect, so that the fear and love can raise the mitzva act. For this reason, even a "good thought" alone, which is unable to connect to deed without God's uniting force, elevates the mitzva to the world of *Beria*. Since the two, thought and deed, have been linked, the mitzva act can rise to the world of consciousness.

אֲבָל בְּלָאו הָכִי נַמִּי עוֹלִים לְעוֹלַם הַיְצִירָה עַל יְדֵי דְחִילוּ וּרְחִימוּ טִבְעִיִּים הַמְסוּתָּרִים בְּלֵב כָּל יִשְׂרָאֵל בְּתוֹלְדוֹתָם,

But even **were they not** united with a good thought, **they would also ascend to the world of *Yetzira* by means of the natural, innate fear and love that are latent in the heart of every Jew,**

Even when a mitzva is not performed perfectly with love and awe, and even when it is not united with a "good thought," still it does not remain in the physical world. Since the Jewish soul contains an innate love and fear of God, this act can be raised to a higher world. Yet this latent love and fear of God do not radiate with consciousness; they are not cognitive, like the good thought that accompanied the less than perfect mitzva, and the emotional experience is only subliminal. Consequently, they elevate the mitzva act to *Yetzira*, the realm of emotions.

כְּמוֹ שֶׁיִּתְבָּאֵר לְקַמָּן בַּאֲרִיכוּת.

as will be explained below at length.

The author of the *Tanya* will go on to explain how every Jew possesses this latent awe and love, no matter his spiritual level, and how they have the power to elevate deeds beyond this physical world.

This chapter described the *beinoni*'s service of God in light of two levels of service: perfect service, infused with authentic love and fear of God, and service that constitutes a "good thought" that God links to an action. In order to attain love and fear of God to the extent that they will influence one to study Torah and perform the commandments, the *beinoni* must toil. He must invest unremitting spiritual effort, employing his intellectual resources – the faculties over which he has control. It is imperative that the awakening he experiences through those faculties does not remain in the dimension of the abstract but trickles down to his soul, to his innate feelings, effecting the appropriate changes.

This is precisely the "perfect service" of the *beinoni* of which the author of the *Tanya* speaks, service in which the *beinoni* serves God with the entire infrastructure of his soul, both the cognitive faculties and the emotive attributes.

The second category of the *beinoni*'s divine service, imperfect service, refers to a scenario where one is unable to generate from his mind's contemplation an emotionally felt love and fear of God. Rather, that love and fear remains only intellectual. Yet even in such a case, this person still possesses a latent love and fear of God, and it is only that he cannot access them fully. In that case, God links these concealed attributes to an action he performs. The author of the *Tanya* dubs these intellectual feelings of love and awe a "good thought," which God links to a "good deed," that is, to the Torah study and mitzvot that he does.

Chapter 17

THE LATTER HALF OF THE PREVIOUS CHAPTER DIScussed the second aspect of the "primary principle" pertaining to the divine service of the *beinoni*: Even one who understands intellectually that it is fitting to love God and fulfill His commandments, yet is unable to translate this understanding into a conscious love for God, is still regarded as serving God perfectly (albeit commensurate with his level). This is reckoned as divine service since he performs God's will and elevates those commandments by means of the love and fear of God that he achieved through his intellectual understanding.

This chapter takes this principle to the next level. It asserts that the very performance of a mitzva testifies to an innate love for God, because without such love, one would not have performed the mitzva. This love, although latent, is still love from the heart, a love that elevates and perfects the *beinoni*'s divine service, transporting it from the realm of action to the heart, from the body to the soul, and from there to the supernal worlds.

After explaining the full scope of the *beinoni*'s service, the author of the *Tanya* concludes the chapter by briefly addressing what transpires on the "other side" – beyond the realm of the *beinoni*.

וּבָזֶה יוּבַן מַה שֶּׁכָּתוּב: "כִּי קָרוֹב אֵלֶיךָ הַדָּבָר מְאֹד בְּפִיךָ וּבִלְבָבְךָ לַעֲשׂוֹתוֹ" (דברים ל, יד)

27 Tevet
4 Shevat (leap year)

With this, that which was discussed in the previous chapter, **we can understand the verse "Rather, the matter is very near to you, in your mouth and in your heart, to perform it"** (Deut. 30:14).

At this point, we can begin to understand this verse, which appears on the title page and is the theme of the entire book.

דִּלְכְאוֹרָה הוּא "בִּלְבָבְךָ" נֶגֶד הַחוּשׁ שֶׁלָּנוּ

On the surface, **it appears that** this statement that the words of the Torah are "**in your heart" is contrary to our experience**

To say that Torah's words are near at hand, not just for us to articulate or to perform, but that they can be near to one's heart, that one can easily feel love and awe for God while fulfilling the Torah and mitzvot, seems unrealistic and very nearly impossible.

[וְהַתּוֹרָה הִיא נִצְחִית],

(**and yet** it is axiomatic that **the Torah is eternal).**

This parenthetical note, which the author of the *Tanya* repeats numerous times, is borrowed from the teachings of the Ba'al Shem Tov.[1] One of the basic tenets of Hasidism, it asserts that the Torah is not limited to a particular time or generation. Rather, it is relevant to all times and individuals. In view of this, one cannot resolve the question by arguing that the verse was intended only for those who left Egypt, stood at Mount Sinai, and received the Torah. The words of the verse must necessarily be understood as applicable to all times and even to each and every one of us today.

שֶׁאֵין קָרוֹב מְאֹד הַדָּבָר לְהַפֵּךְ לִבּוֹ מִתַּאֲווֹת עוֹלָם הַזֶּה לְאַהֲבַת ה' בֶּאֱמֶת,

It is clearly evident **that transforming one's heart from** being focused on **the pleasures of this world to truly loving God is not a "very near matter,"**

Clearly, it is no small thing to transform one's heart, to abandon the love of other things and truly love God. It is no trifling matter for a person who is immersed in worldly affairs, whose heart is occupied with the pleasures of this world, to redirect his heart to the love of God.

---

1. See, e.g., *Ba'al Shem Tov al HaTorah,* beginning of *Parashat Ḥukat.*

וּכְמוֹ שֶׁכָּתוּב בַּגְּמָרָא (ברכות לג, ב): "אַטּוּ יִרְאָה מִילְּתָא זוּטַרְתִּי הִיא?"

as the Talmud asks, "Is fear of Heaven **a minor matter?"** (*Berakhot* 33b),

Regarding the verse "What does the Lord your God ask of you? Only to fear the Lord your God…" (Deut. 10:12), the Talmud asks: Is fear of Heaven a triviality that all God asks is "only" to fear Him? On the contrary, people invest all their strength and dedicate their entire lives to attaining fear of God.

וְכָל שֶׁכֵּן אַהֲבָה.

and all the more so regarding **love.**

It is much more difficult to achieve love of God than fear of Him. Fear is essentially passive. It does not require the effort, transformation, and passion that love does. How can it be said, then, that to fear and, moreover, to love God in our hearts is near at hand? ☞

וְגַם אָמְרוּ רַבּוֹתֵינוּ ז"ל, דְּצַדִּיקִים דַּוְקָא לִבָּם בִּרְשׁוּתָם (בראשית רבה לד, י).

Furthermore, aside from the problem posed by our experience, **our Rabbis stated that only the righteous have their hearts under their control** (*Bereshit Rabba* 34:10).

This implies that anyone who is not righteous does not have his heart under his control, and he must struggle throughout life to escape from

THE UNIQUENESS OF LOVE

☞ Why is it that love is more difficult to attain than fear? In what way do they differ? One reason given is that the ultimate love for God cannot be present in a person without his having first crushed his lusts. By contrast, a person may be afraid of God to the extent that he refrains from committing transgressions, even when he still has an underlying desire to sin. In contrast to love for God, one's fear of mundane matters and the fear of God are not mutually exclusive and can exist within a person simultaneously. Yet one cannot love the pleasures of this world and love God at the same time. Moreover, the proper sequence in the service of God is that fear of God precedes love of Him (see chap. 43). If the first quality is not easy to achieve, all the more so the second (see Rabbi Shlomo Chaim Kesselman's commentary on the *Tanya*).

his heart's dominion. A person cannot immediately reprogram his heart the moment he decides that closeness to God is worthwhile, and it is evident that the Sages were of the opinion that only the righteous have this ability. At any rate, neither the Torah nor this book solely addresses tzaddikim.

אֶלָּא דְ״לַעֲשׂוֹתוֹ״, רוֹצֶה לוֹמַר, הָאַהֲבָה הַמְּבִיאָה לִידֵי עֲשִׂיַּית הַמִּצְוֹת בִּלְבַד,

Rather, the love referred to in the verse is specifically the love regarding which the verse states **"to perform it," meaning, the love that leads merely to the performance of mitzvot,**

This touches on the essential nature of the *beinoni* that the preceding chapters described. The author of the *Tanya* draws a distinction between a state of being that entails inner changes in the heart's emotions and the actions that transpire in the realm of actual deed, the physical action one takes to express his love. It is not uncommon for a person to act a certain way because he understands that it is the proper thing to do, yet he does not necessarily feel that way on an emotional level. The words "The matter is very near to you, in your mouth and in your heart, that you may perform it" are not specifically referring to the ultimate state, to the creation of intense emotions until "in her love you will always be intoxicated" (Prov. 5:19) and "I am lovesick" (Song 2:5). Rather, this is a love that merely leads to action. In this context, "in your heart" does not plumb the emotional profundity and intensity of revealed love, but it is no less love and no less "in your heart."

שֶׁהִיא רְעוּתָא דְלִבָּא שֶׁבְּתַעֲלוּמוֹת לֵב, גַּם כִּי אֵינָהּ בְּהִתְגַּלּוּת לִבּוֹ כְּרִשְׁפֵּי אֵשׁ.

which is the deep **desire of the heart** concealed **in the hidden recesses of** a Jew's **heart, even if it is not manifest in his heart like sparks of fire.**

This is not an experiential love but rather a deep, inner, concealed love that is nestled in the inner recesses of the heart. It is not overt like the fierce love that is felt like sparks of fire, and not everyone is required to evoke the love until they experience it as a fiery love. It is sufficient to arouse the degree of love and inner resolve that inspire the deed.

וְדָבָר זֶה קָרוֹב מְאֹד וְנָקֵל לְכָל אָדָם אֲשֶׁר יֵשׁ לוֹ מוֹחַ בְּקָדְקֳדוֹ,

This matter is very near and simple to achieve **for anyone who possesses a brain in his head,**

Doesn't every person have a brain in his head? Rather, the author of the *Tanya* speaks rhetorically here. He is referring to the dimension of the mind within the soul, to the mind's voice, which differs drastically from the voice of the heart. Whereas the heart cannot contain contradictions, the mind is always able to present an alternative approach, one different from a certain mindset or from an existing emotion. It can say, "This is tempting, yet it is dangerous," or "I am not in the mood, but it is important and the proper thing to do." Therefore, even without overt love in the heart, and even contrary to overt love, one can act differently by virtue of the concealed love in his mind's understanding and the hidden recesses of his heart. ☞

כִּי מוֹחוֹ בִּרְשׁוּתוֹ, וְיָכוֹל לְהִתְבּוֹנֵן בּוֹ כְּכָל אֲשֶׁר יַחְפּוֹץ.

since one's brain is under his control and, as such, **he is capable of using it to ponder whatever he wishes.**

A person has no control over his feelings. To command oneself to love or to hate, to desire or not to desire, is beyond human capability. Yet a person's mind is under his jurisdiction. Through willpower, he can resolve to think about particular matters and not to think of others. His

BRAINS ARE A PREREQUISITE

☞ When speaking of brains, there are various types. Some have the ability to grasp the most sublime abstractions. Others appreciate only simple concepts. Yet even those whose scope of understanding is limited to the most concrete, physical images can nonetheless act in opposition to a feeling within.

A feeling, a person's internal, personal experience, is always a composite of the gamut of his soul's faculties. It follows that one's experience and its outcome will naturally be of equal intensity. For the sublime soul to bear any sort of connection to a physical achievement, to bring about an actionable outcome, there must exist a fine balance among the soul's faculties. When this is achieved, when these faculties are of the same genre, they can then interconnect and interrelate, producing the desired result.

decision, of course, is liable to be undermined by thoughts originating elsewhere, but he is always free to redirect his thoughts as he wishes.

וּכְשֶׁיִּתְבּוֹנֵן בּוֹ בִּגְדוּלַּת אֵין סוֹף בָּרוּךְ הוּא, מִמֵּילָא יוֹלִיד בְּמוֹחוֹ, עַל כָּל פָּנִים, הָאַהֲבָה לַה׳ לְדָבְקָה בּוֹ בְּקִיּוּם מִצְוֹתָיו וְתוֹרָתוֹ,

When one uses his mind **to contemplate the greatness of *Ein Sof*, blessed be He, he automatically generates in his mind, at the very least, the type of love for God** that enables the person **to cleave to Him by fulfilling His commandments and His Torah.**

Any person is capable of compelling himself to meditate on God's greatness, no less than on anything else. In the course of a day, many people go to work and occupy themselves with subjects that do not always interest them, yet they willfully direct their minds to them. So too anyone can focus his mind wherever he chooses. When he intentionally contemplates subjects that arouse his love of God, that love will automatically take form in his mind.

Love in one's mind is not the same as love in one's heart. The former is an awareness that loving Him is fitting. This is not yet an emotional experience but rather an intellectual recognition that this is an appropriate way to feel. Although this is not an emotional tempest that sweeps a person off his feet, it can lead to the same practical conclusions regarding the fulfillment of the Torah and its commandments. As with any matter, once a person realizes that something is beneficial to him, that it is worth doing, he will act accordingly.

5 Shevat (leap year)

וְזֶה כָּל הָאָדָם,

That is all of man,

These words appear in the verse "The end of the matter, everything has been heard: Fear God and observe His commandments, for that is all of man" (Eccles. 12:13). The conclusion of all processes that unfold within the soul takes place in the realm of action, and in the final analysis, it is expected that the action should entail the observance of commandments. Performing the commandments through a desire born of contemplation is "all of man" – it is his whole purpose. There are special expectations for gifted individuals, but for the rest of us, action based on a fiery love of God in the heart is not demanded. It is sufficient for one to fulfill the commandments willingly.

כִּי "הַיּוֹם לַעֲשׂוֹתָם" כְּתִיב (דברים ז, יא), שֶׁהַיּוֹם הוּא עוֹלַם הַמַּעֲשֶׂה דַּוְקָא,

since the verse states, "To perform them today" (Deut. 7:11), **where "today" refers specifically to this world of action,**

"Today" refers to this world, the world of action, a single continuum where one may "perform them." Actions are man's self-expression, as opposed to his feelings and emotions, since they take center stage in human reality. The deciding factor for the objective reality is what we do, not what we feel, and not only in this world: Human actions affect all worlds, the totality of creation. Someone who perpetrates evil, though his innermost heart is lined with good thoughts, is, in the final analysis, an evil person. Someone who performs good actions in this world and encourages others to do likewise, though his inner heart is consumed by doubts and loathsome desires, is a good person.

וּלְמָחָר כו', כְּמוֹ שֶׁנִּתְבָּאֵר בְּמָקוֹם אַחֵר.

while tomorrow, in the ultimate future, is the time to receive reward, **as was explained elsewhere.**

In this world, the world of action, a person cannot fully interconnect all parts of the soul, the thoughts and emotions, with his deeds. Only "tomorrow," in the ultimate future, when one's soul becomes thoroughly integrated with what he has done in this world of action, will it be the "time to receive reward."[2] Were it possible in this world to sense the perfection of good and holiness embodied in a single mitzva that one performs, one would do nothing other than mitzvot. The delight of one mitzva transcends whatever pleasures can be offered by this world, a place not essentially meant for recompense.

In our world, perhaps one in a thousand people can say, "The nearness of God is good" (Ps. 73:28). The closeness of God becomes tangible only "tomorrow," when the soul will receive most of the reward, emotional intensity, and pleasure that the performance of a mitzva entails.

---

2. See *Eiruvin* 22a.

וְהַמּוֹחַ שַׁלִּיט בְּטִבְעוֹ וְתוֹלַדְתּוֹ עַל חָלָל הַשְּׂמָאלִי שֶׁבַּלֵּב, וְעַל פִּיו, וְעַל כָּל הָאֵבָרִים שֶׁהֵם כְּלֵי הַמַּעֲשֶׂה,

The mind, by its inborn nature, controls the left chamber of the heart, as well as one's mouth and all the limbs, which are the implements of action,

The mind governs not only itself, its own thoughts, but it also controls one's emotional experience. This governance does not come about through a divine ordinance but is an integral part of the soul's structure. The mind cannot order the heart to stop desiring those things that the mind considers inappropriate, but it can prevent the heart from developing those desires. It is in man's nature to control the heart to the extent that it will avoid developing feelings and urges that run counter to his awareness.

Of course, there are limits to this mental sovereignty, and if a person allows himself to cultivate such feelings beyond a certain limit, the mind will lose control. The monster he himself creates and nurtures will accept little authority. Yet as long as one is levelheaded, it is possible for him to be master of his heart, mouth, and actions. Mouths cannot speak of their own accord, nor can the limbs act automatically, without a person's conscious will and awareness.

28 Tevet אִם לֹא מִי שֶׁהוּא רָשָׁע בֶּאֱמֶת,

unless he is one who is truly wicked,

Here the author of the *Tanya* adds a somewhat uncommon remark in the broader scope of this book. As the title conveys, this is the *Book of Beinonim,* while this comment pertains to the wicked. It seems that apart from the obvious message for those who are categorized as wicked, this is a lesson that is significant even for the *beinoni.* In the preceding chapters, much attention has been devoted to describing the rank of *beinoni* in relation to that of tzaddik. This present remark delimits the *beinoni* in contrast to lower ranks, the rank of *rasha.*

Until now the author of the *Tanya* was not speaking of exceptional cases but of regular people capable of becoming *beinonim.* Though such a person may not be a complete *beinoni* at the moment, and might even on occasion be considered a *rasha,* he is able to become a *beinoni* at any time because his mind rules his heart and he can direct it as he wishes. This is not the case with someone who is "truly wicked" – someone truly evil, whose iniquity is not characterized only by some misdeed or evil thought.

כְּמַאֲמַר רַבּוֹתֵינוּ זַ"ל: שֶׁהָרְשָׁעִים הֵם בִּרְשׁוּת לִבָּם וְאֵין לִבָּם בִּרְשׁוּתָם כְּלָל (בראשית רבה, לה, י; סז, ח).

in accordance with our Rabbis' statement "The wicked are controlled by their hearts, and they do not control their hearts whatsoever" (*Bereshit Rabba* 34:10, 67:8).

This process parallels drug addiction. A person's intellectual processes may still function at this stage, but he utterly lacks the strength to resist the internal and external forces that now drive him. His heart and his nonintellectual desires and cravings have taken over. Though he may want to reassert control, he cannot. There are individuals who, though not completely wicked, have reached a state in which their hearts are no longer under their control. Rational thought fails against not only their inner urges but even their behavior. They are trapped in a free fall of emotional destruction from which they cannot extricate themselves. Not that they are unaware; they may very well know that they are on the road to destruction. But the mind has lost control of the heart, and the individual finds himself careening down this path with no brakes.

וְזֶה עוֹנֶשׁ עַל גּוֹדֶל וְעוֹצֶם עֲוֹנָם.

This is a punishment for the magnitude and severity of their sinfulness.

When one enters such a cycle of transgression, in which one iniquity follows another and desire leads to desire, this is no longer part of the person's misdeed. Now it is part of his punishment. In this wretched condition, where he is quite aware of how he is destroying himself in this world and the next yet unable to free himself, lies the punishment of one who became so enmeshed in evil. He persisted in his stubbornness, letting out his inner animal and pampering it. Now, in return, the normal ability that the *beinoni* possesses, the ability of his mind to control the heart, is curtailed. At one stage, he relinquished his ability to choose and allowed himself to follow his desires unfettered. Now

God lets him continue to the next stage of this descent, to continue on the path that will lead him to Gehenna.

וְלֹא דִּבְּרָה תּוֹרָה בְּמֵתִים אֵלּוּ שֶׁבְּחַיֵּיהֶם קְרוּיִם מֵתִים.

The Torah does not address these dead people, who even **during their lives are called dead.**

This person's punishment in Gehenna has already begun during his lifetime. Just as a tzaddik can already be living a life of holiness, the life that will be his portion in the World to Come, while clothed in a physical body here in this world, so too can the wicked already reside in Gehenna within their bodily existence in this world.[3] As in Gehenna, where one can change nothing, he becomes a mere spectator, observing how his desires continue to descend and watching how his body and soul fall to ruin. Just as in a nightmare, he can no longer intervene; he cannot be rescued.

כִּי בֶּאֱמֶת אִי אֶפְשָׁר לָרְשָׁעִים לְהַתְחִיל לַעֲבוֹד ה׳ בְּלִי שֶׁיַּעֲשׂוּ תְּשׁוּבָה עַל הֶעָבָר תְּחִלָּה,

Indeed, it is impossible for the wicked to begin serving God without first repenting for the past

Since this person is no longer in control of his heart, it is seemingly impossible for him to break this cycle of evil that generates more evil and to once more choose good. As mentioned, this inability to choose good is a punishment for his actions, a punishment that, like all the punishments in the Torah, transfers him to another state that forces him to break his previous state. It compels him to break the entire being of his soul and to look for something completely different that can extricate him from this negative cycle. In his current situation, the *rasha* truly cannot serve God. He must first rectify the past, change his essential self, and cease his wrongdoings in order to break out of the vicious cycle in which he finds himself.

לְשַׁבֵּר הַקְּלִיפּוֹת שֶׁהֵם מָסָךְ מַבְדִּיל וּמְחִיצָה שֶׁל בַּרְזֶל הַמַּפְסֶקֶת בֵּינָם לַאֲבִיהֶם שֶׁבַּשָּׁמַיִם,

by shattering the *kelippot,* which act as a dividing partition and iron barrier that separate between them **and their Father in Heaven.**

3. See *Berakhot* 18b.

A barrier of transgressions, an "iron curtain" of evil, separates the wicked from God, as the prophet says, "Rather, your iniquities have been separating between you and your God" (Isa. 59:2).[4] It is this partition that the *rasha* must break, or he will remain captive behind it, a prisoner to the cycle of transgressions in which he has allowed himself to fall.

עַל יְדֵי שְׁבִירַת לִבּוֹ וּמְרִירַת נַפְשׁוֹ עַל חֲטָאָיו, כְּמוֹ שֶׁכָּתוּב בַּזֹּהַר עַל פָּסוּק: "זִבְחֵי אֱלֹהִים רוּחַ נִשְׁבָּרָה לֵב נִשְׁבָּר" וגו' (תהלים נא, יט). שֶׁעַל יְדֵי לֵב נִשְׁבָּר - נִשְׁבְּרָה רוּחַ הַטּוּמְאָה דְּסִטְרָא אָחֳרָא [עַיֵּין שָׁם פָּרָשַׁת פִּינְחָס דַּף ר"מ וּפָרָשַׁת וַיִּקְרָא דַּף ח' וְדַף ה' ע"א וּבְפֵירוּשׁ הָרַב מֹשֶׁה זַכּוּת שָׁם].

This is achieved **by means of a broken heart and a bitter soul on account of his transgressions, as it is written in the** ***Zohar*** **regarding the verse "Sacrifices to God are a broken spirit;** You, God will not reject **a broken** and crushed **heart"** (Ps. 51:19). **By having a broken heart, the impure spirit of the** ***sitra aḥara*** **is broken** as well **(see** *Zohar* **there,** ***Parashat Pinḥas*** **240,** ***Parashat Vayikra*** **8, 5a, and the commentary of Rabbi Moshe Zakuto there).**

One can break the *kelippot,* the wall that has formed between oneself and God, by breaking one's heart. Surrounded by impurity, he is caught in a web of social or moral evil that controls him. He is a slave to his urges and desires, to the rhythm of his daily life, in which he does what he does. Yet one escape route remains: a broken heart. When he is overcome by profound bitterness at the realization of how far he has fallen, when he realizes he has touched bottom and his anguish becomes unbearable, then his heart breaks within him. At that moment, all his lusts and desires shatter, together with the evil force that has achieved dominion over him, the *kelippa* separating him from God.[5]

---

4. See *Iggeret HaTeshuva,* chap. 5.
5. See chap. 26 and *Iggeret HaTeshuva,* chap. 7, where the author of the *Tanya* explains this idea at length.

6 Shevat (leap year)

וְהִיא בְּחִינַת תְּשׁוּבָה תַּתָּאָה לְהַעֲלוֹת ה׳ תַּתָּאָה לַהֲקִימָהּ מִנְּפִילָתָהּ שֶׁנָּפְלָה אֶל הַחִיצוֹנִים,

This is the lower level of repentance, which is **to elevate** and restore **the final** ***heh*** in the name of *Havaya* and **erect it from its fallen state when it fell into the** realm of the **external forces** of impurity,

A tormented heart, unable to bear the excruciating pain any longer, is the path to this level of *teshuva,* which entails elevating the final letter *heh* in the name of *Havaya.* This name, spelled *yod-heh-vav-heh,* expresses the drawing down of divinity from the *yod,* which corresponds to the primary source of life in the *sefira* of *Ḥokhma,* to the final *heh,* which corresponds to *Malkhut,* as well as the Divine Presence. The final *heh* – the Divine Presence – fell, so to speak, as a result of man's misdeeds and is torn from its connection to the name of *Havaya,* from its attachment to the source of life in the *yod* of the name. When a person's heart is broken within, the reign of impurity that dominated him also shatters. At that juncture, it becomes possible for him to repent and restore his divine spark, that portion of the Divine Presence, the final *heh,* that is within him, to its place in the name, so that it is reattached to the supernal holiness.

In this sense, repentance is not only an individual affair, a return to one's proper state. It is rather a return of the Divine Presence itself, which the person had pulled down and degraded within his own soul. Through his repentance, the Divine Presence is restored to its heights. ☞

THE TWO LEVELS OF REPENTANCE

☞ In *Iggeret HaTeshuva* (chap. 4), the author of the *Tanya* explains at length that according to a mystical interpretation (see *Zohar* 3:122a), the Hebrew word for repentance, *teshuva,* is comprised of two elements, *tashuv heh,* "restore the *heh,*" meaning, restore the *heh* to its proper place in the name of *Havaya.* Since there are two *hehs* in the name of *Havaya,* there are two corresponding levels of repentance: higher and lower repentance. The higher level of repentance restores the first *heh* in the name of *Havaya* to its rightful place, while the lower level of repentance, the one under discussion here, restores the final, "lower" *heh,* that which represents the Divine Presence, to its rightful place after having descended into the *kelippot* on account of the person's sins.

שֶׁהוּא סוֹד גָּלוּת הַשְּׁכִינָה,

which constitutes the mystic exile of the Divine Presence,

The soul's descent into the realm of the *kelippot,* beyond the iron barrier that separates the Jewish people and their Father in Heaven, constitutes the broader meaning of the concept of the exile of the Divine Presence. The mystic exile of the Divine Presence, the descent of the final *heh* in the name of *Havaya* into the realm of the *kelippot,* is meant to rectify them and elevate them far beyond their initial status. This mystery is the very mystery and meaning of the descent of one's personal soul into the realm of the *kelippot* on account of his sins. A soul's descent into this realm of evil is mysterious because it is not perceivable, just as the true purpose of exile remains unfathomable. It is indeed a mystery why holiness experiences a descent and why it is tormented and suffers. There is meaning to all this, yet it is incomprehensible.

כְּמַאֲמַר רַבּוֹתֵינוּ זַ"ל: "גָּלוּ לֶאֱדוֹם שְׁכִינָה עִמָּהֶם" (ספרי במדבר פד, קסא). דְּהַיְינוּ, כְּשֶׁאָדָם עוֹשֶׂה מַעֲשֵׂה אֱדוֹם

in accordance with our Rabbis' statement "They were exiled to Edom, and **the Divine Presence** went **with them"** (*Sifrei,* Num. 84, 161). **That is** what occurs **when one performs an action** akin to those **of Edom.**

The exile of the Divine Presence also applies to each individual. When a Jew performs an evil act, one akin to that of Edom, he himself becomes Edom, Ishmael, or any other entity that is not part of his essential nature. He is no longer himself. The Jew does not have to physically go forth to the land of Edom in order to go into exile there. He has brought Edom into his own being and internalized it. Not only that, the Divine Presence goes into exile as well.

מוֹרִיד וּמַמְשִׁיךְ לְשָׁם בְּחִינַת וְנִיצוֹץ אֱלֹקוּת הַמְחַיֶּה אֶת נֶפֶשׁ רוּחַ נְשָׁמָה שֶׁלּוֹ, הַמְלוּבָּשִׁים בּוֹ בַּנֶּפֶשׁ הַבַּהֲמִית מֵהַקְּלִיפָּה שֶׁבְּלִבּוֹ שֶׁבֶּחָלָל הַשְּׂמָאלִי, הַמּוֹלֶכֶת בּוֹ

He brings down and channels there the divine spark that sustains his *nefesh, ruaḥ,* **and** *neshama,* **which are clothed in his animal soul,** which stems **from the** *kelippa* **that is in the left chamber of his**

בְּעוֹדוֹ רָשָׁע וּמוֹשֶׁלֶת בָּעִיר בָּעִיר קְטַנָּה שֶׁלוֹ, וְנֶפֶשׁ רוּחַ נְשָׁמָה כְּבוּשִׁים בַּגּוֹלָה אֶצְלָהּ.

heart, and as long as he is wicked, the animal soul **rules over him and governs his small city,** his body and its bodily functions, **and his *nefesh*, *ruaḥ*, and *neshama* are trapped in exile in** the *kelippa*.

When a person sins, he does not only commission the body to execute the transgression but also drags his lofty *nefesh, ruaḥ,* and *neshama* down with it. His *nefesh, ruaḥ,* and *neshama,* components of his divine soul that are clothed within his body and its functions, are exiled. In this sense, one causes his divine soul, the portion of the Divine Presence within him – his divine spark – to descend into exile, no matter how slight the transgression.

וּכְשֶׁנִּשְׁבַּר לִבּוֹ בְּקִרְבּוֹ וְנִשְׁבְּרָה רוּחַ הַטּוּמְאָה וְסִטְרָא אָחֳרָא וַיִּתְפָּרְדוּ וכו׳, הִיא קָמָה מִנְּפִילָתָהּ וְגַם נִצָּבָה, כְּמוֹ שֶׁמְּבוֹאָר בְּמָקוֹם אַחֵר.

When his heart is broken within him, and the spirit of impurity and *sitra aḥara* are broken, resulting in the **scattering** of all evildoers, then **it,** the Divine Presence, the divine spark within him, **rises from its fallen state and stands erect, as explained elsewhere.**

The redemption of the Divine Presence happens within the microcosm, within the individual's soul, whenever he crushes evil, and this comes about through a broken heart, through the bitterness of the soul. That is the door to his soul's redemption.

This chapter dealt chiefly with the verse quoted in the title page of the book: "Rather, the matter is very near to you … to perform it." As explained by the author of the *Tanya,* the "matter that is near to you" refers to the love of God that results from one's contemplation of His greatness. Even in the event that this love does not develop into a fierce, heartfelt emotion but is limited to the sphere of the intellect, it still proves effective since it can, at the very least, move the person to serve God in action. This is true of the *beinoni,* in contrast to the wicked, since the former has gained mastery over his mind and heart.

The chapter concluded by discussing the divine service of the wicked person, a rather rare topic within the greater context of this book, whose primary focus is the *beinoni*. The author of the *Tanya* teaches that the wicked also have a path in the service of God, but in his case "the matter that is near to him to perform it" refers to repentance. Specifically, it refers to the lower level of repentance, which requires a broken heart that will banish the spirit of impurity and release from captivity his hitherto trapped soul, along with the accompanying divine spark within it.

Chapter 18

IN THE PREVIOUS CHAPTER, THE AUTHOR OF THE *TANYA* began to explain the verse that represents a central theme in the book: "Rather, the matter is very near to you, in your mouth and in your heart, to perform it" (Deut. 30:14). This "matter that is very near" relates to the *beinoni,* a rank that "pertains to every person, and each person should strive for it."[1] Yet according to the definition of *beinoni* and what is expected of him, the demand referred to here is no mere mode of behavior, which in itself is not easy, but rather something far more profound, more than thought and more than intent. The *beinoni* is not only expected not to sin, either in deed, speech, or thought, but also these matters should be "in his heart." That is, not only must he do but also feel. The mitzvot he performs should be so rooted in his heart that they evoke genuine, intense love for God. As the *Zohar* states, without awe and love the Torah and commandments cannot ascend above. Without these emotions to give the commandments their wings, their efficacy is minimal and limited. On the surface, it would seem that these matters are not "very near" and certainly not easily attainable by every person.

The author of the *Tanya* goes on to transmute the need for love and awe to be manifest in one's heart to an intellectual love and awe. In place of consciously felt love and awe, there is to be an understanding of the need to love and to fear. It becomes a substitute emotion, perhaps one that does

1. See chap. 14.

not have all the power of living emotion, but it has all the practical implications of conscious, revealed love and awe.

This approach, that one can and should generate internal feelings, or something approximating them, is the *Tanya*'s central proposition. It is a service of God based on practice and training, on the soul's patiently repeated efforts to arrive at authentic, deepfelt emotions that match the more extrinsic intellectual awareness.

This technique conflicts with the nearly universal hasidic demand for spontaneity, for intense and immediately felt emotion. The author of the *Tanya* may have been unique in denying the need for spontaneity, seeing it as nice when possible but not crucial. The model of the *beinoni*, practically speaking, is someone who is not spontaneous, whose love is self-manufactured, and if the love is not actualized, then at least there should be a rationale for love, an inner resolve regarding its necessity. This, says the author of the *Tanya*, is "the matter that is very near to you" – the ability to recognize the need to love and fear God.

In this chapter, the author of the *Tanya* will touch on a deeper level, discussing the case of someone who is unable to achieve even an intellectual love and awe. He can remind himself that he possesses a hidden love, a love so primal and basic to his being that it is hidden within his daily activities. Such a love is manifest only in extraordinary circumstances, those that are above and beyond the intellect.

29 Tevet
7 Shevat (leap year)

וּלְתוֹסֶפֶת בֵּיאוּר בַּאֵר הֵיטֵב מִלַּת "מְאֹד" שֶׁבַּפָּסוּק: "כִּי קָרוֹב אֵלֶיךָ הַדָּבָר מְאֹד" וגו'.

To explain further and more thoroughly the word *me'od*, very, **in the verse "Rather, the matter is very near to you...,"**

The verse not only states that "the matter is near to you," but that it is "very near." The emphasis seems excessive. The matter that is "near," as the previous chapter described, is a product of the mind ruling the heart, "for anyone who possesses a brain in his head." This chapter elucidates how it is "very near" – that is, it is for everyone, even one who is unable to direct his thoughts in this manner.

צָרִיךְ לֵידַע נֶאֱמָנָה כִּי אַף מִי שֶׁדַּעְתּוֹ קְצָרָה בִּידִיעַת ה'	**one must know with certainty that even regarding one whose mind is limited in the knowledge of God**

One way to attain love and awe of God is through intellectual meditation and deep contemplation of the knowledge of God. Obstacles rise, though, and foremost among them is a limited intellect. This is not necessarily an assessment of one's entire capacity. It could be a deficiency specifically in the knowledge of God, an inability to grasp such abstract matters.

Another stumbling block may be a lack of information. To contemplate God's greatness, one needs, besides mental acuity, to know what to contemplate. Perhaps the person has not studied anything that is related to God and His greatness and does not know what he should be contemplating.

וְאֵין לוֹ לֵב לְהָבִין בִּגְדוּלַּת אֵין סוֹף בָּרוּךְ הוּא לְהוֹלִיד מִמֶּנָּה דְּחִילוּ וּרְחִימוּ	**and has no heart to comprehend the greatness of *Ein Sof*, blessed be He, by which to generate fear and love**

One person lacks knowledge of God; another lacks heart. He cannot get past his intellect to the place where meditation translates into feelings of love and fear. The difficulty of transitioning from the intellectual experience to the emotional one, even for one who possesses the brains to do so, is one of the major obstacles in the service of God. ☞

אֲפִילּוּ בְּמוֹחוֹ וּתְבוּנָתוֹ לְבַד,	**even in his mind and intellect alone,**

Not only is he unable to attain love and awe of God in his heart, a forceful emotional experience, or one at least equal in depth to his other feelings, but even an intellectual love and awe is beyond him. This

FROM MIND TO HEART

☞ Much has been written regarding the passage connecting the mind and the heart and about the resulting flaw when this passage is blocked. It is a narrow transit way, corresponding to the throat in the human body, and subject to distortion. A person's experience is an interactive chain of events. Thoughts focus on a topic and create imagery. Images develop and expand until emotion is evoked and action is taken. Between the passages of this chain from initial thought to feeling and deed, the constriction of the throat – otherwise referred to as "Egypt" with its correlative means that an understanding of how to relate, how to love, and what to love, the love and awe "very near to you" described in the previous chapter, are unattainable to him.

אַף עַל פִּי כֵן קָרוֹב אֵלָיו הַדָּבָר מְאֹד, לִשְׁמוֹר וְלַעֲשׂוֹת כָּל מִצְוֹת הַתּוֹרָה, וְתַלְמוּד תּוֹרָה כְּנֶגֶד כּוּלָּן, בְּפִיו וּבִלְבָבוֹ מַמָּשׁ

there is **nevertheless a matter that is very near to him: to observe and perform all the commandments of the Torah, with the study of Torah being equivalent to all** the other mitzvot, **literally in his mouth and heart.**

Although the spiritual work employing the methods explained thus far may not be "near" to this person, there is another possibility that potentially can even be "very near," that is eminently achievable for him.

"chief butler," "chief baker," and "captain of the guard" (see the Arizal's *Likkutei Torah, Parashat Vayeshev*) – is one of the primary obstacles. The blockage stems from a person's connection to his body and the body's desires.

As long as the thoughts of God's greatness remain in the realm of theory, that connection poses no problem. But when they hover too close to emotional realization, they threaten the alleged tranquility of the soul, its web of relationships and agreed-upon compromises with the body. In response, various forces attempt to halt or restrain the energy flow.

Behind them, backing up the throat's constriction, stands Pharaoh himself (the name *Par'o* having the same letters as *ha'oref*, nape of the neck). Next in line, "on the way, upon your exodus from Egypt" (Deut. 25:17), to experiential awareness, to a "good and expansive land," to the expansion of the soul's faculties, stands Amalek. The Hebrew letters comprising the name Amalek can be divided in two, spelling *am malak*, meaning "a nation that severed," based on the Hebrew word *melika*, which refers to the act of severing the head from the body by cutting through the nape (*Torah Or* 85c).

Furthermore, Amalek is the numerical equivalent of *safek*, doubt. Theory is all well and good, but when this has personal and practical implications, Amalek's voice intervenes: "Maybe not?" The idea, he agrees, is wise, persuasive, and convincing. Nevertheless: "Maybe the opposite is true?" This is neither the intellect speaking nor even some particular desire wishing to be heard. It is stiff-necked obstinacy, primal and primitive, and thus Amalek is referred to as "the first of the nations" (Num. 24:20). It is first and foremost of all obstacles and categories of evil inclinations.

Standing opposite him in sanctity is Israel, a "stiff-necked people" (Ex. 34:9), proud and defiant, not because they are wise or mighty, but stiff-necked pure and simple, with a holy stubbornness against the stubbornness of *kelippa*.

This troublesome transit, then, the transformation of intellectual awareness into emotional experience, presents a major challenge to man, and even having brains in his head is no guarantee of achieving love and awe.

That is to perform the mitzvot of the Torah, in particular Torah study. This performance of the mitzvot will not be limited to verbal expression or deed, but is also experienced in the heart and accompanied by actual feelings of love and fear. ☞

מֵעוּמְקָא דְלִבָּא, בֶּאֱמֶת לַאֲמִיתּוֹ,

Moreover, it comes **from the depths of his heart, in absolute truth,**

The depths of the heart is the innermost and deepest seat of emotion. It is the faculty of the heart that is independent of any potentially false experience and as such is an eternal, absolute truth.

בִּדְחִילוּ וּרְחִימוּ, שֶׁהִיא אַהֲבָה מְסוּתֶּרֶת שֶׁבְּלֵב כְּלָלוּת יִשְׂרָאֵל, שֶׁהִיא יְרוּשָּׁה לָנוּ מֵאֲבוֹתֵינוּ.

with the fear and love that is the latent, **concealed love that exists in the heart of the collective of Israel,** bequeathed **as a heritage to us from our forefathers.**

Even someone of limited intellect, incapable of awakening within himself love and awe in his performance of mitzvot, can nevertheless actualize a love of God that stems from his heart's depths. The author of the *Tanya* refers to it as the "concealed love that exists in the heart of the collective of Israel." This love is not something that springs from one's active consciousness but rather from the hereditary connection of every Jew's essence to God, simply because he is a descendant of Abraham, Isaac, and Jacob. Its source is the point at which all Jewish souls unite with the one God, the point known as *Kenesset Yisrael*, the congregation of Israel.

At this junction, one no longer taps into his soul's faculties as they relate to his individual nature. He reaches inside to the deepest root,

THE UNIQUE STATUS OF TORAH STUDY

☞ Torah study, which is "equivalent to all [the other mitzvot]," is not dependent on time or a specific measure, as are the other commandments. It is achievable, and required, even when a person is not obligated to engage in another mitzva. Since man is always obligated to study Torah, he is never in a vacuum because Torah study fills all the otherwise empty spaces. It does not allow neutrality in a person's life. One is always able "to observe and perform all the commandments of the Torah" by means of its study.

to a primal source that can be described paradoxically as the "exalted depths" or "supernal depths,"[2] and from there he draws the strength to serve God. This essential heritage nestled in the depths of the Jewish soul is not something one can create or control, yet its power sustains his own life as it has sustained the Jewish people's existence through all generations. It is the faithfulness of a simple Jew, a quality coming not from intellectual love and awe but from the hidden love that every Jew inherits from his forefathers.

Here the author of the *Tanya* touches on a topic that borders on the dangerous, a power so fundamental and dynamic within every Jew that he can draw on it as an individual and as part of the collective nation without exhausting its source. It is a well so deep, so powerful, that one can draw on it forever. But because it is so very powerful, once manifest it may never again allow for day-to-day existence.

After making every other attempt, we try another source, the most basic, fundamental source, the nucleus of the very existence of matter. We draw power from the atom. But as with the explosion of nuclear energy, the inherent basis of all matter, the potential that is found within each individual, the very foundation of the soul, can be explosive.

As the author of the *Tanya* will go on to explain, this spiritual nuclear bomb comes into play at the moment of martyrdom, the sanctification of God's name. At the moment of the full realization of its potential, life itself is swept away by its overwhelming power. One cannot live with it; it burns through everything in its wake, including life itself. Yet the author of the *Tanya* is telling us that one may tap into this potential for daily life. The conundrum that presents itself is, how does one make use of something so unequivocal, so ultimately yes or no? Without it, one risks emotional vacuity; with it, one leaps beyond all bounds, even that of physical existence. How does one receive from a hidden source that, when revealed, can be devastating? How is one to harness, apportion, and live with it? ☞

רַק שֶׁצָּרִיךְ לְבָאֵר וּלְהַקְדִּים תְּחִלָּה בַּאֵר הֵיטֵב שֹׁרֶשׁ אַהֲבָה זוֹ וְעִנְיָנָהּ, וְאֵיךְ הִיא יְרוּשָּׁה לָנוּ,

But we must first explain and preface how one so limited can evoke this love **with a thorough explanation of the**

2. *Sefer Yetzira*, chap. 1.

וְאֵיךְ נִכְלָל בָּהּ גַּם דְּחִילוּ. **root and idea behind this love, how it is a heritage** bequeathed **to us and how it also incorporates fear.**

The question of how awe is included within the hidden love is no side issue because in a certain sense awe and love are opposites. When we say that within every Jewish heart lies a hidden love, we are speaking of an essential connection and closeness between a Jew and his Father in

A LABOR OF LOVE

☞ Among the unusual qualities of this work, and of Chabad hasidic philosophy in general, are the frequent transitions between intellectuality and cerebral effort, an appreciation of intellectual love and awe, on one hand, and, on the other, a heavy reliance on faculties that are beyond the threshold of consciousness. Compare this to other schools of Hasidism – Kotzk, for example, with its emphasis on sharpening one's emotional aptitude, elevating it to ever-higher levels, with the intention that man live in a constant state of outburst, to live constantly with the love of truth, to the point that it erupts from him unbidden. Such a path is within the realm of possibility. There are people capable of doing this, though they number an elite few.

Then there is another, more down-to-earth hasidic school that demands no revealed love and awe whatsoever, the kind of love and awe that exists in one's awareness, because every Jew possesses a holy soul, and one can rely on the love of God inherent in it.

The author of the *Tanya*'s method attempts to follow both approaches: to rely on the holy soul, the latent love concealed within it, and draw strength from it, while constructing a conscious world of love and awe through the intellect.

The two methods are interrelated. Most avenues of serving God with the intellectually oriented love and awe that this book describes require an additional and deeper foundation that enables a person to come to this way of thinking. Without this basis, even someone quite capable will never be able to contemplate such ideas. At the same time, someone who possesses this capacity for thought and has a supportive environment, even though he may be limited intellectually, can reach the highest levels of thought, a synergy of thought and soul. Though the range of his mind is circumscribed, if he works hard to develop these concepts to their fullest, his self-transformation can dwarf the accomplishments of the wisest of men with their profound knowledge.

Sanctity is not necessarily bound by cerebral ability. The greatest intellect may be housed in the least holy of garments and vice versa. What counts is not the level of thought but the ability to actualize it. Some people have an immense intellectual capacity but have no idea how to tap into it. The power to do this, to enter the world of thought, however lofty, and make proper use of it, flows from that single unfathomable point: the love hidden within every Jew's heart, the inheritance from our forefathers.

Heaven. Awe and fear, by contrast, denote distance. How can someone with this subliminal love for holiness also attain the perspective of distance and the drawing back that follows?

The author of the *Tanya* answers this question only in the next chapter. Now he turns to an explanation of how this love is an inheritance from the forefathers.

8 Shevat (leap year)

וְהָעִנְיָן, כִּי הָאָבוֹת הֵן הֵן הַמֶּרְכָּבָה.

The underlying **idea is that the forefathers are the very chariot** for the Divine Presence.

The designation of the forefathers as the chariot for the Divine tells us that besides their individual identities as Abraham, Isaac, and Jacob, they merited through their service of God to become a chariot for the Divine Presence, a channel for the Divine. They reached a level of self-abnegation before God whereby their bodies and souls became instruments and expressions of Godliness and sanctity within the world.

A chariot is, for its rider, no more than a vehicle, without any will of its own. Its self-nullification with regard to the rider is absolute, greater even than that of the horse to its rider. The intention in calling the forefathers the chariot is that their sense of self had been transmuted. They no longer identified as an individual self but had become the instrument of the Divine Presence. Human dualities, the inclination toward good and the inclination toward evil, the body and soul, ceased to play a role. As chariots of the Divine Presence, their sense of self was as one with the will of God. They became a complete vessel for the divine will, for the divine attributes of love and kindness, restraint and mercy.

The level of chariot, then, bypasses rankings of human virtues. It goes beyond wisdom, love, and awe to any degree. Even the highest level of prophecy is still a quality that relates to an individual, of whom it is said that the Divine Presence speaks through his throat. But the

"THE FOREFATHERS ARE THE VERY CHARIOT"

☞ This expression is borrowed from the Midrash (*Bereshit Rabba* 82:6), where it comments on the verses "And God ascended from upon Abraham" (Gen. 17:22), and "God ascended from upon him [Jacob]" (Gen. 35:13). The Midrash interprets definition of "the forefathers are the very chariot [for the Divine Presence]" is a totally different level, a complete transformation of what it means to be human. The forefathers became a seamless part of the holy and transcendent world of *Atzilut*, not through any specific faculty within their souls but through their very existence. ☞

They therefore merited drawing down for their descendants after them forever a *nefesh*, *ruaḥ*, and *neshama* from the ten holy *sefirot* of the four worlds of *Atzilut*, *Beria*, *Yetzira*, and *Asiya*, each according to his rank and deeds.

וְעַל כֵּן זָכוּ לְהַמְשִׁיךְ נֶפֶשׁ רוּחַ נְשָׁמָה לִבְנֵיהֶם אַחֲרֵיהֶם עַד עוֹלָם מֵעֶשֶׂר סְפִירוֹת דִּקְדוּשָּׁה שֶׁבְּאַרְבַּע עוֹלָמוֹת, אֲצִילוּת בְּרִיאָה יְצִירָה עֲשִׂיָּה, לְכָל אֶחָד וְאֶחָד כְּפִי מַדְרֵגָתוֹ וּכְפִי מַעֲשָׂיו.

The level of chariot is not a rank assigned to a particular individual but rather an essential transformation – a mutation of the person's essence, as it were, that can be passed along to succeeding generations. The forefathers were fundamentally different, and their progeny followed suit with this altered essence. This "new" creation was graced with a unique gift: a soul that stems from the realm of sanctity, a soul that finds expression not only in spiritual, intellectual, or emotional abilities deriving from the rational soul. After all, everything the rational soul is capable of, according to Rambam's yardstick, could be attained by someone like Aristotle. Rather, this is a power unconnected to human comprehension or even prophetic vision. It is an altogether different essence, a vital divine spark that every Jew inherits, unrelated to stature or deeds, wisdom or foolishness, righteousness or evil, closeness to or distance from God. It is the most essential plane of being a Jew, a part of his very essence.

the words "from upon him" in their literal sense, meaning that God was "upon" the forefathers. This follows the interpretation used in reference to the portrayal of the divine chariot in Ezekiel's vision: "Above the firmament that was over their heads was the likeness of a throne…and upon the likeness of the throne was a likeness, like the appearance of a person upon it…" (Ezek. 1:26). In this verse, the throne is the vehicle for the likeness of the person above it, which refers to the divine likeness that sits, or "rides," upon the throne and by which it functions in the worlds. The vehicle is therefore the vessel by which its "rider" functions. The vessel is subordinate to the rider, having no personality or will of its own. Rather, its sole function is that of a vessel for the rider's purposes and self-expression.

This divine spark that passes from the forefathers to their offspring emanates from the sphere of holiness that exists in each of the four worlds. Just as there are ten *sefirot* in the world of *Atzilut*, so there are ten holy *sefirot* in each of the other worlds, through which God manifests that particular world, sustains it, and governs it. The three worlds of created entities – *Beria, Yetzira,* and *Asiya* – parallel the three soul levels present in every Jew, *nefesh, ruaḥ,* and *neshama.* A holy spark from the ten *sefirot* from each of these worlds is drawn down into its corresponding soul level, animating the holiness contained therein. ☞

וְעַל כָּל פָּנִים, אֲפִילוּ לְקַל שֶׁבְּקַלִּים וּפוֹשְׁעֵי יִשְׂרָאֵל **At the very least, even with regard to the most unworthy and the sinners of Israel,**

These individuals do not lead their lives in a manner that is reflective of their holy forebears. Nevertheless, they are still Jewish souls, the

THE INHERITANCE FROM OUR FOREFATHERS

☞ Among the greatest leaders of Israel, we count the seven "shepherds": Abraham, Isaac, Jacob, Moses, Aaron, Joseph, and David. Moses, in a way, transcends them all. The summit of human perfection, he is the greatest of the prophets, regarding whom the verse states, "There has not risen another prophet in Israel like Moses..." (Deut. 34:10). Yet Moses himself is not a chariot.

There are two frames of reference here. From the viewpoint of human greatness, Moses stood at the summit. On the other hand, Abraham, Isaac, and Jacob were chariots for the Divine. A person who is a chariot undergoes a nearly biological metamorphosis. He becomes a progenitor of a new line, a succession that forever transmits this essence to its descendants for all generations.

Jewish tradition also gives tangible expression to this concept. The Torah scholar described in the Talmud is not only one who has studied but one who has become an integral extension of sanctity. He himself constitutes a sanctuary to God. The concept that "whoever brings a gift to a Torah scholar, it is as though he has presented first fruits" (*Ketubot* 105b) relates to the understanding that the forefathers are the chariot, the essential, almost physical, unity with holiness that is every Jew's legacy.

There is a statement attributed to the Ba'al Shem Tov: "No Jew ever became an apostate; no gentile ever converted to Judaism" (see *Iggerot Kodesh*, vol. 8, p. 208). Any Jew who becomes an apostate demonstrates that he is not in essence Jewish, and every gentile who converts was not really a gentile. The statement perhaps undermines principles of biology, yet it defines unequivocally who a Jew is: someone who has by nature and by birth a spark of holiness, regardless of his situation, condition, and status. The proof is that when the moment of truth arrives, he will decide, at whatever cost, that he belongs to God.

progeny of their forefathers, and continue to carry their heritage within them. ☞

נִמְשָׁךְ בְּזִיווּגָם נֶפֶשׁ דְּנֶפֶשׁ דְּמַלְכוּת דַּעֲשִׂיָּה, שֶׁהִיא מַדְרֵגָה הַתַּחְתּוֹנָה שֶׁבִּקְדוּשַּׁת הָעֲשִׂיָּה.

a *nefesh* of the *nefesh* of *Malkhut* of the world of ***Asiya*, namely, the lowest level of holiness in** the world of ***Asiya*, is drawn down as a result of their** act of **coupling.**

The world of *Asiya* is the lowest of the four worlds. In *Asiya* itself are ten *sefirot*, the lowest of which is *Malkhut*. *Malkhut* itself contains the three levels of *nefesh*, *ruaḥ*, and *neshama*, the lowest of which is *nefesh*. In the *nefesh* itself are a *nefesh*, *ruaḥ*, and *neshama*, the lowest level being *nefesh*, which the author of the *Tanya* refers to as a "*nefesh* of the *nefesh* of *Malkhut* [of the world] of *Asiya*." ☞

THE MOST UNWORTHY AND THE SINNERS OF ISRAEL

☞ These two appellations are neither identical nor necessarily coexistent facets of the same person. The most unworthy is a man without a discerning mind, and a sinner of Israel is a wicked individual. The former has a lowly soul, while the latter's soul may be lofty, and it may even be that its loftiness is what caused his sinful behavior. Big souls demand big solutions, and on occasion, whether due to one's background or for other reasons, a person who cannot find the answers in the realm of holiness may direct his formidable energies to the *sitra aḥara*, perhaps out of spite or perhaps in search of what he could not find in sanctity. At any rate, the individual discussed here may be a combination of the two: the most unworthy and a sinner to boot. He transgresses not only out of frivolity but with deliberation and intention.

THE TRAITS WE PASS DOWN

☞ Generally speaking, parents pass along their characteristics to their children. If the parents are frivolous and sinful, the child will follow suit. Nonetheless, even with parents like these, who lacked the right intentions at the moment of conception as well as in whatever education they gave their children, a holy spark passes from them to their offspring. Perhaps the child's soul is the most worthless of the worthless, a "*nefesh* of the *nefesh* of *Malkhut* [of the world] of *Asiya*," but it is still a holy soul, a dwelling place for the divine light, that stems from the ten holy *sefirot*. Every Jew, no matter how lowly, still enables the channeling of Jewish potential to his progeny, regardless of his personal state and unawareness of this transmission.

וְאַף עַל פִּי כֵן, מֵאַחַר שֶׁהִיא מֵעֶשֶׂר סְפִירוֹת קְדוֹשׁוֹת הִיא כְּלוּלָה מִכּוּלָּן,

Yet nevertheless, since Malkhut is one of the ten holy *sefirot*, it is comprised of them all,

Each level incorporates and is comprised of all the other levels, while at the same time maintaining its distinct identity. Thus, even the lowest levels are comprised of the loftiest ones, just as one's toenails are still part of a person and thus contain an element of his comparatively lofty intellect.[3]

The worlds of holiness are distinguished by their interconnectedness and inclusion within each other. This is the natural result of self-negation, which is the mark of sanctity, and contrasts with the self-centeredness of *kelippa*: "My river is mine, and I made myself" (Ezek. 29:3).[4] While *kelippa*'s overriding self-centeredness rules out any possibility of connection with another, the self-abnegation of holiness to supernal sanctity embraces the whole of existence.

גַּם מֵחָכְמָה דַּעֲשִׂיָּה שֶׁבְּתוֹכָהּ מְלוּבֶּשֶׁת חָכְמָה דְּמַלְכוּת דַּאֲצִילוּת, שֶׁבְּתוֹכָהּ חָכְמָה דַּאֲצִילוּת, שֶׁבָּהּ מֵאִיר אוֹר אֵין סוֹף בָּרוּךְ הוּא מַמָּשׁ,

including *Ḥokhma* of the world of ***Asiya*, within which is clothed *Ḥokhma* of *Malkhut*** of the world of ***Atzilut*, within** which is clothed ***Ḥokhma* of *Atzilut*, in which the light of *Ein Sof*, blessed be He, itself shines** (see gloss to chap. 35),

Sanctity, of any level or form, is an all-encompassing constellation unto itself, a complete structure, or *partzuf* in the language of Kabbala. For this reason, the most minuscule unit of sanctity holds within itself boundless universes of holiness. So too the spiritual legacy of a Jew, even if grounded in the lowest levels of sanctity, contains within itself the most sublime heights. The transmission of sanctity, then, does not necessarily follow a neatly organized hierarchy. Every soul, no matter how common, contains the entire world of sanctity and the potential for a direct link to God Himself, even if that potential is nestled in its deepest depths.

This may sound wildly optimistic, a spiritual rags-to-riches story,

3. See commentary on chap. 2.
4. See commentary on chap. 9.

yet "the smallest will become a thousand" (Isa. 60:22), because every Jew bears within himself, as it were, the patriarchs, the chariot itself, though concealed, of reduced dimension, and imperceptible.

כִּדְכְתִיב: "ה' בְּחָכְמָה יָסַד אָרֶץ" (משלי ג, יט)

as it is written, "The Lord founded the earth with wisdom" (Prov. 3:19),

God established the earth with the attribute of *Ḥokhma*, Wisdom. In this sense, *Ḥokhma*, the highest of attributes, where the light of *Ein Sof* itself radiates, is revealed in the earth, which is the level of *Malkhut*, the lowest of the attributes.

וְ"כוּלָּם בְּחָכְמָה עָשִׂיתָ" (תהלים קד, כד).

and "with wisdom You have made them all" (Ps. 104:24).

Wisdom, or *Ḥokhma*, is the vessel through which God operates, and it is revealed within the world of *Asiya*, as the word *asita*, "made," in the verse indicates.

וְנִמְצָא כִּי אֵין סוֹף בָּרוּךְ הוּא מְלוּבָּשׁ בִּבְחִינַת חָכְמָה שֶׁבְּנֶפֶשׁ הָאָדָם, יִהְיֶה מִי שֶׁיִּהְיֶה, מִיִּשְׂרָאֵל.

Thus it follows that *Ein Sof*, blessed be He, is clothed in the faculty of wisdom that is in the soul of a Jew, no matter his status.

As mentioned, every Jew, even the most unworthy and even the sinner of Israel, has inherited a spark of holiness – literally, a portion of God on high – from his forefathers. This spark is clothed within the faculty of wisdom in a person's soul. Consequently, the faculty of wisdom is the starting point for the manifestation of the soul's faculties. This includes not only what is revealed in a person but also what is hidden, including the light of *Ein Sof*.

Elsewhere, the author of the *Tanya* explains why *God* reveals Himself specifically in the faculty of wisdom.[5] Though counted among the soul's cognitive attributes, it stands between consciousness and what soars beyond reality and awareness. In the topology of thought, wisdom is the flash, the spark, that passes from the hidden, unknow-

5. See gloss to chap. 35.

able regions of the intellect into the conscious mind. The threshold between existence and nothingness is no more than a point. Since it is dimensionless, without area or boundaries, it can therefore clothe the light of *Ein Sof.*

וּבְחִינַת הַחָכְמָה שֶׁבָּהּ עִם אוֹר אֵין סוֹף בָּרוּךְ הוּא הַמְלוּבָּשׁ בָּהּ מִתְפַּשֶּׁטֶת בְּכָל בְּחִינוֹת הַנֶּפֶשׁ כּוּלָּהּ לְהַחֲיוֹתָהּ מִבְּחִינַת רֹאשָׁהּ עַד בְּחִינַת רַגְלָהּ, כְּדִכְתִיב: "הַחָכְמָה תְּחַיֶּה בְעָלֶיהָ" (קהלת ז, יב).

The faculty of wisdom in the soul, along **with the light of *Ein Sof,* blessed be He, which is clothed within it, permeates all the faculties of the soul in its entirety, from head to foot, as it were, giving it life, as it is written, "Wisdom grants life to its possessors"** (Eccles. 7:12).

The faculty of wisdom in the soul is the soul's innermost, hidden contact point to the source of life. It is the place where the supernal attribute of *Ḥokhma* illuminates the soul and, as mentioned, is the internal sanctuary for the divine light. This point is the real and true point of life for the soul, giving life to the entire soul from beginning to end. Obscured within lies the hidden facet that was bequeathed by the forefathers, the chariot of the Divine. This is what makes every Jew "a portion of God on high."

As will be explained below, we have no consciousness of it. Normal living precludes its revelation. But the moment a Jew faces an extraordinary situation, it is exposed. The breakthrough is explosive. At that moment, his entire life changes. That flash of clarity does not allow for a return to the routine world of shadows. This connection to the hidden supernal holiness reveals itself particularly when one senses imminent extinction, the end of biological life, or, even more basic, the loss of the soul. At this juncture, one will give up his life rather than be severed from God.

[וְלִפְעָמִים מַמְשִׁיכִים פּוֹשְׁעֵי יִשְׂרָאֵל נְשָׁמוֹת גְּבוֹהוֹת מְאֹד שֶׁהָיוּ בְּעִמְקֵי הַקְּלִיפּוֹת, כְּמוֹ שֶׁכָּתוּב בְּסֵפֶר גִּלְגּוּלִים.]

(**Sometimes** even **sinners of Israel draw down very lofty souls that** were trapped **in the abyss of the *kelippot,* as it is written in *Sefer HaGilgulim.***)

Although this note is somewhat of a non sequitur, it relates to the topic at hand: the essential holiness that is every Jew's legacy. The rule of thumb is that individuals pass along souls similar to theirs to the next generation. On occasion, though, the script changes, and a wholly mysterious process occurs: A sinful individual, the product of lineage seemingly totally removed from sanctity, brings forth a child with a pure and exalted soul. The same hidden facet that can be awakened in any Jew who commits an act of self-sacrifice for the sake of sanctifying God's name can also manifest as a new and holy soul that does not match the soul of its progenitors.

There are sources that describe the lofty souls that fall through the cracks between holiness and impurity. Captives of *kelippa*, they can escape only under unique circumstances. They are like rare gems buried in a garbage dump. Only one who frequents such places – and refined individuals with holy souls avoid such unsavory locations – will ever find them. It is only the sinners of Israel, who are at home in such venues, who can discover and extricate them.

Among the great Jewish leaders in every generation were always those with the most unlikely parentage. One would be hard-pressed to find a more striking example of a noble soul with questionable pedigree than the Messiah, whose family tree is replete with relationships that were on the fringes of impurity: Judah and Tamar, Ruth the Moabite and Na'ama the Ammonite (descendants of Lot's daughters, a flawed lineage in and of itself), and David and Bathsheba. The soul of the Messiah, which itself epitomizes the redemption of sanctity from *kelippa*, can be reached only through these unions that are on the boundary between the sacred and the impure.

As mentioned, the focal point of this sanctity is in the soul's faculty of wisdom. The author of the *Tanya* now explains what this wisdom is, what its function is among the soul's other powers, and why, specifically, the light of *Ein Sof* clothes itself within it.

הִנֵּה הַחָכְמָה הִיא מְקוֹר הַשֵּׂכֶל וְהַהֲבָנָה, וְהִיא לְמַעְלָה מֵהַבִּינָה, שֶׁהוּא הֲבָנַת הַשֵּׂכֶל וְהַשָּׂגָתוֹ, וְהַחָכְמָה הִיא לְמַעְלָה מֵהַהֲבָנָה וְהַהַשָּׂגָה וְהִיא מָקוֹר לָהֶן.

Wisdom is the source of intelligence and understanding. It is above the faculty of **understanding, which constitutes the intellect's understanding and apprehension** of an idea. **Wisdom is above the** level of **understanding and apprehension, and it is their source.**

1 Shevat
9 Shevat (leap year)

Wisdom is not synonymous with the intellect. What we recognize as intellectual comprehension and understanding is the faculty of *bina*, understanding, whereas *ḥokhma*, wisdom, is the source and dynamic that creates the intellect. Wisdom acts as the bridge between a nonconceptualized idea and active intelligence, our perception of the concept. Thought is the process of combination and fusion, of analysis and differentiation. Yet this process can begin only when there is a particular idea for thought to engage, to take apart and reconstruct. The stage at which the idea first appears, before the intellect can start to work on it, is wisdom, which precedes comprehension.

Our thoughts usually unfold so quickly that we miss the chance to both think and meditate on them. We fail to discern their rich layering. Only when the process slows, for whatever reason, are we able to distinguish between the stage at which an idea first appears in wisdom and the subsequent analysis and conceptual reorganization in understanding.

Wisdom is the initial flash of cognition, the first grasp at awareness, neither comprehended nor intellectualized. It is the lightning bolt that illuminates the darkness, delivering its once-only impression. A protracted stage follows in which a person needs to understand what he saw. He disassembles the picture, attempting to integrate it with earlier ones. This is the stage of understanding, in which the intellect comprehends the subject. This is not a onetime impression, like that initial flash, but rather the spark of wisdom flashes and pulsates again and again, like an electric spark that energizes a motor, time after time.

Chabad literature gives another example: Someone is stymied while trying to solve a problem. He sits and examines the issues when, suddenly, lightning flashes. *I found it!* If we were to ask him at that moment, "What did you find?" he could not reply. The flash of wisdom, the source of the intellect, is, by itself, nothing. The dimensions of understanding, their length and breadth, the possibility of exploration and rebuilding, of in-depth study and the discovery of the roots and possible results of things – all these are the intellectual understanding and comprehension that come only after the illumination of wisdom.

וְזֶהוּ לְשׁוֹן חָכְמָה, כֹּ״חַ מָ״ה,

This is the connotation of the term ***ḥokhma,*** whose letters spell ***ko'aḥ ma,*** the potential for what,

Ma, "what," is the term for nothingness, that which is nonexistent. Accordingly, it is an expression for humility and self-negation. As Moses and Aaron said, "And what are we?" (Ex. 16:8). We are nothing. We are not causal factors or influential, and therefore "your complaints are not against us, but against the Lord" (Ex. 16:8). ☞

שֶׁהוּא מַה שֶּׁאֵינוֹ מוּשָּׂג וּמוּבָן וְאֵינוֹ נִתְפָּס בְּהַשָּׂגָה עֲדַיִין.

for it is that which is not apprehended and understood, nor is it yet grasped by the intellect.

We cannot understand what wisdom is. It comes to us as a given fact, a sense of truth that we cannot define. We cannot explain why we feel it is true. At other levels of comprehension, there are systems and criteria. Yet they all depend on that initial conception of objects and ideas emerging from nothingness. Wisdom is therefore *ko'aḥ ma,* "the potential for what," because it draws from within the nothingness, which can neither be defined nor perceived.

וְלָכֵן מִתְלַבֵּשׁ בָּהּ אוֹר אֵין סוֹף בָּרוּךְ הוּא דְּלֵית מַחֲשָׁבָה תְּפִיסָא בֵּיהּ כְּלָל.

Therefore, clothed within it is the light of *Ein Sof,* blessed be He, which no thought can grasp whatsoever.

Wisdom is that element inside us that we cannot fathom. We approach it, only to stand gaping at the inexplicable. We enjoy its end products –

WHAT AND WHO

☞ *Ma* is also a question. The teachings of Kabbala raise two questions: *ma,* what, the query of wisdom, and *mi,* who, the question of understanding. (The Hebrew word *mi,* "who," has the numerical value of fifty, alluding to the fifty gates of *Bina.*)

The two questions are interrelated, as are wisdom and understanding. "What" is the fundamental question confronting the void. "Who" is the question that comes only after there is *ma,* when there is existence. In the words of the *Zohar* (Introduction 1b), it comes only when there is someone about whom it can be asked, "Who?"

intellect, feeling, awareness – without ever knowing their source. The faculty of wisdom is the mysterious point within our being, one that we can neither perceive nor understand. It is beyond the realm of what can be apprehended, although it is the source of human perception, emotion, and living awareness. For this reason, it is the vessel within us that clothes the light of *Ein Sof*, that transcends the thoughts of any created being.

It is axiomatic that whatever a person can perceive in his thoughts is not the light of *Ein Sof*. If it is at all possible, then, for this divine energy to become revealed, it is in the very facet of the soul that itself is beyond knowing. When the Rebbe of Kotzk was once asked about knowing God's path, why He does things one way and not another, he replied, "A God whom some putrid drop can comprehend is hardly worth serving!" Not the most delicate way of putting it, but appropriate nevertheless. Godliness cannot be revealed in anything that can be perceived, measured, or defined within any boundaries but only in that corner of our existence that defies definition. As the verse states, "He who dwells in the shelter of the Most High" (Ps. 91:1) – the Most High dwells in "shelter," in the concealment that we cannot uncover.

וְלָכֵן כָּל יִשְׂרָאֵל, אֲפִילוּ הַנָּשִׁים וְעַמֵּי הָאָרֶץ, הֵם מַאֲמִינִים בַּה׳,

Consequently, every Jew, even women and the ignorant, believe in God,

Even those Jews who never studied and were never educated in Judaism in any depth possess faith in God. The power of faith within every Jew is seen empirically and is described in the talmudic statement "They are believers, children of believers" (*Shabbat* 97a).

שֶׁהָאֱמוּנָה הִיא לְמַעְלָה מִן הַדַּעַת וְהַהַשָּׂגָה,

because faith is beyond knowledge and apprehension,

Where knowledge ends, faith begins. The connection to the Divine by way of faith is possible also for those utterly without understanding and perception of God, because faith is independent of comprehension or knowledge and unaffected by their absence. Faith derives its nurture from a completely different source, one connected to the soul's faculty of wisdom, which is wholly beyond awareness and understanding. For this reason, faith reaches beyond the intellect.

כִּי "פֶּתִי יַאֲמִין לְכָל דָּבָר וְעָרוּם יָבִין" וגו' (משלי יד, טו).

for "the naïf believes everything, and the clever will understand it correctly" (Prov. 14:15).

Understanding requires intelligence, but believing is something that even a simple person can do. The point here is not to extol simplicity but to praise faith, which even an unlettered person can embrace. The demands made of the intellect, the myriad stages of cognition through which one must struggle, have no bearing on faith. One can believe in matters whose complexity far exceeds his understanding. Although comprehension is configured by a thousand perceptual boundaries and dimensions, by the individual's knowledge and intellectual capabilities, faith's borders are free. Free of intellectuality, unrestrained by analysis, faith is unshackled to soar beyond intellect. In no way does this suggest that a man of understanding is disadvantaged in matters of faith, only that faith issues from a source apart from comprehension. To create the internal image of "God standing over him" requires intellect and understanding, whereas the one who has faith needs no pictures. He believes, and his belief requires no understanding of what he believes. ☞

THE LIMITATIONS OF FAITH

☞ Yet the author of the *Tanya* explains elsewhere that one should not be satisfied with faith alone. One who believes everything indiscriminately is liable to misuse faith to throw off all bonds. The *Ein Yaakov* (*Berakhot* 63a) presents the account of a thief who prays to God for success before committing a robbery. This is a clear proof of the thief's faith, without which he would hardly pray, but his faith does little to disturb his choice of profession. Faith does not connect directly to the soul's internal network. It is discrete from everything that we understand, know, and feel. It has no significant influence within the soul. For this reason, it does not influence a person's day-to-day conduct, except for those extraordinary circumstances when business as usual comes to a halt, when all the walls and restrictions collapse.

This is why we must not be content with faith alone in our relationship with God. We must also engage our individual intellectual and meditative capabilities, to build bridges between our faculties of wisdom and understanding, between faith and apprehension – although it should be emphasized that comprehension can only build a link with faith. Faith stands alone, independent and separate, whether one is unschooled or filled with wisdom. Faith comes from the soul's essence, not from its powers of intellect and cognition, from wisdom and not from understanding.

וְלְגַבֵּי הַקָּדוֹשׁ בָּרוּךְ הוּא, שֶׁהוּא לְמַעְלָה מִן הַשֵּׂכֶל וְהַדַּעַת, וְלֵית מַחֲשָׁבָה תְּפִיסָא בֵּיהּ כְּלָל, הַכֹּל כִּפְתָיִים אֶצְלוֹ יִתְבָּרֵךְ,

Relative to the Holy One, blessed be He, who is beyond intellect and knowledge, and no thought can grasp Him at all, everyone is regarded as a "naïf" in His presence,

There are things in which only simple people believe because the intelligent apprehend them through their intellect. Yet in relation to God, everyone is considered simple and "no thought can grasp Him at all." Not only the particular thought of a specific individual but all thought, because God transcends the essential nature of the power of thought on all levels. Consequently, everyone is considered a simple person relative to God.

In those areas where thought is serviceable and where comprehension and understanding can function, simplicity is a disadvantage, and belief is an expression of that shortcoming. But regarding the essence of the Divine, which by definition is incomprehensible and beyond cognition, the fool and the wise man are on the same footing: Neither understands. Both can equally believe. In matters that can be apprehended, they are divided. The wise man comprehends, but the fool does not. By contrast, concerning an unknowable God, all men are fools, with a single gossamer distinction: The simple man cannot fathom the gap, the enormity of the absence of understanding. The wise man at least recognizes his inadequacy.

כִּדְכְתִיב: "וַאֲנִי בַעַר וְלֹא אֵדָע בְּהֵמוֹת הָיִיתִי עִמָּךְ. וַאֲנִי תָמִיד עִמָּךְ" וגו' (תהלים עג, כב-כג), כְּלוֹמַר שֶׁבָּזֶה שֶׁאֲנִי בַּעַר וּבְהֵמוֹת אֲנִי תָּמִיד עִמָּךְ.

as it is written, "I am a boor, unknowing; I am like a beast before You. Yet I am always with You" (Ps. 73:22–23), **meaning,** specifically **by virtue of my being** like **a boor and a beast, I am always with You.**

A person who is open to receiving and believing that which lies beyond comprehension is no longer chained to understanding and perception. Therefore, he is "always with You," whether or not he apprehends what he believes. Moreover, the attempt to perceive that which is not given to understanding, rather than bringing him closer to faith could have distanced him, but since one defines himself as a "boor" and a "beast," he comes to be "always with You," unencumbered by his intellect and knowledge.

Faith, then, is higher than comprehension. Whereas comprehension takes place within the faculty of understanding, faith exists at the precognitive level of wisdom, where one absorbs matters automatically, with the need for neither analysis nor understanding. It is a level present, as mentioned, in the soul of every Jew.

וְלָכֵן אֲפִילוּ קַל שֶׁבַּקַּלִּים וּפוֹשְׁעֵי יִשְׂרָאֵל מוֹסְרִים נַפְשָׁם עַל קְדוּשַּׁת הַשֵּׁם עַל הָרוֹב, וְסוֹבְלִים עִינּוּיִם קָשִׁים שֶׁלֹּא לִכְפּוֹר בַּה׳ אֶחָד, וְאַף אִם הֵם בּוּרִים וְעַמֵּי הָאָרֶץ וְאֵין יוֹדְעִים גְּדוּלַּת ה׳,

Consequently, on the whole, even the most unworthy and the sinners of Israel give up their lives in martyrdom **for the sanctification** of God's **name. They** also **endure severe torture in order to not deny the one God, even if they are boors and ignoramuses and are not knowledgeable in the greatness of God,**

One who is most unworthy is one who makes light of the commandments, who never seriously regarded matters of faith nor gave heed to his actions, while the sinner of Israel is one who has committed numerous transgressions with malicious intent. Yet even they possess within them the potential to sacrifice their lives for the sake of God and would even undergo severe torture to this end.

The *Kuzari*, which bears some resemblance to the *Tanya* in describing the nearly genetic presence of holiness among the Jewish people, attributes their uniqueness to outstanding individuals. According to the *Kuzari*, the verse that refers to Israel as "distinguished from among all the peoples" (Ex. 19:5), indicates that this is the nation of the forefathers. A "kingdom of priests and a holy nation" (Ex. 19:6) is the nation with preeminent prophets and sages who cleave to God.[6] The author of the *Tanya*, by contrast, assigns the sanctity and the uniqueness of the Jewish people to another cause.

6. See *Kuzari* 1:103, 109.

The forefathers and prophets, the *tanna'im* and *amora'im*, were exceptional and holy men, but it is not they who create a kingdom of priests and a holy nation. "For who is a great nation that has God near it?" (Deut. 4:7) does not refer to a nation of prophets and holy individuals who sacrifice themselves for the sanctity of the divine name but to a people that has thieves and ignoramuses who also martyr themselves.

THE HOLY THIEF

☞ Jewish history throughout the generations abounds with such stories, accounts of the unworthy and iniquitous with seemingly no interest in Judaism who, when put to the ultimate test, chose to martyr themselves. It is a matter of record, thousands upon thousands of episodes: In the face of forced conversion, they chose death rather than deny the one God.

In the city of Shpola, Ukraine, there is a gravestone inscribed, "Here lies...the holy thief." The person buried there was an out-and-out thief who was caught red-handed burglarizing a church. In those days, the mid-eighteenth century, the punishment for such a crime, with the additional charge of sacrilege, was death. At his trial, the judges gave him a choice: "Convert to our religion, and we will reduce the charge from sacrilege to theft alone, and that too will be pardoned – or be burned at the stake."

The thief, a simple fellow, the most unworthy of the unworthy, stood and answered, "Indeed, I'm a thief, and I have committed many sins in my life. But to convert? Absolutely not!"

When they lit the fire beneath him, they said, "You can still save yourself from this gruesome death."

The thief replied, "I will burn and endure every torture, but I will never give up my religion!"

In the end, he died at the stake to sanctify God's name.

When I was teaching this subject, a student once asked, "This is all well and good for earlier generations, but how relevant is it today?" I answered that ostensibly it did not appear to be so and he had no answer. The following day, I was to deliver a lecture to a youthful audience in a remote town who were far removed from anything Jewish and who had never received a Jewish education. Their alienation was striking, and employing all my skills, I proceeded to provoke them into acknowledging their deep roots: Their heads were empty; they had cut themselves off from their people. In the middle of his reproach, an incensed young man fired back, "You should know that I'm not religious, and my father is not religious, and my grandfather strayed long ago. But if someone came and ordered me to worship an idol, I would willingly die first!"

The words struck like a thunderbolt. Only the day before, I had been asked this question and could not respond. Today I had received my answer. The young respondent had had a breakthrough. Dormant powers had surfaced because someone had attempted to negate his Jewishness. Perhaps the fact that his entire life he had eaten prohibited foods and done prohibited acts did not particularly bother him, but regarding his link to the Divine he was utterly unwilling to compromise.

What is unique is not that someone scholarly and devout gives his life at the moment of supreme reckoning, though certainly an enormous deed, but that the most unlearned person imaginable, who never opened a book and never once engaged in profound contemplation, also goes to his death to sanctify God's name, revealing an innermost attachment to the sacred that is beyond understanding. This is the true, self-sustained connection to God. ☞

וְגַם בִּמְעַט שֶׁיּוֹדְעִים אֵין מִתְבּוֹנְנִים כְּלָל,

and even the iota that they do know they do not contemplate at all.

Even a limited conceptual grasp can fully permeate a person's character, influencing him in the same manner that a much vaster spectrum affects a greater mind. When a person meditates on what he knows, when he continually probes deeper, this knowledge becoming central to his being, then even if the concept itself is minor, it assumes increasingly greater dimensions and significance in his life.

Among those who sacrificed their lives, suffering all kinds of horrible deaths rather than separate themselves from God, there were also ignorant and boorish individuals who never bothered to contemplate even whatever little they knew.

וְאֵין מוֹסְרִים נַפְשָׁם מֵחֲמַת דַּעַת וְהִתְבּוֹנְנוּת בַּה׳ כְּלָל. אֶלָּא בְּלִי שׁוּם דַּעַת וְהִתְבּוֹנְנוּת, רַק כְּאִלּוּ הוּא דָּבָר שֶׁאִי אֶפְשָׁר כְּלָל לִכְפּוֹר בַּה׳ אֶחָד, בְּלִי שׁוּם טַעַם וְטַעֲנָה וּמַעֲנֶה כְּלָל.

They do not sacrifice their lives in martyrdom **as a result of knowing and meditating upon God at all, but rather** they sacrifice their lives even **without knowledge or meditation, as if denying the one God is something utterly impossible, without rhyme or reason whatsoever.**

Elsewhere, it is explained that self-sacrifice is rooted in the essence of one's being, far beyond the faculty of knowledge or conscious awareness. When a Jew comes to this point, when he must choose between faith and denial of God, there is no room for deliberation. He knows with absolute clarity that he cannot forsake God, whatever the circumstances and at whatever cost. As the author of the *Tanya* goes on to explain, at that moment a flash of certainty enlightens his soul without the slightest internal conflict, though if pressed to debate the issue, he would be mute. This is a feeling as visceral as the fact of his own existence. No proof is required, nor would he be able to provide one.

This perfect assuredness is found within even the most unworthy at the moment of his last and definitive test: to be with God or to deny Him. Whatever his thinking was over a lifetime, whatever his knowledge or lack thereof, none are relevant. As certain as he is of his own existence, so too is his conviction that he cannot sever himself from God.

וְהַיְינוּ מִשּׁוּם שֶׁה׳ אֶחָד מֵאִיר וּמְחַיֶּה כׇּל הַנֶּפֶשׁ עַל יְדֵי הִתְלַבְּשׁוּתוֹ בִּבְחִינַת חׇכְמָה שֶׁבָּהּ שֶׁהִיא לְמַעְלָה מִן הַדַּעַת וְהַשֵּׂכֶל הַמּוּשָּׂג וּמוּבָן.

That is because the one God illuminates and sustains the entire soul by being clothed within its faculty of wisdom, which transcends knowledge and intelligence that are apprehended and understood.

In the instant a Jew senses that his link to supernal holiness is threatened, a very different operating system is initiated, one that is somewhat akin to our survival mechanism in the face of danger. Restraints disappear, together with aches and pains, preconceptions and concerns. In an inelegant analogy, this works like a posthypnotic suggestion. A person receives a sign, hears a particular word, sees a specific sight, and forces beyond his conscious will begin to direct him. His previous life experiences, all that he thought and knew, are pushed aside, and he

DYING IN SANCTIFICATION OF GOD'S NAME

☞ When a Jew sacrifices his life in martyrdom to sanctify God's name, he is on a different plane of being, to the extent that he experiences no torment. A particular book about sixteenth-century Poland incidentally tells of Jews who died in sanctification of God's name (see *Yosef Ometz*, vol. 1, *Dinei Mekadesh Hashem* 482). These Jews were killed in one of the most horrific manners invented by the Tatars: They would seat the victim on a pole until he died in terrible agony. The author writes that during those hours, which should have been hours of indescribable torment, the victims spoke to him with a clear mind, until their souls finally departed.

acts in a completely different manner. At that culminating moment, the faculty of wisdom in the soul inundates his entire being. His thinking moves beyond accustomed patterns; his actions shift to another mode. A previously unknown force surfaces and guides him. ☞

In the chapters that follow, the author of the *Tanya* will direct this potential in every Jew to cleave to God to the extent of martyrdom toward another objective: not only to give up one's life to sanctify God but also to live for Him. To this end, the author places the mindset of sanctifying God as a constant focus throughout life. The attitude toward every commandment – or transgression – is a matter of personal decision: Am I for God or against Him? This decision need not be reserved for extraordinary crises. It is germane to every conclusion one reaches: Is one in favor of the commandment or against it? In favor of the transgression or against it? When one becomes conscious of this, that this too is the moment of truth, his decision is no longer in doubt.

Someone who is ready to die to sanctify God's name will surely be prepared to forgo some desire in his life in order to sanctify Him. Nevertheless, as the author of the *Tanya* will explain, a problem arises. Isolating life's moments second after second, day after day, and basing them on sanctifying God is no easy process. To live with this awareness is hardly effortless, not just for a single moment but constantly, at every instant of one's lifetime.

Chapter 19

IN THE PREVIOUS CHAPTER, THE AUTHOR OF THE *TANYA* gave another interpretation of the verse whose words shape the motif of this work: "The matter is very near to you..." (Deut. 30:14). In particular, he offered an explanation regarding the meaning of the word "very" and explained that "very near" denotes the love that is concealed within the heart of every Jew. In his explanation of this love, the author of the *Tanya* observed that a full understanding of it must be preceded by a clear comprehension of a number of concepts: the root of this love, its nature, how it is our natural inheritance, and how the fear of God is encompassed within it.

The author of the *Tanya* has already dealt with two of these issues: the root of this love and how it came to us as an inheritance from our forefathers. In this chapter, he will explain the two remaining points: the nature of this love and how it is evoked particularly when a person feels under threat of severance from God, as well as how this love contains an element of awe.

וּלְתוֹסֶפֶת בֵּיאוּר צָרִיךְ לְבָאֵר הֵיטֵב מַה שֶּׁכָּתוּב: "נֵר ה' נִשְׁמַת אָדָם" (משלי כ, כז). פֵּירוּשׁ, שֶׁיִּשְׂרָאֵל הַקְּרוּיִים אָדָם - נִשְׁמָתָם הִיא לְמָשָׁל כְּאוֹר הַנֵּר,

2 Shevat

10 Shevat (leap year)

To further elucidate the nature of this concealed love, **it is necessary to properly explain the verse "The soul of man is the candle of the Lord"** (Prov. 20:27). **This means that the soul of** every **Jew, who is referred to as *adam*,** man, **is analogous to the light of a candle,**

This metaphor appears several times in the *Tanya* and has a variety of implications.[1] Fundamentally, the human soul is compared to the flame of a candle, the human body or animal soul to the wick, and the Torah and commandments, whose role is to connect the soul to the body, to the oil, which connects the fire and the wick. As long as there is oil, the fire will continue to burn and will not consume the wick.

שֶׁמִּתְנַעְנֵעַ תָּמִיד לְמַעְלָה בְּטִבְעוֹ מִפְּנֵי שֶׁאוֹר הָאֵשׁ חָפֵץ בְּטֶבַע לִיפָּרֵד מֵהַפְּתִילָה וְלִידָּבֵק בְּשָׁרְשׁוֹ לְמַעְלָה בִּיסוֹד הָאֵשׁ הַכְּלָלִי שֶׁתַּחַת גַּלְגַּל הַיָּרֵחַ, כְּמוֹ שֶׁכָּתוּב בְּ'עֵץ חַיִּים'.

which by nature constantly flickers upward because the flame of a fire naturally desires to part from the wick and cling to its source on high, which is **the universal element of fire** located **below the sphere of the moon, as stated in *Etz Ḥayyim*.**

This image is based on the scientific conception of previous eras,[2] which posited a hierarchy of four basic elements in ascending order: earth, water, wind, and fire. The element of fire thus belongs to the highest stratum of our world and resides just below the sphere of the moon, which is the lowest of the spheres that surround the world.[3] The general principle that the author of the *Tanya* presents here is that these fundamental elements yearn to return to their source. Earth and everything associated with it yearn to return to the element

THE ELEMENTS AND THE CELESTIAL SPHERES

☞ Today, when science views matters differently, this analogy is not as elegant as it once seemed, but not because today's scientific outlook is more correct. The great difference, perhaps the only meaningful one, between the science of today and that of previous eras is that scientists today no longer attempt to arrive at absolute scientific truth. The present-day presumption is that science does not have the tools to reach such a determination. At any rate, any analogy based on a scientific outlook is necessarily limited and dependent on that outlook. Once we understand this, this metaphor loses none of its force. Its intended meaning remains pertinent.

1. See chaps. 35, 53.
2. See notes to *Likkutei Amarim, Mahadura Kamma* (1981), chap. 19, p. 132; Rambam, *Sefer HaMadda, Hilkhot Yesodei HaTorah* 3:10.
3. See Rambam, *Sefer HaMadda, Hilkhot Yesodei HaTorah,* chaps. 3–4.

of earth (thus accounting for the phenomenon of gravity), and anything related to the element of fire yearns to rise to the element of fire above. ☞

There is another, perhaps more relatable analogy that describes the small flame's yearning to be absorbed within the greater flame, its source. When a candle is placed next to a large fire, the small flame of the candle seems drawn to the fire and is extinguished, giving the appearance that it desires to be absorbed into the greater flame and consumed by it.

וְאַף שֶׁעַל יְדֵי זֶה יִכְבֶּה וְלֹא יָאִיר כְּלוּם לְמַטָּה, וְגַם לְמַעְלָה בְּשָׁרְשׁוֹ יִתְבַּטֵּל אוֹרוֹ בִּמְצִיאוּת בְּשָׁרְשׁוֹ, אַף עַל פִּי כֵן בְּכָךְ הוּא חָפֵץ בְּטִבְעוֹ.

Although by doing so the flame **will be extinguished, illuminating nothing below, and also above, in its source, its light will become subsumed within its source, this is nevertheless its natural desire.**

Clearly, the light of the candle does nothing by conscious will. Yet precisely because of that, the use of this analogy is significant in understanding the author of the *Tanya*'s intent. The tendency of the candle's light to annihilate itself in its source contradicts the natural law of inertia, that all entities strive to maintain their basic form, whether or not they possess consciousness. To change the form of an object, or to change its location or destroy it, one must apply pressure from without. The flame of the candle is acting in opposition to that principle, because it desires, as it were, to unite with its source without the imposition of any external force, even though that union would cause it to lose its independent existence. The author of the *Tanya*, then, emphasizes that "this is its natural desire." Although this yearning stands in opposition to the rational principles that we understand, it is embedded within the nature of the candle flame.

A stone too will attempt to connect with its source in the element of earth by falling to the ground, but the stone does not lose its independent existence. When the flame reaches its source, on the other hand, it is entirely nullified, not only in appearance but in fact. This self-nullification is a dual one: surrender of its distinctive identity and, even more, surrender of any independent existence.

כָּךְ נִשְׁמַת הָאָדָם, וְכֵן בְּחִינַת רוּחַ וְנֶפֶשׁ, חֲפֵצָה וְחוֹשֶׁקֶת בְּטִבְעָהּ לִיפָּרֵד וְלָצֵאת מִן הַגּוּף וְלִידָּבֵק בְּשָׁרְשָׁהּ וּמְקוֹרָהּ,

So too a person's *neshama* soul level, as well as his soul levels of *ruaḥ* and *nefesh*, naturally desires and longs to depart and leave the body and cling to its root and source,

This applies not only to the highest level of the soul, the *neshama,* but also to the soul's lower aspects, *ruaḥ* and *nefesh*.[4] Unlike the construct of the self, which is shared by the body and animal soul and which desires to maintain its own independent existence, the divine soul yearns to return to its source, to leave the confines of the body and thereby eliminate the self.

בַּה', חַיֵּי הַחַיִּים בָּרוּךְ הוּא.

in God, the infinite source of life, blessed be He.

Even though the soul infuses a person with life, it itself yearns to be absorbed into the source of life on high. As the author of the *Tanya* will go on to explain, these two aspects of the soul are interdependent. There is only one source of life, and in order that the soul may draw life from the source and give life, that it may be a living soul, it must be absorbed into the one source: God, the "infinite source of life."

הֲגַם שֶׁתִּהְיֶה אַיִן וָאֶפֶס וְתִתְבַּטֵּל שָׁם בִּמְצִיאוּת לְגַמְרֵי וְלֹא יִשָּׁאֵר מִמֶּנָּה מְאוּמָה, מִמַּהוּתָהּ וְעַצְמוּתָהּ הָרִאשׁוֹן,

Although the soul **will become absolute nothingness and will be utterly subsumed there, leaving no trace whatsoever of its original essence and being,**

The soul's yearning for total disengagement from existence is more than a death wish. Death does not eradicate a being's individuality. The soul only changes from one state to another, from containment within a body to a different reality. But the yearning of the soul goes beyond that. Its goal is to completely eliminate itself, knowing that its presence within the source of all life will no longer be the existence

---

4. As mentioned in the previous chapter, even the lowest level of the soul – the "*nefesh* of the *nefesh* of *Malkhut* of *Asiya*" – contains a spark of the Divine (see Rabbi Shmuel Gronem Esterman's commentary on the *Tanya*).

of a self-aware, independent self with its own identity and desires but a radically different state of existence that retains no connection whatsoever to its previous existence and character.

אַף עַל פִּי כֵן זֶה רְצוֹנָהּ וְחֶפְצָהּ בְּטִבְעָהּ. וְטֶבַע זֶה הוּא שֵׁם הַמּוּשְׁאָל לְכָל דָּבָר שֶׁאֵינוֹ בִּבְחִינַת טַעַם וָדַעַת.

this is nevertheless its natural will and desire. This expression, ***teva,*** nature, **is a borrowed term for anything that is not in the realm of reason and logic.**

In all languages, the word "nature" is one of the most obscure. It is used to describe almost anything at all, good or bad, and one would be hard-pressed to find any other word with so little intrinsic meaning. But the very lack of clarity of this word is an indication of its meaning: It is used to characterize a thing's basic makeup for which we have no explanation.

This meaning is inherent in the Hebrew word for nature, *teva,* which means something impressed deeply into an object. Thus, a signet ring, which causes a wax impression, is a *taba'at,* and a coin, whose face is minted, is a *matbe'a*. Nature is the trait, the character, that is imprinted on a thing, or, alternatively, the thing is imprinted in it, and it is not affected by our interface with it.

Although it is possible to derive the laws of nature, it is not possible to explain them. Wherever it is possible to explain why something acts in one way or another, that is no longer a description of nature but of a particular cause that results in a particular action or state. The nature of something is always beyond explanation, beyond rationale.[5] ☞

THE "NATURE" OF THE DIVINE SOUL

☞ The use of the term "nature" to describe the yearning of the soul to connect with its source sheds light on another aspect of this phenomenon. Although seemingly abnormal, this desire of the soul to be subsumed in the infinite source of all life is natural to the divine soul, because it is a portion of God on high. The soul itself is a

5. It was said among hasidim that the word *teva* is related to the Hebrew word *tevia,* drowning, because this word has been used to drown almost every spiritual

וְגַם כָּאן הַכַּוָּנָה שֶׁרָצוֹן וְחֵפֶץ זֶה בַּנֶּפֶשׁ אֵינוֹ בִּבְחִינַת טַעַם וְדַעַת וְשֵׂכֶל מוּשָּׂג וּמוּבָן, אֶלָּא לְמַעְלָה מֵהַדַּעַת וְשֵׂכֶל הַמּוּשָּׂג וְהַמּוּבָן.

Here too the meaning of the word *teva* **is that this will and desire in the soul is not on the level of reason, logic, and intellect** that can be **apprehended and understood. Rather, it is beyond apprehensible and understandable** logic **and intellect.**

The foundation of all rational thought is the self. The concern for the continued existence of the self is the basis and focus of all rational thought. Every rational explanation of human phenomena always returns, in one way or another, directly or indirectly, to the ongoing existence of the self.

This explanation can also be applied to the performance of the mitzvot, as well as to the relationship between man and God in general. They are the result of the yearning of the self to grow to broader and higher realms. But one phenomenon has no rational explanation: the willingness for self-sacrifice. Martyrdom stands in direct opposition to the primary axiom of survival. In this sense, the yearning of the divine soul for self-annihilation is a phenomenon without explanation, beyond rhyme or reason. The manifestation of the concealed love when a person gives up his life to sanctify God's name comes not from

divine spark, and as such it is not destroyed in the Divine, but rather, by returning to its source, it finds completion. Everything, by its nature, desires to complete itself, and this is no less true here. The divine spark within a person yearns constantly to leave the confines of the physical body and return to its original state of being.

The soul and body are not connected to each other willingly but only under mutual duress. The body is interested not in the soul but in physicality. It wants to be even less than an animal, to sink into an eternal torpor, but the soul forces it to live. Nor does the soul desire to be allied with the body, because it wishes to be divine. Together, they are engaged in an unending struggle, and it is that struggle that justifies the existence of these two interlocked opposing entities. By nature, in their essential being, the soul and body wish to be rid of each other, and there must therefore be a constant effort, both physical and spiritual, to maintain the connection between them. Only when such force is applied can this joint existence in reality be maintained.

---

and religious sentiment. Every phenomenon can be explained as expressing a law of nature, so once we label it as such, no rational explanation is sought.

the ego's rational knowledge but from its total self-abnegation, which itself comes from beyond "apprehensible and understandable logic."

This self-sacrifice is total. It is not a selflessness in which a person exchanges one state of existence for another: physical for spiritual, life in this world for life in the Garden of Eden. The continuation of one's existence is essentially the preservation of the self. In this sense, the self continues to exist even in the Garden of Eden, drawing pleasure from the radiance of the Divine Presence. But self-sacrifice is different. It is a yearning for the nullification of the self and not for its continued existence in any form whatsoever. ☞

"I DO NOT WANT EDEN!"

☞ It is told that Rabbi Shneur Zalman of Liadi, the author of the *Tanya*, used to sing the following words when he reached a state of *deveikut*, of attachment to God, in prayer, in his famous melody: "Master of the universe, I do not want Your Eden. I do not want Your World to Come. I want only You!"

Rabbi Shneur Zalman's personality as it comes through in this story – that is, as a man who reached the highest levels of ecstasy – stands in contrast to the portrait of the author that we can glean from the texts of the *Tanya* and his other writings. It stands in contradiction as well to the more restrained Chabad hasidic practice throughout subsequent generations. Other such details are also recorded. It is said that Rabbi Shneur Zalman"s private study was lined with pillows so that he would not hurt himself as he ran back and forth in his fervent devotions. He prayed at such length that more than once he would be left alone for an extended period in the synagogue.

It is told that one time, when those who had left the synagogue returned, they did not find him there. They searched for him until they finally found him outside the city, far from the synagogue. In the midst of his fervent prayers, he had broken off a piece of the *bima* railing, and holding it in his hand while still immersed in his prayers, he had wandered from the synagogue.

Even though this aspect of the author's personality is not visible in his writings, it is important for our understanding. This book is not the work of a cold intellectual fashioning a theological structure but is based in the self-restraint of a man whose nature is not at all in line with such a structure. In a sense, the challenge of such a person is not to reach a state of exalted inspiration but to prevent his soul from leaving his body – to remain in the world and not, like Elijah the prophet, leave it in a storm wind. For a person of this type, life in this world is a constant struggle to be grounded, not a struggle to be elevated.

This personal, open, and overabundant awakening led the author of the *Tanya* to adopt a certain inflexibility and sense of distance in this work. At times, one gets the impression that the author relates to the "most unworthy and the sinners of Israel" as one would relate to creatures of an entirely different species, as though they were a foreign phenomenon that

וְהִיא בְּחִינַת חָכְמָה שֶׁבַּנֶּפֶשׁ, שֶׁבָּהּ אוֹר אֵין סוֹף בָּרוּךְ הוּא.

This will and desire **is clothed in the soul's faculty of wisdom, which contains the light of *Ein Sof*, blessed be He.**

For the concealed love, which is contained in the deepest recesses of the soul, to be manifest and actualized, it is clothed in the soul's faculty of wisdom, where the light of *Ein Sof* shines.[6] Wisdom is the point of awareness that is itself beyond the rational, the passageway within human consciousness between nothingness and existence. Thus it is the point at which the light of *Ein Sof*, which is beyond understanding, may be understood. It is here that the hidden love, which transcends the intellect and rationality, may be found.

3 Shevat וְזֶהוּ כְּלָל בְּכָל סִטְרָא דִקְדוּשָּׁה שֶׁאֵינוֹ אֶלָּא מַה שֶּׁנִּמְשָׁךְ מֵחָכְמָה שֶׁנִּקְרָא 'קוֹדֶשׁ הָעֶלְיוֹן', הַבָּטֵל בִּמְצִיאוּת בְּאוֹר אֵין סוֹף בָּרוּךְ הוּא הַמְלוּבָּשׁ בּוֹ וְאֵינוֹ

This is a general principle with regard to the entire side of holiness, that holiness **constitutes only that which is drawn down from** the faculty of wisdom, **which is called "supernal holiness"** since **its existence is subsumed**

he does not naturally understand. Unlike other hasidic writers (such as his contemporary, who was great in a different way, Rabbi Naḥman of Breslov), whose starting point was in a sense an understanding of the distortions and burdens of such lowly Jews, the author of the *Tanya* writes from a seemingly external perspective – not from an understanding that arises from personal experience but from the analytical gaze of an observer. It is as though he heard from others that such people exist and that they face certain challenges, and he is trying to create a framework in which they might operate, even though his own inner being is built on an entirely different quality.

This point that the author of the *Tanya* makes about self-sacrifice, about the readiness to surrender one's existence and be absorbed into the divine source, about the core of concealed love, was already apparent in himself. From this perspective, he exclaims, as did the prophet, "For I the Lord did not change, and you, sons of Jacob, did not perish" (Mal. 3:6). The author of the *Tanya* interprets this verse as follows: "When you, Israel, contemplate this fact, that I, God, have not changed, that I am the same before the Creation and after the Creation, does this contemplation not cause you to perish? Does the thought of it not cause your soul to expire?"

6. See gloss to chap. 35.

דָּבָר בִּפְנֵי עַצְמוֹ כַּנִּזְכָּר לְעֵיל, וְלָכֵן נִקְרָא כֹּ״חַ מָ״ה.

in the light of *Ein Sof*, blessed be He, which is clothed in it, and it is not a separate entity, as stated above (chap. 6). **It is therefore referred to as *ko'aḥ ma*,** literally, "the potential for what."

Only God Himself can be truly referred to as holy. Therefore, anything that is holy or that is related to holiness can only be drawn from the "supernal holiness," from the faculty of wisdom in which the light of Ein Sof is enclothed.

The faculty of wisdom is also the faculty for self-abnegation, for achieving a state of nothingness. Its essence is that it dissolves into non-being; it becomes nothing. The author of the *Tanya* explained this elsewhere in terms of the mind and its ability to learn.[7] The capacity to learn new things is based on the connection between wisdom and humility: The ability to receive wisdom in one's mind is identified with the self-negating ability to be humble. When a person is filled with his own ideas and knowledge, he cannot arrive at any new understanding but can only assimilate variations on the old. In order to attain new knowledge, he must acquire a state of self-nullification in which the old ideas no longer exist and he can assimilate new concepts.

This is why young children learn so quickly, but as they grow older, their ability diminishes. A young child does not have a developed sense of independent existence, and thus he can more easily absorb new information. But as his sense of self grows, as he recognizes his own independent being, he has less wisdom, less mindfulness of what is going on around him. External reality cannot enter if there is nothing inside to receive it. Wisdom alone constitutes an empty vessel capable of receiving because it is completely nullified before the light of *Ein Sof* and not an independent entity in any way. In this way, wisdom can be a receptacle for holiness, for the boundless *Ein Sof*, which is distinct from everything.

וְהוּא הֵפֶךְ מַמָּשׁ מִבְּחִינַת הַקְּלִיפָּה וְסִטְרָא אָחֳרָא שֶׁמִּמֶּנָּה נַפְשׁוֹת אוּמּוֹת הָעוֹלָם דְּעָבְדִין לְגַרְמַיְיהוּ

This is literally the opposite of the *kelippa* and *sitra aḥara*, from which stem the souls of the gentile **nations of the world, who act for their own** sake

7. See chap. 3.

As the author of the *Tanya* taught in the previous chapter, a Jew is defined as someone who is prepared to give his life for the sake of God. In this sense, holiness in general may be defined as whatever is nullified relative to *Ein Sof*. The fundamental difference between holiness and the *sitra aḥara* is not in external phenomena but in the inner kernel from which everything originates and to which everything returns. When this kernel is solely self-oriented, when the beginning of a human act, no matter what it may be, is for the sake of the self, that act belongs to the *sitra aḥara*. When a person is self-centered, even if he gives charity, acts kindly, or is involved in holy deeds, his actions only enhance his ego and, more generally, magnify the *kelippa*. ☞

SELF-CENTEREDNESS AND THE ROOT OF *KELIPPA*

☞ *Kelippa* in its grossest manifestation can be termed animalistic, carnal, and ignoble. But these are only its coarsest, most unacceptable aspects. At its primal foundation, it is not necessarily linked to those forms but to a point that can be exceedingly subtle, taking the form of a sense of self. The Sages observe that an egotistical person is like one who engages in idolatry, which is the totality of evil and *kelippa* (*Sota* 4b). Haughtiness and egotism inject a person's sense of self into all he does so that his deeds are solely for his own interests. It establishes his sense of self as the center of his universe, and in the end it fills all of existence with his sense of self. Thus the Sages state that God says of a boastful person, "He and I cannot dwell together in the world" (*Sota* 5a). It follows that this is where *kelippa*, the *sitra aḥara*, and idolatry dwell.

The root of *kelippa*, an entity whose essence is that of a being that is separate from the Divine, as it were, is still found even at the source of existence. It emerges from the fact of existence itself, because anything that exists must necessarily possess a "back side." No vessel can have only an inside; it must also possess an outside, or a "back side." In the spiritual realm, the back side constitutes a sense of independence, the sense that it is not a part of the contents that its vessel contains, but rather is an inescapable side effect of existence.

To illustrate, the number five is an abstraction. When the number is written, it has a certain form on the page that expresses its content. But that symbol has other aspects that have no connection at all to its inner content. In this sense, everything in the world has this ancillary condition, which essentially is a self, an "I." Once there is a sense of self, it can turn inward to contemplate itself and act, in a sense, for its own self-interest. Such action does not imply reprehensible behavior but refers to any benefit that a person derives, even the most subtle – even that of a mitzva. Though a person may have good intentions, if his act is for himself alone, it constitutes the initial stage of *kelippa*. It is said that the desire to be a tzaddik is also a type of desire. It may be an elevated desire, one that can be fulfilled only after all other longings have been defeated, but it too is a desire to gain something for oneself, for one's own self-interest.

וְאָמְרִין: "הַב הַב" and say, "Give, give,"

These words are a quotation from the *Zohar* in its description of those who pray solely for themselves, like a dog barking for its food,[8] but the original source is the verse "The leech has two daughters: 'Give, give!' There are three that will not be sated, four that do not say, 'Enough'" (Prov. 30:15). The leech, which sucks blood and is never sated, is an analogy for *kelippa*.[9] While this analogy has several facets, the one expressed here is the demand of the insatiable *kelippa* to receive ("Give, give!"). Unlike holiness, which gives until it has given all of itself, *kelippa* only takes, and even when it gives, it is only making an investment that will return a profit later on, whether in this world or the next. Instead, service to God performed in holiness must be divested of any intention to receive reward. In the words of the Mishna, "Do not be like servants who serve the master in order to receive a reward, but be like servants who serve the master not for the sake of receiving a reward" (*Avot* 1:3). ☞

וְ"הַלְעִיטֵנִי", לִהְיוֹת יֵשׁ וְדָבָר בִּפְנֵי עַצְמוֹ, כַּנִּזְכָּר לְעֵיל, and "Feed me" (Gen. 25:30), **in order to become an independent entity, as stated above** (chap. 6),

On a metaphorical level, the verse in Genesis describes how Esau, who represented *kelippa*, demanded of Jacob, who was symbolic of holiness and the source of life-giving sustenance, to "feed him." He demanded that he direct that sustenance to Esau alone, for his self-aggrandizement.

The contrast between the realm of holiness and the other side is

ALTRUISM IN THE SERVICE OF GOD

☞ For most of his life, the Maggid of Mezeritch lived in abject poverty. When conditions grew especially dire, his wife groaned, and, hearing her, the Maggid groaned as well. At that moment, he heard a proclamation in Heaven that he had lost his portion in the World to Come, because a person of his stature should not have descended to such a level. Joyously, the Maggid exclaimed, "Now I can serve God in truth, without any desire to receive a reward!"

8. *Zohar* 1:111a.
9. See *Torah Or* 5d.

not to be found in their outer manifestations but in a point of great subtlety that resists easy clarification. When the Sages discuss this topic, they enumerate the differences between the disciples of Abraham and the disciples of Bilam but not the differences between Abraham and Bilam themselves.[10] The differences between Abraham and Bilam were in some ways too fine to be discerned by every eye. We must look at their disciples, after these differences had developed by several stages and grown more pronounced.

Bilam was not simply an evil man. He was so great that the Sages comment regarding the verse "There has not risen another prophet in Israel like Moses..." (Deut. 34:10) that another prophet did not rise in Israel, but such a man did rise among the nations, and that was Bilam.[11] In greatness and attainment of the spirit, Bilam was like Moses. But in one inner point, there was a difference between them that changed everything: "The man Moses was very humble, more so than any person on the face of the earth" (Num. 12:3), whereas it is said of Bilam's disciples that they had "an evil eye, a haughty spirit, and a limitless appetite" (Mishna *Avot* 5:19). Even though the greatness of these two men was equal, one man was the root of *kelippa*, and the other was a man of God, without equal in Israel. ☞

HUMILITY IN THE FACE OF LOVING-KINDNESS

☞ In the epistle that the author of the *Tanya* wrote after his liberation from prison (*Iggeret HaKodesh*, epistle 2), he discusses this idea as it is expressed in the words of Jacob: "I am unworthy of all the kindnesses" (Gen. 32:10). The subtle difference between holiness and *kelippa* may be seen in people's reaction to worldly success, to the manifestation of God's loving-kindness. In the realm of *kelippa*, the more a person receives, the greater he grows in his own eyes. The more successful he is, the more assured he is that he deserves success. But in the realm of holiness, a person says, "I am unworthy of all the kindnesses." The more he is given, the smaller he grows in his own eyes. This is not an obvious difference, like the contrast between large and small or beautiful and ugly. It is a very subtle one, which can be recognized only when God bestows kindness: whether one grows haughty and vainglorious – or more humble.

10. See Mishna *Avot* 5:19.
11. *Sifrei*, Deut. 34:10.

הֶפֶךְ בְּחִינַת הַחָכְמָה. which is **the opposite of wisdom.**

The self-centered nature of *kelippa* is antithetical to wisdom. Wisdom is where the human and the Divine meet. This nexus is itself nothingness. Being "something," an independent entity, is the opposite of wisdom, and as such it cannot connect with the Divine.

וְלָכֵן נִקְרָאִים מֵתִים, כִּי "הַחָכְמָה תְּחַיֶּה" (קהלת ז, יב), וּכְתִיב: "יָמוּתוּ וְלֹא בְחָכְמָה" (איוב ד, כא).

Consequently, they are referred to as dead even while alive **because "wisdom grants life** to its possessors" (Eccles. 7:12), **and "they die without wisdom"** (Job 4:21).

Just as wisdom is the source of awareness, it is also the source of life. Accordingly, whatever is not connected to wisdom is not connected to life. Life essentially comes from a single source: holiness. *Kelippa* is thus not an independent source of life but a parasite that takes its life force from holiness. Lacking its own life force, evil constantly attempts to draw that energy from holiness. It attempts to take life ("Give, give") because that is its sole means of survival.

The damage that *kelippa* does to holiness is not purposeful but is the unintended outcome of its desire to exist and live. Because it lacks access to the source of life and existence – that is, the ability to nullify itself before holiness – it clings to holy things, and at times destroys them, in an effort to draw life from them. Yet it does not realize that it is already dead because it is not prepared to nullify itself before holiness. ☞

THE SOMETHING THAT BECOMES EVERYTHING

☞ Idolatry is fundamentally identical with evil. Idolatry is anything that may be considered a god, a separate power, an independent entity. It begins when something is considered to be standing on its own, without the need to answer to a master. At that moment a crack has been opened through which all the evil in the world can pour.

As mentioned elsewhere (see *Torah Or* 57b), the ultimate defilement, the nadir of being, was embodied in Pharaoh, who declared, "My river is mine, and I made myself" (Ezek. 29:3). The statement that "my river is mine" constitutes the beginning of the defilement, when he claimed total ownership over it. The continuation of his statement, "And I made myself," declaring

וְכֵן הָרְשָׁעִים וּפוֹשְׁעֵי יִשְׂרָאֵל קוֹדֶם שֶׁבָּאוּ לִידֵי נִסָּיוֹן לְקַדֵּשׁ הַשֵּׁם, כִּי בְּחִינַת הַחָכְמָה שֶׁבַּנֶּפֶשׁ הָאֱלֹהִית, עִם נִיצוֹץ אֱלֹהוּת מֵאוֹר אֵין סוֹף בָּרוּךְ הוּא הַמְלוּבָּשׁ בָּהּ, הֵם בִּבְחִינַת גָּלוּת בְּגוּפָם בַּנֶּפֶשׁ הַבַּהֲמִית, מִצַּד הַקְּלִיפָּה שֶׁבֶּחָלָל הַשְּׂמָאלִי שֶׁבַּלֵּב הַמּוֹלֶכֶת וּמוֹשֶׁלֶת בְּגוּפָם בְּסוֹד גָּלוּת הַשְּׁכִינָה כַּנִּזְכָּר לְעֵיל.

Likewise, prior to their being confronted with the challenge of dying for the sake of **sanctifying** God's **name, the wicked and sinners of Israel** are also regarded as dead. This is **because the faculty of wisdom in the divine soul,** along **with the spark of the Divine from the light of *Ein Sof,* blessed be He, which is clothed within it, are in a state of exile within their** own **body,** specifically **in the animal soul from the side of *kelippa*** in **the left chamber of the heart, which rules and governs their body,** constituting **the aforementioned mystic exile of the Divine Presence** (see chap. 17).

The exile of the Divine Presence does not constitute the actual absence of God's presence but its involvement in other, unsanctified matters. The Sages state that "when [the Jews] were exiled to Babylonia, the Divine Presence went with them" (*Megilla* 29a). The Divine Presence is with them even in exile, but it is concealed, clothed in sackcloth – in nonholy matters, even in *kelippot.*[12] When it wears this garb, the power

that there was nothing else besides him, was the ultimate in impurity. At its root, *kelippa* does not deny God or wage war against Him. It only declares, "I too am something." But that something grows until it becomes everything.

The nature of holiness, on the other hand, is self-nullification, a state that the divine spark within us enables us to attain. The entire being of great men such as the patriarchs, who were a chariot for the Divine Presence, and Moses, from whose throat God spoke, is actualized self-nullification. But in any Jew, "even the most unworthy and the sinners of Israel," who demonstrates no trace of such self-nullification, a divine spark exists. That spark is the potential in the person to make himself nothing, to give up his life for the sake of God. Yet, paradoxically, this is a person's core of life.

12. See chap. 17; *Iggeret HaKodesh,* epistle 25.

and life force that stems from the Divine Presence can even be turned against holiness itself.

The Ba'al Shem Tov states that there are three stages in the exile of the Divine Presence. The first is the exile of Israel among the nations. The second, and harsher, is the exile of Jews among themselves. The third, and most grievous of all, is the exile of an individual Jew within himself.[13] Here the author of the *Tanya* is speaking of this third stage, when an individual's divine spark, which is found within every person's faculty of wisdom, is obscured by the body and the animal soul.

וְלָכֵן נִקְרֵאת אַהֲבָה זוֹ בַּנֶּפֶשׁ הָאֱלֹהִית, שֶׁרְצוֹנָהּ וְחֶפְצָהּ לְדָבֵק בַּה' חַיֵּי הַחַיִּים בָּרוּךְ הוּא, בְּשֵׁם אַהֲבָה מְסוּתֶּרֶת,

Therefore, this love that is in the divine soul, whose will and desire is to cling to God, the infinite **source of life, blessed be He, is referred to as concealed love,**

The love that is contained in the divine soul is not an operative function or manifestation of the soul on its part but is the essence of its very being. Whom a particular soul belongs to or where it stands is of no account. Every soul constantly yearns to return to its source, and this will and desire is what constitutes the love that is latent in the divine soul.

This love can express itself in a range of emotions, but those emotions are merely manifestations of the soul's yearning and desire to be close to the object of his love, to cling to the infinite source of all life, to surrender itself to the Divine. That is the essential nature of the divine soul. But although every Jew has a divine soul, the love contained within it is not always revealed.

כִּי הִיא מְסוּתֶּרֶת וּמְכוּסָּה בִּלְבוּשׁ שַׂק דִּקְלִיפָּה בְּפוֹשְׁעֵי יִשְׂרָאֵל.

for it is concealed and covered by the sackcloth of *kelippa* in the sinners of Israel.

The *kelippa*'s garment is impenetrable, stymying both this feeling of love for God as well as its practical implementation. This is why, although wicked people too possess this love of God, it is not manifest within

13. See *Ba'al Shem Tov al HaTorah, Parashat Balak* 3 and *Parashat Shemot* 6.

them, since they neither think nor act in a manner whereby this love can be expressed. On the contrary, their lifestyle can even run counter to the divine soul, which sustains them at their essence.[14]

וּמִמֶּנָּה נִכְנַס בָּהֶם רוּחַ שְׁטוּת לַחֲטוֹא, כְּמַאֲמַר רַבּוֹתֵינוּ זַ"ל: "אֵין אָדָם חוֹטֵא" כו'.

From this *kelippa* a spirit of folly enters the sinners of Israel, causing them **to sin, in accordance with our Rabbis' statement "A man does not commit a transgression** unless a spirit of folly enters him" (*Sota* 3a).

A "spirit of folly" appears in a variety of forms. Some are obvious, such as when a person realizes that what he is doing is foolish immediately after sinning or even in the midst of the sin. He recognizes that this act is against his better interests, in conflict with his values, and inconsistent with his nature and will, and yet he does it. Another spirit of folly enters a person when he sins, but this spirit persuades him that what he is doing is not egregious, not even a sin, and that he is not separating himself from God. As a matter of principle, a Jew will deny that he would disconnect himself from God, and he denies that strenuously, even as he takes steps that lead him further and further away from Him. There is also a spirit of folly that tells a person that the prohibition he is violating is not important. It is only symbolic, of mere historical significance, that "the main thing is to be a good Jew in your heart." There can be an intellectual spirit of folly and one that is more simple. All these create the cloak that allows a Jew to live with a paradox: having the power within him to be able to sacrifice his life in order not to be separated from God, while at the same time, he is so distant from Him. ☞

4 Shevat אֶלָּא שֶׁגָּלוּת הַזֶּה לִבְחִינַת חָכְמָה אֵינוֹ אֶלָּא לִבְחִינָה הַמִּתְפַּשֶּׁטֶת מִמֶּנָּה בַּנֶּפֶשׁ כּוּלָּהּ לְהַחֲיוֹתָהּ. אֲבָל שֹׁרֶשׁ וְעִיקַּר

But this exile of the faculty of wisdom applies **only to that aspect that spreads from it into the entire soul to animate it. However, the root and**

14. The same concealing garment covers the latent love of the *beinoni*. The difference is that the *beinoni* has the wherewithal to awaken the hidden love within him to the extent that it can burst through the *kelippa*'s obstructing garment (Rabbi Shmuel Gronem Esterman).

וְאֵינוֹ שֶׁל בְּחִינַת חָכְמָה שֶׁבַּנֶּפֶשׁ הָאֱלֹהִית הוּא בַּמּוֹחִין, וְאֵינָהּ מִתְלַבֶּשֶׁת בִּלְבוּשׁ שַׂק דִּקְלִיפָּה שֶׁבַּלֵּב בֶּחָלָל הַשְּׂמָאלִי בִּבְחִינַת גָּלוּת מַמָּשׁ.

core of wisdom that is in the divine soul is in the brain and does not become clothed in the sackcloth of the *kelippa* that is in the left chamber of the heart in an actual state of exile.

Wisdom is the source of life, so it extends throughout all the parts of a person's being, both spiritual and physical, vivifying it and manifesting itself in a variety of forms. These manifestations of the divine power that extends from the source of life, from the point of wisdom within the soul, may be obscured by the *kelippa* or may emerge from under the *kelippa*'s sackcloth. Yet the core, the fundamental essence of wisdom in the soul, is never truly concealed, is never in actual exile.

רַק שֶׁהִיא בִּבְחִינַת שֵׁינָה בָּרְשָׁעִים

Rather, it is in a state of dormancy within the wicked

There is a difference between exile and sleep. To say that the Divine Presence is in exile is not to say that it ceases to operate. On the contrary, the Divine Presence, the divine force, remains active, but it now operates in mundane areas and for the sake of mundane goals. The Divine Presence is, so to speak, like a slave who is held captive by an enemy. Although he continues to labor, he no longer does so for himself.

In exile, the fundamental being continues to exist and act but is distorted and twisted toward other directions. Although the inner will and power of love and self-sacrifice continue to exist in a Jew's soul even in exile, it finds expression in alien and even hostile forms.

Yet there exists a point within the soul, the point of wisdom within

A CASE OF A SPIRIT OF FOLLY

☞ By way of illustration, a leading Irish politician of the nineteenth century who was perhaps closer than anyone else to gaining Ireland its independence was forced to abandon the political arena at the peak of his career because he had committed adultery. Although this man had fought his entire life on behalf of a cause for which he was willing to give his life, he did what he did knowing that he was destroying his career, his political power, and the independence of his motherland simply because a spirit of folly entered him.

it, that never goes into exile, that never enters servitude, but at most it enters into a state of inactivity that the author of the *Tanya* terms "a state of dormancy." In that state, this core point of wisdom in the soul slumbers. It exists but is inactive, and although it does not express itself in holy forms, neither does it adopt any other. ☞

וְאֵינָהּ פּוֹעֶלֶת פְּעוּלָּתָהּ בָּהֶם כָּל זְמַן שֶׁעֲסוּקִים בְּדַעְתָּם וּבִינָתָם בְּתַאֲוֹת הָעוֹלָם.

and does not exercise its influence within them as long as their faculties of **knowledge and understanding are engaged in** the pursuit of **worldly pleasures.**

As long as a person's thoughts, his intellectual faculties, are applied to the pursuit of mundane pleasures, the inner spark of wisdom remains asleep and inactive. In an essay on the verse "A song of ascents: When God brings about the return to Zion, we were like dreamers" (Ps. 126:1), the author of the *Tanya* wrote that during exile Jewish existence is in a dream state. When God will bring about the Jewish people's return to Zion, we will see that throughout the entire night, during all the years of exile, we were like dreamers.[15]

The question implicit in this thought is, how can a Jew exist in exile? How can that divine spark, the wisdom hidden deep in the soul, which by its nature cannot go into exile, maintain itself during such a time? The answer is that this is possible in a dream. In a dream, everything

THE EXILE OF THE DIVINE PRESENCE IN THE RUSSIAN REVOLUTION

☞ It is well known that the number of Jews involved in the revolutions of the nineteenth century was vastly disproportionate to their numbers in the population at large. These Jews manifested, in a twisted manner, the chosen nature of the Jew. The Divine Presence was present and active in them. The messianic flame, the ideal of the absolute good and the complete rectification of the world, burned in some manner. But the Divine Presence was in exile within them, and the manifestation of its power had no connection to God but instead emerged in other forms, which were indifferent or even hostile to that which is holy. It happened more than once that a father was a rabbi while his son was the "rabbi" of others, and both acted with the same self-sacrifice and "sacred" fervor. That is the Divine Presence in exile, when it actively invests all the good within it against itself.

15. *Torah Or* 28c.

is possible, even for two opposites to coexist. When a person's divine spark is asleep, it can combine two opposites: its existence in exile as its powers spread to other, nonholy realms and its yearning to cling to God alone and to deliver itself to the infinite source of all life. A person can view himself as a faithful Jew even if all his activities are anti-Jewish. That becomes possible when the primary spark, the "root and core of wisdom that is in the divine soul" is slumbering within him.

אַךְ כְּשֶׁבָּאִים לִידֵי נִסָּיוֹן בִּדְבַר אֱמוּנָה, שֶׁהִיא לְמַעְלָה מֵהַדַּעַת, וְנָגְעָה עַד הַנֶּפֶשׁ, לִבְחִינַת חָכְמָה שֶׁבָּהּ - אֲזַי הִיא נֵיעוֹרָה מִשְּׁנָתָהּ וּפוֹעֶלֶת פְּעוּלָּתָהּ בְּכֹחַ ה' הַמְלוּבָּשׁ בָּהּ,

However, when even the wicked **are faced with a test in a matter of faith, which transcends logic, touching the soul,** specifically **the** point of **wisdom within it, then** the point of wisdom **is awakened from its dormant state and exercises its influence through the power of God that is clothed within it,**

When such a person is tested with a challenge of faith, one that he cannot solve by applying his rationale, his cognitive faculties of understanding and knowledge, to decide whether he is in favor or against, whether he has one opinion or another, that is when that spark of wisdom awakens within him.

There is a point beyond which an abnormally strained existence must explode. Every nightmare has a boundary past which the terror is so great that a person awakens from the dream. A person whose divine soul is in exile can build rational structures for himself, philosophical structures on the highest plane or simple structures of a thoughtless life, of eating and drinking for pleasure, with no desire or striving to attain more. But there comes a point when this familiar structure can no longer stand, when none of its rational supports can help – what the author of the *Tanya* calls "a test in a matter of faith."

This point of critical mass, at which all existence must explode, differs in every individual, depending on the time, the place, and the person himself. For some, this point comes when they are told to commit a transgression as minor as moving *muktzeh*, an object prohibited for use, on the Sabbath. For others, it comes when they are about to commit apostasy. But every Jew has a critical point at which he realizes that to go beyond it is to cut himself off from his source, that beyond this point he has severed his ties to his Jewish essence. It is the point at which he must decide whether or not to identify as a Jew. ☞

וּכְמוֹ שֶׁכָּתוּב: ״וַיִּקַץ כְּיָשֵׁן ה׳״ (תהלים עח, סה), **לַעֲמוֹד בְּנִסָּיוֹן בֶּאֱמוּנַת ה׳ בְּלִי שׁוּם טַעַם וָדַעַת וְשֵׂכֶל מוּשָּׂג לוֹ. לְהִתְגַּבֵּר עַל הַקְּלִיפּוֹת וְתַאֲווֹת עוֹלָם הַזֶּה, בְּהֶיתֵּר וּבְאִיסּוּר, שֶׁהוּרְגַּל בָּהֶם, וְלִמְאוֹס בָּהֶם וְלִבְחוֹר לוֹ ה׳ לְחֶלְקוֹ וּלְגוֹרָלוֹ לִמְסוֹר לוֹ נַפְשׁוֹ עַל קְדוּשַּׁת שְׁמוֹ. וְאַף כִּי הַקְּלִיפּוֹת גָּבְרוּ עָלָיו כָּל יָמָיו וְלֹא יָכוֹל לָהֶם, כְּמַאֲמַר רַבּוֹתֵינוּ זַ״ל: שֶׁהָרְשָׁעִים הֵם בִּרְשׁוּת לִבָּם** (בראשית רבה פרשה לד, י ופרשה סז, ח),

as it is written, "Then the Lord awoke as if from sleep" (Ps. 78:65), alluding to the light of *Ein Sof* clothed within the soul's faculty of wisdom. This awakening of wisdom leads the wicked person **to withstand the test of faith in God** and sacrifice his life **without any reason, logic, or intellect that he can apprehend,** and he is prepared **to overpower the *kelippot* and this-worldly lusts, whether they are permitted or prohibited, to which he was accustomed.** Moreover, he is even **repulsed by them and** opts **to choose God as his portion and lot** and **offer his life to** God **for the sanctification of** God's **name, even though the *kelippot* overpowered him his entire life and he was unable to prevail over them in accordance with our Rabbis' statement "The wicked are controlled by their hearts"** (*Bereshit Rabba* 34:10, 67:8).

A HUNGARIAN ARISTOCRAT

☞ In the seventeenth century, a certain Hungarian Jew who was caught up in unsavory affairs eventually became a Christian and a member of the aristocracy. Yet when his fellow Jews were subjected to a blood libel, he gave up his wealth, his status, and his life in order to fight this slander and save the Jewish community. Although he had sold his soul for the sake of his personal pleasures and had converted to Christianity, he could not tolerate such an outrage. For him, standing idly by would have meant that he had turned his back irrevocably on being a Jew. At that moment, his divine spark of wisdom was activated, even if it meant that martyrdom would be involved. Following that episode, the rabbis issued a decree that prohibited anyone from referring to this man as an apostate. His sons, who had remained Jewish, were allowed to be called by his name in the synagogue, and a ban was issued against anyone who would speak of him disparagingly.

A wicked person cannot control his thoughts and feelings, so he stands beyond the bounds of free will. This is not to say that he has been stripped of the ability to choose freely, but that practically speaking he is no longer able to make an informed choice. He is caught within certain modes of living and thought. He no longer possesses the motivation to change his life. He is not able to make decisions that will result in actual change, nor has he any desire to do so. Instead, he slips steadily down a slope that he will not be able to climb again.

מִכָּל מָקוֹם כְּשֶׁבָּא לִידֵי נִסָּיוֹן בִּדְבַר אֱמוּנָה בַּה' אֶחָד, שֶׁיְּסוֹדָתָהּ בְּהַרְרֵי קוֹדֶשׁ, הִיא בְּחִינַת חָכְמָה שֶׁבַּנֶּפֶשׁ הָאֱלֹהִית שֶׁבָּהּ מְלוּבָּשׁ אוֹר אֵין סוֹף בָּרוּךְ הוּא, הֲרֵי כָּל הַקְּלִיפּוֹת בְּטֵלִים וּמְבוּטָּלִים וְהָיוּ כְּלֹא הָיוּ מַמָּשׁ לִפְנֵי ה',

Nevertheless, when faced with a test in a matter of faith in the one God, a faith **whose foundation** is rooted **in the holy mountains, namely, the** faculty of **wisdom in the divine soul, within which is clothed the light of *Ein Sof*, blessed be He, then all the *kelippot* become null and void in the presence of God and vanish as though they never actually existed,**

When a Jew reaches this point, when his faith in the one God is tested, then even if he had lived like a non-Jew his entire life, and even as a wicked non-Jew – even if he had been immersed in his desires and had viewed the world through non-Jewish eyes – at that moment everything that has passed is as nothing, and he performs actions that would never have been expected of him.

כְּדִכְתִיב: "כָּל הַגּוֹיִם כְּאַיִן נֶגְדּוֹ" וגו' (ישעיה מ, יז), וּכְתִיב: "כִּי הִנֵּה אוֹיְבֶיךָ ה' כִּי הִנֵּה אוֹיְבֶיךָ יֹאבֵדוּ יִתְפָּרְדוּ" וגו' (תהלים צב, י), וּכְתִיב: "כְּהִמֵּס דּוֹנַג מִפְּנֵי אֵשׁ יֹאבְדוּ" וגו' (שם סח, ג), וּכְתִיב: "הָרִים כַּדּוֹנַג נָמַסּוּ" (שם צז, ה).

as it is written, "All the nations are as nothing before Him…" (Isa. 40:17), **and it is written, "For behold Your enemies, Lord, behold Your enemies perish;** all evildoers **are scattered"** (Ps. 92:10), **and it is written, "As wax melts before fire, let** the wicked **perish** before God" (Ps. 68:3), **and it is written, "Mountains melt like wax** at the presence of the Lord" (Ps. 97:5).

These verses show that when God is revealed, the enemy automatically has no more power, and evildoers, whether they are outside oneself or within, are no longer significant. A person who was under the control of his heart, who was enmeshed in the web of circumstance and desire that forced him onto a certain path where no solution could be found, who, practically speaking, had lacked the ability to choose good, finds that his world has suddenly been overturned. Now he again is unable to choose, but this time, unable to choose evil.

Such a person experiences a microcosm of the revelation at Mount Sinai, when God, as it were, held the mountain over the heads of the children of Israel, when everything lost all meaning in the face of the divine revelation. This does not mean that he is transformed into a different person altogether, because this revelation has come from within himself, from his own faculties. Still, this revelation is so meaningful that his entire past life is as though it had never been. When holiness shines so strongly, the shadows that create the other side cease to be. The other possibilities melt away, losing their meaning and their force until one lacks the freedom to choose anything but that which is holy.

וְהִנֵּה אוֹר ה' אֵין סוֹף בָּרוּךְ הוּא הַמְלוּבָּשׁ בַּחָכְמָה שֶׁבַּנֶּפֶשׁ - גָּדוֹל וְעָצוּם כֹּחוֹ כָּל כָּךְ לְגָרֵשׁ וְלִדְחוֹת הַסִּטְרָא אָחֳרָא וְהַקְּלִיפּוֹת שֶׁלֹּא יוּכְלוּ יִגְּעוּ אֲפִילּוּ בִּלְבוּשָׁיו, שֶׁהֵם מַחֲשָׁבָה דִּבּוּר וּמַעֲשֶׂה שֶׁל אֱמוּנַת ה' אֶחָד.

The divine light of *Ein Sof*, blessed be He, that is clothed in the faculty of **wisdom in the soul is so great and powerful that it can banish and repel the *sitra aḥara* and the *kelippot* so that they are unable to touch even its garments, namely, the thoughts, speech, and actions** expressing a person's **faith in the one God.**

The power of this revelation is so great that not only does it affect a person's faith, so that he will believe in nothing but God, it even affects his soul's garments. Even though a person knows that certain acts that he is compelled by his enemies to commit are superficial, nonsensical, and meaningless, he will nevertheless sacrifice his life rather than commit them.

דְּהַיְינוּ לַעֲמוֹד בְּנִסָּיוֹן לִמְסוֹר נַפְשׁוֹ אֲפִילּוּ שֶׁלֹּא לַעֲשׂוֹת רַק אֵיזֶה מַעֲשֶׂה לְבַד נֶגֶד אֱמוּנַת ה׳ אֶחָד, כְּגוֹן לְהִשְׁתַּחֲווֹת לַעֲבוֹדָה זָרָה אַף שֶׁאֵינוֹ מַאֲמִין בָּהּ כְּלָל בְּלִבּוֹ.

That is, this person is willing **to withstand the test** of faith and **sacrifice his life even to refuse to perform an isolated action that challenges** his **faith in the one God, such as prostrating** himself **before an idol, even though in his heart he does not believe in it whatsoever.**

For many Jews, the prospect of bowing to a false god, even if they know clearly that they are not professing faith in it and that they would only be performing a purely mechanical act lacking all significance, constitutes the dividing point, the moment when they decide to give their lives rather than bow.

וְכֵן שֶׁלֹּא לְדַבֵּר תּוֹעָה חַס וְשָׁלוֹם עַל אַחְדוּת ה׳, אַף שֶׁאֵין פִּיו וְלִבּוֹ שָׁוִין, רַק לִבּוֹ שָׁלֵם בֶּאֱמוּנַת ה׳.

Similarly, he resolves **to not speak disloyally, God forbid, against the oneness of God, even if his mouth and heart are not congruent, because his heart is whole** in its **faith in God.**

A Jew also will not make superficial and false statements that imply that he accepts another faith. In such cases, his speech would constitute a totally superficial garment that has no connection to his inner being, to his thoughts and feelings. But the process of revelation of the point of wisdom is so powerful that not only does it affect his innermost, fundamental essence, but it reaches his most external and superficial expressions of self. ☞

וְזֶה נִקְרָא דְּחִילוּ הַנִּכְלָל בִּרְחִימוּ,

This is called fear that is integrated with love,

THE JEW WITHIN

☞ Many stories are recorded about people whom no one suspected of being Jewish, but when they had to proclaim themselves one way or another, they could not bring themselves to lie, even if admitting that they were Jewish meant that they were signing their death sentence. Many of them were people who barely knew what a Jew is, for whom the fact of being a Jew had no meaning. Yet when they had to define

Love is a state of closeness and intimacy, whereas fear is one of distance and disconnection. These examples of self-sacrifice are not expressions of closeness but of restraint and distancing from those acts that compel one to deny his Jewish identity. In that sense, they are expressions of fear, or, more precisely, of fear that is contained in love.

Love and fear are not necessarily incompatible. Any love contains fear within it. Whenever there is an object of love, there is also the fear of losing it. On this level, fear of God is not fear of punishment but fear of being disconnected from God. This is "fear that is integrated with love," which is, in a sense, the highest level of the fear of God, a level where love and fear intertwine. This is the foundation and distillation of Jewish life. When we love, we cling to the source of life and are subsumed in it. When we fear, we are afraid that we may be severed from that source, which would mean that we are no longer alive. This point, this juncture, is so precious that every Jew is prepared to die for its sake.

שֶׁהִיא אַהֲבָה הַטִּבְעִית שֶׁבְּנֶפֶשׁ הָאֱלֹהִית שֶׁבִּכְלָלוּת יִשְׂרָאֵל,

which is the innate, concealed **love that is in the divine soul of the collective of Israel,**

The emphasis is on all Jews, because this characteristic is not unique to the forefathers, the prophets, or the greatest among Israel, but belongs to every Jew. The ability to sacrifice one's self, which is the glory of Israel,

themselves under such circumstances as belonging to one side or the other, even if they had lived their entire lives without any interest in Judaism, they made the firm decision to step forward as Jews.

The philosopher Henri Bergson, for instance, grew up in an assimilated home in France and remained far from Judaism throughout his life, even contemplating conversion to Christianity in his later years. But when the Nazis came and ordered the Jews to sign an official list, he, an old man in his eighties, declared himself a Jew.

In the first half of the nineteenth century, many children were forcibly drafted into the Russian army to serve for twenty-five years. They barely knew that they were Jewish, yet these men gave their lives for their religion. Not just a few of them did so. Hundreds died painfully because they were Jews. This was never a matter of thought and rationale. It was never connected to an awareness of their Jewishness. On the contrary, there were instances when people's understanding and rationality interfered with their self-identification as Jews, of realizing the essence of being Jewish.

does not belong only to those who have been educated in Judaism. We can assume that such people would choose martyrdom rather than do something in total contradiction to their lifelong ideals. The wonder and beauty exists particularly in those unlearned people who grew up in a nonreligious environment, even the most unworthy, even those who sin, physically and spiritually. The glory of Israel is found not only in Moses but even in a Jewish thief or reprobate who has given his life for the sake of God. This distinctive characteristic is the element that defines the Jew: a person who contains within himself the ability to give his life for the sake of his Jewishness.

שֶׁחֶפְצָהּ וּרְצוֹנָהּ בְּטִבְעָהּ לִידָּבֵק בְּשָׁרְשָׁהּ וּמְקוֹרָהּ אוֹר אֵין סוֹף בָּרוּךְ הוּא. שֶׁמִּפְּנֵי אַהֲבָה זוֹ וְרָצוֹן זֶה הִיא יְרֵאָה וּמְפַחֶדֶת בְּטִבְעָהּ מִנְּגוֹעַ בִּקְצֵה טוּמְאַת עֲבוֹדָה זָרָה חַס וְשָׁלוֹם, שֶׁהִיא נֶגֶד אֱמוּנַת ה׳ אֶחָד, אֲפִילוּ בִּלְבוּשֶׁיהָ הַחִיצוֹנִים, שֶׁהֵם דִּבּוּר אוֹ מַעֲשֶׂה בְּלִי אֱמוּנָה בַּלֵּב כְּלָל.

whose natural desire and will is to cling to its root and source, the light of *Ein Sof*, blessed be He. On account of this love and this will, the soul **by nature is afraid and terrified lest it brush the tip of the impurity** imparted by **idol worship, God forbid, which** is diametrically **opposed to faith in the one God, even** when it involves only the soul's **outer garments, which are** either **speech or action, without believing** in it **whatsoever in the heart.**

The essence of Jewish identity may be found in the first two of the Ten Commandments: "I am the Lord your God," and "You shall have no other gods" (Ex. 20:2–3). These two precepts express, respectively, attachment to God and love of Him, on one hand, and the repulsion from idolatry, with the attendant fear that one might be disconnected from God, on the other. These are not merely external directives but descriptions of the inner character of the Jewish soul, even if these characteristics are not always apparent.

The author of the *Tanya* will go on to explain at length that every Jew fears and flees idolatry, but because he does not always recognize it, he may engage in an act tinged with idolatry without knowing it. Yet the moment he realizes that he is involved with idolatry, that he has reached the point of severance from the Divine, then all his other internal structures melt away, leaving him with no further doubt. In this sense, the entire Torah comes only to define and explain how to actualize these two precepts: "I am the Lord" and "You shall have no other gods." All the positive commandments are meant to help us come closer to the one God, to fulfill the mitzva of "I am the Lord your God." All the prohibitions express the idea that "you shall have no other gods." We must stay away from idolatry in all its forms and remain distant from anything that might sever our connection to Him. In view of this, one could say that the fulfillment of the Torah as a whole is one extended act of self-sacrifice for the sake of sanctifying the name of God.

In this chapter, the author of the *Tanya* has brought to a close his study of one of the aspects of the concealed love within every Jew. He explained that this love, intrinsic to the Jewish character, serves to define a Jew: one whose divine soul loves God so much that he is willing to die in order to sanctify God's name. The soul yearns to leave the body and, as it clings to God, completely nullify itself. This love is, by nature, concealed; it does not make its presence known in every individual or in every part of one's life. Nevertheless, it unquestionably exists within every Jew. The proof is that even the most unworthy, even the sinners of Israel, will gladly give their life when facing what they believe to be the question of whether or not they stand with God. At that point, an as yet unknown spiritual strength, a strength that expresses the nature of his divine soul and its love and fear of God, directs him to step past the boundaries of his life, to step past his habitual frames of consciousness as he returns to the Jewish self that exists at the core of his being.

The power of this love to totally transform a person and bring him to the pinnacle of self-sacrifice stems from the fact that it is concealed, that it cannot be apprehended rationally. This love comes from the place within the self that exists between nonbeing and being, what we call the point of wisdom that can never be exiled. A person may be living in exile in body or soul, but the spark of wisdom within him can never be displaced. Because that point always expresses the character of his divine soul, it cannot be counterfeited. It can never be anything less than absolutely true. When a Jew reaches a moment of fateful decision, when he stands at the verge of severing himself from holiness, his divine soul breaks out of its concealment and affects him in ways that he might never have dreamed. He may not be conscious of his actions, he may not understand them, he may even ridicule himself, but at that moment he can do nothing else.

The power of this point to cause one's entire soul to be absorbed into the Divine also stems from the fact that the soul itself is a divine spark, a spark of life that vivifies man with the life force that comes from God, the infinite source of all life. A person's slightest deviation from this point would therefore constitute suicide, and no one would accept that without protest. No one would see what appears to be self-destruction without opposing it with all his might.

The intent of this discussion was not merely to celebrate the beauty of the Jewish people's holiness, or to describe the lofty moment of martyrdom, but to enable a person to draw from this ability and accomplish acts that had previously seemed impossible to him. If a person says that he is not fit for such a challenge, that his soul is not ready, this chapter comes to teach him that because he is capable of sacrificing his life for the sake of God, he should also be able to overcome the smaller temptations. Although the fulfillment of mitzvot may seem less significant than the giving up of one's life, essentially it expresses the same desire for connection to God (or, if misused, disconnection from Him). In the final analysis, it is easier to overcome an improper craving than to sacrifice one's entire life and die on the stake.

Chapter 20

THE TWO PRECEDING CHAPTERS DISCUSSED THE LOVE for God inherent in every Jew, what the author of the *Tanya* terms the concealed love. This love does not merely express an individual's relationship with the Divine but also demonstrates the essence of his soul, revolving entirely around a single, yet double-faceted point. The first facet is attachment to God; the second is the feeling of repulsion toward any form of idolatry. The first facet is expressed in the first of the Ten Commandments, "I am the Lord your God" (Ex. 20:2), and the second is expressed in the second precept, "You shall have no other gods" (Ex. 20:3). As the author of the *Tanya* will explain in this chapter, these two precepts comprise more than the distillation of the Torah. They are also the essence of the Jewish soul.

וְהִנֵּה מוּדַעַת זֹאת לַכֹּל כִּי מִצְוַת וְאַזְהָרַת עֲבוֹדָה זָרָה שֶׁהֵם שְׁנֵי דִבְּרוֹת הָרִאשׁוֹנִים: "אָנֹכִי" וְ"לֹא יִהְיֶה לְךָ", הֵם כְּלָלוּת כָּל הַתּוֹרָה כּוּלָּהּ.

5 Shevat

11 Shevat (leap year)

It is well known to all that the positive **commandment** to believe in the one God **and the admonition with regard to idolatry, which are the first two** of the Ten **Commandments, "I am the Lord** your God" **and "You shall have no** other gods before Me," **constitute the totality of the entire Torah,**

The first two precepts deal with one topic: the negation of idolatry in all its forms. The proclamation "I am the Lord your God" is the general negation of the existence of idolatry, and "You shall have no other gods" is the explicit prohibition of its worship. But beyond this specific meaning, these two commandments encompass the entire Torah.

כִּי דִּבּוּר "אָנֹכִי" כּוֹלֵל כָּל רמ"ח מִצְוֹת עֲשֵׂה וְ"לֹא יִהְיֶה לְךָ" כּוֹלֵל כָּל שס"ה מִצְוֹת לֹא תַעֲשֶׂה.

for the precept "I am the Lord your God" **encompasses all the 248 positive commandments, and** the precept **"You shall have no** other gods" **encompasses all 365 prohibitions.**

The positive commandments are the way to connect to the very essence of God until He becomes "the Lord your God," while every transgression is a form of idolatry, a severance from the unity of God by virtue of acting in defiance of His will. At times, this is clearcut, and at others, murky. At times, a transgression results from conscious rebellion. At other times, it comes from a spirit of folly that persuades a person that what he is doing is not quite idolatrous, that he remains a good Jew who is still attached to sanctity. If one were to experience, in its full poignancy and clarity, the truth of "I am the Lord your God" and "You shall have no other gods," one would never be able to sin. ☞

וְלָכֵן שָׁמַעְנוּ "אָנֹכִי" וְ"לֹא יִהְיֶה לְךָ" לְבַד מִפִּי הַגְּבוּרָה, כְּמַאֲמַר רַבּוֹתֵינוּ זַ"ל (מכות כד, א), מִפְּנֵי שֶׁהֵם כְּלָלוּת הַתּוֹרָה כּוּלָּהּ.

Therefore, we heard only the first two precepts, **"I am** the Lord your God" **and "You shall have no** other gods," directly **from the mouth of the Almighty in accordance with our Rabbis' statement** (*Makkot* 24a) **because they constitute the totality of the entire Torah.**

ANGER IS TANTAMOUNT TO IDOLATRY

☞ The Sages state that "when a person grows angry, it is as though he is worshipping idols" (*Zohar* 1:27b; see *Shabbat* 105b). Anger is the emotional expression of idolatry, and essentially, the same holds true for anyone who transgresses a prohibition. An angry person, like any other transgressor, has established his ego as the determining factor of reality: "I want!" "I deserve!" When he does not receive what he wants, he gets angry.

We face a fundamental choice: Either "I made myself" (Ezek. 29:3), and I do all that my heart desires, or God is the Creator and King of the universe, and I connect to Him, knowing that I cannot disengage myself from Him at any time and under any circumstances.

The Jews heard the first two of the Ten Commandments directly from God's mouth and not through the agency of Moses, and the reason for this is "because they constitute the totality of the entire Torah."

A person who completely accepts that "I am the Lord your God" and "You shall have no other gods" accepts the entire Torah. Everything else in the Torah is nothing but a detailed delineation of how to cling to God (embodied by the precept "I am the Lord your God") and how to refrain from idolatry ("You shall have no other gods"). In view of this, every Jew had to hear these commandments directly from God with no intermediary so that these precepts would constitute the primal and direct basis for his existence as a Jew.

At this point, the author of the *Tanya* digresses from the topic of serving God through activating one's concealed love. Over the next few chapters, he embarks on a lengthy discourse on God's unity and one's attachment to Him, a state achieved through divine service and meditation.

In truth, this divergence is not entirely off topic. The very essence and power of the concealed love is entirely rooted in God's oneness and the soul's absolute integration with it. Consequently, it is of the utmost importance at this juncture to elucidate this point, not merely as a speculative exercise, but chiefly in a manner in which one can tangibly meditate on it to the greatest degree possible. The goal set forth here is for one to actively awaken the feeling and power of this concealed love.[1]

וּלְבָאֵר הֵיטֵב עִנְיָן זֶה צָרִיךְ לְהַזְכִּיר תְּחִלָּה בִּקְצָרָה עִנְיַן וּמַהוּת אַחְדּוּתוֹ שֶׁל הַקָּדוֹשׁ בָּרוּךְ הוּא שֶׁנִּקְרָא יָחִיד וּמְיוּחָד,

To thoroughly elucidate this subject, it is necessary to first briefly discuss the idea and essence of the oneness of the Holy One, blessed be He, who is referred to as the one and only.

God's oneness is expressed with the concept of *eḥad*, "one," as we say, when reciting the *Shema*, "The Lord is one." Yet the oneness of God

1. It was the practice of the Chabad spiritual mentor Rabbi Shlomo Ḥayyim Kesselman, when guiding his students to pray with devotion and deep meditation, to instruct them to study and contemplate this section of the *Tanya* (chaps. 20–21) prior to praying.

is more far-reaching than any concept of oneness that exists in all the worlds or that relates to them. This is expressed in the author of the *Tanya*'s description of God as *yaḥid u'meyuḥad*, "one and only."

Elsewhere, the author discusses the meanings of these two terms, *eḥad* and *yaḥid*.[2] In brief, whereas the concept of *eḥad*, that God is one, allows for the existence of an additional being, *yaḥid* denies any possibility of duality, of a second and similar divinity. The author of the *Tanya* then explains why, when reciting the *Shema*, we say that "God is one," *eḥad*, rather than "God is the only one," *yaḥid*, though the meaning of *yaḥid* is apparently more exalted than that of *eḥad*. The reason is that *eḥad* expresses God's oneness in terms of His existence within the worlds, where only He can be truly called one.[3] When reciting the *Shema*, we emphasize the oneness of His all-encompassing being. *Yaḥid*, on the other hand, expresses the singularity and exclusivity of God's essence and being before it was drawn into the worlds. ☞

וְכֹל מַאֲמִינִים שֶׁהוּא לְבַדּוֹ הוּא כְּמוֹ שֶׁהָיָה קוֹדֶם שֶׁנִּבְרָא הָעוֹלָם מַמָּשׁ, שֶׁהָיָה הוּא לְבַדּוֹ,

All believe that He is literally alone just as He was prior to the creation of the world when it was He alone,

We believe that God is singular, that not only is there no other divinity like Him but there is not even any existence outside of Him. "He is

THE ONE AND ONLY

☞ This expression is not merely poetic. Both terms are necessary to imply the absolute, sole existence of God and nothing else. We might, for example, say, "I have one apple," but this does not negate the existence of other apples (or entities in general). In the same vein, were one to merely say that He is "one God," this leaves room for the existence of other entities. It is necessary to append the term "only," yielding the phrase "the one and only," indicating the complete negation of any reality other than God.

2. See, e.g., *Torah Or* 55b, 90c.

3. The word *eḥad* alludes to the one God (represented by the letter *alef* of the word), who exists in the seven heavens and the earth (represented by the *ḥet*, whose numerical value is eight), and the four directions (represented by the *dalet*, whose numerical value is four).

literally alone" means that He alone exists now no differently than before the world was created.

וּכְמוֹ שֶׁאוֹמְרִים: "אַתָּה הוּא עַד שֶׁלֹּא נִבְרָא הָעוֹלָם אַתָּה הוּא מִשֶּׁנִּבְרָא" כו'.

as we say in the morning prayers, "**You are He** who existed **before the world was created,** and **You are He** who exists **since its creation....**"

This odd expression mentions the Creation in the passive voice, without explaining that it was God Himself who created the world. Some prayer books have therefore introduced the alternate wording, "You were He before You created...." But the original wording expresses better the relationship between God and the creation. God is so exalted that we do not explicitly emphasize that He is the Creator of the world in the sense that He actively operates and sustains the world. Rather, "He spoke and it was done" (Ps. 33:9), using the passive voice. He spoke, and it immediately came into existence. God is so elevated, so separate from the world, that He Himself does not change at all as a result of the fact that there is a world. Although it exists and operates as a result of His power, it does not affect Him, and whether or not it exists makes no difference to God.

פֵּירוּשׁ, הוּא מַמָּשׁ בְּלִי שׁוּם שִׁינּוּי, כְּדִכְתִיב: "אֲנִי ה' לֹא שָׁנִיתִי" (מלאכי ג, ו). כִּי עוֹלָם הַזֶּה וְכֵן כָּל הָעוֹלָמוֹת הָעֶלְיוֹנִים אֵינָם פּוֹעֲלִים שׁוּם שִׁנּוּי בְּאַחְדּוּתוֹ יִתְבָּרֵךְ בְּהִבָּרְאָם מֵאַיִן לְיֵשׁ, שֶׁכְּמוֹ שֶׁהָיָה הוּא לְבַדּוֹ הוּא יָחִיד וּמְיוּחָד קוֹדֶם הִבָּרְאָם - כֵּן הוּא לְבַדּוֹ הוּא יָחִיד וּמְיוּחָד אַחַר שֶׁבְּרָאָם,

This means that He is literally without any change, as it is written, "I the Lord did not change" (Mal. 3:6), **for this world, as well as all the higher worlds, effects no change in God's oneness by their having been created from nothingness** and brought forth **into existence. Just He was alone, the one and only, before they were created, so He is alone, the one and only, after He created them.**

When a man fathers a child, he is no longer the same. The existence of the child has altered him. Once there is another, this causes a change in the former. But God is different. We say of Him that He was the same before the world was created, and He has remained the same after the world was created. The creation of the world modified nothing in God. His essence remains immutable, even though the world was created.

מִשּׁוּם דְּכוּלָּא קַמֵּיהּ כְּלָא חֲשִׁיב וּכְאַיִן וְאֶפֶס מַמָּשׁ.

This is **because** in essence **everything is considered as naught, literally like absolute nothingness,** in relation to Him.

The word *ayin*, literally, "nothingness," has a double meaning, depending on whether it refers to the lower unification, the viewpoint from the lower worlds looking up to God, or to the higher unification, the viewpoint from above, gazing downward. From the viewpoint of the lower unification – when we gaze upward – we experience the lower worlds as existing and that which lies beyond them is *ayin*, nothing. But from the standpoint of the higher unification, from above gazing downward, it is actually the lower reality that is absolute nothingness.[4]

In truth, only God alone exists. That which was created, that which appears to be other than God alone, is not real. Even though the world appears to exist, even though it operates in a seemingly independent fashion, that itself expresses the fact that it is, in truth, absolute nothingness.

12 Shevat (leap year)

כִּי הִתְהַוּוּת כָּל הָעוֹלָמוֹת עֶלְיוֹנִים וְתַחְתּוֹנִים מֵאַיִן לְיֵשׁ, וְחַיּוּתָם וְקִיּוּמָם הַמְקַיְּימָם שֶׁלֹּא יַחְזְרוּ לִהְיוֹת אַיִן וָאֶפֶס כְּשֶׁהָיָה, אֵינוֹ אֶלָּא דְּבַר ה׳ וְרוּחַ פִּיו יִתְבָּרֵךְ הַמְלוּבָּשׁ בָּהֶם.

Bringing forth all the higher and lower worlds from nothingness into existence, as well as **their life force and existence that sustains them so that they do not revert to absolute nothingness as they were** before the Creation, **is nothing other than the word of God and the breath of His divine utterance that are clothed within them.**

The creation of the world should not be viewed as the genesis of a new being that emerged from the Divine and is now severed from it. Such

4. See also *Torah Or* 68c; commentary on *Sha'ar HaYiḥud VeHa'emuna*, chap. 7.

a concept would raise three problems: how the world could continue to exist, how it shares existence with the Divine, and what the relationship is between the two. These are questions that have perpetually occupied philosophers and theologians. But our understanding is that the created reality is never separate from the divine being. This is so not only with regard to the life force within the world, but the world's very existence, both its higher and lower realms, is to be understood as nothing but a revelation, a manifestation, of the Divine. As such, there can never be an independent existence that places a barrier before the divine reality. ☞

וּלְמָשָׁל, כְּמוֹ בְּנֶפֶשׁ הָאָדָם **This is analogous to the human soul.** 6 Shevat

THE ONGOING WORD OF GOD

☞ As explained in *Sha'ar HaYiḥud VeHa'emuna*, the second section of the *Tanya*, the creation of the universe was not a one-time event. From the moment it came into being, the world has been continually created anew at every moment. The ongoing existence of the world is an abnormal state, one that demands a consistent, creative force to keep it in existence. Existence requires the constant power of creation to give it life and to construct it at every moment. The utterance of Creation, "Let there be a firmament in the midst of the water" (Gen. 1:6), continues to be spoken, and as long as this is the case, the firmament continues to exist within the waters. God is still declaring, "Let the earth sprout grasses" (Gen. 1:11), and from the power of that utterance, the earth continues to produce vegetation. Were this utterance no longer spoken, that reality would no longer exist. The moment God would cease to speak to the world, it would return to absolute nothingness. The world's vitality and existence are only an expression of "the word of God and the breath of His divine utterance" that are clothed within the world.

The author of the *Tanya* also explains there that when he says that "the word of God and the breath of His divine utterance" causes the world to exist, he is not speaking only in general terms. The divine utterance unfolds, growing increasingly detailed as the letters of the utterance recombine and transmute, bringing into existence the minutest details of reality, degree by degree, from nonspecific to specific. The utterance "Let the earth sprout grasses" generates the general force that causes plant life to sprout from the earth. Its individual letters and their infinite permutations then bring forth the minutest details of each species of plant, of every blade of grass and every leaf. The Sages state that a heavenly force strikes every blade of grass, commanding it, "Grow!" (*Bereshit Rabba* 10:6). This is the word of God compelling the development of each blade of grass and every cell. From the power of that word, the minutiae of the vegetable world grow and endure.

The intent of the author of the *Tanya* is not to elaborate on the existence of the world in and of itself but to discuss the ramifications this has for a person's life. The analogy that follows is meant to clarify the relationship between created being and divine being, between the world and the word of God that vivifies it, in order that one can visualize this concept as much as humanly possible. As we have seen, from God's viewpoint the entire universe is nothing but divine speech. That is, it literally constitutes the ten utterances of Creation. What, then, is the relationship between the Speaker and the spoken? The analogy offers a little clarity.

כְּשֶׁמְּדַבֵּר דִּבּוּר אֶחָד, שֶׁדִּבּוּר זֶה לְבַדּוֹ כְּלֹא מַמָּשׁ אֲפִילּוּ לְגַבֵּי כְּלָלוּת נַפְשׁוֹ הַמְדַבֶּרֶת, שֶׁהוּא בְּחִינַת לְבוּשׁ הָאֶמְצָעִי שֶׁלָּהּ, שֶׁהוּא כֹּחַ הַדִּבּוּר שֶׁלָּהּ,

When a person **utters a single word, that word alone is literally considered as nothing even in relation to his soul's general ability to speak, which is the** soul's **middle garment,** namely, **its faculty of speech,**

In relation to a person's intrinsic nature, any sentence or statement he utters shrinks into insignificance. This is true not only with regard to a person's essence but even in comparison to his soul's ability to speak.

A person's words are insignificant when compared to the ability of his soul to speak. More than that, the ability to speak is merely a garment, and as the author of the *Tanya* explained in previous chapters, the garments of the soul are not the soul itself but only its expression, a particular manifestation. The power of speech is only a garment, and not even an inner garment.

שֶׁיָּכוֹל לְדַבֵּר דִּבּוּרִים לְאֵין קֵץ וְתַכְלִית.

through which one is capable of uttering endless and limitless words.

The soul has three garments: the inner garment, thought; the outer garment, deed; and the middle garment, the power of speech. Speech has its limitations. Certain thoughts and feelings are too subtle and complex to express in words. One cannot speak of some matters but only act on them. But all these limitations concern only speech's ability to express certain thoughts and feelings, not the quantity of speech. They reflect the content of speech, not the act of speech. As an act, speech has no quantitative limitations. The potential of speech in the soul is infinite when compared to any one statement or sentence that a person expresses.[5]

וְכָל שֶׁכֵּן לְגַבֵּי בְּחִינַת לְבוּשׁ הַפְּנִימִי שֶׁלָּהּ שֶׁהוּא הַמַּחֲשָׁבָה, שֶׁמִּמֶּנָּה נִמְשְׁכוּ הַדִּבּוּרִים וְהִיא חַיּוּתָם,

All the more so does this apply **in relation to the** soul's **innermost garment, which is** the faculty of **thought, from which speech flows forth and which is its life force.**

Thought is the innermost garment of the soul and the content of speech, which can communicate only the smallest portion of thought to others. Elsewhere, the author of the *Tanya* distinguishes between various hierarchical levels of thought itself. Two of these strata are speech within thought, or inner monologue, which is relatively close to speech, and, deeper than that, thought within thought, which is thought that constitutes abstract concepts or even preconceptual thought. Clearly, thought on this latter level is remote from speech, and words would be able to express it only in fragmentary fashion.

וְאֵין צָרִיךְ לוֹמַר לְגַבֵּי מַהוּת וְעַצְמוּת הַנֶּפֶשׁ שֶׁהֵן עֶשֶׂר בְּחִינוֹתֶיהָ הַנִּזְכָּרוֹת לְעֵיל חָכְמָה בִּינָה דַּעַת כו׳, שֶׁמֵּהֶן נִמְשְׁכוּ אוֹתִיּוֹת מַחֲשָׁבָה זוֹ הַמְּלוּבָּשׁוֹת בְּדִבּוּר זֶה כְּשֶׁמְּדַבֵּר.

It goes without saying that one's word is considered as naught **when compared to the essence and being of the soul, namely, its aforementioned ten faculties** (see chap. 3), **wisdom, understanding, knowledge, and so forth.** It is **from these** faculties **that the letters of thought are drawn and are** subsequently **clothed in speech when it is spoken,**

Speech is the result of a multileveled process. The sentence a person speaks at the end of that process is the outcome of one's capacity for speech, the ability to communicate to others. That capacity for speech

5. Though one is capable of uttering an infinite number of words and statements, he himself does not live indefinitely. Rabbi Shmuel Gronem Esterman likewise states in his commentary, "The sole reason one can speak only for a span of seventy years is due to the inherent weakness of his body's capacities. As for the soul, it itself is capable of speaking an infinite number of words."

is a result and expression of the power of thought, the ability to engage in internal communication. This power of thought, in turn, is a mere garment, a tool of communication that expresses the faculties of the soul that are revealed in the mind.

Thought stems from the faculties themselves, as well as from the relationships between them – the relationship between wisdom and understanding, for example, and between kindness and restraint. These faculties and their relationships constitute the primary components from which thought is derived. They create the content of a thought and the purpose and direction that guide and activate the thought.

כִּי הַמַּחֲשָׁבָה הִיא גַּם כֵּן בְּחִינַת אוֹתִיּוֹת כְּמוֹ הַדִּבּוּר, רַק שֶׁהֵן רוּחָנִיּוֹת וְדַקּוֹת יוֹתֵר.

for thought, like speech, also consists of letters, only the letters expressing thought **are more spiritual and refined** than those of speech.

Despite the differences between them, thought and speech are both garments of the soul, a means of communication, of transferring ideas from one environment to another. The difference between thought and speech is not qualitative but functional. Thought constitutes internal communication from a person to himself. Speech is outwardly directed. In this sense, writing and hand motions are also speech, whereas if a person is speaking to himself, although he is saying words, he might merely be involved in crystallizing his thoughts without any attempt at outward communication.

The distinction between speech and thought may also be found in descriptions of the nature of prophecy. Our world, the reality that is visible to us all, is the reality of the letters of divine speech. The prophet, on the other hand, sees or hears the letters of divine thought, of God communing with Himself, as it were, as the verse states, "[Moses] heard the voice [of God] speaking to him…" (Num. 7:89). Rashi comments that the word for "speaking," *medaber*, is reflexive, implying that God was speaking to Himself and that Moses overheard.

Like all communication, speech and thought are composed of letters. The letters of speech represent sound waves, whereas the letters of thought are the finer signals expressed by the mind. Like the letters of speech, the letters of thought are vehicles through which the soul is manifest in the organs of the body, whether through the throat or, more subtly, the brain.

אֲבָל עֶשֶׂר בְּחִינוֹת חָכְמָה בִּינָה וָדַעַת כו׳ הֵן שֹׁרֶשׁ וּמְקוֹר הַמַּחֲשָׁבָה וְאֵין בָּהֶם בְּחִינַת אוֹתִיּוֹת עֲדַיִין קוֹדֶם שֶׁמִּתְלַבְּשׁוֹת בִּלְבוּשׁ הַמַּחֲשָׁבָה.

By contrast, the ten attributes, wisdom, understanding, knowledge, and so forth, are the root and source of thought and do not yet possess the element of letters prior to their being clothed in the garment of thought. 13 Shevat (leap year)

A clear distinction is to be drawn between thought, which the author of the *Tanya* views as a partially physical process, and the intellect itself, which is composed of the three cognitive attributes, wisdom, understanding, and knowledge, whose function is purely spiritual. Thought is an activity of the brain, which, although physical, picks up spiritual vibrations and is activated by them. The physical aspect of thought is the letters (described in *Sefer Yetzira* as "stones") that construct thought in the physical world. Needless to say, these letters are not physical in the literal sense, yet they function as vessels housing spiritual content on various levels. As vessels, these letters possess the ability to transmit their contents from one realm to another, similar to the letters of speech, which transmit content from one person to another. Letters allow the spiritual being in the brain to form more than a vague impression. They allow it to create a construct that can become realized in a person's thoughts, speech, and deeds.

לְמָשָׁל, כְּשֶׁנּוֹפֶלֶת אֵיזוֹ אַהֲבָה וְחֶמְדָּה בְּלִבּוֹ שֶׁל אָדָם, קוֹדֶם שֶׁעוֹלָה מֵהַלֵּב אֶל הַמּוֹחַ לַחְשֹׁב וּלְהַרְהֵר בָּהּ - אֵין בָּהּ בְּחִינַת אוֹתִיּוֹת עֲדַיִין רַק חֵפֶץ פָּשׁוּט וַחֲשִׁיקָה בַּלֵּב אֶל הַדָּבָר הַהוּא הַנֶּחְמָד אֶצְלוֹ.

To illustrate **by way of analogy, when a particular** feeling of **love or desire** for something **enters a person's heart, it does not yet possess an element of letters prior to its ascent from the heart to the brain in order that it may think about and ponder it. It is but a simple,** pure **desire and longing in the heart for the object he finds desirable.**

Even prior to thought, even before a person thinks of something in concepts and words, he experiences an initial attraction, a simple desire that cannot be articulated. This attraction is the expression of the direct relationship between the self and the object it desires.

וְכָל שֶׁכֵּן קוֹדֶם שֶׁנָּפְלָה הַתַּאֲוָה וְהַחֶמְדָּה בְּלִבּוֹ לְאוֹתוֹ דָּבָר, רַק הָיְתָה בְּכֹחַ חָכְמָתוֹ וְשִׂכְלוֹ וִידִיעָתוֹ, שֶׁהָיָה נוֹדָע אֶצְלוֹ אוֹתוֹ דָּבָר שֶׁהוּא נֶחְמָד וְנָעִים וְטוֹב וְיָפֶה לְהַשִּׂיגוֹ וְלִידָּבֵק בּוֹ, כְּגוֹן לִלְמוֹד אֵיזוֹ חָכְמָה אוֹ לֶאֱכוֹל אֵיזֶה מַאֲכָל עָרֵב.

All the more so is this the case **before the craving and desire for that object entered his heart, when it existed only in his faculty of wisdom, intellect, and consciousness, when he was aware that this object is desirable, gratifying, good, and pleasant to attain and cling to, such as studying a particular discipline or eating a particular delicacy.**

Even prior to a desire's manifestation as a feeling in one's heart, this desire existed on an inner, more abstract level in the person's soul. This level, that of the intellect, precedes the experience of a sensation in one's heart.

A person cannot desire something of which he has no conceptual awareness. We are not talking necessarily of a sophisticated awareness of all the details of an object but simple recognition. There is no such thing as abstract love. Love must be directed toward a specific object, whether it is an image internalized from the external reality or an image that one initially created in one's mind. There must be an awareness, and there must be an object of which to be aware. It is only when this awareness exists that a relationship is possible. If a person experiences a positive awareness that something is "desirable, gratifying, good, and

"DESIRABLE, GRATIFYING, GOOD, AND PLEASANT"

☞ The author of the *Tanya* uses these descriptions to allude to a dual meaning. On the one hand, this phrase is reminiscent of the statement in the morning prayers praising God's word as "true, established, correct, enduring, straight, faithful, beloved, desired, desirable, and pleasant." On the other hand, it hints at the description in Genesis of the forbidden fruit: "The woman saw that the tree was good for eating and that it was an enticement to the eyes and that the tree was pleasant," he will desire it, whereas a negative awareness will result in feelings of disgust or fear. ☞

Admittedly, this mechanism does not function so simply, and we cannot take for granted that these processes will take place just as we have described them. There can be disruptions on the way, inhibitions and obstacles, whether in our awareness or in the pathways from awareness to emotion. A person may know that a certain object (whether holy or not) is good, yet have no desire for it. But if this framework is properly constructed, it is possible to overcome those barriers.

There are three steps to this process. The first is the awareness that something is good and desirable. This awareness can either be disengaged, or it can be channeled toward the realization that attaining this thing is worthwhile. This can lead to the second step: the desire, the emotion. That emotion leads to the third step: expression in thought, speech, and deed.

Only after the desire and craving entered his heart through his faculty of wisdom, his intellect, and his awareness,	רַק לְאַחַר שֶׁכְּבָר נָפְלָה הַחֶמְדָּה וְהַתַּאֲוָה בְּלִבּוֹ בְּכֹחַ חָכְמָתוֹ, וְשִׂכְלוֹ, וִידִיעָתוֹ,

"His faculty of wisdom, his intellect, and his awareness" describe the three cognitive faculties of wisdom, understanding, and knowledge. Subsequent to the awareness in one's mind facilitated by these faculties,

desirable to apprehend..." (Gen. 3:6). This double allusion teaches us that there is only one psychological mechanism of desire, and one employs it whether he wants a forbidden fruit or God. If he desires the forbidden fruit, he will develop a yearning for it. If, on the other hand, he desires God, he will develop a yearning for God.

In a certain sense, this is the underlying foundation of the philosophy of Chabad Hasidism. When we assume that there are two separate psychological systems, one of evil desires and the other of holy traits, there is no sense in training and refining one's character. But when we accept the axiom that both types of desire operate within the same matrix, then it is possible to channel all desires toward the realm of good. It is the consciousness that decides on the direction, which is a power that the soul can control. A person can direct his thoughts as he desires and create a total awareness of the objects on which he will focus his spiritual faculties.

an emotional connection in the heart is evoked, generating emotions such as love and fear.

וְאַחַר כָּךְ חָזְרָה וְעָלְתָה מֵהַלֵּב לַמּוֹחַ לַחֲשׁוֹב וּלְהַרְהֵר בָּהּ אֵיךְ לְהוֹצִיא תַּאֲוָתוֹ מִכֹּחַ אֶל הַפּוֹעַל, לְהַשִּׂיג הַמַּאֲכָל אוֹ לִמִידַת הַחָכְמָה בְּפוֹעַל, הֲרֵי בְּכָאן נוֹלְדוּ בְּחִינַת אוֹתִיּוֹת בְּמוֹחוֹ,

and only **after** that desire **ascended once more from his heart to his brain so that he might contemplate and ponder how to actualize his craving, to obtain that** delectable **food or to actually study the discipline, only at that point are letters generated in his mind,**

Although born of one's intellectual cognition of the desired object, the desire in the heart is nevertheless unformed, lacking words and letters. It is abstract, without a specific object. Such a desire cannot be realized, or even articulated in speech or thought. It can either remain in this state, disengaged from reality, or it can rise to the mind and become clothed in the letters of thought there. The function of the mind in this second stage is not the same as its function in the initial stage, when it produced the desire. Instead, one could say that it is the intellect born of the desire itself, whose function is to serve and enhance it. This intellect in particular is clothed in letters of thought, letters that are capable of transferring the desire to the next stage: defining the desire and its object in relation to the self and delineating a means of actualizing it.

The distinction between a desire and the words that express it can be demonstrated by considering a language defect, whether in the ability to formulate the letters of thoughts or the capacity to express those thoughts in words. The lack of vocabulary or the lack of ideas and symbols can interfere with one's ability to think of a certain subject or even prevent it.

שֶׁהֵן אוֹתִיּוֹת כִּלְשׁוֹן עַם וָעָם הַמְדַבְּרִים וְהַמְהַרְהֲרִים בָּהֶם כָּל עִנְיְינֵי הָעוֹלָם.

which are the letters spoken **in the** respective **language of each nation, who employ them to speak and ponder all worldly matters.**

In its first stages, before the formulation of letters, the heart's desire is universal. When a person is hungry, even before he thinks that he is hungry, he experiences a sense of hunger, a sensation so abstract and general that all of humanity uniformly shares it. Only after he starts thinking in words and symbols that he is hungry, that he wants to eat, and what and how much he wants to eat, do his desires become specific, distinguishing the thought of one person from that of another. More broadly, the thoughts of one person are distinguished from another, a distinction that is language-specific and based on each individual's manner of expression.

The majority of this chapter, which began by describing God's unity, was devoted to explaining the distance between speech and the inner processes that generate that speech, and between both of these and the essence of the speaker. This description was given as an analogy to give us some idea of the nothingness of this world in relation to God and thereby provide an understanding of God's oneness.

In general, when we hear speech, we do not consider the complex chain of events that produced it. But once we analyze it, it grows clear that speech is not a discrete action but an expression of an inner state that is the outcome of a process, one that begins on the level of wisdom. When we trace back the chain of events from the spoken word to the ability to speak and from that to the powers behind it, proceeding backward from stage to stage until we reach the initial power within a person, his faculty of wisdom, we learn that the divide between speech and thought is so vast that relating one stage to another is practically impossible. As mentioned, all this is presented only in order to bring into sharp relief the relationship between God's word and His essence and being, between a single divine statement and the entire world that it creates, and the chasm that exists between the creation and the Speaker.

However, the purpose of this discussion is not to emphasize how created reality is nothingness in relation to God, but to set forth an understanding of the Torah, its commandments, and God's unity. This understanding is based on the infinite chasm that separates God from the world. If not for this unbridgeable gap, man would be able to take a finite number of steps to reach God. He would need only to learn a certain amount of material, to perform certain deeds, and then be assured of being able to cleave to Him. Since this infinite chasm between

God and man does exist, the matter is not in his hands. Only God can bridge that gulf. Only He, not an angel or seraph, neither illumination nor concealment, can provide us with the way to reach Him.

This bridge is embodied in the concepts contained in the first and second of the Ten Commandments, "I am the Lord your God" and "You shall have no other gods," which were heard from God Himself. The relationship thus formed – composed of 248 positive commandments and 365 prohibitions – is the only way man could relate to the Divine, since it is the sole avenue of God's communication to man. When a person disconnects himself from that relationship, when he does not want to hear, he falls into a deep abyss, the abyss of nothingness, of total cessation and lack of meaning. The moment he abandons this relationship, he abandons any relationship. The moment he ceases to grasp this, he ceases to grasp the whole. Existence in its entirety is expressed in the phrase "There is no other besides Him." All meaning attributed to the creation and existence of man depends on the fact that man has a connection with God who speaks to him, that man has a way of attaching himself to God's unity.

Chapter 21

TO ILLUSTRATE THE CONCEPT OF GOD'S UNITY, HOW He has not changed even in the wake of the world's creation, the previous chapter offered an analogy of the relationship between a person and his speech. The author of the *Tanya* emphasized the contrast between the two, the vast divide between the character and essence of the speaker and his spoken word. The two are bridged by three elements: the initial desires and cravings of the soul that are evoked in the soul by its intellectual faculties before they are crystallized into words and concepts; the desires of the soul as they are defined within verbal, conceptual thought; and the thought itself, which is then expressed in speech.

The divide between a human being and his thoughts is vast, but the divide between God and the ten utterances with which He created heaven and earth is incomparably more vast. In this chapter, the author of the *Tanya* will explore the explanation of the analogy that he brought in the previous chapter.

וְהִנֵּה מִדַּת הַקָּדוֹשׁ בָּרוּךְ הוּא שֶׁלֹּא כְּמִדַּת בָּשָׂר וָדָם.

The attribute of the Holy One, blessed be He, is unlike the attribute of a human being.

7 Shevat

14 Shevat (leap year)

The obvious difference between human speech and divine speech, that human speech is composed of physical sounds and movements, whereas divine speech is not, is not the most important and meaningful difference between the two. The most significant and meaningful distinction between the two is that once expressed, human speech is no longer connected to its source: the soul and its faculties.

שֶׁהָאָדָם כְּשֶׁמְּדַבֵּר דִּבּוּר, הֲרֵי הֶבֶל הַדִּבּוּר שֶׁבְּפִיו הוּא מוּרְגָּשׁ וְנִרְאֶה דָּבָר בִּפְנֵי עַצְמוֹ מוּבְדָּל מִשָּׁרְשׁוֹ, שֶׁהֵן עֶשֶׂר בְּחִינוֹת הַנֶּפֶשׁ עַצְמָהּ.

When a person utters a word, the breath of that utterance in his mouth is tangible and is perceived as an independent entity, separate from its source, namely, the ten faculties of the soul itself.

Broadly defined, speech is the ability to communicate with others. This can occur only because the speech is disconnected from one's being. Speech transfers words from the self, and once expressed, it is no longer part of the self. A word uttered cannot be recalled. A person's being and his speech are thus two separate entities. Speech has its own existence, independent of us. It no longer needs our thoughts and personality in order to exist. As the author of the *Tanya* will note, this reflects the essential difference between speech and thought. Speech is communication with another and therefore is independent of one's soul. Thought, on the other hand, is an inner communication within the bounds of the self. Although not identical to the soul and its faculties, it is not separate from them either.

אֲבָל הַקָּדוֹשׁ בָּרוּךְ הוּא אֵין דִּבּוּרוֹ מוּבְדָּל מִמֶּנּוּ יִתְבָּרֵךְ חַס וְשָׁלוֹם, כִּי אֵין דָּבָר חוּץ מִמֶּנּוּ וְ"לֵית אֲתַר פָּנוּי מִינֵּיהּ" (תיקוני זהר צא, ב), וְלָכֵן אֵין דִּבּוּרוֹ יִתְבָּרֵךְ כְּדִבּוּרֵינוּ חַס וְשָׁלוֹם

But the speech of the Holy One, blessed be He, is not separate from Him, God forbid, for there is nothing outside of Him and "no space is devoid of Him" (*Tikkunei Zohar* 91b). **Consequently, God's speech is not** at all **similar to our speech, God forbid**

God's speech is not independent of Him, because nothing can conceivably be separate from Him. Since there is nothing separate from Him, divine speech too must necessarily be connected to Him. Differentiation between the self and that which is outside the self is relevant only for a human being and has no meaning when applied to God.

This distinction leads to the central point of this chapter: The products of divine speech, which are the universe and everything in it, including humanity, are not independent entities but are always connected to the Divine and to the divine speech that brought them into existence. Just as divine speech is expressed anew at every moment, so is the creation's connection to the divine being, who is thinking and speaking them anew without pause, renewed at every moment.

[כְּמוֹ שֶׁאֵין מַחֲשַׁבְתּוֹ כְּמַחְשְׁבוֹתֵינוּ, כְּדִכְתִיב: "כִּי לֹא מַחְשְׁבוֹתַי מַחְשְׁבוֹתֵיכֶם" (ישעיה נה, ח), וּכְתִיב: "כֵּן גָּבְהוּ דְרָכַי מִדַּרְכֵיכֶם" וגו' (שם פסוק ט)].

(just as His thoughts are not like our thoughts, as it is written, "For My thoughts are not your thoughts," [Isa. 55:8], **and it is written,** "As the heavens are higher than the earth, **so are My ways higher than your ways** and My thoughts than your thoughts" [Isa. 55:9]).

The author of the *Tanya* adds this parenthetical remark, which draws a distinction between man's thoughts and God's thoughts, not only because the notion is explicitly stated in these verses. The concept of man's thoughts and speech is discussed in these chapters for the sole purpose of enabling a more tangible understanding of God's thoughts and speech. In a sense, the analogy drawn here with regard to thoughts is more impactful than that of speech because a person's thoughts too are not distinct from him. Just as God's speech is not distinct from Him, so it is with man's thoughts. One's thoughts exist only as long as one thinks those thoughts. As soon as the thought process is over, those thoughts utterly cease to be. Understanding this enables a more profound grasp of the relationship between this world, a mere expression of God's speech, and God Himself, the one who uttered those words.

וְלֹא נִקְרָא דִּבּוּרוֹ יִתְבָּרֵךְ בְּשֵׁם דִּבּוּר רַק עַל דֶּרֶךְ מָשָׁל.

God's speech is referred to as speech only in a metaphorical sense.

There is a divine process that we call speech because one aspect of that process may be comparable to human speech. But in truth it is unlike our speech in all respects. It is speech only in a metaphorical sense.

כְּמוֹ שֶׁדִּבּוּר הַתַּחְתּוֹן שֶׁבָּאָדָם הוּא מְגַלֶּה לַשּׁוֹמְעִים מַה שֶּׁהָיָה צָפוּן וְנֶעְלָם בְּמַחֲשַׁבְתּוֹ, כָּךְ

Just as the corporeal speech of man reveals to his **listeners that which was hidden and concealed in his thoughts, so it is on high with** respect to ***Ein***

לְמַעְלָה בְּאֵין סוֹף בָּרוּךְ הוּא, יְצִיאַת הָאוֹר וְהַחַיּוּת מִמֶּנּוּ יִתְבָּרֵךְ מֵהַהֶעְלֵם אֶל הַגִּילּוּי לִבְרוֹא עוֹלָמוֹת וּלְהַחֲיוֹתָם נִקְרָא בְּשֵׁם דִּבּוּר.

***Sof,* blessed be He: The emergence of the light and life force from God, from the** state of con**cealment to** that of **manifestation, in order to create worlds and animate them is referred to as speech.**

We cannot, and may not, compare divine speech to human speech with regard to sound, words, and letters, and certainly not in terms of the mechanisms of speech. Human speech and divine speech share only the most fundamental function of the concept of speech: creating a connection in which something that was initially internal and hidden is outwardly revealed. The function of speech is to act as a means of communicating and bonding with another. In broader terms, the purpose of speech is to reveal or express that which was hitherto concealed. It is the transferal of content or information from one level to another, from a deep, incommunicable level to a more external, expressible level. In this sense, one can aptly describe the creative divine power that forms worlds and emerges from the concealment of *Ein Sof*, manifesting itself in the creation, as the speech of God. ☞

וְהֵן הֵן עֲשָׂרָה מַאֲמָרוֹת שֶׁבָּהֶן נִבְרָא הָעוֹלָם,

This constitutes the ten utterances through which the world was created.

The Torah refers to the emergence of light and life force from the Divine in the creation of the worlds as speech. Specifically, it refers to the ten utterances with which God created the world. These are the utterances

THE ROOT OF *DIBBUR*

☞ The Hebrew word for speech, *dibbur*, is linguistically related to the word *dabar*, leader, as in "One leader [*dabar*] for the generation" (*Sanhedrin* 8a), or as in the verse "He subdues [*yadber*] peoples beneath us" (Ps. 47:4). Likewise, a *midbar*, desert, is the setting in which flocks are led. In this sense, speech entails directing the life forces downward into combinations of letters, words, and sentences that create and sustain reality. Similarly, the word *haggada*, which means relating stories or information, revealing that which was not hitherto known, has the same root as another word for leader, *nagid*.

introduced by the ten occurrences of the phrase "God said" in the first chapter of Genesis.[1] ☞

וְכֵן שְׁאָר כָּל הַתּוֹרָה, נְבִיאִים וּכְתוּבִים, שֶׁהִשִּׂיגוּ הַנְּבִיאִים בְּמַרְאֵה נְבוּאָתָם.

Likewise, the rest of the Torah, Prophets, and Writings that the prophets apprehended in their prophetic visions are called divine speech.

Another, deeper form of divine speech is the Torah. Included in this are the words of the Prophets and Writings; they are all a form of divine revelation in the world. In one form of divine expression, the world is revealed, while the words of the Torah and Prophets are revealed in the other.

Obviously God's communication in the Torah and Prophets is not speech as we know it, with our words and letters. When we say that God speaks to a prophet, we mean that He reveals Himself in some manner. The concealed becomes revealed, and the hidden grows more

ANTHROPOMORPHISMS AND DIVINE SPEECH

☞ We know that God's speech is in no way similar to our own. What, then, is the purpose of a phrase such as *vayomer Hashem*, "God said," or *vayedaber Hashem*, "God spoke"?

In *Sha'ar HaYiḥud VeHa'emuna* (chap. 11), the author of the *Tanya* discusses this topic at length, reaching the conclusion that our language allows us no alternative. The human dilemma in every encounter with the Divine is our lack of vocabulary. Words can never express something that is totally abstract. Although words are themselves abstractions, their meaning is always human and material. Consequently, we have no way to directly express an abstraction that is beyond our material human existence. Our only option is to employ metaphor, to apply a word that describes the human condition to a different reality altogether. Clearly, such a metaphorical expression will not express any abstract existence entirely, but our human limitations force us to use it and to attempt to make the metaphor as exact as possible. To define the concept of divine speech, we must use language that we understand.

1. The Talmud (*Rosh HaShana* 32a), as well as numerous hasidic and kabbalistic sources, notes that a careful reading of the text yields only nine such phrases. The Talmud resolves this by counting the first verse in the Torah, "In the beginning, God created the heavens and the earth," as one of the ten utterances of Creation.

clear, but certainly not with human words and our human mechanisms of speech.[2]

15 Shevat (leap year)

וַהֲרֵי דִּבּוּרוֹ וּמַחֲשַׁבְתּוֹ כִּבְיָכוֹל מְיוּחָדוֹת עִמּוֹ בְּתַכְלִית הַיִּחוּד. דֶּרֶךְ מָשָׁל, כְּמוֹ דִּבּוּרוֹ וּמַחֲשַׁבְתּוֹ שֶׁל אָדָם בְּעוֹדָן בְּכֹחַ חָכְמָתוֹ וְשִׂכְלוֹ,

God's **speech and thoughts, as it were, are united with Him in absolute unity, analogous to a person's speech and thought while still in his faculty of wisdom and intellect,**

Human speech differs from divine speech in that it is no longer connected to its speaker from the moment it is spoken but becomes a separate reality. An ancient analogy compares human speech to arrows: "A sharpened arrow is their tongue, speaking deceit" (Jer. 9:7). Just as an arrow, once shot from the bow, cannot be brought back, so too once a person has said something, he cannot retract it. Speech has a life of its own. It does not matter whether the speaker's intent was positive or negative; the words go forth and have their effect with no connection to the thoughts and intent of the person who uttered them.

But divine speech is entirely different. In a sense, a better metaphor for divine speech is not human speech but human thought before it has been articulated, when it is still within consciousness, before it has been articulated through letters and words, the stage at which speech no more than trembles on the verge of coming into being.

אוֹ בִּתְשׁוּקָה וְחֶמְדָּה שֶׁבְּלִבּוֹ קוֹדֶם שֶׁעָלְתָה מֵהַלֵּב לַמּוֹחַ לְהַרְהֵר בָּהּ בִּבְחִינַת אוֹתִיּוֹת,

or as they exist **in a longing and desire in one's heart before they rise from the heart to the brain, where letters are employed in order to contemplate it.**

A thought does not have to be intellectual. It may also be an emotional yearning and desire in the heart, which then signals that it desires something or that it fears or loathes some other thing and wants to avoid it. These signals reach one's mind, which develops them into words and the symbols of thought and speech.

2. See also the commentary on *Sha'ar HaYiḥud VeHa'emuna*, chap. 11.

שֶׁאָז הָיוּ אוֹתִיּוֹת הַמַּחֲשָׁבָה וְהַדִּבּוּר הַזֶּה הַנִּמְשָׁכוֹת מֵחֶמְדָּה וּתְשׁוּקָה זוֹ בְּכֹחַ בַּלֵּב וּמְיוּחָדוֹת שָׁם בְּתַכְלִית הַיִּחוּד בְּשָׁרְשָׁן, שֶׁהֵן הַחָכְמָה וְשֵׂכֶל שֶׁבַּמּוֹחַ וְחֶמְדָּה וּתְשׁוּקָה שֶׁבַּלֵּב.

Then the letters of this thought and speech, which issue from this desire and longing, were in a potential state in the heart, where they were united in absolute unity with their source, **which are** the faculty of **wisdom and intellect in the brain and the desire and longing in the heart.**

The letters and symbols of speech through which the desire later expresses itself first exist in an incipient state in the heart, in the hidden potential of the thought to emerge into speech. The desire or the idea, even before it is verbalized, already has, in potential, the words that can express it. They are already unified with the feeling itself, with the awareness that generates them. Only afterward are they articulated as letters and words, and as the desire grows or the idea takes shape, the words take on an existence of their own. Even if they are not expressed verbally, once an idea is formulated into words, a form of communication takes place. In a way, we are communicating with ourselves. There is an inner speech that is connected with our being, with our desires and ideas. As with divine speech, at a certain point our inner speech is united with our soul. The difference is that divine speech is never separated from the divine being.

וְכָכָה מַמָּשׁ, דֶּרֶךְ מָשָׁל,

So too, figuratively speaking, this is actually analogous 8 Shevat

This expression seems to be self-contradictory. Something cannot be both actual and analogous at one and the same time. To solve this paradox, we must understand the concept of analogy not as diminishing the reality but as providing a means of understanding it: to explain one reality by making reference to another. This phrase underscores two points: It emphasizes that the description of the unity of divine speech with the Divine is exact, not merely a figure of speech. Second, it emphasizes that the comparison between divine speech and human speech is inexact. It does not describe divine speech in its entirety but only by analogy.

מְיוּחָדוֹת דִּבּוּרוֹ וּמַחֲשַׁבְתּוֹ שֶׁל הַקָּדוֹשׁ בָּרוּךְ הוּא בְּתַכְלִית הַיִּחוּד בְּמַהוּתוֹ וְעַצְמוּתוֹ יִתְבָּרֵךְ גַּם אַחַר שֶׁיָּצָא דִּבּוּרוֹ יִתְבָּרֵךְ אֶל הַפּוֹעַל בִּבְרִיאוֹת הָעוֹלָמוֹת, כְּמוֹ שֶׁהָיָה מְיוּחָד עִמּוֹ קוֹדֶם בְּרִיאַת הָעוֹלָמוֹת.

to the speech and thought of the Holy One, blessed be He, which **are united in absolute unity with His essence and being even after His speech emerged in actuality in** the process of **the creation of the worlds, just as** His speech and thoughts **were united with Him before the creation of the worlds.**

Divine speech is never independent from the Divine. It is always connected to God and united with Him, and not even creation separates it. Human speech, on the other hand, is discrete from its speaker because a human being is limited. It is not only an outward revelation of his thoughts but an entity independent of him. None of us contains everything within ourselves. There is existence beyond us, and because of his limited nature, when a person wishes to speak, he must use elements and forces outside himself, which include the body, the air he breathes, and the electrical waves he uses when thinking. In so doing, he creates realities that are detached from his own being.

By contrast, no matter how lofty and distant the divine speech from its source, it is impossible for that speech to become detached from it. This inseparability is not due to a particular aspect of the divine speech itself, but rather by virtue of the infinite nature of God, the Speaker of those words. As a finite being, a person occupies a particular physical space. As such, his words by definition must extend beyond the space he occupies. With respect to God, His infinite nature precludes any concept of something being outside or beyond Him. Those concepts

THE UNITY AND THE DIVIDE

☞ The idea that there is a constant connection between divine speech and the Divine does not contradict the observation regarding the vast distance between the two discussed in the previous chapter, just as the emphasis on the distinction between human and divine speech does not negate the comparable aspects they share. This does not mean to say that divine speech and divine wisdom are identical, but that one is never separate from the other. Divine speech cannot exist and are absurd in relation to God. Even the infinitely gaping chasm between the quintessence of God and His speech and creations does not actually divide them in the slightest. ☞

be actualized unless it maintains an ongoing connection to the divine wisdom and being. At the same time, as the author of the *Tanya* stated in the previous chapter, the distance dividing them is sweeping, incomparably more vast than the distance separating human wisdom from human speech.

Although the metaphor of human speech may not be perfect, it is highly useful, because it gives us some way of understanding the chasm. As the author of the *Tanya* explains elsewhere (*Sha'ar HaYiḥud VeHa'emuna*, chap. 9), the breadth of our human experience and comprehension is the very smallest part of the vast expanses of all the worlds. In the human experience, the process of translating our initial thoughts into practice, the expanse between that first flash of wisdom until it is actualized into the final result, entails five steps: mind, emotion, thought, speech, and deed. But in the larger picture, the expanse of this human process is only one reality amid myriads of myriads, one glimmer in a row of points that recede into the infinite distance.

But those other expanses, those awesome billions, communicate nothing to us despite their undoubted existence. That is because everything beyond that which we can grasp with our mind ceases to be meaningful to us. The power of our comprehension can only encircle the compass of our being. As the author of the *Tanya* stated in *Sha'ar HaYiḥud VeHa'emuna* (chap. 8), "A person can [only] depict in his mind all the concepts that he wishes to conceive and understand as they exist within him."

We can see a rainbow with its palette of colors from indigo to scarlet, but this array comprises only one narrow band of the much broader electromagnetic spectrum, which is invisible to us. Although those electromagnetic waves have various properties, depending on their frequency, they transmit no information to our sense of sight. We speak of black and white as opposites, not because they truly are opposites, but because that is all we can see. In truth, there exist a vast range of waves. Some may be miles long, while others are mere millimicrons in length, yet they are invisible to us.

Like the eye, the human ear is also capable of hearing only a limited part of the sound frequency range. For example, we hear sounds only from a narrow range of the totality of sound. To us, all sounds outside that range are silence.

In the previous chapter, the author of the *Tanya* described the extent of the distance between our mind and our speech. He described our possible range of experience, the part of the spectrum in which we can see and hear. Now imagine, if you will, what it would be like to broaden that range a thousandfold so that we could access realities of much higher frequencies, and then another thousandfold, and another, and then we could fathom just a fraction of the vast expanse of the totality of existence.

וְאֵין שׁוּם שִׁינּוּי כְּלָל לְפָנָיו יִתְבָּרֵךְ, אֶלָּא אֶל הַבְּרוּאִים הַמְקַבְּלִים חַיּוּתָם מִבְּחִינַת דִּבּוּרוֹ יִתְבָּרֵךְ,

There is no change whatsoever with respect to God. Rather, the change exists **only** in relation **to the created beings who receive their life force from God's speech**

For God, there is no difference between the reality that preceded divine speech and the reality created by that speech. There is one stream flowing through all levels of being. The entire range of existence, from one extreme to the other, is merely one aspect of reality. In His eyes, there is no separation between before and after. But for humans, there is a difference, and that difference defines our limits. Divine speech may be God's lowest level of divine revelation, but that speech comprises the highest level of reality that we human beings can perceive. It is the roof of our world, beyond which lies nothingness. From our standpoint, that which is before is beyond comprehension, whereas that which is after can be comprehended. This one-sided and never-ending relationship between the Creator and creation maintains the stasis of the universe throughout the entirety of its existence. God is independent of us, but we depend on Him; He sees us, but we cannot see Him.

Any comprehension that we do achieve is called the revelation of the Divine Presence, which is identical with the attribute of *Malkhut*, or Kingship, also synonymous with the word of God. When a person gains an awareness of the Divine Presence in the world, when he feels how God's glory permeates all of reality, he is cognizant of the divine speech speaking within the world, enlivening it and maintaining its existence. This is the sense that God is King of the world, which is the peak of our human experience. We can reach only up to this point, to the understanding of divine speech, since the divine essence infinitely transcends it. Yet despite the vast divide between God and His speech, His speech is still connected to His being.

When it comes to such subjects, every analogy is necessarily imperfect and so must be understood only in a limited sense. When an adult

PRAYER MADE POSSIBLE

☞ This understanding of the relationship between man and God clearly emphasizes the void that separates us from Him. At the same time, it explains how we are capable talks to a child, the relationship is one-sided. The child can relate only to the words, not to what lies beyond it, which he cannot experience. The adult, on the other hand, is aware of how his words were connected to his mind and the thoughts that generated them. There can be speech that from one aspect is connected to the speaker, yet from another is completely independent of him. ☞

בִּבְחִינַת יְצִיאָתוֹ כְּבָר אֶל הַפּוֹעַל בִּבְרִיאַת הָעוֹלָמוֹת, **through its actualization in the creation of the worlds,**

The divine speech that has been actualized with the creation of the worlds is precisely that which animates the creation. That creation perceives itself as an independent entity of the Creator as a result of the change in reality upon the creation of the world. As mentioned in the previous chapter, there exists a distinction between man's speech when it is actualized and speech still in potentiality in his mind, and even more so deep within his soul. The deeper the speech is nestled within the person, the more it is united and one with him. When it comes to one's thoughts, and certainly the faculties of his soul, the

of connecting to Him, that to beseech God in prayer is not an exercise in futility. Because God is so far from us, it is reasonable to ask why He should pay us any attention. What is the logic in a person with a stomachache asking God to heal him? Doesn't God have more important things to do? On the other hand, everything in the created universe is equally distant from God. We could as easily ask, doesn't God have anything more important to do than to attend to the Milky Way? Although the Milky Way is composed of billions of stars, what is that in God's eyes? He created them merely by saying, "Let there be...." From His viewpoint, a stomachache and the Andromeda Galaxy are equal, falling under the rubric of what the *Zohar* dubs "trivial matters" (*Zohar* 3:149b; see *Likkutei Torah, Vayikra* 22d).

When an adult and child play a game with play money, there is no real difference between a penny and a million dollars. But for the child, who takes the game seriously, it makes a great difference whether he wins one dollar or a hundred, and all his happiness hinges on it. In this sense, God is playing with us in this world, playing King of the universe. However – and this is the crucial point – at the moment that He acknowledges that He is called King, the moment He joins us in the game, He really is King of the universe.

God's word, His speech, is not separate from Him but a part of His very essence. He does not send representatives to play this role; He Himself descends to the very lowest level in order to be the King of the universe. Thus God perceives everything on every level, whether the voice of a child – "the voice of the lad as he is there" (Gen. 21:17) – or that of an angel. To the one who is called King, both are equally inconsequential and equally important.

thinker is prominently present, with no possibility of disconnecting him from the particular thoughts or feelings.

This is in stark contrast to speech that has been expressed and heard by another. The speaker is no longer attached to the words he uttered. Unless one thinks of him and seeks him, he is likely to disappear and lose connection to his words. The same is true of divine speech. Upon becoming actualized by creating the worlds and becoming clothed within them, the infinite divine Speaker disappears, as it were, leaving the creation with a sense of independence and separateness.

שֶׁמִּתְלַבֵּשׁ בָּהֶם לְהַחֲיוֹתָם עַל יְדֵי הִשְׁתַּלְשְׁלוּת מֵעִלָּה לְעָלוּל

when it becomes clothed within them to animate them through a process of cause and effect

The divine light does not descend in a direct fashion, but rather gradually, in a process of cause and effect, like the interconnected links in a chain.

וִירִידַת הַמַּדְרֵגוֹת בְּצִמְצוּמִים רַבִּים וְשׁוֹנִים,

and a descent level by level through numerous and varied constrictions,

At each stage in this process of descent, the divine light is contracted and constricted. Despite the gradual diminution in light, there exists a continual link between the cause and effect, yet that bond is minimal, a shadow of its original intensity.

עַד שֶׁיּוּכְלוּ הַבְּרוּאִים לְקַבֵּל חַיּוּתָם וְהִתְהַוּוּתָם מִמֶּנּוּ וְלֹא יִתְבַּטְּלוּ בִּמְצִיאוּת.

until the created beings can receive their life force and existence from Him and at the same time **not become subsumed in** the divine **reality.**

WORLD AND CONCEALMENT

☞ The wonder of creation is not that existence was brought forth from nothingness but rather that the divine light of *Ein Sof* remains concealed and constricted. The wonder of creation is that in a world that receives its entire existence from God, not only at the original moment of creation but at every moment, we could think that we are self-made. In the words of Pharaoh, "The river is mine, and I have made myself" (Ezek. 29:3). The process of creation is therefore one of concealment, in which we created beings do not realize that essentially "there is no other besides Him"

This unique state, wherein the created being, the "effect," can receive its life force from God, the "cause," yet simultaneously not become subsumed, losing its independent existence, requires a powerful constriction, one that occurs only after myriad other constrictions, through a chain of causes and effects, have occurred. ☞

16 Shevat (leap year)

וְכָל הַצִּמְצוּמִים הֵם בְּחִינַת הֶסְתֵּר פָּנִים לְהַסְתִּיר וּלְהַעְלִים הָאוֹר וְהַחַיּוּת הַנִּמְשָׁךְ מִדִּבּוּרוֹ יִתְבָּרֵךְ שֶׁלֹּא יִתְגַּלֶּה בִּבְחִינַת גִּילּוּי רַב שֶׁלֹּא יוּכְלוּ הַתַּחְתּוֹנִים לְקַבֵּל.

All these **constrictions constitute a concealed countenance,** which is meant **to conceal and hide the light and life force that issue forth from God's speech, so that they will not be manifest through such an intense revelation that the lower worlds would be unable to receive it.**

(Deut. 4:35) but whose primary experience is our sense of self and the seeming existence of the world around us.

Constriction creates a world of concealment. The Hebrew word for creation, *beria*, is a cognate with the word *berei*, meaning to clear out, to make space, alluding to the space God "cleared out" in order to create the world, as in the verse "Go up to the forest and clear for yourself [*bereta*] there" (Josh. 17:15)). The Hebrew word for world, *olam*, connotes concealment, as in the verse "And the matter is concealed [*ne'elam*] from the eyes of the assembly" (Lev. 4:13). Our world is a reality that is not subsumed in the divine light. For such a reality to exist, there must be a vast distance between us and God and a dense concealment of His presence. If we were to be directly aware of God's presence in everything, there would be no more world. The reality of this world is a play of light and shadow, of revelation and concealment of the divine light. The moment that the light is revealed, the game is over. Then there is only the one light.

In the last moments of Rabbi Shneur Zalman's life, as he was fleeing Napoleon and taking refuge in a cabin in an out-of-the-way Russian village called Pyena, he asked his grandson, "What do you see?"

His grandson replied, "I see the cabin, the wooden wall, the beam in the ceiling."

Rabbi Shneur Zalman responded, "And at this moment, I see only the Divine!"

A person who sees only the Divine is no longer a participant in the game. For him, the world is no longer a world, because it no longer conceals the presence of God. Even the greatest tzaddikim need at least the possibility of not seeing the Divine directly. That clear sight will constitute the reality of the end of days, when people will see that "this is our God!" Then there will no longer be any meaning to concepts such as free will or eternal life. The present infrastructure will melt away and lose all its meaning, and the world will become a transformed reality where nothing is hidden.

If the light within divine speech were to be revealed in its full force, it would be too powerful for created beings to receive their vitality from it. The life force that is given to every finite creation cannot exceed that entity's ability to assimilate it, just as a person cannot absorb knowledge beyond his mental capacity, just as an electric cable cannot carry more than a certain voltage, and just as a water hose will burst if too much water passes through it. All these constrictions and concealments are needed to limit the amount of power that is transmitted so that every created being will receive exactly what it is able to sustain and no more.

The mechanism of constriction and concealment is as integral a part of divine speech as divine revelation. Without that mechanism, divine speech would destroy reality rather than construct it. In order for divine speech to be manifest, in order that it may communicate, it must be concealed, bound, and constricted. In this way, it maintains the ongoing existence of the world.

וְלָכֵן גַּם כֵּן נִדְמֶה לָהֶם אוֹר וְחַיּוּת הַדִּבּוּר שֶׁל מָקוֹם בָּרוּךְ הוּא הַמְלוּבָּשׁ בָּהֶם - כְּאִלּוּ הוּא דָּבָר מוּבְדָּל מִמַּהוּתוֹ וְעַצְמוּתוֹ יִתְבָּרֵךְ, רַק שֶׁנִּמְשָׁךְ מִמֶּנּוּ יִתְבָּרֵךְ כְּמוֹ דִּבּוּר שֶׁל אָדָם מִנַּפְשׁוֹ.

Therefore, the light and life force of the speech of God, blessed be He, that is clothed within them also appears to them as if it were an entity distinct from God's essence and being, that it **only issues forth from God just as man's speech** issues forth **from his soul.**

As the author of the *Tanya* stated above, divine speech differs from human speech because it is not disconnected from God, the Speaker. Since there is no divide between the Speaker and the speech, between the Revealer and the reality that is being revealed, there must be a system of concealment in order to constrict the light in the divine speech and to conceal the Speaker in the speech. In this way, the world can receive the speech as though it were separate from the Speaker and the life force without perceiving its Source. The creation appears

DIVINE SPEECH IS CREATION ITSELF

☞ We generally think of the speech that created the world as resembling the outwardly directed words of a person giving orders that some specific action should be to be external, to have emerged from the essence of the Creator and to exist separately from Him. Not everyone believes this, but it is a direct inference based on the evidence of our senses. This perception does not stem from the truth of reality, but because the world is unable to fully receive the divine revelation. ☞ ☞

אַךְ לְגַבֵּי הַקָּדוֹשׁ בָּרוּךְ הוּא אֵין שׁוּם צִמְצוּם וְהֶסְתֵּר וְהֶעְלֵם מַסְתִּיר וּמַעְלִים לְפָנָיו, וְכַחֲשֵׁכָה כָּאוֹרָה, כְּדִכְתִיב: "גַּם חֹשֶׁךְ לֹא יַחְשִׁיךְ מִמֶּךָ" וגו' (תהלים קלט, יב).

However, in relation to the Holy One, blessed be He, there is no constriction, concealment, or hiddenness that conceals or hides anything **from Him.** To God, **darkness is light, as it is written, "Even darkness does not darken for You.** The night, as if day, gives forth light. Darkness and light are the same" (Ps. 139:12).

Elsewhere, the author of the *Tanya* comments that the expression "darkness and light are the same" indicates a total correspondence

carried out outside his being. This notion starkly contrasts with the idea discussed in these chapters (and in greater detail in *Sha'ar HaYiḥud VeHa'emuna*), which explain that the divine speech is itself the very creation, constantly issuing forth and recreating the world from a prior state of nonexistence.

THE GAME OF HIDE-AND-SEEK

☞ Man exists and is active in this world through the awareness that there is both a God and a world. He grasps that his self and God are not identical. To make such an awareness and reality possible, God constricted His light and lowered His speech to such a degree that He exists, so to speak, within the world, which is limited, finite, and cut off from the infinite *Ein Sof* Himself.

By way of analogy, when an adult plays hide-and-seek with a child, the child usually hides where the adult can easily find him, but the adult pretends not to see. He creates the illusion that there is both concealment and visibility, because if everything were revealed, the game would be over. In order that the game may continue, God cannot say, "I know everything," because if He knows everything, why is He playing? In truth, both hide: Can a man hide in concealed places and I will not see him?" (Jer. 23:24) and "Indeed, You are God who conceals Himself" (Isa. 45:15). In this sense, human life consists of man "hiding" from God and God hiding from man. This mutual concealment is a part of the nature of the world, which enables it to continue to exist without being annihilated, because both the Creator and the created can hide from each other. When it grows clear to mankind that the two cannot hide from each other, the world will cease to exist.

between the two: Not only is the dark like the light, but the light is like the dark.[3] For God, not only is that which is concealed completely revealed, but the entire concept of concealment and revelation does not even exist. God exists, as it were, beyond both the realms of light and darkness, in a place that is "not day and not night" (Zech. 14:7).

This can be compared to a one-way mirror. One surface is opaque to some degree, yet the other side is completely transparent. A person who stands on the opaque side sees nothing besides his own image and perhaps vague indications of what lies behind the mirror. But for the person who stands on the transparent side, there is no barrier. He sees clearly that "darkness and light are the same."

Another, more precise analogy appears in the works of the early sages. When a person poses a riddle, all the complexities of the riddle are clear to him because he knows the solution. For him, the question and the solution are one. But the person to whom he poses the riddle is in a different place. This person experiences concealment, a thick curtain separating the riddle from its solution. Both people are engaged in the same question, but to one it is completely opaque. To the other, it is completely transparent.

מִשּׁוּם שֶׁאֵין הַצִּמְצוּמִים וְהַלְּבוּשִׁים דָּבָר נִפְרָד מִמֶּנּוּ יִתְבָּרֵךְ חַס וְשָׁלוֹם, אֶלָּא "כְּהָדֵין קַמְצָא דִּלְבוּשֵׁיהּ מִינֵּיהּ וּבֵיהּ" (בראשית רבה כא, ה),

This is **because the constrictions and garments are not distinct from Him, God forbid. Rather,** they are **akin to "the snail whose garment,** its shell, **is of it and in it"** (*Bereshit Rabba* 21:5),

A person's clothing is not a part of him. He can put it on or take it off as he wishes. But the snail's "garment," its shell, is an inseparable part of it and is integral to its essential nature. In this sense, the garments of divine light are also a part of the divine being. Concealment and constriction are as much a revelation of God as what we usually understand as revelation and manifestation: "Darkness is the same as light."

---

3. *Likkutei Torah*, Lev. 12a.

Without constriction, there would be no space in this world for the revelation of the Divine.[4]

כְּמוֹ שֶׁכָּתוּב: "כִּי ה' הוּא הָאֱלֹהִים" (דברים ד, לה), וּכְמוֹ שֶׁנִּתְבָּאֵר בְּמָקוֹם אַחֵר.

as it is written, "The Lord [*Havaya*], **He is the God** [*Elokim*]" (Deut. 4:35), **as explained elsewhere** (*Sha'ar HaYiḥud VeHa'emuna*, chap. 6).

The four-letter name of *Havaya* and the name *Elokim* each represent different aspects of the same being. The name of *Havaya* indicates God as the one who reveals and emanates from beyond the boundaries of this world, whereas *Elokim* indicates divinity as it is manifest within the world, within nature.[5] In light of this, "The Lord, He is the God" means that "the Lord" manifests Himself within the concealment of nature, that His compassion, represented by the name of *Havaya*, mitigates the strict justice embodied by the name *Elokim*. But it also means more than that. This phrase tells us that in essence there is no difference between the divinity that reveals itself and the divinity that conceals itself, between its immanent essence and its transcendent essence.

וְלָכֵן קַמֵּיהּ כּוּלָּא כְּלָא חָשִׁיב מַמָּשׁ.

Therefore, everything before Him is literally considered as nothingness.

Before God, everything is literally as nothing. The entirety of existence, which perceives itself as a separate entity, is of no consequence whatsoever and has no special, independent existence. Everything is merely an expression of the divine being.

This chapter examined the difference between divine and human speech. Both are a means of communication, a transfer of words from one being to another, from within to the outside, from concealment to revelation. But at their essence, there is a great difference between them. Human speech is separate from the speaker. Once the words have been spoken or written down, they are no longer connected to him. Speaker and spoken are independent entities. Divine speech, on

4. See *Sha'ar HaYiḥud VeHa'emuna*, chap. 6.

5. An allusion to this is found in the shared numerical value of the Hebrew word for "the nature," *hateva*, and the divine name *Elokim*.

the other hand, is not separate from the Divine. Nothing separates the Speaker, the speech, and the reality to which He speaks. To Him, there exists no barrier and nothing outside Himself. Nevertheless, the world is created as a result of the constrictions and concealments that hide the divine light that is embodied in His speech, preventing the divine force within it from being perceived, so that the speech appears separate from Him. This concealment is experienced only by the created beings of the lower worlds. To God, there are no concepts of concealment and revelation. "Darkness is the same as light," because "the Lord, He is the God."

Chapter 22

IN THE PREVIOUS CHAPTER, THE AUTHOR OF THE *TANYA* discussed the concept of divine speech at length, describing how it is bound to God in absolute unity, never separating from the Divine. The creation of our physical world effected no change in the relationship between the Speaker and His spoken word; the unity remains as it was prior to the Creation.

The relationship between the Creator and the created is not a symmetrical one. From God's perspective, everything is transparent. There is no barrier, no concealment, and everything is one. There is only the infinite light of *Ein Sof*. From our human perspective, there are multiple layers of concealment that create a wall, an unbridgeable gulf, between created being and Creator, which manifests as separation, darkness, and the concealment of God's countenance. To put this another way, the distance between the Creator and the creation is not equal to the distance between the creation and the Creator. From the Creator's perspective, He is always intimately close to creation: "Even darkness does not darken for You. The night, as if day, gives forth light. Darkness and light are the same" (Ps. 139:12). But from the viewpoint of created beings, the Creator is infinitely distant.

In the previous chapter, the author of the *Tanya* also provided metaphors and illustrations in an effort to describe the notion of God's perfect oneness so that a person might meditate on the concept and awaken his concealed love to the extent that he is able to attach himself to the divine unity.

This chapter will discuss the other side of the creation's bond with God: the perspective of the creation in a world where God's oneness is hidden and concealed.

9 Shevat
17 Shevat (leap year)

רַק שֶׁהַתּוֹרָה דִּבְּרָה כִּלְשׁוֹן בְּנֵי אָדָם,

The Torah nevertheless speaks in the language of men,

Despite the great divide between human and divine reality, the Torah still calls divine communication speech. Because the Torah is addressing human beings, it uses a language to which they can, in some way, relate.[1] ☞

וְנִקְרָא בַּתּוֹרָה דִּבּוּרוֹ שֶׁל מָקוֹם בָּרוּךְ הוּא בְּשֵׁם דִּבּוּר מַמָּשׁ כְּדִבּוּרוֹ שֶׁל אָדָם.

and the speech of God, blessed be He, is referred to as actual speech in the Torah, like human speech.

Human speech and divine speech are so dissimilar in essence that they should have different names. But because a person can conceive of something only if it relates to his own reality, the Torah calls divine communication by its human counterpart, speech. Thus we are told that God spoke or said, just as human beings such as Moses and Aaron spoke or said.

THE LANGUAGE OF MEN

☞ It is important to note that our relationship to the language of the Torah is necessarily inexact. As human beings, we have a basic problem: If we had an exact concept of divine speech, it would be meaningless to us, and if divine speech has meaning for us, it is necessarily imprecise. The recurring phrase that the author of the *Tanya* uses to express this problematic relationship is "so too, figuratively speaking, this is actually analogous." The wording of the expression literally implies "in the exact same way, as shown in the analogy." The double meaning of this expression communicates the multiple layers behind the Torah's words, which are spoken in the language of human beings. The underlying meaning is actual and exact, but the means of explaining it, the analogy borrowed from human language, is not wholly exact but, rather, an analogy, a figurative manner of speech.

1. See *Berakhot* 31b.

לְפִי שֶׁבֶּאֱמֶת כָּךְ הוּא, דֶּרֶךְ יְרִידַת וְהַמְשָׁכַת הַחַיּוּת לַתַּחְתּוֹנִים בְּצִמְצוּמִים רַבִּים וַעֲצוּמִים

In truth, this is so, that God's speech appears to be separate from Him, **by means of the descent and drawing down of the life force to the lower worlds through numerous, immense constrictions**

From God's perspective, His speech is not separate from Himself, nor does His speech, being a divine power, constitute an actual constriction of the divine light and life force. As explained in *Sha'ar HaYiḥud VeHa'emuna*,[2] since the constriction itself is a divine force, it conceals nothing from God. But from the perspective of His creations, the constriction is real, obscuring the light and life force so that His speech appears to be separate from Him, the Speaker, much like human speech.

The process by which God's speech is constricted by "numerous, immense constrictions" is in many ways comparable to human speech: The speech appears to be distant and separate from the Speaker, a greatly constricted version of the contents of God's thoughts. The essence of the original thought seems to have been broken down into an abundance of details that constitute words, letters, and the various combinations that they form.

The previous chapter discussed speech as a means of transferring meaning from one point to another. Here we explore another quality of speech: the constriction of the original thought. Just as there are states of reality that we cannot conceive, so too there are thoughts that we cannot verbalize. Speech expresses only the lower margins of a thought, only that particular aspect of it that can be constricted through the medium of verbal expression. The greater part of a thought cannot be constricted and so cannot be expressed in speech except as a vague sense of something that floats just beyond the reach of the spoken word.[3]

Constriction is a vital process in every transfer of content from one medium to another. Constriction diminishes the light – the content –

---

2. Chap. 6.
3. See also *Iggeret HaKodesh*, epistle 5.

so that it can fit to the vessel. If there were too much light, the vessel would shatter. This is an exceedingly delicate balance: The more the content suits the vessel, the farther it is from its inner contents, the original, pure concept itself. But the more faithful it remains to the original, the less it conforms to the vessel. ☞

of variations upon variations in order that a vast array of numerous creations may be created through them.

מִינִים מִמִּינִים שׁוֹנִים, לְהִבָּרְאוֹת מֵהֶם בְּרוּאִים רַבִּים מִינִים מִמִּינִים שׁוֹנִים.

The process of constriction can be seen, paradoxically, as multiplicity and expansion. One example of this is the passage from wisdom to understanding. The initial flash of wisdom contains a reality that is not composed of discrete elements but provides a complete picture all at once. When this picture passes to a level of structured understanding, the image is broadened. The one spark of insight expands into a variety of thoughts and ideas, which can be expressed by innumerable words.

There have been people, even great people, who never had more

ON THOUGHTS AND SPEECH

☞ An additional element exists regarding the relationship between thoughts and speech, between the idea and its expression. In terms of the content that passes from thought to words, speech is merely a constricted reflection, a diminution, of the thought. This differs from the standpoint of the vessel. The letters and the words have their own source, one that does not derive from only the thought nor is a constriction of it. It is very possible that the speech will contain more than had been implicit in the thought, because it also contains content beyond the conception of the thought itself.

In terms of the relationship between thought and speech, the passage from thought to speech will always entail the constriction of the original, inner content. By contrast, the instruments of speech, the words and letters, are independent entities possessing particular faculties that can be deeper than those of the conscious thought. It is possible for speech to remove itself, as it were, from the thought-to-speech process and establish itself as an independent entity. For instance, from time to time, we all experience a moment of creativity, in speech or in deed, beyond our normal capabilities. We might make a statement and then be struck by its brilliance.

The relationship between a thought and the spoken word, then, is complex because it flows in both directions. In kabbalistic terms, this mutual relationship is than one idea throughout the course of their lives. All their writings were no more than an attempt to understand and explicate that one illumination of wisdom. That point, that instantaneous comprehension, is transformed on the level of understanding into a thought that can last for years. Yet from a qualitative standpoint, those years of thought and those many books on the topic contain a mere elaboration of what had existed in the primal seed of wisdom.

וְכָל כָּךְ גָּבְרוּ וְעָצְמוּ הַצִּמְצוּמִים וְהֶסְתֵּר פָּנִים הָעֶלְיוֹנִים, עַד שֶׁיּוּכְלוּ לְהִתְהַוּוֹת וּלְהִבָּרְאוֹת גַּם דְּבָרִים טְמֵאִים וּקְלִיפּוֹת וְסִטְרָא אָחֳרָא וּלְקַבֵּל חַיּוּתָם וְקִיּוּמָם מִדְּבַר ה׳ וְרוּחַ פִּיו יִתְבָּרֵךְ בְּהֶסְתֵּר פָּנִים וִירִידַת הַמַּדְרֵגוֹת.

The constrictions and concealment of the supernal countenance are so immensely powerful that even impure entities, the *kelippot*, and the *sitra aḥara* can be brought into existence and created, receiving their life force and existence from the word of God and the breath of His divine utterance through a concealed countenance and a descent through many **levels.**

referred to as the direct light and the returning light. From the standpoint of the direct light, there is always descent and constriction, but it is out of the constriction that the returning light is created (see *Torah Or* 5a), and that returning light rises higher than the original, direct light. A person forms a word, speaks it, and then receives from it. What he receives from the word does not flow entirely from him, because he himself cannot create a thought that is greater than himself.

We can compare this to a horse and its rider (see *Torah Or* 62c; *Likkutei Torah*, Deut. 69c). Although the horse is subject to the will of the rider, the horse's greater strength makes it possible for him to lead the rider to places that the rider could not have reached on his own. The words of speech are the horse, and the thought (the person) is the rider. The letters of speech comprise a vessel of expression for the thought, but the letters have the power to take that thought to new places and raise it higher than it could have risen by itself.

Still, in several places (*Torah Or* 62c; *Ma'amar Admor HaZaken* [5564], p. 25), the author of the *Tanya* makes a point of saying that with regard to a person's service of God, "it is not the might of horses that He desires" (Ps. 147:10) but rather the person's own love and awe. Words are strong. They have a great impact on the soul and can evoke intense emotion, but that is the "might of the horse." Instead, God desires the connection of the person himself, of "those who fear Him, those who long for His kindness" (Ps. 147:11). He desires the direct human relationship, not the enthusiasm fired up by letters and words.

God created everything – "He fashions light and creates darkness, makes peace and creates harm" (Isa. 45:7). There is no other source of life from which the forces of impurity receive their existence and vitality. Everything receives its life force from one and the same source, but creation is inextricably intertwined with constriction. Since there is constriction and concealment of the Divine, it is possible for beings to exist in a reality where the Divine is hidden. These beings see divine speech as, at most, a first cause of their existence but do not comprehend how God is literally giving life to the universe, how His speech directly creates every being without an intermediary at every moment, literally from nothingness. Because the constriction of the divine illumination is so great, it is possible for *kelippa* and the *sitra aḥara* to be created, entities that wage war against Him and even deny His existence even as they receive all their life force from God and God alone.

This concealment is not an end in itself but part of the process of revelation. The purpose of concealment is to reveal that which transcends constriction, a force that will be shattered at some time in the future. In the meantime, constriction and concealment are our reality, to such a degree that we cannot see the vivifying light, and impure entities, *kelippa*, and *sitra aḥara* have come into being. ☞

THE WONDER OF CONCEALMENT

☞ An apparent paradox has come into being. The wonder of the Creation, the strongest proof of the Creator's greatness, lies not in the magnitude and multiplicity of the worlds that He created but in the reality that contains a creature so small and low that it can deny God's existence.

Elsewhere, the author of the *Tanya* discusses the difference between a divine act of creation and that of man (*Sha'ar HaYiḥud VeHa'emuna*, chap. 2). From the moment a craftsman puts the finishing touch to a utensil he has made, it goes on to exist independent of him. But divine creation is continuous and uninterrupted. God's hands are not, as it were, withdrawn from the act of creation, but maintain it and sustain it ceaselessly. He perpetually gives life to the entire universe, and this includes evil and any rebellion this might generate. Even if a person does not desire God, even if he denies Him, God continues to give him life at every moment.

Just as the Creator is omnipotent, so does the power of creation have an omnipotent ability to create infinite worlds, and so does the power of concealment have an omnipotent ability to conceal the power of creation to an infinite degree. Of the two, the power of concealment is the more

וְלָכֵן נִקְרָאִים 'אֱלֹהִים אֲחֵרִים' מִפְּנֵי שֶׁיְּנִיקָתָם וְחַיּוּתָם אֵינָהּ מִבְּחִינַת פָּנִים אֶלָּא מִבְּחִינַת אֲחוֹרַיִים דִּקְדוּשָּׁה.

They are therefore called "other gods" [*elohim aĥerim*], because their nourishment and life force do not derive from the countenance of the Divine **but rather from the back side [*aĥorayim*] of holiness.**

The forces of impurity, the *kelippot* and the *sitra aḥara,* are the root and essence of idolatry and are called "other gods." They are "other" because they do not receive their life force from the inner aspect of the divine sustenance but from the hind part, from the ancillary, from the nonessential, from that which is not God's primary purpose.

וּפֵירוּשׁ אֲחוֹרַיִים, כְּאָדָם הַנּוֹתֵן דָּבָר לְשׂוֹנְאוֹ שֶׁלֹּא בִּרְצוֹנוֹ שֶׁמַּשְׁלִיכוֹ לוֹ כִּלְאַחַר כְּתֵפוֹ, כִּי מַחֲזִיר פָּנָיו מִמֶּנּוּ מִשִּׂנְאָתוֹ אוֹתוֹ.

The meaning of the term ***aĥorayim,*** back side, **can be** illustrated by **a person who begrudgingly gives something to his enemy, tossing it to him over his shoulder while turning away his face from him in his hatred of him.**

wondrous. When we experience a revelation, when we perceive the power of creation, we see creation, not God. Even a great creation reveals only the power of creativity within it. No matter how vast it may be, it is certainly not the Divine. On the other hand, concealment of the Divine, when we do not perceive God, when we do not experience the sense that there is none other than Him, that is the revelation of God Himself.

How can that be? There is a Chabad tune sung to the words "Indeed, You are God who conceals Himself" (Isa. 45:15). Surprisingly, this is a happy, even joyful tune. The Ba'al Shem Tov used to say that any concealment of God's countenance that we recognize as such is no longer a concealment (*Keter Shem Tov* 85). Concealment of God's countenance ceases to be meaningful the moment we know that God is hiding from us and has not gone. As long as a person thinks that God does not exist, he remains in darkness, but when he realizes that God is merely hiding, there is no longer darkness but light. Moreover, in concealment there is a revelation of God's being that is higher than the revelation of God in the worlds.

There is a famous story about the grandson of Rabbi Barukh of Medzibozh who was playing hide-and-seek. When it was the boy's turn to hide, his friends could not find him, so they left. Realizing that no one was looking for him, the child ran to his grandfather and burst into tears. "Grandfather! I hid, but no one is looking for me!" When his grandfather heard this, he was very moved. He said, "This is exactly what God is saying: I hid, but no one is looking for Me."

This is the wonder within the concealment of God: It is a concealment so dense that we forget that Someone is hiding there.

Because the person hates the enemy, he does not want to give him anything. He hates the enemy so much that he does not even want to look at him, so he turns his face away. But he is nevertheless obligated to give, so he throws the object over his shoulder. This illustrates the two types of relationship that could exist between God and His creations: a deep, inner relationship or a relationship of the back side. God desires a deep relationship from the outset, while the back side includes those things that are not desirable from the outset but are necessary to attain God's purpose. They serve as a framework, a vessel that conveys the essence of God's inner intentions.

That the back side exists is not in opposition to God's will. It is a part of the world, even though God does not want it for its own sake. By analogy, hurdles on a racetrack are not an end in themselves, and they seem to interfere with the attainment of the goal. But they are necessary, because the inner intent is that the runner will leap over them in order to advance. In the same way, God sustains the *kelippa*, even though He is not intrinsically interested in its existence. It is a part of the framework of reality, necessary to the world's development until the divine will is fully attained.

כָּךְ לְמַעְלָה בְּחִינַת פָּנִים הוּא פְּנִימִית הָרָצוֹן הָעֶלְיוֹן וְחֶפְצוֹ הָאֲמִיתִּי, אֲשֶׁר חָפֵץ ה׳ לְהַשְׁפִּיעַ חַיּוּת לְכָל הַקָּרוֹב אֵלָיו, מִסִּטְרָא דִקְדוּשָּׁה.

So it is on high with regard to the Divine: **The countenance [*panim*] represents the inner [*penimi*] aspect of the supernal will,** which is **His true desire, God's desire to bestow** His **life force on all those who are close to Him,** all that is **from the side of holiness.**

God's will has an inner and an outer aspect. His inner will, what the author of the Tanya refers to as "God's desire,"[4] is His true, primary, direct will, which is to give of Himself to those who wish to draw close to Him.

אֲבָל הַסִּטְרָא אָחֳרָא וְהַטּוּמְאָה הִיא תּוֹעֲבַת ה׳ אֲשֶׁר שָׂנֵא,

But the *sitra aḥara* and the forces of impurity are abominations to God

4. See also *Torah Or* 59c.

וְאֵינוֹ מַשְׁפִּיעַ לָהּ חַיּוּת מִפְּנִימִית הָרָצוֹן וְחֶפְצוֹ הָאֲמִיתִּי אֲשֶׁר חָפֵץ בָּהּ חַס וְשָׁלוֹם,

that He hates, and He therefore **does not bestow them** with the **life force of His inner will and true desire in which He delights, God forbid,**

When God gives vitality to the powers of evil and the *sitra aḥara,* He does not do so because He desires this or gets pleasure from it. He does not desire their existence as an end in itself. They are vital for God's true desire, His true intent, and that is the sole reason He sustains them. But He sustains them begrudgingly, so to speak, and not out of His true, deepest desire. If the other side were to receive more than the absolute minimum it requires for its existence, were it to benefit from God's inner will, it would break loose of its constraints and morph into "other gods" and idolatry itself.

כִּי אִם כְּמַאן דְּשָׁדֵי בָּתַר כַּתְפוֹי לְשׂוֹנְאוֹ שֶׁלֹּא בִּרְצוֹנוֹ,

but rather as one who begrudgingly tosses an object **over his shoulder to his enemy.**

When a person wants to realize an inner desire, he has to do many things he does not want to do. For example, when someone wants an item, he goes to the store and buys it. He does not pay for it out of an inner desire to give away his money. On the contrary, he hates parting with it. He pays because that is the external means of attaining that which he desires.

רַק כְּדֵי לְהַעֲנִישׁ אֶת הָרְשָׁעִים וְלִיתֵּן שָׂכָר טוֹב לַצַּדִּיקִים דְּאַכְפְּיָין לְסִטְרָא אָחֳרָא. וְזֶה נִקְרָא בְּחִינַת אֲחוֹרַיִים דִּרְצוֹן הָעֶלְיוֹן בָּרוּךְ הוּא.

The function of the *sitra aḥara* and the forces of impurity is **only in order to punish the wicked and grant a good reward to the righteous, who subdue the** *sitra aḥara*. **This is referred to as the back side of God's supernal will.**

The author of the *Tanya* now goes into greater detail concerning the purpose of the *sitra aḥara* and the forces of impurity. The *sitra aḥara* is the "other" aspect of all reality, which includes man himself. The existence of this other side in us makes possible the existence of tzaddikim and *resha'im,* free will, and reward and punishment.

Evil punishes the wicked. As the verse states, "Evil causes the death of the wicked" (Ps. 34:22), indicating that the evil that a wicked person does eventually kills him. At the same time, it elevates the righteous, "who subdue the *sitra aḥara*," raising them even higher than they were originally. Evil is a strainer that clarifies whether a person will be righteous or wicked, whether he will rise to the heights or descend to the depths. ☞

10 Shevat וְהִנֵּה רָצוֹן הָעֶלְיוֹן בִּבְחִינַת פָּנִים הוּא מְקוֹר הַחַיִּים הַמְחַיֶּה אֶת כָּל הָעוֹלָמוֹת.

The supernal will, in its aspect as the divine **countenance, is the source of life that sustains all the worlds.**

God's inner will, which the author of the *Tanya* refers to as the countenance of the supernal will, the deep, inner content of all external, trivial wills, is the true source of life. It is the root of all types and levels of life by which the worlds are sustained. This inner will is manifest only in the realm of holiness, since the side of holiness is precisely that which clothes and expresses God's inner will. ☞

וּלְפִי שֶׁאֵינוֹ שׁוֹרֶה כְּלָל עַל הַסִּטְרָא אָחֳרָא, וְגַם בְּחִינַת אֲחוֹרַיִים שֶׁל רָצוֹן הָעֶלְיוֹן אֵינוֹ מְלוּבָּשׁ בְּתוֹכָהּ מַמָּשׁ

Yet since it is not bequeathed upon the *sitra aḥara* **whatsoever, and even the back side of the supernal will is not actually clothed within** the *sitra aḥara*

THE EXISTENCE OF EVIL

☞ The existence of evil in this world is one of the greatest enigmas, evoking unanswerable questions: How is it possible? Why? What is the purpose? The discussion revolving around this topic presented here is a mere tip of the iceberg since it is not the purpose of this book. Yet this topic must be broached because it is an essential element for a proper understanding of God's oneness, which is the focus of these chapters.

This subject is not simply an intellectual exercise. It is intended to help one contemplate and internalize God's unity, applying it in a practical manner to his everyday life. Living in our physical world, we are also witness to its less beautiful and not-so-holy aspects. Although they may not offer a complete resolution to all the above questions, the explanations presented here allow us to integrate the concept of God's unity into our tangible world. These explanations help equip us with the ability to take the broad picture of this world, including what we perceive as bad, and surrender it to God's absolute oneness.

Even the "back side" of the supernal will, described above as being tossed begrudgingly over the shoulder, is not actually enclothed within the reality of the *sitra aḥara*. Were that the case, the inner will would also become intermingled within it, implying its tacit consent, so to speak, to the forces of evil.

אֶלָּא מַקִּיף עָלֶיהָ מִלְמַעְלָה, לְכָךְ הִיא מְקוֹם הַמִּיתָה וְהַטּוּמְאָה, ה' יִשְׁמְרֵנוּ. כִּי מְעַט מִזְּעֵר אוֹר וְחַיּוּת שֶׁיּוֹנֶקֶת וּמְקַבֶּלֶת לְתוֹכָהּ מִבְּחִינַת אֲחוֹרַיִים דִּקְדוּשָּׁה שֶׁלְּמַעְלָה,

but rather encompasses it from above, it is therefore the abode of death and impurity, may God protect us. The minuscule amount of light and life force that it derives and absorbs within itself from the back side of the holiness on high

The realm of the *sitra aḥara* is the abode of death and impurity because the divine light, the divine life force, is not manifest there. Death is the total lack of life, and impurity is the spiritual corollary of death and emptiness, of nonexistence in all its aspects. God does not desire the existence of the *sitra aḥara*. Therefore, His divine will does not instill life within it but only surrounds it from without, so that it receives its life force in an almost automatic fashion. In this sense, the powers of evil lack inner life. They are silent powers, corpses, beings of terror and impurity that inhabit existence.

Two types of life force exist on the side of holiness, corresponding to the divine will that surrounds all worlds and the divine speech that permeates all worlds. Corresponding to these two forces on the side of holiness, the divine will and the divine speech, there are two types of life forces that exist on the side of impurity. We have already seen the first, the back side of the divine will, which surrounds it from above. The second is "the minuscule amount of light and life force" that

LIFE AND THE SOURCE OF LIFE

☞ As Rabbi Shmuel Gronem Esterman explains in his commentary on the *Tanya*, God's word, which permeates all worlds, is referred to as "life" because it is this that is enclothed within each created being, sustaining and vivifying it. But the power to bestow life and sustain it is powered by the aspect of God's "encompassing all worlds," which is called the source of life. That is what the author of the *Tanya* refers to as God's "supernal will, [which is] His true desire."

nourishes the realm of impurity. This life force, which vivifies the side of impurity from within itself, is a spark of the lowest level of holiness that has been absorbed into the side of impurity.[5]

הוּא בִּבְחִינַת גָּלוּת מַמָּשׁ בְּתוֹכָהּ בְּסוֹד גָּלוּת הַשְּׁכִינָה הַנִּזְכָּר לְעֵיל.

is literally in a state of exile within it, this **being the mystic exile of the Divine Presence discussed above** (chaps. 6, 17, 19).

God gives life to the lower worlds, including the *sitra aḥara* and the forces of impurity, even though they do not recognize this, do not nullify themselves before Him, and even deny the very essence of His existence and rebel against Him. This constitutes the exile of the Divine Presence. Although the Divine Presence is captive within these evil realms and gives them life, it is not manifest within them. It exists there in exile and estrangement, enabling them to attack it even as they use the very life force that continuously nourishes them.

וְלָכֵן נִקְרָא בְּשֵׁם 'אֱלֹהִים אֲחֵרִים', שֶׁהִיא עֲבוֹדָה זָרָה מַמָּשׁ וּכְפִירָה בְּאַחְדוּתוֹ שֶׁל מֶלֶךְ מַלְכֵי הַמְּלָכִים הַקָּדוֹשׁ בָּרוּךְ הוּא.

The *kelippa* **is therefore referred to as "other gods," for it constitutes actual idolatry and the denial of the oneness of the King of kings, the Holy One, blessed be He.**

We already know that the realm of *kelippa* is a world of darkness, far from the source of life, a world of shadows in which signs of life may be detected only with difficulty. Now we learn something new: Hidden within the world of *kelippa* lies the first seed of idolatry.

There in the *sitra aḥara,* holiness lies in exile, captured by forces that no longer recognize the source of their sustenance but see themselves as independent beings with access to a source of life that is not connected with holiness. Here is where, whether consciously or not, the denial of God's unity begins. The doorway to idolatry has been opened. The existence of the *sitra aḥara* as a force, as a state of being,

5. This low-level spark is from *Malkhut* of *Malkhut* of the world of *Asiya,* which is enclothed within the *kelippot* and animates them (based on Rabbi Shmuel Gronem Esterman's commentary on the *Tanya*).

or as people who see themselves as detached, in whatever way, from the realm of holiness postulates that a source of life exists that is not drawn from holiness. The acts that come from this assumption, whether they have led to idolatrous faith or whether, more subtly, they have led to the belief in any kind of independent, core existence, are at any rate based in the belief in the existence of other gods and the denial of God's all-encompassing unity.

כִּי מֵאַחַר שֶׁאוֹר וְחַיּוּת דִּקְדוּשָּׁה הוּא בִּבְחִינַת גָּלוּת בְּתוֹכָהּ,

Since the light and life force of holiness are in a state of exile within the *kelippa,*

The divine life force exists in *kelippa* in a state of exile. There, where the essence and will of the divine life force are not manifest but hidden and subjugated, the *kelippa* sees itself as an entity independent of holiness.

אֵינָהּ בְּטֵילָה כְּלָל לְגַבֵּי קְדוּשַּׁת הַקָּדוֹשׁ בָּרוּךְ הוּא, וְאַדְּרַבָּה מַגְבִּיהַּ עַצְמָהּ כַּנֶּשֶׁר לוֹמַר: "אֲנִי וְאַפְסִי עוֹד" (ישעיה מז, ח), וּכְמַאֲמַר: "יְאוֹר לִי וַאֲנִי עֲשִׂיתִנִי".

it is not nullified whatsoever in relation to the holiness of the Holy One, blessed be He. On the contrary, the *kelippa* **raises itself** like a soaring **eagle, saying, "It is I, and there is none like me"** (Isa. 47:8), **and as in the statement "The river is mine, and I made myself."**

Pharaoh, the epitome of haughtiness, symbolizes the *kelippa.* First, he feels a sense of ownership: "The river is mine." Next, he claims to have made the Nile and all of existence. Finally, he claims, "I made myself!"[6]

---

6. The expression that the author of the *Tanya* quotes, "The river is mine, and I made myself," is actually a composite of two verses: "The Nile is mine and I made [it]" (Ezek. 29:9) and "My river is mine, and I made myself" (Ezek. 29:3). This begs the obvious question: Why the composite form? The Lubavitcher Rebbe, Rabbi Menaḥem Mendel Schneerson, explains that the two verses express two distinct points. The first verse describes Pharaoh's act of hubris when he exclaimed that he made the Nile. Even this act, essentially a denial of God's involvement in the world, is sufficient to deserve harsh divine punishment. The second verse

This is the ultimate *kelippa,* the ultimate arrogance. He has become an entity that denies all connection to the Divine.

וְלָכֵן אָמְרוּ רַבּוֹתֵינוּ ז״ל (סוטה ד, ב), שֶׁגַּסּוּת הָרוּחַ שְׁקוּלָה כַּעֲבוֹדָה זָרָה מַמָּשׁ.

Therefore, our Rabbis stated that arrogance is equivalent to actual idolatry (*Sota* 4b),

It may seem surprising that a sin as grave as idolatry should be equated with arrogance, which is at most a character failing or a moral flaw. But idolatry and haughtiness essentially share the same root. Haughtiness and egotism are the opposite of self-nullification. Their root is not the denial of God but the viewpoint that the "I," the self, is also an independent being.

כִּי עִיקַּר וְשֹׁרֶשׁ עֲבוֹדָה זָרָה הוּא מַה שֶּׁנֶּחְשָׁב לְדָבָר בִּפְנֵי עַצְמוֹ, נִפְרָד מִקְּדוּשָּׁתוֹ שֶׁל מָקוֹם, וְלֹא כְּפִירָה בַּה׳ לְגַמְרֵי,

because the core and root of idolatry is that it is regarded as an independent entity, distinct from the holiness of God but not necessarily **a total denial of God,**

The essence and starting point of idolatry is not necessarily the denial of God but the assumption of an independent status separate from His holiness. Of course, denial of God is also idolatry, but it is an outcome of the original premise.

כִּדְאִיתָא בַּגְּמָרָא: ״דְּקָרוּ לֵיהּ אֱלָהָא דֶּאֱלָהַיָּא״ (מנחות קי, א), אֶלָּא שֶׁגַּם הֵם מַחֲשִׁיבִים עַצְמָם לְיֵשׁ וְדָבָר בִּפְנֵי עַצְמוֹ.

as the Talmud states, "They call Him the God of gods" (*Menaĥot* 110a), **yet,** at the same time, **they also regard themselves as independent beings and entities.**

Even idolaters call God the "God of gods." In other words, even the *kelippot,* the forces of impurity, and the *sitra aḥara* admit that God is

---

describes the extent of Pharaoh's hubris: He denied the existence of God altogether, as he claimed, "I made myself." However, in other sources, the author of the *Tanya* does cite the original form of the verse: "My river is mine, and I made myself" (see note to *Tikkun Ḥatzot* in the author of the *Tanya*'s prayer book; *Likkutei Torah,* s.v. "*zot ḥukat*"; *Likkutei Torah, Song, s.v.* "*yonati*").

superior to all. Yet in opposition to the awareness of the side of holiness that "the Lord is the God" and there is no other, the understanding of the *kelippa* consciousness is that there is another. That is to say, they consider themselves to be self-sufficient, not originating from God nor dependent on Him. If they want, they will accept God's sovereignty to a greater or lesser extent, but they may choose not to do so, because they do not see themselves as an inseparable part of the Divine.

וּבָזֶה מַפְרִידִים אֶת עַצְמָם מִקְּדוּשָּׁתוֹ שֶׁל מָקוֹם בָּרוּךְ הוּא, מֵאַחַר שֶׁאֵין בְּטֵלִים לוֹ יִתְבָּרֵךְ, כִּי אֵין קְדוּשָּׁה עֶלְיוֹנָה שׁוֹרָה אֶלָּא עַל מַה שֶּׁבָּטֵל לוֹ יִתְבָּרֵךְ, כַּנִּזְכָּר לְעֵיל.

It is with this sense of independence **that they separate themselves from the holiness of God, blessed be He, since they are not nullified to Him, for the supernal holiness rests only upon that which is nullified to God, as stated above.**

As the author of the *Tanya* said earlier, holiness cannot enter into partnership with anything else. Whatever is connected to holiness cannot retain an independent, separate being. Rather, the only state of holiness is self-nullification before the divine being, and so holiness cannot reside wherever there is even a trace of autonomy. The opposite is true as well: The more complete one's nullification to the Divine, the more profound the presence of that which is holy.

וְלָכֵן נִקְרָאִים "טוּרֵי דִפְרוּדָא" בַּזֹּהַר הַקָּדוֹשׁ (חלק א קנח, א).

They are therefore referred to in the holy *Zohar* (1:158a) **as "mountains of separation."**

The lower worlds, which sustain the existence of evil and impurity, are called "mountains of separation."[7] This refers to the "mountains" that elevate themselves and view themselves as separate from the Divine. They experience themselves as autonomous units and inflate themselves with the boast "I will rule!" They separate themselves from the divine light and conceal themselves from it, as it were. Therefore,

7. See *Torah Or* 116b, which describes these "mountains of separation" as being the angelic forces that oversee idolaters.

beyond them and receiving energy from them are the "mountains of darkness," entities that exist in a pitch-black environment where there is no revelation of the divine light.

וַהֲרֵי זוֹ כְּפִירָה בְּאַחְדוּתוֹ הָאֲמִיתִּית, דְּכוּלָּא קַמֵּיהּ כְּלָא חָשִׁיב וּבָטֵל בֶּאֱמֶת לוֹ יִתְבָּרֵךְ וְלִרְצוֹנוֹ הַמְחַיֶּה אֶת כּוּלָּם וּמְהַוֶּה אוֹתָם מֵאַיִן לְיֵשׁ תָּמִיד.

This, then, constitutes the denial of His true oneness, because everything before Him is considered as nothingness and is truly nullified to God and His will, which sustains them all and constantly brings them forth from nothingness to existence.

The mountains of separation cast a shadow over everything that is nourished from them. They create the image of an illusory world, a world that appears to be independent, a world that sees itself as separate and autonomous, even as it draws its energy and gains its existence only from holiness. This is a world that does not know that holiness is the sole source of life, because in this world the divine life force is in exile, as it were, not ruling but ruled.

Continuing the theme of the previous chapter, this chapter addressed the concept of divine speech. After delineating the qualitative difference between human and divine speech, it went on to discuss their similarities and explained divine speech in terms of our understanding of human speech. Just as human speech is a means of transferring content from the concealed to the revealed, from within outward, divine speech is a means of drawing the divine life force to the lower worlds after a great many powerful constrictions, until it arrives at worlds that are, in a sense, alien to it and estranged from it.

However, as the author of the *Tanya* repeatedly emphasizes, divine speech is not really like ours, and from His perspective there is not, nor can there ever be, anything outside Him. It only appears to created beings, which receive their life force from the divine speech through many constrictions and concealments, that divine speech is separate from the Divine.

This concept, of existence outside the Divine, that even a scintilla of anything exists that is not nullified before the Divine, is the root of all idolatry, because the essence of holiness on every level is the nullification of that level within the supernal holiness. Since everything that is holy is defined by being connected to the Divine, holiness cannot claim any intrinsic value without the Divine.

Another, somewhat tangential theme discussed in this chapter is the divine concealment in the creation and the resultant spawning of the realms of *kelippa* and *sitra aĥara*. This thematic divergence from the topic of God's unity is actually another way of understanding that oneness. The intent of the author of the *Tanya* is to explain that these elements of evil are actually only a mirage stemming from our finite perception. In truth, the oneness of God is absolute. This chapter thus helps us understand that even though we may experience hardships at times, we are still able to perceive, at the very least, a glimpse of God's profound oneness.

Chapter 23

THE PREVIOUS CHAPTER DISCUSSED THE CONSTRICTIONS and layers of concealment represented by divine speech, a process taken so far that the *kelippot* and the *sitra aḥara*, which receive their life force from the "back side" of holiness, not from its inner aspect, can come into being. This chapter will discuss how the inner core of holiness finds expression in Torah study and in the performance of the mitzvot.

וְעִם כָּל הַנִּזְכָּר לְעֵיל, יוּבַן וִיבוֹאַר הֵיטֵב בְּתוֹסֶפֶת בֵּיאוּר מַה שֶּׁאָמְרוּ בַּזֹּהַר: דְּאוֹרַיְיתָא וְקֻדְשָׁא בְּרִיךְ הוּא כּוּלָּא חַד. וּבַתִּיקּוּנִים (תיקוני זהר עד, א) פֵּירְשׁוּ דְּרמ"ח פִּיקּוּדִין אִינּוּן רמ"ח אֵבָרִין דְּמַלְכָּא. לְפִי שֶׁהַמִּצְוֹת הֵן פְּנִימִיּוּת רָצוֹן הָעֶלְיוֹן וְחֶפְצוֹ הָאֲמִיתִּי,

11 Shevat

18 Shevat (leap year)

Based on all that has been said above, we can thoroughly understand and further elucidate the *Zohar*'s **statement** that **the Torah and the Holy One, blessed be He, are entirely one. The *Tikkunei*** *Zohar* (74a) **explains that the 248** positive **commandments comprise the 248 limbs of the King,** that is, God, **because the commandments constitute the inner** aspect of God's **supernal will and His true desire,**

Everything that was discussed in the previous chapter, that God's word and all of creation are in reality subsumed in their divine source and only appear to possess an independent identity, can be elucidated by the concept that God and His Torah are one.[1]

1. See *Zohar* 1:24a; see also chap. 4, where this statement is also cited; *Likkutei Torah*, Deut. 46a.

Whatever exists in the world does so only because God wills it, and the commandments in the Torah are the expression of that supreme will and desire. The reality of the universe encompasses multitudes of entities of an infinite variety. All of them express the will of God. If God did not will them into being, they would not exist. Yet only a select few express the inner essence of His will, His true desire. The majority of creation lacks any inner intrinsic purpose and is simply part of the sum total of existence, there only to keep the universe in operation. Only a few components of reality express God's true will, not the will that maintains the framework of existence but the ultimate and inner purpose of reality, and these components are the commandments. They are the expression of God's utmost will and true desire.

which is clothed in all the higher and lower worlds, giving them life,

הַמְלוּבָּשׁ בְּכָל הָעוֹלָמוֹת הָעֶלְיוֹנִים וְתַחְתּוֹנִים לְהַחֲיוֹתָם.

The commandments in the Torah are God's will, that which He truly desires from all the worlds on the most profound level. They are the inner force that brings all the worlds into being and vitalizes them. To illustrate, if one decides to build a house, what he really wants is the house itself. Even so, there are so many steps the builder must take, steps that he does not want to do just for their own sake, but they are necessary for the construction. He must demolish the old house, gather building materials, pour cement, set up scaffolding, and all the rest. Those actions accord with his desire, but they are not the intent and goal itself, and they are no more than the means to reach that goal. It is for the primary desire that he takes these steps, that he demolishes the old edifice, that he pours cement, that he acquires building materials, and it is that inner desire that vivifies and maintains them.

God too wishes to build a structure in this world that will express His inner desire. To do so, He requires an entire universe to help realize His will in the most perfect fashion. This inner essence of His will is the commandments. Everything else in all the worlds, from the very highest to the very lowest, are no more than tools to help make that inner intent a reality.

כִּי כָּל חַיּוּתָם וְשִׁפְעָם תָּלוּי בְּמַעֲשֵׂה הַמִּצְוֹת שֶׁל הַתַּחְתּוֹנִים כַּנּוֹדָע.

for all the life force and life-giving **sustenance** of the higher and lower worlds **is contingent on the performance of the mitzvot by the creations in the lower worlds, as is known.**

A mitzva that is performed in this world justifies the continued existence of our world, as well as the higher worlds. No mitzvot exist in those supernal realms. The higher worlds are only supporting structures that operate mechanically, as it were. They are no more than tools that make possible the existence of this, our lower world. Only here does the performance of a mitzva possess any meaning, for only here does the possibility of mitzva and sin exist.

וְנִמְצָא שֶׁמַּעֲשֵׂה הַמִּצְוֹת וְקִיּוּמָן הוּא לְבוּשׁ הַפְּנִימִי לִפְנִימִית רָצוֹן הָעֶלְיוֹן,

It follows that the performance and fulfillment of mitzvot constitutes the inner garment for the inner aspect of God's **supernal will,**

All the worlds are instruments, or garments, that express the divine will that is found within them all. But a mitzva act is the inner garment and instrument in which the divine intent itself is crystallized. Indeed, it is the expression of the inner core of the supernal will.

שֶׁמִּמַּעֲשֶׂה זֶה נִמְשָׁךְ אוֹר וְחַיּוּת רָצוֹן הָעֶלְיוֹן לְהִתְלַבֵּשׁ בָּעוֹלָמוֹת.

because as a result of this act, the light and life force of the supernal will are drawn down and clothed within the worlds.

When a person performs a mitzva in this world, he clothes the inner core of the highest will in the worlds. He is giving the supernal will a form in which it may manifest in this world. At that moment, the divine will expresses itself within the person performing the mitzva and is drawn into the world in which the mitzva is being performed.

וְלָכֵן נִקְרָאִים "אֵבָרֵי דְמַלְכָּא", דֶּרֶךְ מָשָׁל, כְּמוֹ שֶׁאֵבְרֵי גוּף

Therefore, the mitzvot **are referred to** 19 Shevat (leap year)
as the "limbs of the King," just as, by way of analogy, the limbs of a person's

הָאָדָם הֵם לְבוּשׁ לְנַפְשׁוֹ וּבְטֵלִים לְגַמְרֵי אֵלֶיהָ מִכֹּל וָכֹל.

body serve as garments for his soul and are completely and totally subservient to it.

In a sense, a person's body is his soul's garment. Every physical limb is a tool that serves a function of the soul: The eye clothes the power of sight, the ear clothes the faculty of hearing, the foot, the soul's ability to walk. A tool lacks its own will and serves only as an instrument of the person wielding it. Similarly, the limbs of the body are not independent beings. Their entire existence is dedicated to serving the soul so that it may function through them.

כִּי מִיָּד שֶׁעוֹלֶה בִּרְצוֹנוֹ שֶׁל אָדָם לִפְשׁוֹט יָדוֹ אוֹ רַגְלוֹ, הֵן נִשְׁמָעוֹת לִרְצוֹנוֹ תֵּכֶף וּמִיָּד בְּלִי שׁוּם צִוּוּי וַאֲמִירָה לָהֶן וּבְלִי שׁוּם שְׁהִיָּה כְּלָל, אֶלָּא כְּרֶגַע מַמָּשׁ כְּשֶׁעָלָה בִּרְצוֹנוֹ.

We know this to be true, **for the moment a person wishes to extend his arm or foot, they immediately and instantaneously obey his will without** requiring **any command or directive and without the slightest delay whatsoever, but rather the exact instant it arose in his will** to do so.

Commands and persuasions are employed when another is involved, someone with his own mind and will. Such a process, which bridges one will to another, one personality to another, involves a moment, or more, of hesitation. But when there is no other being and no other will, when there exists only one will, there is no transition and no time gap. The limb of the body does not have its own will. Its action is dictated and flows directly, totally, from the inner will of the soul.

כָּךְ דֶּרֶךְ מָשָׁל, הַחַיּוּת שֶׁל מַעֲשֵׂה הַמִּצְוֹת וְקִיּוּמָן הוּא בָּטֵל לְגַמְרֵי לְגַבֵּי רָצוֹן הָעֶלְיוֹן הַמְּלוּבָּשׁ בּוֹ וְנַעֲשֶׂה לוֹ מַמָּשׁ כְּגוּף לִנְשָׁמָה.

So too this is analogous to the life force of the performance and fulfillment of the mitzvot. It is utterly subservient to God's **supernal will, which is clothed within it, and** that life force **literally becomes like the body** in relation **to the soul.**

A mitzva is the divine, inner, and primal will of all of existence. When this will is expressed in the performance of a mitzva in this world, it traverses all of existence and connects the act to the supernal will itself. Other objects and actions in the world are merely external garments, garments needed for the reality to exist. But the mitzvot are the specific instruments, the particular means that the divine self, as it were, uses to express itself in the world. The mitzva act is not an independent entity. It is entirely nullified in relation to the highest will clothed within it, just as the limbs of the body are nullified in relation to the soul clothed within them.

וְכֵן הַלְּבוּשׁ הַחִיצוֹן שֶׁל נֶפֶשׁ הָאֱלֹהִית שֶׁבָּאָדָם, הַמְקַיֵּים וְעוֹשֶׂה הַמִּצְוָה, שֶׁהוּא כֹּחַ וּבְחִינַת הַמַּעֲשֶׂה שֶׁלָּהּ,

Likewise, the same applies to **the outer garment of the divine soul within the person fulfilling and performing the mitzva, which is its faculty of action.**

20 Shevat (leap year)

Not only is the mitzva act nullified to God's supernal will, but also the person performing the mitzva is completely subservient to His will. In its broader sense, the term "person" in this context refers to his soul, its garments, and his physical body, all of which function to manifest the person and his actions in this world.

As the author of the *Tanya* mentioned above,[2] the divine soul expresses itself and acts in the world through its garments: the thoughts, speech, and deeds of the Torah's 613 commandments. Thought is the innermost garment, speech the middle one, and deed the outer garment.

הוּא מִתְלַבֵּשׁ בַּחַיּוּת שֶׁל מַעֲשֵׂה הַמִּצְוָה, וְנַעֲשֶׂה גַּם כֵּן כְּגוּף לִנְשָׁמָה לָרָצוֹן הָעֶלְיוֹן וּבָטֵל אֵלָיו לִגְמְרֵי.

It is clothed in the life force of the performance of the mitzva and also becomes like the body in relation **to the soul, completely subservient to the divine will.**

Just as the limbs of the physical body express the soul's will in the physical world, not as external tools, recipients of commands, but as part of the soul's inner being, so does a person performing a mitzva express the inner essence of the divine will in this physical world. When a person fulfills a commandment, he is transformed at that moment

2. Chap. 4.

into a part of the commandment, totally nullified in relation to the divine will that is acting through him.

וְעַל כֵּן גַּם אֶבְרֵי גוּף הָאָדָם הַמְקַיְּימִים הַמִּצְוָה, שֶׁכֹּחַ וּבְחִינַת הַמַּעֲשֶׂה שֶׁל נֶפֶשׁ הָאֱלֹהִית מְלוּבָּשׁ בָּהֶם בִּשְׁעַת מַעֲשֵׂה וְקִיּוּם הַמִּצְוָה, הֵם נַעֲשׂוּ מֶרְכָּבָה מַמָּשׁ לָרְצוֹן הָעֶלְיוֹן.

Therefore, the person's limbs that fulfill the mitzva, in which the divine soul's faculty of action is clothed during the performance and fulfillment of the mitzva, also become an actual chariot for the divine will,

When a person performs a mitzva, it is not only the soul's faculty of action that is nullified in relation to the divine will, but also the limbs of his body become a tool that enables the supreme will to express itself within existence. In becoming a vessel for the revelation of the divine will, the part of the body that becomes a tool for the will is called, in hasidic and kabbalistic literature, a chariot. The imagery of a chariot is based on the account of the divine chariot recorded in the book of Ezekiel, and it implies, in the simplest sense, a tool that serves the rider's will and brings him to his destination. Since a mitzva is what we might call a "limb of the King," a tool that expresses the divine will within the reality of this world, our physical limbs become the chariot through which the heavenly will is actualized when we perform a mitzva.

כְּגוֹן: הַיָּד הַמְחַלֶּקֶת צְדָקָה לַעֲנִיִּים אוֹ עוֹשָׂה מִצְוָה אַחֶרֶת, וְרַגְלַיִם הַמְהַלְּכוֹת לִדְבַר מִצְוָה, וְכֵן הַפֶּה וְלָשׁוֹן שֶׁמְּדַבְּרִים דִּבְרֵי תוֹרָה, וְהַמּוֹחַ שֶׁמְּהַרְהֵר בְּדִבְרֵי תוֹרָה וְיִרְאַת שָׁמַיִם וּבִגְדוּלַּת ה׳ בָּרוּךְ הוּא.

such as the hand that distributes charity to the poor or performs another mitzva, or the feet that walk for a matter pertaining to a mitzva, and similarly the mouth and tongue that speak words of Torah, and the brain that meditates on words of Torah, the fear of Heaven, and the greatness of God, blessed be He.

The hand of a person distributing charity becomes a vehicle of the Divine. It becomes, as it were, a particular instrument of the hand of God, a limb of the King, and at that moment, it is nullified in relation to the divine will. At that juncture, it is literally like God's own hand. Likewise, every one of a person's limbs that performs a mitzva becomes a tool for the divine will and is thus directly connected to the Divine.

וְזֶהוּ שֶׁאָמְרוּ רַבּוֹתֵינוּ זַ"ל: הָאָבוֹת הֵן הֵן הַמֶּרְכָּבָה (בראשית רבה פב, ו), שֶׁכָּל אֵבְרֵיהֶם כּוּלָּם הָיוּ קְדוֹשִׁים וּמוּבְדָּלִים מֵעִנְיְינֵי עוֹלָם הַזֶּה, וְלֹא נַעֲשׂוּ מֶרְכָּבָה רַק לָרָצוֹן הָעֶלְיוֹן לְבַדּוֹ כָּל יְמֵיהֶם.

This is the meaning of our Rabbis' statement "The forefathers are the very chariot for the Divine Presence" (*Bereshit Rabba* 82:6): **that all their limbs were sanctified and separated from** mundane **matters of this world so that they became a vehicle only for the supernal will throughout their lives.**

A person can live in this world yet not be subjugated to it. This world comprises only a framework, a field of action, whereas a person's inner intent, his inner will, can ceaselessly be directed elsewhere, connected to the divine will. The forefathers lived and functioned in this world, yet their inner desire and will were constantly nullified in the face of the divine will. For this reason, the Sages say that "the forefathers are the very chariot [for the Divine Presence]." When the forefathers achieved a total nullification in relation to the divine will, there no longer existed any separation between the divine chariot, the throne of glory above, and the forefathers below. True, there exists a hierarchical difference: there is a chariot, above it a throne, above that another throne, extending into the infinite heights. Yet on every plane, there exists a state of being that is nothing less than self-nullification in relation to God and actualization of the divine will. That is the chariot, bearing the revelation of God's will within existence.

12 Shevat

21 Shevat (leap year)

אַךְ הַמַּחֲשָׁבָה וְהַהִרְהוּר בְּדִבְרֵי תוֹרָה שֶׁבַּמּוֹחַ וְכֹחַ הַדִּבּוּר בְּדִבְרֵי תוֹרָה שֶׁבַּפֶּה, שֶׁהֵם לְבוּשִׁים הַפְּנִימִיִּם שֶׁל נֶפֶשׁ הָאֱלֹהִית, וְכָל שֶׁכֵּן נֶפֶשׁ הָאֱלֹהִית עַצְמָהּ הַמְלוּבֶּשֶׁת בָּהֶם, כּוּלָּם מְיוּחָדִים מַמָּשׁ

However, the thought and contemplation of words of Torah within the brain, and the faculty of speech employed in speaking words of Torah, which is in the mouth, which are the inner garments of the divine soul, and certainly the divine soul itself that is clothed within them, are all literally

בְּיִחוּד גָּמוּר בִּרְצוֹן הָעֶלְיוֹן, וְלֹא מֶרְכָּבָה לְבַד.

unified in absolute unity with the supernal will and are not merely a chariot.

Until this point, the author of the *Tanya* has discussed the outermost garment of the divine soul, the garment of action, which becomes a vehicle for the Divine Presence when entirely woven of a mitzva act. When a person performs a mitzva, the limbs of his body become a vehicle for the divine will. When his hand distributes charity, it performs God's will as though it were literally His hand. When a person dons *tefillin,* his hand and head function as the servants of the divine will, which desires that *tefillin* should be worn. But when one thinks and speaks words of Torah, when his soul is connected to the Torah through the soul's inner garments, its speech and thoughts, then his connection to the divine will is even more profound than the rider-chariot connection.

Ultimately, the vehicle is separate from the rider, just as the body is separate from the soul. But the unification of the soul with Torah through study is comparable to the unification of the soul with the mind, where the soul uses the mind to literally contemplate the divine will. The commandments are limbs of the King, but Torah study is more than a limb of the King. Rather, "Torah and the Holy One, blessed be He, are entirely one."

כִּי רְצוֹן הָעֶלְיוֹן הוּא הוּא הַדְּבַר הֲלָכָה עַצְמָהּ שֶׁמְּהַרְהֵר וּמְדַבֵּר בָּהּ. שֶׁכָּל הַהֲלָכוֹת הֵן פְּרָטֵי הַמְשָׁכוֹת פְּנִימִיּוּת רָצוֹן הָעֶלְיוֹן עַצְמוֹ, שֶׁכָּךְ עָלָה בִּרְצוֹנוֹ יִתְבָּרֵךְ, שֶׁדָּבָר זֶה מוּתָּר אוֹ כָּשֵׁר אוֹ פָּטוּר אוֹ זַכַּאי אוֹ לְהֵפֶךְ.

The supernal will is synonymous with the halakhic matter itself that one contemplates and of which one speaks since all the *halakhot* are the specific extensions of the inner aspect of God's **supernal will itself, for God willed it that this item be permitted or rendered fit** or that this person be **exempt or** found **innocent, or vice versa.**

The divine will is itself the *halakha* being studied, the idea of what to do and how to do it. Thinking about a halakhic issue and discussing it is not only the realization of the divine will (as is the observance of the *halakha*), but it comprises the divine will in and of itself. It is an expression and documentation of what God wants, in which way and under what conditions. When a person studies *halakha*, whether or not it has practical ramifications for him, he is living the very idea of the *halakha*. At that moment, even if he performs no action, his mind and soul identify with God's will. He is relating not to a deed brought to completion in actuality but to God's plan, His inner thought.

To give an analogy, when an architect plans a building, he considers all its details, visualizes the plans, and writes instructions. Then workers come, receive those directives, and carry them out. When a person performs a mitzva, he is like a worker constructing a building. But when a person studies Torah, he is involved with the building plans themselves. He is, so to speak, considering the instructions anew together with the Architect Himself. The person performing the commandment is in the action stage, but the person studying Torah is at the planning stage. The connection with the planner at the planning stage is deeper and more intimate than it is at the action stage.

A person who studies and contemplates *halakha*, what is permitted or kosher, is at that moment thinking God's thoughts, so to speak. He is not merely an instrument for the performance of the divine thought but a partner in that thought. That is the meaning of the Sages' statement regarding the verse "They are the potters and the inhabitants of Neta'im and Gedera; they dwelt there in the king's employ" (I Chron. 4:23), that the souls of the righteous were together with God at the time of the creation of the world, not just at the action stage but at the stage when it was orchestrated.[3] In the same vein, the thoughts of those who study *halakha* are with the King in His work.

וְכֵן כָּל צֵרוּפֵי אוֹתִיּוֹת תּוֹרָה נְבִיאִים כְּתוּבִים **Likewise, all the letter combinations of the Torah, Prophets, and Writings**

The language of the *Tanya* is precise. The implication here is that the divine revelation within the Written Torah lies not only in the words and sentences but also in the letters. The Mishna and Talmud are also holy, but the revelation of holiness within them is inherent in the

3. *Bereshit Rabba* 8:6.

concepts, in the words and sentences that express the ideas, not in the letters, which are the mere vehicles for that expression.[4] In the Written Torah, on the other hand, the revelation of holiness lies primarily in the letters, and the meaning of the words that the letters comprise is secondary. In light of this, the Written Torah should be viewed as a collection of letters, six hundred thousand symbols, each of which is an independent code. Although the letters combine into meaningful words and sentences, that is only a second-tier communication. ☞

הֵן הַמְשָׁכַת רְצוֹנוֹ וְחָכְמָתוֹ הַמְיוּחָדוֹת בְּאֵין סוֹף בָּרוּךְ הוּא בְּתַכְלִית הַיִּחוּד, שֶׁהוּא הַיּוֹדֵעַ וְהוּא הַמַּדָּע כו׳. וְזֶהוּ שֶׁאָמְרוּ:

are extensions of God's will and wisdom, which are united with *Ein Sof*, blessed be He, in absolute unity, for He is the knower, He is the known, and He is the knowledge itself. **This**

THE LETTER COMBINATIONS OF THE WRITTEN TORAH

☞ In the introduction to his commentary on the Torah, Ramban states that one's initial approach to the Written Torah must be based on the axiom learned from the earliest sages that the entire Torah consists of the names of God (see *Zohar* 3:35b). These names may be arranged in groups that convey a certain meaning, but those meanings are only the form, not the essence.

To illustrate, when we look at the Hebrew alphabet, we see that it can be divided at various points to make meaningful words. These combinations are certainly not the principal meaning of the order of the alphabet since it is not intended to be a combination of such words. If the letters combine to form some meaning that helps someone remember the alphabet, so much the better. But that is not the letters' essential meaning.

By contrast, the meaning of the terms "permitted," "kosher," "exempt," or "innocent" forms the content of the Oral Torah. Its essence and basis is its comprehensible meaning, concepts that a human being can grasp and understand. But in the Written Torah, which is analogous to the alphabet, the comprehensible meaning is not its essence. A person learning the Written Torah is only, as it were, reviewing a code of holy names, which he is not obligated to, or even able to, truly understand. For instance, the words *bereshit bara*, the opening words of the Written Torah, essentially consist of a row of letters: *bet, resh, alef, shin, yod, tav, bet, resh, alef*. The parsing of these letters into *bereshit bara* is only one of many meaningful possibilities (see *Sukka* 49a).

Some espionage codes are composed in a double or even triple layer of complexity. A seemingly innocent missive may be a code containing an entirely different mes-

4. See *Ba'al Shem Tov al HaTorah, Parashat Noaḥ, Amud HaTefilla* 23.

דְּאוֹרַיְיתָא וְקֻדְשָׁא בְּרִיךְ הוּא כּוּלָּא חַד, וְלֹא אֵבָרִין דְּמַלְכָּא לְחוּד כְּפִיקּוּדִין.

is the meaning of **the statement "The Torah and the Holy One, blessed be He, are entirely one," and not merely the "limbs of the King," as are the mitzvot.**

The 248 positive commandments are the 248 limbs of the King, but the Torah is one with Him. The Torah in its entirety, not just the mandates in it, is the direct expression of God's will. It itself is God's will and wisdom. True, when a person studies Torah, he does not arrive at a complete understanding of God's will at its deepest level. In the language of the philosophers, "If I were to understand Him, I would be Him." If a person were to completely understand God's wisdom, he himself would be God. But still, when a person learns even one detail of the Torah, no matter how incomplete and peripheral, at that moment he is united with the divine will. Every detail of God's will is

sage, which itself may conceal a code concealing yet a third message. The Torah narrative is, as it were, the first code. Perfect in its execution, it is so well built as a narrative, with a surface meaning that can be understood on almost any level, that it does not reveal itself to be a code. But below this stratum, there is always a submerged message, and that is itself a code to an even deeper layer of meaning.

The Torah is said to be an orchard, a *pardes*, the word *pardes* an acronym for *peshat*, *remez*, *derush*, and *sod*: plain meaning, allusion, homiletic exposition, and mystical aspects. The Torah does not have a single meaning but a simultaneous multiplicity of meanings: one tale within another, one signification within another.

In his introduction to *Guide of the Perplexed*, Rambam cites the verse "A well-turned phrase is like golden apples in silver ornaments" (Prov. 25:11). The "golden apples in silver ornaments," he explains, are an ornament in the form of a golden apple placed in a net of silver. At first glance, the ornament appears to be the silver net, but a second observation shows that the silver is merely the setting for the apple. The same is true of "a well-turned phrase": Wisdom must be expressed in such a way that there is wisdom in both the inner meaning and the parable. Even the parable should be something precious. The silver net, the means of expression, is finely crafted. But that is not the ultimate intent; it is not the "golden apples."

The meaning that we extract from the Written Torah's stories, ethical instruction, content, and even the words and sentences is merely the setting, the silver net. The essential meaning lies in the letters themselves, which are the fundamental message of the Written Torah.

a microcosm of the will as a whole, not only an instrument through which the will expresses itself. When a person studies Torah, when he meditates on even the smallest part of the Creator's will and wisdom, he is united not only with the creation, but with the Creator Himself.

22 Shevat (leap year)

וּמֵאַחַר שֶׁרָצוֹן הָעֶלְיוֹן, הַמְיוּחָד בְּאֵין סוֹף בָּרוּךְ הוּא בְּתַכְלִית הַיִּחוּד, הוּא בְּגִילּוּי לְגַמְרֵי וְלֹא בְּהֶסְתֵּר פָּנִים כְּלָל וּכְלָל בַּנֶּפֶשׁ הָאֱלֹהִית וּלְבוּשֶׁיהָ הַפְּנִימִים, שֶׁהֵם מַחֲשַׁבְתָּהּ וְדִבּוּרָהּ, בְּאוֹתָהּ שָׁעָה שֶׁהָאָדָם עוֹסֵק בְּדִבְרֵי תוֹרָה,

Since God's **supernal will, which is united in absolute unity with *Ein Sof*, blessed be He, is in** a state of **complete revelation within the divine soul and its inner garments, namely, thought and speech, while a person studies words of Torah and is not** in a state of **concealed countenance whatsoever,**

Even though a person cannot apprehend the infinite nature of the divine will, one's desires align with the divine will itself and one's mind is in line with the divine intellect when he studies Torah. The part of the divine will that is expressed in that section of the Torah that he is studying is manifest in his soul, in the thoughts and speech that he employs for study.

הֲרֵי גַּם הַנֶּפֶשׁ וּלְבוּשֶׁיהָ אֵלּוּ מְיוּחָדִים מַמָּשׁ בְּאֵין סוֹף בָּרוּךְ הוּא בְּאוֹתָהּ שָׁעָה בְּתַכְלִית הַיִּחוּד, כְּיִחוּד דִּבּוּרוֹ וּמַחֲשַׁבְתּוֹ שֶׁל הַקָּדוֹשׁ בָּרוּךְ הוּא בְּמַהוּתוֹ וְעַצְמוּתוֹ כַּנִּזְכָּר לְעֵיל. כִּי אֵין שׁוּם דָּבָר נִפְרָד כִּי אִם בְּהֶסְתֵּר פָּנִים כַּנִּזְכָּר לְעֵיל.

then, at that time, the soul and these inner **garments** of thought and speech **are also literally united in absolute unity with *Ein Sof*, blessed be He, just like the unity of the speech and thought of the Holy One, blessed be He, with His essence and being, as stated above** (chap. 21), **for in truth there is nothing that** appears **separate** from the Divine **except when in** a state of **concealed countenance, as stated above** (chap. 21).

Nothing is separate from the divine essence. All of existence depends on and flows from the divine will that functions within it. The difference that we perceive between one object and another stems not from the power that gives them life, but from the degree to which the Divine is concealed within them. In our world, the divine will is hidden so that it seems as if the world exists and acts independently. By contrast, the Torah expresses God's will explicitly and openly. We do not entirely and genuinely comprehend all levels of the divine will and wisdom disclosed in the Torah, but at every stage and in every part that we can understand, the Torah expresses this divine inner will, which is totally and completely united with God's essence and being.

Furthermore, just as the Torah is one with the divine will, so is the person who studies it. Since the Torah is God's wisdom, it is an expression of its constant state of unity with the Divine, and one who studies Torah will discover, sooner or later, that through his study he will achieve a state of absolute unity and oneness with God. ☞

UNITING WITH GOD THROUGH TORAH

☞ When a person studies Torah properly, on whatever level, he is in harmony with the entire spectrum of the Torah, not just with that one specific level. It has been said about many of the greatest rabbis that their halakhic decisions were aimed at the truth on both the revealed and esoteric planes, even if they had never studied the mystical aspects of the Torah. Since they studied for the sake of Heaven, the conclusions they reached were true on all the myriad levels of the Torah. If a person operates in line with a certain model, as long as the model is accurate, the conclusions he reaches about the model will also be true for the original that this model represents, as well as for other similar models.

Unlike the world, nothing in the Torah is distorted, and there is no exile of the Divine Presence in relation to it. Although God has constricted the Torah from its original form into various thought forms and letter forms, the Torah itself has not been distorted or changed. In every plane of existence, the Torah is revealed in its purity. A law in our world may concern an ox goring a cow; in other realms, it may speak to other realities. Yet it makes no difference: The law is true on every level of existence. Although the Torah in our physical world is not the entire Torah in all its possible manifestations, it is entirely true.

The Torah we possess is not merely a metaphor for other truths nor only a means of expressing one specific matter. It is a multilayered, multifaceted truth. It is total, unadulterated truth on every level in which it is revealed. In the realm of human reality, the Torah is connected both to our souls and to our deeds. It is a revelation of the divine will on every plane of existence.

Whenever one studies Torah, on whatever level, he becomes one with the divine will. Then, together with God, he contemplates and creates the structure of the world. This partnership can take place at any level, lofty or low. Even a young boy who has just started learning to read "In the beginning" reaches a point where he can identify with the divine will. Merely by pronouncing these first letters of the Torah, as long as he says them properly, he is on the same level as the greatest of Torah scholars. Although he does not understand every layer of meaning, what he does understand is absolutely true.

Knowledge of a simple electric device is not only knowledge on one level. There is a superficial knowledge of how to use the device, and then there are increasingly deeper levels of understanding regarding the device's makeup and the theory of electricity. But every level of knowledge, even the simplest, is equally true. The knowledge of how to use the device is total truth no less than the knowledge of its inner workings. One person may know more about the device than another, but that knowledge is not any more true.

Similarly, when a person studies *halakha* in even the most elementary and cursory manner, he knows the divine will at that moment, with a knowledge that is completely true on every level. When a person studying Torah thinks divine thoughts and desires that which God desires, then he is united with the divine will to the highest degree.

This explains why every Jew is expected to study Torah. One is not necessarily expected to study Torah on all its levels, for not everyone has the intellectual and spiritual abilities to do so. But every person is capable of at least pronouncing the holy words. If a person recites Psalms even without understanding the words he is saying, he is fulfilling the commandment "You shall ponder it day and night" (Josh. 1:8). He forms the same connection with the Divine as does the wisest Torah scholar. Although there is a difference between a simple person reciting Psalms and a scholar studying the most profound passages of the Talmud, it is not clear who has the advantage. The person reciting Psalms may not understand the words, but he may recite them with total self-abnegation. On the other hand, the scholar who understands what he is learning is liable to be inflated with feelings of pride, and then it might have been preferable had he only been reciting Psalms without understanding them.

This was one of the issues that brought about the persecution of the Ba'al Shem Tov's first hasidim. Because they stressed the essential value of studying Torah for the sake of unification with the divine will, their opponents believed that they were denigrating the value of scholarship. When a person studies Torah for the sake of unifying with God's will, it is no longer the sole province of scholars. Now one need merely "touch" the Torah, one need merely recite the words, as long as one does so with the nullification of his self.

The unification that Torah study brings about is not necessarily an experience that a person can sense, and it has no bearing at all on one's subjective feelings. In a previous chapter (chap. 4), the author illustrated this insight with an analogy: One can embrace the king whether the king is wearing few clothes or many. Although there will be a difference in one's subjective feeling of touch, one is embracing the king in either case. The difference between one who studies Torah in a state of heightened awareness and another who, although he reads the letters, feels nothing, is in their personal perceptions alone. The experiences of connection are different, but the connection itself is the same.

The person who feels a union with the divine will in every word of Torah that he studies is fortunate. But the union itself does not flow from that feeling, nor is it dependent on it. That experience is a gift that a person might or might not receive. Our ancient teachings point out that the expression "union" can be applied either to the spiritual realm or to the physical act of reproduction. A unification in the latter sense can be accompanied by a variety of physical and emotional sensations, but any connection between those sensations and the creation of a child is tenuous at best. In the spiritual realm as well, even if we have powerful and profound experiences, they are tangential and have little bearing on the actual creation of a tie to the Divine.

But does this connection to the Divine, which may be found at every level of Torah study, exist even when errors are made in the course of the study? The answer is yes, as long as that error is part of an earnest effort. But if a person errs as a result of injecting egotistical motives into his study, his text ceases to be God's Torah and becomes instead his own. Whether it deals with mystical insights or oxen goring cows, it is no longer truth but speculation, and speculation does not engender a connection with God. Once the tie to the divine will and divine thought is severed, then the will is one's own and not God's. The thoughts are one's own and not God's.

But a person may well err as he clarifies his thoughts in the dialectic process that is often inherent in the study of Torah. In that event, he is still studying Torah. Not only the answers are Torah, but the questions too are Torah, perhaps on a lower plane but Torah nevertheless. When an architect draws plans for a building, he first draws preliminary sketches. Later he will erase these lines, but while they exist, they are part of the process of his creation. Similarly, the Torah is the blueprint of the world, and every "sketch," every question and every discussion, even if it is in error, is a part of the Torah.

A tzaddik known as the good Jew of Neustadt, who was considered a simple person, lived near Rabbi Chaim Halberstam of Sanz, one of the greatest Torah scholars of his day. One time Rabbi Chaim was close to completing a cycle of studying the entire Talmud, but he could not understand a passage in the commentary of *Tosafot*. He went to the good Jew of Neustadt and presented him with the problem.

The good Jew responded, "I can't even conceive how it is possible to learn the entire Talmud. I myself can barely read through the book of Psalms, and that only with great difficulty."

Nevertheless, Rabbi Chaim prevailed on him to look at the passage of *Tosafot*. The good Jew took the Talmud volume in his hand and began to read aloud. As he did so, he ended a sentence at a point where Rabbi Chaim had not thought to do so, and at once the topic became clear to him.

It is said that Rabbi Chaim later asked the good Jew, "Would you be willing to exchange my completion of the Talmud for your completion of Psalms?" But it appeared to Rabbi Chaim that the good Jew was not interested. The trade, he thought, was not worthwhile.

It would seem that the story is telling us of two unequal levels of Torah study. On one hand, there is the great scholar who has studied all of the Talmud, and on the other hand, there is the simple man who can barely recite Psalms. But Rabbi Chaim of Sanz realized that the true connection to God through Torah study is not at all contingent on one's intellectual level but rather on what kind of instrument one is for the Torah. This Jew reciting Psalms was a vehicle for divine wisdom, whether or not he understood what he was saying, and so Rabbi Chaim was sure that he would be able to read the *Tosafot* correct-

וְלֹא עוֹד אֶלָּא שֶׁיִּחוּדָם הוּא בְּיֶתֶר שְׂאֵת וְיֶתֶר עָז מִיִּחוּד אוֹר אֵין סוֹף בָּרוּךְ הוּא בְּעוֹלָמוֹת עֶלְיוֹנִים.

Moreover, their unity, the unity of the person studying Torah with the divine light, **is of greater magnitude and greater power than the unity of the light of *Ein Sof*, blessed be He, with the higher worlds**

Though in the higher worlds God is welcomed on a higher level and with greater clarity, it is nevertheless merely an illumination, a reflection of the divine will. In our world, where the Torah was given, the revelation is more profound and tangible.

מֵאַחַר שֶׁרָצוֹן הָעֶלְיוֹן הוּא בְּגִילּוּי מַמָּשׁ בַּנֶּפֶשׁ וּלְבוּשֶׁיהָ הָעוֹסְקִים בַּתּוֹרָה, שֶׁהֲרֵי הוּא הוּא הַתּוֹרָה עַצְמָהּ, וְכָל הָעוֹלָמוֹת הָעֶלְיוֹנִים מְקַבְּלִים חַיּוּתָם מֵאוֹר וְחַיּוּת הַנִּמְשָׁךְ מֵהַתּוֹרָה, שֶׁהִיא רְצוֹנוֹ וְחָכְמָתוֹ יִתְבָּרֵךְ, כְּדִכְתִיב: "כּוּלָּם בְּחָכְמָה עָשִׂיתָ" (תהלים קד, כד).

since the supernal will is literally manifest in the soul and its garments that are engaged in Torah study, **for** the divine will **is the very Torah itself.** By contrast, **all the higher worlds receive their life force** only **from the light and life force drawn down from the Torah, which is the will and wisdom of God, as it is written, "With wisdom You have made them all"** (Ps. 104:24).

All of existence was created and constructed by divine wisdom. It is the instrument with which God created the world. That wisdom is synonymous with the Torah, as the *Zohar* (2:121a) states, "The Torah emanates from wisdom."

וְאִם כֵּן הַחָכְמָה, שֶׁהִיא הַתּוֹרָה, לְמַעְלָה מִכּוּלָּם, וְהִיא הִיא רְצוֹנוֹ

If so, it follows that **the** divine **wisdom, which is the Torah, transcends all** the

ly. This Jew, Rabbi Chaim believed, resonated with the divine wisdom. He was not as certain about himself.

One person may have a more perfect connection to the Divine and another a less perfect connection. But as long as one is not making purposeful errors, as long as one is not inserting his ego into his Torah study, he is still involved in Torah study, which is itself a heavenly endeavor.

יִתְבָּרֵךְ הַנִּקְרָא סוֹבֵב כָּל עָלְמִין,

worlds **and is synonymous with God's will, which is described as encompassing all worlds**

The Torah is not merely a blueprint of the worlds, a spiritual inventory detailing all events past, present, and future. It is the transcendent essence of the world that gives life and meaning to everything therein, the manifestation of the divine will that is completely united with the divine essence and being, a will that is beyond any constraints of rationale or reality.

שֶׁהִיא בְּחִינַת מַה שֶּׁאֵינוֹ יָכוֹל לְהִתְלַבֵּשׁ בְּתוֹךְ עָלְמִין, רַק מְחַיֶּה וּמֵאִיר לְמַעְלָה בִּבְחִינַת מַקִּיף.

in the sense that it is that which cannot be clothed within the worlds but rather sustains and illuminates them **from above as an encompassing** light.

All the worlds, higher and lower, receive their life force only from the divine radiance and illumination that emits from the Divine Presence. But when a person studies Torah, at that moment he is a part of the Divine itself, a part of the light itself that creates and sustains the world. More than that, as he studies Torah he is connected to the divine will, to the divine essence that cannot be revealed in the worlds because it is so immense, so enormous, that the universe cannot bear it and so it exists, as it were, beyond the universe and not within it.

All the worlds are mere instruments for expressing God's will. But the Torah is the will itself. When a person studies Torah on any level, he is no longer connected to creation but to the Creator.

וְהִיא הִיא הַמִּתְלַבֶּשֶׁת בְּנֶפֶשׁ וּלְבוּשֶׁיהָ בִּבְחִינַת גִּילּוּי מַמָּשׁ כְּשֶׁעוֹסְקִים בְּדִבְרֵי תוֹרָה,

It is precisely this level of encompassing light **that is clothed within the soul and its garments in a revealed state when** a person **studies words of Torah,**

The divine will that cannot be revealed because it is too immense to be clothed in any world is clothed and revealed in the soul of a person studying Torah. This is because the Torah itself is the divine will, that which God truly and absolutely wants, and a person studying Torah unveils that divine will within his own soul.

וְאַף עַל גַּב דְּאִיהוּ לָא חָזֵי כו'

and although he himself **does not see it,** the root of his soul does see it.

The book of Daniel recounts that Daniel had a vision through the agency of an angel. Afterward he reported, "I, Daniel, alone saw the vision, and the men who were with me did not see the vision; however, a great trembling overcame them, and they fled into hiding" (Dan. 10:7). The Talmud asks, "Since they did not see the vision, what is the reason that they were frightened?" The answer is that "even though they did not see the vision, the root of their souls saw it" (*Megilla* 3a).

It is possible for a person to experience fear without knowing why. Although his conscious sensibilities have not registered anything, on a higher and hidden level of his being some understanding does exist that causes him to feel terror, so much so that he flees, that he attempts to escape from this situation. In the same way, a person studying Torah does not sense through his conscious sensibilities, his intellect and emotions, the essence of what he is studying even though it is literally being manifest and clothed in his body and soul.

[וּמִשּׁוּם הָכִי יָכוֹל לִסְבּוֹל, מִשּׁוּם דְּלָא חָזֵי, מַה שֶּׁאֵין כֵּן בָּעֶלְיוֹנִים].

(**It is due to this inability to see** the encompassing light **that one can tolerate** its intensity, **which is not the case with regard to the higher creations.**)

Man exists in this lower world, where God is concealed. A person's body houses his soul, and in this world the soul can comprehend reality only through the body's abilities and senses. But it is precisely because we are in this lower realm, with our bodies and evil inclinations, that we can engage in lofty matters without our souls being obliterated. Although a person may not be sensitive to holiness, he can involve himself with holiness. Although he does not sense the essence of the Torah, which is a "consuming fire," the revelation of divine essence itself, he can study the Torah without being consumed.

A welder must shield his eyes and filter the blowtorch's blazing flame so as not to be blinded. But the heavenly beings, creatures of the higher realms, cannot shield their eyes. Since their eyes are open, they cannot bear even a little of the light of Torah, and so they cannot be the instruments to draw it to themselves. Mortal men, with their physical bodies, can study the Torah, whose essence transcends every reality that exists, because that essence is obscured to them.

Some tzaddikim tell a parable about a king who ordered an extraordinary and unique royal crown encrusted with gold and jewels. The greatest artisan toiled to fashion it, but when he had to place the most precious stone in the centerpiece, his fingers trembled so much that he was unable to do so. He understood what it meant to be handling the king's crown. He summoned a simple villager who knew nothing about the king or the crown and told him to put the stone in its place, which the villager easily did.

Like that villager, we are able to study Torah only because we are unaware, to some extent, of what we are doing. A person studies a passage about an ox that gored a cow, and he does not sense the essence of the inner divine intent, whose revelation cannot be borne by any world. Only here in the lower world, where our eyes are covered, can we freely deal with that which transcends all of reality.

וּבָזֶה יוּבַן לָמָּה גְּדוֹלָה מְאֹד מַעֲלַת הָעֵסֶק בַּתּוֹרָה יוֹתֵר מִכָּל הַמִּצְוֹת, וַאֲפִילּוּ מִתְּפִלָּה שֶׁהִיא יִחוּד עוֹלָמוֹת עֶלְיוֹנִים

Now we can understand why the value of studying Torah is vastly superior to all the other **mitzvot, and even more than prayer, which unifies the higher worlds.**

13 Shevat
23 Shevat (leap year)

The purpose of prayer, when man's words ascend from below on high and draw down divine life-giving sustenance from above, is to unite worlds and join them together. It is "a ladder set on the earth and its top reaching to the heavens."[5] Yet, like all the mitzvot, prayer is only an action within the world that serves as an instrument for the divine will. Torah study, on the other hand, is unification with the divine will itself. A person who studies Torah is connected with the Creator, not with His tools, with the will itself and not with its expression. ☞

TORAH AND MITZVOT

☞ Although Torah study is loftier than the other mitzvot, the general relationship between Torah, the mitzvot, and prayer has additional aspects. From the perspective of man's purpose in the world, though the Torah is indeed the highest level, the

5. See Gen. 28:12.

[וְהָא דְּמִי שֶׁאֵין תּוֹרָתוֹ אוּמָּנְתּוֹ צָרִיךְ לְהַפְסִיק, הַיְינוּ מֵאַחַר דְּמַפְסִיק וּמְבַטֵּל בְּלָאו הָכִי].

(**Although** the *halakha* states that **one whose Torah** study **is not his** entire **occupation is required to interrupt** his studies in order to pray, **this is because in any event he interrupts** his Torah study **and squanders** his time on mundane matters.)

The *halakha* states that if a person whose Torah study is not his full-time occupation is studying and the time for prayer arrives, he must set aside his study in order to pray.[6] But if Torah study is on a higher plane than all the other commandments, including prayer, why should it be set aside in favor of prayer?

The answer is because this person's Torah study is not his full-time occupation. A person who studies Torah night and day should not interrupt his studies in order to pray. But if he does not occupy himself with Torah study full-time, then even if a person does not interrupt his studies for prayer, he will inevitably interrupt them for something else. It is certainly preferable that he interrupt his studies for a mitzva and not for some mundane matter.

וּמִזֶּה יוּכַל הַמַּשְׂכִּיל לְהַמְשִׁיךְ עָלָיו יִרְאָה גְּדוֹלָה בְּעָסְקוֹ בַּתּוֹרָה, כְּשֶׁיִּתְבּוֹנֵן אֵיךְ שֶׁנַּפְשׁוֹ וּלְבוּשֶׁיהָ שֶׁבְּמוֹחוֹ וּבְפִיו הֵם מְיוּחָדִים מַמָּשׁ בְּתַכְלִית הַיִּחוּד בִּרְצוֹן הָעֶלְיוֹן, וְאוֹר אֵין סוֹף בָּרוּךְ הוּא מַמָּשׁ הַמִּתְגַּלֶּה בָּהֶם.

Based on this, the intelligent person can evoke in himself a great fear of God **while studying Torah by meditating on how his soul and its garments** of thought and speech, **which are found in his brain and in his mouth, are literally united in absolute unity with the supernal will and the actual light of** ***Ein Sof*****, which is manifest in them.**

mitzvot are a necessity. Though the mitzvot are relatively lower on the scale, a particular mitzva can be performed only by a particular human being in this world, whereas Torah study, although it is higher on the scale, is not the sole province of any particular person.

6. *Mishneh Torah, Sefer HaAhava, Hilkhot Tefilla 6:8; Shulḥan Arukh, Oraḥ Ḥayyim* 106:3.

When a person meditates on the meaning of Torah study, he can attain a concomitant feeling: a great fear. This feeling, which emerges from his Torah study itself, is not fear of punishment but an awe that stems from an awareness of God's greatness.[7] ☞

מַה שֶּׁכָּל הָעוֹלָמוֹת עֶלְיוֹנִים וְתַחְתּוֹנִים כְּלָא חֲשִׁיבֵי קַמֵּיהּ וּכְאַיִן וָאֶפֶס מַמָּשׁ עַד שֶׁאֵינוֹ מִתְלַבֵּשׁ בְּתוֹכָם מַמָּשׁ, אֶלָּא סוֹבֵב כָּל עָלְמִין בִּבְחִינַת מַקִּיף, לְהַחֲיוֹתָם עִיקַּר חַיּוּתָם.

In comparison to the supernal will and divine light, **all the higher and lower worlds are literally considered as absolute nothingness to the extent that** the supernal will **is not actually clothed in them but rather** transcends and **encompasses all worlds** and affects them **as an encompassing** light, **granting them their primary life force.**

THE THIRST FOR CONNECTION

☞ Elsewhere (see, e.g., chap. 40), the author of the *Tanya* quotes the verse "Ho, everyone thirsty, go to water" (Isa. 55:1). Why should the prophet exhort someone who is thirsty to go to water, a self-evident proposition? By analogy, because "water refers only to the study of Torah" (*Bava Kamma* 17a), if a person wants to study Torah, why is it necessary to tell him to do so? If he wants to study, he will do so of his own volition. Rather, the prophet means to say the following:

"Ho, everyone thirsty," those who are thirsty for God, then "go to water" – go study Torah, because that is the way you will come close to God and unite with Him. A person's soul may be thirsty to connect with God, to forge a relationship with *Ein Sof*. He wants to rise to Heaven, to do something great and awesome. The prophet comes and tells him, "It is not, as you imagine, that there is some wondrous path that you must climb in order to attain transcendent experiences. Rather, 'go to water!' Go learn about an ox that gored a cow." Even if this appears to have no connection to the Divine, a wise person will recognize that it is precisely in this way that he will arrive at a true and unparalleled union with God. Moreover, in meditating on this, he will evoke in himself great fear of God, even greater than the fear that could be attained in prayer and in performing the other mitzvot.

---

7. The Lubavitcher Rebbe, Rabbi Menaḥem Mendel Schneerson, suggests that the novel insight that the author of the *Tanya* offers here is that the sense of awe generated through Torah study is even more significant than the oneness with the divine will that one achieves. This is because the purpose of the mitzvot and Torah study, and the oneness achieved thereby, is to fear God, as the author of the *Tanya* will state presently. It follows that the greater one's fear of God, the closer one is to performing the mitzvot with love and awe, as the verse states, "Rather, the matter is very near to you, in your mouth and in your heart, to perform it" (Deut. 30:14).

The worlds cannot contain the divine light. Though it is not clothed in the worlds, it pours energy onto them. The inner will of the Creator at the transcendent level of encompassing all the worlds is too distant and mighty to be clothed in the minutiae of creation, within created beings. But the life force that it infuses in them and that encompasses them is the essence of their vitality. It is the first and basic cause of their existence.

רַק אֵיזוֹ הֶאָרָה מִתְלַבֶּשֶׁת בְּתוֹכָם, מַה שֶּׁיְכוֹלִים לִסְבּוֹל, שֶׁלֹּא יִתְבַּטְּלוּ בִּמְצִיאוּת לְגַמְרֵי.

Only a glimmer of the divine light **is clothed in** the worlds, **just enough that they can endure** it **without becoming utterly nullified from existence.**

The Divine cannot, as it were, exist within the world because the world cannot bear it. In order not to be nullified by the overwhelming light, the created world receives only an illumination of an illumination, a weak echo of the divine, infinite being.

וְזֶהוּ שֶׁכָּתוּב: "וַיְצַוֵּנוּ ה' אֶת כָּל הַחוּקִּים הָאֵלֶּה לְיִרְאָה אֶת ה'" וגו' (דברים ו, כד)

This is the meaning of the verse "The Lord commanded us to perform **all these statutes, to fear the Lord..."** (Deut. 6:24).

The purpose of the mandate to keep the laws is that we will fear God. The mandate is the tool, the means, to attaining a great and extraordinary awe of God. When a person studies the words of Torah that speak of this commandment, when he thinks the divine thought and desires the divine will that is beyond all worlds, he arrives at a fear of God that is greater than anything else.

Within this world that cannot bear the divine light is something extraordinary, something that affords a revelation of the Divine, and that is the Torah. As the hasidic teachings put it, it is not just that the Torah comes from Heaven but that the Torah is Heaven itself. Nothing is greater than sitting and studying Torah. The tzaddikim sit in the Garden of Eden and take pleasure in the radiance of the Divine Presence, but they derive that pleasure only from a glimmer of the divine light shining in a particular plane. When a person studies Torah, even if he is living in the physical world, even if he derives no pleasure from it at all, he is involved in something that is above and beyond not only the radiance of the Divine Presence but the Divine Presence itself. When a person ponders this, that he is touching a light that no world is able to bear, that he is connected to the divine essence, which transcends every revelation and every world, he will experience an immense feeling of awe as he studies Torah.

[וְעַל יִרְאָה גְדוֹלָה זוֹ אָמְרוּ: "אִם אֵין חָכְמָה אֵין יִרְאָה" (אבות פרק ג משנה יז), וְהַתּוֹרָה נִקְרֵאת אֶצְלָהּ "תַּרְעָא לְדַרְתָּא", כְּמוֹ שֶׁנִּתְבָּאֵר בְּמָקוֹם אַחֵר].

(**With regard to this great fear,** the Sages **state, "If there is no wisdom, there is no fear"** [Mishna *Avot* 3:17], **while the Torah is referred to as a "gate to the courtyard," as explained elsewhere** [chap. 43].)

In a later chapter, the author engages in a broad discussion of the relationship between fear and wisdom:[8] Which takes precedence? Which is preferable? Which is more profound? The Sages do not give a clear answer to these questions. Sometimes they describe fear as only a means to preparing one to fulfill the Torah. At other times, they consider fear to be a very lofty level, in which case the Torah is a "gate to the courtyard," the means of attaining that fear.[9]

This paradox is solved when we realize that the Sages are discussing two levels of fear. The first is a lower level of fear, regarding which it is said, "If there is no fear, there is no wisdom." Without fear, there is no possibility of studying Torah. In order to study Torah properly, one must relate to it as the Torah of God. To do so, one must begin with a simple and basic fear of God. This will make it possible to receive God's wisdom.

The second level is a higher level of fear. Regarding this, the Sages said, "If there is no wisdom, there is no fear." This is a fear that one attains through wisdom. The "great fear" referred to by the author of the *Tanya* is this higher level of fear. In order to evoke it within oneself, one must be wise in Torah and understand what it means to study "all

8. Chap. 43; see also *Likkutei Torah*, Lev. 6d, Num. 15b, 21a, 88a.
9. See *Shabbat* 31b; *Yoma* 72b, and Rashi ad loc.

these statutes" that God has commanded. This fear flows from one's consciousness as a person stands before the divine will itself, before the being that has no name and that cannot be defined, before whom all the worlds are as nothingness.[10] ☞

אֶלָּא דְלָאו כָּל מוֹחָא סָבִיל דָא, יִרְאָה כָּזוֹ. **Yet not every mind can tolerate such** a level of **fear.**

Not every mind can contain this fear, which does not stem from a thing that frightens but from contact with the essence of the divine will. This fear is dependent on an apprehension of the highest level, an apprehension that not every mind is sensitive and perfected enough to attain, even partially.

THE GREAT FEAR

☞ This great fear, for which the Torah is the gateway, was described by the students of the Ba'al Shem Tov. "When we studied Torah with the Ba'al Shem Tov," they said, "it was with thunder and lightning and the sound of the *shofar*, as when the Torah was given on Mount Sinai, when 'all the people were seeing the thunder...and the people saw and trembled and stood at a distance" (Ex. 20:15).'"

The Mount Sinai experience was transcendental, beyond the boundaries of time and space, that would endure forever. Like the creation of the world, it is a permanent state, not a onetime act but an ongoing activity. Whenever one sits and studies Torah properly, he hears the voice of God, "a great voice that did not cease" (Deut. 5:19). Torah study is the gateway, and when one passes through it, a great fear falls upon him. This is the fear that results from Torah study, that is evoked when one understands that the Torah is one with the divine wisdom and that when one engages in such study, God Himself speaks out of one's throats (see *Torah Or* 67b).

This is the "great fear," a perfect and exalted awe of God's greatness, which can be attained only after connecting with wisdom, the wisdom of the Torah.

---

10. The Lubavitcher Rebbe, Rabbi Menaḥem Mendel Schneerson, points out that the verse that the author of the *Tanya* quotes to convey this idea, "The Lord commanded us to perform all these statutes, to fear the Lord...," seems to be counterintuitive. It implies that one achieves fear of God only as a result of performing His mitzvot, while the very opposite would seem to be the case, that fear of God must motivate the performance of the mitzvot. He explains that the verse is in fact referring to the higher level of fear of God, and this "great fear" is not only a result of studying His statutes but is their ultimate purpose.

אַךְ גַּם מַאן דְּלָא סָבִיל מוֹחוֹ כְּלָל יִרְאָה זוֹ, לֹא מִינָּהּ וְלֹא מִקְצָתָהּ, מִפְּנֵי פְּחִיתוּת עֵרֶךְ נַפְשׁוֹ בְּשָׁרְשָׁהּ וּמְקוֹרָהּ בְּמַדְרֵגוֹת תַּחְתּוֹנוֹת דְּעֶשֶׂר סְפִירוֹת דַּעֲשִׂיָּה,

However, even one whose mind cannot tolerate this level of **fear at all, not even a minute aspect of it, because of his soul's inferior rank at its root and source in the lowest levels of the ten *sefirot* of** the world of ***Asiya,***

Some people's souls are more responsive to holiness, while others may be relatively insensitive to feelings of holiness so that they are not touched by this great fear. But if one possesses intellectual and other capabilities, one can understand that such a great fear exists and that other people can experience it, even if he himself, because of the quality of his soul, cannot. ☞

אֵין יִרְאָה זוֹ מְעַכֶּבֶת בּוֹ לְמַעֲשֶׂה, כְּמוֹ שֶׁיִּתְבָּאֵר לְקַמָּן.

the lack of **this fear is not indispensable for his performance** of Torah and mitzvot, **as will be explained below** (chap. 41).

God does not demand of us anything beyond our capabilities. The feeling of great fear that the author of the *Tanya* has described is granted to certain people. It can be a welcome gift or a burden that is difficult to bear. In either case, whether or not a person possesses it does not affect his responsibility to fulfill his obligations. If a person has not had

THE QUALITY OF A SOUL

☞ The author of the *Tanya* seems to make a distinction between those with loftier souls and those with lower-ranking souls. But this evaluation relates only to a sensitivity to holiness: The loftier the soul, the greater its sensitivity to holiness, to an awareness of higher states of existence, and the greater its ability to subtly touch the hidden presence of the sacred. If a soul is on a lower level, it lacks that ability to sense holiness. Yet that in no way affects the soul's other qualities. It is possible for the wisest of sages to have a lowly soul and for a person who in every other way is extremely simple to possess the loftiest of souls. If someone is a great musician, that tells us nothing about his intellect or his personal attributes. It only tells us that he is sensitive to sounds that someone else cannot hear and that he responds to sounds that others cannot appreciate.

such an experience, that is unfortunate, but it does not detract from his obligations with regard to the Torah, nor does it detract from his true connection with it. That essential connection, that unity with the divine will, exists whether or not he is sensitive to it.

A person may be a Torah scholar out of whose throat the Divine Presence speaks and yet be unaware of it. He may perform mitzvot yet not sense the holiness of his own actions. The great physicist Hertz could analyze exactly how a violin produces sound and how to perfect its tone even though he himself had never heard a violin because he was deaf. Similarly, a person may achieve great things on which the continued existence of the world depends and yet have no experiential knowledge or understanding of that fact.

In this chapter, the author of the *Tanya* explained that the Torah and its mitzvot reveal the deep connection to the Divine that is interwoven into the world's existence and that of each individual. This was not only a theoretical discussion but the construction of a foundation that will make it possible for a person to connect to this profound reality and act accordingly. As the author of the *Tanya* will explain in the ensuing chapters, every Jew contains within him the ability to decide in favor of a mitzva and against a transgression. This is because each mitzva or transgression expresses a person's basic connection to the Divine and to his own soul. The problem is when one belittles, intellectually and otherwise, this meaning of the Torah and mitzvot, and he loses the power to make choices in real life. The purpose of these chapters, and in a sense of this entire work, is an educational one: to give us the tools for contemplation. Through contemplation, the Torah and commandments are accorded their profound and incomparable importance. Then we will come to the practical decision "to learn and to teach, to guard and to do."

Chapter 24

THE PREVIOUS CHAPTER DISCUSSED THE ATTACHMENT with the Divine that is achieved through performance of mitzvot and Torah study. This chapter will deal with the converse: disconnection from the Divine caused by transgression of the Torah's prohibitions. Just as attachment to the Divine is disproportionately greater than any alternative means of attachment, so the disconnection from the Divine as a result of committing a transgression disproportionately exceeds the disconnection inherent in the *kelippot* themselves.

14 Shevat
24 Shevat (leap year)

וְזֶה לְעוּמַּת זֶה, הֵן שס״ה מִצְוֹת לֹא תַעֲשֶׂה דְּאוֹרַיְיתָא וְכָל אִיסּוּרֵי דְּרַבָּנָן, מֵאַחַר שֶׁהֵן נֶגֶד רְצוֹנוֹ וְחָכְמָתוֹ יִתְבָּרֵךְ

Corresponding to the positive commandments **are the 365 biblical prohibitions and all rabbinically mandated prohibitions since they are the opposite of God's will and wisdom**

The positive commandments are the most profound revelation of the divine will. They are God's ultimate desire, that which He wishes us to do. Their counterparts are the prohibitions, actions that God does not want us to do, even though, within the framework of our world, God gives us the freedom to choose.

וְהֶפְכָּם מַמָּשׁ.

and are literally antithetical to them.

Not only are the prohibitions not the will of God, but they are the exact opposite of His will. It is His desire that we choose not to do these actions.

הֵם נִפְרָדִים מִיִּחוּדוֹ וְאַחְדּוּתוֹ יִתְבָּרֵךְ בְּתַכְלִית הַפֵּירוּד מַמָּשׁ, כְּמוֹ הַסִּטְרָא אָחֳרָא וְהַקְּלִיפָּה הַנִּקְרֵאת עֲבוֹדָה זָרָה וֵאלֹהִים אֲחֵרִים, מֵחֲמַת הֶסְתֵּר פָּנִים שֶׁל רָצוֹן הָעֶלְיוֹן כַּנִּזְכָּר לְעֵיל.

These prohibitions **are literally and utterly separate from God's unity and oneness, just as the** ***sitra aḥara*** **and** ***kelippa,*** **referred to as idolatry and other gods,** are separated from God **due to the concealed countenance** of God's **supernal will, as discussed above** (chap. 22).

Every transgression, whether in violation of a biblical prohibition or a rabbinic decree, is essentially an act of idolatry, the worship of something alien, an entity that is not God. When a person commits a transgression, whatever its nature, he disconnects himself from the divine will, from the source of life, from all goodness and holiness. There is no neutral space: Either something is connected and united with God, or it is not. Everything in our lives belongs either to the sacred or to *kelippa.* There is no middle ground.

Because a transgression is a part of the realm of *kelippa,* it incorporates within itself all the characteristics of *kelippa*: betrayal, disloyalty, and rebellion against the Divine. Although different degrees of gravity exist between one transgression and another as measured by halakhic standards or by the punishments that various transgressions incur, all transgressions share a common denominator: Every transgression causes disconnection from the Divine and association with the *sitra aḥara.* Because of this, every transgression is essentially a form of idolatry, a total abandonment of the realm of holiness.

וְכֵן ג׳ לְבוּשֵׁי הַנֶּפֶשׁ שֶׁמִּקְּלִיפַּת נוֹגַהּ שֶׁבְּיִשְׂרָאֵל, שֶׁהֵם מַחֲשָׁבָה דִּבּוּר וּמַעֲשֶׂה הַמְּלוּבָּשִׁים בְּשס״ה לֹא תַעֲשֶׂה דְּאוֹרַיְיתָא וּדְרַבָּנָן, וְכֵן מַהוּת הַנֶּפֶשׁ עַצְמָהּ הַמְּלוּבֶּשֶׁת בִּלְבוּשֶׁיהָ - כּוּלָּם מְיוּחָדִים מַמָּשׁ בְּסִטְרָא אָחֳרָא וּקְלִיפָּה זוֹ הַנִּקְרֵאת עֲבוֹדָה זָרָה.

Likewise, the three garments of a Jew's soul that stem from ***kelippat noga,*** **which are the thoughts, speech, and actions that are clothed within the 365 biblically and rabbinically mandated prohibitions, as well as the essence of the soul itself that is clothed in its garments, are all literally unified with this** ***sitra aḥara*** **and** ***kelippa,*** **which is referred to as idolatry.**

When a person commits a transgression, the parts of his soul that are a partner to the deed – the faculties of speech, thought, and deed, as well as the soul that gives life to those forces – are unified with the realm of *kelippa* and *sitra aḥara*. When a person performs a mitzva, which is a limb of the King, he himself becomes a "limb of the King." He unites with God and becomes part of the world of holiness.

וְלֹא עוֹד, אֶלָּא שֶׁבְּטֵלִים וּטְפֵלִים אֵלֶיהָ,

Moreover, they are secondary and subordinate to the *kelippa*

The person who transgressed has totally surrendered to *kelippa*. He is no more than a utensil, a tool, to actualizing the *kelippa* in the world.

וּגְרוּעִים וּפְחוּתִים מִמֶּנָּה מְאֹד, כִּי הִיא אֵינָהּ מְלוּבֶּשֶׁת בְּגוּף חוּמְרִי,

and considerably inferior and lower than it because it is not clothed in a corporeal body.

The *kelippa* is not a material reality and in itself cannot create anything in the world. But when a person clings to it, he gives it a physical and substantive body. He creates a palpable reality of actual evil. Therefore, when a person clings to the *kelippa*, he becomes even lower than the *kelippa* itself.

וְיוֹדַעַת אֶת רִבּוֹנָהּ, וְאֵינָהּ מוֹרֶדֶת בּוֹ לִפְעוֹל פְּעוּלָּתָהּ בְּמִשְׁלַחַת מַלְאֲכֵי רָעִים שֶׁלָּהּ שֶׁלֹּא בִּשְׁלִיחוּתוֹ שֶׁל מָקוֹם בָּרוּךְ הוּא חַס וְשָׁלוֹם,

It is aware of its Master and does not rebel against Him by performing its mission and employing its band of destroying angels without the directive of the Holy One, blessed be He, God forbid,

There is another reason that a person who commits a transgression is lower than the *kelippa*. At the end of the day, the *kelippa* recognizes its Master. All the powers of evil – terror and destruction, death and idolatry – do not act on their own. They only fulfill a role, one that may not be pleasing or agreeable but that constitutes a part of the structure of the world, and its agents are among the servants of God, as the verse states, "The children of the great came to stand before the Lord, and the accuser too came among them" (Job 1:6). Yet when a human being connects with the powers of evil, the situation is different. By engaging in evil, a person is not acting as an agent of God. Rather, he is functioning on his own, voluntarily, in a manner directly opposed to God. A person can choose differently, and if he delivers himself to *kelippa,* he is essentially lower than the *kelippa,* because it is fulfilling its mission, but he is not. ☞

וּכְמַאֲמַר בִּלְעָם: "לֹא אוּכַל לַעֲבוֹר אֶת פִּי ה'" וגו' (במדבר כב, יח).

as Bilam stated, "I would be unable to violate the directive of the Lord my God, to perform a small or a great matter" (Num. 22:18).

Bilam was connected to the depth of *kelippa.* He was the prophet of *kelippa,* the exact opposite of Moses. Yet even he knew that ultimately he was only an agent of God and that he himself possessed no intrinsic power, in neither his curses nor his blessings.

וְאַף שֶׁנִּקְרָא עֲבוֹדָה זָרָה, הָא קָרוּ לֵיהּ אֱלָהָא דֶּאֱלָהַיָּא.

Although the *kelippot* **are referred to as idolatry, they** nevertheless **refer to** God **as the "God of gods."**

The *kelippa* apparently proclaims itself to be a god, an independent being. Yet idolaters call God the "God of gods"[1] because idolatry itself

EVIL AS AN AGENT OF GOD

☞ In one of his most audacious parables, the Ba'al Shem Tov tells about a king who wanted to learn whether his subjects were loyal. He clothed one of his servants in royal garments and told him, "Go out and incite a rebellion." The servant proclaimed a rebellion against the king, and the king waited to see how the people would react. Those who were wicked joined the rebellion, while those who were worthy fought against it. But there was one righteous and wise man who did not involve himself in the conflict at all. Instead, he approached the servant and told him, "I know as well as you do that you are only a servant of the king and that you have no standing of your own." Immediately, the entire rebellion came to an end. After such an insight, there is no Satan, no angel of death, and no evil inclination (see *Ba'al Shem Tov al HaTorah, Parashat Bereshit* 141).

1. See *Menaḥot* 110a.

recognizes that God is the highest, the utmost force, the God higher than all other gods, the source of them all.

וְאֵינָם יְכוֹלִים לַעֲבוֹר כְּלָל עַל רְצוֹנוֹ יִתְבָּרֵךְ, כִּי יוֹדְעִים וּמַשִּׂיגִים שֶׁהוּא חַיּוּתָם וְקִיּוּמָם שֶׁיּוֹנְקִים מִבְּחִינַת אֲחוֹרַיִים דַּאֲחוֹרַיִים שֶׁל רָצוֹן הָעֶלְיוֹן בָּרוּךְ הוּא הַמַּקִּיף עֲלֵיהֶם.

They are incapable of transgressing God's will whatsoever because they know and apprehend that He is their life force and sustenance, for **they suckle from the back side of the back side of God's supernal will, which encompasses them.**

Though the *kelippot* appear to be a source of power and strength, they cannot transgress God's will because He is the source of their life force. Yet they do not receive their life force from the inner aspect of the divine will since they do not express the divine will but rather constitute only the framework of the world – the back side of the divine will. They are the support beams but not the main structure, the primary purpose of the world's existence.

This "back side of the back side" is so removed from the inner aspect of the divine will that not only do the *kelippot,* which they nourish, not perceive God, but they are unaware of this lack of perception. It follows that not only do they not serve God, but they serve foreign gods instead.

אֶלָּא שֶׁיְּנִיקָתָם וְחַיּוּתָם שֶׁבְּתוֹכָם הִיא בִּבְחִינַת גָּלוּת בְּתוֹכָם לְהַחְשִׁיב עַצְמָן אֱלֹהוּת,

Rather, the nourishment and life force within them are in a state of exile within them so that they regard themselves as divine,

The *kelippot* do not draw sustenance from that inner place where the light is plentiful and creates a clear sense of dependency. Where the light is not plentiful, because the vitality flowing down is indirect, coming from the "back side of the back side," this generates the sense that the Divine Presence is in exile. The *kelippa* no longer senses the Divine Presence that is giving it life, so it experiences itself as an independent being. This is the Divine Presence in exile.

וַהֲרֵי זוֹ כְּפִירָה בְּאַחְדוּתוֹ.

which is a denial of God's **oneness.**

At the root of idolatry, there may be an acknowledgment that everything is dependent on the God of gods, but it is an indirect acknowledgment of God's existence that still allows for the existence of other entities. Although the act of idolatry does not deny God's existence, it denies His singularity. That God is one means that there is no other than Him. But idolatry allows for the possibility of an additional, independent entity that can act with its own autonomous motives.

אֲבָל מִכָּל מָקוֹם אֵינָן כּוֹפְרִים וְכִחֲשׁוּ בַּה' לְגַמְרֵי וְלוֹמַר "לֹא הוּא", אֶלָּא דְּקָרוּ לֵיהּ אֱלָהָא דֶּאֱלָהַיָּא, דְּהַיְינוּ חַיּוּתָם וְקִיּוּמָם הַנִּמְשָׁךְ וְיוֹרֵד עֲלֵיהֶם מֵרְצוֹנוֹ יִתְבָּרַךְ, וְלָכֵן אֵינָן עוֹבְרִין רְצוֹנוֹ יִתְבָּרַךְ לְעוֹלָם.

Yet nevertheless they do not completely deny or repudiate God by saying "He is not." Rather, they refer to Him as the "God of gods," meaning, they are aware that **their life force and sustenance that issue forth and descend to them** stem **from His will. Consequently, they never transgress His will.**

Ultimately, no *kelippa*, not even idolatry, can ever be totally opposed to God. The *kelippa* has a sense of itself, yet somehow it knows that it has limitations. It may not know how to define those limitations, but neither can it act knowingly and directly against the divine will.

וְאִם כֵּן, הָאָדָם הָעוֹבֵר עַל רְצוֹנוֹ יִתְבָּרַךְ הוּא גָּרוּעַ וּפָחוּת הַרְבֵּה מְאֹד מֵהַסִּטְרָא אָחֳרָא וּקְלִיפָּה הַנִּקְרֵאת עֲבוֹדָה זָרָה וֵאלֹהִים אֲחֵרִים, וְהוּא בְּתַכְלִית הַפֵּירוּד מִיִּחוּדוֹ וְאַחְדּוּתוֹ שֶׁל הַקָּדוֹשׁ בָּרוּךְ הוּא יוֹתֵר מִמֶּנָּה, וּכְאִלּוּ כּוֹפֵר בְּאַחְדּוּתוֹ יוֹתֵר מִמֶּנָּה חַס וְשָׁלוֹם,

If so, a person who transgresses God's will is exceedingly worse than and inferior to the *sitra aḥara* and *kelippa*, which are called idolatry and other gods. The sinner **is utterly separated from the unity and oneness of the Holy One, blessed be He, more so than** the *kelippa*, **and it is as if he denies His oneness more than** the *kelippa*, **God forbid.**

When a person commits a transgression, whatever it may be, he sins against God's will. He rebels against the supernal will, against the God of gods, whom even the *sitra aḥara* and the *kelippa* of idolatry acknowledge and to whom they are subservient. His denial, then, is even more profound than that of *kelippa*. Idolatry denies that there is no other besides Him, but a person who commits a transgression denies God Himself.

וְכָמוֹ שֶׁכָּתוּב בְּעֵץ חַיִּים שַׁעַר מ״ב סוֹף פֶּרֶק ד׳, שֶׁהָרַע שֶׁבָּעוֹלָם הַזֶּה הַחוּמְרִי הוּא שְׁמָרֵי הַקְּלִיפּוֹת הַגַּסּוֹת כו׳,

As it is written in *Etz Ḥayyim* 42, at the end of the fourth chapter, the evil in this material world constitutes the dregs of the coarse *kelippot*, and so forth,

The evil that a person does in the world is not only of the *kelippa* but of the dregs, the concentrated and most foul distillation of evil, in comparison to which there is nothing coarser.

וְהוּא תַּכְלִית הַבֵּירוּר וכו׳,

and it is where **the ultimate refinement** occurs, **and so on.**

Since the holiness within this evil is so concealed, here the ultimate purification process can take place. It is the very lowest level from which goodness can still be extracted.

וְלָכֵן כָּל מַעֲשֵׂה עוֹלָם הַזֶּה קָשִׁים וְרָעִים וְהָרְשָׁעִים גּוֹבְרִים בּוֹ וכו׳.

Therefore, all matters of this world are harsh and evil, and the wicked hold sway in it, and so forth.

The physical world, where man exists and functions, is the lowest of all worlds. Here the divine light is so concealed that it can go completely unnoticed, and it is possible for a person to disconnect himself from the divine will and engage in evil so complete that it is lower than *kelippa* itself.

A cholera bacteria may be an agent of evil, it may be fatal, but it is not intrinsically evil. Since it is part of the natural framework, it is connected, if only indirectly, to the divine will. Only man, who transgresses of his own free will against the divine will, can be lower than that. Because such a thing can exist in our world, it is the worst of all the worlds.

Our reality is constructed in such a way that concealment is stronger than revelation, evil appears to prevail, and the wicked appear to dominate. Evil seems to grow ever stronger and the darkness ever thicker. Ours is not the best of all possible worlds. It would be more accurate to say that ours is the lowest of all worlds, but with one important caveat: It is the lowest of all worlds that can be rectified. Our world stands in a delicate balance, at the final verge. It is the lowest stage where the possibility of ascent still exists. Had it been just a little bit worse, ours would have been a world without hope, a world that is itself Gehenna.

Judaism is said to be optimistic. That is so, but its optimism must be understood against this framework. It is an optimism that does not claim that this world is entirely fine and good. It acknowledges that the world is entirely black and evil. But this world can nevertheless be rectified. It still has hope – and that is true optimism.

15 Shevat

וְלָכֵן אָמְרוּ רַבּוֹתֵינוּ ז״ל (סוטה ג, א) עַל פָּסוּק (במדבר ה, יב): ״כִּי תִשְׂטֶה אִשְׁתּוֹ״, אֵין אָדָם עוֹבֵר עֲבֵירָה וכו׳. דַּאֲפִילּוּ אִשָּׁה הַמְנָאֶפֶת, שֶׁדַּעְתָּהּ קַלָּה, הָיְתָה מוֹשֶׁלֶת בְּרוּחַ תַּאֲוָתָהּ לוּלֵי רוּחַ שְׁטוּת שֶׁבָּהּ הַמְכַסֶּה וּמַסְתִּיר וּמַעֲלִים אֶת הָאַהֲבָה מְסוּתֶּרֶת שֶׁבְּנַפְשָׁהּ הָאֱלֹהִית, לְדָבְקָה בֶּאֱמוּנַת ה׳ וְיִחוּדוֹ וְאַחְדוּתוֹ וְלֹא לִיפָּרֵד חַס וְשָׁלוֹם מֵאַחְדוּתוֹ, אֲפִילּוּ נוֹטְלִים אֶת נַפְשָׁהּ מִמֶּנָּה לַעֲבוֹד עֲבוֹדָה זָרָה חַס וְשָׁלוֹם,

Therefore, our Rabbis stated regarding the verse "If any man's **wife goes astray"** (Num. 5:12) that **"a man commits a transgression only** if a spirit of folly enters him" (*Sota* 3a). **Even an adulteress, who is weak minded, would control her spirit of lust were it not for the spirit of folly within her that covers, conceals, and hides the latent love in her divine soul** whose desire is **to cleave to faith in God and His unity and oneness and not to separate from His oneness, God forbid, and commit idolatry, God forbid, even if it means losing her life.**

After concluding a lengthy discussion of both the revealed and concealed aspects of God's unity that spanned the previous few chapters,[2] the author of the *Tanya* revisits the subject he addressed

2. Chaps. 20–24.

before he embarked on this subject: that of the concealed love for God within every Jew.[3] This latent love is the sole yearning and raison d'être of a Jew's divine soul – a veritable piece of the divine oneness itself. So powerful is this love that the soul is willing to sacrifice its very own existence to become fused with the Divine, never again to disconnect.

In light of this, if even an adulteress who gave in to her temptations were compelled to serve an idol, she would do as so many others have done and choose a martyr's death. It is well known that during the pogroms of the Middle Ages, even men and women at the lowest fringes of Jewish society preferred martyrdom to apostasy together with the rest of the community.

וַאֲפִילוּ בְּהִשְׁתַּחֲוָאָה לְבַדָּהּ בְּלִי שׁוּם אֱמוּנָה בַּלֵּב כְּלָל,

She would sacrifice her life **even if** she were compelled **to perform a mere** act of **prostration without possessing an iota of** idolatrous **belief in** her **heart at all,**

Jews throughout the generations have given their lives not only to defend the fundamentals of their faith but even to avoid the most superficial of wrongdoings. From a Jewish perspective, all the idolatrous rites that violate our faith are meaningless. Yet in order to not be involved even in a mere ritual that they found meaningless, even the most frivolous of society would be ready to die. This is not only a theory. Many have done so throughout the ages. Men and women who during their lifetimes were debased sinners, to whom religion should have meant nothing, clearly showed that it was so important to them that they were ready to die rather than transgress.

וְכָל שֶׁכֵּן לִכְבּוֹשׁ הַיֵּצֶר וְתַאֲוַת הַנִּיאוּף, שֶׁהֵם יִסּוּרִים קַלִּים מִמִּיתָה, ה׳ יִשְׁמְרֵנוּ.

and all the more so would she be able **to vanquish the evil inclination and the lust for adultery, which constitute suffering that is less severe than death, may God protect us.**

3. See chaps. 19–20.

It is certainly easier to conquer one's physical drives than to die a violent death. Nevertheless, even though this woman is prepared to face martyrdom rather than worship a false god, when it comes to the prohibition against adultery, she does not attempt to conquer her lusts.

וְהַהֶפְרֵשׁ שֶׁאֶצְלָהּ בֵּין אִיסּוּר נִיאוּף לְאִיסּוּר הִשְׁתַּחֲוָאָה לַעֲבוֹדָה זָרָה הוּא גַּם כֵּן רוּחַ שְׁטוּת דִּקְלִיפָּה הַמַּלְבֶּשֶׁת לַנֶּפֶשׁ הָאֱלֹהִית,

The distinction she makes between the prohibition against adultery and that against prostrating to an idol is also due to **the spirit of folly** stemming **from *kelippa*, which clothes the divine soul**

Even though adultery conceals the divine unity as much as idolatry does, a spirit of foolishness tells a person that the two are not the same. It persuades the woman that committing this act of adultery will not detach her from the source of holiness, that she can still remain connected. As absurd as the proposition may be on a cognitive level, she believes that she can sin and still remain a faithful Jew. She foolishly persuades herself that even though she is rebelling against the divine will, she remains an upstanding Jew, no different from one who convinces himself that he is a kettle or a goose.

עַד בְּחִינַת חָכְמָה שֶׁבָּהּ וְלֹא עַד בִּכְלָל, מִפְּנֵי אוֹר ה׳ הַמְלוּבָּשׁ בְּחָכְמָה כַּנִּזְכָּר לְעֵיל.

up to but not including the faculty of wisdom within it on account of the light of God that is clothed within the faculty of **wisdom, as mentioned above** (chap. 19).

The spirit of foolishness can clothe and conceal the divine soul. But the foolishness can only reach so far and cannot conceal the soul completely. There is a point in the soul, one point, where there is an identification between man and God. At this point of contact, there is no barrier, no garment concealing the soul from the light of God. When this point is reached, there is a sort of explosion. The structure of falsehood collapses, garment after garment falls away, and a person stands naked before one stark choice: life and goodness as opposed to death and evil, connection to the source of life or severance from life. There is no room for compromise or discussion, for emotions or calculations.

People who have reached this point have acted in ways that defy all rational calculation, all estimations of whether or not the action is worthwhile, in practical or even in spiritual terms. Contradicting all the principles they held throughout their lives, their actions now flow solely from the reality of this point, and thus they went forward to meet the most horrible of deaths as martyrs.

As the author of the *Tanya* has said earlier, the definition of a Jew is that there exists within his soul, whether in a revealed or a concealed state, a point of connection with the source of life, with *Ein Sof*. Whenever a Jew, no matter who he may be, touches this point, he is literally transformed into a part of the Divine.

אֲבָל בֶּאֱמֶת לַאֲמִיתּוֹ, אֲפִילּוּ עֲבֵירָה קַלָּה, הֲרֵי הָעוֹבְרָהּ עוֹבֵר עַל רָצוֹן הָעֶלְיוֹן בָּרוּךְ הוּא, וְהוּא בְּתַכְלִית הַפֵּירוּד מִיִּחוּדוֹ וְאַחְדּוּתוֹ יִתְבָּרֵךְ, יוֹתֵר מִסִּטְרָא אָחֳרָא וּקְלִיפָּה הַנִּקְרֵאת אֱלֹהִים אֲחֵרִים וַעֲבוֹדָה זָרָה מַמָּשׁ.

But the truth of the matter is that even one who commits a minor transgression transgresses the supernal will and is utterly separated from God's unity and oneness even **more than the *sitra aḥara* and *kelippa*, which are referred to as other gods and actual idolatry,**

As noted above, a person who commits a sin is even lower than *kelippa* itself. At its root, *kelippa* is a part of the larger structure of existence, whereas a person who commits a sin is no longer a part of the holy reality but a contradiction to it. In the larger framework of reality, there are not only angels, seraphim, and holy *ḥayot* but also demons and all kinds of beings that harm man. As long as a person leaves these negative forces alone, they do no more than preserve the framework of reality. They pose a threat, but they are not actively evil.

In one sense, these forces of evil are comparable to a policeman on his beat. He holds no interest to the law-abiding citizen, to whom he is no different from any other person on the street. But to a criminal, the policeman is an agent of punishment, instigating terror and flight.[4] The

4. Obviously this is not a perfect analogy, because the role of the *kelippa* is not

mechanism of evil does not act independently. Although it comprises the potential for evil, it itself does not desire evil, nor is it capable of committing evil on its own.

Kelippa, the source of evil, is a part of the total structure of the world. The powers of evil themselves know that they have a Master, that they do not possess an independent existence. In light of this, when a person commits a transgression and thus rebels against God, he is worse than kelippa.

וְיוֹתֵר מִכָּל הַדְּבָרִים הַנִּשְׁפָּעִים מִמֶּנָּה בָּעוֹלָם הַזֶּה, שֶׁהֵם בְּהֵמוֹת טְמֵאוֹת וְחַיּוֹת וְעוֹפוֹת טְמֵאִים וּשְׁקָצִים וּרְמָשִׂים,

and more than all things that issue forth from *kelippa* in this world, such as impure domesticated and undomesticated animals, impure birds, detestable things, and crawling creatures,

An impure worm is not as impure as a person committing a sin. As long as one does not eat the worm, it does not cause evil. Even if someone eats it, this creature is not to blame. Similarly, a pig is an animal created by God. It is the Jew who eats pork who defies God's will.

וּכְמַאֲמַר: "יַתּוּשׁ קְדָמְךָ" (סנהדרין לח, א).

in accordance with the Sages' statement **"The mosquito preceded you"** (*Sanhedrin* 38a).

The Sages ask why man was created last during the six days of Creation, on Friday afternoon. They answer that if a man grows proud, he can be told, "The mosquito preceded you in the acts of Creation." The simple meaning of this statement is that the mosquito was created before man and so has a better lineage than does a human being. A human being's superiority is not dependent on the order of creation. Rather, it is dependent on his doing the will of his Creator. If he sins and loses that unique superiority, he becomes a creature like any other, and then he is inferior even to the mosquito, which was created before he was.

This is the simple understanding of this talmudic statement. The author of the *Tanya* will soon examine this saying more deeply and

---

only that of the policeman. It is not only the angel of death. It plays multiple roles: "He is the evil inclination, he is the Satan, he is the angel of death" (*Bava Batra* 16a).

teach that "the mosquito preceded you" refers not only to the fact that it was created earlier but also to an essential superiority that even the *kelippa* of a mosquito possesses over any evil that a human being has committed.

פֵּירוּשׁ, דְּאַף יַתּוּשׁ שֶׁמַּכְנִיס וְאֵינוֹ מוֹצִיא, שֶׁהִיא קְלִיפָּה הַיּוֹתֵר תַּחְתּוֹנָה וּרְחוֹקָה מִבְּחִינַת הַקְּדוּשָּׁה הַמַּשְׁפַּעַת בְּתַכְלִית הָרִיחוּק,	**This means that even a mosquito, which ingests but does not excrete, signifying the lowest and furthest *kelippa* from the realm of holiness, which gives sustenance** even **to that which is the most remote** from it,

The mosquito sucks in blood, but it does not excrete anything that is useful to others.[5] It is the symbol of a parasite, a being that lives at the expense of others, entirely self-centered, giving no sustenance of any kind to another.

The *kelippot*, the powers of evil and harm, are the spiritual parasites of man. Because they cannot exist independently, they strive with all their might to attach themselves to holiness, to a place of life, in order to draw life to themselves. The lower and more remote the *kelippa* is

THE PARASITIC NATURE OF *KELIPPA*

☞ A parasite loves and desires its host but in a twisted manner, for it also destroys him. The more it grows, the more harm it causes. The more harm it generates, the more it weakens its own source of life. This sheds light on the verse "Whenever man controlled man, it was to his detriment" (Eccles. 8:9). This verse refers to the dominion of evil over good. Ultimately that is to the detriment of the *kelippa*, for beyond a certain stage, the host can no longer sustain the parasite. Together with its source of sustenance, evil destroys itself (see *Iggeret HaKodesh*, epistles 25–26).

In essence, evil acts as a parasite. It punishes the person who clings to it, because after draining him of life and power, it gives him nothing in return. In itself, evil is total negativity and nothingness, and so in essence its touch perverts the relationship of all life to holiness.

The *kelippa* does not have an independent source of life. Instead, it strives to cling to holiness and draw life from it. The holier a person is, the more he serves as a target and source of life for *kelippa*. This is why "anyone who is greater than another, his [evil] inclination is greater than his" (*Sukka* 52a). The higher a person's level, the more desirable he is to the forces of evil and his battles are correspondingly greater and fiercer. By contrast, a baser

5. See *Gittin* 56b.

from a source of holiness, the more opaque it is, obstructing the holy light from penetrating and sustaining it. Consequently, its only source of sustenance is the person onto whom it leeches and from whom it sucks its nourishment. ☞ ☞

קוֹדֶמֶת לָאִישׁ הַחוֹטֵא, בְּהִשְׁתַּלְשְׁלוּת וִירִידַת הַחַיּוּת מֵרָצוֹן הָעֶלְיוֹן בָּרוּךְ הוּא.

precedes the sinner in the chain of progression and descent of the life force that emanates **from God's supernal will.**

person is easier prey for the powers of evil and the blandishments of his evil inclination, but evil does not gain much from him. The higher a person has climbed on the ladder of holiness, the more powerfully evil is drawn to him, even though he has many more ways to protect himself.

This model also applies to crime in the sociological sense. A criminal is a parasite who draws from life and creates evil, who perverts the societal structure with his very touch: robbing, killing, cheating, and generally being destructive. As in the world of the *kelippa* as a whole, such evil has no independent means of ongoing existence. A society composed solely of thieves and murderers could not endure for long. Between that underworld and society at large, certain bridges transfer the means of existence to the underworld: dealers in stolen goods, lawyers, theoreticians, all of whom make it possible for evil to flourish. Theoretically, in the absence of such contacts, if these transfer points would be sealed, evil too would cease to exist.

There is a fixed correlation between a society's health and ability to protect itself and the degree of criminal behavior it contains. The weaker and poorer a society, the weaker and more moderate its evildoers, its thieves and cheats, because they have no one from whom to take. Criminality always seeks to attach itself to a flourishing and wealthy society, even if that society's powers of self-preservation are stronger.

THE STERILE NATURE OF *KELIPPA*

☞ The characteristic of holiness is that it gives, and the characteristic of *kelippa* is that it cannot give, that it has nothing of its own. The *Zohar* states that the *sitra aḥara* is sterile and does not bear fruit (*Zohar* 2:103a). The power of creation, of fruitfulness, of giving, is the essence of the power of holiness. In his tales, Rabbi Naḥman of Breslov frequently presents evil in the image of a merchant: He creates nothing and has nothing of his own; he only buys and sells the merchandise of others.

The incomplete *kelippa*, which has an admixture of good, exists in a sort of ecological balance, taking and giving, though it takes more than it gives. But in its depths, in its ultimate, polluted abyss, the *kelippa* takes and gives nothing. That is the *kelippa* of the mosquito, the lowest stage, at the farthest remove from holiness, which absorbs from others but gives nothing of its own.

From the viewpoint of the divine will, a mosquito is higher than a sinner. Although it is a lowly creature that does base things, it does not rebel against God, because the mosquito is a necessary part of the structure of the world, unlike the sinner. The person who transgresses is only a possibility that exists in the structure, and this possibility is subservient to a person's free will. If he chooses to sin, he does so not in order to fulfill his mission but voluntarily, of his own choice, in rebellion against the divine sovereignty.

וְכָל שֶׁכֵּן שְׁאָר בַּעֲלֵי חַיִּים הַטְּמֵאִים, וַאֲפִילוּ חַיּוֹת רָעוֹת, שֶׁכּוּלָּם אֵינָם מְשַׁנִּים תַּפְקִידָם, וּפְקוּדָּתוֹ יִתְבָּרֵךְ שָׁמְרָה רוּחָם,

All the more so is the sinner lower than **the other impure animals, and even wild,** predatory **beasts, none of whom deviate from their purpose** in this world, as **their spirit preserves God's command.**

The leopard is not evil. Although it preys on other animals, though it kills and maims, it is only doing the will of the Creator, following the role it has been assigned. ☞

וְאַף עַל גַּב דְּאִיהוּ לָא חָזֵי.

Although they do not see it, their spiritual root does see it,

This statement was cited in the previous chapter in reference to people. In the present context, the author of the *Tanya* extends the dictum to include animals. In this world, the leopard lacks the intelligence to know that it is serving as an agent of the Divine. But at its root and source in the upper world, it has that awareness. Thus, as it roams this

SUPERIOR TO HUMANS

☞ *Perek Shira* relates that once, as King David was walking alongside a river, he grew proud of having composed so many songs and praises to God. A frog emerged from the river and told him, "I praise God more than you do!" But how could that be? Rabbi Tzadok HaKohen notes that unlike the frog, King David possessed wisdom and an understanding of holiness. But simply by virtue of carrying out its tasks without changing them, the frog proclaims, with its every croak, "I exist and do only the will of God!" This is something that King David could not say. In this one aspect, the frog, which has no intelligence of its own and is thus nullified to God, is superior to a human being.

world, where it carries out tasks and missions on God's behalf, it cannot actually damage that which is holy since its actions all derive from the power of holiness. If it injures a person, it is because that was the divine will. The leopard is the agent, the executioner, that must carry out God's decree against that particular person. Although the leopard is not aware of this, it is impelled to act as it does, because it always carries out the will of God.

וּכְמוֹ שֶׁכָּתוּב: "וּמוֹרַאֲכֶם וְחִתְּכֶם יִהְיֶה עַל כָּל חַיַּת הָאָרֶץ" (בראשית ט, ב), וּכְפֵירוּשׁ רַבּוֹתֵינוּ ז"ל, שֶׁאֵין חַיָּה רָעָה מוֹשֶׁלֶת בָּאָדָם אֶלָּא אִם כֵּן נִדְמֶה לָהּ כִּבְהֵמָה (סנהדרין לח, ב).

as it is written, "And fear of you and dread of you shall be upon every beast of the earth" (Gen. 9:2), regarding which **our Rabbis explain that "a wild animal does not have power over a person unless** that person **seems to** the wild animal **like an animal"** (*Sanhedrin* 38b).

It would seem from the verse that animals should be afraid of man. So why do they sometimes prey on people?

An animal will harm a person only if it does not recognize him as a human being. The animal does not discern as we do. When a person conforms to the will of God, when he thinks and speaks of divine wisdom, he manifests the divine image in which he was created, instilling fear in the animal. But if a person has made himself a part of the zoological matrix, he becomes subject to the laws of zoology, laws such as survival of the fittest, at which point the wild animal may fearlessly attack him. It does not know that the person has a doctorate or that he was the subject of a newspaper article. To the animal, here is just another type of gorilla on whom it may prey.

וְהַצַּדִּיקִים שֶׁאֵין צֶלֶם אֱלֹהִים מִסְתַּלֵּק מֵעַל פְּנֵיהֶם, כָּל חַיּוֹת רָעוֹת אִתְכַּפְיָין קַמַּיְיהוּ, כְּמוֹ שֶׁכָּתוּב בַּזֹּהַר (חלק א קצא, א) גַּבֵּי דָּנִיֵּאל בְּגוֹב אֲרָיוֹת.

But in the presence of the righteous, from whose visages the image of God never departs, all wild beasts are tame, as it is written in the *Zohar* (1:191a) **regarding Daniel in the lions' den.**

When a person is not a part of the framework to which animals relate, he is no longer their prey. Daniel did not need a special angel to be sent to protect him from the lions. His personality was sufficient in itself. Since he was clearly created in the image of God, the lions would not harm him. It is not that animals rationally understand such a thing, but their spiritual root knows that their mission does not pertain to such a person, that their mission concerns other things and other places.

וְאִם כֵּן, הַחוֹטֵא וְעוֹבֵר רְצוֹנוֹ יִתְבָּרֵךְ אֲפִילּוּ בַּעֲבֵירָה קַלָּה בִּשְׁעַת מַעֲשֶׂה - הוּא בְּתַכְלִית הָרִיחוּק מִקְּדוּשָּׁה הָעֶלְיוֹנָה, שֶׁהִיא יִחוּדוֹ וְאַחְדּוּתוֹ יִתְבָּרֵךְ, יוֹתֵר מִכׇּל בַּעֲלֵי חַיִּים הַטְּמֵאִים וּשְׁקָצִים וּרְמָשִׂים הַמּוּשְׁפָּעִים מִסִּטְרָא אָחֳרָא וּקְלִיפַּת עֲבוֹדָה זָרָה.

This being the case, one who sins and transgresses the will of God even with a minor transgression is, at that moment, at the furthest point from the supernal holiness, namely, God's unity and oneness, more so than all the impure animals, detestable things, and crawling creatures that receive their sustenance from the *sitra aḥara* and the *kelippa* of idolatry.

A sin is a disconnection from holiness, an attack on the oneness of God. Every sin is an act of idolatry, an act of rebellion, where a person casts off the yoke of Heaven and removes himself from the source of life. From this standpoint, there is no difference between a major or a minor rebellion, between an insignificant misdemeanor or a grave betrayal. When there is an act of rebellion, it makes no essential difference what the specific deed entails.

וּמַה שֶּׁפִּקּוּחַ נֶפֶשׁ דּוֹחֶה שְׁאָר עֲבֵירוֹת, וְגַם "יַעֲבוֹר וְאַל יֵהָרֵג",

Although we find that saving a life overrides other prohibitions, and also that one must **transgress** a prohibition **rather than be killed,** 16 Shevat

In essence, no distinction can be drawn between minor and major sins. But if that is so, why does saving a life override the Sabbath to the extent that one may desecrate the Sabbath or engage in other transgressions in order to save a life? If Sabbath may be overridden in certain cases, does this mean its desecration is not so stringent? If there can be no distinction between types of sin, why is it that for idolatry, forbidden sexual relations, and murder, the law is that one must choose death rather than commit the transgression, while for other sins, the rule is that one should transgress rather than be killed?[6]

הַיְינוּ כְּפֵירוּשׁ חֲכָמֵינוּ זַ"ל: אָמְרָה תוֹרָה, חַלֵּל עָלָיו שַׁבָּת אַחַת כְּדֵי שֶׁיִּשְׁמוֹר שַׁבָּתוֹת הַרְבֵּה (שבת קנא, ב, ויומא פה, ב),

this must be understood in light of our Sages' explanation that **"the Torah says: Desecrate one Sabbath on his behalf so that he will observe many Sabbaths"** (*Shabbat* 151b; *Yoma* 85b)

Saving someone's life overrides the Sabbath, not because violating the Sabbath is not as important as saving a human life but because in the long term the Sabbath itself profits, as it were. If a person were to die because the Sabbath could not be violated on his behalf, he would not be able to keep many future Sabbaths. This is not a comparison of the worth of one commandment with that of another, but the calculation of the gain and loss with regard to a specific mitzva. If the holiness of the Sabbath had not been desecrated on his behalf this one time, many future Sabbaths will not be sanctified by him.

וְלֹא מִשּׁוּם קַלּוּת הָעֲבֵירוֹת וְחוּמְרָן

and not in terms of the leniency or stringency of the relevant **prohibitions.**

The reason that one should commit certain sins rather than give up one's life, while one should choose death rather than commit certain other sins, is not that there are minor and major sins. There is no objective scale for the relative severity of sins. There are only calculations that at times justify committing a certain sin for a certain purpose and at other times do not justify transgressing. But these calculations have

6. It is matter of debate among the halakhic authorities whether one is absolutely obligated to transgress a prohibition rather than be killed or if is it merely an option, so that should one decide to give up his life rather than transgress, he is permitted to do so. See the Lubavitcher Rebbe, Rabbi Menaḥem Mendel Schneerson, *Iggerot Kodesh*, vol. 1, letter 165.

no connection to the essential nature of the sin. Each sin is inherently as serious as idolatry.

[תֵּדַע שֶׁהֲרֵי שַׁבָּת חֲמוּרָה וּשְׁקוּלָה כַּעֲבוֹדָה זָרָה לְעִנְיַן שְׁחִיטַת מוּמָר לְדָבָר אֶחָד, בְּיוֹרֶה דֵּעָה סִימָן ב׳,

(**Know** that this is true, **because** desecration of **the Sabbath is a severe violation and tantamount to idolatry with regard to the** halakhic status of **ritual slaughter performed by one who habitually violates one particular** Torah **precept,** as stated **in** *Shulḥan Arukh*, ***Yoreh De'a* 2.**

An animal that is ritually slaughtered by a person who rejects the entire Torah is not kosher, and it is just as if it had been slaughtered by a gentile. What if a person acts as a gentile regarding just one commandment? In that case, his ritual slaughter is kosher. However, there is an exception: If the one sin he commits involves either the public desecration of the Sabbath or idolatry, such a person is considered like one who has rejected the entire Torah. Though he may fulfill all the other mitzvot, he is regarded as an apostate, and his ritual slaughter is regarded as if it were performed by a gentile.

מַה שֶּׁאֵין כֵּן בְּמוּמָר לְגִילּוּי עֲרָיוֹת,

This is not the case concerning one who habitually violates prohibitions against illicit relations.

A person who transgresses the laws of prohibited sexual relations commits a grave transgression, regarding which one must choose death rather than sin. Yet this sin in itself is not sufficient to place him in the category of a person who has rejected the entire Torah and whose ritual slaughter is not kosher.

וַאֲפִילוּ הָכִי, פִּיקּוּחַ נֶפֶשׁ דּוֹחֶה שַׁבָּת וְלֹא גִּילּוּי עֲרָיוֹת.

Yet, nevertheless, *halakha* dictates that **saving a life overrides the Sabbath but not the prohibitions against illicit relations.**

The desecration of the Sabbath is more egregious with regard to ritual slaughter than the sin of illicit relations, yet the Sabbath prohibitions may be overridden to save a life. We see that there is no single scale for determining the relative gravity of sins. With regard to defining a person as an apostate, one who is no longer considered a member of the Jewish community and who has rebelled against God, violating the Sabbath is literally as grave as idolatry, and it is worse than illicit relations. But in another respect, illicit relations are more severe: One can violate the Sabbath to save someone's life, whereas one cannot engage in illicit relations for this purpose. It is clear that the legal distinctions between sins is not connected with the relative leniency or gravity of the sin.

אֶלָּא דִּגְזֵירַת הַכָּתוּב הוּא.]

Rather, it is only **because of a Torah edict** that the prohibitions against illicit relations cannot be overridden to save a life.)

ESTIMATING THE VALUE OF MITZVOT

☞ We cannot categorize sins by their relative importance. They are all equally serious, because each is an expression of rebellion against the Divine. The difference between them, when one should or should not commit a transgression, depends on other factors, such as the directive to "desecrate one Sabbath on his behalf so that he will observe many Sabbaths."

When taking into account these factors, we differentiate not only between one sin and another (for example, between Sabbath desecration and idolatry) but also between different circumstances with regard to the same sin. For instance, there have been times when Jews were forced to transgress the Sabbath and eat non-kosher food in order to survive. In such cases, we say, "Let him transgress and not be killed." But during a time when Jews are persecuted for their faith, and the gentile nation's intent is to force the Jew to abandon his faith, the Jew must choose death rather than transgress. In such circumstances, it makes no difference which sin is at issue. Every sin is a proclamation of rebellion, a statement of lack of faith in God, whether it is an act of idolatry, Sabbath desecration, or even violating a Jewish custom. Even if it is something as minor as how a sandal strap is fastened, where a proper Jewish custom is involved and one is commanded to change it in order to appear similar to gentiles, one must be ready to die rather than transgress (*Sanhedrin* 74b). At a time of forced conversion, one may not transgress any sin, no matter what its nature. At such a time, any act that a person commits in order to cast off the yoke of the kingdom of Heaven and accept a different master is a denial of God, and so "that person shall be excised from among his people" (Num. 15:30).

The author of the *Tanya* suggests a resolution to the apparent inconsistencies with regard to the various *halakhot* mentioned. He posits that the reason one should choose death rather than commit illicit relations is not by virtue of the egregiousness of adultery in relation to other prohibitions. Essentially, no distinctions are made between prohibitions, since each transgression constitutes a spiritual death of sorts, and a Jew must feel that he is going to die by transgressing a particular prohibition. Rather, the distinctions made in these *halakhot* are a result of a biblical decree, beyond human logic. ☞

אֶלָּא שֶׁלְּאַחַר מַעֲשֵׂה הַחֵטְא, **However, after the sin has been committed,**

The differences that nonetheless exist between various types of sins may be considered after the sin has been committed. Before that, when a person is on the verge of committing a sin, he faces a choice: Is he for God or against Him? If he is against God, he is rebelling against God's sovereignty at that moment, and it makes no difference whether his rebellion is big or small. There are situations, as in wartime, when people are killed for the most minor offenses. If a person does not acknowledge a password, if he disobeys an order, he is shot, regardless of whether he had a reason for his action or not. No one will give him a hearing, and the question of extenuating circumstances is of no interest to anyone. There is no room for flexibility, no place to distinguish between a major and a minor misdeed, between one person and another. Everyone must be completely alert and totally responsible, because any deviation will result in the collapse of the entire system. In such a situation, the system itself acts as judge and jury.

If the offender was not summarily punished, then after the fact, when the war is over, he is court-martialed. He is entitled to defend himself, and the court will determine his guilt or innocence based on the circumstances of the case. In this sense, when a person is about to sin, when he is in the midst of the battle, he faces one question only: What side am I on? Am I connected to holiness or to *kelippa*? Here there is no middle ground, no rationalization of minor and major. But after the sin has been committed, when the individual is no longer transgressing, there is room to distinguish between one sin and another.

אִם הִיא מֵעֲבֵירוֹת שֶׁאֵין בָּהֶן כָּרֵת וּמִיתָה בִּידֵי שָׁמַיִם, שֶׁאֵין נַפְשׁוֹ הָאֱלֹהִית מֵתָה לְגַמְרֵי וְנִכְרֶתֶת מִשָּׁרְשָׁהּ בֵּאלֹהִים חַיִּים, רַק שֶׁנִּפְגַּם קְצָת דְּבֵיקוּתָהּ וַאֲחִיזָתָהּ בְּשָׁרְשָׁהּ בְּחֵטְא זֶה,

if it was one of the transgressions that incurs neither *karet* nor death at the hand of Heaven, in which case his divine soul does not die completely nor is utterly **severed from its root in the living God, but rather its connection and attachment to its source has been slightly damaged by this sin,** then the animal soul can still elevate itself and connect with the Divine.

With every sin that a person commits, he severs the connection between himself and God. There are certain grave sins for which the punishment is *karet* – excision from the World to Come or premature death – and death at the hand of Heaven, because by committing such transgressions one causes a total disconnection. Other sins cut off only a part of that connection.

In *Iggeret HaTeshuva*,[7] the author of the *Tanya* offers a parable based on the verse "For the portion of the Lord is His people; Jacob, the allotment [*ḥevel*] of His inheritance" (Deut. 32:9). The word *ḥevel* can also mean cord. There is a cord, much like an umbilical cord, that connects a person to the source of life.[8] That rope is woven of 613 strands, corresponding to the 613 commandments. If a person commits a sin, he cuts one strand. If he commits a few sins, he cuts more strands. But if he transgresses a prohibition punishable by *karet*, he cuts the entire cord and excises himself from his life force, from the silver cord that draws down holiness and life from above.

Consequently, sins differ considerably with regard to the nature of the damage caused by the act and the manner of its rectification, and it is important to know which strands have been cut and which must be reconnected, whether the connection is only damaged or entirely severed.

---

7. Chap. 5.

8. Ecclesiastes offers a similar image describing the end of life: "Before the silver cord is severed..." (Eccles. 12:6).

הַגָּהָה: וּלְפִי עֵרֶךְ וְחִלּוּקֵי בְּחִינַת הַפְּגָם בַּנֶּפֶשׁ **Gloss: Corresponding to the degree and distinction between various types of blemishes in the soul**

Once a sin has been committed, it is possible to make distinctions about its nature. A sin that incurs *karet* or death by the hand of Heaven indicates that the sin was such that the perpetrator's soul becomes completely severed from its divine source. On the other hand, there are sins that do not cause a complete severance, but only a slight nick in the cord connecting the soul to its divine source. The question is, why is this information necessary after the fact? What difference does it make to know the severity of a sin and the damage it incurred once it already happened?

Here the author of the *Tanya* will explain that this information is imperative in order for the person who committed the act to know how to make his way back to his pristine original state. The ability to rectify one's ways and return is only possible when a person knows how far he strayed.

וּבְשָׁרְשָׁהּ בָּעֶלְיוֹנִים, **and in its root in the higher worlds**

Every transgression damages the soul. Because each mitzva corresponds to a particular limb, each transgression damages that limb and the corresponding part of the soul. Moreover, the transgression not only damages the soul in the body but also the root of the soul in the higher realms. The transgression affects the entire framework of the worlds, from the loftiest heights to the lowest depths. The nature and force of that impact depends on the nature of the transgression.

כָּךְ הֵם חִלּוּקֵי בְּחִינוֹת הַמֵּירוּק וְהָעוֹנֶשׁ בַּגֵּיהִנֹּם אוֹ בָּעוֹלָם הַזֶּה, לְכָל עָוֹן וְחֵטְא עוֹנֶשׁ מְיוּחָד לְמָרֵק וּלְהַעֲבִיר הַלִּכְלוּךְ וְהַפְּגָם. **are the various types of scouring and punishments** that the soul must undergo either **in Gehenna or in this world. For each category of iniquity or sin, there is a specific punishment** the soul must undergo **in order to scour and remove the filth and blemish.**

Just as each physical disease causes a different type of physical damage, and each has its specific remedy (though some medicines can treat a number of related illnesses), so too regarding spiritual illnesses, the rectification for one transgression is not the same as that for another.

וְכֵן בְּחַיָּיבֵי מִיתָה וְכָרֵת - אֵין פּוֹגְמִין כּוּלָּם בְּשָׁוֶה.

Similarly, those sins **that are liable for death** by the hand of Heaven **or** by ***karet*** **do not inflict equal** degrees of **damage** to the soul.

As the author of the *Tanya* explains in *Iggeret HaTeshuva*,[9] even if a person has committed a sin punishable by *karet*, the disconnection does not occur immediately. If it did, the person would die at that instant. In actuality, there is a delay during which he continues to live. Because the "impression" of the divine soul still remains, one can continue living for as many as fifty or sixty years. In light of this, even if a person has committed a transgression and damaged his soul, even if he has polluted and contaminated it, and even if he has severed it from its source of life, he can still reattach himself to God. Though his descent has been unfathomably deep, his soul can return and recreate the connection that has been lost. As long as a person is alive, he can renew his connection with the living God.

הֲרֵי גַּם נַפְשׁוֹ הַחִיּוּנִית הַבַּהֲמִית הַמְלוּבֶּשֶׁת בְּגוּפוֹ, וְכֵן גּוּפוֹ - חוֹזְרִים וְעוֹלִים מֵהַסִּטְרָא אָחֳרָא וּקְלִיפָּה זוֹ, וּמִתְקָרְבִים לִקְדוּשַּׁת נֶפֶשׁ הָאֱלֹהִית הַמְלוּבֶּשֶׁת בָּהֶם הַמַּאֲמִינָה בַּה' אֶחָד.

If one has not committed a sin that incurs *karet* or death by the hand of Heaven, **then,** after he repents, **both his vital animal soul, which is clothed within his body, as well as his body** itself, **return and ascend from this *sitra aḥara* and *kelippa* and draw closer to the holiness of the divine soul that is clothed in them and believes in the one God.**

When a person commits a sin, he is situated within *kelippa*, gives expression to *kelippa*, and channels life force to the powers of evil. But after the fact, when he disconnects from the sin, and certainly after he repents completely, his animal soul and body return to the holiness of the divine soul.

9. Chap. 4.

This process must be seen within a matrix of four dimensions – the three spatial dimensions and time. At the time of the sin's commission, at a certain point of time within this matrix, the sinner is completely disconnected from God and is a part of the other side, the *sitra aḥara*. This point remains as a stain both within his own existence and within the world's existence. At the next juncture, in the coming moment, he returns to his original state, to the side of life, perhaps as a fine, honest, and even holy person.

Even at the moment the sin was committed, the divine soul **remained faithful to God,**

וְגַם בִּשְׁעַת הַחֵטְא הָיְתָה בְּאֱמוּנָה אִתּוֹ יִתְבָּרֵךְ,

The divine soul within a person never strays. It is the point at which God may be found within every person. Whatever one does, even while committing a transgression, one cannot remove this single point in which God resides.

only it was in an actual state of exile in the animal soul, which stems **from the *sitra aḥara* that causes the body to sin and drags it down with it into the abyss of the netherworld,**

רַק שֶׁהָיְתָה בִּבְחִינַת גָּלוּת מַמָּשׁ תּוֹךְ נֶפֶשׁ הַבַּהֲמִית מִסִּטְרָא אָחֳרָא הַמַּחֲטִיאָה אֶת הַגּוּף וּמוֹרִידָתוֹ עִמָּהּ בְּעִמְקֵי שְׁאוֹל,

We cannot say that only a part of a person performs a mitzva or commits a sin. The divine soul is a part of the person, and when a person sins, the divine soul is forced, as it were, to participate in that sin. Thus, even the core of the soul that believes in the one God is dragged along, against its will, together with the other parts of the soul. Exiled, concealed, faint, semiconscious, it descends with the animal soul, with the body, to the depths of the netherworld.

to the deepest depths, even **lower than the impurity of the *sitra aḥara* and the *kelippa* of idolatry, may God protect us.**

לְמַטָּה מַטָּה תַּחַת טוּמְאַת הַסִּטְרָא אָחֳרָא וּקְלִיפַּת עֲבוֹדָה זָרָה, ה׳ יִשְׁמְרֵנוּ.

As mentioned above, the powers of evil in and of themselves, and even idolatry, are not as debased as the person committing a transgression.

Even the *kelippa* of idolatry knows that it is not an independent entity. It knows that there is a "God of gods," and it never goes so far as to rebel against Him. But a sinner, who rebels against God, not only joins the side of evil, he even outdoes it. He descends even lower than the depths of the impurity itself.

וְאֵין לְךָ גָּלוּת גָּדוֹל מִזֶּה "מֵאִיגְּרָא רָמָה" כו' וּכְמוֹ שֶׁנִּתְבָּאֵר לְעֵיל דְּשֹׁרֶשׁ וּמְקוֹר נַפְשׁוֹת כָּל בֵּית יִשְׂרָאֵל הוּא מֵחָכְמָה עִילָּאָה, וְהוּא יִתְבָּרֵךְ וְחָכְמָתוֹ אֶחָד וכו',

You do not find an exile of greater magnitude than this, which entails a descent **from a high roof** to a deep pit. **As was explained above** (chap. 2), **the root and source of all the souls of the Jewish people stems from** God's **supernal wisdom, and God and His wisdom are one** and the same, **and so forth.**

Within the divine soul, the wisdom of God reveals itself, and within that wisdom, the very light of *Ein Sof* is revealed. When a person sins, he takes the spark of his soul in which the light of *Ein Sof* is revealed, in which he identifies with God, and drags it down with the body into the sin.

וְהוּא כִּמְשַׁל הָאוֹחֵז בְּרֹאשׁוֹ שֶׁל מֶלֶךְ וּמוֹרִידוֹ לְמַטָּה וְטוֹמֵן פָּנָיו בְּתוֹךְ בֵּית הַכִּסֵּא מָלֵא צוֹאָה שֶׁאֵין לְךָ עֶלְבּוֹן גָּדוֹל מִזֶּה,

This sinful act **is analogous to one who grabs the king's head, pushes it down, and buries it in a latrine full of excrement, the ultimate disgrace,**

The sin not only disgraces the sinner, but it also disgraces God. The divine soul is not only a part of the world, one of God's servants doing His will, but an extension of God Himself. When a person sins, it is as if he pulls God down and forces Him, as it were, to participate in the sin. The outrage, whether for the one causing shame or for the One being shamed, is the greatest possible.

אֲפִילּוּ עוֹשֶׂה כֵּן לְפִי שָׁעָה,

even if he does this only **for a moment,**

Even if one does not drag down the head of the king continuously but only from time to time, when his evil disposition overpowers him, once a day or once a month, that does not mitigate the disgrace. Since the outrage is so great, nothing can excuse, explain, or alleviate it. Here the nature of the sin, whether it is of greater or smaller measure, whether significant or insignificant, is of no relevance. Every sin, at any time, to any degree, and in every situation, is an unparalleled disgrace.

שֶׁהַקְּלִיפּוֹת וְסִטְרָא אָחֳרָא נִקְרָאוֹת "קִיא צוֹאָה" כַּנּוֹדָע.

for the *kelippot* and *sitra aḥara* are referred to as "vomit and excrement," as is known.

These terms used to refer to *kelippa* and *sitra aḥara*[10] are the terms we use to define waste products of higher levels of existence, the excrescence of digestion, that which could not undergo the process of assimilation. In this sense, the *kelippot* are the remnants of higher realities. Parts of our world can rise and be assimilated into holiness, and other parts cannot be absorbed, and it is to there that a person drags down the holiness of God when he commits a transgression.

In a previous chapter,[11] the author of the *Tanya* stated that the first two of the Ten Commandments, "I am God" and "You shall have no other gods," comprise the entirety of the Torah. They are the axis around which the sum total of Jewish life revolves. Just as every positive commandment expresses the concept that "I am the Lord your God," so too every transgression violates the prohibition "You shall have no other gods." Essentially, every sin is an act of idolatry.

In this chapter, the author described how every sin causes disconnection from the one God. Every sin is comparable to idolatry, which drags down the body and the animal soul and, with them, the divine soul and the divine spark within man, until they are lower than *kelippa* and the *sitra aĥara* themselves.

Yet it is precisely because every sin is comparable to idolatry that the hidden love that exists within every Jew may be revealed. With the revelation of this love, every Jew has the strength to sacrifice not only a passing pleasure but life in this world in its entirety, to sacrifice his own

---

10. Based on Isa. 28:8; *Zohar* 2:154a–b.
11. Chap. 20.

life. This has occurred time after time when Jews, wherever they were, accepted martyrdom, not from deep insight or elevated sensibility but out of a clear awareness that they could not allow themselves to be separated from the living God.

Chapter 25

IN THE PREVIOUS CHAPTERS, THE AUTHOR OF THE *Tanya* discussed two aspects of the commandments: attachment to the Divine as a result of performing the positive commandments and severance from the Divine as a result of violating prohibitions. Both aspects essentially express the same idea: that the commandments are not only details and that their observance is not merely a question of good deeds or bad deeds. Rather, they embody our entire relationship with God: Are we for or against Him?

At the end of the previous chapter, the author of the *Tanya* connected this concept to the concealed love inherent in every Jew. This refers to a love so potent that it empowers one to cleave to God and never become separated from Him, even at the cost of sacrificing his very life. In this chapter, the author of the *Tanya* develops this idea into a methodical approach to divine service.

Though this love exists within every Jew, it is latent. At the same time, a person is constantly challenged by a spirit of folly driven by other forces and passions that are active within his soul. To overcome these counterforces and uncover one's concealed love for God through Torah study and the performance of mitzvot, one must wage war against these forces. Precisely how to do so and how to emerge victorious are the subjects of this chapter.

וְזֶהוּ שֶׁכָּתוּב: "כִּי קָרוֹב אֵלֶיךָ הַדָּבָר מְאֹד" וגו' (דברים ל, יד), שֶׁבְּכָל עֵת וּבְכָל שָׁעָה בְּיָדוֹ שֶׁל

This is the meaning of the verse "Rather, the matter is very near to you..." (Deut. 30:14): **that at any**

17 Shevat / 25 Shevat (leap year)

אָדָם וּבִרְשׁוּתוֹ הוּא לְהַעֲבִיר רוּחַ שְׁטוּת וְהַשִּׁכְחָה מִקִּרְבּוֹ, וְלִזְכּוֹר וּלְעוֹרֵר אַהֲבָתוֹ לַה' אֶחָד, הַמְסוּתֶּרֶת בְּוַדַּאי בְּלִבָּבוֹ בְּלִי שׁוּם סָפֵק. וְזֶהוּ שֶׁכָּתוּב: "וּבִלְבָבְךָ" (שם).

given moment a person is capable of removing the spirit of folly and forgetfulness from within him so that he may remember and rouse his love for the one God that is certainly concealed in his heart, without a shadow of a doubt. This is the meaning of the continuation of **the verse "and in your heart."**

The author of the *Tanya* is not referring here to the love that is evoked when one contemplates God's greatness, because that love is not equally accessible to all, nor is it available at all times. Rather, when put to the test, every Jew clearly demonstrates that he possesses a constant, innate love for God that enables him to overcome the spirit of folly that attempts to thwart his divine service. Even if he ordinarily cannot rouse this love, even if he cannot express it in his thoughts and in his feelings, even if a sword must be pressed against his throat before he can feel anything, that love is always present. As the verse continues, it is "in your mouth and in your heart, to perform it."

Beyond the feelings that a person is aware of, he possesses an inner readiness, which entertains no doubts, to bring this love into actual expression. In one way or another, it is "in your heart" in truth and not the product of the imagination.

וְנִכְלָל בָּהּ גַּם דְּחִילוּ, דְּהַיְינוּ שֶׁלֹּא לִיפָּרֵד בְּשׁוּם אוֹפֶן מִיִּחוּדוֹ וְאַחְדּוּתוֹ יִתְבָּרֵךְ אֲפִילוּ בִּמְסִירַת נֶפֶשׁ מַמָּשׁ

Encompassed in this hidden love **is also fear, that is, that one should not become separated, by any means, from God's unity and oneness, even** if it means **literally giving up one's life**

The love of God, whether it is concealed or revealed, is the desire and the ability to cling to God. This love encompasses the awe of God, that is, the fear of losing one's connection with God, the object of this love.[1] The love of God gives man the strength to refrain from transgressing,

1. See also *Sha'ar HaYiḥud VeHa'emuna*, chap. 6.

because it inspires a person to sanctify God's name, even if it means that he must pay the ultimate price.

בְּלִי שׁוּם טַעַם וְשֵׂכֶל מוּשָּׂג, אֶלָּא בְּטֶבַע אֱלֹהִי.

without any reason or logic but rather by virtue of one's divine nature.

When a person engages in such self-sacrifice, he himself might not know why he does so. The power behind this self-sacrifice does not flow from his rational mind. He is not acting from his own capacity but from the divine force within him, even if he is completely unaware of it.

וְכָל שֶׁכֵּן בִּשְׁבִירַת הַתַּאֲווֹת, הַקַּלָּה מִיסּוּרֵי מִיתָה,

All the more so with regard to subduing one's lusts, which entails lighter **suffering than the torments of death,**

Because a person has the strength to refuse to commit a sin even at the cost of his life, he certainly has the strength to resist all of life's other temptations, because nothing can be as terrible as the threat of death and nothing as seductive as the will to live.

שֶׁקָּרוֹב אֵלָיו הַדָּבָר יוֹתֵר לִכְבּוֹשׁ הַיֵּצֶר, הֵן בִּבְחִינַת 'סוּר מֵרָע' אֲפִילוּ מֵעֲבֵירָה קַלָּה שֶׁל דִּבְרֵי סוֹפְרִים, שֶׁלֹּא לַעֲבוֹר עַל רְצוֹנוֹ יִתְבָּרֵךְ מֵאַחַר שֶׁנִּפְרָד בָּהּ מִיִּחוּדוֹ וְאַחְדוּתוֹ כְּמוֹ בַּעֲבוֹדָה זָרָה מַמָּשׁ בִּשְׁעַת מַעֲשֶׂה.

it is easier to subjugate one's evil **inclination, to turn away from evil, even** from violating **a minor prohibition of rabbinic origin, in order to not transgress the will of God, since at that moment** that he commits a transgression **he is separated from God's unity and oneness, as if** he **literally** committed **idolatry.**

The difference between various transgressions is meaningful only after they have been committed, not at the time of the act itself. At that moment, every sin, no matter what it is, constitutes disloyalty toward God. Whether the person has transgressed a biblical prohibition or a rabbinic edict, his action contradicts the divine will. If he has failed to fulfill a mitzva because he had no desire to do so, whether he lacked the will or the ability, he has made the choice as to which side he belongs. If his decision is not to stand with God, then the details of his failure are irrelevant. At that moment, he has sunk far lower than any impure *kelippa*.

וַהֲרֵי גַּם בַּעֲבוֹדָה זָרָה יָכוֹל לַעֲשׂוֹת תְּשׁוּבָה אַחַר כָּךְ.

In truth, **one can subsequently repent for** the sin of **idolatry as well.**

After the fact, a person can repent and rectify his misdeeds, whatever their nature. In light of this, a person might tell himself from the outset that even were he to sin, he would not be completely cut off from God because afterward he could atone for it. In a certain sense, the possibility of sin is predicated on the assumption that one will have the opportunity to repent later. From this perspective, even idolatry is not substantially different from any other sin.

In the final analysis, no sin precludes the possibility of repentance. It makes no difference whether a person decides to violate a seemingly minor rabbinic enactment or to worship an idol. He might conclude that in either case he will not suffer complete and absolute disconnection from the Divine even if he decides from the outset to sin.

26 Shevat (leap year)

וְאַף שֶׁהָאוֹמֵר: 'אֶחֱטָא וְאָשׁוּב' - אֵין מַסְפִּיקִין כו' (יומא פרק ח משנה ט), הַיְינוּ שֶׁאֵין מַחֲזִיקִים יָדוֹ לִהְיוֹת לוֹ שְׁעַת הַכּוֹשֶׁר לַעֲשׂוֹת תְּשׁוּבָה.

Though the Mishna states regarding **one who says, "I will sin and** then **I will repent,"** that "Heaven **does not provide** him **the opportunity** to repent" (*Yoma* 8:9), **this** merely **means that they do not provide him an opportune occasion to repent.**

Some sins, such as idolatry, obviously sever the link between a person and God, and a person could commit such a sin only by explicitly telling himself that afterward he will repent. But such a strategy apparently would not be effective since the Sages state that if a person sins with such a plan in mind, he should not rely on his intention to atone for it afterward. Yet the author of the *Tanya* tells us that the Sages do not mean to say that the person will find it impossible to repent. Rather, he is not provided the opportunity to repent.

Generally speaking, after a person sins, he is given the proper circumstances, whether it his environs or his spirits, that inspire him to repent. But if a person decided to sin from the outset, relying on the fact that he will atone for it afterward, he is not provided such opportunities. ☞

אֲבָל אִם דָּחַק הַשָּׁעָה וְעָשָׂה תְּשׁוּבָה - אֵין לְךָ דָּבָר שֶׁעוֹמֵד בִּפְנֵי הַתְּשׁוּבָה.

But if he forces the moment and repents, nothing stands in the way of repentance.

NO OPPORTUNITY TO REPENT

☞ When a person decides that he will sin and afterward repent, he makes the assumption that he will have the time to do so. Because he is always sure that he will have time to repent in the future, he will always see himself as having the chance to commit another minor transgression in the meantime. The very assumption that he will be able to repent after he sins prevents him from repenting.

We can understand this behavior by comparing a time in a person's life when everything seems possible, and as a result, he does nothing. Because he knows that the door of opportunity is always open, he never bothers to walk through it.

But if, after having committed a sin, a person is so upset that he cannot look at himself in the mirror, if he feels that he cannot continue to live with himself, then he has no time to commit another transgression. He feels that he must atone this instant. He feels that he has been flung deep into the abyss from which he cannot climb out, that he does not know how he will go on. Because he feels this way, he will seek any crack, even one as small as the eye of a needle, and seize the opportunity to repent.

Another implication of this idea is mentioned in several places in the name of the Ba'al Shem Tov (see *Toledot Yaakov Yosef, Parashat Aḥarei Mot*). The penitent has the possibility of repentance when he is on a higher level of consciousness than he was at the time he committed the sin. Because he now knows what he did not know earlier, he can evaluate his misdeed, and then, as it were, he can retrieve the situation in which he sinned and recreate the original events as if the sin had not occurred.

For instance, let us say that a person unwittingly committed a transgression – for example, because he overslept. When he awakes, his consciousness is at a higher level, having emerged from his slumbering state. A person who sinned unwittingly did so because he lacked certain necessary information. Once he has acquired that knowledge, he can repent. Even if a person deliberately sinned, he nevertheless gains the new knowledge of the possibility of repentance. But when a person commits a sin with the intent to repent afterward, his state of awareness is no higher after sinning than it was before. When he transgressed, he knew that what he was doing was wrong and he was aware of the power of repentance. He had already then arrived at the highest level of awareness, as it were, that he cannot afterward surpass in order to repent.

If a person decides to sin and afterward repent, he is not provided with the opportunities to do so. Nevertheless, if he is unyielding and does repent, that repentance is authentic.

It follows that a person can repent not only for presumably minor transgressions but even for a sin as grave as idolatry. Even if he said, "I will sin, and then I will repent," so that he was not provided with favorable circumstances to do so, he can still genuinely repent. It makes no actual difference whether a person has committed a minor sin and still feels that he is a good Jew or whether he has engaged in idolatry and realizes that he is separated from God.

וְאַף עַל פִּי כֵן, כָּל אִישׁ יִשְׂרָאֵל מוּכָן וּמְזוּמָּן לִמְסוֹר נַפְשׁוֹ עַל קְדוּשַּׁת ה׳, שֶׁלֹּא לְהִשְׁתַּחֲווֹת לַעֲבוֹדָה זָרָה אֲפִילוּ לְפִי שָׁעָה וְלַעֲשׂוֹת תְּשׁוּבָה אַחַר כָּךְ.

Despite this, every Jew is ready and willing to give up his life for the sake of sanctifying God's name rather than prostrate himself before an idol even for a moment with the intention of repenting afterward.

Although a person can repent for any sin, no matter how vile and depraved, there are some sins a Jew will never commit, not even with the knowledge of the possibility of repentance. At the moment of the sin, he would be like an actual apostate, cut off from God, and his concealed love of the Divine cannot allow him to be separated from God for even a moment.

וְהַיְינוּ מִפְּנֵי אוֹר ה׳ הַמְלוּבָּשׁ בְּנַפְשָׁם כַּנִּזְכָּר לְעֵיל, שֶׁאֵינוֹ בִּבְחִינַת זְמַן וְשָׁעָה כְּלָל אֶלָּא לְמַעְלָה מֵהַזְּמַן, וְשַׁלִּיט וּמוֹשֵׁל עָלָיו כַּנּוֹדָע.

This is on account of God's light that is clothed within their souls, as explained above (chap. 19). This light **is not bound by the realm of time at all, but rather transcends time and** even **controls and governs it, as is well known.**

The reality in which we live is bound by time, and likewise, both mitzvot and transgressions are committed within the bounds of time. A person can sin, telling himself that later he will repent, because he assumes that afterward he will have the time to do so. But certain deeds, certain circumstances, are such that the question of what will happen later loses all meaning. When a person must choose whether or not to commit idolatry, when the question is whether he is with or against God, at that moment all the garments covering his soul fall away and the reality that he faces is illuminated by the light of *Ein Sof* that had been clothed within him. At that moment, he faces a decision that transcends time, and the question of what will happen afterward does not concern him and has no meaning for him. ☞

TO LIVE WITH SELF-SACRIFICE

☞ Almost every sophisticated instrument contains an override device. When this device is activated, usually in the face of danger, it takes control of the entire instrument and all its systems, stopping all operations,, breaking its contacts, and initiating a completely different procedure.

We find the same phenomenon at work almost everywhere in nature. Most animals are triggered by certain highly important cues to react in certain ways, to adopt a different order of priorities and a completely different set of reactions and responses. A wolf, due to training, nature, or instinct, would not ordinarily attack a grizzly bear. But if the bear threatens the wolf's pups, the override system in the wolf's brain is triggered, and the wolf now attacks. A higher order of priorities has taken over, and everything that the wolf has known or been accustomed to in its life is forgotten and is no longer taken into account.

This phenomenon is particularly dramatic in domesticated animals. Despite years (and sometimes generations) of training, a tame dog can, if its puppies are threatened, suddenly revert to a feral ferocity reminiscent of its wild ancestors. Such override mechanisms exist even in human beings, who rely on instinct less than animals do. If a mother sees that her child is in danger, she is capable of extraordinary feats of strength and heroism, which would ordinarily have been completely beyond her capabilities and, if viewed rationally, would have seemed impossible.

Every Jew reacts in the same nonrational way, with the same unleashed strength, when faced with the challenge of sanctifying God's name. A person makes his way in the world directed by a complex combination of education, dreams, drives, and free will. All these lead him on until, step by step, he may find himself in the deepest abyss. Yet at any moment, if he senses the trigger "You are abandoning the one God!" – all his normal mechanisms, all that he knew, all that he thought, all that he felt, all that he was taught, shut down, and he begins to act on a totally different and nonrational plane. The new mechanism that now impels him is not rational. It does not contrast the reward for a mitzva against the punishment for a sin, because his considerations do not take the future into account. In this realm, a person cannot say, "In a half hour, I will repent." There is no other time than this moment in which one must make a crucial decision.

This is the mechanism of self-sacrifice, with no other considerations, because if one were to engage in such considerations (*How serious? How painful? What will be tomorrow?*), one would never sacrifice his life for the sake of God's name.

18 Shevat
27 Shevat (leap year)

וְהֵן בִּבְחִינַת 'וַעֲשֵׂה טוֹב'

Likewise, this can be accomplished **by doing good,**

Until now, the author of the *Tanya* has discussed "turning away from evil," by using the ability concealed within oneself to sacrifice one's life rather than commit a transgression. The author now adds that this ability for self-sacrifice also exists with regard to doing good.

לְהִתְגַּבֵּר כַּאֲרִי בִּגְבוּרָה וְאוֹמֶץ הַלֵּב נֶגֶד הַיֵּצֶר הַמַּכְבִּיד אֶת גּוּפוֹ וּמַפִּיל עָלָיו עַצְלָה, מִבְּחִינַת יְסוֹד הֶעָפָר שֶׁבַּנֶּפֶשׁ הַבַּהֲמִית, מִלְּהַטְרִיחַ גּוּפוֹ בִּזְרִיזוּת בְּכָל מִינֵי טוֹרַח וַעֲבוֹדַת מַשָּׂא בַּעֲבוֹדַת ה' שֶׁיֵּשׁ בָּהּ טוֹרַח וְעָמָל,

by steeling oneself like a lion with might and a courageous heart against the evil **inclination, which encumbers his body and casts over him** a feeling of **laziness that stems from the element of earth in the animal soul** (see chap. 1). This laziness prevents **his body from enthusiastically expending all types of effort and labor in the service of God, which entails exertion and toil,**

Theoretically, this person could have taken that extreme step before. A person possesses rational free will throughout his life. Just as he is now prepared to sacrifice his life, he could have engaged in self-sacrifice in the past as well, even if less dramatically. Even as he pursued his desires, he hypothetically could have changed direction, but the other mechanisms in his life were too strong and did not allow him to realize this possibility.

At the other extreme, when this person is ready to give up his life for the sanctification of God's name rather than commit a certain sin, there still exists the theoretical possibility that he will decide not to sacrifice his life but commit the sin and repent afterward. Yet the mechanism of self-sacrifice that is now at work does not take this possibility into account. It acts with such great force that nothing can limit or stop it. In a sense, it takes away a person's free will and forces him to act in a certain way, even if that action contradicts his every rational consideration.

The superiority of this self-sacrifice mechanism, as the author of the *Tanya* states repeatedly, is not only its powerful and unfettered potency but the fact that it already exists in the soul and no training is necessary in order to acquire it. Training is required, however, in order to integrate self-sacrifice into one's daily life, in order to live by it and not just die by it. This can be compared to atomic energy. An atomic bomb can release all its energy in a split second, but to provide power on a functional basis, atomic energy must be controlled and channeled day by day. Here too the issue is how to channel the power of self-sacrifice into the decisions of daily life and learn to live with self-sacrifice for the sanctification of God's name.

Just as a person's evil inclination urges him to commit evil, so does it dissuade him from doing good. The same evil inclination that energizes him to act with the alacrity of a deer to commit sins weighs him down and removes his desire and enthusiasm for performing mitzvot.

כְּגוֹן לַעֲמוֹל בַּתּוֹרָה בְּעִיּוּן וּבַפֶּה, לָא פָּסִיק פּוּמֵיהּ מִגִּירְסָא, וְכַמַּאֲמַר רַבּוֹתֵינוּ זַ"ל: "לְעוֹלָם יָשִׂים אָדָם אֶת עַצְמוֹ עַל דִּבְרֵי תוֹרָה כְּשׁוֹר לְעוֹל וְכַחֲמוֹר לְמַשְּׂאוֹי" (עבודה זרה ה, ב).

such as toiling in Torah with in-depth study and orally so that one's mouth does not pause from Torah **study, in accordance with our Rabbis' statement "A person should always make himself** subjugated **to matters of Torah like an ox to a yoke and like a donkey to a burden"** (*Avoda Zara* 5b).

One does not always experience or sense the Divine that is manifest in the Torah he studies. He must study in any case, just as an ox pulls its load, guided by its yoke. The ox has no understanding as to the importance of its act of pulling. It simply does so with all its might because that is its duty; it is the will of its master.

Moreover, Torah study demands more than time. It requires diligence, perseverance, concentration, and vocalization of the words. Beyond ability and the amount of time that a person invests in his Torah study, he must have an intense relationship with it. If he devotes his mind and his entire being to acquiring the knowledge of the topics that he desires to study, the time he puts into his study will have a far greater value than it would otherwise. ☞

A MORE PROFOUND DEMAND

☞ The reader should keep in mind that this is the *Book of Beinonim*. The author of the *Tanya* does not discuss people whose struggles are in the realm between mitzva and sin, whether or not to violate the Sabbath or to commit adultery, for example. The author is well aware that such people exist, but he intentionally begins his discourse on a higher plane. He speaks of a person who performs mitzvot, who does not sin, and who engages in Torah study, but his Torah study is apathetic and his performance of mitzvot is bereft of meaning. In fact, this person's inner self may identify not with mitzvot but with sin.

In this book, the author of the *Tanya* demands repeatedly that such a person's relationship to the Torah and to God be much more profound and fiery. As the author of the *Tanya* states in his introduction,

וְכֵן לִתְפִלָּה בְּכַוָּנָה בְּכָל כֹּחוֹ מַמָּשׁ,

Likewise, with regard to **praying with intent,** one should pray **literally with all one's might,**

The ability to focus in prayer is generally connected with a person's desire to pray correctly and the amount of intentional effort that he invests, but sometimes this devotion and intensity occur spontaneously. When a person prays for something that matters deeply to him, or when he is intensely moved, his concentration is automatic and profound. In general, though, if a person does not exert himself to focus on his prayers, he will not be able to maintain his concentration.

The intensity in prayer that is demanded of us does not stem from the illumination that occasionally shines down from above but from the difficult work of focusing one's attention and harnessing all one's strength to concentrating on the words and their meaning. It is not enough to make an effort. A person must immerse his entire soul in prayer and disengage from everything else.

וְכֵן בַּעֲבוֹדַת ה' שֶׁהִיא בְּדָבָר שֶׁבְּמָמוֹן כְּמוֹ עֲבוֹדַת הַצְּדָקָה,

and also with regard to **serving God in monetary matters, such as the service** of giving **charity,**

Giving charity is not merely an act. It is categorized as "service," a part of one's divine service. When a person acts generously, with his actions or with his money, he is engaged in the difficult service of giving of himself.[2] ☞

this work is intended for readers whose souls yearn to serve God, who do not struggle against the "alien demons," the urges to openly transgress, but who struggle within the realm of Jewish practice, of divine service, that it should be entirely for the sake of Heaven in an authentic, intense, and powerful way.

2. Rabbi Shmuel Gronem Esterman points out that this is the third of a triad of divine services that fall under the rubric of "doing good" that the author of the *Tanya* mentions here: Torah study, prayer, and charity. See Mishna *Avot* 1:2, where these three facets of divine service are referred to as the three pillars.

וְכַיּוֹצֵא בָּאֵלּוּ מִמִּלְחֲמוֹת הַיֵּצֶר וְתַחְבּוּלוֹתָיו לְקָרֵר נֶפֶשׁ הָאָדָם שֶׁלֹּא לְהַפְקִיר מָמוֹנוֹ וּבְרִיאוּת גּוּפוֹ.

and similar matters where one must confront **battle tactics and stratagems employed by the** evil **inclination** intended **to cool** the passions of **a person's soul so that he will not forfeit his money and** sacrifice his **physical health.** 28 Shevat (leap year)

A person might not relish having to get up early and expose himself to the cold for the sake of attending morning services, after which he must study Torah and, in general, serve God with intensity and great spiritual tension, none of which contribute to his mental tranquility or physical well-being. The evil inclination uses these concerns to quench the fire of a person's love of God and desire to serve Him. Everyone experiences such struggles, in one form or another.

THE SERVICE OF GIVING CHARITY

☞ For the followers of the author of the *Tanya*, the service of giving charity was a significant act of devotion. The demand for generosity was not a matter of donating a small amount of money to charity, nor even contributing the normative 10 percent, nor even a generous 20 percent (the upper limit normally prescribed by Jewish law). As the author of the *Tanya* explains in *Iggeret HaTeshuva* (chap. 3), in addition to his normative obligation to give charity, if a person has sinned, he must give additional money as a substitute for the self-mortification and fasting that he would otherwise have to undergo. For this, no upper limit exists, because this type of charity is the equivalent of spending money on one's health, for which a person will pay whatever is necessary.

There was also a special category of charity earmarked for supporting the Jewish community in the Land of Israel. That too was in addition to the usual sum that the author of the *Tanya* and his followers set aside for charity. Besides that, as the author of the *Tanya* says elsewhere, all the limitations of how much one is allowed to spend on charity apply only when people's incomes are relatively equal. But when that is not the case, when some people enjoy luxury while others go hungry, then there is no limit to giving charity. Even though the great majority of hasidim in the author's day were terribly poor, they raised great sums of money for charity. If there was no money left to give, women would give away their household utensils, and bridegrooms would donate the dowries that their brides brought to the marriage.

We see that the author's requirements for charity are extremely rigorous and demand that a person train himself so strictly that he will even deprive himself of the basic necessities.

שֶׁלַּעֲמוֹד נֶגְדּוֹ וּלְכָבְשׁוֹ קָרוֹב מְאֹד אֶל הָאָדָם כְּשֶׁיָּשִׂים אֶל לִבּוֹ שֶׁלְּנַצֵּחַ הַיֵּצֶר בְּכָל זֶה, וְיוֹתֵר מִזֶּה וְלַעֲשׂוֹת הֶפְכּוֹ מַמָּשׁ, קַל מְאֹד מִיִּסּוּרֵי מִיתָה, ה' יִשְׁמְרֵנוּ.

It is very easy to oppose and subjugate one's evil inclination **when a person carefully considers that prevailing over the** evil **inclination in all these** instances, **and, moreover, actually acting in opposition** to this inclination, **entails much lighter suffering than the torments of death, may God protect us.**

A person should do more than remain indifferent to the advice of his evil inclination. When he feels tired and dejected, he must not only overcome these feelings and persist in his service to God, but he must increase his intensity and enthusiasm. All this is easier than suffering the torments of death.

וְיִסּוּרֵי מִיתָה, ה' יִשְׁמְרֵנוּ, הָיָה מְקַבֵּל בְּאַהֲבָה וּבְרָצוֹן שֶׁלֹּא לִיפָּרֵד מִיִּחוּדוֹ וְאַחְדּוּתוֹ יִתְבָּרַךְ, אֲפִילוּ לְפִי שָׁעָה, לְהִשְׁתַּחֲוֹת לַעֲבוֹדָה זָרָה חַס וְשָׁלוֹם. וְכָל שֶׁכֵּן שֶׁיֵּשׁ לוֹ לְקַבֵּל בְּאַהֲבָה וּבְרָצוֹן, כְּדֵי לְדָבְקָה בּוֹ לְעוֹלָם וָעֶד.

Yet one would lovingly and willingly accept upon himself **the torments of death, may God protect us, so as not to become separated from God's unity and oneness, even momentarily, by prostrating oneself before an idol, God forbid. All the more so should one have the ability to lovingly and willingly accept** upon himself to do the will of God **in order to cleave to God for eternity.**

We see that a person is prepared to give up his life, unfettered by any rational considerations, in order to sanctify God's name. Despite the loss, despite the fear, despite the terrible suffering it entails, he has the strength and spiritual capability to do this. If that is the case, then he certainly has the ability to apply that strength in other ways, such as carrying out God's will with fierce love and desire. As the author of the *Tanya* explained in previous chapters, the performance of the mitzvot and Torah study constitute an unequaled attachment to God. If a person is prepared to die rather than leave God for even a moment, how much more so does he have the strength to toil in the study of Torah and the performance of the mitzvot in order to cleave to Him in life.

דְּהַיְינוּ כְּשֶׁיַּעֲשֶׂה רְצוֹנוֹ יִתְבָּרֵךְ בַּעֲבוֹדָה זוֹ, יִתְגַּלֶּה בָּהּ פְּנִימִית רָצוֹן הָעֶלְיוֹן בִּבְחִינַת פָּנִים וְגִילּוּי רַב וְלֹא בְּהֶסְתֵּר כְּלָל.

That is, when one fulfills the will of God through this service of performing mitzvot with love, **the inner aspect of** God's **supernal will is profoundly revealed in** that service **internally, without any concealment whatsoever.**

God's inner will exists within the mitzvot. Thus, when one performs the will of God "through this service [of performing mitzvot with love]," this will is manifest with no obstructions whatsoever.

וּכְשֶׁאֵין שׁוּם הֶסְתֵּר פָּנִים בָּרָצוֹן הָעֶלְיוֹן, אֲזַי אֵין דָּבָר נִפְרָד כְּלָל וּכְלָל לִהְיוֹת יֵשׁ וְדָבָר בִּפְנֵי עַצְמוֹ.

When there is no concealment of countenance in God's **supernal will, then nothing is separated** from Him **in the slightest, having its own existence and substance.**

A mitzva cuts through the veil that obscures all the worlds. The structure of the worlds is built on levels, one beneath the other, one veil after the other, masking the Divine in ever more opaque concealments. This process of concealment makes possible the existence of the world, the *olam*, which itself connotes the *he'elam*, the concealment. The complex system of revelation and concealment, of concealment enfolded within concealment, makes up the existing framework of the universes and creates the delicate balance of this world's existence, hovering between concealment and revelation. Yet within this system, passing through all its levels of concealment, one transfer point is open on both sides: the doorway of the mitzvot. Here on earth, a person might not sense the divine revelation within a mitzva, but at the moment of its fulfillment, a person is no longer bound within the concealment of God's countenance. ☞

WINDOWS TO THE DIVINE

☞ Within all of existence, there is one positive point: the immanent divine essence. This is the point of true being that exists in all of reality as reality. Yet reality as we know it is one of concealment, composed of a multitude of *kelippot:* constriction, concealment, leaps between one world and another (a degree of descent that brings about another layer of detachment from the previous level to serve as a vehicle for concealment), and changes, all of which cloak this point of the original divine intent. As a result, the reality of this world cannot relate directly to the one who created it, and it is possible for a person to plumb the greatest depths of profundity yet never find God. The map of the world, its road signs, do not lead directly to that divine point. A distortion in the essence of creation, in the constriction of the divine light, in the existence of the forces of evil, prevents the world from directly proclaiming the glory of God. Granted, the verse states that "the heavens declare the glory of God" and "day to day gives utterance" (Ps. 19:2–3), but this does not mean that the creation itself reveals the Divine. Rather, the Divine is revealed through the prism of man's perception of the creation, a perception that can easily be clouded.

To reach that which lies beyond the world, its distortions must be rectified. Rabbi Naḥman's tale "The Prince and the Maidservant's Son" describes a country (the world) that needs to regain its original name, its pristine state before the constriction and concealment. To accomplish this, the prince in the story (who represents man) must arrange certain aspects of reality in order to remove the distortion, so that divine guidance (the heavenly throne or chariot) may manifest. After the prince transfers a number of items from one spot to another, they begin to sing a wondrous tune. The harmony of all the elements of the world returns, and the point of divine existence within them is revealed. Then everything sings of the glory of God. Everything is an instrument of divine revelation, of praise and glorification of the Divine.

When a person can see the undistorted relationships in our present world, when he can make his way directly to the Divine, he touches on a reality in which the forefathers are the chariot – a reality in which the forefathers intuitively fulfilled the entire Torah even before it was given. Of course, now that it has been given, we follow its directives rather than our intuitions, because the Torah contains the pattern of the rectified world. The Torah is the key, the map, in which reality appears as it should be, in which God Himself appears without the constriction and distortion of the created world.

As a rough analogy, a lock is built in a specific pattern. A good lock contains a row of teeth that are out of alignment, that are purposely "distorted," as it were. The key that opens the lock has a configuration that fits with teeth in the lock, making it possible to open the lock. To a person who does not have the key, the door remains closed. Similarly, without the key, the map, to reality, the existence of this world is closed, and we cannot see the Divine beyond it. There is no connection between one level and the next leading directly to God. But the mitzvot create a direct link between creation and Creator, a connection to the highest level, with no distortion.

In this sense, the performance of a mitzva completes the circle of creation. Such performance consists of three parts: the will of God, which is the mitzva itself; the performance of the mitzva; and the person who performs it. The mitzva in and of itself has no force. When *tefillin* lie in their container, they are merely leather boxes. They complete the holy circle only when a person who is fit for the task puts them on. At that moment, the circle is complete, from the beginning of beginnings to our reality, and the divine nature of the object employed in the mitzva is revealed. Then there is nothing separate from the Divine, no independent entity.

וְלָזֹאת, תִּהְיֶינָה נַפְשׁוֹ הָאֱלֹהִית וְהַחִיּוּנִית, וּלְבוּשֵׁיהֶן כּוּלָּן, מְיוּחָדוֹת בְּתַכְלִית הַיִּחוּד בִּרְצוֹן הָעֶלְיוֹן וְאוֹר אֵין סוֹף בָּרוּךְ הוּא כַּנִּזְכָּר לְעֵיל.

As such, both **the divine and vital** animal **souls** of the person who performs a mitzva **and their garments,** thought, speech, and action, **will all be unified in perfect unity with the supernal will and the light of *Ein Sof*, blessed be He, as explained above** (chap. 23).

The moment there is a revelation of man's will intertwined with God's will, when the innermost part of a person clings to the innermost part of God's will, then the soul of the person who performs a mitzva is unified with God.

This is a unification of both the divine and animal souls, along with their garments, the thoughts, speech, and deeds employed by the body. All are perfectly aligned with the supernal will. At that moment, there is no concealment of God's countenance to mask the divine will. The crooked is made straight, concealments disappear, and man's spiritual and physical existence becomes transparent to his inner being. At that moment, a complete union is forged between man and God.

29 Shevat (leap year)

וְיִחוּד זֶה לְמַעְלָה הוּא נִצְחִי לְעוֹלָם וָעֶד, כִּי הוּא יִתְבָּרֵךְ וּרְצוֹנוֹ לְמַעְלָה מֵהַזְּמַן.

In the upper spheres, this unity is eternal, for God and His will transcend time.

This union, this point of contact, between man and God is, from a human standpoint, temporal, lasting only as long as a person is involved in the mitzva. But from God's standpoint, the matter is entirely different. A mitzva is the will of God, and, like Him, it transcends time.

Similarly, while a person is entirely absorbed in his performance of the mitzva, completely unified with the divine will, he is connected to the eternal, to that which transcends time. The word *mitzva* shares a root with the word *tzavta,* which means bond. A mitzva represents a bond with the eternal. It is as if a piece of the fabric of eternity stretches from the Divine, beyond time and space, and envelops both the reality of the mitzva in this world and the person performing it. Even though here on earth the mitzva is performed at a specific time, in itself it contains no element of time. Though the person performing the mitzva serves as a vehicle for the Divine in this world only during the time that he performs the mitzva, the connection to the eternal that is forged does not last only during the time of its performance. The connection with *Ein Sof* ultimately lies beyond the boundaries of time. ☞

וְכֵן גִּילּוּי רְצוֹנוֹ שֶׁבְּדִבּוּרוֹ, שֶׁהִיא הַתּוֹרָה - הוּא נִצְחִי. וּכְמוֹ שֶׁכָּתוּב: "וּדְבַר אֱלֹהֵינוּ יָקוּם לְעוֹלָם" (ישעיה מ, ח), "וּדְבָרָיו חַיִּים וְקַיָּימִים" כו', וְ"לֹא יַחֲלִיף וְלֹא יָמִיר דָּתוֹ לְעוֹלָמִים" כו'.

Likewise, the manifestation of His will through His speech, the Torah, is eternal, as it is written, "But the word of our God will stand forever" (Isa. 40:8), and it is written in the prayer service, **"His words are alive and enduring"** and "God **will never exchange nor alter His law...."**

If the word of God were limited by time, it might change with the passage of time. But the divine statement is eternal. The Ten Commandments are not merely utterances that were relevant at a particular moment but an ongoing revelation at every moment of existence: "a great voice that did not cease" (Deut. 5:19). That voice continues unceasingly throughout all time, without change, without the boundaries of time and place.

19 Shevat אֶלָּא שֶׁלְּמַטָּה הוּא תַּחַת הַזְּמַן, וּבְאוֹתָהּ שָׁעָה לְבַדָּהּ שֶׁעוֹסֵק בָּהּ בַּתּוֹרָה אוֹ בְּמִצְוָה,

Below, however, in our world, **this** unity **is subject to the constraints of time, and it** occurs **only while one is engaged in Torah** study **or** the fulfillment of **a mitzva,**

BEYOND TIME

☞ This is somewhat analogous to a father who is playing a game with his young child. The game has certain rules and guidelines that the two follow as they play. During the game, the child becomes totally engrossed in it, and it becomes his entire world. But for the father, it is merely a game, and although it may appear as though he is completely ensconced in it, he is obviously not. If, during the game, the child says something that penetrates his father's personal world, such as "I love you, Daddy," it has a profound impact, beyond the limited world of the game. For the child, these words are simply part of the game – his world for the moment – yet for the father, that declaration, along with the image of his beloved child, will forever be ingrained in his heart, long after the game has ended.

In the higher realms, where the source of the soul clings to the Torah, the connection is eternal and boundless, but in this world, which exists within time and is subordinate to changes brought about by time, the mitzva is also subject to the boundaries of time. When a person is engaged in Torah study and mitzvot, he is living in two different realities. Part of him stands within the boundaries of time and space, and he therefore performs the mitzva within a certain span of time, from this moment to that moment. But another part of him unites with eternity, so that there is no difference between one period of time and another, and the concept of time ceases to have any meaning whatsoever. ☞

This duality causes an apparent contradiction: A person forms a connection with eternity, yet this does not invest him with eternity. In this world, man is chained to the matrixes of time and space; he cannot reside in eternity at the same time. Yet the Torah he studies or the mitzva he performs has no such temporal or spatial limitations. The mitzva continues to exist in the realm of the eternal even when its performer goes on to engage in other activities, and even though he may change, it does not.

THE ATOMIZATION OF LIFE

☞ One can say that the concept of life in this work is based on viewing life as an atomized process, composed of units of time, and the only relevant unit is the one that occurs at this very moment. What will occur tomorrow or next week or in twenty years is not important. At this very moment, man is being tested, and he must decide: Am I for or against God? At this moment, he decides unequivocally: I am for God! At this moment, he does not have to know what will occur a moment later.

It has been said that the difference between a tzaddik and a *rasha*, a righteous person and a wicked one, is whom each addresses when he says, "Wait a moment." When a tzaddik is challenged by his evil desires, he does not necessarily have to give an unequivocal no. He can tell that temptation, "Wait a moment." A *rasha*, on the other hand, tells his good inclination to "wait a moment."

This is not only a pragmatic concept. It describes the nature of reality itself. In just one moment of sin, an entire world is lost. But in one moment of performing a mitzva, a person acquires eternal life. One must act in the present moment. He need make no decision now regarding the one that follows. We are able to endure life's battles because we do not have to decide what we will do over the course of the coming year but only in the coming moment. If a person considers the extent of his entire life, he will not be able to bear the burden. He will be unable to come to any resolution; he will be incapable of acting. The burden is so heavy that it can be borne only for a single moment more. But this one moment suffices, because in the present one does not have to consider the moment that follows.

In this sense, every mitzva, whether great or small, is a moment of contact with God, and that is equal to life itself. This is the source of the power of self-sacrifice, the readiness to give one's life, the very essence of life, for the sake of every mitzva. ☞

כִּי אַחַר כָּךְ, אִם עוֹסֵק בְּדָבָר אַחֵר - נִפְרָד מֵהַיִּחוּד הָעֶלְיוֹן לְמַטָּה,

because afterward, if he engages in something else, he is separated from the supernal union in our world **below,**

High above, at the primal root, time has no meaning, and unification with God is eternal. But here in this world, where the soul inhabits a time-bound body, we are liable at some moment to be separated from God and to instead connect ourselves to other concerns.

וְהַיְינוּ, כְּשֶׁעוֹסֵק בִּדְבָרִים בְּטֵלִים לְגַמְרֵי שֶׁאֵין בָּהֶם צוֹרֶךְ כְּלָל לַעֲבוֹדַת ה'.

that is, when he engages in utterly purposeless matters that are not at all necessary for the service of God.

The heavenly union created by the performance of a mitzva is not severed when a person ceases to engage in that mitzva performance but only when he engages in completely worthless endeavors. No one

THE REWARD OF A MITZVA

☞ It is told that the great hasidic Rebbe Rabbi Yitzḥak Meir of Gur, the author of *Ḥiddushei HaRim*, was taken for a carriage ride by a heretic who lived in his city. The man mockingly said to Rabbi Yitzḥak Meir, "Tell me, Rabbi, it is written in the *Shema* that if a person sins, the clouds will not give their rain, the earth will not give its fruit, and he will quickly disappear from the earth. But I have been committing sins my entire life, and I do not perform any commandments, yet my land is fruitful, I am wealthy and honored, and I lack nothing."

"It is clear from your question that you have recited the *Shema* at least once in your life," Rabbi Yitzḥak Meir told him. "You should be aware that all the good in this world is not enough to reward you for the one time that you recited the *Shema*. As for your sins, that will be subject to a different reckoning."

Some explain the statement of the Sages that "there is no reward for commandments in this world" (*Kiddushin* 39b) in the same way. Our limited world is too small to contain the reward of a mitzva, because a mitzva is a unification with the infinite *Ein Sof*, and nothing in this limited world can compare with that.

can be engaged in Torah study and mitzvot twenty-four hours a day. One must sleep, eat, and take care of his other earthly concerns. But as long as he carries out his obligations, even when he is not studying Torah or performing mitzvot, the unification with God does not cease. It continues to exist above, although it does not grow any stronger nor is the person below severed from it.

The Talmud states that even if a person has recited just one paragraph of the *Shema,* once in the morning and once in the evening, he has fulfilled the obligation of Torah study as mandated in the verse "This book of the Torah shall not depart from your mouth" (Josh. 1:8).[3] More than that, it is considered as though he were immersed in study the entire day, as the continuation of the verse states: "And you shall ponder it day and night." Yet this is true only if from the time he recited the *Shema* in the morning to the time he recited it at night, he was involved solely in vital, meaningful activities. If he also engaged in completely meaningless activities, not necessarily sins but matters having no connection, even indirectly, to God and to His Torah, then the connection to the supernal is severed.

וְאַף עַל פִּי כֵן, כְּשֶׁחוֹזֵר וְשָׁב לַעֲבוֹדַת ה׳ אַחַר כָּךְ, לְתוֹרָה וְלִתְפִלָּה, וּמְבַקֵּשׁ מְחִילָה מֵה׳ עַל שֶׁהָיָה אֶפְשָׁר לוֹ לַעֲסוֹק אָז בַּתּוֹרָה וְלֹא עָסַק - ה׳ יִסְלַח לוֹ,

Nevertheless, when he subsequently repents and returns to the service of God, through Torah study **and prayer, and asks God to forgive him for the Torah he could have studied yet did not,** then **God will forgive him,**

It is true that he involved himself in matters that have no connection to God and His Torah. But as long as he did not commit a transgression, he did no damage. He only suspended the connection of the ultimate unification, and for that, God will forgive him.

כְּמַאֲמַר רַבּוֹתֵינוּ ז״ל: ״עָבַר עַל מִצְוַת עֲשֵׂה וְשָׁב - לֹא זָז מִשָּׁם עַד שֶׁמּוֹחֲלִין לוֹ״ (יומא פו, א).

in accordance with our Rabbis' statement "If one violates a positive commandment and repents, he is forgiven immediately, **even before he moves** from his place" (*Yoma* 86a).

3. *Menaḥot* 99b.

The person did not violate a prohibition; he did not cause harm. All that can be said is that he could have done better. Because he caused no damage, there is nothing to rectify. Once he repents, there is no need for anything more, He is immediately forgiven and returns to the state of unification with the Divine.

וְלָזֶה תִּקְּנוּ בִּרְכַּת "סְלַח לָנוּ", שָׁלֹשׁ פְּעָמִים בְּכָל יוֹם, עַל עֲוֹן בִּיטּוּל תּוֹרָה, שֶׁאֵין אָדָם נִיצּוֹל מִמֶּנּוּ בְּכָל יוֹם,

It is for this reason that the Sages **instituted the blessing** that begins "**Forgive us**" in the *Amida* **three times daily: It is on account of the sin of neglecting Torah** study, a sin **from which a person is not spared even a single day.**

This blessing is recited in the morning, afternoon, and evening *Amida* prayer. But the question arises: Does a person sin so frequently between one prayer service and the next that he needs to seek forgiveness each time?

It is impossible to avoid the sin of neglecting Torah study entirely. The obligation to study Torah is not limited to certain times, places, or conditions. One is obligated to study Torah, in some manner, at any time and in all circumstances, and almost no one can fulfill this requirement every day and every moment of his life. That is why a person must ask forgiveness three times a day.

This applies not only to Torah study but to the commandments of loving and fearing God as well, which are also universally applicable. Whenever a person is disconnected from the love and fear of God, he is severed from the divine unification, and for this too he must ask forgiveness three times a day.

וּכְמוֹ הַתָּמִיד שֶׁהָיָה מְכַפֵּר עַל מִצְוֹת עֲשֵׂה.

This blessing is **similar to the daily** offering, **which atoned for** neglect of **a positive commandment.**

The daily sacrifice, the *tamid*, which was offered in the Temple in the morning and late afternoon, atoned for unperformed and improperly performed positive commandments.

וְאֵין זֶה 'אֶחֱטָא וְאָשׁוּב',

This is not regarded as a case of "**I will sin and** then **I will repent,**"

The notion of requesting forgiveness constantly and predictably may seem no different from the idea of intending to sin and afterward repent, regarding which the Talmud says that a person is not given the opportunity to repent. But the two are not the same. The category of intending to sin and afterward repent applies only under certain conditions.

אֶלָּא אִם כֵּן שֶׁבִּשְׁעַת הַחֵטְא מַמָּשׁ הוּא סוֹמֵךְ עַל הַתְּשׁוּבָה - וּלְכָךְ חוֹטֵא, כְּמוֹ שֶׁנִּתְבָּאֵר בְּמָקוֹם אַחֵר.

unless during the act of the transgression itself **one relied on the** subsequent **repentance, and it is on account of this that he sinned, as explained elsewhere** (*Iggeret HaTeshuva*, chap. 11).

Saying "I will sin and then I will repent" is not the same as knowing that repentance is possible. A person need not have totally forgotten the concept of repentance in order to eventually repent. Rather, we are talking about a person who could have overcome his urges, who could have in some way emerged from his confusion, yet nevertheless he sinned. Such a person, one who sins because he thinks that he can repent afterward, is not given the means to do so. When repentance is a part of the very mechanism of the sin, when it makes it easier for a person to transgress, then he will find it harder to repent.

However, people generally do not neglect Torah study intentionally and with forethought. They get distracted, and other matters weigh on their minds. Neglecting Torah study is therefore a sin that people stumble into. Although they do not intend to be remiss, it is human nature to err in such matters. It is for this that a person requests "Forgive us" three times a day.

וּבָזֶה יוּבַן לָמָּה צִוָּה מֹשֶׁה רַבֵּינוּ עָלָיו הַשָּׁלוֹם בְּמִשְׁנֵה תּוֹרָה לַדּוֹר שֶׁנִּכְנְסוּ לָאָרֶץ לִקְרוֹת קְרִיאַת שְׁמַע פַּעֲמַיִם בְּכָל יוֹם, לְקַבֵּל עָלָיו מַלְכוּת שָׁמַיִם בִּמְסִירַת נֶפֶשׁ. וַהֲלֹא הִבְטִיחַ לָהֶם: "פַּחְדְּכֶם וּמוֹרַאֲכֶם יִתֵּן ה'" וגו' (דברים יא,כה)? אֶלָּא

In light of this, we can understand why we find **in** the book of **Deuteronomy** that **Moses, our teacher, commanded the generation** of Jews **entering the Land** of Israel **to recite the *Shema* twice daily, so that they might accept the yoke of Heaven with self-sacrifice. But did** Moses **not promise them,** "No man will stand before you; **the Lord** — 30 Shevat (leap year)

מִשּׁוּם שֶׁקִּיּוּם הַתּוֹרָה וּמִצְוֹתֶיהָ תָּלוּי בָּזֶה שֶׁיִּזְכּוֹר תָּמִיד עִנְיַן מְסִירַת נַפְשׁוֹ לַה' עַל יִחוּדוֹ, שֶׁיִּהְיֶה קָבוּעַ בְּלִבּוֹ תָּמִיד מַמָּשׁ, יוֹמָם וָלַיְלָה, לֹא יָמִישׁ מִזִּכְרוֹנוֹ. כִּי בָּזֶה יוּכַל לַעֲמוֹד נֶגֶד יִצְרוֹ לְנַצְּחוֹ תָּמִיד בְּכָל עֵת וּבְכָל שָׁעָה, כַּנִּזְכָּר לְעֵיל.

your God will place terror of you and fear of you upon the entire land on which you will tread" (Deut. 11:25)? **Rather, it is because the fulfillment of the Torah and its commandments are contingent on this, that one must constantly remember the matter of sacrificing one's life to God for the sake of His unity. This must be fixed permanently in one's heart, literally day and night, never slipping his mind. It is through this that one will be able to stand in opposition to his** evil **inclination, constantly vanquishing it at every given moment, as mentioned above.**

The generation that entered the Land of Israel needed the strength of self-sacrifice, not for the external war that it would wage against the land's inhabitants, but for the inner daily battles that each individual would face. The readiness and spiritual ability to sacrifice themselves in the course of sanctifying God's name would form the foundation of everything they would be confronted with in life, in this "land" of life to which they were coming. It is for this reason that this command was given to the generation who entered the land, not to the wilderness generation. A person who is ready to give his life for God and whose consciousness of this is "fixed permanently in one's heart" can perform the same act of self-sacrifice in countless small ways in his regular life.

This chapter concludes the series of chapters (from chapter 18 onward) that focus on the concealed love embedded in the heart of every Jew. This love serves as the driving force behind a Jew's readiness for self-sacrifice for the sake of God. The author of the *Tanya* uses the spirit of self-sacrifice again and again to create the image of the *beinoni*. This strength, which is rooted in a Jew's concealed love of God, is connected to his divine soul. It is the love and expression of the divine soul, which is a part of the divine spark that exists in every Jew, whether a great tzaddik or a simple person. The ability to overcome obstacles and to truly live every day for the sake of God depends on keeping in mind this power that is concealed within, this ability to sacrifice oneself, even to die if necessary, in order to sanctify God's name.

The self-sacrifice entailed in sanctifying God's name, in its most dramatic fashion, provides the impetus for a different kind of self-sacrifice, less dramatic but much more common: overcoming one's negative urges, whatever they may be, in whatever degree. Whenever a person's urges interfere with his life, either pressing him to do evil or to refrain from doing good, he should have the clear knowledge "fixed permanently in his heart day and night" that he has the power to sacrifice his life in order to not be disconnected from God for even an instant. From that moment on, the world is transformed. Nothing is impossible for him anymore.

Chapter 26

AFTER CONCLUDING THAT EVERY JEW HAS THE ABILITY to stave off his evil inclination, to apply himself to the service of God with uncompromising dedication and to always emerge victorious, the author of the *Tanya* now embarks on a discussion of the more practical aspects of this campaign. At the center of this topic stands one of the central tenets of Hasidism: the total eradication of sadness and the positive value of joy.

בְּרַם כְּגוֹן דָּא צָרִיךְ לְאוֹדוֹעֵי כְּלָל גָּדוֹל, כִּי כְּמוֹ שֶׁנִּצָּחוֹן לְנַצֵּחַ דָּבָר גַּשְׁמִי, כְּגוֹן שְׁנֵי אֲנָשִׁים הַמִּתְאַבְּקִים זֶה עִם זֶה, לְהַפִּיל זֶה אֶת זֶה, הִנֵּה אִם הָאֶחָד הוּא בְּעַצְלוּת וּכְבֵדוּת יְנוּצַּח בְּקַל וְיִפּוֹל, גַּם אִם הוּא גִּבּוֹר יוֹתֵר מֵחֲבֵירוֹ,

But the following fundamental principle must be made known: Just as with achieving a physical victory, such as when **two people are wrestling with one another, one attempting to throw down the other, if one of them is lazy and lethargic, he will be easily defeated and will fall, even if he is stronger than his opponent,**

20 Shevat

1 Adar I (leap year)

A variety of factors determine the outcome of every struggle, aside from the relative strength of the contestants. If, for instance, a wrestler is awkward, if he does not move or respond quickly, then even if he is stronger than his opponent, he will likely be defeated.

כָּכָה מַמָּשׁ בְּנִצְחוֹן הַיֵּצֶר, אִי אֶפְשָׁר לְנַצְּחוֹ בְּעַצְלוּת וּכְבֵדוּת, הַנִּמְשָׁכוֹת מֵעַצְבוּת וְטִמְטוּם הַלֵּב כְּאֶבֶן,

it is precisely the same with regard to vanquishing the evil **inclination. It is impossible to vanquish it** when one is in a state of **laziness and lethargy, which stem from sadness and a stone-like numbness of the heart,**

Two factors cause indolence and sluggishness of the soul: sadness and a dulled heart. Sadness paralyzes the soul, making it unable to act, and a dulled heart paralyzes one's feelings, making them inaccessible. A dulled heart is not identical to a dulled mind. The latter is the consequence of a constricted and closed intellect. It is essentially an inability to respond appropriately to intellectual challenges. But a dulled heart is a heart that is closed, an inability to respond to emotional stimuli. Although a person with a dulled heart may have experiences that are joyful or sad, upsetting or exalting, he does not respond appropriately.

but rather with alacrity, which stems from joy and an open heart that is pure of any trace of worry and sadness in the world.

כִּי אִם בִּזְרִיזוּת הַנִּמְשֶׁכֶת מִשִּׂמְחָה וּפְתִיחַת הַלֵּב וְטָהֳרָתוֹ מִכָּל נִדְנוּד דְּאָגָה וְעֶצֶב בָּעוֹלָם.

Only when a person lives and acts with alacrity can he conquer his evil inclination. This alacrity cannot emerge from sadness. It comes only from joy, when everything is open, when there is no anxiety, no sense of oppressiveness. Quickness in action relates to the quickness of the soul, and that emanates from a positive spirit, from a person's positive sense about what he is doing and about what he must do.

As for the verse that states, "In all sadness there will be an advantage" (Prov. 14:23)**, meaning that** sadness **will result in a certain advantage and virtue, this expression,** "there will be," **implies that, on the contrary, sadness possesses no virtue of its own, only that a certain advantage will come** as a result **of it.**

וּמַה שֶּׁכָּתוּב: "בְּכָל עֶצֶב יִהְיֶה מוֹתָר" (משלי יד, כג), פֵּירוּשׁ שֶׁיִּהְיֶה אֵיזֶה יִתְרוֹן וּמַעֲלָה מִזֶּה, הִנֵּה אַדְּרַבָּה, מִלָּשׁוֹן זֶה מַשְׁמַע שֶׁהָעֶצֶב מִצַּד עַצְמוֹ אֵין בּוֹ מַעֲלָה, רַק שֶׁיַּגִּיעַ וְיָבֹא מִמֶּנּוּ אֵיזֶה יִתְרוֹן.

Sadness in and of itself is always negative, always a failure, always toxic. But sometimes we must use it, only with great caution. If a person falls unconscious, he may need to be injected with a small amount of a toxic substance in order to be revived. Although it is ordinarily a deadly poison, he needs it in order to return to consciousness, to regain movement in his limbs and be restored to life. The same applies to a person's soul. At times, when our senses are asleep, it is necessary to use a trace of sadness to awaken the soul and inject it with the spirit of life.

וְהַיְינוּ הַשִּׂמְחָה הָאֲמִיתִּית בַּה' אֱלֹהָיו הַבָּאָה אַחַר הָעֶצֶב הָאֲמִיתִּי

This ultimate advantage **is the true joy in God that follows true sadness,**

Even when used for holy purposes, sadness is not healthy. But at times, it must be used, just as a pathogen may be used, to effect an extreme reaction. When the heart has been saddened by something truly upsetting, such as one's wickedness or sins, and the person can, as a result, break the power of evil and cleanse himself of the falsehood within himself, then he can experience true joy.

By way of example, the digestive system cannot tolerate an emetic, and it is unpleasant to ingest. But if one's digestive system is blocked and needs to be cleaned out, such a drug is beneficial. More precisely, it is not the emetic itself that is useful, it does not give the body any nourishment, but it is its function that provides the benefit: It helps the body discharge the waste matter. Once sadness purges our system of its spiritual wastes, we come to the next stage: the relief of true joy. That is the meaning of "In all sadness there will be an advantage."

לְעִתִּים מְזוּמָּנִים עַל עֲוֹנוֹתָיו בְּמַר נַפְשׁוֹ וְלֵב נִשְׁבָּר,

which one experiences **with a bitter soul and a broken heart over his sins at specific,** appropriate **times.**

Like any powerful drug, sadness must be carefully controlled and used only in the right way and at the right time. A person must manage his sadness, not the other way around, and the way to accomplish this is to designate specific times in which to allow himself to be sad. ☞

THE TIME AND PLACE FOR SADNESS

☞ The ability to manage one's sadness hinges on focusing on the right place and time for it. Prayer books of earlier times used to instruct, "Here one weeps." People's difficult circumstances and bitter lives always provided sufficient reason for tears. But a person could not cry all the time, so at certain points in prayer permission was

שֶׁעַל יְדֵי זֶה נִשְׁבָּרָה רוּחַ הַטּוּמְאָה וְסִטְרָא אָחֳרָא וּמְחִיצָה שֶׁל בַּרְזֶל הַמַּפְסֶקֶת בֵּינוֹ לְאָבִיו שֶׁבַּשָּׁמַיִם,

Through this sadness caused by a broken heart, **the spirit of impurity and the *sitra aḥara*, as well as the** resultant **iron barrier that interposes between him and his Father in Heaven, are broken,**

At times, a person cannot evoke his emotions. Something is in the way, a curtain dividing him from God, but it is the person himself who creates this curtain, as the verse states, "Rather, your iniquities have been separating between you and your God" (Isa. 59:2). From God's standpoint, there is no barrier. That wall of sin, of the spirit of impurity and the *sitra aḥara*, can be an impenetrable iron curtain. Behind it, a person goes through life pleased with himself, pleased with his accomplishments, pleased with his plans, and he never engages in the slightest bit of self-reflection. He may read devotional tracts on the fear and love of God, he may attend lectures delivering ethical reproof, and he may even deliver such lectures. But none of this affects him, because a wall stands between him and such feelings, preventing them from reaching him.

When a person reaches this state of "you became fat, you thickened, you grew obese" (Deut. 32:15), he is covered in a layer of "the fat that covers the innards" (Ex. 29:13), an opacity that coats his heart and allows no vital emotion to penetrate. He may know everything intellectually, he may even know that something is wrong, but the unending routine of his life does not allow him to truly relate to this.

given, and at those points people would weep copiously.

Everyone has sufficient reason to experience sadness and bitterness. But he must set that aside for the appropriate time. Sadness should not arise spontaneously, at the times that are convenient for one's evil inclination, but should be summoned when one desires it.

As the author of the *Tanya* will soon explain, when such sadness arises spontaneously, that is usually a distinct sign that it is being generated by one's evil inclination. A tzaddik said, "Once, when I was about to recite my prayers, I began to grieve over my sins: What kind of person am I? I am so contemptible, so wretched, so sinful. But then it occurred to me: Do I have such thoughts when I am about to eat? I understood then that this was nothing other than an artifice of my evil inclination."

Even though he acknowledges the importance of the love and fear of God, they remain external to him. A person in such a situation has to break down this wall, which can be broken only when he is totally shattered.

At times, a person is given divine assistance, and Heaven sends him the means to a breakdown, not that he should seek it or take pride in it, but there may be no other way. Such a breakdown in one's life may be tragic, but it will affect the person more than endless words of reproof. Many people have discovered that only after a negative event, only after a crisis, were they open to a new insight, to faith, and that then, for perhaps the first time in their lives, they experienced a feeling of genuine joy.

What does a crisis accomplish? It breaks the iron curtain and allows a person to feel. Many people in the world act, speak, go through the motions of life, yet are unable to truly experience either love of others or love of God. They are unable to experience fear, whether the fear of others or the fear of God. They conduct the entire cycle of their lives on one plane. Such a person comes and goes, enters a scene and leaves a scene. Things in his life are constantly changing, but he never has a genuine experience. Only a crisis can challenge such a state. Only then is a person open to the possibility of relating to others, to the world around him, to God. From the moment he experiences his pain, he can begin to experience the entire world. In the end, perhaps, he will see the world as it is and people as they are. But prior to that, behind the iron curtain, his relationships are mechanical, without a true connection to others or to God. After the crisis, he is like a person who has suffered a burn. As the old skin peels, he begins to feel with the new skin that was concealed underneath it. Although he feels pain, he has pleasant sensations as well. A new sensitivity has been created, open to everything. ☞

PIERCING THE IRON CURTAIN

☞ Unlike the tenets of several optimistic philosophies, it seems that it is more difficult to arrive at authentic feeling through positive experiences than through negative ones. This is not a pleasant thought to contemplate, but negative experiences are more effective at piercing the iron curtain. Positive experiences only increase a person's self-satisfaction because they indicate to him that everything is well and

כְּמוֹ שֶׁכָּתוּב בַּזֹּהַר (חלק ג רמ, א) עַל פָּסוּק: "רוּחַ נִשְׁבָּרָה, לֵב נִשְׁבָּר" וגו' (תהלים נא, יט).

as it is written in the *Zohar* (3:240a) **regarding the verse** "Sacrifices to God are **a broken spirit;** You, God, will not reject **a broken** and crushed **heart**" (Ps. 51:19).

The spirit of impurity, the iron curtain, is built on the sense that "I am, and there is nothing besides me." But when a person's heart is broken and contrite, that feeling dissipates. The spirit of impurity melts away, and the iron curtain shatters.

The hasidim of Kotzk used to recount paradoxical statements such as "There is nothing straighter than a bent ladder," "There is nothing blacker than white shrouds," and "There is nothing more whole than a broken heart." This book states that God desires us to be whole, that He "does not inhabit a blemished place."[1] Yet even though it may appear paradoxical, God does inhabit a broken heart, because only a broken heart is truly whole. A broken heart is true, whereas an unbroken heart is lacking at its very essence. In a sense, a person without a broken heart has no heart at all because he does not feel, and in order to feel, his heart must be broken.

וַאֲזַי יְקוּיַּם בּוֹ רֵישֵׁיהּ דִּקְרָא: "תַּשְׁמִיעֵנִי שָׂשׂוֹן וְשִׂמְחָה" וגו'

Then the preceding verses will be fulfilled through him: "Make me hear

that he can proceed as usual. But a negative event, a crisis, wakes him up. Because it is difficult, because he cannot bear it, he is forced to change.

The author of the *Tanya* discusses this elsewhere (see, e.g., chap. 45) with regard to the verse "So says the Lord to the house of Jacob that redeemed Abraham" (Isa. 29:22). Abraham is the spirit of love, and Jacob is the spirit of compassion. At times, a person cannot arouse a love for God within himself. He is not in a state in which love of God has any meaning for him. At such a moment, it is possible that Jacob will redeem Abraham because even if a person cannot love God, he can, at the very least, have compassion for himself. Even if he cannot sense love, he can say to himself, "If this is the case, how far has my soul fallen? How far have I dragged God down with me?"

A person is galvanized more quickly and more powerfully by such thoughts than by a feeling of love. Then, when he comes to a true experience of being connected, when he shatters the iron curtain, he can come to love. This is the meaning of "the house of Jacob that redeemed Abraham."

1. See chap. 32.

(תהלים נא, י), "הָשִׁיבָה לִּי שְׂשׂוֹן יִשְׁעֶךָ וְרוּחַ נְדִיבָה" וגו' (שם פסוק יד).

joy and gladness; let the bones that You crushed rejoice" (Ps. 51:10) and "**Restore the joy of Your salvation to me;** sustain me **with a generous spirit**" (Ps. 51:14).

A broken, dejected heart does not give a person a joyous feeling. A person with a broken heart grows aware of his offensiveness, his impure spirit, his wretchedness, and this feeling has nothing positive about it. Nevertheless, such a feeling of sadness and brokenness can be beneficial if it leads to feelings of joy. In order for a person to attain such "joy and gladness," he must first experience "crushed bones"; in order to feel that God "sustains me with a generous spirit," he himself must be entirely a "broken heart."

It is not that joy must always be experienced as a consequence of crisis or as a counter to sadness. Rather, at its essence, it stems from an ability to arrive at an experience of truth. If a person lives his entire life in falsehood, never once having a genuine experience, he may deceive himself into thinking that he is having true experiences, but they are in reality delusions. He has not felt true joy or even any genuine emotion. For this reason, it is only after he experiences a sufficiently earthshaking ordeal that can he begin to comprehend what it means to feel and truly experience anything.

The story is told about an intellectual Jew, a distinguished scientist, who once, in the course of conversation with a rabbi, said, "See, Rabbi, I too ask questions. I too think of God from time to time."

The rabbi asked him, "But tell me, how many times were you unable to sleep at night because you were thinking about God?"

When a person can sleep well at night and eat in tranquility, he cannot say that his soul thirsts for God. But if he should experience a true anxiety, when he knows what it means to be unable to sleep for three nights in a row because his thoughts do not give him respite, then he can understand what it means to think about God. ☞

IF YOU SEEK IT LIKE SILVER

☞ Rabbi Moses Ḥayyim Luzzatto discusses this idea in the introduction to his *Mesillat Yesharim*, citing the verses "If you seek it like silver and search for it like for

וְזֶהוּ טַעַם הַפָּשׁוּט לְתִיקּוּן הָאֲרִ"י ז"ל לוֹמַר מִזְמוֹר זֶה אַחַר תִּיקּוּן חֲצוֹת

This is the simple reason, apart from the deeper, esoteric ones, **that the Arizal instituted the recitation of this psalm,** Psalms 51, **after** ***Tikkun Ĥatzot***

Sadness is dangerous and must be employed in a controlled fashion: at a prescribed time and in a prescribed manner. As the author of the *Tanya* explains elsewhere,[2] the proper time and framework is the time of the recitation of *Tikkun Ḥatzot*. This is a time when a person meditates on the exile of the Divine Presence in relation to God, and in relation to the entire world. It is also appropriate for him to think of his own private exile of the Divine Presence, his own troubles and distance from God.

Other works state that every tragedy, every misfortune, represents the exile of the Divine Presence. Every trouble that an individual suffers is part of the world's imperfection. When a person feels his own private suffering, he should associate it with the greater context of the exile of the Divine Presence. The moment his private suffering becomes a part of the universal exile of the Divine Presence, he achieves rectification.

hidden treasures, then you will understand fear of the Lord, and you will find knowledge of God" (Prov. 2:4–5). Everyone desires the fear of God, yet why doesn't everyone have it? The answer is that the fear of God is attained only when one seeks it in the same way that others seek silver and hidden treasures, with the same fervor and consistency.

Yet people often invest only desultory effort in this realm, expecting to receive an incommensurate reward. The story is told of a famous merchant who was traveling for business. One cold and rainy night, he entered the home of his Rebbe, and as he dried himself next to the oven, he began to think about his life. He said, "Rebbe, look at what I enjoy in this world. What can I hope for in the World to Come?"

The Rebbe said to him, "Learn from your dealings in this world. If, in this world, in which you have invested so much, this is what you get in return, how much do you expect to get in the World to Come, in which you are not investing?"

If we invest our lives in those things that touch our soul, we receive a return commensurate with our investment. But if nothing touches us, we must scour away the veneer in order to arrive at some emotion. Although there is no need to invite external suffering, it is necessary to set aside time during which one experiences bitterness over his inner state. This will break a person's heart, making it possible for him to feel.

2. *Iggeret HaTeshuva*, chap. 7; see also the note to *Tikkun Ḥatzot* in *Siddur Admor HaZaken*.

At the same time, when a person's suffering ceases to be his private affair and is transformed into a part of the universal suffering, an emotional change also takes place. A person can pray, but as long as he remains focused on himself and his own needs, demanding, "Give! Give! I need such and such!" his every request is judged by the question, Does he deserve it or not? But when a person says, "Master of the universe, something is missing in Your world, and therefore suffering exists. The Divine Presence is in exile and needs salvation," that is no longer his private affair. When his affairs are those of the Divine Presence, when his suffering is the suffering of the Divine Presence, then that is the proper time to weep over his private distress as well.

Tikkun Ḥatzot is thus a time of sadness and is properly followed by the recitation of Psalm 51.[3]

קוֹדֶם הַלִּימּוּד, כְּדֵי לִלְמוֹד בְּשִׂמְחָה אֲמִיתִּית בַּה׳ הַבָּאָה אַחַר הָעֶצֶב.

and just **prior to Torah study, so that one will study** Torah **with genuine joy in God,** a feeling **that follows the sadness** evoked during *Tikkun Ḥatzot*.

Sadness must be followed by a transitional stage leading to joy, and that process is expressed in Psalms 51, which describes the joy that follows the sadness. This crossing from sadness to joy is dealt with extensively in hasidic literature. A person does not have to immerse himself in sadness, even if it is, as it were, justified. Once he feels remorse over his sins and his abased condition, he must cast aside the sadness and any thought of his transgressions and embrace the joy that results from having broken the iron curtain, because now he sees the light.

שֶׁיֵּשׁ לְשִׂמְחָה זוֹ יִתְרוֹן כְּיִתְרוֹן הָאוֹר הַבָּא מִן הַחֹשֶׁךְ דַּוְקָא, כְּמוֹ שֶׁכָּתוּב בַּזֹּהַר (חלק ג מז, ב) **עַל פָּסוּק: ״וְרָאִיתִי שֶׁיֵּשׁ יִתְרוֹן לַחָכְמָה מִן הַסִּכְלוּת כְּיִתְרוֹן הָאוֹר״ כו׳** (קהלת ב, יג),

This type of **joy has an advantage, akin to the advantage inherent in light that specifically follows darkness, as it is written in the *Zohar*** (3:47b) **regarding the verse "I saw that there is advantage to wisdom over folly, like the advantage of light** over darkness" (Eccles. 2:13).

3. See *Pri Etz Ḥayyim, Sha'ar Tikkun Ḥatzot*, chap. 4.

A light that emerges from the darkness, that banishes the darkness, is superior to light that follows light. There is an advantage to wisdom that follows foolishness, that comes when foolishness is shattered, similar to the advantage of light that shines when darkness is shattered. This light is unique in that it can illuminate only through darkness. It may not be greater than other types of light, but it is more precious to a person because it touches the primal foundation of his existence, the border between light and dark, between being and nonbeing. This is the advantage of joy that results from sadness.

Other texts discuss the power of pleasure, which is the soul's highest faculty. Although this faculty may be felt through a variety of pleasures, its most perfect expression is the delight of life itself, of being alive. Most of us do not sense this pleasure, because we have been born with life and have grown up with it. It is possible to feel this pleasure only in the way one appreciates light that has been generated through darkness. A person on death row who has been given a reprieve or a person who has recovered from a terminal disease can, at a certain moment, feel the pure delight of being alive. Only after this gift has been withheld can one appreciate what he possesses.

Similarly, after one has experienced sadness as a result of recognizing his sins, his lowliness and insignificance, after he has come to recognize that he deserves nothing, then he can say, "Nevertheless, I can still turn to God!" This basic connection with the Divine, so natural to us, which exists because we exist, because we are Jews, comes to a person in a revelation of unparalleled joy because, for a time, it had seemed that it might be taken away.

עַיֵּין שָׁם, וְדַי לַמֵּבִין. **See there. This is sufficient for one who understands** the esoteric wisdom.

This discussion touches on the mystical concept of elevating sparks of holiness from the *kelippa* and the redeeming of good from evil and imperfection. These topics that deal with the borderline where good and evil touch should not be discussed at length. For those who understand these concepts, this discussion should suffice.

וּמִקְרָא מָלֵא דִּבֵּר הַכָּתוּב: "תַּחַת אֲשֶׁר לֹא עָבַדְתָּ אֶת ה' אֱלֹהֶיךָ בְּשִׂמְחָה" וגו' (דברים כח, מז), וְנוֹדָע לַכֹּל פֵּירוּשׁ הָאֲרִ"י ז"ל עַל פָּסוּק זֶה.

Furthermore, **the Torah categorically states, "Because you did not serve the Lord your God with joy** and with gladness of heart, due to the abundance of everything" (Deut. 28:47), **and everyone knows the Arizal's interpretation of this verse.**

This verse, "Because you did not serve the Lord your God with joy…," which appears in Moses's rebuke of the Jewish people, is generally understood in the context of the verse that follows: "Because you did not serve the Lord…you will serve your enemies, whom the Lord will dispatch against you, in hunger and in thirst and in nakedness and in the lack of everything…" (Deut. 28:48). In other words, because you did not serve God in joy, you will serve other nations in grief. But by citing the first verse by itself without reference to its continuation, the Arizal arrives at a much more expansive explanation.[4] All the punishments described in the rebuke, he says, are inflicted only because the Jews' service to God lacked joy. The stress is not on serving God but on the joy that should accompany this service. The threatened plagues and sufferings will come not because "you did not serve" but because "you did not serve with joy." ☞

SERVING GOD JOYOUSLY

☞ The meaning and importance of serving God with joy is the profound connection to the Divine that it implies. It is not a connection based on a legal contract and its clauses but a connection that is personal and intimate. It is serving God for the sake of it.

The early hasidim expressed this idea in a parable about a king who sent out his general to conduct a military campaign. When the general suffered defeat, the king wondered whether his general was incompetent or disloyal. To determine the truth, he sent another general to take his place. When this general was successful, the king monitored the reaction of the first general. If he was happy, that would indicate that his defeat had been nothing but bad luck. But if he was upset, that would indicate that he was, in fact, disloyal.

The same applies to the battle against the evil inclination. If a person sinned, was

4. See the preface to *Sha'ar HaMitzvot*.

21 Shevat

וְהִנֵּה עֵצָה הַיְעוּצָה לְטַהֵר לִבּוֹ מִכָּל עֶצֶב וְנִדְנוּד דְּאָגָה מִמִּילֵּי דְעָלְמָא, וַאֲפִילוּ בָּנֵי חַיֵּי וּמְזוֹנֵי.

The following is the counsel offered to cleanse one's heart of any trace of sadness and worry about mundane matters, even matters pertaining to **children,** length of **life, and livelihood.**

These are the three fundamental items on the human agenda, the spur to our aspirations and the source of our greatest suffering. "Children" refers to a person's wish to have children and his ensuing anxiety about how they will turn out. "Life" refers to one's desire for a long, healthy life. "Livelihood" refers to one's concern for his livelihood. Anxiety about these basics is not foolish. The question is, how can a person disregard these issues and divest his heart of any last trace of sadness and worry?

מוּדַעַת זֹאת לַכֹּל מַאֲמַר רַבּוֹתֵינוּ ז"ל: "כְּשֵׁם שֶׁמְּבָרֵךְ עַל הַטּוֹבָה" כו' (ברכות פרק ט משנה ה), וּפֵירְשׁוּ בַּגְּמָרָא (שם ס, ב): לְקַבּוֹלֵי בְּשִׂמְחָה, כְּמוֹ שִׂמְחַת הַטּוֹבָה הַנִּגְלֵית וְנִרְאֵית,

This advice is contained in the **well-known statement of our Rabbis: "Just as one recites a blessing for a positive event,** so too one recites a blessing for a calamity" (Mishna *Berakhot* 9:5). **The Talmud explains that one should accept** the calamity **with joy, just as one rejoices over a clearly perceived positive event** (*Berakhot* 60b),

it because he could not withstand temptation or because his fundamental personal connection to God was impaired? To learn the answer, we need only look at how he relates to others who are successful in their personal struggle. Is he glad for them or upset? Does he hate them because they succeeded where he failed, or is he glad that someone, even if not himself, succeeded? If this battle on behalf of God is truly his battle, then he is glad that it is being waged successfully, no matter how and no matter by whom.

This difference in attitude has been compared to the contrast between one's son and an employee. A worker has a contract that outlines his responsibilities and the scope of his duties, and the attitude toward him is based purely on utilitarian considerations. But a son is connected to his father in an altogether different way: with a bond of love. He will always do as much as he can, and therefore there is joy in this relationship even if the son has not done the work perfectly, because he is motivated by an innate desire that wells from the core of his being and is propelled by his love.

The Talmud is not saying that we recite the same blessing for good news – "Blessed is He who is good and does good" – as for the bad. The blessing to be recited over bad news is entirely different: "Blessed is the true Judge." The intent is that we should recite both blessings with the same feeling.

This concept is difficult to absorb – and that much harder to implement. The dilemma is illustrated in a story about Rabbi Dov Berish Meisels, a pious Torah scholar who later became the rabbi of Krakow and Warsaw. At a younger age, he was the head of a yeshiva and, simultaneously, a wealthy lumber merchant. In those days, logs were lashed together onto rafts and floated down the Vistula River to the sea. When river traffic went well, the profits were great. From time to time, the melting snow or other natural conditions destroyed these rafts, and then the logs would be lost and the merchants were ruined.

One day the news came that the worst had happened: All the logs had sunk. This meant that Rabbi Meisels, a man who had grown up in a wealthy family and who had lived a life of luxury, was now destitute. His relatives did not know how to break the news to him. Finally, they asked one of his students to break the news in such a way that he would not collapse.

The student approached Rabbi Meisels with a tractate of the Talmud and said to him, "Rabbi, there is a passage here that I don't understand," and he showed him the passage about reciting a blessing over evil tidings in exactly the same way that one says a blessing over good news.

The rabbi explained the passage, but the student repeated, "Rabbi, I still don't understand. How can one accept bad news joyfully?"

The rabbi explained the passage again according to its simple meaning and then according to its esoteric meaning. But the student asked again, "Rabbi, I still can't understand. If you were told that all of your rafts had been lost, would you dance with joy?"

The rabbi told him, "Certainly."

To this, the student replied, "If so, you may begin dancing, because your rafts have, in fact, been lost."

When Rabbi Meisels heard this, he fainted. It is said that the first thing he said when he recovered was "Now I too do not understand this passage."

This story does not solve the problem but expresses its basic difficulty: There is a difference between theoretical knowledge that God is good and one's personal feelings when one suffers a loss. Nevertheless, there are doubtless many stories about people who really did exemplify this teaching of accepting misfortune with joy.

כִּי גַם זוֹ לְטוֹבָה, רַק שֶׁאֵינָהּ נִגְלֵית וְנִרְאֵית לְעֵינֵי בָשָׂר.

because it too is for good, only it is not yet **clearly perceivable** as such **to the human eye.**

Hasidism has adopted an extreme stance toward the understanding of divine providence: Everything, down to the most microscopic level, is under God's direct control. In this context, the question of accepting suffering with joy and the meaning of evil takes on additional force. The explanation here reaches a depth of profundity far beyond the usual explanations. The basis of this approach is the Sages' teaching that "nothing evil descends from on high" (*Bereshit Rabba* 51:5), which may be understood on a number of levels.

One approach, cited in the name of the Ba'al Shem Tov, is that evil is a seat for good. That is to say, evil does not act independently but is always an instrument for good. In a broader sense, "evil defines good" (*Sefer Yetzira* 1:2). Evil indicates where good ends so that through evil good can be clearly recognized. In this sense, everything evil is a tool that we can use to reach goals that are good. According to this understanding, any seeming victory of evil is only a way station on the road toward good. Every descent is a descent for the purpose of ascent. Evil is one of the tools of universal good. It is the pedestal, the base on which all good stands on display. This approach aligns with several of our Sages' teachings, such as the concept that God uses evil as a means by which to punish the wicked and by which to exact retribution upon the righteous for their paucity of sins in this world in order that they merit unadulterated reward in the next.

The author of the *Tanya* offers an additional, more profound explanation. That which appears evil, the author explains, is not essentially evil but a good that we cannot see. Although certain events may appear to be evil, this does not express their essential character but only reflects our insufficient understanding. This can be compared to one who is being addressed lovingly but in a language he does not understand. No matter how many affectionate words are spoken to him, he may experience anger, frustration, the feeling that he is wasting his time. He does not sense the love in the words, only the pain. Similarly, because our understanding is limited, certain levels of goodness that God draws down to us appear imperfect and evil.

This explanation concurs with the attitude of the talmudic Sage Naḥum Ish Gam Zu,[5] who responded to every event in his life, "This too is for the good," not as a way of accepting harsh judgment but because he saw that what other people experience as a descent is, in reality, an elevation.

This realization can be attained to varying degrees. The simplest, which is readily apparent, is that exemplified by the story about Rabbi Akiva, who, while traveling, bedded down for the night in a field with an oil lamp, a rooster, and a donkey.[6] The wind blew out the light, a cat came and ate the rooster, and a lion came and ate the donkey. As each occurrence took place, Rabbi Akiva responded, "All that the Holy One, blessed be He, has done, He has done for the good." Later that night, bandits attacked and looted the nearby town. Only Rabbi Akiva, whose presence was not betrayed by his light, rooster, or donkey, was untouched.

Sometimes the connection between the apparent evil and the true good is not so direct and grows clear only after the passage of a year, twenty years, or an entire lifetime, when one realizes that the events that had appeared evil were actually a hidden good. But it really makes no difference whether a person realizes this right away or after twenty years, or even if he never realizes it at all. In essence, there is no qualitative difference between good and evil. All that comes from above is good, although not of the same type. It is easy to recite a blessing of thanksgiving on something that is good and appears to be good. It is more difficult to recite a blessing on something that appears negative. To bless God even under difficult circumstances, one needs a broad mind, a certain degree of refinement, and mental preparation.

---

5. See *Ta'anit* 21a.
6. See *Berakhot* 60b.

Unfortunately, not everyone is given their set of challenges at a time when they are prepared to accept it. ☞

כִּי הִיא מֵעָלְמָא דְּאִתְכַּסְיָא, שֶׁלְּמַעְלָה מֵעָלְמָא דְּאִתְגַּלְיָא,

This is **because it stems from the concealed world, which is higher than the revealed world,**

There is yet a further level of understanding, even deeper and more profound, that sees evil not only as a hidden good but as an especially elevated good. Concealed good comes from the hidden world, which is more elevated than the revealed world and thus more difficult to understand. Some things are easy for anyone to grasp, such as when God speaks simply, as it were, in the language of wealth, honor, children, long life, and a good income. Everyone will agree that these things are good. But when the revelation comes from a higher level, from the hidden world, in which good is given in a different manner, a person has no clear understanding of what is happening to him. In order to see and experience that good, one must possess faith and a certain emotional maturity. Art for the masses is something that everyone, even the most uneducated, can appreciate. Good art is necessarily complex and subtle, and a person who is not sufficiently trained cannot fully appreciate it.

Those experiences that are superficially good, that are easy to understand, come from a lower world. When we ourselves are on a relatively low level, that is enough for us. Higher messages require greater effort

THE TASTE OF BITTERNESS

☞ There are some flavors, such as sweetness, that everyone, even an infant, can agree are good, but in order to appreciate more sophisticated flavors, one needs to have acquired an educated palate. The story is told of two brothers who, as small children, were brought to a certain Rebbe. He put a glass of beer before each one. The older brother tasted the beer and put it down, complaining that it was bitter. The younger brother tasted it, then drank the entire cup and said, "It's bitter, but it's good." The Rebbe said of them, quoting the verse about the brothers Ephraim and Manasseh, that the older one "shall be great; however, his younger brother shall be greater than he" (Gen. 48:19).

So it was. The boy who understood that though there are bitter experiences in life, everything will be fine, grew up to be great. The boy who understood that something can be both bitter and good grew to become even greater.

to accept. They are liable to come in ways that are inexplicable, ways that, because they come from the hidden world, appear in our revealed world as darkness.

שֶׁהוּא ו״ה מִשֵּׁם הֲוָיָ״ה בָּרוּךְ הוּא, וְעָלְמָא דְּאִתְכַּסְיָא הוּא י״ה.

which derives from the letters ***vav*** and ***heh*** **of God's name of *Havaya*, while the world of concealment** derives from the letters ***yod*** and ***heh*** of the name of *Havaya*.

The reality exists wholly through the four-letter name of *Havaya*, which gives existence to all. This name is composed of four letters. The first letters are the letters *yod* and *heh*, which give existence to the concealed world, and the final two letters are the letters *vav* and *heh*, which give existence to the revealed world.

וְזֶהוּ שֶׁכָּתוּב: ״אַשְׁרֵי הַגֶּבֶר אֲשֶׁר תְּיַסְּרֶנּוּ יָ״הּ״ וגו׳ (תהלים צד, יב).

This is the meaning of the verse "Blessed is the man whom You chastise, Lord…" (Ps. 94:12), where the name of God is spelled with a *yod* and *heh*.

Suffering devolves from the first and higher (and therefore hidden) half of the name of *Havaya*, from the *yod* and *heh*, not from the lower (and therefore revealed) part of the name, *vav* and *heh*. Thus, "Blessed is the man…" because in the end he receives more. Even though it appears that he is the recipient of pain and suffering, he is in fact receiving goodness, but goodness on such a high plane that he cannot, at that moment, recognize it as such.

But the discussion cannot stop here, because suffering hurts and is unwanted. In some versions of the *Viduy*, the prayer of confession, we ask God to forgive us and remove our sins, but "not through suffering and disease."[7] In truth, we know that suffering is a profound and genuine good. Nothing genuine can come without suffering, as the Sages state, "The Land of Israel, the Torah, and the World to Come were given only by means of suffering" (*Berakhot* 5a). Yet at times we cannot stop ourselves from asking, "Master of the universe, do not relate to us

7. See *Berakhot* 17a; *Yoma* 87b.

as tzaddikim and sages but as simple and lowly creatures. We cannot comprehend the great goodness that is hidden within suffering. We want You to speak to us in a simpler, more understandable language."

In view of all this, there is something paradoxical in the fact that a wicked person is afflicted with suffering, because it is actually a gift for him: Suffering is his chance to escape the closed circle of evil. Some suggest that an evildoer's true punishment comes not with his suffering but with its cessation.

This idea informs one interpretation of the punishment that the serpent in the Garden of Eden received when God cursed it, "Dust you shall eat all the days of your life" (Gen. 3:14). One might think that there could be no greater boon than this. Since dust is everywhere, the serpent will always have food to eat. While others grow weary of seeking nourishment, the serpent need not make the slightest effort. But this is the meaning of God's words: "I am giving you everything so that you will never grow tired, you will never have to worry, you will never have any problems, because I do not want to see you again. You will never have to turn to Me. You will never need to pray to Me."

An element of this exists in every gift we receive from God. Success generally breeds self-satisfaction, as the verse states, "You became fat, you thickened, you grew obese" (Deut. 32:15). It takes great wisdom to know how to truly and correctly receive those things for which we have prayed.[8] On a certain level, success and a good and pleasant life are dangerous. They lead a person to a thoughtless life, to an island of tranquility far from any inspiration and exaltation of the spirit. Yet we pray for these things and do not pray for suffering. This is the paradox of the juxtaposition "Blessed is the man whom You chastise, Lord."

In a certain sense, this is like the paradox inherent in how we treat children. A misbehaving child receives more attention and time than a good child, and he receives more than the good child in the end. Similarly, the Talmud tells us, "Had Israel not sinned, they would have been given the five books of the Torah and the book of Joshua alone" (*Nedarim* 22b). In a way, we must be grateful for the sins of our forefathers, which resulted in the writing of the greater part of *Tanakh*. Our history and the subject matter of our prophets are our misdeeds,

8. See commentary on *Iggeret HaKodesh*, epistle 2.

sins, and rebelliousness because, in a sense, all these require a higher level of God's involvement. A person who is wicked will, as it were, attain God's attention, because only God's personal intervention will be able to heal him. ☞ ☞

RABBI AKIVA'S TRUE LOVE

☞ Medicine is more precious than food, but it is also more bitter. Like children, we do not want bitter medicine. We want things to be as sweet and pleasant as possible. To mature and leave this childlike stage behind, to learn to desire those things that are bitter but good, is extraordinarily difficult. Only rare individuals reach the stage at which they can honestly ask for suffering.

One such person was Rabbi Akiva. When the Romans raked his flesh with iron combs, causing him excruciating suffering, Rabbi Akiva felt that at long last he had attained the fulfillment of his dreams: to truly recite the *Shema* "with all your heart and with all your soul and with all your might" (Deut. 6:5). He said, "All my days I have been troubled by the verse 'with all your soul,' meaning, even if God takes your soul. I said to myself: When will the [opportunity] be afforded me to fulfill this [verse]?" (*Berakhot* 61b).

Throughout Rabbi Akiva's life, he lacked this one thing, and he suffered because he could not fully express his love of God. Only when his flesh was raked with iron combs could he, for perhaps the first time in his life, reach a sense of fulfillment in his love, a pleasure in terrible suffering until, as Rabbi Akiva recited the word *eḥad* in the *Shema*, his soul left his body.

A RIGHTEOUS PERSON WHO PROSPERS

☞ Unlike the author of the *Tanya*'s definition of a righteous person who prospers, or, as he understands it, a righteous person who possesses only good (see chap. 1), the simple understanding of this talmudic phrase is a person who has it good in life, who is immune from experiencing bad. He sees things differently than we generally do, seeing not what he lacks but what he has.

This is a different spiritual construct, a different way of living, a state of being in which it is impossible to suffer. This is not to say that in an objective sense such a person does not experience troubles and ills but that he does not suffer. Rabbi Naḥman of Breslov, certainly not a naïve man, suffered from tuberculosis at the end of his life. He never complained about having contracted this disease, but expressed great pleasure if, between coughing and spitting up blood, he was able to say a few words.

True, this level of consciousness is not normal, because in general a tzaddik is not a normative figure. When a normal person receives this gift of "Blessed is the man whom You chastise, Lord," he feels the pain. His challenge, then, is whether he can receive it as a gift. The point is not to derive pleasure from suffering, which no one enjoys. What is important is whether or not a person is prepared to accept that suffering, to learn from it, and to go forward.

When a person accepts suffering, he is prepared to receive blessing. If not, the

וְלָכֵן אָמְרוּ רַבּוֹתֵינוּ ז"ל (יומא כג, א) כִּי הַשְּׂמֵחִים בְּיִסּוּרִים - עֲלֵיהֶם הַכָּתוּב אוֹמֵר: "וְאוֹהֲבָיו כְּצֵאת הַשֶּׁמֶשׁ בִּגְבוּרָתוֹ" (שופטים ה, לא). כִּי הַשִּׂמְחָה הִיא מֵאַהֲבָתוֹ קִרְבַת ה' יוֹתֵר מִכָּל חַיֵּי הָעוֹלָם הַזֶּה, כְּדִכְתִיב: "כִּי טוֹב חַסְדְּךָ מֵחַיִּים" וגו' (תהלים סג, ד).

In this vein, our Rabbis taught (*Yoma* 23a) **that the verse states with regard to those who are happy** even **in** their **suffering, "May all those who love Him be like the sun coming out in its might"** (Judg. 5:31), **for this joy** in suffering **stems from one's love for closeness to God more than all the life in this world, as it is written, "For your kindness is better than life…"** (Ps. 63:4).

Why is this verse quoted here to refer specifically to those who rejoice in their suffering? What is the relationship between those who rejoice in their suffering and "those who love him like the sun coming out in its might"?

In a sense, God's kindness and our mundane lives are diametrically opposed, and man must choose between them. In its highest form, divine kindness does not always appear in the form of life, in the form of obvious pleasure and goodness. Someone with a tangible love of God can say that "Your kindness is better than life," because he can

suffering has been wasted on him. So we read repeatedly in the rebuke in the Torah: "And if with this you do not heed Me, and you walk contrarily with Me, I will walk with you in furious contrariness" (Lev. 26:27–28). If the suffering does not teach us anything, if we do not read its message but say that everything has been mere coincidence, then it will return. As long as people are not prepared to accept it, it will come back again and again.

When a person accepts suffering as a gift from God, and as a result begins to grow, he no longer suffers. At that moment, the medicine is having its effect. As the verse states, "Blessed is the man whom You chastise, Lord, whom You instruct with Your teaching." When a person learns from his suffering, then "blessed is the man." But if he does not learn, if he considers his suffering as mere coincidence, and it does not bring him to a state where "You instruct with Your teaching" – where he learns from his suffering – then he is not a blessed man. The blessed man describes someone who has experienced suffering and learned from it. He has received grave and exalted circumstances from the hidden world, matters that are, as it were, from the world of God, which is concealed in our world, and yet he can, in some way, relate to them and grow from them.

choose the kindness of God and closeness to Him over the apparent and visible good of this world.

וְקָרְבַת ה׳ הִיא בְּיֶתֶר שְׂאֵת וּמַעֲלָה לְאֵין קֵץ בְּעָלְמָא דְּאִתְכַּסְיָא כִּי שָׁם חֶבְיוֹן עוּזּוֹ, וְיוֹשֵׁב בְּסֵתֶר עֶלְיוֹן.

Closeness to God is of an infinitely greater magnitude and quality in the concealed world, for there is the hiding place of His might, and the Most High dwells in concealment.

The more elevated the Divine, the more it is hidden. A person is therefore closest to God when the flow of divine energy descends from the hidden world, even though he can hardly understand that language. In the relationship between a teacher and student, the student might feel more comfortable if his teacher speaks to him with words and concepts that he readily understands. But if he truly wishes to learn new things, he must strain to grasp a difficult language, even if he can barely understand it. Similarly, when God talks to us in a familiar language and with familiar concepts, with the goodness that we recognize and the evil that we know, God is speaking to us in a simplistic language. But when God speaks to us in a more difficult language, one not so easily understood, a language that can at times cause us pain and suffering, God is conversing with us in a higher language, and we are in turn immeasurably closer to the Divine.

The more profound the inner meaning, the more difficult it is to understand. It is sometimes so difficult that we only sense the difficulty and must, as it were, chew on this bitter herb until we at last understand its goodness, its rationale, its content. One who rejoices in suffering, who feels that God speaks to him through suffering no less than He does through those things ordinarily considered good and positive, knows that closeness to God in the hidden world is much greater than ordinary good, because "Your kindness is better than life." Closeness to God is better and sweeter than the life of this world.

וְעַל כֵּן זוֹכֶה לְ״צֵאת הַשֶּׁמֶשׁ בִּגְבוּרָתוֹ״ לֶעָתִיד לָבֹא, שֶׁהִיא יְצִיאַת חַמָּה מִנַּרְתֵּקָהּ שֶׁהִיא מְכוּסָּה

Therefore, this person **merits** experiencing **"the sun when it goes forth in its might" in the World to Come, namely, the emergence of the sun**

בּוֹ בָּעוֹלָם הַזֶּה, וְלֶעָתִיד תִּתְגַּלֶּה מִכִּסּוּיָהּ. דְּהַיְינוּ שֶׁאָז יִתְגַּלֶּה עָלְמָא דְּאִתְכַּסְיָא

from its sheath within which it was concealed in this world and which will ultimately be removed from its casing. That is, in the World to Come, **the world of concealment will be revealed**

The Sages note that the sun is now concealed within a sheath, whereas in the messianic era its light will be completely revealed, as the verse states, "The light of the moon will be like the light of the sun, and the light of the sun will be sevenfold, like the light of the seven days" (Isa. 30:26).[9]

Our world operates in almost total blackness. That which we perceive is the minimal amount of light passing through the sheath, the concealing filter. But in the messianic era, our world will experience a total revolution. The hidden world will be transformed into a revealed world.

וְיִזְרַח וְיָאִיר בְּגִילּוּי רַב וְעָצוּם לְכָל הַחוֹסִים בּוֹ בָּעוֹלָם הַזֶּה וּמִסְתּוֹפְפִים בְּצִלּוֹ צֵל הַחָכְמָה, שֶׁהוּא בְּחִינַת צֵל וְלֹא אוֹרָה וְטוֹבָה נִרְאֵית, וְדַי לַמֵּבִין.

and will shine forth and radiate in a mighty and awesome revelation for all those **who take refuge in** God **in this world and lodge in His shadow, the shadow of wisdom, which possesses the quality of a shadow as opposed to perceivable light and good. This is sufficient for one who understands** esoteric wisdom.

At present, God's utmost wisdom is hidden, operating in shadow. One who is prepared to sit in that shadow while in this reality will, in the messianic era, attain the light of wisdom and see the sun as it rises in its full might. Elsewhere, the Sages say that in the messianic era, God will remove the sun from its sheath, and the righteous will be healed by it and the wicked will be punished by it.[10] The tzaddik who was prepared to receive the sunlight while it was sheathed will receive it when it is

9. See *Bereshit Rabba* 3:6, 6:6; *Pesaḥim* 68a.

10. *Nedarim* 8b.

revealed as well. But a person who was not prepared to receive it when it was sheathed will be burned by its naked rays. ☞

אַךְ הָעַצְבוּת מִמִּילֵי דִשְׁמַיָּא, צָרִיךְ לָשִׁית עֵצוֹת בְּנַפְשׁוֹ לִיפָּטֵר מִמֶּנָּה.

Yet with regard to **sadness** deriving **from** 22 Shevat
heavenly matters, one must devise stratagems for himself to rid himself of it.

This refers to sadness that results from a person's degeneration in any or all spiritual pursuits. Until this point, the author of the *Tanya* has discussed the unhappiness that results from mundane concerns: child-rearing, life and health, and livelihood. But sometimes a person suffers not because he lacks anything of this world but because of his lowly spiritual state. This sadness too is not desirable, and he must do all he can to relieve himself of it.

אֵין צָרִיךְ לוֹמַר בִּשְׁעַת עֲבוֹדָה שֶׁצָּרִיךְ לַעֲבוֹד ה' בְּשִׂמְחָה וּבְטוּב לֵבָב,

Needless to say, during the **service** of God **one is required to serve God with joy and with gladness of heart.**

GRAPPLING WITH THE VICISSITUDES OF LIFE

☞ The question of why one suffers is not theoretical. When a person is suffering, he is not open to consolation based on promises of spiritual reward in the future. He is not in a state of mind to philosophize or to accept the standard solace of conventional faith. He wants to know how to relate to the gist of the matter, the existence of his pain, and his present suffering and neediness.

The author of the *Tanya* approaches the subject of suffering by describing it as a gift from God. We receive gifts from Heaven, and they are always positive, even though at first glance that is not always apparent. Sometimes we must give them a second or even a third look before we are able to learn how to relate to them as gifts.

Although this explanation does not solve a person's pain, it removes his sadness. Although it does not resolve the problem, it removes his worries.

What the author of the *Tanya* attempts here is to draw a distinction between suffering and the concealment of God's countenance. Even if a person cannot solve the problem of his suffering, he can still undo the problem of the concealment of God's countenance. Disease, pain, suffering, and all the afflictions that man experiences are part of the structure of our world. Our experience of them is a part of our reality. But when pain and suffering do not appear to us as a concealment of the divine countenance, their meaning is totally transformed.

One must always serve God, whether through prayer or mitzva performance, with joy and gladness, never with sadness and worry, not even worry about one's sins or pangs of conscience.

אֶלָּא אֲפִילּוּ מִי שֶׁהוּא בַּעַל עֲסָקִים וְדֶרֶךְ אֶרֶץ, אִם נוֹפֵל לוֹ עֶצֶב וּדְאָגָה מִמִּילֵי דִשְׁמַיָּא בִּשְׁעַת עֲסָקָיו,

Yet even with regard to **one who engages in business or work, if in the course of his business affairs, he has a sudden thought of sadness or worry pertaining to heavenly matters,**

A person might be in the midst of his business affairs or work when suddenly his mind is filled with thoughts about his poor spiritual condition, how he does not study Torah, is not involved in serving God, and cannot even call himself a man.

בְּיָדוּעַ שֶׁהוּא תַּחְבּוּלַת הַיֵּצֶר, כְּדֵי לְהַפִּילוֹ אַחַר כָּךְ בְּתַאֲווֹת חַס וְשָׁלוֹם, כַּנּוֹדָע.

it is clearly an act of **subterfuge** employed **by the** evil **inclination to cause him to ultimately fall** prey **to** his **lusts, God forbid, as is known.**

He must realize that this is not a sign of holiness but a manifestation of the evil inclination. The sadness that seemingly relates to great and elevated matters does not stem from holiness but from impurity. When a person's evil inclination attempts to overwhelm him with sadness, the cause of that sadness does not matter. The deeper the sadness, the more a person will grow depressed until he succumbs to a temptation of one kind or another.

This is a well-known psychological phenomenon: When a person berates himself for his sinfulness, he is liable to become so depressed that in his despair he paradoxically commits a sin graver than any he already committed. Even if one's sadness seems motivated by the desire to rectify his life, its ultimate outcome discloses its true identity, that it is the cunning of the evil inclination, intended to cast a person to the depths.

שֶׁאִם לֹא כֵן, מֵאַיִן בָּאָה לוֹ עַצְבוּת אֲמִיתִּית מֵחֲמַת אַהֲבַת ה׳ אוֹ יִרְאָתוֹ בְּאֶמְצַע עֲסָקָיו?

If it were not the ploy of the evil inclination, **where did** this **genuine sadness, which stems from love or fear of God, come from in the midst of his business affairs?**

The source of genuine sadness is a genuine love and fear of God. If the sadness one feels comes from that source of holiness, then one would expect to be conscious of that source. But if a person is in the middle of his everyday affairs when overcome by sadness, then what connection does he have at that point to the genuine love and fear of God and the subsequent genuine sadness or joy that results? Clearly his thoughts of sadness do not come from the love and fear of God. Rather, they are a stratagem of the evil inclination, intended to dishearten him and leave him vulnerable to the siren call of further sin.

וְהִנֵּה בֵּין שֶׁנָּפְלָה לוֹ הָעַצְבוּת בִּשְׁעַת עֲבוֹדָה, בְּתַלְמוּד תּוֹרָה אוֹ בִּתְפִלָּה, וּבֵין שֶׁנָּפְלָה לוֹ שֶׁלֹּא בִּשְׁעַת עֲבוֹדָה - זֹאת יָשִׂים אֶל לִבּוֹ, כִּי אֵין הַזְּמַן גְּרָמָא כָּעֵת לְעַצְבוּת אֲמִתִּית, אֲפִילּוּ לְדַאֲגַת עֲוֹנוֹת חֲמוּרִים חַס וְשָׁלוֹם.

Whether the feeling of **sadness came over him during** his divine **service,** such as **while studying Torah or praying, or whether it came over him not during** his **service, he must be well aware that now is an inappropriate time for genuine sadness** and **even for worrying about egregious sins** that he has committed, **God forbid.**

Whenever a person experiences heaviness, a feeling of descent, whether while serving God or while involved in other affairs, even if the reason is a true one, even if this distress is a consequence of his distance from God, he must tell himself, "This is not the time!"

רַק לָזֹאת צָרִיךְ קְבִיעוּת עִתִּים

Rather, this requires fixed times

This is not to say that a person should never ponder his flaws or that he must forget that he ever transgressed. Rather, everything has its time. Just as there is a time to examine one's accounts, there is a time to examine one's soul. When a person has such a thought, but not at the proper time, he must reject it as an unwelcome intrusion.

וּשְׁעַת הַכּוֹשֶׁר בְּיִשּׁוּב הַדַּעַת, לְהִתְבּוֹנֵן בִּגְדוּלַּת ה׳ אֲשֶׁר חָטָא לוֹ, כְּדֵי שֶׁעַל יְדֵי זֶה יִהְיֶה לִבּוֹ נִשְׁבָּר בֶּאֱמֶת, בִּמְרִירוּת אֲמִתִּית, וְכַמְבוֹאָר עֵת זוֹ

and an appropriate time frame, as well as **a composed mind** with which **to contemplate the greatness of God against whom he sinned, so that he** may ultimately **achieve a truly broken heart accompanied by true bitterness.**

בְּמָקוֹם אַחֵר. וְשָׁם נִתְבָּאֵר גַּם כֵּן כִּי מִיָּד אַחַר שֶׁנִּשְׁבַּר לִבּוֹ בְּעִתִּים קְבוּעִים הָהֵם - אֲזַי יָסִיר הָעֶצֶב מִלִּבּוֹ לְגַמְרֵי

This time for remorse **is described elsewhere** (*Iggeret HaTeshuva,* chaps. 7, 11), **where it is also explained that immediately upon achieving a broken heart at those fixed times, one must completely remove the** feelings of **sadness from his heart,**

This contemplation must be well timed and more than a thought that suddenly appears in one's mind without any knowledge of its source. In order to develop the correct perspective, one should begin one's reflection not with a monotonous recitation on the theme "I am wicked, I am a sinner" but with a meditation on the grandeur of God.

Once he has contemplated the greatness of God, he can evaluate himself within this context, and then he will truly come to a broken heart. He will arrive at a sadness that is not generated by his evil inclination but that is genuine bitterness, which, as the author will explain, has its time and place.

Having examined one's soul and concluded that one indeed stands at the lowest rung, having attained a genuine state of broken-heartedness, one may not remain in that state. He must immediately and completely remove the sadness from his heart.

There is a time to engage in such a reckoning, and that reckoning must be candid and authentic. If a person appears to himself to be wretched, base, and abject, he must gaze unflinchingly at that self-portrait and allow his heart to break. But that heartbreak cannot be permanent, because a broken soul does no one any good. Once he knows himself, once he has achieved a broken heart, it is time to move on to a new surge of devotion and constructiveness.

וְיַאֲמִין אֱמוּנָה שְׁלֵימָה כִּי ה' הֶעֱבִיר חַטָּאתוֹ וְרַב לִסְלוֹחַ.

and believe wholeheartedly that God has removed his sin and forgives abundantly.

This new momentum is, to the degree that his self-examination was unreserved and honest, pure and whole. The more profoundly his heart was broken, the more profoundly is his present rectification based on a deep, wholehearted faith that God forgives whatever it is possible to forgive, in any way that it is possible to forgive. From this vantage point of pure faith, at the genuine end of one phase in his life and a true beginning of another, one must begin anew his service of God.

וְזוֹ הִיא הַשִּׂמְחָה הָאֲמִיתִּית בַּה' הַבָּאָה אַחַר הָעֶצֶב, כַּנִּזְכָּר לְעֵיל.

This is the true joy in God that follows genuine **sadness, as mentioned above.**

One does not have to constantly make such a reckoning. Endless involvement in such self-examination prevents a person from fulfilling his obligations, particularly if his reckoning leads him to conclude that his sins outweigh his merits. Yet it is necessary to engage from time to time in an honest reckoning, which might cause a person temporary worry or sadness. But one may not wallow in the sadness, even if justified. As soon as one recognizes one's weak and problematic points, one must rouse oneself once again to renewed service of God.

An old folk saying says that making a reckoning is half of the punishment. Although this reckoning is an important step, it is only a temporary one. The sadness that results is necessary, but it must be followed by joy.

At the outset of this chapter, the author of the *Tanya* pointed out that true joy is that which follows sadness, as the verse states, "In all sadness, there will be an advantage." After seeing oneself at the very nadir, after stripping oneself of all false joy, when one believes that God forgives and absolves a person of his sins, he is ready to attain a genuine joy in God Himself, and with this strength to begin anew.

Chapter 27

THE PREVIOUS CHAPTER DEALT WITH THE STRUGGLE to overcome sadness and eradicate it from the heart, no matter what the cause, whether mundane or spiritual. There is no room for sadness in one's life, with a few specific exceptions, such as when one uses sadness as a vehicle to transport one to authentic joy in the service of God. This chapter continues the discussion of various types of sadness, including that which seems to have its roots in holiness, and offers advice on how to relate to painful thoughts and wrongful desires.

וְאִם הָעַצְבוּת אֵינָהּ מִדַּאֲגַת עֲוֹנוֹת, אֶלָּא מֵהִרְהוּרִים רָעִים וְתַאֲווֹת רָעוֹת שֶׁנּוֹפְלוֹת בְּמַחֲשַׁבְתּוֹ,

If the sadness is not a result of worry over sins that one committed **but rather a result of evil thoughts and evil lusts that suddenly enter one's mind,** 23 Shevat

2 Adar I (leap year)

In the previous chapter, the author of the *Tanya* stated that sadness, even that which is caused by dwelling on one's sins, does not play a role in the service of God and is entirely unhelpful. Here he adds that this is true both when one reflects on the past and when one reacts to the negative thoughts and desires of the moment.

Every individual who serves God must sooner or later encounter the universal and fundamental problem that nothing in one's spiritual growth is assured. A person could dedicate his whole life to holiness and engage only in sanctified deeds, words, and thoughts, when he is suddenly assailed by doubts in his faith and by profane desires.

If one were to judge his life at such a moment, he might well deem it a hopeless failure. He might question what his service of God had accomplished and whether he had grown spiritually in any way at all since he is still capable of entertaining such lowly thoughts and feelings. At such a moment, he is liable to experience a sadness more harmful than any sin he has ever committed.

הִנֵּה אִם נוֹפְלוֹת לוֹ שֶׁלֹּא בִּשְׁעַת הָעֲבוֹדָה, אֶלָּא בְּעֵת עָסְקוֹ בַּעֲסָקָיו וְדֶרֶךְ אֶרֶץ וּכְהַאי גַּוְונָא, אַדְּרַבָּה, יֵשׁ לוֹ לִשְׂמוֹחַ בְּחֶלְקוֹ.

then if they suddenly occur to him not during his service of God **but rather while he is engaged in his** business **affairs and mundane activities and the like, he should, on the contrary, be happy with his portion.**

If spiritual doubts and harmful desires arise when a person is not engaged in studying Torah, performing mitzvot, or praying, but rather when he is doing such things as earning a living or eating and drinking, rather than growing despondent that he experienced such thoughts, he should be glad.

שֶׁאַף שֶׁנּוֹפְלוֹת לוֹ בְּמַחֲשַׁבְתּוֹ - הוּא מַסִּיחַ דַּעְתּוֹ מֵהֶן, לְקַיֵּים מַה שֶּׁנֶּאֱמַר: "וְלֹא תָתוּרוּ אַחֲרֵי לְבַבְכֶם וְאַחֲרֵי עֵינֵיכֶם אֲשֶׁר אַתֶּם זוֹנִים אַחֲרֵיהֶם" (במדבר טו, לט).

Although they suddenly enter his mind, he may divert his mind from them, fulfilling what it states in the verse **"You shall not rove after your heart and after your eyes, after which you stray"** (Num. 15:39).

When a person's mind is invaded by these unwanted thoughts, he has the opportunity to fulfill the precept not to follow after his heart and eyes by diverting his mind from them. For this reason, he should be happy, not fall into depression.[1]

1. The Lubavitcher Rebbe, Rabbi Menaḥem Mendel Schneerson, points out that if he does not divert his attention from these sudden thoughts, then the sadness that results is in the same category as that which is evoked because he worries about the sins of his past, which the author of the *Tanya* discussed in the previous chapter. There he said that one must immediately transform such sadness into joy and not dwell on it at all.

וְאֵין הַכָּתוּב מְדַבֵּר בְּצַדִּיקִים לִקְרָאָם זוֹנִים חַס וְשָׁלוֹם,

The verse is not addressing the righteous, referring to them as those who stray, God forbid,

Clearly, the phrase "after which you stray" is not speaking of tzaddikim, who do not experience temptation in their daily lives.

אֶלָּא בְּבֵינוֹנִים כַּיּוֹצֵא בּוֹ, שֶׁנּוֹפְלִים לוֹ הִרְהוּרֵי נִיאוּף בְּמַחֲשַׁבְתּוֹ, בֵּין בְּהֶיתֵּר כו'.

but rather *beinonim* like himself, in whose mind illicit thoughts enter unwittingly, whether they are thoughts of that which is **permitted** or prohibited acts of sexuality.

A licentious thought of an innocent nature involves someone with whom relations are permitted, whether one's spouse or a woman whom it is permitted to marry. Forbidden thoughts involve a woman whom one is prohibited from marrying.

וּכְשֶׁמֵּסִיחַ דַּעְתּוֹ מְקַיֵּים לָאו זֶה,

When one diverts his mind from such thoughts, **he fulfills** the mitzva of avoiding **this prohibition,**

Even if a person does not fully succeed in averting his mind but at least lessens the time or intensity of the thought, he fulfills the prohibition of turning away from evil.[2]

וְאָמְרוּ רַבּוֹתֵינוּ ז"ל: "יָשַׁב וְלֹא עָבַר עֲבֵירָה, נוֹתְנִים לוֹ שָׂכָר כְּאִלּוּ עָשָׂה מִצְוָה" (קידושין לט, ב). וְעַל כֵּן צָרִיךְ לִשְׂמוֹחַ בְּקִיּוּם הַלָּאו כְּמוֹ בְּקִיּוּם מִצְוַת עֲשֵׂה מַמָּשׁ.

and our Rabbis stated, "**If one sits and does not transgress, he receives a reward as one who performs a mitzva**" (*Kiddushin* 39b). **Therefore, one should rejoice in** his **fulfillment of** the mitzva of avoiding **the prohibition just as** one does **when fulfilling an actual positive commandment.**

The Talmud explains that one does not fulfill a prohibition all the time that one does not sin but rather only when there is an opportunity to sin and one refrains from doing so. The prohibition of "You shall not rove after your heart" presents itself only when a person has the desire

2. Rambam, *Sefer HaMitzvot*, prohibition 47.

and does not yield. When he restrains himself and overcomes his desire, he merits fulfilling the mitzva. If so, why should this person be depressed about such thoughts? He now has the opportunity to fulfill a mitzva by refraining from transgressing a prohibition, which is no less meaningful than the performance of any other mitzva.

3 Adar I (leap year)

וְאַדְּרַבָּה, הָעַצְבוּת הִיא מִגַּסּוּת הָרוּחַ שֶׁאֵינוֹ מַכִּיר מְקוֹמוֹ,

On the contrary, this sadness stems from arrogance, a result of the fact **that he does not recognize his place.**

A person may think that his sadness is an expression of holiness. But it actually comes from the *kelippa* of overweening pride. He feels proud and so he estimates himself too highly.

וְעַל כֵּן יֵרַע לִבָבוֹ עַל שֶׁאֵינוֹ בְּמַדְרֵגַת צַדִּיק, שֶׁלְּצַדִּיקִים בְּוַדַּאי אֵין נוֹפְלִים לָהֶם הִרְהוּרֵי שְׁטוּת כָּאֵלּוּ.

Consequently, his heart is troubled because he is not on the level of tzaddik, for such foolish thoughts do not occur to the righteous.

Since he considers himself a tzaddik, he grows dispirited when he has such thoughts. This mood originates not in holiness but in egotism. He may also grow angry that others do not recognize him as a tzaddik. Feeling insulted that he must still struggle, he may lash out. He may wonder why he is fated to repeat his hard work having already gained spiritual victory.

כִּי אִילּוּ הָיָה מַכִּיר מְקוֹמוֹ שֶׁהוּא רָחוֹק מְאֹד מִמַּדְרֵגַת צַדִּיק,

Were he to recognize his place, namely, **that he is exceedingly far from** having attained **the level of tzaddik,**

The rank of tzaddik is extraordinarily lofty. It is attained by an elite few in each generation. No one else, not even those who have served God in a spirit of holiness for all their lives, can realistically strive to achieve it.

וְהַלְוַאי הָיָה בֵּינוֹנִי וְלֹא רָשָׁע כָּל יָמָיו, אֲפִילּוּ שָׁעָה אַחַת, הֲרֵי זֹאת הִיא מִדַּת הַבֵּינוֹנִים

and if only he were to strive **to be a** *beinoni* **and not a wicked person his entire life, even for one moment, then**

וַעֲבוֹדָתָם - לִכְבּוֹשׁ הַיֵּצֶר וְהַהִרְהוּר הָעוֹלֶה מֵהַלֵּב לַמּוֹחַ וּלְהַסִּיחַ דַּעְתּוֹ לְגַמְרֵי מִמֶּנּוּ וְלִדְחוֹתוֹ בִּשְׁתֵּי יָדַיִם, כַּנִּזְכָּר לְעֵיל.

he would recognize that **this is the lot and task of *beinonim*,** namely, **to subdue the** evil **inclination and any** evil **thought that rises from the heart to the brain, completely diverting his mind from it and utterly rejecting it, as discussed above** (chap. 12).

Rather than attempt to become a tzaddik, a person must strive to be a *beinoni*. When he sets this as his goal, he will not be upset or disheartened if he has evil urges and foolish thoughts. A *beinoni* has not solved any problems at their root. He has not transformed his character in any fundamental sense. He still has the inclinations, desires, and weaknesses of his past. But unlike a wicked person, he has the ability to control these qualities. The *beinoni* has not yet ended the battle but remains in the midst of the fray. He constantly struggles to push away the many temptations that assail him, but invariably he emerges victorious.

4 Adar I (leap year)

וּבְכָל דְּחִיָּה וּדְחִיָּה שֶׁמַּדְחֵהוּ מִמַּחֲשַׁבְתּוֹ,

Each and every time he successfully **repels** the thought **from his mind,**

The *beinoni* lacks the ability to control his heart. Rather, his power rests in his mind. When temptation arises and moves from the heart to the brain, he can push away the thought so that he will neither consider nor commit the unholy deed.

אִתְכַּפְיָא סִטְרָא אָחֳרָא לְתַתָּא,

the *sitra aḥara* is subdued below, in our world.

He subjugates the *sitra aḥara*, the force of impurity as it exists on our plane, as will be explained below.

וּבְאִתְעָרוּתָא דִּלְתַתָּא אִתְעָרוּתָא דִּלְעֵילָּא, וְאִתְכַּפְיָא סִטְרָא אָחֳרָא דִּלְעֵילָּא,

By means of an awakening from below, a reciprocal **awakening from above** is generated, **and the *sitra aḥara* on high,** at its root, **is subdued** as well.

Whatever occurs in our world also occurs in the higher world in an even more powerful and encompassing form. When the *sitra aḥara* is subdued in this world, it is also subdued at its source.

הַמַּגְבִּיהַּ עַצְמָהּ כַּנֶּשֶׁר, לְקַיֵּים מַה שֶּׁנֶּאֱמַר: "אִם תַּגְבִּיהַּ כַּנֶּשֶׁר וגו', מִשָּׁם אוֹרִידְךָ נְאֻם ה'" (עובדיה א, ד).

The root of impurity lies in the fact that **it raises itself like a** soaring **eagle to fulfill what is stated in the verse "If you raise yourself like the eagle,** or place your nest among the stars, **from there I will bring you down – the utterance of the Lord"** (Obad. 1:4).

The root and source of *kelippa* is that it elevates itself to become an entity in itself, separated from God.

וּכְמוֹ שֶׁהִפְלִיג בַּזֹּהַר פָּרָשַׁת תְּרוּמָה [דַּף קכח] בְּגוֹדֶל נַחַת רוּחַ לְפָנָיו יִתְבָּרֵךְ כַּד אִתְכַּפְיָא סִטְרָא אָחֳרָא לְתַתָּא, דְּאִסְתַּלֵּק יְקָרָא דְקֻדְשָׁא בְּרִיךְ הוּא לְעֵילָּא עַל כּוֹלָּא, יַתִּיר מִשְּׁבָחָא אָחֳרָא, וְאִסְתַּלְּקוּתָא דָא יַתִּיר מִכּוֹלָּא וכו'.

The *Zohar* on *Parashat* **Teruma (p. 128) extolls the great sense of gratification that God derives when the** *sitra aḥara* **is subdued below,** stating **that the glory of the Holy One, blessed be He, is elevated above all, more than by** any **other praise, and** that **this elevation is greater than all else and so on.**

The subjugation of evil constitutes God's praise because He is then glorified in all the worlds.[3] This is the greatest praise possible, since it is expressed as the fulfillment of the ultimate purpose of the world's creation. It is specifically for this purpose that God created a vastly complex structure that encompasses multiple worlds. The divine service of an angel is a loftier level of worship and more complete than anything a human being could achieve. But since an angel exists solely in the higher worlds, it cannot relate to physical entities, created on a comparatively lower level, and so it cannot fulfill the highest purpose of creation. Only imperfect mortal man, who struggles with himself

3. For further elaboration, see *Torah Or* 114b; *Likkutei Torah*, Ex. 3b, Num. 65c; *Ma'amar Bati LeGani* (1950), chap. 1.

and who can yield to the *sitra aḥara* and become lower than everything, can in turn cause God's glory to rise beyond all other praise, toward the original purpose of existence and beyond it, when he makes the choice to subjugate the *sitra aḥara.* ☞

SUBDUING AND TRANSFORMING

☞ Hasidic texts discuss at length two basic paths or levels in serving God: subduing the *sitra aḥara* and transforming the *sitra aḥara.* In subduing the *sitra aḥara,* a person is in a spiritual state where, left to his own devices, he would act as he pleases, even if contrary to God's will. In this path of divine service, one must compel himself to subdue his own inclinations and refrain from acting on his impulses. As soon as a person sincerely desires to do God's will, there is no need to compel himself to subdue his inclinations.

On the other hand, when a person, no matter his spiritual standing, transforms the *sitra aḥara,* he transforms his deepest desires so that they become one with God's will. He transforms his attraction to the mundane into a love of the Divine. This is not a novel love that did not exist before but rather a complete transformation of his preexisting love. Where before he was drawn to material pleasures, or even to more refined pursuits, this love is now channeled solely toward God.

The distinction between these two paths may be found in *Pirkei Avot* (2:4): "Make His will like your will, so that He will make your will like His will, and nullify your will before His will so that He will nullify the will of others before your will." "Make His will like your will" refers to one who would otherwise desire the wrong things and would act on those desires but instead compels himself to do God's will as though it were his own. "Nullify your will" means that a person completely erases his own will and instead aligns all his desires with the divine will. If a person on this level were allowed to do as he wished, he would do exactly what God wants (see *Likkutei Torah*, Num. 2a).

The path of transformation is usually considered the superior course. It is a level of expanded consciousness based on an inner identification with the Divine. The path of subjugation is a spiritually undeveloped level, void of this divine identification. Yet the hasidic literature also presents the opposite view and finds that subjugation can sometimes surpass transformation. This perspective focuses not on the level to which a person's consciousness and emotions have evolved but rather on the spiritual energy that he is able to muster and manifest in his service of God.

When one transforms his desires, he achieves enlightenment, a true understanding that his inner being and outer deeds are one. But for this very reason, the relationship is limited by one's ability to comprehend. One can never understand beyond one's capacity. But when a person subjugates his desire, when his actions are not the expression of his inner understanding, it is possible for him to be affected beyond the limits of his personality and of his understanding in general.

A child's mind is limited compared to that of an adult. This limited ability is known as *moḥin dekatnut*, a constricted or undeveloped consciousness. A child's

24 Shevat וְלָכֵן אַל יִפּוֹל לֵב אָדָם עָלָיו וְלֹא יֵרַע לְבָבוֹ מְאֹד גַּם אִם יִהְיֶה כֵּן כׇּל יָמָיו בְּמִלְחָמָה זוֹ, כִּי אוּלַי לְכָךְ נִבְרָא וְזֹאת עֲבוֹדָתוֹ לְאַכְפְּיָא לְסִטְרָא אָחֳרָא תָּמִיד.

Therefore, there is no need for a person to be saddened or unduly distressed at heart, even if he is to be engaged his entire life in this battle. Perhaps it is for this that he was created, and this is his divine **service** that is demanded of him: **to constantly subdue the *sitra aḥara*.**

We all want to attain the level where we no longer experience certain thoughts and desires and are free to engage in other matters. But it is very possible that we will never reach that point, that we are by nature

mind is not as developed physically and spiritually as an adult's, and he cannot understand matters as deeply as an adult could. Yet it is precisely because of this limitation that a child can learn new languages more easily than adults can. He is capable of absorbing information without the barriers formed by previous misconceptions, while for an adult such an endeavor would take years of dedicated study. The adult, on the other hand, uses concepts that are shaped by the language in which he thinks. He may find it difficult, sometimes even impossible, to shift from one conceptual framework to another – in this example, from one language to another. Although a child may not understand as the adult does, he can at any rate absorb the material more readily.

Many hasidic teachings discuss the difference between a child of God, who walks on the path of transformation, and a servant of God, who travels the course of subjugation (see chap. 41; see also *Torah Or* 114b; *Likkutei Torah*, Num. 39a, 73a). A child does his father's will because he loves his father and identifies with him, so he nullifies his own will to that of the father. A servant, on the other hand, does the will of his master because he is forced to do so.

Without question, the son is on a higher plane than the servant, and a person who serves God as a slave must strive with all his might to become a child of God. Even so, in one sense, the servant is superior to the child, because "the hand of a slave is like the hand of his master" (*Gittin* 77b). A servant is not an independent being but the master's tool. When it comes to divine service, a person who takes on the role of servant accepts the yoke of God's sovereignty with an unthinking, unconditional submission. In this, the servant's self-nullification to God is superior to that of a son. The servant does not understand a thing, he has no conceptual limits, so he can arrive at the highest level where there are no limitations, a reality far loftier than any mind can grasp. Thus, the phrase "servant of the Lord" (see Deut. 34:5) refers to a person who has reached the highest level that a person can attain.

To put it bluntly, on the path of transformation, one who works at transforming his character to align it with holiness does so, in a certain sense, out of egotistical motives since he is elevating himself of his own volition rather than constantly submitting to the divine will even counter to his own. His motivations may be elevated and refined and resonate with holiness, but he is still acting on his own behalf. On this path, his ego continues to exist and is even stressed far more. Even when he is growing and striv-

beinonim who must engage in this struggle our entire lives. A *beinoni* is a professional soldier who is constantly engaged in some aspect of battle, on one front or another. He was not created to live in a safe, protected haven. His job is to serve as a warrior of God, subduing the *sitra aḥara* within himself.

ing toward the highest spiritual attainments, it is his ego that desires them.

We motivate a child by offering candy, yet we do not incentivize an adult with candy, because it is not enticing for him. The adult is attracted by the prospect of honor, and even more so by the appeal of spiritual reward destined for him in the Garden of Eden. Although the incentive changes, at its root it remains one and the same: the acquisition of something for himself.

On the other hand, a person who subjugates his will to that of God sets aside his own desires. He does not identify with the divine will (among other reasons, because he has no sense of self, no ego that can identify with the other). But precisely because of that, he truly serves God, because he is subjugating himself and his being to the Divine. His sense of self has not changed. It has not been transformed. He still wishes to fulfill his desires, yet he does God's will by controlling them. At that moment, his sense of self is nullified.

This correspondence between subjugation and transformation is similar, although not identical, to that of the love of God and the fear of God (see *Likkutei Torah*, Num. 73a). Fear of God, whether an exalted awe or a fear of punishment, parallels the act of subjugation and the role of the servant. It holds an advantage over the love of God, which mirrors the act of transformation and the role of the son. At its base, all love is an expansion of the lover's personality. His "self" loves, grows, and spreads outward so that he becomes a self of two people, of two groups, of the entire world. Any love for another always begins with a sense of self, which becomes the very thing that limits that love. That sense of self may reach great heights, but it does not reach the heavens.

Fear, on the other hand, is a constriction, a gathering inward. A person who fears attempts to withdraw and hide. The result of fear is self-nullification. Even when it comes from nonenlightened impulses, it is still a nullification of an individual's personality in a way that does not limit the flow from above.

The story is told of two great people who were once conversing. One said, "I have reached the seventh heaven!"

The other replied, "I am so small that the seventh heaven comes down to me."

No one is great enough to reach Heaven. Indeed, the greater a person is, the more he prevents Heaven from descending to him. However, when a person is small, Heaven can reach him.

The core of any mitzva (whether the word is translated as "commandment" or "bond") is based on this concept. If the mitzvot were nothing more than good advice, we could relate to them and understand them in some way. But in that case, the mitzvot would not help us forge a bond with God. The creation of a connection, of a bridge across a gap of utter otherness, of a chasm that cannot be crossed, can be achieved only by the connection formed when one fulfills a commandment that is not dependent on understanding. It is only through a connection that we cannot identify, a connection that exists solely in the realm of subjugation, that we can make the transition to the transcendent Divine.

One danger that such a soldier faces is the feeling that he is wasting his life. While he may progress, he never feels that his problems have been resolved, that he has reached the end of the journey. Feeling powerless, unable to gain a clear victory, he may be led to the greatest defeat, and sin, of all: being incapacitated by dejection. The author of the *Tanya* therefore explains that the *beinoni*'s existence does have meaning, that a life of insoluble problems, of striving with an inability to arrive at an end, has its own value and is an existence worthy of his aspirations.

וְעַל זֶה אָמַר אִיּוֹב: "בָּרָאתָ רְשָׁעִים" (בבא בתרא טז, א).

Regarding this, Job said, "You created righteous people, and **You created wicked people**" (*Bava Batra* 16a).

In chapter 1, the author of the *Tanya* expressed surprise at this deterministic statement, since it runs contrary to the axiomatic notion that whether one is wicked or righteous is solely a result of one's own choosing. The author addresses his question later, in chapter 14, where he explained that the concept of God creating righteous people means that He grants only a select few the ability to choose to be righteous. The author of the *Tanya* will now explain the continuation of Job's statement, "You created wicked people."

וְלֹא שֶׁיִּהְיוּ רְשָׁעִים בֶּאֱמֶת חַס וְשָׁלוֹם,

It is **not that they will be** created **wicked in truth, God forbid,**

Job was not saying that God creates wicked people, because whether a person will be wicked or not depends entirely on one's power of free choice. If a person wishes to sin, there is nothing to stop him. If he wishes to descend, there are many paths he can take, yet such a descent is not preordained.

In this vein, this world is compared to the Hebrew letter *heh*, which has two openings, one toward the top and one at the bottom. This symbolizes how a person can choose which path to take. The opening at the bottom is always open, and one can always step through it, but no one is forced to descend into sin.

אֶלָּא שֶׁיַּגִּיעַ אֲלֵיהֶם כְּמַעֲשֵׂה הָרְשָׁעִים, בְּמַחְשַׁבְתָּם וְהִרְהוּרָם לְבַד, וְהֵם יִהְיוּ נִלְחָמִים תָּמִיד לְהַסִּיחַ דַּעְתָּם מֵהֶם כְּדֵי לְאַכְפְּיָא לְסִטְרָא אָחֳרָא.

but rather that in their minds and thoughts alone enter that which occurs to the wicked, and they must constantly engage in battle to divert their minds from these evil impulses **in order to subdue the *sitra aḥara*.**

These people are created with the character and temperament of the wicked, with an evil inclination that cannot be completely eradicated, as well as a constitution of emotional faculties that are capable of sin. But although they cannot change their nature, they can overcome it by waging an internal battle against it. They can decide that they wish to do good and not evil and live by their commitment.

וְלֹא יוּכְלוּ לְבַטְּלָהּ מִכֹּל וָכֹל, כִּי זֶה נַעֲשֶׂה עַל יְדֵי צַדִּיקִים.

They will never be able to totally nullify the *sitra aḥara,* **for this is** a feat **accomplished by the righteous.**

Only the tzaddik can nullify the *sitra aḥara* so that it is no longer a part of his life and experience. The *beinoni,* who cannot accomplish this, must constantly work to overcome it. It is true that as a member of the Jewish people, particularly if he is a leader, a tzaddik knows that evil exists. Yet this is not an internal, intimate knowledge but rather an external awareness, just as one can know about the world of animals without being an animal oneself. A tzaddik knows that evil exists, and he is able to empathize with those who suffer because they are wicked, but he himself cannot experience these troubles. Although he recognizes the existence of such a problem, he himself is not a part of that problem. Since it is not his task to battle the *sitra ahara,* he is not meant to conquer it.

In this light, when Job speaks of the righteous and the wicked, he is referring to two types of people who will always be different: those who can become tzaddikim and those who will at best become *beinonim.*

וּשְׁנֵי מִינֵי נַחַת רוּחַ לְפָנָיו יִתְבָּרֵךְ לְמַעְלָה.

There are two types of divine gratification on high. 5 Adar I (leap year)

A deeper analysis will show that the two levels, subduing the *sitra aḥara* and transforming it, are not hierarchically placed. One is not superior to the other, but they are equal in stature. If God had a single, hierarchical value system, with some people superior to others, it would be unfair of Him to have created people who could never actualize their potential to the fullest extent. The existence of such imperfect beings would mean a defect in the work of creation. But the author of the *Tanya* tells us, "There are two types of divine gratification on high." Just as God desires the existence of tzaddikim, so He desires the existence of *beinonim* and makes different demands of each.

The distinction between the tzaddik and *beinoni* is similar in this regard to that of non-priest and a priest. God did not create Jews born as non-priests so that they would be transformed into priests. He desires both and does not in any way wish that all Jews be priests.

Both tzaddikim and *beinonim* give God gratification, although not in the same way. They cannot be judged by the same measure, just as an ox and a donkey cannot be treated equally and just as different substances cannot be judged by the same yardstick. Wood and metal cannot be expected to resist the same level of pressure. Each has its own properties and its distinct advantages.

אֶחָד, מִבִּיטּוּל הַסִּטְרָא אָחֳרָא לְגַמְרֵי וְאִתְהַפְּכָא מִמְּרִירוּ לְמִתְקָא וּמֵחֲשׁוֹכָא לִנְהוֹרָא עַל יְדֵי הַצַּדִּיקִים.

One is from the utter nullification of the *sitra aḥara* and its transformation from bitter to sweet and from darkness to light, accomplished **by the righteous.**

TRANSFORMING BITTER TO SWEET

☞ The tzaddik changes both himself and everything around him. Whatever he touches is transformed to sweetness and light. Just as King Midas's touch turned everything to gold, whatever the tzaddik touches is transformed to good. In this vein, the Talmud states, "The righteous person who prospers is completely righteous" (*Berakhot* 7a). This does not mean that a complete tzaddik never experienc-

A person who was born a tzaddik can progress until he attains perfection, when he completely transforms his nature from evil to good. This wondrous phenomenon, the transformation of bitter to sweet, of dark to light, is a source of gratification for God. ☞

es challenging times. But such difficulties do not cause him to suffer. He does not feel the evil in them.

In this spirit, the story is told of two Torah scholars who asked the Maggid of Mezeritch about the talmudic dictum "One recites a blessing for the bad just as he does for the good" (*Berakhot* 60b). The Maggid sent them to his student, Reb Zusha of Anipoli.

Throughout his life, Reb Zusha lived in dire poverty. When these two men came to him with their question, he replied, "I do not understand why the Rebbe sent you to me. I have never had a bad moment in my life."

Events occur on one plane of existence, while we relate to them on another plane, one that is usually confused, snarled, and tangled. That is not the experience of a tzaddik. On the contrary, it is said of a tzaddik that "no evil dwells with You" (Ps. 5:6). The tzaddik turns all darkness that he experiences into light and turns bitterness into sweet.

The tzaddik's experience changes the valence and meaning of things even in the sense of absolute good and evil. From this perspective, a tzaddik is superior to an angel (see *Bava Batra* 75b). An angel is a one-dimensional being since it is only spiritual, while a tzaddik also has a physical aspect. He has a double perspective of reality that is deeper and more meaningful than that of an angel.

The superiority of the tzaddik to an angel exists in the quintessence of reality and is not merely confined to the realm of the intellect. By means of his corporeal body, the righteous individual bears a connection to the physical world and the evil inclination. An angel possesses no evil inclination and is aware of it only from literary sources, so to speak. The tzaddik, by contrast, is fully aware of it due to his very existence in this physical world. Consequently, by dint of his transforming his evil inclination, from bitter to sweet and from darkness to light, he literally transforms and elevates himself and his entire milieu.

In a sense, the superiority of man over angel relates also to the *beinoni*. But the *beinoni*'s ties to the body and to this world are so strong that they are almost impossible to break. The *beinoni* cannot relate to his environment in a way that makes it possible for him to transform it entirely. Only the tzaddik, who is not bound by the physical, can transform the *sitra aḥara*. Since he is not connected to the framework of evil, since he is on the outside looking in, he can bring about the complete transformation from dark to light and bitter to sweet.

The idea that a tzaddik can change reality is first found in God's statement to Abimelech that Abraham "is a prophet, and he shall pray for you, and you will live" (Gen. 20:7). Every generation has unique individuals whose prayers are answered and who can transform bitter to sweet and dark to light.

וְהַשֵּׁנִית, כַּד אִתְכַּפְיָא הַסִּטְרָא אָחֳרָא, בְּעוֹדָהּ בְּתָקְפָּהּ וּגְבוּרָתָהּ וּמַגְבִּיהַּ עַצְמָהּ כַּנֶּשֶׁר - וּמִשָּׁם מוֹרִידָהּ ה׳ בְּאִתְעָרוּתָא דִלְתַתָּא עַל יְדֵי הַבֵּינוֹנִים.

The second is when the *sitra aḥara* is subdued while in its full **potency and strength and raises itself like a** soaring **eagle. God drags it down from** those heights **through an awakening from below initiated by the *beinonim*.**

The *beinoni* subjugates, struggles, and conquers. The tzaddik does not struggle and cannot be a victor in the same way. For him, the enemy has turned into an ally, and the war is over. There is no battle against evil because evil has dissipated before him as darkness gives way to light. Light does not need to battle against the dark. The light only needs to exist for darkness to be vanquished.

The *beinoni* is different: He must struggle with the *sitra aḥara*. For him, the *sitra aḥara* is not a shadow but a demon, not an illusion but a real and malevolent force. The tzaddik has succeeded in overpowering the predatory beasts, while the *beinoni* still struggles with their savagery. When the *beinoni* overcomes the *sitra aḥara* at its most powerful, equal in size to the entire universe, he shatters evil on all levels and in all worlds.

וְזֶהוּ שֶׁאָמַר הַכָּתוּב: ״וַעֲשֵׂה לִי מַטְעַמִּים כַּאֲשֶׁר אָהַבְתִּי״ (בראשית כז, ד). ״מַטְעַמִּים״ - לְשׁוֹן רַבִּים, שְׁנֵי מִינֵי נַחַת רוּחַ. וְהוּא מַאֲמַר הַשְּׁכִינָה לְבָנֶיהָ כְּלָלוּת יִשְׂרָאֵל, כִּדְפֵירֵשׁ בַּתִּיקּוּנִים (תיקוני זהר נא, ב).

This is the deeper **meaning of the verse "Prepare for me tasty food** [*matamim*], **such as I like"** (Gen. 27:4). The word ***matamim* is in the plural,** referring to the **two types of gratification. This is the directive of the Divine Presence to its children, the collective of Israel, as explained in *Tikkunei* Zohar** (51b),

This verse is understood as God's request of mankind. He wants us to give Him two delicacies, two types of pleasure.

וּכְמוֹ שֶׁבְּמַטְעַמִּים גַּשְׁמִיִּים דֶּרֶךְ מָשָׁל יֵשׁ שְׁנֵי מִינֵי מַעֲדַנִּים: אֶחָד מִמַּאֲכָלִים עֲרֵבִים וּמְתוּקִים

just as with tasty physical food, for example, there are two kinds of delicacies, one of delectable and sweet food and the second of sharp or sour

וְהַשֵּׁנִי מִדְּבָרִים חֲרִיפִים אוֹ חֲמוּצִים, רַק שֶׁהֵם מְתוּבָּלִים וּמְתוּקָּנִים הֵיטֵב עַד שֶׁנַּעֲשׂוּ מַעֲדַנִּים לְהָשִׁיב הַנֶּפֶשׁ.

ingredients but they are spiced and well prepared until they have become delicacies sufficiently tasty **to restore the soul.**

There are foods that are inherently sweet and tasty, and others that are sharp or sour but when spiced properly taste delicious. The tzaddik is like a sweet food. His personality is completely developed, and his traits all express themselves in complete harmony. The *beinoni*, on the other hand, has sharp and sour elements, ingredients that reflect his active evil inclination. When he conquers that inclination, the sharp and the sour are no longer repulsive and evil but pleasant.

Although the *beinoni* cannot always transform his reality into sweetness, he can mitigate it. The sharpness still exists, but it enters a new framework and moves in a different direction. The sharpness is rectified so that it becomes edible, even a delicacy.

This idea may be applied to beauty as well. There is a beauty in perfection, in harmony of form and color. On the other hand, there is the beauty of something that lacks perfection, something twisted and flawed yet so cunningly made that it has its own aesthetic and serves as a counterpart to the classically beautiful.

וְזֶהוּ שֶׁאָמַר הַכָּתוּב: "כֹּל פָּעַל ה' לַמַּעֲנֵהוּ וְגַם רָשָׁע לְיוֹם רָעָה" (משלי טז, ד). פֵּירוּשׁ, שֶׁיָּשׁוּב מֵרִשְׁעוֹ וְיַעֲשֶׂה הָרַע שֶׁלּוֹ יוֹם וְאוֹר לְמַעְלָה, כַּד אִתְכַּפְיָא סִטְרָא אָחֳרָא וְאִסְתַּלֵּק יְקָרָא דְקֻדְשָׁא בְּרִיךְ הוּא לְעֵילָּא.

This is conveyed by the verse "Everything done by the Lord is for its own sake, even the wicked for the evil day" (Prov. 16:4). **This means that one should repent his wickedness and turn his evil** nature **into day and light on high by subduing the *sitra aḥara* and elevating the glory of the Holy One, blessed be He, on high.**

Subjugating evil, and fighting the battle, when it is at the height of its power is an end in itself, not just one stage on the way to converting the evil inclination into good. It is the fulfillment of an end goal that cannot be done in any other way, and only then does the glory of God become exalted.

It is the *beinoni*, not the tzaddik, who can accomplish this. Since the tzaddik does not suffer from evil, he does not battle against it. For him, reality is all good, and he has no personal reason to fight. The *beinoni* does not succumb to evil, which remains an ongoing and very real temptation, but he constantly suffers and is pained by evil (although this never leads him to be ungrateful and deny God's goodness). A *beinoni* must see himself as a soldier in God's war. A soldier does not view his struggle as a sign of inferiority. Confronting the enemy is not a mark that he has fallen or failed. Instead, the confrontation proves that he is actively engaged in the work assigned to him.[4]

25 Shevat
6 Adar I (leap year)

וְלֹא עוֹד, אֶלָּא אֲפִילּוּ בִּדְבָרִים הַמּוּתָּרִים לְגַמְרֵי. כָּל מַה שֶּׁהָאָדָם זוֹבֵחַ יִצְרוֹ אֲפִילּוּ שָׁעָה קַלָּה

Moreover, one must subdue the ***sitra aḥara*** **even with regard to completely permissible matters.** This is achieved **any time one slaughters his inclination, even for but a brief moment,**

The *sitra aḥara* must be subjugated not only in the battle against total evil, against what is expressly prohibited, but even when it comes to permissible matters, such as when a person eats in a moderate and proper manner.

וּמִתְכַּוֵּין לְאַכְפְּיָא לְסִטְרָא אָחֳרָא שֶׁבֶּחָלָל הַשְּׂמָאלִי,

and focuses on subduing the *sitra aḥara* in the left chamber of his heart,

A person can have many reasons for restraining himself. But when he has the intention of overcoming his evil inclination so that he is not a slave to its urges, he is vanquishing the *sitra aḥara*.

כְּגוֹן, שֶׁחָפֵץ לֶאֱכוֹל וּמְאַחֵר סְעוּדָּתוֹ עַד לְאַחַר שָׁעָה אוֹ פָּחוֹת,

for instance, when he wishes to eat yet postpones his meal by an hour or even **less**

4. In a certain sense, as explained in *Ḥinukh Katan*, the author of the *Tanya*'s introduction to *Sha'ar HaYiḥud VeHa'emuna*, it also indicates ascent and revival.

The meal will be the same, and he will eat it in the same manner. The only difference is that he controls himself for a brief period.

וְעוֹסֵק בַּתּוֹרָה בְּאוֹתָהּ שָׁעָה.

and studies Torah during that time.

He must intentionally dedicate the delay in satisfying his desires to a holy endeavor. Otherwise, he is not engaged in overcoming the *sitra aḥara* and transforming its darkness to light.

כִּדְאִיתָא בַּגְּמָרָא (שבת י, א): "שָׁעָה רְבִיעִית - מַאֲכַל כָּל אָדָם. שָׁעָה שִׁשִּׁית - מַאֲכַל תַּלְמִידֵי חֲכָמִים". וְהָיוּ מַרְעִיבִים עַצְמָם שְׁתֵּי שָׁעוֹת לְכַוָּונָה זוֹ, אַף שֶׁגַּם אַחַר הַסְּעוּדָה הָיוּ לוֹמְדִים כָּל הַיּוֹם.

As the Talmud states, "The **fourth hour** is the time of **eating for all people.** The **sixth hour** is the time of **eating for Torah scholars"** (*Shabbat* 10a). Torah scholars **would go hungry for two hours with this intention** of subduing their nature, **even though after the meal they would study** Torah **the entire day.**

The regular time for the daytime meal was the fourth hour of the day – about ten in the morning. We see that Torah scholars delayed their meal by two hours to overcome the evil inclination. But they did not avoid eating just to have more time to study Torah, since in any event they were engaged in Torah study the entire day. They delayed their mealtime for one purpose only: to gain victory over temptation by overcoming and shattering the evil inclination instead of eating the moment they became hungry.

A hasidic saying advises, "What is forbidden is forbidden, and as for what is permissible – it is not mandatory."[5] When a person wants something, whether it is eating or engaging in mundane conversation, even though it is permissible and even necessary, the evil inclination must be involved. When a person delays such an action, even if only for a short while, it is then that he overcomes the *sitra aḥara*.

וְכֵן אִם בּוֹלֵם פִּיו מִלְּדַבֵּר דְּבָרִים שֶׁלִּבּוֹ מִתְאַוֶּה מְאֹד לְדַבְּרָם, מֵעִנְיְינֵי הָעוֹלָם,

Likewise, if one restrains his mouth from speaking of matters pertaining to mundane affairs about which he very much desires to converse,

5. Cited in the name of the author of the *Tanya* in *HaYom Yom,* 25 Adar II.

We do not battle the *sitra aḥara* solely in the arena of physical desires and needs. The *sitra aḥara* can clothe itself in the subtlest garments of speech and thought, and not only ugly and prohibited speech but even words that are permissible and necessary. When a person feels driven to speak, he must instead restrain himself and overcome his inclination.

This is one reason that we recite a blessing prior to eating. Before a person has the benefit of the food, before he experiences the gustatory pleasure, he must pause. Instead of immediately satisfying his desire, he spends a moment in the service of holiness.

וְכֵן בְּהִרְהוּרֵי מַחֲשַׁבְתּוֹ, אֲפִילּוּ בִּמְעַט מִזְּעֵיר. דְּאִתְכַּפְיָא סִטְרָא אָחֳרָא לְתַתָּא, אִסְתַּלֵּק יְקָרָא דְקֻדְשָׁא בְּרִיךְ הוּא וּקְדוּשָּׁתוֹ לְעֵילָּא הַרְבֵּה.

and the same applies to the thoughts in one's mind, that one should restrain them **even for the slightest bit, for when the** ***sitra aḥara*** **is subdued** here **below,** even only slightly, **the glory and holiness of the Holy One, blessed be He, is exceedingly elevated on high.**

When a person prevents himself from thinking about some topic, or at the least delays the thought, he has succeeded, to some degree, in suppressing his evil inclination. That is to say, in everything, in deed, speech, and even in thought, if he overcomes it, that is a victory. The victory is the same whether he exerts much effort or a little, as long as he has this purpose in mind. Whether a person eventually eats after a delay of two hours or of three is of no intrinsic significance. One can get used to anything, and habits of behavior have no meaning. To do something consequential, a person must always challenge himself. That is where victory lies. That is where he overcomes the *sitra aḥara*.

7 Adar I (leap year)

וּמִקְּדוּשָּׁה זוֹ נִמְשֶׁכֶת קְדוּשָּׁה עֶלְיוֹנָה עַל הָאָדָם לְמַטָּה לְסַיְּיעוֹ סִיּוּעַ רַב וְעָצוּם לַעֲבוֹדָתוֹ יִתְבָּרֵךְ.

From this holiness, a supernal holiness is drawn down on the person below to afford him a great and immense degree of **assistance in his service of God.**

The holiness a person creates when he subdues the *sitra aḥara* in his struggle and in the change that he brings into his life infuses him with a great spiritual influence. When a person does a holy act below, even if it is something minuscule, he awakens a greater degree of holiness from above that in turn will give him considerable power to grow stronger and rise higher.

וְזֶהוּ שֶׁאָמְרוּ רַבּוֹתֵינוּ ז״ל: ״אָדָם מְקַדֵּשׁ עַצְמוֹ מְעַט לְמַטָּה - מְקַדְּשִׁין אוֹתוֹ הַרְבֵּה מִלְמַעְלָה״ (יומא לט, ב),

This is the meaning of our Rabbis' statement "A person who **sanctifies himself a bit** here **below, they sanctify him** and assist him **greatly from on high"** (*Yoma* 39b).

When a person overcomes the *sitra aḥara,* he puts into motion a mechanism of holiness, creating a wheel of circumstances that carries him forward to the realm of holiness. On the other hand, there are paths of evil, of one sin leading to another, on which a person descends, unable to free himself. As soon as he makes the slightest movement to accomplish something holy, he walks on a different path. At that moment, a light shines on him from above, giving him the strength to leave one pathway and rise to another. The more he sanctifies himself below, the more he is sanctified above. With that new power, he can consecrate himself still more in the world below.

לְבַד מַה שֶּׁמְּקַיֵּים מִצְוַת עֲשֵׂה שֶׁל תּוֹרָה: ״וְהִתְקַדִּשְׁתֶּם״ וכו׳ (ויקרא יא, מד) כְּשֶׁמְּקַדֵּשׁ עַצְמוֹ בְּמוּתָּר לוֹ.

This is **apart from the fact that one fulfills the biblically mandated positive commandment "Sanctify yourselves** and you will be sanctified..." (Lev. 11:44), **when one sanctifies himself** even **with regard to that which is permissible for him.**

The author of the *Tanya* refers here to the second of two facets of subduing one's inclination. The first facet was the subjugation of one's inclination in the realm of avoiding evil, where one curbs his inclination, whether it is in the realm of the prohibited or that which is permitted. The author now turns his attention to the second aspect: that of actively doing something to increase one's sanctity, a facet embodying the aspect of doing good.

The commandment to "sanctify yourselves" serves as the source for increased vigilance when performing the mitzvot.[6] It does not only constitute the avoidance of prohibited behavior, because adhering to such minimal requirements would make it possible for a person to fulfill the precepts of the Torah yet be entirely reprobate and dissolute, surrendering wholly to his desires. Instead, the commandment refers to those undefined areas that have no specific halakhic parameters. To be sanctified, one must strengthen oneself by doing even that which one is not obligated to do.

There is no real challenge in avoiding those matters that are clearly prohibited, every individual on his level. The battle to overcome the *sitra aḥara* takes place in the realm where matters are neither prohibited nor obligatory. That is where the *sitra aḥara* gains its strength. That is where a person must fight to overcome it and perform the Torah commandment of "Sanctify yourselves and you will be sanctified."

וּפֵירוּשׁ "וְהִתְקַדִּשְׁתֶּם" – שֶׁתַּעֲשׂוּ עַצְמְכֶם קְדוֹשִׁים.

"Sanctify yourselves" means that you shall make yourselves holy.

The underlying question is that since the verse begins with the injunction to "sanctify yourselves," why the need for the continuation of the verse, "and you will be sanctified"? Surely one will become sanctified when he sanctifies himself.

The author of the *Tanya* explains, somewhat implicitly, that the verb employed by the verse for "sanctify yourselves," *vehitkadishtem,* is reflexive, referring to an action one does to himself, as in *hitḥala,* which

6. According to the author of *Halakhot Gedolot,* this verse is a specific commandment counted among the 613 mitzvot, while Rambam considers this verse a general injunction to fulfill the entire Torah (see *Sefer HaMitzvot, shoresh* 4). The Lubavitcher Rebbe, Rabbi Menaḥem Mendel Schneerson, notes that the author of the *Tanya* is adding another virtue to the rank of the *beinoni* that does not apply to the righteous: Not only does the *beinoni* please God by subduing his inclination, by avoiding evil, but he also does so by fulfilling this positive commandment to sanctify himself.

indicates that one makes himself ill. In our context, the Torah enjoins every Jew to make himself as though he were holy by acting as such.

כְּלוֹמַר, אַף שֶׁבֶּאֱמֶת אֵינוֹ קָדוֹשׁ וּמוּבְדָּל מִסִּטְרָא אָחֳרָא, כִּי הִיא בְּתָקְפָּהּ וּבִגְבוּרָתָהּ כְּתוֹלַדְתָּהּ בֶּחָלָל הַשְּׂמָאלִי,

That is to say, although in truth one is not holy and separate from the *sitra aḥara,* since it maintains its innate potency and strength in the left chamber of the heart,

A person who is sanctifying himself is not truly sanctified but only acts as if he is holy. Although one who makes himself as though holy through his actions perhaps feels somewhat holy and disentangled from the *sitra aḥara,* he is not completely holy.

The *beinoni*'s character cannot change. He cannot become a tzaddik, utterly holy and separated from the evil inclination. The *sitra aḥara* operates within him constantly, even if he is not aware of it. A person might do only good his entire life, he might be a genuine leader whose life serves as a model to others, but he still retains the potential to be completely wicked.

Moreover, the Talmud states, "Anyone who is greater than another, his evil inclination is greater than his" (*Sukka* 52a), meaning that in a certain sense, the greater one's spiritual level, the greater is his potential to become wicked.[7] By extrapolation, this spiritually reciprocal relationship indicates that one who possesses a powerful evil inclination concomitantly possesses the potential to become that much greater.

It is told that Rabbi Levi Yitzḥak of Berditchev succeeded in causing a wayward Jew to return to God by applying this concept. He once approached a wicked person and said, "I am envious of you, as we know that if one repents out of love for God, his deliberate sins are reckoned as merits. If so, how spiritually great will you become when you repent!" The sinner took Rabbi Levi Yitzḥak's words to heart and ultimately repented wholeheartedly.

---

7. See Rabbi Tzadok HaKohen of Lublin, *Divrei Sofrim* 19.

רַק שֶׁכּוֹבֵשׁ יִצְרוֹ וּמְקַדֵּשׁ עַצְמוֹ, "וְהִיִיתֶם קְדוֹשִׁים". כְּלוֹמַר, סוֹפוֹ לִהְיוֹת קָדוֹשׁ וּמוּבְדָּל בֶּאֱמֶת מֵהַסִּטְרָא אָחֳרָא, עַל יְדֵי שֶׁמְּקַדְּשִׁים אוֹתוֹ הַרְבֵּה מִלְמַעְלָה וּמְסַיְּיעִים אוֹתוֹ לְגָרְשָׁהּ מִלִּבּוֹ מְעַט מְעַט.

and **he merely conquers his** evil **inclination and sanctifies himself,** as if making himself holy, he can still attain the level of **"You will be sanctified." In other words, he will ultimately become truly holy and separate from the *sitra aḥara* by being greatly sanctified from on high and being assisted in banishing it from his heart, bit by bit.**

Despite the *beinoni*'s inability to completely transform his evil inclination into good, but only subdue it by acting as though he were holy, he can nevertheless attain the level of "You will be sanctified." The *beinoni* cannot become a tzaddik. He can never completely resolve all his issues and live an uncomplicated life, one without struggle. On the other hand, he can, with divine help, achieve a level where his struggles are less severe. Slowly but surely, he can attain a state in which he will no longer suffer the acute feelings of bitterness and spiritual numbness previously experienced.

The *beinoni* is capable of developing habits, of calibrating the faculties of his soul, and creating a lifestyle whereby the performance of the mitzvot and attainment of holiness become easier for him, almost as if they are second nature. By sanctifying himself and receiving divine assistance as a consequence, what initially seemed to him as an overwhelming burden and an impossible task will ultimately become less intimidating and even a pleasant experience. What began as a fierce struggle can, step by step, become a spiritual ascent along a most gentle path.

This can be compared to the vicissitudes of battle. The righteous person effects a total victory, completely obliterating the enemy. By contrast, the *beinoni* is forever threatened by the enemy, yet under this constant threat there are different situations. One is where the *beinoni* finds himself in imminent danger, while there are times when he is captured by the enemy. Yet another situation is one in which the *beinoni* gains the upper hand. Even then, while the *beinoni* enjoys a respite from fighting, the enemy will regroup and once again pose a serious threat. Nevertheless, when the *beinoni* does have the upper hand, he can feel a certain degree of calm.

In light of this, we must recall one of the opening sentences of the *Tanya*: "Even if the entire world says to you, 'You are righteous,' consider yourself like a wicked person." The *beinoni* must constantly be aware that the forces of evil are embedded within him, waiting for the exact moment to strike. He must exercise extreme caution and maintain constant vigilance, ever prepared to mobilize his spiritual forces in a counterattack.

In this chapter, the author of the *Tanya* explained that even if it seems that the *beinoni*'s chances of victory in the battle against his evil inclination are hopeless, and even though it appears that his unremitting struggles yield no tangible results, he must never lose hope. Depression and sadness have no place in his world. Of all character traits, these are the most detrimental, because they completely destroy one's ability to muster his inner resources and strength to counter his evil inclination, so that he could end up being dragged down into the abyss of sin and depravity.

Even if, for example, one is engaged in his business affairs when the evil inclination within him rears its ugly head, poised for attack, and he is visited without warning by lustful and inappropriate thoughts, it should nevertheless be no cause for sadness. On the contrary, this very scenario affords him the opportunity to subdue his evil inclination, fulfilling the mitzva of avoiding the prohibition of actualizing one's lusts. He should not view such thoughts as a sign of spiritual degeneration. Instead, this is the telltale sign of a *beinoni*. He ought to view the upsurge of evil within him as another struggle, as part of a lifelong process, another step on the path toward spiritual progress embodied by the Torah's directive "Sanctify yourselves, and you will be sanctified."

Some people can be categorized as a soldier of God. God desires this individual's spiritual struggle and wants him stationed on the front lines, fighting valiantly, enjoying no respite, and progressing from one victory to the next. Every victory achieved, every subjugation of the evil inclination, effects an unparalleled elevation of God's glory on high.

Chapter 28

THE PREVIOUS CHAPTERS DEALT WITH THE TRAIT OF sadness: its modalities, causes, and cures. Chapter 27 discussed sadness that comes as a reaction to sinful thoughts and desires. When a person is beset by such thoughts during the day, he has no cause to be upset. Instead, he should rejoice that he has been given the chance to fulfill the commandment "You shall not rove after your heart and after your eyes..." (Num. 15:39). When a person is immersed in the affairs of this world, far removed from holiness, such thoughts and desires allow him the opportunity to break through the matrix of the mundane and propel him to engage in God's battle against the *sitra aĥara*. In this way, he can subdue it and establish, despite all obstacles, a relationship with holiness of unprecedented vigor.

The present chapter also discusses sadness that comes as a reaction to experiencing foreign thoughts, but this time in the context of one's Torah study or intense prayer (prayer that lacks such intensity is merely a mundane activity). Such an experience should not bring about despair or idleness. On the contrary, it should serve as a springboard to strengthen one's service of God.

וַאֲפִילּוּ אִם נוֹפְלִים לוֹ הִרְהוּרֵי תַאֲוֹות וּשְׁאָר מַחֲשָׁבוֹת זָרוֹת בִּשְׁעַת הָעֲבוֹדָה בַּתּוֹרָה אוֹ בִּתְפִלָּה בְּכַוָּונָה,

Even if lustful musings and other foreign thoughts suddenly **occur to someone during his** divine **service,** while he is engaged **in Torah** study **or** while **praying with concentration,**

26 Shevat

8 Adar I (leap year)

Whereas the previous chapter explored unwanted thoughts that occur to someone while engaged in mundane affairs, the foreign thoughts discussed here beset a person while engaged in Torah study and prayer. These thoughts concern us for two reasons: They interrupt a person's service of God, and they occur even though he is engaged in a holy endeavor. That alone can dishearten a person and cast him down from the spiritual level he has already achieved. ☞

let him pay them no attention but divert his mind from them immediately.	אַל יָשִׁית לֵב אֲלֵיהֶן, אֶלָּא יַסִּיחַ דַּעְתּוֹ מֵהֶן כְּרֶגַע.

This principle holds true whether one is engaged in one's personal affairs or in serving God. A person who handles filth gets soiled; a person who struggles with perverse instincts becomes defiled. Any contact with these drives, whether of attraction or repulsion, creates a bond through which energy flows. The only solution is to disconnect oneself immediately.

To do so, one should take his mind off the negative thoughts while also, and principally, focusing on something positive, since a person cannot entertain two thoughts simultaneously. Even this technique will not prevent random foreign musings from occasionally entering one's mind, yet it will undoubtedly prevent continued focus and analysis of such thoughts.

FOREIGN THOUGHTS DURING PRAYER

☞ The time of prayer is a unique breeding ground for unwanted thoughts. There is a well-known anecdote concerning a Jew who came to his rabbi to confide in him a particular worry. He explained that he had cheated the local landowner in a business venture and was now worried that the latter would reconsider the deal and realize the deception. To this the rabbi replied, "You have nothing to fear. The landowner is a gentile and does not recite the *Amida* prayer, and as such, he will never have the opportunity to recall the incident."

This story is more than a mere witticism. It calls to attention a fundamental issue. As a person stands in silent prayer, he clears his mind of all active thought, so there is nothing to compartmentalize other thoughts, to prevent them from entering his mind. He is consequently visited by all sorts of extraneous thoughts, the bills he must pay, his business affairs, worries both great and small of which he cannot rid himself.

וְגַם אַל יְהִי שׁוֹטֶה לַעֲסוֹק בְּהַעֲלָאַת הַמִּדּוֹת שֶׁל הַמַּחֲשָׁבָה זָרָה כַּנּוֹדָע.

Also, one should not be so foolish as to engage in elevating the attributes of the foreign thought, as is known,

The early works of Hasidism speak at length of serving God by elevating foreign thoughts.[1] This approach, based on the notion of paying specific attention to a foreign thought with the aim of rectifying and elevating it, seemingly stands in direct opposition to the advice offered here by the author of the *Tanya*. Yet since this is a generally accepted fundamental approach in hasidic thought, the author of the *Tanya* felt it necessary to include several remarks here that are critical for a proper understanding of both his unique approach in hasidic thought and his personal conceptualization of Hasidism from which he developed this outlook. ☞

ELEVATING A FOREIGN THOUGHT

☞ At the core of this practice is the concept that every impulse, every desire, comprises two factors: a drive to acquire or repel the desire and the object of that desire. It goes without saying that to engage in this discipline, to rectify and elevate a foreign thought, one must be able to distinguish between these two components and see the object of one's mundane desire as a mask that he must remove to find the true reality. For instance, a person who desires something of beauty must get beyond the object to the primary source of all beauty. He can then ask himself, "Why should I chase something that is only a sliver, a dim copy, when I can chase and embrace the source of beauty and eternity – God himself?"

One elevates a foreign thought, then, by delving into it in order to change its direction, to focus on the attribute motivating the thought rather than the object of the thought. If the object of one's desire and love is a physical thing, he should focus on the fact that its physical constitution is merely a mask obscuring its true essence. Once the mask is removed, the attribute, in this case love, which at its root is good, will be elevated and rectified to the extent that it becomes transformed into a love that connects the person to holiness and brings him to a love for God. It is told of a number of hasidic masters that they would see only the deepest root of things, the quintessential good, and the resultant scope of meaning it gave things. This is the work of elevating foreign thoughts.

1. See *Keter Shem Tov* 171; *Degel Maḥaneh Efrayim, Parashat Beha'alotekha*; Maggid of Mezeritch, *Likkutei Amarim* 37; *Ma'or Einayim, Parashat Shemot*; *Ba'al Shem Tov al HaTorah, Parashat Noaḥ, Amud HaTefilla* 102ff.

כִּי לֹא נֶאֶמְרוּ דְּבָרִים הָהֵם, אֶלָּא לַצַּדִּיקִים שֶׁאֵין נוֹפְלִים לָהֶם מַחֲשָׁבוֹת זָרוֹת שֶׁלָּהֶם כִּי אִם מִשֶּׁל אֲחֵרִים.

for such matters apply only to the righteous, to whom do not occur foreign thoughts of their own but rather those of others.

When a foreign thought occurs to a non-tzaddik as he prays or studies Torah, that thought is actually his own. But when such a thought occurs to a tzaddik, it is not his; he is sensing the mind of someone else.[2] Because it is possible to rectify a foreign thought only if it is truly foreign, if it is not one's own, the hasidic teachings on elevating and rectifying such thoughts pertains solely to tzaddikim, or, at the very least, to one who is categorized as a righteous person with regard to that foreign thought, where at that moment the thought is not his own but is extrinsic to him.

To understand a thought, desire, or fear objectively, to remove their external casings and penetrate their essence, a person must stand outside them. If he is imprisoned within them, he cannot do so and thus cannot elevate them. A person can pull his friend out of the mud, yet he cannot pull himself out by yanking at his own hair. If he is already immersed in foreign thoughts, the more he engages in them, the more he will sink down into them, rendering himself incapable of elevating them.

This applies to every area of life. We can relate to the pristine essence of any object, feeling, or thought through deep contemplation only when we are not distracted by its outer image, by the way it appears to us. Imagine, for example, a work of art depicting an attack dog so realistic that it leaves us terrified. A person who is overwhelmed by the image is not able to assess the picture as a work of art.

---

2. This statement of the author of the *Tanya* has perplexed many a great sage, since it seems to run counter to the teachings of the Ba'al Shem Tov in a number of places (see, e.g., *Ba'al Shem Tov al HaTorah, Parashat Noaḥ, Amud HaTefilla* 285, 286, 335). Rabbi Yehoshua Mondshine discusses this topic at length in his essay "Elevating the Attributes of a Foreign Thought" (*Pardes Chabad* 1 [Adar I 5757]: 71–115). In summation, Rabbi Mondshine concludes that despite the apparent lack of congruity between the sources, it is specifically the approach presented here by the author of the *Tanya* that is widely accepted by Chabad mentors when counseling their students as to the proper path in the service of God.

The evil inclination has an outer appearance: a thought, a desire. When a person is under its influence, he cannot step back and relate to it objectively. He can only be objective when he himself has no desire for it, when he is dealing with someone else's evil inclination and not his own. It is particularly the tzaddik, then, who has no evil inclination. who can sense the foreign thoughts of others as he leads the community and guides individuals. These thoughts appear in his mind in an abstract fashion, as experiences that are not his own. Since they are not his, he can distance himself enough to analyze them successfully and elevate them to holiness.

אֲבָל מִי שֶׁנּוֹפֵל לוֹ מִשֶּׁלּוֹ, מִבְּחִינַת הָרַע שֶׁבְּלִבּוֹ בֶּחָלָל הַשְּׂמָאלִי, אֵיךְ יַעֲלֵהוּ לְמַעְלָה, וְהוּא עַצְמוֹ מְקוּשָּׁר לְמַטָּה?

But one who is visited by a foreign thought of **his own,** which stems **from the element of evil situated in the left chamber of his heart, how can he elevate it when he himself is still bound** here **below** to the whims of his animal soul?

A person cannot raise something higher than the spiritual rung on which he stands. The *beinoni,* who coexists with his animal soul, with its thoughts and impulses, should not engage these foreign thoughts at all. The best he can do is ignore and disavow them. Should he attempt to raise them to holiness, even if he begins with the purest intentions, he is liable to be drawn into the maelstrom of impurity.

The author of the *Tanya* now returns to the central theme of this chapter: not to become depressed on account of these foreign thoughts.

אַךְ אַף עַל פִּי כֵן אַל יִפּוֹל לִבּוֹ בְּקִרְבּוֹ, לִהְיוֹת מִזֶּה עָצֵב נִבְזֶה בִּשְׁעַת הָעֲבוֹדָה, שֶׁצָּרִיךְ לִהְיוֹת בְּשִׂמְחָה רַבָּה.

Nevertheless, he should not be downhearted nor feel dejected or degraded because of this occurrence of foreign thoughts **during his** divine **service, when he should be very joyous.**

Assailed by foreign thoughts while praying or studying Torah, a person may be disappointed in himself and sink into sadness and depression. That sadness constitutes a more serious problem than the foreign thoughts themselves. A person stands and prays in a holy place on a holy day, and everything seems so beautiful, so holy, and so promising. Suddenly a thought enters his mind that is so abominable that he himself is ashamed. At that moment, he may come to think that whatever he felt before, the closeness and the holiness, was completely in vain, a lie and a sham. He may fall into despair, feeling enervated and unable to go on. The author of the *Tanya* says that such a person should not be discouraged. He should remain buoyant and positive, particularly in his worship of God.

אֶלָּא אַדְּרַבָּה, יִתְחַזֵּק יוֹתֵר וְיוֹסִיף אוֹמֶץ בְּכָל כֹּחוֹ בְּכַוָּונַת הַתְּפִלָּה בְּחֶדְוָה וְשִׂמְחָה יְתֵירָה, בְּשׂוּמוֹ אֶל לִבּוֹ כִּי נְפִילַת הַמַּחֲשָׁבָה זָרָה הִיא מֵהַקְּלִיפָּה שֶׁבֶּחָלָל הַשְּׂמָאלִי, הָעוֹשָׂה מִלְחָמָה בַּבֵּינוֹנִי עִם נֶפֶשׁ אֱלֹקִית שֶׁבּוֹ.

On the contrary, he should strengthen himself even more and exert all his might to intensify his concentration in prayer with even greater joy and happiness. This is accomplished **when he realizes that the** sudden **occurrence of the foreign thought stems from the *kelippa* in the left chamber** of his heart, **which wages war in the *beinoni* against the divine soul within him.**

It is precisely when a person's divine soul is elevated through the study of Torah or through prayer that an opposing reaction is triggered in his animal soul. A *beinoni* must recognize that the other side will be ever present within him, and he will never succeed in completely vanquishing the essence of the evil epitomized by this *sitra aḥara*. Its counterattack is not a proof that his Torah study and prayer have been in vain. Rather, the *sitra aḥara* reflects his inner struggle. He has succeeded so well in his spiritual work that the forces of evil have been awakened to wage a renewed battle. This is not cause for sadness. Instead, it should be a reason for joy and a renewed commitment to prayer and Torah study so that he can maintain, and even transcend, the level he has already attained.

The true battle is not about one or another thought but about one's way of life in general. The purpose of a foreign thought, in particular when it comes during Torah study or prayer, is to hold back or halt a person's spiritual progress. Every such thought is an obstacle on the path, yet it is also a part of the path. It is part of the life of a *beinoni* to confront and overcome impediments. The greatest danger is to be dismayed by obstacles and see them as signs of defeat. If such a reaction leads a person to fall into sadness, despair, and inactivity, he leaves the path of serving God and spirals downward so that one sin leads to another, and his descent grows ever more precipitous.

וְנוֹדָע דֶּרֶךְ הַנִּלְחָמִים וְכֵן הַנֶּאֱבָקִים יַחַד, כְּשֶׁאֶחָד מִתְגַּבֵּר אֲזַי הַשֵּׁנִי מִתְאַמֵּץ לְהִתְגַּבֵּר גַּם כֵּן, בְּכָל מַאֲמַצֵּי כֹּחוֹ.

It is well known that the way of combatants and, likewise, wrestlers is that when one begins to **overpower** his opponent, **the other also uses all his strength and exerts effort to gain the upper hand.**

In all struggles, when one side grows stronger, the adversary exerts a corresponding upsurge of strength.[3]

וְלָכֵן כְּשֶׁנֶּפֶשׁ הָאֱלוֹקִית מִתְאַמֶּצֶת וּמִתְגַּבֶּרֶת לְהִתְפַּלֵּל, אֲזַי גַּם הַקְּלִיפָּה מִתְגַּבֶּרֶת כְּנֶגְדָּהּ לְבַלְבְּלָהּ וּלְהַפִּילָהּ בְּמַחֲשָׁבָה זָרָה שֶׁלָּהּ.

Therefore, when the divine soul exerts effort and strengthens itself to pray with concentration, **the *kelippa* also strengthens itself in opposition to confuse and topple it with a foreign thought of its own.**

When someone experiences a random foreign thought while involved in mundane affairs, it is readily understood that this thought is a direct consequence of this involvement. On the other hand, a foreign thought that arises while one is serving God is a natural reaction of the *kelippa* to a holy action that breaks free of the former status quo set in place by

3. Rabbi Shmuel Gronem Esterman points out that the terms "combatants" and "wrestlers" are not merely synonyms, but rather they allude to two distinct types of divine service. The term "combatants" connotes those who are fighting to kill one another, while "wrestlers" connotes a fight yet not to the death. So it is in the realm of divine service: "The way of combatants" alludes to a fight over a forbidden lust, while the term "wrestlers" alludes to one's struggle with a permitted desire.

the limitations of the *kelippa*. When a person strives toward holiness, the *sitra aḥara* is thus awakened and orchestrates a counterattack. The fact that one's holiness has increased does not lessen the strength of the *sitra aḥara*'s reaction. On the contrary, its reaction grows more forceful and intense.

27 Shevat

וְלֹא כְּטָעוּת הָעוֹלָם שֶׁטּוֹעִים לְהוֹכִיחַ מִנְּפִילַת הַמַּחֲשָׁבָה זָרָה, מִכְּלָל שֶׁאֵין תְּפִלָּתָם כְּלוּם, שֶׁאִילּוּ הִתְפַּלֵּל כָּרָאוּי וְנָכוֹן לֹא הָיוּ נוֹפְלִים לוֹ מַחֲשָׁבוֹת זָרוֹת. וְהָאֱמֶת הָיָה כְּדִבְרֵיהֶם אִם הָיְתָה נֶפֶשׁ אַחַת לְבַדָּהּ, הִיא הַמִּתְפַּלֶּלֶת וְהִיא הַמְּחַשֶּׁבֶת וּמְהַרְהֶרֶת הַמַּחֲשָׁבוֹת זָרוֹת.

This refutes **a common misconception, where people mistakenly** attempt to **prove that the occurrence of a foreign thought** during prayer, for instance, **implies that their prayer is worthless.** These people claim **that if one were to pray properly and correctly, no foreign thoughts would have occurred to him. Their assertion would be true if there were only one soul that both prays and thinks and reflects upon foreign thoughts.**

If a person were one-dimensional, all the qualities of his soul would be in harmony and his actions open to only one interpretation. Then he would be right to believe that foreign thoughts during or after prayer reflect badly on him and his prayers. But man is multidimensional. When one aspect within him grows stronger, another reacts to redress the imbalance. This is something that the *beinoni* cannot control. The more he struggles to intensify his prayer and the higher he reaches, the more other forces within him are awakened. The greater his struggle to study Torah with pure intent and exclusive focus, the greater the temptations of the *sitra aḥara* become.

Some say that this was Rebecca's concern when she went to seek God.[4] At the time, she was pregnant and could feel a struggle within her womb. She thought that she was carrying a single child and that this struggle was a bad omen, signaling that her child would be unable to control his baser instincts. Once told that she was carrying twins,[5] she was relieved. She realized that this struggle was a sign of a battle between two separate beings.

---

4. See Gen. 25:22; commentary on chaps. 9, 13.
5. See Gen. 25:23

אֲבָל בֶּאֱמֶת לַאֲמִיתּוֹ הֵן שְׁתֵּי נְפָשׁוֹת הַנִּלְחָמוֹת זוֹ עִם זוֹ בְּמוֹחוֹ שֶׁל אָדָם, כָּל אַחַת חֶפְצָהּ וּרְצוֹנָהּ לִמְשׁוֹל בּוֹ וְלִהְיוֹת הַמּוֹחַ מְמוּלָּא מִמֶּנָּה לְבַדָּהּ. וְכָל הִרְהוּרֵי תוֹרָה וְיִרְאַת שָׁמַיִם - מִנֶּפֶשׁ הָאֱלוֹקִית, וְכָל מִילֵּי דְעָלְמָא - מִנֶּפֶשׁ הַבַּהֲמִית, רַק שֶׁהָאֱלוֹקִית מְלוּבֶּשֶׁת בָּהּ.

But the truth of the matter is that there are two souls that engage in battle with one another in a person's mind. The wish and desire of each one is to control the mind and permeate it exclusively. All thoughts of Torah and fear of Heaven derive from the divine soul, while all mundane matters derive from the animal soul, except that the divine soul is clothed within it, the animal soul.

The soul of the *beinoni* has two parts, two different souls stemming from separate sources and acting independently. One soul is involved with mundane desires, fears, and foreign thoughts, and the other soul is filled with holy longing, with the love and fear of God. These two souls, with their diametrically opposed sensibilities, can coexist only in the realm of the subconscious. In the realm of the conscious, the two souls are engaged in a never-ending struggle.

Only the tzaddik can prevent thoughts, whether good or evil, from entering his mind. Though the *beinoni* may have the appearance of a tzaddik, he still suffers from foreign thoughts and evil desires. A *rasha,* on the other hand, who is under the influence of evil, is beset by foreign thoughts of his own: thoughts that stem from the side of holiness that evoke in him regret for his misdeeds and the desire to repent.[6]

We may conclude that a person who has foreign thoughts while he is studying Torah or praying intently should not view this as a crisis of his human existence. Rather, the thoughts are the reaction of his animal soul to the growing strength of his divine soul. ☞

THE TWO SOULS WITHIN

☞ Although the two souls within a person are separate from each other and in a sense not responsible toward one another, they are bound together in a person's awareness and in his every deed. The animal soul, like the body, does not derive its

6. See chap. 11; *Shevet Mussar,* chap. 25.

וְהוּא כְּמָשָׁל אָדָם הַמִּתְפַּלֵּל בְּכַוָּנָה וְעוֹמֵד לְנֶגְדּוֹ עָרֵל רָשָׁע וּמֵשִׂיחַ וּמְדַבֵּר עִמּוֹ כְּדֵי לְבַלְבְּלוֹ,

This is like a person who is praying with concentration, and in front of him stands a wicked gentile who chatters incessantly **and speaks to him in order to distract him.**

A person must reframe a foreign thought so that it is something outside himself, as though it were introduced by an uninvited stranger whom he cannot dismiss, someone standing in front of him and pestering him. Of course, the stranger does not literally stand outside but within, because the thought comes from one's own animal soul. But since it is not part of the divine soul, the thought should be treated as a disturbance from outside.

שֶׁזֹּאת עֲצָתוֹ בְּוַדַּאי, שֶׁלֹּא לְהָשִׁיב לוֹ מִטּוֹב וְעַד רָע, וְלַעֲשׂוֹת עַצְמוֹ כְּחֵרֵשׁ לֹא יִשְׁמַע, וּלְקַיֵּים מַה שֶּׁכָּתוּב: "אַל תַּעַן כְּסִיל כְּאִוַּלְתּוֹ פֶּן תִּשְׁוֶה לּוֹ גַם אָתָּה" (משלי כו, ד). כָּךְ אַל יָשִׁיב מְאוּמָה, וְשׁוּם טַעֲנָה וּמַעֲנֶה נֶגֶד הַמַּחֲשָׁבָה זָרָה,

In this case, the advice to the one praying **would certainly be not to respond to him either good or bad but rather to pretend as though one were deaf, unable to hear, in fulfillment of the verse "Do not answer a fool according to his folly, lest you too resemble him"** (Prov. 26:4)**. Likewise, he should neither answer at all nor should he offer any counterclaim or response to the foreign thought,**

If a wicked gentile were trying to keep a person from praying, the best advice would be for him to pay him no heed. Just as a *beinoni* cannot successfully argue with a malicious heathen by telling him how to act or how not to act, so he cannot influence a distracting foreign thought. There is simply no point in trying to give a response. If he argues, that

existence directly from the source of life but through the divine soul clothed within it. On the other hand, the divine soul functions in the body only by way of the animal soul, which is embodied in the blood (see chap. 35). The totality of a human being, and his every expression of that totality, is a complex structure composed of man and beast, of the divine soul and the animal soul bound together.

will only distract him from his Torah study and prayer. If he pretends to agree, that is false and serves no benefit. The only proper response is not to react, to act as though he is deaf, as though he hears nothing and thus has no need to respond. ☞

The more a person ignores such disturbances, the sooner they will fade away. Paying them attention will only cause them to persist. Even if a confrontation succeeds this time, the next foreign thought may react more strongly, with a different strategy, under different circumstances, and then he might not be adequately prepared. A person may enjoy a long period of tranquility, perhaps even for years, either because he has achieved spiritual success or because he is living a life of spiritual mediocrity where evil has succeeded and he is not even conscious of the fact. Yet when it seems to him that he has overcome all his internal conflicts and personal obstacles, a wave of challenges engulfs him. This is particularly likely to happen if he imagines himself to be a tzaddik, if he believes that he has removed his evil inclination once and for all. But that is not realistic. A *beinoni* will never eradicate the evil within himself. It will remain with him forever and will at most change form.

As a *beinoni* rises from level to level, as he overcomes the evil in one arena, he may for a limited time enjoy a tranquil period, released from his usual conflicts. But it is only a matter of time before his temptations and foreign thoughts return. Then he will discover a new form of the

THE WICKED GENTILE

☞ There are no foreign elements, nothing extraneous or wicked, in a righteous person. By definition, then, he experiences no foreign thoughts. Instead, such thoughts become part and parcel of his divine nature so that they become elevated and perfected.

By contrast, a *beinoni* will forever experience unbidden thoughts that are foreign to him, just as his animal soul forever remains foreign to his divine soul, and nothing can change that. Sooner or later, these foreign thoughts will adversely influence him, dragging him into a state of depression or causing him to succumb to his lusts. The author of the *Tanya* therefore advises the *beinoni* not to pay any attention to these thoughts, in which case they will remain absolutely separate and foreign to him, as if they are literally another person, a separate entity from him. A person cannot separate himself from himself, but he can separate himself from another person. The more he ignores these thoughts, the more separate and distant they become, and, at least for those moments, they dissolve into oblivion.

evil inclination, one that he does not yet know how to handle and overcome.

כִּי הַמִּתְאַבֵּק עִם מְנוּוָּל - מִתְנַוֵּול גַּם כֵּן.

for anyone who wrestles with a vile person becomes vile himself.

Any contact between two opponents, even if it is one of struggle, forges a relationship. If a person wrestles with his foreign thoughts, he only becomes entangled in them and increases his involvement with them.

רַק יַעֲשֶׂה עַצְמוֹ כְּלֹא יוֹדֵעַ וְלֹא שׁוֹמֵעַ הַהִרְהוּרִים שֶׁנָּפְלוּ לוֹ וִיסִירֵם מִדַּעְתּוֹ, וְיוֹסִיף אוֹמֶץ בְּכֹחַ כַּוָּונָתוֹ.

Instead, he should pretend as though he neither knows nor hears the foreign **thoughts that occurred to him, and he should remove them from his mind by increasing the strength and power of his concentration.**

The proper response to a foreign thought involves two aspects. The first is passive: Rather than dwell on the thought, one should ignore it. The second is active: One should renew and intensify his focus on his prayers. This can be achieved by focusing on the meaning of the words and increasing his concentration, in whatever manner that resonates with him and that he finds meaningful.

It is all but impossible to consciously shake off a thought. When a person knows that he is forbidden to think about something, he will usually think only of that. What can be done is first and foremost to be conscious of the circular process. The more aware he is, the more easily he will deal with such challenges.

Practically speaking, it is best to replace one thought with another, since a person cannot think of two matters at once. As long as a person's mind remains unoccupied, a foreign thought can enter. But when he focuses on another topic, the foreign thought will not be able to intrude, or, at the very least, it will be deprived of the ability to grow and develop.

Changing the direction and quality of a thought is very difficult, almost impossible. But it is possible to change the subject of one's thought. Just as one can choose to talk exclusively about a certain topic, so can one choose to think a certain thought and nothing else. ☞

וְאִם יִקְשֶׁה לוֹ לַהֲסִירָם מִדַּעְתּוֹ מִפְּנֵי שֶׁטּוֹרְדִים דַּעְתּוֹ מְאֹד בְּחָזְקָה,

If it is difficult for him to rid his mind of them because they disrupt his thoughts with an overwhelming intensity,

When a foreign thought is clearly foolish or fleeting, a person can dismiss it by turning to something else. But if he suffers from a fixation or is impelled by an urgent desire, he may not be able to refocus his attention.

PREPARATION FOR PRAYER

☞ In general, preparation creates a momentum for prayer. It paves the way for the proper mindset, an internal space free of worry, fear, and disturbance. One way to create this mindset (a method used primarily by non-Chabad hasidim) is to make one's mundane reality a springboard for holiness. This can be done by telling a joke or a story or performing some action. Sometimes such a catalyst creates a quiet moment and displaces a person's worries more effectively than reproof could.

This method is not used only by hasidim. The Talmud tells us that when Elijah the prophet was asked who had earned a place in the World to Come, he pointed to a few simple men. Elijah explained that these men had spent their time cheering up sad people (*Ta'anit* 22a). Such individuals deserve their place in the World to Come because they make it possible for others to transcend this world.

The Talmud also tells us that before Rabba began teaching, he would make his students laugh and so free their minds from worry (*Pesaḥim* 117a). Only then did Rabba enter a serious state of mind, one befitting the transmission of Torah.

An even more far-reaching story is told of the hasidic master, Rabbi Moshe Leib of Sassov. He once learned that a certain man had made an assignation with a married woman. He invited the man to play cards with him. Each time the man tried to get up, the Rebbe stopped him: "You can't go now. You're winning, and I need a chance to win my money back," or "You just lost. You deserve a chance to get your money back." They played cards until the time set for the rendezvous had passed, and only then did the Rebbe let him go.

Sometimes all one needs to be freed of a compulsion is some time to redirect one's thoughts. Anything that helps, no matter how trivial, is worthwhile.

Yet many authorities are uneasy with this approach, because if a person is not exceedingly careful, it can pull him down. They believe that only someone whose foreign thoughts truly come from without, someone who does not himself gain pleasure from the joke he tells, someone who is careful to fill each moment with holiness but plays a game solely to help another, can succeed this way. Therefore, the author of the *Tanya* recommends a different method that hasidim employ: to prepare for prayer by studying a hasidic text that will inspire his mind and heart. He will then become tranquil, free from his usual concerns, desires, and foreign thoughts, and his heart will be ready to concentrate on his prayers.

אֲזַי יַשְׁפִּיל נַפְשׁוֹ לַה׳ וְיִתְחַנֵּן לוֹ יִתְבָּרֵךְ בְּמַחֲשַׁבְתּוֹ לְרַחֵם עָלָיו בְּרַחֲמָיו הַמְּרוּבִּים

then he should humble himself before God and plead with Him in his thoughts to have compassion on him in His abundant mercy.

When one feels that he cannot win the struggle himself, he should seek help, pleading with God to have compassion on him. The author of the *Tanya* emphasizes that he should do this in his thoughts since he is in the midst of praying.

כְּרַחֵם אָב עַל בָּנִים הַנִּמְשָׁכִים מִמּוֹחוֹ,

Just as a father has compassion on his children, who issue forth from his brain,

A father's relationship with his children is, in a sense, with himself. The father has compassion for his children because they are a part of him. In the words of the Sages, "The son is a limb of the father" (*Eiruvin* 70b). Just as the limbs of the body are part of the body itself, so the son is to some extent an expression of the father's essential being.

וְכָכָה יְרַחֵם ה׳ עַל נַפְשׁוֹ הַנִּמְשֶׁכֶת מֵאִתּוֹ יִתְבָּרֵךְ, לְהַצִּילָהּ מִמַּיִם הַזֵּדוֹנִים, וּלְמַעֲנוֹ יַעֲשֶׂה, כִּי חֵלֶק ה׳ מַמָּשׁ עַמּוֹ.

so will God have compassion on his soul, which issues forth from Him, and rescue it from the seething waters, the illicit thoughts. God **will do it for His sake because the portion of the Lord is literally His people.**

In the prayer of *Avinu Malkenu*, we ask God to help us first in the merit of our prayers, then in the merit of our children, next in the merit of our dedication and self-sacrifice, and finally as a final plea against which there is no argument: "Act for Your own sake and save us!" It is as if we are saying, "Act for Your own sake, for this is Your affair because we are a part of You!" ☞

Continuing the theme of the preceding chapters, this chapter dealt with various methods to be employed in divine service, particularly how to overcome sadness and heavyheartedness in order to emerge victorious in the battle between one's animal soul and divine soul. The sadness discussed in this chapter is one that besets a person on account of unbidden foreign thoughts that enter his mind while he is praying or studying Torah. The author of the *Tanya* urges him not to succumb to the sadness but rather to rejoice in the opportunity to struggle against it. As part of this discussion, the author of the *Tanya*

ACT FOR YOUR OWN SAKE!

☞ The hasidic texts speak a great deal about what is expected of one who is having troubles. A person who is in serious distress tends to think more about himself and less of others, which encourages egotism. His suffering can then have the effect of ruining his soul and degrading his character. To prevent this, the sufferer must see his own problem as more than a personal sorrow and place it instead within the context of the entire Jewish people and the Divine Presence. When an individual Jew suffers, the Divine Presence weeps, and God, as it were, suffers (see chap. 26). Therefore, the person should beseech God, "Act for Your own sake!"

This idea is expressed in almost every Jewish prayer and blessing, so that the prayer does not remain solely on the individual level. When we pray on behalf of a particular sick person, we do so "in the midst of the other sick of Israel." We take the problem out of its private context and intercede on behalf of the individual as a part of the Jewish people. We present our petition on behalf of the Divine Presence, which cries out for its children. "Our Father, our King," we say, "act for Your own sake!"

A person's evil inclination attacks him at his weakest moments. When he studies Torah or prays and feels that he has reached heavenly heights, that awareness is his Achilles' heel, because it inflates his ego. When he congratulates himself on his talent, on his good fortune, on how righteous he is in Torah and prayer, he gives a hand to all the vermin to rise and get hold of him. Therefore, he must lower his ego and address God: "I myself am not important. I am not unusually gifted or exceptionally learned. But I am a portion, a spark, of the Divine. So I ask You to act for Your own sake." When a person turns to God in this way, the rectification has been made.

Temptations affect a person only when they have something to hold on to. But when a person effaces himself by identifying with the Divine Presence, the temptations have nothing to grasp. When a person prays for his livelihood or health, he is judged on whether he is deserving of this gift. But when he says, "Act for Your own sake," the reckoning is no longer about him.

We see that foreign thoughts are no reason to grow depressed. Even when they come to a person while he is serving God, while studying Torah or praying, there is no need to see them as a sign of failure. Instead, they indicate that he has been growing spiritually and therefore has elicited a negative reaction from his animal soul. Now that he has advanced, he must attain a new equilibrium of freedom and choice. That is why the awakening of holiness is balanced by an awakening of the *sitra aḥara*.

set forth a general approach to dealing with foreign thoughts that occur during prayer or Torah study.

An additional point that this chapter offered is that one's internal battles share the same dynamic as all struggles. In a war, the enemy's fierce attacks are not a sign of failure but a sign that the battle has reached a new and more decisive phase. The experience may not be pleasant, but it cannot be regarded as a failure.

A person must know how to persevere. He must know how to take refuge and ask God for help. He should never surrender to sadness, to bitterness, which leads to spiritual decline and lethargy. Even after years of Torah study, prayer, and good deeds, the *beinoni* can stumble. The *beinoni* struggles against an indefatigable enemy, seldom experiencing moments of respite. It is the *beinoni*'s fate to be embattled, because he is God's warrior. The war may at times be fierce, even unbearable, but the knowledge that this is his lot should encourage him as he is confronted with foreign thoughts and other stumbling blocks on the path of serving God. The fact that the *beinoni* has joined the fray is itself a victory. By doing so, he is bound with God's absolute oneness in which all the worlds exist.

Chapter 29

THE STRUGGLE BETWEEN THE DIVINE SOUL AND THE animal soul may be compared to two men wrestling with each other. In the spiritual struggle, as in the physical struggle, a person will not win if he feels sad and despondent. In the previous chapters, several types of sadness were discussed, as well as solutions for how to extricate oneself from them. This chapter will deal with the second type of obstacle, one even more entrenched and systemic than sadness: a blocked heart unable to experience emotion.

28 Shevat

9 Adar I (leap year)

אַךְ עוֹד אַחַת צָרִיךְ לָשִׁית עֵצוֹת בְּנַפְשׁוֹת הַבֵּינוֹנִים, אֲשֶׁר לִפְעָמִים וְעִתִּים רַבִּים יֵשׁ לָהֶם טִמְטוּם הַלֵּב,

However, those who possess **the soul of a *beinoni* must internalize yet another** piece of **advice: that at times, and** perhaps even **frequently, they experience a dullness of the heart,**

Sometimes a person's mind closes down, and he finds himself unable to absorb information, unable even to grasp the obvious, to absorb what he is seeing and hearing. There is also an emotional type of shutting down, an internal blockage that the author of the *Tanya* refers to as a "dullness of the heart." This is an emotional deadness, an inability to experience feelings and to develop emotional relationships. A blocked mind and a dull heart do not have to come hand in hand. Sometimes a person's emotional numbness stands in stark contrast to his mind's comprehension of a particular matter. A person's mind may be sensitive and open so that he understands a topic fully, yet it makes no emotional impression on him.

Both conditions interfere with a person's life, including his service of God. But since this is the *Book of Beinonim,* and a *beinoni* is by definition someone who is in control of his mind, the *Tanya*'s focus will confine itself to the problem of a dull heart.[1]

שֶׁנַּעֲשָׂה כָּאֶבֶן וְלֹא יָכוֹל לִפְתּוֹחַ לִבּוֹ בְּשׁוּם אוֹפֶן לַעֲבוֹדָה שֶׁבַּלֵּב זוֹ תְּפִלָּה.

so that it becomes stone-like, and he is unable, under any circumstances, to open his heart to engage in **the service of the heart, which is prayer.**

This imagery of the heart of stone actually appears in *Tanakh*: "I will remove the heart of stone from their flesh, and I will give them a heart of flesh" (Ezek. 11:19).[2]

Although one with a dull heart, with the "stone-like" heart, may thoroughly understand the liturgy in the prayer book that discusses God's greatness, his heart is not moved. There is no change in his emotional life because of this understanding. He remains as he had been, unchanged, as though he were a stone.

A dull heart is chiefly an obstruction to one's spiritual work in the realm of prayer, described by the Sages as the "service of the heart."[3] This service refers primarily to the deep, inner devotion required of the one praying. Mechanically reciting the words in the prayer book, even if one knows their meaning, is a far cry from the deep spiritual work required of one truly engaged in prayer. One must profoundly know what he is saying and feel it in his heart. It follows that dullness of the heart is not necessarily an obstacle to one's performance of mitzvot or Torah study, but it does, by definition, constitute an utter impediment to the service of the heart, to prayer.

---

1. The Lubavitcher Rebbe, Rabbi Menaḥem Mendel Schneerson, points out that this holds true despite the discussion regarding the other type of blockage, a dullness of mind, a few lines below. He explains that the context in which the author of the *Tanya* mentions dullness of mind is simply elucidating a lesson of the *Zohar,* which is not limited to the *beinoni,* but is also clearly referring to the wicked. The author of the *Tanya* mentions dullness of the mind in that context, but it is not his main focus.
2. See also Ezek. 36:26.
3. *Ta'anit* 2a.

וְגַם לִפְעָמִים לֹא יוּכַל לְהִלָּחֵם עִם הַיֵּצֶר, לְקַדֵּשׁ עַצְמוֹ בַּמּוּתָּר לוֹ, מִפְּנֵי כְּבֵדוּת שֶׁבְּלִבּוֹ.

Also, there are times when one is unable to wage war against the evil **inclination** and **to sanctify oneself through that which is permitted to him due to the heaviness in his heart.**

The same deep, inner spiritual work necessary to succeed in prayer is required in any area of divine service wherein one struggles to overpower the wiles of his evil inclination. Engaging in divine service by simply relying on habit or even on one's knowledge that this is "the right thing to do" is doomed from the outset. The ingredient for success is the heart's thirsting and yearning to engage in such work.

Such divine work entails "sanctifying oneself through that which is permitted."[4] We must bear in mind that the *Tanya* speaks to the *beinoni,* who has already mastered the art of refraining from prohibited behavior. His rank is such that he need not struggle, at least too intensely, with the evil inclination. He lives his life in strict compliance with the dictates of the *halakha.* But to curb permissible behavior, he needs to overcome his nature, transcend his habits, and go beyond the letter of the law. This is a difficult battle that cannot be won if his heart is not fully engaged, fully present, but is instead stone-like and unreceptive to the fear and love of God. This battle can be waged only by one who is buoyant and vibrant, so it is essential that he overcome the pitfalls of sadness and a dull heart.

וְזֹאת הִיא עֵצָה הַיְעוּצָה בַּזֹּהַר הַקָּדוֹשׁ (חלק ג קסח, א): דְּאָמַר רַב מְתִיבְתָּא בְּגַן עֵדֶן: "אָעָא דְּלָא סָלִיק בֵּיהּ נְהוֹרָא - מְבַטְּשִׁין לֵיהּ כוּ'. גּוּפָא דְּלָא סָלִיק בֵּיהּ נְהוֹרָא דְּנִשְׁמְתָא - מְבַטְּשִׁין לֵיהּ" כוּ'.

This is the recommended counsel that the holy *Zohar* (3:168a) offers: "The president of the academy in the Garden of Eden said, 'A beam of **wood that cannot catch fire must be broken** into smaller pieces. Similarly, **a body that the light of the soul cannot penetrate must be broken....'"**

4. See *Yevamot* 20a; Rashi, Deut. 14:21.

A person with a dull heart is emotionally dead. Instead of feeling, instead of being moved and responsive, he is apathetic and torpid. This dullness is like a large log that will not catch fire. But if one chops it down into smaller pieces, they will easily burn. Similarly, a person must break his sense of perfection, the feeling that he has no need to strive, because it is only when this feeling is splintered that the soul's light can penetrate those broken pieces and ignite them.

The "light of the soul" refers to the light of the soul that illuminates the **intellect, which does not shine to the extent that it governs the corporeality of the body. Although one may use his intellect to understand and contemplate the greatness of God,** his understanding **is not grasped and embedded in his brain to the extent that it can govern the corporeality of the heart, because of** the brain and heart's **crudeness and coarseness.**

פֵּירוּשׁ, נְהוֹרָא דְּנִשְׁמְתָא - שֶׁאוֹר הַנְּשָׁמָה וְהַשֵּׂכֶל אֵינוֹ מֵאִיר כׇּל כָּךְ לִמְשׁוֹל עַל חוּמְרִיּוּת שֶׁבַּגּוּף. וְאַף שֶׁמֵּבִין וּמִתְבּוֹנֵן בְּשִׂכְלוֹ בִּגְדוּלַּת ה׳, אֵינוֹ נִתְפָּס וְנִדְבָּק בְּמוֹחוֹ כׇּל כָּךְ שֶׁיּוּכַל לִמְשׁוֹל עַל חוּמְרִיּוּת הַלֵּב, מֵחֲמַת חוּמְרִיּוּתָן וְגַסּוּתָן.

The light emitted by the soul that illuminates the intellect is the initial revelation of the soul in the body. Note that the author of the *Tanya* distinguishes between the intellect and the brain. The intellect is a spiritual faculty that the human soul possesses,[5] while the brain is a physical organ with which a person thinks, in much the same way that he walks with his legs.

Like the brain, the heart is also a physical organ, and with it a person feels the faculties contained in the soul. Rooted even more deeply than the spiritual faculties of the intellect and the emotions is the light of the divine soul itself. This light that is rooted in the soul unites it with the Divine above. When a person experiences dullness of the heart, the light of the soul does not shine directly into the limbs of his body, unable to be absorbed by the physicality of the brain and heart and exert an influence on them. Even when the light of the soul shines into

5. See chap. 3 and commentary there.

a person's mind, his understanding is muddled, so that the divine light is prevented from being grasped by the physical brain. The soul's light does not shine at its fullest capacity so that the brain cannot transfer this understanding to the emotions of the physical heart.

10 Adar I (leap year)

וְהַסִּיבָּה הִיא גַּסּוּת הַקְּלִיפָּה שֶׁמַּגְבִּיהַּ עַצְמָהּ עַל אוֹר קְדוּשַּׁת נֶפֶשׁ הָאֱלֹהִית וּמַסְתֶּרֶת וּמַחְשִׁיכָה אוֹרָהּ.

The cause of the dull heart **is the coarseness of the *kelippa*, which raises itself above the light of the holiness of the divine soul, utterly obscuring its light.**

The reason that the heart is closed off is not only because there is *kelippa* in a person – in every *beinoni* there is some trace of *kelippa* that never disappears completely – but because the *kelippa* is very coarse. To be able to absorb abstract topics and be moved by them, the soul must be refined. To apprehend subtle matters, even outside the realm of holiness, one must have not only the intellectual capacity but also the emotional capacity. This is something that a person dominated by a coarse *kelippa*, whose senses are obscured and whose light is concealed, cannot attain.

וְלָזֹאת צָרִיךְ לְבַטְּשָׁהּ, וּלְהַשְׁפִּילָהּ לֶעָפָר,

For this reason, one must crush the *kelippa* **and cast it to the dust.**

Kelippa is essentially the idea of something that regards itself as an independent entity, expressed by the author of the *Tanya* as "raising" itself up in arrogance, casting a shadow over the divine light of the soul. As the author of the *Tanya* proceeds to explain, one must crush this arrogance by humbling himself and lowering the conceited sense of self "to the dust," that is, until it is no longer recognizable as an independent entity.

דְּהַיְינוּ לִקְבּוֹעַ עִתִּים, לְהַשְׁפִּיל עַצְמוֹ לִהְיוֹת "נִבְזֶה בְּעֵינָיו נִמְאָס" (תהלים טו, ד), כַּכָּתוּב.

This means that one must fix specific **times to humble himself so that he is "despised and repugnant in his own eyes"** (Ps. 15:4)**, as it is written.**

The individual suffering a dull heart is temporarily under the influence of *kelippa,* but *kelippa* is too abstract a concept to tackle directly. One cannot relate to it or affect it with feelings or actions. One can overcome it only by facing it within himself. The way to do this is by humbling himself. He must lower himself and shatter his perfect self-image and haughtiness. As soon as he feels that his self is lowered and yielding, his heart will open, and the flame of his soul will enter and burn brightly.

A broken heart leads to **a broken spirit, which is the** ***sitra aḥara.***

וְלֵב נִשְׁבָּר רוּחַ נִשְׁבָּרָה הִיא הַסִּטְרָא אָחֳרָא,

When a person's heart is broken, the spirit of impurity within him is also broken; his ego is shattered.

In the case of ***beinonim,*** **that constitutes the very person himself, for the vital,** animal **soul that gives life to the body is at its** full **innate potency in the heart** of the *beinoni.* **It follows that** the animal soul **constitutes the very person himself.**

שֶׁהִיא הִיא הָאָדָם עַצְמוֹ בַּבֵּינוֹנִים. שֶׁנֶּפֶשׁ הַחִיּוּנִית הַמְחַיָּה הַגּוּף הִיא בְּתָקְפָּהּ כְּתוֹלַדְתָּהּ בְּלִבּוֹ, נִמְצָא הִיא הִיא הָאָדָם עַצְמוֹ.

Initially and naturally, a *beinoni* is identified with the perspective of the animal soul. In order to break the coarseness of that animal soul, which is the *sitra aḥara* within, the *beinoni* must in a sense break his ego. ☞

THE ESSENCE OF THE *BEINONI*

☞ The Lubavitcher Rebbe, Rabbi Menaḥem Mendel Schneerson, explains that the statement here that the animal soul constitutes the *beinoni* refers only to the external sense. On the deepest level, all Jews, even those on the lowest spiritual rungs, possess the innate resolve to sacrifice their lives for the sake of God (see chap. 19). The true essence of a Jew's existence and identity, then, is his divine soul, the source of this unstoppable inner resolve.

וְעַל נֶפֶשׁ הָאֱלֹהִית שֶׁבּוֹ נֶאֱמַר: "נְשָׁמָה שֶׁנָּתַתָּ בִּי טְהוֹרָה הִיא" - "שֶׁנָּתַתָּ בִּי" דַּיְיקָא, מִכְּלַל שֶׁהָאָדָם עַצְמוֹ אֵינֶנּוּ הַנְּשָׁמָה הַטְּהוֹרָה,

As for the divine soul within him, it states in the prayer book, **"The soul that You gave me is pure."** The phrase **"that You gave me" is precise, implying that the person himself is not** synonymous with **the pure soul.**

Since on a conscious level this person is identified with his animal soul, the divine soul is "the soul that You gave me," implying a distinction between his self and his soul.

כִּי אִם בְּצַדִּיקִים, שֶׁבָּהֶם הוּא לְהֶפֶךְ, שֶׁ'נְּשָׁמָה הַטְּהוֹרָה' שֶׁהִיא נֶפֶשׁ הָאֱלֹהִית - הוּא הָאָדָם, וגוּפָם נִקְרָא 'בְּשַׂר אָדָם'.

Yet for the righteous, with them the opposite is the case: The "pure soul," that is, the divine soul, is synonymous with **the person, while their body is referred to as "the flesh of man."**

The tzaddik identifies himself with his divine soul, not with his body and his animal soul. For him, the body is mere material, flesh and bones – the "flesh of man."[6] It belongs to him, but it is not identical to him, just as his clothes and his house belong to him but are not actually him.

וּכְמַאֲמַר הִלֵּל הַזָּקֵן לְתַלְמִידָיו, כְּשֶׁהָיָה הוֹלֵךְ לֶאֱכוֹל הָיָה אוֹמֵר שֶׁהוּא הוֹלֵךְ לִגְמוֹל חֶסֶד עִם הָעֲלוּבָה וַעֲנִיָּה, הוּא גּוּפוֹ, כִּי כְּמוֹ זָר נֶחְשָׁב אֶצְלוֹ. וְלָכֵן אָמַר שֶׁהוּא גּוֹמֵל חֶסֶד עִמּוֹ בַּמֶּה שֶׁמַּאֲכִילוֹ, כִּי הוּא עַצְמוֹ אֵינוֹ רַק נֶפֶשׁ הָאֱלֹהִית לְבַד, כִּי הִיא לְבַדָּהּ מְחַיָּה גּוּפוֹ וּבְשָׂרוֹ.

This is illustrated by **a statement of Hillel the Elder to his disciples. When he went to eat, he would say that he was going to bestow kindness on the "scorned and impoverished one," meaning his body, because he regarded** his body as a **foreign entity in relation to him. He therefore said that he was bestowing kindness on it by giving it** something **to eat, because he himself was nothing but the divine soul, for that alone animated his body and flesh** (see chap. 9). 11 Adar I (leap year)

6. See *Zohar* 1:20b; *Keter Shem Tov* 194.

Hillel regarded his body as some other being with which he had a relationship and for which he was responsible, but he did not identify himself with it.[7]

שֶׁהָרַע שֶׁהָיָה בַּנֶּפֶשׁ הַחִיּוּנִית הַמְלוּבֶּשֶׁת בְּדָמוֹ וּבְשָׂרוֹ נִתְהַפֵּךְ לְטוֹב, וְנִכְלַל בִּקְדוּשַּׁת נֶפֶשׁ הָאֱלֹהִית מַמָּשׁ בַּצַּדִּיקִים.

That is, in the righteous the evil that was within the vital animal **soul, which is clothed in his blood and flesh, has been transformed into good and is literally subsumed in the holiness of the divine soul.**

In general, a person identifies himself with the animal soul that is clothed within the body and animates it. But the tzaddik, who has perfected his animal soul to the extent that it is absorbed into his divine soul, identifies with his holy divine soul. He relates to the desires of the body, and even its needs, from a distance, as though they belong to someone else.

29 Shevat אֲבָל בַּבֵּינוֹנִי, מֵאַחַר שֶׁמַּהוּתָהּ וְעַצְמוּתָהּ שֶׁל נֶפֶשׁ הַחִיּוּנִית, הַבַּהֲמִית, שֶׁמִּסִּטְרָא אָחֳרָא, הַמְלוּבֶּשֶׁת בְּדָמוֹ וּבְשָׂרוֹ – לֹא נֶהֱפַּךְ לְטוֹב,

As for the *beinoni*, since the essence and being of the vital animal soul, which stems **from the *sitra aḥara* and is clothed in his blood and flesh, has not been transformed into good,**

The *beinoni* controls his animal soul, but he does not rectify it. That control is thus only superficial, because it does not express the animal soul's inner will. His vital soul's essence remains the animal soul, the soul connected to physicality. Since its wants and desires are still drawn after the *sitra aḥara*, so are those of the *beinoni*.

הֲרֵי הִיא הָאָדָם עַצְמוֹ.

it is synonymous with **the very person himself.**

The person's self, his simple, natural, initial awareness, is identified with the animal soul.

7. See *Vayikra Rabba* 34:3.

12 Adar I (leap year)

וְאִם כֵּן הוּא רָחוֹק מֵה׳ בְּתַכְלִית הָרִיחוּק, שֶׁהֲרֵי כֹּחַ הַמִּתְאַוֶּה שֶׁבְּנַפְשׁוֹ הַבַּהֲמִית יָכוֹל גַּם כֵּן לְהִתְאַוּוֹת לִדְבָרִים הָאֲסוּרִים, שֶׁהֵם נֶגֶד רְצוֹנוֹ יִתְבָּרֵךְ.

If so, he is utterly distant from God, since the faculty of desire in his animal soul is also capable of desiring things that are prohibited, which are contrary to God's will.

Above, the author of the *Tanya* explained that a person's animal soul can have desires that run counter to God's will, a feat that even the *sitra aḥara* itself cannot achieve.[8] Such an individual is identified with his animal soul and its whims, both antithetical to God's will. Ironically, it is the divine will that gives life to this individual and the entire world at the very moment that his desires are utterly distant from that divine will, forming an unparalleled remoteness between himself and God.

אַף שֶׁאֵינוֹ מִתְאַוֶּה לַעֲשׂוֹתָם בְּפוֹעַל מַמָּשׁ חַס וְשָׁלוֹם,

Although he does not desire to actually and literally act on them, God forbid,

The *beinoni* is not a person who overcomes evil only fitfully. He is someone who has profoundly worked on himself. Though he may desire things that are prohibited, he does not actually plan to act on them. They remain mere fleeting thoughts, an opinion that the body occasionally expresses and that the *beinoni* unequivocally rejects.[9]

רַק שֶׁאֵינָם מְאוּסִים אֶצְלוֹ בֶּאֱמֶת כְּבְצַדִּיקִים, כְּמוֹ שֶׁנִּתְבָּאֵר לְעֵיל [פֶּרֶק יב].

they are nevertheless not truly repugnant to him as they are to the righteous, as explained above (chapter 12).

The difference between a tzaddik and a *beinoni* is usually not apparent to the eye, neither to others nor even at times to the tzaddik himself. Still, in one respect, they are demonstrably different, and that is in how they relate to that which is prohibited. Although the *beinoni* would never think of committing sins, he still does not find them completely

8. See chap. 24.
9. See chap. 13.

repugnant, since he still has a covert attraction toward them.[10] On the other hand, the forbidden never even enters the tzaddik's mind. In his eyes, the temptation to sin is a perversion that disgusts him.

וּבָזֶה הוּא גָּרוּעַ וּמְשׁוּקָּץ וּמְתוֹעָב יוֹתֵר מִבַּעֲלֵי חַיִּים הַטְּמֵאִים וּשְׁקָצִים וּרְמָשִׂים כַּנִּזְכָּר לְעֵיל,

In this regard, he is inferior, more detestable, and more abominable than impure animals, detestable things, and crawling creatures, as mentioned above (chap. 24),

Impure animals and even the *kelippa* itself are incapable of transgressing God's will and even of wanting to do so. The most loathsome crawling creatures do exactly what God programmed them to do. In this regard, a person can be their inferior. If a person eats an impure animal, food that is prohibited, or simply craves to eat it, he has become its inferior. In fact, by eating it, he does the animal an injustice. The purpose of eating is to elevate food spiritually, and when he eats that impure creature, he casts it downward.

וּכְמוֹ שֶׁכָּתוּב: "וְאָנֹכִי תוֹלַעַת וְלֹא אִישׁ" וגו' (תהלים כב, ז)

as it is written, "But I am a worm and not a man..." (Ps. 22:7).

The worm is a worm, as it should be. But a person who disgraces himself is "a worm and not a man" – a worm, although he was meant to be a man. As a worm, a worm does God's will; as a worm, a man transgresses God's will. A worm is incapable of defying God. But a person, even a *beinoni*, can flout the divine will, and then, as he descends to evil, he is more base than the worm.

[וְגַם כְּשֶׁמִּתְגַּבֶּרֶת בּוֹ נַפְשׁוֹ הָאֱלֹקִית, לְעוֹרֵר הָאַהֲבָה לַה' בִּשְׁעַת הַתְּפִלָּה,

(Even when his divine soul prevails over him to awaken the love for God during prayers,

Although the *beinoni* is capable of desiring prohibited things, at other times, such as prayer, he can be inspired toward holiness. Then his divine soul rules his entire being, his wants, thoughts, and senses,

10. See chap. 10.

until his self at its core identifies with the divine soul, its purposes and wishes.

אֵינָהּ בֶּאֱמֶת לַאֲמִיתּוֹ לְגַמְרֵי, מֵאַחַר שֶׁחוֹלֶפֶת וְעוֹבֶרֶת אַחַר הַתְּפִלָּה, כַּנִּזְכָּר לְעֵיל סוֹף פֶּרֶק יג.]

this identity with holiness **is not completely, absolutely true, since it vanishes and passes** immediately **after the prayer, as mentioned above at the end of chapter 13.)**

If that inspiration were completely genuine, if it were carved into the core of the *beinoni*'s soul, it would not disappear as soon as his prayers are done. Even after he has closed his prayer book, the wellsprings of his soul would continue to flow. Had he achieved true awareness, he would have lit a flame that does need not be reignited. When a person realizes he is sitting next to a venomous snake, he does not need to contemplate his plight in efforts to continuously reawaken feelings of fear and panic within himself. But if, after the spiritual height of prayer, the *beinoni* quickly forgets how the flame of love for God had burned within him, the authenticity of his love for God is in question. It is not that he consciously deceives himself. Rather, his soul is unable to authentically, appropriately, and perfectly incorporate that love within himself.

וּבִפְרָט כְּשֶׁיִּזְכּוֹר טוּמְאַת נַפְשׁוֹ בְּחַטַּאת נְעוּרִים,

One can also humble himself **when he recalls, in particular, the spiritual impurity** caused to **his soul as a result of the sin of** his **youth,** 13 Adar I (leap year)

The author of the *Tanya* now recommends another technique that the *beinoni* can use to fulfill the words of the *Zohar* that one should so thoroughly humble himself that he considers himself despicable and contemptible. That technique is to look upon himself as he had been in the past. Although it may be that at present he does not find any faults or deficiencies within himself, a mature self-assessment of his past self, after years of soul work, will undoubtedly reveal that he was in a lower spiritual state in his youth.

Usually, as a person matures into adulthood, he leaves this problem behind. But a person can maintain a clear awareness of that phase of his life and the negative consequences of his actions. The "sin of [his] youth" in particular refers to sexual misconduct, most notably the wasting of seed.[11]

וְהַפְּגַם שֶׁעָשָׂה בָּעֶלְיוֹנִים. **and the blemish he wrought in the higher worlds.**

From the person's subjective point of view, past events, which may have occurred thirty or forty years ago, have little relevance in the present. He has left them behind, and they do not touch him now. But each sinful deed creates a blemish in the higher worlds, and at times in this world as well, which generates its own set of problems.

וְשָׁם הוּא לְמַעְלָה מֵהַזְּמַן, כְּאִלּוּ פָּגַם וְנִטְמָא הַיּוֹם חַס וְשָׁלוֹם מַמָּשׁ. There, a realm **that transcends time, it is as if he literally caused the blemish and defiled himself this day, God forbid.**

The existence of time begins on the spiritual plane of *Malkhut*, from which this physical world stems. Everything above that plane transcends time.[12] If someone sinned ten or twenty years ago, in the higher worlds it is as though he committed the sin at this very moment. From the perspective of the higher worlds, there is no past. There is only today, only the present. Just as the effect of a mitzva in the higher worlds is eternal, transcending time, so is the blemish caused by a sin.[13]

וְאַף שֶׁכְּבָר עָשָׂה תְּשׁוּבָה נְכוֹנָה, **Even if he has repented properly,**

This is speaking of a *beinoni*, who has repented and rectified everything that required rectification, as explained in *Iggeret HaTeshuva*.[14]

---

11. See *Reshit Ḥokhma, Sha'ar HaTeshuva*, chap. 3, p. 109c.
12. See *Derekh Mitzvotekha*, p. 151; commentary on the *Zohar* by the Tzemaḥ Tzedek, p. 257.
13. It appears that the author's reference to the higher worlds incorporates even the worlds of *Beria, Yetzira,* and *Asiya*. Therefore, the phrase "transcends time" should be explained to mean beyond time as it exists in our reality. See *HaTomim*, p. 358a.
14. Chap. 4.

הֲרֵי עִיקַּר הַתְּשׁוּבָה בַּלֵּב,

repentance is primarily accomplished **in the heart,**

As the author of the *Tanya* explains in *Iggeret HaTeshuva*,[15] the essence of repentance is not a specific action. It is not a recipe that one follows: so much charity, so many self-afflictions, so many fasts. Essentially, repentance is a feeling in the heart, constituting regret over the past and a resolution for the future, where one resolves to henceforth act properly.

וְהַלֵּב יֵשׁ בּוֹ בְּחִינוֹת וּמַדְרֵגוֹת רַבּוֹת, וְהַכֹּל לְפִי מַה שֶּׁהוּא אָדָם וּלְפִי הַזְּמַן וְהַמָּקוֹם, כַּיָּדוּעַ לַיּוֹדְעִים.

and the heart contains many facets and levels, all depending on the person, time, and place, as is known to those who are knowledgeable in the esoteric wisdom of Kabbala.

In the human heart there are many degrees and facets; it is home to a broad range of depths.[16] At every stage of life, according to one's personal development and depending on the time and place in which he lives, the society and the environment, he will experience a different layer of his heart. Each time, the events of his life will take on a new form and weight, which will also require of him to reevaluate his relationship toward them.

These matters are not known to everyone because only the person himself can recognize the state of his heart, and even then, only when he can assess himself honestly at every moment and in every circumstance. When a person views his soul in this way, so that he knows it and senses it, the heartfelt sentiments of regret and repentance that had been enough at an earlier age and at a different level of being will now seem superficial and unsatisfactory. The deeper he delves into his own mind, and the more developed his personality, the more clearly the person can recognize his problems and the more profoundly he can see each deficiency. Then his previous repentance may no longer

15. Chap. 4.

16. This is alluded to in the verse "Out of the depths I call to You…" (Ps. 130:1). "Depths" is written in the plural, indicating deeper and variegated degrees of depths (Rabbi Shmuel Gronem Esterman).

seem to be enough. It may be that his previous repentance had not been able to reach the deeper levels of imperfections. ☞

וְלָכֵן עַכְשָׁיו, בְּשָׁעָה זוֹ, שֶׁרוֹאֶה בְּעַצְמוֹ דְּלָא סָלִיק בֵּיהּ נְהוֹרָא דְּנִשְׁמְתָא, מִכְּלָל שֶׁהַיּוֹם לֹא נִתְקַבְּלָה תְּשׁוּבָתוֹ, וַעֲוֹנוֹתָיו מַבְדִּילִים,

Consequently, now, at this moment, when one observes about himself that the light of the soul does not permeate him, it is evident that his repentance was not accepted today, and his past **sins are** still **separating** him from God,

His past repentance no longer suffices now, today. Although he has already rectified his sins and even forgotten them, they are like an old fracture, which can begin to hurt again even years after it healed. No matter how well the bone was set, the reconstruction cannot be perfect. With a change of conditions – a different age or a stormier climate – the pain can return.

אוֹ שֶׁרוֹצִים לְהַעֲלוֹתוֹ לִתְשׁוּבָה עִילָּאָה יוֹתֵר מֵעוּמְקָא דְּלִבָּא יוֹתֵר.

or it is desired that he be elevated to a higher level of **repentance,** deriving **from a deeper place in his heart.**

It is possible that an individual truly has committed no sins that separate him from God, and it is not on account of past sins that he is now required to repent. Rather, it was decided on high that this person be elevated to a higher spiritual rank and achieve a greater degree of perfection through an awakening from above.[17] In truth, this individual's soul already shines into him from that higher level of its own accord,

PERSON, TIME, AND PLACE

☞ These three aspects constitute the three archetypal dimensions mentioned in Kabbala: soul, year, and world (see *Sefer Yetzira*, chap. 3). According to hasidic literature, these three aspects are forever interconnected and intertwined. A change that occurs to one effects a change in the other, essentially creating a new reality for the person. A different time and place result in a different person.

17. This corresponds to the talmudic principle "The left hand drives away, and the right draws near" (*Sanhedrin* 107b). There are instances where one receives a boost of heavenly assistance to repent, the "right drawing near," as we find in the

yet it cannot take permanent hold of the person's corporeal body and fully permeate it since the body does not share the refinement and level of the soul. In order for this to occur, the individual is required to repent from a deeper level in his heart.[18]

וְלָכֵן אָמַר דָּוִד: "וְחַטָּאתִי נֶגְדִּי תָמִיד" (תהלים נא, ה).

For this reason, David said, "My sin is always before me" (Ps. 51:5).

King David was constantly ascending in holiness, from one level to the next. Whenever he arrived at a higher level, he realized that his previous repentance had been incomplete, that his sin was before him still, and that he must repent anew.[19]

30 Shevat

14 Adar I (leap year)

וְגַם מִי שֶׁהוּא נָקִי מֵחַטֹּאות נְעוּרִים הַחֲמוּרִים יָשִׂים אֶל לִבּוֹ לְקַיֵּים מַאֲמַר זֹהַר הַקָּדוֹשׁ (חלק ג קעח, א) לִהְיוֹת מִמָּארֵי דְחוּשְׁבְּנָא, דְּהַיְינוּ לַעֲשׂוֹת חֶשְׁבּוֹן עִם נַפְשׁוֹ מִכָּל הַמַּחֲשָׁבוֹת וְהַדִּיבּוּרִים וְהַמַּעֲשִׂים שֶׁחָלְפוּ וְעָבְרוּ מִיּוֹם הֱיוֹתוֹ עַד הַיּוֹם הַזֶּה, אִם הָיוּ

Even one who is innocent of egregious sins of his **youth should resolve to fulfill the teaching of the holy** ***Zohar*** (3:178a) **to become a master of introspection. That is,** he should **make an accounting with his soul of all the thoughts, words, and actions that transpired from the day he came into existence**

case of Rabbi Elazar ben Durdaya. But here the author of the *Tanya* is discussing the experience of the "left hand driving away," in which the divine love is withheld, with the ultimate intent of making the person aware that he is being called upon to achieve a higher level of repentance (*Likkutei Biurim*).

18. As the author of the *Tanya* explains elsewhere, what we call repentance, or *teshuva*, which literally means to return, refers primarily to one's spiritual ascent and return to the source of his soul in the Divine and not necessarily repentance on account of a sin. See *Likkutei Torah*, Num. 19a.

19. The Lubavitcher Rebbe, Rabbi Menaḥem Mendel Schneerson, explains that this does not mean that there was a sin or deficiency for which King David had to atone. As noted in chapter 1, King David serves as the paradigm of a truly righteous person, since he "killed" his evil inclination by fasting, as alluded to in the verse "And my heart is dead within me" (Ps. 109:22). Rather, the idea being conveyed here is that which was mentioned above, that it was decided on high that King David had to achieve a higher level of repentance.

כּוּלָם מִצַּד הַקְּדוּשָּׁה אוֹ מִצַּד הַטּוּמְאָה רַחֲמָנָא לִיצְּלָן.

until this day, ascertaining **whether they were all from the side of holiness or from the side of impurity, may the Merciful One save us.**

Even one who has not committed sins during his youth and cannot therefore crush the haughtiness to which the *beinoni* is susceptible should still make an accounting of his behavior.

We should remember that the author of the *Tanya* is not speaking of a sinner or even an average man. His words are directed at people of great spiritual stature, whether they are actual *beinonim* or at the least have some connection to that exalted spiritual plane. When they examine themselves, such people will not always find sins and blemishes. They will have nothing to contemplate that can help them shatter their spirit and break their heart. Therefore, they must be "master accountants" and take the trouble to keep a precise accounting of their lives over the course of many years.

דְּהַיְינוּ, כָּל הַמַּחֲשָׁבוֹת וְהַדִּיבּוּרִים וְהַמַּעֲשִׂים אֲשֶׁר לֹא לַה' הֵמָּה וְלִרְצוֹנוֹ וְלַעֲבוֹדָתוֹ, שֶׁזֶּהוּ פֵּירוּשׁ לְשׁוֹן "סִטְרָא אָחֳרָא" כַּנִּזְכָּר לְעֵיל [בְּפֶרֶק ו].

This, the side of impurity, **includes any thoughts, words, or actions that are not directed to God, His will, or His service. This is the meaning of the term *sitra aḥara*, as mentioned above (in chapter 6).**

The *sitra aḥara*, or the other side, is not limited to a carefully delineated, isolated provenance, of outright prohibited and detestable things. It also incorporates any thoughts, words, or actions unrelated to holiness.

Broadly speaking, the other side has no relationship with the side of holiness. As the author of the *Tanya* stated above, there is no middle ground between holiness and impurity.[20] Whatever is not holy is, by default, impurity and *kelippa*. A person is either on one side or the other. When a person takes stock, he will discover that many areas in his life had no relationship with holiness. They were not necessarily

20. See chap. 6 and commentary there.

outright sins but were occasions when he did not direct his actions solely to God, His Torah, and His service.

וּמוּדַעַת זֹאת כִּי כָּל עֵת שֶׁהָאָדָם מְחַשֵּׁב מַחֲשָׁבוֹת קְדוֹשׁוֹת, נַעֲשָׂה מֶרְכָּבָה בְּעֵת זוֹ לְהֵיכָלוֹת הַקְּדוּשָּׁה שֶׁמֵּהֶן מוּשְׁפָּעוֹת מַחֲשָׁבוֹת הַלָּלוּ.

It is known that every time a person thinks holy thoughts, he becomes a vehicle, at that moment, for the sanctums of holiness from which these thoughts issue forth.

Similarly, when one acts and speaks in a holy manner, he becomes a vehicle for the emanation of holiness. At that moment, his body and soul become the instruments through which that holiness is revealed in this world.

וְכֵן לְהֵפֶךְ, נַעֲשָׂה מֶרְכָּבָה טְמֵאָה בְּעֵת זוֹ לְהֵיכָלוֹת הַטּוּמְאָה שֶׁמֵּהֶן מוּשְׁפָּעוֹת כָּל מַחֲשָׁבוֹת רָעוֹת, וְכֵן בְּדִבּוּר וּמַעֲשֶׂה.

Conversely, when one thinks unholy thoughts, **he becomes an impure vehicle, at that moment, for the sanctums of impurity from which all evil thoughts issue forth. The same applies to speech and action.**

The reckoning that the "master of introspection" makes is not merely a weighing of good deeds and sins. It also takes into account the so-called middle ground that contains neither explicit sin nor unqualified good deeds but permissible activities that are attached to the *sitra aḥara* because they are not directed toward God's service. After a precise accounting, even a person who cannot find within himself sinful blemishes in thought and deed that contravene the will of God and His Torah will surely discover many instances in his life that were not dedicated to the service of the Divine. He can use these to attain the broken heart, the feeling of humility, that is the key to breaking open the dull heart.

עוֹד יָשִׂים אֶל לִבּוֹ רוֹב חֲלוֹמוֹתָיו, שֶׁהֵם הֶבֶל וּרְעוּת רוּחַ,

Moreover, one should consider his dreams, which are mostly futile and baseless, 15 Adar I (leap year)

Here the author of the *Tanya* offers another means of breaking a dull heart. When the *beinoni* is awake and engaged in Torah and mitzvot, he may sense nothing untoward in himself. The author of the *Tanya* advises him to pursue humility and a broken heart when he is asleep, in his dreams, which are mostly "futile and baseless," and some are downright repugnant.

In his waking hours, a *beinoni* can fully suppress the aspects within himself that remain "other." He can impose a framework on them and restrict their expression. But in a dream, when he does not wield complete control over himself, these aspects of his character are no longer contained. They break forth and express themselves freely, whether to reveal his hidden desires or as a perverse caricature of his inner being.

מִשּׁוּם שֶׁאֵין נַפְשׁוֹ עוֹלָה לְמַעְלָה. וּכְמוֹ שֶׁכָּתוּב: "מִי יַעֲלֶה בְהַר ה' נְקִי כַפַּיִם" וגו' (תהלים כד, ג-ד).

because his soul does not ascend on high while he sleeps, **as it is written, "Who may ascend the mountain of the Lord?** Who may stand in His holy place? **He who has clean hands** and a pure heart" (Ps. 24:3–4).

If his soul rose upward as he slept, it would not experience such dreams. The soul of a person who has "clean hands and a pure heart" rises when he sleeps, and his dreams are connected solely to holiness. But when his dreams are "futile and baseless," his soul is not rising upward. This demonstrates that he does not have a pure heart, that he is not a tzaddik, perfect in everything, but blemished and deficient.

וְ"אִינוּן סִטְרִין בִּישִׁין אָתְיָין וּמִתְדַּבְּקָן בֵּיהּ וּמוֹדְעִין לֵיהּ בְּחֶלְמָא מִילִּין דְּעָלְמָא וכו'.

Moreover, "**those evil aspects come and attach themselves to him and inform him of mundane affairs in** his **dreams....**

When a person's dreams do not originate from the side of holiness, the forces of the *sitra aḥara* cling to him in his dreams, speaking to him of the mundane world. When he is awake, he is involved only in holy matters, but that does not prove that he has "clean hands and a pure heart," that all the chambers of his soul have been cleansed of the evil inclination, that he is a tzaddik whose "heart is dead within him." In his dream, the parts of his inner being that he has cast to the edges of waking consciousness come to the fore and let him know that although they are usually concealed, they are still part of who he is.

וּלְזִמְנִין, דְּחַיְיכָן בֵּיהּ וְאַחֲזִיאוּ לֵיהּ מִילֵּי שֶׁקֶר וְצַעֲרִין לֵיהּ בְּחֶלְמֵיהּ" כו׳, כְּמוֹ שֶׁכָּתוּב בַּזֹּהַר וַיִּקְרָא [דַּף כה עַמּוּד א וְעַמּוּד ב], עַיֵּין שָׁם בַּאֲרִיכוּת.

Sometimes they mock him and show him false things and torment him in his dream…," as it is written in the ***Zohar*** **on** ***Vayikra*** **(25a–b). See there at length.**

A person is not responsible for his dreams, and he does not have to atone for them. But they do serve as a measure of his inner being. They can show him aspects of himself that he would not otherwise see. On a conscious level, the *beinoni* functions in a familiar realm of perfection that he constructs within certain limited parameters, within a life marked by definite boundaries. But in a dream, he sees a different image, one that contains falsehood, perversion, and worse. Still, his dreams are useful, because they provide him with a rough representation of his true spiritual state.

וְהִנֵּה כָּל מַה שֶּׁיַּאֲרִיךְ בְּעִנְיָנִים אֵלּוּ בְּמַחֲשַׁבְתּוֹ,

The longer one considers these mat-ters, that is, the advice offered here to humble oneself, by contemplating them **in one's thoughts,** 1 Adar

Each person must contemplate these matters in light of his own state of being. It is not enough to read about such things in books. As the author of the *Tanya* explained in his introduction above, no text, including this one, can teach a person how to transform his traits and emotions. Only "the heart knows the bitterness of itself" (Prov. 14:10). No one knows a person's imperfections as well as he does, and only he can reflect on them properly. As for this book, it presents no more than a general prescription meant to inspire a person to think on his own.

וְגַם בְּעִיּוּנוֹ בִּסְפָרִים,

as well as by perusing books written on the subject,

This is a reference to ethical works that describe the gravity of sin and the blemishes that exist in all things that are not directed toward God. Even after a person recognizes his imperfections, he is not always impacted by his knowledge until he reads such works.

לִהְיוֹת לִבּוֹ נִשְׁבָּר בְּקִרְבּוֹ וְ״נִבְזֶה בְּעֵינָיו נִמְאָס״ כַּכָּתוּב (תהלים טו, ד), בְּתַכְלִית הַמִּיאוּס וְלִמְאֹס חַיָּיו מַמָּשׁ,

in order for his heart to be broken within him and be **"despised and repugnant in his own eyes,"** as **stated** in Psalms (15:4), to the extent that he is **utterly repulsive** in his own eyes **and literally despises his life,**

This self-introspection must be carried out with great precision and acceptance of responsibility, so that even if a person has not committed obvious sins, he will be "despised and repugnant in his own eyes."

הֲרֵי בָּזֶה מְמָאֵס וּמְבַזֶּה הַסִּטְרָא אַחֲרָא,

the more he thereby repulses and despises the *sitra aḥara*,

The *beinoni* must despise and degrade himself because in so doing he despises and degrades the *sitra aḥara*. This does not mean that he devalues himself or makes nothing of the holiness he possesses within. On the contrary, he is downgrading the sense of self, the ego, that permeates him, and in so doing, he overcomes and crushes the *sitra aḥara*, so that the light of holiness may still shine.

וּמַשְׁפִּילָהּ לֶעָפָר וּמוֹרִידָהּ מִגְּדוּלָּתָהּ וְגַסּוּת רוּחָהּ וְגַבְהוּתָהּ, שֶׁמַּגְבִּיהַּ אֶת עַצְמָהּ עַל אוֹר קְדוּשַּׁת נֶפֶשׁ הָאֱלֹהִית לְהַחֲשִׁיךְ אוֹרָהּ.

throwing it to the dust and lowering it from its self-proclaimed **greatness, arrogance, and haughtiness with which it exalts itself above the light of the divine soul's holiness to obscure its radiance.**

Dullness of the heart is an impure sheath enveloping a person's heart. It is made of self-satisfaction and an egotistical sense of being. It so completely covers the heart that it prevents the divine soul from shining brightly within it, and then the heart does not receive its life force and vitality from holiness. A person must crack this sheath, and he does so by humbling himself and shattering the gestalt of self-satisfaction.

וְגַם יַרְעִים עָלֶיהָ בְּקוֹל רַעַשׁ וְרוֹגֶז לְהַשְׁפִּילָהּ,

He should also thunder at it with a loud and raging voice in order to humble it,

At times, a person must relate to his spirit, his being, as if it were something outside of himself. He must shout at it as he would shout at another person.

כְּמַאֲמַר רַבּוֹתֵינוּ ז"ל (ברכות ה, א): "לְעוֹלָם יַרְגִּיז אָדָם יֵצֶר טוֹב עַל יֵצֶר הָרָע, שֶׁנֶּאֱמַר: 'רִגְזוּ' וגו'" (תהלים ד, ה)". דְּהַיְינוּ לִרְגּוֹז עַל נֶפֶשׁ הַבַּהֲמִית שֶׁהִיא יִצְרוֹ הָרָע

in accordance with our Rabbis' statement (*Berakhot* 5a) **"One should always incite his good inclination against his evil inclination, as the verse states, 'Rage,** and do not sin' (Ps. 4:5)." **That is,** he ought **to rage against his animal soul, which is his evil inclination,**

A person must rouse himself and rage against the dull heart, the painful lack of feeling, the inability to arouse emotion despite one's prayers and performance of mitzvot, and confront the sly impurity that conceals the divine vitality and causes it to slumber. He cannot allow himself to sink but must set his good inclination against his bad.

בְּקוֹל רַעַשׁ וְרוֹגֶז בְּמַחֲשַׁבְתּוֹ,

with a loud and raging voice, in his mind,

He does not have to speak aloud. It suffices to shout in his thoughts. The author of the *Tanya* emphasizes that this raging shout take place in the mind because this anger is directed toward oneself. It is no great feat to express feelings of bitterness and anger by screaming at another person (even if that person cannot hear those vitriolic words). But to direct such intense anger inward in the hope of proving efficacious in helping the individual make a genuine self-assessment, he must confine that voice to his mind.

לוֹמַר לוֹ: אַתָּה רַע וְרָשָׁע וּמְשׁוּקָּץ וּמְתוֹעָב וּמְנוּוָּל וכו׳, כְּכָל הַשֵּׁמוֹת שֶׁקְּרָאוּ לוֹ חֲכָמֵינוּ ז״ל,

telling it, "You are evil, wicked, despicable, loathsome, vile...," using all **the epithets our Sages called it,**

When a person faints, we slap him in the face in order to rouse him. A dulled heart is similarly immobile. The heart had been smothered beneath *kelippot* that have made it unable to respond. It requires a strong shock to awaken it and break its complacent air. The *kelippot* conceal and hide this person's heart because he identifies with them and views them as being part and parcel of himself. In order to shake the person, to break through bland smugness, to crack his veneer of perfection, we must shout and insult. The evil inclination disguises itself in beauty so that we will feel a kinship with it. To overcome that, and expose it for what it truly is, we must call it by every foul name that our Sages have used,[21] and even add our own: evil, wicked, disgusting, and so on.

בֶּאֱמֶת.

feeling this **in truth.**

One must feel the truth of this statement, telling one's evil inclination, "You are truly evil, truly wicked," and so on. At its root, it may possess an entirely different quality, as indicated in the parable of the harlot that the author of the *Tanya* relates at the end of the chapter, which teaches that at its core, even evil is good. But here the person must focus on the present reality, and in the present, the evil inclination is truly pernicious. One who possesses a deep understanding and sense of the true essence of evil, that at its core it is good, will not be motivated to destroy it by berating it vehemently, nor for that matter will he be motivated to achieve a greater degree of holiness. In order to successfully crush the evil inclination, one must feel the truth of what he is saying.

עַד מָתַי תַּסְתִּיר לְפָנַי אוֹר אֵין סוֹף בָּרוּךְ הוּא הַמְמַלֵּא כָּל עָלְמִין, הָיָה הֹוֶה וְיִהְיֶה בְּשָׁוֶה, גַּם בְּמָקוֹם זֶה שֶׁאֲנִי עָלָיו, כְּמוֹ

He must confront it, saying, **"How long will you conceal from me the light of *Ein Sof*, blessed be He, which permeates all worlds, which was, is, and will** always **be the same, even in this place**

21. See *Sukka* 52a.

שֶׁהָיָה אוֹר אֵין סוֹף בָּרוּךְ הוּא לְבַדּוֹ קוֹדֶם שֶׁנִּבְרָא הָעוֹלָם בְּלִי שׁוּם שִׁינּוּי. כְּמוֹ שֶׁכָּתוּב: "אֲנִי ה' לֹא שָׁנִיתִי" (מלאכי ג, ו), כִּי הוּא לְמַעְלָה מֵהַזְּמַן וכו'.

where I am, just as the light of *Ein Sof* was alone, utterly unchanged, before the world was created, as it is written, 'I the Lord did not change' (Mal. 3:6), **for He transcends time, and so on?**

The divine light does not exist in some other place but resides within all the worlds, here and everywhere. The same applies to time. Time does not change God. He is the same today as He was yesterday and as He was before the world was created. The divine light that filled all of existence before the creation of the world fills it now to an equal extent. From God's point of view, the existence of the world does not conceal His light. Such concealment exists only from the human perspective. A human being does not see the Divine but the world. Rather than seeing the One who acts, he sees only what has been acted on.

וְאַתָּה מְנוּוָּל וכו' מַכְחִישׁ הָאֱמֶת הַנִּרְאֶה לָעֵינַיִם, דְּכוּלָּא קַמֵּיהּ כְּלָא מַמָּשׁ בֶּאֱמֶת, בִּבְחִינַת רְאִיָּיה חוּשִׁיִּית.

But you, animal soul, **vile one, and so on, deny the truth that is plainly evident: that everything is literally and truly as nothingness in His presence,** a truth that can be **tangibly seen."**

It is possible to see directly with our own eyes the existence of God in the world, how His glory completely fills the world, and how it is He alone who gives life and sustains all the entities of the universe. This world and everything it contains therein is something we can see with our physical eyes, not to mention our other physical senses. It follows that meditating on the divine source, the fact that God constantly brings the world into existence, is essentially a truth experienced through our physical sense of sight. ☞

TANGIBLE FAITH

☞ The commandment to believe in God is not a commandment to believe in His existence. The concept of faith, more precisely understood, relates to believing something about the divine essence, the fact that "the Lord, He is the God" (Deut. 4:39). That is to say, that the transcendental and the immanent are one (see *Likkutei Torah*, Deut. 4a).

"I am the Lord your God" (Ex. 20:2),

וְהִנֵּה עַל יְדֵי זֶה יוֹעִיל לְנַפְשׁוֹ הָאֱלֹהִית, לְהָאִיר עֵינֶיהָ בֶּאֱמֶת יִחוּד אוֹר אֵין סוֹף,

Through this he will help his divine soul, by enlightening it with the truth of the unity of the light of *Ein Sof*

the commandment to believe in God (see *Sefer HaMitzvot*, positive commandment 1), is thus not a commandment to believe in the existence of a Creator but rather to believe in the unique connection between the unfathomable being beyond all existence and, as the commandment continues, "the Lord your God, who took you out of the land of Egypt" – the omnipotent, active operating power in the world.

On the other hand, awareness of the existence of God, the Supreme Power, Creator, and Operator of all of existence, is related not to faith but to vision: "From my flesh I will view God" (Job 19:26). We can perceive Him with a palpable consciousness in the same way that we see physical objects. This is why the Torah does not command us to believe in the existence of God, just as it does not command us to believe in the existence of our souls and bodies: because we can sense these on our own. We do not need to be commanded.

On every level of his being, a human being is a sort of amphibian, living simultaneously in two worlds: the world of matter and the world of the spirit. This does not mean that every individual lives on a high spiritual plane but that the life of every human being is a composite of material and nonmaterial experiences. People love, hate, are offended, and generally live rich internal lives.

In this sense, the definition of reality is largely subjective. Is an object real only when we can touch it with our hands? Or does it also include that which we think or feel? Or does reality also include the power of the Creator in what has been created?

As easily as we have accepted the notion that what we sense physically is reality, so we can accept the concept that the divine power acting through the world is also tangible. Unfortunately, the animal soul within a person builds constructs that ascribe reality only to what he can see and touch.

We generate the image of a physical world that is self-sustained and independent, divorced from the spirit and thus disconnected from the power that creates and impels it. In this image, we acknowledge only those objects that we have already decided are real, and we do not see those things that the animal soul wishes to remain invisible.

It is written, "The scoundrel says in his heart: There is no God. They have been corrupted and have acted abominably" (Ps. 53:2). This verse can be interpreted as saying: Why does the degenerate individual say in his heart that there is no God? It is so that he may afterward allow himself to act in a corrupt and perverse manner (see *Sanhedrin* 63b).

A person's intellectual and emotional awareness of the existence of God hampers his impulse to sin, so he denies that awareness in order to loosen his inhibitions. Driven by the desire to do wrong, a person's animal soul creates a mental structure that perverts and conceals this primal perception. Even if he is intelligent, cultured, and enlightened, he will be unable to see what even small children or members of the most primitive tribes can perceive.

When a person shouts at himself – that is, at the animal soul – in order to humble it and reveal its falsehood, its perverseness, its false appearance, and deceit, it will prove beneficial in helping his divine soul perceive the truth of divine unity. That truth is that He is one and unique, that He is now and will be in the future no different than He was before the world was created, for He never changes at all.

בִּרְאִיָּה חוּשִׁיִּית וְלֹא בִּבְחִינַת שְׁמִיעָה וַהֲבָנָה לְבַדָּהּ, **with tangible sight and not merely** through **hearing or** cognitive **understanding.**

The difference between seeing and hearing is in a sense the difference between a direct relationship and one maintained via one or two intermediaries.[22] We have heard of the unity of the light of *Ein Sof*, and to some degree we even comprehend it. However, to see it and relate to it directly, we must destroy the complex structure that shields us from that awareness. When we remove that obstacle, we arrive at a direct understanding of it, one corresponding to sight.

This is not a mystical state or an elevated experience of an extraordinary nature that can be reached only after study and preparation. It is the simplest, most generalized awareness of even an untutored Jew, to whom it is starkly obvious that God exists. ☞

SEEING VERSUS HEARING

☞ It is possible for a Jew to pray, learn, and perform other activities at a distant remove. His hand moves to perform a mitzva, his mouth prays, but he does not truly experience it. Then one day, perhaps after decades have gone by, he realizes that he himself is performing the mitzva, that it is he who is standing and speaking to God. This is not because he now possesses information he did not have before, because he has acquired new theories, but because now he is directly experiencing his actions. Suddenly he actually "sees" what he is doing. This is the difference between a person who knows something because he read it in a textbook, who knows it theoretically, and someone who sees it for himself.

22. See, e.g., *Iggeret HaKodesh*, epistle 19; *Torah Or* 65a. Some explain that this distinction is represented in the unique qualities inherent in the *sefirot* of *Ḥokhma* and *Bina*, where *Ḥokhma* represents the sense of sight, while *Bina* signifies the sense of hearing.

כְּמוֹ שֶׁנִּתְבָּאֵר בְּמָקוֹם אַחֵר שֶׁזֶּהוּ שֹׁרֶשׁ כָּל הָעֲבוֹדָה.

As explained elsewhere (chap. 36), **this** clear perception of the unity of the divine light **is the root of all** divine **service.**

There are two aspects to serving God. The first is to do His will. The second, which we are discussing here, is to work on oneself in order to be able to see the Divine as fully as one is able to see it. A person achieves this by overcoming the images created by the senses of the body and animal soul. He must conquer and cast down the animal soul, breaking down and removing the sensory images that prevent him from seeing the divine light. When a person successfully overcomes this structure of falsehood, of the world's illusions and its material nature, his divine soul can perceive the divine light even within the animal soul with a vital and genuine feeling that will remain active within him at every moment of existence.

2 Adar וְהַטַּעַם, לְפִי שֶׁבֶּאֱמֶת אֵין שׁוּם מַמָּשׁוּת כְּלָל בְּסִטְרָא אָחֳרָא, שֶׁלָּכֵן נִמְשְׁלָה לְחֹשֶׁךְ שֶׁאֵין בּוֹ שׁוּם מַמָּשׁוּת כְּלָל

The reason this shouting is effective **is because in truth, there is no substance to the** ***sitra aḥara*** **whatsoever, which is why it is analogous to darkness, which also possesses no substance at all**

Someone once asked Rabbi Tzvi Hirsch Eichenstein, the founding leader of the Ziditchov hasidic dynasty, what was so innovative about the hasidic movement. He answered with a parable:

A traveler once returned from a remote foreign land and reported that he had seen a bird with a human face and cow's legs. Only a few people believed this outlandish tale. Later, another traveler came from that same land and described the same bird but in a more abstract manner: Its face bore only a certain similarity to that of a human being, and its legs a certain resemblance to a cow's legs. More people were prepared to accept that explanation, but there were still many skeptics. Finally, a third traveler arrived and brought one of those birds with him, which he showed to everyone.

This story is an allegory alluding to the three stages in the revelation of the Torah's mysteries. The first traveler represents Rabbi Shimon bar Yoḥai, whose work, the *Zohar*, is filled with depictions of various heavenly figures and images. The second traveler is the Ari, who explained and arranged the material in a more comprehensible manner. The third traveler is the Ba'al Shem Tov, who demonstrated: Here is God! There was nothing new in the Ba'al Shem Tov teachings. The only difference was in the relationship to that knowledge. The Ba'al Shem Tov pointed out that the things that everyone had already heard about could be seen with their own eyes.

Why should shouting at oneself be effective although one says nothing new? How is it that simply breaking the evil without any active, positive work brings a person to a fresh and true apprehension of holiness?

It is because in truth we do not believe in the existence of an independent power that stands in opposition to holiness. The entire existence of the *sitra aḥara* is darkness, without substance and so, as the author of the *Tanya* goes on to say, it dissipates when faced with that truth.

וּמִמֵּילָא נִדְחֶה מִפְּנֵי הָאוֹר.

and is therefore **automatically dispelled by light.**

Darkness cannot exist in the presence of light, since it is no more than the absence of light. It cannot battle against light in order to defend itself and protect its existence, because when there is light, there cannot be darkness. When one merely uncovers the divine light, the *sitra aḥara* ceases to exist and so ceases to obscure it.

The Hebrew word for created, *bara,* implies the formation of a vacuum, like a clearing in the forest.[23] Related words are *bor,* pit, and *be'er,* well. In light of this, one can understand the verse that states that God "fashions light and creates darkness, makes peace and creates evil" (Isa. 45:7). God "creates darkness" by making a vacuum within light. Similarly, He "creates evil," which results from a vacuum made within the divine light.

However, there can be no true vacuum in the divine and infinite light. The reality of the *sitra aḥara* is an illusion, a mirage. When it dissipates, the divine light is revealed and the imaginary matrix of evil disappears.

וְכָךְ הַסִּטְרָא אָחֳרָא, אַף שֶׁיֵּשׁ בָּהּ חַיּוּת הַרְבֵּה לְהַחֲיוֹת כָּל בַּעֲלֵי חַיִּים הַטְּמֵאִים וְנַפְשׁוֹת אוּמּוֹת הָעוֹלָם, וְגַם נֶפֶשׁ הַבַּהֲמִית שֶׁבְּיִשְׂרָאֵל כַּנִּזְכָּר לְעֵיל, מִכָּל מָקוֹם, הֲרֵי כָּל חַיּוּתָהּ אֵינָהּ מִצַּד עַצְמָהּ חַס

Likewise, although the *sitra aḥara* possesses an abundance of life force to give life to all impure animals, the souls of the gentile **nations of the world, and the Jew's animal soul, as mentioned above** (chaps. 6, 7, 24), **its entire life force is nevertheless**

23. See Josh. 17:15; *HaKetav VeHakabbala,* Gen. 1:1.

וְשָׁלוֹם אֶלָּא מִצַּד הַקְּדוּשָּׁה כַּנִּזְכָּר לְעֵיל.

not its own, God forbid, but rather derives from the side of holiness, as mentioned above (chaps. 6, 7, 24).

Apparently, the *sitra aḥara* in one form or another seems to give life to the majority of the world. In truth, it possesses no inherent power of life. It is only the element of holiness within it that empowers it to create and build. In this sense, evil is a perversion, the exploitative misuse of holiness. This creates an illusion, a false world that misuses the force of life and the truth of holiness to support its existence.

Complete falsehood is an abstract concept. To exist, a lie must possess a grain of truth, not only to be persuasive but also so that one will be able to express it. It is akin to a shadow that cannot exist without the light that surrounds it. In this sense, the existence of evil is not its own, not intrinsic, but drawn from holiness. ☞

וְלָכֵן הִיא בְּטֵלָה לְגַמְרֵי מִפְּנֵי הַקְּדוּשָּׁה, כְּבִיטּוּל הַחֹשֶׁךְ מִפְּנֵי הָאוֹר הַגַּשְׁמִי.

Therefore, it is completely nullified in the presence of holiness, just as darkness is nullified in the presence of physical light.

The existence of darkness depends on the existence of light. When light is concealed, a world of shadows is created, a world whose entire existence ceases to exist the moment the light shines once more. Light has no need to battle against darkness. When it appears, the darkness dissipates.

THE VIRULENCE OF EVIL

☞ According to one theory about the structure of microscopic organisms, a virus is no more than a genetic code. This virus attaches itself to an existing biological structure and perverts it in accordance with its particular code. In essence, the existence of the virus is perversion. In itself, it cannot germinate. It possesses no more than the ability to parasitically attach itself and create forms within others. With that power it lives, and with that power it twists its world in order to create, as it were, a world of illusion.

This virus does not wage war against the body, and it does not have specific programs and stratagems with regard to the body. It simply grows and develops, and as it does so, it increasingly perverts and destroys the organism to which it is attached.

Evil too is a parasite. If it were isolated and separated from holiness, it would cease to live and exist. Whatever it has is not its own, and what is its own is nothing.

That being the case, why does evil continue to exist within a person who possesses holiness?

רַק שֶׁלְּגַבֵּי קְדוּשַּׁת נֶפֶשׁ הָאֱלֹהִית שֶׁבָּאָדָם - נָתַן לָהּ הַקָּדוֹשׁ בָּרוּךְ הוּא רְשׁוּת וִיכוֹלֶת לְהַגְבִּיהַּ עַצְמָהּ כְּנֶגְדָּהּ

It is only with regard to the holiness of the divine soul within a person that the Holy One, blessed be He, granted the ***sitra aḥara*** **the permission and ability to raise itself against it**

Evil in man is totally different from evil in the rest of existence, and that is due to man's unique status as a "portion of God from on high." Man has the ability to choose freely between good and evil. This ability is a divine and almost unbounded gift, unchained by the laws of cause and effect, and the source from which the evil in man receives its existence. In order that man may exercise free will, for the "portion of God from on high" to make moral choices, evil is given the power to constantly challenge the divine soul.

כְּדֵי שֶׁהָאָדָם יִתְעוֹרֵר לְהִתְגַּבֵּר עָלֶיהָ

in order that the person will be awakened to overpower it

If the evil in man would melt in the face of the good within him, there would be no struggle. As explained above at length, our human existence and greatness flourish in the soil of the battle between good and evil. Our goodness gains strength as a result of its unending struggle against the *sitra aḥara* and its ultimate victory over it. This victory, whether it is in the realm of the emotions or the intellect, and no matter to what degree, propels the victor to ever loftier spiritual levels, essentially far beyond his known limits. Despite the apparent insignificance of the victor's successes below, his resultant ascent to the Divine demonstrates man's advantage over the rest of God's creations, which can never push beyond their God-given limitations.

לְהַשְׁפִּילָהּ עַל יְדֵי שִׁפְלוּת וּנְמִיכַת רוּחוֹ, וְ"נִבְזֶה בְּעֵינָיו נִמְאָס" (תהלים טו, ד).

and **to humble it through the humility and abnegation of his spirit and by being "despised and repugnant in his own eyes"** (Ps. 15:4).

That a person must humble himself does not mean that he humbles his divine holiness. Rather, he humbles his perception of himself as a separate, independent being. In doing so, he humbles the animal soul, or the *sitra aḥara,* within him and thus opens the possibility for his divine soul to shine.

וּבְאִתְעֲרוּתָא דִלְתַתָּא - אִתְעֲרוּתָא דִלְעֵילָא,

The awakening from below causes a reciprocal **awakening from above,**

A person needs to do what he can, even he is not able to vanquish his animal soul completely. He should humble himself to the best of his ability right now and trust that God will do the rest. As the Ba'al Shem Tov comments on the verse "The Lord is your shadow by your right hand" (Ps. 121:5), God acts as our shadow, as it were.[24] When a person lifts his hand, the shadow of his hand also rises. Similarly, when a person acts kindly, God correspondingly acts kindly. When a person acts to the fullest capacity of his ability, although he is unable to completely nullify his being, God completes his efforts, in their entire breadth and fullness.

לְקַיֵּים מַה שֶּׁנֶּאֱמַר: "מִשָּׁם אוֹרִידְךָ נְאֻם ה'" (עובדיה א, ד). דְּהַיְינוּ שֶׁמְּסִירָהּ מִמֶּמְשַׁלְתָּהּ וִיכָלְתָּהּ וּמְסַלֵּק מִמֶּנָּה הַכֹּחַ וּרְשׁוּת שֶׁנָּתַן לָהּ לְהַגְבִּיהַּ עַצְמָהּ נֶגֶד אוֹר קְדוּשַּׁת נֶפֶשׁ הָאֱלֹהִית, וַאֲזַי מִמֵּילָא בְּטֵילָה וְנִדְחֵית כְּבִיטּוּל הַחֹשֶׁךְ מִפְּנֵי אוֹר הַגַּשְׁמִי.

fulfilling the verse "If you raise yourself like the eagle, or place your nest among the stars, **from there I will bring you down – the utterance of the Lord**" (Obad. 1:4). **That is, God strips** the *sitra aḥara* **of its dominion and power and removes from it the strength and authority He** originally **granted it to raise itself against the light of the divine soul's holiness. Then it is automatically nullified and repelled, similar to the nullification of darkness in the presence of physical light.**

24. See *Ba'al Shem Tov al HaTorah, Parashat Kedoshim 21–23; Kedushat Levi, Parashat Beshalaḥ.*

The battle between good and evil within man rages to the extent that God permits it. Evil that continues to exist in the presence of good is an anomaly, yet God allows that anomaly to exist because it is the true means of spiritual advancement.

In a certain sense, just as light defines darkness, so does darkness define light: "Good delineates evil, [and] evil delineates good" (*Sefer Yetzira* 6:4). *Oneg*, or delight, is the highest level of holiness, yet its letters, when reversed, spell *nega*, plague. The polarities of good and evil, of black and white, define each other, making up a single, interdependent construct. God allows this structure to exist as long as it is needed. The moment that it is no longer needed it will cease to exist.

To return to the previous analogy, from the moment a person is immunized against a virus, the virus no longer has a function and so ceases to exist within him. The same applies to the function of evil in the world. When a person fulfills his destiny as best he can, God brings the rest to fruition. When one proves that he has withstood the test, the test ceases to be meaningful, and there is no reason for it to continue. There is no need for the continuation of the drama; the show comes to an end and the lights come on. This is not something that a person can accomplish by himself, but the moment he fulfills his obligation, God withdraws the freedom that He had given to the *sitra aḥara*, which thus ceases entirely to exist, like darkness retreating before light.

The battle between good and evil begins in the realm of shadow, where the precise locations of good and evil are not clearly recognizable. The moment certainty exists, the moment there is a face-to-face confrontation and a person cries out upon recognizing the evil, "You are evil, wicked, disgusting, loathsome, and abhorrent!" the battle has been decided, the lamp has been lit, and the shadows fade. The moment a person pushes through the illusions, God completely removes the *sitra aḥara*'s power of misdirection. When it ceases to mold itself into the shapes of the world, it no longer possesses form and immediately dissipates before the divine light.

וּכְמוֹ שֶׁמָּצִינוּ דָּבָר זֶה מְפוֹרָשׁ בַּתּוֹרָה	**We find this matter stated explicitly in the Torah**

The author of the *Tanya* finds it necessary to bring support for his thesis, since it is such a striking claim, that simply by shouting at himself, without attaining any new awareness, a person can cause a new light to shine on his soul, which can completely change his behavior.

גַּבֵּי מְרַגְּלִים, שֶׁמִּתְּחִלָּה אָמְרוּ: "כִּי חָזָק הוּא מִמֶּנּוּ" (במדבר יג, לא). "אַל תִּקְרֵי 'מִמֶּנּוּ'" כו' - שֶׁלֹּא הֶאֱמִינוּ בִּיכוֹלֶת ה'.

with regard to the spies, who, upon their return from the Land of Israel, **initially said,** "We will not be able to go up against the people, **for they are stronger than we are** [***mimenu***]**...**" (Num. 13:31). Our Sages state, **"Do not read** the phrase as 'stronger **than we are,'** but rather read it as 'stronger than Him'" (*Sota* 35a) – meaning **that they did not have faith in God's ability** to bring them into the Land of Israel.

The Hebrew word *mimenu* in the verse cited bears two possible interpretations. It can be read either in the first-person plural form, in which case it means "than us." Alternatively, it can be read in third-person singular and so means "than Him." The Sages understood *mimenu* in the latter sense, as though the spies were saying that God Himself was incapable of removing the other nations from the Holy Land. This was a profoundly blasphemous statement, since the spies were claiming that the inhabitants of the land were stronger than God.

וְאַחַר כָּךְ, חָזְרוּ וְאָמְרוּ: "הִנֶּנּוּ וְעָלִינוּ" וגו' (במדבר יד, מ). וּמֵאַיִן חָזְרָה וּבָאָה לָהֶם הָאֱמוּנָה בִּיכוֹלֶת ה'?

Subsequently, they retracted their statement **and said, "Here we are, and we will go up...**" (Num. 14:40). **From where did their faith in God's ability return to them?**

A few verses later, after Moses expressed his anger toward them, the spies retracted their blasphemous words, eager to demonstrate their newfound trust in God and enter the Land of Israel. Initially, they felt that they were unable to accomplish anything, that not even God could help them. Yet now they were filled with such self-confidence that they were prepared to rise and enter into battle even without God.

הֲרֵי לֹא הֶרְאָה לָהֶם מֹשֶׁה רַבֵּינוּ עָלָיו הַשָּׁלוֹם שׁוּם אוֹת וּמוֹפֵת עַל זֶה בֵּנְתַיִים,

Moses, our teacher, may he rest in peace, had not shown them any sign or miracle with regard to this, with God's ability to bring them to the land, **in the interim.**

Moses showed the spies no signs or wonders, no new creations, as in the case of Koraḥ and his company, no fire descending from God, as in the case of Elijah on Mount Carmel. He did not even tell them anything they had not previously known.

רַק שֶׁאָמַר לָהֶם אֵיךְ שֶׁקָּצַף ה׳ עֲלֵיהֶם וְנִשְׁבַּע שֶׁלֹּא לַהֲבִיאָם אֶל הָאָרֶץ. וּמַה הוֹעִיל זֶה לָהֶם אִם לֹא הָיוּ מַאֲמִינִים בִּיכוֹלֶת ה׳ חַס וְשָׁלוֹם לִכְבּוֹשׁ ל״א מְלָכִים וּמִפְּנֵי זֶה לֹא רָצוּ כְּלָל לִיכָּנֵס לָאָרֶץ?

He merely told them how God was angry with them and had sworn not to bring them into the land. Of what benefit was this to them if they lacked faith in God's ability, God forbid, to vanquish the thirty-one kings who ruled the land **and on account of which they had absolutely no desire to enter the land?**

After the spies expressed their doubts about God's ability to vanquish the inhabitants of the land, God seemed to prove them right by stating, "As I live – the utterance of the Lord – surely as You spoke in My ears, so I shall do to you. Your carcasses shall fall in this wilderness…" (Num. 14:28–29). They should have drawn the logical inference and declared their intention to return to Egypt. Yet it was precisely at this point that they changed their minds and declared, "We will go up!" (Num. 14:40). What caused them to change their minds so radically?

אֶלָּא וַדַּאי מִפְּנֵי שֶׁיִּשְׂרָאֵל עַצְמָן הֵם "מַאֲמִינִים בְּנֵי מַאֲמִינִים" (שבת צז, א), רַק שֶׁהַסִּטְרָא אָחֳרָא הַמְלוּבֶּשֶׁת בְּגוּפָם הִגְבִּיהָּ עַצְמָהּ עַל אוֹר קְדוּשַּׁת נַפְשָׁם הָאֱלֹהִית בְּגַסּוּת רוּחָהּ וְגַבְהוּתָהּ, בְּחוּצְפָּה בְּלִי טַעַם וָדַעַת.

Rather, it is certainly because the Jewish people themselves are "believers, descendants of believers" (*Shabbat* 97a). **It is only because the *sitra aḥara* clothed in their bodies raised itself, in its arrogance and haughtiness, against the light of the holiness of their divine souls, with inexplicable audacity.**

It was because of the influence of the *sitra aḥara* that the Jewish people said, "They are stronger than Him." The *sitra aḥara*'s entire power rests in the fact that it has no need to explain itself. It can make statements without logic, mock and doubt without reason. From the very start, it does not possess true power but only haughtiness, pride, and arrogance, which have no tangible basis.

וְלָכֵן מִיָּד שֶׁקָּצַף ה׳ עֲלֵיהֶם וְהִרְעִים בְּקוֹל רַעַשׁ וְרוֹגֶז: ״עַד מָתַי לָעֵדָה הָרָעָה הַזֹּאת״ וגו׳ (במדבר יד, כז), **״בַּמִּדְבָּר הַזֶּה יִפְּלוּ פִגְרֵיכֶם״ וגו׳** (פסוק כט), **״אֲנִי ה׳ דִּבַּרְתִּי אִם לֹא זֹאת אֶעֱשֶׂה לְכָל הָעֵדָה הָרָעָה הַזֹּאת״ וגו׳** (פסוק לה). **וּכְשֶׁשָּׁמְעוּ דְּבָרִים קָשִׁים אֵלּוּ נִכְנַע וְנִשְׁבַּר לִבָּם בְּקִרְבָּם, כִּדְכְתִיב: ״וַיִּתְאַבְּלוּ הָעָם מְאֹד״** (פסוק לט),

Therefore, immediately afterward God became angry at them and thundered loudly and angrily, "How long will it be with this evil congregation... ?" (Num. 14:27); **"Your carcasses shall fall in this wilderness"** (Num. 14:29); **"I am the Lord, I have spoken; surely I will do this to this entire evil congregation..."** (Num. 14:35). **When they heard these harsh words, their hearts became subdued and broken within them, as it is written, "And the people mourned greatly"** (Num. 14:39).

The spies were great men and outstanding leaders. As such, they did not realize to what extent they were filled with a sense of self, a sense that increasingly colored their reality until they saw nothing wrong in speaking against God and His appointed leader. But the instant that this haughtiness, which has no substance, was crushed, they realized how very small and lowly they were.

וּמִמֵּילָא נָפְלָה הַסִּטְרָא אָחֳרָא מִמֶּמְשַׁלְתָּהּ וְגַבְהוּתָהּ וְגַסּוּת רוּחָהּ, וְיִשְׂרָאֵל עַצְמָן הֵם מַאֲמִינִים.

Consequently, the *sitra aḥara* fell from its dominion, from its **haughtiness and arrogance, while** the children of **Israel themselves** remained **believers.**

When the haughtiness is broken, when the *sitra aḥara* falls from its dominion, there is no need for a new doctrine to guide a person step by step toward an awareness of the truth. The divine light automatically shines from within.

In this sense, a person's entire work is to overcome the animal soul's sense of self. Rabbi Yeḥiel Michel of Zlotchov is quoted as interpreting the verse "I was standing between the Lord and you…" (Deut. 5:5) as implying that a person's sense of self, no matter how learned, important, and outstanding he is, stands between him and God. When this insubstantial illusion is shattered, the divine light immediately floods his entire being.

וּמִזֶּה יָכוֹל לִלְמוֹד כָּל אָדָם שֶׁנּוֹפְלִים לוֹ בְּמַחֲשַׁבְתּוֹ סְפֵיקוֹת עַל אֱמוּנָה, כִּי הֵם דִּבְרֵי רוּחַ הַסִּטְרָא אָחֳרָא לְבַדָּהּ, הַמַּגְבִּיהַּ עַצְמָהּ עַל נַפְשׁוֹ.

Every person whose mind is plagued with doubts pertaining to faith can extrapolate from this that they are merely the empty words of the *sitra aḥara,* which raises itself against his divine **soul.**

The power of these doubts lies not in their content or in their certainty but only in the questions about faith that they raise. Their only strength is in evoking the possibility of disbelief, posing random, vapid questions: "Maybe not?" "Why is it so?" These doubts do not depend on proof. They merely muddy the waters and weaken a person's certitude until he knows nothing clearly.

Everyone has had the experience of repeating a word over and over until its meaning grows unclear and it sounds like mere nonsense. In this way, a person can come to doubt the reality of something that he has known all his life: the name of a person or place, for example, or a telephone number. The more he dwells on the matter, the more uncertain and confused he becomes. For this dilemma, rational struggle will not help, since this is not a matter of logic and has nothing to do with refutable argument.

This is a sickly process, which only leads a person down to the abyss. It seizes on a particular point and begins to question whether it is correct, whether it is credible – whether it even exists. No rational argument will succeed in dispelling these doubts, since the doubts themselves are not rational. ☞

A WALL OF DOUBT

☞ One tzaddik observed that when Heaven decides to cast a person down, he is presented with doubts about tzaddikim. When he falls further, he is presented

אֲבָל יִשְׂרָאֵל עַצְמָן הֵם מַאֲמִינִים כו'.

But the Jewish people themselves are believers, descendants of believers.

Since the construct of doubts is entirely illusory, the foundation of "believers, descendants of believers" is automatically revealed when it falls away: a simple, clear faith that does not require in-depth study, demonstrations, or proofs.

In that case, the correction for such doubts is to disengage from them entirely. Then one will see clearly that he has no need to fight or dispute them.

וְגַם הַסִּטְרָא אָחֳרָא עַצְמָהּ אֵין לָהּ סְפֵיקוֹת כְּלָל בֶּאֱמוּנָה, רַק שֶׁנִּיתַּן לָהּ רְשׁוּת לְבַלְבֵּל הָאָדָם בְּדִבְרֵי שֶׁקֶר וּמִרְמָה לְהַרְבּוֹת שְׂכָרוֹ,

Even the *sitra aḥara* itself has no doubts whatsoever pertaining to faith. It was merely granted the authority to confuse a person with lies and deceit in order to increase the person's **reward,**

Not only do the Jewish people believe in God, but even the *sitra aḥara* itself believes. It knows that it is a servant of God alone. It has no doubts. But it misleads a person in order to give him the opportunity to gain reward when he overcomes the confusion and serves God despite his doubts.

כְּפִיתּוּיֵי הַזּוֹנָה לְבֶן הַמֶּלֶךְ בְּשֶׁקֶר וּמִרְמָה בִּרְשׁוּת הַמֶּלֶךְ, כְּמוֹ שֶׁכָּתוּב בַּזֹּהַר הַקָּדוֹשׁ (חלק ב קסג, א).

like the harlot's seduction of the king's son with lies and deceit under the king's authority, as recounted in the holy *Zohar* (2:163a).

with doubts about his friends. In light of this, it sometimes happens that a person's relationship with a friend, brother, or relative changes for no reason, as though something has shifted. A part of the soul has been poisoned, and the relationship cannot revert to what it had been. He entertains suspicions, and the more he suspects, the more those suspicions grow, until a wall arises that separates him from the other person. Likewise, in the spiritual realm, a wall can arise that separates him from God. That wall cannot be fixed. It can only be broken down.

In the parable, a king who wished to test his son sent a harlot to seduce him. She made every effort to do so, even though she knew that the king would be happier if she failed.

God has given the *sitra aḥara* the authority to confuse a person with lies and falsehoods. The *sitra aḥara* attempts to confuse him by claiming that God does not exist, even as it knows that its own existence comes only from God. At the very moment that the *sitra aḥara* entices a person to act against that will, it knows itself to be doing God's will.

This chapter dealt with a great spiritual problem: the phenomenon of a dull heart, which is the inability to experience emotion of any kind. In the realm of divine service, dullness of the heart represents the difficulty of opening one's heart and allowing holiness entry.

The author of the *Tanya* examined the causes of a dull heart and suggested that the way to liberate oneself is by breaking the heart. The source of a dull heart is a feeling of self-satisfaction, and that is destroyed when one humbles oneself and crushes his ego. This chapter therefore discussed the ways by which one may achieve an unassuming spirit and a broken heart in comparison to others.

Chapter 30

THE PRECEDING CHAPTER DISCUSSED ONE OF THE MOST difficult challenges a *beinoni* will face: the phenomenon of a dull heart. The unique challenge of a dull heart is that one cannot resolve it through the cognitive process. Since a dull heart exists independently of a person's intellectual awareness, he cannot transfer his rational comprehension to the realm of emotional experience. This is not because of any lack of understanding or insufficient devotions on his part but because his vitality has been attenuated. His heart is weary and ossified, unable to feel, respond to stimulation, and blossom.

The only solution is for the *beinoni* to break his heart. In a sense, this entails breaking himself by crushing his self-centeredness and ego. Only then can he emerge from his torpor to reach a state of inspiration, devotion, and renewed vitality.

This chapter will continue exploring this theme, though from a different angle. The approach presented here is one in which an individual suffering from a dulled heart shatters an illusory sense of perfection by recognizing his lowly status in comparison to everyone else. This is accomplished by reexamining his perceptions of himself and others, both of which are typically the reverse of his original assessment.

עוֹד זֹאת יָשִׂים אֶל לִבּוֹ לְקַיֵּים מַאֲמַר רַבּוֹתֵינוּ ז״ל: ״וֶהֱוֵי שְׁפַל רוּחַ בִּפְנֵי כָל הָאָדָם״ (אבות פרק ד משנה י). וֶהֱוֵי - בֶּאֱמֶת לַאֲמִיתּוֹ.

3 Adar | 16 Adar I (leap year)

In addition, one should ensure that one fulfills our Rabbis' teaching "Be of humble spirit in the presence of all people" (Mishna *Avot* 4:10). The expression **"be"** implies being humble **in the truest sense.**

This dictum is difficult to properly understand and fulfill.[1] The author of the *Tanya* explains that this statement places emphasis on the imperative "be," indicating that a person must do more than act humbly. It should not just be expressed in his behavior, but rather he must possess an internal, intrinsic sense of humility.

בִּפְנֵי כָּל הָאָדָם - מַמָּשׁ, אֲפִילּוּ בִּפְנֵי קַל שֶׁבַּקַּלִּים.

The phrase **"in the presence of all people"** is to be taken **literally** so that one is humble **even in the presence of the most unworthy.**

One should feel humble not only in the presence of people greater than he but in the company of everyone else, even the most unworthy people. This begs the question: How can a God-fearing Torah scholar, punctilious in his performance of the mitzvot, view himself as less than the "most unworthy"? ☞

וְהַיְינוּ עַל פִּי מַאֲמַר רַבּוֹתֵינוּ ז"ל: "אַל תָּדִין אֶת חֲבֵירְךָ עַד שֶׁתַּגִּיעַ לִמְקוֹמוֹ" (אבות פרק

This is achieved **by** adhering to **our Rabbis' teaching "Do not judge your fellow man until you have reached his**

EGOTISM: NOT ONLY FOR THE *BEINONI*

☞ When a person breaks his heart, he breaks his ego, his self-satisfaction and insistence on his worth. It would seem, then, that this effort is particularly relevant to the *beinoni*, who is liable to mistake himself for a flawless tzaddik.

In truth, the problem of self-satisfaction and a dull heart is not unique to the *beinoni*. Even someone with little to recommend him, with no reason to be prideful, can suffer from smugness and egotistical self-aggrandizement. That is pride's unique failing: It requires no basis in reality to exist. An adulterer must have a willing consort and a measure of opportunity; a slanderer requires a friend to listen to what he wants to say. But the sin of pride demands no contextual reality. The most foolish, impoverished, and unappealing person in the world can harbor a grandiose conception of his importance.

1. The author of the *Tanya* cites this dictum with the definite article "the" affixed to the word *adam*, "people," so that the literal reading of the statement is "Be of humble spirit in the presence of all *the* people." The actual expression in the Mishna is *kol adam*, with the definite article omitted. For a possible explanation of this variant reading, see *Iggerot Kodesh* by the Lubavitcher Rebbe, Rabbi Menaḥem Mendel Schneerson, vol. 2, letter 219.

ב משנה ד). כִּי מְקוֹמוֹ גּוֹרֵם לוֹ לַחֲטוֹא, לִהְיוֹת פַּרְנָסָתוֹ לֵילֵךְ בַּשּׁוּק כָּל הַיּוֹם וְלִהְיוֹת מִיּוֹשְׁבֵי קְרָנוֹת,

place" (Mishna *Avot* 2:4), **for it is his place that causes him to sin, to walk through the marketplace every day for his livelihood and be among those who sit on street corners.**

"Place" in this context is to be understood in both the abstract sense of a person's spiritual attainments and in the concrete sense of his physical environment. He does not have the option of sitting in a secluded corner of the study hall amid God-fearing individuals. He must make his way through the marketplace and the streets. Even if he is not just being idle, like some who spend their days on the street corners,[2] at the very least, such is the company he keeps.

וְעֵינָיו רוֹאוֹת כָּל הַתַּאֲווֹת, וְהָעַיִן רוֹאָה וְהַלֵּב חוֹמֵד,

Consequently, **his eyes see all** sorts of **temptations,** and it is axiomatic that **the eye sees and the heart covets,**

The world in which we live subjects us to unrelenting temptation. Such constant, formidable pressure applied over an extended period is very difficult to withstand. This is not an occasional and temporary desire that can be dismissed with relative ease but the pervading influence of the environment at all times. In that atmosphere, even someone ordinarily immune to such temptations finds that over the course of time, as "the eye sees," eventually "the heart covets."[3]

וְיִצְרוֹ בּוֹעֵר כְּתַנּוּר בּוֹעֲרָה מֵאוֹפֶה, כְּמוֹ שֶׁכָּתוּב בְּהוֹשֵׁעַ: "הוּא בוֹעֵר כְּאֵשׁ לֶהָבָה" וגו' (ז, ו).

and certainly if he is **one whose** evil **inclination burns** within him **like an oven fired by a baker, as it is written in Hosea,** "For in their ambush, they prepared their heart like an oven. Their baker sleeps all night; in the morning **it burns like a blazing fire"** (Hos. 7:6).

The environment influences all individuals. Even one who is intrinsically on a high level may capitulate, so the environment will certainly

2. See *Berakhot* 28b.

3. See Rashi, Num. 15:39; *Bemidbar Rabba* 10:2.

affect a person who has strong passions. Some people have an evil inclination that burns hot as an oven, and not an oven found in the average home but that of a baker, which burns red hot twenty-four hours a day.

מַה שֶּׁאֵין כֵּן מִי שֶׁהוֹלֵךְ בַּשּׁוּק מְעַט, וְרוֹב הַיּוֹם יוֹשֵׁב בְּבֵיתוֹ,

This is not the case concerning one who seldom walks through the marketplace and stays at home most of the day,

A person who spends the day at home or in the study hall is not distracted by sights that tempt him. When the eye does not see, the heart does not covet so strongly. This kind of person has no authority to judge those who find themselves in circumstances that unceasingly inflame their evil inclination. The person who dedicates all his time to Torah study cannot claim superiority on the grounds that such temptations do not drive him to sin.

וְגַם אִם הוֹלֵךְ כָּל הַיּוֹם בַּשּׁוּק, יָכוֹל לִהְיוֹת שֶׁאֵינוֹ מְחוּמָּם כָּל כָּךְ בְּטִבְעוֹ,

and even if the *beinoni* **does walk through the marketplace all day, it is possible that he is not so passionate by nature,**

Even if the *beinoni* were surrounded by every manner of temptation, yet still does not sin, that is still not proof that he has a superior character. It is possible that he is naturally indifferent to worldly allurements. Although his eyes see, his heart does not covet. For someone with such a nature, his immunity to temptation cannot be attributed to any spiritual triumphs or purity on his part. It is only on account of his dispassionate nature that he is impervious to the surrounding enticements.

כִּי אֵין הַיֵּצֶר שָׁוֶה בְּכָל נֶפֶשׁ, יֵשׁ שֶׁיִּצְרוֹ כו׳, כְּמוֹ שֶׁנִּתְבָּאֵר בְּמָקוֹם אַחֵר.

for the evil **inclination is not the same in every person. There are those whose** evil **inclination** is more passionate and some less so, **as explained elsewhere** (*Likkutei Torah*, Lev. 2d).

No two people are alike, and this includes their inclinations. Some people are unaffected by tempting stimuli that others find impossible to resist. There are those who are lustful, while others' inclinations burn for money. Those who are by nature not easily impassioned should not feel superior. Like a blind person who cannot congratulate himself on not being tempted by his eyes, a dispassionate person cannot view his lack of passion as a sign of superiority.[4]

וְהִנֵּה בֶּאֱמֶת גַּם מִי שֶׁהוּא מְחוּמָּם מְאֹד בְּטִבְעוֹ, וּפַרְנָסָתוֹ הִיא לִהְיוֹת מִיּוֹשְׁבֵי קְרָנוֹת כָּל הַיּוֹם, אֵין לוֹ שׁוּם הִתְנַצְּלוּת עַל חֲטָאָיו! וּמִיקְּרֵי רָשָׁע גָּמוּר עַל אֲשֶׁר "אֵין פַּחַד אֱלֹהִים לְנֶגֶד עֵינָיו" (תהלים לו, ב). כִּי הָיָה לוֹ לְהִתְאַפֵּק וְלִמְשׁוֹל עַל רוּחַ תַּאֲוָתוֹ שֶׁבְּלִבּוֹ מִפְּנֵי פַּחַד ה' הָרוֹאֶה כָּל מַעֲשָׂיו,

17 Adar I (leap year)

In truth, even someone who is extremely passionate by nature, and his livelihood forces him **to sit on street corners all day has no excuse whatsoever for his sins. He is categorized as a completely wicked person, for "there is no fear of God before him"** (Ps. 36:2). **He should have restrained himself and controlled the spirit of lust in his heart due to the fear of God, who sees all his actions,**

Although this argument mitigates our judgment of an individual overcome by temptation, the fact that he possesses strong drives and has the opportunity to do wrong in no way justifies sinful behavior. At times there are circumstances in which a person who possesses powerful desires is compelled to sit at street corners for his livelihood and is therefore constantly beset by temptations. It would seem that succumbing to these temptations is, at least to a certain degree, justified. Yet the author of the *Tanya* vehemently rejects this notion, asserting that there is no justification for his failure to subdue his evil inclination. In fact, the moment he sins, he is considered completely wicked.[5] Even

4. The Ba'al Shem Tov points out that the phrase "his inclination," as in "Who is mighty? He who subdues his inclination" (Mishna *Avot* 4:1), alludes that one is regarded as mighty only when subduing "his" inclination. It is no act of valor when not succumbing to a matter that tempts, not him, but another.

5. See chap. 1.

when a person is overwhelmed by temptation, he must control himself and his inclination. If he does sin, he is liable.

כְּמוֹ שֶׁנִּתְבָּאֵר לְעֵיל, כִּי הַמּוֹחַ שַׁלִּיט עַל הַלֵּב בְּתוֹלַדְתּוֹ.

a feat attainable by all, **as explained above** (chap. 12), **since it is the innate nature of the mind to control the heart.**

Temptations overcome a person only when some measure of conscious complicity exists. Feelings, holy or otherwise, do not arise in a vacuum. They develop within one's conscious awareness, within the image of the world as one understands it.

Even if a person cannot dominate his feelings – his heart – he can control his intellect. He can use his mind to visualize God gazing at all he does until this awareness becomes part of his worldview, a tangible component of his reality. If this image is sufficiently robust, he will develop correspondingly powerful feelings that can, at the very least, stand in staunch opposition to the urges that threaten to overwhelm him. These newfound feelings will give him the strength to overcome both the evil inclination that surges within him and the great temptations that assail him from without, ultimately leading him to victory.

18 Adar I (leap year)

וְהִנֵּה בֶּאֱמֶת שֶׁהִיא מִלְחָמָה גְּדוֹלָה וַעֲצוּמָה לִשְׁבּוֹר הַיֵּצֶר הַבּוֹעֵר כְּאֵשׁ לֶהָבָה מִפְּנֵי פַּחַד ה׳,

In truth, it is a great and intense battle to break the evil **inclination, which burns** within **like a blazing fire, through one's fear of God**

Though the sinner has no excuse because he could have overcome the temptation, it is wrong to disparage such a person and feel superior to him. The sinner must struggle to overpower his fiery passion through a conscious fear of God. A person who does not experience such passion, who is not susceptible to the fire of lust burning in his blood and overwhelming his senses, cannot understand that struggle, what it means to withstand temptation and declare, "Because I fear God, I will not sin!"

וּכְמוֹ נִסָּיוֹן מַמָּשׁ.

and must be viewed **as a true test.**

The fierceness of the battle could be equated to the challenge of martyrdom. The temptation to sin is as strong as the desire for life in a person who must accept death to avoid desecrating God's name.

וְהִלְכָּךְ צָרִיךְ כָּל אָדָם לְפִי מַה שֶּׁהוּא מְקוֹמוֹ וּמַדְרֵגָתוֹ בַּעֲבוֹדַת ה׳,

Therefore, every person, according to his place and rank in the service of God,

Every Jew, from the most unworthy, from the most deliberate sinner, to the *beinoni*, who fulfills all the mitzvot and justifiably sees himself as being on a higher level than they, must nevertheless take careful stock of his divine service.

לִשְׁקוֹל וְלִבְחוֹן בְּעַצְמוֹ אִם הוּא עוֹבֵד ה׳ בְּעֵרֶךְ וּבְחִינַת מִלְחָמָה עֲצוּמָה כָּזוֹ וְנִסָּיוֹן כָּזֶה.

must weigh and assess himself, determining **whether he serves God according to the quality and nature of such an intense battle and test.**

When a person is judged, whether by himself or others, that assessment cannot take into account superficial criteria alone. To compare people and judge fairly, it is not enough to merely align one person's deeds with those of another. The true assessment of two people can be reached only by taking their inner struggles and challenges into consideration and comparing them both. A person's character is determined, not by his objective accomplishments alone, but also by his subjective efforts.

A *beinoni* should therefore not disparage someone who has failed and sinned but should consider the struggles the person has endured. Rather than diminish the sinner, the *beinoni* should ask himself if he would be able to withstand similar challenges. Has he faced his own desires and struggles with the same degree of self-sacrifice that he expects of others?

בִּבְחִינַת ׳וַעֲשֵׂה טוֹב׳, כְּגוֹן בַּעֲבוֹדַת הַתְּפִלָּה בְּכַוָּונָה לִשְׁפּוֹךְ נַפְשׁוֹ לִפְנֵי ה׳ בְּכָל כֹּחוֹ מַמָּשׁ, עַד מִיצּוּי הַנֶּפֶשׁ

As for the aspect of doing good, such as in the service of prayer with concentration, so that he pours out his soul before God literally with all his might until he exhausts his soul,

Although the *beinoni*'s struggle does not involve either withstanding actual sin or neglect of performing mitzvot, he too faces unyielding demands and must engage in a remorseless battle in order to do good and turn aside from evil. In the realm of doing good, he will face challenges in the service of prayer, which demands intense and constant concentration. The service of prayer is not only worship in the ceremonial sense, such as the service of the Temple,[6] but also an effort that draws on the powers of the body and soul. That work must be done with such intent and concentration that it results in "exhaustion of the soul," when a person can draw forth nothing more from within himself.[7]

וּלְהִלָּחֵם עִם גּוּפוֹ וְנֶפֶשׁ הַבַּהֲמִית שֶׁבּוֹ, הַמּוֹנְעִים הַכַּוָּנָה בְּמִלְחָמָה עֲצוּמָה,

the *beinoni* **must wage war against his body and the animal soul within it, which thwart his concentration, in an intense battle,**

The *Zohar* states that "the time of prayer is a time of war" (*Zohar* 3:243a). When one prays, he is assailed by the body and animal soul, which divert his focus so that the divine soul struggles to rise upward against their downward pull.

וּלְבַטְּשָׁם וּלְכַתְּתָם כֶּעָפָר קוֹדֶם הַתְּפִלָּה שַׁחֲרִית וְעַרְבִית, מִדֵּי יוֹם בְּיוֹם.

crushing and pulverizing them like dust each and every day prior to the morning and evening prayers.

A person lays the groundwork for successful prayer first by breaking the egocentric and coarse nature of his body and animal soul, so that he will be able to approach his prayers with the proper mindset and maintain that state throughout his prayers.

וְגַם בִּשְׁעַת הַתְּפִלָּה לְיַיגֵּעַ עַצְמוֹ בִּיגִיעַת נֶפֶשׁ וִיגִיעַת בָּשָׂר, כְּמוֹ שֶׁיִּתְבָּאֵר לְקַמָּן בַּאֲרִיכוּת.

Also, while praying, one must exert himself with exertion of the soul and the exertion of the flesh, as will be explained below at length (chap. 42).

6. See *Sifrei*, Deut. 11:13.

7. This expression is found in *Sifrei*, Deut. 6:5; see also *Iggeret HaKodesh*, epistle 1.

It is not enough to engage in battle before prayer. Even when a person has prepared properly by crushing his animal soul and grinding it into dust, that is no guarantee that he will pray well and without struggle. Prayer is more than the recitation of the words in the prayer book, which is no great struggle. It is a time of battle between mighty forces as the soul wrestles with all the opposing forces assailing it. This is a spiritual and physical effort in which one concentrates all his thoughts and attention, oblivious to everything else. The combination of such unswerving focus with the effort to arrive at a higher level of union with the Divine demands a strenuous battle. To wage this battle on a continuous and daily basis, one requires "the exertion of the soul and the exertion of the flesh."

וְכֹל שֶׁלֹּא הִגִּיעַ לִידֵי מִדָּה זוֹ, לְהִלָּחֵם עִם גּוּפוֹ מִלְחָמָה עֲצוּמָה כָּזוֹ, עֲדַיִין לֹא הִגִּיעַ לִבְחִינַת וְעֵרֶךְ מִלְחֶמֶת הַיֵּצֶר הַבּוֹעֵר כְּאֵשׁ לֶהָבָה לִהְיוֹת נִכְנָע וְנִשְׁבָּר מִפְּנֵי פַּחַד ה׳.

Anyone who has not attained this state, that of waging such an intense battle with his body, has not yet experienced the quality and dimension of the battle waged by the most unworthy **against the** evil **inclination that burns** within them **like a blazing fire so that it may be subdued and broken through fear of God.**

4 Adar

19 Adar I (leap year)

The demand that every prayer be an instance of union with the Divine, of an outpouring of one's soul, that one's physicality should be stripped away,[8] is a very exalted one. It is a demand for an intense war engaged in daily to overcome one's nature and habits.

It would be understandable if a person were to declare himself incapable of such laborious effort, to declare, "I cannot do this." But the author of the *Tanya* states that this seemingly exalted and extreme expectation is actually less than that which is required of the simplest person, "the most unworthy," in his battle with his evil inclination. For such a person, whose livelihood compels him to engage in a world rife with temptations, his struggle presents a much greater difficulty than for one who is fortunate to spend his days in spiritual devotion and thus is guarded against the outside world. If a person finds the demand

8. See *Shulḥan Arukh, Oraḥ Ḥayyim* 91:1.

to pray with perfect divine union until his soul is exhausted to be too overwhelming, he should not demand the same of the person who makes his living in the marketplace, filled with desires and surrounded by temptations. He has no right to view the one deemed "the most unworthy" in a condescending manner.

וְכֵן בְּעִנְיַן בִּרְכַּת הַמָּזוֹן וְכָל בִּרְכוֹת הַנֶּהֱנִין וְהַמִּצְוֹת בְּכַוָּנָה,

So too with regard to concentration during the Grace after Meals and all blessings, whether those recited **over food or over** the performance of **mitzvot,**

The demand for concentration, for focusing and clinging to God, pertains not only to prayer but also to the Grace after Meals and to every blessing that a person recites in the course of the day. In a sense, reciting a brief blessing with concentration is even more difficult than praying with concentration. Blessings are said often and in a variety of settings, usually when neither place nor time is conducive to proper focus.

וְאֵין צָרִיךְ לוֹמַר כַּוָּנַת הַמִּצְוֹת לִשְׁמָן.

and it goes without saying that proper **concentration** is required **in the authentic** performance of **the mitzvot.**

If a blessing over a mitzva must be recited with concentration, how much more so the performance of the mitzva itself.

וְכֵן בְּעִנְיַן עֵסֶק לִימּוּד הַתּוֹרָה, לִלְמוֹד הַרְבֵּה יוֹתֵר מֵחֶפְצוֹ וּרְצוֹנוֹ לְפִי טִבְעוֹ וּרְגִילוּתוֹ, עַל יְדֵי מִלְחָמָה עֲצוּמָה עִם גּוּפוֹ. כִּי הַלּוֹמֵד מְעַט יוֹתֵר מִטִּבְעוֹ, הֲרֵי זוֹ מִלְחָמָה קְטַנָּה וְאֵין לָהּ עֵרֶךְ וְדִמְיוֹן עִם מִלְחֶמֶת הַיֵּצֶר הַבּוֹעֵר כְּאֵשׁ,

Likewise, with regard to engaging in Torah study, the battle one must wage **to study far more than one's natural and habitual desire and will is by means of an intense battle with his body.** Although **studying** only a **bit more than** the desire of **his innate nature** demands effort, **it is a minor struggle, bearing no parallel or comparison to the battle against the** evil **inclination that burns like fire** within,

Studying Torah according to one's nature and habit, even if one studies a great amount in this way, does not entail a struggle. Likewise, studying just a bit more than one is accustomed does not constitute an "intense battle," since it does not at all compare to the supreme struggle required of one to overcome one's evil inclination, defined above as "a great and intense battle" and a "true test."

דִּמְקְרֵי רָשָׁע גָּמוּר אִם אֵינוֹ מְנַצֵּחַ יִצְרוֹ לִהְיוֹת נִכְנָע וְנִשְׁבָּר מִפְּנֵי ה׳.

for which one is regarded as a completely wicked person if he does not conquer his evil **inclination so that it is subdued and broken before God** (see chap. 1).

It makes no difference whether the struggle with the evil inclination is over something great or something small, whether one struggles to withstand sinning or one struggles to exert effort in his service. In either case, the battle could be of equal intensity and importance. A person who has studied Torah for eight or ten hours may feel unable to continue and is absolutely convinced that he needs a break. At that moment, the effort to go on is a battle no less demanding than the war against the evil inclination's most fiery desires.

In the final analysis, there is no qualitative difference between a person who sins because he gave in to the distractions of the streets and a scholar who does not increase his study schedule or pray with concentration. Neither is prepared to struggle, and neither steps beyond his limitations.

וּמַה לִּי בְּחִינַת ׳סוּר מֵרָע׳ וּמַה לִּי בְּחִינַת ׳וַעֲשֵׂה טוֹב׳.

What difference is there between turning away from evil and doing good?

The man on the temptation-filled street, whose evil inclination burns like fire, struggles to "turn away from evil" and refrain from sinning. The person who sits undisturbed in the study hall and whose temperament is naturally indifferent struggles to increase his Torah study and pray with concentration – to "do good." In either case, the battle is the same.

הַכֹּל הִיא מִצְוַת הַמֶּלֶךְ הַקָּדוֹשׁ, יָחִיד וּמְיוּחָד בָּרוּךְ הוּא.

Everything is ultimately **a commandment of the holy King, the one and only, blessed be He.**

At the root of everything stands the will of God, infinite, one, and unique. Disobedience of God's will is equally serious whether a person commits a wrongdoing or refrains from acting correctly, violating either the injunction to "turn away from evil" or "do good," and whether his is a major or minor infraction. In the face of the fact that he has opposed God's will, the particulars do not matter. Once he has rebelled, it is not important exactly how he has done so.

וְכֵן בִּשְׁאָר מִצְוֹת,

So too with regard to the other mitzvot,

This goes beyond Torah study alone. It does not suffice to fulfill one's duty. A person must do more, whether quantitatively or qualitatively.

וּבִפְרָט בְּדָבָר שֶׁבְּמָמוֹן, כְּמוֹ עֲבוֹדַת הַצְּדָקָה וּכְהַאי גַוְונָא.

particularly concerning monetary matters, such as the service of giving **charity and the like.**

Like the mitzva of Torah study, by Torah law the mitzva of giving charity is not limited in any sense. It can be performed at all times and in all circumstances and is not bound by any qualitative or quantitative constraints. In light of this, a person must struggle against an innate miserliness and give more than he is accustomed to giving beyond his normal ability.

20 Adar I (leap year)

וַאֲפִילוּ בִּבְחִינַת 'סוּר מֵרָע' יָכוֹל כָּל אִישׁ מַשְׂכִּיל לִמְצוֹא בְּנַפְשׁוֹ שֶׁאֵינוֹ סָר לְגַמְרֵי מֵהָרַע בַּכֹּל מִכֹּל כֹּל

Even with regard to turning away from evil, any intelligent person may find within himself that he has not completely and utterly turned away from evil

The *beinoni* may feel that he is almost perfect and thus superior to the "most unworthy." But if he were to compare how difficult it is to pray well with the effort that they must expend to refrain from sinning, he would realize that he is not intrinsically superior to them even in terms of turning aside from evil.

בְּמָקוֹם שֶׁצָּרִיךְ לְמִלְחָמָה עֲצוּמָה כָּעֵרֶךְ הַנִּזְכָּר לְעֵיל, וַאֲפִילוּ פָּחוֹת מֵעֵרֶךְ הַנִּזְכָּר לְעֵיל, כְּגוֹן: לְהַפְסִיק בְּאֶמְצַע שִׂיחָה נָאָה,

in a circumstance that requires an intense battle of the degree described above, or even of a lesser degree than that described above. For example, he may not be able **to stop in the middle of a pleasant,** though pointless, **conversation,**

Above, the author of the *Tanya* explained that the *beinoni* must not regard himself as superior to the "most unworthy" in the arena of doing good. The amount of effort they require simply to not succumb to their evil inclination is by no means matched by the *beinoni* in his effort to fulfill a mitzva perfectly.

Now the author of the *Tanya* suggests that if the *beinoni* performs a careful self-examination, he will realize that he is not superior to the "most unworthy" even with regard to turning away from evil. For example, he may find it difficult to cut short a meaningless but permissible conversation that gives him pleasure.

אוֹ סִיפּוּר בִּגְנוּת חֲבֵירוֹ וַאֲפִילוּ גְּנַאי קָטָן וְקַל מְאֹד, אַף שֶׁהוּא אֱמֶת, וַאֲפִילוּ כְּדֵי לְנַקּוֹת עַצְמוֹ,

or while recounting **an incident disgracing another, even** if it is only **a minor and very trivial disparaging remark, even if it is true, and even if** the purpose of the remark is **to exonerate himself,**

In these examples, the individual is not speaking purposelessly or for his personal gain but clearing himself of some innuendo. Still, it is considered a wrongdoing from which he should have refrained.

כַּנּוֹדָע מֵהָא דְּאָמַר רַבִּי שִׁמְעוֹן לְאָבִיו, רַבֵּינוּ הַקָּדוֹשׁ: לָאו אֲנָא כְּתַבְתֵּיהּ אֶלָּא יְהוּדָא חַיָּיטָא כְּתַבֵיהּ. וְאָמַר לוֹ: כַּלֵּךְ מִלָּשׁוֹן הָרָע [עַיֵּין שָׁם בַּגְּמָרָא רֵישׁ פֶּרֶק י' דְּבָבָא בָּתְרָא (קסד, ב)].

as is known from Rabbi Shimon's statement to his father, the saintly Rabbeinu, Rabbi Yehuda HaNasi, concerning a problematic bill of divorce: **"I did not write it but rather Yehuda Ḥayyata wrote it."** Rabbi Yehuda HaNasi **said to** his son, **"Turn away from** uttering this kind of **malicious speech." (See the talmudic passage there at the beginning of chapter 10 of *Bava Batra* [164b].)**

Although Rabbi Shimon made his statement only to exonerate himself, and it was not merely a purposeless remark, his father castigated him for slandering another. For a person on Rabbi Shimon's level, such a statement is considered slander, a grave sin that one must firmly avoid. The struggle to refrain from such a remark is as difficult as that faced by someone else who must withstand the burning desire to transgress an explicit Torah-mandated prohibition.

וְכְהַאי גַּוְונָא כַּמָּה מִילֵּי דִּשְׁכִיחֵי טוּבָא,

The same applies to many similar matters that frequently occur,

This is a reference to matters that seem unimportant but require attention and "a great and intense battle" if one is to properly turn aside from evil. These may be between a person and God or between one person and another, such as disparaging speech, gaining honor at the expense of others, or financial impropriety.

וּבִפְרָט בְּעִנְיַן לְקַדֵּשׁ עַצְמוֹ בַּמּוּתָּר לוֹ,

particularly those pertaining to sanctifying oneself with regard to permitted matters,

For the *beinoni*, the struggle to turn aside from evil applies specifically with regard to matters that are technically permitted. In such cases, he is enjoined to sanctify himself by avoiding overindulgence, regarding such an act as strictly prohibited. A person becomes sanctified by separating himself from worldly matters, even in circumstances where these matters are completely kosher and permissible. For some people, it is a struggle to sanctify themselves by making moral choices as to how they will engage in these activities.

שֶׁהוּא מִדְּאוֹרַיְיתָא, כְּמוֹ שֶׁכָּתוּב: "קְדוֹשִׁים תִּהְיוּ" וגו' (ויקרא יט, ב). "וְהִתְקַדִּשְׁתֶּם" וגו' (שם יא, מד),

which is a biblical mandate, as it is written, "You shall be holy…" (Lev. 19:2), and it states, **"And you shall sanctify yourselves…"** (Lev. 11:44).

In his commentary on the verse "You shall be holy…," Ramban explains that this mitzva demands that a person sanctify himself particularly with those things that are permitted to him so that he will not be "a degenerate with the Torah's sanction." An individual's holiness or spiritual decadence is defined by how he conducts himself when confronted with something that by Torah law is permissible yet if misused could potentially lead to a spiritual downfall. Faced with such a challenge, this person is invited to assess the situation and make the appropriate moral choices by exercising his free will. This call for higher moral conduct is not a mere suggestion but is the actual mitzva entailed by the verse "You shall be holy." ☞

וְגַם דִּבְרֵי סוֹפְרִים חֲמוּרִים מִדִּבְרֵי תוֹרָה וכו'.

Also, injunctions of the Sages are more severe than prohibitions of the Torah and so on,

Even though rabbinic decrees would seem to be less important than biblical laws, the Sages tell us that in some ways one must be more stringent with regard to rabbinic injunctions.[9] Moreover, a person who transgresses the words of the Sages is sometimes punished more severely than one who violates the Torah's commandments.

אֶלָּא שֶׁכָּל אֵלּוּ וְכַיּוֹצֵא בָּהֶן הֵן מֵעֲוֹונוֹת שֶׁהָאָדָם דָּשׁ בַּעֲקֵבָיו,

yet all these and the like are among the sins that a person tends to disregard,

THE GREATER CHALLENGE

☞ The Torah allows the consumption of meat and wine, yet it is not only what one eats but how one eats that matters. A person may, while eating only kosher foods, even simple foods, become obsessed with gratifying his palate. Someone may be honest, yet immersed in the pursuit of money with such utter self-abandon that it becomes his personal idol.

Regarding the verse "You shall not commit adultery" (Ex. 20:13), Rashi comments that "adultery applies only to a married woman." The Kotzker Rebbe adds that this also includes one's own wife. Even if one follows all the halakhic guidelines pertaining to relations with one's wife, he can still, at his core, be regarded as an adulterer since he has yet to overpower and bridle his evil inclination.

It is by far a greater challenge to control oneself and not fall prey to one's lusts with regard to matters that are permitted than it is to do so in the face of unequivocally prohibited matters. To properly conduct oneself in a state of holiness, one must brace himself for this unremitting and difficult challenge.

9. *Eiruvin* 21b; *Sanhedrin* 88b.

For a variety of reasons, people consider some commandments and prohibitions, even those that are grave, to be of little account. This may be because a certain commandment is widely ignored, so the sinner does not sense the shame of his behavior. The relative assessment of commandments and prohibitions fluctuates based on any given circumstance. Each society creates an illusory frame of reference as to what is important and necessary and what is of little worth. Once a sin has been defined as insignificant, the prohibition against it is disregarded and forgotten.

וְגַם נַעֲשׂוּ כְּהֶיתֵּר, מֵחֲמַת שֶׁעָבַר וְשָׁנָה וכו׳.

and they come to be regarded by him **as if they are permitted since he committed** these transgressions **repeatedly and so on.**

The first time a person commits a sin, he trembles to the depths of his being. But as he repeats his behavior, the offense appears less grave, and the shock grows less dire. The sense that he is harming himself, polluting and blemishing his soul, loses its power. It is not only the feeling of trepidation that dissipates but even his assessment of the act as egregious.[10]

Even when a person knows that he is committing a prohibited and perhaps even grave offense, he gradually ceases to feel that he is sinning or that his worth has been diminished. The breach remains unrepaired for so long that it becomes a comfortable way station.

21 Adar I (leap year)

אֲבָל בֶּאֱמֶת אִם הוּא יוֹדֵעַ סֵפֶר וּמַחֲזִיק בְּתוֹרַת ה׳, וְקִרְבַת אֱלֹקִים יֶחְפָּץ,

In truth, however, if he is a scholar, upholds God's Torah, and desires closeness to God,

A Torah scholar is aware of the true value of the fulfillment of mitzvot and the gravity of transgressing prohibitions. Moreover, since he is primarily occupied with Torah study, he defines his life mission as an ongoing attempt to come closer to God.

גָּדוֹל עֲוֹנוֹ מִנְּשׂוֹא וְאַשְׁמָתוֹ גָּדְלָה בְּכִפְלֵי כִפְלַיִים, בַּמֶּה שֶׁאֵינוֹ נִלְחָם וּמִתְגַּבֵּר עַל יִצְרוֹ

his sin is unbearably great, and his guilt is magnified exponentially because he did not battle and overcome his evil **inclination**

10. See *Yoma* 86b.

בְּעֵרֶךְ וּבְחִינַת מִלְחָמָה עֲצוּמָה הַנִּזְכֶּרֶת לְעֵיל,

commensurate with the degree and nature of the intense battle described above.

This intense battle refers to the great struggle that a passionate person in the prime of life experiences, particularly if he finds himself in an environment where everything is permitted and easily available. He must struggle to control his thoughts and deeds due to the fear of God and His glory.

But the need to engage in ferocious battle applies as well to the one who is not disturbed by such desires, who confines himself to the study hall, untroubled by outside distractions. Yet even he must protect his soul vociferously against his particular temptations, precisely because he is a scholar. If he fails, he will be deemed guiltier than the man of passion. Since he knows more, his misdeed is that much more willful.

מֵאַשְׁמַת קַל שֶׁבַּקַּלִּים מִיּוֹשְׁבֵי קְרָנוֹת הָרְחוֹקִים מֵה׳ וְתוֹרָתוֹ, וְאֵין אַשְׁמָתָם גְּדוֹלָה כָּל כָּךְ בַּמֶּה שֶׁאֵינָם כּוֹבְשִׁים יִצְרָם הַבּוֹעֵר כְּאֵשׁ לֶהָבָה, מִפְּנֵי פַּחַד ה׳ הַמֵּבִין וּמַבִּיט אֶל כָּל מַעֲשֵׂיהֶם,

His guilt is greater **than the guilt of the most unworthy, than those who sit on street corners, who are distant from God and His Torah. Their guilt for not overpowering their** evil **inclination, which burns like a blazing fire, through fear of God, who understands and sees all their deeds, is not as great**

The further a sinner is from God and His Torah, the less drastic his descent and guilt. Since such people are not scholars, they lack the tools they need to contemplate and attain fear of God, which would lead them to conquer their inclinations. Granted, such a person cannot justify himself. He too could have overcome his evil inclination and is expected to do so. But guilt is bound up with awareness, and this person lacks the clear understanding, illuminated by the fear of God, of the consequences of his actions. He is not even aware that he should call on his fear of God in order to overpower his evil inclination. On the contrary, he finds the concept altogether foreign.

כְּאַשְׁמַת "כָּל הַקָּרֵב הַקָּרֵב" אֶל ה׳ וְאֶל תּוֹרָתוֹ וַעֲבוֹדָתוֹ,

as the guilt of one who draws close to God, His Torah, and His service.

In contrast to one who is unlearned, the Torah scholar is well aware of his actions. The closer a person comes to God and increases his fear of Heaven, and the more he devotes his time to Torah study and increases his piety, the more he is responsible for his actions and the more liable he is if he transgresses.

וּכְמוֹ שֶׁאָמְרוּ רַבּוֹתֵינוּ ז״ל גַּבֵּי 'אַחֵר' שֶׁיָּדַע בִּכְבוֹדִי וכו' (על פי עין יעקב חגיגה טו, א).

As our Rabbis said concerning the apostate **Aḥer**, Elisha ben Avuya, "**He knew My glory** yet rebelled against Me" (see *Ein Yaakov, Ḥagiga* 15a).

Elisha ben Avuya was one of the greatest Sages of his time until he strayed and became an apostate and so became known as Aḥer, "other." It is true that others who acted as egregiously as he did found atonement. But since Aḥer was a scholar of the first rank and one of the leaders of the generation, who even gazed at the mystic chariot, his guilt was that much worse, to the extent that he could no longer find atonement.

וְלָכֵן אָמְרוּ רַבּוֹתֵינוּ ז״ל עַל עַמֵּי הָאָרֶץ, שֶׁ״זְדוֹנוֹת נַעֲשׂוּ לָהֶם כִּשְׁגָגוֹת״ (בבא מציעא לג, ב).

Therefore, our Rabbis stated concerning the ignorant that "their **intentional transgressions become for them tantamount to unwitting transgressions**" (*Bava Metzia* 33b).

Even if an unlettered person purposely commits a sin or neglects to perform a mitzva, his sin is considered unintentional and minor because it lacks the basic element of complete willfulness: rebellion, denial of a supreme Master, and a conscious turning away from God's will. A person who is distant from God and His Torah cannot be considered a purposeful sinner. This person does not truly understand the significance of holiness and the mitzvot. He is thus considered to be acting unwittingly, like a child who breaks an expensive item whose value he cannot appreciate. Even when such a person acts knowingly, his knowledge does not extend to a full understanding.

To be willful, a person must be aware. When his consciousness is on a low level, when he does not adequately understand the significance of a transgression and the value of a mitzva, he cannot be judged on the same scale as someone who does know and comprehend.

This chapter began by proposing that the *beinoni* acquire a broken heart and lowly spirit as a remedy for a dull heart, thus adhering to the Sages' dictum "Be humble of spirit in the presence of all people." Even though the *beinoni* fulfills the mitzvot and does not sin, he should feel humble even when compared to the "most unworthy." How does the *beinoni* attain authentic humility when comparing himself to sinners and unworthy people?

As the author of the *Tanya* goes on to explain, at the end of the day people cannot be judged by their external deeds but only by the measure of spiritual effort they are prepared to exert. One for whom a certain matter poses no temptation, whether due to his outstanding self-discipline or due to his nature, has no right to be disdainful of someone who is enamored by that same thing. Someone who takes no pleasure in gambling does not have the right to disparage another person who is enveloped in that culture. Instead of looking down at the card player, comparing his waste of time with one's own important and perhaps even holy endeavors, a person must ask himself if he would be willing to wage a spiritual fight as difficult as the one the gambler must face in order to stop gambling.

Before passing judgment on another, one must carefully consider the other person's struggle against his evil inclination, taking into account his personal life circumstances and his evil inclination's potency. He must then consider his own personal struggle against his evil inclination. After considering the struggles of the simple individual, which might be compared with another's willingness to accept martyrdom, he should ask himself if he is prepared to wage such an intense battle to overcome his own challenges, and he might arrive at a newfound humility. He might learn that the person whom he considered to be a sinner nevertheless endeavors to remain within a framework of goodness, perhaps even more than he himself, and is able to muster his strength in order to improve his character and overcome his imperfections.

Once, Rabbi Dovid of Lelov described with great feeling an extraordinary example of the fear of Heaven that he himself witnessed. He was traveling through the forest when he saw a young man standing over his father with an ax in his hand and yelling, "Father, if I were not afraid of God, I would chop off your head!"

Rabbi Dovid stood there for a long time contemplating this man's fear of Heaven and was deeply impressed because he realized that the man had to engage in a great struggle to overcome his urge to kill. Rabbi Dovid recognized in him a dedication to overpower his primal urges, a dedication he did not see even in his closest disciples, in whom that would have translated into a willingness to sacrifice something that they deeply desired due to their fear of God.

Someone who looks at others from this perspective will truly feel humble before every man, even if he himself is a great Jewish leader.

Chapter 31

THE PRECEDING CHAPTERS DISCUSSED REMEDIES FOR healing a dull heart, a state of being caused by self-satisfaction, even if only sensed in the subconscious alone, and marked by a loss of emotions. The heart grows progressively insensible, layered and encrusted with a sense of self, until one becomes unresponsive. To rejuvenate himself, a person must first break down that smug sense of self, just as a log is chopped into small pieces so that they can be set ablaze.

To crush that smugness, the author of the *Tanya* recommended a method of exhaustive self-examination that takes into account not only the sins and mitzvot visible to the outside world, but also the hidden perplexities of the heart, the internal effort one is willing to expend in his spiritual struggle. When a person carries out such an honest self-assessment, he may learn that contrary to his demanding expectations of others, he is not prepared to face his own personal challenges. He may also learn that his service of God is inferior to that of those whom he had previously disparaged.

Such contemplation, considering one's own inadequacies, may bring a person to sadness. Yet sadness and dullness of the heart are the very traits that these chapters tell us how to eradicate. Why would the author of the *Tanya* encourage behavior that leads to sadness if it must be avoided? The author of the *Tanya* will explain in this chapter that the sadness that results from acknowledging one's deficiencies is not the ugly feeling of sadness that paralyzes a person and prevents him from advancing in his spiritual endeavors.

Rather, It is the feeling of bitterness that causes a person to stand up and fight, to go out and struggle. This feeling does not stem from the *sitra aĥara,* but in fact has the opposite effect: It pushes a person toward holiness.

5 Adar

22 Adar I (leap year)

וְהִנֵּה אַף אִם כְּשֶׁיַּאֲרִיךְ הַרְבֵּה לְהַעֲמִיק בָּעִנְיָנִים הַנִּזְכָּרִים לְעֵיל, כְּשָׁעָה וּשְׁתַּיִם, לִהְיוֹת בִּנְמִיכַת רוּחַ וְלֵב נִשְׁבָּר - יָבֹא לִידֵי עַצְבוּת גְּדוֹלָה, לֹא יָחוּשׁ.

Even if the deep and lengthy contemplation of the aforementioned matters lasting **for an hour or two, in order to be humble of spirit and contrite of heart, leads to great sadness, one should not be concerned.**

When a person compares himself to others, he may find that he has no reason to consider himself superior. On the contrary, he may see much that is worth emulating. It is possible, for instance, that a Torah scholar is making no effort to improve, while an unremarkable individual, even one who might be considered most unworthy, is valiantly struggling against sweeping passions. When the scholar realizes this, he is liable to grow dejected. Yet the sadness and dejection that results from such contemplation is not a reason for concern.

וְאַף שֶׁעַצְבוּת הִיא מִצַּד קְלִיפַּת נוֹגַהּ, וְלֹא מִצַּד הַקְּדוּשָּׁה. כִּי בְּצַד הַקְּדוּשָּׁה כְּתִיב: "עֹז וְחֶדְוָה בִּמְקוֹמוֹ" (דברי הימים א טז, כז), וְאֵין הַשְּׁכִינָה שׁוֹרָה אֶלָּא מִתּוֹךְ שִׂמְחָה,

It is true that sadness stems from the side of *kelippat noga* and not from the side of holiness, for concerning holiness the verse states, "Might and joy are His place" (I Chron. 16:27)**, and the Divine Presence rests** upon an individual **only from** a state of **joy,**

Sadness generally stems from *kelippa,* from the side of evil, or at the very least from *kelippat noga,* which is neither good nor evil. Moreover, the sources cited by the author of the *Tanya* teach that joy is required in the performance of any area of divine service. There is no place for sadness or depression when engaging in holy matters. This holds true particularly with regard to prayer, since its function is to reveal the Divine Presence, which rests upon a person and his surroundings only when a person is in a state of joy.

וְכֵן לִדְבַר הֲלָכָה וכו׳, **and the same applies with regard to** the study of **a matter of *halakha* and so on,**

Our Sages teach that since the Divine Presence abides with a person when he is joyous and not depressed, one should also study *halakha* in a state of joy and self-abnegation, so that God Himself will be present as he studies.[1] On a simple level, this dictum teaches that joy is conducive to a proper understanding of the subject matter being studied.

אֶלָּא שֶׁאִם הָעַצְבוּת הִיא מִמִּילֵּי דִשְׁמַיָּא - הִיא מִבְּחִינַת טוֹב שֶׁבְּנוֹגַהּ **but if the sadness is due to heavenly matters,** that is, if one is sad due to his sins, **it stems from the good inherent in** the *kelippa* of ***noga.***

The *kelippa* of *noga* contains a glimmer of light, a trace of goodness.[2] Generally speaking, dejection comes from the realm of *kelippa*. But that is the dejection caused by mundane concerns, such as monetary loss or a thwarted attempt to commit a sin. Such sadness stems from the evil within *kelippat noga*. On the other hand, dejection due to one's spiritual failures, such as when one does not study Torah properly or one has failed to perform a mitzva correctly, comes from the good within *kelippat noga*.

(וְלָכֵן כָּתַב הָאֲרִ"י ז"ל שֶׁאֲפִילּוּ דַּאֲגַת הָעֲוֹנוֹת אֵינָהּ רְאוּיָה כִּי אִם בִּשְׁעַת הַוִּידּוּי, **(Therefore, the Arizal wrote that even worrying about** one's **sins is inappropriate except during the time of confession,**

Even though worry about spiritual matters comes from the good aspect contained within *kelippat noga*, at the end of the day it still stems from *kelippa*. In light of this, one should indulge in such contemplations

1. *Shabbat* 30b.
2. This is the *noga*, which means glow or glimmer, in the *kelippa*. See, e.g., chaps. 1, 7.

only at the appropriate point in the prayer service, when one confesses his sins.[3]

וְלֹא בִּשְׁעַת הַתְּפִלָּה וְתַלְמוּד תּוֹרָה, שֶׁצָּרִיךְ לִהְיוֹת בְּשִׂמְחָה שֶׁמִּצַּד הַקְּדוּשָּׁה דַּוְוקָא.]

and not during prayer or Torah study, which must be performed **with joy stemming specifically from the side of holiness.**)

The joy referred to here is that which is experienced when performing a holy act, to the exclusion of frivolity and other such meaningless behavior.

אַף עַל פִּי כֵן, הֲרֵי כָּךְ הִיא הַמִּדָּה - לְאַכְפְּיָא לְסִטְרָא אָחֳרָא בְּמִינָהּ וְדוּגְמָתָהּ, כְּמַאֲמַר רַבּוֹתֵינוּ ז״ל: ״מִינֵּיהּ וּבֵיהּ אַבָּא לִשְׁדְּיֵיהּ בֵּיהּ נַרְגָּא״ (סנהדרין לט, ב),

Nevertheless, since sadness derives from *kelippa,* **this is the approach: to subdue the *sitra aḥara* using its own methods and tools in accordance with our Rabbis' statement "From and within the forest comes the ax** handle that fells it" (*Sanhedrin* 39b),

The forest itself provides the handle for the ax used to fell its own trees. The proper way to battle the *sitra aĥara* is by using its own weapons. In our context, we intentionally employ the negative trait of depression to combat evil. From evil itself we carve the weapon with which we will ultimately destroy it.

וּ״פָּגַע בּוֹ כַּיּוֹצֵא בוֹ״ (שבת קכא, ב).

and, in a different context, **"One of its type killed it"** (*Shabbat* 121b).

The Talmud there recounts that after a snake was found in the study hall on the Sabbath, and a Nabatean killed it, Rabbi Yehuda HaNasi stated that "one of its type killed it." In other words, a dangerous person killed the dangerous snake. To fight evil, we must use something that comes

3. See *Pri Etz Ḥayyim, Sha'ar Olam HaAsiya,* end of chap. 1.

from evil and appears similar to it. We need only change its direction so that it will act on behalf of good.[4]

וְעַל זֶה נֶאֱמַר: "בְּכָל עֶצֶב יִהְיֶה מוֹתָר" (משלי יד, כג). וְהַיִּתְרוֹן הִיא הַשִּׂמְחָה הַבָּאָה אַחַר הָעֶצֶב כִּדִּלְקַמָּן.

With regard to this, the verse states, "In all sadness there will be an advantage" (Prov. 14:23). **The advantage is the joy that follows the sadness, as** will be explained **below.**

Although sadness is intrinsically an evil trait, it can, if properly employed, present an advantage in the realm of sanctity.[5] Sadness in itself has nothing to recommend it, but it can elevate a person to a state of joy greater than he had previously experienced. Following a period of sadness, an unprecedented upsurge of joy, which one could not have otherwise attained, bursts forth. Thus, even though sadness is generally undesirable since it stems from *kelippa*, at times it may be used to attain positive ends.

The author of the *Tanya* now proceeds to explain that this sadness

---

4. The Lubavitcher Rebbe, Rabbi Menaḥem Mendel Schneerson, points out that the author of the *Tanya* intentionally selected these talmudic dictums because they parallel the lessons taught in the preceding two chapters. In chapter 29, the author described how one must break the evil within that manifests itself as a dull heart by meditating on the ephemerality of the body and material world, both realms in which his soul is mired. The corporeal body and the physical world are not inherently evil, and so are not included in the three utterly evil *kelippot*. Rather, they are an expression of *kelippat noga*, the neutral realm that lies between holiness and impurity. It follows that *kelippat noga* is merely a type of *kelippa*, but not entirely so. This fits well with the example of the ax handle and the forest. The handle is not the instrument that actually fells the trees. It merely connects the wielder with the blade, the actual instrument that ultimately does the deed. Chapter 30 focuses on the battle waged against the evil inclination by contemplating the sins that one has transgressed, such as engaging in idle conversation or prohibited speech (depending on a person's level), where unintentional sins are considered to have been committed wittingly. This parallels the second talmudic dictum, "One of its type killed it." Here the battle waged is against the utterly impure *kelippa* by means of reflecting on those very transgressions.

5. See also chap. 26, where this verse and advantage is discussed.

under discussion, that which rectifies evil and ultimately leads to happiness, is not true sadness at all.

אַךְ בֶּאֱמֶת אֵין לֵב נִשְׁבָּר וּמְרִירוּת הַנֶּפֶשׁ עַל רִיחוּקָהּ מֵאוֹר פְּנֵי ה׳ וְהִתְלַבְּשׁוּתָהּ בְּסִטְרָא אָחֳרָא נִקְרָאִים בְּשֵׁם עַצְבוּת כְּלָל בִּלְשׁוֹן הַקּוֹדֶשׁ. כִּי עַצְבוּת הִיא שֶׁלִּבּוֹ מְטוּמְטָם כָּאֶבֶן וְאֵין חַיּוּת בְּלִבּוֹ.

In truth, however, a broken heart and bitterness of the soul due to its remoteness from the light of God's countenance and its being clothed in the *sitra aḥara* is not at all referred to as *atzvut*, sadness, in biblical Hebrew, for *atzvut* is a state **where one's heart is dull as a stone, possessing no vitality.**

The sense of humility, the contrite heart and bitterness of the soul, that results from the awareness of one's distance from God is attained after a thorough self-introspection, as discussed in the preceding chapters. The author of the *Tanya* now points out that bitterness of the soul does not denote sadness in Hebrew. Although these two states appear similar, they are not at all identical.

Atzvut denotes melancholy or depression, a state that renders a person unresponsive and unable to act. It deprives him of his capabilities and strips him of his energy. A person who is depressed is caught up in himself, in his thoughts and feelings, with no desire to escape. He nurses the awareness of his misfortunes, comfortable in the thought of his incapacity, neither initiating nor welcoming communication.

אֲבָל מְרִירוּת וְלֵב נִשְׁבָּר, אַדְּרַבָּה, הֲרֵי יֵשׁ חַיּוּת בְּלִבּוֹ לְהִתְפַּעֵל וּלְהִתְמַרְמֵר,

But bitterness of the soul **and a broken heart** demonstrate **that on the contrary, there is vitality in his heart motivating him to become embittered,**

One does not indulge in self-pity as a result of realizing his distance from God. He only grows determined to change. When his broken heart cries out, "Why am I so far from God?" that is not a pretext for self-pity but the expression of impatience with himself, even anger. His bitterness impels him to ask searching questions: "Where do I stand? Where am I headed?"

This sentiment is not one of a lack of vitality, of foundering and death. On the contrary, his soul is vibrant and awakened. Whereas a sad person is overwhelmed and unable to do anything, a bitter person is driven by the need to rise to the occasion, the imperative to act.

רַק שֶׁהִיא חַיּוּת מִבְּחִינַת גְּבוּרוֹת קְדוֹשׁוֹת - וְהַשִּׂמְחָה מִבְּחִינַת חֲסָדִים,

except that this vitality stems from the holy aspects of *Gevura* (Restraint), **while joy** stems **from the** holy **aspects of *Ḥesed*** (Kindness),

The force of life always flows from what is good and holy, from "life and good" versus "death and evil."[6] But it can come in one of two ways. There is a vitality that is pleasing, permeated with advancement, a joyous aliveness that flows from holy kindness. But there is a second kind of vitality as well that comes from bitterness, from a broken heart, and that flows from holy aspects of *Gevura*, the attribute of restraint. The full-fledged experience of severity is never easy or pleasant. But a person who undergoes that painful experience is alive.

כִּי הַלֵּב כָּלוּל מִשְּׁתֵּיהֶן.

for the heart comprises both attributes.

The heart, the seat of emotion in the soul, contains both aspects of restraint and aspects of kindness. Anger and depression are aspects of the attribute of *Gevura* rooted in *kelippa*, and as such, these feelings have no place in the holy divine soul. By contrast, the sense of bitterness over one's distance from God, though rooted in the aspects of *Gevura*, is regarded as holy, and so has a place in the divine soul. At the same time, joy, which stems from the holy aspects of *Ḥesed*, may also claim a place in the realm of holiness. Although the emotions of bitterness and joy are dissimilar, both bear an essential bond with the divine soul.[7]

---

6. See Deut. 30:15.

7. The shared bond of joy and bitterness with the divine soul accounts for the phenomenon of their simultaneous expression. In the words of the *Zohar* (3:75a), "Weeping is lodged in this side of my heart, and joy is lodged in the other." See also chap. 34 below; *Iggeret HaTeshuva*, chap. 11; *Sefer HaMa'amarim* 5700, p. 145.

וְהִנֵּה לְעִתִּים צָרִיךְ לְעוֹרֵר בְּחִינַת גְּבוּרוֹת הַקְּדוֹשׁוֹת

It is sometimes necessary to evoke the holy aspects of *Gevura*

Normally, we prefer to avoid the side of *Gevura*. Since it limits and confines the essence of things, it can be unpleasant to experience. It may even be dangerous because it exposes us to fearsome forces, such as anger or war. Nevertheless, for certain purposes and at certain times, we must evoke in the depths of our heart the aspects of this attribute that stem from the side of holiness, generating the bitterness of the soul.

כְּדֵי לְהַמְתִּיק הַדִּינִים,

in order to mitigate, literally, "sweeten," **the** harsh **judgments** stemming from the aspects of *Gevura,*

The Hebrew word for mitigate, *lehamtik,* literally means to sweeten, as when bitter waters are sweetened and become potable. To sweeten something is to completely transform and rectify it. In the service of God, this constitutes transforming the essence of the animal soul to good.[8]

External factors can uproot and eradicate evil. But sweetening entails rectifying something from itself and within itself. There is a change at its essence that brings a deeper understanding and hence a correction of behavior.

שֶׁהֵם בְּחִינַת נֶפֶשׁ הַבַּהֲמִית וְיֵצֶר הָרַע, כְּשֶׁשּׁוֹלֵט חַס וְשָׁלוֹם עַל הָאָדָם.

which are the animal soul and the evil inclination whenever the evil inclination **dominates a person, God forbid,**

Judgments in this context refer to life challenges and the concealment of the Divine, whether those affecting mundane matters, such as one's livelihood or health, or those challenging one's spiritual ascent. In spiritual terms, a person is affected by severe judgments when his animal soul rules over his divine soul. On a physical level, a person visited by such judgments suffers through calamities visited upon his children,

8. Rabbi Shmuel Gronem Esterman.

his well-being, and his livelihood.[9] When such judgments inundate a person, the way to "sweeten" or mitigate them is by employing the very same force they themselves engender. One should harness the power of the bitter emotions he feels when beset by these troubles and use them to sweeten the bitterness inherent in the harsh judgments. The anger and disappointment he feels at being distant from God are the very tools he may employ in assuaging those judgments. ☞

כִּי אֵין הַדִּינִים נִמְתָּקִין אֶלָּא בְּשָׁרְשָׁן. for harsh **judgments can be sweetened only at their source.**

These judgments, which are an aspect of the animal soul and the evil inclination, can be rectified only at their source, the holy aspects of *Gevura,* because at their root they are not evil. When we uncover the good at the source, all the harshness that emerged from it is rectified as well.

Although judgment may also be rectified by kindness, that is merely external and partial, the equivalent of making a bitter food palatable by adding honey to it. Judgment is truly sweetened only at its source, and to attain that, the power of judgment itself is needed.[10] When a psychologist eases his patient's guilty feelings, he will also be easing his

SWEETENING HARSH JUDGMENTS

☞ A person under the influence of harsh judgments, who is enveloped by the animal soul and the evil inclination, which obscure the light of the Divine, suffers from a dull heart. To sweeten these judgments, to shine the light on them, one has to crack open this cover. This act of breaking employs the power of harshness as well, though in this context it is through the holy aspects of *Gevura.*

9. These two manifestations of judgments are interdependent, the spiritual judgments leading to this-worldly judgments. As the verse states, "Is it not because my God is not in my midst that these evils found me?" (Deut. 31:17). Judgments are ameliorated when a person transforms his animal soul so that it attains a divine nature, which he does by giving his "strength to Torah study" (*Bava Metzia* 84a) – that is, by devoting his passions to Torah study and mitzvot. This is why it is said that the penitent is greater than the completely righteous individual (Rabbi Shmuel Gronem Esterman).

10. See *Beitza* 25b; *Likkutei Torah* by the Arizal, *Parashat Behar.*

patient's overwrought symptoms. But to completely solve the patient's problem, he must uncover its cause at its source.

וְלָכֵן אָמְרוּ רַבּוֹתֵינוּ ז"ל: "לְעוֹלָם יַרְגִּיז אָדָם יֵצֶר הַטּוֹב" (ברכות ה, א),

It is for this reason that **our Rabbis** state, **"One should always incite his good inclination** against his evil inclination" (*Berakhot* 5a),

One fulfills this talmudic dictum by conducting a spiritual self-assessment and crushing the egotistical natures of his animal soul and evil inclination. Essentially, by executing judgment on oneself by means of this self-assessment, one effectively sweetens the harsh judgments set upon him from above at their root.

וְהַיְינוּ בְּכָל עֵת שֶׁרוֹאֶה בְּנַפְשׁוֹ שֶׁצָּרִיךְ לְכָךְ.

meaning any time he sees that he requires it.

The expression *le'olam*, "always," in the abovementioned talmudic passage is not meant to be taken literally. It does not mean that a person must break his heart and experience a bitterness of soul at every moment. That is not the way to serve God or attain holiness. Rather, a person must do so only at certain times.

A principled person may grow proud and pleased with himself. At times, this may inspire him to progress with a sense of joy. At other times, this feeling brings on smugness that prevents him from seeing his flaws, and as a result he does nothing to improve. Such a person is rotting within, sinking into the torpor of the dull heart. It is then that he must incite his good nature against his evil inclination by exploring whatever is broken and damaged, by examining himself. In this way, he may awaken with a renewed vitality.

AN OPPORTUNE TIME FOR BITTERNESS

☞ Several reasons are suggested as to why one is encouraged to transform bitterness over mundane problems to those of holiness. The most basic reason is that since in general one ought to be in a state of happiness, it behooves a person to utilize his predicament, his state of bitterness or sadness, as a springboard for holiness. In this case, he should seize the opportunity to convert those sad feelings he experiences on account of mundane matters into sadness he feels on account of holy matters.

Additionally, we know that the divine

אַךְ שְׁעַת הַכּוֹשֶׁר, שֶׁהִיא שָׁעָה הַמְיוּחֶדֶת וּרְאוּיָה לְכָךְ לְרוֹב בְּנֵי אָדָם, הִיא בְּשָׁעָה שֶׁהוּא עָצֵב בְּלָאו הָכִי, מִמִּילֵי דְעָלְמָא אוֹ כָּךְ בְּלִי שׁוּם סִבָּה.

However, the fitting time to be bitter or brokenhearted, **the opportune and appropriate time for this for most people, is when one is already sad over mundane matters, or** he feels **this way for no** explicable **reason whatsoever.**

These "mundane matters" are worries that cause a person to be sad, such as monetary problems, loss, anxiety, and insults. On the other hand, people go through cycles of emotions and may grow sad without any clear reason. Whatever the cause, when a person is sad, that is a good opportunity to channel the sadness and bitterness toward the realm of holiness. ☞

אֲזַי הִיא שְׁעַת הַכּוֹשֶׁר לְהַפֵּךְ הָעֶצֶב, לִהְיוֹת מִמָּרֵי דְּחוּשְׁבָּנָא הַנִּזְכָּרִים לְעֵיל,

This is a fitting time to transform the sadness and **to be one of the aforementioned masters of introspection** (see chap. 29)

When a person is sad for whatever reason, that is the right time to do soul-searching so that the introspection will lead to a bitterness of the soul and a feeling of dejection about his spiritual concerns. This can

soul is clothed within the animal soul. The implication of such an arrangement is that the divine soul can become manifest and expressed in the physical world only by mimicking the nature and composition of the animal soul. When the animal soul experiences happiness over mundane matters, it is a propitious time for the divine soul to evoke joy over holy matters. For example, drinking wine and consuming meat are a means by which to express and experience joy on the holidays (see *Pesaḥim* 109a).

Finally, some suggest that the true underlying cause of sadness and depression is that at that very moment one is being judged on high. This is alluded to in the verse "The heart knows the bitterness of itself" (Prov. 14:10). The root of a person's soul in the higher realms is acutely aware of the heavenly proceedings on high, that, as the Talmud states, a person is judged every day (*Rosh HaShana* 16a). Even if the person himself may not be aware of these heavenly proceedings, the root of his soul is aware (*Megilla* 3a). This is liable to cause a person to feel bitter and depressed. The author of the *Tanya* therefore teaches that if one feels depressed or sad, he should utilize the opportunity to "pass judgment" on himself by feeling bitter that he is distant from God. The principle is that a judgment below obviates the need for a judgment on high (Rabbi Shmuel Gronem Esterman).

change his mood from a sadness that is pulling him downward to a bitterness of the soul that can lift him up. ☞

וּלְקַיֵּים מַאֲמַר רַבּוֹתֵינוּ ז״ל: ״לְעוֹלָם יַרְגִּיז״ וכו׳, כַּנִּזְכָּר לְעֵיל, וּבָזֶה יִפָּטֵר מֵהָעַצְבוּת שֶׁמִּמִּילֵי דְעָלְמָא.

and to thereby **fulfill our Rabbis' statement "One should always incite** his good inclination against his evil inclination" (*Berakhot* 5a), **as mentioned above. Through this, he will be released from the sadness brought on by mundane matters**

When a person first experiences a bitterness of the spirit regarding heavenly matters, he is no longer saddened by the concerns of this world. That kind of sadness comes from feeling slighted, from the sense that one is not getting what one deserves, that one is receiving unfair treatment.

After introspection and seeing his flaws, a person understands that he deserves no better than he has received. He may feel pained, he may be upset, but he will not feel slighted, nor will he be sad. He will not assume that he is worthy of more; he will no longer ask why bad things happen to him. As a result, such matters will no longer depress him.

6 Adar וְאַחַר כָּךְ יָבֹא לִידֵי שִׂמְחָה אֲמִיתִּית,

and will subsequently arrive at true joy.

WAYS TO SELF-INTROSPECT

☞ One can conduct a self-introspection in a number of ways. But however one proceeds, one must make sure that it will be elevating and energizing and not the opposite. Unfortunately, many people take the wrong approach. With regard to mundane matters, they compare themselves to those who are better off than they are and as a result grow depressed and envious. In the realm of the spirit, they compare themselves to their inferiors and as a result become self-satisfied and dull-hearted. Instead, in the realm of the mundane, a person should compare himself to those who are less fortunate and learn how to be satisfied with less. In the realm of the spirit, by contrast, one should compare himself to his betters, realizing how imperfect he is and motiving him to become more holy (see *HaYom Yom*, 30 Sivan).

After he has been crushed by the bitterness of the soul, after reflection has revealed his imperfections and exposed his heart to pain, he can attain true joy.

דְּהַיְינוּ שֶׁזֹּאת יָשִׁיב אֶל לִבּוֹ לְנַחֲמוֹ בְּכִפְלַיִים, אַחַר הַדְּבָרִים וְהָאֱמֶת הָאֵלֶּה הַנִּזְכָּרִים לְעֵיל,

That is, in the wake of these aforementioned matters, the results of his soul-searching, **and** confronting **the truth, he can console himself to a much greater degree**

After an accounting of the soul, when a person finds that he is lacking and blemished, he can console himself even more than he could have before experiencing this bitterness of the soul.

לֵאמֹר לְלִבּוֹ: אֱמֶת הוּא כֵּן בְּלִי סָפֵק שֶׁאֲנִי רָחוֹק מְאֹד מֵה' בְּתַכְלִית, וּמְשׁוּקָּץ וּמְתוֹעָב כו',

by telling his heart, "It is undoubtedly true that I am exceedingly far from God, despicable, loathsome, and so on.

This is not mere rhetoric or an act of pretension. When a person examines himself honestly, he truly experiences himself in this way.

אַךְ כָּל זֶה הוּא אֲנִי לְבַדִּי, הוּא הַגּוּף עִם נֶפֶשׁ הַחִיּוּנִית שֶׁבּוֹ.

But all this is applicable to myself alone, meaning **my body and the vital soul** that is clothed **in it.**

As explained above, the animal soul that gives life to the body is the *beinoni*'s sense of self.[11] Therefore, the part that is "despicable and loathsome" is the body and the animal soul that gives life to the body.

אֲבָל מִכָּל מָקוֹם יֵשׁ בְּקִרְבִּי חֵלֶק ה' מַמָּשׁ, שֶׁיֶּשְׁנוֹ אֲפִילּוּ בְּקַל שֶׁבְּקַלִּים, שֶׁהִיא נֶפֶשׁ הָאֱלֹקִית עִם נִיצוֹץ אֱלֹקוּת מַמָּשׁ הַמְלוּבָּשׁ בָּהּ לְהַחֲיוֹתָהּ,

Yet nevertheless there is within me an actual part of God that exists even in the most unworthy: the divine soul along **with an actual spark of Godliness that is clothed within it, animating it.**

11. See chap. 29.

Something divine, a soul that is a spark of God's illumination, exists in the Jew's very persona, even though it is the animal soul and even if he is the most worthless of individuals.

רַק שֶׁהִיא בִּבְחִינַת גָּלוּת.

It is only hidden because it is **in a state of exile** within me.

A person must be aware of this soul within him. If he cannot sense it, that is because his divine soul is in exile. He has kept it from having dominion over him and has sent it into exile. When it is revealed at all, it is not on its own behalf but to benefit the body and the animal soul.

וְאִם כֵּן אַדְּרַבָּה, כָּל מַה שֶּׁאֲנִי, בְּתַכְלִית הָרִיחוּק מֵה' וְהַתִּיעוּב וְשִׁיקּוּץ, הֲרֵי נֶפֶשׁ הָאֱלֹקִית שֶׁבִּי בְּגָלוּת גָּדוֹל יוֹתֵר

If so, on the contrary, the more that I, my body and animal soul, **am utterly distant from God, and** the more **loathsome and despicable, the deeper in exile is the divine soul within me,**

The lower the person descends, the further the divine soul clothed within him descends into exile. Wherever a person goes with his body and animal soul, he draws along his divine soul, the Godly spark within him.

וְהָרַחֲמָנוּת עָלֶיהָ גְּדוֹלָה מְאֹד.

and all the more so is it to be pitied.

Such pity is an awareness of the gap between the soul's divine source and its present distance and concealment from the Divine. There is pity when someone finds himself cast below his station. If a person feels that he is getting what he deserves, he may suffer, but that is all. He pities himself only when he believes that he has been deprived (and the same holds true regarding his perceptions of others).

וְלָזֶה אָשִׂים כָּל מְגַמָּתִי וְחֶפְצִי לְהוֹצִיאָהּ וּלְהַעֲלוֹתָהּ מִגָּלוּת זֶה לַהֲשִׁיבָהּ אֶל בֵּית אָבִיהָ כִּנְעוּרֶיהָ קוֹדֶם שֶׁנִּתְלַבְּשָׁה

It is to this end that I direct my entire goal and desire toward extricating it and raising it out of this exile and returning it to its father's house as in its youth, that is, to its source and

בְּגוּפִי, שֶׁהָיְתָה נִכְלֶלֶת בְּאוֹרוֹ יִתְבָּרֵךְ וּמְיוּחֶדֶת עִמּוֹ בְּתַכְלִית.

root, **before it was clothed in my body, when it was subsumed in God's light and totally united with Him.**

Bitterness, unlike sadness, leads to resolve. In this case, one becomes motivated to redeem the divine soul from its imprisonment and suffering. The expression the author of the *Tanya* uses here, "returning it to its father's house as in its youth" is borrowed from the verse "But if a priest's daughter is a widow or a divorcée, and she has no offspring, and she returns to her father's house as in her youth, from the food of her father she may partake…" (Lev. 22:13). In the context of the *Tanya*, the phrase refers to the return of the divine soul to its original source.

Along these lines, the *Zohar* states that the "priest's daughter" is the divine soul, which is also called the daughter of the king. When the divine soul is "a widow or a divorcée," separated from the body, it "returns to its father's house," to God, "as in its youth" – that is, to its original state, as it was before it descended to the body.[12]

וְגַם עַתָּה כֵּן תְּהֵא כְּלוּלָה וּמְיוּחֶדֶת בּוֹ יִתְבָּרֵךְ, כְּשֶׁאָשִׂים כָּל מְגַמָּתִי בְּתוֹרָה וּמִצְוֹת, לְהַלְבִּישׁ בָּהֶן כָּל עֶשֶׂר בְּחִינוֹתֶיהָ, כַּנִּזְכָּר לְעֵיל,

Now too it will be incorporated and united with God, when I set my entire focus on Torah study **and** the fulfillment of **mitzvot in which to clothe all its ten faculties, as mentioned above** (chap. 4),

A person's entire focus must be to liberate his divine soul from its exile and raise it up to God. The way to do this is to turn one's attention to Torah study and the performance of mitzvot so that the soul's ten faculties will become clothed in them. In exile, the divine soul is clothed in the filthy garments of the animal soul, the *kelippa*. It is redeemed when we clothe it in Torah and mitzvot, which are its essential garments, the way in which it expresses its essence. By studying Torah and fulfilling

12. *Zohar* 3:7a; see also *Or HaḤayyim*, Lev. 22:12; *Iggeret HaKodesh*, epistle 12.

mitzvot, by allowing the soul's inner essence to shine through, the soul returns to its source in the Divine, "returning to its father's house as in its youth."

וּבִפְרָט בְּמִצְוַת תְּפִלָּה, לִצְעוֹק אֶל ה׳ בַּצַּר לָהּ מִגָּלוּתָהּ בְּגוּפִי הַמְשׁוּקָּץ לְהוֹצִיאָהּ מִמַּסְגֵּר וּלְדָבְקָה בּוֹ יִתְבָּרֵךְ.

particularly the mitzva of prayer, by crying out to God regarding its distress from its exile in my despicable body so that it may be extricated from its confinement and cleave to God."

The function of prayer is to express the outcry of the divine soul, freeing it from the boundaries of the body and returning it to "its Father's house as in its youth."

וְזוֹ הִיא בְּחִינַת "תְּשׁוּבָה וּמַעֲשִׂים טוֹבִים" (אבות פרק ד משנה יז), שֶׁהֵן מַעֲשִׂים טוֹבִים שֶׁעוֹשֶׂה כְּדֵי לְהָשִׁיב חֵלֶק ה׳ לִמְקוֹרָא וְשָׁרְשָׁא דְּכָל עָלְמִין.

This constitutes "repentance and good deeds" (Mishna *Avot* 4:17), **which are the good deeds one does in order to restore** this **part of God,** the divine soul, **to the root and source of all worlds.**

Repentance in this sense does not refer to repenting for a sin. The author of the *Tanya* is, after all, discussing the *beinoni,* who has never sinned. The literal meaning of the Hebrew word for repentance, *teshuva,* is to return. This could entail the return of the world to God or the return of the divine soul to its source, which is also the source and root of all the worlds. We achieve such atonement when we perform "good deeds" – when we study Torah and fulfill the mitzvot.

7 Adar וְזֹאת תִּהְיֶה עֲבוֹדָתוֹ כָּל יָמָיו בְּשִׂמְחָה רַבָּה, הִיא שִׂמְחַת הַנֶּפֶשׁ בְּצֵאתָהּ מֵהַגּוּף הַמְתוֹעָב וְשָׁבָה אֶל בֵּית אָבִיהָ כִּנְעוּרֶיהָ בִּשְׁעַת הַתּוֹרָה וְהָעֲבוֹדָה,

This should be one's lifelong service of God, to perform mitzvot **with great joy, which is the joy of the soul as it leaves the loathsome body and returns to its father's house as in its youth during** one's **Torah** study **and** divine **service,**

This comprehensive *teshuva* is comprised of Torah study and divine service, particularly prayer. A person engages in that service with great joy, because it represents the soul's liberation from the body, from its sensory perceptions and desires, and brings about renewal and emergence into the freedom of divine holiness.

וּכְמַאֲמַר רַבּוֹתֵינוּ ז״ל, לִהְיוֹת "כָּל יָמָיו בִּתְשׁוּבָה" (שבת קנג, א).

in accordance with our Rabbis' statement that one should "spend his entire life in a state of repentance" (*Shabbat* 153a).

A person who is in a "state of repentance" throughout his life is not someone who must atone for a particular sin. If he is constantly in a state of repentance, on account of which sin is he repenting?[13] Rather, he is constantly striving to return to God, to the source and root of his soul, becoming ever closer and growing ever more intimately connected with Him, walking on a path that reaches to infinity, a path without end on which one walks forever, "spending his entire life in a state of repentance."

וְאֵין לְךָ שִׂמְחָה גְּדוֹלָה כְּצֵאת מֵהַגָּלוּת וְהַשִּׁבְיָה,

There is no greater joy than that of being released from exile and captivity,

The greater one's distance from God, the greater the joy upon being brought close to Him once more. It is only the pain associated with that sense of distance that has the ability to evoke the degree of joy one feels when reunited with God. A person who perpetually enjoys a high-quality lifestyle is not always consciously joyous over his comfortable circumstances. It is typically only upon experiencing distance – that is, pain and hardship – that this person can once again appreciate and rejoice in his original station in life.

כְּמָשָׁל בֶּן מֶלֶךְ שֶׁהָיָה בַּשִּׁבְיָה וְטוֹחֵן בְּבֵית הָאֲסוּרִים וּמְנוּוָּל בָּאַשְׁפָּה, וְיָצָא לְחָפְשִׁי אֶל בֵּית אָבִיו הַמֶּלֶךְ.

as in the parable of a prince who was held in captivity and, having been tasked with **grinding** wheat **in prison,** became **a filthy wretch, whereupon he was set free** and returned **to the house of his father, the king.**

13. Lubavitcher Rebbe, Rabbi Menaḥem Mendel Schneerson.

There is no greater joy than emerging from rock bottom and rising to the highest realm of existence, from a world of disgrace and enslavement to the house of one's father and king. When the divine soul leaves the exile of the body, there is joy in its broadest sense, the joy that comes with the nullification of self, with leaving behind the vessels of the body and animal soul, for "might and joy are in His place" (I Chron. 16:27).[14]

וְאַף שֶׁהַגּוּף עוֹמֵד בְּשִׁיקּוּצוֹ וְתִיעוּבוֹ,

Indeed, his body remains despicable and loathsome,

When a person is immersed in Torah and mitzvot, his divine soul is liberated from the bonds of the body and clings to God. The soul can experience no greater joy than that. This is so even if his self-identification with his body and animal soul remains unchanged, in its contemptible and abominable state.

וּכְמוֹ שֶׁכָּתוּב בַּזֹּהַר (תיקוני זהר בהקדמה י, ב ותיקון כא מח, ב) דְּנִקְרָא מַשְׁכָּא דְחִוְיָא,

and as the *Zohar* states (*Tikkunei Zohar* 10b, 48b), the body is **called the skin of a serpent**

The serpent itself represents the three unclean *kelippot*, which can never emerge from their polluted state. The skin of the serpent is the outer part of the three unholy *kelippot*, which is the *kelippa* of *noga*, the body.[15]

כִּי מַהוּתָהּ וְעַצְמוּתָהּ שֶׁל הַנֶּפֶשׁ הַבַּהֲמִית לֹא נֶהְפַּךְ לְטוֹב לִיכָּלֵל בַּקְּדוּשָּׁה,

since the essence and being of the animal soul has not transformed into good so that it may be absorbed into the realm of **holiness.**

Just as the body remains a body, so does the animal soul always remain animal-like. This in part defines the *beinoni*, who cannot change the nature of his animal soul.[16] ☞

14. This is reminiscent of Isaac's laughter, as well as the verse "There ships go; and the leviathan, which You created to frolic with" (Ps. 104:26). See also chap. 33; *Torah Or* 17c; *Likkutei Torah*, Num. 77c.

15. For a fuller treatment of this idea, see the Tzemaḥ Tzedek's essay in *Sefer HaḤakira*, entitled "*Vatipakaḥna*," p. 136; see also *Me'orei Or* 8:12.

16. See chap. 12.

מִכָּל מָקוֹם, תֵּיקַר נַפְשׁוֹ בְּעֵינָיו לִשְׂמוֹחַ בְּשִׂמְחָתָהּ יוֹתֵר מֵהַגּוּף הַנִּבְזֶה, שֶׁלֹּא לְעָרֵב וּלְבַלְבֵּל שִׂמְחַת הַנֶּפֶשׁ בְּעַצְבוֹן הַגּוּף.

Yet his divine **soul should nevertheless be more precious to him than his loathsome body,** and the ensuing feelings of sadness associated with it, **so that he rejoices in** his soul's **joy without mingling and confusing the joy of the** divine **soul with the sadness of the body.**

Since a person is composed of both the animal and the divine souls, why does he identify himself with the body and animal soul? Why should he rejoice or concern himself with his body alone? He should be able to rejoice when his divine soul is freed, when it rises with every holy word and deed he performs, and he should be able to do this without concerning himself with his body, which is certainly cause for his sense of inadequacy. If a person occupies himself with the divine soul's joy, which is the joy of God himself, there is no room for his private sorrows.

וְהִנֵּה בְּחִינָה זוֹ הִיא בְּחִינַת יְצִיאַת מִצְרַיִם, שֶׁנֶּאֱמַר בָּהּ: "כִּי בָרַח הָעָם" (שמות יד, ה).

This is reminiscent of the exodus from Egypt, regarding which the verse states, "The people had fled" (Ex. 14:5).

Escape from one's limitations, as one hides oneself from evil, parallels the exodus. Such escape does not constitute a denial of the reality of evil. On the contrary, for such a person, evil is very real and very strong, which is precisely why he is fleeing from it.

ALLEGIANCE TO THE DIVINE SOUL

☞ Even when a person truly feels the utter lowliness of his animal soul, that does not bar him from holy thoughts and actions. On the contrary, it is specifically after a person sees himself as having descended to the lowest level that he can awaken with the awareness that he has the capacity to elevate himself. In a sense, one renounces his allegiance to his body and animal soul and transfers his loyalty to his divine soul. It is only through this that he is capable of emerging from his state of sadness and transforming his bitterness to joy. When one turns away from the bitterness and sadness associated with his animal soul, and instead studies Torah, prays, or performs any act of holiness vitalized by his divine soul, then his divine soul is released and is able to come close to the light of the Divine.

The notion of hiding oneself from evil refers to his disregarding and disengaging from it. He flees from evil instead of confronting it. He tries to build something holy despite the existence of evil and despite its persistence in being evil. This is not a conscious attempt to perfect the self, the totality of reality as he knows it. He does no more than give his divine soul a chance, an illumination of some point of light, to gain its freedom.

דִּלְכְאוֹרָה הוּא תָּמוּהַ, לָמָּה הָיְתָה כָּזֹאת? וְכִי אִילּוּ אָמְרוּ לְפַרְעֹה לְשַׁלְּחָם חָפְשִׁי לְעוֹלָם, לֹא הָיָה מוּכְרָח לְשַׁלְּחָם?

On the surface, this is perplexing. Why was it so, that the people had to flee from Egypt? **Had they told Pharaoh to set them free forever, would he not have been forced to do so?**

Why was it that the exodus from Egypt took the form of flight? Why didn't they leave "with a high hand" (Ex. 14:8) at the outset? Why did they need to use tricks, to pretend that they were only leaving temporarily, telling Pharaoh, "We will go for a three-day journey" (Ex. 8:23)? After all, Pharaoh would have been forced to give in to any conditions that they set.

אֶלָּא מִפְּנֵי שֶׁהָרַע שֶׁבְּנַפְשׁוֹת יִשְׂרָאֵל עֲדַיִין הָיָה בְּתָקְפּוֹ בֶּחָלָל הַשְּׂמָאלִי,

Rather, the reason they had to escape Egypt is **because the evil in the souls of the Israelites was still at its** full **potency in the left chamber** of their hearts,

The exodus came about from on high and not through the refined, inner powers within the Israelites' souls. Their souls had not yet undergone a deeply transformative experience, so they were completely unprepared to bring about the exodus on their own.

כִּי לֹא פָּסְקָה זוּהֲמָתָם עַד מַתַּן תּוֹרָה,

for their contamination did not cease until the giving of the Torah.

From the time of Adam's sin, all human souls were compromised until the souls of the Jewish people standing at Mount Sinai were perfected. The Sages say that the serpent injected venom into Eve, which lodged within all humanity until the Jewish people stood at Mount Sinai, whereupon their souls were rectified.[17]

רַק מְגַמָּתָם וְחֶפְצָם הָיְתָה לָצֵאת נַפְשָׁם הָאֱלוֹקִית מִגָּלוּת הַסִּטְרָא אָחֳרָא, הִיא טוּמְאַת מִצְרַיִם,

Yet their focus and desire was that their divine souls be extricated from the exile of the *sitra aḥara,* namely, the defilement of Egypt,

A sojourn in Egypt did not merely entail residing in a foreign country. The Jews were also partners in its degradation, in a land that was the epitome of impurity, a part of the *sitra aĥara*. Thus, when a person leaves behind his own personal Egypt, he leaves behind the *sitra aḥara*.

וּלְדָבְקָה בוֹ יִתְבָּרֵךְ, וּכְדִכְתִיב: "ה' עוּזִּי וּמָעוּזִּי וּמְנוּסִי בְּיוֹם צָרָה" וגו' (ירמיה טז, יט), "מִשְׂגַּבִּי וּמְנוּסִי" וגו' (שמואל ב כב, ג), וְ"הוּא מָנוֹס לִי" וגו'.

and cleave to God, as it is written, "Lord, my strength, my stronghold, and my refuge on the day of trouble…" (Jer. 16:19), and **"my stronghold and my refuge…"** (II Sam. 22:3), and it says, **"He is my escape…."**

The word *manos* used in these verses not only means refuge but also denotes escape. The Jewish people had to escape from Egypt because of the Egypt within their souls and not because of Pharaoh. As long as they were spiritual slaves to Egypt, they could leave and come to cleave to God only through a quick escape.

The same concept applies to all of us. If a person is not on a level where he sincerely wants to leave Egypt and all its temptations, the only way to escape it is to flee. He cannot solve all the problems that the animal soul presents, but while he cannot fully resolve all the challenges associated with the self, he can at least flee from them and run toward God. That itself is something great because it is in this way that the divine soul proceeds along its own exodus to Mount Sinai.

17. *Shabbat* 146a.

וְלָכֵן לֶעָתִיד, כְּשֶׁיַּעֲבִיר ה׳ רוּחַ הַטּוּמְאָה מִן הָאָרֶץ, כְּתִיב: ״וּבִמְנוּסָה לֹא תֵלֵכוּן כִּי הוֹלֵךְ לִפְנֵיכֶם ה׳״ וגו׳ (ישעיה נב, יב).

Therefore, with regard to the final redemption in **the future, when God will remove the spirit of impurity from the earth, it is written, "You will not go in flight, for the Lord will go before you…"** (Isa. 52:12).

In the future, during the final redemption, there will be no need to flee. When the Jewish people left Egypt, they had to escape in great haste. Had they gone slowly, they would not have ended up leaving, or they would have turned around and returned to Egypt, as the verse states, "Lest the people reconsider when they see war and return to Egypt" (Ex. 13:17). But once the spirit of impurity is removed from the earth, the march toward holiness will become clear and whole, without hesitation or interruption. It will then be possible to proceed at leisure. There will be nothing to fear, nothing to hide from, no need to flee.

Until this point, the author of the *Tanya* has discussed the joy that results when the divine soul is liberated from the dungeon of exile. Now he will discuss a deeper reason for this joy that follows in the wake of bitterness.

8 Adar וְלִהְיוֹת בְּחִינַת תְּשׁוּבָה זוֹ בְּיֶתֶר שְׂאֵת וְיֶתֶר עָז מֵעוּמְקָא דְלִבָּא, וְגַם שִׂמְחַת הַנֶּפֶשׁ תִּהְיֶה בְּתוֹסֶפֶת אוֹרָה וְשִׂמְחָה,

One will be able to add a greater magnitude of power to this repentance from the depths of the heart, as well as adding a greater measure of light and joy to the joy of his soul

There is a direct link between repentance, the restoration of the soul to its source, and joy. The deeper one's atonement as it arises from humility and bitterness, the greater will be one's joy.[18]

18. This level of repentance refers not only to the restoration of the divine soul but also to that of the animal soul and body. Even they are elevated and literally absorbed within the essence of God's supernal will by means of Torah study and the fulfillment of mitzvot (see chaps. 23, 35, 37).

כַּאֲשֶׁר יָשִׁיב אֶל לִבּוֹ דַּעַת וּתְבוּנָה לְנַחֲמוֹ מֵעִצְּבוֹנוֹ וִיגוֹנוֹ, לֵאמֹר כַּנִּזְכָּר לְעֵיל, הֵן אֱמֶת כוּ'.

by reflecting in his heart with **knowledge and understanding, in order to console it from its sadness and sorrow, saying that which was mentioned above** (chap. 29): **"It is true** that I am full of imperfections, **and so on,**

He will, as it were, speak to himself in order to arrive at the awakening described above, that "all of my imperfections, blemishes, and flaws, which I sensed amid the bitterness of my soul, truly exist. My self-introspection, assuming it to be accurate, has condemned me."

The greater a person is, the more clearly he can see his faults. The higher his spiritual level and the longer he has been there, the more clearly he can see the superficiality of his good deeds, their lack of inner drive. Although he may appear to others, and even to himself, as an important person, as someone both humble and holy, he is still lowly and deficient.[19]

אַךְ אֲנִי לֹא עָשִׂיתִי אֶת עַצְמִי!

but I did not create myself!

Essentially, when a person is weighed in the balance and found wanting, that is not because he has used his free will wrongly but because of the basic, inborn structure of the soul. One enters the world with a soul and body that already have desires and a certain way of viewing the world. One perceives the world with his senses and interprets it with tacit assumptions. Whether through nature or nurture, a person's first and direct understanding of the world is physical, and this understanding does not have to be learned but is innate.

To arrive at a sense of the spiritual, on the other hand, one must always push beyond one's boundaries. Because the self has a direct and intimate relationship with the body and its senses, a piece of bread always seems more real than the Divine. The ability to relate to a nonphysical reality requires effort and a dramatic change in one's

19. See *Iggeret HaKodesh*, epistle 2: "The greater one's closeness to God … the more humble that person ought to be."

perception of the world. It is not because he is wicked that a person first finds it easy to sin. Generally speaking, it is because sins take a tangible form, while the realization of holiness requires education, refinement, and elevation. ☞

וְלָמָּה עָשָׂה ה׳ כָּזֹאת, לְהוֹרִיד חֵלֶק מֵאוֹרוֹ יִתְבָּרֵךְ הַמְמַלֵּא וְסוֹבֵב כָּל עָלְמִין, וְכוּלָּא קַמֵּיהּ כְּלָא חָשִׁיב, וְהִלְבִּישׁוֹ בְּמַשְׁכָּא דְחִוְיָא וְטִפָּה סְרוּחָה?

Yet why did God do such a thing and cause the divine soul, **a portion of His light, which permeates and encompasses all worlds and in relation to which everything is considered as nothingness, to descend and be clothed in the serpent's skin and a putrid drop** of semen?

The skin of the serpent is the depths of *kelippa* that was created as a result of Adam's sin. That *kelippa* is more intrinsic than the body because it is the garment of the innermost feelings of the animal soul. In addition, man is created from a drop of semen, which is the distillation of the human body, a piece of flesh no different from the flesh of any other creature.

Why did God take the divine soul, which is even higher than the angels, and clothe it in such a lowly garment?

אֵין זֶה כִּי אִם יְרִידָה זוֹ הִיא צוֹרֶךְ עֲלִיָּה -

It must be that this descent is necessary only for a subsequent **ascent,**

This descent should not be seen as punishment but as a means of accomplishing a goal: to ultimately cause the animal soul and all its garments to ascend to God.

THE REALITY OF THIS WORLD

☞ Rabbi Levi Yitzḥak of Berditchev would say, "Master of the world, You did not make the world correctly. You placed temptations before our eyes and hid the concept of Gehenna in the text of *Reshit Ḥokhma*. Had You done the opposite, so that people would see Gehenna and read about temptations in *Reshit Ḥokhma*, I swear to you by my beard that no Jew would ever sin." This is essentially what the author of the *Tanya* is expressing here: "I did not create myself!" (see *Torat Menaḥem*, vol. 2, p. 20, and vol. 19, p. 295).

לְהַעֲלוֹת לַה׳ כָּל נֶפֶשׁ הַחִיּוּנִית הַבַּהֲמִית שֶׁמִּקְּלִיפַּת נוֹגַהּ, וְכָל לְבוּשֶׁיהָ, הֵן בְּחִינַת מַחֲשָׁבָה דִּבּוּר וּמַעֲשֶׂה שֶׁלָּהּ,

to cause the entire vital, animal soul, which stems from *kelippat noga*, along with **all its garments, which are its thoughts, speech, and actions, to ascend to God**

Just as a drill pierces the earth and exposes its hidden treasures so they can be recovered, so the divine soul penetrates the animal soul and everything connected with it, its thoughts, speech, and deeds, in order to uncover the holiness within and raise it up.

עַל יְדֵי הִתְלַבְּשׁוּתָן בְּמַעֲשֶׂה דִּבּוּר וּמַחְשֶׁבֶת הַתּוֹרָה

by being clothed in the actions, speech, and thoughts of the Torah."

A person cannot think, speak, or act without his body and animal soul. When he studies Torah and performs mitzvot, which require thoughts, speech, and actions, the animal soul participates. At that moment, willingly or not, it is garbed in holiness so that it too rises. As the divine soul gains its freedom and attains its personal exodus, it merits tranquility. The entire scope of the self, including the body, animal soul, and garments of the animal soul, joins that divine illumination.

God has placed the divine soul in this world to be enveloped and immersed in physicality. In this sense, our divine soul is God's investment, just as a farmer sows seeds in order to harvest a bountiful crop or a businessman invests in merchandise in order to make a profit.[20]

The purpose of the ascent that follows the descent is not to return to the previous status, which would bring the divine soul back to its original divine source and leave the body and animal soul behind on earth.[21] Instead, the ascent is meant to raise the animal soul together with the divine soul.

The process of return is not one of separation. Separation is essentially death, wherein the soul leaves the body and proceeds to its next destination. The true, inherent liberation of the soul does not depend on cutting itself off from the body but on its unification with God. This does not require leaving the body. In a sense, the divine soul must act

20. See *Torah Or* 26c.

21. See Eccles. 3:21.

through the body, the vehicle that performs mitzvot and provides the context of human, physical life in which the Torah and mitzvot can exist. The divine soul itself cannot function unless it acts together with the animal soul within the body. When the divine soul returns to God, it must take the body and the animal soul along with it.

When we harness an animal to a plow, it walks forward for its own purposes. But as the animal seeks food or a place of rest, it operates the tool. In another analogy, when we build a dam to generate electricity, our goal is not to hold back the water and then allow it to flow as it did before. We want it to cascade vigorously and, as it moves, also activate the turbine.

Similarly, the divine soul yearns for connection and a relationship with the Divine. But God binds the divine soul to the body and the animal soul in a manner that it cannot escape without them. As long as the divine soul remains within the body, it cannot express itself on its own, since all it does must pass through the body and the animal soul. The divine soul cannot even think without the intermediary of the body, since thought is a function of the physical brain. If the divine soul wishes to cling to God in thought, it must do so through the brain. The brain must then change its own nature in order to think of holy things and not other matters. The same is true of speech and deed.

This difficult process, which involves effort and struggle, makes it possible for the divine soul to free itself and for the animal soul to rise. Then the divine soul itself attains an even higher level than it had originally occupied.

[וּכְמוֹ שֶׁיִּתְבָּאֵר לְקַמָּן עִנְיַן הָעֲלָאָה זוֹ בַּאֲרִיכוּת, אֵיךְ שֶׁהִיא תַּכְלִית בְּרִיאַת הָעוֹלָם].

(**The concept of this ascent** and **how it is the purpose of the world's creation will be explained further below at length** [chaps. 35–37].)

The elevation of the animal soul together with its garments is not only a nice thing, something positive and beneficial. It actually fulfills the first and overarching goal of the world's creation.

The world was not created for the sake of the divine soul but for the animal soul and the body to be elevated through the divine soul. The makeup of the world is one of raw material, of *kelippa*, within which the divine force operates. The purpose of this construct is so that this divine force acts to such an extent that the light contained therein is uncovered and elevated to the realm of holiness. This, then, is the purpose of existence: a descent for the sake of a subsequent ascent.

וְאִם כֵּן אֵיפוֹא, זֹאת אֶעֱשֶׂה וְזֹאת תִּהְיֶה כָּל מְגַמָּתִי כָּל יְמֵי חֶלְדִּי, לְכֹל בָּהֶן חַיֵּי רוּחִי וְנַפְשִׁי, וּכְמוֹ שֶׁכָּתוּב: "אֵלֶיךָ ה' נַפְשִׁי אֶשָּׂא" (תהלים כה, א),

"If that is the case, then this I will do, and that will be my entire focus for the duration of my existence: to infuse them, my Torah study and mitzva performance, **with the life of my spirit and soul, as it is written, 'To You, Lord, I lift my soul'** (Ps. 25:1).

As mentioned above, a person must tell himself, "I did not create myself!" God joined the divine soul, literally a portion of God that is loftier than everything else, with the animal soul and the physical body. After experiencing the bitterness of the soul, after the self-hatred, one must recognize that he was not the one who joined these elements together. One is not held responsible for this pairing. Moreover, this was God's specific intent. At times, we do the same. Whether for educational or other purposes, we pair two individuals of opposing natures, one very good and the other very bad, in the hope that the better half of the pair will influence its partner for the good. The same applies to pairing two horses of different strengths. The danger always exists that the opposite will occur, that the inferior element will corrupt the better. Still, the good part is not supposed to isolate itself from the other. Rather, the role of the good is to strengthen the bond so that with time the worse half will identify with its better half.

In that sense, the essential purpose of creation is the existence of the body and the animal soul, not the existence of the divine soul. Even though the great effort that we must invest in them is neither pleasant nor easy, it is our mission to do so. It is the reason we exist and the world as a whole exists.[22]

---

22. The verse from Psalms that the author of the *Tanya* quotes – "To You, Lord, I lift my soul" – is quite apropos, since the chapter from which it is taken is recited in the Arizal's version of *nefilat apayim*, the penitent's prayer. This prayer alludes to

דְּהַיְינוּ לְקַשֵּׁר מַחֲשַׁבְתִּי וְדִבּוּרִי בְּמַחֲשַׁבְתּוֹ וְדִבּוּרוֹ יִתְבָּרֵךְ, וְהֵן הֵן גּוּפֵי הֲלָכוֹת הָעֲרוּכוֹת לְפָנֵינוּ וְכֵן מַעֲשֶׂה בְּמַעֲשֵׂה הַמִּצְוֹת,

This means binding my thoughts and speech to God's thoughts and speech, which constitute the very corpus of *halakhot* that have been set forth before us. Similarly, I wish to bind my **actions with** God's **actions by** fulfilling **the mitzvot."**

The Torah and the mitzvot constitute God's will and wisdom. When a person is engaged in fulfilling them, he unites with God since he is essentially thinking His thoughts and speaking His words. Since this unity encompasses thoughts, speech, and deeds, which are expressed by the body and the animal soul, it incorporates a person's animal soul. The animal soul is the instrument through which we act. It is through the animal soul that holy thoughts are contemplated, holy words are spoken, and holy deeds are performed.

שֶׁלָּכֵן נִקְרֵאת הַתּוֹרָה "מְשִׁיבַת נָפֶשׁ" (תהלים יט, ח). **פֵּירוּשׁ, לִמְקוֹרָהּ וְשָׁרְשָׁהּ.**

For this reason, the Torah is described as "restoring the soul" (Ps. 19:8), **meaning,** it restores the soul **to its root and source.**

The usual explanation of the phrase "restoring the soul" is that the Torah revives the soul, giving a person the strength to live. But it can also be understood as saying that the Torah returns the soul "to its father's house as in its youth." The Torah is a path on which the soul returns to its source.

וְעַל זֶה נֶאֱמַר: "פִּקּוּדֵי ה' יְשָׁרִים מְשַׂמְּחֵי לֵב" (שם פסוק ט).

With regard to this, it states, "The precepts of the Lord are upright, gladdening the heart" (Ps. 19:9).

The heart rejoices in the mitzvot because they enable the soul to return to its source and experience joy. The "precepts of the Lord gladden the heart" because they are the path on which the soul returns to unite with

---

the soul's descent into the lower worlds in order to elevate the sparks of holiness trapped therein and in the animal soul. See also *Likkutei Torah*, Deut. 33c.

its Maker. And when this occurs, the soul justifies its own existence and that of all reality.

This chapter discussed the question of how to emerge from the sadness and bitterness of the soul, a state in which one knowingly placed himself. As explained in the previous chapter, a person does this in order to break the egotistical sense of smugness that, particularly for the *beinoni*, leads to a dull, unfeeling heart and at times to a dull, unthinking mind. A person achieves this by conducting an honest self-assessment, the results of which may be disturbing and upsetting. He realizes that even if he has been engaged in Torah study and mitzvot all his life, he is no better than others and in some ways worse.

However, although this bitterness and sadness may be justified, he must ultimately move beyond them since a person needs to serve God joyfully. But he cannot emerge from his state of sadness by denying reality. Once he has judged himself honestly and found himself wanting and flawed, he cannot avoid the conclusions. He must find joy despite his reflection and even as a result of it.

In this chapter, the author of the *Tanya* tells us that such a person can rejoice in his divine soul as it returns to its source and as he sets aside his concerns for his animal soul. Just as during the exodus "the people had fled," his holy soul is liberated as it flees his self – his body and animal soul – which remains low, contemptible, and abhorrent.

Yet a solution exists on a larger scale, one that involves the liberation of all of existence and fulfills the goal of creation, thus justifying the world's existence. This solution involves shifting one's awareness and way of thinking so that one's sense of self is no longer of prime importance, not only with regard to selfish motives but even to supposedly holy intentions. The person moves from a world in which his sense of self and attainments are central to an objective world where the center is occupied by God.

In light of this, the question of whether or not a person's self, with all its needs and problems, is deserving is of no account. All that matters is one's service of God and the reality on which one has to work. Instead of examining himself, asking, "Have I progressed? Have I attained purity?" – questions that can only aggravate his bitterness

– he focuses on the world outside himself, on the concerns of God. Rather than ask who is achieving, he asks what has been achieved. In that broader context, all the worlds come ever closer to fulfilling their ultimate purpose.

From this perspective, this expanded outlook, a person's deeds are of momentous account, because they literally affect reality, and that is deserving of joy.

Chapter 32

THE PRECEDING CHAPTER DISCUSSED THE PATH THAT brings a person from a state of sadness and bitterness to a state of joy that results from that sadness. This transformation occurs when a person breaks free of his ego's grasp and experiences the delight of the divine soul alone, putting aside the concerns of his animal soul. The path that leads from sadness to joy is synonymous with that on which one moves from living within his body to living within his holy soul. This is achieved when one relocates the center of his focus, of his whole existence, from his physical, individual sense of self to a loftier, universal sense of self, one that constitutes the source of the divine soul, which is literally a portion of God on high.

The theme of this chapter presents other implications of this relocation, how it takes a person beyond his own self and connects him to all of Israel and to the God of Israel, a bond that is known as *ahavat Yisrael,* love of a fellow Jew.

Although the theme of loving a fellow Jew is a derivative of the subject matter treated in the preceding chapters, its placement here is chiefly tangential, rather than serving as a segue to the chapters that follow. In fact, this chapter is entirely missing from the manuscript editions of the *Tanya* and was added only subsequently in the printed editions. The Lubavitcher Rebbe, Rabbi Menaḥem Mendel Schneerson, posits a reason for its later insertion: "'It is well known that loving one's fellow Jew is one of the core tenets of Hasidism.'[1]

1. See *Likkutei Dibburim* by the sixth Lubavitcher Rebbe, Rabbi Yosef Yitzḥak

Notice how the chapter of the *Tanya*, the Written Law of Chabad Hasidism, that speaks of *ahavat Yisrael* is chapter 32 [in Hebrew, *lamed-bet*, which spells *lev*, the Hebrew word for heart], for it constitutes the very heart of Hasidism."[2]

9 Adar
23 Adar I (leap year)

וְהִנֵּה עַל יְדֵי קִיּוּם הַדְּבָרִים הַנִּזְכָּרִים לְעֵיל לִהְיוֹת גּוּפוֹ נִבְזֶה וְנִמְאָס בְּעֵינָיו,

Implementing the aforementioned ideas (in chaps. 29–31), **by viewing one's body as vile and despicable**

In the previous chapters, the author of the *Tanya* recommended that one conduct a self-assessment of his own deeds and spiritual level. If the introspection is honest, he will become aware that not only is he no better than others, but he is beneath them on the spiritual ladder. This self-assessment is efficacious in arousing the good inclination against the evil inclination, so that one comes to despise his body, along with his sense of self, which comprises his animal soul.

רַק שִׂמְחָתוֹ תִּהְיֶה שִׂמְחַת הַנֶּפֶשׁ לְבַדָּהּ,

and **rejoicing only in the joy of the** divine **soul alone**

One's animal, physical soul is not yet worthy of giving one joy. This is not a joy that is individual, that stems from a fulfillment of the body's needs, but rather a rejoicing in being part of a whole, a portion of God on high. This joy is not a joy of the self but rather a rejoicing in the achievement of the goal, in one's accomplishments and what remains to be done, and in the divine will that continuously desires one's service. When a person attains this joy, he can overcome all suffering, because in the bigger picture, all considerations of the individual sense of self are of secondary importance.

הֲרֵי זוֹ דֶּרֶךְ יְשָׁרָה וְקַלָּה לָבֹא לִידֵי קִיּוּם מִצְוַת "וְאָהַבְתָּ לְרֵעֲךָ כָּמוֹךָ" (ויקרא יט, יח)

is a direct and easy path leading to the fulfillment of the commandment "You shall love your neighbor as yourself" (Lev. 19:18),

---

Schneerson, 2 Adar 5705.

2. See *Likkutei Siḥot*, vol. 9, p. 156.

This mitzva is not only important on its own terms, but it also gives us a means of assessing our spiritual progress. A person who cannot love his fellow as himself is equally unable to love God.[3]

לְכָל נֶפֶשׁ מִיִּשְׂרָאֵל לְמִגָּדוֹל וְעַד קָטָן.

which includes **every Jew, from great to small.**

It is easy to love people with sterling qualities or to whom we owe a debt of gratitude. But we are commanded to love every individual, great or small, good or wicked, worthy or reprehensible.

24 Adar I (leap year)

כִּי מֵאַחַר שֶׁגּוּפוֹ נִמְאָס וּמְתוֹעָב אֶצְלוֹ, וְהַנֶּפֶשׁ וְהָרוּחַ מִי יוֹדֵעַ גְּדוּלָּתָן וּמַעֲלָתָן בְּשָׁרְשָׁן וּמְקוֹרָן בֵּאלֹקִים חַיִּים,

For one's body is already viewed as despicable and abominable, and as for the soul and spirit, who can know their greatness and quality at their source and root, the living God?

When a person identifies with his physical self, when he dwells on his desires, yearnings, and material achievements, he is likely to compare himself to others and judge himself against them. He may view himself as superior, as having superlative virtues. But when a person views his body, and in a sense himself, as deserving of only scorn and contempt, he can no longer see himself as anyone else's superior. Even in his successes he will see only imperfection, how much he has fallen short in realizing his true potential commensurate with his talents and capabilities. When he disregards his body, and, consequently, the bodies of others, he comes to value the soul, the spirit infused in him from God. In that realm, assessments and comparisons are irrelevant. Only achievements can be measured, but it is impossible to assess a person by his soul. ☞

BREAKING FREE OF THE BODY

☞ What divides people? What causes one person to look down on another? What accounts for the all too familiar phenomenon that people cannot tolerate one

3. See discourse of the Lubavitcher Rebbe, Rabbi Menaḥem Mendel Schneerson, delivered on 18 Elul 5710. This idea is not unique to Chabad Hasidism; see, e.g., *Ohev Yisrael, Parashat Ḥayei Sara,* s.v. "*veYitzḥak*"; *Tiferet Shlomo, Parashat Tetzaveh.*

בְּשֶׁגַּם שֶׁכּוּלָּן מַתְאִימוֹת וְאָב אֶחָד לְכוּלָּנָה.

Moreover, all Jewish souls are **alike and all have one father.**

It is not just that we do not have the means of evaluating and ranking souls. Rather, all souls are equal, connected to each other as equal branches stemming from one root.

וְלָכֵן נִקְרְאוּ כָּל יִשְׂרָאֵל אַחִים מַמָּשׁ, מִצַּד שׁוֹרֶשׁ נַפְשָׁם בַּה' אֶחָד,

Consequently, all Jews are literally called brothers on account of their collective **soul's** common **root in the one God.**

another? The author of the *Tanya* explains here that people generally evaluate themselves and others in terms of their physical being.

When we speak of individual differences in the physical realm, we do not mean only those distinctive qualities that we can see. There is an entire spectrum of traits that stem from the body yet are intangible, power, influence, and honor among them. Just as one person's body is separate from the bodies of others, so one's character and personality are distinct from those of others. We may be envious, we may quarrel, and we may even hate because a particular drive or attribute is found in us and not in another. It is difficult to love others when one feels differently and even in opposition to them.

To move beyond these obstacles, a person must erase those qualities from his image of himself and others, beginning with himself. As hasidim say, one cannot begin by nullifying someone else's ego.

Such a reevaluation happens in every area and stage in life. Children make friends based on their particular preference, on a certain set of criteria. As they grow older, those criteria become less important. They begin to evaluate others according to their own set of values, not according to that of others. There are always particulars that one does not take into consideration, since one does not consider them to be important. Such considerations are affected by differences in culture, age, gender, and personality. To one person the shape of someone's nose may be a primary focus, while to someone else it is completely irrelevant.

One can construct a set of values in which all physical attributes are as unimportant as the size of a person's nose. In such a framework, it is possible to relate to others solely in terms of their souls, and those traits that divide us, such as jealousy and hatred, become completely inconsequential. This is not because people are truly equal but because the differences between them are of no account.

The more we judge others based on the body and its characteristics, the more unequal society becomes. When we believe that one person is somehow superior to another, true equality is impossible. Under these circumstances, there cannot be real love between one person and another.

Hasidic society was, and in many ways still is, a very egalitarian society. Hasidim have considered distinctions such as

Like the children of one father, like branches that come from one root, so all the souls of Israel are the outgrowth of one inclusive soul, the "congregation of Israel."

The collective soul of Israel is to be found deep within each individual, where there exists only one shared soul, a soul that is not intrinsically divided but only seems that way, just as a ray refracted by polished glass splits into thousands of flickering lights and varied hues. At their source, that one ray of light, there is no difference between great and small, between one color and another.

Elsewhere, the bond between one Jew and another is likened to the connection between the limbs of a single body. We think of the body as a single organic entity rather than a collection of its parts. We would not consider six hundred chairs as an organic entity, but the 613 limbs of the body and the 613 mitzvot belong to the same infrastructure as one single organism.[4]

youth and old age, poverty and wealth, and scholarship and illiteracy to be of relatively little importance. It is not that one ignores the facts. It is a matter of relationship: How important are these elements in creating relations between people?

Among the Kotzker hasidim, the spirit of equality reached an extreme. When Rabbi Leibele Eiger, a grandson of Rabbi Akiva Eiger, one of the great masters of Torah, became a hasid, his family sent someone to Kotzk to determine the extent of the "calamity."

When the traveler arrived in Kotzk, he asked for Rabbi Leibele by his usual titles, but no one had heard of such a person. At last the traveler realized that in Kotzk he was referred to no differently than the simplest of Jews. When he at last found Rabbi Leibele, he saw him dressed as a simple Jew and sitting with the hasidim as an equal among equals. At that moment, an ordinary Jew dressed in ragged clothing approached, and the hasidim rose to meet him.

The visitor asked, "Is that a great Torah scholar?"

The hasidim replied, "No, he can barely learn a chapter of Mishna."

"Is he from a great family, then?"

"He is the son of a laborer."

"Is he wealthy, at least?"

"You yourself can see how he is dressed."

"So why do you honor him?"

"Because he is humble."

When the traveler returned and told this story, Rabbi Leibele's relatives laughed and said, "If he is not learned, from a great family, or wealthy, why shouldn't he be humble?"

But when that retort made its way back to Kotzk, someone commented, "No, if he is not learned, wealthy, or from a great family, then the fact that he is humble is truly remarkable."

4. See *Derekh Mitzvotekha, Mitzvat Ahavat Yisrael,* p. 28; *Likkutei Torah,* Deut. 47b.

Such an organism must fulfill three conditions. First, the combination of parts is not arbitrary. They cannot be increased or reduced at random. Second, the parts relate to each other and to the total being. Finally, the function of each part serves the entire body.

Each member of the Jewish people is meaningful and vital to every other member. One can never dissociate himself from another, from their needs, troubles, or illnesses, just as the head cannot say, "What happens to the finger is none of my concern."

This perspective leads to a love of a fellow Jew that is not necessarily emotional but essentially one of caring. No Jew can divorce himself from another because he knows that someone else's problem is essentially his own. If one were to feel detached from one of his limbs or a part of his personality, he would be considered severely ill, suffering from schizophrenia or something worse.

This concept goes beyond the idea of mutual responsibility. As a single organism, each part can be found in every other part, so that whatever occurs to one affects the others. This applies not only to the saintly and the righteous. When a Jew suffers, even when a guilty Jew is condemned to death, the Divine Presence cries out, "I am distressed about My head. I am distressed about My arm" (Mishna *Sanhedrin* 6:5). Because the Divine Presence is synonymous with the congregation of Israel, with the totality of all Jewish souls, the pain of each member is the pain of the Divine Presence. ☞ ☞

It is only their bodies that are distinct from one another.

רַק שֶׁהַגּוּפִים מְחוּלָּקִים.

ONE COMPLETE STRUCTURE

☞ The Jewish people as a whole is considered one complete structure. But it is not a structure made up of a random collection of points but rather a combination of elements that takes shape and, if incomplete, grows deformed. If the third story of a house collapses, it would become a two-story house. But if one's head were removed, one would no longer be a person. When we speak of an organic entity such as the congregation of Israel, what is partial is flawed to the point that it cannot maintain its identity.

A parable may help us understand this idea. Someone injured in a traffic accident was visited at the hospital by his relatives. When they entered the room, they saw that he had lost his eyes. Lifting the sheet, they saw that he had lost his hands, and lifting it still further, they saw that he had lost his feet. But the doctor entered and reassured them, "You have nothing to worry about. His heart is fine!"

When one limb and then another is removed from the Jewish collective, the mind and heart may still be functioning, but the totality has been grievously affected. Some Jews correspond to the heart or mind. As long as they remain alive, then theoretically the Jewish people can continue to exist. But if the Jewish collective is missing hands, feet, or eyes, the structure is no longer the same. Jews are missing from the whole, the problem is not just demographic but qualitative.

There are hundreds of thousands of Jews across the world without whom the principal centers of Jewish life can continue to exist, but only like the man who lies in the hospital without eyes, hands, or feet. If a limb is so diseased that it is liable to cause one's death, it must be amputated, but the consequence will be far from trivial. Such an operation is not like taking out the trash. One is amputating a limb from a body. Though the body may have been salvaged, it is now a body without that limb.

The Ba'al Shem Tov waged a fierce battle against the Frankists throughout his life. Yet when they had converted to Catholicism, he grew deeply upset and exclaimed that "the Divine Presence cries out for their sake." He explained that as long as a limb is connected to the body, even if it has shriveled, it may still recover. But once the limb is severed, it is gone forever, and every Jew is a limb of the Divine Presence.

This analogy of the complete, organic structure of the Jewish people has a more far-reaching implication as well: Not only is the well-being of each limb dependent on the soundness of the others, but each is also intimately interrelated with every other. They are deeply intertwined, each existing within the other, appearing in it, influencing it, and being influenced by it.

A seasoned dentist once said that a person's tooth bears an imprint of all the experiences he has undergone, and when a tooth is pulled and analyzed, one can tell that he broke his hand at a certain age, the various diseases from which he has suffered, and so forth. An impression of all of these is left on each tooth. Similarly, whatever happens to any Jew, physically or spiritually, affects every other Jew wherever he may be, even if that effect is not consciously perceived.

JEWISH HEADS

☞ A Jewish leader is called "the head of Israel" (see, e.g., I Sam. 15:17) since he is like the head, which cannot say, "It makes no difference to me if a foot has been amputated." There is clearly something wrong with a head that is unaware that a leg was amputated from the very body they share.

If a corpse is found in a field and the identity of its murderer is unknown, the elders of the nearest town gather and declare, "Our hands did not shed this blood" (Deut. 21:7). Nowadays, were a corpse found without knowing the identity of its murderer, the police would detain all known convicts in the area until they provide a valid alibi. Why, then, does God place the onus specifically on the venerable sages of the nearest town?

Our Sages explain that we do not truly believe that these elders committed murder. But still they make this declaration, since as the heads of Israel, they bear some responsibility. Thus they must confess that "our hands did not shed this blood" (Mishna *Sota* 9:6).

Differences between people, whether in status, physical location, and so forth, result from their physical nature. Bodies cannot become unified with each other. They can use each other to gain benefit, but they cannot become one entity. On the other hand, in its inner being, a person's soul is one with all other Jewish souls. Distance and division arise only when the soul expresses itself through the thoughts and deeds of the body.

וְלָכֵן הָעוֹשִׂים גּוּפָם עִיקָּר וְנַפְשָׁם טְפֵלָה, אִי אֶפְשָׁר לִהְיוֹת אַהֲבָה וְאַחֲוָה אֲמִיתִּית בֵּינֵיהֶם, אֶלָּא הַתְּלוּיָה בְּדָבָר לְבַדָּהּ.

Therefore, those who consider their bodies primary and their souls secondary cannot experience true love and brotherhood among themselves but only love **that is dependent on something.**

The inner meaning and significance of the mitzva of loving one's fellow Jew can be seen as an indicator of the soul's progress. A true love of others is impossible as long as one views the body as one's essential being. The body is separate, gaining benefit for itself and by itself. It has no sympathy for others. Only its own gain rates its attention. This kind of love is a "love that is dependent on something" (Mishna *Avot* 5:16), where one loves others as long as they serve one's interests, whether those interests are simple and coarse or more refined.

That love is no more than an appreciation of the usefulness that someone else may provide. But true love, one not dependent on anything, exists only when one identifies with the soul as one's essence and center of being, so that a loving relationship between souls exists without the divisive self-centeredness of the physical self.

25 Adar I (leap year)

וְזֶהוּ שֶׁאָמַר הִלֵּל הַזָּקֵן עַל קִיּוּם מִצְוָה זוֹ: "זֶהוּ כָּל הַתּוֹרָה כּוּלָּהּ, וְאִידָךְ פֵּירוּשָׁא הוּא" כו׳ (שבת לא, א).

This is the meaning of Hillel the Elder's statement with regard to the fulfillment of this mitzva, "That is the entire Torah, and the rest is its interpretation..." (*Shabbat* 31a),

When a non-Jew proposed to convert to Judaism on the condition that Hillel teach him the entire Torah as he stood on one foot, Hillel told him, "That which is hateful to you do not do to another. That is the entire Torah." Hillel's expression "That which is hateful to you do not do to others," appears in the Aramaic translation of the verse "You shall love your neighbor as yourself" (Lev. 19:18).[5] This mitzva, says Hillel, is the foundation of the Torah. In that sense, everything else is mere commentary.[6] ☞

כִּי יְסוֹד וְשׁוֹרֶשׁ כָּל הַתּוֹרָה הוּא לְהַגְבִּיהַּ וּלְהַעֲלוֹת הַנֶּפֶשׁ עַל הַגּוּף, מַעְלָה מַעְלָה, עַד עִיקָּרָא וְשָׁרְשָׁא דְּכָל עָלְמִין,

for the foundation and root of the entire Torah is to exalt and elevate the soul above and beyond the body to the source and root of all the worlds

The aim of the Torah is to enable the soul to overcome the body's impediments and free itself from having to depend on the body's perceptions and desires, so that it may rise and bond with its source.[7]

THE FOUNDATION OF THE ENTIRE TORAH

☞ Why is it that the mitzva of loving one's fellow Jews is regarded as the bedrock of the entire Torah? One could claim that the other commandments that deal with human relations are no more than details of this mitzva. But that does not take into account the many mitzvot between man and God.

Rashi answers the question with a reference to the verse "Do not forsake your friend or your father's friend" (Prov. 27:10), interpreting "your friend and your father's friend" as a reference to God.[6] In light of this, Hillel's statement can also be read, "That which is hateful to you do not do to God."

But this explanation is unsatisfactory, since Hillel's principle implies mutuality, and there can be no mutual relationship between man and God, of whom the verse states, "If you are righteous, what have you given Him?" (Job 35:7). Therefore, at the very outset of this discussion, the author of the *Tanya* describes the mitzva of loving one's fellow Jew as transcending the purely interpersonal social sphere and involving one soul as an expression of divinity interacting with another soul that is an expression of divinity.

---

5. See *Targum Yonatan* there. This is obviously not a direct translation of the verse but instead expresses the flip side of fulfilling the positive commandment to love a fellow Jew: refraining from doing something unsavory to another. See Maharsha, *Shabbat* 31a; *Derekh Mitzvotekha, Mitzvat Ahavat Yisrael*, p. 29.

6. *Shabbat* 31a.

7. It is for this reason that prior to the morning prayers, it is customary to accept upon oneself the mitzva of loving a fellow Jew, since that is the very mitzva whereby one's soul is elevated during prayers (Rabbi Shmuel Gronem Esterman).

וְגַם לְהַמְשִׁיךְ אוֹר אֵין סוֹף בָּרוּךְ הוּא בִּכְנֶסֶת יִשְׂרָאֵל, כְּמוֹ שֶׁיִּתְבָּאֵר לְקַמָּן.

and also to draw down the light of *Ein Sof*, blessed be He, into the congregation of Israel, as will be explained below (chap. 41).

One goal of the Torah is to raise a person heavenward, to the source of all souls and all worlds. The second is to draw down the divine life-giving vitality from *Ein Sof*, who is entirely beyond worlds, to the point that is the source of the worlds and of all Jewish souls known as *Kenesset Yisrael*, the congregation of Israel, and thenceforth to the worlds themselves.

דְּהַיְינוּ בִּמְקוֹר נִשְׁמוֹת כָּל יִשְׂרָאֵל, לְמֶהֱוֵי אֶחָד בְּאֶחָד דַּוְקָא וְלֹא כְּשֶׁיֵּשׁ פֵּירוּד חַס וְשָׁלוֹם בַּנְּשָׁמוֹת,

This refers to drawing down the light **into the root of the souls of every Jew so that the One,** God, **may be united with one, but** this is **not** possible **when there is disunity among the souls, God forbid,**

As noted above, the congregation of Israel is the collective soul of the Jewish people, which encompasses all the individual souls that emerge from it like branches sprouting from the root. At their source, the souls of Israel are united as one. When they rise to that point, when they are united with each other, the one God unites with them.

This is the goal of existence, of the creation of the worlds, to arrive at the place where "the One is united with one," where the one God unites with the unified congregation of Israel at their root. But when there is division among souls, the congregation of Israel is flawed, and there can be no unity with the Divine.

דְּקֻדְשָׁא בְּרִיךְ הוּא לָא שַׁרְיָא בַּאֲתַר פְּגִים.

for the Holy One, blessed be He, does not dwell in a place that is blemished.

When the souls of Israel are divided, when there is a lack of coordination and connection among souls, then the congregation of Israel is an imperfect place. At that moment, God and His life-giving vitality cannot dwell among them.[8]

8. See *Zohar* 1:216b.

The flow from above must be preceded by an elevation from below. That elevation is an offering, whether an animal brought to the Temple or one's soul dedicated to the one God. The offering must be perfect and whole, as the verse states, "It shall be unblemished to be accepted" (Lev. 22:21). Nothing flawed can rise to God, whether a worm-infested log used for the altar pyre, spoiled wine for libations, or a blemished animal, or a person who is not completely connected to the other souls of Israel.

When we cry out, "Hear, Israel, the Lord is our God, the Lord is One," we are making three statements. The first, "Hear, Israel," is a call to gather together the people as one.[9] When a person says, "Hear, Israel," he is in effect stating, "I love each Jew. All of us constitute one unified people." The second statement, "The Lord is our God," proclaims that we accept the yoke of the kingdom of Heaven. The third statement, "The Lord is one," expresses the absolute oneness of God and resultant absence of any other entity in existence.

The second and third phrases imply self-sacrifice, raising an offering to God. They are preceded by "Hear, Israel" because without the unity of Israel, there is a flaw in Israel, and when the offering is blemished, it cannot rise to "the Lord our God, the Lord is One." For this reason, the Arizal instituted the custom of preceding one's prayers with the statement "I hereby accept upon myself the positive commandment of 'You shall love your neighbor as yourself.'"[10]

וּכְמוֹ שֶׁאוֹמְרִים: ״בָּרְכֵנוּ אָבִינוּ כּוּלָּנוּ כְּאֶחָד בְּאוֹר פָּנֶיךָ״, וּכְמוֹ שֶׁמְּבוֹאָר בְּמָקוֹם אַחֵר בַּאֲרִיכוּת.

The same applies to prayer, **as we recite** in the *Amida* prayer, **"Bless us, our Father, all of us as one, with the light of Your countenance," as explained elsewhere at length.**

The core of prayer, and in a sense any blessing, is "Blessed are You, the Lord." A blessing's function is to draw the Divine down to our reality. But since God does not cause His presence to rest in a flawed place, we ask that all the imperfections of all Jews, whether in health, wisdom, livelihood, or any other area, be rectified.[11] Moreover, it is only when

9. See, e.g., I Sam. 15:4.

10. See *Pri Etz Ḥayyim, Sha'ar Olam HaAsiya*, chap. 1.

11. It is for this reason that our Sages say that prophecy, which requires the

we are "all of us as one" that we can receive God's blessing. But when we are divided, so that each individual is alone, that blessing cannot come to fruition through us. The Jewish people must attain unity before the divine light can dwell on the congregation of Israel and thus on the world as a whole.

There are varied degrees to loving a fellow Jew. On one level, it is a testimony to a person's rank. The extent of a Jew's love of the Jewish people reflects how much he has freed himself of the body's dominion and so can relate to others through his soul alone. It is, after all, only through the soul that one can love all Jews.

On a deeper level, loving one's fellow Jew is the vessel through which the Divine Presence rests in the world. Thus the love of a fellow Jew is both an indicator of one's love of God and the result of one's love of God. It is both a sign that a person has attained a certain level and is also his reward.

10 Adar | 26 Adar I (leap year)

וּמַה שֶּׁאָמְרוּ בַּגְּמָרָא שֶׁמִּי שֶׁרוֹאֶה בַּחֲבֵירוֹ שֶׁחָטָא - מִצְוָה לִשְׂנֹאותוֹ (פסחים קיג, ב),

As for the talmudic statement that when one sees his fellow Jew commit a transgression, it is a mitzva to hate him (*Pesaḥim* 113b),

Other statements of our Sages apparently do not agree that the love of Israel is limitless and directed to every Jew. Regarding the verse "If you see the donkey of your enemy crouching under its burden…" (Ex. 23:5), the Talmud asks, is it possible to have an enemy? That would seemingly contradict the commandment "You shall not hate your brother in your heart" (Lev. 19:17).

The answer to this question is that when a person sees something sinful in another, it is a mitzva to hate him.

וְגַם לוֹמַר לְרַבּוֹ שֶׁיִּשְׂנָאֵהוּ,

and also that it is permitted **to tell** that person's **teacher to hate him,**

Not only is it a mitzva to hate that person, but he can also tell others who trust him to hate that person.

---

prophet to have perfected himself, comes only to those who are wise, mighty, and wealthy. See *Shabbat* 92a.

The author of the *Tanya* specifically chose the example of one's teacher because the *halakha* forbids a single witness to testify since testimony by one witness is merely gossip and thus prohibited.[12] But reporting to one's teacher who is also the other person's teacher is not gossip, since it is information that the teacher must have in order to educate that student properly.

At any rate, this seemingly grants permission, albeit limited, to hate another Jew.

הַיְינוּ בַּחֲבֵירוֹ בְּתוֹרָה וּמִצְוֹת, **that** applies only **to his fellow,** his equal, **in Torah** study **and** the fulfillment of **mitzvot.**

The author of the *Tanya* now offers a resolution to this apparent contradiction. He explains that the Talmud is teaching that one may hate only someone with a similar way of life and perspective on the world. One may not hate a person who is not one's equal in Torah and mitzvot. Even if such a person knows that something is prohibited, that knowledge affects him less than it does a more learned person. He easily makes excuses for himself, saying that he is not religious or that he is unaware of the obligation. In that case, it is prohibited to hate him.

One has permission only to hate someone who acts willfully, and one can assume that a person equal to oneself in Torah and mitzvot is acting willfully and understands as well as he does the significance of his deeds.

The halakhic definition of one who acts willfully is a subject for another discussion. But when it comes to a sinner who is not one's "fellow in Torah [study] and [the fulfillment of] mitzvot," one must assume that when he commits a sin, he does so in a different way and from a different perspective, and so one may not hate him. Only a person who is aware of the meaning of his deeds can commit an act of rebellion against God. Only such a sinner is considered to be casting his soul to the depths, to be contaminating himself with a greater measure of defilement than that inherent in an impure creeping animal. But if a person lacks such an awareness, his situation is altogether different.

---

12. *Pesaḥim* 113b.

In light of this, before one makes it his business to assess the sin of another, he needs to make certain they share the exact same points of view, education, and general approach to life. If these diverge in any way, not only is there no mitzva to hate the other person, but one is prohibited from doing so.

וּכְבָר קִיֵּים בּוֹ מִצְוַת "הוֹכֵחַ תּוֹכִיחַ אֶת עֲמִיתֶךָ" (שם) - "עִם שֶׁאִתְּךָ בְּתוֹרָה וּבְמִצְוֹת" (שבועות ל, א), וְאַף עַל פִּי כֵן לֹא שָׁב מֵחֶטְאוֹ, כְּמוֹ שֶׁכָּתוּב בְּסֵפֶר חֲרֵדִים (פרק לה).

Also, he has to have filled the commandment "You shall rebuke your neighbor" (Lev. 19:17), referring to "one who is **with you in** the observance of **Torah and in** the fulfillment of **mitzvot**" (*Shevuot* 30a), **and nevertheless he has not repented for his sin, as it is written in *Sefer Ĥaredim*** (chap. 35).

In addition, even if the sinner is one's equal in the fulfillment of the Torah and mitzvot, one should still not hate him, as the verse states, "You shall not hate your brother in your heart" (Lev. 19:17). This holds true unless one has fulfilled the injunction to rebuke him, contained in the continuation of that very verse.

The mitzva of rebuke does not pertain to every Jew. Our Sages infer this from the very makeup of the word *amitekha* in the verse, translated as "your neighbor." They understand it as a composite of the two words *im* and *itekha*, literally, "together with you," implying "one who is together with you in the observance of the Torah."

The term *amitekha*, "your neighbor," is not the same as *aḥikha*, "your brother," a term that appears frequently in the Torah. Whereas "your brother" refers to any Jew, "your neighbor" implies an extra measure of intimacy. It is someone who has the perspective and engages in the deeds characteristic of a fully observant Jew.

Since accepting rebuke is a delicate and complex matter, giving rebuke requires a great deal of tact. One can only chastise someone with whom one shares a relationship, a soulful connection that remains strong despite the criticism. This is so difficult an undertaking that our Sages state, "It would be very surprising were we to find anyone in this generation capable of accepting rebuke" (*Arakhin* 16b), with the sole exception of Rabbi Akiva. Only then, when one has already chastised this person who is classified as his friend and neighbor and who nevertheless did not repent, only then is it said that one is commanded to hate him.

אֲבָל מִי שֶׁאֵינוֹ חֲבֵירוֹ וְאֵינוֹ מְקוֹרָב אֶצְלוֹ,

But concerning one who is neither his friend nor one with whom he is on close terms, it is forbidden to hate him. 27 Adar I (leap year)

For one to rebuke another and hate him under certain conditions, the latter must be his friend and neighbor, one who is on close terms. If these conditions are not met, and his words of rebuke will not be received well, he has no moral right to hate and reject the other person.

הִנֵּה עַל זֶה אָמַר הִלֵּל הַזָּקֵן: "הֱוֵי מִתַּלְמִידָיו שֶׁל אַהֲרֹן, אוֹהֵב שָׁלוֹם וכו' אוֹהֵב אֶת הַבְּרִיּוֹת וּמְקָרְבָן לַתּוֹרָה" (אבות פרק א משנה יב). לוֹמַר שֶׁאַף הָרְחוֹקִים מִתּוֹרַת ה' וַעֲבוֹדָתוֹ, וְלָכֵן נִקְרָאִים בְּשֵׁם בְּרִיּוֹת בְּעָלְמָא,

It is with regard to this that Hillel the Elder said, "Be among the disciples of Aaron, loving peace and pursuing peace, **loving creatures and drawing them close to the Torah"** (Mishna *Avot* 1:12). **That is to say, even with regard to those who are distant from God's Torah and His service, and are therefore referred to simply as "creatures,"**

The author of the *Tanya* understands the Mishna's use of the word *beriyot*, creatures, as alluding to those who are distant from God. Hillel the Elder is thus stressing that one must love not only the righteous but even the "creatures." This is not to be interpreted in a derogatory sense but as a generic term used to describe even the lowest, most unworthy people, those possessing no notable qualities apart from their being created by God. ☞

MERE CREATURES

☞ The prophet Elijah was once asked why God created rodents and other crawling creatures. He replied that when God looks at His world and sees the evil of

צָרִיךְ לְמָשְׁכָן בְּחַבְלֵי עֲבוֹתוֹת אַהֲבָה, וְכוּלַי הַאי וְאוּלַי, יוּכַל לְקָרְבָן לַתּוֹרָה וַעֲבוֹדַת ה׳. וְהֵן לָא, לֹא הִפְסִיד שְׂכַר מִצְוַת אַהֲבַת רֵיעִים.

one must draw them toward God's Torah **with thick cords of love, and perhaps, by means of all this** love, **he will be able to bring them close to the Torah and God's service. Even if** he is **not** successful, **he does not lose the reward for the mitzva of loving one's fellow** Jew.

Hillel the Elder states that we must engage in two distinct actions: First we are to "love creatures" and afterward "bring them close to the Torah." The love of others is not just a means of bringing them close to the Torah. It is a goal in itself, with its own intrinsic importance.

If a person can come to a mutual love and understanding of others so that he brings them close to the Torah, he has fully performed the injunction "Be of the disciples of Aaron." But if one has not succeeded in drawing such people close to the Torah, he has performed perfectly the mitzva of loving a Jew, and that is sufficient.

The love of a Jew is by definition "a love that is not dependent on anything," not even on drawing him close to the Torah. One has to love others simply, without cause, because that is the Torah's directive. That love does not depend on the qualities of the recipient but on those of the giver. When a person has reached a level where he can see the soul, his love is no longer limited. The soul of a person whose abilities or deeds are lowly may at its core be fine and elevated. When one considers the source of the soul, one may well reverse one's initial, negative judgment of that person. Then he will be able to love those who are only "creatures," even if he fails to bring them close to the Torah.

Thus the mitzva to hate someone is extremely limited. There is certainly no carte blanche to hate people for failing to reach a certain

human beings and wishes to destroy them, He considers those rodents and says, "Fine, so there are some more critters and crawling creatures. Just as I maintain the actual rodents, I'll maintain these others as well" (*Seder Eliyahu Rabba* 1).

There are people whose only saving grace is that they are no different from the other lowly creatures that exist. Hillel the Elder tells us that even such people possess a spark of Godliness, though it may be deeply hidden, and so it is a mitzva to love them and bring them close to the Torah.

level or because they do not keep the Torah and mitzvot fully. At its core, then, this mitzva does not stand in contradiction to the mitzva of loving one's fellow Jews.

וְגַם הַמְקוֹרָבִים אֵלָיו, וְהוֹכִיחָם וְלֹא שָׁבוּ מֵעֲוֹנוֹתֵיהֶם, שֶׁמִּצְוָה לִשְׂנוֹאתָם - מִצְוָה לְאַהֲבָם גַּם כֵּן,

Even in those instances where one may hate, since they are **those who are close to him, and he rebuked them yet they did not repent for their sins, in which case it is a mitzva to hate them, it is a mitzva to love them as well.** 28 Adar I (leap year)

The mitzvot of love and hate are not mutually exclusive. Even when it is a mitzva to hate someone, one must love him at the same time.

וּשְׁתֵּיהֶן הֵן אֱמֶת:

Both feelings **are genuine:**

One is not pretending to love or hate. These feelings are genuine. In a sense, this approach is based on the premise that one cannot judge others completely and absolutely. Only God is the absolute judge of one's guilt or innocence, righteousness or wickedness. The earthly courts must at times determine the law and judge whether to impose a fine or imprisonment. But the court does no more than impose a form of punishment that Torah laws prescribe. The proof is that after a person accepts his punishment, he is again considered righteous, but we ourselves do not have the tools to measure who is actually righteous and who is wicked.

In view of this, in the special case that one's friend, someone to whom one is close emotionally and ideologically, is sinning and continues to sin, so that one is commanded to hate him, that is not a confirmation that he is wicked. That is not up to us to decide. When this is one's basic approach toward others, it is possible for hate and love to coexist.

שִׂנְאָה - מִצַּד הָרַע שֶׁבָּהֶם, וְאַהֲבָה - מִצַּד בְּחִינַת הַטּוֹב הַגָּנוּז שֶׁבָּהֶם, שֶׁהוּא נִיצוֹץ אֱלֹקוּת שֶׁבְּתוֹכָם הַמְחַיֶּה נַפְשָׁם הָאֱלֹקִית.

hatred on account of the evil within them and love on account of the aspect of good hidden within them, which is the divine spark in them that animates their divine soul.

In essence, every person possesses two souls: the animal, physical soul and the divine soul, a portion of God above. The fact that a human being is a portion of the Divine is not obscured by the fact that he sins. That portion must be respected and loved in every individual. In that portion, all of us are brothers, the children of one Father. We are all limbs of one body, one being, the congregation of Israel. ☞ ☞

וְגַם לְעוֹרֵר רַחֲמִים בְּלִבּוֹ עָלֶיהָ, כִּי הִיא בִּבְחִינַת גָּלוּת בְּתוֹךְ הָרַע, מִסִּטְרָא אָחֳרָא הַגּוֹבֵר עָלֶיהָ בָּרְשָׁעִים.

One must also evoke compassion for it, the sinner's divine soul, **for it is in exile within the evil that stems from the** ***sitra aḥara*****, which overpowers** the divine soul **in the wicked.**

A person's relationship with his fellow must be based not solely on love or hatred. Even as the left hand rejects, the right hand embraces. He must maintain his relationship with the third, mediating trait, compassion, and so must ask God to have mercy on his fellow's soul. When a person sees that his friend has sinned, he must, in addition to hating the evil and loving the holy in him, have compassion on this person who has descended to such a low and sinful state.

Compassion is different from the attribute of strict judgment, or hatred in this context, and it differs from the attribute of kindness, or love. Like judgment, it accepts facts as they are; but unlike judgment, it does not pass sentence on them. It is also different from love, which essentially has no interest at all in the objective facts of a case. Love wishes to give, but it does not take into account what may be lacking in the beloved. The feeling of love is not directed to a particular person so much as it constitutes the expression of the soul toward that which is outside itself.

LIKE FAMILY

☞ In every intimate relationship, between parents and children or between close friends, love and hatred or frustration exist simultaneously. One may feel angry and upset at the flaws one sees in another, yet the intimacy of the relationship also involves love. This is not the same as hating someone's evil deeds and loving his good deeds. In this case, the person's deeds might be entirely evil. Yet as much as it is possible to hate, it is impossible not to love. One does not preclude the other. They exist, as it were, on two separate planes.

Compassion, on the other hand, is a complex emotion that encompasses judgment and the recognition of imperfection. That awareness does not generate hatred or abhorrence. Rather, it creates even more closeness. The more one is aware of the other's flaws, the more one feels compassion toward him.

וְהָרַחֲמָנוּת מְבַטֶּלֶת הַשִּׂנְאָה וּמְעוֹרֶרֶת הָאַהֲבָה,	**Compassion nullifies the hatred and evokes love,**

When we have compassion for someone, we cannot hate him because it is possible to see a person at his core and love him. It is hard to love someone whom one despises. But compassion breaks down judgment and distance, and then love can flourish.

כַּנּוֹדָע מִמַּה שֶּׁכָּתוּב: 'לְיַעֲקֹב אֲשֶׁר פָּדָה אֶת אַבְרָהָם' (ישעיה כט, כב).	**as is known from the verse "Jacob who redeemed Abraham"** (Isa. 29:22).

LOVING ANOTHER AS ONE LOVES HIMSELF

☞ How is it possible to love a sinner? The hasidic literature addresses this question, and the answer is derived from the verse "Love your neighbor as yourself." One must love others just as one loves himself despite his intimate knowledge of his own imperfections and flaws and even though he may simultaneously hate himself for them.

This idea is expressed in the verse "Love covers all transgressions" (Prov. 10:12). Love does not conceal the facts, but rather it changes the evaluation of those facts. Although a person recognizes his own sins, his love mitigates their severity and hatefulness. In that sense, "Love your neighbor as yourself" is the challenge to see another as one sees oneself. It is not that one does not see the sin, but one sees it from a different perspective, and then one's entire attitude toward it changes.

Many stories in this vein are told of the great champion of the Jewish people, Rabbi Levi Yitzḥak of Berditchev. In some of these stories, the shift in focus is so radical as to appear humorous and almost absurd. For instance, when Rabbi Levi Yitzḥak looked out his window one morning, he saw a wagon driver reciting the morning prayers dressed in a prayer shawl and *tefillin*, even as he was greasing his wagon wheels. Rabbi Levi Yitzḥak exclaimed, "Master of the world, look! Even when a Jew greases his wagon wheels, he prays!"

Rabbi Levi Yitzḥak was able to reverse his perspective of the incident. Instead of being appalled at the apparent irreverence of the wagon driver, he was inspired by the man's devotion to God.

It is well known that Abraham epitomized the trait of love and Jacob that of compassion. When the trait of Abraham is, as it were, imprisoned so that it cannot appear, we arouse the trait of compassion and its power to liberate the love. It may be impossible to love a person because there are so many reasons to hate him. Yet for those very reasons, we must have compassion on him – and when we have compassion, it is possible to love as well.

[וְלֹא אָמַר דָּוִד הַמֶּלֶךְ עָלָיו הַשָּׁלוֹם: "תַּכְלִית שִׂנְאָה שְׂנֵאתִים" וגו׳ (תהלים קלט, כב) אֶלָּא עַל הַמִּינִים וְהָאֶפִּיקוֹרְסִים, שֶׁאֵין לָהֶם חֵלֶק בֵּאלֹקֵי יִשְׂרָאֵל, כִּדְאִיתָא בַּגְּמָרָא רֵישׁ פֶּרֶק טז דְּשַׁבָּת (קטז, א).]

(King David, of blessed memory, stated, "I hate them with utter hatred" (Ps. 139:22), **only with regard to heretics and apostates, who have no portion in the God of Israel, as the Talmud states at the beginning of chapter 16 of** tractate **Shabbat** [116a].)

The phrase "utter hatred" reflects an absolute animosity toward a person whose wickedness is also absolute. When a person knowingly and completely divorces himself from the God of Israel and attempts to lead other Jews away from God as well, he severs his kinship with the Jewish people. As long as some connection remains, it justifies and even demands a mutual relationship. But when there is no longer a shared bond, any hope of rebuilding that relationship dies away.

The question as to when the divorce becomes final remains unsolved. But the author of the *Tanya* focuses not on that split but on hatred. Even when that hatred is an "utter hatred," it is not yet absolute and final. On the contrary, in a certain sense, that very hatred indicates the existence of a connection of some sort.

One of the descriptions given to the Messiah is that he loves righteousness and hates wickedness.[13] Love of righteousness and hatred of wickedness are apparently opposites. But there is undoubtedly a genuine relationship between them. The more love there is in a person, the more it is possible that he will have a real relationship with hatred.

13. See Ps. 45:8.

On the other hand, a person who does not hate evil lacks the capacity to love good completely. The ability to build a relationship, distant or close, bad or good, assumes a concern with others. When that concern does not exist, a person can neither love the righteous nor hate the wicked. He can only relate to others as objects, as neither enemies nor friends.

A person who does not care for others can distance himself from them, act with great courtesy, use them, and take his leave of them. The shocking and cruel enormities that occurred in our generation, unlike any known before, were not committed by people who possessed a passionate hatred but by people who were indifferent, people who acted mechanically and were able to view people as things. But when the "other" is a human being – in our case, a Jew – whom it is possible to hate, it is also possible to love him.

There is a living connection between the two polarities of love and hate. Hatred, even a consummate hatred, testifies to an ongoing relationship. "I hate them with utter hatred," because they bother me, because they harm me, for they are still an integral part of me.

This chapter is a self-contained discussion of the love of Israel. The first half of the chapter dealt with the theoretical aspect of that love, discussing the closeness among souls that demands that we love every Jew, even someone very different from us and seemingly distant. It defined this mitzva as the basis of the entire Torah and the foundation of our connection with God.

The second half of the chapter dealt with the parameters of the mitzva. Does it have limitations, and if so, what are they? May one Jew hate another? The author of the *Tanya* declared that the mitzva of loving Jews has no boundaries, that one must love every Jew without exception and unconditionally. Even the unusual circumstance that requires a person to hate a Jew does not remove the obligation to love him.

Glossary

Abaye A prominent fourth-generation talmudic Sage from Babylonia

aggadot The nonlegalistic teachings of the Midrash and Talmud, often containing maxims, anecdotes, and parables

alef First letter of the Hebrew alphabet

Amida Silent prayer recited three times daily

amora (pl. amora'im) Sages of the Talmud who lived from approximately 200 to 500 CE

Arizal Rabbi Yitzḥak Luria of Tzefat (1534–1572), the most influential kabbalist of modern times

Asiya The world of Action, the fourth and lowest of the spiritual worlds

Atzilut The world of Emanation, the highest of the four spiritual worlds and closest to the source of creation

Ba'al Shem Tov Rabbi Yisrael ben Eliezer (1698–1760), founder of the hasidic movement

baraita (pl. beraitot) A teaching of the Sages that was not included in the Mishna

beinoni (pl. beinonim) Literally, "intermediate"; a person who is on a level where he is neither wicked nor righteous

Beit Hillel Literally, "House of Hillel"; a school of thought named after the mishnaic Sage Hillel, who founded it

Beit Shammai Literally, "House of Shammai"; a school of thought named after the mishnaic Sage Shammai, who founded it

Beria The world of Creation, the second of the four spiritual worlds

bet The second letter of the Hebrew alphabet

Bina Understanding, one of the ten divine attributes known as *sefirot*

Chabad An acronym of the three cognitive attributes, *Ḥokhma*, *Bina*, and *Da'at*; the name attributed to Lubavitch Hasidism, founded by Rabbi Shneur Zalman of Liadi

Da'at Knowledge, one of the ten divine attributes known as *sefirot*

dalet The fourth letter of the Hebrew alphabet

derush Homiletic exposition

dinar A coin that was common in the times of the Talmud, the term attributed to several coins

Ein Sof God's infinite being

Elokim The name of God that embodies the attribute of judgment

Gehenna Literally, "Valley of Hinnom"; the spiritual realm where souls are purified of sin after death

Gevura Restraint, one of the ten divine attributes known as *sefirot*

gimmel The third letter of the Hebrew alphabet

halakha (pl. halakhot) Jewish law

hasid (pl. hasidim) Literally, "pious individual"; a follower of Hasidism, the movement initiated by the Ba'al Shem Tov

Havaya A reference to the four-letter name of God known as the Tetragrammaton

ḥaya The second highest of the five soul levels

ḥayot Angelic creatures that appear in Ezekiel's mystical vision

heh The fifth letter of the Hebrew alphabet

Ḥesed Kindness, one of the ten divine attributes known as *sefirot*

ḥet The eighth letter of the Hebrew alphabet

Hod Splendor, one of the ten divine attributes known as *sefirot*

Ḥokhma Wisdom, one of the ten divine attributes known as *sefirot*

Ibn Ezra Abraham ben Meir ibn Ezra (c.1092–1167), a Spanish poet, grammarian, and biblical commentator

Kabbala The mystical teachings of the Torah

kaf (or khaf) The eleventh letter of the Hebrew alphabet

karet The punishment of premature death and excision from the World to Come

kelippa (pl. kelippot) Literally, "husk"; the aspect of the universe that is unholy and conceals the Divine

kelippat noga Literally, "glowing husk"; a form of *kelippa* that contains an element of goodness that can be elevated

Keter Crown, one of the ten divine attributes known as *sefirot*

Kiddush Benediction and prayer recited over a cup of wine immediately before the meal on the Sabbath or a festival
kof The nineteenth letter of the Hebrew alphabet
lamed The twelfth letter of the Hebrew alphabet
lulav Palm frond, one of the four species waved on the festival of Sukkot
Maggid of Dubno Rabbi Yaakov Kranz (1741–1804), who served as the *maggid* (preacher) of the city Dubno, known for his parables
Maggid of Mezeritch Rabbi Dovber (d. 1772), a disciple of the Ba'al Shem Tov and the teacher of Rabbi Shneur Zalman of Liadi, author of the *Tanya,* who strengthened the Hasidism of his master, anchoring it firmly in Jewish thought and practice
Maharal An acronym for Rabbi Yehudah Loew of Prague (1525–1609), one of the outstanding scholars and Jewish leaders of the sixteenth century
Maharsha An acronym for *Morenu HaRav Shmuel Eidels,* "our teacher, Rabbi Shmuel Eidels" (1555–1631), a talmudist renowned for his commentary on the Talmud
Malkhut Kingship, one of the ten divine attributes known as *sefirot*
mem The thirteenth letter of the Hebrew alphabet
Midrash Collection of homiletic interpretations of the Scriptures by the Sages of the Talmud
Mishna A concise summary of the teachings of the Sages on all topics of Torah, which was redacted in the beginning of the third century CE by Rabbi Yehuda HaNasi
mitzva (pl. mitzvot) A Torah commandment
mussar Literally, "reproof"; ethical instruction and self-improvement
nefesh The soul; specifically, the lowest of the five levels of the soul
Ne'ila The concluding prayer service of Yom Kippur
neshama The soul; specifically, the third of the five soul levels
Netzaḥ Dominance, one of the ten divine attributes known as *sefirot*
nun The fourteenth letter of the Hebrew alphabet
Or HaḤayyim Rabbi Hayyim ibn Attar (1696–1743), a Moroccan kabbalist and scholar, known as the Or HaḤayyim after his commentary on the Torah by the same name
parasha (pl. parashot) Torah portion

partzufim Literally, "divine countenances"; particular arrangements of the ten *sefirot*

peh The seventeenth letter of the Hebrew alphabet

peshat The plain meaning

Pumbedita Ancient Babylonian city that was home to the great talmudic academy known by the same name

Rabba Rabba bar Naḥmani (died c. 320 CE), a prominent third-generation talmudic Sage from Babylon

Rabbi Ḥayyim Vital Master kabbalist of Tzefat and Damascus (1543–1620) and a primary disciple of the Arizal

Rabbi Moses Ḥayyim Luzzatto Also known as the Ramḥal (1707–1747), an Italian rabbi best known for his kabbalistic writings

Rabbi Yosef Karo A prominent scholar and mystic of Tzefat (1488–1575 CE), most famous as the author of the halakhic masterwork *Shulḥan Arukh*

Ramak Rabbi Moshe Kordevero (1522–1570), one of the greatest kabbalists of Tzefat

Ramaz Rabbi Moshe Zakuto (c. 1620–1697), Italian kabbalist and poet

Rambam Maimonides; Rabbi Moses ben Maimon (1138–1204), a leading halakhic authority and philosopher

Ramban Nachmanides; Rabbi Moses ben Naḥman (1194–1270), renowned for his commentary on the Torah and Talmud

rasha Wicked individual

Rashi Rabbi Shlomo Yitzḥaki (1040–1105), one of the foremost commentators of the Torah and Talmud

remez Allusion

resh The twentieth letter of the Hebrew alphabet

ruaḥ Second of the five soul levels

ruaḥ hakodesh Prophetic intuition, a level of perception akin to prophecy

samekh The fifteenth letter of the Hebrew alphabet

Seder Ceremonial meal held on the first or the first and second nights of Passover commemorating the exodus from Egypt.

sefira (pl. sefirot) One of the ten divine attributes with which God creates, sustains, and directs the worlds

Shema Prayer recited three times daily in which one declares one's faith in the oneness of God

shin Twenty-first letter of the Hebrew alphabet
shofar Ram's horn sounded on the festival of Rosh HaShana
sitra aḥara Literally, "the other side"; a general term for evil, including all aspects of the universe that counter the Divine
sod Mystical aspects of the Torah
sukka Hut or shelter with a roof of branches and leaves used as a temporary residence during the festival of Sukkot
Sukkot The harvest festival celebrated in the fall during which Jews leave their houses to live in temporary shelters
tallit Prayer shawl
Tanakh An acronym for *Torah, Nevi'im, Ketuvim* (Torah, Prophets, Writings), comprising the twenty-four books of the Scriptures
tanna (pl. tanna'im) Sages who lived in the period spanning 332 BCE to 220 CE whose views were recorded in the Mishna
tav Twenty-second letter of the Hebrew alphabet
tefillin Leather boxes worn on the arm and forehead containing certain biblical passages that declare the unity of God and the miracles of the exodus from Egypt
teshuva Repentance
tet Ninth letter of the Hebrew alphabet
Tiferet Beauty, one of the ten divine attributes known as *sefirot*
Tikkun Ḥatzot Prayer recited after midnight, lamenting the destruction of the Temple in Jerusalem
Tosafot Medieval commentators of the Talmud
tzaddik (pl. tzaddikim) Righteous individual; a person born with the extraordinary ability and brilliance to perceive God
tzadi Eighteenth letter of the Hebrew alphabet
tzitzit Strings that are affixed to four-cornered garments
vav The sixth letter of the Hebrew alphabet
yeḥida The highest of the five soul levels
yeshiva An academy dedicated to the study of Torah
Yesod Foundation, one of the ten divine attributes known as *sefirot*
Yetzira The world of Formation, the second of the four spiritual worlds
yod The tenth letter of the Hebrew alphabet
Yom Kippur The Day of Atonement, when the Jewish people engage in fasting, prayer, and repentance
zayin The seventh letter of the Hebrew alphabet

Works Cited in This Volume

Ba'al Shem Tov al HaTorah A compendium of teachings on the Torah and the festivals by the founder of the hasidic movement, anthologized by Shimon Menaḥem Mendel Vodnik

Beit Rebbe Biography of the author of the *Tanya*, Rabbi Shneur Zalman of Liadi (1745–1812), and his successors by Chaim Meir Heilman

Bereshit Rabba Midrash comprising a collection of homiletical interpretations of the book of Genesis

Degel Maḥaneh Efrayim a work of hasidic teachings on the Torah by Rabbi Moshe Ḥayyim Efrayim of Sudilkov (c. 1737–1800)

Derekh Mitzvotekha Hasidic discourses on the esoteric meaning of the mitzvot by the third Lubavitcher Rebbe, Rabbi Menaḥem Mendel Schneerson (1789–1866), also known as the Tzemaḥ Tzedek

Divrei Sofrim A work of hasidic teachings and insights by Rabbi Tzadok HaKohen Rabinowitz of Lublin (1823–1900)

Ein Yaakov A sixteenth-century compilation of all aggadic material in the Talmud together with commentaries

Etz Ḥayyim The fundamental work of the Arizal's Kabbala, compiled by his disciple, Rabbi Ḥayyim Vital

Gevurot Hashem Commentary on the exodus from Egypt and the Passover Haggada by Rabbi Judah Loew, the Maharal of Prague (c.1520–1609)

Guide of the Perplexed Classic work of Jewish philosophy by Rambam (1138–1204)

Halakhot Gedolot A work on Jewish law dating from the Geonic period (589–1038)

HaLekaḥ VeHalibbuv A commentary on the *Tanya* by Rabbi Alexander Sender Yudeson (d. 1983)

HaTomim A periodical published in Warsaw between 1935 and 1938 by the association of students of the Chabad yeshiva network

HaYom Yom An anthology of hasidic aphorisms and customs arranged according to the days of the year, complied by Rabbi Menaḥem Mendel Schneerson, the Lubavitcher Rebbe

Ḥiddushei HaRim Work of hasidic teachings by Rabbi Yitzḥak Meir Rothenberg Alter (1799–1866), the first Rebbe of Gur

Ḥovot HaLevavot A classical work on Jewish ethics authored by Rabbi Baḥya ben Yosef ibn Paquda in around 1161

Idra Rabba A section of the *Zohar* on *Parashat Naso* where kabbalistic mysteries that Rabbi Shimon bar Yoḥai revealed to nine of his students are transcribed

Iggeret HaKodesh The fourth section of the *Tanya* containing the compiled epistles of Rabbi Shneur Zalman of Liadi to his disciples

Iggerot Kodesh A comprehensive collection of correspondence written by Rabbi Menaḥem Mendel Schneerson, the Lubavitcher Rebbe (1902–1994)

Jerusalem Talmud Written in the Land of Israel, an extensive work built upon the foundation of the Mishna like its better-known counterpart, the Babylonian Talmud

Kedushat Levi A classic hasidic work on the Torah by Rabbi Levi Yitzḥak of Berditchev (1740–1810)

Ketav VeHakabbala A commentary on the Torah by Rabbi Yaakov Tzvi of Mecklenberg (1785–1865)

Keter Shem Tov Collection of teachings of the Ba'al Shem Tov (c. 1698–1760), compiled from the works of his disciples, by Rabbi Aharon Hacohen

Kitzurim VeHe'arot LeSefer Likkutei Amarim A pamphlet containing the letters of the Tzemaḥ Tzedek, the third Lubavitcher Rebbe, pertaining to the *Tanya*

Kitzur Shulḥan Arukh A condensed version of the *Shulḥan Arukh,* the authoritative code of Jewish law, authored by Rabbi Shlomo Gantzfreid (1804–1886)

Likkutei Amarim Also known as *Maggid Devarav LeYaakov,* a collection of teachings of Rabbi Dov Ber, the maggid of Mezeritch (c.1700–1770), compiled by his disciple, Rabbi Shlomo of Lutzk

Likkutei Biurim LaTanya Explanations on the *Tanya* culled from other works of Chabad Hasidism, including the discourses of the seventh Lubavitcher Rebbe, Rabbi Menaḥem Mendel Schneerson (1902–1994), compiled by Rabbi Yehoshua Karp

Likkutei Dibburim A series of books containing the teachings of the sixth Lubavitcher Rebbe, Rabbi Yosef Yitzḥak Schneerson (1880–1950)

Likkutei Hagahot LeTanya A collection of marginalia from various copies of the *Tanya* transcribed by illustrious figures

Likkutei Moharan The magnum opus of Rebbe Naḥman of Breslov (1772–1810) containing all his major lessons

Likkutei Siḥot The collected discourses of the seventh Lubavitcher Rebbe, Rabbi Menaḥem Mendel Schneerson (1902–1994) on the Torah and festivals

Likkutei Torah Hasidic discourses by the author of the *Tanya*, Rabbi Shneur Zalman of Liadi (1745–1812) on the last three books of the Torah and the festivals

Likkutei Torah A collection of mystical teachings of the Arizal (1534–1572) on the Torah (not to be confused with the work written by the author of the *Tanya* of the same name)

Ma'amar Bati LeGani The title of the last hasidic discourse of the sixth Lubavitcher Rebbe, Rabbi Yosef Yitzḥak Schneerson (1880–1950), and the first, as well as subsequent, discourses of his successor Rabbi Menaḥem Mendel Schneerson

Ma'amarei Admor HaZaken The collected discourses of the author of the *Tanya*

Ma'or Einayim Hasidic teachings on the Torah by Rabbi Menaḥem Naḥum Twersky of Chernobyl (1730–1798)

Maharsha Commentary on the Talmud by Rabbi Shmuel Eliezer Eidels (1555–1631)

Me'orei Or Kabbalistic reference book by Rabbi Meir Paprish (1624–1662)

Mesillat Yesharim A classic ethical *mussar* text by Rabbi Moshe Ḥayyim Luzzatto (1707–1746)

Midrash Mishlei The aggadic Midrash to the book of Proverbs

Midrash Talpiyot A collection of homiletic teachings by Rabbi Eliyahu HaKohen of Izmir (d. 1729), arranged alphabetically by topic

Milḥamot Hashem Commentary of Nachmanides (1194–1270) to the *halakhot* codified by the Rif, Rabbi Yitzḥak Alfasi

Mishnat Ḥasidim Exposition of the Arizal's kabbalistic teachings by Rabbi Raphael Immanuel Hai Ricchi (1687–1743)

Mishneh Torah Code of Jewish law composed by Rambam (1138–1204), containing fourteen books, including *Sefer HaMadda* (the Book of Knowledge), which addresses fundamentals of Judaism

Ohev Yisrael Hasidic teachings on the Torah by Rabbi Avraham Yehoshua Heshel of Apta (1748–1825)

Pardes Rimmonim The primary exposition of the kabbalistic system of Rabbi Moshe Kordevero, famously known as the Ramak (1522–1570)

Perek Shira Ancient text in which phenomena of creation use biblical and rabbinic verses to sing God's praises

Pirkei Avot Literally, "Chapters of the Fathers"; a tractate of the Mishna dealing with ethics and piety

Pitḥei Teshuva An anthology of halakhic rulings from responsa compiled according to the order of the Shulḥan Arukh by Rabbi Avraham Tzvi Hirsch Eisenstadt (1813–1865)

Pri Etz Ḥayyim Mystical teachings of the Arizal on rituals and holidays as recorded by his disciple Rabbi Hayyim Vital

Raya Meheimna Subsection of the *Zohar* presenting a kabbalistic exposition of the commandments and prohibitions of the Torah

Reshit Ḥokhma Work of Kabbala, ethics, and morality written by Rabbi Eliyahu de Vidas (1518–1587)

Sefer HaGilgulim Kabbalistic work on the concept of reincarnation from the teachings of the Arizal (1534–1572), edited by Rabbi Meir Popperos

Sefer HaḤakira Tract on foundations of faith by the third Lubavitcher Rebbe, the Tzemaḥ Tzedek

Sefer HaMitzvot Work by Rambam (1138–1204), listing and briefly describing all the commandments of the Torah

Sefer Ḥaredim Treatise on the 613 commandments by Rabbi Elazar Ezkari (1533–1600) of Tzefat

Sefer HaToledot A series of biographical works on the founders of Hasidism and the Rebbes of Chabad edited by Rabbi Avraham Ḥanokh Glitzenstein (1929–2015)

Sefer Yetzira Ancient mystical work attributed to the biblical Abraham

Sha'ar HaKedusha (Sha'arei Kedusha) Mystical work on piety by Rabbi Ḥayyim Vital (1542–1620)

Sha'ar HaMitzvot The fifth section of the work *Shemoneh She'arim*, containing the kabbalistic teachings of the Arizal on the commandments

Shemot Rabba Midrash comprising a collection of homiletical interpretations of the book of Exodus

Shenei Luḥot HaBerit Work of Kabbala, ethics, and halakha by Rabbi Yeshaya HaLevi Horowitz, famously known as the Shelah (c. 1655–1730)

Shevet Mussar Prominent ethical work by Eliyahu HaKohen HaItamri (1659–1729)

Shulḥan Arukh The most important and influential codification of Jewish law, compiled by Rabbi Yosef Karo of Tzefat (1488–1575)

Shulḥan Arukh HaRav The code of Jewish law compiled by the author of the *Tanya*

Siddur Admor HaZaken Prayer book edited in accordance with the teachings of the author of the *Tanya*, Rabbi Shneur Zalman of Liadi (1745–1812)

Sifrei Midrash containing halakhic exegesis on the books of Numbers and Deuteronomy

Ta'amei HaMitzvot Treatise containing kabbalistic teachings of the Arizal on the commandments of the Torah

Tanna deVei Eliyahu A compilation of midrashic teachings ascribed to the prophet Elijah

Tiferet Shlomo Hasidic teachings on the Torah by Rabbi Shlomo Rabinowitz of Radomsk (1803–1866)

Tikkunei Zohar Also known as the *Tikkunim*, an appendix to the *Zohar* consisting of seventy commentaries on the opening word of the Torah, *bereshit*

Toledot Yaakov Yosef The first hasidic work ever published containing the teachings of the Ba'al Shem Tov as recorded by his disciple, Yaakov Yosef of Polonne (1710–1784)

Torah Or Hasidic discourses by the author of the *Tanya*, Rabbi

Shneur Zalman of Liadi (1745–1812), on the books of Genesis and Exodus, as well as on Hanukkah and the book of Esther

Torat Ḥayyim The collected discourses of the second Lubavitcher Rebbe, Rabbi Dovber Schneerson (1773–1827), on the books of Genesis and Exodus

Torat Menaḥem The comprehensive collection of discourses and speeches of the seventh Lubavitcher Rebbe, Rabbi Menahem Mendel Schneerson (1902–1994)

Torat Shalom The collected speeches of the fifth Lubavitcher Rebbe, Rabbi Sholom Dovber Schneerson (1860–1920)

Vayikra Rabba Midrash comprising a collection of homiletical interpretations of the book of Leviticus

Yahel Or Hasidic commentary to the book of Psalms by the third Lubavitcher Rebbe, the Tzemaḥ Tzedek (1789–1866)

Yalkut Shimoni A collection of homiletic teachings on the books of *Tanakh*, compiled between the eleventh and fourteenth centuries

Yeshuot Yaakov Halakhic work on the Shulḥan Arukh by Rabbi Yaakov Orenstein (1775–1839)

Yosef Ometz Treatise on Ashkenazic customs and practices by Rabbi Yosef Han Neerlingen of Frankfurt (1570–1637)

Zohar One of the fundamental texts of Kabbala (Jewish mysticism) that consists of the teachings of Rabbi Shimon bar Yoḥai (second century CE), as recorded by his close disciples

Zohar Ḥadash A section of the *Zohar* containing material that was not included in the first edition

יט כסלו פשוטה

יט כסלו מעוברת

ספר

לקוטי אמרים

חלק ראשון

הנקרא בשם

ספר של בינונים

מלוקט מפי ספרים ומפי סופרים קדושי עליון נ"ע מיוסד על פסוק כי קרוב אליך הדבר מאוד בפיך ובלבבך לעשותו. לבאר היטב איך הוא קרוב מאד בדרך ארוכה וקצרה בעזה"י.

הסכמת

הרב החסיד המפורסם איש אלהי קדוש
יאמר לו מוהר״ר משולם זוסיל מאניפאלי:

הנה בראותי את הכתבים של הרב האי גאון איש אלקים קדוש וטהור אספקלריא המאירה וטוב אשר עשה ואשר הפליא ה׳ חסדו ונתן בלבו הטהור לעשות את כל אלה להראות עם ה׳ דרכיו הק׳. ורצונו היה שלא להעלות את הכתבים ההם לבית הדפוס מחמת שאין דרכו בכך. רק מחמת התפשטות הקונטרסים ההם בקרב כל ישראל בהעתקות רבות מידי סופרים משונים ומחמת ריבוי העתקות שונות רבו הט״ס במאד. והוכרח להביא הקונטרסים ההם לבית הדפוס. והעיר ה׳ את רוח השותפים ה״ה הרבני המופלג הותיק מוהר״ר שלום שכנא במהור״ר נח וה״ה הרבני המופלג הותיק מהור״ר מרדכי במהור״ר שמואל הלוי להביא הקונטרסים ההם לבית הדפוס בסלאוויטא ולפעלא טבא אמרתי יישר חילא אך עלו בלבם מגור מסביב מן הדפוסים אשר רבו שדרכן להזיק ולקלקל המאושרים אי לזאת גמרנו בלבינו ליתן הסכמה לבל ירים איש את ידו ואת רגלו לגרום להמדפיסים הנ״ל שום היזק חס ושלום בהשגת גבול בשום אופן. ואסור לשום אדם לדפוס הספר הנ״ל בלתי ידיעת המדפיסים הנ״ל עד משך חמש שנים רצופים מיום דלמטה ושומע לדברי אלה יבא עליו ברכת טוב הכ״ד הדורש זאת לכבוד התורה היום יום ג׳ שנכפל בו כי טוב פ׳ תבא שנת פדותינו לפ״ק.

הקטן משולם זוסיל מאניפאלי.

הסכמת

הרב החסיד המפורסם איש אלהי קדוש
יאמר לו מהור״ר יהודא ליב הכהן:

חכמת אדם תאיר פני הארץ בראותי ידי קדש המחבר הרב הגאון איש אלקים קדוש וטהור חסיד ועניו אשר מכבר נגלה מסתריו יושב בשבת תחכמוני אצל אדונינו מורינו ורבינו גאון עולם ודלה מים מבאר מים חיים וכעת ישמח ישראל בהגלות דברי קדשו המחובר להביא לבית הדפוס ללמד לעם ה׳ דרכי קדש כאשר כל אחד יחזה בפנימיות דבריו והמפורסם אין צריך ראיה רק מחשש קלקול הדבר שלא יגרום היזק למדפיסים באתי ליתן תוקף ואזהרה לבל ירים איש את ידו ורגלו לדפוס עד משך חמש שנים מיום דלמטה ושומע לדברי אלה יבוא עליו ברכת טוב הכ״ד המדבר זאת לכבוד התורה היום יום ג׳ פרשה תבא תקנ״ו לפ״ק.

יהודא ליב הכהן.

הסכמת

כ כסלו מעוברת

הרבנים שי' בני הגאון המחבר ז"ל נ"ע.

היות שהוסכם אצלינו ליתן רשות והרמנא להעלות על מכבש הדפוס לזכרון לבנ"י כתוב דברי יושר ואמת דברי אלקים חיים של א"א מו"ר ז"ל כתובים בכתב ידו הקדושה בעצמו ולשונו הקדוש שכל דבריו כגחלי אש בוערות ילהיבו הלבבות לקרבן לאביהן שבשמים. ובשם אגרת הקדש נקראו שרובם היו אגרת שלוח מאת כ"ק להורות לעם ה' הדרך ילכו בה והמעשה אשר יעשון ומחמת שבכמה מקומות הציב לו ציונים בס' לקוטי אמרים שלו וד"ת עניים במקום אחד ועשירים במ"א ומה גם בשביל דבר שנתחדש בו קונטרס אחרון על איזה פרקים אשר כתב בעת חיברו הס' לק"א פלפול ועיון עמוק על מאמרי זהר וע"ח ופע"ח שנראים כסותרים זא"ז וברוח מבינתו מישבם כל דיבור על אופניו שכתב בלק"א ראו ראינו שראוי ונכון לחברם עם ספר לקוטי אמרים ואגה"ת של כ"ק א"א מו"ר ז"ל. אי לזאת באנו להטיל גודא רבה וגזרת נח"ש דרבנן דלית לה אסוותא שלא ירים איש את ידו להדפיס כתבניתם או זה בלא זה משך חמשה שנים מיום דלמטה ברם כגון דא צריך לאודועי שבעו"ה ספו תמו כתבי ידו הקדושה בעצמו אשר היו בדקדוק גדול לא חסר ולא יתר אות א' ולא נשאר כ"א זה המעט מהרבה אשר נלקטו אחד לאחד מהעתקות המפוזרים אצל התלמידים ואם המצא תמצא איזה טעות שגיאות מי יבין ימצא הטעות דמוכח מטעות סופר והכוונה תהיה ברורה:

נאום דוב בער בא"א מו"ר הגאון החסיד
קדוש ישראל מרנא ורבנא שניאור זלמן ז"ל נבג"מ.

ונאום חיים אברהם בא"א מו"ר הגאון החסיד
מרנא ורבנא שניאור זלמן זצ"ל נבג"מ.

ונאום משה בא"א מו"ר הגאון החסיד שניאור זלמן ז"ל נבג"מ.

כ כסלו פשוטה
כא כסלו מעוברת

הקדמת המלקט

והיא אגרת השלוחה לכללות אנשי שלומינו יצ"ו:

אליכם אישים אקרא שמעו אלי רודפי צדק מבקשי ה' וישמע אליכם אלקים למגדול ועד קטן כל אנ"ש דמדינתינו וסמוכות שלה איש על מקומו יבוא לשלום וחיים עד העולם נס"ו אכי"ר:

הנה מודעת זאת כי מרגלא בפומי דאינשי בכל אנ"ש לאמר כי אינה דומה שמיעת דברי מוסר לראייה וקריאה בספרים שהקורא קורא לפי דרכו ודעתו ולפי השגת ותפיסת שכלו באשר הוא שם ואם שכלו ודעתו מבולבלים ובחשיכה יתהלכו בעבודת ה' בקושי יכול לראות את האור כי טוב הגנוז בספרים אף כי מתוק האור לעינים ומרפא לנפש ובר מן דין הנה ספרי היראה הבנויים ע"פ שכל אנושי בוודאי אינן שוין לכל נפש כי אין כל השכלים והדעות שוות ואין שכל אדם זה מתפעל ומתעורר ממה שמתפעל ומתעורר שכל חבירו וכמו שארז"ל גבי ברכת חכם הרזים על ששים ריבוא מישראל שאין דעותיהם דומות זו לזו וכו' וכמ"ש הרמב"ן ז"ל במלחמות שם בפירוש הספרי גבי יהושע שנאמר בו איש אשר רוח בו שיכול להלוך נגד רוחו של כל אחד ואחד וכו'. אלא אפילו בספרי היראה אשר יסודותם בהררי קודש מדרשי חז"ל אשר רוח ה' דבר בם ומלתו על לשונם ואורייתא וקב"ה כולא חד וכל ששים רבוא נשמות כללות ישראל ופרטיהם ופרטי פרטיהם עד ניצוץ קל שבקלים ופחותי הערך שבעמינו ב"י כולהו מתקשראן באורייתא ואורייתא היא המקשרת אותן להקב"ה כנודע בזה"ק הרי זה דרך כללות לכללות ישראל ואף שניתנה התורה לידרש בכלל ופרט ופרטי פרטות לכל נפש פרטית מישראל המושרשת בה הרי אין כל אדם זוכה להיות מכיר מקומו הפרטי שבתורה: והנה אף בהלכות איסור והיתר הנגלות לנו ולבנינו מצאנו ראינו מחלוקת תנאים ואמוראים מן הקצה אל הקצה ממש ואלו ואלו דברי אלהים חיים לשון רבים על שם מקור החיים לנשמות ישראל הנחלקות דרך כלל לשלשה קוין ימין ושמאל ואמצע שהם חסד וגבורה וכו' ונשמות ששרשן ממדת חסד הנהגתן גם כן להטות כלפי חסד להקל כו' כנודע וכ"ש וק"ו בהנסתרות לה' אלהינו דאינון דחילו ורחימו דבמוחא ולבא דכל חד וחד לפום שיעורא דיליה לפום מה דמשער בליביה כמ"ש בזה"ק על פסוק נודע בשערים בעלה וגו':

כא כסלו פשוטה

כב כסלו מעוברת

אך ביודעיי ומכיריי קאמינא הם כל אחד ואחד מאנ"ש שבמדינתינו וסמוכות שלה אשר היה הדבור של חיבה מצוי בינינו וגילו לפני כל תעלומות לבם ומוחם בעבודת ה' התלויה בלב אליהם תטוף מלתי ולשוני עט סופר בקונטריסים אלו הנקראים בשם לקוטי אמרים מלוקטים מפי ספרים ומפי סופרים קדושי עליון נשמתם עדן המפורסמים אצלינו וקצת מהם נרמזין לחכימין באגרות הקדש מרבותינו שבאה"ק תובב"א. וקצתם שמעתי מפיהם הקדוש בהיותם פה עמנו וכולם הן תשובות על שאלות רבות אשר שואלין בעצה כל אנ"ש דמדינתינו תמיד כל אחד לפי ערכו לשית עצות בנפשם בעבודת ה' להיות כי אין הזמן גרמא עוד להשיב לכל אחד ואחד על שאלתו בפרטות וגם השכחה מצויה על כן רשמתי כל התשובות על כל השאלות למשמרת לאות להיות לכל אחד וא' לזכרון בין עיניו ולא ידחוק עוד ליכנס לדבר עמי ביחידות כי בהן ימצא מרגוע לנפשו ועצה נכונה לכל דבר הקשה עליו בעבודת ה' ונכון יהיה לבו בטוח בה' גומר בעדינו: ומי שדעתו קצרה להבין דבר עצה מתוך קונטריסים אלו יפרש שיחתו לפני הגדולים שבעירו והם יבוננוהו ואליהם בקשתי שלא לשום יד לפה להתנהג בענוה ושפלות של שקר ח"ו וכנודע עונש המר על מונע בר וגודל השכר ממאמר רז"ל ע"פ מאיר עיני שניהם ה' כי יאיר ה' פניו אליהם אור פני מלך חיים. ומחיה חיים יזכנו ויחיינו לימים אשר לא ילמדו עוד איש את רעהו וגו' כי כולם ידעו אותי וגו' כי מלאה הארץ דעה את ה' וגו' אכי"ר:

כג כסלו מעוברת

והנה אחר שנתפשטו הקונטריסים הנ"ל בקרב כל אנ"ש הנ"ל בהעתקות רבות מידי סופרים שונים ומשונים הנה ע"י ריבוי ההעתקות שונות רבו כמו רבו הט"ס במאוד מאוד ולזאת נדבה רוחם של אנשים אפרתים הנקובים הנ"ל מע"ל לטרוח בגופם ומאודם להביא את קונטריסים הנ"ל לבית הדפוס מנוקים מכל סיג וט"ס ומוגהים היטב ואמינא לפעלא טבא יישר חילא ולהיות כי מקרא מלא דבר הכתוב ארור מסיג גבול רעהו וארור בו קללה בו נידוי ח"ו וכו' ע"כ כיהודה ועוד לקרא קאתינא למשדי גודא רבא על כל המדפיסים שלא להדפיס קונטריסים הנ"ל לא על ידי עצמן ולא על ידי גירא דילהון בלתי רשות הנקובים הנ"ל משך חמש שנים מיום כלות הדפוס ולשומעים יונעם ותבוא עליהם ברכת טוב כה דברי המלקט ליקוטי אמרים הנ"ל:

כב כסלו פשוטה
כד כסלו מעוברת

פרק א תניא [בספ"ג דנדה] משביעים אותו תהי צדיק ואל תהי רשע ואפי' כל העולם כולו אומרים לך צדיק אתה היה בעיניך כרשע וצריך להבין דהא תנן [אבות פ"ב] ואל תהי רשע בפני עצמך וגם אם יהיה בעיניו כרשע ירע לבבו ויהיה עצב ולא יוכל לעבו' ה' בשמחה ובטוב לבב ואם לא ירע לבבו כלל מזה יכול לבוא לידי קלות ח"ו. אך הענין כי הנה מצינו בגמרא ה' חלוקות. צדיק וטוב לו צדיק ורע לו רשע וטוב לו רשע ורע לו ובינוני. ופירשו בגמרא צדיק וטוב לו צדיק גמור צדיק ורע לו צדיק שאינו גמור וברעיא מהימנא פ' משפטים פי' צדיק ורע לו שהרע שבו כפוף לטוב וכו' ובגמרא ספ"ט דברכות צדיקים יצ"ט שופטן כו' רשעים יצה"ר שופטן בינונים זה וזה שופטן וכו' אמר רבה כגון אנא בינוני א"ל אביי לא שביק מר חיי לכל בריה וכו' ולהבין כל זה באר היטב וגם להבין מה שאמר איוב [ב"ב פ"א] רבש"ע בראת צדיקי' בראת רשעי' כו' והא צדיק ורשע לא קאמר. וגם להבין מהות מדרגת הבינוני שבודאי אינו מחצה זכיות ומחצה עונות שא"כ איך טעה רבה בעצמו לומר שהוא בינוני ונודע דלא פסיק פומיה מגירסא עד שאפי' מלאך המות לא היה יכול לשלוט בו ואיך היה יכול לטעות במחצה עונות ח"ו. ועוד שהרי בשעה שעושה עונות נקרא רשע גמור [ואם אח"כ עשה תשובה נקרא צדיק גמור] ואפילו העובר על איסור קל של דברי סופרים מקרי רשע כדאיתא בפ"ב דיבמות ובפ"ק דנדה ואפילו מי שיש בידו למחות ולא מיחה נק' רשע [בפ"ו דשבועו'] וכ"ש וק"ו במבטל איזו מ"ע שאפש' לו לקיימה כמו כל שאפשר לו לעסוק בתורה ואינו עוסק שעליו דרשו רז"ל כי דבר ה' בזה וגו' הכרת תכרת וגו' ופשיטא דמקרי רשע טפי מעובר איסור דרבנן וא"כ ע"כ הבינוני אין בו

כג כסלו פשוטה
כה כסלו מעוברת

אפי' עון ביטול תורה ומש"ה טעה רבה בעצמו לומר שהוא בינוני* והא דאמרי' בעלמא דמחצ' על מחצה מקרי בינוני ורוב זכיות מקרי צדיק הוא שם המושאל לענין שכר ועונש לפי שנדון אחר רובו ומקרי צדיק בדינו מאחר שזוכה בדין אבל לענין אמיתת שם התואר והמעלה של מעלת ומדרגות חלוקות צדיקים ובינונים ארז"ל צדיקים יצ"ט שופטן שנא' ולבי חלל בקרבי שאין לו יצה"ר כי הרגו בתענית אבל כל מי שלא הגיע למדרגה זו אף שזכיותיו מרובים על עונותיו אינו במעלת ומדרגת צדיק כלל ולכן ארז"ל במדרש ראה הקב"ה בצדיקים שהם מועטים עמד ושתלן בכל דור ודור וכו' וכמ"ש וצדיק יסוד עולם: אך ביאור הענין על פי מ"ש הרח"ו ז"ל

הגהה

* (ומ"ש בזהר ח"ג ד' רל"א כל שממועטין עונותיו וכו' היא שאלת רב המנונא לאליהו אבל לפי תשובת אליהו שם פי' צדיק ורע לו הוא כמ"ש בר"מ פרשה משפטים דלעיל ושבעים פנים לתורה):

בשער הקדושה [ובע״ח שער נ׳ פ״ב] דלכל איש ישראל אחד צדיק ואחד רשע יש שתי נשמות וכדכתיב ונשמות אני עשיתי שהן שתי נפשות נפש אחת מצד הקליפה וסטרא אחרא והיא המתלבשת בדם האדם להחיות הגוף וכדכתיב כי נפש הבשר בדם היא וממנה באות כל המדות רעות מארבע יסודות רעים שבה דהיינו כעס וגאוה מיסוד האש שנגבה למעלה. ותאות התענוגים מיסוד המים כי המים מצמיחים כל מיני תענוג. והוללות וליצנות והתפארות ודברים בטלים מיסוד הרוח. ועצלות ועצבות מיסוד העפר. וגם מדות טובות שבטבע כל ישראל בתולדותם כמו רחמנות וג״ח באות ממנה כי בישראל נפש זו דקליפה היא מקליפ׳ נוגה שיש בה ג״כ טוב והיא מסוד עץ הדעת טוב ורע: משא״כ נפשות אומות העולם הן משאר קליפות טמאות שאין בהן טוב כלל כמ״ש בע״ח שער מ״ט פ״ג וכל טיבו דעבדין האומות לגרמייהו עבדין וכדאיתא בגמרא ע״פ וחסד לאומים חטאת שכל צדקה וחסד שאומות העולם עושין אינן אלא להתייהר כו׳:

כד כסלו פשוטה
כו כסלו מעוברת

פרק ב ונפש השנית בישראל היא חלק אלוה ממעל ממש כמ״ש ויפח באפיו נשמת חיים ואתה נפחת בי וכמ״ש בזהר מאן דנפח מתוכיה נפח פי׳ מתוכיותו ומפנימיותו שתוכיות ופנימיות החיות שבאדם מוציא בנפיחתו בכח: כך עד״מ נשמות ישראל עלו במחשבה כדכתיב בני בכורי ישראל בנים אתם לה׳ אלהיכם פי׳ כמו שהבן נמשך ממוח האב כך כביכול נשמת כל איש ישראל נמשכה ממחשבתו וחכמתו ית׳ דאיהו חכים ולא בחכמה ידיעא אלא הוא וחכמתו א׳ וכמ״ש הרמב״ם*: שהוא המדע והוא היודע כו׳ ודבר זה אין ביכולת האדם להבינו על בוריו כו׳ כדכתיב החקר אלוה תמצא וכתיב כי לא מחשבותי מחשבותיכם וגו׳ ואף שיש רבבות מיני חלוקי מדרגות בנשמו׳ גבוה מעל גבוה לאין קץ כמו גודל מעלת נשמות האבות ומשה רבינו ע״ה על נשמות דורותינו אלה דעקבי משיח׳ שהם בחי׳ עקביים ממש לגבי המוח והראש וכן בכל דור ודור יש ראשי אלפי ישראל שנשמותיהם הם בחי׳ ראש ומוח לגבי נשמות ההמון וע״ה וכן נפשות לגבי נפשות כי כל נפש כלולה מנפש רוח ונשמה מכל מקום שרש כל הנפש רוח ונשמה כולם מראש כל המדריגות עד סוף כל דרגין המלובש בגוף עמי הארץ וקל שבקלים נמשך ממוח העליון שהיא חכמה עילאה כביכול כמשל

הגהה

* הגהה והודו לו חכמי הקבלה כמ״ש בפרדס מהרמ״ק וגם לפי קבלת האר״י ז״ל יציבא מילתא בסוד התלבשות אור א״ס ב״ה על ידי צמצומים רבים בכלים דחב״ד דאצילו׳ אךלא למעלה מהאצילו׳ וכמ״ש במ״א שא״ס ב״ה מרומם ומתנשא רוממות אין קץ למעלה מעלה ממהות ובחי׳ חב״ד עד שמהות ובחי׳ חב״ד נחשבת כעשייה גופניית אצלו ית׳ כמ״ש כולם בחכמה עשית:

הבן הנמשך ממוח האב שאפי׳ צפרני רגליו נתהוו מטפה זו ממש ע״י שהייתה תשעה חדשים בבטן האם וירדה ממדרגה למדרגה להשתנות ולהתהוו׳ ממנה צפרנים ועם כל זה עודנה קשורה ומיוחדת ביחוד נפלא ועצום במהותה ועצמותה הראשון שהיתה טפת מוח האב וגם עכשיו בבן יניקת הצפרנים והיותם נמשכת מהמוח שבראש כדאיתא בגמ׳ [נדה שם לובן שממנו גידים ועצמות וצפרנים [וכמ״ש בע״ח שער החשמל בסוד לבושים של אדם הראשון בגן עדן שהיו צפרנים מבחי׳ מוח תבונה] וככה ממש כביכול בשרש כל הנפש רוח ונשמה של כללות ישראל למעלה בירידתו ממדרגה למדרגה על ידי השתלשלות העולמות אבי״ע מחכמתו ית׳ כדכתיב כולם בחכמה עשית נתהוו ממנו נפש רוח ונשמה של עמי הארץ ופחותי הערך ועם כל זה עודינה קשורות ומיוחדות ביחוד נפלא ועצום במהותן ועצמותן הראשון שהיא המשכת חכמה עילאה כי יניקת וחיו׳ נפש רוח ונשמה של עמי הארץ הוא מנפש רוח ונשמה של הצדיקים והחכמים ראשי בני ישראל שבדורם: ובזה יובן מאמר רז״ל על פסוק ולדבקה בו שכל הדבק בת״ח מעלה עליו הכתוב כאלו נדבק בשכינה ממש כי ע״י דביקה בתלמידי חכמים קשורות נפש רוח ונשמה של עמי הארץ ומיוחדות במהותן הראשון ושרשם שבחכמה עילאה שהוא ית׳ וחכמתו א׳ והוא המדע כו׳ [והפושעים ומורדים בתלמידי חכמים יניקת נפש רוח ונשמה שלהם מבחי׳ אחוריים של נפש רוח ונשמת ת״ח] ומ״ש בזהר ובזהר חדש שהעיקר תלוי שיקדש עצמו בשעת תשמיש דווקא משא״כ בני עמי הארץ כו׳ היינו משום שאין לך נפש רוח ונשמה שאין לה לבוש מנפש דעצמות אביו ואמו וכל המצות שעושה הכל ע״י אותו הלבוש כו׳ ואפי׳ השפע שנותנים לו מן השמים הכל ע״י לבוש זה ואם יקדש את עצמו ימשיך לבוש קדוש לנשמת בנו ואפילו היא נשמה גדולה צריכה לקידוש אביו כו׳ אבל הנשמה עצמה הנה לפעמים נשמת אדם גבוה לאין קץ בא להיות בנו של אדם נבזה ושפל כו׳ כמ״ש האר״י ז״ל כל זה בליקוטי תורה פ׳ וירא ובטעמי מצות פ׳ בראשית:

כה כסלו פשוטה
כז כסלו מעוברת

פרק ג והנה כל בחי׳ ומדרגה משלש אלו נפש רוח ונשמה כלולה מעשר בחי׳ כנגד עשר ספירות עליונות שנשתלשלו מהן הנחלקות לשתים שהן שלש אמות ושבע כפולות פי׳ חכמה בינה ודעת ושבעת ימי הבנין חסד גבורה תפארת כו׳ וכך בנפש האדם שנחלקת לשתים שכל ומדות. השכל כולל חכמה בינה ודעת. והמדות הן אהבת ה׳ ופחדו ויראתו ולפארו כו׳ וחב״ד נקראו אמות ומקור למדות כי המדות הן תולדות חב״ד: וביאור הענין כי הנה השכל שבנפש המשכל׳ שהוא המשכיל כל דבר נקרא בשם חכמה כ״ח מ״ה וכשמוציא כחו אל הפועל שמתבונן בשכלו להבין דבר לאשורו ולעמקו מתוך איזה דבר חכמה המושכל בשכלו

כו כסלו פשוטה
כח כסלו מעוברת

נקרא בינה והן הם אב ואם המולידות אהבת ה׳ ויראתו ופחדו כי השכל שבנפש המשכלת כשמתבונן ומעמיק מאד בגדולת ה׳ איך הוא ממלא כל עלמין וסובב כל עלמין וכולא קמיה כלא חשיב נולדה ונתעוררה מדת יראת הרוממות במוחו ומחשבתו לירא ולהתבושש מגדולתו ית׳ שאין לה סוף ותכלית ופחד ה׳ בלבו ושוב יתלהב לבו באהבה עזה כרשפי אש בחשיקה וחפיצה ותשוקה ונפש שוקקה לגדולת אין סוף ב״ה והיא כלות הנפש כדכתיב נכספה וגם כלתה נפשי וגו׳ וכתיב צמאה נפשי לאלהים וגו׳ וכתיב צמאה לך נפשי וגו׳ והצמאון הוא מיסוד האש שבנפש האלהית וכמ״ש הטבעיים וכ״ה בע״ח שיסוד האש הוא בלב ומקור המים והליחות מהמוח וכמ״ש בע״ח שער נ׳ שהיא בחי׳ חכמה שנקרא מים שבנפש האלהית ושאר המדות כולן הן ענפי היראה והאהבה ותולדותיהן כמ״ש במקום אחר. והדעת הוא מלשון והאדם ידע את חוה והוא לשון התקשרות והתחברות שמקשר דעתו בקשר אמיץ וחזק מאוד ויתקע מחשבתו בחוזק בגדולת אין סוף ב״ה ואינו מסיח דעתו כי אף מי שהוא חכם ונבון בגדולת א״ס ב״ה הנה אם לא יקשר דעתו ויתקע מחשבתו בחוזק ובהתמדה לא יוליד בנפשו יראה ואהבה אמיתית כי אם דמיונות שוא ועל כן הדעת הוא קיום המדות וחיותן והוא כולל חסד וגבורה פי׳ אהבה וענפיה ויראה וענפיה:

כז כסלו פשוטה
כט כסלו מעוברת

פרק ד ועוד יש לכל נפש אלהית שלשה לבושים שהם מחשבה דבור ומעשה של תרי״ג מצות התורה שכשהאדם מקיים במעשה כל מצות מעשיות ובדבור הוא עוסק בפירוש כל תרי״ג מצות והלכותיהן ובמחשבה הוא משיג כל מה שאפשר לו להשיג בפרד״ס התורה

ל כסלו מעוברת

הרי כללות תרי״ג אברי נפשו מלובשים בתרי״ג מצות התורה ובפרטות בחי׳ חב״ד שבנפשו מלובשות בהשגת התורה שהוא משיג בפרד״ס כפי יכולת השגתו ושרש נפשו למעלה. והמדות שהן יראה ואהבה וענפיהן ותולדותיהן מלובשות בקיום המצות במעשה ובדבור שהוא ת״ת שכנגד כולן כי האהבה היא שרש כל רמ״ח מ״ע וממנה הן נמשכות ובלעדה אין להן קיום אמיתי כי המקיימן באמת הוא האוהב את שם ה׳ וחפץ לדבקה בו באמת ואי אפשר לדבקה בו באמת כי אם בקיום רמ״ח פקודין שהם רמ״ח אברין דמלכא כביכול כמ״ש במקום אחר והיראה היא שרש לשס״ה לא תעשה כי ירא למרוד במלך מלכי המלכים הקב״ה. או יראה פנימית מזו שמתבושש מגדולתו למרות עיני כבודו ולעשות הרע בעיניו כל תועבת ה׳ אשר שנא הם הקליפות וסטרא אחרא אשר יניקתם מהאדם התחתון

כח כסלו פשוטה
א טבת מעוברת

ואחיזתם בו הוא בשס״ה מצות לא תעשה. והנה שלשה לבושים אלו מהתורה ומצותיה אף שנקראים לבושים לנפש רוח ונשמה עם כל זה גבהה וגדלה מעלתם לאין קץ וסוף על מעלת נפש רוח ונשמה עצמן כמ״ש בזהר

דאורייתא וקב"ה כולא חד פי' דאורייתא היא חכמתו ורצונו של הקב"ה והקב"ה בכבודו ובעצמו כולא חד כי הוא היודע והוא המדע וכו' כמ"ש לעיל בשם הרמב"ם. ואף דהקב"ה נקרא אין סוף ולגדולתו אין חקר ולית מחשבה תפיסא ביה כלל וכן ברצונו וחכמתו כדכתיב אין חקר לתבונתו וכתי' החקר אלוה תמצא וכתיב כי לא מחשבותי מחשבותיכם הנה על זה אמרו במקום שאתה מוצא גדולתו של הקב"ה שם אתה מוצא ענותנותו וצמצם הקב"ה רצונו וחכמתו בתרי"ג מצות התורה ובהלכותיהן ובצרופי אותיות תנ"ך ודרשותיהן שבאגדות ומדרשי חכמינו ז"ל בכדי שכל הנשמה או רוח ונפש שבגוף האדם תוכל להשיגן בדעתה ולקיימן כל מה שאפשר לקיים מהן במעשה דבור ומחשבה וע"י זה תתלבש בכל עשר בחינותיה
בשלשה לבושים אלו. ולכן נמשלה התורה למים מה מים יורדים ממקום ב טבת מעוברת
גבוה למקום נמוך כך התורה ירדה ממקום כבודה שהיא רצונו וחכמתו יתברך ואורייתא וקודשא בריך הוא כולא חד ולית מחשבה תפיסא ביה כלל. ומשם נסעה וירדה בסתר המדרגות ממדרגה למדרגה בהשתלשלות העולמות עד שנתלבשה בדברים גשמיים ועניני עולם הזה שהן רוב מצות התורה ככולם והלכותיהן ובצרופי אותיות גשמיות בדיו על הספר עשרים וארבעה ספרים שבתורה נביאים וכתובים כדי שתהא כל מחשבה תפיסא בהן ואפי' בחי' דבור ומעשה שלמטה ממדרגת מחשבה תפיסא בהן
ומתלבשת בהן ומאחר שהתורה ומצותיה מלבישים כל עשר בחי' הנפש כט כסלו פשוטה
וכל תרי"ג אבריה מראשה ועד רגלה הרי כולה צרורה בצרור החיים את ה' ממש ואור ה' ממש מקיפה ומלבישה מראשה ועד רגלה כמ"ש צורי אחסה בו וכתיב כצנה רצון תעטרנו שהוא רצונו וחכמתו יתברך המלובשים בתורתו
ומצותיה. ולכן אמרו יפה שעה אחת בתשובה ומעשים טובים בעולם הזה ג טבת מעוברת
מכל חיי עולם הבא כי עולם הבא הוא שנהנין מזיו השכינה שהוא תענוג ההשגה ואי אפשר לשום נברא אפי' מהעליונים להשיג כי אם איזו הארה מאור ה' ולכן נקרא בשם זיו השכינה אבל הקב"ה בכבודו ובעצמו לית מחשבה תפיסא ביה כלל כי אם כאשר תפיסא ומתלבשת בתורה ומצותיה
אזי היא תפיסא בהן ומתלבשת בהקב"ה ממש דאורייתא וקב"ה כולא חד. בכ"י ליתא תיבת בהן
ואף שהתורה נתלבשה בדברים תחתונים גשמיים הרי זה כמחבק את המלך ד"מ שאין הפרש במעלת התקרבותו ודביקותו במלך בין מחבקו כשהוא לבוש לבוש אחד בין שהוא לבוש כמה לבושים מאחר שגוף המלך בתוכם. וכן אם המלך מחבקו בזרועו גם שהיא מלובשת תוך מלבושיו כמ"ש וימינו תחבקני שהיא התורה שנתנה מימין שהיא בחי' חסד ומים:

ל כסלו פשוטה | ד טבת מעוברת

פרק ה ולתוספת ביאור באר היטב לשון תפיסא שאמר אליהו לית מחשבה תפיסא בך כו'. הנה כל שכל

כשמשכיל ומשיג בשכלו איזה מושכל הרי השכל תופס את המושכל ומקיפו בשכלו והמושכל נתפס ומוקף ומלובש בתוך השכל שהשיגו והשכילו וגם השכל מלובש במושכל בשעה שמשיגו ותופסו בשכלו ד"מ כשאדם מבין ומשיג איזו הלכה במשנה או בגמרא לאשורה על בוריה הרי שכלו תופס ומקיף אותה וגם שכלו מלובש בה באותה שעה. והנה הלכה זו היא חכמתו ורצונו של הקב"ה שעלה ברצונו שכשיטען ראובן כך וכך דרך משל ושמעון כך וכך יהיה הפסק ביניהם כך וכך ואף אם לא היה ולא יהיה הדבר הזה לעולם לבא למשפט על טענות ותביעות אלו מכל מקום מאחר שכך עלה ברצונו וחכמתו של הקב"ה שאם יטעון זה כך וזה כך יהיה הפסק כך הרי כשאדם יודע ומשיג בשכלו פסק זה כהלכה הערוכה במשנה או גמרא או פוסקים הרי זה משיג ותופס ומקיף בשכלו רצונו וחכמתו של הקב"ה דלית מחשבה תפיסא ביה ולא ברצונו וחכמתו כי אם בהתלבשותם בהלכות הערוכות לפנינו וגם שכלו מלובש בהם והוא יחוד נפלא שאין יחוד כמוהו ולא כערכו נמצא כלל בגשמיות להיות לאחדים ומיוחדים ממש מכל צד ופנה. וזאת מעלה יתרה גדולה ונפלאה לאין קץ א טבת פשוטה
אשר במצות ידיעת התורה והשגתה על כל המצות מעשיות ואפי' על מצות התלויות בדבור ואפי' על מצות תלמוד תורה שבדבור כי ע"י כל המצות שבדבור ומעשה הקב"ה מלביש את הנפש ומקיפה אור ה' מראשה ועד רגלה. ובידיעת התורה מלבד שהשכל מלובש בחכמת ה' הנה גם חכמת ה' בקרבו מה שהשכל משיג ותופס ומקיף בשכלו מה שאפשר לו לתפוס ולהשיג מידיעת התורה איש כפי שכלו וכח ידיעתו והשגתו בפרד"ס. ולפי שבידיעת התורה התורה מלובשת בנפש האדם ושכלו ומוקפת בתוכם לכן נקראת בשם לחם ומזון הנפש כי כמו שהלחם הגשמי זן את הגוף כשמכניסו בתוכו וקרבו ממש ונהפך שם להיות דם ובשר כבשרו ואזי יחיה ויתקיים כך בידיעת התורה והשגתה בנפש האדם שלומדה היטב בעיון שכלו עד שנתפסת בשכלו ומתאחדת עמו והיו לאחדים נעשה מזון לנפש וחיים בקרבה מחיי החיים אין סוף ברוך הוא המלובש בחכמתו ותורתו שבקרבה וז"ש ותורתך בתוך מעי וכמ"ש בע"ח שער מ"ד פ"ג שלבושי הנשמות בגן עדן הן המצות והתורה היא המזון לנשמות שעסקו בעולם הזה בתורה לשמה וכמ"ש בזהר ויקהל דף ר"י ולשמה היינו כדי לקשר נפשו לה' ע"י השגת התורה איש כפי שכלו כמ"ש בפרע"ח [והמזון היא בחי' אור פנימי והלבושים בחי' מקיפים ולכן אמרו רז"ל שתלמוד תורה שקול כנגד כל המצות לפי שהמצות הן לבושים לבד והתורה היא מזון וגם לבוש לנפש המשכלת שמתלבש בה בעיונה ולימודה וכל שכן כשמוציא בפיו בדבור שהבל הדבור נעשה בחי' אור מקיף כמ"ש בפרע"ח]:

פרק ו והנה זה לעומת זה עשה אלהים כי כמו שנפש האלהית כלולה ב טבת פשוטה
מעשר ספירות קדושות ומתלבשת בשלשה לבושים ה טבת מעוברת
קדושים כך הנפש דסטרא אחרא מקליפות נוגה המלובשת בדם האדם
כלולה מעשר כתרין דמסאבותא שהן שבע מדות רעות הבאות מארבע
יסודות רעים הנ"ל ושכל המולידן הנחלק לשלש שהן חכמה בינה ודעת
מקור המדות כי המדות הן לפי ערך השכל כי הקטן חושק ואוהב דברים
קטנים פחותי הערך לפי ששכלו קטן וקצר להשיג דברים יקרים יותר מהם.
וכן מתכעס ומתקצף מדברים קטנים וכן בהתפארות ושאר מדות ועשר
בחי' אלו הטמאות כשאדם מחשב בהן או מדבר או עושה הרי מחשבתו
שבמוחו ודבורו שבפיו וכח המעשיי שבידיו ושאר איבריו נקראים לבושי
מסאבו לעשר בחי' אלו הטמאות שמתלבשות בהן בשעת מעשה או דבור
או מחשבה והן הם כל המעשים אשר נעשים תחת השמש אשר הכל הבל
ורעות רוח וכמ"ש בזהר בשלח שהן תבירו דרוחא כו' וכן כל הדבורים וכל ו טבת מעוברת
המחשבות אשר לא לה' המה ולרצונו ולעבודתו שזהו פי' לשון סטרא
אחרא פי' צד אחר שאינו צד הקדושה וצד הקדושה אינו אלא השראה
והמשכה מקדושתו של הקב"ה ואין הקב"ה שורה אלא על דבר שבטל
אצלו יתב' בין בפועל ממש כמלאכים עליונים בין בכח ככל איש ישראל
למטה שבכחו להיות בטל ממש לגבי הקב"ה במסירת נפשו על קדושת ה'.
ולכן אמרו רז"ל שאפי' אחד שיושב ועוסק בתורה שכינה שרויה כו' וכל
בי עשרה שכינתא שריא לעולם אבל כל מה שאינו בטל אצלו ית' אלא ג טבת פשוטה
הוא דבר נפרד בפני עצמו אינו מקבל חיות מקדושתו של הקב"ה מבחי'
פנימית הקדושה ומהותה ועצמותה בכבודה ובעצמה אלא מבחי' אחוריים
שיורדים ממדרגה למדרגה רבבות מדרגות בהשתלשלות העולמות דרך
עלה ועלול וצמצומים רבים עד שנתמעט כל כך האור והחיות מיעוט אחר
מיעוט עד שיכול להתצמצם ולהתלבש בבחי' גלות תוך אותו דבר הנפרד
להחיותו ולקיימו מאין ליש שלא יחזור להיות אין ואפס כבתחלה מקודם
שנברא ולכן נקרא עולם הזה ז טבת מעוברת
ומלואו עולם הקליפות וסטרא
אחרא ולכן כל מעשה עוה"ז
קשים ורעים והרשעים גוברים בו
כמ"ש בע"ח שער מ"ב סוף פ"ד*:
אלא שהקליפות הן נחלקות
לשתי מדרגות זו למטה מזו
המדרגה התחתונה היא שלש
קליפו' הטמאות ורעות לגמרי ואין

הגהה

* עם היות בתוכו עשר ספי' דעשיה דקדושה וכמ"ש בע"ח שער מ"ג ובתוך עשר ספי' דעשיה אלו הן עשר ספי' דיצירה ובתוכן עשר ספי' דבריאה ובתוכן עשר ספי' דאצילות שבתוכן אור א"ס ב"ה ונמצא אור א"ס ב"ה מלא כל הארץ הלזו התחתונה על ידי התלבשותו בעשר ספי' דארבע עולמות אבי"ע כמ"ש בע"ח שער מ"ז פ"ב ובספר גלגולים פרק כ':

בהם טוב כלל ונקראו במרכבת יחזקאל רוח סערה וענן גדול וגו׳ ומהן נשפעות ונמשכות נפשות כל אומות העולם וקיום גופם ונפשות כל בעלי חיים הטמאים ואסורים באכילה וקיום גופם וקיום וחיות כל מאכלות אסורות מהצומח כמו ערלה וכלאי הכרם כו׳ וכמ״ש בע״ח שער מ״ט פ״ו וכן קיום וחיות כל המעשה דבור ומחשבה של כל שס״ה לא תעשה וענפיהן כמ״ש שם סוף פ״ה:

ד טבת פשוטה

ח טבת מעוברת

פרק ז אך נפש החיונית הבהמית שבישראל שמצד הקליפה המלובשת בדם האדם כנ״ל ונפשות בהמות וחיות ועופות ודגים טהורים ומותרים באכילה וקיום וחיות כל הדומם וכל הצומח המותר באכילה וכן קיום וחיות כל המעשה דבור ומחשבה בענייני עוה״ז שאין בהם צד איסור לא שרש ולא ענף משס״ה מצות לא תעשה וענפיהן דאורייתא ודרבנן רק שאינן לשם שמים אלא רצון הגוף וחפצו ותאותו ואפי׳ הוא צורך הגוף וקיומו וחיותו ממש אלא שכוונתו אינה לשם שמים כדי לעבוד את ה׳ בגופו לא עדיפי מעשה דבור ומחשבות אלו מנפש החיונית הבהמית בעצמה והכל כאשר לכל נשפע ונמשך ממדרגה השנית שבקליפות וסטרא אחרא שהיא קליפה רביעית הנקראת קליפת נוגה שבעולם הזה הנקרא עולם העשיה רובו ככולו רע רק מעט טוב מעורב בתוכה [שממנה באות מדות טובות שבנפש הבהמית שבישראל כמ״ש לעיל] והיא בחי׳ ממוצעת בין שלש קליפות הטמאות לגמרי ובין בחי׳ ומדרגת הקדושה ולכן פעמים שהיא נכללת בשלש קליפות הטמאות [כמ״ש בע״ח שער מ״ט ריש פ״ד בשם הזהר] ופעמים שהיא נכללת ועולה בבחי׳ ומדרגת הקדושה דהיינו כשהטוב המעורב בה נתברר מהרע וגובר ועולה ונכלל בקדושה כגון ד״מ האוכל בשרא שמינא דתורא ושותה יין מבושם להרחיב דעתו לה׳ ולתורתו כדאמר רבא חמרא וריחא כו׳ או בשביל כדי לקיים מצות ענג שבת וי״ט אזי נתברר חיות הבשר והיין שהיה נשפע מקליפת נוגה ועולה לה׳ כעולה וכקרבן. וכן האומר מילתא דבדיחותא לפקח דעתו ולשמח לבו לה׳ ולתורתו ועבודתו שצריכים להיות בשמחה וכמו שעשה רבא לתלמידיו שאמר לפניהם מילתא דבדיחותא תחלה ובדחי רבנן. אך מי שהוא בזוללי בשר וסובאי יין למלאת ה טבת פשוטה
תאות גופו ונפשו הבהמית שהוא בחי׳ יסוד המים מארבע יסודות הרעים ט טבת מעוברת
שבה שממנו מדת התאוה הנה ע״י זה יורד חיות הבשר והיין שבקרבו ונכלל לפי שעה ברע גמור שבשלש קליפות הטמאות וגופו נעשה להן לבוש ומרכבה לפי שעה עד אשר ישוב האדם ויחזור לעבודת ה׳ ולתורתו כי לפי שהיה בשר היתר ויין כשר לכך יכולים לחזור ולעלות עמו בשובו לעבודת ה׳ שזהו לשון היתר ומותר כלומר שאינו קשור ואסור בידי החיצונים שלא יוכל לחזור ולעלות לה׳ רק שהרשימו ממנו נשאר בגוף ועל כן צריך הגוף

לחיבוט הקבר כמ"ש לקמן וכן החיות שבטפות זרע שיצאו ממנו בתאוה בהמית שלא קדש עצמו בשעת תשמיש עם אשתו טהורה מה שאין כן במאכלות אסורות וביאות אסורות שהן משלש קליפות הטמאות לגמרי הם אסורים וקשורים בידי החיצונים לעולם ואין עולים משם עד כי יבא יומם ויבולע המות לנצח כמ"ש ואת רוח הטומאה אעביר מן הארץ או עד שיעשה תשובה גדולה כל כך שזדונות נעשו לו כזכיות ממש שהיא תשובה מאהבה מעומקא דלבא באהבה רבה וחשיקה ונפש שוקקה לדבקה בו ית' וצמאה נפשו לה' כארץ עיפה וציה להיות כי עד הנה היתה נפשו בארץ ציה וצלמות היא הסטרא אחרא ורחוקה מאור פני ה' בתכלית ולזאת צמאה נפשו ביתר עז מצמאון נפשות הצדיקים כמאמרם ז"ל במקום שבעלי תשובה עומדים כו' ועל תשובה מאהבה רבה זו אמרו שזדונות נעשו לו כזכיות הואיל ועל ידי זה בא לאהבה רבה זו אבל תשובה שלא מאהבה זו אף שהיא תשובה נכונה וה' יסלח לו מכל מקום לא נעשו לו כזכיות ואין עולים מהקליפה לגמרי עד עת קץ שיבולע המות לנצח. אך החיות שבטפות זרע שיצאו ממנו לבטלה אף שירדה ונכללה בשלש קליפות הטמאות הרי זו עולה משם בתשובה נכונה ובכוונה עצומה בקריאת שמע שעל המטה כנודע מהאר"י ז"ל ומרומז בגמרא כל הקורא קריאת שמע על מטתו כאלו אוחז חרב של שתי פיות כו' להרוג גופות החיצונים שנעשו לבוש לחיות שבטפות ועולה החיות מהם כידוע לי"ח. ולכן לא הוזכר עון זרע לבטלה בתורה בכלל ביאות אסורות אף שחמור מהן וגדול עונו בבחי' הגדלות ורבוי הטומאה והקליפות שמוליד ומרבה במאד מאד בהוצאת זרע לבטלה יותר מביאות אסורות רק שבביאות אסורות מוסיף כח וחיות בקליפה טמאה ביותר עד שאינו יכול להעלות משם החיות בתשובה:* אא"כ יעשה תשובה מאהבה רבה כל כך עד שזדונות נעשו לו כזכיות ובזה יובן מאמר רז"ל איזהו מעוות שלא יוכל לתקון זה שבא על הערוה והוליד ממזר שאז גם אם יעשה תשובה גדולה כל כך אי אפשר לו להעלות החיות לקדושה מאחר שכבר ירדה לעולם הזה ונתלבשה בגוף בשר ודם:

ו טבת פשוטה

י טבת מעוברת

הגה"ה

* (מפני שנקלטה ביסוד דנוקבא דקליפה המקבלת וקולטת החיות מהקדושה משא"כ בזרע לבטלה שאין שם בחי' נוקבא דקליפה רק שכחותיה וחיילותיה מלבישים לחיות שבטפות כידוע לי"ח):

ז טבת פשוטה

יא טבת מעוברת

פרק ח ועוד זאת במאכלות אסורות שלכך נקראים בשם איסור מפני שאף מי שאכל מאכל איסור בלא הודע לשם שמים לעבוד ה' בכח אכילה ההיא וגם פעל ועשה כן וקרא והתפלל בכח אכילה ההיא

אין החיות שבה עולה ומתלבשת בתיבות התורה והתפלה כמו ההיתר מפני איסורה בידי הס"א משלש קליפות הטמאות ואפי' הוא איסור דרבנן שחמורים דברי סופרים יותר מדברי תורה כו' ולכן גם היצר הרע וכח המתאוה לדברים האסורים הוא שד משדין נוכראין שהוא יצר הרע של אומות העולם שנפשותיהם משלש קליפות הטמאות משא"כ היצה"ר וכח המתאוה לדברים המותרים למלאת תאותו הוא שד משדין יהודאין לפי שיכול לחזור לקדושה כדלעיל. אך מ"מ קודם שחזר לקדושה הוא ס"א וקליפה וגם אח"כ הרשימו ממנו נשאר דבוק בגוף להיות כי מכל מאכל ומשקה נעשה תיכף דם ובשר מבשרו ולכן צריך הגוף לחיבוט הקבר לנקותו ולטהרו מטומאתו שקיבל בהנאת עולם הזה ותענוגיו מטומאת קליפת נוגה ושדין יהודאין אא"כ מי שלא נהנה מעוה"ז כל ימיו כרבינו הקדוש. ועל דברים בטלים בהיתר כגון ע"ה שאינו יכול ללמוד צריך לטהר ח טבת פשוטה
נפשו מטומאה זו דקליפה זו ע"י גלגולה בכף הקלע כמ"ש בזהר פ' בשלח דף נ"ט. אבל לדיבורים אסורים כמו ליצנות ולשון הרע וכיוצא בהם שהן משלש קליפות הטמאות לגמרי אין כף הקלע [לבדו] מועיל לטהר ולהעביר טומאתו מהנפש רק צריכה לירד לגיהנם. וכן מי שאפשר לו לעסוק בתורה ועוסק בדברים בטלים אין כף הקלע לבדו מועיל לנפשו למרקה ולזככה רק עונשים חמורים שמענישים על ביטול תורה בפרטות מלבד עונש הכללי לכל ביטול מ"ע מחמת עצלות בגיהנם של שלג כמבואר במ"א וכן העוסק בחכמות אומות העולם בכלל דברים בטלים יחשב לענין עון ביטול תורה כמ"ש בהלכות תלמוד תורה ועוד זאת יתרה טומאתה של חכמת האומות על טומאת דברים בטלים שאינו מלביש ומטמא רק המדות מיסוד הרוח הקדוש שבנפשו האלהית בטומאת קליפת נוגה שבדברים בטלים הבאים מיסוד הרוח הרע שבקליפה זו בנפשו הבהמית כדלעיל ולא בחי' חב"ד שבנפשו מאחר שהם דברי שטות ובורות שגם השוטים וע"ה יכולים לדבר כן. משא"כ בחכמת האומות הוא מלביש ומטמא בחי' חב"ד שבנפשו האלהית בטומאת קליפת נוגה שבחכמות אלו שנפלו שמה בשבירת הכלי' מבחי' אחוריים של חכמה דקדושה כידוע ליודעי חן אלא א"כ עושה אותן קרדום לחתוך בהן דהיינו כדי להתפרנס מהן בריוח לעבוד ה' או שיודע להשתמש בהן לעבודת ה' או לתורתו וזהו טעמו של הרמב"ם ורמב"ן ז"ל וסיעתן שעסקו בהן:

פרק ט והנה מקום משכן נפש הבהמית שמקליפת נוגה בכל איש ישראל הוא בלב בחלל שמאלי שהוא מלא דם וכתיב כי ט טבת פשוטה / יב טבת מעוברת
הדם הוא הנפש ולכן כל התאות והתפארות וכעס ודומיהן הן בלב ומהלב הן מתפשטות בכל הגוף וגם עולה למוח שבראש לחשב ולהרהר בהן

ולהתחכם בהן כמו שהדם מקורו בלב ומהלב מתפשט לכל האברים וגם עולה להמוח שבראש. אך מקום משכן נפש האלהית הוא במוחין שבראש ומשם מתפשטת לכל האברים וגם בלב בחלל הימני שאין בו דם וכמ״ש לב חכם לימינו והיא אהבת ה׳ כרשפי שלהבת מתלהבת בלב משכילים המבינים ומתבוננים בדעתם אשר במוחם בדברים המעוררים את האהבה. וכן שמחת לבב בתפארת ה׳ והדר גאונו כאשר עיני החכם אשר בראשו במוח חכמתו ובינתו מסתכלים ביקרא דמלכא ותפארת גדולתו עד אין חקר ואין סוף ותכלית כמבואר במקום אחר וכן שאר מדות קדושות שבלב הן מחב״ד שבמוחין. אך הנה כתיב ולאום מלאום יאמץ כי הגוף נקרא עיר י טבת פשוטה | יג טבת מעוברת
קטנה וכמו ששני מלכים נלחמים על עיר אחת שכל אחד רוצה לכבשה ולמלוך עליה דהיינו להנהיג יושביה כרצונו ושיהיו סרים למשמעתו בכל אשר יגזור עליהם. כך שתי הנפשות האלהית והחיונית הבהמית שמהקליפה נלחמות זו עם זו על הגוף וכל אבריו שהאלהית חפצה ורצונה שתהא היא לבדה המושלת עליו ומנהיגתו וכל האברים יהיו סרים למשמעתה ובטלים אצלה לגמרי ומרכבה אליה ויהיו לבוש לעשר בחינותיה וג׳ לבושיה הנ״ל שיתלבשו כולם באברי הגוף ויהיה הגוף כולו מלא מהם לבדם ולא יעבור זר בתוכם ח״ו דהיינו תלת מוחין שבראש יהיו ממולאים מחב״ד שבנפש האלהית שהיא חכמת ה׳ ובינתו להתבונן בגדולתו אשר עד אין חקר ואין סוף ולהוליד מהן על ידי הדעת היראה במוחו ופחד ה׳ בלבו ואהבת ה׳ כאש בוערה בלבו כרשפי שלהבת להיות נכספה וגם כלתה נפשו בחשיקה וחפיצה לדבקה בו בא״ס ב״ה בכל לב ונפש ומאד מעומקא דלבא שבחלל הימני שיהיה תוכו רצוף אהבה מלא וגדוש עד שתתפשט גם לחלל השמאלי לאכפיא לס״א יסוד המים הרעים שבה שהיא התאוה שמקליפת נוגה לשנותה ולהפכה מתענוגי עולם הזה לאהבת ה׳ כמ״ש בכל לבבך בשני יצריך והיינו שיעלה ויבא ויגיע למדרגת אהבה רבה וחיבה יתרה ממדרגת אהבה עזה כרשפי אש והיא הנקראת בכתוב אהבה בתענוגים להתענג יד טבת מעוברת
על ה׳ מעין עולם הבא והענג הוא במוח חכמה ושכל המתענג בהשכלת ה׳ וידיעתו כפי השגת שכלו וחכמתו והוא בחי׳ המים וזרע אור זרוע שבקדושת נפש האלהית המהפכת לטוב את בחי׳ המים שבנפש הבהמית שמהם באו תאות תענוגי עוה״ז מתחלה וכמ״ש בע״ח שער נ׳ פרק ג׳ בשם הזהר שהרע נהפך להיות טוב גמור כמו יצר טוב ממש בהסיר הבגדים הצואים ממנו שהם תענוגי עוה״ז שהוא מלובש בהם וכן שאר כל המדות שבלב שהן ענפי היראה והאהבה יהיו לה׳ לבדו וכל כח הדבור שבפה והמחשבה שבמוח יהיו ממולאים מן לבושי המחשבה והדבור של נפש האלהית לבדה שהן מחשבת ה׳ ותורתו להיות שיחתו כל היום לא פסיק פומיה מגירסא וכח המעשיי שבידי׳ ושאר רמ״ח אבריו יהיה במעשה המצות לבד שהוא לבוש

השלישי של נפש האלהית אך נפש הבהמית שמהקליפה רצונה להפך ממש לטובת האדם שיתגבר עליה וינצחנה כמשל הזונה שבזה״ק:

יא טבת פשוטה **פרק י והנה** כשהאדם מגביר נפשו האלהית ונלחם כל כך עם הבהמית
טו טבת מעוברת עד שמגרש ומבער הרע שבה מחלל השמאלי כמ״ש
ובערת הרע מקרבך ואין הרע נהפך לטוב ממש נקרא צדיק שאינו גמור וצדיק ורע לו דהיינו שיש בו עדיין מעט מזער רע בחלל השמאלי אלא שכפוף ובטל לטוב מחמת מיעוטו ולכן נדמה לו כי ויגרשהו וילך לו כולו לגמרי אבל באמת אלו חלף והלך לו לגמרי כל הרע שבו היה נהפך לטוב ממש. וביאור הענין כי הנה צדיק גמור שנהפך הרע שלו לטוב ולכן נקרא צדיק וטוב לו הוא ע״י הסרת הבגדים הצואים לגמרי מהרע דהיינו למאוס מאד בתענוגי עוה״ז להתענג בם בתענוגות בני אדם למלאת תאות הגוף בלבד ולא לעבודת ה׳ מפני היותם נמשכים ונשפעים מהקליפה וס״א וכל מה שהוא מהס״א הצדיק גמור הוא שונאו בתכלית השנאה מחמת גודל אהבתו לה׳ וקדושתו באהבה רבה בתענוגים וחיבה יתרה הנ״ל כי הם זה לעומת זה כדכתיב תכלית שנאה שנאתים לאויבים היו לי חקרני ודע לבבי וגו׳ וכפי ערך גודל האהבה לה׳ כך ערך גודל השנאה לס״א והמיאוס ברע
טז טבת מעוברת בתכלית כי המיאוס הוא הפך האהבה ממש כמו השנאה. וצדיק שאינו גמור הוא שאינו שונא הס״א בתכלית השנאה ולכן אינו מואס ג״כ ברע בתכלית וכל שאין השנאה והמיאוס בתכלית ע״כ נשאר איזה שמץ אהבה ותענוג לשם ולא הוסרו הבגדים הצואים לגמרי מכל וכל ולכן לא נהפך לטוב ממש מאחר שיש לו איזה אחיזה עדיין בבגדים הצואים אלא שהוא בטל במיעוטו וכלא חשיב ולכן נקרא צדיק ורע כפוף ובטל לו. ועל כן גם
יב טבת פשוטה אהבתו לה׳ אינה בתכלית ולכן נקרא צדיק שאינו גמור. והנה מדרגה זו מתחלקת לרבבות מדרגות בענין בחי׳ מיעוט הרע הנשאר מאחת מארבע יסודות הרעים ובענין ביטולו במיעוטו בששים עד״מ או באלף ורבבה וכיוצא עד״מ והן הם בחי׳ צדיקים הרבים שבכל הדורות כדאיתא בגמ׳ דתמניסר אלפי צדיקי קיימי קמי׳ הקב״ה אך על מעלת צדיק גמור הוא שאמר רשב״י ראיתי בני עליה והם מועטים כו׳ שלכן נקראים בני עליה שמהפכין הרע ומעלים אותו לקדושה כדאיתא בזהר בהקדמה שכשרצה רבי חייא לעלות להיכל ר״ש בן יוחאי שמע קלא נפיק ואמר מאן מנכון די חשוכא מהפכן לנהורא וטעמין מרירו למיתקא עד לא ייתון הכא וכו׳:
יז טבת מעוברת ועוד נקראים בני עליה מפני שגם עבודתם בבחי׳ ועשה טוב בקיום התורה ומצותיה הוא לצורך גבוה ומעלה מעלה עד רום המעלות ולא כדי לדבקה בו ית׳ בלבד לרוות צמאון נפשם הצמאה לה׳ כמ״ש הוי כל צמא לכו למים וכמ״ש במ״א אלא כדפירשו בתיקונים איזהו חסיד המתחסד עם קונו עם

קן דיליה לייחדא קב"ה ושכינתי' בתחתונים וכמ"ש ברעי' מהימנא פ' תצא כברא דאשתדל בתר אבוי ואימיה דרחים לון יתיר מגרמיה ונפשיה ורוחיה ונשמתי' כו' ומסר גרמיה למיתה עלייהו למיפרק לון כו' וכמ"ש במ"א. [ושניהם עולים בקנה אחד כי ע"י הבירורים שמבררים מנוגה מעלים מיין נוקבין ונעשי' יחודים עליונים להוריד מיין דכורין שהם הם מימי החסדים שבכל מצוה ומצוה מרמ"ח מצות עשה שכולן הן בחי' חסדים ומיין דכורין דהיינו המשכת קדושת אלהותו יתברך מלמעלה למטה להתלבש בתחתונים כמ"ש במ"א]:

יג טבת פשוטה

יח טבת מעוברת

פרק יא וזה לעומת זה רשע וטוב לו לעומת צדיק ורע לו דהיינו שהטוב שבנפשו האלהי' שבמוחו ובחלל הימני שבלבו כפוף ובטל לגבי הרע מהקליפה שבחלל השמאלי וזה מתחלק גם כן לרבבות מדרגות חלוקות בענין כמות ואיכות הביטול וכפיפת הטוב לרע ח"ו יש מי שהכפיפה והביטול אצלו מעט מזער ואף גם זאת אינו בתמידות ולא תדיר לפרקים קרובים אלא לעתים רחוקים מתגבר הרע על הטוב וכובש את העיר קטנה הוא הגוף אך לא כולו אלא מקצתו לבד שיהיה סר למשמעתו ונעשה לו מרכבה ולבוש להתלבש בו א' משלשה לבושיה הנ"ל דהיינו או במעשה לבד לעשות עבירות קלות ולא חמורות ח"ו או בדיבור לבד לדבר אבק לשון הרע וליצנות וכהאי גוונא או במחשבה לבד הרהורי עבירה הקשים מעבירה וגם אם אינו מהרהר בעבירה לעשותה אלא בענין זיווג זכר ונקיבה בעולם שעובר על אזהרת התורה ונשמרת מכל דבר רע שלא יהרהר ביום כו' או שהיא שעת הכושר לעסוק בתורה והוא מפנה לבו לבטלה כדתנן באבות הניעור בלילה כו' ומפנה לבו כו' שבאחת מכל אלה וכיוצא בהן נקרא רשע בעת ההיא שהרע שבנפשו גובר בו ומתלבש בגופו ומחטיאו ומטמאו ואח"כ גובר בו הטוב שבנפשו האלהי' ומתחרט ומבקש מחילה וסליחה מה' וה' יסלח לו אם שב בתשובה הראויה על פי עצת חכמינו ז"ל בשלשה חלוקי כפרה שהיה ר' ישמעאל דורש כו' כמ"ש במ"א. ויש מי שהרע גובר בו יותר ומתלבשי' בו כל שלשה לבושים של הרע ומחטיאו בעבירות חמורות יותר ובעתים קרובים יותר אך בינתיים מתחרט ובאים לו הרהורי תשובה מבחי' הטוב שבנפשו שמתגבר קצת בינתיים אלא שאין לו התגברות כל כך לנצח את הרע לפרוש מחטאיו לגמרי להיות מודה ועוזב ועל זה אמרו רז"ל רשעים מלאים חרטות שהם רוב הרשעים שיש בחי' טוב בנפשם עדיין. אך מי שאינו מתחרט לעולם ואין באים לו הרהורי תשובה כלל נקרא רשע ורע לו שהרע שבנפשו הוא לבדו נשאר בקרבו כי גבר כל כך על הטוב עד שנסתלק מקרבו ועומד בבחי' מקיף עליו מלמעלה ולכן ארז"ל אכל בי עשרה שכינתא שריא:

יד טבת פשוטה / יט טבת מעוברת

פרק יב והבינוני הוא שלעולם אין הרע גובר כל כך לכבוש את העיר קטנ׳ להתלבש בגוף להחטיאו דהיינו ששלש׳ לבושי נפש הבהמית שהם מחשבה דבור ומעשה שמצד הקליפ׳ אין גוברים בו על נפש האלהית להתלבש בגוף במוח ובפה ובשאר רמ״ח אברים להחטיאם ולטמאם ח״ו רק שלשה לבושי נפש האלהית הם לבדם מתלבשים בגוף שהם מחשבה דבור ומעשה של תרי״ג מצות התורה ולא עבר עבירה מימיו ולא יעבור לעולם ולא נקרא עליו שם רשע אפי׳ שעה אחת ורגע אחד כל ימיו

כ טבת מעוברת

אך מהות ועצמות נפש האלהית שהן עשר בחינותיה לא להן לבדן המלוכה והממשלה בעיר קטנה כי אם בעתים מזומנים כמו בשעת קריאת שמע ותפלה שהיא שעת מוחין דגדלות למעלה וגם למטה היא שעת הכושר לכל אדם שאז מקשר חב״ד שלו לה׳ להעמיק דעתו בגדולת א״ס ב״ה ולעורר את האהבה כרשפי אש בחלל הימני שבלבו לדבקה בו בקיום התורה ומצותיה מאהבה שזהו ענין המבואר בקריאת שמע דאורייתא וברכותיה שלפניה ולאחריה שהן מדרבנן הן הכנה לקיום הק״ש כמ״ש במ״א ואז הרע שבחלל השמאלי כפוף ובטל לטוב המתפשט בחלל הימני מחב״ד שבמוח המקושרים בגדולת א״ס ב״ה. אבל אחר התפלה בהסתלקות המוחין דגדלות א״ס ב״ה הרי הרע חוזר וניעור בחלל השמאלי ומתאוה תאוה

טו טבת פשוטה / כא טבת מעוברת

לתאות עוה״ז ותענוגיו. רק מפני שלא לו לבדו משפט המלוכה והממשלה בעיר אינו יכול להוציא תאותו מכח אל הפועל להתלבש באברי הגוף במעשה דבור ומחשבה ממש להעמיק מחשבתו בתענוגי עוה״ז איך למלאת תאות לבו כי המוח שליט על הלב [כמ״ש בר״מ פ׳ פינחס] בתולדתו וטבע יצירתו שכך נוצר האדם בתולדתו שכל אדם יכול ברצונו שבמוחו להתאפק ולמשול ברוח תאותו שבלבו שלא למלאת משאלות לבו במעשה דבור ומחשבה ולהסיח דעתו לגמרי מתאות לבו אל ההפך לגמרי ובפרט אל צד הקדושה כדכתיב וראיתי שיש יתרון לחכמה מן הסכלות כיתרון האור מן החושך פי׳ כמו שהאור יש לו יתרון ושליטה וממשלה על החושך שמעט אור גשמי דוחה הרבה מן החשך שנדחה ממנו מאליו וממילא כך נדחה ממילא סכלות הרבה של הקליפה וס״א שבחלל השמאלי [כמאמר רז״ל אלא אם כן נכנס בו רוח שטות וכו׳] מפני החכמה שבנפש האלהית שבמוח אשר רצונה למשול לבדה בעיר ולהתלבש בשלשה לבושיה הנ״ל בכל הגוף כולו כנ״ל שהם מחשבה דבור ומעשה של תרי״ג מצות התורה כנ״ל

טז טבת פשוטה / כב טבת מעוברת

ואעפ״כ אינו נקרא צדיק כלל מפני שיתרון הזה אשר לאור נפש האלהית על החושך וסכלות של הקליפה הנדחה ממילא אינו אלא בשלשה לבושי׳ הנ״ל ולא במהותה ועצמותה על מהותה ועצמותה של הקליפה כי מהותה ועצמותה של נפש הבהמית שמהקליפה שבחלל השמאלי לא נדחה כלל

ממקומו בבינוני אחר התפלה שאין רשפי אש אהבת ה׳ בהתגלות לבו בחלל הימני כי אם תוכו רצוף אהבה מסותרת שהיא אהבה הטבעית שבנפש האלהית כמ״ש לקמן ואזי יכול להיות סכלות הכסיל הרע בהתגלו׳ לבו בחלל השמאלי להתאות תאוה לכל ענייני גשמיות עוה״ז בין בהיתר בין באיסור ח״ו כאלו לא התפלל כלל אלא שבדבר איסור אינו עולה בדעתו לעשות האיסור בפועל ממש ח״ו אלא הרהורי עבירה הקשים מעבירה יכולים לפעול לעלות למוחו ולבלבלו מתורה ועבודה וכמארז״ל ג׳ עבירות אין אדם ניצול מהן בכל יום הרהור עבירה ועיון תפלה כו׳ רק שלזה מועיל הרשימו במוחין ויראת ה׳ ואהבתו המסותרת בחלל הימני להתגבר ולשלוט על הרע הזה המתאוה תאוה שלא להיות לו שליטה וממשלה בעיר להוציא תאותו מכח אל הפועל להתלבש באברי הגוף ואפי׳ במוח לבדו להרהר ברע אין לו שליטה וממשלה להרהר ח״ו ברצונו שבמוחו שיקבל ברצון ח״ו הרהור זה הרע העולה מאליו מהלב למוח כנ״ל אלא מיד בעלייתו לשם דוחהו בשתי ידים ומסיח דעתו מיד שנזכר שהוא הרהור רע ואינו מקבלו ברצון אפי׳ להרהר בו ברצון וכ״ש להעלותו על הדעת לעשותו ח״ו או אפי׳ לדבר בו כי המהרהר ברצון נק׳ רשע באותה שעה והבינוני אינו רשע אפי׳ שעה אחת לעולם. וכן בדברים שבין אדם לחבירו מיד שעולה לו מהלב למוח איזו טינא ושנאה ח״ו או איזו קנאה או כעס או קפידא ודומיהן אינו מקבלן כלל במוחו וברצונו ואדרבה המוח שליט ומושל ברוח שבלבו לעשות ההפך ממש להתנהג עם חבירו במדת חסד וחיבה יתרה מודעת לו לסבול ממנו עד קצה האחרון ולא לכעוס ח״ו וגם שלא לשלם לו כפעלו ח״ו אלא אדרבה לגמול לחייבים טובות כמ״ש בזהר ללמוד מיוסף עם אחיו: יז טבת פשוטה | כג טבת מעוברת

פרק יג ובזה יובן לשון מאמרז״ל בינונים זה וזה שופטן [פי׳ יצר טוב ויצר הרע] דכתיב כי יעמוד לימין אביון להושיע משופטי נפשו ולא אמרו זה וזה מושלים ח״ו כי כשיש איזו שליטה וממשלה ליצר הרע בעיר קטנה אפי׳ לפי שעה קלה נקרא רשע באותה שעה אלא היצה״ר אינו רק עד״מ כמו שופט ודיין האומר דעתו במשפט ואעפ״כ יכול להיות שלא יהיה פסק הלכה כך למעשה מפני שיש עוד שופט ודיין החולק עליו וצריך להכריע ביניהם והלכה כדברי המכריע כך היצה״ר אומר דעתו בחלל השמאלי שבלב ומהלב עולה למוח להרהר בו ומיד חולק עליו השופט השני שהוא הנפש האלהית שבמוח המתפשט בחלל הימני שבלב מקום משכן היצר טוב והלכה כדברי המכריע הוא הקב״ה העוזרו להיצר טוב כמאמר רז״ל אלמלא הקב״ה עוזרו אין יכול לו והעזר יח טבת פשוטה | כד טבת מעוברת

היא ההארה שמאיר אור ה׳ על נפש האלהית להיות לה יתרון ושליטה
על סכלות הכסיל ויצה״ר כיתרון האור מן החושך כנ״ל. אך מאחר שהרע כה טבת מעוברת
שבחלל השמאלי בבינוני הוא בתקפו כתולדתו להתאות תאוה לכל תענוגי
עוה״ז ולא נתבטל במיעוט לגבי הטוב ולא נדחה ממקומו כלל רק שאין לו
שליטה וממשלה להתפשט באברי הגוף מפני הקב״ה העומד לימין אביון
ועוזר ומאיר לנפש האלהית לכן נקרא כרשע כמארז״ל אפילו כל העולם
כולו אומרים לך צדיק אתה היה בעיניך כרשע ולא רשע ממש אלא
שיחזיק עצמו לבינוני ולא להאמין להעולם שאומרים שהרע שבו נתבטל
לגבי הטוב שזו מדרגת צדיק אלא יהיה בעיניו כאלו מהותו ועצמותו של
הרע הוא בתקפו ובגבורתו בחלל השמאלי כתולדתו ולא חלף והלך ממנו
מאומה ואדרבה נתחזק יותר בהמשך הזמן שנשתמש בו הרבה באכילה
ושתיה ושאר ענייני עוה״ז ואף מי שבתורת ה׳ חפצו ויהגה בה יומם ולילה יט טבת פשוטה
לשמה אין זו הוכחה כלל שנדחה הרע ממקומו אלא יכול להיות שמהותו
ועצמותו הוא בתקפו ובגבורתו במקומו בחלל השמאלי רק שלבושיו שהם
מחשבה דבור ומעשה של נפש הבהמית אינן מתלבשים במוח והפה והידים
ושאר אברי הגוף מפני ה׳ שנתן שליטה וממשלה למוח על הלב ולכן נפש
האלהית שבמוח מושלת בעיר קטנה אברי הגוף כולם שיהיו לבוש ומרכבה
לשלש׳ לבושיה שיתלבשו בהם שהם מחשבה דבור ומעשה של תרי״ג מצות
התורה אבל מהותה ועצמותה של נפש האלהית אין לה שליטה וממשלה
על מהותה ועצמותה של נפש הבהמית בבינוני כי אם בשעה שאהבת ה׳
הוא בהתגלות לבו בעתים מזומנים כמו בשעת התפלה וכיוצא בה ואף גם
זאת הפעם אינה רק שליטה וממשלה לבד כדכתיב ולאום מלאום יאמץ
כשזה קם זה נופל וכשזה קם כו׳ שנפש האלהית מתאמצת ומתגברת על
נפש הבהמית במקור הגבורות שהיא בינה להתבונן בגדולת ה׳ א״ס ב״ה
ולהוליד אהבה עזה לה׳ כרשפי אש בחלל הימני שבלבו ואז אתכפיא ס״א
שבחלל השמאלי אבל לא נתבטל לגמרי בבינוני אלא בצדיק שנאמר בו
ולבי חלל בקרבי והוא מואס ברע ושונאו בתכלית השנאה והמיאוס או
שלא בתכלית השנאה כנ״ל. אבל בבינוני הוא ד״מ כאדם שישן שיכול
לחזור וליעור משנתו כך הרע בבינוני הוא כישן בחלל השמאלי בשעת
ק״ש ותפלה שלבו בוער באהבת ה׳ ואח״כ יכול להיות חוזר וניעור. ולכן
היה רבה מחזיק עצמו כבינוני אף דלא פסיק פומיה מגירסא ובתורת ה׳
חפצו יומם ולילה בחפיצה וחשיקה ותשוקה ונפש שוקקה לה׳ באהבה רבה
כבשעת ק״ש ותפלה ונדמה בעיניו כבינוני המתפלל כל היום וכמאמר רז״ל
הלואי שיתפלל אדם כל היום כולו: והנה מדת אהבה זו האמורה בבינונים כ טבת פשוטה
בשעת התפלה ע״י התגברות הנפש האלהית כו׳ הנה לגבי מדרגת הצדיקים

עובדי ה׳ באמת לאמיתו אין בחי׳ אהבה זו נקראת בשם עבודת אמת כלל מאחר שחולפת ועוברת אחר התפלה וכתיב שפת אמת תכון לעד ועד ארגיעה לשון שקר ואעפ״כ לגבי מדרגת הבינונים נקראת עבודה תמה באמת לאמיתו שלהם איש איש כפי מדרגתו במדרגת הבינונים והריני קורא באהבתם שבתפלתם ג״כ שפת אמת תכון לעד הואיל ובכח נפשם האלהית לחזור ולעורר בחי׳ אהבה זו לעולם בהתגברותה בשעת התפלה מדי יום ביום ע״י הכנה הראויה לכל נפש כפי ערכה ומדרגת׳ כי הנה מדת אמת היא מדתו של יעקב הנקרא בריח התיכון המבריח מן הקצה אל הקצה מרום המעלות ומדרגות עד סוף כל דרגין ובכל מעלה ומדרגה מבריח תוך נקודה האמצעית שהיא נקודת ובחי׳ מדת אמת שלה ומדת אמת היא נחלה בלי מצרים ואין לה שיעור למעלה עד רום המעלות וכל מעלות ומדרגות שלמטה הם כאין לגבי מעלות ומדרגות שלמעלה מהן [כידוע לי״ח שבחי׳ ראש ומוחין של מדרגות תחתונות הן למטה מבחי׳ עקביים ורגלי מדרגות עליונות מהן וכמאמר רז״ל רגלי החיות כנגד כולן]:

פרק יד והנה מדת הבינוני היא מדת כל אדם ואחריה כל אדם ימשוך שכל אדם יכול להיות בינוני בכל עת ובכל שעה כי הבינוני אינו מואס ברע שזהו דבר המסור ללב ולא כל העתים שוות אלא סור מרע ועשה טוב דהיינו בפועל ממש במעשה דבור ומחשבה שבהם הבחירה והיכולת והרשות נתונה לכל אדם לעשות ולדבר ולחשוב גם מה שהוא נגד תאות לבו והפכה ממש כי גם בשעה שהלב חומד ומתאוה איזו תאוה גשמיית בהיתר או באיסור ח״ו יכול להתגבר ולהסיח דעתו ממנה לגמרי באמרו ללבו אינני רוצה להיות רשע אפי׳ שעה אחת כי אינני רוצה להיות מובדל ונפרד ח״ו מה׳ אחד בשום אופן כדכתיב עונותיכם מבדילים וגו׳ רק אני רוצה לדבקה בו נפשי רוחי ונשמתי בהתלבשן בשלשה לבושיו ית׳ שהם מעשה דבור ומחשבה בה׳ ותורתו ומצותיו מאהבה מסותרת שבלבי לה׳ כמו בלב כללו׳ ישראל שנקראו אוהבי שמך ואפי׳ קל שבקלים יכול למסור נפשו על קדושת ה׳ ולא נופל אנכי ממנו בודאי אלא שנכנס בו רוח שטות ונדמה לו שבעביר׳ זו עודנו ביהדותו ואין נשמתו מובדלת מאלהי ישראל וגם שוכח אהבתו לה׳ המסותרת בלבו אבל אני אינני רוצה להיות שוטה כמוהו לכפור האמת. משא״כ בדבר המסור ללב דהיינו שיהא הרע מאוס ממש בלב ושנאוי בתכלית שנאה או אפי׳ שלא בתכלית שנאה הנה זה אי אפשר שיהיה באמת לאמיתו אלא ע״י גודל ותוקף האהבה לה׳ בבחי׳ אהבה בתענוגים להתענג על ה׳ מעין עוה״ב. ועל זה אמרו רז״ל עולמך תראה בחייך כו׳ ואין כל אדם זוכה לזה כי זהו כעין קבול שכר

כא טבת פשוטה
כו טבת מעוברת
כז טבת מעוברת

וכדכתיב עבודת מתנה אתן את כהונתכם וגו׳ כמ״ש במ״א. ולכן אמר איוב בראת צדיקים כו׳ וכדאיתא בתיקונים שיש בנשמות ישראל כמה מיני מדרגות ובחי׳. חסידים גבורים המתגברים על יצרם מארי תורה נביאים כו׳ צדיקים כו׳ ע״ש: ובזה יובן כפל לשון השבועה תהי צדיק ואל תהי רשע דלכאורה תמוה כי מאחר שמשביעים אותו תהי צדיק למה צריכים להשביעו עוד שלא יהיה רשע. אלא משום שאין כל אדם זוכה להיות צדיק ואין לאדם משפט הבחירה בזה כל כך להתענג על ה׳ באמת ושיהיה הרע מאוס ממש באמת ולכן משביעים שנית אל תהי רשע עכ״פ שבזה משפט הבחירה והרשות נתונה לכל אדם למשול ברוח תאותו שבלבו ולכבוש יצרו שלא יהיה רשע אפי׳ שעה אחת כל ימיו בין בבחי׳ סור מרע בין בבחי׳ ועשה טוב ואין טוב אלא תורה דהיינו תלמוד תורה שכנגד כולן. אך אעפ״כ צריך לקבוע לו עתים גם כן לשית עצות בנפשו להיות מואס ברע כגון בעצת חכמינו ז״ל אשה חמת מלאה צואה כו׳. וכהאי גוונא. וכן כל מיני מטעמים ומעדנים נעשים כך חמת מלא כו׳. וכן כל תענוגי עוה״ז החכם רואה הנולד מהן שסופן לרקוב ולהיות רמה ואשפה וההפך להתענג ולשמוח בה׳ ע״י התבוננות בגדולת א״ס ב״ה כפי יכולתו אף שיודע בנפשו שלא יגיע למדרגה זו באמת לאמיתו כי אם בדמיונות אעפ״כ הוא יעשה את שלו לקיים את השבועה שמשביעים תהי צדיק וה׳ יעשה הטוב בעיניו. ועוד שההרגל על כל דבר שלטון ונעשה טבע שני. וכשירגיל למאס את הרע יהיה נמאס קצת באמת וכשירגיל לשמח נפשו בה׳ ע״י התבוננות בגדולת ה׳ הרי באתערותא דלתתא אתערותא דלעילא וכולי האי ואולי יערה עליו רוח ממרום ויזכה לבחי׳ רוח משרש איזה צדיק שתתעבר בו לעבוד ה׳ בשמחה אמיתית כדכתיב שמחו צדיקים בה׳ ותתקיים בו באמת השבועה שמשביעים תהי צדיק:

כב טבת פשוטה | כח טבת מעוברת

פרק טו

ובזה יובן מ״ש ושבתם וראיתם בין צדיק לרשע בין עובד אלהים לאשר לא עבדו שההפרש בין עובד אלהים לצדיק הוא שעובד הוא לשון הוה שהוא באמצע העבודה שהיא המלחמה עם היצה״ר להתגבר עליו ולגרשו מהעיר קטנה שלא יתלבש באברי הגוף שהוא באמת עבודה ועמל גדול להלחם בו תמיד והיינו הבינוני. אבל הצדיק נקרא עבד ה׳ בשם התואר כמו שם חכם או מלך שכבר נעשה חכם או מלך כך זה כבר עבד וגמר לגמרי עבודת המלחמה עם הרע עד כי ויגרשהו וילך לו ולבו חלל בקרבו. ובבינוני יש ג״כ שתי מדרגות עובד אלהים ואשר לא עבדו ואעפ״כ אינו רשע כי לא עבר מימיו שום עבירה קלה וגם קיים כל המצות שאפשר לו לקיימן ותלמוד תורה כנגד כולם ולא פסיק פומיה מגירסא אלא שאינו עושה שום מלחמה עם היצר לנצחו ע״י אור ה׳ המאיר

כג טבת פשוטה | כט טבת מעוברת

א שבט מעוברת

על נפש האלהית שבמוח השליט על הלב כנ״ל מפני שאין יצרו עומד לנגדו כלל לבטלו מתורתו ועבודתו ואין צריך ללחום עמו כלל כגון שהוא מתמיד בלמודו בטבעו מתולדתו על ידי תגבורת המרה שחורה וכן אין לו מלחמה מתאות נשים מפני שהוא מצונן בטבעו וכן בשאר תענוגי עוה״ז הוא מחוסר הרגש הנאה בטבעו ולכן אין צריך להתבונן כל כך בגדולת ה׳ להוליד מבינתו רוח דעת ויראת ה׳ במוחו להשמר שלא לעבור על מצות ל״ת ואהבת ה׳ בלבו לדבקה בו בקיום המצות ות״ת כנגד כולן אלא די לו באהבה מסותרת אשר בלב כללות ישראל שנקראו אוהבי שמו ולכן אינו נקרא עובד כלל כי אהבה זו המסותרת אינה פעולתו ועבודתו כלל אלא היא ירושתנו מאבותינו לכלל ישראל וכמ״ש לקמן. וכן אף מי שאינו מתמיד בלמודו בטבעו רק שהרגיל עצמו ללמוד בהתמדה גדולה ונעשה ההרגל לו טבע שני די לו באהבה מסותרת זו אא״כ רוצה ללמוד יותר מרגילותו ובזה יובן מ״ש בגמרא דעובד אלהים היינו מי ששונה פרקו מאה פעמים ואחד ולא עבדו היינו מי ששונה פרקו מאה פעמים לבד והיינו משום שבימיהם היה הרגילות לשנות כל פרק מאה פעמים כדאיתא התם בגמרא משל משוק של חמרים שנשכרים לעשר פרסי בזוזא ולאחד עשר פרסי בתרי זוזי מפני שהוא יותר מרגילותם. ולכן זאת הפעם המאה ואחת היתרה על הרגילות שהורגל מנעוריו שקולה כנגד כולן ועולה על גביהן ביתר שאת ויתר עז להיות נקרא עובד אלהים מפני שכדי לשנות טבע הרגילות צריך לעורר את האהבה לה׳ ע״י שמתבונן בגדולת ה׳ במוחו לשלוט על הטבע שבחלל השמאלי המלא דם הנפש הבהמית שמהקליפה שממנה הוא הטבע וזו היא עבודה תמה לבינוני. או לעורר את האהבה המסותרת שבלבו למשול על ידה על הטבע שבחלל השמאלי שזו נקרא ג״כ עבודה להלחם עם הטבע והיצר ע״י שמעורר האהבה המסותרת בלבו משא״כ כשאין לו מלחמה כלל אין אהבה זו מצד עצמה נקראת עבודתו כלל:

כד טבת פשוטה | ב שבט מעוברת

פרק טז וזה

כה טבת פשוטה | ג שבט מעוברת

כלל גדול בעבודת ה׳ לבינונים העיקר הוא למשול ולשלוט על הטבע שבחלל השמאלי ע״י אור ה׳ המאיר לנפש האלהית שבמוח ולשלוט על הלב כשמתבונן במוחו בגדולת א״ס ב״ה להוליד מבינתו רוח דעת ויראת ה׳ במוחו להיות סור מרע דאורייתא ודרבנן ואפילו איסור קל של דבריהם ח״ו ואהבת ה׳ בלבו בחלל הימני בחשיקה וחפיצה לדבקה בו בקיום המצות דאורייתא ודרבנן ות״ת שכנגד כולן. ויתר על כן צריך לידע כלל גדול בעבודה לבינונים שגם אם אין יד שכלו ורוח בינתו משגת

הגהה

› (והסיבה לזה היא מפני היות המוחין שלו ונר״נ שלו מבחי׳ עיבור והעלם תוך התבונה ולא מבחי׳ לידה והתגלות כידוע לי״ח):

להוליד אהבת ה׳ בהתגלו׳ לבו שיהיה לבו בוער כרשפי אש וחפץ בחפיצה וחשיקה ותשוקה מורגשת בלב לדבקה בו רק האהבה מסותרת במוחו ותעלומות לבו:* דהיינו שהלב מבין ברוח חכמה ובינ׳ שבמוחו גדולת א״ס ב״ה דכולא קמיה כלא חשיב ממש אשר על כן יאתה לו יתב׳ שתכלה אליו נפש כל חי לידבק ולהכלל באורו. וגם נפשו ורוחו אשר בקרבו כך יאתה להן להיות כלות אליו בחשיקה וחפיצה לצאת מנרתקן הוא הגוף לדבקה בו רק שבע״כ חיות הנה בתוך הגוף וצרורות בו כאלמנות חיות ולית מחשבה דילהון תפיסא ביה כלל כי אם כאשר תפיסא ומתלבשת בתורה ובמצותי׳ כמשל המחבק את המלך הנ״ל. ואי לזאת יאתה להן לחבקו בכל לב ונפש ומאד דהיינו קיום התרי״ג מצות במעשה ובדבור ובמחשבה שהיא השגת וידיעת התורה כנ״ל הנה כשמעמיק בענין זה בתעלומות תבונות לבו ומוחו ופיו ולבו שוין שמקיים כן בפיו כפי אשר נגמר בתבונת לבו ומוחו דהיינו להיות בתורת ה׳ חפצו ויהגה בה יומם ולילה בפיו וכן הידים ושאר אברים מקיימים המצות כפי מה שנגמר בתבונת לבו ומוחו הרי תבונה זו מתלבשת במעשה דבור ומחשבת התורה ומצותיה להיות להם בחי׳ מוחין וחיות וגדפין לפרחא לעילא כאלו עסק בהם בדחילו ורחימו ממש אשר בהתגלות לבו [בחפיצה וחשיקה ותשוקה מורגשת בלבו ונפשו הצמאה לה׳ מפני רשפי אש אהבתו שבלבו כנ״ל] הואיל ותבונה זו שבמוחו ותעלומות לבו היא המביאתו לעסוק בהם ולולי שהיה מתבונן בתבונה זו לא היה עוסק בהם כלל אלא בצרכי גופו לבד [וגם אם הוא מתמיד בלמודו בטבעו אעפ״כ אוהב את גופו יותר בטבעו] וזה רמזו רז״ל באמרם מחשבה טובה הקב״ה מצרפה למעשה והוה ליה למימר מעלה עליו הכתוב כאלו עשאה. אלא הענין כי דחילו ורחימו שבהתגלות לבו הם המתלבשים במעשה המצות להחיותם לפרחא לעילא כי הלב הוא ג״כ חומרי כשאר אברים שהם כלי המעשה אלא שהוא פנימי וחיות להם ולכן יכול להתלבש בהם להיות להם גדפין להעלותם. אך הדחילו ורחימו שבתבונות מוחו ותעלומות לבו הנ״ל גבהו דרכיהם למעלה מעלה מבחי׳ המעשה ואי אפשר להם להתלבש בבחי׳ מעשה המצות להיות להם בחי׳ מוחין וחיות להעלותן לפרחא לעילא אם לא שהקב״ה מצרפן ומחברן לבחי׳ המעשה והן נקראות בשם מחשבה טובה כי אינן דחילו ורחימו ממש בהתגלות לבו כי אם בתבונת מוחו ותעלומות לבו כנ״ל:* אך צירוף זה מצרף הקב״ה כדי להעלות מעשה המצות ועסק התורה הנעשים על

כו טבת פשוטה

הגהה

* (וכמ״ש בזוהר וע״ח דתבונה אותיות ב״ן וב״ת שהן דחילו ורחימו ולפעמים התבונה יורדת להיות מוחין בנוק׳ דזעיר אנפין שהן אותיות התורה והמצות והמשכיל יבין):

ידי מחשבה טובה הנ״ל עד עולם הבריאה מקום עליית התורה והמצות הנעשים ע״י דחילו ורחימו שכליים אשר בהתגלו׳ לבו ממש אבל בלא״ה נמי עולים לעולם היציר׳ ע״י דחילו ורחימו טבעיים המסותרים בלב כל ישראל בתולדותם כמ״ש לקמן באריכות:

כז טבת פשוטה
ד שבט מעוברת

פרק יז ובזה יובן מ״ש כי קרוב אליך הדבר מאד בפיך ובלבבך לעשותו דלכאורה הוא בלבבך נגד החוש שלנו [והתורה היא נצחית] שאין קרוב מאד הדבר להפך לבו מתאוות עוה״ז לאהבת ה׳ באמת וכמ״ש בגמרא אטו יראה מילתא זוטרתי היא וכל שכן אהבה. וגם אמרו רז״ל דצדיקים דוקא לבם ברשותם. אלא דלעשותו ר״ל האהבה המביאה לידי עשיית המצות בלבד שהיא רעותא דלבא שבתעלומות לב גם כי אינה בהתגלות לבו כרשפי אש ודבר זה קרוב מאד ונקל לכל אדם אשר יש לו מוח בקדקדו כי מוחו ברשותו ויכול להתבונן בו בכל אשר יחפוץ וכשיתבונן בו בגדולת א״ס ב״ה ממילא יוליד במוחו על כל פנים האהבה
ה שבט מעוברת
לה׳ לדבקה בו בקיום מצותיו ותורתו וזה כל האדם כי היום לעשותם כתיב שהיום הוא עולם המעשה דוקא ולמחר כו׳ כמ״ש במ״א. והמוח שליט בטבעו ותולדתו על חלל השמאלי שבלב ועל פיו ועל כל האברים שהם כלי המעשה
כח טבת פשוטה
אם לא מי שהוא רשע באמת כמארז״ל שהרשעים הם ברשות לבם ואין לבם ברשותם כלל וזה עונש על גודל ועוצם עונם ולא דברה תורה במתים אלו שבחייהם קרוים מתים כי באמת אי אפשר לרשעים להתחיל לעבוד ה׳ בלי שיעשו תשובה על העבר תחלה לשבר הקליפו׳ שהם מסך מבדיל ומחיצה של ברזל המפסקת בינם לאביהם שבשמים ע״י שבירת לבו ומרירת נפשו על חטאיו כמ״ש בזהר על פסוק זבחי אלהים רוח נשברה לב נשבר וגו׳ שע״י לב נשבר נשברה רוח הטומאה דס״א [ע״ש פ׳ פינחס ד׳ ר״מ ופ׳
ו שבט מעוברת
ויקרא ד׳ ח׳ וד׳ ה׳ ע״א ובפי׳ הרמ״ז שם] והיא בחי׳ תשובה תתאה להעלות ה׳ תתאה להקימה מנפילתה שנפלה אל החיצוני׳ שהוא סוד גלות השכינה כמארז״ל גלו לאדום שכינה עמהם דהיינו כשאדם עושה מעשה אדום מוריד וממשיך לשם בחי׳ וניצוץ אלהות המחיה את נר״נ שלו המלובשים בו בנפש הבהמית מהקליפה שבלבו שבחלל השמאלי המולכת בו בעודו רשע ומושלת בעיר קטנה שלו ונר״נ כבושי׳ בגולה אצלה וכשנשבר לבו בקרבו ונשברה רוח הטומאה וס״א ויתפרדו כו׳ היא קמה מנפילתה וגם נצבה כמ״ש במ״א:

כט טבת פשוטה
ז שבט מעוברת

פרק יח ולתוספת ביאור באר היטב מלת מאד שבפסוק כי קרוב אליך הדבר מאד וגו׳ צריך לידע נאמנה כי אף

מי שדעתו קצרה בידיעת ה׳ ואין לו לב להבין בגדולת א״ס ב״ה להוליד
ממנה דחילו ורחימו אפי׳ במוחו ותבונתו לבד אעפ״כ קרוב אליו הדבר
מאד לשמור ולעשות כל מצות התורה ות״ת כנגד כולן בפיו ובלבבו ממש
מעומקא דלבא באמת לאמיתו בדחילו ורחימו שהיא אהבה מסותרת
שבלב כללות ישראל שהיא ירושה לנו מאבותינו רק שצריך לבאר ולהקדי׳
תחלה באר היטב שרש אהבה זו ועניינה ואיך היא ירושה לנו ואיך נכלל
בה גם דחילו. והענין כי האבות הן הן המרכבה ועל כן זכו להמשיך נר״נ ח שבט מעוברת
לבניהם אחריהם עד עולם מעשר ספירות דקדושה שבארבע עולמות
אבי״ע לכל אחד ואחד כפי מדרגתו וכפי מעשיו ועל כל פנים אפי׳ לקל
שבקלים ופושעי ישראל נמשך בזיווגם נפש דנפש דמלכות דעשיה שהיא
מדרגה התחתונה שבקדושת העשיה ואעפ״כ מאחר שהיא מעשר ספירות
קדושות היא כלולה מכולן גם מחכמה דעשי׳ שבתוכה מלובשת חכמה
דמלכות דאצילות שבתוכה חכמה דאצילות שבה מאיר אור א״ס ב״ה
ממש כדכתיב ה׳ בחכמה יסד ארץ וכולם בחכמה עשית ונמצא כי אין סוף
ב״ה מלובש בבחי׳ חכמה שבנפש האדם יהיה מי שיהיה מישראל ובחי׳
החכמה שבה עם אור א״ס ב״ה המלובש בה מתפשטת בכל בחי׳ הנפש
כולה להחיותה מבחי׳ ראשה עד בחי׳ רגלה כדכתיב החכמה תחיה בעליה
[ולפעמים ממשיכים פושעי ישראל נשמות גבוהות מאד שהיו בעמקי
הקליפות כמ״ש בספר גלגולים]: הנה החכמה היא מקור השכל וההבנה א שבט פשוטה
והיא למעלה מהבינה שהוא הבנת השכל והשגתו והחכמה היא למעלה ט שבט מעוברת
מההבנה וההשגה והיא מקור להן וזהו לשון חכמה כ״ח מ״ה שהוא מה
שאינו מושג ומובן ואינו נתפס בהשגה עדיין ולכן מתלבש בה אור א״ס
ב״ה דלית מחשבה תפיסא ביה כלל ולכן כל ישראל אפילו הנשים ועמי
הארץ הם מאמינים בה׳ שהאמונה היא למעלה מן הדעת וההשג׳ כי פתי
יאמין לכל דבר וערום יבין וגו׳ ולגבי הקב״ה שהוא למעלה מן השכל
והדעת ולית מחשבה תפיסא ביה כלל הכל כפתיים אצלו ית׳ כדכתיב
ואני בער ולא אדע בהמות הייתי עמך ואני תמיד עמך וגו׳ כלומר שבזה
שאני בער ובהמות אני תמיד עמך ולכן אפי׳ קל שבקלים ופושעי ישראל
מוסרים נפשם על קדושת ה׳ על הרוב וסובלים עינוים קשים שלא לכפור
בה׳ אחד ואף אם הם בורים ועמי הארץ ואין יודעים גדולת ה׳. וגם במעט
שיודעים אין מתבונני׳ כלל ואין מוסרי׳ נפשם מחמת דעת והתבוננות בה׳
כלל. אלא בלי שום דעת והתבוננות רק כאלו הוא דבר שאי אפשר כלל
לכפור בה׳ אחד בלי שום טעם וטענה ומענה כלל והיינו משום שה׳ אחד
מאיר ומחיה כל הנפש ע״י התלבשותו בבחי׳ חכמה שבה שהיא למעלה
מן הדעת והשכל המושג ומובן:

פרק יט ולתוספת ביאור צריך לבאר היטב מ״ש נר ה׳ נשמת אדם ב שבט פשוטה
פי׳ שישראל הקרוים אדם נשמתם היא למשל י שבט מעוברת
כאור הנר שמתנענע תמיד למעלה בטבעו מפני שאור האש חפץ בטבע ליפרד מהפתילה ולידבק בשרשו למעלה ביסוד האש הכללי שתחת גלגל הירח כמ״ש בע״ח ואף שע״י זה יכבה ולא יאיר כלום למטה וגם למעלה בשרשו יתבטל אורו במציאות בשרשו אעפ״כ בכך הוא חפץ בטבעו. כך נשמת האדם וכן בחי׳ רוח ונפש חפצה וחשקה בטבעה ליפרד ולצאת מן הגוף ולידבק בשרשה ומקורה בה׳ חיי החיים ב״ה הגם שתהיה אין ואפס ותתבטל שם במציאות לגמרי ולא ישאר ממנה מאומה ממהותה ועצמותה הראשון אעפ״כ זה רצונה וחפצה בטבעה וטבע זה הוא שם המושאל לכל דבר שאינו בבחי׳ טעם ודעת וגם כאן הכוונה שרצון וחפץ זה בנפש אינו בבחי׳ טעם ודעת ושכל מושג ומובן אלא למעלה מהדעת ושכל המושג
ג שבט פשוטה והמובן והיא בחי׳ חכמה שבנפש שבה אור א״ס ב״ה. וזהו כלל בכל סטרא דקדושה שאינו אלא מה שנמשך מחכמה שנק׳ קודש העליון הבטל במציאות באור א״ס ב״ה המלובש בו ואינו דבר בפני עצמו כנ״ל ולכן נקרא כ״ח מ״ה והוא הפך ממש מבחי׳ הקליפה וס״א שממנה נפשות אומות העולם דעבדין לגרמייהו ואמרין הב הב והלעיטני להיות יש ודבר בפני עצמו כנ״ל הפך בחי׳ החכמה ולכן נקראים מתים כי החכמה תחיה וכתיב ימותו ולא בחכמה. וכן הרשעים ופושעי ישראל קודם שבאו לידי נסיון לקדש השם כי בחי׳ החכמה שבנפש האלהית עם ניצוץ אלהות מאור א״ס ב״ה המלובש בה הם בבחי׳ גלות בגופם בנפש הבהמית מצד הקליפה שבחלל השמאלי שבלב המולכת ומושלת בגופם בסוד גלות השכינה כנ״ל. ולכן נקראת אהבה זו בנפש האלהית שרצונה וחפצה לדבק בה׳ חיי החיים ברוך הוא בשם אהבה מסותרת כי היא מסותרת ומכוסה בלבוש שק דקליפה בפושעי ישראל וממנה נכנס בהם רוח שטות לחטוא כמאמר רז״ל אין אדם
ד שבט פשוטה חוטא כו׳ אלא שגלות הזה לבחי׳ חכמה אינו אלא לבחי׳ המתפשטת ממנה בנפש כולה להחיותה אבל שרש ועיקר של בחי׳ חכמה שבנפש האלהית הוא במוחין ואינה מתלבשת בלבוש שק דקליפה שבלב בחלל השמאלי בבחי׳ גלות ממש. רק שהיא בבחי׳ שינה ברשעים ואינה פועלת פעולתה בהם כל זמן שעסוקים בדעתם ובינתם בתאות העולם. אך כשבאים לידי נסיון בדבר אמונה שהיא למעלה מהדעת ונגעה עד הנפש לבחי׳ חכמה שבה אזי היא ניעורה משנתה ופועלת פעולתה בכח ה׳ המלובש בה. וכמ״ש ויקץ כישן ה׳ לעמוד בנסיון באמונת ה׳ בלי שום טעם ודעת ושכל מושג לו להתגבר על הקליפות ותאוות עוה״ז בהיתר ובאיסור שהורגל בהם ולמאוס בהם ולבחור לו ה׳ לחלקו ולגורלו למסור לו נפשו על קדושת שמו ואף כי

הקליפות גברו עליו כל ימיו ולא יכול להם כמארז״ל שהרשעים הם ברשות לבם מ״מ כשבא לידי נסיון בדבר אמונה בה׳ אחד שיסודתה בהררי קודש היא בחי׳ חכמה שבנפש האלהית שבה מלובש אור א״ס ב״ה הרי כל הקליפות בטלים ומבוטלים והיו כלא היו ממש לפני ה׳ כדכתיב כל הגוים כאין נגדו וגו׳ וכתיב כי הנה אויביך ה׳ כי הנה אויביך יאבדו יתפרדו וגו׳ וכתיב כהמס דונג מפני אש יאבדו וגו׳ וכתיב הרים כדונג נמסו. והנה אור ה׳ א״ס ב״ה המלובש בחכמה שבנפש גדול ועצום כל כך לגרש ולדחות הס״א והקליפות שלא יוכלו יגעו אפי׳ בלבושיו שהם מחשבה דבור ומעשה של אמונת ה׳ אחד דהיינו לעמוד בנסיון למסור נפשו אפי׳ שלא לעשות רק איזה מעשה לבד נגד אמונת ה׳ אחד כגון להשתחות לעבודה זרה אף שאינו מאמין בה כלל בלבו וכן שלא לדבר תועה ח״ו על אחדות ה׳ אף שאין פיו ולבו שוין רק לבו שלם באמונת ה׳ וזה נקרא דחילו הנכלל ברחימו שהיא אהבה הטבעית שבנפש האלהית שבכללות ישראל שחפצה ורצונה בטבעה לידבק בשרשה ומקורה אור א״ס ב״ה שמפני אהבה זו ורצון זה היא יראה ומפחדת בטבעה מנגוע בקצה טומאת ע״ז ח״ו שהיא נגד אמונת ה׳ אחד אפילו בלבושיה החיצונים שהם דבור או מעשה בלי אמונה בלב כלל:

ה שבט פשוטה
יא שבט מעוברת

פרק כ והנה מודעת זאת לכל כי מצות ואזהרת ע״ז שהם שני דברות הראשונים אנכי ולא יהיה לך הם כללות כל התורה כולה.
כי דבור אנכי כולל כל רמ״ח מצות עשה. ולא יהיה לך כולל כל שס״ה מצות ל״ת ולכן שמענו אנכי ולא יהיה לך לבד מפי הגבורה כמארז״ל מפני שהם כללות התורה כולה. ולבאר היטב ענין זה צריך להזכיר תחלה בקצרה ענין ומהות אחדותו של הקב״ה שנקרא יחיד ומיוחד וכל מאמינים שהוא לבדו הוא כמו שהיה קודם שנברא העולם ממש שהיה הוא לבדו וכמ״ש אתה הוא עד שלא נברא העולם אתה הוא משנברא כו׳ פי׳ הוא ממש בלי שום שינוי כדכתיב אני ה׳ לא שניתי כי עוה״ז וכן כל העולמות העליונים אינם פועלים שום שינוי באחדותו ית׳ בהבראם מאין ליש שכמו שהיה הוא לבדו הוא יחיד ומיוחד קודם הבראם כן הוא לבדו הוא יחיד ומיוחד אחר
יב שבט מעוברת
שבראם משום דכולא קמיה כלא חשיב וכאין ואפס ממש כי התהוות כל העולמ׳ עליונים ותחתונים מאין ליש וחיותם וקיומם המקיימם שלא יחזרו להיות אין ואפס כשהיה אינו אלא דבר ה׳ ורוח פיו ית׳ המלובש בהם.
ו שבט פשוטה
ולמשל כמו בנפש האדם כשמדבר דבור אחד שדבור זה לבדו כלא ממש אפי׳ לגבי כללות נפשו המדברת שהוא בחי׳ לבוש האמצעי שלה שהוא כח הדבור שלה שיכול לדבר דבורי׳ לאין קץ ותכלית וכ״ש לגבי בחי׳ לבוש הפנימי שלה שהוא המחשבה שממנה נמשכו הדבורים והיא חיותם וא״צ

לומר לגבי מהות ועצמות הנפש שהן עשר בחינותיה הנ"ל חב"ד כו' שמהן נמשכו אותיות מחשבה זו המלובשות בדבור זה כשמדבר כי המחשבה היא ג"כ בחי' אותיות כמו הדבור רק שהן רוחניות ודקות יותר אבל עשר בחי' חב"ד כו' הן שרש ומקור המחשבה ואין בהם בחי' אותיות עדיין קודם שמתלבשות בלבוש המחשבה. למשל כשנופלת איזו אהבה וחמדה בלבו של אדם קודם שעולה מהלב אל המוח לחשב ולהרהר בה אין בה בחי' אותיות עדיין רק חפץ פשוט וחשיקה בלב אל הדבר ההוא הנחמד אצלו וכ"ש קודם שנפלה התאוה והחמדה בלבו לאותו דבר רק היתה בכח חכמתו ושכלו וידיעתו שהיה נודע אצלו אותו דבר שהוא נחמד ונעים וטוב ויפה להשיגו ולידבק בו כגון ללמוד איזו חכמה או לאכול איזה מאכל ערב רק לאחר שכבר נפלה החמדה והתאוה בלבו בכח חכמתו ושכלו וידיעתו ואח"כ חזרה ועלתה מהלב למוח לחשב ולהרהר בה איך להוציא תאותו מכח אל הפועל להשיג המאכל או למידת החכמה בפועל הרי בכאן נולדו בחי' אותיות במוחו שהן אותיות כלשון עם ועם המדברים והמהרהרים בהם כל ענייני העולם:

יג שבט מעוברת

פרק כא והנה מדת הקב"ה שלא כמדת בשר ודם שהאדם כשמדבר דבור הרי הבל הדבור שבפיו הוא מורגש ונראה דבר בפני עצמו מובדל משרשו שהן עשר בחי' הנפש עצמה אבל הקב"ה אין דבורו מובדל ממנו ית' ח"ו כי אין דבר חוץ ממנו ולית אתר פנוי מיני' ולכן אין דבורו ית' כדבורינו ח"ו [כמו שאין מחשבתו כמחשבתינו כדכתיב כי לא מחשבותי מחשבותיכם וכתיב כן גבהו דרכי מדרכיכם וגו'] ולא נקרא דבורו ית' בשם דבור רק עד"מ כמו שדבור התחתון שבאדם הוא מגלה לשומעים מה שהיה צפון ונעלם במחשבתו כך למעלה בא"ס ב"ה יציאת האור והחיות ממנו ית' מההעלם אל הגילוי לברוא עולמות ולהחיותם נק' בשם דבור והן הן עשרה מאמרות שבהן נברא העולם וכן שאר כל התורה נביאים וכתובים שהשיגו הנביאים במראה נבואתם. והרי דבורו ומחשבתו כביכול מיוחדות עמו בתכלית היחוד ד"מ כמו דבורו ומחשבתו של אדם בעודן בכח חכמתו ושכלו או בתשוקה וחמדה שבלבו קודם שעלתה מהלב למוח להרהר בה בבחי' אותיות שאז היו אותיות המחשבה והדבור הזה הנמשכות מחמדה ותשוקה זו בכח בלב ומיוחדות שם בתכלית היחוד בשרשן שהן החכמה ושכל שבמוח והחמדה ותשוקה שבלב. וככה ממש ד"מ מיוחדות דבורו ומחשבתו של הקב"ה בתכלית היחוד במהותו ועצמותו ית' גם אחר שיצא דבורו ית' אל הפועל בבריאות העולמות כמו שהיה מיוחד עמו קודם בריאת העולמו' ואין שום שינוי כלל לפניו ית' אלא אל הברואים המקבלים חיותם מבחי' דבורו ית' בבחי' יציאתו כבר אל הפועל

ז שבט פשוטה
יד שבט מעוברת
טו שבט מעוברת
ח שבט פשוטה

בבריאת העולמות שמתלבש בהם להחיותם ע״י השתלשלו׳ מעלה לעלול
וירידת המדרגו׳ בצמצומים רבים ושונים עד שיוכלו הברואים לקבל חיותם
טז שבט מעוברת והתהוותם ממנו ולא יתבטלו במציאות וכל הצמצומים הם בחי׳ הסתר פנים
להסתיר ולהעלים האור והחיות הנמשך מדבורו ית׳ שלא יתגלה בבחי׳
גילוי רב שלא יוכלו התחתונים לקבל ולכן ג״כ נדמה להם אור וחיות הדבור
של מקום ב״ה המלובש בהם כאלו הוא דבר מובדל ממהותו ועצמותו ית׳
רק שנמשך ממנו ית׳ כמו דבור של אדם מנפשו. אך לגבי הקב״ה אין שום
צמצום והסתר והעלם מסתיר ומעלים לפניו וכחשכה כאורה כדכתיב גם
חשך לא יחשיך ממך וגו׳ משום שאין הצמצומים והלבושי׳ דבר נפרד ממנו
ית׳ ח״ו אלא כהדין קמצא דלבושי׳ מיניה וביה כמ״ש כי ה׳ הוא האלהים
וכמ״ש במ״א ולכן קמיה כולא כלא חשיב ממש:

ט שבט פשוטה **פרק כב רק** שהתורה דברה כלשון ב״א ונקרא בתורה דבורו של
יז שבט מעוברת מקו׳ ב״ה בשם דבור ממש כדבורו של אדם לפי שבאמת
כך הוא דרך ירידת והמשכת החיות לתחתונים בצמצומים רבים ועצומים
מינים ממינים שונים להבראות מהם ברואים רבים מינים ממינים שונים
וכ״כ גברו ועצמו הצמצומים והסתר פנים העליונים עד שיוכלו להתהוות
ולהבראות גם דברים טמאים וקליפות וס״א ולקבל חיותם וקיומם מדבר
ה׳ ורוח פיו ית׳ בהסתר פנים וירידת המדרגות ולכן נקראים אלהים אחרים
מפני שיניקתם וחיותם אינה מבחי׳ פנים אלא מבחי׳ אחוריים דקדושה
ופי׳ אחוריים כאדם הנותן דבר לשונאו שלא ברצונו שמשליכו לו כלאחר
כתפו כי מחזיר פניו ממנו משנאתו אותו כך למעלה בחי׳ פנים הוא פנימית
הרצון העליון וחפצו האמיתי אשר חפץ ה׳ להשפיע חיות לכל הקרוב
אליו מסטרא דקדושה אבל הס״א והטומאה היא תועבת ה׳ אשר שנא
ואינו משפיע לה חיות מפנימית הרצון וחפצו האמיתי אשר חפץ בה ח״ו
כ״א כמאן דשדי בתר כתפוי לשונאו שלא ברצונו רק כדי להעניש את
הרשעים וליתן שכר טוב לצדיקי׳ דאכפיין לס״א וזה נקרא בחי׳ אחוריים
י שבט פשוטה דרצון העליון ב״ה. והנה רצון העליון בבחי׳ פנים הוא מקור החיים המחיה
את כל העולמות ולפי שאינו שורה כלל על הס״א וגם בחי׳ אחוריים של
רצון העליון אינו מלובש בתוכה ממש אלא מקיף עליה מלמעלה לכך היא
מקום המיתה והטומאה ה׳ ישמרנו כי מעט מזער אור וחיות שיונקת ומקבלת
לתוכה מבחי׳ אחוריים דקדושה שלמעלה הוא בבחי׳ גלות ממש בתוכה
בסוד גלות השכינה הנ״ל ולכן נקרא בשם אלהים אחרים שהיא ע״ז ממש
וכפירה באחדותו של ממ״ה הקב״ה כי מאחר שאור וחיות דקדושה הוא
בבחי׳ גלות בתוכה אינה בטילה כלל לגבי קדושת הקב״ה ואדרבה מגביה

עצמה כנשר לומר אני ואפסי עוד וכמאמר יאור לי ואני עשיתני ולכן אמרו רז"ל שגסות הרוח שקולה כע"ז ממש כי עיקר ושרש ע"ז הוא מה שנחשב לדבר בפני עצמו נפרד מקדושתו של מקום ולא כפירה בה' לגמרי כדאיתא בגמ' דקרו ליה אלהא דאלהיא אלא שגם הם מחשיבים עצמם ליש ודבר בפני עצמו ובזה מפרידים את עצמם מקדושתו של מקום ב"ה מאחר שאין בטלים לו ית' כי אין קדושה עליונה שורה אלא על מה שבטל לו ית' כנ"ל ולכן נקראי' טורי דפרודא בזה"ק והרי זו כפירה באחדותו האמיתית דכולא קמיה כלא חשיב ובטל באמת לו ית' ולרצונו המחיה את כולם ומהוה אותם מאין ליש תמיד:

פרק כג ועם כל הנ"ל יובן ויבואר היטב בתוספ' ביאור מה שאמרו יא שבט פשוטה
בזהר דאורייתא וקב"ה כולא חד ובתיקוני' פירשו דרמ"ח יח שבט מעוברת
פיקודין אינון רמ"ח אברין דמלכא לפי שהמצות הן פנימיות רצון העליון וחפצו האמיתי המלובש בכל העולמו' העליוני' ותחתוני' להחיותם כי כל חיותם ושפעם תלוי במעשה המצות של התחתוני' כנודע. ונמצא שמעשה המצות וקיומן הוא לבוש הפנימי לפנימית רצון העליון שממעשה זה נמשך
אור וחיות רצון העליון להתלבש בעולמות ולכן נקרא' אברי דמלכא ד"מ יט שבט מעוברת
כמו שאברי גוף האדם הם לבוש לנפשו ובטלים לגמרי אליה מכל וכל כי מיד שעולה ברצונו של אדם לפשוט ידו או רגלו הן נשמעות לרצונו תכף ומיד בלי שום צווי ואמירה להן ובלי שום שהייה כלל אלא כרגע ממש כשעלה ברצונו. כך ד"מ החיות של מעשה המצות וקיומן הוא בטל לגמרי לגבי
רצון העליון המלובש בו ונעשה לו ממש כגוף לנשמה. וכן הלבוש החיצון כ שבט מעוברת
של נפש האלהית שבאדם המקיים ועושה המצוה שהוא כח ובחי' המעשה שלה הוא מתלבש בחיות של מעשה המצוה ונעשה ג"כ כגוף לנשמה לרצון העליון ובטל אליו לגמרי ועל כן גם אברי גוף האדם המקיימים המצוה שכח ובחי' המעשה של נפש האלהית מלובש בהם בשעת מעשה וקיום המצוה הם נעשו מרכבה ממש לרצון העליון כגון היד המחלקת צדקה לעניים או עושה מצוה אחרת. ורגלים המהלכות לדבר מצוה וכן הפה ולשון שמדברי' דברי תורה והמוח שמהרהר בד"ת וי"ש ובגדולת ה' ב"ה. וזהו שארז"ל האבות הן הן המרכבה שכל אבריהם כולם היו קדושים ומובדלים מענייני
עוה"ז ולא נעשו מרכבה רק לרצון העליון לבדו כל ימיהם: אך המחשבה יב שבט פשוטה
וההרהור בד"ת שבמוח וכח הדבור בד"ת שבפה שהם לבושי' הפנימים של כא שבט מעוברת
נפש האלהית וכ"ש נפש האלהית עצמה המלובשת בהם כולם מיוחדים ממש ביחוד גמור ברצון העליון ולא מרכבה לבד כי רצון העליון הוא הוא הדבר הלכה עצמה שמהרהר ומדבר בה שכל ההלכות הן פרטי המשכות

פנימיות רצון העליון עצמו שכך עלה ברצונו ית׳ שדבר זה מותר או כשר
או פטור או זכאי או להפך וכן כל צרופי אותיות תנ״ך הן המשכת רצונו
וחכמתו המיוחדו׳ בא״ס ב״ה בתכלית היחוד שהוא היודע והוא המדע כו׳
כב שבט מעוברת וז״ש דאורייתא וקב״ה כולא חד ולא אברין דמלכא לחוד כפיקודין. ומאחר
שרצון העליון המיוחד בא״ס ב״ה בתכלית היחוד הוא בגילוי לגמרי ולא
בהסתר פנים כלל וכלל בנפש האלהית ולבושיה הפנימים שהם מחשבתה
ודבורה באותה שעה שהאדם עוסק בדברי תורה הרי גם הנפש ולבושיה
אלו מיוחדים ממש בא״ס ב״ה באותה שעה בתכלית היחוד כיחוד דבורו
ומחשבתו של הקב״ה במהותו ועצמותו כנ״ל כי אין שום דבר נפרד כי
אם בהסתר פנים כנ״ל ולא עוד אלא שיחודם הוא ביתר שאת ויתר עז
מיחוד אור א״ס ב״ה בעולמות עליונים מאחר שרצון העליון הוא בגילוי
ממש בנפש ולבושיה העוסקים בתורה שהרי הוא הוא התורה עצמה וכל
העולמות העליונים מקבלים חיותם מאור וחיות הנמשך מהתורה שהיא
רצונו וחכמתו ית׳ כדכתיב כולם בחכמה עשית וא״כ החכמה שהיא התורה
למעלה מכולם והיא היא רצונו ית׳ הנק׳ סובב כל עלמין שהיא בחי׳ מה
שאינו יכול להתלבש בתוך עלמין רק מחיה ומאיר למעלה בבחי׳ מקיף
והיא היא המתלבשת בנפש ולבושיה בבחי׳ גילוי ממש כשעוסקים בד״ת
ואע״ג דאיהו לא חזי כו׳ [ומשו׳ הכי יכול לסבול משום דלא חזי משא״כ
יג שבט פשוטה בעליונים]. ובזה יובן למה גדלה מאד מעלת העסק בתורה יותר מכל המצות
ואפי׳ מתפלה שהיא יחוד עולמות עליונים [והא דמי שאין תורתו אומנתו
כג שבט מעוברת צריך להפסיק היינו מאחר דמפסיק ומבטל בלא״ה]. ומזה יוכל המשכיל
להמשיך עליו יראה גדולה בעסקו בתורה כשיתבונן איך שנפשו ולבושיה
שבמוחו ובפיו הם מיוחדי׳ ממש בתכלית היחוד ברצון העליון ואור א״ס
ב״ה ממש המתגלה בהם מה שכל העולמות עליונים ותחתונים כלא חשיבי
קמיה וכאין ואפס ממש עד שאינו מתלבש בתוכם ממש אלא סובב כל
עלמין בבחי׳ מקיף להחיות׳ עיקר חיותם רק איזו הארה מתלבשת בתוכם
מה שיכולים לסבול שלא יתבטלו במציאות לגמרי. וז״ש ויצונו ה׳ את כל
החוקים האלה ליראה את ה׳ וגו׳ [ועל יראה גדולה זו אמרו אם אין חכמה
אין יראה והתורה נקראת אצלה תרעא לדרתא כמ״ש במ״א] אלא דלאו
כל מוחא סביל דא יראה כזו. אך גם מאן דלא סביל מוחו כלל יראה זו
לא מינה ולא מקצתה מפני פחיתות ערך נפשו בשרשה ומקורה במדרגות
תחתונות דעשר ספירות דעשיה אין יראה זו מעכבת בו למעשה כמ״ש לקמן:

יד שבט פשוטה / כד שבט מעוברת **פרק כד וזה** לעומת זה הן שס״ה מצות לא תעשה דאורייתא וכל
איסורי דרבנן מאחר שהן נגד רצונו וחכמתו ית׳ והפכם

ממש הם נפרדים מיחודו ואחדותו ית׳ בתכלית הפירוד ממש כמו הס״א והקליפה הנק׳ ע״ז ואלהים אחרים מחמת הסתר פנים של רצון העליון כנ״ל. וכן ג׳ לבושי הנפש שמקליפת נוגה שבישראל שהם מחשבה דבור ומעשה המלובשי׳ בשס״ה ל״ת דאורייתא ודרבנן וכן מהות הנפש עצמה המלובשת בלבושיה כולם מיוחדים ממש בס״א וקליפ׳ זו הנק׳ ע״ז ולא עוד אלא שבטלים וטפלים אליה וגרועים ופחותים ממנה מאד כי היא אינה מלובשת בגוף חומרי ויודעת את רבונה ואינה מורדת בו לפעול פעולתה במשלחת מלאכי רעים שלה שלא בשליחותו של מקום ב״ה ח״ו וכמאמר בלעם לא אוכל לעבור את פי ה׳ וגו׳ ואף שנקרא ע״ז הא קרו ליה אלהא דאלהיא ואינם יכולי׳ לעבור כלל על רצונו ית׳ כי יודעי׳ ומשיגים שהוא חיותם וקיומם שיונקים מבחי׳ אחוריים דאחוריי׳ של רצון העליון ב״ה המקיף עליהם אלא שיניקתם וחיותם שבתוכם היא בבחי׳ גלות בתוכם להחשיב עצמן אלהות והרי זו כפירה באחדותו אבל מ״מ אינן כופרים וכחשו בה׳ לגמרי ולומר לא הוא אלא דקרו ליה אלהא דאלהיא דהיינו חיותם וקיומם הנמשך ויורד עליהם מרצונו ית׳ ולכן אינן עוברין רצונו ית׳ לעולם. וא״כ האדם העובר על רצונו ית׳ הוא גרוע ופחות הרבה מאד מהס״א וקליפה הנקראת ע״ז ואלהים אחרים והוא בתכלי׳ הפירוד מיחודו ואחדותו של הקב״ה יותר ממנה וכאלו כופר באחדותו יותר ממנה ח״ו. וכמ״ש בע״ח שער מ״ב סוף פ״ד שהרע שבעוה״ז החומרי הוא שמרי הקליפות הגסות כו׳ והוא תכלית הבירור וכו׳ ולכן כל מעשה עוה״ז קשים ורעים והרשעים גוברים בו וכו׳:

ולכן אמרו רז״ל על פסוק כי תשטה אשתו אין אדם עובר עבירה וכו׳ דאפי׳ טו שבט פשוטה
אשה המנאפת שדעתה קלה היתה מושלת ברוח תאותה לולי רוח שטות שבה המכסה ומסתיר ומעלי׳ את האהבה מסותרת שבנפשה האלהית לדבקה באמונת ה׳ ויחודו ואחדותו ולא ליפרד ח״ו מאחדותו אפי׳ נוטלים את נפשה ממנה לעבוד ע״ז ח״ו ואפי׳ בהשתחואה לבדה בלי שום אמונה בלב כלל וכ״ש לכבוש היצר ותאות הניאוף שהם יסורים קלים ממיתה ה׳ ישמרנו וההפרש שאצלה בין איסור ניאוף לאיסור השתחואה לע״ז הוא ג״כ רוח שטות דקליפה המלבשת לנפש האלהית עד בחי׳ חכמה שבה ולא עד בכלל מפני אור ה׳ המלובש בחכמה כנ״ל. אבל באמת לאמיתו אפי׳ עבירה קלה הרי העוברה עובר על רצון העליון ב״ה והוא בתכלית הפירוד מיחודו ואחדותו ית׳ יותר מס״א וקליפה הנקרא׳ אלהים אחרי׳ וע״ז ממש ויותר מכל הדברים הנשפעים ממנה בע״הז שהם בהמות טמאות וחיות ועופות טמאים ושקצים ורמשים וכמאמר יתוש קדמך פי׳ דאף יתוש שמכנים ואינו מוציא שהיא קליפ׳ היותר תחתונה ורחוקה מבחי׳ הקדושה המשפעת בתכלית הריחוק קודמת לאיש החוטא בהשתלשלות וירידת החיות מרצון

העליון ב"ה וכ"ש שאר בעלי חיים הטמאים ואפי' חיות רעות שכולם אינם
משנים תפקידם ופקודתו ית' שמרה רוחם ואע"ג דאיהו לא חזי כו'. וכמ"ש
ומוראכם וחתכם יהיה על כל חית הארץ וכפי' רז"ל שאין חיה רעה מושלת
באדם אא"כ נדמה לה כבהמה. והצדיקים שאין צלם אלהים מסתלק מעל
פניהם כל חיות רעות אתכפיין קמייהו כמ"ש בזהר גבי דניאל בגוב אריות.
וא"כ החוטא ועובר רצונו ית' אפי' בעבירה קלה בשעת מעשה הוא בתכלית
הריחוק מקדושה העליונה שהיא יחודו ואחדותו ית' יותר מכל בעלי חיים
הטמאי' ושקצי' ורמשים המושפעים מס"א וקליפת ע"ז ומה שפיקוח נפש טז שבט פשוטה
דוחה שאר עבירות וגם יעבור ואל יהרג היינו כפי' חז"ל אמרה תורה חלל
עליו שבת אחת כדי שישמור שבתות הרבה ולא משו' קלות העבירות
וחומרן [תדע שהרי שבת חמורה ושקולה כע"ז לענין שחיטת מומר לדבר
אחד בי"ד סי' ב' משא"כ במומר לגילוי עריות ואפי' הכי פיקוח נפש דוחה
שבת ולא ג"ע אלא דגזירת הכתוב הוא] אלא שלאחר מעשה החטא אם
היא מעבירות שאין בהן כרת ומיתה בידי שמים שאין נפשו האלהית מתה
לגמרי ונכרתת משרשה באלהים חיים רק שנפגם קצת דביקותה ואחיזתה
בשרשה בחטא זה:* הרי גם נפשו החיוני' הבהמית המלובש' בגופו וכן גופו
חוזרים ועולים מהס"א וקליפה זו ומתקרבים לקדושת נפש האלהית המלובשת בהם המאמינה בה' אחד וגם בשעת החטא היתה באמנה אתו ית' רק שהיתה בבחי' גלות ממש תוך נפש הבהמית מס"א המחטיאה את הגוף
ומורידתו עמה בעמקי שאול למטה מטה תחת טומאת הס"א וקליפת ע"ז
ה' ישמרנו ואין לך גלות גדול מזה מאיגרא רמה כו' וכמש"ל דשרש ומקור
נפשו כל בית ישראל הוא מחכמה עילאה והוא ית' וחכמתו אחד וכו' והוא
כמשל האוחז בראשו של מלך ומורידו למטה וטומן פניו בתוך בית הכסא
מלא צואה שאין לך עלבון גדול מזה אפי' עושה כן לפי שעה שהקליפות
וס"א נקראות קיא צואה כנודע:

הגהה

* (ולפי ערך וחלוקי בחי' הפגם בנפש ובשרשה בעליונים כך הם חלוקי בחי' המירוק והעונש בגיהנם או בעוה"ז לכל עון וחטא עונש מיוחד למרק ולהעביר הלכלוך והפגם וכן בחייבי מיתה וכרת אין פוגמין כולם בשוה):

פרק כה

וזהו שכתוב כי קרוב אליך הדבר מאד וגו' שבכל עת ובכל יז שבט פשוטה
שעה בידו של אדם וברשותו הוא להעבי' רוח שטות כה שבט מעוברת
והשכחה מקרבו ולזכור ולעורר אהבתו לה' אחד המסותרת בודאי בלבבו
בלי שום ספק. וז"ש ובלבבך ונכלל בה גם דחילו דהיינו שלא ליפרד בשום
אופן מיחודו ואחדותו יתברך אפי' במסירת נפש ממש בלי שום טעם ושכל

מושג אלא בטבע אלהי וכ״ש בשבירת התאוות הקלה מיסורי מיתה שקרוב
אליו הדבר יותר לכבוש היצר הן בבחי׳ סור מרע אפי׳ מעבירה קלה של
דברי סופרים שלא לעבור על רצונו ית׳ מאחר שנפרד בה מיחודו ואחדותו
כמו בע״ז ממש בשעת מעשה והרי גם בע״ז יכול לעשות תשובה אח״כ. ואף כו שבט מעוברת
שהאומר אחטא ואשוב אין מספיקין כו׳ היינו שאין מחזיקים ידו להיות לו
שעת הכושר לעשות תשובה אבל אם דחק השעה ועשה תשובה אין לך
דבר שעומד בפני התשובה. ואעפ״כ כל איש ישראל מוכן ומזומן למסור
נפשו על קדושת ה׳ שלא להשתחוות לע״ז אפי׳ לפי שעה ולעשות תשובה
אח״כ והיינו מפני אור ה׳ המלובש בנפשם כנ״ל שאינו בבחי׳ זמן ושעה כלל
אלא למעלה מהזמן ושליט ומושל עליו כנודע. והן בבחי׳ ועשה טוב להתגבר יח שבט פשוטה
כארי בגבורה ואומץ הלב נגד היצר המכביד את גופו ומפיל עליו עצלה כז שבט מעוברת
מבחי׳ יסוד העפר שבנפש הבהמית מלהטריח גופו בזריזות בכל מיני טורח
ועבוד׳ משא בעבודת ה׳ שיש בה טורח ועמל כגון לעמול בתורה בעיון ובפה
לא פסיק פומיה מגירסא וכמארז״ל לעולם ישים אדם עצמו על דברי תורה
כשור לעול וכחמור למשאוי וכן לתפלה בכונה בכל כחו ממש וכן בעבודת
ה׳ שהיא בדבר שבממון כמו עבודת הצדקה וכיוצא באלו ממלחמות היצר כח שבט מעוברת
ותחבולותיו לקרר נפש האדם שלא להפקיר ממונו ובריאות גופו שלעמוד
נגדו ולכבשו קרוב מאד אל האדם כשישים אל לבו שלנצח היצר בכל זה
ויותר מזה ולעשות הפכו ממש קל מאד מיסורי מיתה ה׳ ישמרנו ויסורי מיתה
ה׳ ישמרנו היה מקבל באהבה וברצון שלא ליפרד מיחודו ואחדותו ית׳ אפי׳
לפי שעה להשתחות לע״ז ח״ו וכ״ש שיש לו לקבל באהבה וברצון כדי לדבקה
בו לעולם ועד דהיינו כשיעשה רצונו ית׳ בעבודה זו יתגלה בה פנימית רצון
העליון בבחי׳ פנים וגילוי רב ולא בהסתר כלל וכשאין שום הסתר פנים ברצון
העליון אזי אין דבר נפרד כלל וכלל להיות יש ודבר בפני עצמו ולזאת תהיינה
נפשו האלהית והחיונית ולבושיהן כולן מיוחדות בתכלית היחוד ברצון
העליון ואור א״ס ב״ה כנ״ל. ויחוד זה למעלה הוא נצחי לעולם ועד כי הוא כט שבט מעוברת
ית׳ ורצונו למעלה מהזמן וכן גילוי רצונו שבדבורו שהיא התורה הוא נצחי
וכמ״ש ודבר אלהינו יקום לעולם ודבריו חיים וקיימים כו׳ ולא יחליף ולא ימיר
דתו לעולמים כו׳. אלא שלמטה הוא תחת הזמן ובאותה שעה לבדה שעוסק יט שבט פשוטה
בה בתור׳ או במצוה כי אח״כ אם עוסק בדבר אחר נפרד מהיחוד העליון
למטה. והיינו כשעוסק בדברים בטלים לגמרי שאין בהם צורך כלל לעבודת
ה׳ ואעפ״כ כשחוזר ושב לעבודת ה׳ אח״כ לתורה ולתפלה ומבקש מחילה
מה׳ על שהיה אפשר לו לעסוק אז בתורה ולא עסק ה׳ יסלח לו כמארז״ל
עבר על מצות עשה ושב לא זז משם עד שמוחלין לו. ולזה תקנו ברכת סלח
לנו שלש פעמים בכל יום על עון ביטול תורה שאין אדם ניצול ממנו בכל

יום וכמו התמיד שהיה מכפר על מצות עשה. ואין זה אחטא ואשוב אא״כ
ל שבט מעוברת
שבשעת החטא ממש הוא סומך על התשובה ולכך חוטא כמ״ש במ״א: ובזה יובן למה צוה משה רבינו ע״ה במשנה תורה לדור שנכנסו לארץ לקרות ק״ש פעמים בכל יום לקבל עליו מלכות שמים במסירת נפש והלא הבטיח להם פחדכם ומוראכם יתן ה׳ וגו׳ אלא משום שקיום התורה ומצותיה תלוי בזה שיזכור תמיד ענין מסירת נפשו לה׳ על יחודו שיהיה קבוע בלבו תמיד ממש יומם ולילה לא ימיש מזכרונו כי בזה יוכל לעמוד נגד יצרו לנצחו תמיד בכל עת ובכל שעה כנ״ל:

כ שבט פשוטה
א אדר א מעוברת

פרק כו ברם כגון דא צריך לאודועי כלל גדול כי כמו שנצחון לנצח דבר גשמי כגון שני אנשים המתאבקים זה עם זה להפיל זה את זה. הנה אם האחד הוא בעצלות וכבדות ינוצח בקל ויפול גם אם הוא גבור יותר מחבירו ככה ממש בנצחון היצר אי אפשר לנצחו בעצלות וכבדות הנמשכות מעצבות וטמטום הלב כאבן כ״א בזריזות הנמשכת משמחה ופתיחת הלב וטהרתו מכל נדנוד דאגה ועצב בעולם. ומ״ש בכל עצב יהיה מותר פי׳ שיהיה איזה יתרון ומעלה מזה הנה אדרבה מלשון זה משמע שהעצב מצד עצמו אין בו מעלה רק שיגיע ויבא ממנו איזה יתרון והיינו השמחה האמיתית בה׳ אלהיו הבאה אחר העצב האמיתי לעתים מזומנים על עונותיו במר נפשו ולב נשבר שע״י זה נשברה רוח הטומאה וס״א ומחיצה של ברזל המפסקת בינו לאביו שבשמים כמ״ש בזהר ע״פ רוח נשברה לב נשבר וגו׳ ואזי יקוים בו רישיה דקרא תשמיעני ששון ושמחה וגו׳ השיבה לי ששון ישעך ורוח נדיבה וגו׳ וזהו טעם הפשוט לתיקון האר״י ז״ל לומר מזמור זה אחר תיקון חצות קודם הלימוד כדי ללמוד בשמחה אמיתית בה׳ הבאה אחר העצב שיש לשמחה זו יתרון כיתרון האור הבא מן החשך דוקא כמ״ש בזהר על פסוק וראיתי שיש יתרון לחכמה מן הסכלות כיתרון האור כו׳ ע״ש וד״ל ומקרא מלא דבר הכתוב תחת אשר לא עבדת את ה׳ אלהיך בשמחה וגו׳ ונודע לכל פי׳ האר״י ז״ל על פסוק
כא שבט פשוטה
זה: והנה עצה היעוצה לטהר לבו מכל עצב ונדנוד דאגה ממילי דעלמא ואפי׳ בני חיי ומזוני מודעת זאת לכל מאמר רז״ל כשם שמברך על הטובה כו׳ ופירשו בגמ׳ לקבולי בשמחה כמו שמחת הטובה הנגלית ונראית כי גם זו לטובה רק שאינה נגלית ונראית לעיני בשר כי היא מעלמא דאתכסי׳ שלמעלה מעלמא דאתגלייא שהוא ו״ה משם הוי״ה ב״ה ועלמא דאתכסיא הוא י״ה וז״ש אשרי הגבר אשר תיסרנו י״ה וגו׳ ולכן ארז״ל כי השמחים ביסורים עליהם הכתוב אומר ואוהביו כצאת השמש בגבורתו כי השמחה היא מאהבתו קרבת ה׳ יותר מכל חיי העוה״ז כדכתיב כי טוב חסדך מחיים וגו׳ וקרבת ה׳ היא ביתר שאת ומעלה לאין קץ בעלמא דאתכסיא כי שם

חביון עוזו ויושב בסתר עליון ועל כן זוכה לצאת השמש בגבורתו לעתיד לבא שהיא יציאת חמה מנרתקה שהיא מכוסה בו בעוה״ז ולעתיד תתגלה מכסויה דהיינו שאז יתגלה עלמא דאתכסיא ויזרח ויאיר בגילוי רב ועצום לכל החוסים בו בעוה״ז ומסתופפים בצלו צל החכמה שהוא בחי׳ צל ולא אורה וטובה ונראית וד״ל: אך העצבות ממילי דשמיא צריך לשית עצות כב שבט פשוטה
בנפשו ליפטר ממנה אין צריך לומר בשעת עבודה שצריך לעבוד ה׳ בשמחה ובטוב לבב אלא אפילו מי שהוא בעל עסקים ודרך ארץ אם נופל לו עצב ודאגה ממילי דשמיא בשעת עסקיו בידוע שהוא תחבולת היצר כדי להפילו אח״כ בתאוות ח״ו כנודע שאל״כ מאין באה לו עצבות אמיתית מחמת אהבת ה׳ או יראתו באמצע עסקיו. והנה בין שנפלה לו העצבות בשעת עבודה בת״ת או בתפלה ובין שנפלה לו שלא בשעת עבודה זאת ישים אל לבו כי אין הזמן גרמא כעת לעצבות אמיתית אפי׳ לדאגת עונות חמורים ח״ו. רק לזאת צריך קביעות עתים ושעת הכושר בישוב הדעת להתבונן בגדול׳ ה׳ אשר חטא לו כדי שע״י זה יהיה לבו נשבר באמת במרירות אמיתית וכמבואר עת זו במ״א ושם נתבאר ג״כ כי מיד אחר שנשבר לבו בעתים קבועים ההם אזי יסיר העצב מלבו לגמרי ויאמין אמונה שלימה כי ה׳ העביר חטאתו ורב לסלוח וזו היא השמחה האמיתית בה׳ הבאה אחר העצב כנ״ל:

פרק כז ואם העצבות אינה מדאגת עונות אלא מהרהורים רעים כג שבט פשוטה
ותאוות רעות שנופלות במחשבתו. הנה אם נופלות ב אדר א מעוברת
לו שלא בשעת העבודה אלא בעת עסקו בעסקיו ודרך ארץ וכהאי גוונא אדרבה יש לו לשמוח בחלקו שאף שנופלות לו במחשבתו הוא מסיח דעתו מהן לקיים מה שנאמר ולא תתורו אחרי לבבכם ואחרי עיניכם אשר אתם זונים אחריהם. ואין הכתוב מדבר בצדיקי׳ לקראם זונים ח״ו אלא בבינונים כיוצא בו שנופלים לו הרהורי ניאוף במחשבתו בין בהיתר כו׳ וכשמסיח דעתו מקיים לאו זה ואמרו רז״ל ישב ולא עבר עבירה נותנים לו שכר כאלו עשה מצוה ועל כן צריך לשמוח בקיום הלאו כמו בקיום מצות עשה
ממש ואדרבה העצבות היא מגסות הרוח שאינו מכיר מקומו ועל כן ירע ג אדר א מעוברת
לבבו על שאינו במדרגת צדיק שלצדיקים בודאי אין נופלים להם הרהורי שטות כאלו כי אילו היה מכיר מקומו שהוא רחוק מאד ממדרגת צדיק והלואי היה בינוני ולא רשע כל ימיו אפי׳ שעה אחת הרי זאת היא מדת הבינונים ועבודתם לכבוש היצר וההרהור העולה מהלב למוח ולהסיח
דעתו לגמרי ממנו ולדחותו בשתי ידים כנ״ל ובכל דחיה ודחיה שמדחהו ד אדר א מעוברת
ממחשבתו אתכפיא ס״א לתתא ובאתערותא דלתתא אתערותא דלעילא ואתכפיא ס״א דלעילא המגביה עצמה כנשר לקיים מ״ש אם תגביה כנשר

וגו׳ משם אורידך נאם ה׳ וכמו שהפליג בזהר פ׳ תרומה [דף קכח] בגודל
נחת רוח לפניו ית׳ כד אתכפיא ס״א לתתא דאסתלק יקרא דקב״ה לעילא
על כולא יתיר משבח׳ אחרא ואסתלקות׳ דא יתיר מכולא וכו׳. ולכן אל כד שבט פשוטה
יפול לב אדם עליו ולא ירע לבבו מאד גם אם יהיה כן כל ימיו במלחמה זו
כי אולי לכך נברא וזאת עבודתו לאכפיא לס״א תמיד. ועל זה אמר איוב
בראת רשעים ולא שיהיו רשעים באמת ח״ו אלא שיגיע אליהם כמעשה
הרשעים במחשבתם והרהורם לבד והם יהיו נלחמים תמיד להסיח דעתם
מהם כדי לאכפי׳ לס״א ולא יוכלו לבטלה מכל וכל כי זה נעשה ע״י צדיקים.
ושני מיני נחת רוח לפניו ית׳ למעלה. א׳ מביטול הס״א לגמרי ואתהפכא ה אדר א מעוברת
ממרירו למתקא ומחשוכא לנהורא ע״י הצדיקים. והשנית כד אתכפיא
הס״א בעודה בתקפה וגבורתה ומגביה עצמה כנשר ומשם מורידה ה׳
באתערותא דלתתא ע״י הבינונים. וז״ש הכתוב ועשה לי מטעמים כאשר
אהבתי מטעמים לשון רבים שני מיני נחת רוח והוא מאמר השכינה לבניה
כללות ישראל כדפי׳ בתיקונים. וכמו שבמטעמים גשמיים ד״מ יש שני מיני
מעדנים אחד ממאכלים ערבים ומתוקים. והשני מדברים חריפים או חמוצי׳
רק שהם מתובלים ומתוקני׳ היטב עד שנעשו מעדנים להשיב הנפש. וז״ש
הכתו׳ כל פעל ה׳ למענהו וגם רשע ליום רעה פי׳ שישוב מרשעו ויעשה הרע
שלו יום ואור למעלה כד אתכפיא ס״א ואסתלק יקרא דקב״ה לעילא. ולא כה שבט פשוטה
עוד אלא אפי׳ בדברים המותרים לגמרי כל מה שהאדם זובח יצרו אפי׳ שעה ו אדר א מעוברת
קלה ומתכוין לאכפיא לס״א שבחלל השמאלי כגון שחפץ לאכול ומאחר
סעודתו עד לאחר שעה או פחות ועוסק בתורה באותה שעה. כדאיתא
בגמ׳ שעה רביעית מאכל כל אדם שעה ששית מאכל ת״ח. והיו מרעיבים
עצמם שתי שעות לכוונה זו אף שגם אחר הסעודה היו לומדים כל היום.
וכן אם בולם פיו מלדבר דברים שלבו מתאוה מאד לדברם מענייני העולם
וכן בהרהורי מחשבתו אפי׳ במעט מזעיר דאתכפיא ס״א לתתא אסתלק
יקרא דקב״ה וקדושתו לעילא הרבה ומקדושה זו נמשכת קדושה עליונה ז אדר א מעוברת
על האדם למטה לסייעו סיוע רב ועצום לעבודתו ית׳. וז״ש רז״ל אדם מקדש
עצמו מעט למטה מקדשין אותו הרבה מלמעלה לבד מה שמקיים מצות
עשה של תורה והתקדשתם וכו׳ כשמקדש עצמו במותר לו ופי׳ והתקדשתם
שתעשו עצמכם קדושים כלומר אף שבאמת אינו קדוש ומובדל מס״א כי
היא בתקפה ובגבורתה כתולדתה בחלל השמאלי רק שכובש יצרו ומקדש
עצמו. והייתם קדושים כלומר סופו להיות קדוש ומובדל באמת מהס״א ע״י
שמקדשים אותו הרבה מלמעלה ומסייעים אותו לגרשה מלבו מעט מעט:

כו שבט פשוטה

פרק כח ואפילו אם נופלים לו הרהורי תאוות ושאר מחשבות זרות ח אדר א מעוברת
בשעת העבודה בתורה או בתפלה בכוונה אל ישית

לב אליהן אלא יסיח דעתו מהן כרגע. וגם אל יהי שוטה לעסוק בהעלאת המדות של המחשבה זרה כנודע כי לא נאמרו דברים ההם אלא לצדיקים שאין נופלים להם מחשבות זרות שלהם כ״א משל אחרים. אבל מי שנופל לו משלו מבחי׳ הרע שבלבו בחלל השמאלי איך יעלהו למעלה והוא עצמו מקושר למטה: אך אעפ״כ אל יפול לבו בקרבו להיות מזה עצב נבזה בשעת העבודה שצריך להיות בשמחה רבה אלא אדרבה יתחזק יותר ויוסיף אומץ בכל כחו בכוונת התפלה בחדוה ושמחה יתירה בשומו אל לבו כי נפילת המחשבה זרה היא מהקליפה שבחלל השמאלי העושה מלחמה בבינוני עם נפש אלהית שבו. ונודע דרך הנלחמים וכן הנאבקים יחד כשאחד מתגבר אזי השני מתאמץ להתגבר ג״כ בכל מאמצי כחו. ולכן כשנפש האלהית מתאמצת ומתגברת להתפלל אזי גם הקליפה מתגברת כנגדה לבלבלה ולהפילה במחשב׳ זרה שלה ולא כטעות העולם שטועים להוכיח מנפילת המחשבה זרה מכלל שאין תפלתם כלום שאילו התפלל כראוי ונכון לא היו נופלים לו מחשבות זרות. והאמת היה כדבריהם אם היתה נפש אחת לבדה היא המתפללת והיא המחשבת ומהרהרת המחשבות זרות. אבל באמת לאמיתו הן שתי נפשות הנלחמו׳ זו עם זו במוחו של אדם כל אחת חפצה ורצונה למשול בו ולהיות המוח ממולא ממנה לבדה. וכל הרהורי תורה ויראת שמים מנפש האלהית וכל מילי דעלמא מנפש הבהמית רק שהאלהית מלובשת בה. והוא כמשל אדם המתפלל בכוונ׳ ועומד לנגדו ערל רשע ומשיח ומדבר עמו כדי לבלבלו שזאת עצתו בודאי שלא להשיב לו מטוב ועד רע ולעשות עצמו כחרש לא ישמע ולקיים מה שכתו׳ אל תען כסיל באולתו פן תשוה לו גם אתה כך אל ישיב מאומה ושום טענה ומענה נגד המחשבה זרה כי המתאבק עם מנוול מתנוול ג״כ רק יעשה עצמו כלא יודע ולא שומע ההרהורי׳ שנפלו לו ויסירם מדעתו ויוסיף אומץ בכח כוונתו ואם יקשה לו להסירם מדעתו מפני שטורדים דעתו מאד בחזקה אזי ישפיל נפשו לה׳ ויתחנן לו ית׳ במחשבתו לרחם עליו ברחמיו המרובים כרחם אב על בנים הנמשכים ממוחו וככה ירחם ה׳ על נפשו הנמשכת מאתו ית׳ להצילה ממים הזדונים ולמענו יעשה כי חלק ה׳ ממש עמו:

כז שבט פשוטה

פרק כט

אך עוד אחת צריך לשית עצות בנפשו׳ הבינונים אשר לפעמים ועתים רבים יש להם טמטום הלב שנעשה כאבן ולא יכול לפתוח לבו בשום אופן לעבודה שבלב זו תפלה. וגם לפעמים לא יוכל להלחם עם היצר לקדש עצמו במותר לו מפני כבדות שבלבו וזאת היא עצה היעוצה בזהר הקדוש דאמר רב מתיבתא בגן עדן אעא דלא סליק ביה נהורא מבטשין ליה כו׳. גופא דלא סליק ביה נהורא דנשמתא מבטשין ליה כו׳ פי׳ נהורא דנשמתא שאור הנשמה והשכל אינו מאיר כל

כח שבט פשוטה

ט אדר א מעוברת

כך למשול על חומריות שבגוף. ואף שמבין ומתבונן בשכלו בגדולת ה׳ אינו
נתפס ונדבק במוחו כל כך שיוכל למשול על חומריו׳ הלב מחמת חומריותן
וגסותן והסיבה היא גסות הקליפה שמגביה עצמה על אור קדושת נפש י אדר א מעוברת
האלהית ומסתרת ומחשיכה אורה. ולזאת צריך לבטשה ולהשפילה לעפר
דהיינו לקבוע עתים להשפיל עצמו להיות נבזה בעיניו נמאס ככתוב ולב
נשבר רוח נשברה היא הס״א שהיא היא האדם עצמו בבינונים שנפש
החיונית המחיה הגוף היא בתקפה כתולדתה בלבו נמצא היא היא האדם
עצמו. ועל נפש האלהית שבו נאמר נשמה שנתת בי טהורה היא שנתת
בי דייקא מכלל שהאדם עצמו איננו הנשמה הטהורה כי אם בצדיקים
שבהם הוא להפך שנשמה הטהורה שהיא נפש האלהית הוא האדם
וגופם נקרא בשר אדם. וכמאמר הלל הזקן לתלמידיו כשהיה הולך לאכול יא אדר א מעוברת
היה אומר שהוא הולך לגמול חסד עם העלובה ועניה הוא גופו כי כמו זר
נחשב אצלו ולכן אמר שהוא גומל חסד עמו במה שמאכילו כי הוא עצמו
אינו רק נפש האלהית לבד כי היא לבדה מחיה גופו ובשרו שהרע שהיה
בנפש החיונית המלובשת בדמו ובשרו נתהפך לטוב ונכלל בקדושת נפש
האלהית ממש בצדיקים. אבל בבינוני מאחר שמהותה ועצמותה של נפש כט שבט פשוטה
החיונית הבהמית שמס״א המלובשת בדמו ובשרו לא נהפך לטוב הרי
היא היא האדם עצמו וא״כ הוא רחוק מה׳ בתכלית הריחוק שהרי כח יב אדר א מעוברת
המתאוה שבנפשו הבהמית יכול ג״כ להתאוות לדברי׳ האסורים שהם
נגד רצונו ית׳ אף שאינו מתאוה לעשותם בפועל ממש ח״ו רק שאינם
מאוסים אצלו באמת כבצדיקים כמש״ל [פ׳ יב]. ובזה הוא גרוע ומשוקץ
ומתועב יותר מבעלי חיים הטמאים ושקצים ורמשים כנ״ל וכמ״ש ואנכי
תולעת ולא איש וגו׳ [וגם כשמתגברת בו נפשו האלהית לעורר האהבה
לה׳ בשעת התפלה אינה באמת לאמיתו לגמרי מאחר שחולפת ועוברת
אחר התפלה כנ״ל ספי״ג] ובפרט כשיזכור טומאת נפשו בחטאת נעורים יג אדר א מעוברת
והפגם שעשה בעליוני׳ ושם הוא למעלה מהזמן וכאלו פגם ונטמא היום
ח״ו ממש ואף שכבר עשה תשובה נכונה הרי עיקר התשובה בלב והלב
יש בו בחי׳ ומדרגות רבות והכל לפי מה שהוא אדם ולפי הזמן והמקום
כידוע ליודעים ולכן עכשיו בשעה זו שרואה בעצמו דלא סליק ביה נהורא
דנשמתא מכלל שהיום לא נתקבלה תשובתו ועונותיו מבדילים או שרוצים
להעלותו לתשובה עילאה יותר מעומקא דלבא יותר ולכן אמר דוד וחטאתי
נגדי תמיד. וגם מי שהוא נקי מחטאות נעורים החמורים ישים אל לבו לקיים ל שבט פשוטה
מאמר זה״ק להיות ממארי דחושבנא דהיינו לעשו׳ חשבון עם נפשו מכל יד אדר א מעוברת
המחשבות והדיבורים והמעשים שחלפו ועברו מיום היותו עד היום הזה
אם היו כולם מצד הקדושה או מצד הטומאה ר״ל דהיינו כל המחשבות

והדיבורים והמעשים אשר לא לה׳ המה ולרצונו ולעבודתו שזהו פי׳ לשון
ס״א כנ״ל [בפ״ו] ומודעת זאת כי כל עת שהאדם מחשב מחשבות קדושות
נעשה מרכבה בעת זו להיכלות הקדושה שמהן מושפעות מחשבות הללו
וכן להפך נעשה מרכבה טמאה בעת זו להיכלות הטומאה שמהן מושפעות
כל מחשבות רעות וכן בדבור ומעשה. עוד ישים אל לבו רוב חלומותיו שהם טו אדר א מעוברת
הבל ורעות רוח משום שאין נפשו עולה למעלה וכמ״ש מי יעלה בהר ה׳
נקי כפים וגו׳ ואינון סטרין בישין אתיין ומתדבקן ביה ומודעין ליה בחלמא
מילין דעלמא וכו׳ ולזמנין דחייכן ביה ואחזיאו ליה מילי שקר וצערין ליה
בחלמיה כו׳ כמ״ש בזהר ויקרא [ד׳ כ״ה ע״א וע״ב] ע״ש באריכות. והנה א אדר פשוטה
כל מה שיאריך בעניינים אלו במחשבתו וגם בעיונו בספרים להיות לבו
נשבר בקרבו ונבזה בעיניו נמאס ככתוב בתכלית המיאוס ולמאס חייו ממש
הרי בזה ממאס ומבזה הס״א ומשפילה לעפר ומורידה מגדולתה וגסות
רוחה וגבהותה שמגביה את עצמה על אור קדושת נפש האלהית להחשיך
אורה. וגם ירעים עליה בקול רעש ורוגז להשפילה כמאמר רז״ל לעולם ירגיז
אדם יצ״ט על יצ״הר שנאמר רגזו וגו׳ דהיינו לרגוז על נפש הבהמית שהיא
יצרו הרע בקול רעש ורוגז במחשבתו לומר לו אתה רע ורשע ומשוקץ
ומתועב ומנוול וכו׳ ככל השמות שקראו לו חכמינו ז״ל באמת עד מתי
תסתיר לפני אור א״ס ב״ה הממלא כל עלמין היה הוה ויהיה בשוה גם
במקום זה שאני עליו כמו שהיה אור א״ס ב״ה לבדו קודם שנברא העולם
בלי שום שינוי כמ״ש אני ה׳ לא שניתי כי הוא למעלה מהזמן וכו׳ ואתה
מנוול וכו׳ מכחיש האמת הנראה לעינים דכולא קמיה כלא ממש באמת
בבחי׳ ראייה חושיית. והנה על ידי זה יועיל לנפשו האלהית להאיר עיניה
באמת יחוד אור אין סוף בראייה חושיית ולא בחי׳ שמיעה והבנה לבדה
כמ״ש במ״א שזהו שרש כל העבודה והטעם לפי שבאמת אין שום ממשות ב אדר פשוטה
כלל בס״א שלכן נמשלה לחשך שאין בו שום ממשות כלל וממילא נדחה
מפני האור וכך הס״א אף שיש בה חיות הרבה להחיות כל בעלי חיים
הטמאים ונפשות אומות העולם וגם נפש הבהמית שבישראל כנ״ל מ״מ
הרי כל חיותה אינה מצד עצמה ח״ו אלא מצד הקדושה כנ״ל ולכן היא
בטלה לגמרי מפני הקדושה כביטול החשך מפני האור הגשמי רק שלגבי
קדושת נפש האלהית שבאדם נתן לה הקב״ה רשות ויכולת להגביה עצמה
כנגדה כדי שהאדם יתעורר להתגבר עליה להשפילה ע״י שפלות ונמיכת
רוחו ונבזה בעיניו נמאס ובאתערותא דלתתא אתערותא דלעילא לקיים
מ״ש משם אורידך נאם ה׳ דהיינו שמסירה מממשלתה ויכלתה ומסלק
ממנה הכח ורשות שנתן לה להגביה עצמה נגד אור קדושת נפש האלהית
ואזי ממילא בטילה ונדחית כביטול החשך מפני אור הגשמי. וכמו שמצינו

דבר זה מפורש בתורה גבי מרגלים שמתחלה אמרו כי חזק הוא ממנו אל תקרי ממנו כו׳ שלא האמינו ביכולת ה׳ ואח״כ חזרו ואמרו הננו ועלינו וגו׳ ומאין חזרה ובאה להם האמונה ביכולת ה׳ הרי לא הראה להם משרע״ה שום אות ומופת על זה בנתיים רק שאמ׳ להם איך שקצף ה׳ עליהם ונשבע שלא להביאם אל הארץ ומה הועיל זה להם אם לא היו מאמינים ביכולת ה׳ ח״ו לכבוש ל״א מלכי׳ ומפני זה לא רצו כלל ליכנס לארץ אלא ודאי מפני שישראל עצמן הם מאמינים בני מאמינים רק שהס״א המלובשת בגופם הגביה עצמה על אור קדושת נפשם האלהית בגסות רוחה וגבהות׳ בחוצפה בלי טעם ודעת ולכן מיד שקצף ה׳ עליהם והרעים בקול רעש ורוגז עד מתי לעדה הרעה הזאת וגו׳ במדבר הזה יפלו פגריכם וגו׳ אני ה׳ דברתי אם לא זאת אעשה לכל העדה הרעה הזאת וגו׳ וכששמעו דברים קשים אלו נכנע ונשבר לבם בקרבם כדכתיב ויתאבלו העם מאד וממילא נפלה הס״א מממשלתה וגבהותה וגסות רוחה וישראל עצמן הם מאמינים ומזה יכול ללמוד כל אדם שנופלים לו במחשבתו ספיקות על אמונה כי הם דברי רוח הס״א לבדה המגביה עצמה על נפשו אבל ישראל עצמן הם מאמינים כו׳ וגם הס״א עצמה אין לה ספיקות כלל באמונה רק שניתן לה רשות לבלבל האדם בדברי שקר ומרמה להרבות שכרו כפיתויי הזונה לבן המלך בשקר ומרמה ברשות המלך כמ״ש בזה״ק:

פרק ל עוד זאת ישים אל לבו לקיים מאמר רז״ל והוי שפל רוח בפני כל האדם. והוי באמת לאמיתו בפני כל האדם ממש אפי׳ ג אדר פשוטה / טז אדר א מעוברת
בפני קל שבקלים. והיינו ע״פ מארז״ל אל תדין את חבירך עד שתגיע למקומו. כי מקומו גורם לו לחטוא להיות פרנסתו לילך בשוק כל היום ולהיות מיושבי קרנות ועיניו רואות כל התאוות והעין רואה והלב חומד ויצרו בוער כתנור בוערה מאופה כמ״ש בהושע הוא בוער כאש להבה וגו׳. משא״כ מי שהולך בשוק מעט ורוב היום יושב בביתו וגם אם הולך כל היום בשוק יכול להיות שאינו מחומם כ״כ בטבעו כי אין היצר שוה
בכל נפש יש שיצרו כו׳ כמ״ש במ״א. והנה באמת גם מי שהוא מחומם יז אדר א מעוברת
מאד בטבעו ופרנסתו היא להיות מיושבי קרנות כל היום אין לו שום התנצלות על חטאיו ומיקרי רשע גמור על אשר אין פחד אלהי׳ לנגד עיניו. כי היה לו להתאפק ולמשול על רוח תאוותו שבלבו מפני פחד ה׳ הרואה
כל מעשיו כמש״ל כי המוח שליט על הלב בתולדתו. והנה באמת שהיא יח אדר א מעוברת
מלחמה גדולה ועצומ׳ לשבור היצר הבוער כאש להבה מפני פחד ה׳ וכמו נסיון ממש. והלכך צריך כל אדם לפי מה שהוא מקומו ומדרגתו בעבודת ה׳ לשקול ולבחון בעצמו אם הוא עובד ה׳ בערך ובחי׳ מלחמה עצומה כזו ונסיון כזה בבחי׳ ועשה טוב כגון בעבודת התפלה בכוונה לשפוך נפשו

לפני ה׳ בכל כחו ממש עד מיצוי הנפש ולהלחם עם גופו ונפש הבהמית שבו
המונעים הכוונה במלחמה עצומה ולבטשם ולכתתם כעפר קודם התפלה
שחרית וערבית מדי יום ביום וגם בשעת התפלה לייגע עצמו ביגיעת נפש
ויגיעת בשר כמ״ש לקמן באריכות. וכל שלא הגיע לידי מדה זו להלחם עם ד אדר פשוטה
גופו מלחמה עצומה כזו עדיין לא הגיע לבחי׳ וערך מלחמת היצר הבוער יט אדר א מעוברת
כאש להבה להיות נכנע ונשבר מפני פחד ה׳. וכן בענין ברכת המזון וכל
ברכות הנהנין והמצות בכונה ואצ״ל כונת המצות לשמן. וכן בענין עסק
לימוד התורה ללמוד הרבה יותר מחפצו ורצונו לפי טבעו ורגילותו ע״י
מלחמה עצומה עם גופו. כי הלומד מעט יותר מטבעו ה״ז מלחמה קטנה
ואין לה ערך ודמיון עם מלחמת היצר הבוער כאש דמקרי רשע גמור אם
אינו מנצח יצרו להיות נכנע ונשבר מפני ה׳. ומה לי בחי׳ סור מרע ומה
לי בחי׳ ועשה טוב הכל היא מצות המלך הקדוש יחיד ומיוחד ב״ה. וכן
בשאר מצות ובפרט בדבר שבממון כמו עבודת הצדקה וכה״ג. ואפי׳ בבחי׳ כ אדר א מעוברת
סור מרע יכול כל איש משכיל למצוא בנפשו שאינו סר לגמרי מהרע בכל
מכל כל במקום שצריך למלחמה עצומה כערך הנ״ל ואפי׳ פחות מערך
הנ״ל כגון להפסיק באמצע שיחה נאה או סיפור בגנות חבירו ואפי׳ גנאי
קטן וקל מאד אף שהוא אמת ואפי׳ כדי לנקות עצמו כנודע מהא דאר״ש
לאביו רבינו הקדוש לאו אנא כתבי׳ אלא יהודא חייטא כתביה וא״ל כלך
מלה״ר [ע״ש בגמרא רפ״י דב״ב]. וכה״ג כמה מילי דשכיחי טובא ובפרט
בענין לקדש עצמו במותר לו שהוא מדאוריית׳ כמ״ש קדושים תהיו וגו׳
והתקדשתם וגו׳. וגם ד״ס חמורים מד״ת וכו׳. אלא שכל אלו וכיוצא בהן
הן מעוונות שהאדם דש בעקביו וגם נעשו כהיתר מחמת שעבר ושנה וכו׳.
אבל באמת אם הוא יודע ספר ומחזיק בתורת ה׳ וקרבת אלקי׳ יחפץ גדול כא אדר א מעוברת
עונו מנשוא ואשמתו גדלה בכפלי כפליים במה שאינו נלחם ומתגבר על
יצרו בערך ובחי׳ מלחמה עצומה הנ״ל מאשמת קל שבקלים מיושבי קרנות
הרחוקים מה׳ ותורתו ואין אשמתם גדולה כ״כ במה שאינם כובשים יצרם
הבוער כאש להבה מפני פחד ה׳ המבין ומביט אל כל מעשיהם כאשמת
כל הקרב הקרב אל ה׳ ואל תורתו ועבודתו וכמשארז״ל גבי אחר שידע
בכבודי וכו׳ ולכן ארז״ל על ע״ה שזדונות נעשו להם כשגגות:

פרק לא והנה אף אם כשיאריך הרבה להעמיק בענייני׳ הנ״ל כשעה ה אדר פשוטה
ושתי׳ להיות בנמיכת רוח ולב נשבר יבא לידי עצבות כב אדר א מעוברת
גדולה לא יחוש ואף שעצבות היא מצד קליפת נוגה ולא מצד הקדושה
כי בצד הקדושה כתיב עוז וחדוה במקומו ואין השכינה שורה אלא מתוך
שמחה וכן לדבר הלכה וכו׳ אלא שאם העצבות היא ממילי דשמיא היא
מבחי׳ טוב שבנוגה [ולכן כתב האר״י ז״ל שאפי׳ דאגת העונות אינה ראויה

כ״א בשעת הוידוי ולא בשעת התפלה ות״ת שצ״ל בשמחה שמצד הקדושה
דווקא] אעפ״כ הרי כך היא המדה לאכפיא לס״א במינה ודוגמתה.
כמארז״ל מיניה וביה אבא לשדי׳ ביה נרגא ופגע בו כיוצא בו. וע״ז נאמר
בכל עצב יהיה מותר והיתרון היא השמחה הבאה אחר העצב כדלקמן. אך
באמת אין לב נשבר ומרירות הנפש על ריחוקה מאור פני ה׳ והתלבשותה
בס״א נקראים בשם עצבות כלל בלשון הקודש כי עצבות היא שלבו
מטומטם כאבן ואין חיות בלבו אבל מרירות ולב נשבר אדרבה הרי יש חיות
בלבו להתפעל ולהתמרמר רק שהיא חיות מבחי׳ גבורות קדושות והשמחה
מבחי׳ חסדים כי הלב כלול משתיהן. והנה לעתים צריך לעורר בחי׳ גבורות
הקדושות כדי להמתיק הדינים שהם בחי׳ נפש הבהמי׳ ויצה״ר כששולט
ח״ו על האדם כי אין הדינים נמתקין אלא בשרשן ולכן ארז״ל לעולם ירגיז
אדם יצ״הט והיינו בכל עת שרואה בנפשו שצריך לכך אך שעת הכושר
שהיא שעה המיוחדת וראויה לכך לרוב בני אדם היא בשעה שהוא עצב
בלא״ה ממילי דעלמא או כך בלי שום סבה אזי היא שעת הכושר להפך
העצב להיות ממרי דחושבנא הנ״ל ולקיים מארז״ל לעולם ירגיז וכו׳ כנ״ל
ובזה יפטר מהעצבות שממילי דעלמא ואח״כ יבא לידי שמחה אמיתית ו אדר פשוטה
דהיינו שזאת ישיב אל לבו לנחמו בכפליים אחר הדברי׳ והאמת האלה
הנ״ל לאמר ללבו אמת הוא כן בלי ספק שאני רחוק מאד מה׳ בתכלית
ומשוקץ ומתועב כו׳ אך כל זה הוא אני לבדי הוא הגוף עם נפש החיונית
שבו אבל מ״מ יש בקרבי חלק ה׳ ממש שישנו אפי׳ בקל שבקלים שהיא
נפש האלהית עם ניצוץ אלקות ממש המלובש בה להחיותה רק שהיא בבחי׳
גלות וא״כ אדרבה כל מה שאני בתכלי׳ הריחוק מה׳ והתיעוב ושיקוץ הרי
נפש האלהית שבי בגלות גדול יותר והרחמנות עליה גדולה מאד ולזה
אשים כל מגמתי וחפצי להוציאה ולהעלותה מגלות זה להשיבה אל בית
אביה כנעורי׳ קודם שנתלבשה בגופי שהיתה נכללת באורו ית׳ ומיוחדת
עמו בתכלית וגם עתה כן תהא כלולה ומיוחדת בו ית׳ כשאשים כל מגמתי
בתור׳ ומצות להלביש בהן כל עשר בחינותיה כנ״ל ובפרט במצות תפלה
לצעוק אל ה׳ בצר לה מגלותה בגופי המשוקץ להוציאה ממסגר ולדבקה
בו ית׳ וזו היא בחי׳ תשובה ומעשים טובים שהן מעשים טובים שעושה כדי
להשיב חלק ה׳ למקורא ושרשא דכל עלמין. וזאת תהיה עבודתו כל ימיו ז אדר א פשוטה
בשמחה רבה היא שמחת הנפש בצאתה מהגוף המתועב ושבה אל בית
אביה כנעוריה בשעת התורה והעבודה וכמארז״ל להיות כל ימיו בתשובה
ואין לך שמחה גדולה כצאת מהגלות והשביה כמשל בן מלך שהיה בשביה
וטוחן בבית האסורים ומנוול באשפה ויצא לחפשי אל בית אביו המלך
ואף שהגוף עומד בשיקוצו ותיעובו וכמ״ש בזהר דנקרא משכא דחויא

כי מהותה ועצמותה של הנפש הבהמית לא נהפך לטוב ליכלל בקדושה
מ״מ תיקר נפשו בעיניו לשמוח בשמחתה יותר מהגוף הנבזה שלא לערבב
ולבלבל שמחת הנפש בעצבון הגוף. והנה בחי׳ זו היא בחי׳ יציאת מצרים
שנאמר בה כי ברח העם דלכאור׳ הוא תמוה למה היתה כזאת וכי אילו
אמרו לפרעה לשלחם חפשי לעולם לא היה מוכרח לשלחם אלא מפני שהרע
שבנפשות ישראל עדיין היה בתקפו בחלל השמאלי כי לא פסקה זוהמתם
עד מתן תורה רק מגמתם וחפצם היתה לצאת נפשם האלהית מגלות הס״א
היא טומאת מצרים ולדבקה בו ית׳ וכדכתיב ה׳ עוזי ומעוזי ומנוסי ביום
צרה וגו׳ משגבי ומנוסי וגו׳ והוא מנוס לי וגו׳ ולכן לעתיד כשיעביר ה׳ רוח
הטומאה מן הארץ כתיב ובמנוסה לא תלכון כי הולך לפניכם ה׳ וגו׳. ולהיות ח אדר פשוטה
בחי׳ תשובה זו ביתר שאת ויתר עז מעומקא דלבא וגם שמחת הנפש תהיה
בתוספת אורה ושמחה כאשר ישיב אל לבו דעת ותבונה לנחמו מעצבונו
ויגונו לאמר כנ״ל הן אמת כו׳ אך אני לא עשיתי את עצמי. ולמה עשה ה׳
כזאת להוריד חלק מאורו ית׳ הממלא וסובב כל עלמין וכולא קמי׳ כלא
חשיב והלבישו במשכא דחויא וטפה סרוחה אין זה כי אם ירידה זו היא
צורך עליה להעלות לה׳ כל נפש החיונית הבהמית שמקליפת נוגה וכל
לבושיה הן בחי׳ מחשבה דבור ומעשה שלה ע״י התלבשותן במעשה דבור
ומחשבת התורה [וכמ״ש לקמן ענין העלאה זו באריכות איך שהיא תכלית
בריאת העולם] וא״כ איפוא זאת אעשה וזאת תהיה כל מגמתי כל ימי
חלדי לכל בהן חיי רוחי ונפשי וכמ״ש אליך ה׳ נפשי אשא דהיינו לקשר
מחשבתי ודבורי במחשבתו ודבורו ית׳ והן הן גופי הלכות הערוכו׳ לפנינו
וכן מעשה במעשה המצות שלכן נקראת התורה משיבת נפש פי׳ למקורה
ושרשה וע״ז נאמ׳ פקודי ה׳ ישרים משמחי לב:

פרק לב והנה ע״י קיום הדברי׳ הנ״ל להיות גופו נבזה ונמאס בעיניו ט אדר פשוטה
רק שמחתו תהיה שמחת הנפש לבדה הרי זו דרך כג אדר א מעוברת
ישרה וקלה לבא לידי קיום מצות ואהבת לרעך כמוך לכל נפש מישראל
למגדול ועד קטן. כי מאחר שגופו נמאס ומתועב אצלו והנפש והרוח מי כד אדר א מעוברת
יודע גדולתן ומעלתן בשרשן ומקורן באלקי׳ חיים. בשגם שכולן מתאימות
ואב א׳ לכולנה ולכן נקראו כל ישראל אחים ממש מצד שורש נפשם בה׳
אחד רק שהגופים מחולקי׳. ולכן העושי׳ גופם עיקר ונפשם טפלה אי אפשר
להיות אהבה ואחוה אמיתית ביניהם אלא התלויה בדבר לבדה. וז״ש הלל כה אדר א מעוברת
הזקן על קיום מצוה זו זהו כל התורה כולה ואידך פירושא הוא כו׳. כי
יסוד ושורש כל התורה הוא להגביה ולהעלו׳ הנפש על הגוף מעלה מעלה
עד עיקרא ושרשא דכל עלמין וגם להמשיך אור א״ס ב״ה בכנסת ישראל

כמ״ש לקמן דהיינו במקור נשמות כל ישראל למהוי אחד באחד דוקא ולא
כשיש פירוד ח״ו בנשמות דקב״ה לא שריא באתר פגים וכמ״ש ברכנו אבינו
י אדר פשוטה כולנו כאחד באור פניך וכמ״ש במ״א באריכות: ומ״ש בגמ׳ שמי שרואה
כו אדר א מעוברת בחבירו שחטא מצוה לשנאותו וגם לומר לרבו שישנאהו. היינו בחבירו
בתורה ומצות וכבר קיים בו מצות הוכח תוכיח את עמיתך עם שאתך
כד אדר א מעוברת בתורה ובמצות ואעפ״כ לא שב מחטאו כמ״ש בס׳ חרדים אבל מי שאינו
חבירו ואינו מקורב אצלו הנה ע״ז אמר הלל הזקן הוי מתלמידיו של אהרן
אוהב שלום וכו׳ אוהב את הבריות ומקרבן לתורה. לומר שאף הרחוקים
מתורת ה׳ ועבודתו ולכן נקראי׳ בשם בריות בעלמא צריך למשכן בחבלי
עבותו׳ אהבה וכולי האי ואולי יוכל לקרבן לתורה ועבודת ה׳ והן לא לא
כח אדר א מעוברת הפסיד שכר מצות אהבת ריעים וגם המקורבים אליו והוכיחם ולא שבו
מעונותיהם שמצוה לשנאותם מצוה לאהבם ג״כ ושתיהן הן אמת שנאה
מצד הרע שבהם ואהבה מצד בחי׳ הטוב הגנוז שבהם שהוא ניצוץ אלקות
שבתוכם המחיה נפשם האלקית וגם לעורר רחמים בלבו עליה כי היא בבחי׳
גלות בתוך הרע מס״א הגובר עליה ברשעי׳ והרחמנות מבטלת השנאה
ומעוררת האהבה כנודע ממ״ש ליעקב אשר פדה את אברהם [ולא אמר
דה״עה תכלית שנאה שנאתים וגו׳ אלא על המינים והאפיקורסים שאין
להם חלק באלהי ישראל כדאיתא בגמרא ר״פ ט״ז דשבת]: